The LATEX Companion

Second Edition

Addison-Wesley Series on Tools and Techniques for Computer Typesetting

This series focuses on tools and techniques needed for computer typesetting and information processing with traditional and new media. Books in the series address the practical needs of both users and system developers. Initial titles comprise handy references for LaTeX users; forthcoming works will expand that core. Ultimately, the series will cover other typesetting and information processing systems, as well, especially insofar as those systems offer unique value to the scientific and technical community. The series goal is to enhance your ability to produce, maintain, manipulate, or reuse articles, papers, reports, proposals, books, and other documents with professional quality.

Ideas for this series should be directed to the editor: mittelbach@aw.com.
Send all other comments to the publisher: awprofessional@aw.com.

Series Editor

Frank Mittelbach
Manager LaTeX3 Project, Germany

Editorial Board

Jacques André
Irisa/Inria-Rennes, France

Barbara Beeton
Editor, TUGboat, USA

David Brailsford
University of Nottingham, UK

Tim Bray
Textuality Services, Canada

Peter Flynn
University College, Cork, Ireland

Leslie Lamport
Creator of LaTeX, USA

Chris Rowley
Open University, UK

Richard Rubinstein
Human Factors International, USA

Paul Stiff
University of Reading, UK

Series Titles

Guide to LaTeX, Fourth Edition, by Helmut Kopka and Patrick W. Daly

The LaTeX Companion, Second Edition, by Frank Mittelbach and Michel Goossens with Johannes Braams, David Carlisle, and Chris Rowley

The LaTeX Graphics Companion, by Michel Goossens, Sebastian Rahtz, and Frank Mittelbach

The LaTeX Web Companion, by Michel Goossens and Sebastian Rahtz

Also from Addison-Wesley:

LaTeX: A Document Preparation System, Second Edition, by Leslie Lamport

The Unicode Standard, Version 4.0, by the Unicode Consortium

The LaTeX Companion

Second Edition

Frank Mittelbach
LaTeX3 Project, Mainz, Germany

Michel Goossens
CERN, Geneva, Switzerland

with Johannes Braams, David Carlisle,
and Chris Rowley

and contributions by
Christine Detig and Joachim Schrod

✦ Addison-Wesley

Boston • San Francisco • New York • Toronto • Montreal
London • Munich • Paris • Madrid
Capetown • Sydney • Tokyo • Singapore • Mexico City

Many of the designations used by manufacturers and sellers to distinguish their products are claimed as trademarks. Where those designations appear in this book, and Addison-Wesley was aware of a trademark claim, the designations have been printed with initial capital letters or in all capitals.

The authors and publisher have taken care in the preparation of this book, but make no expressed or implied warranty of any kind and assume no responsibility for errors or omissions. No liability is assumed for incidental or consequential damages in connection with or arising out of the use of the information or programs contained herein.

The publisher offers discounts on this book when ordered in quantity for bulk purchases and special sales. For more information, please contact:

U.S. Corporate and Government Sales
(800) 382-3419
corpsales@pearsontechgroup.com

For sales outside of the U.S., please contact:

International Sales
(317) 581-3793
international@pearsontechgroup.com

Visit Addison-Wesley on the Web: www.awprofessional.com

Library of Congress Cataloging-in-Publication Data

Mittelbach, Frank.
  The LaTeX Companion.- 2nd ed. / Frank Mittelbach and Michel Goossens,
with Johannes Braams, David Carlisle, and Chris Rowley.
      p. cm.
  Goossens' name appears first on the earlier edition.
  Includes bibliographical references and index.
  ISBN 0-201-36299-6 (pbk. : alk. paper)
 1. LaTeX (Computer file) 2. Computerized typesetting. I. Goossens,
Michel. II. Rowley, Chris, 1948- III. Title.
  Z253.4.L38G66 2004
  686.2'2544536-dc22

                                                      2003070810

ISBN 0-201-36299-6
Text printed on recycled paper

1 2 3 4 5 6 7 8 9 10—CRW—0807060504

First printing, April 2004

We dedicate this book to the memory of Michael Downes (1958–2003), a great friend and wonderful colleague on the LaTeX Team. His thoughtful contributions to our work and our lives are diverse and profound. Moreover, he brightens the lives of countless grateful (LA)TEX users through the wisdom built into his support for all aspects of mathematical typesetting—very many *masterpieces of the publishing art* will stand for ever as superb memorials to his quiet but deep insights.

Contents

List of Figures

List of Tables

Preface

A full decade has passed since the publication of the first edition of *The LaTeX Companion*—a decade during which some people prophesied the demise of TeX and LaTeX and predicted that other software would take over the world. There have been a great many changes indeed, but neither prediction has come to pass: TeX has not vanished and the interest in LaTeX has not declined, although the approach to both has gradually changed over time.

When we wrote the *Companion* in 1993 [55], we intended to describe what is usefully available in the LaTeX world (though ultimately we ended up describing what was available at CERN in those days). As an unintentional side effect, the first edition *defined* for most readers what should be available in a then-modern LaTeX distribution. Fortunately, most of the choices we made at that time proved to be reasonable, and the majority (albeit not all) of the packages described in the first edition are still in common use today. Thus, even though "the book shows its age, it still remains a solid reference in most parts", as one reviewer put it recently.

Nevertheless, much has changed and a lot of new and exciting functionality has been added to LaTeX during the last decade. As a result, while revising the book we ended up rewriting 90% of the original content and adding about 600 additional pages describing impressive new developments.

What you are holding now is essentially a new book—a book that we hope preserves the positive aspects of the first edition even as it greatly enhances them, while at the same time avoiding the mistakes we made back then, both in content and presentation (though doubtless we made some others). For this book we used the CTAN archives as a basis and also went through the `comp.text.tex` news group archives to identify the most pressing questions and queries.

In addition to highlighting a good selection of the contributed packages available on the CTAN archives, the book describes many aspects of the basic LATEX system that are not fully covered in the *LATEX Manual*, Leslie Lamport's *LATEX: A Document Preparation System* [104]. Note, however, that our book is not a replacement for the *LATEX Manual* but rather a companion to it: a reader of our book is assumed to have read at least the first part of that book (or a comparable introductory work, such as the *Guide to LATEX* [101]) and to have some practical experience with producing LATEX documents.

The second edition has seen a major change in the authorship; Frank took over as principal author (so he is to blame for all the faults in this book) and several members of the LATEX3 project team joined in the book's preparation, enriching it with their knowledge and experience in individual subject areas.

Thanks to a great guy! The preparation of the book was overshadowed by the sudden death of our good friend, colleague, and prospective co-author Michael Downes, whose great contributions to LATEX, and AMS-LATEX in particular, are well known to many people. We dedicate this book to him and his memory.

*   *   *

We first of all wish to thank Peter Gordon, our editor at Addison-Wesley, who not only made this book possible, but through his constant encouragement also kept us on the right track (just a few years late). When we finally went into production, Elizabeth Ryan was unfailingly patient with our idiosyncrasies and steered us safely to completion.

We are especially indebted to Barbara Beeton, David Rhead, Lars Hellström, and Walter Schmidt for their careful reading of individual parts of the manuscript. Their numerous comments, suggestions, corrections, and hints have substantially improved the quality of the text.

Our very special thanks go to our contributing authors Christine Detig and Joachim Schrod for their invaluable help with Chapter 11 on index preparation.

Haunted package authors Those who keep their ears to the ground for activities in the LATEX world may have noticed an increased number of new releases of several well-established packages in 2002 and 2003. Some of these releases were triggered by our questions and comments to the package authors as we were preparing the manuscript for this second edition. Almost all package authors responded favorably to our requests for updates, changes, and clarifications, and all spent a considerable amount of time helping us with our task. We would particularly like to thank Jens Berger (jurabib), Axel Sommerfeldt (caption), Steven Cochran (subfig), Melchior Franz (soul, euro), and Carsten Heinz (listings) who had to deal with the bulk of the nearly 6000 e-mail messages that have been exchanged with various package authors.

Hearty thanks for similar reasons go to Alexander Rozhenko (manyfoot), Bernd Schandl (paralist), David Kastrup (perpage), Donald Arseneau (cite, relsize, threeparttable, url), Fabrice Popineau (TEX Live CD), Frank Bennett, Jr. (camel), Gerd Neugebauer (bibtool), Harald Harders (subfloat), Hideo Umeki (geometry), Hubert Gäßlein (sidecap,pict2e), Javier Bezos (titlesec, titletoc), Jean-Pierre Drucbert (minitoc), Jeffrey Goldberg (endfloat, lastpage), John Lavagnino (endnotes), Markus Kohm (typearea), Martin Schröder (ragged2e), Matthias Eckermann (parallel), Michael Covington (upquote), Michel Bovani (fourier), Patrick Daly (custom-bib, natbib), Peter Heslin (ellipsis), Peter Wilson (layouts), Piet van Oostrum (extramarks,fancyhdr), Rei Fukui (tipa), Robin Fairbairns (footmisc), Rolf Niepraschk (sidecap,pict2e), Stephan Böttcher (lineno), Thomas Esser (teTeX distribution), Thomas Henlich (marvosym), Thorsten Hansen (bibunits), and Walter Schmidt (fix-cm, PSNFSS). Our apologies if we missed someone.

We gratefully recognize all of our many colleagues in the (LA)TeX world who developed the packages—not only those described here, but also the hundreds of others—that aim to help users meet the typesetting requirements for their documents. Without the continuous efforts of these enthusiasts, LaTeX would not be the magnificent and flexible tool it is today.

We would also like to thank Blenda Horn from Y&Y and Michael Vulis from MicroPress for supplying the fonts used to typeset the pages of this book.

The picture of Chris Rowley, taken after a good lunch at Kai Tek airport, Hong Kong, appears courtesy of Wai Wing. The picture of Michael Downes, taken at the TeX 2000 conference, Oxford, appears courtesy of Alan Wetmore.

* * *

We would like to thank our families and friends for the support given during the preparation of this book—though this may sound like an alibi sentence to many, it never felt truer than with this book.

Chris would like to thank the Open University, United Kingdom, for supporting his work on LaTeX and the School of Computer Science and Engineering, University of New South Wales, for providing a most pleasant environment in which to complete his work on this book.

Frank Mittelbach
Michel Goossens
Johannes Braams
David Carlisle
Chris Rowley

February 2004

## CHAPTER 1

Introduction

LaTeX is not just a system for typesetting mathematics. Its applications span the one-page memorandum, business and personal letters, newsletters, articles, and books covering the whole range of the sciences and humanities, ... right up to full-scale expository texts and reference works on all topics. Nowadays, versions of LaTeX exist for practically every type of computer and operating system. This book provides a wealth of information about its many present-day uses but first provides some background information.

The first section of this chapter looks back at the origins and subsequent development of LaTeX.[1] The second section gives an overview of the file types used by a typical current LaTeX system and the rôle played by each. Finally, the chapter offers some guidance on how to use the book.

1.1 A brief history

In May 1977, Donald Knuth of Stanford University [94] started work on the text-processing system that is now known as "TeX and METAFONT" [82–86]. In the *In the Beginning ...* foreword of *The TeXbook* [82], Knuth writes: "TeX [is] a new typesetting system intended for the creation of beautiful books—and especially for books that contain a lot of mathematics. By preparing a manuscript in TeX format, you will be telling a computer exactly how the manuscript is to be transformed into pages whose typographic quality is comparable to that of the world's finest printers."

---

[1] A more personal account can be found in *The LaTeX legacy: 2.09 and all that* [148].

In 1979, Gordon Bell wrote in a foreword to an earlier book, *TeX and META-FONT, New Directions in Typesetting* [80]: "Don Knuth's Tau Epsilon Chi (TeX) is potentially the most significant invention in typesetting in this century. It introduces a standard language in computer typography and in terms of importance could rank near the introduction of the Gutenberg press."

In the early 1990s, Donald Knuth officially announced that TeX would not undergo any further development [96] in the interest of stability. Perhaps unsurprisingly, the 1990s saw a flowering of experimental projects that extended TeX in various directions; many of these are coming to fruition in the early 21st century, making it an exciting time to be involved in automated typography.

The development of TeX from its birth as one of Don's "personal productivity tools" (created simply to ensure the rapid completion and typographic quality of his then-current work on *The Art of Computer Programming*) [88] was largely influenced and nourished by the American Mathematical Society on behalf of U.S. research mathematicians.

... and Lamport saw that it was Good.

While Don was developing TeX, in the early 1980s, Leslie Lamport started work on the document preparation system now called LaTeX, which used TeX's typesetting engine and macro system to implement a declarative document description language based on that of a system called Scribe by Brian Reid [142]. The appeal of such a system is that a few high-level LaTeX declarations, or commands, allow the user to easily compose a large range of documents without having to worry much about their typographical appearance. In principle at least, the details of the layout can be left for the document designer to specify elsewhere.

The second edition of *LaTeX: A Document Preparation System* [104] begins as follows: "LaTeX is a system for typesetting documents. Its first widely available version, mysteriously numbered 2.09, appeared in 1985." This release of a stable and well-documented LaTeX led directly to the rapid spread of TeX-based document processing beyond the community of North American mathematicians.

LaTeX was the first widely used language for describing the logical structure of a large range of documents and hence introducing the philosophy of logical design, as used in Scribe. The central tenet of "logical design" is that the author should be concerned only with the logical content of his or her work and not its visual appearance. Back then, LaTeX was described variously as "TeX for the masses" and "Scribe liberated from inflexible formatting control". Its use spread very rapidly during the next decade. By 1994 Leslie could write, "LaTeX is now extremely popular in the scientific and academic communities, and it is used extensively in industry." But that level of ubiquity looks quite small when compared with the present day when it has become, for many professionals on every continent, a workhorse whose presence is as unremarkable and essential as the workstation on which it is used.

Going global

The worldwide availability of LaTeX quickly increased international interest in TeX and in its use for typesetting a range of languages. LaTeX 2.09 was (deliberately) not globalized but it was globalizable; moreover, it came with documentation worth translating because of its clear structure and straightforward style. Two pivotal conferences (Exeter UK, 1988, and Karlsruhe Germany, 1989) established clearly the widespread adoption of LaTeX in Europe and led directly to International LaTeX [151] and to work led by Johannes Braams [25] on more general support for using a wide variety of languages and switching between them (see Chapter 9).

Note that in the context of typography, the word *language* does not refer exclusively to the variety of natural languages and dialects across the universe; it also has a wider meaning. For typography, "language" covers a lot more than just the choice of "characters that make up words", as many important distinctions derive from other cultural differences that affect traditions of written communication. Thus, important typographic differences are not necessarily in line with national groupings but rather arise from different types of documents and distinct publishing communities.

Another important contribution to the reach of LaTeX was the pioneering work of Frank Mittelbach and Rainer Schöpf on a complete replacement for LaTeX's interface to font resources, the New Font Selection Scheme (NFSS) (see Chapter 7). They were also heavily involved in the production of the $\mathcal{A}_{\mathcal{M}}\mathcal{S}$-LaTeX system that added advanced mathematical typesetting capabilities to LaTeX (see Chapter 8). *The Next Generation*

As a reward for all their efforts, which included a steady stream of bug reports (and fixes) for Leslie, by 1991 Frank and Rainer had "been allowed" to take over the technical support and maintenance of LaTeX. One of their first acts was to consolidate International LaTeX as part of the kernel[1] of the system, "according to the standard developed in Europe". Very soon Version 2.09 was formally frozen and, although the change-log entries continue for a few months into 1992, plans for its demise as a supported system were already far advanced as something new was badly needed. The worldwide success of LaTeX had by the early 1990s led in a sense to too much development activity: under the hood of Leslie's "family sedan" many TeXnicians had been laboring to add such goodies as super-charged, turbo-injection, multi-valved engines and much "look-no-thought" automation. Thus, the announcement in 1994 of the new standard LaTeX, christened LaTeX 2_ε, explains its existence in the following way: *Too much of a Good Thing*[TM]

> "Over the years many extensions have been developed for LaTeX. This is, of course, a sure sign of its continuing popularity but it has had one unfortunate result: incompatible LaTeX formats came into use at different sites. Thus, to process documents from various places, a site maintainer was forced to keep LaTeX (with and without NFSS), SLITeX, $\mathcal{A}_{\mathcal{M}}\mathcal{S}$-LaTeX, and so on. In addition, when looking at a source file it was not always clear for which format the document was written.
>
> To put an end to this unsatisfactory situation a new release of LaTeX was produced. It brings all such extensions back under a single format and thus prevents the proliferation of mutually incompatible dialects of LaTeX 2.09."

---

[1] *Kernel* here means the core, or center, of the system.

Standard LaTeX The development of this "New Standard LaTeX" and its maintenance system was started in 1993 by the LaTeX3 Project Team [126], which soon comprised Frank Mittelbach, Rainer Schöpf, Chris Rowley, Johannes Braams, Michael Downes, David Carlisle, Alan Jeffrey, and Denys Duchier, with some encouragement and gentle bullying from Leslie. Although the major changes to the basic LaTeX system (the kernel) and the standard document classes (styles in 2.09) were completed by 1994, substantial extra support for colored typography, generic graphics, and fine positioning control were added later, largely by David Carlisle. Access to fonts for the new system incorporated work by Mark Purtill on extensions of NFSS to better support variable font encodings and scalable fonts [30–32].

The 21st century Although the original goal for this new version was consolidation of the wide range of models carrying the LaTeX marquee, what emerged was a substantially more powerful system with both a robust mechanism (via LaTeX packages) for extension and, importantly, a solid technical support and maintenance system. This provides robustness via standardization and maintainability of both the code base and the support systems. This system remains the current standard LaTeX system that is described in this book. It has fulfilled most of the goals for "a new LaTeX for the 21st Century", as they were envisaged back in 1989 [129, 131].

The specific claims of the current system are "... better support for fonts, graphics and color; actively maintained by the LaTeX3 Project Team". The details of how these goals were achieved, and the resulting subsystems that enabled the claims to be substantially attained, form a revealing study in distributed software support: The core work was done in at least five countries and, as is illustrated by the bugs database [106], the total number of active contributors to the technical support effort remains high.

The package system Although the LaTeX kernel suffered a little from feature creep in the late 1990s, the package system together with the clear development guidelines and the legal framework of the LaTeX Project Public License (LPPL) [111] have enabled LaTeX to remain almost completely stable while supporting a wide range of extensions. These have largely been provided by a similarly wide range of people who have, as the project team are happy to acknowledge and the on-line catalogue [169] bears witness, enhanced the available functionality in a vast panoply of areas.

Development work All major developments of the base system have been listed in the regular issues of *LaTeX News* [107]. At the turn of the century, development work by the LaTeX3 Project Team focused on the following areas: supporting multi-language documents [120]; a "Designer Interface for LaTeX" [123]; major enhancements to the output routine [121]; improved handling of inter-paragraph formatting; and the complex front-matter requirements of journal articles. Prototype code has been made available; see [124].

No new features . . . One thing the project team steadfastly refused to do was to unnecessarily "enhance" the kernel by providing additional features as part of it, thereby avoiding the trap into which LaTeX 2.09 fell in the early 1990s: the disintegration into incompatible dialects where documents written at one site could not be successfully processed at another site. In this discussion it should not be forgotten that LaTeX serves not only to produce high-quality documents, but also to enable collaboration and exchange by providing a lingua franca for various research communities.

With LaTeX 2_ε, documents written in 1996[1] can still be run with today's LaTeX. New documents run on older kernel releases if the additional packages used are brought up-to-date—a task that, in contrast to updating the LaTeX kernel software, is easily manageable even for users working in a multiuser environment (e.g., in a university or company setting).

But a stable kernel is not identical to a standstill in software development; of equally crucial importance to the continuing relevance and popularity of LaTeX is *... but no standstill* the diverse collection of contributed packages building on this stable base. The success of the package system for non-kernel extensions is demonstrated by the enthusiasm of these contributors—many thanks to all of them! As can be easily appreciated by visiting the highly accessible and stable Comprehensive TeX Archive Network (see Appendix C) or by reading this book (where more than 250 of these "Good Guys"[2] are listed on page 1080), this has supported the existence of an enormous treasure trove of LaTeX packages and related software.

The provision of services, tools, and systems-level support for such a highly distributed maintenance and development system was itself a major intellectual *The back office* challenge, because many standard working methods and software tools for these tasks assume that your colleagues are in the next room, not the next continent (and in the early days of the development, e-mail and FTP were the only reliable means of communication). The technical inventiveness and the personalities of everyone involved were both essential to creating this example of the friendly face of open software maintenance, but Alan Jeffrey and Rainer Schöpf deserve special mention for "fixing everything".

A vital part of this system that is barely visible to most people is the regression testing system with its vast suite of test files [119]. It was devised and set up by Frank and Rainer with Daniel Flipo; it has proved its worth countless times in the never-ending battle of the bugs.

Some members of the project team have built on the team's experience to extend their individual research work in document science beyond the current *Research* LaTeX structures and paradigms. Some examples of their work up to 2003 can be found in the following references: [33–36, 117, 127, 138, 147, 149].

Meanwhile, the standard LaTeX system will have two major advantages over anything else that will emerge in the next 10 years to support fully automated *Until 2020?* document processing. First, it will efficiently provide high-quality formatting of a large range of elements in very complex documents of arbitrary size. Second, it will be robust in both use and maintenance and hence will have the potential to remain in widespread use for at least a further 15 years.[3]

---

[1]The time between 1994 and 1996 was a consolidation time for LaTeX 2_ε, with major fixes and enhancements being made until the system was thoroughly stable.

[2]Unfortunately, this is nearly the literal truth: You need a keen eye to spot the nine ladies listed.

[3]One of the authors has publicly staked a modest amount of beer on TeX remaining in general use (at least by mathematicians) until at least 2010.

…and into the future An important spin-off from the research work was the provision of some interfaces and extensions that are immediately usable with standard LATEX. As more such functionality is added, it will become necessary to assess the likelihood that merely extending LATEX in this way will provide a more powerful, yet still robust and maintainable, system. This is not the place to speculate further about the future of LATEX but we can be sure that it will continue to develop and to expand its areas of influence whether in traditional publishing or in electronic systems for education and commerce.

1.2 Today's system

This section presents an overview of the vast array of files used by a typical LATEX system with its many components. This overview will also involve some descriptions of how the various program components interact. Most users will never need to know anything of this software environment that supports their work, but this section will be a useful general reference and an aid to understanding some of the more technical parts of this book.

Although modern LATEX systems are most often embedded in a project-oriented, menu-driven interface, behind the scenes little has changed from the file-based description given here. The stability of LATEX over time also means that an article by Joachim Schrod on *The Components of TEX* [153] remains the best source for a more comprehensive explanation of a TEX-based typesetting system. The following description assumes familiarity with a standard computer file system in which a "file extension" is used to denote the "type of a file".

In processing a document, the LATEX program reads and writes several files, some of which are further processed by other applications. These are listed in Table 1.1, and Figure 1.1 shows schematically the flow of information behind the scenes (on pages 8 and 9).

Document input The most obviously important files in any LATEX-based documentation project are the *input source files*. Typically, there will be a master file that uses other subsidiary files (see Section 2.1). These files most often have the extension `.tex` (code documentation for LATEX typically carries the extension `.dtx`; see Chapter 14); they are commonly known as "plain text files" since they can be prepared with a basic text editor. Often, external graphical images are included in the typeset document utilizing the `graphics` interface described in Section 10.2.

Structure and style LATEX also needs several files containing structure and layout definitions: *class* files with the extension `.cls`; *option* files with the extension `.clo`; *package* files with the extension `.sty` (see Appendix A). Many of these are provided by the basic system set-up, but others may be supplied by individual users. LATEX is distributed with five standard document classes: article, report, book, slides, and letter. These document classes can be customized by the contents of other files specified either by class options or by loading additional packages as described in Section 2.1. In addition, many LATEX documents will implicitly input *language definition files* of the babel system with the extension .ldf (see Chapter 9) and *encoding definition files* of the inputenc/fontenc packages with the extension .def (see Chapter 7).

The information that LaTeX needs about the glyphs to be typeset is found in *Font resources* *TeX font metric* files (extension .tfm). This does not include information about the shapes of glyphs, only about their dimensions. Information about which font files are needed by LaTeX is stored in *font definition* files (extension .fd). Both types are loaded automatically when necessary. See Chapter 7 for further information about font resources.

A few other files need to be available to TeX, but you are even less likely to come across them directly. An example includes the LaTeX format file latex.fmt *The LaTeX format* that contains the core LaTeX instructions, precompiled for processing by the TeX formatter. There are some situations in which this format needs to be recompiled—for example, when changing the set of hyphenation rules available to LaTeX (configured in language.dat; see Section 9.5.1) and, of course, when a new LaTeX kernel is made available. The details regarding how such formats are generated differ from one TeX implementation to the next, so they are not described in this book.

The output from LaTeX itself is a collection of *internal* files (see below), plus one very important file that contains all the information produced by TeX about the typeset form of the document.

TeX's own particular representation of the formatted document is that of a *device-independent* file (extension .dvi). TeX positions glyphs and rules with a *Formatted output* precision far better than $0.01\,\mu m$ (1/4,000,000 inch). Therefore, the output generated by TeX can be effectively considered to be independent of the abilities of any physical rendering device—hence the name. Some variants of the TeX program, such as pdfTeX [159, 161] and VTeX [168], can produce other device-independent output forms in proprietary languages such the Page Description Format (PDF) (extension .pdf).

The .dvi file format specifies only the names/locations of fonts and their glyphs—it does not contain any rendering information for those glyphs. The .pdf file format can contain such rendering information.

Some of the *internal* files contain code needed to pass information from *Cross-references* one LaTeX run to the next, such as for cross-references (the *auxiliary* file, extension .aux; see Section 2.3) and for typesetting particular elements of the document such as the table of contents (extension .toc) and the lists of figures (extension .lof) and of tables (extension .lot). Others are specific to particular packages (such as minitoc, Section 2.3.6, or endnotes, Section 3.2.7) or to other parts of the system (see below).

Finally, TeX generates a transcript file of its activities with the extension .log. This file contains a lot of information, such as the names of the files read, the *Errors, warnings,* numbers of the pages processed, warning and error messages, and other pertinent *and information* data that is especially useful when debugging errors (see Appendix B).

A file with the extension .idx contains individual unsorted items to be indexed. These items need to be sorted, collated, and unified by a program like *Indexing* makeindex or xindy (see Chapter 11). The sorted version is typically placed into

	File Type	*Common File Extension(s)*
Document Input	text	`.tex .dtx .ltx`
	bibliography	`.bbl`
	index / glossary	`.ind` / `.gnd`
Graphics	internal	`.tex`
	external	`.ps .eps .tif .png .jpg .gif .pdf`
Other Input	layout and structure	`.clo .cls .sty`
	encoding definitions	`.def`
	language definitions	`.ldf`
	font access definitions	`.fd`
	configuration data	`.cfg`
Internal Communication	auxiliary	`.aux`
(Input and Output)	table of contents	`.toc`
	list of figures / tables	`.lof` / `.lot`
Low-level TEX Input	format	`.fmt`
	font metrics	`.tfm`
Output	formatted result	`.dvi .pdf`
	transcript	`.log`
Bibliography (BIBTEX)	input / output	`.aux` / `.bbl`
	database / style / transcript	`.bib` / `.bst` / `.blg`
Index (MakeIndex)	input / output	`.idx` / `.ind`
	style / transcript	`.ist` / `.ilg`

Table 1.1: Overview of the file types used by TEX and LATEX

a file (extension `.ind`) that is itself input to LATEX. For makeindex, the *index style information* file has an extension of `.ist` and its transcript file has an extension `.ilg`; in contrast xindy appears not to use any predefined file types.

Citations and bibliography Information about bibliographic citations (see Chapter 12) in a document is normally output by LATEX to the *auxiliary* file. This information is used first to extract the necessary information from a bibliographic database and then to sort it; the sorted version is put into a *bibliography* file (extension `.bbl`) that is itself input to LATEX. If the system uses BIBTEX (see Chapter 13) for this task, then the *bibliographic database* files will have an extension of `.bib`, and information about the process will be in a *bibliography style* file (extension `.bst`). Its transcript file has the extension `.blg`.

Using \specials Because of the limitations of TEX, especially its failure to handle graphics, it is often necessary to complete the formatting of some elements of the typeset document after TEX has positioned everything and written this information to the `.dvi` file. This is normally done by attaching extra information and handling instructions at the correct "geometrical position in the typeset document", using

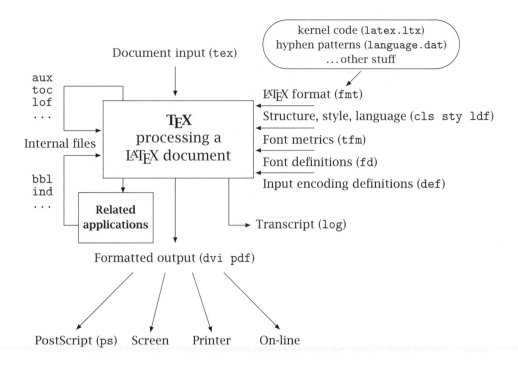

Figure 1.1: Data flow in the LATEX system

TEX's \special primitive that simply puts this information at the correct place in the .dvi file (see Chapter 10). This information may be simply the name of a graphics file to be input; or it may be instructions in a graphics language. Currently the most common such secondary formatter is a PostScript interpreter. To use this method, all information output by TEX to the .dvi file, including that in the \specials, must be transformed into PostScript code; applications to do this form part of all LATEX systems.   *PostScript*

Once the document has been successfully processed by TEX (and possibly transformed into PostScript), you will probably want to take a look at the format-   *Seeing is believing* ted text. This is commonly done on screen, but detailed inspection of printed output should always be performed via printing on paper at the highest available resolution. The applications available for viewing documents on screen still (as of late 2003) vary quite a lot from system to system. Some require a .dvi file, while others use a .ps file. A current favorite approach is to use a .pdf file, especially when electronic distribution of the formatted document is required. Occasionally you will find that some applications will produce much better quality screen output than others; this is due to limitations of the different technologies and the availability of suitable font resources.

1.3 Working with this book

This final section of Chapter 1 gives an overview of the structure of this book, the typographic conventions used, and ways to use the examples given throughout the book.

1.3.1 What's here

Following is a summary of the subject areas covered by each chapter and appendix. In principle, the remaining chapters can be read independently since, when necessary, pointers are given to where necessary supplementary information can be found in other parts of the book.

Chapter 1   gives a short introduction to the LaTeX system and this book.

Chapter 2   discusses document structure markup, including sectioning commands and cross-references.

Chapter 3   describes LaTeX's basic typesetting commands.

Chapter 4   explains how to influence the visual layout of the pages in various ways.

Chapter 5   shows how to lay out material in columns and rows, on single and multiple pages.

Chapter 6   discusses floating material and caption formatting.

Chapter 7   discusses in detail LaTeX's Font Selection Scheme and shows how to access new fonts.

Chapter 8   reviews mathematical typesetting, particularly the packages supported by the American Mathematical Society.

Chapter 9   describes support for using LaTeX with multiple languages, particularly the babel system.

Chapter 10 covers the simpler extensions of LaTeX for graphics, including the use of PostScript.

Chapter 11 discusses the preparation and typesetting of an index; the programs makeindex and xindy are described.

Chapter 12 describes LaTeX's support for the different bibliographical reference schemes in common use.

Chapter 13 explains how to use bibliographical databases in conjunction with LaTeX and how to generate typeset bibliographies according to publishers' expectations.

Chapter 14 shows how to document LaTeX files and how to use such files provided by others.

Appendix A reviews how to handle and manipulate the basic LaTeX programming structures and how to produce class and package files.

Appendix B discusses how to trace and resolve problems.

Appendix C explains how to obtain the packages and systems described in this book and the support systems available.

Appendix D briefly introduces the TLC2 TeX CD-ROM (at the back of the book).

Some of the material covered in the book may be considered "low-level" TeX that has no place in a book about LaTeX. However, to the authors' knowledge, much of this information has never been described in the "LaTeX" context though it is important. Moreover, we do not think that it would be helpful simply to direct readers to books like *The TeXbook*, because most of the advice given in books about Plain TeX is either not applicable to LaTeX or, worse, produces subtle errors if used with LaTeX. In some sections we have, therefore, tried to make the treatment as self-contained as possible by providing all the information about the underlying TeX engine that is relevant and useful within the LaTeX context.

1.3.2 Typographic conventions

It is essential that the presentation of the material conveys immediately its function in the framework of the text. Therefore, we present below the typographic conventions used in this book.

Throughout the text, LaTeX command and environment names are set in mono-spaced type (e.g., \caption, enumerate, \begin{tabular}), while names of package and class files are in sans serif type (e.g., article). Commands to be typed by the user on a computer terminal are shown in monospaced type and are underlined (e.g., This is user input). *Commands, environments, packages, ...*

The syntax of the more complex LaTeX commands is presented inside a rectan-gular box. Command arguments are shown in italic type: *Syntax descriptions*

\titlespacing*{*cmd*}{*left-sep*}{*before-sep*}{*after-sep*}[*right-sep*]

In LaTeX, optional arguments are denoted with square brackets and the star indicates a variant form (i.e., is also optional), so the above box means that the \titlespacing command can come in four different incarnations:

```
\titlespacing{cmd}{left-sep}{before-sep}{after-sep}
\titlespacing{cmd}{left-sep}{before-sep}{after-sep}[right-sep]
\titlespacing*{cmd}{left-sep}{before-sep}{after-sep}
\titlespacing*{cmd}{left-sep}{before-sep}{after-sep}[right-sep]
```

For some commands, not all combinations of optional arguments and/or star forms are valid. In that case the valid alternatives are explicitly shown together, as, for example, in the case of LaTeX's sectioning commands:

```
\section*{title}      \section[toc-entry]{title}
```

Here the optional *toc-entry* argument can be present only in the unstarred form; thus, we get the following valid possibilities:

```
\section*{title}
\section{title}
\section[toc-entry]{title}
```

Code examples … Lines containing examples with LaTeX commands are indented and are typeset in a monospaced type at a size somewhat smaller than that of the main text:

```
\addtocontents{lof}{\protect\addvspace{10pt}}
\addtocontents{lot}{\protect\addvspace{10pt}}
```

… with output … However, in the majority of cases we provide complete examples together with the output they produce side by side:

The right column shows the input text to be treated by LaTeX with preamble material shown in blue. In the left column one sees the result after typesetting.

```
\usepackage{ragged2e}

The right column shows the input text to be treated by
\LaTeX{} with preamble material shown in blue. In the
left column one sees the result after typesetting.
```

1-3-1

Note that all preamble commands are always shown in blue in the example source.

… with several pages … In case several pages need to be shown to prove a particular point, (partial) "page spreads" are displayed and usually framed to indicate that we are showing material from several pages.

1-3-2

1   A TEST
1   A test
Some text for our page which might get reused over and over again.
Page 6 of 7

1   A TEST
Some text for our page which might get reused over and over again.
Page 7 of 7

```
\usepackage{fancyhdr,lastpage}
\pagestyle{fancy}
\fancyhf{} % --- clear all fields
\fancyhead[RO,LE]{\leftmark}
\fancyfoot[C]{Page \thepage\
              of \pageref{LastPage}}
% \sample defined as before
\section{A test}
\sample \par \sample
```

A number of points should be noted here:

- We usually arrange the examples to show pages 6 and 7 so that a double spread is displayed.

- We often use the command \sample to hold a short piece of text to keep the example code short (the definition for this command is either given as part of the example or, as indicated here, repeated from an earlier example—which in this example is simply a lie as \sample is not defined).

- The output may or may not show a header and footer. In the above case it shows both.

For large examples, where the input and output cannot be shown conveniently alongside each other, the following layout is used:

... with large output ...

```
\usepackage{ragged2e}
This is a wide line, whose input commands and output result cannot
be shown nicely in two columns.
```

Depending on the example content, some additional explanation might appear between input and output (as in this case).

1-3-3

This is a wide line, whose input commands and output result cannot be shown nicely in two columns.

Chapter 8 shows yet another example format, where the margins of the example are explicitly indicated with thin blue vertical rules. This is done to better show the precise placement of displayed formulas and their tags in relation to the text margins.

... or with lines indicating the margins

1-3-4

(1) $(a + b)^2 = a^2 + 2ab + b^2$

```
\usepackage[leqno]{amsmath}
\begin{equation} (a+b)^2 = a^2+2ab+b^2 \end{equation}
```

All of these examples are "complete" if you mentally add a \documentclass line (with the article class[1] as an argument) and surround the body of the example with a document environment. In fact, this is how all of the (nearly 1000) examples in this book were produced. When processing the book, special LATEX commands take the source lines for an example and writes them to an external file, thereby automatically adding the \documentclass and the document environment lines. This turns each example into a small but complete LATEX document. These documents are then externally processed (using a mechanism that runs each example as often as necessary, including the generation of a bibliography through BIBTEX). The result is converted into small EPS graphics, which are then loaded in the appropriate place the next time LATEX is run on the whole book. More details on the actual implementation of this scheme can be found in Section 3.4.3 on page 162.

Throughout the book, blue notes are sprinkled in the margin to help you easily find certain information that would otherwise be hard to locate. In a few cases these notes exhibit a warning sign, indicating that you should probably read this information even if you are otherwise only skimming through the particular section.

Watch out for these

---

[1]Except for examples involving the \chapter command, which need the report or book class.

1.3.3 Using the examples

Our aim when producing this book was to make it as useful as possible for our readers. For this reason the book contains nearly 1000 complete, self-contained examples of all aspects of typesetting covered in the book.

These examples are made available in source format on CTAN in `info/ examples/tlc2` and are also provided on the accompanying CD-ROM in `Books/ tlc2/examples`. The examples are numbered per section, and each number is shown in a small box in the inner margin (e.g., 1-3-4 for the example on the preceding page). These numbers are also used for the external file names by appending `.ltx` (single-page examples) or `.ltx2` (double-page examples).

To reuse any of the examples it is usually sufficient to copy the preamble code (typeset in blue) into the preamble of your document and, if necessary, adjust the document text as shown. In some cases it might be more convenient to place the preamble code into your own package (or class file), thus allowing you to load this package in multiple documents using `\usepackage`. If you want to do the latter, there are two points to observe:

- Any use of `\usepackage` in the preamble code should be replaced by `\RequirePackage`, which is the equivalent command for use in package and class files (see Section A.4.5).

- Any occurrence of `\makeatletter` and `\makeatother` *must* be removed from the preamble code. This is very important because the `\makeatother` would stop correct reading of such a file.

So let us assume you wish to reuse the code from the following example:

1-3-5

1 Equations...

$$(a + b)^2 = a^2 + 2ab + b^2 \quad (1.1)$$

$$(a - b)^2 = a^2 - 2ab + b^2 \quad (1.2)$$

2 ...per section

$$(a + b)(a - b) = a^2 - b^2 \quad (2.1)$$

```
\makeatletter % '@' now normal "letter"
\@addtoreset{equation}{section}
\makeatother  % '@' is restored as "non-letter"
\renewcommand\theequation{\oldstylenums{\thesection}%
                 .\oldstylenums{\arabic{equation}}}
\section{Equations\ldots}
\begin{equation} (a+b)^2 = a^2 + 2ab + b^2\end{equation}
\begin{equation} (a-b)^2 = a^2 - 2ab + b^2\end{equation}

\section{\ldots per section}
\begin{equation} (a+b)(a-b) = a^2 -  b^2  \end{equation}
```

You have two alternatives: You can copy the preamble code (i.e., code colored blue) into your own document preamble or you can place that code—but without the `\makeatletter` and `\makeatother`—in a package file (e.g., `reseteqn.sty`) and afterwards load this "package" in the preamble of your own documents with `\usepackage{reseteqn}`.

CHAPTER 2

The Structure of a LaTeX Document

One of the ideas behind LaTeX is the separation between layout and structure (as far as possible), which allows the user to concentrate on content rather than having to worry about layout issues [104]. This chapter explains how this general principle is implemented in LaTeX.

The first section of this chapter shows how document class files, packages, options, and preamble commands can affect the structure and layout of a document. The logical subdivisions of a document are discussed in general, before explaining in more detail how sectioning commands and their arguments define a hierarchical structure, how they generate numbers for titles, and how they produce running heads and feet. Different ways of typesetting section titles are presented with the help of examples. It is also shown how the information that is written to the table of contents can be controlled and how the look of this table, as well as that of the lists of tables and figures, can be customized. The final section introduces LaTeX commands for managing cross-references and their scoping rules.

2.1 The structure of a source file

You can use LaTeX for several purposes, such as writing an article or a letter, or producing overhead slides. Clearly, documents for different purposes may need different logical structures, i.e., different commands and environments. We say that a document belongs to a *class* of documents having the same general structure (but not necessarily the same typographical appearance). You specify the class to which your document belongs by starting your LaTeX file with a \documentclass command, where the mandatory parameter specifies the name of the *document class*. The document class defines the available logical commands and environments (for example, `\chapter` in the `report` class) as well as a default formatting for those elements. An optional argument allows you to modify the formatting of those elements by supplying a list of *class options*. For example, `11pt` is an option recognized by most document classes that instructs LaTeX to choose eleven point as the basic document type size.

Many LaTeX commands described in this book are not specific to a single class but can be used with several classes. A collection of such commands is called a package and you inform LaTeX about your use of certain packages in the document by placing one or more `\usepackage` commands after `\documentclass`.

Just like the `\documentclass` declaration, `\usepackage` has a mandatory argument consisting of the name of the package and an optional argument that can contain a list of *package options* that modify the behavior of the package.

The document classes and the packages reside in external files with the extensions `.cls` and `.sty`, respectively. Code for class options is sometimes stored in files (in this case with the extension `.clo`) but is normally directly specified in the class or package file (see Appendix A for information on declaring options in classes and packages). However, in case of options, the file name can differ from the option name. For example, the option `11pt` might be related to `art11.clo` when used in the `article` class and to `bk11.clo` inside the `book` class.

The document preamble Commands placed between `\documentclass` and `\begin{document}` are in the so-called *document preamble*. All style parameters must be defined in this preamble, either in package or class files or directly in the document *before* the `\begin{document}` command, which sets the values for some of the global parameters. A typical document preamble could look similar to the following:

```
\documentclass[twocolumn,a4paper]{article}
\usepackage{multicol}
\usepackage[german,french]{babel}
\addtolength\textheight{3\baselineskip}
\begin{document}
```

This document preamble defines that the class of the document is `article` and that the layout is influenced by the formatting request `twocolumn` (typeset in two columns) and the option `a4paper` (print on A4 paper). The first `\usepackage` declaration informs LaTeX that this document contains commands and structures provided by the package `multicol`. In addition, the `babel` package with the options `german` (support for German language) and `french` (support for French language) is loaded. Finally, the default height of the text body was enlarged by three lines for this document.

Generally, nonstandard LaTeX package files contain modifications, extensions, or improvements[1] with respect to standard LaTeX, while commands in the pream-

---

[1] Many of these packages have become de facto standards and are described in this book. This

ble define changes for the current document. Thus, to modify the layout of a document, you have several possibilities:

- Change the standard settings for parameters in a class file by options defined for that class.

- Add one or more packages to your document and make use of them.

- Change the standard settings for parameters in a package file by options defined for that package.

- Write your own local packages containing special parameter settings and load them with \usepackage after the package or class they are supposed to modify (as explained in the next section).

- Make final adjustments inside the preamble.

If you want to get deeper into LaTeX's internals, you can, of course, define your own general-purpose packages that can be manipulated with options. You will find additional information on this topic in Appendix A.

2.1.1 Processing of options and packages

Today's LaTeX makes a clear distinction between declared options (of a class or package) and general-purpose package files. The latter have to be specified using the \usepackage command. Think of options as properties of the whole document (when used in \documentclass) or as properties of individual packages (if specified in \usepackage).

You can specify options in a \usepackage command only if these options are declared by the package. Otherwise, you will receive an error message, informing you that your specified option is unknown to the package in question. Options to the \documentclass are handled slightly differently. If a specified option is not declared by the class, it will be assumed to be a "global option".

All options to \documentclass (both declared and global ones) are automatically passed as class options to all \usepackage declarations. Thus, if a package file loaded with a \usepackage declaration recognizes (i.e., declares) some of the class options, it can take appropriate actions. If not, the class options will be ignored while processing that package. Because all options have to be defined inside the class or package file, their actions are under the control of the class or package (an action can be anything from setting internal switches to reading an external file). For this reason their order in the optional argument of \documentclass or \usepackage is (usually) irrelevant.

---

does not mean, however, that packages that are not described here are necessarily less important or useful, of inferior quality, or should not be used. We merely concentrated on a few of the more established ones; for others, we chose to explain what functionality is possible in a given area.

If you want to use several packages, all taking the same options (for example, none), it is possible to load them all with a single \usepackage command by specifying the package names as a comma-separated list in the mandatory argument. For example,

```
\usepackage[german]{babel}     \usepackage[german]{varioref}
\usepackage{multicol}          \usepackage{epic}
```

is equivalent to

```
\usepackage[german]{babel,varioref} \usepackage{multicol,epic}
```

Specifying german as a global option to the class can further shorten the \usepackage declaration as german will be passed to all loaded packages and thus will be processed by those packages that declare it.

```
\documentclass[german]{book}
\usepackage{babel,varioref,multicol,epic}
```

Of course, this assumes that neither multicol nor epic changes its behavior when german is passed as a class option.

Finally, when the \begin{document} is reached, all global options are checked to see whether each has been used by at least one package; if not, a warning message is displayed. It is usually a spelling mistake if your option name is never used; another possibility is the removal of a \usepackage command loading a package that used this option previously.

If you want to make some modifications to a document class or a package (for example, changing parameter values or redefining some commands), you should put the relevant code into a separate file with the extension .sty. Then load this file with a \usepackage command after the package whose behavior you wish to modify (or the document class, if your modifications concern class issues).

Alternatively, you can insert the modifications directly into the preamble of your document. In that case, you may have to bracket them with \makeatletter and \makeatother if they contain internal LaTeX commands (i.e., those with an @ sign in their names). For more details see the discussion on page 843 concerning internal commands in the preamble.

2.1.2   Splitting the source file into parts

LaTeX source documents can be conveniently split into several parts by using \include commands. Moreover, documents can be reformatted piecewise by specifying as arguments of an \includeonly command only those files LaTeX has to reprocess. For the other files that are specified in \include statements, the counter information (page, chapter, table, figure, equation, ...) will be read from the corresponding .aux files as long as they have been generated during a previous run.

Partial processing

In the following example, the user wants to reprocess only files `chap1.tex` and `appen1.tex`:

```
\documentclass{book}        % the document class ''book''
\includeonly{chap1,appen1} % only include chap1 and appen1
\begin{document}
\include{chap1}             % input chap1.tex
\include{chap2}             % input chap2.tex
\include{chap3}             % input chap3.tex
\include{appen1}            % input appen1.tex
\include{appen2}            % input appen2.tex
\end{document}
```

Be aware that LaTeX only issues a warning message like "No file xxx.tex" when it cannot find a file specified in an `\include` statement, not an error message, and continues processing.

If the information in the `.aux` files is up-to-date, it is possible to process only part of a document and have all counters, cross-references, and pages be corrected in the reformatted part. However, if one of the counters (including the page number for cross-references) changes in the reprocessed part, then the complete document might have to be rerun to get the index, table of contents, and bibliographic references consistently correct.

Note that each document part loaded via `\include` starts on a new page and finishes by calling `\clearpage`; thus, floats contained therein will not move outside the pages produced by this part. So natural candidates for `\include` are whole chapters of a book but not necessarily small fractions of text.

While it is certainly an advantage to split a larger document into smaller parts and to work on more manageable files with a text editor, partial reformatting should be used only with great care and when still in the developing stage for one or more chapters. When a final and completely correct copy is needed, the only safe procedure is to reprocess the complete document. If a document is too large to process in a single run, it can be subdivided into parts that can be run separately. However, in this case, the pieces must be processed *in the correct sequence* (if necessary several times), to ensure that the cross-references and page numbers are correct.

If you intend to work with `\include` commands, consider using the small package askinclude created by Pablo Straub. It interactively asks you which files *Interactive inclusion* to include. You can then specify the files as a comma-separated list (i.e., what you would put into the `\includeonly` argument). If the Enter button is pressed in response, then the files from the previous run are included automatically (except on the first run, where this response means to include all files). If the answer is a *, then all files are included; a – means no files should be included. This way you do not have to modify your master source to process different parts of your document (a very useful feature during the production of this book).

Excluding instead An extension to the \include mechanism is provided by the package
of including excludeonly created by Dan Luecking and Donald Arseneau. It offers the command \excludeonly, which takes a comma-separated list of \include file names
and prevents their inclusion. If both \includeonly and \excludeonly are used,
then only the files permitted by both declarations are used. For example,

```
\includeonly{chap1,chap2,chap3,appen1}
\excludeonly{chap2,chap3,appen2}
```

results in only chap1 and appen1 being included. This behavior actually contra-
dicts the package name, which indicates that "only" the given list is excluded. You
can achieve effect this by calling the package with the option only, in which case
an \includeonly declaration is ignored.

This package redefines the internal \@include command, so it will not work
with packages or classes that redefine this command as well. Known conflicts are
with the document classes paper and thesis by Wenzel Matiaske.

2.1.3 Combining several files

When sending a LATEX document to another person you may have to send local or
uncommon package files (e.g., your private modifications to some packages) along
with the source. In such cases it is often helpful if you can put all the information
required to process the document into a single file.

For this purpose, LATEX provides the environment filecontents. This environment takes one argument, the name of a file;[1] its body consists of the contents
of this file. It is only allowed to appear before a \documentclass declaration. The
\begin and \end tags should be placed on lines of their own in the source. In
particular, there should be no material following them, or you will get LATEX errors.

If LATEX encounters such an environment, it will try to find the mentioned file
name. If it cannot, it will write the body of the environment verbatim into a file
in the current directory and inform you about this action. Conversely, if a file
with the given name was found by LATEX, it will inform you that it has ignored this
instance of the filecontents environment because the file is already present on
the file system.

The generated file will get a few comment lines (using % as a comment character) added to the top to announce that this file was written by a filecontents
environment:

```
%% LaTeX2e file 'foo.txt'
%% generated by the 'filecontents' environment
%% from source 'test' on 2003/04/16.
```

---

[1]If no extension is specified, the actual external file name will be the one LATEX would read if you
used this name as an argument to \input, e.g., typically adding the extension .tex.

If this is not appropriate—for example, if the file is not a LATEX file—use the `filecontents*` environment instead, which does not produce such extra lines.

To get a list of (nearly) all files used in your document (so that you know what you might have to pack together), specify the command `\listfiles` in the preamble.

2.1.4 optional—Providing variants in the document source

Sometimes it is useful to keep several versions of a document together in a single source, especially if most of the text is shared between versions. This functionality is provided by the optional package by created Donald Arseneau.

The variant text parts are specially marked in the source using the command `\opt`, and during formatting some of them are selected. The command takes two arguments: a label (or a comma-separated list of labels) that describes to which variant the optional text belongs, and the text to be conditionally printed. Because the text is given in an argument, it cannot contain `\verb` commands and must have balanced braces. This approach works well enough for shorter texts. With longer parts to be optionally printed, however, it is usually best to store them in an external file and conditionally load this file using the `\opt` command, as was done in the example below.

There are a number of ways to select which variants are to be printed. The following example shows the non-interactive way, where the variants to be printed are specified by selecting them as options on the `\usepackage` declaration.

Typeset this if option code was declared. Typeset this for either doc or code. Typeset this always.

`2-1-1`

```
\usepackage[code]{optional}
\opt{doc}{Typeset this if option doc was declared.}
\opt{code}{Typeset this if option code was declared.}
\opt{doc,code}{Typeset this for either doc or code.}
Typeset this always.      \opt{}{and this never!}
\opt{doc}{\input{examples}}
```

Alternatively, you can prompt the user each time for a list of options by including the declaration `\AskOptions` in the preamble, though that can become tedious if used too often. To help the person select the right options interactively you can define the command `\ExplainOptions`—if defined, its replacement text will be displayed on the terminal prior to asking for a list of options.

If your LATEX implementation supports passing LATEX code instead of a file name to the program, there is a third way to select the variants. If you invoke LATEX with the line

```
latex "\newcommand\UseOption{doc,code}\input{file}"
```

then the variants with the labels doc and code will be used (in addition to those specified on the `\usepackage`, if any). The example command line above would be suitable for a UN*X system; on other platforms, you might need different quotes.

The optional package selects the variants to process during the LaTeX formatting. Depending on the application, it might be better to use a different approach involving a preprocessor that extracts individual variants from the master source. For example, the docstrip program can be successfully used for this purpose; in contrast to other preprocessors, it has the advantage that it will be usable at every site that has an installed LaTeX system (see Section 14.2 for details).

2.2   Sectioning commands

The standard LaTeX document classes (i.e., article, report, and book) contain commands and environments to define the different hierarchical structural units of a document (e.g., chapters, sections, appendices). Each such command defines a nesting level inside a hierarchy and each structural unit belongs to some level.

A typical document (such as an article) consists of a title, some sections with probably a multilevel nested substructure, and a list of references. To describe such a structure the title-generating command \maketitle, sectioning commands such as \section and \subsection, and the thebibliography environment are used. The commands should be correctly nested. For example, a \subsection command should be issued only after a previous \section.

Longer works (such as reports, manuals, and books) start with more complex title information, are subdivided into chapters (and parts), provide cross-reference information (table of contents, list of figures, list of tables, and indexes), and probably have appendices. In such a document you can easily distinguish the *front matter*, *body*, and *back matter*. In LaTeX's book class these three parts can be explicitly marked up using the commands \frontmatter, \mainmatter, and \backmatter. In other classes you often find only the command \appendix, which is used to separate the body matter from the back matter.

In the front matter the so-called *starred form* of the \section or \chapter sectioning command is normally used. This form suppresses the numbering of a heading. Sectional units with fixed names, such as "Introduction", "Index", and "Preface", are usually not numbered. In the standard classes, the commands \tableofcontents, \listoftables, and \listoffigures, and the theindex and thebibliography environments internally invoke the command (\section or \chapter) using their starred form.

Standard LaTeX provides the set of sectioning commands shown in Table 2.1. The \chapter command defines level zero of the hierarchical structure of a document, \section defines level one, and so on, whereas the optional \part command defines the level minus one (or zero in classes that do not define \chapter). Not all of these commands are defined in all document classes. The article class does not have \chapter and the letter class does not support sectioning commands at all. It is also possible for a package to define other sectioning commands, allowing either additional levels or variants for already supported levels.

\part (in book and report)	level −1	\part (in article)	level 0
\chapter (only book and report)	level 0	\section	level 1
\subsection	level 2	\subsubsection	level 3
\paragraph	level 4	\subparagraph	level 5

Table 2.1: LATEX's standard sectioning commands

Generally, the sectioning commands automatically perform one or more of the following typesetting actions:

- Produce the heading number reflecting the hierarchical level.

- Store the heading as an entry for a table of contents (into the .toc file).

- Save the contents of the heading to be (perhaps) used in a running head and/or foot.

- Format the heading.

All sectioning commands have a common syntax as exemplified here by the \section command:

| \section*{*title*}   \section[*toc-entry*]{*title*} |

The starred form (e.g., \section*{...}) suppresses the numbering for a title and does not produce an entry in the table of contents or the running head. In the second form the optional argument *toc-entry* is used when the text string for the table of contents and the running head and/or foot is different from the printed title. If this variant is used, numbering depends on the current value of the counter secnumdepth (discussed in the next section).

If you try to advise TEX on how to split the heading over a few lines using the "~" symbol or the \\ command, then side effects may result when formatting the table of contents or generating the running head. In this case the simplest solution is to repeat the heading text without the specific markup in the optional parameter of the sectioning command.

Problems with explicit formatting

The remainder of this section discusses how the appearance of headings can be modified. It explains how to define a command like \section that has the above syntax, produces a table of contents entry if desired, but has a thick rule above its heading text or uses a normal-sized *italic* font rather than a large **bold** one.

First, some examples show how to change the numbering of headings. Next, examples demonstrate how to enter information about headings into the table of contents. Finally, changes to the general layout of headings are discussed, showing what LATEX offers to define them.

2.2.1 Numbering headings

To support numbering, LaTeX uses a counter for each sectional unit and composes the heading number from these counters.

Numbering no headings

Perhaps the change desired most often concerning the numbering of titles is to alter the nesting level up to which a number should be produced. This is controlled by a counter named `secnumdepth`, which holds the highest level with numbered headings. For example, some documents have none of their headings numbered. Instead of always using the starred form of the sectioning commands, it is more convenient to set the counter `secnumdepth` to `-2` in the document preamble. The advantages of this method are that an entry in the table of contents can still be produced, and that arguments from the sectioning commands can produce information in running headings. As discussed above, these features are suppressed in the starred form.

Numbering all headings

To number all headings down to `\subparagraph` or whatever the deepest sectioning level for the given class is called, setting the counter to a high enough value (e.g., a declaration such as `\setcounter{secnumdepth}{10}` should normally be sufficient).

Finally, the `\addtocounter` command provides an easy way of numbering more or fewer heading levels without worrying about the level numbers of the corresponding sectioning commands. For example, if you need one more level with numbers, you can place `\addtocounter{secnumdepth}{1}` in the preamble of your document without having to look up the right value.

Every sectioning command has an associated counter, which by convention has the same name as the sectioning command (e.g., the command `\subsection` has a corresponding counter `subsection`). This counter holds the current (formatted) number for the given sectioning command. Thus, in the report class, the commands `\chapter`, `\section`, `\subsection`, and so on represent the hierarchical structure of the document and a counter like `subsection` keeps track of the number of `\subsection`s used inside the current `\section`. Normally, when a counter at a given hierarchical level is stepped, then all lower-level counters (i.e., those with higher-level numbers) are reset. For example, the report class file contains the following declarations:

```
\newcounter{part}                       % (-1)  parts
\newcounter{chapter}                     % (0)   chapters
\newcounter{section}[chapter]            % (1)   sections
\newcounter{subsection}[section]         % (2)   subsections
\newcounter{subsubsection}[subsection]   % (3)   subsubsections
\newcounter{paragraph}[subsubsection]    % (4)   paragraphs
\newcounter{subparagraph}[paragraph]     % (5)   subparagraphs
```

These commands declare the various counters. The level one (`section`) counter is reset when the level zero (`chapter`) counter is stepped. Similarly, the level two (`subsection`) counter is reset whenever the level one (`section`) counter is

stepped. The same mechanism is used down to the \subparagraph command.
Note that in the standard classes the part counter is decoupled from the other
counters and has no influence on the lower-level sectioning commands. As a consequence, \chapters in the book or report class or \sections in article will be
numbered consecutively even if a \part command intervenes. Changing this is
simple—you just replace the corresponding declaration of the chapter counter
with:

```
\newcounter{chapter}[part]
```

The behavior of an already existing counter can be changed with the command
\@addtoreset (see Appendix A.1.4), for example,

```
\@addtoreset{chapter}{part}
```

Recall that the latter instruction, because of the presence of the @ character,
can be issued only inside a package file or in the document preamble between
\makeatletter and \makeatother commands, as explained on page 843.

Every counter in LaTeX, including the sectioning counters, has an associated
command constructed by prefixing the counter name with \the, which generates
a typeset representation of the counter in question. In case of the sectioning commands this representation form is used to produce the full number associated
with the commands, as in the following definitions:

```
\renewcommand\thechapter{\arabic{chapter}}
\renewcommand\thesection{\thechapter.\arabic{section}}
\renewcommand\thesubsection{\thesection.\arabic{subsection}}
```

In this example, \thesubsection produces an Arabic number representation of
the subsection counter prefixed by the command \thesection and a dot. This
kind of recursive definition facilitates modifications to the counter representations because changes do not need to be made in more than one place. If, for
example, you want to number sections using capital letters, you can redefine the
command \thesection:

A Different-looking section

```
\renewcommand\thesection{\Alph{section}}
```

A.1 Different-looking subsection

Due to the default definitions not only the numbers
on sections change, but lower-level sectioning commands also show this representation of the section
number.

```
\section{Different-looking section}
\subsection{Different-looking subsection}
Due to the default definitions not only the
numbers on sections change, but lower-level
sectioning commands also show this
representation of the section number.
```

2-2-1

Thus, by changing the counter representation commands, it is possible to
change the number displayed by a sectioning command. However, the representa-

tion of the number cannot be changed arbitrarily by this method. Suppose you want to produce a subsection heading with the number surrounded by a box. Given the above examples one straightforward approach would be to redefine \thesubsection, e.g.,

```
\renewcommand\thesubsection{\fbox{\thesection.\arabic{subsection}}}
```

But this is not correct, as one sees when trying to reference such a section.

3.1 A mistake

Referencing a subsection in this format produces a funny result as we can see looking at subsection 3.1. We get a boxed reference.

```
\renewcommand\thesubsection
    {\fbox{\thesection.\arabic{subsection}}}
\setcounter{section}{3}
\subsection{A mistake}\label{wrong}
Referencing a subsection in this format
produces a funny result as we can see
looking at subsection~\ref{wrong}.
We get a boxed reference.
```

2-2-2

In other words, the counter representation commands are also used by LaTeX's cross-referencing mechanism (the \label, \ref commands; see Section 2.4). Therefore, we can only make small changes to the counter representation commands so that their use in the \ref command still makes sense. To produce the box around the heading number without spoiling the output of a \ref, we have to redefine LaTeX's internal command \@seccntformat, which is responsible for typesetting the counter part of a section title. The default definition of \@seccntformat typesets the \the representation of the section counter (in the example above, it uses the \thesection command), followed by a fixed horizontal space of 1 em. Thus, to correct the problem, the previous example should be rewritten as follows:

```
\makeatletter
\renewcommand\@seccntformat[1]{\fbox
  {\csname the#1\endcsname}\hspace{0.5em}}
\makeatother
\section{This is correct}\label{sec:OK}
Referencing a section using this
definition generates the correct result
for the section reference~\ref{sec:OK}.
```

1 This is correct

Referencing a section using this definition generates the correct result for the section reference 1.

2-2-3

The framed box around the number in the section heading is now defined only in the \@seccntformat command, and hence the reference labels come out correctly.[1] Also note that we reduced the space between the box and the text to 0.5 em

---

[1] The command \@seccntformat takes as an argument the section level identifier, which is appended to the \the prefix to generate the presentation form needed via the \csname, \endcsname command constructor. In our example, the \@seccntformat command is called with the section argument and thus the replacement text \fbox{\csname thesection\endcsname\hspace{0.5em}} is generated. See the *TeXbook* [82] for more details about the \csname command.

(instead of the default 1 em). The definition of \@seccntformat applies to all headings defined with the \@startsection command (which is described in the next section). Therefore, if you wish to use different definitions of \@seccntformat for different headings, you must put the appropriate code into every heading definition.

2.2.2   Formatting headings

LaTeX provides a generic command called \@startsection that can be used to define a wide variety of heading layouts. To define or change a sectioning command one should find out whether \@startsection can do the job. If the desired layout is not achievable that way, then \secdef can be used to produce sectioning formats with arbitrary layout.

Headings can be loosely subdivided into two major groups: display and run-in headings. A display heading is separated by a vertical space from the preceding and the following text—most headings in this book are of this type.

A run-in heading is characterized by a vertical separation from the preceding text, but the text following the title continues on the same line as the heading itself, only separated from the latter by a horizontal space.

Run-in headings.   The present example shows what a run-in heading looks like. Text in the paragraph following the heading continues on the same line as the heading.

```
\paragraph{Run-in headings.}
The present example shows what a run-in
heading looks like. Text in the paragraph
following the heading continues on the
same line as the heading.
```

2-2-4

The generic command \@startsection allows both types of headings to be defined. Its syntax and argument description are as follows:

\@startsection{*name*}{*level*}{*indent*}{*beforeskip*}{*afterskip*}{*style*}

name   The name used to refer to the heading counter[1] for numbered headings and to define the command that generates a running header or footer (see page 218). For example, *name* would be the counter name, \the*name* would be the command to display the current heading number, and *name*mark would be the command for running headers. In most circumstances the *name* will be identical to the name of the sectioning command being defined, without the preceding backslash—but this is no requirement.

level   A number denoting the depth level of the sectioning command. This level is used to decide whether the sectioning command gets a number (if the level is less than or equal to secnumdepth; see Section 2.2.1 on page 24) or shows up in the table of contents (if the value is less or equal to tocdepth, see Section 2.3.2 on page 49). It should therefore reflect the position in the command

---
[1] This counter must exist; it is not defined automatically.

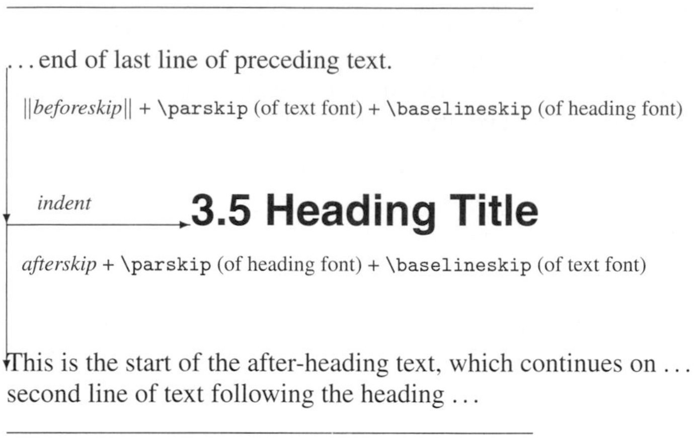

...end of last line of preceding text.

$\|beforeskip\|$ + \parskip (of text font) + \baselineskip (of heading font)

indent   **3.5 Heading Title**

afterskip + \parskip (of heading font) + \baselineskip (of text font)

This is the start of the after-heading text, which continues on ...
second line of text following the heading ...

2-2-5

Figure 2.1: The layout for a display heading (produced by layouts)

hierarchy of sectioning commands, where the outermost sectioning command has level zero.[1]

indent The indentation of the heading with respect to the left margin. By making the value negative, the heading will start in the outer margin. Making it positive will indent all lines of the heading by this amount.

beforeskip The absolute value of this parameter defines the space to be left in front of the heading. If the parameter is negative, then the indentation of the paragraph following the heading is suppressed. This dimension is a rubber length, that is, it can take a stretch and shrink component. Note that LaTeX starts a new paragraph before the heading, so that additionally the value of \parskip is added to the space in front.

afterskip The space to be left following a heading. It is the vertical space after a display heading or the horizontal space after a run-in heading. The sign of *afterskip* controls whether a display heading ($afterskip \geq 0$) or a run-in heading ($afterskip < 0$) is produced. In the first case a new paragraph is started so that the value of \parskip is added to the space after the heading. An unpleasant side effect of this parameter coupling is that it is impossible to define a display heading with an effective "after space" of less than \parskip using the \@startsection command. When you try to compensate for a positive \parskip value by using a negative *afterskip*, you change the display heading into a run-in heading.

style The style of the heading text. This argument can take any instruction that influences the typesetting of text, such as \raggedright, \Large, or \bfseries (see the examples below).

---

[1] In the book and report classes, the \part command actually has level -1 (see Table 2.1).

... end of last line of preceding text.

$\|beforeskip\|$ + \parskip (of text font) + \baselineskip (of heading font)

indent

afterskip (< 0)

3.5 Heading Title _____ Start of text ...

second line of text following the heading ...

2-2-6

Figure 2.2: The layout for a run-in heading (produced by layouts)

Figures 2.1 and 2.2 show these parameters graphically for the case of display and run-in headings, respectively.

Next we show how these arguments are used in practice to define new sectioning commands. Suppose that you want to change the \subsection command of a class like article to look roughly like this:

... some text above.

4.1 Example of a Section Heading

The heading is set in normal-sized italic and the separation from the preceding text is exactly one baseline. The separation from the text following is one-half baseline and this text is not indented.

2-2-7

```
% redefinition of \subsection shown below
\setcounter{section}{4} % simulate previous
                                   % sections

\ldots\ some text above.
\subsection{Example of a Section Heading}
The heading is set in normal-sized italic
and the separation from the preceding text
is exactly one baseline. The separation
from the text following is one-half
baseline and this text is not indented.
```

In this case the following redefinition for \subsection is needed:

```
\makeatletter
\renewcommand\subsection{\@startsection
  {subsection}{2}{0mm}%              % name, level, indent
  {-\baselineskip}%                  % beforeskip
  {0.5\baselineskip}%                % afterskip
  {\normalfont\normalsize\itshape}}% % style
\makeatother
```

The first argument is the string subsection to denote that we use the corresponding counter for heading numbers. In the sectional hierarchy we are at level two. The third argument is 0mm because the heading should start at the left margin. The absolute value of the fourth argument (*beforeskip*) specifies that a distance equal to one baseline must be left in front of the heading and, because the parameter is negative, that the indentation of the paragraph following the heading should be suppressed. The absolute value of the fifth parameter (*after-skip*) specifies that a distance equal to one-half baseline must be left following the heading and, because the parameter is positive, that a display heading has to be produced. Finally, according to the sixth parameter, the heading should be typeset in an italic font using a size equal to the normal document type size.

In fact, the redefinition is a bit too simplistic because, as mentioned earlier, on top of the absolute value of *beforeskip* and *afterskip*, LaTeX always adds the current value of \parskip. Thus, in layouts where this parameter is nonzero, we need to subtract it to achieve the desired separation.

Another layout, which is sometimes found in fiction books, is given by the following definition:

```
\makeatletter
\renewcommand\section{\@startsection
  {section}{1}{1em}%                        % name, level, indent
  {\baselineskip}%                          % beforeskip
  {-\fontdimen2\font                        % afterskip
    plus -\fontdimen3\font
    minus -\fontdimen4\font
  }%
  {\normalfont\normalsize\scshape}}%        % style
\makeatother
```

This defines a run-in heading using small capitals. The space definition for the horizontal *afterskip* deserves an explanation: it is the value of the stretchable space between words taken from the current font, negated to make a run-in heading. Details about \fontdimens can be found in Section 7.10.3 on page 426. The result is shown in the next example.

... some text above.

THE MAN started to run away from the truck. He saw that he was followed by

```
% redefinition of \section shown above
\setcounter{secnumdepth}{-2}

\ldots\ some text above.
\section{The man}
started to run away from the truck. He
saw that he was followed by
```

2-2-8

Of course, for such a layout one should turn off numbering of the headings by setting the counter secnumdepth to -2.

Simple heading style changes   Which commands can be used for setting the styles of the heading texts in the *style* argument of the \@startsection command? Apart from the font-changing directives (see Chapter 7), few instructions can be used here. A \centering command produces a centered display heading and a \raggedright declaration makes the text left justified. The use of \raggedleft is possible, but may give somewhat strange results. You can also use \hrule, \medskip, \newpage, or

similar commands that introduce local changes. The next example shows some
possible variations.

```
\makeatletter
\newcommand\Csub{\@startsection{subsection}{2}%
 {0pt}{-\baselineskip}{.2\baselineskip}%
 {\centering\itshape}}
\newcommand\Lsub{\@startsection{subsection}{2}%
 {0pt}{-\baselineskip}{.2\baselineskip}%
 {\raggedright\sffamily}}
\newcommand\Rsub{\@startsection{subsection}{2}%
 {0pt}{-\baselineskip}{.2\baselineskip}%
 {\raggedleft\MakeUppercase}}
\newcommand\Hsub{\@startsection{subsection}{2}%
 {0pt}{-\baselineskip}{.2\baselineskip}%
 {\hrule\medskip\itshape}}
\makeatother
```

1   A very long heading that shows the default behavior of LaTeX's sectioning commands

1.1   A subsection heading

The heading is centered using an italic font.

1.2   A subsection heading

The heading is left-justified using a sans serif font.

```
\section{A very long heading that shows
         the default behavior of \LaTeX's
         sectioning commands}
\Csub{A subsection heading}
The heading is centered using an italic font.
\Lsub{A subsection heading}
The heading is left-justified using a sans
serif font.
\Rsub{A subsection heading}
The heading is right-justified and uses
uppercase letters.
\Hsub{A subsection heading}
This heading has a horizontal rule above
the text.
```

1.3   A SUBSECTION HEADING

The heading is right-justified and uses upper-case letters.

1.4   A subsection heading

This heading has a horizontal rule above the
text.

2-2-9

In the standard LaTeX document classes, words in long headings are justified
and, if necessary, hyphenated as can be seen in the previous example. If this is
not wanted, then justification can be turned off by using \raggedright in the
style part of the \@startsection command. If line breaks are manually adjusted
using \\, then one has to repeat the heading title, without the extra formatting
instruction, in the optional argument. Otherwise, the line breaks will also show up
in the table of contents.

*Hyphenation
and line breaks
in headings*

1   A very long heading that shows the default behavior of LaTeX's sectioning commands

```
\makeatletter
\renewcommand\section{\@startsection{section}%
 {1}{0pt}{-\baselineskip}{.2\baselineskip}%
 {\normalfont\Large\bfseries\raggedright}}
\makeatother
\section{A very long heading that shows
         the default behavior of \LaTeX's
         sectioning commands}
```

2-2-10

Indentation after   Finally, a few words about the suppression of the indentation for the first
a heading   paragraph after a display heading. Standard LaTeX document classes, following
(American) English typographic tradition, suppress the indentation in this case.
All first paragraphs after a display heading can be indented by specifying the
package indentfirst (David Carlisle).

In the standard LaTeX classes the highest-level sectioning commands \part
Complex heading   and \chapter produce their titles without using \@startsection since their lay-
layout definitions   out cannot be produced with that command. Similarly, you may also want to construct sectioning commands without limitations. In this case you must follow a
few conventions to allow LaTeX to take all the necessary typesetting actions when
executing them.

The command \secdef can help you when defining such commands by providing an easy interface to the three possible forms of section headings, as shown
in the case of the \part command. With the definition

```
\newcommand\part{\secdef\cmda\cmdb}
```

the following actions take place:

\part{*title*}	will invoke	\cmda[*title*]{*title*}
\part[*toc-entry*]{*title*}	will invoke	\cmda[*toc-entry*]{*title*}
\part*{*title*}	will invoke	\cmdb{*title*}

The commands you have to provide are a (re)definition[1] of \part and a definition
of the commands labeled \cmda or \cmdb, respectively. Note that \cmda has an
optional argument containing the text to be entered in the table of contents .toc
file, while the second (mandatory) argument, as well as the single argument to
\cmdb, specifies the heading text to be typeset. Thus, the definitions must have
the following structure:

```
\newcommand\part{ ... \secdef \cmda \cmdb }
\newcommand\cmda[2][default]{ ... }
\newcommand\cmdb[1]{ ... }
```

An explicit example is a simplified variant of \appendix. It redefines the
\section command to produce headings for appendices (by invoking either the
\Appendix or \sAppendix command), changing the presentation of the section
counter and resetting it to zero. The modified \section command also starts a
new page, sets a special format for the first page (see Chapter 4), prohibits floats
from appearing at the top of the first page, and suppresses the indentation of the
first paragraph in a section.

---

[1] Redefinition in case you change an existing heading command such as \part in the preamble of
your document.

```
\renewcommand\appendix{%
  \renewcommand\section{%                    Redefinition of \section
      \newpage\thispagestyle{plain}%
      \secdef\Appendix\sAppendix}%
  \setcounter{section}{0}%
  \renewcommand\thesection{\Alph{section}}%
}
```

In the definition below you can see how \Appendix advances the section
counter using the \refstepcounter command (the latter also resets all subsidiary counters and defines the "current reference string"; see Section 2.4). It
writes a line into the .toc file with the \addcontentsline command, performs
the formatting of the heading title, and saves the title for running heads and/or
feet by calling \sectionmark.

```
\newcommand\Appendix[2][?]{%   Complex form
    \refstepcounter{section}%
    \addcontentsline{toc}{appendix}%
        {\protect\numberline{\appendixname~\thesection} #1}%
    {\flushright\large\bfseries\appendixname\ \thesection\par
     \centering#2\par}%
    \sectionmark{#1}\addvspace{\baselineskip}}
```

The \sAppendix command (starred form) performs only the formatting.

```
\newcommand\sAppendix[1]{%                  Simplified (starred) form
      {\flushright\large\bfseries\appendixname\par
       \centering#1\par}%
      \addvspace{\baselineskip}}
```

Applying these definitions will produce the following output:

Appendix A
The list of all commands

Then follows the text of the first section
in the appendix. Some more text in the appendix. Some more text in the appendix.

```
%% Example needs commands introduced above!
\appendix
\section{The list of all commands}
```

```
Then follows the text of the first section in
the appendix.  Some more text in the appendix.
Some more text in the appendix.
```

2-2-11

Do not forget that the example shown above represents only a simplified version of a redefined \section command. Among other things, we did not take
into account the secnumdepth counter, which contains the numbering threshold.
You might also have to foresee code dealing with various types of document formats, such as one- and two-column output, or one- and two-sided printing (see
Chapter 4).

Command	Default
\abstractname	Abstract
\appendixname	Appendix
\bibname	Bibliography
\chaptername	Chapter
\contentsname	Contents
\indexname	Index
\listfigurename	List of Figures
\listtablename	List of Tables
\partname	Part
\refname	References

Table 2.2: Language-dependent strings for headings

2.2.3   Changing fixed heading texts

Some of the standard heading commands produce predefined texts. For example, \chapter produces the string "Chapter" in front of the user-supplied text. Similarly, some environments generate headings with predefined texts. For example, by default the abstract environment displays the word "Abstract" above the text of the abstract supplied by the user. LaTeX defines these strings as command sequences (see Table 2.2) so that you can easily customize them to obtain your favorite names. This is shown in the example below, where the default name "Abstract", as defined in the article class, is replaced by the word "Summary".

Summary

This book describes how to modify the appearance of documents produced with the LaTeX typesetting system.

```
\renewcommand\abstractname{Summary}
\begin{abstract}
 This book describes how to modify the
 appearance of documents produced with
 the \LaTeX{} typesetting system.
\end{abstract}
```

2-2-12

The standard LaTeX class files define a few more strings. See Section 9.1.3, and especially Table 9.2 on page 547, for a full list and a discussion of the babel system, which provides translations of these strings in more than twenty languages.

2.2.4   fncychap—Predefined chapter heading layouts

For those who wish to have fancy chapter headings without much work there exists the package fncychap (Ulf Lindgren). It provides six distinctive layout styles for the \chapter command that can be activated by loading the package with one of the following options: Sonny, Lenny, Glenn, Conny, Rejne, or Bjarne. Because the package is intended for modifying the \chapter command, it works only with document classes that provide this command (e.g., report and book, but not article and its derivatives). As an example we show the results of using the option Lenny.

```
┌──────────            ──────────────┐
│           1                        │
│                                    │
Chapter   1     ────────────────────┘
```

2-2-13   **A Package Test**

```
\usepackage[Lenny]{fncychap}
\chapter{A Package Test}
```

The package also offers several commands to modify the layouts in various ways. It comes with a short manual that explains how to provide your own layouts.

2.2.5 quotchap—Mottos on chapters

Another way to enhance \chapter headings is provided by the quotchap package created by Karsten Tinnefeld. It allows the user to specify quotation(s) that will appear on the top left of the chapter title area.

The quotation(s) for the next chapter are specified in a savequote environment; the width of the quotation area can be given as an optional argument defaulting to 10cm. Each quotation should finish with a \qauthor command to denote its source, though it would be possible to provide your own formatting manually.

The default layout produced by the package can be described as follows: the quotations are placed flush left, followed by vertical material stored in the command \chapterheadstartvskip. It is followed by a very large chapter number, typeset flush right in 60% gray, followed by the chapter title text, also typeset flush right. After a further vertical separation, taken from the command \chapterheadendvskip, the first paragraph of the chapter is started without indentation.

The number can be printed in black by specifying the option nogrey to the package. To print the chapter number in one of the freely available PostScript fonts, you can choose among a number of options, such as charter for Bitstream's Charter BT or times for Adobe's Times. By default, Adobe's Bookman is chosen. Alternatively, you could redefine the \chapnumfont command, which is responsible for selecting the font for the chapter number. Finally, the font for the chapter title can be influenced by redefining the \sectfont command as shown in the example.

This, together with the possibilities offered by redefining the commands \chapterheadstartvskip and \chapterheadendvskip, allows you to produce a number of interesting layouts. The example below uses a negative vertical skip to move the quotation on the same level as the number (in Avantgarde) and set the title and quotation in Helvetica.

Cookies! Give me some cookies!
Cookie Monster

A Package Test

```
\usepackage[avantgarde]{quotchap}
\renewcommand\chapterheadstartvskip
                {\vspace*{-5\baselineskip}}
% select Helvetica for title and quote
\usepackage{helvet}
\renewcommand\sectfont{\sffamily\bfseries}
\begin{savequote}[10pc]
 \sffamily
 Cookies! Give me some cookies!
 \qauthor{Cookie Monster}
\end{savequote}
\chapter{A Package Test}
```

Adding this package changes the chapter heading dramatically.

Adding this package changes the chapter heading dramatically.

2-2-14

If you want quotations on your chapters but prefer one of the layouts provided by fncychap, you can try to combine both packages. Load the latter package *after* quotchap. Of course, the customization possibilities described above are then no longer available but savequote will still work, although the quotations will appear always in a fixed position above the heading.

2.2.6 titlesec—A different approach to headings

The information presented so far in this chapter has focused on the tools and mechanisms provided by the LaTeX kernel for defining and manipulating headings, as well as a few packages that provide some extra features, such as predefined layouts, built on top of the standard tools.

The titlesec package created by Javier Bezos approaches the topic differently by providing a complete reimplementation for the heading commands. Javier's approach overcomes some of the limitations inherent in the original tools and provides a cleaner and more generic interface. The disadvantage is that this package might introduce some incompatibilities with extensions based on the original interfaces. Whether this possibility turns out to be a real issue clearly depends on the task at hand and is likely to vanish more or less completely the moment this interface comes into more widespread use.

The package supports two interfaces: a simple one for smaller adjustments, which is realized mainly by options to the package, and an extended interface to make more elaborate modifications.

The basic interface

The basic interface lets you modify the font characteristics of all headings by specifying one or more options setting a font family (rm, sf, tt), a font series (md, bf), or a font shape (up, it, sl, sc). The title size can be influenced by selecting one of the following options: big (same sizes as for standard LATEX classes), tiny (all headings except for chapters in text size), or medium or small, which are layouts between the two extremes. The alignment is controlled by raggedleft, center, or raggedright, while the vertical spacing can be reduced by specifying the option compact.

To modify the format of the number accompanying a heading, the command \titlelabel is available. Within it \thetitle refers to the current sectioning number, such as \thesection or \thesubsection. The declaration applies to all headings, as can be seen in the next example.

1. A section

1.1. A subsection

1.1.1. A subsubsection

Three headings following each other, a situation you will not see often ...

2-2-15

```
\usepackage[sf,bf,tiny,center]{titlesec}
\titlelabel{\thetitle.\enspace}
\section{A section}
\subsection{A subsection}
\subsubsection{A subsubsection}
Three headings following each other, a situation you
will not see often \ldots
```

<big>\titleformat*{*cmd*}{*format*}</big>

The basic interface offers one more command, \titleformat*, that takes two arguments. The first argument (*cmd*) is a sectioning command we intend to modify. The second argument (*format*) contains the formatting instruction that should be applied to this particular heading. This declaration works on individual sectioning commands, and its use overwrites all font or alignment specifications given as options to the package (i.e., the options rm, it, and raggedleft in the following example). The last command used in the second argument can be a command with one argument—it will receive the title text if present. In the next example we use this feature to set the \subsubsection title in lowercase (though this looks rather ugly with full-sized numbers).

1   A section

1.1   A subsection

1.1.1   A SUBSUBSECTION

Three headings following each other, a situation you will not see often ...

2-2-16

```
\usepackage[rm,it,raggedleft,tiny,compact]{titlesec}
\titleformat*{\subsubsection}{\scshape\MakeLowercase}
\section{A section}
\subsection{A subsection}
\subsubsection{A subsubsection}
Three headings following each other, a situation you
will not see often \ldots
```

The \part heading is not influenced by settings for the basic interface. If you want to modify it, you must use the extended interface described below.

The extended interface

The extended interface consists of two major commands, \titleformat and
\titlespacing. They allow you to declare the "inner" format (i.e., fonts, label,
alignment, ...) and the "outer" format (i.e., spacing, indentation, etc.), respectively.
This scheme was adopted because people often wish to alter only one or the other
aspect of the layout.

\titleformat{*cmd*} [*shape*] {*format*}{*label*}{*sep*}{*before-code*} [*after-code*]

The first argument (*cmd*) is the heading command name (e.g., \section) whose
format is to be modified. In contrast to \@startsection this argument requires
the command name—that is, with the backslash in front. The remaining arguments have the following meaning:

shape   The basic shape for the heading. A number of predefined shapes are available: hang, the default, produces a hanging label (like \section in standard
classes); display puts label and heading text on separate lines (like standard
\chapter); while runin produces a run-in title (like standard \paragraph).
In addition, the following shapes, which have no equivalents in standard LaTeX,
are provided: frame is similar to display but frames the title; leftmargin
puts the title into the left margin; while rightmargin places it into the right
margin. The last two shapes might conflict with \marginpar commands, that
is, they may overlap.
A general-purpose shape is block, which typesets the heading as a single
block. It should be preferred to hang for centered layouts.
Both drop and wrap wrap the first paragraph around the title, with drop using
a fixed width for the title and wrap using the width of the widest title line (automatically breaking the title within the limit forced by the *left-sep* argument
of \titlespacing).
As the interface is extensible (for programmers), additional shapes may be
available with your installation.

format   The declarations that are applied to the whole title—label and text. They
may include only vertical material, which is typeset following the space above
the heading. If you need horizontal material, it should be entered in the *label*
or *before-code* argument.

label   The formatting of the label, that is, the heading number. To refer to the
number itself, use \thesection or whatever is appropriate. For defining
\chapter headings the package offers \chaptertitlename, which produces
\chaptername or \appendixname, depending on the position of the heading
in the document.

sep   Length whose value determines the distance between the label and title text.
Depending on the *shape* argument, it might be a vertical or horizontal separa-

tion. For example, with the `frame` shape, it specifies the distance between the frame and heading text.

before-code   Code executed immediately preceding the heading text. Its last command can take one argument, which will pick up the heading text and thus permits more complicated manipulations (see Example 2-2-19).

after-code   Optional code to be executed after formatting the heading text (still within the scope of the declarations given in *format*). For `hang`, `block`, and `display`, it is executed in vertical mode; with `runin`, it is executed in horizontal mode. For other shapes, it has no effect.

If the starred form of a heading is used, the *label* and *sep* arguments are ignored because no number is produced.

The next example shows a more old-fashioned run-in heading, for which we define only the format, not the spacing around the heading. The latter is manipulated with the `\titlespacing` command.

```
\usepackage{titlesec}
\titleformat{\section}[runin]{\normalfont\scshape}
        {\S\,\oldstylenums{\thesection}.}{.5em}{}[.\quad]
\section{The Title}
The heading is separated from the section text by
a dot and a space of one quad.
```

§ 1. THE TITLE.   The heading is separated from the section text by a dot and a space of one quad.

2-2-17

By default, LATEX's `\section` headings are not indented (they are usually of *shape* hang). If you prefer a normal paragraph indentation with such a heading, you could add `\indent` before the `\S` sign or specify the indentation with the `\titlespacing` declaration, described next.

`\titlespacing*{`*cmd*`}{`*left-sep*`}{`*before-sep*`}{`*after-sep*`}[`*right-sep*`]`

The starred form of the command suppresses the paragraph indentation for the paragraph following the title, except with shapes where the heading and paragraph are combined, such as `runin` and `drop`. The *cmd* argument holds the heading command name to be manipulated. The remaining arguments are as follows:

left-sep   Length specifying the increase of the left margin for headings with the `block`, `display`, `hang`, or `frame` shape. With `...margin` or `drop` shapes it specifies the width of the heading title, with `wrap` it specifies the maximum width for the title, and with `runin` it specifies the indentation before the title (negative values would make the title hang into the left margin).

before-sep   Length specifying the vertical space added above the heading.

after-sep   Length specifying the separation between the heading and the following paragraph. It can be a vertical or horizontal space depending on the shape deployed.

right-sep Optional length specifying an increase of the right margin, which is supported for the shapes block, display, hang, and frame.

The *before-sep* and *after-sep* arguments usually receive rubber length values to allow some flexibility in the design. To simplify the declaration you can alternatively specify *f* (where *f* is a decimal factor). This is equivalent to *f* ex with some stretchability as well as a small shrinkability inside *before-sep*, and an even smaller stretchability and no shrinkability inside *after-sep*.

. . . some text before . . .

───── SECTION 1 ─────
A Title Test

Some text to prove that this paragraph is not indented and that the title has a margin of 1pc on either side.

```
\usepackage{titlesec}
\titleformat{\section}[frame]{\normalfont}
    {\footnotesize \enspace SECTION \thesection
     \enspace}{6pt}{\large\bfseries\filcenter}
\titlespacing*{\section}{1pc}{*4}{*2.3}[1pc]

\ldots some text before \ldots
\section{A Title Test}
Some text to prove that this paragraph is not indented
and that the title has a margin of 1pc on either side.
```

2-2-18

Spacing tools for headings

The previous example introduced \filcenter, but there also exist \filleft, \filright, and \fillast—the latter produces an adjusted paragraph but centers the last line. These commands should be preferred to \raggedleft or \raggedright inside \titleformat, as the latter would cancel *left-sep* or *right-sep* set up by the \titlespacing command. Alternatively, you can use \filinner or \filouter, which resolve to \filleft or \filright, depending on the current page. However, due to TEX's asynchronous page makeup algorithm, they are only supported for headings that start a new page—for example, \chapter in most designs. See Example 2-2-21 on page 43 for a solution to this problem for other headings. Another useful spacing command is \wordsep, which refers to the interword space (including stretch and shrink) of the current font.

Indentation after heading

The paragraph indentation for the first paragraph following the headings can alternatively be globally specified using the package options indentafter or noindentafter, bypassing the presence or absence of a star in \titlespacing.

Spacing between consecutive headings

By default, the spacing between two consecutive headings is defined to be the *after-sep* of the first one. If this result is not desired you can change it by specifying the option largestsep, which will put the spacing to the maximum of *after-sep* from the first heading and *before-sep* of the second.

Headings at page bottom

After a heading LATEX tries to ensure that at least two lines from the following paragraph appear on the same page as the heading title. If this proves impossible the heading is moved to the next page. If you think that two lines are not enough, try the option nobottomtitles or nobottomtitles*, which will move headings to a new page whenever the remaining space on the page is less than the current value of \bottomtitlespace. (Its default is .2\textheight; to change its value, use \renewcommand rather than \setlength.) The starred version is preferred, as it computes the remaining space with more accuracy, unless you use headings with `drop`, `margin`, or `wrap` shapes, which may get badly placed when deploying the starred option.

In most heading layouts the number appears either on top or to the left of the heading text. If this placement is not appropriate, the *label* argument of `\titleformat` cannot be used. Instead, one has to exploit the fact that the *before-code* can pick up the heading text. In the next example, the command `\secformat` has one argument that defines the formatting for the heading text and number; we then call this command in the *before-code* argument of `\titleformat`. Note that the font change for the number is kept local by surrounding it with braces. Without them the changed font size might influence the title spacing in some circumstances.

Handling unusual layouts

```
\usepackage{titlesec}
\newcommand\secformat[1]{%
  \parbox[b]{.5\textwidth}{\filleft\bfseries #1}%
  \quad\rule[-12pt]{2pt}{70pt}\quad
  {\fontsize{60}{60}\selectfont\thesection}}
\titleformat{\section}[block]
  {\filleft\normalfont\sffamily}{}{0pt}{\secformat}
\titlespacing*{\section}{0pt}{*3}{*2}[1pc]
\section{A Title\\ on Two Lines}
In this example the heading number appears to
the right of the heading text.
```

A Title on Two Lines │ **1**

In this example the heading number appears to the right of the heading text.

2-2-19

The same technique can be applied to change the heading text in other ways. For example, if we want a period after the heading text we could define

```
\newcommand\secformat[1]{#1.}
```

and then call `\secformat` in the *before-code* of the `\titleformat` declaration as shown in the previous example.

The `wrap` shape has the capability to measure the lines in the title text and return the width of the widest line in `\titlewidth`. This capability can be extended to three other shapes (`block`, `display`, and `hang`) by loading the package with the option `calcwidth` and then using `\titlewidth` within the arguments of `\titleformat`, as needed.

Measuring the width of the title

For rules and leaders the package offers the `\titlerule` command. Used without any arguments it produces a rule of height `.4pt` spanning the full width of the column (but taking into account changes to the margins as specified with the `\titlespacing` declaration). An optional argument lets you specify a height for the produced rule. The starred form of `\titlerule` is used to produce leaders (i.e., repeated objects) instead of rules. It takes an optional *width* argument and a mandatory *text* argument. The *text* is repeatedly typeset in boxes with its natural width, unless a different *width* is specified in the optional argument. In that case,

Rules and leaders

only the first and the last boxes retain their natural widths to allow for proper alignment on either side.

The command \titleline lets you add horizontal material to arguments of \titleformat that expect vertical material. It takes an optional argument specifying the alignment and a mandatory argument containing the material to typeset. It produces a box of fixed width taking into account the marginal changes due to the \titlespacing declaration. Thus, either the material needs to contain some rubber space, or you must specify an alignment through the optional argument (allowed values are l, r, and c).

The \titleline* variant first typesets the material from its mandatory argument in a box of width \titlewidth (so you may have to add rubber space to this argument) and then uses this box as input to \titleline (i.e., aligns it according to the optional argument). Remember that you may have to use the option calcwidth to ensure that \titlewidth contains a sensible value.

In the next somewhat artificial example, which is worth studying though better not used in real life, all of these tools are applied together:

```
\usepackage[noindentafter,calcwidth]{titlesec}
\titleformat{\section}[display]
  {\filright\normalfont\bfseries\sffamily}
  {\titleline[r]{Section \Huge\thesection}}{1ex}
  {\titleline*[l]{\titlerule[1pt]}\vspace{1pt}%
   \titleline*[l]{\titlerule[2pt]}\vspace{2pt}}
  [{\titleline*[l]{\titlerule*{\tiny\LaTeX}}}]
\titlespacing{\section}{1pc}{*3}{*2}

\section{Rules and Leaders}
Note that the last \verb=\titleline*= is
surrounded by braces. Without them its
optional argument would prematurely end the
outer optional argument of \verb=\titleformat=.
```

Section 1

Rules and Leaders
LATEX LATEX LATEX LATEX LATEX LATEX LATEX

Note that the last \titleline* is surrounded by braces. Without them its optional argument would prematurely end the outer optional argument of \titleformat.

2-2-20

Standard LaTeX considers the space before a heading to be a good place to break the page unless the heading immediately follows another heading. The penalty to break at this point is stored in the internal counter \@secpenalty and in many classes it holds the value -300 (negative values are bonus places for breaking). As only one penalty value is available for all heading levels, there is seldom any point in modifying its setting. With titlesec, however, you can exert finer control: whenever a command *name*break is defined (where *name* is the name of a sectioning command, such as \sectionbreak), the latter will be used instead of adding the default penalty. For example,

Breaking before a heading

```
\newcommand\sectionbreak{\clearpage}
```

would result in sections always appearing on top of a page with all pending floats being typeset first.

In some layouts the space above a heading must be preserved, even if the *Always keeping the* heading appears on top of a page (by default, such spaces vanish at page breaks). *space above a* This can be accomplished using a definition like the following: *heading*

```
\newcommand\sectionbreak{\addpenalty{-300}\vspace*{0pt}}
```

The `\addpenalty` command indicates a (good) break point, which is followed by a zero space that cannot vanish. Thus, the "before" space from the heading will appear as well at the top of the page if a break is taken at the penalty.

Conditional heading layouts

So far we have seen how to define fixed layouts for a heading command using `\titleformat` and `\titlespacing`. The titlesec package also allows you to conditionally change the layout on verso and recto pages, and to use special layouts for numberless headings (i.e., those produced by the starred form of the heading command).

This is implemented through a keyword/value syntax in the first argument of `\titleformat` and `\titlespacing`. The available keys are name, page (values odd or even), and numberless (values true or false). In fact, the syntax we have seen so far, `\titleformat{\section}{..}...`, is simply an abbreviation for the general form `\titleformat{name=\section}{..}...`.

In contrast to the spacing commands `\filinner` and `\filouter`, which can only be used with headings that start a new page, the page keyword enables you to define layouts that depend on the current page without any restriction. To specify the layout for a verso (left-hand) page, use the value even; for a recto (right-hand) page, use the value odd. Such settings only affect a document typeset in twoside mode. Otherwise, all pages are considered to be recto in LaTeX. In the following example we use a block shape and shift the heading to one side, depending on the current page. In a similar fashion you could implement headings that are placed in the margin by using the shapes leftmargin and rightmargin.

```
\usepackage{titlesec}
\titleformat{name=\section,page=odd}[block]
    {\normalfont}{\thesection.}{6pt}{\bfseries\filleft}
\titleformat{name=\section,page=even}[block]
    {\normalfont}{\thesection.}{6pt}{\bfseries\filright}
\section{A Head}
Some text to fill the page. Some text to fill the page.
\newpage
Some text to fill the page.
\section{Another}
Some text to fill the page.
```

1. A Head

Some text to fill the page. Some text to fill the page.

Some text to fill the page. Some text to fill the page.

2. Another

Some text to fill the page.

2-2-21

Similarly, the numberless key is used to specify that a certain `\titleformat` or `\titlespacing` declaration applies only to headings with (or without) numbers. By default, a heading declaration applies to both cases, so in the example the second declaration actually overwrites part of the first declaration. To illustrate what is possible the example uses quite different designs for the two cases—do not mistake this for an attempt to show good taste. It is important to realize that neither the *label* nor the *sep* argument is ignored when numberless is set to true as seen in the example—in normal circumstances you would probably use {}{0pt} as values.

1. A Head
 	
Some text to fill the page. Some text to fill the page.
 	
    ***   *Another*
 	
Some text to fill this line.
	``
	\usepackage{titlesec}
	\titleformat{name=\section}[block]
	   {\normalfont}{\thesection.}{6pt}{\bfseries\filright}
	\titleformat{name=\section,numberless=true}[block]
	   {\normalfont}{***}{12pt}{\itshape\filcenter}
	``

```
\section{A Head}
Some text to fill the page. Some text to fill the page.
\section*{Another}
Some text to fill this line.
```

2-2-22

Changing the heading hierarchy

The commands described so far are intended to adjust the formatting and spacing of existing heading commands. With the \titleclass declaration it is possible to define new headings.

```
\titleclass{cmd}{class}
\titleclass{cmd}{class}[super-level-cmd]
\titleclass{cmd}[start-level]{class}              (with loadonly option)
```

There are three classes of headings: the page class contains headings that fill a full page (like \part in LaTeX's report and book document classes); the top class contains headings that start a new page and thus appear at the top of a page; and all other headings are considered to be part of the straight class.

Used without any optional argument the \titleclass declaration simply changes the heading class of an existing heading *cmd*. For example,

```
\titleclass\section{top}
```

would result in sections always starting a new page.

If this declaration is used with the optional *super-level-cmd* argument, you introduce a new heading level below *super-level-cmd*. Any existing heading command at this level is moved one level down in the hierarchy. For example,

```
\titleclass\subchapter{straight}[\chapter]
```

introduces the heading \subchapter between \chapter and \section. The declaration does not define any layout for this heading (which needs to be defined by an additional \titleformat and \titlespacing command), nor does it initialize the necessary counter. Most likely you also want to update the counter representation for \section:

```
\titleformat{\subchapter}{..}...      \titlespacing{\subchapter}{..}...
\newcounter{subchapter}
\renewcommand\thesubchapter{\thechapter.\arabic{subchapter}}
\renewcommand\thesection{\thesubchapter.\arabic{section}}
```

The third variant of \titleclass is needed only when you want to build a heading structure from scratch—for example, when you are designing a completely new document class that is not based on one of the standard classes. In that case load the package with the option loadonly so that the package will make no attempt to interpret existing heading commands so as to extract their current layout. You can then start building heading commands, as in the following example:

```
\titleclass\Ahead[0]{top}
\titleclass\Bhead{straight}[\Ahead]
\titleclass\Chead{straight}[\Bhead]
\newcounter{Ahead} \newcounter{Bhead} \newcounter{Chead}
\renewcommand\theBhead{\theAhead-\arabic{Bhead}
\renewcommand\theBhead{\theBhead-\arabic{Chead}
\titleformat{name=\Ahead}{..}...   \titlespacing{name=\Ahead}{..}...
\titleformat{name=\Bhead}{..}...        ...
```

The *start-level* is usually 0 or –1; see the introduction in Section 2.2 for its meaning. There should be precisely one \titleclass declaration that uses this particular optional argument.

If you intend to build your own document classes in this way, take a look at the documentation accompanying the titlesec package. It contains additional examples and offers further tips and tricks.

2.3   Table of contents structures

A *table of contents* (TOC) is a special list in which the titles of the section units are listed, together with the page numbers indicating the start of the sections. This list can be rather complicated if units from several nesting levels are included, and it should be formatted carefully because it plays an important rôle as a navigation aid for the reader.

Similar lists exist containing reference information about the floating elements in a document—namely, the *list of tables* and the *list of figures*. The structure of these lists is simpler, as their contents, the captions of the floating elements, are normally all on the same level (but see Section 6.5.2).

Standard LaTeX can automatically create these three contents lists. By default, LaTeX enters text generated by one of the arguments of the sectioning commands into the .toc file. Similarly, LaTeX maintains two more files, one for the list of figures (.lof) and one for the list of tables (.lot), which contain the text specified as the argument of the \caption command for figures and tables.

The information written into these files during a previous LaTeX run is read and typeset (normally at the beginning of a document) during a subsequent LaTeX run by invoking these commands: \tableofcontents, \listoffigures, and \listoftables.

A TOC needs two, sometimes even three, LaTeX runs To generate these cross-reference tables, it is always necessary to run LaTeX at least twice—once to collect the relevant information, and a second time to read back the information and typeset it in the correct place in the document. Because of the additional material to be typeset in the second run, the cross-referencing information may change, making a third LaTeX run necessary. This is one of the reasons for the tradition of using different page-numbering systems for the front matter and the main text: in the days of hand typesetting any additional iteration made the final product much more expensive.

The following sections will discuss how to typeset and generate these contents lists. It will also be shown how to enter information directly into one of these auxiliary files and how to open and write into a supplementary file completely under user control.

2.3.1 Entering information into the contents files

Normally the contents files are generated automatically by LaTeX. With some care this interface, which consists of the \addcontentsline and \addtocontents commands, can also be used to enter information directly.

`\addcontentsline{`*ext*`}{`*type*`}{`*text*`}`

The \addcontentsline command writes the *text* together with some additional information, such as the page number of the current page, into a file with the extension *ext* (usually .toc, .lof, or .lot). Fragile commands within *text* needed to be protected with \protect. The *type* argument is a string that specifies the kind of contents entry that is being made. For the table of contents (.toc), it is usually the name of the heading command without a backslash; for .lof or .lot files, figure or table is normally specified.

The \addcontentsline instruction is normally invoked automatically by the document sectioning commands or by the \caption commands within the float environments. Unfortunately, the interface has only one argument for the variable text, which makes it awkward to properly identify an object's number if present. Since such numbers (e.g., the heading number) typically need special formatting in the contents lists, this identification is absolutely necessary. The trick used by the current LaTeX kernel to achieve this goal is to surround such a number with the command `\numberline` within the *text* argument as follows:

```
\protect\numberline{number}heading
```

For example, a `\caption` command inside a `figure` environment saves the caption text for the figure using the following line:

```
\addcontentsline{lof}{figure}
        {\protect\numberline{\thefigure}caption text}
```

Because of the `\protect` command, `\numberline` will be written unchanged into the external file, while `\thefigure` will be executed along the way so that the actual figure number will end up in the file.

Later on, during the formatting of the contents lists, `\numberline` can be used to format the number in a special way, such as by providing extra space or a different font. The downside of this approach is that it is less general than a version that takes a separate argument for this number (e.g., you cannot easily do arbitrary transformation on this number) and it requires a suitable definition for `\numberline`—something that is unfortunately not always available (see the discussion in Section 2.3.2 on page 49).

Sometimes `\addcontentsline` is used in the source to complement the actions of standard LaTeX. For instance, in the case of the starred form of the section commands, no information is written to the `.toc` file. If you do not want a heading number (starred form) but you do want an entry in the `.toc` file, you can use `\addcontentsline` with or without `\numberline` as shown in the following example.

Contents

Foreword	**1**
1 Thoughts	**2**
1.1 Contact info . .	2
References	**2**

Foreword

A starred heading with the TOC entry manually added. Compare this to the form used for the bibliography.

2-3-1   1

---

1   Thoughts

We find all in [1].

1.1   Contact info

E-mail Ben at [2].

References

[1] Ben User, Some day will never come, 2010

[2] BUser@earth.info

2

```
\tableofcontents
\section*{Foreword}
\addcontentsline{toc}{section}
 {\protect\numberline{}Foreword}
A starred heading with the TOC
entry manually added. Compare
this to the form used for the
bibliography.
\section{Thoughts}
We find all in \cite{k1}.
\subsection{Contact info}
E-mail Ben at \cite{k2}.
\begin{thebibliography}{9}
\addcontentsline{toc}
        {section}{\refname}
\bibitem{k1} Ben User, Some
    day will never come, 2010
\bibitem{k2} BUser@earth.info
\end{thebibliography}
```

Using \numberline as in the "Foreword" produces an indented "section" entry in the table of contents, leaving the space where the section number would go free. Omitting the \numberline command (as was done for the bibliography entry) would typeset the heading flush left instead. Adding a similar line after the start of the theindex means that the "Index" will be listed in the table of contents. Unfortunately, this approach cannot be used to get the list of figures or tables into the table of contents because \listoffigures or \listoftables might generate a listing of several pages and consequently the page number picked up by \addcontentsline might be wrong. And putting it before the command does not help either, because often these list commands start a new page. One potential solution is to copy the command definition from the class file and put \addcontentsline directly into it.

Bibliography or index in table of contents
In case of standard classes or close derivatives you can use the tocbibind package created by Peter Wilson to get the "List of...", "Index", or "Bibliography" section listed in the table of contents without further additions to the source. The package offers a number of options such as notbib, notindex, nottoc, notlof, and notlot (do not add the corresponding entry to the the table of contents) as well as numbib and numindex (number the corresponding section). By default the "Contents" section is listed within the table of contents, which is seldom desirable; if necessary, use the nottoc option to disable this behavior.

> \addtocontents{*ext*}{*text*}

The \addtocontents command does not contain a *type* parameter and is intended to enter special formatting information not directly related to any contents line. For example, the \chapter command of the standard classes places additional white space in the .lof and .lot files to separate entries from different chapters as follows:

```
\addtocontents{lof}{\protect\addvspace{10pt}}
\addtocontents{lot}{\protect\addvspace{10pt}}
```

By using \addvspace at most 10 points will separate the entries from different chapters without producing strange gaps if some chapters do not contain any figures or tables.

Potential problems with \addvspace
This example, however, shows a certain danger of the interface: while the commands \addcontentsline, \addtocontents, and \addvspace appear to be user-level commands (they do not contain any @ signs in their names), they can easily produce strange errors.[1] In particular, \addvspace can be used only in vertical mode, which means that a line like the above works correctly only if an earlier \addcontentsline ends in vertical mode. Thus, you need to understand

---

[1] For an in-depth discussion of \addvspace, see Appendix A.1.5, page 858.

how such lines are actually processed to be able to enter arbitrary formatting instructions between them. This is the topic of the next section.

If either \addcontentsline or \addtocontents is used within the source of a document, one important restriction applies: neither command can be used at the same level as an \include statement. That means, for example, that the sequence Potential problems
with \include

```
\addtocontents{toc}{\protect\setcounter{tocdepth}{1}}
\include{sect1}
```

with sect1.tex containing a \section command would surprisingly result in a .toc file containing

```
\contentsline {section}{\numberline {1}Section from sect1}{2}
\setcounter {tocdepth}{1}
```

showing that the lines appear out of order. The solution is to move the \addtocontents or \addcontentsline statement into the file loaded via \include or to avoid \include altogether.

2.3.2   Typesetting a contents list

As discussed above, contents lists are generated by implicitly or explicitly using the commands \addcontentsline and \addtocontents. Thereby, the result of

```
\addcontentsline{ext}{type}{text}
```

is to place the line

```
\contentsline{type}{text}{page}
```

into the auxiliary file with extension *ext*, where *page* is the current page number in the document. The command \addtocontents{*ext*}{*text*} is simpler: it just puts *text* into the auxiliary file. Thus, a typical contents list file consists of a number of \contentsline commands, possibly interspersed with further formatting instructions added as a result of \addtocontents calls. It is also possible for the user to create a table of contents by hand with the help of the command \contentsline.

A typical example is shown below. Note that most (though not all) heading numbers are entered as a parameter of the \numberline command to allow formatting with the proper indentation. LaTeX is unfortunately not consistent here; the standard classes do not use \numberline for \part headings but instead specify the separation between number and text explicitly. Since the 2001/06/01 release you can also use \numberline in this place, but with older releases the formatting will be unpredictable. *Inconsistency*
with \part

```
\setcounter{tocdepth}{3}
\contentsline {part}{I\hspace{1em}Part}{2}
\contentsline{chapter}{\numberline{1}A-Head}{2}
\contentsline{section}{\numberline{1.1}B-Head}{3}
\contentsline{subsection}%
    {\numberline{1.1.1}C-Head}{4}
\contentsline{subsection}%
    {\numberline{}With Empty Number}{5}
\contentsline{subsection}{Unnumbered C-Head}{6}
```

2-3-2

The `\contentsline` command is implemented to take its first argument *type*, and then use it to call the corresponding `\l@`*type* command, which does the actual typesetting. One separate command for each of the types must be defined in the class file. For example, in the report class you find the following definitions:

```
\newcommand\l@section       {\@dottedtocline{1}{1.5em}{2.3em}}
\newcommand\l@subsection     {\@dottedtocline{2}{3.8em}{3.2em}}
\newcommand\l@subsubsection{\@dottedtocline{3}{7.0em}{4.1em}}
\newcommand\l@paragraph      {\@dottedtocline{4}{10em}{5em}}
\newcommand\l@subparagraph {\@dottedtocline{5}{12em}{6em}}
\newcommand\l@figure        {\@dottedtocline{1}{1.5em}{2.3em}}
\newcommand\l@table          {\l@figure}
```

By defining `\l@`*type* to call `\@dottedtocline` (a command with five arguments) and specifying three arguments (*level*, *indent*, and *numwidth*), the remaining arguments, *text* and *page*, of `\contentsline` will be picked up by `\@dottedtocline` as arguments 4 and 5.

Note that some section levels build their table of contents entries in a somewhat more complicated way, so that the standard document classes have definitions for `\l@part` and `\l@chapter` that do not use `\@dottedtocline`. Generally they use a set of specific formatting commands, perhaps omitting the ellipses and typesetting the title in a larger font.

So to define the layout for the contents lists, we have to declare the appropriate `\l@`*type* commands. One easy way to do this, as shown above, is to use `\@dottedtocline`, an internal command that we now look at in some detail.

`\@dottedtocline{`*level*`}{`*indent*`}{`*numwidth*`}{`*text*`}{`*page*`}`

The last two parameters of `\@dottedtocline` coincide with the last parameters of `\contentsline`, which itself usually invokes a `\@dottedtocline` command. The other parameters are the following:

level   The command `\contentsline` nesting level of an entry. This parameter allows the user to control how many nesting levels will be displayed. Levels greater than the value of counter tocdepth will not appear in the table of contents.

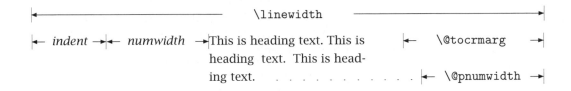

Figure 2.3: Parameters defining the layout of a contents file

indent   The total indentation from the left margin.

numwidth   The width of the box that contains the number if *text* has a \numberline command. It is also the amount of extra indentation added to the second and later lines of a multiple-line entry.

Additionally, the command \@dottedtocline uses the following global formatting parameters, which specify the visual appearance of all entries:

\@pnumwidth   The width of the box in which the page number is set.

\@tocrmarg   The indentation of the right margin for all but the last line of multiple-line entries. Dimension, but changed with \renewcommand!

\@dotsep   The separation between dots, in mu (math units).[1] It is a pure number (like 1.7 or 2). By making this number large enough you can get rid of the dots altogether. To be changed with \renewcommand!

A pictorial representation of the effects described is shown in Figure 2.3. The field identified by *numwidth* contains a left-justified section number, if present. You can achieve the proper indentation for nested entries by varying the settings of *indent* and *numwidth*.

One case in which this is necessary, while using a standard class (article, report, or book), arises when you have ten or more sections and within the later *Problem with many* ones more than nine subsections. In that case numbers and text will come too *headings on one* close together or even overlap if the *numwidth* argument on the corresponding *level* calls to \@dottedtocline is not extended, as seen in the following example.

10 A-Head   **3**   \contentsline{section}{\numberline{10}A-Head}{3}
   10.9 B-Head   4   \contentsline{subsection}{\numberline{10.9}B-Head}{4}
   10.10B-Head   4   \contentsline{subsection}{\numberline{10.10}B-Head}{4}

2-3-3

---

[1]There are 18 mu units to an em, where the latter is taken from the \fontdimen2 of the math symbol font symbols. See Section 7.10.3 for more information about \fontdimens.

Redefining `\l@subsection` to leave more space for the number (third argument to `\@dottedtocline`) gives a better result in this case. You will probably
have to adjust the other commands, such as `\l@subsubsection`, as well to produce a balanced look for the whole table.

```
\makeatletter
\renewcommand\l@subsection{\@dottedtocline{2}{1.5em}{3em}}
\makeatother
```

<table>
<tr><td>**10 A-Head**</td><td></td><td>**3**</td><td>`\contentsline{section}{\numberline{10}A-Head}{3}`</td></tr>
<tr><td>10.9   B-Head</td><td>. . . .</td><td>4</td><td>`\contentsline{subsection}{\numberline{10.9}B-Head}{4}`</td></tr>
<tr><td>10.10 B-Head</td><td>. . . .</td><td>4</td><td>`\contentsline{subsection}{\numberline{10.10}B-Head}{4}`</td></tr>
</table>

2-3-4

Another example that requires changes is the use of unusual page numbering.
For example, if the pages are numbered by part and formatted as "A-78", "B-328",
and so on, then the space provided for the page number is probably too small,
resulting at least in a large number of annoying "Overfull hbox" warnings, but
more likely in some bad spacing around them. In that case the remedy is to set
`\@pnumwidth` to a value that fits the widest entry—for example, via

```
\makeatletter \settowidth\@pnumwidth{\textbf{A--123}} \makeatother
```

The level down to which the heading information is displayed in the table of
contents is controlled by the counter `tocdepth`. It can be changed, for example,
with the following declaration:

```
\setcounter{tocdepth}{2}
```

In this case section heading information down to the second level (e.g., in the
report class part, chapter, and section) will be shown.

2.3.3   Combining contents lists

By default, LaTeX produces separate lists for the table of contents, the list of figures, and the list of tables, available via `\tableofcontents`, `\listoffigures`,
and `\listoftables`, respectively. None of the standard classes support combining those lists, such as having all tables and figures in a single list, or even combining all three in a single table of contents as is sometimes requested.

How could such a request be fulfilled? The first requirement is that
we make LaTeX write to the appropriate auxiliary file when it internally uses
`\addcontentsline`. For example, all `\caption` commands need to write to a single file if we want to combine figures and tables in a single list. Looking at the LaTeX
sources reveals that this goal is easy to achieve: figure captions write to a file with
the extension specified by `\ext@figure`, while table captions use `\ext@table` for
this purpose.

So using an appropriate redefinition of, say, `\ext@table` we can force LaTeX to assemble all references to figures and tables in the `.lof` file. But is this enough? The example clearly shows that it is probably not enough to force the entries together. When looking at the generated list we cannot tell which entry refers to a figure or a table. The only indication that something is amiss is given by the identical numbers on the left.

A figure

Figure 1: Figure-Caption

Figures and Tables

1   A Section

Some text . . . Some text referencing figure 1 . . .

A table

Table 1: Table-Caption

```
\makeatletter
\renewcommand\ext@table{lof}
\makeatother
\renewcommand\listfigurename
            {Figures and Tables}
\listoffigures
\section{A Section}
Some text \ldots
\begin{table}[b]
  \centering
  \fbox{\scriptsize A table}
  \caption{Table-Caption}
\end{table}
Some text referencing
figure~\ref{fig} \ldots
\begin{figure}
  \centering
  \fbox{\scriptsize A figure}
  \caption{Figure-Caption}\label{fig}
\end{figure}
```

2-3-5

The situation would be slightly better if the figures and tables share the same counter, so that we do not end up with identical numbers in the left column of the list. Unfortunately, this result is fairly difficult to achieve, because one must directly manipulate the low-level float definitions.

Another possible remedy is to define `\l@figure` and `\l@table` in such a way that this information is present. The example on the following page shows a possible solution that appends the string "(figure)" or "(table)" to each entry. In theory it would also be possible to annotate the number to indicate the type of float, but that would require redefining a lot of LaTeX's internals such as `\numberline`.

What happens if we force all entries into a single list—that is, into the table of contents? In that case we get a list ordered according to the final appearance of the objects in the document, which may not be what we would expect to see. In the next example, the figure, which actually came last in the source, shows up before the section in which it is referenced, because the float algorithm places it on the top of the page. This outcome might be acceptable within books or reports where the major heading starts a new page and prevents top floats on the heading page, but is probably not desirable in other cases.

A figure

Figure 1: Figure-Caption

Contents

1 Figure-Caption (figure) 1

1 A Section 1

1 Table-Caption (table) 1

1 A Section

Some text ... Some text referencing figure 1 ...

A table

Table 1: Table-Caption

```
\makeatletter
\renewcommand\ext@figure{toc}
\renewcommand\ext@table{toc}
\renewcommand\l@figure[2]{\@dottedtocline
    {1}{1.5em}{2.3em}{#1~(figure)}{#2}}
\renewcommand\l@table [2]{\@dottedtocline
    {1}{1.5em}{2.3em}{#1~(table)}{#2}}
\makeatother
\tableofcontents
\section{A Section}
Some text \ldots
\begin{table}[b]
 \centering \fbox{\scriptsize A table}
 \caption{Table-Caption}
\end{table}
Some text referencing
figure~\ref{fig} \ldots
\begin{figure}
 \centering \fbox{\scriptsize A figure}
 \caption{Figure-Caption}\label{fig}
\end{figure}
```

2-3-6

In summary, while it is possible to combine various types of contents lists, the results may not be what one would expect. In any case such an approach requires a careful redesign of all `\l@`*type* commands so that the final list will be useful to the reader.

2.3.4 Providing additional contents files

If you want to make a list comprising all of the examples in a book, you need to create a new contents file and then make use of the facilities described above. First, two new commands must be defined. The first command, `\ecaption`, associates a caption with the current position in the document by writing its argument and the current page number to the contents file. The second command, `\listofexamples`, reads the information written to the contents file on the previous run and typesets it at the point in the document where the command is called.

The `\listofexamples` command invokes `\@starttoc{`*ext*`}`, which reads the external file (with the extension *ext*) and then reopens it for writing. This command is also used by the commands `\tableofcontents`, `\listoffigures`, and `\listoftables`. The supplementary file could be given an extension such as `xmp`. A command like `\chapter*{List of examples}` can be put in front or inside of `\listofexamples` to produce a title and, if desired, a command `\addcontentsline` can signal the presence of this list to the reader by entering it into the `.toc` file.

The actual typesetting of the individual entries in the `.xmp` file is controlled by `\l@example`, which needs to be defined. In the example below, the captions are typeset as paragraphs followed by an italicized page number.

```
\newcommand\ecaption[1]
            {\addcontentsline{xmp}{example}{#1}}
\makeatletter \newcommand\listofexamples
            {\section*{Comments}\@starttoc{xmp}}
 \newcommand\l@example[2]
    {\par\noindent#1,~\textit{#2}\par}    \makeatother
\section{Selection of recordings}
Ravel's Bol\'ero by Jacques Loussier
Trio.\ecaption{Loussier: A strange experience}

Davis' Blue in Green by Cassandra
Wilson.\ecaption{Wilson: A wonderful version}
\listofexamples
```

1   Selection of recordings

Ravel's Boléro by Jacques Loussier Trio.

   Davis' Blue in Green by Cassandra Wilson.

Comments

Loussier: A strange experience, *1*

Wilson: A wonderful version, *1*

2-3-7

The float package described in Section 6.3.1 on page 291 implements the above mechanism with the command `\listof`, which generates a list of floats of the type specified as its argument.

2.3.5   shorttoc—Summary table of contents

With larger documents it is sometimes helpful to provide a summary table of contents (with only the major sections listed) as well as a more detailed one. This can be accomplished with the shorttoc package created by Jean-Pierre Drucbert.

```
\shorttableofcontents{title}{depth}
```

This `\shorttableofcontents` command (or `\shorttoc` as a synonym) must be specified before the `\tableofcontents` command; otherwise, the summary table of contents will be empty. The table's heading is given by the *title* argument and the *depth* down to which contents entries are shown is defined by second argument. Thus, to show only chapters and sections in the summary and everything down to subsubsections in the detailed table of contents, you would specify:

```
\shorttableofcontents{Summary table of contents}{1}
\setcounter{tocdepth}{3}
\tableofcontents
```

The package supports two options, `loose` (default) and `tight`, that deal with the vertical spacing of the summary table.

2.3.6   minitoc—**Multiple tables of contents**

The minitoc package, originally written by Nigel Ward and Dan Jurafsky and completely redesigned by Jean-Pierre Drucbert, enables the creation of mini-tables of contents (a "minitoc") for chapters, sections, or parts. It also supports the creation of mini-tables for the list of figures and list of tables contained in a chapter, section, or part. A similar functionality, albeit using a completely different approach, is provided by the titletoc package described in Section 2.3.7.

Here we describe in some detail the use of the package to generate such tables on a per-chapter basis. The generation of per-section or per-part tables is completely analogous (using differently named commands); an overview appears at the end of the section.

The package supports almost all language options of the babel system (see Section 9.1.3), which predefine the heading texts used. In addition, the formatting of the generated tables can be influenced by the options `loose` (default) or `tight` and `dotted` (default) or `undotted`. Further control over the appearance is provided by a number of parameters that can be set in the preamble (see Table 2.3 on the next page).

To initialize the minitoc system, you place a `\dominitoc` command before the `\tableofcontents` command. If you do not want a full table of contents but only mini-tables, replace the latter command with `\faketableofcontents`. Mini-lists of figures or tables are initialized similarly, by using `\dominilof` or `\dominilot`, if necessary together with `\fakelistoffigures` or `\fakelistoftables`.

The `\domini...` commands accept one optional argument to denote the position of the table titles: `l` for left (default), `c` for center, `r` for right, or `n` for no title (a supported synonym is `e` for empty). The declaration is global for all tables in the document.

The actual mini-tables of contents are then generated by putting the command `\minitoc` in suitable places (typically directly after a `\chapter` command) inside the document. The actual placement is at your discretion. For instance, you may put some text before it or place a box around it. If one of the tables is empty, the package suppresses the heading and issues a warning to alert you about possible formatting problems due to the material added by you around the command.

If you want to generate mini-lists of figures or tables, you use `\minilof` or `\minilot` after initializing the system as explained above.

For each mini-table of contents, an auxiliary file with the extension `.mtc`$\langle n \rangle$, where $\langle n \rangle$ is the chapter number, will be created.[1] For mini-lists of figures and tables, files with the extensions `.mlf`$\langle n \rangle$ and `.mlt`$\langle n \rangle$ are created, respectively.

By default, the mini-tables contain only references to sections and subsections. The `minitocdepth` counter, similar to `tocdepth`, allows the user to modify this behavior. The fonts used for individual entries can also be modified by chang-

---

[1]A different scheme is automatically used for operating systems in which file extensions are limited to three characters, like MS-DOS or Windows. It can be explicitly requested using the option `shortext` on the `\usepackage` command.

`minitocdepth`	A LaTeX counter that indicates how many levels of headings will be displayed in the mini-table (default value is 2).
`\mtcindent`	The length of the left/right indentation of the mini-table (default value is 24pt).
`\mtcfont`	Command defining the default font that is used for the mini-table entries (default definition is a small Roman font).
`\mtcSfont`	Command defining the font that is used for `\section` entries (default definition is a small bold Roman font).
`\mtcSSfont`	If defined, font used for `\subsection` entries (default is to use `\mtcfont` for this and the following).
`\mtcSSSfont`	If defined, font used for `\subsubsection` entries.
`\mtcPfont`	If defined, font used for `\paragraph` entries.
`\mtcPSfont`	If defined, font used for `\subparagraph` entries.
`\mtctitle`	Title text for the mini-table of contents (preset by language option).
`\nomtcrules`	Declaration that disables rules above and below the mini-tables (`\mtcrules` enables them).
`\nomtcpagenumbers`	Declaration that suppresses page numbers in the mini-tables (`\mtcpagenumbers` enables them).

Table 2.3: A summary of the minitoc parameters

ing the definitions of `\mtcfont` and its companions shown in Table 2.3. You can influence the use of rules around the mini-tables by specifying `\mtcrule` (default) or `\nomtcrule` in the preamble or before individual mini-tables. Similarly, you can request the use of page numbers in the mini-table by using the `\mtcpagenumbers` declaration (default) or their suppression by using `\nomtcpagenumbers`.

As the mini-tables and mini-lists take up room within the document, their use will alter the page numbering. Therefore, three runs normally are needed to ensure correct information in the mini-table of contents.

For mini-tables and mini-lists on the `\part` level, commands similar to those in Table 2.3 are provided. The only difference is that their names contain the string part instead of mini or ptc instead of mtc. Thus, you would use `\doparttoc` to initialize the system, `\partoc` to print a mini-table, `\noptcrules` to suppress rules, and so on. The only addition is the declaration `\ptcCfont`, which defines the font to use for chapter entries and which naturally has no equivalent. *Mini-tables on part or section level*

For mini-tables and mini-lists on the `\section` command level, the situation is again similar: replace mini by sect or mtc by stc— for example, use `\dosecttoc`,

\secttoc, and \stcfont. If \sectlof or \sectlot commands are used, you may want to try the option placeins, which confines floats to their sections by using the placeins package with its options below and section (see Section 6.2.1 on page 288).

1   Afghanistan

1.1   Geography . .   1
1.1.1   Total area   . .   1
1.1.2   Land area   . .   1
1.2   History   2

1.1   Geography

1.1.1   Total area

647,500 km2

1.1.2   Land area

647,500 km2

1

1.2   History

. . .

2   Albania

2.1   Geography . .   2
2.1.1   Total area   . .   2
2.1.2   Land area   . .   3
2.2   History   3

2.1   Geography

2.1.1   Total area

28,750 km2

2

```
\usepackage{minitoc}
\setlength\stcindent{0pt}
\renewcommand\stctitle{}
\renewcommand\stcfont
            {\footnotesize}
\setcounter{secttocdepth}{3}
\dosecttoc \faketableofcontents

\section{Afghanistan}\secttoc
\subsection{Geography}
\subsubsection{Total area}
    647,500 km2
\subsubsection{Land area}
    647,500 km2
\subsection{History} \ldots

\section{Albania} \secttoc
\subsection{Geography}
\subsubsection{Total area}
    28,750 km2
\subsubsection{Land area}
    27,400 km2
\subsection{History} \ldots
```

2-3-8

To turn off the \minitoc commands, merely replace the package minitoc with mtcoff on your \usepackage command. This step ensures that all minitoc-related commands in the source will be ignored.

2.3.7   titletoc—A different approach to contents lists

The titletoc package written by Javier Bezos was originally developed as a companion package to titlesec but can be used on its own. It implements its own interface to lay out contents structures, thereby avoiding some of the limitations of the original LaTeX code.

Relation to standard LaTeX The actual generation of external contents files and their syntax is left unchanged so that it works nicely with other packages generating such files. There is one exception, however: contents files should end with the command \contentsfinish. For the standard file extensions .toc, .lof, and .lot, this is handled automatically. But if you provide your own type of contents lists (see

Section 2.3.4), you have to announce it to titletoc, as in the following example:

```
\contentsuse{example}{xmp}
```

As explained in Section 2.3.2 a contents file consists of \contentsline commands that are sometimes separated by some arbitrary code due to the use of \addtocontents. To format such contents lines with standard LaTeX we had to define commands of the form \l@*type*; with titletoc, this step is no longer needed. Instead, we declare the desired formatting using the \titlecontents declaration (for vertically oriented entries) or its starred form (for run-in entries).

\titlecontents{*type*}[*left-indent*]{*above-code*}{*numbered-entry-format*}
                {*numberless-entry-format*}{*page-format*}[*below-code*]

The first argument of \titlecontents contains the *type* of contents line for which we set up the layout—it corresponds to the first argument of \contentsline. In other words, for each *type* of sectioning command that can appear in the document, we need one \titlecontents declaration.[1] The remaining arguments have the following meaning:

left-indent   Argument that specifies the indentation from the left margin for all lines of the entry. It is possible to place material (e.g., the heading number) in this space. Even though this argument has to be given in square brackets, it is *not* optional in the current package release!

above-code   Code to be executed before the entry is typeset. It can be used to provide vertical space, such as by using \addvspace, and to set up formatting directives, such as font changes, for the whole entry. You can also use \filleft, \filright, \filcenter, or \fillast, already known from the titlesec package, at this point.

numbered-entry-format   Code to format the entry including its number. It is executed in horizontal mode (after setting up the indentation). The last token can be a command with one argument, in which case it will receive the entry *text* as its argument. The unformatted heading number is available in the command \thecontentslabel, but see below for other possibilities to access and place it.

numberless-entry-format   Code to format the entry if the current entry does not contain a number. Again the last token may be a command with one argument.

page-format   Code that is executed after formatting the entry but while still being in horizontal mode. It is normally used to add some filling material, such as a dotted line, and to attach the page number stored in \thecontentspage. You can use the \titlerule command, discussed on page 41, to produce leaders.

---

[1]The package honors existing \l@*type* declarations made, for example, by the document class. Thus, it can be used to change the layout of only some types.

below-code An (optional) argument used to specify code to be executed in vertical mode after the entry is typeset—for example, to add some extra vertical space after the entry.

To help with placing and formatting the heading and page numbers, the titletoc package offers two useful tools: `\contentslabel` and `\contentspage`.

> `\contentslabel[`*text*`]{`*size*`}`

The purpose of the `\contentslabel` command is to typeset the *text* (which by default contains `\thecontentslabel`) left aligned in a box of width *size* and to place that box to the left of the current position. Thus, if you use this command in the *numbered-entry-format* argument of `\titlecontents`, then the number will be placed in front of the entry text into the margin or indentation set up by *left-indent*. For a more refined layout you can use the optional argument to specify your own formatting usually involving `\thecontentslabel`.

Package options The package offers three options to influence the default outcome of the `\contentslabel` command when used without the *text* argument. With `rightlabels` the heading number is right aligned in the space. The default, `leftlabels`, makes it left aligned. With `dotinlabels` a period is added after the number.

> `\contentspage[`*text*`]`

In similar fashion `\contentspage` typesets *text* (which by default contains `\thecontentspage`) right aligned in a box and arranges for the box to be placed to the right of the current position but without taking up space. Thus, if placed at the right end of a line, the box will extend into the margin. In this case, however, no mandatory argument specifies the box size: it is the same for all entries. Its value is the same as the space found to the right of all entries and can be set by the command `\contentsmargin` described below.

A note on the examples in this section For the examples in this section we copied some parts of the original `.toc` file generated by LaTeX for this book (Chapter 2 and parts of Chapter 3) into the file `partial.toc`. Inside the examples we then loaded this file with `\input` and manually added `\contentsfinish`. Of course, in a real document you would use the command `\tableofcontents` instead, so that the `.toc` file for *your* document is loaded and processed.

In our first example we provide a new formatting for chapter entries, while keeping the formatting for the section entries as defined by the standard LaTeX document class. The chapter entries are now set ragged right (`\filright`) in bold typeface, get one pica space above, followed by a thick rule. The actual entry is indented by six picas. In that space we typeset the word "Chapter" in small caps followed by a space and the chapter number (`\thecontentslabel`) using the `\contentslabel` directive with its optional argument. There is no special handling for entries without numbers, so they would be formatted with an indentation of six picas. We fill the remaining space using `\hfill` and typeset the page number in the margin via `\contentspage`. Finally, after the entry we add another two points of space so that the entry is slightly separated from any section entry following.

```
\usepackage[dotinlabels]{titletoc}
\titlecontents{chapter} [6pc]
  {\addvspace{1pc}\bfseries
   \titlerule[2pt]\filright}
  {\contentslabel
     [\textsc{\chaptername}\
     \thecontentslabel]{6pc}}
  {}{\hfill\contentspage}
  [\addvspace{2pt}]
% Show only chapter/section entries:
\setcounter{tocdepth}{1}
\input{partial.toc}
\contentsfinish
```

2-3-9

Instead of indenting the whole entry and then moving some material into the left margin using `\contentslabel`, you can make use of `\contentspush` to achieve a similar effect.

`\contentspush{`*text*`}`

This command typesets *text* and then increases the *left-indent* by the width of *text* for all additional lines of the entry (if any). As a consequence, the indentation will vary if the width of the *text* changes. In many cases such variation is not desirable, but in some cases other solutions give even worse results. Consider the case of a document with many chapters, each containing dozens of sections. A rigid *left-indent* needs to be able to hold the widest number, which may have five or six digits. In that case a label like "1.1" will come out unduly separated from its entry text. Given below is a solution that grows with the size of the entry number.

```
\usepackage{titletoc}
\titlecontents{section}[0pt]{\addvspace{2pt}\filright}
             {\contentspush{\thecontentslabel\ }}
             {}{\titlerule*[8pt]{.}\contentspage}
```

```
\contentsline{section}{\numberline{12.8}Some section that
                is wrapped in the TOC}{87}
\contentsline{section}{\numberline{12.9}Another section}{88}
\contentsline{section}{\numberline{12.10}And yet another
                wrapping section}{90}
\contentsline{section}{\numberline{12.11}Final section}{92}
\contentsfinish
```

2-3-10

```
\contentsmargin [correction] {right-sep}
```

The right margin for all entries can be set to *right-sep* using the `\contentsmargin` declaration. The default value for this margin is `\@pnumwidth`, which is set by the standard classes to be wide enough to contain up to three digits. The optional *correction* argument will be added to all lines of an entry except the last. This argument can, for example, be used to fine-tune the contents layout, so that dots from a row of leaders align with the text of previous lines in a multiple-line entry.

Contents entries combined in a paragraph

Standard LaTeX only supports contents entries formatted on individual lines. In some cases, however, it is more economical to format lower-level entries together in a single paragraph. With the titletoc package this becomes possible.

```
\titlecontents*{type} [left-indent] {before-code}{numbered-entry-format}
                {numberless-entry-format}{page-format} [mid-code]
\titlecontents*{type}...{page-format} [mid-code] [final-code]
\titlecontents*{type}...{page-format} [start-code] [mid-code] [final-code]
```

The `\titlecontents*` declaration is used for entries that should be formatted together with other entries of the same or lower level in a single paragraph. The first six arguments are identical to those of `\titlecontents` described on page 59. But instead of a vertically oriented *below-code* argument, `\titlecontents*` provides one to three optional arguments that handle different situations that can happen when entries are about to be joined horizontally. All three optional arguments are by default empty. The joining works recursively as follows:

- If the current entry is the first entry to participate in joining, then its *start-code* is executed before typesetting the entry.
- Otherwise, there has been a previous entry already participating.
  - If both entries are on the same level, then the *mid-code* is inserted.
  - Otherwise, if the current entry is of a lower level, then the *start-code* for it is inserted and we recourse.
  - Otherwise, the current entry is of a higher level. First, we execute for each level that has ended the *final-code* (in reverse order). Then, if the current entry is not participating in joining, we are done. Otherwise, the *mid-code* for the entry is executed, as a previous entry of the same level should already be present (assuming a hierarchically structured document).

If several levels are to be joined, then you have to specify any paragraph layout information in the *before-code* of the highest level participating. Otherwise, the scope of your settings will not include the paragraph end and thus will not be applied. In the following example, `\footnotesize` applies only to the section entries—the `\baselineskip` for the whole paragraph is still set in `\normalsize`.

This artifical example shows how one can join two different levels using the three optional arguments. Note in particular the spaces added at the beginning of some arguments to get the right result when joining.

```
\usepackage{titletoc}
\contentsmargin{0pt}
\titlecontents*{chapter}[0pt]{\sffamily}
      {}{}{, \thecontentspage}[ \textbullet\ ][~\P]
\titlecontents*{section}[0pt]{\footnotesize\slshape}
      {}{}{}[ \{][; ][\}]
\contentsline{chapter}{\numberline{1}A first}{1}
\contentsline{chapter}{\numberline{2}A second}{4}
\contentsline{section}{\numberline{2.1}sec-A}{5}
\contentsline{section}{\numberline{2.2}sec-B}{6}
\contentsline{chapter}{\numberline{3}A third}{8}
\contentsline{section}{\numberline{3.1}sec-C}{8}
\contentsfinish
```

A first, 1 • A second, 4 *{sec-A; sec-B}* •
A third, 8 *{sec-C}* ¶

2-3-11

Let us now see how this works in practice. In the next example we join the section level, separating entries by a bullet surrounded by some stretchable space (\xquad) and finishing the list with a period. The chapter entries are interesting as well, because we move the page number to the left. Both types omit the heading numbers completely in this design. As there are no page numbers at the right, we also set the right margin to zero.

15 The Structure of a LaTeX Document

The structure of a source file, 15 • Sectioning commands, 22 • Table of contents structures, 45 • Managing references, 66.

79 Basic Formatting Tools

Phrases and paragraphs, 80 • Footnotes, endnotes, and marginals, 109 • List structures, 128 • Simulating typed text, 151.

```
\usepackage{titletoc}
\contentsmargin{0pt}
\titlecontents{chapter}[0pt]
      {\addvspace{1.4pc}\bfseries}
      {{\Huge\thecontentspage\quad}}{}{}
\newcommand\xquad
      {\hspace{1em plus.4em minus.4em}}
\titlecontents*{section}[0pt]
      {\filright\small}{}{}
      {,~\thecontentspage}
      [\xquad\textbullet\xquad][.]
\setcounter{tocdepth}{1}
\input{partial.toc}\contentsfinish
```

2-3-12

As a second example we look at a set-up implementing a layout close to the one used in *Methods of Book Design* [170]. This design uses non-lining digits, something we achieve by using the eco package. The \chapter titles are set in small capitals. To arrange that we use \scshape and turn all letters in the title to lower-case using \MakeLowercase (remember that the last token of the *numbered-entry-format* and the *numberless-entry-format* arguments can be a command with one argument to receive the heading text). The sections are all run together in a paragraph with the section number getting a § sign prepended. Separation between entries is a period followed by a space, and the final section is finished with a period as well.

```
\usepackage{eco,titletoc}
\contentsmargin{0pt}
\titlecontents{chapter}[1.5pc]
  {\addvspace{2pc}\large}
  {\contentslabel{2pc}%
   \scshape\MakeLowercase}
  {\scshape\MakeLowercase}
  {\hfill\thecontentspage}
  [\vspace{2pt}]
\titlecontents*{section}[1.5pc]
  {\small}{\S\thecontentslabel\ }{}
  {,~\thecontentspage}[. ][.]
\setcounter{tocdepth}{1}
\input{partial.toc}
\contentsfinish
```

2-3-13

Generating partial table of contents lists

It is possible to generate partial contents lists using the titletoc package; it provides four commands for this purpose.

> \startcontents [*name*]

A partial table of contents is started with \startcontents. It is possible to collect data for several partial TOCs in parallel, such as one for the current \part as well as one for the current \chapter. In that case the optional *name* argument allows us to distinguish between the two (its default value is the string default). Concurrently running partial TOCs are allowed to overlap each other, although normally they will be nested. All information about these partial TOCs is stored in a single file with the extension .ptc; this file is generated once a single \startcontents command is executed.

> \printcontents [*name*] {*prefix*} {*start-level*} {*toc-code*}

This command prints the current partial TOC started earlier by \startcontents; if the optional *name* argument is used, then a partial contents list with that *name* must have been started.[1]

It is quite likely that you want to format the partial TOC differently from the main table of contents. To allow for this the *prefix* argument is prepended to any entry *type* when looking for a layout definition provided via \titlecontents or its starred form. In the example below we used p- as the *prefix* and then defined a formatting for p-subsection to format \subsection entries in the partial TOC.

---

[1] The package is currently (as of 2003) quite unforgiving if you try to print a contents list without first starting it—you will receive an unspecific low-level TeX error.

The *start-level* argument defines the first level that is shown in the partial TOC; in the example we used the value 2 to indicate that we want to see all subsections and lower levels.

The depth to which we want to include entries in the partial TOC can be set in *toc-code* by setting the `tocdepth` to a suitable value. Other initializations for typesetting the partial TOC can be made there as well. In the example we cancel any right margin, because the partial TOC is formated as a single paragraph.

Integrating partial TOCs in the heading definitions so that there is no need to change the actual document is very easy when titletoc is used together with the titlesec package. Below we extend Example 2-2-18 from page 40 so that the `\section` command now automatically prints a partial TOC of all its subsections. This is done by using the optional *after-code* argument of the `\titleformat` declaration. We first add some vertical space, thereby ensuring that no page break can happen at this point. We next (re)start the `default` partial TOC with `\startcontents`. We then immediately typeset it using `\printcontents`; its arguments have been explained above. Finally, we set up a formatting for subsections in a partial TOC using `\titlecontents*` to run them together in a justified paragraph whose last line is centered (`\fillast`). Stringing this all together gives the desired output without any modification to the document source. Of course, a real design would also change the look and feel of the subsection headings in the document to better fit those of the sections.

```
\usepackage{titlesec,titletoc}
\titleformat{\section}[frame]{\normalfont}
   {\footnotesize \enspace SECTION \thesection
    \enspace}{6pt}{\large\bfseries\filcenter}
   [\vspace*{5pt}\startcontents
    \printcontents{p-}{2}{\contentsmargin{0pt}}]
\titlespacing*{\section}{1pc}{*4}{*2.3}[1pc]
\titlecontents*{p-subsection}[0pt]
   {\small\itshape\fillast}{}{}{}[ --- ][.]
\section{A Title Test}
Some text to prove that this paragraph is not indented.
\subsection{A first}  Some text       \ldots \newpage
\subsection{A longer second} Some more text.
\stopcontents  \subsection{A third}  \resumecontents
\subsection{An even longer fourth}
```

— SECTION 1 —

A Title Test

A first — A longer second — An even longer fourth.

Some text to prove that this paragraph is not indented.

1.1 A first

2-3-14 Some text ...

If necessary, one can temporarily (or permanently) stop collecting entries for a partial TOC. We made use of this feature in the previous example by suppressing the third subsection.

`\stopcontents` [*name*]	`\resumecontents` [*name*]

The `\stopcontents` command stops the entry collection for the `default` partial TOC or, if used with the *name* argument, for the TOC with that *name*. At a later point the collection can be restarted using \resumecontents. Note that this is quite different from calling \startcontents, which starts a *new* partial TOC, thereby making the old entries inaccessible.

2.4   Managing references

LaTeX has commands that make it easy to manage references in a document. In particular, it supports *cross-references* (internal references between elements within a document), *bibliographic* citations (references to external documents), and *indexing* of selected words or expressions. Indexing facilities will be discussed in Chapter 11, and bibliographic citations in Chapters 12 and 13.

To allow cross-referencing of elements inside a document, you should assign a "key" (consisting of a string of ASCII letters, digits, and punctuation) to the given structural element and then use that key to refer to that element elsewhere.

```
\label{key}   \ref{key}   \pageref{key}
```

The \label command assigns the *key* to the currently "active" element of the document (see below for determining which element is active at a given point). The \ref command typesets a string, identifying the given element—such as the section, equation, or figure number—depending on the type of structural element that was active when the \label command was issued. The \pageref command typesets the number of the page where the \label command was given. The *key* strings should, of course, be unique. As a simple aid it can be useful to prefix them with a string identifying the structural element in question: sec might represent sectional units, fig would identify figures, and so on.

```
\section{A Section} \label{sec:this}

A reference to this section looks
like this:  ``see section~\ref{sec:this}
on page~\pageref{sec:this}''.
```

4   A Section

A reference to this section looks like this: "see section 4 on page 6".

2-4-1

Restrictions on the characters used in keys
There is a potential danger when using punctuation characters such as a colon. In certain language styles within the babel system (see Chapter 9), some of these characters have special meanings and behave essentially like commands. The babel package tries hard to allow such characters as part of \label keys but this can fail in some situations. Similarly, characters outside the ASCII range, made available through packages such as inputenc, are not officially supported in such keys and are likely to produce errors if used.

For building cross-reference labels, the "currently active" structural element of a document is determined in the following way. The sectioning commands (\chapter, \section, ...), the environments equation, figure, table, and the theorem family, as well as the various levels of the enumerate environment, and

\footnote set the *current reference string*, which contains the number generated by LaTeX for the given element. This reference string is usually set at the beginning of an element and reset when the scope of the element is exited.

Notable exceptions to this rule are the table and figure environments, where the reference string is defined by the \caption commands. This allows several \caption and \label pairs inside one environment.[1] As it is the \caption directive that generates the number, the corresponding \label command must *follow* the \caption command in question. Otherwise, an incorrect number will be generated. If placed earlier in the float body, the \label command will pick up the *current reference string* from some earlier entity, typically the current sectional unit.

Problems with wrong references on floats

The problem is shown clearly in the following example, where only the labels "fig:in2" and "fig:in3" are placed correctly to generate the needed reference numbers for the figures. In the case of "fig:in4" it is seen that environments (in this case, center) limit the scope of references, since we obtain the number of the current section, rather than the number of the figure.

3   A section

3.1   A subsection

Text before is referenced as '3.1'.

+--------------------+
| ... figure body ... |
+--------------------+

Figure 1: First caption

+--------------------+
| ... figure body ... |
+--------------------+

Figure 2: Second caption

The labels are: 'before' (3.1), 'fig:in1' (3.1), 'fig:in2' (1), 'fig:in3' (2), 'fig:in4' (3.1), 'after' (3.1).

2-4-2

```
\section{A section}
\subsection{A subsection}\label{sec:before}
Text before is referenced as '\ref{sec:before}'.

\begin{figure}[ht]            \label{fig:in1}
 \begin{center}
   \fbox{\ldots{} figure body \ldots}
   \caption{First caption}    \label{fig:in2}
   \bigskip
   \fbox{\ldots{} figure body \ldots}
   \caption{Second caption}   \label{fig:in3}
 \end{center}                 \label{fig:in4}
\end{figure}
\label{sec:after}

\raggedright
The labels are: 'before' (\ref{sec:before}),
'fig:in1' (\ref{fig:in1}), 'fig:in2'
(\ref{fig:in2}), 'fig:in3' (\ref{fig:in3}),
'fig:in4' (\ref{fig:in4}), 'after'
(\ref{sec:after}).
```

For each *key* declared with \label{*key*}, LaTeX records the current reference string and the page number. Thus, multiple \label commands (with different key identifiers *key*) inside the same sectional unit will generate an identical reference string but, possibly, different page numbers.

---

[1]There are, however, good reasons for not placing more than one \caption command within a float environment. Typically proper spacing is difficult to achieve and, more importantly, future versions of LaTeX might make this syntax invalid.

2.4.1 showkeys—**Displaying the reference keys**

When writing a larger document many people print intermediate drafts. With such drafts it would be helpful if the positions of \label commands as well as their keys could be made visible. This becomes possible with the showkeys package written by David Carlisle.

When this package is loaded, the commands \label, \ref, \pageref, \cite, and \bibitem are modified in a way that the used key is printed. The \label and \bibitem commands normally cause the key to appear in a box in the margin, while the commands referencing a key print it in small type above the formatted reference (possibly overprinting some text). The package tries hard to position the keys in such a way that the rest of the document's formatting is kept unchanged. There is, however, no guarantee for this, and it is best to remove or disable the showkeys package before attempting final formatting of the document.

sec

1   An example

Section~1 shows the use of the showkeys package with a reference to equation (1).

$$a = b \qquad (1)$$

eq

```
\usepackage{showkeys}
\section{An example}\label{sec}
Section~\ref{sec} shows the use of the
\texttt{showkeys} package with a
reference to equation~(\ref{eq}).
\begin{equation}
  a = b \label{eq}
\end{equation}
```

2-4-3

The package supports the fleqn option of the standard classes and works together with the packages of the $\mathcal{A}_{\mathcal{M}}S$-LaTeX collection, varioref, natbib, and many other packages. Nevertheless, it is nearly impossible to ensure its safe working with all packages that hook into the reference mechanisms.

If you want to see only the keys on the \label command in the margin, you can suppress the others by using the package option notref (which disables the redefinition of \ref, \pageref, and related commands) or the option notcite (which does the same for \cite and its cousins from the natbib and harvard packages). Alternatively, you might want to use the option color to make the labels less obstructive.

Finally, the package supports the options draft (default) and final. While the latter is useless when used on the package level, because you can achieve the same result by not specifying the showkeys package, it comes in handy if final is specified as a global option on the class.

2.4.2 varioref—**More flexible cross-references**

In many cases it is helpful, when referring to a figure or table, to put both a \ref and a \pageref command into the document, especially when one or more pages separate the reference and the object. Some people use a command like

```
\newcommand\fullref[1]{\ref{#1} on page~\pageref{#1}}
```

to reduce the number of keystrokes necessary to make a complete reference. But because one never knows with certainty where the referenced object finally falls, this method can result in a citation to the current page, which is disturbing and should therefore be avoided. The package varioref, written by Frank Mittelbach, tries to solve that problem. It provides the commands \vref and \vpageref to deal with single references, as well as \vrefrange and \vpagerefrange to handle multiple references. In addition, its \labelformat declaration offers the ability to format references differently depending on the counter used in the reference.

| `\vref*{`*key*`}` |

The command \vref is like \ref when the reference and \label are on the same page. If the label and reference differ by one page, \vref creates one of these strings: "on the facing page", "on the preceding page", or "on the following page". The word "facing" is used when both label and reference fall on a double spread. When the difference is larger than one page, \vref produces both \ref and \pageref. Note that when a special page numbering scheme is used instead of the usual Arabic numbering (for example, \pagenumbering{roman}), there will be no distinction between being one or many pages off.

There is one other difference between \ref and \vref: the latter removes any preceding space and inserts its own. In some cases, such as after an opening parenthesis, this is not desirable. In such cases, use \vref*, which acts like \vref but does not add any space before the generated text.

| `\vpageref*[`*samepage*`] [`*otherpage*`]{`*key*`}` |

Sometimes you may only want to refer to a page number. In that case, a reference should be suppressed if you are citing the current page. For this purpose the \vpageref command is defined. It produces the same strings as \vref except that it does not start with \ref, and it produces the string saved in \reftextcurrent if both label and reference fall on the same page.

Defining \reftextcurrent to produce something like "on this page" ensures that text like

```
... see the diagram \vpageref{ex:foo} which shows ...
```

does not come out as "... see the diagram which shows ...", which could be misleading.

You can put a space in front of \vpageref; it will be ignored if the command does not create any text at all. If some text is added, an appropriate space is automatically placed in front of the text. The variant form \vpageref* removes preceding white space before the generated text but does not reinsert its own. Use it if the space otherwise generated poses a problem.

In fact, \vpageref and \vpageref* allow even more control when used with their two optional arguments. The first argument specifies the text to be used if the label and reference fall on the same page. This is helpful when both are close together, so that they may or may not be separated by a page break. In such a case, you will usually know whether the reference comes before or after the label so that you can code something like the following:

```
... see the diagram \vpageref[above]{ex:foo} which shows ...
```

The resultant text will be "... see the diagram above which shows ..." when both are on the same page, or "... see the diagram on the page before which shows ..." (or something similar, depending on the settings of the \reftext..before and \reftext..after commands) if they are separated by a page break. Note, however, that if you use \vpageref with the optional argument to refer to a figure or table, depending on the float placement parameters, the float may show up at the top of the current page and therefore before the reference, even if it follows the reference in the source file.[1]

Maybe you even prefer to say "... see the above diagram" when both diagram and reference fall on the same page—that is, reverse the word order compared to our previous example. In fact, in some languages the word order automatically changes in that case. To allow for this variation the second optional argument *otherpage* can be used. It specifies the text preceding the generated reference if both object and reference do not fall on the same page. Thus, one would write

```
... see the \vpageref[above diagram][diagram]{ex:foo} which shows ...
```

to achieve the desired effect.

The amsmath package provides a \eqref command to reference equations. It automatically places parentheses around the equation number. To utilize this, one could define

```
\newcommand\eqvref[1]{\eqref{#1}\ \vpageref{#1}}
```

to automatically add a page reference to it.

> \vrefrange [*here-text*] {*start-key*}{*end-key*}

This command is similar to \vref but takes two mandatory arguments denoting a range of objects to refer to (e.g., a sequence of figures or a sequence of equations). It decides what to say depending on where the two labels are placed in

---

[1]To ensure that a floating object always follows its place in the source use the flafter package, which is described in Section 6.2.

relation to each other; it is essentially implemented using \vpagerefrange (described below). The optional argument that the command may take is the text to use in case both labels appear on the current page. Its default is the string stored in \reftextcurrent.

---

1 Test

Observe equations 1.1 to 1.3 on pages 6–7 and in particular equations 1.2 to 1.3 on the facing page.

$$a = b + c \qquad (1.1)$$

2-4-4   6

Here is a second equation...

$$b = a + c \qquad (1.2)$$

...and finally one more equation:

$$c = a + b \qquad (1.3)$$

7

```
\usepackage{varioref}
\renewcommand\theequation
     {\thesection.\arabic{equation}}
\section{Test}
Observe equations~\vrefrange{A}{C} and
in particular equations~\vrefrange{B}{C}.
\begin{equation}
      a=b+c\label{A}     \end{equation}
Here is a second equation\ldots
\begin{equation}
      b=a+c\label{B}     \end{equation}
\ldots and finally one more equation:
\begin{equation}
      c=a+b\label{C}     \end{equation}
```

> **\vpagerefrange*[*here-text*]{*start-key*}{*end-key*}**

This command is similar to \vpageref but takes two mandatory arguments—two labels denoting a range. If both labels fall on the same page, the command acts exactly like \vpageref (with a single label); otherwise, it produces something like "on pages 15–18" (see the customization possibilities described below). Like \vrefrange it has an optional argument that defaults to the string stored in \reftextcurrent and is used if both labels appear on the current page.

Again there exists a starred form, \vpagerefrange*, which removes preceding white space before the generated text without reinserting its own space.

A reference via \ref produces, by default, the data associated with the corresponding \label command (typically a number); any additional formatting must *Fancy labels* be provided by the user. If, for example, references to equations are always to be typeset as "equation (*number*)", one has to code "equation (\ref{*key*})".

> **\labelformat{*counter*}{*formatting-code*}**

With \labelformat the varioref package offers a possibility to generate such frills automatically.[1] The command takes two arguments: the name of a counter and its representation when referenced. Thus, for a successful usage, one has to know the counter name being used for generating the label, though in practice this should not pose a problem. The current counter number (or, more exactly, its representation) is picked up as an argument, so the second argument should contain #1.

---

[1] This command is also available separately with the fncylab package written by Robin Fairbairns.

A side effect of using \labelformat is that, depending on the defined formatting, it becomes impossible to use \ref at the beginning of a sentence (if its replacement text starts with a lowercase letter). To overcome this problem varioref introduces the commands \Ref and \Vref (including starred forms) that behave like \ref and \vref except that they uppercase the first token of the generated string. In the following example (which you should compare to Example 2-4-3 on page 68), you can observe this behavior when "section" is turned into "Section".

1   An example

Section 1 shows the use of the \labelformat declaration with a reference to equation (1).

$$a = b \qquad (1)$$

```
\usepackage{varioref}
\labelformat{section}{section~#1}
\labelformat{equation}{equation~(#1)}
\section{An example}\label{sec}
\Ref{sec} shows the use of the \verb=\labelformat=
declaration with a reference to \ref{eq}.
\begin{equation} a = b \label{eq} \end{equation}
```

2-4-5

To make \Ref or \Vref work properly the first token in the second argument of \labelformat has to be a simple ASCII letter; otherwise, the capitalization will fail or, even worse, you will end up with some error messages. If you actually need something more complicated in this place (e.g., an accented letter), you have to explicitly surround it with braces, thereby identifying the part that needs to be capitalized. For example, for figure references in the Hungarian language you might want to write \labelformat{figure}{{\'a}bra~\thefigure}.

As a second example of the use of \labelformat consider the following situation: in the report or book document class, footnotes are numbered per chapter. Referencing them would normally be ambiguous, given that it is not clear whether we refer to a footnote in the current chapter or to a footnote from a different chapter. This ambiguity can be resolved by always adding the chapter information in the reference, or by comparing the chapter number in which the \label with the current chapter number and adding extra information if they differ. This is achieved by the following code:

```
\usepackage{ifthen,varioref}
\labelformat{footnote}{#1\protect\iscurrentchapter{\thechapter}}
\newcommand\iscurrentchapter[1]{%
    \ifthenelse{\equal{#1}{\thechapter}}{}{ in Chapter~#1}}
```

The trick is to use \protect to prevent \iscurrentchapter from being evaluated when the label is formed. Then when the \ref command is executed, \iscurrentchapter will compare its argument (i.e., the chapter number current when the label was formed) to the now current chapter number and, when they differ, typeset the appropriate information.

Providing your own reference commands   The package also provides the \vrefpagenum command, which allows you to write your own small commands that implement functions similar to those provided by the two previous commands. It takes two arguments: the second is a label (i.e., as used in \label or \ref) and the first is an arbitrary command name (make sure you use your own) that receives the page number related to this label. Thus, if you have two (or more) labels, you could retrieve their page numbers, compare them, and then decide what to print.

The next example shows a not very serious application that compares two equation labels and prints out text depending on their relative positions. Compare the results of the tests on the first page with those on the second.

Test: the equations 1 and 2 on this page

Test: the equation 1 on the current page and 3 on page 8

$$a = b + c \qquad (1)$$

$$b = a + c \qquad (2)$$

Test: the equations 1 and 2 on the preceding page

Test: the equation 1 on the facing page and 3 on the next page

6

7

```
\usepackage{varioref,ifthen}
\newcommand\veqns[2]{%
  \vrefpagenum\firstnum{#1}%
  \vrefpagenum\secondnum{#2}%
  the equation%
  \ifthenelse
    {\equal\firstnum\secondnum}%
    {s \ref{#1}}%
    { \ref{#1}\vpageref{#1}}%
  \space and \ref{#2}\vpageref{#2}%
}
Test: \veqns{A}{B} \par Test: \veqns{A}{C}
\begin{equation} a=b+c \label{A}\end{equation}
\begin{equation} b=a+c \label{B}\end{equation}
\newpage
Test: \veqns{A}{B} \par Test: \veqns{A}{C}
\newpage
\begin{equation} c=a+b \label{C}\end{equation}
```

2-4-6

The package supports the options defined by the babel system (see Section 9.1.3); thus a declaration like \usepackage[german]{varioref} will produce texts suitable for the German language. In addition, the package supports the options final (default) and draft; the latter changes certain error messages (described on page 75) into warnings. This ability can be useful during the development of a document.

Package options

To allow further customization, the generated text strings (which will be predefined by the language options) are all defined via macros. Backward references use \reftextbefore if the label is on the preceding page but invisible, and \reftextfacebefore if it is on the facing page (that is, if the current page number is odd).

Individual customization

Similarly, \reftextafter is used when the label comes on the next page but one has to turn the page, and \reftextfaceafter when it is on the next, but facing, page. These four strings can be redefined with \renewcommand.

The command \reftextfaraway is used when the label and reference differ by more than one page, or when they are non-numeric. This macro is a bit different from the preceding ones because it takes one argument, the symbolic reference string, so that you can make use of \pageref in its replacement text. For instance, if you wanted to use your macros in German language documents, you would define something like:

```
\renewcommand\reftextfaraway[1]{auf Seite~\pageref{#1}}
```

The `\reftextpagerange` command takes two arguments and produces the text that describes a page range (the arguments are keys to be used with `\pageref`). See below for the English language default.

Similarly, `\reftextlabelrange` takes two arguments and describes the range of figures, tables, or whatever the labels refer to. The default for English is "`\ref{#1} to~\ref{#2}`".

To allow some random variation in the generated strings, you can use the command `\reftextvario` inside the string macros. This command takes two arguments and selects one or the other for printing depending on the number of `\vref` or `\vpageref` commands already encountered in the document.

The default definitions of the various macros described in this section are shown below:

```
\newcommand\reftextfaceafter
        {on the \reftextvario{facing}{next} page}
\newcommand\reftextfacebefore
        {on the \reftextvario{facing}{preceding} page}
\newcommand\reftextafter
        {on the \reftextvario{following}{next} page}
\newcommand\reftextbefore
        {on the \reftextvario{preceding page}{page before}}
\newcommand\reftextcurrent
        {on \reftextvario{this}{the current} page}
\newcommand\reftextfaraway    [1]{on page~\pageref{#1}}
\newcommand\reftextpagerange [2]{on pages~\pageref{#1}--\pageref{#2}}
\newcommand\reftextlabelrange[2]{\ref{#1} to~\ref{#2}}
```

If you want to customize the package according to your own preferences, just write appropriate redefinitions of the above commands in a file with the extension `.sty` (e.g., `vrflocal.sty`). If you also put `\RequirePackage{varioref}` (see Section A.4 on page 877) at the beginning of this file, then your local package will automatically load the varioref package. If you use the babel system, redefinitions for individual languages should be added using `\addto`, as explained in Section 9.5.

Some people do not like textual references to pages but want to automatically suppress a page reference when both label and reference fall on the same page. This can be achieved with the help of the `\thevpagerefnum` command as follows:

```
\renewcommand\reftextfaceafter {on page~\thevpagerefnum}
\renewcommand\reftextfacebefore{on page~\thevpagerefnum}
\renewcommand\reftextafter     {on page~\thevpagerefnum}
\renewcommand\reftextbefore    {on page~\thevpagerefnum}
```

Within one of the `\reftext...` commands, `\thevpagerefnum` evaluates to the current page number if known, or to two question marks otherwise.

Defining commands, like the ones described above, poses some interesting problems. Suppose, for example, that a generated text like "on the next page" *A few warnings* gets broken across pages. If this happens, it is very difficult to find an acceptable algorithmic solution and, in fact, this situation can even result in a document that will always change from one state to another (i.e., inserting one string; finding that this is wrong; inserting another string on the next run which makes the first string correct again; inserting ...). The current implementation of the package varioref considers the end of the generated string as being relevant. For example,

> Table 5 on the current ⟨*page break*⟩ page

would be true if Table 5 were on the page containing the word "page", not the one containing the word "current". However, this behavior is not completely satisfactory, and in some cases may actually result in a possible loop (where LaTeX is requesting an additional run over and over again). Therefore, all such situations will produce a LaTeX error message, so that you can inspect the problem and perhaps decide to use a `\ref` command in that place.

Also, be aware of the potential problems that can result from using `\reftextvario`: if you reference the same object several times in nearby places, the change in wording every second time will look strange.

A final warning: every use of `\vref` or `\vpageref` internally generates two macro names. As a result, you may run out of name space or main memory if you make heavy use of this command on a small TeX installation. For this reason the command `\fullref` is also provided. It can be used whenever you are sure that both label and reference cannot fall on nearby pages.

2.4.3   prettyref—**Adding frills to references**

One problem with LaTeX's cross-referencing mechanism is that it only produces the element number (or the page number) but leaves the surrounding formatting as the responsibility of the author. This means that uniform references are difficult to achieve. For example, if the publisher's house style requires that figures be referenced as "Fig.xx" one has to manually go through the source document and change all references to that format.

The prettyref package written by Kevin Ruland provides automatic support for such additional formatting strings, provided the *keys* used on the `\label` commands obey a certain structure. They have to be of the form "⟨*prefix*⟩:⟨*name*⟩" with neither *prefix* nor *name* containing a colon (e.g., `fig:main`), a form used by many people anyway. The extra formatting strings are produced when using the command `\prettyref`; standard `\ref` and `\pageref` are not affected by the package. Note that this is different from the `\labelformat` declaration, as provided by varioref, which changes the display of the reference labels in all circumstances.

> `\newrefformat{`*prefix*`}{`*code*`}`

This command defines the formatting for references having the *prefix* as the prefix in their key. The *code* argument uses #1 to refer to the key used so that it can be passed to `\ref`, `\vref`, and so on. This format can be accessed when using the *key* with the command `\prettyref`.

4   A Section

A reference to the equation in this section looks like: "see (1) in Section 4".

$$a = b \tag{1}$$

```
\usepackage{prettyref}
\newrefformat{sec}{Section~\ref{#1}}

\section{A Section}\label{sec:this}
A reference to the equation in this section looks like:
``see \prettyref{eq:a} in \prettyref{sec:this}''.
\begin{equation} a = b \label{eq:a} \end{equation}
```

2-4-7

The example shows that the prettyref package has formatting for the ⟨*prefix*⟩ "eq" already built in. In fact, it knows about several other predefined formats, but since most of them allow breaking between the generated text and the number you should probably define your own.

Because this package does not make any distinction between references used at the beginning of a sentence and references used in mid-sentence, it may not be usable in all circumstances. It is also impossible to replace the colon that separates ⟨*prefix*⟩ and ⟨*name*⟩, which means that it cannot be combined with some language packages that use the colon in special ways. In that case you might consider using the fancyref package written by Axel Reichert, which provides a similar functionality but internally uses a much more complex set-up.

2.4.4   titleref—Non-numerical references

In some documents it is required to reference sections by displaying their title texts instead of their numbers, either because there is no number to refer to or because the house style asks for it. This functionality is available through the titleref package written by Donald Arseneau, which provides the command `\titleref` to cross-reference the titles of sections and float captions.

For numbered sections and floats with captions, the titles are those that would be displayed in the contents lists (regardless of whether such a list is actually printed). That is, if a short title is provided via the optional argument of a sectioning command or caption, then this title is printed by `\titleref`. Unnumbered sections take their title reference from the printed title. As a consequence, all arguments of `\caption` and the sectioning commands are turned into moving arguments, which will cause weird errors if they contain un`\protected` fragile commands.

All arguments become moving arguments

A `\titleref` to a label unrelated to a title (e.g., a label in a footnote, or an enumeration item) will simply pick up any earlier title, typically the one from the surrounding section.

As shown in the next example, the title of the current section is available through \currenttitle, independently of whether it was associated with a \label key. The example also shows that \titleref and \ref can coexist.

1   Textual References

In section "Textual References" we prove that it is possible to reference unnumbered sections by referencing section "Example".

A Small Example

2-4-8   The current section is referenced in section 1.

```
\usepackage{titleref}
\setcounter{secnumdepth}{1}

\section{Textual References}\label{num}
In section ``\currenttitle{}'' we prove that
it is possible to reference unnumbered sections
by referencing section ``\titleref{ex}''.

\subsection[Example]{A Small Example}\label{ex}
The current section is referenced in
section~\ref{num}.
```

The format of the title reference can be controlled by redefining the command \theTitleReference. It takes two arguments: a *number* as it would be displayed by \ref, and a *title*. If a document contains references to unnumbered titles, the *number* argument should not be used in the replacement text as it will contain an arbitrary number. For instance, the \titleref command in the next example displays "1", even though the reference is to an unnumbered section.

1   Textual References

In section *1 Textual References* we prove that it is possible to reference unnumbered sections by referencing section *1 Example*.

A Small Example

2-4-9   The current section is referenced in section 1.

```
\usepackage{titleref}
\renewcommand\theTitleReference[2]{\emph{#1\ #2}}
\setcounter{secnumdepth}{1}

\section{Textual References}\label{num}
In section \currenttitle{} we prove that
it is possible to reference unnumbered
sections by referencing section \titleref{ex}.

\subsection[Example]{A Small Example}\label{ex}
The current section is referenced in
section~\ref{num}.
```

By default, the package works by inserting additional code into commands that are typically used to build headings, captions, and other elements. If combined with other packages that provide their own methods for typesetting titles, it might create conflicts. In that case you can tell the package to use a completely different approach by specifying the option usetoc. As the name implies, it directs the package to record the titles from the data written to the contents lists by redefining \addcontentsline. A consequence of this approach is that the \label command is not allowed within the *title* argument but has to follow it. In addition, no \addcontentsline command is allowed to intervene between heading and label. As starred sectioning commands do not generate contents entries, they are still redefined. This can be prevented by additionally specifying the option nostar, although then one can no longer refer to their titles.

Conflicts with other packages

2.4.5 hyperref—Active references

Sebastian Rahtz has developed the package hyperref, which makes it possible to turn all cross-references (citations, table of contents, and so on) into hypertext links. It works by extending the existing commands with functionality to produce \special commands that suitably equipped drivers can use to turn the references into hypertext links. The package is described in detail in [56, pp.35–67] and comes with its own manual, which itself contains hypertext links produced using the package.

The usage of hyperref can be quite easy. Just including it in your list of loaded packages (as the *last* package) suffices to turn all cross-references in your document into hypertext links. The package has a number of options to change the way the hypertext links look or work. The most important options are colorlinks, which makes the text of the link come out in color instead of with a box around it, and backref, which inserts links in the bibliography pointing to the place where an entry was cited.

The package offers a number of ways to influence the behavior of the PDF file produced from your document as well as ways to influence the behavior of the PDF viewer, such as the Acrobat Reader.

2.4.6 xr—References to external documents

David Carlisle, building on earlier work of Jean-Pierre Drucbert, developed a package called xr, which implements a system for external references.

If, for instance, a document needs to refer to sections of another document—say, other.tex—then you can specify the xr package in the main file and give the command \externaldocument{other} in the preamble. Then you can use \ref and \pageref to refer to anything that has been defined with a \label command in either other.tex or your main document. You may declare any number of such external documents.

If any of the external documents or the main document uses the same \label key, then a conflict will occur because the key will have been multiply defined. To overcome this problem, \externaldocument takes an optional argument. If you declare \externaldocument[A-]{other}, then all references from the file other.tex are prefixed by A-. So, for instance, if a section in the file other.tex had a \label{intro}, then it could be referenced with \ref{A-intro}. The prefix need not be A-; it can be any string chosen to ensure that all the labels imported from external files are unique.

Note, however, that if one of the packages you are using declares certain active characters (e.g., : in French or " in German), then these characters should not be used inside \label commands. Similarly, you should not use them in the optional argument to \externaldocument.

The package does not work together with the hyperref package because both modify the internal reference mechanism. Instead, you can use the xr-hyper package, which is a reimplementation tailored to work with hyperref.

## CHAPTER 3

Basic Formatting Tools

The way information is presented visually can influence, to a large extent, the message as it is understood by the reader. Therefore, it is important that you use the best possible tools available to convey the precise meaning of your words. It must, however, be emphasized that visual presentation forms should aid the reader in understanding the text, and should not distract his or her attention. For this reason, visual consistency and uniform conventions for the visual clues are a must, and the way given structural elements are highlighted should be the same throughout a document. This constraint is most easily implemented by defining a specific command or environment for each document element that has to be treated specially and by grouping these commands and environments in a package file or in the document preamble. By using exclusively these commands, you can be sure of a consistent presentation form.

This chapter explains various ways for highlighting parts of a document. The first part looks at how short text fragments or paragraphs can be made to stand out and describes tools to manipulate such elements.

The second part deals with the different kind of "notes", such as footnotes, marginal notes, and endnotes, and explains how they can be customized to conform to different styles, if necessary.

Typesetting lists is the subject of the third part. First, the various parameters and commands controlling the standard LaTeX lists, enumerate, itemize, and description, are discussed. Then, the extensions provided by the paralist package and the concept of "headed lists" exemplified by the amsthm package are presented. These will probably satisfy the structure and layout requirements of most readers. If not, then the remainder of this part introduces the generic list environment and explains how to build custom layouts by varying the values of the parameters controlling it.

The fourth part explains how to simulate "verbatim" text. In particular, we have a detailed look at the powerful packages fancyvrb and listings.

The final part presents packages that deal with line numbering, handling of columns, such as parallel text in two columns, or solving the problem of producing multiple columns.

3.1   Phrases and paragraphs

In this section we deal with small text fragments and explain how they can be manipulated and highlighted in a consistent manner by giving them a visual appearance different from the one used for the main text.

We start by discussing how to define commands that take care of the space after them, then show a way to produce professional-looking marks of omission.

For highlighting text you can customize the font shape, weight, or size (see Section 7.3.1 on page 338). Text can also be underlined, or the spacing between letters can be varied. Ways for performing such operations are offered by the four packages relsize, textcase, ulem, and soul.

The remainder of this section then turns to paragraph-related issues, such as producing large initial letters at the start of a paragraph, modifying paragraph justification, altering the vertical spacing between lines of a paragraph, and introducing rectangular holes into it, that can be filled with small pictures, among other things.

3.1.1   xspace—Gentle spacing after a macro

The small package xspace (by David Carlisle) defines the \xspace command, for use at the end of macros that produce text. It adds a space unless the macro is followed by certain punctuation characters.

The \xspace command saves you from having to type \␣ or {} after most occurrences of a macro name in text. However, if either of these constructs follows \xspace, a space is not added by \xspace. This means that it is safe to add \xspace to the end of an existing macro without making too many changes in your document. Possible candidates for \xspace are commands for abbreviations such as "e.g.," and "i.e.,".

```
\newcommand\eg{e.g.,\xspace}
\newcommand\ie{i.e.,\xspace}
\newcommand\etc{etc.\@\xspace}
```

Notice the use of the \@ command to generate the correct kind of space. If used to the right of a punctuation character, it prevents extra space from being added: the dot will not be regarded as an end-of-sentence symbol. Using it on the left forces LaTeX to interpret the dot as an end-of-sentence symbol.

   Sometimes `\xspace` may make a wrong decision and add a space when it is not required. In such cases, follow the macro with `{}`, which will suppress this space.

Great Britain was unified in 1707. Great Britain, the United States of America, and Canada have close cultural links.

```
\usepackage{xspace}
\newcommand\USA{United States of America\xspace}
\newcommand\GB {Great Britain\xspace}

\GB was unified in 1707.\\ \GB, the \USA, and
Canada have close cultural links.
```

3-1-1

3.1.2   ellipsis, lips—**Marks of omission**

Omission marks are universally represented by three consecutive periods (also known as an *ellipsis*). Their spacing, however, depends on house style and typographic conventions, and significant difference are observed. In French, according to Hart [63] or *The Chicago Manual of Style* [38], "points de suspension" are set close together and immediately follow the preceding word with a space on the right:

   C'est une chose... bien difficile.

In German, according to the Duden [44], "Auslassungspunkte" have space on the left *and* right unless they mark missing letters within a word or a punctuation after them is kept:

   Du E... du! Scher dich zum ...!

Elsewhere, such as in British and American typography, the dots are sometimes set with full word spaces between them and rather complex rules determine how to handle other punctuation marks at either end.

   LaTeX offers the commands `\dots` and `\textellipsis` to produce closely spaced omission marks. Unfortunately, the standard definition (inherited from plain TeX) produces uneven spacing at the left and right—unsuitable to typeset some of the above examples properly. The extra thin space at the right of the ellipsis is correct in certain situations (e.g., when a punctuation character follows). If the ellipsis is followed by space, however, it looks distinctly odd and is best canceled as shown in the example below (though removing the space in the second instance brings the exclamation mark a bit too close).

Compare the following:
Du E... du! Scher dich zum ...!
Du E...du! Scher dich zum ...!

```
\newcommand\lips{\dots\unkern}
Compare the following:\\
  Du E\dots\ du! Scher dich zum \dots!\\
  Du E\lips\ du! Scher dich zum \lips!
```

3-1-2

This problem is addressed in the package ellipsis written by Peter Heslin, which redefines the \dots command to look at the following character to decide whether to add a final separation. An extra space is added if the following character is listed in the command \ellipsispunctuation, which defaults to ",.:;!?". When using some of the language support packages that make certain characters active, this list may have to be redeclared afterwards to enable the package to still recognize the characters.

The spacing between the periods and the one possibly added after the ellipsis can be controlled through the command \ellipsisgap. To allow for automatic adjustments depending on the font size use a font-dependent unit like em or a fraction of a \fontdimen (see page 428).

Compare the following:
Du E... du! Scher dich zum ...!
Du E...du! Scher dich zum ...!
Du E...du! Scher dich zum ...!

```
\usepackage{ellipsis}
Compare the following:\\
  Du E\dots\ du! Scher dich zum \dots!\\
\renewcommand\ellipsisgap{1.5\fontdimen3\font}
  Du E\dots\ du! Scher dich zum \dots!\\
\renewcommand\ellipsisgap{0.3em}
  Du E\dots\ du! Scher dich zum \dots!
```

3-1-3

For the special case when you need an ellipsis in the middle of a word (or for other reasons want a small space at either side), the package offers the command \midwordellipsis. If the package is loaded with the option mla (Modern Language Association style), the ellipsis is automatically bracketed without any extra space after the final period.

If one follows *The Chicago Manual of Style* [38], then an ellipsis is set with full word spaces between the dots. For this, one can deploy the lips package[1] by Matt Swift. It implements the command \lips, which follows the recommendations in this reference book. For example, an ellipsis denoting an omission at the end of a sentence should, according to [38, §10.48–63], consist of four dots with the *first* dot being the sentence period.[2] The \lips command implements this by interpreting "\lips." like ".\lips", as can be seen in the next example.

Elsewhere ... the dots are normally set with full word spaces between them. ... An example would be this paragraph.

```
\usepackage{moredefs,lips}
Elsewhere \lips the dots are normally set with
full word spaces between them \lips. An example
would be this paragraph.
```

3-1-4

The \lips command looks for punctuation characters following it and ensures that in case of ,.:;?!)']/ the ellipsis and the punctuation are not separated by a line break. In other cases (e.g., an opening parenthesis), a line break would be possible. The above list is stored in \LPNobreakList and can be adjusted if

---

[1] lips is actually part of a larger suite of packages. If used on a stand-alone basis, you also have to load the package moredefs by the same author.

[2] Not that the authors of this book can see any logic in this.

necessary. To force an unbreakable space following \lips, follow the command with a tie (~).

When applying the mla option the ellipsis generated will be automatically bracketed and a period after the \lips command will not be moved to the front. If necessary, \olips will produce the original unbracketed version.

3-1-5

Elsewhere . . . the dots are normally set with full word spaces between them [. . .]. An example would be this paragraph.	``` \usepackage{moredefs}\usepackage[mla]{lips} Elsewhere \olips the dots are normally set with full word spaces between them \lips. An example would be this paragraph. ```

3.1.3   amsmath—**Nonbreaking dashes**

The amsmath package, extensively discussed in Chapter 8, also offers one command for use within paragraphs. The command \nobreakdash suppresses any possibility of a line break after the following hyphen or dash. A very common use of \nobreakdash is to prevent undesirable line breaks in usages such as "p-adic" but here is another example: if you code "Pages 3–9" as Pages 3\nobreakdash--9 then a line break will never occur between the dash and the 9.

This command must be used *immediately* before a hyphen or dash (-, --, or ---). The following example shows how to prohibit a line break after the hyphen but allow normal hyphenation in the following word (it suffices to add a zero-width space after the hyphen). For frequent use, it's advisable to make abbreviations, such as \p. As a result "dimension" is broken across the line, while a break after "p-" is prevented (resulting in a overfull box in the example) and "3–9" is moved to the next line.

3-1-6

The generalization to the n-dimensional case (using the standard p-adic topology) can be found on Pages 3–9 of Volume IV.	``` \usepackage{amsmath} \newcommand\p{p\nobreakdash}% "\p-adic" \newcommand\Ndash{\nobreakdash--}% "3\Ndash 9" \newcommand\n[1]{n\nobreakdash-\hspace{0pt}} % "\n-dimensional" \noindent The generalization to the \n-dimensional case (using the standard \p-adic topology) can be found on Pages 3\Ndash 9 of Volume IV. ```

3.1.4   relsize—**Relative changes to the font size**

Standard LaTeX offers 10 predefined commands that change the overall font size (see Table 7.1 on page 342). The selected sizes depend on the document class but are otherwise absolute in value. That is, \small will always select the same size within a document regardless of surrounding conditions.

However, in many situations it is desirable to change the font size relative to the current size. This can be achieved with the relsize package, originally developed by Bernie Cosell and later updated and extended for LaTeX 2_ε by Donald Arseneau and Matt Swift.

The package provides the declarative command \relsize, which takes a number as its argument denoting the number of steps by which to change the size. For example, if the current size is \large then \relsize{-2} would change to \small. If the requested number of steps is not available then the smallest (i.e., \tiny) or largest (i.e., \Huge) size command is selected. This means that undoing a relative size change by negating the argument of \relsize is not guaranteed to bring you back to the original size—it is better to delimit such changes by a brace group and let LaTeX undo the modification.

The package further defines \smaller and \larger, which are simply abbreviations for \relsize with the arguments −1 and 1, respectively. Convenient variants are \textsmaller and \textlarger, whose argument is the text to reduce or enlarge in size. These four commands take as an optional argument the number of steps to change if something different from 1 (the default) is needed.

Some large text with a
few small words inside.

Small Caps (faked)
Small Caps (real; compare the running length and stem thickness to previous line).

```
\usepackage{relsize}
\Large Some large text with  a few
    {\relsize{-2} small words} inside.
\par\medskip
\normalsize\noindent
S\textsmaller[2]{MALL} C\textsmaller[2]{APS} (faked)\\
\textsc{Small Caps} (real; compare the running length
    and stem thickness to previous line).
```

3-1-7

In fact, the above description for \relsize is not absolutely accurate: it tries to increase or decrease the size by 20% for each step and selects the LaTeX font size command that is closest to the resulting target size. It then compares the selected size and target size. If they differ by more than the current value of \RSpercentTolerance (interpreted as a percentage), the package calls \fontsize with the target size as one of the arguments. If this happens it is up to LaTeX's font selection scheme to find a font matching this request as closely as possible. By default, \RSpercentTolerance is an empty macro, which is interpreted as 30 (percent) when the current font shape group is composed of only discrete sizes (see Section 7.10.3), and as 5 when the font shape definition covers ranges of sizes.

Using a fixed factor of 1.2 for every step may be too limiting in certain cases. For this reason the package additionally offers the more general declarative command \relscale{*factor*} and its variant \textscale{*factor*}{*text*}, to select the size based on the given *factor*, such as 1.3 (enlarge by 30%).

There are also two commands, \mathsmaller and \mathlarger, for use in math mode. LaTeX recognizes only four different math sizes, of which two (\displaystyle and \textstyle) are nearly identical for most symbols, so the application domain of these commands is somewhat limited. With exscale additionally loaded the situation is slightly improved: the \mathlarger command, when used in \displaystyle, will then internally switch to a larger text font size and afterwards select the \displaystyle corresponding to that size.

3-1-8

$$\sum \neq \sum$$

and $\frac{1}{2} \neq \frac{1}{2}$ but $N = N$

```
\usepackage{exscale,relsize}
\[ \sum \neq \mathlarger{\sum} \]
and $\frac{1}{2} \neq \frac{\mathlarger 1}
{2}$ but $N = \mathlarger {N}$
```

These commands will attempt to correctly attach superscripts and subscripts to large operators. For example,

3-1-9

$$\sum_{i=1}^{n} \neq \sum_{i=1}^{n} \neq \sum_{i=1}^{n} \qquad \int_0^\infty \neq \int_0^\infty \neq \int_0^\infty$$

```
\usepackage{exscale,relsize}
\[ \mathsmaller\sum_{i=1}^n \neq
   \sum_{i=1}^n \neq \mathlarger\sum_{i=1}^n
\qquad  \mathsmaller\int_0^\infty \neq
   \int_0^\infty \neq \mathlarger\int_0^\infty
\]
```

Be aware that the use of these commands inside formulas will hide the true nature of the math atoms inside the argument, so that the spacing in the formula, without further help, might be wrong. As shown in following example, you may have to explicitly use \mathrel, \mathbin, or \mathop to get the correct spacing.

3-1-10

$$a \times b \neq a \times b \neq a \times b$$

```
\usepackage{exscale,relsize}
\[ a \times b \neq  a \mathlarger{\times} b \neq
   a \mathbin{\mathlarger\times} b \]
```

Due to these oddities, the \mathlarger and \mathsmaller commands should not be trusted blindly, and they will not be useful in every instance.

3.1.5 textcase—Change case of text intelligently

The standard LATEX commands \MakeUppercase and \MakeLowercase change the characters in their arguments to uppercase or lowercase, respectively, thereby expanding macros as needed. For example,

```
\MakeUppercase{On \today}
```

will result in "ON 28TH OF JULY 2003". Sometimes this will change more characters than desirable. For example, if the text contains a math formula, then uppercasing this formula is normally a bad idea because it changes its meaning. Similarly, arguments to the commands \label, \ref, and \cite represent semantic information, which, if modified, will result in incorrect or missing references, because LATEX will look for the wrong labels.

> \MakeTextUppercase{*text*}   \MakeTextLowercase{*text*}

The package **textcase** by David Carlisle overcomes these defects by providing two alternative commands, \MakeTextUppercase and \MakeTextLowercase, which recognize math formulas and cross-referencing commands and leave them alone.

1   Textcase example

TEXT IN SECTION 1, ABOUT $a = b$ AND $\alpha \neq a$

```
\usepackage{textcase}
\section{Textcase example}\label{exa}
\MakeTextUppercase{Text in section~\ref{exa},
    about $a=b$ and \(\alpha \neq a \) }
```
3-1-11

Sometimes portions of text should be left unchanged for one reason or another. With \NoCaseChange the package provides a generic way to mark such parts. For instance:

SOME TEXT Some More TEXT

```
\usepackage{textcase}
\MakeTextUppercase{Some text
    \NoCaseChange{Some More} text}
```
3-1-12

If necessary, this method can be used to hide syntactic information, such as

```
\NoCaseChange{\begin{tabular}{ll}} ... \NoCaseChange{\end{tabular}}
```

thereby preventing `tabular` and `ll` from incorrectly being uppercased.

All this works only as long as the material is on the top level. Anything that is inside a group of braces (other than the argument braces to \label, \ref, \cite, or \NoCaseChange) will be uppercased or lowercased regardless of its nature.

BOTH OF THESE WILL **FAIL** $A + B = C$
UNFORTUNATELY

```
\usepackage{textcase}
\MakeTextUppercase{Both of these will
    \textbf{fail $a+b=c$}
    \emph{\NoCaseChange{unfortunately}}}
```
3-1-13

In the above case you could avoid this pitfall by taking the formula out of the argument to \textbf and moving \emph inside the argument to \NoCaseChange. In other situations this kind of correction might be impossible. In such a case the (somewhat cumbersome) solution is to hide the problem part inside a private macro and protect it from expansion during the case change; this method works for the standard LaTeX commands as well, as shown in the next example.

BUT THIS WILL **WORK** $a + b = c$ ALWAYS

```
\newcommand\mymath{$a+b=c$}
\MakeUppercase{But this will
    \textbf{work \protect\mymath} always}
```
3-1-14

Some classes and packages employ \MakeUppercase internally—for example, in running headings. If you wish to use \MakeTextUppercase instead, you should load the `textcase` package with the option `overload`. This option will replace the standard LATEX commands with the variants defined by the package.

3.1.6 `ulem`—Emphasize via underline

LATEX encourages the use of the `\emph` command and the `\em` declaration for marking emphasis, rather than explicit font-changing declarations, such as `\bfseries` and `\itshape`. The `ulem` package (by Donald Arseneau) redefines the command `\emph` to use underlining, rather than italics. It is possible to have line breaks and even primitive hyphenation in the underlined text. Every word is typeset in an underlined box, so automatic hyphenation is normally disabled, but explicit discretionary hyphens (`\-`) can still be used. The underlines continue between words and stretch just like ordinary spaces do. As spaces delimit words, some difficulty may arise with syntactical spaces (e.g., `"2.3 pt"`). Some effort is made to handle such spaces. If problems occur you might try enclosing the offending command in braces, since everything inside braces is put inside an `\mbox`. Thus, braces suppress stretching and line breaks in the text they enclose. Note that nested emphasis constructs are not always treated correctly by this package (see the gymnastics performed below to get the interword spaces correct in which each nested word is put separately inside an `\emph` expression).

No, I did <u>not</u> act in the movie <u>The Persecution and Assassination of Jean-Paul Marat</u>, as performed by the Inmates of the Asylum of Charenton under the direction of the Marquis de Sade! But I <u>did</u> see it.

```
\usepackage{ulem}
No, I did \emph{not} act in the movie
\emph{\emph{The} \emph{Persecution} \emph{and}
\emph{Assassination} \emph{of} \emph{Jean-Paul}
\emph{Marat}, as performed  by the Inmates of
the Asylum of Charenton under the direc\-tion of
the Marquis de~Sade!} But I \emph{did} see it.
```

3-1-15

Alternatively, underlining can be explicitly requested using the `\uuline` command. In addition, a number of variants are available that are common in editorial markup. These are shown in the next example.

Double underlining (under-line),
a wavy underline (under-wave),
a line through text (~~strike out~~),
crossing out text (▨▨▨▨▨▨),

```
\usepackage{ulem}
Double underlining  (\uuline{under-line}),\\
a wavy underline    (\uwave{under-wave}), \\
a line through text (\sout{strike out}),  \\
crossing out text (\xout{cross out, X out}),
```

3-1-16

The redefinition of `\emph` can be turned off and on by using `\normalem` and `\ULforem`. Alternatively, the package can be loaded with the option `normalem` to suppress this redefinition. Another package option is `UWforbf`, which replaces `\textbf` and `\bfseries` by `\uwave` whenever possible.

The position of the line produced by `\uline` can be set explicitly by specifying a value for the length `\ULdepth`. The default value is font-dependent, denoted by the otherwise senile value `\maxdimen`. Similarly, the thickness of the line can be controlled via `\ULthickness`, which, for some historical reason, needs to be redefined using `\renewcommand`.

3.1.7 soul—**Letterspacing or stealing sheep**

Frederic Goudy supposedly said, "Anyone who would letterspace black letter would steal sheep". Whether true or a myth, the topic of letterspacing clearly provokes heated discussions among typographers and is considered bad practice in most situations because it changes the "grey" level of the text and thus disturbs the flow of reading. Nevertheless, there are legitimate reasons for undertaking letterspacing. For example, display type often needs a looser setting and in most fonts uppercased text is improved this way. You may also find letterspacing being used to indicate emphasis, although this exhibits the grey-level problem.

TₑX is ill equipped when it comes to supporting letterspacing. In theory, the best solution is to use specially designed fonts rather than trying to solve the problem with a macro package. But as this requires the availability of such fonts, it is not an option for most users. Thus, in practice, the use of a macro-based solution is usually easier to work with, even though it means dealing with a number of restrictions. Some information about the font approach can be found in the documentation for the fontinst package [74, 75].

The soul package written by Melchior Franz provides facilities for letterspacing and underlining, but maintains TₑX's ability to automatically hyphenate words, a feature not available in ulem. The package works by parsing the text to be letterspaced or underlined, token by token, which results in a number of peculiarities and restrictions. Thus, users who only wish to underline a few words and do not need automatic hyphenation are probably better off with ulem, which is far less picky about its input.

`\caps{`*text*`}`	`\hl{`*text*`}`	`\so{`*text*`}`	`\st{`*text*`}`	`\ul{`*text*`}`

The use of the five main user commands of soul are shown in the next example. In cases where TₑX's hyphenation algorithm fails to find the appropriate hyphenation points, you can guide it as usual with the `\-` command. If the color package is loaded, `\hl` will work like a text marker, coloring the background using yellow as the default color; otherwise, it will behave like `\ul` and underline its argument.

With the soul package you can l e t t e r - s p a c e w o r d s a n d p h r a s e s. Capitals are LETTERSPACED with a different command. Interfaces for underlining, ~~strike-outs~~, and highlighting are also provided.

```
\usepackage{soul,color}
With the \textttt{soul} package you can
\so{letter\-space words and phrases}. Capitals
are \caps{LETTERSPACED} with a different
command. Interfaces for \ul{underlining},
\st{strikeouts}, and \hl{highlighting} are
also provided.
```

3-1-17

Normally, the soul package interprets one token after another in the argument of \so, \st, and so on. However, in case of characters that are represented by more than one token (e.g., accented characters) this might fail with some low-level TeX error messages. Fortunately, the package already knows about all common accent commands, so these are handled correctly. For others, such as those provided by the textcomp package, you can announce them to soul with the help of a \soulaccent declaration. The alternative is to surround the tokens by braces.

ä ù Õ X̀ Y̆

```
\usepackage{soul} \usepackage{textcomp}
\soulaccent[\capitalgrave]
\Huge \st{\"a \`u \~O \capitalgrave X {\capitalbreve Y}}
```

3-1-18

The soul package already knows that quotation characters, en dash, and em dash consist of several tokens and handles them correctly. In case of other syntactical ligatures, such as the Spanish exclamation mark, you have to help it along with a brace group.

"S o t h e r e ," he said.
¡HOLA—MY **FRIEND**!

```
\usepackage{soul}
\so{``So there,''} he said. \caps{{!`}Hola---my \textbf{friend}!}
```

3-1-19

The soul package also knows about math formulas as long as they are surrounded by $ signs (the form \(...\) is not supported) and it knows about all standard font-changing commands, such as \textbf. If you have defined your own font-switching command or use a package that provides additional font commands, you have to register them with soul using \soulregister. This declaration expects the font command to be registered as its first argument and the number of arguments (i.e., 0 or 1) for that command to appear as its second argument. Within the soul commands none of the font commands inserts any (necessary) italic correction. If needed, one has to provide it manually using \/.

H e r e w e s e e **soul**
in $action$: $x \neq y$ O K ?

```
\newcommand\textsfbf[1]{\textsf{\bfseries#1}}
\usepackage{soul} \soulregister{\textsfbf}{1}
\so{Here we see \textsfbf{soul} in \emph{action}: $x\neq y$ OK?}
```

3-1-20

If you look carefully, you will see that the font commands suppress letterspacing directly preceding and following them, such as between "action" and the colon. This can be corrected by adding \>, which forces a space.

b l o **oo** d y v i z. b l o **oo** d y

```
\usepackage{soul}
\so{bl\textbf{oo}dy  viz. bl\>\textbf{oo}\>dy}
```

3-1-21

Text inside a brace group is regarded as a single object during parsing and is therefore not spaced out. This is handy if certain ligatures are to be kept intact inside spaced-out text. However, this method works only if the text inside the brace group contains no hyphenation points. If it does, you will receive the package error message "Reconstruction failed". To hide such hyphenation points you need to put the text inside an \mbox, as shown in the second text line of the next example (TeX would hyphenate this as "Es-cher"—that is, between the "sch" that we try to keep together). You can also use \soulomit to achieve this effect, but then your text will work only when the soul package is loaded.

𝔖 𝔠𝔥𝔲𝔱𝔷𝔳𝔬𝔯𝔯𝔦𝔠𝔥𝔱𝔲𝔫𝔤
G ö d e l , E sch e r , B a c h
Temporarily disabling the scanner

```
\usepackage{soul,yfonts} \usepackage[latin1]{inputenc}
\textfrak{\so{S{ch}u{tz}vorri{ch}tung}} \par
\so{Gödel, E\mbox{sch}er, Bach}            \par
\ul{Temporarily dis\soulomit{abl}ing the scanner}
```
3-1-22

One of the most important restrictions of the above commands is that they cannot be nested; any attempt to nest soul commands will result in low-level TeX errors. If you really need nesting you will have to place the inner material in a box, which means you lose the possibility to break the material at a line ending.

This i s h e l l for all of us!

```
\usepackage{soul}  \newsavebox\soulbox
\sbox\soulbox{\so{ is hell }}
\ul{This\mbox{\usebox{\soulbox}}for all of us!}
```
3-1-23

A few other commands are special within the argument of \so and friends. Spacing out at certain points can be canceled using \< or forced with \> as we saw above. As usual with LaTeX a ~ will produce an unbreakable space. The \\ command is supported, though only in its basic form—no star, no optional argument. You can also use \linebreak to break a line at a certain point, but again the optional argument is not supported. Other LaTeX commands are likely to break the package—some experimentation will tell you what is safe and what produces havoc. The next example shows applications of these odds and ends.

"S o t h e r e" h e s a i d . L e t ' s
p r o d u c e   a   s p a c e d   o u t   l i n e ,
O K ?

```
\usepackage{soul}
\so{''\<So there\<'' he said.  Let's\\
    produce a spaced out line\>,\linebreak OK?}
```
3-1-24

\sodef{*cmd*}{*font*}{*inter-letter space*}{*word space*}{*outer space*}

The \sodef declaration allows you to define your own letterspacing commands. It can also be used to overwrite the defaults for \so.

The letterspacing algorithm works by putting a certain *inter-letter space* between characters of a word, a certain *word space* between words, and a certain *outer space* at the beginning and end of the letterspaced text section. The latter space is added only if it is appropriate at that point. The default values for these spaces are adjusted for typesetting texts in Fraktur fonts but with the help of the \sodef declaration it is easy to adjust them for your own needs. The *font* argument allows you to specify font attributes; in most cases it will be empty. Rather than using explicit dimensions in the other arguments it is advisable to resort to em values, thereby making your definition depend on the current font and its size.

```
\usepackage{soul}
\sodef\sobf{\bfseries}{.3em}{1em plus .1em}
                      {1.3em plus.1em minus.2em}
```

3-1-25   Here we **e m p h a s i z e   w o r d s** a lot.   `Here we \sobf{emphasize words} a lot.`

While \so or any new command defined via \sodef simply retrieves and executes its stored definition, the \caps command works somewhat differently. It examines the current font and tries to find it (or a close match) in an internal database. It then uses the letterspacing values stored there. You can extend this database using the \capsdef declaration by providing values for individual fonts or groups of fonts. In this way you can fine-tune the letterspacing—for example, for text in headings. It is even possible to keep several such databases and change them on the fly within a document.

> \capsdef{*match spec*}{*font*}{*inter-letter space*}{*word space*}{*outer space*}

Apart from the first argument, which is totally different, the other arguments to \capsdef are identical to those of \sodef. The first argument, *match spec*, defines the font (or fonts) to which the current declaration applies.

Its syntax is *encoding*, *family*, *series*, *shape*, and *size* separated by slashes using the naming conventions of NFSS. Empty values match anything, so //// matches any font, /ptm///10 matches all Times fonts in 10 points, and OT1/cmr/m/n/ matches Computer Modern (cmr) medium series (m) normal shape (n) encoded in OT1 in any size. It is also possible to specify size ranges. For example, 5–14 means $5\,\text{pt} \le size < 14\,\text{pt}$ and 14– matches all sizes equal or greater 14 pt. Refer to the tables in Chapter 7 for details on the NFSS font naming conventions.

As with \sodef, in most declarations the *font* argument will be empty. On some occasions it may make sense to use \scshape in this place, such as to change the font shape to small caps before applying letterspacing.

Because \caps uses the first matching entry in its database, the order of \capsdef declarations is important. Later declarations are examined first so that it is possible to overwrite or extend existing declarations.

```
\usepackage{titlesec,soul}
\newcommand\allcaps[1]{\MakeUppercase{\caps{#1}}}
\titleformat{\section}[block]{\centering\sffamily}
                      {\thesection.}{.5em}{\allcaps}
\titlespacing*{\section}{0pt}{8pt}{3pt}
\capsdef{/phv///}{\scshape}{.17em}{.55em}{.4em}
```

A SAMPLE HEADING

The \capsdef declaration applies here, because the heading definition specifies sans serif and our examples are typeset with
3-1-26   Times and Helvetica (phv).

```
\section*{A Sample Heading}
The \verb=\capsdef= declaration applies here, because the
heading definition specifies sans serif and our examples
are typeset with Times and Helvetica (\texttt{phv}).
```

The previous example also contained an interesting combination of \caps and \MakeUppercase: the command \allcaps changes its argument to uppercase and then uses \caps to letterspace the result.

| \capssave{*name*}   \capsselect{*name*}   \capsreset |

Customized letterspacing for different occasions

With \capsreset the database is restored to its initial state containing only a generic default. You can then add new entries using \capsdef. The current state of the \caps database can be stored away under a *name* by using \capssave. You can later retrieve this state by recalling it with \capsselect. If you use the capsdefault option when loading the package, then all uses of \caps that have no matching declaration are flagged by underlining the text.

```
\usepackage{titlesec} \usepackage[capsdefault]{soul}
\capsdef{/phv///}{\scshape}{.17em}{.55em}{.4em}
\capssave{display}     \capsreset
\capsdef{/phv///}{\scshape}{.04em}{.35em}{.35em}
\titlespacing*{\section}{0pt}{8pt}{3pt}
\titleformat{\section}[block]{\centering\sffamily}
            {\thesection.}{.5em}{\capsselect{display}\caps}
\section*{A Sample Heading}
Notice the different letterspacing in the heading and
\textsf{\caps{Running Text}}. For Times we have no
definition above so that the \caps{default} will match.
```
3-1-27

A SAMPLE HEADING

Notice the different letterspacing in the heading and RUNNING TEXT. For Times we have no definition above so that the DEFAULT will match.

Customizing underlining

The position and the width of the line produced by the \ul command can be customized using either \setul or \setuldepth. The command \setul takes two dimensions as arguments: the position of the line in relation to the baseline and the width of the line. Alternatively, \setuldepth can be used to specify that the line should be positioned below the text provided as an argument. Finally, \resetul will restore the default package settings.

Here we test
a number of
different settings.
And back to normal!

```
\usepackage{soul}
\setul{0pt}{.4pt}  \ul{Here we test}          \par
\setul{-.6ex}{.3ex} \ul{a number of}           \par
\setuldepth{g}      \ul{different settings.} \par
\resetul            \ul{And back to normal!}
```
3-1-28

Both \ul and \st use a black rule by default. If you additionally load the color package, you can use colored rules instead and, if desired, modify the highlighting color:

Rules can be in black blue.

```
\usepackage{soul,color}
\sethlcolor{green} \setulcolor{blue} \setstcolor{red}
Rules \hl{can} be in \st{black} \ul{blue}.
```
3-1-29

3.1.8   url—Typesetting URLs, path names, and the like

E-mail addresses, URLs, path or directory names, and similar objects usually require some attention to detail when typeset. For one thing, they often contain characters with special significance to LaTeX, such as ~, #, &, {, or }. In addition, breaking them across lines should be avoided or at least done with special care. For example, it is usually not wise to break at a hyphen, because then it is not clear whether the hyphen was inserted because of the break (as it would be the case with normal words) or was already present. Similar reasons make breaks at a space undesirable. To help with these issues, Donald Arseneau wrote the url package, which attempts to solve most of these problems.

> \url{*text*}   \url!*text*!   \path{*text*}   \path=*text*=

The base command provided by the package is `\url`, which is offered in two syntax variants: the *text* argument either can be surrounded by braces (in which case the *text* must not contain unbalanced braces) or, like `\verb`, can be delimited by using an arbitrary character on both sides that is not used inside *text*. (The syntax box above uses ! and = but these are really only examples.) In that second form one can have unbalanced braces in the argument.

   The `\path` command is the same except that it always uses typewriter fonts (`\ttfamily`), while `\url` can be customized as we will see below. The argument to both commands is typeset pretty much verbatim. For example, `\url{~}` produces a tilde. Spaces are ignored by default, as can be seen in the following example.

<table>
<tr><td>

   The LaTeX project web pages are at <code>http: //www.latex-project.org</code> and my home directory is <code>~frank</code> (sometimes).

</td><td>

```
\usepackage{url}
The \LaTeX{} project web pages are at
\url{http://www . latex-project . org} and my
home directory is \path+~frank+ (sometimes).
```

</td></tr>
</table>

3-1-30

   Line breaks can happen at certain symbols (by default, not between letters or hyphens) and in no case can the commands add a hyphen at the break point. Whenever the *text* contains either of the symbols % or #, or ends with \, it cannot be used in the argument to another command without producing errors (just like the `\verb` command). Another case that does not work properly inside the argument of another command is the use of two ^ characters in succession. However, the situation is worse in that case because one might not even get an error but simply incorrect output[1] as the next example shows.

<table>
<tr><td>

   ^frank and ^frank (OK)
   ^^frank but &rank (bad)

</td><td>

```
\usepackage{url}
\url{^frank}   and \mbox{\url{^frank}}  (OK)\par
\url{^^frank} but \mbox{\url{^^frank}} (bad)
```

</td></tr>
</table>

3-1-31

---

[1] It depends on the letter that is following. An uppercase `F` instead of the lowercase `f` would produce an error.

Even if the *text* does not contain any critical symbols, it is always forbidden to use such a command inside a moving argument—for instance, the argument of a \section. If used there, you will get the error message

```
! Undefined control sequence.
\Url Error ->\url used in a moving argument.
```

followed by many strange errors. Even the use of \protect will not help in that case. So what can be done if one needs to cite a path name or a URL in such a place? If you are prepared to be careful and only use "safe" characters inside *text*, then you can enable the commands for use in moving arguments by specifying the option allowmove when loading the package. But this does not help if you actually need a character like "#". In that case the solution is to record the information first using \urldef and then reuse it later.

\urldef{*cmd*}{*url-cmd*}{*text*}   \urldef{*cmd*}{*url-cmd*}=*text*=

The declaration \urldef defines a new command *cmd* to contain the *url-cmd* (which might be \url, \path, or a newly defined command—see below) and the *text* in a way such that they can be used in any place, including a moving argument. The *url-cmd* is not executed at this point, which means that style changes can still affect the typesetting (see Example 3-1-33 on the facing page). Technically, what happens is that the \catcodes of characters in *text* are frozen during the declaration, so that they cannot be misinterpreted in places like arguments.

1   ^^frank~#$\ **works?**

It does—in contrast to the earlier example.

```
\usepackage{url}
\urldef\test\path{^^frank~#$\}
\section{\test{} works?}
It does---in contrast to the earlier example.
```

3-1-32

\urlstyle{*style*}

We have already mentioned style changes. For this task the url package offers the \urlstyle command, which takes one mandatory argument: a named *style*. Predefined styles are rm, sf, tt, and same. The first three select the font family of that name, while the same style uses the current font and changes only the line breaking.

     The \url command uses whatever style is currently in force (the default is tt, i.e., typewriter), while \path internally always switches to the tt style. In the following example we typeset a URL saved in \lproject several times using differ-ent styles. The particular example may look slightly horrifying, but imagine how it would have looked if the URL had not been allowed to split at all in this narrow measure.

> *Zapf Chancery!* http://www.latex-project.org *(default setup)* http://www.latex-project.org *(CM Roman)* http://www.latex-project.org *(CM Sans Serif)* http://www.latex-project.org *(CM Typewriter)* *http://www.latex-project.org (Zapf Chancery)*

```
\usepackage[hyphens]{url}
\urldef\lproject\url{http://www.latex-project.org}
\fontfamily{pzc}\selectfont Zapf Chancery!
              \lproject\     (default setup) \quad
\urlstyle{rm}\lproject\     (CM Roman)        \quad
\urlstyle{sf}\lproject\     (CM Sans Serif)   \quad
\urlstyle{tt}\lproject\     (CM Typewriter)   \quad
\urlstyle{same}\lproject\ (Zapf Chancery)
```

If you studied the previous example closely you will have noticed that the option hyphens was used. This option allows breaking at explicit hyphens, something normally disabled for \url-like commands. Without this option breaks would have been allowed only at the periods, after the colon, or after "//".

As mentioned earlier spaces inside *text* are ignored by default. If this is not desired one can use the option obeyspaces. However, this option may introduce spurious spaces if the \url command is used inside the argument of another command and *text* contains any "\" character. In that case \urldef solves the problem. Line breaks at spaces are not allowed unless you also use the option spaces.

Spaces in the argument

The package automatically detects which font encoding is currently in use. In case of T1 encoded fonts it will make use of the additional glyphs available in this encoding, which improves the overall result.

The package offers two hooks, \UrlLeft and \UrlRight, that by default do nothing but can be redefined to typeset material at the left or right of *text*. The material is typeset in the same fashion as the *text*. For example, spaces are ignored unless one uses \␣ or specifies obeyspaces as an option. If the commands are redefined at the top level, they act on every \url-like command. See Example 3-1-34 on the next page for a possibility to restrict their scope.

Appending material at left or right

\DeclareUrlCommand{*cmd*}{*style-information*}

It is sometimes helpful to define your own commands that work similarly to \url or \path but use their own fonts, and so on. The command \DeclareUrlCommand can be used to define a new \url-like command or to modify an existing one. It takes two arguments: the command to define or change and the *style-information* (e.g., \urlstyle).

Defining URL-like commands

In the next example, we define \email to typeset e-mail addresses in rm style, prepending the string "e-mail: " via \UrlLeft. The example clearly shows that the scope for this redefinition is limited to the \email command. If you look closely,

you can see that a space inside \UrlLeft (as in the top-level definition) has no
effect, while \␣ produces the desired result.

```
\usepackage{url}
\renewcommand\UrlLeft{<url: }
\renewcommand\UrlRight{>}
\DeclareUrlCommand\email{\urlstyle{rm}%
    \renewcommand\UrlLeft{e-mail:\ }%
    \renewcommand\UrlRight{}}
```

<url:http://www.latex-project.org>   \url{http://www.latex-project.org}   \par
e-mail: frank.mittelbach@latex-project.org   \email{frank.mittelbach@latex-project.org} \par
<url:$HOME/figures> oops, wrong!   \path{$HOME/figures} oops, wrong!   `3-1-34`

The url package offers a number of other hooks that influence line breaking,
among them \UrlBreaks, \UrlBigBreaks, and \UrlNoBreaks. These hooks can
be redefined in the *style-information* argument of \DeclareUrlCommand to set up
new or special conventions. For details consult the package documentation, which
can be found at the end of the file url.sty.

3.1.9 euro—**Converting and typesetting currencies**

To ease the calculations needed to convert between national units and the euro,
Melchior Franz developed the package euro. In fact, the package converts arbitrary currencies using the euro as the base unit. The calculations are done with
high precision using the fp package written by Michael Mehlich. The formatting
is highly customizable on a per-currency basis, so that this package can be used
for all kind of applications involving currencies whether or not conversions are
needed.

> \EURO{*from-currency*}[*to-currency*]{*amount*}

The main command \EURO converts an *amount* in *from-currency* into *to-currency*
or, if this optional argument is missing, into euros. The arguments *from-currency*
and *to-currency* are denoted in ISO currency codes, as listed in Table 3.1 on the facing page. When inputting the *amount* a dot must separate the integer value from
any fractional part, even if the formatted number uses a different convention.

With the default settings the *amount* is displayed in the *from-currency* with
the converted value in the *to-currency* shown in parentheses.

```
\usepackage{euro}
\EURO{DEM}[FRF]{7}\quad \EURO{FRF}[DEM]{23.48}
\\
\EURO{EUR}[DEM]{10.00}\quad \EURO{DEM}{20}
```

7 DM (23,48 FRF)   23,48 FRF (7 DM)
10 Euro (19,56 DM)   20 DM (10,23 Euro)   `3-1-35`

EUR	Europe	GRD	Greece
ATS	Austria	IEP	Ireland
BEF	Belgium	ITL	Italy
DEM	Germany	LUF	Luxembourg
ESP	Spain	NLG	The Netherlands
FIM	Finland	PTE	Portugal
FRF	France		

Table 3.1: ISO currency codes of the *euro* and the 12 *euro-zone* countries

The package offers a number of options to influence the general style of the output (unless overwritten by the more detailed formatting declarations discussed *The package options* below). With `eco` the ISO codes precede the value and no customized symbols are used; with `dots` a period is inserted between every three-digit group (the default is to use a small space).

By default, integer amounts are printed as such, without adding a decimal separator and a (zero) fractional part. If the `table` option is specified this behavior is globally changed and either a — (option `emdash`, also the default), a – (option `endash`), or the right number of zeros (option `zeros`) is used.

DEM 7,– (FRF 23,48)   FRF 23,48 (DEM 7,–)
EUR 10,– (DEM 19,56)   DEM 20,– (EUR 10,23)

3-1-36

```
\usepackage[eco,table,endash]{euro}
\EURO{DEM}[FRF]{7}\quad \EURO{FRF}[DEM]{23.48}
\\ \EURO{EUR}[DEM]{10.00}\quad \EURO{DEM}{20}
```

The more detailed output customizations, which we discuss below, can be placed anywhere in the document. It is, however, advisable to keep them together in the preamble, or even to put them into the file `euro.cfg`, which is consulted upon loading the package.

The monetary symbols typeset can be adjusted with a `\EUROSYM` declaration; as defaults the package uses the ISO codes for most currencies. The example below changes the presentation for lira and euro using the currency symbols from the `textcomp` package. It also uses `dots` to help with huge lira amounts.

10.000 £ (5,16 €)   1.000 DM (989.999 £)

3-1-37

```
\usepackage{textcomp}\usepackage[dots]{euro}
\EUROSYM{ITL}{\textlira}\EUROSYM{EUR}{\texteuro}
\EURO{ITL}{10000}\quad \EURO{DEM}[ITL]{1000}
```

The package is well prepared for new countries to join the euro-zone. In fact, it is well prepared to deal with conversions from and to any currency as long as the conversion rate to the euro is known. To add a new currency use the `\EUROADD` declaration, which takes three arguments: the ISO currency code, the symbol or text to display for the currency, and the conversion rate to the euro. The next example makes the British pound available. Note the abbreviation \GBP, which makes the input a bit easier.

14,90 £ (23,29 €)
10 £ (102,54 FRF)
10 € (6,40 £)

```
\usepackage{eurosans,euro}
\EUROADD{GBP}{\textsterling}{0.6397} % 2002/12/21
\newcommand*\GBP{\EURO{GBP}} \EUROSYM{EUR}{\euro}
\noindent \GBP{14.9}\\ \GBP[FRF]{10}\\ \EURO{EUR}[GBP]{10}
```
3-1-38

The conversion rates for the national currencies of the euro-zone countries are fixed (and predefined by the package). With other currencies the rates may change hourly, so you have to be prepared for frequent updates.

The package allows you to tailor the presentation via \EUROFORMAT declarations, either to provide new defaults or to adjust the typesetting of individual currencies. The first argument specifies which part of the formatting should be adjusted, and the second argument describes the formatting.

The main format specifies how the source and target currencies are to be arranged using the reserved keywords \in and \out to refer to the source and target currencies, respectively. In the example below the first line implements a format close to the default, the second line displays the result of the conversion, and the third line does not show the conversion at all (although it happens behind the scenes). The latter is useful if you want to make use of the currency formatting features of the package without being interested in any conversion.

1 000 DM (= 3 353,85 FRF)
3 353,85 FRF
1 000 DM

```
\usepackage{euro}
\EUROFORMAT{main}{\in\ (=\,\out)} \EURO{DEM}[FRF]{1000}\par
\EUROFORMAT{main}{\out}          \EURO{DEM}[FRF]{1000}\par
\EUROFORMAT{main}{\in}           \EURO{DEM}    {1000}
```
3-1-39

The in and out formats specify how the source and target currencies should be formatted using the reserved keywords \val (monetary amount), \iso (currency code), and \sym (currency symbol if defined; ISO code otherwise).

DM 1 000 (FRF 3 353,85)

```
\usepackage{euro}
\EUROFORMAT{in}{\sym~\val} \EUROFORMAT{out}{\iso~\val}
\EURO{DEM}[FRF]{1000}
```
3-1-40

Perhaps more interesting are the possibilities to influence the formatting of monetary amounts, for which the package offers five declarations to be used in the second argument to \EUROFORMAT. The \round declaration specifies where to round the monetary amount: positive values round to the integer digits and negative values to the fractional digits. For example, \round{-3} means show and round to three fractional digits. The \form declaration takes three arguments: the integer group separator (default \,), the decimal separator (default a comma), and the fractional group separator (default \,).

The first argument can be either `all` to define the default number formatting or an ISO currency code to modify the formatting for a single currency.

1,022·5838 Euro
−335·3855 FRF
9,900,000 Lit.

```
\usepackage{euro} \EUROFORMAT{main}{\out}
\EUROFORMAT{all}{\round{-4}\form{,}{\textperiodcentered}{}}
\EUROFORMAT{ITL}{\round{2}}

\noindent \EURO{DEM}{2000}\\ \EURO{DEM}[FRF]{-100}\\
\EURO{DEM}[ITL]{10000}
```

The `\minus` declaration formats negative values by executing its first argument before the number and its second argument after it (default `\minus{$-$}{}`). The number itself is typeset unsigned, so that a minus sign has to be supplied by the declaration. The `\plus` declaration is the analogue for dealing with positive numbers (default `\plus{}{}`).

+1 022,58 Euro   −335,39 FRF

```
\usepackage{color,euro} \EUROFORMAT{main}{\out}
\EUROFORMAT{all}{\plus{$+$}{}\minus{\color{blue}$-$}{}}
\EURO{DEM}{2000}\quad \EURO{DEM}[FRF]{-100}
```

The `\zero` declaration takes three arguments to describe what to do if everything is zero, the integer part is zero, or the fractional part is zero. In the first and third arguments, the decimal separator has to be entered as well, so it should correspond to the default or the value given in the `\form` command.

0,00 €   0,51 €   1,– €

```
\usepackage{eurosans,euro}
\EUROFORMAT{main}{\out} \EUROSYM{EUR}{\euro}
\EUROFORMAT{all}{\zero{0,00}{0}{,--}}
\EURO{DEM}{0}\quad \EURO{DEM}{1}\quad \EURO{EUR}{1}
```

3.1.10   lettrine—Dropping your capital

In certain types of publications you may find the first letter of some paragraphs being highlighted by means of an enlarged letter often dropped into the paragraph body (so that the paragraph text flows around it) and usually followed by the first phrase or sentence being typeset in a special font. Applications range from chapter openings in novels, or indications of new thoughts in the text, to merely decorative elements to produce lively pages in a magazine. This custom can be traced back to the early days of printing, when such initials were often hand-colored after the printing process was finished. It originates in the manuscripts of the Middle Ages; that is, it predates the invention of printing.

`\lettrine[key/val-list]{initial}{text}`

The package lettrine written by Daniel Flipo lets you create such initials by providing the command `\lettrine`. In its simplest form it takes two arguments: the letter to become an initial and the follow-up text to be typeset in a special font, by default in \scshape.

L A MOITIÉ DES PASSAGERS, affaiblis, expirants de ces angoisses inconcevables que le roulis d'un vaisseau porte dans les nerfs et dans toutes les humeurs du corps agitées en sens contraire, . . .

```
\usepackage{lettrine} \usepackage[latin1]{inputenc}
\usepackage[french]{babel}

\lettrine{L}{a moitié des passagers,} affaiblis,
expirants de ces angoisses inconcevables que le
roulis d'un vaisseau porte dans les nerfs et
dans toutes les humeurs du corps agitées en sens
contraire, \ldots
```
3-1-44

The font used for the initial is, by default, a larger size of the current text font. Alternatively, you can specify a special font family by redefining the command \LettrineFontHook using standard NFSS commands. Similarly, the font used for the text in the second argument can be modified by changing \LettrineTextFont.

Because the \lettrine command calculates the initial size to fit a certain number of lines, you need scalable fonts to obtain the best results. As the examples in this book are typeset in Adobe Times and Helvetica by default, we have no problems here. Later examples use Palatino, which is also a scalable Type 1 font. But if you use a bitmapped font, such as Computer Modern, you might have to use special .fd files (see Chapter 7, pages 419ff) to achieve acceptable results.

L A MOITIÉ DES PASSAGERS, affaiblis, expirants de ces angoisses inconcevables que le roulis d'un vaisseau porte dans les nerfs et dans toutes les humeurs du corps agitées en sens contraire, . . .

```
\usepackage{lettrine} \usepackage[latin1]{inputenc}
\usepackage[french]{babel}
\renewcommand\LettrineFontHook{\sffamily\bfseries}
\renewcommand\LettrineTextFont{\sffamily\scshape}
\lettrine{L}{a moitié des passagers,} affaiblis,
expirants de ces angoisses inconcevables que le
roulis d'un vaisseau porte dans les nerfs et
dans toutes les humeurs du corps agitées en sens
contraire, \ldots
```
3-1-45

Many books on typography give recommendations about how to best set large initials with respect to surrounding text. For highest quality it is often necessary to manually adjust the placement depending on the shape of the initial. For example, it is often suggested that letters with a projecting left stem should overhang into the margin. The \lettrine command caters to this need by supporting an optional argument in which you can specify adjustments in the form of a comma-separated list of key/value pairs.

The size of the initial is calculated by default to have a height of two text lines (stored in \DefaultLines); with the keyword lines you can change this value to a different number of lines. There is an exception: if you specify lines=1 the initial is still made two lines high, but instead of being dropped is placed onto the baseline of the first text line.

If you want a dropped initial that also extends above the first line of text, then use the keyword `loversize`. A value of `.2` would enlarge the initial by 20%. The default value for this keyword is stored in `\DefaultLoversize`. This keyword is also useful in conjunction with `lraise` (default 0 in `\DefaultLraise`). In case of an initial with a large descender such as a "Q" you may have to raise the initial to avoid it overprinting following lines. In that case `loversize` can be used to reduce the height so as to align the initial properly.

With the keyword `lhang` you specify how much the initial extends into the margin. The value is specified as a fraction—that is, between 0 and 1. Its document default is stored in `\DefaultLhang`.

QUAND ILS FURENT revenus un peu à eux, ils marchèrent vers Lisbonne ; il leur restait quelque argent, avec lequel ils espéraient se sauver de la faim après avoir échappé à la tempête . . .

```
\usepackage{palatino,lettrine}
\usepackage[latin1]{inputenc}
\usepackage[french]{babel}

\lettrine[lines=3, loversize=-0.1, lraise=0.1,
  lhang=.2]{Q}{uand ils furent} revenus un peu à eux,
ils marchèrent vers Lisbonne ; il leur restait quelque
argent, avec lequel ils espéraient se sauver de la
faim après avoir échappé à la tempête \ldots
```

3-1-46

The distance between the initial and the following text in the first line is controlled by the command `\DefaultFindent` (default 0pt) and can be overwritten using the keyword `findent`. The indentation of following lines is by default `0.5em` (stored in `\DefaultNindent`) but can be changed through the keyword `nindent`. If you want to specify a sloped indentation you can use the keyword `slope`, which applies from the third line onward. Again the default value can be changed via the command `\DefaultSlope`, though it seems questionable that you would ever want anything different than 0pt since a slope is normally only used for letters like "A" or "V".

À PEINE ONT-ILS MIS le pied dans la ville en pleurant la mort de leur bienfaiteur, qu'ils sentent la terre trembler sous leurs pas ; . . .

```
\usepackage{palatino,lettrine}
\usepackage[latin1]{inputenc}
\usepackage[french]{babel}

\lettrine[lines=4, slope=0.6em, findent=-1em,
  nindent=0.6em]{À} { peine ont-ils mis} le pied dans
la ville en pleurant la mort de leur bienfaiteur,
qu'ils sentent la terre trembler sous leurs pas; \ldots
```

3-1-47

The example above clearly demonstrates that the size calculation for the initial does not take accents into account, which is normally the desired behavior. It is nevertheless possible to manually adjust the size using `loversize`.

To attach material to the left of the initial, such as some opening quote, you can use the keyword `ante`. It is the only keyword for which no command exists to set the default.

By modifying the default settings you can easily adapt the package to typeset initials the way you like. This can be done either in the preamble or in a file with the name `lettrine.cfg`, which is loaded if found.

3.1.11 Paragraph justification in LaTeX

For formatting paragraphs LaTeX deploys the algorithms already built into the TeX program, which by default produce justified paragraphs. In other words, spaces between words will be slightly stretched or shortened to produce lines of equal length. TeX achieves this outcome with an algorithm that attempts to find an optimal solution for a whole paragraph, using the current settings of about 20 internal parameters. They include aspects such as trying to produce visually compatible lines, such that a tight line is not followed by one very loosely typeset, or considering several hyphens in a row as a sign of bad quality. The interactions between these parameters are very subtle and even experts find it difficult to predict the results when tweaking them. Because the standard settings are suitable for nearly all applications, we describe only some of the parameters in this book. Appendix B.3.3 discusses how to trace the algorithm. If you are interested in delving further into the matter of automatic paragraph breaking, refer to *The TeXbook* [82, chap. 14], which describes the algorithm in great of detail, or to the very interesting article by Michael Plass and Donald Knuth on the subject, which is reprinted in [98].

The downside of the global optimizing approach of TeX, which you will encounter sooner or later, is that making small changes, like correcting a typo near the end of a paragraph, can have drastic and surprising effects, as it might affect the line breaking of the whole paragraph. It is possible, and not even unlikely, that, for example, the *removal* of a word might actually result in making a paragraph one line *longer*. This behavior can be very annoying if you are near the end of finishing an important project (like the second edition of this book) and a correction wreaks havoc on your already manually adjusted page breaks. In such a situation it is best to place \linebreak or \pagebreak commands into strategic places to force TeX to choose a solution that it would normally consider inferior. To be able to later get rid of such manual corrections you can easily define your own commands, such as

```
\newcommand\finallinebreak{\linebreak}
```

rather than using the standard LaTeX commands directly. This helps you to distinguish the layout adjustments for a particular version from other usages of the original commands—a method successfully used in the preparation of this book.

The interword spacing in a justified paragraph (the white space between individual words) is controlled by several TeX parameters—the most important ones are \tolerance and \emergencystretch. By setting them suitably for your document you can prevent most or all of the "Overfull box" messages without any manual line breaks. The \tolerance command is a means for setting how much the interword space in a paragraph is allowed to diverge from its optimum value.[1] This command is a TeX (not LaTeX) counter and therefore it has an uncommon

---

[1] The optimum is font defined; see Section 7.10.3 on page 428.

assignment syntax—for example, \tolerance=500. Lower values make TeX try harder to stay near the optimum; higher values allow for loose typesetting. The default value is often 200. When TeX is unable to stay in the given tolerance you will find overfull boxes in your output (i.e., lines sticking out into the margin like this). Enlarging the value of \tolerance means that TeX will also consider poorer but still acceptable line breaks, instead of turning the problem over to you for manual intervention. Sensible values are between 50 and 9999. Do not use 10000 or higher, as it allows TeX to produce arbitrary bad lines (like   this   one).

Careful with TeX's idea about infinitely bad

If you really need fully automated line breaking, it is better to set the length parameter \emergencystretch to a positive value. If TeX cannot break a paragraph without producing overfull boxes (due to the setting of \tolerance) and \emergencystretch is positive, it will add this length as stretchable space to every line, thereby accepting line-breaking solutions that have been rejected before. You may get some underfull box messages because all the lines are now set in a loose measure, but this result will still look better than a single horrible line in the middle of an otherwise perfectly typeset paragraph.

LaTeX has two predefined commands influencing the above parameters: \fussy, which is the default, and \sloppy, which allows for relatively bad lines. The \sloppy command is automatically applied by LaTeX in some situations (e.g., when typesetting \marginpar arguments or p columns in a tabular environment) where perfect line breaking is seldom possible due to the narrow measure.

Unjustified text

While the theory on producing high-quality justified text is well understood (even though surprisingly few typesetting systems other than TeX use algorithms that can produce high quality other than by chance), the same cannot be said for the situation when unjustified text is being requested. This may sound strange at first hearing. After all, why should it be difficult to break a paragraph into lines of different length? The answer lies in the fact that we do not have quantifiable quality measures that allow us to easily determine whether a certain breaking is good or bad. In comparison to its work with justified text, TeX does a very poor job when asked to produce unjustified paragraphs. Thus, to obtain the highest quality we have to be prepared to help TeX far more often by adding explicit line breaks in strategic places. A good introduction to the problems in this area is given in an article by Paul Stiff [154].

The main type of unjustified text is the one in which lines are set flush left but are unjustified at the right. For this arrangement LaTeX offers the environment flushleft. It typesets all text in its scope "flush left" by adding very stretch-able white space at the right of each line; that is, it sets the internal parameter \rightskip to 0pt plus 1fil. This setting often produces very ragged-looking paragraphs as it makes all lines equally good independent of the amount of text they contain. In addition, hyphenation is essentially disabled because a hyphen adds to the "badness" of a line and, as there is nothing to counteract it, TEX's paragraph-breaking algorithm will normally choose line breaks that avoid them.

"The LaTeX document preparation system is a special version of Donald Knuth's TEX program. TEX is a sophisticated program designed to produce high-quality typesetting, especially for mathematical text."

```
\begin{flushleft}
''The \LaTeX{} document preparation system is a special
version of Donald Knuth's \TeX{} program.  \TeX{} is a
sophisticated program designed to produce high-quality
typesetting, especially for mathematical text.''
\end{flushleft}
```

3-1-48

In summary, LaTeX's `flushleft` environment is not particularly well suited to continuous unjustified text, which should vary at the right-hand boundary only to a certain extent and where appropriate should use hyphenation (see the next section for alternatives). Nevertheless, it can be useful to place individual objects, like a graphic, flush left to the margin, especially since this environment adds space above and below itself in the same way as list environments do.

Another important restriction is the fact that the settings chosen by this environment have no universal effect, because some environments (e.g., `minipage` or `tabular`) and commands (e.g., `\parbox`, `\footnote`, and `\caption`) restore the alignment of paragraphs to full justification. That is, they set the `\rightskip` length parameter to 0pt and thus cancel the stretchable space at the right line endings. A way to automatically deal with this problem is provided by the package `ragged2e` (see next section).

Other ways of typesetting paragraphs are flush right and centered, with the `flushright` and `center` environments, respectively. In these cases the line breaks are usually indicated with the `\\` command, whereas for ragged-right text (the `flushleft` environment discussed above) you can let LaTeX do the line breaking itself (if you are happy with the resulting quality).

The three environments discussed in this section work by changing declarations that control how TEX typesets paragraphs. These declarations are also available as LaTeX commands, as shown in the following table of correspondence:

environment:	center	flushleft	flushright
command:	\centering	\raggedright	\raggedleft

The commands neither start a new paragraph nor add vertical space, unlike the corresponding environments. Hence, the commands can be used inside other environments and inside a `\parbox`, in particular, to control the alignment in p columns of an `array` or `tabular` environment. Note, however, that if they are used in the last column of a `tabular` or `array` environment, the `\\` is no longer available to denote the end of a row. Instead, the command `\tabularnewline` can be used for this purpose (see also Section 5.2.1).

3.1.12 `ragged2e`—Enhancing justification

The previous subsection discussed the deficiencies of LaTeX's `flushleft` and `flushright` environments. The package `ragged2e` written by Martin Schröder sets out to provide alternatives that do not produce such extreme raggedness. This venture is not quite as simple as it sounds, because it is not enough to set `\rightskip` to something like `0pt plus 2em`. Notwithstanding the fact that this would result in TeX trying hard to keep the line endings within the 2em boundary, there remains a subtle problem: by default, the interword space is also stretchable for most fonts. Thus, if `\rightskip` has only finite stretchability, TeX will distribute excess space equally to all spaces. As a result, the interword spaces will have different width, depending on the amount of material in the line. The solution is to redefine the interword space so that it no longer can stretch or shrink by specifying a suitable (font-dependent) value for `\spaceskip`. This internal TeX parameter, if nonzero, represents the current interword space, overwriting the default that is defined by the current font.

By default, the package does not modify the standard LaTeX commands and environments discussed in the previous section, but instead defines its own using the same names except that some letters are uppercased.[1] The new environments and commands are given in the following correspondence table:

environment:	Center	FlushLeft	FlushRight
command:	\Centering	\RaggedRight	\RaggedLeft

They differ from their counterparts of the previous section not only in the fact that they try to produce less ragged output, but also in their attempt to provide additional flexibility by easily letting you change most of their typesetting aspects.

As typesetting the mixed-case commands and environments is somewhat tedious, you can overload the original commands and environments, such as `\raggedright`, with the new definitions by supplying the `newcommands` option when loading the package.   *Overloading the original commands*

The package offers a large number of parameters to define the exact behavior of the new commands and environments (see Table 3.2 on the next page). For `\RaggedRight` or `FlushLeft` the white space added at the right of each line can be specified as `\RaggedRightRightskip`, the one at the left can be specified as `\RaggedRightLeftskip`, the paragraph indentation to use is available as `\RaggedRightParindent`, and even the space added to fill the last line is available as `\RaggedRightParfillskip`. Similarly, the settings for `\Centering` and `\RaggedLeft` can be altered; just replace `RaggedRight` in the parameter names with either `Centering` or `RaggedLeft`.

To set a whole document unjustified, specify `document` as an option to the `ragged2e` package. For the purpose of justifying individual paragraphs the   *Unjustified setting as the default*

---

[1]This is actually against standard naming conventions. In most packages mixed-case commands indicate interface commands to be used by designers in class files or in the preamble, but not commands to be used inside documents.

\RaggedLeftParindent	0pt	\RaggedLeftLeftskip	0pt plus 2em
\RaggedLeftRightskip	0pt	\RaggedLeftParfillskip	0pt
\CenteringParindent	0pt	\CenteringLeftskip	0pt plus 2em
\CenteringRightskip	0pt plus 2em	\CenteringParfillskip	0pt
\RaggedRightParindent	0pt	\RaggedRightLeftskip	0pt
\RaggedRightRightskip	0pt plus 2em	\RaggedRightParfillskip	0pt plus 1fil
\JustifyingParindent	1 em	\JustifyingParfillskip	0pt plus 1fil

Table 3.2: Parameters used by ragged2e

package offers the command \justifying and the environment justify. Both can be customized using the length parameters \JustifyingParindent and \JustifyingParfillskip.

Thus, to produce a document with a moderate amount of raggedness and paragraphs indented by 12pt, you could use a setting like the one in the following example (compare it to Example 3-1-48 on page 104).

"The LaTeX document preparation system is a special version of Donald Knuth's TeX program. TeX is a sophisticated program designed to produce high-quality typesetting, especially for mathematical text."

```
\usepackage[document]{ragged2e}
\setlength\RaggedRightRightskip{0pt plus 1cm}
\setlength\RaggedRightParindent{12pt}
``The \LaTeX{} document preparation system is a special
version of Donald Knuth's \TeX{} program.  \TeX{} is a
sophisticated program designed to produce high-quality
typesetting, especially for mathematical text.''
```

3-1-49

Unjustified settings in narrow columns
In places with narrow measures (e.g., \marginpars, \parboxes, minipage environments, or p-columns of tabular environments), the justified setting usually produces inferior results. With the option raggedrightboxes, paragraphs in such places are automatically typeset using \RaggedRight. If necessary, \justifying can be used to force a justified paragraph in individual cases.

The default values
The use of em values in the defaults (see Table 3.2) means that special care is needed when loading the package, as the em is turned into a real dimension at this point! The package should therefore be loaded *after* the body font and size have been established—for example, after font packages have been loaded.

Instead of using the defaults listed in Table 3.2, one can instruct the package to mimic the original LaTeX definitions by loading it with the option originalparameters and then changing the parameter values as desired.

3.1.13 setspace—Changing interline spacing

The \baselineskip command is TeX's parameter for defining the *leading* (normal vertical distance) between consecutive baselines. Standard LaTeX defines a leading approximately 20% larger than the design size of the font (see Section 7.9.1 on page 413). Because it is not recommended to change the setting of \baselineskip directly, LaTeX provides the \baselinestretch command to allow for changing \baselineskip at all sizes globally.

Be aware that after the \renewcommand{\baselinestretch}{1.5} command is issued, the leading will not increase immediately. A font size changing command (e.g., \small, \Large) must be executed to make the new value take effect.

The package setspace (by Geoffrey Tobin and others) provides commands and environments for typesetting with variable spacing (primarily double and one-and-a-half). Three commands—\singlespacing, \onehalfspacing, and \doublespacing—are available for use in the preamble to set the overall spacing for the document. Alternatively, a different spacing value can be defined by placing a \setstretch command in the preamble. It takes the desired spacing factor as a mandatory argument. In the absence of any of the above commands, the default setting is single spacing.

To change the spacing inside a document three specific environments—singlespace, onehalfspace, and doublespace—are provided. They set the spacing to single (default), one-and-a-half, and double spacing, respectively. These environments cannot be nested.

In the beginning God created the heaven and the earth. Now the earth was unformed and void, and darkness was upon the face of the deep; and the spirit of God hovered over the face of the waters.

`3-1-50`

```
\usepackage{setspace}
\begin{doublespace}
In the beginning God created the heaven
and the earth. Now the earth was unformed
and void, and darkness was upon the face
of the deep; and the spirit of God
hovered over the face of the waters.
\end{doublespace}
```

For any other spacing values the generic environment spacing should be used. Its mandatory parameter is the value of \baselinestretch for the text enclosed by the environment.

In the beginning God created the heaven and the earth. Now the earth was unformed and void, and darkness was upon the face of the deep; and the spirit of God hovered over the face of the waters.

`3-1-51`

```
\usepackage{setspace}
\begin{spacing}{2.0}
In the beginning God created the heaven
and the earth. Now the earth was unformed
and void, and darkness was upon the face
of the deep; and the spirit of God
hovered over the face of the waters.
\end{spacing}
```

In the above example the coefficient "2.0" produces a larger leading than the "double spacing" (doublespace environment) required for some publications. With the spacing environment the leading is increased twice—once by \baselineskip (where LaTeX already adds about 20% space between baselines) and a second time by setting \baselinestretch. "Double spacing" means that the vertical distance between baselines is about twice as large as the font size.

spacing	10pt	11pt	12pt
one and one-half	1.25	1.21	1.24
double	1.67	1.62	1.66

Table 3.3: Effective \baselinestretch values for different font sizes

Since \baselinestretch refers to the ratio between the desired distance and the \baselineskip, the values of \baselinestretch for different document base font sizes (and at two different optical spacings) can be calculated and are presented in Table 3.3.

3.1.14   picinpar—**Making rectangular holes**

The package picinpar (created by Friedhelm Sowa based on earlier work by Alan Hoenig) allows "windows" to be typeset inside paragraphs. The basic environment is window. It takes one mandatory argument specified in contrast to LATEX conventions in square brackets, in the form of a comma-separated list of four elements. These elements are the number of lines before the window starts; the alignment of the window inside the paragraph (l for left, c for centered, and r for right); the material shown in the window; and explanatory text about the contents in the window (e.g., the caption).

```
\usepackage{picinpar}
\begin{window}[1,c,%
    \fbox{\shortstack{H\\e\\l\\l\\o}},]
In this case we center a word printed
vertically inside the paragraph. It is not
difficult to understand that tables can also
be easily included with the \texttt{tabwindow}
environment.\par When a paragraph ends, like
here, and the window is not yet finished,
then it just continues past the paragraph
boundary, right into the next one(s).
\end{window}
```

In this case we center a word printed vertically inside the paragraph. It is not difficult to understand that tables can also be easily included with the tabwindow environment. When a paragraph ends, like here, and the window is not yet finished, then it just continues past the paragraph boundary, right into the next one(s).

H
e
l
l
o

3-1-52

If you look at the above example you will notice that the second paragraph is not properly indented. You can fix this defect by requesting an explicit indentation using \par\indent, if necessary.

Centering a window as in the previous example works only if the remaining text width on either side is still suitably wide (where "suitably" means larger than one inch). Otherwise, the package will simply fill it with white space.

The package also provides two variant environments, figwindow and tabwindow. They can format the explanatory text as a caption, by adding a caption number. You should, however, be careful when mixing such "nonfloating" floats with standard `figure` or `table` environments, because the latter might get deferred and this way mess up the numbering of floats.

The next example shows such an embedded figure—a map of Great Britain placed inside a paragraph. Unfortunately, the caption formatting is more or less hard-wired into the package; if you want to change it, you have to modify an internal command named `\@makewincaption`.

Is this a dagger which I see before me, The handle toward my hand? Come, let me clutch thee. I have thee not, and yet I see thee still. Art thou not, fatal vision, sensible To feeling as to sight? or art thou but A dagger of the mind, a false creation, Proceeding from the heat-oppressed brain? I see thee yet, in form as palpable As this which now I draw. Thou marshall'st me the way that I was going; And such an instrument I was to use. Mine eyes are made the fools o' the other senses, Or else worth all the rest; I see thee still, And on thy blade and dudgeon gouts of blood, Which was not so before. (*Macbeth*, Act II, Scene 1).

Figure 1: United Kingdom

3-1-53

```
\usepackage{picinpar,graphicx}
\begin{figwindow}[3,1,%
 \fbox{\includegraphics[width=30mm]{ukmap}},%
            {United Kingdom}]
Is this a dagger which I see before me, The
handle toward my hand? Come, let me clutch
thee. I have thee not, and yet I see thee
still.  Art thou not, fatal vision,
sensible To feeling as to sight?  or art
thou but A dagger of the mind, a false
creation, Proceeding from the
heat-oppressed brain?  I see thee yet, in
form as palpable As this which now I draw.
Thou marshall'st me the way that I was
going; And such an instrument I was to use.
Mine eyes are made the fools o' the other
senses, Or else worth all the rest; I see
thee still, And on thy blade and dudgeon
gouts of blood, Which was not so before.
(\emph{Macbeth}, Act II, Scene 1).
\end{figwindow}
```

3.2   Footnotes, endnotes, and marginals

LaTeX has facilities to typeset "inserted" text, such as marginal notes, footnotes, figures, and tables. The present section looks more closely at different kinds of notes, while Chapter 6 describes floats in more detail.

We start by discussing the possibilities offered through standard LaTeX's footnote commands and explain how (far) they can be customized. For two-column documents, a special layout for footnotes is provided by the ftnright package, which moves all footnotes to the bottom of the right column. This is followed by a presentation of the footmisc package, which overcomes most of the limitations of the standard commands and offers a wealth of additional features. The manyfoot package (which can be combined with footmisc) extends the footnote support for disciplines like linguistics by providing several independent footnote commands.

Support for endnotes is provided through the package endnotes, which allows for mixing footnotes and endnotes and can also be used to provide chapter notes, as required by some publishers. The section concludes with a discussion of marginal notes, which are already provided by standard LaTeX.

3.2.1 Using standard footnotes

A sharp distinction is made between footnotes in the main text and footnotes inside a `minipage` environment. The former are numbered using the `footnote` counter, while inside a `minipage` the `\footnote` command is redefined to use the `mpfootnote` counter. Thus, the representation of the footnote mark is obtained by the `\thefootnote` or the `\thempfootnote` command depending on the context. By default, it typesets an Arabic number in text and a lowercase letter inside a `minipage` environment. You can redefine these commands to get a different representation by specifying, for example, footnote symbols, as shown in the next example.

text text text[*] text text[†] text.

```
\renewcommand\thefootnote
               {\fnsymbol{footnote}}
text text text\footnote{The first}
text text\footnote{The second} text.
```

3-2-1

---

[*]The first
[†]The second

Peculiarities inside a minipage Footnotes produced with the `\footnote` command inside a `minipage` environment use the `mpfootnote` counter and are typeset at the bottom of the parbox produced by the `minipage`. However, if you use the `\footnotemark` command in a `minipage`, it will produce a footnote mark in the same style and sequence as the main text footnotes—that is, stepping the `footnote` counter and using the `\thefootnote` command for the representation. This behavior allows you to produce a footnote inside your `minipage` that is typeset in sequence with the main text footnotes at the bottom of the page: you place a `\footnotemark` inside the `minipage` and the corresponding `\footnotetext` after it.

... main text ...

Footnotes in a minipage are numbered using lowercase letters.[a]
This text references a footnote at the bottom of the page.[1] And another[b] note.

---

[a]Inside minipage
[b]Inside again

---

[1]At bottom of page

```
\noindent\ldots{} main text \ldots
\begin{center}
 \begin{minipage}{.7\linewidth}
   Footnotes in a minipage are numbered using
   lowercase letters.\footnote{Inside minipage}
   \par This text references a footnote at the
   bottom of the page.\footnotemark{}
   And another\footnote{Inside again} note.
 \end{minipage}\footnotetext{At bottom of page}
\end{center}
\ldots{} main text \ldots
```

3-2-2

As the previous example shows, if you need to reference a `minipage` footnote several times, you cannot use `\footnotemark` because it refers to footnotes typeset at the bottom of the page. You can, however, load the package footmisc and then use \mpfootnotemark in place of \footnotemark. Just like \footnotemark, the \mpfootnotemark command first increments its counter and then displays its value. Thus, to refer to the previous value you typically have to decrement it first, as shown in the next example.

Main text ...

Footnotes in a minipage are numbered using lowercase letters.[a]
This text references the previous footnote.[a] And another[b] note.

---

[a]Inside minipage
[b]Inside as well

3-2-3

```
\usepackage{footmisc}
\noindent Main text \ldots \begin{center}
 \begin{minipage}{.7\linewidth}
 Footnotes in a minipage are numbered using
 lowercase letters.\footnote{Inside minipage}
 \par This text references the previous
 footnote.\addtocounter{mpfootnote}{-1}%
        \mpfootnotemark{}
 And another\footnote{Inside as well} note.
 \end{minipage}
\end{center} \ldots{} main text \ldots
```

LaTeX does not allow you to use a \footnote inside another \footnote command, as is common in some disciplines. You can, however, use the \footnotemark command inside the first footnote and then put the text of the footnote's footnote as the argument of a \footnotetext command. For other special footnote requirements consider using the manyfoot package (described below).

Some[1] text and some more text.

---

[1]A sample[2] footnote.
[2]A subfootnote.

3-2-4

```
Some\footnote{A sample\footnotemark{}
footnote.}\footnotetext{A subfootnote.}
text and some more text.
```

What if you want to reference a given footnote? You can use LaTeX's normal \label and \ref mechanism, although you may want to define your own command to typeset the reference in a special way. For instance:

This is some text.[1]
... as shown in footnote (1) on page 6,...

---

[1]Text inside referenced footnote.

3-2-5

```
\newcommand\fnref[1]{\unskip~(\ref{#1})}
This is some text.\footnote{Text inside
referenced footnote\label{fn:myfoot}.}\par
\ldots as shown in footnote\fnref{fn:myfoot}
on page~\pageref{fn:myfoot},\ldots
```

Standard LaTeX does not allow you to construct footnotes inside tabular material. Section 5.8 describes several ways of tackling that problem.

3.2.2   Customizing standard footnotes

Footnotes in LaTeX are generally simple to use and provide a quite powerful mechanism to typeset material at the bottom of a page.[1] This material can consist of several paragraphs and can include lists, inline or display mathematics, tabular material, and so on.

LaTeX offers several parameters to customize footnotes. They are shown schematically in Figure 3.1 on the next page and are described below:

\footnotesize   The font size used inside footnotes (see also Table 7.1 on page 342).

\footnotesep   The height of a strut placed at the beginning of every footnote. If it is greater than the \baselineskip used for \footnotesize, then additional vertical space will be inserted above each footnote. See Appendix A.2.3 for more information about struts.

\skip\footins   A low-level TeX length parameter that defines the space between the main text and the start of the footnotes. You can change its value with the \setlength or \addtolength command by putting \skip\footins into the first argument:

```
\addtolength{\skip\footins}{10mm plus 2mm}
```

\footnoterule   A macro to draw the rule separating footnotes from the main text that is executed right after the vertical space of \skip\footins. It should take zero vertical space; that is, it should use a negative skip to compensate for any positive space it occupies. The default definition is equivalent to the following:

```
\renewcommand\footnoterule{\vspace*{-3pt}%
    \hrule width 2in height 0.4pt \vspace*{2.6pt}}
```

Note that TeX's \hrule command and not LaTeX's \rule command is used. Because the latter starts a paragraph, it would be difficult to calculate the spaces needed to achieve a net effect of zero height. For this reason producing a fancier "rule" is perhaps best done by using a zero-sized picture environment to position the rule object without actually adding vertical space.

In the report and book classes, footnotes are numbered inside chapters; in article, footnotes are numbered sequentially throughout the document. You can change the latter default by using the \@addtoreset command (see Appendix A.1.4). However, do not try to number your footnotes within pages with

---

[1] An interesting and complete discussion of this subject appeared in the French TeX Users' Group magazine *Cahiers GUTenberg* [10, 133].

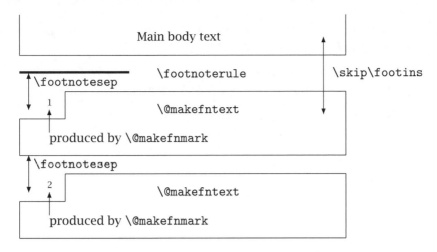

Figure 3.1: Schematic layout of footnotes

the help of this mechanism. LaTeX is looking ahead while producing the final pages, so your footnotes would most certainly be numbered incorrectly. To number foot- notes on a per-page basis, use the footmisc or perpage package (described below).

The command `\@makefnmark` is normally used to generate the footnote mark. One would expect this command to take one argument (the current footnote num- ber), but in fact it takes none. Instead, it uses the command `\@thefnmark` to indi- rectly refer to that number. The reason is that depending on the position (inside or outside of a minipage) a different counter needs to be accessed. The definition, which by default produces a superscript mark, looks roughly as follows:

```
\renewcommand\@makefnmark
            {\mbox{\textsuperscript{\normalfont\@thefnmark}}}
```

The `\footnote` command executes `\@makefntext` inside a `\parbox`, with a width of `\columnwidth`. The default version looks something like:

```
\newcommand\@makefntext[1]
            {\noindent\makebox[1.8em][r]{\@makefnmark}#1}
```

This will place the footnote mark right aligned into a box of width 1.8em directly followed by the footnote text. Note that it reuses the `\@makefnmark` macro, so any change to it will, by default, modify the display of the mark in both places. If you want the text set flush left with the number placed into the margin, then you could use the redefinition shown in the next example. Here we do not use `\@makefnmark` to format the mark, but rather access the number via `\@thefnmark`. As a result, the mark is placed onto the baseline instead of being raised. Thus, the marks in the text and at the bottom are formatted differently.

text text text[1] text text[2] text.

```
\makeatletter
\renewcommand\@makefntext[1]%
   {\noindent\makebox[0pt][r]{\@thefnmark.\,}#1}
\makeatother
text text text\footnote{The first}
text text\footnote{The second} text.
```

3-2-6

---

1. The first
2. The second

3.2.3   ftnright—**Right footnotes in a two-column environment**

It is sometimes desirable to group all footnotes in a two-column document at the bottom of the right column. This can be achieved by specifying the ftnright package written by Frank Mittelbach. The effect of this package is shown in Figure 3.2 on the facing page—the first page of the original documentation (including its spelling errors) of the ftnright implementation. It is clearly shown how the various footnotes collect in the lower part of the right-hand column.

The main idea for the ftnright package is to assemble the footnotes of all columns on a page and place them all together at the bottom of the right column. The layout produced allows for enough space between footnotes and text and, in addition, sets the footnotes in smaller type.[1] Furthermore, the footnote markers are placed at the baseline instead of raising them as superscripts.[2]

This package can be used together with most other class files for LaTeX. Of course, the ftnright package will take effect only with a document using a two-column layout specified with the twocolumn option on the \documentclass command. In most cases, it is best to use ftnright as the very last package to make sure that its settings are not overwritten by other options.

3.2.4   footmisc—**Various footnotes styles**

Since standard LaTeX offers only one type of footnotes and only limited (and somewhat low-level) support for customization, several people developed small packages that provided features otherwise not available. Many of these earlier efforts were captured by Robin Fairbairns in his footmisc package, which supports, among other things, page-wise numbering of footnotes and footnotes formatted as a single paragraph at the bottom of the page. In this section we describe the features provided by this package, showing which packages it supersedes whenever applicable.

---

[1] Some journals use the same size for footnotes and text, which sometimes makes it difficult to distinguish footnotes from the main text.

[2] Of course, this is done only for the mark preceding the footnote text and not the one used within the main text, where a raised number or symbol set in smaller type will help to keep the flow of thoughts uninterrupted.

Footnotes in a multi-column layout*

Frank Mittelbach

August 10, 1991

1 Introduction

The placement of footnotes in a multi-column layout always bothered me. The approach taken by LaTeX (i.e., placing the footnotes separately under each column) might be all right if nearly no footnotes are present. But it looks clumsy when both columns contain footnotes, especially when they occupy different amounts of space.

In the multi-column style option [5], I used page-wide footnotes at the bottom of the page, but again the result doesn't look very pleasant since short footnotes produce undesired gaps of white space. Of course, the main goal of this style option was a balancing algorithm for columns which would allow switching between different numbers of columns on the same page. With this feature, the natural place for footnotes seems to be the bottom of the page[1] but looking at some of the results it seems best to avoid footnotes in such a layout entirely.

Another possibility is to turn footnotes into endnotes, i.e., printing them at the end of every chapter or the end of the entire document. But I assume everyone who has ever read a book using such a layout will agree with me, that it is a pain to search back and forth, so that the reader is tempted to ignore the endnotes entirely.

When I wrote the article about "Future extensions of TeX" [6] I was again dissatisfied with the outcome of the footnotes, and since this article should show certain aspects of high quality typesetting, I decided to give the footnote problem a try and modified the LaTeX output routine for this purpose. The layout I used was inspired by the yearbook of the Gutenberg Gesellschaft Mainz [1]. Later on, I found that it is also recommended by Jan White [9]. On the layout of footnotes I also consulted books by Jan Tschichold [8] and Manfred Simoneit [7], books, I would recommend to everyone being able to read German texts.

1.1 Description of the new layout

The result of this effort is presented in this paper and the reader can judge for himself whether it was successful or not.[2] The main idea for this layout is to assemble the footnotes of all columns on a page and place them all together at the bottom of the right column. Allowing for enough space between footnotes and text, and in addition, setting the footnotes in smaller type[3] I decided that one could omit the footnote separator rule which is used in most publications prepared with TeX.[4] Furthermore, I decided to place the footnote markers[5] at the baseline instead of raising them as superscripts.[6]

All in all, I think this generates a neat layout, and surprisingly enough, the necessary changes to the LaTeX output routine are nevertheless astonishingly simple.

1.2 The use of the style option

This style option might be used together with any other style option for LaTeX which does not change the three internals changed by ftnright.sty.[7] In most cases, it is best to use this style option as the very last option in the \documentstyle command to make sure that its settings are not overwritten by other options.[8]

---

*. The LaTeX style option ftnright which is described in this article has the version number v1.0d dated 92/06/19. The documentation was last revised on 92/06/19.

[1] You can not use column footnotes at the bottom, since the number of columns can differ on one page.

[2] Please note, that this option only changed the placement of footnotes. Since this article also makes use of the doc option [4], that assigns tiny numbers to code lines sprincled throughout the text, the resulting design is not perfect.

[3] The standard layout in *TUGboat* uses the same size for footnotes and text, giving the footnotes, in my opinion, much too much prominence.

[4] People who prefer the rule can add it by redefining the command \footnoterule [2, p. 156]. Please, note, that this command should occupy no space, so that a negative space should be used to compensate for the width of the rule used.

[5] The tiny numbers or symbols, e.g., the '5' in front of this footnote.

[6] Of course, this is only done for the mark preceeding the footnote text and not the one used within the main text where a raised number or symbol set in smaller type will help to keep the flow of thoughts uninterrupted.

[7] These are the macros \@startcolumn, \@makecol and \@outputdblcol as we will see below. Of course, the option will take only effect with a document style using a twocolumn layout (like ltugboat) or when the user additionally specifies twocolumn as a document style option in the \documentstyle command.

[8] The ltugboat option (which is currently set up as a style option instead of a document style option which it actually is) will overwrite

1

Figure 3.2: The placement of text and footnotes with the ftnright package

The interface for footmisc is quite simple: nearly everything is customized by specifying options when the package is loaded, though in some cases further control is possible via parameters.

In the article class, footnotes are numbered sequentially throughout the document; in report and book, footnotes are numbered inside chapters. Sometimes, however, it is more appropriate to number footnotes on a per-page basis. This can be achieved by loading footmisc with the option perpage. The package footnpag (by Joachim Schrod) provides the same feature with a somewhat different implementation as a stand-alone package. A generalized implementation for resetting counters on a per-page basis is provided by the package perpage (see Section 3.2.5 on page 120). Since TeX's page-building mechanism is asynchronous, it is always necessary to process the document at least twice to get the numbering correct. Fortunately, the package warns you via "Rerun to get cross-references right" if the footnote numbers are incorrect. The package stores information between runs in the .aux file, so after a lot of editing this information is sometimes not even close to reality. In such a case deleting the .aux file helps the package to find the correct numbering faster.[1]

Some text* with a footnote. More† text.	Even more text.* And even† more text. Some	

───────── *First. †Second.	───────── *Third. †Fourth.	`\usepackage[perpage,symbol]{footmisc}`
		`Some text\footnote{First.} with a footnote.`
		`More\footnote{Second.} text. Even more`
		`text.\footnote{Third.} And even\footnote`
		`{Fourth.} more text. Some final text.`

3-2-7

For this special occasion our example shows two pages side by side, so you can observe the effects of the perpage option. The example also shows the effect *Counter too large* of another option: symbol will use footnote symbols instead of numbers. As only *errors* a limited number of such symbols are available, you can use this option only if there are few footnotes in total or if footnote numbers restart on each page. There are six different footnote symbols and, by duplicating some, standard LaTeX supports nine footnotes. By triplicating some of them, footmisc supports up to 16 footnotes (per page or in total). If this number is exceeded you will get a LaTeX error message.

In particular with the perpage option, this behavior can be a nuisance because the error could be spurious, happening only while the package is still trying to determine which footnotes belong on which page. To avoid this problem, you can use the variant option symbol*, which also produces footnote symbols but numbers footnotes for which there are no symbols left with Arabic numerals. In that case you will get a warning at the end of the run that some footnotes were out of range and detailed information is placed in the transcript file.

`\setfnsymbol{`*name*`}`   `\DefineFNsymbols*{`*name*`}[`*type*`]{`*symbol-list*`}`

If the symbol or symbol* option is selected, a default sequence of footnote symbols defined by Leslie Lamport is used. Other authorities suggest different se-

───────────────

[1] In fact, during the preparation of this chapter I managed to confuse footmisc (by changing the \textheight in an example) so much that it was unable to find the correct numbering thereafter and kept asking for a rerun forever. Removing the .aux file resolved the problem.

lamport	*	†	‡	§	¶	‖	**	††	‡‡	§§	¶¶	***	†††	‡‡‡	§§§	¶¶¶
bringhurst	*	†	‡	§	‖	¶										
chicago	*	†	‡	§	‖	#										
wiley	*	**	†	‡	§	¶	‖									

Table 3.4: Footnote symbol lists predefined by footmisc

quences, so footmisc offers three other sequences to chose from using the declaration \setfnsymbol (see Table 3.4).

In addition, you can define your own sequence using the \DefineFNsymbols declaration in the preamble. It take two mandatory arguments: the *name* to access the list later via \setfnsymbol and the *symbol-list*. From this list symbols are taken one after another (with spaces ignored). If a symbol is built from more than one glyph, it has to be surrounded by braces. If the starred form of the declaration is used, LATEX issues an error message if it runs out of symbols. Without it, you will get Arabic numerals and a warning at the end of the LATEX run.

Due to an unfortunate design choice, footnote symbols (as well as some other text symbols) were originally added to the math fonts of TEX, rather than to the text fonts, with the result that they did not change when the text font is modified. In LATEX this flaw was partly corrected by adding these symbols to the text symbol encoding (TS1; see Section 7.5.4). However, for compatibility reasons the footnote symbols are still taken by default from the math fonts, even though this choice is not appropriate if one has changed the text font from Computer Modern to some other typeface. By using the optional *type* argument with the value text, you can tell footmisc that your list consist of text symbols. Note that all predefined symbol lists consists of math symbols and may need redeclaring if used with fonts other than Computer Modern.

Some text* with a footnote. More** text.
Even more text.*** And even**** more text.
Some more text to finish up.

```
\usepackage[symbol]{footmisc}
\DefineFNsymbols{stars}[text]{* {**} {***} {****}}
\setfnsymbol{stars}

Some text\footnote{First.} with a footnote.
More\footnote{Second.} text. Even more
text.\footnote{Third.} And even\footnote{Fourth.}
more text. Some more text to finish up.
```

---

*First.
**Second.
***Third.
****Fourth.

3-2-8

If you have many short footnotes then their default placement at the bottom of the page, stacked on top of each other, is perhaps not completely satisfactory. A typical example would be critical editions, which contain many short footnotes.[1] The layout of the footnotes can be changed using the para option, which formats

---

[1] See, for example, the ledmac package [171] the kinds of footnotes and endnotes that are common in critical editions. This package is a reimplementation of the EDMAC system [112] for LATEX and was recently made available by Peter Wilson. See also the bigfoot package by David Kastrup.

them into a single paragraph. If this option is chosen then footnotes never split across pages. The code for this option is based on work by Chris Rowley and Dominik Wujastyk (available as the package fnpara), which in turn was inspired by an example in *The TEXbook* by Donald Knuth.

Some text with a footnote.[1] More text.[2] Even more text.[3] Some final text.

---
[1] A first.   [2] A second.   [3] A third.

```
\usepackage[para]{footmisc}
Some text with a footnote.\footnote{A first.}
More text.\footnote{A second.}  Even more
text.\footnote{A third.}  Some final text.
```
3-2-9

Another way to deal with footnotes is given by the option side. In this case footnotes are placed into the margin, if possible on the same line where they are referenced. What happens internally is that special \marginpar commands are used to place the footnote text, so everything said in Section 3.2.8 about the \marginpar commands is applicable. This option cannot be used together with the para option, described earlier, but can be combined with most others.

[1]A first.

[2]A second.

[3]A third.

[4]A fourth.

Some text with a footnote.[1] A lot of additional text here with a footnote.[2] Even more text and then another footnote.[3] Some more text.[4] A lot of additional lines of text here to fill up the space on the left.

```
\usepackage[side,flushmargin]{footmisc}
Some text with a footnote.\footnote{A first.}
A lot of additional text here with a
footnote.\footnote{A second.}
Even more text and then another
footnote.\footnote{A third.}
Some more text.\footnote{A fourth.} A lot of
additional lines of text here to fill up the
space on the left.
```
3-2-10

The option flushmargin used in the previous example makes the footnote text start at the left margin with the footnote marker protruding into the margin; by default, the footnote text is indented. For obvious reasons this option is incompatible with the para option. A variant form is called marginal. If this option is used then the marker sticks even farther into the margin, as shown in the example below.

Some text[1] with a footnote. More text.[2] Even more text.[3] Some final text.

---
[1] A first.
[2] A second.
[3] A third.

```
\usepackage[marginal]{footmisc}
Some text\footnote{A first.} with a
footnote. More text.\footnote{A second.}
Even more text.\footnote{A third.} Some
final text.
```
3-2-11

Instead of using one of the above options, the position of the footnote marker can be directly controlled using the parameter \footnotemargin. If set to a negative value the marker is positioned in the margin. A value of 0pt is equivalent to using the option flushmargin. A positive value means that the footnote text is indented by this amount and the marker is placed flush right in the space produced by the indentation.

Some text[1] with a footnote. More text.[2] Even more text.[3] Some final text.

---
[1] A first.
[2] A second.
[3] A third.

3-2-12

```
\usepackage{footmisc}
\setlength\footnotemargin{10pt}
Some text\footnote{A first.} with a
footnote. More text.\footnote{A second.}
Even more text.\footnote{A third.} Some
final text.
```

By default, the footnote text is adjusted but this does not always give satisfactory results, especially with the options para and side. In case of the para option nothing can be done, but for other layouts you can switch to ragged-right typesetting by using the option ragged. The next example does not specify flushmargin, so we get an indentation of width \footnotemargin—compare this to Example 3-2-10 on the preceding page.

[1] In the margin ragged right often looks better.

Some text[1] with a footnote A lot of additional text here to fill up the space in the example. A lot of additional text here to fill up the space in the example.

3-2-13

```
\usepackage[side,ragged]{footmisc}
Some text\footnote{In the margin ragged
right often looks better.} with a footnote
A lot of additional text here to fill
up the space in the example. A lot of
additional text here to fill up the space
in the example.
```

The two options norule and splitrule (courtesy of Donald Arseneau) modify the rule normally placed between text and footnotes. If norule is specified, then the separation rule will be suppressed. As compensation the value of \skip\footins is slightly enlarged. If a footnote does not fit onto the current page it will be split and continued on the next page, unless the para option is used (as it does not support split footnotes). By default, the rule separating normal and split footnotes from preceding text is the same. If you specify the option splitrule, however, it becomes customizable: the rule above split footnotes will run across the whole column while the one above normal footnotes will retain the default definition given by \footnoterule. More precisely, this option will introduce the commands \mpfootnoterule (for use in minipages), \pagefootnoterule (for use on regular pages), and \splitfootnoterule (for use on pages starting with a split footnote). By modifying their definitions, similar to the example given earlier for the \footnoterule command, you can customize the layout according to your needs.

Some text with a footnote.[1] More text.[2] Even more text.[3] Some final text.

---
[1] A first.   [2] A second.   [3] A third.

3-2-14

```
\usepackage[norule,para]{footmisc}
Some text with a footnote.\footnote{A first.}
More text.\footnote{A second.}  Even more
text.\footnote{A third.}  Some final text.
```

In classes such as article or report in which \raggedbottom is in effect, so that columns are allowed to be of different heights, the footnotes are attached at a distance of \skip\footins from the column text. If you prefer them aligned at the bottom, so that any excess space is put between the text and the footnotes, specify the option bottom. In classes for which \flushbottom is in force, such as book, this option does nothing.

In some documents, e.g., literary analysis, several footnotes may appear at a single point. Unfortunately, LaTeX's standard footnote commands are not able to handle this situation correctly: the footnote markers are simply clustered together so that you cannot tell whether you are to look for the footnotes 1 and 2, or for the footnote with the number 12.

Some text[12] with two footnotes. Even more text.[3]

---
[1] A first.   [2] A second.   [3] A third.

```
\usepackage[para]{footmisc}
Some text\footnote{A first.}\footnote{A second.} with
two footnotes. Even more text.\footnote{A third.}
```

3-2-15

This problem will be resolved by specifying the option multiple, which ensures that footnotes in a sequence will display their markers separated by commas. The separator can be changed to something else, such as a small space, by changing the command \multfootsep.

Some text[1,2] with two footnotes. Even more text.[3]

---
[1] A first.   [2] A second.   [3] A third.

```
\usepackage[multiple,para]{footmisc}
Some text\footnote{A first.}\footnote{A second.} with
two footnotes. Even more text.\footnote{A third.}
```

3-2-16

The footmisc package deals with one other potential problem: if you put a footnote into a sectional unit, then it might appear in the table of contents or the running header, causing havoc. Of course, you could prevent this dilemma (manually) by using the optional argument of the heading command; alternatively, you could specify the option stable, which prevents footnotes from appearing in such places.

3.2.5 perpage—Resetting counters on a "per-page" basis

As mentioned earlier, the ability to reset arbitrary counters on a per-page basis is implemented in the small package perpage written by David Kastrup.

```
\MakePerPage[start]{counter}
```

The declaration \MakePerPage defines *counter* to be reset on every page, optionally requesting that its initial starting value be *start* (default 1). For demonstration we repeat Example 3-2-7 on page 116 but start each footnote marker sequence with the second symbol (i.e., "†" instead of "*").

<table>
<tr><td>

Some text† with a footnote. More‡ text.

_____
†First.
†Second.
</td><td>

Even more text.† And even‡ more text. Some

_____
†Third.
†Fourth.
</td><td>

```
\usepackage[symbol]{footmisc}
\usepackage{perpage}
\MakePerPage[2]{footnote}
```
Some text\footnote{First.} with a footnote.
More\footnote{Second.} text. Even more
text.\footnote{Third.} And even\footnote
{Fourth.} more text. Some final text.
</td></tr>
</table>

3-2-17

The package synchronizes the numbering via the .aux file of the document, thus requiring at least two runs to get the numbering correct. In addition, you may get spurious "Counter too large" error messages on the first run if \fnsymbol or \alph is used for numbering (see the discussion of the symbol* for the footmisc package on page 116).

Among LaTeX's standard counters probably only footnote can be sensibly modified in this way. Nevertheless, one can easily imagine applications that provide, say, numbered marginal notes, which could be defined as follows:

```
\newcounter{mnote}
\newcommand\mnote[1]{{\refstepcounter{mnote}%
   \marginpar[\itshape\small\raggedleft\themnote.\ #1]%
          {\itshape\small\raggedright\themnote.\ #1}}}
\usepackage{perpage} \MakePerPage{mnote}
```

We step the new counter mnote outside the \marginpar so that it is executed only once;[1] we also need to limit the scope of the current redefinition of \label (through \refstepcounter) so we put braces around the whole definition. Notes on left-hand pages should be right aligned, so we use the optional argument of \marginpar to provide different formatting for this case.

<table>
<tr><td>

1. First.   Some text with a
       footnote. More[1] text.
2. Third! Even more text. And

_____
[1]Second as footnote.
</td><td>

even more text. Some   *1. Fourth.*
final text.[2]

_____
[2]Fifth!
</td><td>

```
% code as above
```
Some text\mnote{First.} with a
footnote. More\footnote{Second
as footnote.} text. Even more
text.\mnote{Third!} And even
more\mnote {Fourth.} text. Some
final text.\footnote{Fifth!}
</td></tr>
</table>

3-2-18

Another application for the package is given in Example 3-2-24 on page 125, where several independent footnote streams are all numbered on a per-page basis.

_____
[1]If placed in both arguments of \marginpar it would be executed twice. It would work if placed in the optional argument only, but then we would make use of an implementation detail (that the optional argument is evaluated first) that may change.

3.2.6 manyfoot—**Independent footnotes**

Most documents have only a few footnotes, if any. For them LaTeX's standard commands plus the enhancements offered by footmisc are usually sufficient. However, certain applications, such as critical editions, require several independently numbered footnote streams. For these situations the package manyfoot by Alexander Rozhenko can provide valuable help.[1]

\DeclareNewFootnote[*fn-style*]{*suffix*}[*enum-style*]

This declaration can be used to introduce a new footnote level. In its simplest form you merely specify a *suffix* such as "B". This allocates a new counter footnote⟨*suffix*⟩ that is used to automatically number the footnotes on the new level. The default is to use Arabic numerals; by providing the optional argument *enum-style*, some other counter style (e.g., roman or alph) can be selected.

The optional *fn-style* argument defines the general footnote style for the new level; the default is plain. If the package was loaded with the para or para* option, then para can also be selected as the footnote style.

The declaration will then automatically define six commands for you. The first three are described here:

\footnote⟨*suffix*⟩[*number*]{*text*} Same as \footnote but for the new level. Steps the footnote⟨*suffix*⟩ counter unless the optional *number* argument is given. Generates footnote markers and puts *text* at the bottom of the page.

\footnotemark⟨*suffix*⟩[*number*] Same as \footnotemark but for the new level. Steps the corresponding counter (if no optional argument is used) and prints a footnote marker corresponding to its value.

\footnotetext⟨*suffix*⟩[*number*]{*text*} Same as \footnotetext but for the new level. Puts *text* at the bottom of the page using the current value of footnote⟨*suffix*⟩ or the optional argument to generate a footnote marker in front of it.

In all three cases the style of the markers depends on the chosen *enum-style*.

The remaining three commands defined by \DeclareNewFootnote for use in the document are \Footnote⟨*suffix*⟩, \Footnotemark⟨*suffix*⟩, and \Footnotetext⟨*suffix*⟩ (i.e., same names as above but starting with an uppercase F). The important difference to the previous set is the following: instead of the optional *number* argument, they require a mandatory *marker* argument allowing you to specify arbitrary markers if desired. Some examples are given below.

The layout of the footnotes can be influenced by loading the footmisc package in addition to manyfoot, except that the para option of footmisc cannot be used. In the next example we use the standard footnote layout for top-level footnotes and the run-in layout (option para) for the second level. Thus, if all footnote levels should produce run-in footnotes, the solution is to avoid top-level footnotes

---

[1]A more comprehensive package, bigfoot, is currently being developed by David Kastrup.

completely (e.g., \footnote) and provide all necessary levels through manyfoot. Note how footmisc's multiple option properly acts on all footnotes.

Some text[1],[a] with footnotes. Even more text.[b] Some text[2],[*] with footnotes. Even more text.[c]

---

[1]A first.
[2]Another main note.

[a]B-level.   [b]A second.   [*]A manual marker.
[c]Another B note.

```
\usepackage[multiple]{footmisc}
\usepackage[para]{manyfoot}
\DeclareNewFootnote[para]{B}[alph]
Some text\footnote{A first.}\footnoteB{B-level.}
with footnotes. Even more text.\footnoteB{A second.}
Some text\footnote{Another main note.}%
\FootnoteB{*}{A manual marker.} with footnotes.
Even more text.\footnoteB{Another B note.}
```

3-2-19

In the following example the top-level footnotes are moved into the margin by loading footmisc with a different set of options. This time manyfoot is loaded with the option para*, which differs from the para option used previously in that it suppresses any indentation for the run-in footnote block. In addition, the second-level notes are now numbered with Roman numerals. For comparison the example typesets the same input text as Example 3-2-19 but it uses a different measure, as we have to show marginal notes now.

[1]A first.
[2]Another main note.

Some text[1],[i] with footnotes. Even more text.[ii] Some text[2],[*] with footnotes. Even more text.[iii]

---

[i]B-level.   [ii]A second.   [*]A manual marker.
[iii]Another B note.

```
\usepackage[side,flushmargin,ragged,multiple]
    {footmisc}
\usepackage[para*]{manyfoot}
\DeclareNewFootnote[para]{B}[roman]
Some text\footnote{A first.}\footnoteB{B-level.}
with footnotes. Even more text.\footnoteB{A
second.} Some text\footnote{Another main note.}%
\FootnoteB{*}{A manual marker.} with footnotes.
Even more text.\footnoteB{Another B note.}
```

3-2-20

The use of run-in footnotes, with either the para or the para* option, is likely to produce one particular problem: very long footnotes near a page break will not be split. To resolve this problem the manyfoot package offers a (semi)manual solution: at the point where you wish to split your note you place a \SplitNote command and end the footnote. You then place the remaining text of the footnote one paragraph farther down in the document in a \Footnotetext⟨*suffix*⟩ using an empty *marker* argument.

Some[1] text with two footnotes.[i] More text.[ii] Even more text.

---

[1]A first.

[i]A second.   [ii]This is a very very long footnote that

Some text here and[2] even more there. Some text for this block to fill the page.

---

[2]Another first.

is continued here.

```
\usepackage[para]{manyfoot}
\DeclareNewFootnote[para]{B}[roman]
Some\footnote{A first.} text with two
footnotes.\footnoteB{A second.} More
text.\footnoteB{This is a very very long
footnote that\SplitNote} Even more text.

Some\FootnotetextB{}{is continued here.}
text here and\footnote{Another first.}
even more there. \sample % as elsewhere
```

3-2-21

If both parts of the footnote fall onto the same page after reformatting the document, the footnote parts get correctly reassembled, as we prove in the next example, which uses the same example text but a different measure. However, if the reformatting requires breaking the footnote in a different place, then further manual intervention is unavoidable. Thus, such work is best left until the last stage of production.

Some[1] text with two footnotes.[i] More text.[ii] Even more text.

Some text here and[2] even more there. Some text for this block to fill the page.

---

[1] A first.

[2] Another first.

[i] A second.　　[ii] This is a very very long footnote that is continued here.

```
\usepackage[para]{manyfoot}
\DeclareNewFootnote[para]{B}[roman]
Some\footnote{A first.} text with two
footnotes.\footnoteB{A second.} More
text.\footnoteB{This is a very very long
footnote that\SplitNote} Even more text.

Some\FootnotetextB{}{is continued here.}
text here and\footnote{Another first.}
even more there. \sample % as elsewhere
```
3-2-22

The vertical separation between a footnote block and the previous one is specified by \skip\footins⟨*suffix*⟩. By default, it is equal to \skip\footins (i.e., the separation between main text and footnotes). Initially the extra blocks are only separated by such spaces, but if the option ruled is included a \footnoterule is used as well. In fact, arbitrary material can be placed in that position by redefining the command \extrafootnoterule—the only requirement being that the typeset result from that command does not take up any additional vertical space (see the discussion of \footnoterule on page 112 for further details). It is even possible use different rules for different blocks of footnotes; consult the package documentation for details.

Some text[1,*] with a footnote. Even more text.[A] Some text[†] with a footnote.[B] Some more text for the example.

---

[1] A first.

---

[*] A second.

[†] A sample.

[A] A third.

[B] Another sample.

```
\usepackage[marginal,multiple]{footmisc}
\usepackage[ruled]{manyfoot}
\DeclareNewFootnote{B}[fnsymbol]
\DeclareNewFootnote{C}[Alph]
\setlength{\skip\footinsB}{5pt minus 1pt}
\setlength{\skip\footinsC}{5pt minus 1pt}
Some text\footnote{A first.}\footnoteB{A second.}
with a footnote. Even more text.\footnoteC{A third.}
Some text\footnoteB{A sample.} with a
footnote.\footnoteC{Another sample.} Some more
text for the example.
```
3-2-23

Number the footnotes per page　The previous example deployed two additional *enum-style*s, Alph and fnsymbol. However, as only a few footnote symbols are available in both styles, that choice is most likely not a good one, unless we ensure that these footnote streams are numbered on a per-page basis. The perpage option of footmisc will not help here, as it applies to only the top-level footnotes. We can achieve the desired effect either by using \MakePerPage from the perpage package on the counters footnoteB and footnoteC (as done below), or by using the perpage option of manyfoot (which calls on the perpage package to do the job, which will number all new footnote levels defined on a per-page basis). Note that the top-level footnotes are still numbered sequentially the way the example was set up.

Some text[1] with a footnote. Even more[*],[A] text. Some

text[A] with a foot-note here.[B] Some more text. And[2],[*] a

> [1] A first.
>
> [*] Second.
>
> [A] Third.

> [2] Again.
>
> [*] A last.
>
> [A] A sample.
> [B] Another sample.

```
\usepackage[multiple]{footmisc}
\usepackage{manyfoot,perpage}
\DeclareNewFootnote{B}[fnsymbol]
\DeclareNewFootnote{C}[Alph]
\MakePerPage{footnoteB}\MakePerPage{footnoteC}

Some text\footnote{A first.} with a footnote.
Even more\footnoteB{Second.}\footnoteC{Third.}
text. Some text\footnoteC{A sample.} with a
footnote here.\footnoteC{Another sample.} Some
more text. And\footnote{Again.}\footnoteB{A
    last.} a last note.
```

3-2-24

3.2.7 endnotes—An alternative to footnotes

Scholarly works usually group notes at the end of each chapter or at the end of the document. Such notes are called endnotes. Endnotes are not supported in standard LaTeX, but they can be created in several ways.

The package endnotes (by John Lavagnino) provides its own \endnote command, thus allowing footnotes and endnotes to coexist.

The document-level syntax is modeled after the footnote commands if you replace foot with end—for example, \endnote produces an endnote, \endnotemark produces just the mark, and \endnotetext produces just the text. The counter used to hold the current endnote number is called endnote and is stepped whenever \endnote or \endnotemark without an optional argument is used.

All endnotes are stored in an external file with the extension .ent and are made available when you issue the command \theendnotes.

This is simple text.[1] This is simple text.[2] Some more text with a mark.[1]

Notes

> [1] The first endnote.
> [2] The second endnote.

3-2-25

```
\usepackage{endnotes}
This is simple text.\endnote{The first endnote.}
This is simple text.\endnote{The second endnote.}
Some more text with a mark.\endnotemark[1]

\theendnotes    % output endnotes here
```

This process is different from the way the table of contents is built; the endnotes are written directly to the file, so that you will see only those endnotes which are defined earlier in the document. The advantage of this approach is that you can have several calls to \theendnotes, for example, at the end of each chapter.

To additionally restart the numbering you have to set the `endnote` counter to zero after calling `\theendnotes`.

The heading produced by `\theendnotes` can be controlled in several ways. The text can be changed by modifying `\notesname` (default is the string `Notes`). If that is not enough you can redefine `\enoteheading`, which is supposed to produce the sectioning command in front of the notes.

The layout for endnote numbers is controlled through `\theendnote`, which is the standard way LaTeX handles counter formatting. The format of the mark is produced from `\makeenmark` with `\theenmark`, holding the formatted number for the current mark.

This is simple text.[a)] This is simple text.[b)] Some more text with a mark.[a)]

Chapter Notes

[a)]The first endnote.
[b)]The second endnote.

```
\usepackage{endnotes}
\renewcommand\theendnote{\alph{endnote}}
\renewcommand\makeenmark{\textsuperscript{\theenmark)}}
\renewcommand\notesname {Chapter Notes}

This is simple text.\endnote{The first endnote.}
This is simple text.\endnote{The second endnote.}
Some more text with a mark.\endnotemark[1]
\theendnotes
```

3-2-26

The font size for the list of endnotes is controlled through `\enotesize`, which defaults to `\footnotesize`. Also, by modifying `\enoteformat` you can change the display of the individual endnotes within their list. This command is supposed to set up the paragraph parameters for the endnotes and to typeset the note number stored in `\theenmark`. In the example we start with no indentation for the first paragraph and with the number placed into the margin.

This is simple text.[1] This is simple text.[2] Some more text with a mark.[1]

Notes

1. The first endnote with a lot of text to produce two lines.
    And even a second paragraph.
2. The second endnote.

```
\usepackage{endnotes}
\renewcommand\enoteformat{\noindent\raggedright
  \setlength\parindent{12pt}\makebox[0pt][r]{\theenmark.\,}}
\renewcommand\enotesize{\scriptsize}

This is simple text.\endnote{The first endnote with a lot
    of text to produce two lines.\par And even a second
    paragraph.}
This is simple text.\endnote{The second endnote.}
Some more text with a mark.\endnotemark[1]
\theendnotes
```

3-2-27

3.2.8 Marginal notes

The standard LaTeX command `\marginpar` generates a marginal note. This command typesets the text given as its argument in the margin, with the first line being at the same height as the line in the main text where the `\marginpar` command occurs. When only the mandatory argument is specified, the text goes to the right margin for one-sided printing; to the outside margin for two-sided printing;

and to the nearest margin for two-column formatting. When you also specify an optional argument, its text is used if the left margin is chosen, while the second (mandatory) argument is used for the right margin.

This placement strategy can be reversed (except for two-column formatting) using `\reversemarginpar`, which acts on all marginal notes from there on. You can return to the default behavior with `\normalmarginpar`.

There are a few important things to understand when using marginal notes. First, the `\marginpar` command does not start a paragraph. Thus, if it is used before the first word of a paragraph, the vertical alignment will not match the beginning of the paragraph. Second, the first word of its argument is not automatically hyphenated. Thus, for a narrow margin and long words (as in German), you may have to precede the first word by a `\hspace{0pt}` command to allow hyphenation of that word. These two potential problems can be eased by defining a command like `\marginlabel`, which starts with an empty box `\mbox{}`, typesets a marginal note ragged left, and adds a `\hspace{0pt}` in front of the argument.

Some text with a marginal note. Some more text. Another text with a marginal note. Some more text. A lot of additional text here to fill up the space in the example on the left.

ASuperLongFirstWord with problems ASuperLong-Firstword without problems

```
\newcommand\marginlabel[1]{\mbox{}\marginpar
    {\raggedright\hspace{0pt}#1}}
Some\marginpar{ASuperLongFirstWord with problems}
text with a marginal note. Some more text.
Another\marginlabel{ASuperLongFirstword without
problems}  text with a marginal note. Some more
text. A lot of additional text here to fill
up the space in the example on the left.
```

3-2-28

Of course, the above definition can no longer produce different texts depending on the chosen margin. With a little more finesse this problem could be solved, using, for example, the `\ifthenelse` constructs from the ifthen package.

The LaTeX kernel tries hard (without producing too much processing overhead) to ensure that the contents of `\marginpar` commands always show up in the correct margin and in most circumstances will make the right decisions. In some cases, however, it will fail. If you are unlucky enough to stumble across one of them, a one-off solution is to add an explicit `\pagebreak` to stop the page generation from looking too far ahead. Of course, this has the disadvantage that the correction means visual formatting and has to be undone if the document changes. A better solution is to load the package mparhack written by Tom Sgouros and Stefan Ulrich. Once this package is loaded all `\marginpar` positions are tracked (internally using a label mechanism and writing the information to the `.aux` file). You may then get a warning "Marginpars may have changed. Rerun to get them right", indicating that the positions have changed in comparison to the previous LaTeX run and that a further run is necessary to stabilize the document.

Incorrectly placed `\marginpars`

As explained in Table 4.2 on page 196, there are three length parameters to customize the style of marginal notes: `\marginparwidth`, `\marginparsep`, and `\marginparpush`.

	Command	Default Definition	Representation
First Level	\labelitemi	\textbullet	•
Second Level	\labelitemii	\normalfont\bfseries \textendash	–
Third Level	\labelitemiii	\textasteriskcentered	*
Fourth Level	\labelitemiv	\textperiodcentered	·

Table 3.5: Commands controlling an `itemize` list environment

3.3 List structures

Lists are very important LaTeX constructs and are used to build many of LaTeX's display-like environments. LaTeX's three standard list environments are discussed in Section 3.3.1, where we also show how they can be customized. Section 3.3.2 starting on page 132 provides an in-depth discussion of the `paralist` package, which introduces a number of new list structures and offers comprehensive methods to customize them, as well as the standard lists. It is followed by a discussion of "headed lists", such as theorems and exercises. Finally, Section 3.3.4 on page 144 discusses LaTeX's general list environment.

3.3.1 Modifying the standard lists

It is relatively easy to customize the three standard LaTeX list environments `itemize`, `enumerate`, and `description`, and the next three sections will look at each of these environments in turn. Changes to the default definitions of these environments can either be made globally by redefining certain list-defining parameters in the document preamble or can be kept local.

Customizing the `itemize` list environment

For a simple unnumbered `itemize` list, the labels are defined by the commands shown in Table 3.5. To create a list with different-looking labels, you can redefine the label-generating command(s). You can make that change local for one list, as in the example below, or you can make it global by putting the redefinition in the document preamble. The following simple list is a standard `itemize` list with a marker from the PostScript Zapf Dingbats font (see Section 7.6.4 on page 378) for the first-level label:

```
\usepackage{pifont}
\newenvironment{MYitemize}{\renewcommand\labelitemi
        {\ding{43}}\begin{itemize}}{\end{itemize}}
```

☞ Text of the first item in the list.

☞ Text of the first sentence in the second item of the list. And the second sentence.

```
\begin{MYitemize}
\item Text of the first item in the list.
\item Text of the first sentence in the second
        item of the list. And the second sentence.
\end{MYitemize}
```

3-3-1

Customizing the enumerate **list environment**

LaTeX's enumerated (numbered) list environment enumerate is characterized by the commands and representation forms shown in Table 3.6 on the next page. The first row shows the names of the counter used for numbering the four possible levels of the list. The second and third rows are the commands giving the representation of the counters and their default definition in the standard LaTeX class files. Rows four, five, and six contain the commands, the default definition, and an example of the actual enumeration string printed by the list.

A reference to a numbered list element is constructed using the \theenumi, \theenumii, and similar commands, prefixed by the commands \p@enumi, \p@enumii, etc., respectively. The last three rows in Table 3.6 on the following page show these commands, their default definition, and an example of the representation of such references. It is important to consider the definitions of both the representation and reference-building commands to get the references correct.

We can now create several kinds of numbered description lists simply by applying what we have just learned.

Our first example redefines the first- and second-level counters to use capital Roman digits and Latin characters. The visual representation should be the value of the counter followed by a dot, so we can use the default value from Table 3.6 on the next page for \labelenumi.

```
\renewcommand\theenumi     {\Roman{enumi}}
\renewcommand\theenumii    {\Alph{enumii}}
\renewcommand\labelenumii{\theenumii.}
\begin{enumerate}
  \item \textbf{Introduction}           \label{q1}
  \begin{enumerate}
    \item \textbf{Applications}  \\
      Motivation for research and applications
      related to the subject.          \label{q2}
    \item \textbf{Organization}  \\
      Explain organization of the report, what
      is included, and what is not.  \label{q3}
  \end{enumerate}
  \item \textbf{Literature Survey}    \label{q4}
\end{enumerate}
q1=\ref{q1} q2=\ref{q2} q3=\ref{q3} q4=\ref{q4}
```

I. **Introduction**

   A. **Applications**
     Motivation for research and applications related to the subject.

   B. **Organization**
     Explain organization of the report, what is included, and what is not.

II. **Literature Survey**

3-3-2   q1=I q2=IA q3=IB q4=II

After these redefinitions we get funny-looking references; to correct this we have to adjust the definition of the prefix command \p@enumii. For example, to get a reference like "I-A" instead of "IA" as in the previous example, we need

```
\makeatletter \renewcommand\p@enumii{\theenumi--} \makeatother
```

because the reference is typeset by executing \p@enumii followed by \theenumii.

	First Level	*Second Level*	*Third Level*	*Fourth Level*
Counter	enumi	enumii	enumiii	enumiv
Representation	\theenumi	\theenumii	\theenumiii	\theenumiv
Default Definition	\arabic{enumi}	\alph{enumii}	\roman{enumiii}	\Alph{enumiv}
Label Field	\labelenumi	\labelenumii	\labelenumiii	\labelenumiv
Default Form	\theenumi.	(\theenumii)	\theenumiii.	\theenumiv.
Numbering Example	1., 2.	(a), (b)	i., ii.	A., B.

Reference representation

	First Level	*Second Level*	*Third Level*	*Fourth Level*
Prefix	\p@enumi	\p@enumii	\p@enumiii	\p@enumiv
Default Definition	{}	\theenumi	\theenumi(\theenumii)	\p@enumiii\theenumiii
Reference Example	1, 2	1a, 2b	1(a)i, 2(b)ii	1(a)iA, 2(b)iiB

Table 3.6: Commands controlling an enumerate list environment

Note that we need \makeatletter and \makeatother because the command name to redefine contains an @ sign. Instead of this low-level method, consider using \labelformat from the varioref package described in Section 2.4.2.

You can also decorate an enumerate field by adding something to the label field. In the example below, we have chosen for the first-level list elements the paragraph sign (§) as a prefix and a period as a suffix (omitted in references).

§1. text inside list, more text inside list

§2. text inside list, more text inside list

§3. text inside list, more text inside list

w1=§1 w2=§2 w3=§3

```
\renewcommand\labelenumi{\S\theenumi.}
\usepackage{varioref} \labelformat{enumi}{\S#1}
\begin{enumerate}
\item \label{w1} text inside list, more text inside list
\item \label{w2} text inside list, more text inside list
\item \label{w3} text inside list, more text inside list
\end{enumerate}
w1=\ref{w1}   w2=\ref{w2}   w3=\ref{w3}
```

3-3-3

You might even want to select different markers for consecutive labels. For instance, in the following example, characters from the PostScript font ZapfDingbats are used. In this case there is no straightforward way to automatically make the \ref commands produce the correct references. Instead of \theenumi simply producing the representation of the enumi counter, we define it to calculate from the counter value which symbol to select. The difficulty here is to create this definition in a way such that it survives the label-generating process. The trick is to add the \protect commands so that \setcounter and \ding are not executed when the label is written to the .aux file, yet to ensure that the current value of the counter is stored therein. The latter goal is achieved by prefixing \value by the (internal)

TEX command \the within \setcounter (but not within \ding!); without it the
references would all show the same values.[1]

```
\usepackage{calc,pifont}  \newcounter{local}
\renewcommand\theenumi{\protect\setcounter{local}%
    {171+\the\value{enumi}}\protect\ding{\value{local}}}
\renewcommand\labelenumi{\theenumi}
```

① text inside list, text inside list, text
    inside list, more text inside list;

② text inside list, text inside list, text
    inside list, more text inside list;

③ text inside list, text inside list, text
    inside list, more text inside list.

```
\begin{enumerate}
\item text inside list, text inside list, \label{l1}
     text inside list, more text inside list;
\item text inside list, text inside list, \label{l2}
     text inside list, more text inside list;
\item text inside list, text inside list, \label{l3}
     text inside list, more text inside list.
\end{enumerate}
```

3-3-4   l1=① l2=② l3=③   `l1=\ref{l1}   l2=\ref{l2}   l3=\ref{l3}`

The same effect is obtained with the dingautolist environment defined
in the pifont package, which is part of the PSNFSS system (see Section 7.6.4 on
page 378).

Customizing the description list environment

With the description environment you can change the \descriptionlabel command that generates the label. In the following example the font for typesetting
the labels is changed from boldface (default) to sans serif.

```
\renewcommand\descriptionlabel[1]%
               {\hspace{\labelsep}\textsf{#1}}
\begin{description}
```

A. text inside list, text inside list, text
    inside list, more text inside list;

B. text inside list, text inside list, text
    inside list, more text inside list;

```
\item[A.] text inside list,  text inside list,
     text inside list, more text inside list;
\item[B.] text inside list,  text inside list,
     text inside list, more text inside list;
\end{description}
```

3-3-5

The standard LATEX class files set the starting point of the label box in a
description environment at a distance of \labelsep to the left of the left margin of the enclosing environment. Thus, the \descriptionlabel command in the
example above first adds a value of \labelsep to start the label aligned with the
left margin (see page 147 for detailed explanations).

---

[1] For the TEXnically interested: LATEX's \value command, despite its name, is not producing the
"value" of a LATEX counter but only its internal TEX register name. In most circumstances this can
be used as the value but unfortunately not inside \edef or \write, where the internal name rather
than the "value" will survive. By prefixing the internal register name with the command \the, we get
the "value" even in such situations.

3.3.2   paralist—Extended list environments

The paralist package created by Bernd Schandl provides a number of new list environments and offers extensions to LaTeX's standard ones that make their customization much easier. Standard and new list environments can be nested within each other and the enumeration environments support the \label/\ref mechanism.

Enumerations

All standard LaTeX lists are display lists; that is, they leave some space at their top and bottom as well as between each item. Sometimes, however, one wishes to enumerate something within a paragraph without such visual interruption. The inparaenum environment was developed for this purpose. It supports an optional argument that you can use to customize the generated labels, the exact syntax of which is discussed later in this section.

We may want to enumerate items within a paragraph to (a) save space (b) make a less prominent statement, or (c) for some other reason.

```
\usepackage{paralist}
We may want to enumerate items within a paragraph to
\begin{inparaenum}[(a)]
  \item save space
  \item make a less prominent statement, or
  \item for some other reason.
\end{inparaenum}
```

3-3-6

But perhaps this is not precisely what you are looking for. A lot of people like to have display lists but prefer them without much white space surrounding them. In that case compactenum might be your choice, as it typesets the list like enumerate but with all vertical spaces set to 0pt.

On the other hand we may want to enumerate like this:
 i) still make a display list
 ii) format items as usual but with less vertical space, that is
 iii) similar to normal enumerate.

```
\usepackage{paralist}
On the other hand we may want to enumerate like this:
\begin{compactenum}[i)]
 \item still make a display list
 \item format items  as usual but with less
    vertical space, that is
 \item similar to normal \textttt{enumerate}.
\end{compactenum}
```

3-3-7

Actually, our previous statement was not true—you can customize the vertical spaces used by compactenum. Here are the parameters: \pltopsep is the space above and below the environment, \plpartopsep is the extra space added to the previous space when the environment starts a paragraph on its own, \plitemsep is the space between items, and \plparsep is the space between paragraphs within an item.

A final enumeration alternative is offered with the `asparaenum` environment, which formats the items as individual paragraphs. That is, their first line is indented by `\parindent` and following lines are aligned with the left margin.

Or perhaps we may want to enumerate like this:

    1) still make a display list

    2) format items as paragraphs with turnover lines not indented, that is

    3) similar to normal `enumerate`.

```
\usepackage{paralist}

Or perhaps we may want to enumerate like this:
\begin{asparaenum}[1)]
\item still make a display list \item format items
 as paragraphs with turnover lines not indented,
 that is \item similar to normal \texttt{enumerate}.
\end{asparaenum}
```

3-3-8

As seen in the previous examples all enumeration environments support one optional argument that describes how to format the item labels. Within the argument the tokens A, a, I, i, and 1 have a special meaning: they are replaced by the enumeration counter displayed in style `\Alph`, `\alph`, `\Roman`, `\roman`, or `\arabic`, respectively. All other characters retain their normal meanings. Thus, the argument `[(a)]` will result in labels like (a), (b), (c), and so on, while `[\S i:]` will produce §i:, §ii:, §iii:, and so on.

You have to be a bit careful if your label contains text strings, such as labels like Example 1, Example 2, ... In this case you have to hide the "a" inside a brace group—that is, use an argument like `[{Example} 1]`. Otherwise, you will get strange results, as shown in the next example.

Item b shows what can go wrong:

Example a: On the first item we will not notice it but

Exbmple b: the second item then shows what happens if a special character is mistakenly matched.

```
\usepackage{paralist}

Item~\ref{bad} shows what can go wrong:
\begin{asparaenum}[Example a:]
\item On the first item we will not notice it
but \item the second item then shows what
happens if a special character is mistakenly
matched. \label{bad}
\end{asparaenum}
```

3-3-9

Fortunately, the package usually detects such incorrect input and will issue a warning message. A consequence of hiding special characters by surrounding them with braces is that an argument like `[\textbf{a)}]` will not work either, because the "a" will not be considered as special any more. A workaround for this case is to use something that does not require braces, such as `\bfseries`.

As can be seen above, referencing a `\label` will produce only the counter value in the chosen representation but not any frills added in the optional argument. This is the case for all enumeration environments.

It is not possible with this syntax to specify that a label should show the outer as well as the inner enumeration counter, because the special characters always refer to the current enumeration counter. There is one exception: if you load the package with the option `pointedenum` or with the option `pointlessenum`, you will get labels like those shown in the next example.

```
\usepackage[pointedenum]{paralist}
\begin{compactenum}
\item First level.
 \begin{compactenum}
 \item Second level.
  \begin{compactenum} \item Third level. \end{compactenum}
 \item Second level again.
 \end{compactenum}
\end{compactenum}
```

1. First level.
  1.1. Second level.
    1.1.1. Third level.
  1.2. Second level again.

3-3-10

The difference between the two options is the presence or absence of the trailing period. As an alternative to the options you can use the commands \pointedenum and \pointlessenum. They enable you to define your own environments that format labels in this way while other list environments show labels in different formats. If you need more complicated labels, such as those involving several enumeration counters from different levels, then you have to construct them manually using the methods described in Section 3.3.1 on page 129.

The optional argument syntax for specifying the typesetting of enumeration labels was first implemented in the `enumerate` package by David Carlisle, who extended the standard `enumerate` environment to support such an optional argument. With `paralist` the optional argument is supported for all enumeration environments, including the standard `enumerate` environment (for which it is an upward-compatible extension).

If an optional argument is used on any of the enumeration environments, then by default the left margin will be made only as wide as necessary to hold the labels. More exactly, the indentation is adjusted to the width of the label as it would be if the counter value is currently seven. This produces a fairly wide number (vii) if the numbering style is "Roman" and does not matter otherwise. This behavior is shown in the next example. For some documents this might be the right behavior, but if you prefer a more uniform indentation use the option `neverdecrease`, which will ensure that the left margin is always at least as wide as the default setting.

```
\usepackage{paralist}
The left margin may vary if we are not careful.
\begin{enumerate}
\item An item in a normal \texttt{enumerate}.
\end{enumerate}
\begin{compactenum}
\item Same left margin in \item this case.
\end{compactenum}
\begin{compactenum}[i)]
\item But a different one \item here.
\end{compactenum}
```

The left margin may vary if we are not careful.

1. An item in a normal enumerate.

1. Same left margin in
2. this case.
 i) But a different one
ii) here.

3-3-11

On the other hand, you can always force that kind of adjustment, even for environments without an optional argument, by specifying the option `alwaysadjust`.

Here we force the shortest possible indentation always:

1. An item in a normal enumerate.

   i) But a different
  ii) indentation
 iii) here.
1. Same left margin as
2. in the first case.

```
\usepackage[alwaysadjust]{paralist}
Here we force the shortest possible indentation always:
\begin{enumerate}
\item An item in a normal \texttt{enumerate}.
\end{enumerate}
\begin{compactenum}[i)]
\item But a different \item indentation \item here.
\end{compactenum}
\begin{compactenum}[1.]
\item Same left margin as \item in the first case.
\end{compactenum}
```

3-3-12

Finally, with the option `neveradjust` the standard indentation is used in all cases. Thus, labels that are too wide will extend into the left margin.

With this option the label is pushed into the margin.

  1. An item in a normal
     enumerate.

Task A) Same left indentation in
Task B) this case.
  1) And the same indentation
  2) here.

```
\usepackage[neveradjust]{paralist}
With this option the label is pushed into the margin.
\begin{enumerate}
\item An item in a normal\\ \texttt{enumerate}.
\end{enumerate}
\begin{compactenum}[{Task} A)]
\item Same left indentation in \item this case.
\end{compactenum}
\begin{compactenum}[1)]
\item And the same indentation \item here.
\end{compactenum}
```

3-3-13

Itemizations

For itemized lists the paralist package offers the environments `compactitem`, which is a compact version of the standard `itemize` environment; `asparaitem` which formats the items as paragraphs; and `inparaitem`, which produces an in-line itemization. The last environment was added mainly for symmetry reasons. All three environments accept an optional argument, that specifies the label to be used for each item.

Producing itemized lists with special labels is easy.
  ⋆ This example uses the package option `neverdecrease`.
  ⋆ Without it the left margin would be smaller.

```
\usepackage[neverdecrease]{paralist}
Producing itemized lists with special labels is easy.
\begin{compactitem}[$\star$]
\item This example uses the package option
      \texttt{neverdecrease}.
\item Without it the left margin would be smaller.
\end{compactitem}
```

3-3-14

The three label justification options `neverdecrease`, `alwaysadjust`, and `neveradjust` are also valid for the itemized lists, as can be seen in the previous example. When the `paralist` package is loaded, LaTeX's `itemize` environment is extended to also support that type of optional argument.

Descriptions

For descriptions the `paralist` package introduces three additional environments: `compactdesc`, which is like the standard LaTeX `description` environment but with all vertical spaces reduced to zero (or whatever you specify as a customization); `asparadesc`, which formats each item as a paragraph; and `inparadesc`, which allows description lists within running text.

Because description-type environments specify each label at the `\item` command, these environments have no need for an optional argument.

Do you like inline description lists? Try them out!

paralist A useful package as it supports **compact...** environments that have zero vertical space, **aspara...** environments formatted as paragraphs, and **inpara...** environments as inline lists.

enumerate A package that is superseded now.

```
\usepackage{paralist}
Do you like inline description lists? Try them out!
\begin{compactdesc}
\item[paralist] A useful package as it supports
 \begin{inparadesc} \item[compact\ldots] environments
  that have zero vertical space, \item[aspara\ldots]
  environments  formatted as paragraphs, and
  \item[inpara\ldots] environments as inline lists.
 \end{inparadesc}
\item[enumerate] A package that is superseded now.
\end{compactdesc}
```

3-3-15

Adjusting defaults

Besides providing these useful new environments the `paralist` package lets you customize the default settings of enumerated and itemized lists.

You can specify the default labels for different levels of itemized lists with the help of the `\setdefaultitem` declaration. It takes four arguments (as four levels of nesting are possible). In each argument you specify the desired label (just as you do with the optional argument on the environment itself) or, if you are satisfied with the default for the given level, you specify an empty argument.

• Outer level is using the default label.

  • On the second level we use again a bullet.

    ⋆ And on the third level a star.

```
\usepackage{paralist} \setdefaultitem{}{\textbullet}{$\star$}{}
\begin{compactitem}
\item Outer level is using the default label.
  \begin{compactitem}
  \item On the second level we use again a bullet.
    \begin{compactitem}
    \item And on the third level a star.
    \end{compactitem}
  \end{compactitem}
\end{compactitem}
```

3-3-16

The changed defaults apply to all subsequent itemized environments. Normally, such a declaration is placed into the preamble, but you can also use it to change the defaults mid-document. In particular, you can define environments that contain a \setdefaultitem declaration which would then apply only to that particular environment—and to lists nested within its body.

You will probably not be surprised to learn that a similar declaration exists for enumerations. By using \setdefaultenum you can control the default look and feel of such environments. Again, there are four arguments corresponding to the four levels. In each you either specify your label definition (using the syntax explained earlier) or you leave it empty to indicate that the default for this level should be used.

1) All levels get a closing parenthesis in this example.
   a) Lowercase letters here.
      i) Roman numerals here.
      ii) Really!

```
\usepackage{paralist}  \setdefaultenum{1)}{a)}{i)}{A)}
\begin{compactenum}
\item All levels get a closing parenthesis in this example.
  \begin{compactenum}
  \item Lowercase letters here.
    \begin{compactenum}
    \item Roman numerals here. \item Really!
    \end{compactenum}
  \end{compactenum}
\end{compactenum}
```

3-3-17

There is also the possibility of adjusting the indentation for the various list levels using the declaration \setdefaultleftmargin. However, this command has six arguments (there are a total of six list levels in the standard LaTeX classes), each of which takes either a dimension denoting the increase of the indention at that level or an empty argument indicating to use the current value as specified by the class or elsewhere. Another difference from the previous declarations is that in this case we are talking about the absolute list levels and not about relative levels related to either enumerations or itemizations (which can be mixed). Compare the next example with the previous one to see the difference.

1) All levels get a closing parenthesis in this example.
   a) Lowercase letters here.
      i) Roman numerals here.
      ii) Really!

```
\usepackage{paralist}
\setdefaultenum{1)}{a)}{i)}{A)}
\setdefaultleftmargin{\parindent}{\parindent}
                     {\parindent}{}{}{}
\begin{compactenum}
\item All levels get a closing parenthesis in this example.
  \begin{compactenum}
  \item Lowercase letters here.
    \begin{compactenum}
    \item Roman numerals here. \item Really!
    \end{compactenum}
  \end{compactenum}
\end{compactenum}
```

3-3-18

By default, enumeration and itemized lists set their labels flush right. This behavior can be changed with the help of the option `flushleft`.

As described earlier, the label of the standard `description` list can be adjusted by modifying `\descriptionlabel`, which is also responsible for formatting the label in a `compactdesc` environment. With `inparadesc` and `asparadesc`, however, a different command, `\paradescriptionlabel`, is used for this purpose. As these environments handle their labels in slightly different ways, they do not need adjustments involving `\labelsep` (see page 147). Thus, its default definition is simply:

```
\newcommand*\paradescriptionlabel[1]{\normalfont\bfseries #1}
```

Finally, the `paralist` package supports the use of a configuration file named `paralist.cfg`, which by default is loaded if it exists. You can prevent this by specifying the option `nocfg`.

3.3.3   amsthm—Providing headed lists

The term "headed lists" describes typographic structures that, like other lists such as quotations, form a discrete part of a section or chapter and whose start and finish, at least, must be clearly distinguished. This is typically done by adjusting the vertical space at the start or adding a rule, and in this case also by including some kind of heading, similar to a sectioning head. The end may also be distinguished by a rule or other symbol, maybe within the last paragraph, and by extra vertical space.

Another property that distinguishes such lists is that they are often numbered, using either an independent system or in conjunction with the sectional numbering.

Perhaps one of the more fruitful sources of such "headed lists" is found in the so-called "theorem-like" environments. These had their origins in mathematical papers and books but are equally applicable to a wide range of expository material, as examples and exercises may take this form whether or not they contain mathematical material.

Because their historical origins lie in the mathematical world, we choose to describe the amsthm package [7] by Michael Downes from the American Mathematical Society (AMS) as a representative of this kind of extension.[1] This package provides an enhanced version of standard LaTeX's `\newtheorem` declaration for specifying theorem-like environments (headed lists).

As in standard LaTeX, environments declared in this way take an optional argument in which extra text, known as "notes", can be added to the head of the environment. See the example below for an illustration.

---

[1] When the amsthm package is used with a non-AMS document class and with the amsmath package, amsthm must be loaded *after* amsmath. The AMS document classes incorporate both packages.

```
\newtheorem*{name}{heading}
```

The \newtheorem declaration has two mandatory arguments. The first is the environment name that the author would like to use for this element. The second is the heading text.

If \newtheorem* is used instead of \newtheorem, no automatic numbers will be generated for the environments. This form of the command can be useful if you have only one lemma or exercise and do not want it to be numbered; it is also used to produce a special named variant of one of the common theorem types.

Lemma 1 (Main). *The LaTeX Companion complements any LaTeX introduction.*

Mittelbach's Lemma. *The LaTeX Companion contains packages from all application areas.*

```
\usepackage{amsthm}
\newtheorem{lem}{Lemma}
\newtheorem*{ML}{Mittelbach's Lemma}
\begin{lem}[Main] The \LaTeX{} Companion
  complements any \LaTeX{} introduction.
\end{lem}
\begin{ML} The \LaTeX{} Companion contains
  packages from all application areas.
\end{ML}
```

3-3-19

In addition to the two mandatory arguments, \newtheorem has two mutually exclusive optional arguments. They affect the sequencing and hierarchy of the numbering.

```
\newtheorem{name}[use-counter]{heading}
\newtheorem{name}{heading}[number-within]
```

By default, each kind of theorem-like environment is numbered independently. Thus, if you have lemmas, theorems, and some examples interspersed, they will be numbered something like this: Example 1, Lemma 1, Lemma 2, Theorem 1, Example 2, Lemma 3, Theorem 2. If, for example, you want the lemmas and theorems to share the same numbering sequence—Example 1, Lemma 1, Lemma 2, Theorem 3, Example 2, Lemma 4, Theorem 5—then you should indicate the desired relationship as follows:

```
\newtheorem{thm}{Theorem}    \newtheorem{lem}[thm]{Lemma}
```

The optional *use-counter* argument (value thm) in the second statement means that the lem environment should share the thm numbering sequence instead of having its own independent sequence.

To have a theorem environment numbered subordinately within a sectional unit—for example, to get exercises numbered Exercise 2.1, Exercise 2.2, and so on, in Section 2—put the name of the parent counter in square brackets in the final position:

```
\newtheorem{exa}{Exercise}[section]
```

With the optional argument [section], the exa counter will be reset to 0 whenever the parent counter section is incremented.

Defining the style of headed lists

The specification part of the amsthm package supports the notion of a current theorem style, which determines the formatting that will be set up by a collection of \newtheorem commands.[1]

> \theoremstyle{*style*}

The three theorem styles provided by the package are plain, definition, and remark; they specify different typographical treatments that give the environments a visual emphasis corresponding to their relative importance. The details of this typographical treatment may vary depending on the document class, but typically the plain style produces italic body text and the other two styles produce Roman body text.

To create new theorem-like environments in these styles, divide your \newtheorem declarations into groups and preface each group with the appropriate \theoremstyle. If no \theoremstyle command is given, the style used will be plain. Some examples follow:

Definition 1. A typographical challenge is a problem that cannot be solved with the help of *The LATEX Companion*.

Theorem 2. *There are no typographical challenges.*

Remark. The proof is left to the reader.

```
\usepackage{amsthm}
\theoremstyle{plain}         \newtheorem{thm}{Theorem}
\theoremstyle{definition}    \newtheorem{defn}[thm]{Definition}
\theoremstyle{remark}        \newtheorem*{rem}{Remark}
\begin{defn}
 A typographical challenge is a problem that cannot be
 solved with the help of \emph{The \LaTeX{} Companion}.
\end{defn}
\begin{thm}There are no typographical challenges.\end{thm}
\begin{rem}The proof is left to the reader.\end{rem}
```

3-3-20

Note that the fairly obvious choice of "def" for the name of a "Definition" environment does not work, because it conflicts with the existing low-level TEX command \def.

Number swapping   A fairly common style variation for theorem heads is to have the theorem number on the left, at the beginning of the heading, instead of on the right. As this variation is usually applied across the board regardless of individual \theoremstyle changes, swapping numbers is done by placing a \swapnumbers declaration at the beginning of the list of \newtheorem statements that should be affected.

---

[1] This was first introduced in the now-superseded theorem package by Frank Mittelbach.

Advanced customization

More extensive customization capabilities are provided by the package through the \newtheoremstyle declaration and through a mechanism for using package options to load custom theorem style definitions.

```
\newtheoremstyle{name}{space-above}{space-below}{body-font}{indent}
        {head-font}{head-after-punct}{head-after-format}{head-full-spec}
```

To set up a new style of "theorem-like" headed list, use this declaration with the nine mandatory arguments described below. For many of these arguments, if they are left empty, a default is used as listed here.

name   The name used to refer to the new style.

space-above   The vertical space above the headed list, a rubber length (default \topsep).

space-below   The vertical space below the headed list, a rubber length (default \topsep).

body-style   A declaration of the font and other aspects of the style to use for the text in the body of the list (default \normalfont).

indent   The extra indentation of the first line of the list, a non-rubber length (default is no extra indent).

head-style   A declaration of the font and other aspects of the style to use for the text in the head of the list (default \normalfont).

head-after-punct   The text (typically punctuation) to be inserted after the head text, including any note text.

head-after-space   The horizontal space to be inserted after the head text and "punctuation", a rubber length. It cannot be completely empty. As two very special cases it can contain either a single space character to indicate that just a normal interword space is required or, more surprisingly, just the command \newline to indicate that a new line should be started for the body of the list.

head-full-spec   A non-empty value for this argument enables a complete specification of the setting of the head itself to be supplied; an empty value means that the layout of the "plain" theorem style is used. See below for further details.

Any extra set-up code for the whole environment is best put into the *body-style* argument, although care needs to be taken over how it will interact with what is set up automatically. Anything that applies only to the head can be put in *head-style*.

In the example below we define a `break` theorem style, which starts a new line after the heading. The heading text is set in bold sans serif, followed by a colon and outdented into the margin by 12 pt. Since the book examples are typeset in a very small measure, we added `\RaggedRight` to the *body-style* argument.

```
\usepackage{ragged2e,amsthm}
\newtheoremstyle{break}%
   {9pt}{9pt}%                        Space above and below
   {\itshape\RaggedRight}%   Body style
   {-12pt}%                           Heading indent amount
   {\sffamily\bfseries}{:}% Heading font and punctuation after it
   {\newline}%             Space after heading (\newline = linebreak)
   {}%                     Head spec (empty = same as 'plain' style)
\theoremstyle{break}
\newtheorem{exa}{Exercise}
\begin{exa}[Active author]
   Find the author responsible for the largest number of
   packages  described in The \LaTeX{} Companion.
\end{exa}
```

Exercise 1 (Active author):
Find the author responsible for the largest number of packages described in The ℝTEX Companion.

3-3-21

Specifying the heading format

The *head-full-spec* argument, if non-empty, becomes the definition part of an internal command that is used to typeset the (up to) three bits of information contained in the head of a theorem-like environment: its number (if any), its name, and any extra notes supplied by the author when using the environment. Thus, it should contain references to three arguments that will then be replaced as follows:

#1 The fixed text that is to be used in the head (for example, "Exercises"), It comes from the `\newtheorem` used to declare an environment.

#2 A representation of the number of the element, if it should be numbered. It is conventionally left empty if the environment should not be numbered.

#3 The text for the optional note, from the environment's optional argument.

Assuming all three parts are present, the contents of the *head-full-spec* argument could look as follows:

```
#1 #2 \textup{(#3)}
```

Although you are free make such a declaration, it is normally best not to use these arguments directly as this might lead to unwanted extra spaces if, for example, the environment is unnumbered.

To account for this extra complexity, the package offers three additional commands, each of which takes one argument: `\thmname`, `\thmnumber`, and `\thmnote`. These three commands are redefined at each use of the environment so as to process their arguments in the correct way. The default for each of them is simply to "typeset the argument". Nevertheless, if, for example, the particular occurrence is unnumbered, then \thmnumber gets redefined to do no typesetting. Thus, a better definition for the *head-full-spec* argument would be

```
\thmname{#1}\thmnumber{ #2}\thmnote{ \textup{(#3)}}
```

which corresponds to the set-up used by the default plain style. Note the spaces within the last two arguments: they provide the interword spaces needed to separate the parts of the typeset head but, because they are inside the arguments, they are present only if that part of the head is typeset.

In the following example we provide a "Theorem" variation in which the whole theorem heading has to be supplied as an optional note, such as for citing theorems from other sources.

```
\usepackage{amsthm}
\newtheoremstyle{citing}%   Name
  {3pt}{3pt}%                         Space above and below
  {\itshape}%                         Body font
  {\parindent}{\bfseries}% Heading indent and font
  {.}%                                Punctuation after heading
  { }%    Space after head (" " = normal interword space)
  {\thmnote{#3}}%                     Typeset note only, if present
\theoremstyle{citing}   \newtheorem*{varthm}{}
\begin{varthm}[Theorem 3.16 in \cite{Knuth90}]
By focusing on small details, it is possible to
understand the deeper significance of a passage.
\end{varthm}
```

Theorem 3.16 in [87]. *By focusing on small details, it is possible to understand the deeper significance of a passage.*

3-3-22

Proofs and the QED symbol

Of more specifically mathematical interest, the package defines a proof environment that automatically adds a "QED symbol" at the end. This environment produces the heading "Proof" with appropriate spacing and punctuation.[1]

An optional argument of the proof environment allows you to substitute a different name for the standard "Proof". If you want the proof heading to be, for example, "Proof of the Main Theorem", then put this in your document:

```
\begin{proof}[Proof of the Main Theorem]
   ...
\end{proof}
```

A "QED symbol" (default □) is automatically appended at the end of a proof environment. To substitute a different end-of-proof symbol, use \renewcommand to redefine the command \qedsymbol. For a long proof done as a subsection or

---

[1]The proof environment is primarily intended for short proofs, no more than a page or two in length. Longer proofs are usually better done as a separate \section or \subsection in your document.

section, you can obtain the symbol and the usual amount of preceding space by using the command \qed where you want the symbol to appear.

Automatic placement of the QED symbol can be problematic if the last part of a proof environment is, for example, tabular or a displayed equation or list. In that case put a \qedhere command at the somewhat earlier place where the QED symbol should appear; it will then be suppressed from appearing at the logical end of the proof environment. If \qedhere produces an error message in an equation, try using \mbox{\qedhere} instead.

Proof (sufficiency). This proof involves a list:

1. because the proof comes in two parts —

2. — we need to use \qedhere. □

```
\usepackage{amsthm}
\begin{proof}[Proof (sufficiency)]
This proof involves a list:
\begin{enumerate}
 \item because the proof comes in two parts ---
 \item --- we need to use \verb|\qedhere|. \qedhere
\end{enumerate}
\end{proof}
```

3-3-23

3.3.4 Making your own lists

Most lists in LaTeX, including those we have seen previously, are internally built using the generic list environment. It has the following syntax:

\begin{list}{*default-label*}{*decls*} *item-list* \end{list}

The argument *default-label* is the text to be used as a label when an \item command is found without an optional argument. The second argument, *decls*, can be used to modify the different geometrical parameters of the list environment, which are shown schematically in Figure 3.3 on the next page.

The default values of these parameters typically depend on the type size and the level of the list. Those being vertically oriented are rubber lengths, meaning that they can stretch or shrink. They are set by the list environment as follows: upon entering the environment the internal command \@list⟨*level*⟩ is executed, where ⟨*level*⟩ is the list nesting level represented as a Roman numeral (e.g., \@listi for the first level, \@listii for the second, \@listiii for the third, and so on). Each of these commands, defined by the document class, holds appropriate settings for the given level. Typically, the class contains separate definitions for each major document size available via options. For example, if you select the option 11pt, one of its actions is to change the list defaults. In the standard classes this is done by loading the file size11.clo, which contains the definitions for the 11 pt document size.

In addition, most classes contain redefinitions of \@listi (i.e., first-level list defaults) within the size-changing commands \normalsize, \small, and \footnotesize, the assumption being that one might have lists within "small"

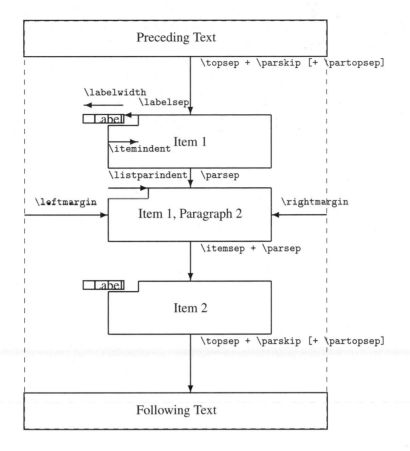

3-3-24

\topsep rubber space between first item and preceding paragraph.

\partopsep extra rubber space added to \topsep when environment starts a new paragraph.

\itemsep rubber space between successive items.

\parsep rubber space between paragraphs within an item.

\leftmargin space between left margin of enclosing environment (or of page if top-level list) and left margin of this list. Must be non-negative. Its value depends on the list level.

\rightmargin similar to \leftmargin but for the right margin. Its value is usually 0pt.

\listparindent extra indentation at beginning of every paragraph of a list except the one started by \item. Can be negative, but is usually 0pt.

\itemindent extra indentation added to the horizontal indentation of the text part of the first line of an item. The starting position of the label is calculated with respect to this reference point by subtracting the values of \labelsep and \labelwidth. Its value is usually 0pt.

\labelwidth the nominal width of the box containing the label. If the natural width of the label is ≤\labelwidth, then by default the label is typeset flush right inside a box of width \labelwidth. Otherwise, a box of the natural width is employed, which causes an indentation of the text on that line. It is possible to modify the way the label is typeset by providing a definition for the \makelabel command.

\labelsep the space between the end of the label box and the text of the first item. Its default value is 0.5 em.

Figure 3.3: Parameters used by the list environment

or "footnote-sized" text. However, since this is a somewhat incomplete set-up, strange effects are possible if you

- Use nested lists in such small sizes (the nested lists get the standard defaults intended for \normalsize),
- Jump from \small or \footnotesize directly to a large size, such as \huge (a first-level list now inherits the defaults from the small size, since in this set-up \huge does not reset the list defaults).

With a more complex set-up these defects could be mended. However, since the simpler set-up works well in most practical circumstances, most classes provide only this restricted support.

Global changes are difficult   Because of this size- and nesting-dependent set-up for the list parameters, it is not possible to change any of them globally in the preamble of your document. For global changes you have to provide redefinitions for the various \@list.. commands discussed above or select a different document class.

Page breaking around lists   Page breaking around and within a list structure is controlled by three TEX counters: \@beginparpenalty (for breaking before the list), \@itempenalty (for breaking before an item within the list), and \@endparpenalty (for breaking the page after a list). By default, all three are set to a slightly negative value, meaning that it is permissible (and even preferable) to break a page in these places compared to other break points. However, this outcome may not be appropriate. You may prefer to discourage or even prevent page breaks directly before a list. To achieve this, assign a high value to \@beginparpenalty (10000 or more prohibits the break in all circumstances), for example:

```
\makeatletter  \@beginparpenalty=9999  \makeatother
```

TEX counters need this unusual assignment form and since all three contain an @ sign in their name, you have to surround them with \makeatletter and \makeatother if the assignment is done in the preamble.

Many environments are implemented as lists   It is important to realize that such a setting is global to all environments based on the generic list environment (unless it is made in the *decls* argument) and that several LATEX environments are defined with the help of this environment (for example, quote, quotation, center, flushleft, and flushright). These environments are "lists" with a single item, and the \item[] command is specified in the environment definition. The main reason for them to be internally defined as lists is that they then share the vertical spacing with other display objects and thus help achieve a uniform layout.

As an example, we can consider the quote environment, whose definition gives the same left and right margins. The simple variant Quote, shown below, is identical to quote apart from the double quote symbols added around the text. Note the special precautions, which must be taken to eliminate undesirable white space in front of (\ignorespaces) and following (\unskip) the text. We also placed the quote characters into boxes of zero width to make the quotes hang into the margin. (This trick is worth remembering: if you have a zero-width box and align the contents with the right edge, they will stick out to the left.)

```
\newenvironment{Quote}%
 {\begin{list}{}%
                {\setlength\rightmargin{\leftmargin}}%
  \item[]\makebox[0pt][r]{``}\ignorespaces}%
 {\unskip\makebox[0pt][l]{''}\end{list}}
```

... text before.

"Some quoted text, followed
by more quoted text."

Text following ...

```
\ldots\ text before.
\begin{Quote}
  Some quoted text, followed by more quoted text.
\end{Quote}
Text following \ldots
```

3 3 25

In the remainder of this section we will construct a number of different "description" lists, thereby explaining the various possibilities offered by the generic list environment. We start by looking at the default definition of the description environment as it can be found in LATEX's standard classes such as article or report.[1]

```
\newenvironment{description}
   {\begin{list}{}{\setlength\labelwidth{0pt}%
                   \setlength\itemindent{-\leftmargin}%
                   \let\makelabel\descriptionlabel}}
   {\end{list}}
```

To understand the reasoning behind this definition recall Figure 3.3 on page 145, which explains the relationship between the various list parameters. The parameter settings start by setting \labelwidth to zero, which means that we do not reserve any space for the label. Thus, if the label is being typeset, it will move the text of the first line to the right to get the space it needs. Then the \itemindent parameter is set to the negation of \leftmargin. As a result, the starting point for the first text line is moved to the enclosing margin but all turnover lines are still indented by \leftmargin. The last declaration makes \makelabel identical to the command \descriptionlabel. The command \makelabel is called by the list environment whenever it has to format an item label. It takes one argument (the label) and is supposed to produce a typeset version of that argument. So the final task to finish the definition of the description environment is to provide a suitable definition for \descriptionlabel. This indirection is useful because it allows us to change the label formatting without modifying the rest of the environment definition.

How should \descriptionlabel be defined? It has to provide the formatting for the label. With the standard description environment this label is supposed

---

[1] If you look into article.cls or report.cls you will find a slightly optimized coding that uses, for example, low-level assignments instead of \setlength. However, conceptually, the definitions are identical.

to be typeset in boldface. But recall that the label is separated from the following text by a space of width \labelsep. Due to the parameter settings given above this text starts at the outer margin. Thus, without correction our label would end up starting in the margin (by the width of \labelsep). To prevent this outcome the standard definition for the \descriptionlabel command has the following curious definition, in that it first moves to the right and then typesets the label:

```
\newcommand*\descriptionlabel[1]
    {\hspace{\labelsep}\normalfont\bfseries #1}
```

To remove this dependency, one would need to change the setting of \itemindent to already take the \labelsep into account, which in itself would not be difficult. You may call this behavior an historical artifact, but many documents rely on this somewhat obscure feature. Thus, it is difficult to change the setting in the LaTeX kernel without breaking those documents.

With the parameter settings of the standard description environment, in case of short labels the text of the first line starts earlier than the text of remaining lines. If we always want a minimal indentation we can try a definition similar to the one in the following example, where we set \labelwidth to 40pt and \leftmargin to \labelwidth plus \labelsep. This means that \makelabel has to concern itself only with formatting the label. However, given that we now have a positive nominal label width, we need to define what should happen if the label is small. By using \hfill we specify where extra white space should be inserted.

```
\usepackage{calc}
\newenvironment{Description}
   {\begin{list}{}{\let\makelabel\Descriptionlabel
       \setlength\labelwidth{40pt}%
       \setlength\leftmargin{\labelwidth+\labelsep}}}%
   {\end{list}}
\newcommand*\Descriptionlabel[1]{\textsf{#1:}\hfil}
\begin{Description}
\item[Description]
  Returns from a function. If issued at top level,
  the interpreter simply terminates, just as if
  end of input had been reached.
\item[Errors]   None.
\item[Return values]
  \mbox{}\\
  Any arguments in effect are passed back to the
  caller.
\end{Description}
```

Description: Returns from a function. If issued at top level, the interpreter simply terminates, just as if end of input had been reached.

Errors: None.

Return values:
            Any arguments in effect are passed back to the caller.

3-3-26

This example shows a typical problem with description-like lists when the text in the label (*term*) is wider than the width of the label. Our definition lets the text of the term continue into the text of the *description* part. This is often not desired, and to improve the visual appearance of the list we have started one of the description parts on the next line. A new line was forced by putting an empty box on the same line, followed by the '\\' command.

   In the remaining part of this section various possibilities for controlling the width and mutual positioning of the term and description parts will be investigated. The first method changes the width of the label. The environment is declared with an argument specifying the desired width of the label field (normally chosen to be the widest term entry). Note the redefinition of the \makelabel command where you specify how the label will be typeset. As this redefinition is placed inside the definition[1] of the altDescription environment, the argument placeholder character # must be escaped to ## to signal LATEX that you are referring to the argument of the \makelabel command, and not to the argument of the outer environment. In such a case, \labelwidth is set to the width of the environment's argument after it is processed by \makelabel. This way formatting directives for the label that might change its width are taken into account.

```
\usepackage{calc}
\newenvironment{altDescription}[1]
  {\begin{list}{}%
    {\renewcommand\makelabel[1]{\textsf{##1:}\hfil}%
     \settowidth\labelwidth{\makelabel{#1}}%
     \setlength\leftmargin{\labelwidth+\labelsep}}}%
  {\end{list}}
\begin{altDescription}{Return values}
\item[Description]
    Returns from a function.  If issued at top level,
    the interpreter simply terminates, just as if end
    of input had been reached.
\item[Errors]
    None.
\item[Return values]
    Any arguments in effect are passed back to the
    caller.
\end{altDescription}
```

Description: Returns from a function. If issued at top level, the interpreter simply terminates, just as if end of input had been reached.

Errors: None.

Return values: Any arguments in effect are passed back to the caller.

3-3-27

A similar environment (but using an optional argument) is shown in Example A-1-9 on page 850. However, having several lists with varying widths for the label field on the same page might look typographically unacceptable. Evaluating the width of the term is another possibility that avoids this problem. If the width is wider than \labelwidth, an additional empty box is appended with the effect that the description part starts on a new line. This matches the conventional method for displaying options in UN*X manuals.

   To illustrate this method we reuse the Description environment defined

---

[1] This is done for illustration purposes. Usually the solution involving an external name is preferable, as with \Descriptionlabel in Example 3-3-26 on the preceding page.

in Example 3-3-26 but provide a different definition for the \Descriptionlabel command as follows:

```
\usepackage{calc,ifthen}    \newlength{\Mylen}
% definition of Description environment as before
\newcommand*\Descriptionlabel[1]{%
   \settowidth\Mylen{\textsf{#1:}}%   determine width
   \ifthenelse{\lengthtest{\Mylen > \labelwidth}}%
       {\parbox[b]{\labelwidth}%          term > labelwidth
          {\makebox[0pt][l]{\textsf{#1:}}\\}}%
       {\textsf{#1:}}%                    term < labelwidth
   \hfill}
\begin{Description}
\item[Description]  Returns from a function.
 If issued at top level, the interpreter simply
 terminates, just as if end of input had been reached.
\item[Errors]    None.
\item[Return values]
 Any arguments in effect are passed back to the caller.
\end{Description}
```

Description:
   Returns from a function. If issued at top level, the interpreter simply terminates, just as if end of input had been reached.

Errors: None.

Return values:
   Any arguments in effect are passed back to the caller.

3-3-28

The definition of \Descriptionlabel sets the length variable \Mylen equal to the width of the label. It then compares that length with \labelwidth. If the label is smaller than \labelwidth, then it is typeset on the same line as the description term. Otherwise, it is typeset in a zero-width box with the material sticking out to the right as far as needed. It is placed into a bottom-aligned \parbox followed by a forced line break so that the description term starts one line lower. This somewhat complicated maneuver is necessary because \makelabel, and thus \Descriptionlabel, are executed in a strictly horizontal context in which vertical spaces or \\ commands have no effect.

Yet another possibility is to allow multiple-line labels.

```
\usepackage{calc}
% definition of Description environment as before
\newcommand*\Descriptionlabel[1]
   {\raisebox{0pt}[1ex][0pt]%
      {\makebox[\labelwidth][l]%
         {\parbox[t]{\labelwidth}%
                     {\hspace{0pt}\textsf{#1:}}}}}
\begin{Description}
\item[Description]  Returns from a function.
 If issued at top level, the interpreter simply
 terminates, just as if end of input had been reached.
\item[Errors]    None.
\item[Return\\values]
 Any arguments in effect are passed back to the caller.
\end{Description}
```

Descrip-   Returns from a function. If
tion: issued at top level, the interpreter simply terminates, just as if end of input had been reached.

Errors: None.

Return   Any arguments in effect are
values: passed back to the caller.

3-3-29

In the previous example, we once again used the Description environment as a basis, with yet another redefinition of the \Descriptionlabel command. The idea here is that large labels may be split over several lines. Certain precautions have to be taken to allow hyphenation of the first word in a paragraph, and therefore the \hspace{0pt} command is introduced in the definition. The material gets typeset inside a paragraph box of the correct width \labelwidth, which is then top and left aligned into a box that is itself placed inside a box with a height of 1 ex and no depth. In this way, LATEX does not realize that the material extends below the first line.

The final example deals with the definition of enumeration lists. An environment with an automatically incremented counter can be created by including a \usecounter command in the declaration of the list environment. This function is demonstrated with the Notes environment, which produces a sequence of notes. In this case, the first parameter of the list environment is used to provide the automatically generated text for the term part.

After declaring the notes counter, the default label of the Notes environment is defined to consist of the word NOTES in small caps, followed by the value of the notes counter, using as its representation an Arabic numeral followed by a dot. Next \labelsep is set to a relatively large value and \itemindent, \leftmargin, and \labelwidth are adjusted in a way such that the label nevertheless starts out at the left margin. Finally, the already-mentioned \usecounter declaration ensures that the notes counter is incremented for each \item command.

```
\newcounter{notes}
\newenvironment{Notes}
    {\begin{list}{\textsc{Note} \arabic{notes}.}%
                {\setlength\labelsep{10pt}%
                 \setlength\itemindent{10pt}%
                 \setlength\leftmargin{0pt}%
                 \setlength\labelwidth{0pt}%
                 \usecounter{notes}}}%
    {\end{list}}
\begin{Notes}
\item This is the text of the first note item.
        Some more text for the first note item.
\item This is the text of the second note item.
        Some more text for the second note item.
\end{Notes}
```

NOTE 1.   This is the text of the first note item. Some more text for the first note item.

NOTE 2.   This is the text of the second note item. Some more text for the second note item.

3-3-30

3.4   Simulating typed text

It is often necessary to display information verbatim—that is, "as entered at the terminal". This ability is provided by the standard LATEX environment verbatim. However, to guide the reader it might be useful to highlight certain textual strings in a particular way, such as by numbering the lines. Over time a number of packages have appeared that addressed one or the other extra feature—unfortunately, each with its own syntax.

In this section we will review a few such packages. Since they have been used extensively in the past, you may come across them in document sources on the Internet or perhaps have used them yourself in the past. But we then concentrate on the package fancyvrb written by Timothy Van Zandt, which combines all such features and many more under the roof of a single, highly customizable package.

This coverage is followed by a discussion of the listings package, which provides a versatile environment in which to pretty print computer listings for a large number of computer languages.

3.4.1 Simple verbatim extensions

The package alltt (by Leslie Lamport) defines the `alltt` environment. It acts like a `verbatim` environment except that the backslash "\" and braces "{" and "}" retain their usual meanings. Thus, other commands and environments can appear inside an `alltt` environment. A similar functionality is provided by the fancyvrb environment keyword `commandchars` (see page 161).

```
One can have font changes, like
emphasized text.
Some special characters: # $ % ^ & ~ _
```
```
\usepackage{alltt}
\begin{alltt}
One can have font changes, like
\emph{emphasized text}.
Some special characters: # $ % ^ & ~ _
\end{alltt}
```
3-4-1

In documents where a lot of \verb commands are needed the source soon becomes difficult to read. For this reason the doc package, described in Chapter 14, introduces a shortcut mechanism that lets you use a special character to denote the start and stop of verbatim text, without having to repeatedly write \verb in front of it. This feature is also available in a stand-alone package called shortvrb. With fancyvrb the same functionality is provided, unfortunately using a slightly different syntax (see page 167).

```
The use of \MakeShortVerb can make
sources much more readable.   And with the
declaration \DeleteShortVerb{\|} we can
return the | character back to normal.
```
```
\usepackage{shortvrb}
\MakeShortVerb{\|}
The use of |\MakeShortVerb| can make sources
much more readable.
\DeleteShortVerb{\|}\MakeShortVerb{\+}
And with the declaration +\DeleteShortVerb{\|}+
we can return the +|+ character back to normal.
```
3-4-2

The variant form, \MakeShortVerb*, implements the same shorthand mechanism for the \verb* command. This is shown in the next example.

<table>
<tr><td>3-4-3</td><td>Instead of ␣ we can now write ␣.</td><td>

```
\usepackage{shortvrb}   \MakeShortVerb*{\+}
Instead of \verb*/ / we can now write + +.
```
</td></tr>
</table>

The package verbatim (by Rainer Schöpf) reimplements the LATEX environments verbatim and verbatim*. One of its major advantages is that it allows arbitrarily long verbatim texts, something not possible with the basic LATEX versions
of the environments. It also defines a comment environment that skips all text
between the commands \begin{comment} and \end{comment}. In addition, the
package provides hooks to implement user extensions for defining customized
verbatim-like environments.

A few such extensions are realized in the package moreverb (by Angus Dug-
gan). It offers some interesting verbatim-like commands for writing to and reading
from files as well as several environments for the production of listings and dealing with tab characters. All of these extensions are also available in a consistent
manner with the fancyvrb package, so here we only give a single example to show
the flavor of the syntax used by the moreverb package.

Text before listing environment.

```
   The␣listing␣environment␣numbers␣the
 4 lines␣in␣it.␣␣It␣takes␣an␣optional
   argument,␣which␣is␣the␣step␣between
 6 numbered␣lines␣(line␣1␣is␣always
   numbered␣if␣present),␣and␣a␣required
 8 argument,␣which␣is␣the␣starting␣line.
   The␣star␣form␣makes␣blanks␣visible.
```

Text between listing environments.

```
10 This listingcont environment continues
   where the previous listing environment
12 left off.  Both the listing and
   listingcont environments expand tabs
14 with a default tab width of 8.
```

3-4-4   Text following listing environments.

```
\usepackage{verbatim,moreverb}
Text before listing environment.
\begin{listing*}[2]{3}
The listing environment numbers the
lines in it.  It takes an optional
argument, which is the step between
numbered lines (line 1 is always
numbered if present), and a required
argument, which is the starting line.
The star form makes blanks visible.
\end{listing*}
Text between listing environments.
\begin{listingcont}
This listingcont environment continues
where the previous listing environment
left off.  Both the listing and
listingcont environments expand tabs
with a default tab width of 8.
\end{listingcont}
Text following listing environments.
```

3.4.2   upquote—Computer program style quoting

The Computer Modern Typewriter font that is used by default for typesetting
"verbatim" is a very readable monospaced typeface. Due to its small running length
it is very well suited for typesetting computer programs and similar material. See
Section 7.7.4 for a comparison of this font with other monospaced typefaces.

There is, however, one potential problem when using this font to render computer program listings and similar material: most people expect to see a (right) quote in a computer listing represented with a straight quote character (i.e., ') and a left or back quote as a kind of grave accent on its own (i.e., `). The Computer Modern Typewriter font, however, displays real left and right curly quote characters (as one would expect in a normal text font). In fact, most other typewriter fonts when set up for use with LATEX follow this pattern. This produces somewhat unconventional results that many people find difficult to understand. Consider the following example, which shows the standard behavior for three major typewriter fonts: LuxiMono, Courier, and Computer Modern Typewriter.

```
                                     \usepackage[scaled=0.85]{luximono}
                                     \raggedright
                                     \verb+TEST='ls -l |awk '{print $3}''+
TEST='ls -l |awk '{print $3}''        \par \renewcommand\ttdefault{pcr}
TEST='ls -l |awk '{print $3}''        \verb+TEST='ls -l |awk '{print $3}''+
TEST='ls -l |awk '{print $3}''        \par \renewcommand\ttdefault{cmtt}
                                     \verb+TEST='ls -l |awk '{print $3}''+         3-4-5
```

This behavior can be changed by loading the package upquote (written by Michael Covington), which uses the glyphs \textasciigrave and \textquotesingle from the textcomp package instead of the usual left and right curly quote characters within \verb or the verbatim environment. Normal typewriter text still uses the curly quotes, as shown in the last line of the example.

```
                                     \usepackage[scaled=0.85]{luximono}
                                     \usepackage{upquote}
                                     \raggedright
                                     \verb+TEST='ls -l |awk '{print $3}''+
TEST=`ls -l |awk '{print $3}'`        \par \renewcommand\ttdefault{pcr}
TEST=`ls -l |awk '{print $3}'`        \verb+TEST='ls -l |awk '{print $3}''+
TEST=`ls -l |awk '{print $3}'`        \par \renewcommand\ttdefault{cmtt}
but 'text' is unaffected!             \verb+TEST='ls -l |awk '{print $3}''+
                                     \par \texttt{but 'text' is unaffected!}      3-4-6
```

The package works well together with "verbatim" extensions as described in this chapter, except for the listings package; it conflicts with the scanning mechanism of that package. If you want this type of quoting with listings simply use the \lstset keyword upquote.

```
                                     \usepackage{textcomp}
                                     \usepackage{listings} \lstset{upquote}
                                     \begin{lstlisting}[language=ksh]
                                     TEST='ls -l |awk '{print $3}''
TEST=`ls -l |awk '{ print $3}'`       \end{lstlisting}                            3-4-7
```

3.4.3 fancyvrb—**Highly customizable verbatim environments**

The fancyvrb package by Timothy Van Zandt (these days maintained by Denis Girou and Sebastian Rahtz) offers a highly customizable set of environments and commands to typeset and manipulate verbatim text.

It works by parsing one line at a time from an environment or a file (a concept pioneered by the verbatim package), thereby allowing you to preprocess lines in various ways. By incorporating features found in various other packages it provides a truly universal production environment under a common set of syntax rules.

The main environment provided by the package is the Verbatim environment, which, if used without customization, behaves similarly to standard LaTeX's verbatim environment. The main difference is that it accepts an optional argument in which you can specify customization information using a key/value syntax. However, there is one restriction to bear in mind: the left bracket of the optional argument must appear on the same line as \begin. Otherwise, the optional argument will not be recognized but instead typeset as verbatim text.

More than 30 keywords are available, and we will discuss their use and possible values in some detail.

A number of variant environments and commands will be discussed near the end of this section as well. They also accept customization via the key/value method. Finally, we cover possibilities for defining your own variants in a straightforward way.

Customization keywords for typesetting

To manipulate the fonts used by the verbatim environments of the fancyvrb package, four environment keywords, corresponding to the four axes of NFSS, are available. The keyword fontfamily specifies the font family to use. Its default is Computer Modern Typewriter, so that when used without keywords the environments behave in similar fashion to standard LaTeX's verbatim. However, the value of this keyword can be any font family name in NFSS notation, such as pcr for Courier or cmss for Computer Modern Sans, even though the latter is not a monospaced font as would normally be used in a verbatim context. The keyword also recognizes the special values tt, courier, and helvetica and translates them internally into NFSS nomenclature.

Because typesetting of verbatim text can include special characters like "\" you must be careful to ensure that such characters are present in the font. This should be no problem when a font encoding such as T1 is active, which could be loaded using the fontenc package. It is, however, not the case for LaTeX's default font encoding OT1, in which only some monospaced fonts, such as the default typewriter font, contain all such special characters. The type of incorrect output you might encounter is shown in the second line of the next example.

```
\usepackage{fancyvrb}
\usepackage[OT1,T1]{fontenc}
\fontencoding{OT1}\selectfont
\begin{Verbatim}[fontfamily=tt]
Family 'tt' is fine in OT1: \sum_{i=1}^n
\end{Verbatim}
\begin{Verbatim}[fontfamily=helvetica]
But 'helvetica' fails in OT1: \sum_{i=1}^n
\end{Verbatim}
\fontencoding{T1}\selectfont
\begin{Verbatim}[fontfamily=helvetica]
...   while it works in T1: \sum_{i=1}^n
\end{Verbatim}
```

Family 'tt' is fine in OT1: \sum_{i=1}^n

But 'helvetica' fails in OT1: "sum˙–i=1˜n

... while it works in T1: \sum_{i=1}^n

3-4-8

Since all examples in this book are typeset using the T1 encoding this kind of problem will not show up elsewhere in the book. Nevertheless, you should be aware of this danger. It represents another good reason to use T1 in preference to TeX's original font encoding; for a more in-depth discussion see Section 7.2.4 on page 336.

The other three environment keywords related to the font set-up are fontseries, fontshape, and fontsize. They inherit the current NFSS settings from the surrounding text if not specified. While the first two expect values that can be fed into \fontseries and \fontshape, respectively (e.g., bx for a bold extended series or it for an *italic* shape), the fontsize is special. It expects one of the higher-level NFSS commands for specifying the font size—for example, \small. If the relsize package is available then you could alternatively specify a change of font size relative to the current text font by using something like \relsize{-2}.

```
\usepackage{relsize,fancyvrb}
\begin{Verbatim}[fontsize=\relsize{-2}]
  \sum_{i=1}^n
\end{Verbatim}
A line of text to show the body size.
\begin{Verbatim}[fontshape=sl,fontsize=\Large]
  \sum_{i=1}^n
\end{Verbatim}
```

\sum_{i=1}^n

A line of text to show the body size.

$\sum\_{i=1}^n$

3-4-9

A more general form for customizing the formatting is available through the environment keyword formatcom, which accepts any LaTeX code and executes it at the start of the environment. For example, to color the verbatim text you could pass it something like \color{blue}. There is also the possibility to operate on each line of text by providing a suitable redefinition for the command \FancyVerbFormatLine. This command is executed for every line, receiving the text from the line as its argument. In the next example every second line is

colored in blue, a result achieved by testing the current value of the counter
FancyVerbLine. This counter is provided automatically by the environment and
holds the current line number.

```
\usepackage{ifthen,color,fancyvrb}
\renewcommand\FancyVerbFormatLine[1]
  {\ifthenelse{\isodd{\value{FancyVerbLine}}}%
                  {\textcolor{blue}{#1}}{#1}}
\begin{Verbatim}[gobble=2]
  This line should become blue while
    this one will be black. And here
  you can observe that gobble removes
  not only blanks but any character.
\end{Verbatim}
```

```
This line should become blue while
  this one will be black. And here
u can observe that gobble removes
t only blanks but any character.
```

3-4-10

As shown in the previous example the keyword gobble can be used to remove
a number of characters or spaces (up to nine) from the beginning of each line. This
is mainly useful if all lines in your environments are indented and you wish to get
rid of the extra space produced by the indentation. Sometimes the opposite goal is
desired: every line should be indented by a certain space. For example, in this book
all verbatim environments are indented by 24pt. This indentation is controlled by
the keyword xleftmargin. There also exists a keyword xrightmargin to specify
the right indentation, but its usefulness is rather limited, since verbatim text is
not broken across lines. Thus, its only visible effect (unless you use frames, as
discussed below) are potentially more overfull box messages[1] that indicate that
your text overfloods into the right margin. Perhaps more useful is the Boolean keyword resetmargins, which controls whether preset indentations by surrounding
environments are ignored.

```
\usepackage{fancyvrb}
\begin{itemize}  \item  Normal indentation left:
  \begin{Verbatim}[frame=single,xrightmargin=2pc]
A verbatim line of text!
  \end{Verbatim}
  \item No indentation at either side:
  \begin{Verbatim}[resetmargins=true,
                  frame=single]
A verbatim line of text!
  \end{Verbatim}
\end{itemize}
```

- Normal indentation left:

  ```
  A verbatim line of text!
  ```

- No indentation at either side:

```
A verbatim line of text!
```

3-4-11

The previous example demonstrates one use of the frame keyword: to draw a
frame around verbatim text. By providing other values for this keyword, different-

---

[1]Whether overfull boxes inside a verbatim environment are shown is controlled the hfuzz keyword, which has a default value of 2pt. A warning is issued only if boxes protrude by more than the
keywords's value into the margin.

looking frames can be produced. The default is none, that is, no frame. With `topline`, `bottomline`, or `leftline` you get a single line at the side indicated;[1] `lines` produces a line at top and bottom; and `single`, as we saw in Example 3-4-11, draws the full frame. In each case, the thickness of the rules can be customized by specifying a value via the `framerule` keyword (default is `0.4pt`). The separation between the lines and the text can be controlled with `framesep` (default is the current value of `\fboxsep`).

If the color package is available, you can color the rules using the environment keyword `rulecolor` (default is black). If you use a full frame, you can also color the separation between the frame and the text via `fillcolor`.

```
\usepackage{color,fancyvrb}
\begin{Verbatim}[frame=single,rulecolor=\color{blue},
    framerule=3pt,framesep=1pc,fillcolor=\color{yellow}]
A framed verbatim line!
\end{Verbatim}
```

3-4-12

Unfortunately, there is no direct way to fill the entire background. The closest you can get is by using `\colorbox` inside `\FancyVerbFormatLine`. But this approach will leave tiny white rules behind the lines and—without forcing the lines to be of equal length, such as via `\makebox`—will also result in colored blocks of different widths.

```
\usepackage{color,fancyvrb}
\renewcommand\FancyVerbFormatLine[1]
    {\colorbox{green}{#1}}
\begin{Verbatim}
Some verbatim lines with a
background color.
\end{Verbatim}
\renewcommand\FancyVerbFormatLine[1]
    {\colorbox{yellow}{\makebox[\linewidth][l]{#1}}}
\begin{Verbatim}
Some verbatim lines with a
background color.
\end{Verbatim}
```

3-4-13

It is possible to typeset text as part of a frame by supplying it as the value of the `label` keyword. If this text contains special characters, such as brackets, equals sign, or comma, you have to hide them by surrounding them with a brace group. Otherwise, they will be mistaken for part of the syntax. The text appears by default at the top, but is printed only if the frame set-up would produce a line in that position. Alternate positions can be specified by using `labelposition`, which accepts none, `topline`, `bottomline`, or `all` as values. In the last case the text is printed above and below. If the label text is unusually large you may need

---

[1] There is no value to indicate a line at the right side.

to increase the separation between the frame and the verbatim text by using the keyword `framesep`. If you want to cancel a previously set label string, use the value `none`—if you really need "none" as a label string, enclose it in braces.

```
                                        \usepackage{fancyvrb}
  ┌─────────────────────────────┐       \begin{Verbatim}[frame=single,label=\fbox{Example code},
  │  Some verbatim text framed  │                      framesep=5mm,labelposition=bottomline]
  │        ┌──────────────┐     │       Some verbatim text framed
3-4-14 ────┤ Example code ├──── │       \end{Verbatim}
  └────────┴──────────────┴─────┘
```

You can, in fact, provide different texts to be placed at top and bottom by surrounding the text for the top position with brackets, as shown in the next example. For this scheme to work `frame` needs to be set to either `single` or `lines`.

```
                                        \usepackage{fancyvrb}
  ────────── Start of code ──────────   \begin{Verbatim}[frame=lines,framesep=5mm,
                                                       label={[Start of code]End of code}]
      A line of code                    A line of code
3-4-15 ────────── End of code ──────────  \end{Verbatim}
```

By default, the typeset output of the verbatim environments can be broken across pages by LaTeX if it does not fully fit on a single page. This is even true in cases where a frame surrounds the text. If you want to ensure that this cannot happen, set the Boolean keyword `samepage` to `true`.

The vertical spacing between lines in a verbatim environment is the same as in normal text, but if desired you can enlarge it by a factor using the keyword `baselinestretch`. Shrinking so that lines overlap is not possible. If you want to revert to the default line separation, use the string `auto` as a value.

```
                                            \usepackage{fancyvrb}
This text is more or less double-spaced.    \begin{Verbatim}[baselinestretch=1.6]
                                            This text is more or less double-spaced.
See also the discussion about the           See also the discussion about the
                                            setspace package elsewhere.
3-4-16 setspace package elsewhere.          \end{Verbatim}
```

When presenting computer listings, it is often helpful to number some or all of the lines. This can be achieved by using the keyword `numbers`, which accepts `none`, `left`, or `right` as a value to control the position of the numbers. The distance between the number and the verbatim text is 12pt by default but it can be adjusted by specifying a different value via the keyword `numbersep`. Usually, numbering restarts at 1 with each environment, but by providing an explicit number with the keyword `firstnumber` you can start with any integer value, even a negative one. Alternatively, this keyword accepts the word `last` to indicate that numbering should resume where it had stopped in the previous `Verbatim` instance.

```
\usepackage{fancyvrb}
\begin{Verbatim}[numbers=left,numbersep=6pt]
Verbatim lines can be numbered
at either left or right.
\end{Verbatim}
Some intermediate text\ldots
\begin{Verbatim}[numbers=left,firstnumber=last]
Continuation is possible too
as we can see here.
\end{Verbatim}
```

```
1  Verbatim lines can be numbered
2  at either left or right.

   Some intermediate text...

3  Continuation is possible too
4  as we can see here.
```

3-4-17

Some people prefer to number only some lines, and the package caters to this possibility by providing the keyword stepnumber. If this keyword is assigned a positive integer number, then only line numbers being an integer multiple of that number will get printed. We already learned that the counter that is used internally to count the lines is called FancyVerbLine, so it comes as no surprise that the appearance of the numbers is controlled by the command \theFancyVerbLine. By modifying this command, special effects can be obtained; a possibility where the current chapter number is prepended is shown in the next example. It also shows the use of the Boolean keyword numberblanklines, which controls whether blank lines are numbered (default is false, i.e., to not number them).

```
\usepackage{fancyvrb}
\renewcommand\theFancyVerbLine{\footnotesize
   \thechapter.\arabic{FancyVerbLine}}
\begin{Verbatim}[numbers=left,stepnumber=2,
                   numberblanklines=true]
Normally empty lines in
in a verbatim will not receive
numbers---here they do!

Admittedly using stepnumber
with such a redefinition of
FancyVerbLine looks a bit odd.
\end{Verbatim}
```

```
     Normally empty lines in
3.2  in a verbatim will not receive
     numbers---here they do!
3.4
     Admittedly using stepnumber
3.6  with such a redefinition of
     FancyVerbLine looks a bit odd.
```

3-4-18

In some situations it helps to clearly identify white space characters by displaying all blanks as ␣. This can be achieved with the Boolean keyword showspaces or, alternatively, the Verbatim* variant of the environment.

Another white space character, the tab, plays an important rôle in some programming languages, so there may be a need to identify it in your source. This is achieved with the Boolean keyword showtabs. The tab character displayed is defined by the command \FancyVerbTab and can be redefined, as seen below. By default, tab characters simply equal eight spaces, a value that can be changed with the keyword tabsize. However, if you set the Boolean keyword obeytabs to true, then each tab character produces as many spaces as necessary to move to the next

integer multiple of `tabsize`. The example input contains tabs in each line that are
displayed on the right as spaces with the default `tabsize` of 8. Note in particular
the difference between the last input and output line.

```
\usepackage{fancyvrb}
\begin{Verbatim}[showtabs=true]
12345678901234567890123456789 0
Two        default tabs
\end{Verbatim}
\begin{Verbatim}[obeytabs=true,showtabs=true]
Two        real    tabs
\end{Verbatim}
\renewcommand\FancyVerbTab{$\triangleright$}
\begin{Verbatim}[obeytabs=true,showtabs=true]
Two        new     tabs
\end{Verbatim}
\begin{Verbatim}[obeytabs=true,tabsize=3,showtabs=true]
Using   a           special tab      size
\end{Verbatim}
```

```
12345678901234567890123456789 0
Two         ⊣default           ⊣tabs

Two      ⊣real    ⊣tabs

Two      ▷new     ▷tabs

Using▷a ▷special tab▷size
```

3-4-19

If you wish to execute commands within the verbatim text, then you need one
character to act as an escape character (i.e., to denote the beginning of a command
name) and two characters to serve as argument delimiters (i.e., to play the rôle
that braces normally play within LaTeX). Such special characters can be specified
with the `commandchars` keyword as shown below; of course, these characters then
cannot appear as part of the verbatim text. The characters are specified by putting
a backslash in front of each one so as to mask any special meaning they might
normally have in LaTeX. The keyword `commentchar` allows you to define a comment
character, which will result in ignoring everything following it until and including
the next new line. Thus, if this character is used in the middle of a line, this line
and the next will be joined together. If you wish to cancel a previous setting for
`commandchars` or `commentchar`, use the string value "none".

```
\usepackage{fancyvrb}
\begin{Verbatim}[commandchars=\|\[\],commentchar=\!]
We can |emph[emphasize] text
! see above (this line is invisible)
Line with label|label[linea] ! removes new line
is shown here.
\end{Verbatim}
On line~\ref{linea} we see\ldots
```

```
We can emphasize text
Line with label is shown here.

On line 2 we see...
```

3-4-20

If you use `\label` within the verbatim environment, as was done in the previous example, it will refer to the internal line number whether or not that number is
displayed. This requires the use of the `commandchars` keyword, a price you might
consider too high because it deprives you of the use of the chosen characters in
your verbatim text.

Two other keywords let you change the parsing and manipulation of verbatim data: `codes` and `defineactive`. They allow you to play some devious tricks but their use is not so easy to explain: one needs a good understanding of TeX's inner workings. If you are interested, please check the documentation provided with the fancyvrb package.

Limiting the displayed data

Normally, all lines within the verbatim environment are typeset. But if you want to display only a subset of lines, you have a number of choices. With the keywords `firstline` and `lastline`, you can specify the start line and (if necessary) the final line to typeset. Alternatively, you can specify a start and stop string to search for within the environment body, with the result that all lines between (but this time *not* including the special lines) will be typeset. The strings are specified in the macros `\FancyVerbStartString` and `\FancyVerbStopString`. To make this work you have to be a bit careful: the macros need to be defined with `\newcommand*` and redefined with `\renewcommand*`. Using `\newcommand` will *not* work! To cancel such a declaration is even more complicated: you have to `\let` the command to `\relax`, for example,

```
\let\FancyVerbStartString\relax
```

or ensure that your definition is confined to a group—everything else fails.

```
\usepackage{fancyvrb}
\newcommand*\FancyVerbStartString{START}
\newcommand*\FancyVerbStopString{STOP}
\begin{Verbatim}
  A verbatim line not shown.
START
  Only the third line is shown.
STOP
  But the remainder is left out.
\end{Verbatim}
```

```
Only the third line is shown.
```

3-4-21

You may wonder why one would want to have such functionality available, given that one could simply leave out the lines that are not being typeset. With an environment like `Verbatim` they are indeed of only limited use. However, when used together with other functions of the package that write data to files and read it back again, they offer powerful solutions to otherwise unsolvable problems.

How the book examples have been produced

For instance, all examples in this book use this method. The example body is written to a file together with a document preamble and other material, so that the resulting file will become a processable LaTeX document. This document is then externally processed and included as an EPS graphic image into the book. Beside it, the sample code is displayed by reading this external file back in but displaying only those lines that lie between the strings `\begin{document}`

and \end{document}. This accounts for the example lines you see being typeset in black. The preamble part, which is shown in blue, is produced in a
similar fashion: for this the start and stop strings are redefined to include
only those lines lying between the strings \StartShownPreambleCommands and
\StopShownPreambleCommands. When processing the example externally, these
two commands are simply no-ops; that is, they are defined by the "example" class
(which is otherwise close to the article document class) to do nothing. As a consequence, the example code will always (for better or worse) correspond to the
displayed result.[1]

   To write data verbatim to a file the environment VerbatimOut is available.
It takes one mandatory argument: the file name into which to write the data.
There is, however, a logical problem if you try to use such an environment inside your own environments: the moment you start the VerbatimOut environment, everything is swallowed without processing and so the end of your environment is not recognized. As a solution the fancyvrb package offers the command
\VerbatimEnvironment, which, if executed within the \begin code of your environment, ensures that the end tag of your environment will be recognized in
verbatim mode and the corresponding code executed.

   To read data verbatim from a file, the command \VerbatimInput can be used.
It takes an optional argument similar to the one of the Verbatim environment (i.e.,
it accepts all the keywords discussed previously) and a mandatory argument to
specify the file from which to read. The variant \BVerbatimInput puts the typeset
result in a box without space above and below. The next example demonstrates
some of the possibilities: it defines an environment example that first writes its
body verbatim to a file, reads the first line back in and displays it in blue, reads
the file once more, this time starting with the second line, and numbers the lines
starting with the number 1. As explained above, a similar, albeit more complex
definition was used to produce the examples in this book.

```
\usepackage{fancyvrb,color}
\newenvironment{example}
  {\VerbatimEnvironment\begin{VerbatimOut}{test.out}}
  {\end{VerbatimOut}\noindent
   \BVerbatimInput[lastline=1,formatcom=\color{blue}]{test.out}%
   \VerbatimInput[numbers=left,firstnumber=1,firstline=2]{test.out}}
\begin{example}
A blue line.
Two lines
with numbers.
\end{example}
```

A blue line.

1 Two lines
2 with numbers.

3-4-22

   An interesting set of sample environments can be found in the package
fvrb-ex written by Denis Girou, which builds on the features provided by fancyvrb.

---

[1]In the first edition we unfortunately introduced a number of mistakes when showing code in
text that was not directly used.

Variant environments and commands

So far, all examples have used the `Verbatim` environment, but there also exist a number of variants that are useful in certain circumstances. `BVerbatim` is similar to `Verbatim` but puts the verbatim lines into a box. Some keywords discussed above (notably those dealing with frames) are not supported, but two additional ones are available. The first, `baseline`, denotes the alignment point for the box; it can take the values `t` (for top), `c` (for center), or `b` (for bottom—the default). The second, `boxwidth`, specifies the desired width of the box; if it is missing or given the value `auto`, the box will be as wide as the widest line present in the environment. We already encountered `\BVerbatimInput`; it too, supports these additional keywords.

```
\usepackage{fancyvrb}
\begin{BVerbatim}[boxwidth=4pc,baseline=t]
first line
second line
\end{BVerbatim}
\begin{BVerbatim}[baseline=c]
first line
second line
\end{BVerbatim}
```

```
                  first line
first line        second line
second line
```

3-4-23

All environments and commands for typesetting verbatim text also have star variants, which, as in the standard LATEX environments, display blanks as ␣. In other words, they internally set the keyword `showspaces` to `true`.

Defining your own variants

Defining customized variants of verbatim commands and environments is quite simple. For starters, the default settings built into the package can be changed with the help of the `\fvset` command. It takes one argument, a comma-separated list of key/value pairs. It applies them to every verbatim environment or command. Of course, you can still overwrite the new defaults with the optional argument on the command or environment. For example, if nearly all of your verbatim environments are indented by two spaces, you might want to remove them without having to deploy `gobble` on each occasion.

```
\usepackage{fancyvrb}    \fvset{gobble=2}
\noindent A line of text to show the left margin.
\begin{Verbatim}
  The new 'normal' case.
\end{Verbatim}
\begin{Verbatim}[gobble=0]
We now need to explicitly
cancel gobble occasionally!
\end{Verbatim}
```

A line of text to show the left margin.

```
The new 'normal' case.

We now need to explicitly
cancel gobble occasionally!
```

3-4-24

However, \fvset applies to all environments and commands, which may not be what you need. So the package offers commands to define your own verbatim environments and commands or to modify the behavior of the predefined ones.

```
\CustomVerbatimEnvironment      {new-env}{base-env}{key/val-list}
\RecustomVerbatimEnvironment{change-env}{base-env}{key/val-list}
\CustomVerbatimCommand          {new-cmd}{base-cmd}{key/val-list}
\RecustomVerbatimCommand        {change-cmd}{base-cmd}{key/val-list}
```

These declarations take three arguments: the name of the new environment or command being defined, the name of the environment or command (without a leading backslash) on which it is based, and a comma-separated list of key/value pairs that define the new behavior. To define new structures, you use \CustomVerbatimEnvironment or \CustomVerbatimCommand and to change the behavior of existing environments or commands (predefined ones as well as those defined by you), you use \RecustomVerbatimEnvironment or \RecustomVerbatimCommand. As shown in the following example, the default values, set in the third argument, can be overwritten as usual with the optional argument when the environment or command is instantiated.

```
\usepackage{fancyvrb}
\CustomVerbatimEnvironment{myverbatim}{Verbatim}
        {numbers=left,frame=lines,framerule=2pt}

\begin{myverbatim}
The normal case with thick
rules and numbers on the left.
\end{myverbatim}
\begin{myverbatim}[numbers=none,framerule=.6pt]
The exception without numbers
and thinner rules.
\end{myverbatim}
\RecustomVerbatimEnvironment{myverbatim}{Verbatim}
        {numbers=left,frame=none,showspaces=true}
\begin{myverbatim}
And from here on the environment
behaves differently again.
\end{myverbatim}
```

```
1  The normal case with thick
2  rules and numbers on the left.


   The exception without numbers
   and thinner rules.


1  And␣from␣here␣on␣the␣environment
2  behaves␣differently␣again.
```

3-4-25

Miscellaneous features

LaTeX's standard \verb command normally cannot be used inside arguments, because in such places the parsing mechanism would go astray, producing incorrect results or error messages. A solution to this problem is to process the verbatim data outside the argument, save it, and later use the already parsed data in such dangerous places. For this purpose the fancyvrb package offers the commands \SaveVerb and \UseVerb.

> \SaveVerb[*key/val-list*]{*label*}= *data* =   \UseVerb*[*key/val-list*]{*label*}

The command \SaveVerb takes one mandatory argument, a *label* denoting the storage bin in which to save the parsed data. It is followed by the verbatim *data* surrounded by two identical characters (= in the syntax example above), in the same way that \verb delimits its argument. To use this data you call \UseVerb with the *label* as the mandatory argument. Because the data is only parsed but not typeset by \SaveVerb, it is possible to influence the typesetting by applying a list of key/value pairs or a star as with the other verbatim commands and environments. Clearly, only a subset of keywords make sense, irrelevant ones being silently ignored. The \UseVerb command is unnecessarily fragile, so you have to \protect it in moving arguments.

Contents

1   Real \danger

Real␣\danger is no longer dangerous and can be reused as often as desired.

Real \danger

```
\usepackage{fancyvrb}
\SaveVerb{danger}=Real \danger=

\tableofcontents

\section{\protect\UseVerb{danger}}

\UseVerb*{danger} is no longer dangerous
and can\marginpar{\UseVerb[fontsize=\tiny]
                        {danger}}
be reused as often as desired.
```

3-4-26

It is possible to reuse such a storage bin when it is no longer needed, but if you use \UseVerb inside commands that distribute their arguments over a large distance you have to be careful to ensure that the storage bin still contains the desired contents when the command finally typesets it. In the previous example we placed \SaveVerb into the preamble because the use of its storage bin inside the \section command eventually results in an execution of \UseVerb inside the \tableofcontents command.

\SaveVerb also accepts an optional argument in which you can put key/value pairs, though again only a few are relevant (e.g., those dealing with parsing). There is one additional keyword aftersave, which takes code to execute immediately after saving the verbatim text into the storage bin. The next example shows an application of this keyword: the definition of a special variant of the \item command that accepts verbatim text for display in a description environment. It also supports an optional argument in which you can put a key/value list to influence the formatting. The definition is worth studying, even though the amount of mixed braces and brackets seems distressingly complex at first. They are necessary to ensure that the right brackets are matched by \SaveVerb, \item, and \UseVerb—the usual problem, since brackets do not nest like braces do in TeX.[1] Also note the use of \textnormal, which is needed to cancel the \bfseries implicitly issued

---

[1] The author confesses that it took him three trials (close to midnight) to make this example work.

by the \item command. Otherwise, the \emph command in the example would not show any effect since no Computer Modern bold italic face exits.

\ddanger Dangerous beast; found in TEXbooks.

\danger Its small brother, still dangerous.

\dddanger{*arg*} The ultimate horror.

3-4-27

```
\usepackage{fancyvrb}
\newcommand\vitem[1][]{\SaveVerb[commandchars=\|\<\>,%
    aftersave={\item[\textnormal{\UseVerb[#1]{vsave}}]}]{vsave}}
\begin{description}
\vitem+\ddanger+   Dangerous beast;\\ found in \TeX books.
\vitem[fontsize=\tiny]+\danger+ Its small brother,
                                still dangerous.
\vitem+\dddanger{|emph<arg>}+   The ultimate horror.
\end{description}
```

In the same way you can save whole verbatim environments using the environment SaveVerbatim, which takes the name of a storage bin as the mandatory argument. To typeset them, \UseVerbatim or \BUseVerbatim (boxed version) with the usual key/value machinery can be used.

Even though verbatim commands or environments are normally not allowed inside footnotes, you do not need to deploy \SaveVerb and the like to get verbatim text into such places. Instead, place the command \VerbatimFootnotes at the beginning of your document (following the preamble!) and from that point onward, you can use verbatim commands directly in footnotes. However, this was only implemented for footnotes—for other commands, such as \section, you still need the more complicated storage bin method described above.

A bit of text to give us a reason to use a footnote.[1] Was this good enough?

─────────────

3-4-28   [1] Here is proof: \danger{%_^}

```
\usepackage{fancyvrb}
\VerbatimFootnotes
A bit of text to give us a reason to use a
footnote.\footnote{Here is proof: \verb=\danger{%_^}=}
Was this good enough?
```

The fancyvrb version of \verb is called \Verb, and it supports all applicable keywords, which can be passed to it via an optional argument as usual. The example below creates \verbx as a variant of \Verb with a special setting of commandchars so that we can execute commands within its argument. We have to use \CustomVerbatimCommand for this purpose, since \verbx is a new command not available in standard LATEX.

\realdanger{*emph<arg>*}
3-4-29 \realdanger{*arg*}

```
\usepackage{fancyvrb}
\CustomVerbatimCommand\verbx{Verb}{commandchars=\|\<\>}
\Verb[fontfamily=courier]+\realdanger{|emph<arg>}+ \\
\verbx[fontfamily=courier]+\realdanger{|emph<arg>}+
```

As already mentioned, fancyvrb offers a way to make a certain character denote the start and stop of verbatim text without the need to put \verb in front. The command to declare such a delimiting character is \DefineShortVerb.

Like other fancyvrb commands it accepts an optional argument that allows you to set key/value pairs. These influence the formatting and parsing, though this time you cannot overwrite your choices on the individual instance. Alternatively, \fvset can be used, since it works on all verbatim commands and environments within its scope. To remove the special meaning from a character declared with \DefineShortVerb, use \UndefineShortVerb.

The use of \DefineShortVerb can make sources much more readable—or unreadable!
And with \UndefineShortVerb{\|} we can return the | character back to normal.

```
\usepackage{fancyvrb}
\DefineShortVerb[fontsize=\tiny]{\|}
The use of |\DefineShortVerb| can make sources
much more readable---or unreadable! \par
\UndefineShortVerb{\|}\DefineShortVerb{\+}
\fvset{fontfamily=courier}
And with +\UndefineShortVerb{\|}+
we can return the +|+ character back to normal.
```

3-4-30

Your favorite extensions or customizations can be grouped in a file with the name fancyvrb.cfg. After fancyvrb finishes loading, the package will automatically search for this file. The advantage of using such a file, when installed in a central place, is that you do not have to put your extensions into all your documents. The downside is that your documents will no longer be portable unless you distribute this file in tandem with them.

3.4.4 listings—Pretty-printing program code

A common application of verbatim typesetting is presenting program code. While on can successfully deploy a package like fancyvrb to handle this job, it is often preferable to enhance the display by typesetting certain program components (such as keywords, identifiers, and comments) in a special way.

Two major approaches are possible: one can provide commands to identify the logical aspects of algorithms or the programming language, or the application can (try to) analyze the program code behind the scenes. The advantage of the first approach is that you have potentially more control over the presentation; however, your program code is intermixed with TeX commands and thus may be difficult to maintain, unusable for direct processing, and often rather complicated to read in the source. Examples of packages classified into this category are alg and algorithmic. Here is an example:

if $i \leq 0$ **then**
 $i \leftarrow 1$
else
 if $i \geq 0$ **then**
  $i \leftarrow 0$
 end if
end if

```
\usepackage{algorithmic}
\begin{algorithmic}
\IF {$i\leq0$} \STATE $i\gets1$ \ELSE
\IF {$i\geq0$} \STATE $i\gets0$ \ENDIF
\ENDIF
\end{algorithmic}
```

3-4-31

ABAP (R/2 4.3, R/2 5.0, R/3 3.1, R/3 4.6C, R/3 6.10)	Haskell	PHP
ACSL	HTML	PL/I
Ada (83, 95)	IDL (empty, CORBA)	POV
Algol (60, 68)	Java (empty, AspectJ)	Prolog
Assembler (x86masm)	ksh	Python
Awk (gnu, POSIX)	Lisp (empty, Auto)	R
Basic (Visual)	Logo	Reduce
C (ANSI, Objective, Sharp)	Make (empty, gnu)	S (empty, PLUS)
C++ (ANSI, GNU, ISO, Visual)	Mathematica (1.0, 3.0)	SAS
Caml (light, Objective)	Matlab	Scilab
Clean	Mercury	SHELXL
Cobol (1974, 1985, ibm)	MetaPost	Simula (67, CII, DEC, IBM)
Comal 80	Miranda	SQL
csh	Mizar	tcl (empty, tk)
Delphi	ML	TeX (AlLaTeX, common, LaTeX, plain, primitive)
Eiffel	Modula-2	
Elan	MuPAD	VBScript
erlang	NASTRAN	Verilog
Euphoria	Oberon-2	VHDL (empty, AMS)
Fortran (77, 90, 95)	OCL (decorative, OMG)	VRML (97)
GCL	Octave	XML
Gnuplot	Pascal (Borland6, Standard, XSC)	
	Perl	

Table 3.7: Languages supported by listings (Winter 2003); blue indicates default dialect

The second approach is exemplified in the package listings[1] written by Carsten Heinz. This package first analyzes the code, decomposes it into its components, and then formats those components according to customizable rules. The package parser is quite general and can be tuned to recognize the syntax of many different languages (see Table 3.7). New languages are regularly added, so if your target language is not listed it might be worth checking the latest release of the package on CTAN. You may even consider contributing the necessary declarations yourself, which involves some work but is not very difficult.

The user commands and environments in this package share many similarities with those in fancyvrb. Aspects of parsing and formatting are controlled via key/value pairs specified in an optional argument, and settings for the whole document or larger parts of it can be specified using \lstset (the corresponding fancyvrb command is \fvset). Whenever appropriate, both packages use the same keywords so that users of one package should find it easy to make the transition to the other.

---

[1] The package version described here is 1.0. Earlier releases used a somewhat different syntax in some cases, so please upgrade if you find that certain features do not work as advertised.

After loading the package it is helpful to specify all program languages needed in the document (as a comma-separated list) using \lstloadlanguages. Such a declaration does not select a language, but merely loads the necessary support information and speeds up processing.

Program fragments are included inside a lstlisting environment. The language of the fragment is specified with the language keyword. In the following example we set this keyword via \lstset to C and then overwrite it later in the optional argument to the second lstlisting environment.

A "for" loop in C:

```
int sum;
int i; /* for  loop  variable */
sum=0;
for (i=0;i<n;i++) {
  sum += a[i];
}
```

Now the same loop in Ada:

```
Sum: Integer;
-- no decl for I necessary
Sum := 0;
for I in 1..N loop
  Sum := Sum + A(I);
end loop;
```

```
\usepackage{listings}
\lstloadlanguages{C,Ada}
\lstset{language=C,commentstyle=\scriptsize}
A ''for'' loop in C:
\begin{lstlisting}[keywordstyle=\underbar]
int sum;
int i; /*for loop variable*/
sum=0;
for (i=0;i<n;i++) {
   sum += a[i];
}
\end{lstlisting}
Now the same loop in Ada:
\begin{lstlisting}[language=Ada]
Sum: Integer;
-- no decl for I necessary
Sum := 0;
for I in 1..N loop
   Sum := Sum + A(I);
end loop;
\end{lstlisting}
```

3-4-32

This example also uses the keyword commentstyle, which controls the layout of comments in the language. The package properly identifies the different syntax styles for comments. Several other such keywords are available as well—basicstyle to set the overall appearance of the listing, stringstyle to format strings in the language, and directivestyle to format compiler directives, among others.

To format the language keywords, keywordstyle and ndkeywordstyle (second order) are used. Other identifiers are formatted according to the setting of identifierstyle. The values for the "style" keywords (except basicstyle) accept a one-argument LATEX command such as \textbf as their last token. This scheme works because the "identifier text" is internally surrounded by braces and can thus be picked up by a command with an argument.

Thus, highlighting of keywords, identifiers, and other elements is done automatically in a customizable way. Nevertheless, you might want to additionally emphasize the use of a certain variable, function, or interface. For this purpose you can use the keywords `emph` and `emphstyle`. The first gets a list of names you want to emphasize; the second specifies how you want them typeset.

```
\usepackage{listings,color}
\lstset{emph={Sum,N},emphstyle=\color{blue},
         emph=[2]I,emphstyle=[2]\underbar}
\begin{lstlisting}[language=Ada]
Sum: Integer;    Sum := 0;
for I in 1..N loop
   Sum := Sum + A(I);
end loop;
\end{lstlisting}
```

Sum: Integer;   Sum := 0;
for I **in** 1..N **loop**
   Sum := Sum + A(I);
end loop;

3-4-33

If you want to typeset a code fragment within normal text you can use the command `\lstinline`. The code is delimited in the same way as with the `\verb` command, meaning that you can choose any character (other than the open bracket) that is not used within the code fragment and use it as delimiter. An open bracket cannot be used because the command also accepts an optional argument in which you can specify a list of key/value pairs.

```
\usepackage{listings}  \lstset{language=C}
The \lstinline[keywordstyle=\underbar]!for!
loop is specified as \lstinline!i=0;i<n;i++!.
```

The for loop is specified as i=0;i<n;i++.

3-4-34

Of course, it is also possible to format the contents of whole files; for this purpose you use the command `\lstinputlisting`. It takes an optional argument in which you can specify key/value pairs and a mandatory argument in which you specify the file name to process. In the following example, the package identifies keywords of case-insensitive languages, even if they are written in an unusual mixed-case (WrItE) manner.

```
\usepackage{listings}
\begin{filecontents*}{pascal.src}
for i:=1 to maxint do
begin
   WrItE('This is stupid');
end.
\end{filecontents*}
\lstinputlisting[language=Pascal]{pascal.src}
```

for i:=1 **to maxint do**
begin
   WrItE('This␣is␣stupid');
end.

3-4-35

Spaces in strings are shown as ␣ by default. This behavior can be turned off by setting the keyword `showstringspaces` to `false`, as seen in the next example. It is also possible to request that all spaces be displayed in this way by setting the keyword `showspaces` to `true`. Similarly, tab characters can be made visible by using the Boolean keyword `showtabs`.

Line numbering is possible, too, using the same keywords as employed with fancyvrb: numbers accepts either `left`, `right`, or `none` (which turns numbering on or off), numberblanklines decides whether blank lines count with respect to numbering (default `false`), numberstyle defines the overall look and feel of the numbers, stepnumber defines which line numbers will appear (0 means no numbering), and numbersep defines the separation between numbers and the start of the line. By default, line numbering starts with 1 on each `\lstinputlisting` but this can be changed using the firstnumber keyword. If you specify `last` as a special value to firstnumber, numbering is continued.

Some text before ...

```
10  for i:=1 to maxint do
    begin
12      WrItE('This is stupid');
    end.
```

```
\usepackage{listings}
% pascal.src as defined before
\lstset{numberstyle=\tiny,numbers=left,
    stepnumber=2,numbersep=5pt,firstnumber=10,
    xleftmargin=12pt,showstringspaces=false}
\noindent Some text before \ldots
\lstinputlisting[language=Pascal]{pascal.src}
```

3-4-36

An overall indentation can be set using the xleftmargin keyword, as shown in the previous example, and gobble can be used to remove a certain number of characters (hopefully only spaces) from the left of each line displayed. Normally, indentations of surrounding environments like itemize will be honored. This feature can be turned off using the Boolean keyword resetmargin. Of course, all such keywords can be used together. To format only a subrange of the code lines you can specify the first and/or last line via firstline and lastline; for example, `lastline=10` would typeset a maximum of 10 code lines.

Another way to provide continued numbering is via the name keyword. If you define "named" environments using this keyword, numbering is automatically continued with respect to the previous environment with the same name. This allows independent numbering if the need arises.

```
Sum: Integer;                      1
```

The second fragment continues the numbering.

```
Sum := 0;                          2
for I in 1..N loop                 3
    Sum := Sum + A(I);             4
end loop;                          5
```

```
\usepackage{listings} \lstset{language=Ada,numbers=right,
    numberstyle=\tiny,stepnumber=1,numbersep=5pt}
\begin{lstlisting}[name=Test]
Sum: Integer;
\end{lstlisting}
The second fragment continues the numbering.
\begin{lstlisting}[name=Test]
Sum := 0;
for I in 1..N loop
    Sum := Sum + A(I);
end loop;
\end{lstlisting}
```

3-4-37

If a listing contains very long lines they may not fit into the available measure. In that case listings will produce overfull lines sticking out to the right, just like a `verbatim` environment would do. However, you can direct it to break long lines at spaces or punctuation characters by specifying the keyword `breaklines`. Wrapped lines are indented by 20pt, a value that can be adjusted through the keyword `breakindent`.

If desired, you can add something before (keyword `prebreak`) and after (keyword `postbreak`) the break to indicate that the line was artifically broken in the listing. We used this ability below to experiment with small arrows and later on with the string "(cont.)" in tiny letters. Both keywords are internally implemented as a TEX `\discretionary`, which means that they accept only certain input (characters, boxes, and kerns). For more complicated material it would be best to wrap everything in an `\mbox`, as we did in the example. In case of color changes, even that is not enough: you need an extra level of braces to prevent the color `\special` from escaping from the box (see the discussion in Appendix A.2.5).

The example exhibits another feature of the breaking mechanism—namely, if spaces or tabs appear in front of the material being broken, then these spaces are by default repeated on continuation lines. If this behavior is not desired, set the keyword `breakautoindent` to `false` as we did in the second part of the example.

```
\usepackage{color,listings}
\lstset{breaklines=true,breakindent=0pt,
          prebreak=\mbox{\tiny$\searrow$},
          postbreak=\mbox{{\color{blue}\tiny$\rightarrow$}}}
\begin{lstlisting}
Text at left margin
        /*A long string is broken across the line!*/
\end{lstlisting}
\begin{lstlisting}[breakautoindent=false,
                    postbreak=\tiny (cont.)\,]
        /*A long string is broken across the line!*/
\end{lstlisting}
```

3-4-38

You can put frames or rules around listings using the `frame` keyword, which takes the same values as it does in fancyvrb (e.g., `single`, `lines`). In addition, it accepts a subset of the string `trblTRBL` as its value. The uppercase letters stand for double rules the lowercase ones for single rules. There are half a dozen more keywords: to influence rule widths, create separation from the text, make round corners, and so on—all of them are compatible with fancyvrb if the same functionality is provided.

```
\usepackage{listings}
% pascal.src as defined before
\lstset{frame=trBL,framerule=2pt,framesep=4pt,
          rulesep=1pt,showspaces=true}
\lstinputlisting[language=Pascal]{pascal.src}
```

3-4-39

You can specify a caption for individual listings using the keyword `caption`. The captions are, by default, numbered and prefixed with the string Listing stored in `\lstlistingname`. The counter used is `lstlisting`; thus, to change its appearance you could modify `\thelstlisting`. The caption is positioned either above (default) or below the listing, and this choice can be adjusted using the keyword `captionpos`.

To get a list of all captions, put the command `\lstlistoflistings` at an appropriate place in your document. It produces a heading containing the words stored in `\lstlistlistingname` (default is Listings). If you want the caption text in the document to differ from the caption text in the list of listings, use an optional argument as shown in the following example. Note that in this case you need braces around the value to hide the right bracket. To prevent the caption from appearing in the list of listings, use the keyword `nolol` with a value of `true`. By using the keyword `label` you can specify a label for referencing the listing number via `\ref`, provided you have not suppressed the number.

Listings

The Pascal code in listing 1 shows...

```
for i:=1 to maxint do
begin
  WrItE('This is stupid');
end.
```
Listing 1: Pascal

```
\usepackage{listings}
% pascal.src as defined before
\lstset{frame=single,frameround=tftt,
        language=Pascal,captionpos=b}
\lstlistoflistings
          %
\bigskip  % normally the above is in the
\noindent % front matter section, but here ...
          %
The Pascal code in listing~\ref{foo} shows\ldots
\lstinputlisting
    [caption={[Pascal listing]Pascal},label=foo]
    {pascal.src}
```
3-4-40

The keyword `frameround` used in the previous example allows you to specify round corners by giving `t` for true and `f` for false, starting with the upper-right corner and moving clockwise. This feature is not available with fancyvrb frames.

Instead of formatting your listings within the text, you can turn them into floats by using the keyword `float`, typically together with the `caption` keyword. Its value is a subset of `htbp` specifying where the float is allowed to go (using it without a value is equivalent to `tbp`). You should, however, avoid mixing floating and nonfloating listings as this could sometimes result in captions being numbered out of order, as in Example 6-3-5 on page 296.

By default, listings only deals with input characters in the ASCII range; unexpected 8-bit input can produce very strange results, like the misordered letters in the following example. By setting `extendedchars` to `true` you can enable the use of 8-bit characters, which makes the package work harder, but (usually) produces

the right results. Of course, if you use an extended character set you would normally add the keyword to the `\lstset` declaration instead of specifying it every
time on the environment. It is also possible to specify an input encoding for the
code fragments (if different from the input encoding used for the remainder of
the document) by using the keyword `inputencoding`. This keyword can be used
only if the inputenclistings package is loaded.

```
\usepackage[latin1]{inputenc}
\usepackage{listings}
\lstset[language=C,commentstyle=\scriptsize]
\begin{lstlisting}
int i; /*für die äußere Schleife*/
\end{lstlisting}
\begin{lstlisting}[extendedchars=true]
int i; /*für die äußere Schleife*/
\end{lstlisting}
```

```
int  i;  /*üfr  die  äßuere  Schleife*/
```
```
int  i;  /* für  die  äußere  Schleife */
```

3-4-41

The package offers many more keys to influence the presentation. For instance, you can escape to LATEX for special formatting tricks, display tab or form-
feed characters, index certain identifiers, or interface to hyperref so that clicking
on some identifier will jump to the previous occurrence. Some of the features are
still considered experimental and you have to request them using an optional argument during package loading. These are all documented in great detail in the
manual (roughly 50 pages) accompanying the package.

As a final example of the kind of treasures you can find in that manual, look at
the following example. It shows code typesetting as known from Donald Knuth's
literate programming conventions.

```
\usepackage{listings}
\lstset{literate={:=}{{$\gets$}}1
 {<=}{{$\leq$}}1 {>=}{{$\geq$}}1 {<>}{{$\neq$}}1}
\begin{lstlisting}[gobble=2]
  var i:integer;
  if (i<=0) i := 1;
  if (i>=0) i := 0;
  if (i<>0) i := 0;
\end{lstlisting}
```

```
var  i : integer ;
if  ( i≤0 )  i ←  1;
if  ( i≥0 )  i ←  0;
if  ( i≠0 )  i ←  0;
```

3-4-42

3.5 Lines and columns

In the last part of this chapter we present a few packages that help in manipulating
the text stream in its entirety. The first package deals with attaching line numbers
to paragraphs, supporting automatic references to them. This can be useful in
critical editions and other scholarly works.

The second package deals with the problem of presenting two text streams side by side—for example, some original and its translation. We will show how both packages can be combined in standard cases.

The third package deals with layouts having multiple columns. It allows switching between different numbers of columns on the same page and supports balancing textual data. Standard LaTeX already offers the possibility of typesetting text in one- or two-column mode, but one- and two-column output cannot be mixed on the same page.

We conclude by introducing a package that allows you to mark the modifications in your source with vertical bars in the margin.

3.5.1 lineno—**Numbering lines of text**

In certain applications it is useful or even necessary to number the lines of paragraphs to be able to refer to them. As TeX optimizes the line breaking over the whole paragraph, it is ill equipped to provide such a facility, since technically line breaking happens at a very late stage during the processing, just before the final pages are constructed. At that point macro processing, which could add the right line number or handle automatic references, has already taken place. Hence, the only way to achieve line numbering is by deconstructing the completed page line by line in the "output routine" (i.e., the part of LaTeX, that normally breaks the paragraph galley into pages and adds running headers and footers) and attaching the appropriate line numbers at that stage.

This approach was taken by Stephan Böttcher in his lineno package. Although one would expect such an undertaking to work only in a restricted environment, his package is surprisingly robust and works seamlessly with many other packages—even those that modify the LaTeX output routine, such as ftnright, multicol, and wrapfig. It also supports layouts produced with the twocolumn option of the standard LaTeX classes.

`\linenumbers*[`*start-number*`]`   `\nolinenumbers`

Loading the lineno package has no direct effect: to activate line numbering, a `\linenumbers` command must be specified in the preamble or at some point in the document. The command `\nolinenumbers` deactivates line numbering again. Line numbering works on a per-paragraph basis. Thus, when LaTeX sees the end of a paragraph, it checks whether line numbering is currently requested and, if so, attaches numbers to *all* lines of that paragraph. It is therefore best to put these commands between paragraphs rather than within them.

The `\linenumbers` command can take an optional argument that denotes the number to use for the first line. If used without such an argument, it continues from where it stopped numbering previously. You can also use a star form, which is a shorthand for \linenumbers[1].

```
\usepackage{lineno}
\newcommand\para{ Some text to experiment
                   with line numbering.\par}
No line numbers here.\para
\linenumbers
But here we get line numbers. \para
And here too. \para
\linenumbers[-10]
Restart with a negative number. \para
```

No line numbers here. Some text to experiment with line numbering.

But here we get line numbers. Some text to experiment with line numbering.

And here too. Some text to experiment with line numbering.

Restart with a negative number. Some text to experiment with line numbering.

3-5-1

Rather than starting or stopping line numbering with the above commands, you can use the environment linenumbers to define the region that should get line numbers. This environment will automatically issue a \par command at the end to terminate the current paragraph. If line numbers are needed only for short passages, the environment form (or one of the special environments numquote and numquotation described later) is preferable.

As the production of line numbers involves the output routine, numbering will take place only for paragraphs being built and put on the "main vertical list" but not for those built inside boxes (e.g., not inside a \marginpar or within the body of a float). However, the package offers some limited support for numbering lines in such places via the \internallinenumbers command. Restrictions are that the baselines within such paragraphs need to be a fixed distance apart (otherwise, the numbers will not get positioned correctly) and that you may have to end such paragraphs with explicit \par commands. The \internallinenumbers command accepts a star and an optional argument just as \linenumbers does. However, the starred form not only ensures that line numbering is (re)started with 1, but also that the line numbers do not affect line numbering in the main vertical list; compare the results in the two \marginpars below.

Numbering boxed paragraphs

```
\usepackage{lineno}
% \para defined as before
\linenumbers
Some text on the main vertical list!
\marginpar{\footnotesize
           \internallinenumbers* \para}
\para \para In this paragraph we use
a second marginal note affecting the
\marginpar{\footnotesize
           \internallinenumbers  \para}
line numbers this time. \para
```

Some text on the main vertical list! Some text to experiment with line numbering.

Some text to experiment with line numbering.

In this paragraph we use a second marginal note affecting the line numbers this time. Some text to experiment with line numbering.

3-5-2

The line numbers in the second \marginpar continue the numbering on the main vertical list (the last line of first paragraph was 5) and the second paragraph then continues with line number 9. Such \marginpar commands are processed before the paragraph containing them is broken into lines, which explains the ordering of the numbers.

Handling display math As lineno needs \par to attach line numbers when the output routine is invoked, a TEXnical problem arises when certain display math constructs are used: the partial paragraph above such a display is broken into lines by TEX without issuing a \par. As a consequence, without further help such a partial paragraph will not get any line numbers attached. The package's solution, as illustrated in the next example, is to offer the environment linenomath, which, if it surrounds such a display, will take care of the line numbering problem. It also has a starred form that also numbers the display lines.

No line number before the display:

$$x \neq y$$

1 Some text to experiment with line numbering.
2   But line numbers in this case:

$$x \neq y$$

3 Some text to experiment with line numbering.

```
\usepackage{lineno} \linenumbers
\newcommand\sample{ Some text to
          experiment with line numbering.}
No line number before the display:
\[ x \neq y \] \sample \par
But line numbers in this case:
\begin{linenomath}
  \[ x \neq y \]
\end{linenomath}
\sample\par
```

3-5-3

If there are many such displays the need for surrounding each of them with a linenomath environment is cumbersome. For this reason the package offers the option displaymath, which redefines the basic LATEX math display environments so that they internally use linenomath environments. The option mathlines will make linenomath behave like its starred form so that the displayed mathematical formulas get line numbers as well.

1   Some text to experiment with line numbering.

2                   $$x \neq y$$

3 Some text to experiment with line numbering.
4   Some text to experiment with line numbering.

5                   $$x \neq y$$

6 Some text to experiment with line numbering.

```
\usepackage[displaymath,mathlines]
                {lineno}
\linenumbers
% \sample as defined before
\sample \[ x \neq y \] \sample\par
\sample
\begin{displaymath}
  x \neq y
\end{displaymath}
\sample
```

3-5-4

Cross-references to line numbers To reference line numbers put a \linelabel into the line and then refer to it via \ref or \pageref, just as with other references defined using \label. The exception is that \linelabel can only be used on the main vertical list and should only be used within paragraphs that actually carry numbers. If it is used elsewhere, you get either a bogus reference (if the current line does not have a line number) or an error message (in places where \linelabel is not allowed).

1 Some text to experiment with line num- 2 bering. Some text to experiment with line 3 numbering. Some text to experiment with 4 line numbering. Some text to experiment 5 with line numbering. Some text to exper- 6 iment with line numbering. 7 In the text on lines 2, 3, up to and includ- 8 ing line 5 we see to refer to individual lines 9 ...	``` \usepackage{lineno} \linenumbers % \sample as defined before \sample\linelabel{first} \sample \sample \sample\linelabel{second} \sample In the text on lines~\ref{first}, \lineref[1]{first}, up to and including line~\ref{second} we see to refer to individual lines \ldots ```

3-5-5

It is also possible to refer to a line that carries no \linelabel, by using the \lineref command with an optional argument specifying the offset. This ability can be useful if you need to refer to a line that cannot be easily labeled, such as a math display, or if you wish to refer to a sequence of lines, as in the previous example.

There are several ways to customize the visual appearance of line numbers. Specifying the option modulo means that line numbers will only appear on some lines (default is every fifth). This effect can also be achieved by using the command \modulolinenumbers. Calling this command with an optional argument attaches numbers to lines that are multiples of the specified number (in particular, a value of 1 corresponds to normal numbering). Neither command nor option initiates line numbering mode, for that a \linenumbers command is still necessary.

Labeling only some lines

1   Some text to experiment with line num-
2 bering. Some text to experiment with line
3 numbering. Some text to experiment with
4 line numbering.
    And now a paragraph with numbers on
6 every second line. Some text to experiment
  with line numbering. Some text to experi-
8 ment with line numbering. Some text to ex-
  periment with line numbering.
	``
	\usepackage{lineno}
	\linenumbers
	% \sample defined as before
	
	\sample \sample \sample \par
	\modulolinenumbers[2]
	And now a paragraph with numbers on every
	second line. \sample \sample \sample \par
	``

3-5-6

The font for line numbers is controlled by the hook \linenumberfont. Its default definition is to use tiny sans serif digits. The numbers are put flush right in a box of width \linenumberwidth. This box is separated from the line by the value stored in \linenumbersep. To set the number flush left you have to dig deeper, but even for this case you will find hooks like \makeLineNumberRight in the package. Although changing the settings in the middle of a document is usually not a good idea, it was done in the next example for demonstration purposes.

The option "right" changes the line number position. Some text to experiment with line numbering. Some text to experiment with line numbering.

Now we use a different font and a bigger separation. Some text to experiment with line numbering. Some text to experiment with line numbering.

```
\usepackage[right]{lineno}
\linenumbers
% \sample defined as before
The option ``right'' changes the line
number position. \sample \sample \par
\renewcommand\linenumberfont
  {\normalfont\footnotesize\ttfamily}
\setlength\linenumbersep{20pt}
Now we use a different font and a bigger
separation. \sample \sample \par
```

3-5-7

For special applications the package offers two environments that provide line numbers automatically: numquote and numquotation. They are like their LaTeX cousins quote and quotation, except that their lines are numbered. They accept an optional argument denoting the line number with which to start (if the argument is omitted, they restart with 1) and they have starred forms that will suppress reseting the line numbers.

The main difference from their LaTeX counterparts (when used together with the \linenumbers command) is the positioning of the numbers, which are indented inward. Thus, their intended use is for cases when only the quoted text should receive line numbers that can be referenced separately.

1 Some text to experiment with line
2 numbering.

3 Some text to experiment with line number-
4 ing. Some text to experiment with line num-
5 bering.

1 Some text to experiment with line
2 numbering.

3 Some more text.

```
\usepackage{lineno}
\linenumbers
% \sample defined as before
\begin{quote}
 \sample
\end{quote}
\sample \sample
\begin{numquote}
  \sample
\end{numquote}
Some more text.
```

3-5-8

Providing your own extensions   Using the machinery provided by the package material, it is fairly easy to develop your own environments that attach special items to each line. The main macro to customize is \makeLineNumber, which gets executed inside a box of zero width at the left edge of each line (when line numbering mode is turned on). The net effect of your code should take up no space, so it is best to operate with \llap or \rlap. Apart from that you can use basically anything. You should only remember that the material is processed and attached after the paragraph has been broken into lines and normal macro-processing has finished, so, you should not expect it to interact with data in mid-paragraph. You can produce the current line number with the \LineNumber command, which will supply the number or nothing, depending on whether line numbering mode is on.

The following example shows the definition and use of two new environments that (albeit somewhat crudely, as they do not care about setting fonts and the like) demonstrate some of the possibilities. Note that even though the second environment does not print any line numbers, the lines are internally counted, so that line numbering resumes afterwards with the correct value.

```
\usepackage{lineno} \linenumbers
% \sample defined as before
\newenvironment{numarrows}
    [{\renewcommand\makeLineNumber
            {\llap{\LineNumber$\rightarrow$ }}}
  {\par}
\newenvironment{arrows}{\renewcommand\makeLineNumber
    {\rlap{\hspace{\textwidth} $\leftarrow$}}}{\par}
\begin{numarrows}  \sample  \end{numarrows}
\begin{arrows} \sample \sample \end{arrows}
\sample
\begin{numarrows}  \sample  \end{numarrows}
```

1→   Some text to experiment
2→ with line numbering.
           Some text to experiment ←
       with line numbering. Some text ←
       to experiment with line number- ←
       ing.   ←
7→   Some text to experiment
8→ with line numbering. Some text
9→ to experiment with line number-
10→ ing.

3-5-9

The appearance and behavior of the line numbers can be further controlled by a set of options or, alternatively, by a set of commands equivalent to the options (see the package documentation for details on the command forms). With the options `left` (default) and `right`, you specify in which margin the line numbers should appear. Using the option `switch` or `switch*`, you get them in the outer and inner margins, respectively.

At least two LaTeX runs of the document are required before the line numbers will appear in the appropriate place. Unfortunately, there is no warning about the need to rerun the document, so you have to watch out for this issue yourself.

You can also request that numbers restart on each page by specifying the option `pagewise`. This option needs to come last.

3.5.2   parallel—Two text streams aligned

Sometimes it is necessary to typeset something in parallel columns, such as when presenting some text and its translation. Parallel in this context means that at certain synchronization points the two text streams are vertically (re)aligned. This type of layout is normally not supported by LaTeX (which by default only works with a single text stream), but it can be achieved by using Matthias Eckermann's parallel package.

This package provides the `Parallel` environment, which surrounds the material to be typeset in parallel. It takes two mandatory arguments: the widths of the left and right columns. Their sum should be less than `\textwidth`; otherwise, the text in the two columns will touch or even overlap. To ease usage, one or both arguments can be left empty, in which case the appropriate width for the column(s) will be calculated automatically, using the current value of `\ParallelUserMidSkip` as the column separation. To mark up the left and the right text streams, you use

\verb *is allowed* \ParallelLText and \ParallelRText, respectively. Although both commands expect the text as an argument, it is nevertheless possible to use \verb or a verbatim environment inside, as the following example shows.

```
\usepackage{parallel}
\begin{Parallel}{}{}
  \ParallelLText{This is text in the English
    language explaining the command \verb=\foo=.}
  \ParallelRText{Dies ist Text in deutscher Sprache,
    der das Kommando \verb=\foo= erl\"autert.}
\end{Parallel}
```

This is text in the English language explaining the command \foo.

Dies ist Text in deutscher Sprache, der das Kommando \foo erläutert.

3-5-10

To align certain lines of text you split the two text streams at appropriate points by using pairs of \ParallelLText and \ParallelRText commands and separating each pair with \ParallelPar. If you forget one of the \ParallelPar commands, some of your text will get lost without warning. Moreover, as its name suggests, the \ParallelPar command introduces a paragraph break, so that alignment is possible only at paragraph boundaries. Additional paragraph breaks inside the argument of an \Parallel..Text command are also possible but in that case no alignment is attempted.

In the next example, displaying a few "direct" translations of computer lingua into German (taken from [54] with kind permission by Eichborn Verlag), we define a shorthand command \LR to make it easier to input the text. If such a shorthand is used, \verb can no longer be used in the argument. Thus, if you need \verb, use the package commands directly. We also use the lineno package since line numbers can be useful when talking about a text and its translation.

```
\usepackage{parallel,lineno}
\linenumbers \modulolinenumbers[2]
\setlength\linenumbersep{1pt}
\newcommand\LR[2]{\ParallelLText{#1}%
                  \ParallelRText{#2}\ParallelPar}
\begin{Parallel}{.45\linewidth}{}
\raggedright   \setlength\leftskip{10pt}
               \setlength\parindent{-10pt}
\LR{I just go online and download an update.}{Ich
  geh mal eben auf den Strich und lade mir ein
  Auffrisch herunter.}  \LR{This laptop is missing
  several interfaces.} {Dieser Scho\ss\-spitze
  fehlt so manches Zwi\-schen\-ge\-sicht.}
\LR{Microsoft Office on floppy disks.}{Kleinweich
  B\"uro auf Schlabberscheiben.}
\end{Parallel}
```

I just go online
2 and download
an update.

4

6 This laptop is
missing
8 several
interfaces.

10

Microsoft Office
12 on floppy
disks.

Ich geh mal eben
auf den Strich
und lade mir
ein Auffrisch
herunter.

Dieser
Schoßspitze
fehlt so
manches Zwi-
schengesicht.

Kleinweich Büro
auf Schlabber-
scheiben.

3-5-11

As you can see, it is possible to adjust paragraph parameters within the scope of the Parallel environment. The negative \parindent cancels the positive \leftskip so that each paragraph starts flush left but following lines are indented by \leftskip (and both must be changed *after* calling \raggedright, as the latter also sets these registers).

The Parallel environment works by aligning line by line, which has a surprising consequence when one block contains unusually large objects, such as a display. Thus, the method is suitable only for normal text lines.

This is text that contains:
$$\sum_{n=1}^{x} 2a_n$$

And here is the explanation showing some surprising effect.

```
\usepackage{parallel}
\begin{Parallel}{}{}
\ParallelLText{This is text that contains:
             \[ \sum_{n=1}^x2 a_n \]}
\ParallelRText{And here is the explanation
             showing some surprising effect.}
\end{Parallel}
```

3-5-12

Footnotes within the parallel text are not placed at the bottom of the current page, but rather are typeset directly after the end of the current Parallel environment and separated from it by the result of executing \ParallelAtEnd, which is a command defined to do nothing. You can, however, redefine it to place something between footnotes and preceding text. If the redefinition should apply only to a single Parallel environment, place it within the scope of the environment.

Footnotes in parallel text

The presentation of the footnotes is controlled by four package options: OldStyleNums sets footnote numbers using old-style numerals, RaiseNums generates raised footnote numbers, and ItalicNums produces italic numbers. If none of these options is given, then Arabic numerals at the baseline position are used. The options affect only the numbers in front of the footnote text; the markers within the parallel text are always raised Arabic numerals. The fourth option, SeparatedFootnotes, can be combined with one of the three other options and indicates that footnotes in each column should be independently numbered. The numbers from the right column are then postfixed with \ParallelDot, which by default produces a centered dot. In the next example its definition is slightly modified so that the dot itself does not take up any space.

This is text in the English language[1] explaining the command \foo.

Dies ist Text[1] in deutscher Sprache[2], der das Kommando \foo erläutert.

---
[1] We hope!

[1·] Ein Satz.

[2·] Schlechter Stil!

```
\usepackage[OldStyleNums,SeparatedFootnotes]{parallel}
\renewcommand\ParallelAtEnd{\vspace{7pt}\footnoterule}
\renewcommand\ParallelDot
             {\makebox[0pt][l]{\textperiodcentered}}
\begin{Parallel}[v]{}{} \raggedright
\ParallelLText{This is text in the English
   language\footnote{We hope!} explaining the
   command \verb=\foo=.}
\ParallelRText{Dies ist Text\footnote{Ein Satz.} in
   deutscher Sprache\footnote{Schlechter Stil!}, der
   das Kommando \verb=\foo= erl\"autert.}
\end{Parallel}
```

3-5-13

The Parallel environment can sport an optional argument before the mandatory ones, whose value can be c (make two columns—the default), v (separate columns with a vertical rule as shown in the previous example), or p (put left text on left-hand pages and right text on right-hand pages). If the "page" variant is chosen it is possible that you get empty pages. For example, if you are on a verso page the environment has to skip to the next recto page in order to display the texts on facing pages.

3.5.3 multicol—A flexible way to handle multiple columns

With standard LaTeX it is possible to produce documents with one or two columns (using the class option twocolumn). However, it is impossible to produce only parts of a page in two-column format as the commands \twocolumn and \onecolumn always start a fresh page. Additionally, the columns are never balanced, which sometimes results in a slightly weird distribution of the material.

The multicol package[1] by Frank Mittelbach solves these problems by defining an environment, multicols, with the following properties:

- Support is provided for 2–10 columns, which can run for several pages.
- When the environment ends, the columns on the last page are balanced so that they are all of nearly equal length.
- The environment can be used inside other environments, such as figure or minipage, where it will produce a box containing the text distributed into the requested number of columns. Thus, you no longer need to hand-format your layout in such cases.
- Between individual columns, vertical rules of user-defined widths can be inserted.
- The formatting can be customized globally or for individual environments.

\begin{multicols}{*columns*} [*preface*] [*skip*]

Normally, you can start the environment simply by specifying the number of desired columns. By default paragraphs will be justified, but with narrow measures— as in the examples—they would be better set unjustified as we show later on.

Here is some text to be distributed over several columns. If the columns are very narrow try typesetting ragged right.

```
\usepackage{multicol}
\begin{multicols}{3}
 Here is some text to be distributed over
 several columns. If the columns are very
 narrow try typesetting ragged right.
\end{multicols}
```

3-5-14

---

[1]For historical reasons the copyright of the multicol package, though distributed under LPPL (LaTeX Project Public License) [111], contains an additional "moral obligation" clause that asks commercial users to consider paying a license fee to the author or the LaTeX3 fund for their use of the package. For details see the head of the package file itself.

```
\premulticols    50.0pt          \postmulticols   20.0pt
\columnsep       10.0pt          \columnseprule    0.0pt
\multicolsep     12.0pt plus 4.0pt minus 3.0pt
```

Table 3.8: Length parameters used by `multicols`

You may be interested in prefixing the multicolumn text with a bit of single-column material. This can be achieved by using the optional *preface* argument. LaTeX will then try to keep the text from this argument and the start of the multi-column text on the same page.

```
\usepackage{multicol}
\begin{multicols}{2}
          [\section*{Some useful advice}]
Here is some text to be distributed over
several columns. If the columns are very
narrow try typesetting ragged right.
\end{multicols}
```

Some useful advice

Here is some text to be distributed over several columns. If the columns are very narrow try typesetting ragged right.

3-5-15

The `multicols` environment starts a new page if there is not enough free space left on the current page. The amount of free space is controlled by a global parameter. However, when using the optional argument the default setting for this parameter may be too small. In this case you can either change the *global* default (see below) or adjust the value for the *current* environment by using a second optional *skip* argument as follows:

```
\begin{multicols}{3}[\section*{Index}][7cm]
   Text Text Text Text ...
\end{multicols}
```

This would start a new page if less than 7cm free vertical space was available.

The `multicols` environment balances the columns on the last page (it was originally developed for exactly this purpose). If this effect is not desired you can use the `multicols*` variant instead. Of course, this environment works only in the main vertical galley, since inside a box one has to balance the columns to determine a column height.

Preventing balancing

The `multicols` environment recognizes several formatting parameters. Their meanings are described in the following sections. The default values can be found in Table 3.8 (dimensions) and Table 3.9 (counters). If not stated otherwise, all changes to the parameters have to be placed before the start of the environment to which they should apply.

The `multicols` environment first checks whether the amount of free space left on the page is at least equal to \premulticols or to the value of the second optional argument, when specified. If the requested space is not available, a

The required free space

\multicolpretolerance	−1	\multicoltolerance	9999
columnbadness	10000	finalcolumnbadness	9999
collectmore	0	unbalance	0
tracingmulticols	0		

Table 3.9: Counters used by `multicols`

\newpage is issued. A new page is also started at the end of the environment if the remaining space is less than \postmulticols. Before and after the environment, a vertical space of length \multicolsep is placed.

Column width and separation   The column width inside the `multicols` environment will automatically be calculated based on the number of requested columns and the current value of \linewidth. It will then be stored in \columnwidth. Between columns a space of \columnsep is left.

Adding vertical lines   Between any two columns, a rule of width \columnseprule is placed. If this parameter is set to 0pt (the default), the rule is suppressed. If you choose a rule width larger than the column separation, the rule will overprint the column text.

```
\usepackage{multicol,ragged2e}
\setlength\columnseprule{0.4pt}
\addtolength\columnsep{2pt}

\begin{multicols}{3}
\RaggedRight
  Here is some text to be distributed over
  several columns. In this example ragged-right
  typesetting is used.
\end{multicols}
```

Here is some | over several | ragged-right
text to be | columns. In | typesetting
distributed | this example | is used.

3-5-16

Column formatting

By default (the \flushcolumns setting), the `multicols` environment tries to typeset all columns with the same length by stretching the available vertical space inside the columns. If you specify \raggedcolumns the surplus space will instead be placed at the bottom of each column.

Paragraphs are formatted using the default parameter settings (as described in Sections 3.1.11 and 3.1.12) with the exception of \pretolerance and \tolerance, for which the current values of \multicolpretolerance and \multicoltolerance are used, respectively. The defaults are −1 and 9999, so that the paragraph-breaking trial without hyphenation is skipped and relatively bad paragraphs are allowed (accounting for the fact that the columns are typically very narrow). If the columns are wide enough, you might wish to change these defaults to something more restrictive, such as

```
\multicoltolerance=3000
```

Note the somewhat uncommon assignment form: \multicoltolerance is an internal TeX counter and is controlled in exactly the same way as \tolerance.

Balancing control

At the end of the multicols environment, remaining text will be balanced to produce columns of roughly equal length. If you wish to place more text in the left columns you can advance the counter unbalance. This counter determines the number of additional lines in the columns in comparison to the number that the balancing routine has calculated. It will automatically be restored to zero after the environment has finished. To demonstrate the effect, the next example uses the text from Example 3-5-16 on the facing page but requests one extra line.

```
\usepackage{multicol,ragged2e}
\addtolength\columnsep{2pt}
\begin{multicols}{3}
\RaggedRight
\setcounter{unbalance}{1}
  Here is some text to be distributed over
  several columns. In this example ragged-right
  typesetting is used.
\end{multicols}
```

Here is some   columns. In   is used.
text to be   this example
distributed   ragged-right
over several   typesetting

3-5-17

Column balancing is further controlled by the two counters columnbadness and finalcolumnbadness. Whenever LaTeX is constructing boxes (such as a column) it will compute a badness value expressing the quality of the box—that is, the amount of excess white space. A zero value is optimal, and a value of 10000 is infinitely bad in LaTeX's eyes.[2] While balancing, the algorithm compares the badness of possible solutions and, if any column except the last one has a badness higher than columnbadness, the solution is ignored. When the algorithm finally finds a solution, it looks at the badness in the last column. If it is larger than finalcolumnbadness, it will typeset this column with the excess space placed at the bottom, allowing it to come out short.

Collecting material

To be able to properly balance columns the multicols environment needs to collect enough material to fill the remaining part of the page. Only then does it cut the collected material into individual columns. It tries to do so by assuming that not more than the equivalent of one line of text per column vanishes into the margin due to breaking at vertical spaces. In some situations this assumption is incorrect and it becomes necessary to collect more or less material. In such a case

---

[1]Very bad for reading but too good to fix: this problem of a break-stack with "the" four times in a row will not be detected by TeX's paragraph algorithm—only a complete paragraph rewrite would resolve it.

[2]For an overfull box the badness value is set to 100000 by TeX, to mark this special case.

you can adjust the default setting for the counter `collectmore`. Changing this counter by one means collecting material for one more (or less) `\baselineskip`.

There are, in fact, reasons why you may want to reduce that collection. If your document contains many footnotes and a lot of surplus material is collected, there is a higher chance that the unused part will contain footnotes, which could come out on the wrong page. The smallest sensible value for the counter is the negative number of columns used. With this value `multicols` will collect exactly the right amount of material to fill all columns as long as no space gets lost at a column break. However, if spaces are discarded in this set up, they will show up as empty space in the last column.

Tracing the algorithm

You can trace the behavior of the multicol package by loading it with one of the following options. The default, `errorshow`, displays only real errors. With `infoshow`, multicol becomes more talkative and you will get basic processing information such as

```
Package multicol: Column spec: 185.0pt = indent + columns + sep =
(multicol)        0.0pt + 3 x 55.0pt + 2 x 10.0pt on input line 32.
```

which is the calculated column width.

With `balancingshow`, you get additional information on the various trials made by `multicols` when determining the optimal column height for balancing, including the resulting badness of the columns, reasons why a trial was rejected, and so on.

Using `markshow` will additionally show which marks for the running header or footer are generated on each page. Instead of using the options you can (temporarily) set the counter `tracingmulticols` to a positive value (higher values give more tracing information).

Manually breaking columns

Sometimes it is necessary to overrule the column-breaking algorithm. We have already seen how the `unbalance` counter is used to influence the balancing phase. But on some occasions one wishes to explicitly end a column after a certain line. In standard LaTeX this can be achieved with a `\pagebreak` command, but this approach does not work within a `multicols` environment because it will end the collection phase of `multicols` and thus end *all* columns on the page. As an alternative the command `\columnbreak` is provided. If used within a paragraph it marks the end of the current line as the desired breakpoint. If used between paragraphs it forces the next paragraph into the next column (or page) as shown in the following example. If `\flushcolumns` is in force, the material in the column is vertically stretched (if possible) to fill the full column height. If this effect is not desired one can prepend a `\vfill` command to fill the bottom of the column with white space.

Here is some text to be distributed over several columns.

With the help of the \columnbreak command this paragraph was forced into the second column.

```
\usepackage{multicol,ragged2e}
\begin{multicols}{2}  \RaggedRight
Here is some text to be distributed over several
columns. \par \vfill\columnbreak
With the help of the \verb=\columnbreak= command
this paragraph was forced into the second column.
\end{multicols}
```

3-5-18

Floats and footnotes in multicol

Floats (e.g., figures and tables) are only partially supported within `multicols`. You can use starred forms of the float environments, thereby requesting floats that span all columns. Column floats and \marginpars, however, are not supported.

Footnotes are typeset (full width) on the bottom of the page, and not under individual columns (a concession to the fact that varying column widths are supported on a single page).

Under certain circumstances a footnote reference and its text may fall on subsequent pages. If this is a possibility, `multicolst` produces a warning. In that case, you should check the page in question. If the footnote reference and footnote text really are on different pages, you will have to resolve the problem locally by issuing a \pagebreak command in a strategic place. The reason for this behavior is that `multicols` has to look ahead to assemble material and may not be able to use all material gathered later on. The amount of looking ahead is controlled by the `collectmore` counter.

3.5.4 changebar—Adding revision bars to documents

When a document is being developed it is sometimes necessary to (visually) indicate the changes in the text. A customary way of doing that is by adding bars in the margin, the known as "changebars". Support for this functionality is offered by the `changebar` package, originally developed by Michael Fine and Neil Winton, and now supported by Johannes Braams. This package works with most PostScript drivers, but in particular `dvips`, which is the default driver when the package is loaded. Other drivers can be selected by using the package option mechanism. Supported options are `dvitoln03`, `dvitops`, `dvips`, `emtex`, `textures`, and `vtex`.

Supported printer drivers

\begin{changebar}[*barwidth*] \cbstart[*barwidth*] ... \cbend

When you add text to your document and want to signal this fact, you should surround it with the `changebar` environment. Doing so ensures that LATEX will warn you when you forget to mark the end of a change. This environment can be (properly) nested within other environments. However, if your changes start within one LATEX environment and end inside another the environment form cannot be used as this would result in improperly nested environments. Therefore, the package also provides the commands \cbstart and \cbend. These should be used with care, because there is no check that they are properly balanced. Spaces after them might get ignored.

If you want to give a single bar a different width you may use the optional argument and specify the width as a normal LaTeX length.

> `\cbdelete[`*`barwidth`*`]`

Text that has been removed can be indicated by inserting the `\cbdelete` command. Again, the width of the bar can be changed.

```
\usepackage{changebar}
\cbstart
This is the text in the first paragraph.
This is the text in the first paragraph.\cbend

This is the text in the second paragraph.
\cbdelete
This is the text in the second paragraph.

\setcounter{changebargrey}{35}
\begin{changebar}[4pt]
This is paragraph three. \par
This is paragraph four.
\end{changebar}
```

This is the text in the first paragraph. This is the text in the first paragraph.

This is the text in the second paragraph. This is the text in the second paragraph.

This is paragraph three.

This is paragraph four.

3-5-19

> `\nochangebars`

When your document has reached the final stage you can remove the effect of using the changebar package by inserting the command `\nochangebars` in the preamble of the document.

Customizations

Changing the width If you want to change the width of *all* changebars you can do so by changing the value of `\changebarwidth` via the command `\setlength`. The same can be done for the deletion bars by changing the value of `\deletebarwidth` .

Positioning changebars By default, the changebars will show up in the "inner margin", but this can be changed by using one of the following options: `outerbars`, `innerbars`, `leftbars`, or `rightbars`.

The distance between the text and the bars is controlled by `\changebarsep`. It can can be changed only in the preamble of the document.

Coloring changebars The color of the changebars can be changed by the user as well. By default, the option `grey` is selected so the changebars are grey (grey level 65%). The drivers `dvitoln03` and `emtex` are exceptions that will produce black changebars.

The "blackness" of the bars can be controlled with the help of the LaTeX counter `changebargrey`. A command like `\setcounter{changebargrey}{85}` changes that value. The value of the counter is a percentage, where 0 yields black bars, and 100 yields white bars.

The option color makes it possible to use colored changebars. It internally loads dvipsnames, so you can use a name when selecting a color.

\cbcolor{*name*}

The color to use when printing changebars is selected with the command \cbcolor, which accepts the same arguments as the \color command from the color package [57, pp. 317–326].

```
\usepackage[rightbars,color]{changebar}
\cbcolor{blue}
\setlength\changebarsep{10pt}

\cbstart
This is the text in the first paragraph.
This is the text in the first paragraph.\cbend

This is the text in the second paragraph.
\cbdelete
This is the text in the second paragraph.

\begin{changebar}
This is paragraph three. \par
This is paragraph four.
\end{changebar}
```

This is the text in the first paragraph. This is the text in the first paragraph.

This is the text in the second paragraph. This is the text in the second paragraph.

This is paragraph three.

This is paragraph four.

3-5-20

You can trace the behavior of the changebar package by loading it with one of the following options. The default, traceoff, displays the normal information LaTeX always shows. The option traceon informs you about the beginning and end points of changebars being defined. The *additional* option tracestacks adds information about the usage of the internal stacks.

Tracing the algorithm

## CHAPTER 4

The Layout of the Page

In this chapter we will see how to specify different page layouts. Often a single document requires several different page layouts. For instance, the layout of the first page of a chapter, which carries the chapter title, is generally different from that of the other pages in that chapter.

We first introduce LaTeX's dimensional parameters that influence the page layout and describe ways to change them and visualize their values. This is followed by an in-depth discussion of the packages typearea and geometry, both of which provide sophisticated ways to implement page layout specifications. The third section deals with the LaTeX concepts used to provide data for running headers and footers. This is followed by a section that explains how to format such elements, including many examples deploying the fancyhdr package and others. The fifth section then introduces commands that help in situations when the text does not fit into the layout and manual intervention is required. The chapter concludes with a brief look at two generic classes that go a long way toward providing almost full control over the page layout specification process.

4.1 Geometrical dimensions of the layout

The text of a document usually occupies a rectangular area on the paper—the so-called *type area* or *body*. Above the text there might be a *running header* and below it a *running footer*. They can consist of one or more lines containing the page number; information about the current chapter, section, time, and date; and possibly other markers. If they are visually heavy and closely tied to the text, then

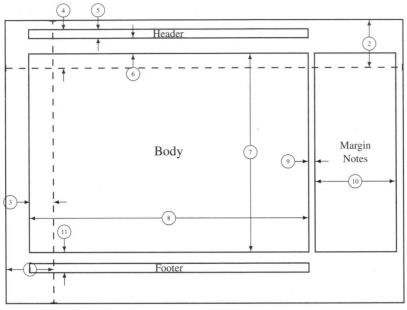

1	one inch + \hoffset	2	one inch + \voffset
3	\oddsidemargin = -36pt	4	\topmargin = -58pt
5	\headheight = 12pt	6	\headsep = 25pt
7	\textheight = 296pt	8	\textwidth = 418pt
9	\marginparsep = 11pt	10	\marginparwidth = 121pt
11	\footskip = 30pt		\marginparpush = 5pt (not shown)
	\hoffset = 0pt		\voffset = 0pt
	\paperwidth = 597pt		\paperheight = 423pt

4-1-1

\paperheight Height of the paper to print on.

\paperwidth Width of the paper to print on.

\textheight Height of the body (without header and footer).

\textwidth Width of the body.

\columnsep Width of space between columns of text in multicolumn mode.

\columnseprule Width of a vertical line separating the two adjacent columns in multicolumn output (default 0pt, i.e., no visible rule).

\columnwidth Width of a single column in multicolumn mode. Calculated by LATEX from \textwidth and \columnsep as appropriate.

\linewidth Width of the current text line. Usually equals \columnwidth but might get different values in environments that change the margins.

\evensidemargin For two-sided printing, the extra space added at the left of even-numbered pages.

\oddsidemargin For two-sided printing, the extra space added at the left of odd-numbered pages; otherwise the extra space added at the left of all pages.

\footskip Vertical distance separating the baseline of the last line of text and the baseline of the footer.

\headheight Height of the header.

\headsep Vertical separation between header and body.

\topmargin Extra vertical space added at the top of the header.

\marginparpush Minimal vertical space between two successive marginal notes (not shown in the figure).

\marginparsep Horizontal space between body and marginal notes.

\marginparwidth Width of marginal notes.

Figure 4.1: Page layout parameters and visualization

letterpaper	$8^{1}/_{2} \times$	11	inches	
legalpaper	$8^{1}/_{2} \times$	14	inches	
executivepaper	$7^{1}/_{4} \times 10^{1}/_{2}$		inches	
a4paper	$\approx 8^{1}/_{4} \times 11^{3}/_{4}$		inches	210×297 mm
a5paper	$\approx 5^{7}/_{8} \times$	$8^{1}/_{4}$	inches	148×210 mm
b5paper	≈ 7	$\times$ $9^{7}/_{8}$	inches	176×250 mm

Table 4.1: Standard paper size options in LATEX

these elements are considered to belong to the type area; this is often the case for running headers, especially when underlined. Otherwise, they are considered to belong to the top or bottom *margins*. This distinction is important when interpreting size specifications.

The fields to the left and the right of the body are also called *margins*. Usually they are left blank, but small pieces of text, such as remarks or annotations—so-called *marginal notes*—can appear there.

In general one talks about the *inner* and the *outer* margins. For two-sided printing, inner refers to the middle margins—that is, the left margin on recto (odd-numbered) pages and the right margin on verso (even-numbered) ones. For one-sided printing, inner always indicates the left margin. In a book spread, odd-numbered pages are those on the right-hand side.

The size, shape, and position of these fields and margins on the output medium (paper or screen) and the contents of the running headers and footers are collectively called a *page layout*.

The standard LATEX document classes allow document formatting for recto–verso (*two-sided*) printing. Two-sided layouts can be either asymmetrical or symmetrical (the LATEX default). In the latter case the type areas of recto and verso pages are positioned in such a way that they overlap if one holds a sheet to the light. Also, marginal notes are usually swapped between left/right pages.

The dimensional parameters controlling the page layout are described and shown schematically in Figure 4.1 on the facing page.[1] The default values of these parameters depend on the paper size. To ease the adjustments necessary to print on different paper sizes, the LATEX class files support a number of options that set those parameters to the physical size of the requested paper as well as adjust the other parameters (e.g., \textheight) that depend on them.

Table 4.1 shows the paper size options known to standard LATEX classes together with the corresponding page dimensions. Table 4.2 on the following page presents the page layout parameter values for the letterpaper paper size option, the default when no explicit option is selected. They are identical for the three standard LATEX document classes (article, book, and report). If a different paper size option is selected the values may change. Thus, to print on A4 paper, you can simply specify \documentclass[a4paper]{article}.

---

[1]The graphical presentation was produced with the layouts package, described in Section 4.2.1.

Parameter	Two-sided printing			One-sided printing		
	10pt	11pt	12pt	10pt	11pt	12pt
\oddsidemargin	44pt	36pt	21pt	63pt	54pt	39pt
\evensidemargin	82pt	74pt	59pt	63pt	54pt	39pt
\marginparwidth	107pt	100pt	85pt	90pt	83pt	68pt
\marginparsep	11pt	10pt	10pt	ditto		
\marginparpush	5pt	5pt	7pt	ditto		
\topmargin	27pt	27pt	27pt	ditto		
\headheight	12pt	12pt	12pt	ditto		
\headsep	25pt	25pt	25pt	ditto		
\footskip	30pt	30pt	30pt	ditto		
\textheight	43	38	36	ditto		
	$\times$\baselineskip					
\textwidth	345pt	360pt	390pt	ditto		
\columnsep	10pt	10pt	10pt	ditto		
\columnseprule	0pt	0pt	0pt	ditto		

Table 4.2: Default values for the page layout parameters (letterpaper)

Additional or different options may be available for other classes. Nevertheless, there seems to be little point in providing, say, an a0paper option for the book class that would produce incredibly wide text lines.

Most of the layout parameters in LaTeX class files are specified in terms of the physical page size. Thus, they automatically change when \paperwidth or \paperheight is modified via one of the paper size options. Changing these two parameters in the preamble of your document does not have this effect, since by then the values for the other parameters are already calculated.

One-inch default margins Standard-conforming dvi drivers place the reference point for TeX one inch down and to the right of the upper-left corner of the paper. These one-inch offsets are called *driver margins*. The reference point can be shifted by redefining the lengths \hoffset and \voffset. By default, their values are zero. In general, the values of these parameters should never be changed. They provide, however, a convenient way to shift the complete page image (body, header, footer, and marginal notes) on the output plane without disturbing the layout. The driver margins are inherited from TeX, and are not needed in LaTeX's parameterization of the page layout. A change to \topmargin shifts the complete text vertically, while changes to \oddsidemargin and \evensidemargin shift it horizontally.

Note that some dvi drivers introduce their own shifts in the placement of the text on paper. To make sure that the reference point is properly positioned, you can run the test file `testpage.tex` (by Leslie Lamport, with modifications by Stephen Gildea) through LaTeX and the `dvi` driver in question. The resulting output page will show the position of the reference point with respect to the edges of the paper. For LaTeX 2_ε this file was rewritten by Rainer Schöpf to allow the specification of a paper size option.

4.2   Changing the layout

When you want to redefine the value of one or more page layout parameters, the `\setlength` and `\addtolength` commands should be used. It is important to keep in mind that changes to the geometrical page layout parameters should be made only in class or package files and/or in the preamble (i.e., before the `\begin{document}` command). Although changing them in mid-document is not absolutely impossible, it will most likely produce havoc, due to the inner workings of TeX, which involve a number of subtle dependencies and timing problems. For example, if you change the `\textwidth` you might find that the running header of the previous page is changed.

Change parameters only in the preamble

Initially, it is advisable to use TeX's `\baselineskip` parameter for setting vertical distances. This parameter is the distance between the baselines of two consecutive lines of text set in the "normal" document type size inside a paragraph. The `\baselineskip` parameter may be considered to be the height of one line of text. Therefore, the following setting always means "two lines of text":

```
\normalsize                          % set normal \baselineskip
\setlength\headheight{2\baselineskip}  % Height of heading
```

To guarantee that `\baselineskip` is set properly, first set up the fonts used in the document (if necessary), and then invoke `\normalsize` to select the type size corresponding to the document base size.

Sometimes it is convenient to calculate the page layout parameters according to given typographic rules. For example, the requirement "the text should contain 50 lines" can be expressed using the command given below. It is assumed that the height of all (except one) lines is `\baselineskip` and the height of the top line of the text body is `\topskip` (this is TeX's `\baselineskip` length parameter for the first line with a default value of 10pt). Note that the examples in this chapter use the LaTeX package calc (which simplifies the calculational notation) and the extended control structures of LaTeX 2_ε (see Appendix A, Sections A.3.1 and A.3.2).

```
\setlength\textheight{\baselineskip*49+\topskip}
```

A requirement like "the height of the body should be 198mm" can be met in a similar way, and the calculation is shown below. First calculate the number of lines that the body of the desired size can contain. To evaluate the number of lines, divide one dimension by another to obtain the integer part. As TeX is unable to perform this kind of operation directly, the dimensions are first assigned to counters. The latter assignment takes place with a high precision because sp units are used internally.

```
\newcounter{tempc} \newcounter{tempcc}   % define two temporary counters
\setlength\textheight                    % subtract top line
        {198mm-\topskip}                 %   from desired size
\setcounter{tempc}{\textheight}          % assign counter 1
\setcounter{tempcc}{\baselineskip}       % assign counter 2
\setcounter{tempc}%                       % divide counters
        {\value{tempc}/\value{tempcc}}
\setlength\textheight{\baselineskip*\value{tempc}+\topskip}
```

The value of the vertical distance, \topmargin, can also be customized. As an example, suppose you want to set this margin so that the space above the text body is two times smaller than the space below the text body. The following calculation shows how to determine the needed value in the case of A4 paper (the paper height is 297 mm).

```
\setlength\topmargin
  {(297mm-\textheight)/3 - 1in - \headheight - \headsep}
```

In general, when changing the page layout you should take into account some elementary rules of legibility (see, for example, [150]). Studies of printed material in the English language have shown that a line should not contain more than 10–12 words, which corresponds to not more than 60–70 characters per line.

The number of lines on a page depends on the type size being used. The code below shows one way of calculating a \textheight that depends on the document base size. Use the fact that in most document classes the internal LaTeX command \@ptsize holds the number 0, 1, or 2 for the base font size 10 pt, 11 pt, or 12 pt, respectively. This command is set when you select an option such as 11pt.

```
\ifthenelse{\@ptsize = 0}%      10 point typeface as base size
  {\setlength\textheight{53\baselineskip}}{}
\ifthenelse{\@ptsize = 1}%      11 point typeface as base size
  {\setlength\textheight{46\baselineskip}}{}
\ifthenelse{\@ptsize = 2}%      12 point typeface as base size
  {\setlength\textheight{42\baselineskip}}{}
\addtolength\textheight{\topskip}
```

Another important parameter is the amount of white space surrounding the text. As printed documents are likely to be bound or stapled, enough white space should be left in the inner margin of the text to allow for this possibility. If

\oddsidemargin is fixed, then the calculation of \evensidemargin for two-sided printing is based on the following relationship:

```
width_of_paper =
    (1in+\hoffset)*2+\oddsidemargin+\textwidth+\evensidemargin
```

In most classes two-sided printing is turned on by specifying the twoside class option, which sets the Boolean register @twoside to true. Using commands from the Ifthen package we can set parameters depending on the value of this Boolean register, also taking into account the selected document base size:

```
\ifthenelse{\@ptsize = 0}%          10 point typeface as base size
    {\setlength\textwidth{5in}%
     \setlength\marginparwidth{1in}%
     \ifthenelse{\boolean{@twoside}}%
         {\setlength\oddsidemargin {0.55in}%        two-sided
          \setlength\evensidemargin{0.75in}}%
         {\setlength\oddsidemargin {0.55in}%        one-sided
          \setlength\evensidemargin{0.55in}}%
    }{}
\ifthenelse{\@ptsize = 1}{...}%    11 point typeface as base size
\ifthenelse{\@ptsize = 2}{...}%    12 point typeface as base size
```

Similarly, when a document contains a lot of marginal notes, it is worthwhile changing the layout to increase the margins. As an example, the (obsolete) a4 package defines a command \WideMargins. This macro modifies the geometrical parameters in such a way that the width reserved for marginal notes is set to 1.5 inches by decreasing the width of the text body.

4.2.1 layouts—Displaying your layout

To visualize your layout parameter settings and help you experiment with different values there are two packages available. The package layout (originally written by Kent McPherson and converted to LaTeX2_ε by Johannes Braams) provides the command \layout, which produces a graphical representation of the current page parameters with all sizes reduced by a factor of two. If the class option twoside is used then two pages are produced.

A more flexible solution is provided by the package layouts written by Peter Wilson. This package can be used for two purposes: to produce an abstract graphical representation of the layout parameters (not reflecting the current settings) via \pagediagram (as shown in the next example) or to produce trial layouts that show the effect of setting parameters to trial values and then applying the command \pagedesign. In either mode \setlayoutscale sets the scale factor to the specified value.

The circle is at 1 inch from the top and left of the page. Dashed lines represent (\hoffset + 1 inch) and (\voffset + 1 inch) from the top and left of the page.

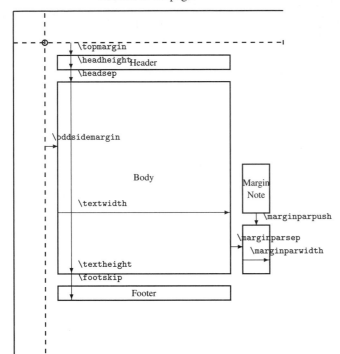

```
\usepackage{layouts}
\setlayoutscale{0.33}
\setparametertextfont
            {\scriptsize}
\setlabelfont{\scriptsize}
\pagediagram
```

4-2-1

To produce a trial layout you first have to specify suitable values for all page layout parameters. For each parameter *param*, there exists a declaration \try⟨*param*⟩ that accepts the trial values for this parameter as an argument. For example, \tryheadsep{18pt} would produce a layout with \headsep set to 18pt.

In addition, there are four Boolean-like declarations: \oddpagelayoutfalse produces an "even page" (default is to produce odd pages), the declaration \twocolumnlayouttrue produces a two-column layout (default is a single-column layout). The command \reversemarginpartrue mimics the result of LaTeX's \reversemarginpar, and \marginparswitchfalse prevents marginal notes from changing sides between verso and recto pages (a suitable setting for asymmetrical layouts, which are easily produced using the geometry package; see page 208).

To facilitate the specification of trial values you can start your trial by specifying \currentpage. It sets all trial values and Boolean switches to the values currently used in your document.

By default, the footer has a height of one line, as LaTeX has no explicit parameter to change the box size of the footer. However, depending on the page style used this choice might not be appropriate, as the footer box defined by the page style might have an exceptionally large depth. To produce a diagram that is (approximately) correct in this case, one can set the footer box height and depth explicitly using \setfootbox as we do in the example below.

This example also shows that you can combine this package with the calc package to allow arithmetic expressions in your trial declarations.

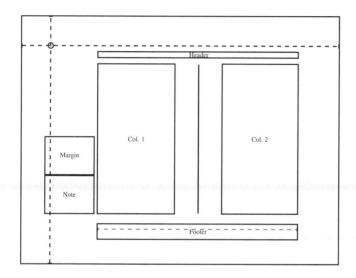

Lengths are to the nearest pt.

page height = 614pt	page width = 795pt
\hoffset = 0pt	\voffset = 0pt
\evensidemargin = 120pt	\topmargin = 16pt
\headheight = 12pt	\headsep = 18pt
\textheight = 370pt	\textwidth = 500pt
\footskip = 40pt	\marginparsep = 11pt
\marginparpush = 5pt	\columnsep = 120pt
\columnseprule = 3.0pt	

4-2-2

```
\usepackage{calc,layouts}
\setlayoutscale{0.3}
\currentpage
\oddpagelayoutfalse
\twocolumnlayouttrue

\trypaperwidth{11in}
\trypaperheight{8.5in}
\trytextwidth{500pt}
\trytextheight{\topskip
        + 30\baselineskip}
\trycolumnsep{120pt}
\trycolumnseprule{3pt}

\tryheadheight{12pt}
\tryheadsep{18pt}
\tryfootskip{40pt}

\tryevensidemargin{120pt}

\setfootbox{12pt}{24pt}

\setlabelfont{\tiny}
\drawdimensionsfalse
\printheadingsfalse
\pagedesign
```

A number of display control statements influence the visual representation of the printed page designs, some of which were used in the previous example. The most important are discussed here, whilst others are described in the documentation accompanying the package. *Controlling the presentation*

With the \setlabelfont declaration the font size used for the textual labels can be changed. Similarly, \setparametertextfont influences the font sizes for parameters if they are shown (e.g., Example 4-2-1 on the preceding page).

The heading text displayed on top of the example can be suppressed with \printheadingsfalse. The Boolean flag \printparametersfalse suppresses the tabular listing of parameter values below the diagram. A similar table can be generated separately using the command \pagevalues.

With \drawdimensionstrue arrows are drawn to indicate where parameters apply (by default, this feature is turned on in \pagediagram and off when \pagedesign is used).

Visualizing other layout objects The layouts package is not restricted to page layouts. It also supports the visualization of other objects. Eight "diagram" commands can be used to show the general behavior of other LATEX layout parameters. The \listdiagram command visualizes the list-related parameter (it is used in in Figure 3.3 on page 145). The \tocdiagram command shows which parameters influence table of content lists and how they relate to each other. Float-related parameters are visualized using \floatdiagram and \floatpagediagram. Parameters for sectioning commands are displayed with \headingdiagram, and parameters related to footnotes and general paragraphs can be shown with \footnotediagram and \paragraphdiagram. Finally, the \stockdiagram command produces a page layout diagram similar to \pagediagram but displays parameters available only in the memoir document class and its derivatives (see Section 4.6.2 on page 237).

There also exist corresponding "design" commands, such as \listdesign, \tocdesign, \floatdesign, \floatpagedesign, \headingdesign, and so on, that allow you to experiment with different parameter settings. For each parameter a declaration \try⟨param⟩ allows you to set its value for visualization. The full list of parameters supported this way is given in the package documentation. But if you know the applicable LATEX parameters (or look them up on the "diagram" command results) you can start experimenting straight away.

4.2.2 A collection of page layout packages

Because the original LATEX class files were based on American page sizes, European users developed several packages that adapt the page layout parameters for metric sizes. All such packages are superseded by the typearea or geometry package (described in the next two sections) and for new documents we recommend that you use these packages. As you will find the original attempts still in the archives, we mention them here in passing.

Examples of such packages are a4, which generates rather small pages; a4dutch (by Johannes Braams and Nico Poppelier), which is well documented; and a4wide (by Jean-François Lamy), which produces somewhat longer lines. Moreover, often there exist locally developed files under such names. For A5 pages one has the package files a5 and a5comb (by Mario Wolczko). The problem with all of these early packages was that they allowed little to no customization with respect to the size and placement of the text area and, for some of them, incompatible implementations exist.

A more general approach was taken by the vmargin package written by Volker Kuhlmann. His package supports a variety of paper sizes and allows you to specify a number of layout parameters with a single declaration, calculating others from the input (a number of variant declarations exist). In the example below the margins are specified and the text area is calculated.

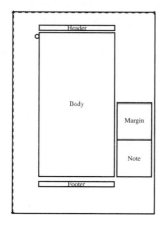

```
\usepackage{vmargin}
\setpapersize[portrait]{A5}
\setmarginsrb{80pt}{40pt}%  left, top
             {120pt}{80pt}%  right, bottom
             {12pt}{10pt}%  head height, sep
             {12pt}{30pt}%  foot height, sep
\setlength\marginparwidth{100pt}
% Code to display the resulting layout:
\usepackage{layouts}
\newcommand\showpage{%
  \setlayoutscale{0.25}\setlabelfont{\tiny}%
  \printheadingsfalse\printparametersfalse
  \currentpage\pagedesign}
\showpage
```

4-2-3

The package internally cancels the default offset of one inch (added normally by TeX output devices) by using a negative \hoffset and \voffset, a fact that can cause some surprise. This behavior can be seen in the example, where the dashed lines normally indicating this offset have vanished behind the page border and only the circle at (1 inch, 1 inch) remains.

4.2.3 typearea—A traditional approach

In books on typography one usually finds a section that deals with page layout, often describing construction methods for placing the text body and providing one or the other criteria for selecting text width, number of text lines, relationship between margins, and other considerations.

The package typearea by Markus Kohm and Frank Neukam, which is distributed as part of the KOMA-Script bundle, offers a simple way to deploy one of the more traditional page layout construction methods that has been used for many books since the early days of printing.

In a nutshell, the page layout generated by typearea provides a text body with the same spatial relationship as given by the paper size on which the document is being printed. In addition, the outer margin will be twice as wide as the inner margin and the bottom margin will be twice as wide as the top margin.

The construction method works by dividing the paper horizontally and vertically into n equal slices and then using one slice at the top and inner edges and two slices at the bottom and outer edges for the margins. By default, the variable n is calculated automatically by the package. It can also be requested explicitly (for example, to overwrite a configuration setting in the file typearea.cfg) by using the option DIVcalc. This option works by examining the document font and selecting a value that results in approximately 60–70 characters per text line, assuming a portrait page. Alternatively, one can explicitly set the value of n by specifying the option DIVn, resulting in n slices. As a third possibility, one can specify the option DIVclassic, which results in a page layout close to that found in certain types of medieval books.

The page height resulting from the chosen or calculated DIV value is automatically adjusted to produce an integral number of text lines. For this approach to work, the effective \baselineskip used throughout the document has to be established first. Thus, when using a package like setspace or applying the command \linespread this step should be taken prior to loading typearea.

For defining the paper typearea offers all of the paper size options of LaTeX's standard classes (see Table 4.1 on page 195) as well as all sizes of the ISO-A, ISO-B, and ISO-C series (e.g., a0paper or c5paper). To change the text orientation use landscape, as in the example below.

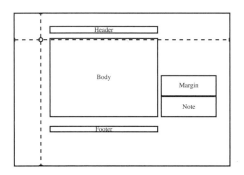

```
\usepackage[a5paper,landscape,DIVcalc]{typearea}
% to display the resulting layout:
\usepackage{layouts}
\newcommand\showpage{%
  \setlayoutscale{0.27}\setlabelfont{\tiny}%
  \printheadingsfalse\printparametersfalse
  \currentpage\pagedesign}
\showpage
```

4-2-4

The calculated DIV value is recorded in the .log file of the LaTeX run together with the values chosen for other page parameters. In the above example this value was 7, so instead of DIVcalc we could have used DIV7.

Determining the body area
So far, we have explained how the package chooses the text body dimensions and how it places that body on the page, but we have not discussed whether the running header and footer participate in that calculation. This issue must be decided depending on their content. If, for example, the running header contains a lot of material, perhaps even with a rule underlining it, and thus contributes considerably to the grey value of the page, it is best regarded as part of the page body. In other cases it might be more appropriate to consider it as being part of the margin (e.g., if it is unobstructive text in small type). For the same reason a footer holding only the page number should normally be considered as lying outside the text body and not contributing to the placement calculations.

The choices for a particular document can be explicitly specified with the options headinclude, footinclude, headexclude, and footexclude. The latter two options are used by default. With large DIV values (i.e., small margins), excluding the header or footer might make it fall off the page boundary so you may have to adjust one or the other setting.

In a similar fashion (using mpinclude or mpexclude), one can include or exclude the \marginpar area into the calculation for left and right margins. This, too, is turned off by default but it might be appropriate to include it for layouts with many objects of this type.

The header size is by default 1.25 text lines high. This value can be adjusted by using an option of the type *num*headlines, where *num* is a decimal number, such as 2.3, denoting the number of text lines the header should span.

The next example has header and marginals included and the header is size enlarged to 2.5 lines. Compare this example to the layout in Example 4-2-4 on the preceding page, where header, footer, and marginals are excluded.

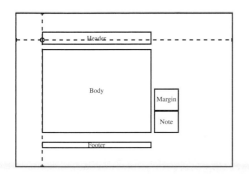

```
\usepackage[a5paper,landscape,
            2.5headlines,
            headinclude,mpinclude,
            DIVcalc]{typearea}
\usepackage{layouts}
% \showpage as previously defined
\showpage
```

4-2-5

Depending on the type of binding for the final product, more or less of the inner margin will become invisible. To account for this loss of white space the package supports the option BCOR⟨*val*⟩, where *val* is the amount of space (in any LATEX unit) taken up by the binding method. For example, BCOR1.2cm would subtract 1.2 centimeters from the page width prior to doing the page layout calculations.

As an alternative to customizing the layout through options to the package, one can the parameter calculations with the command \typearea. This ability is useful, for example, if a document class, such as one of the classes in the KOMA-Script bundle, already loads the typearea package and you want to use an unusual body font by loading it in the preamble of the document. In that case the layout calculations need to be redone to account for the properties of the chosen font.

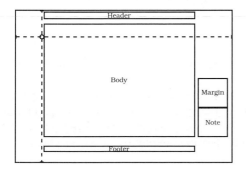

```
\usepackage[a5paper,landscape]{typearea}
\usepackage{bookman}
\typearea[10mm]{11}
\usepackage{layouts}
% \showpage as previously defined
\showpage
```

4-2-6

4.2.4 geometry—Layout specification with auto-completion

The geometry package written by Hideo Umeki provides a comprehensive and easy-to-use interface to all geometrical aspects of the page layout. It deploys the keyval package so that all parameters (and their values) can be specified as options to the \usepackage declaration.

In contrast to the typearea package, geometry does not implement a certain typographical concept but rather carries out specifications as requested. It knows, however, about certain relationships between various page parameters and in case of incomplete specifications can calculate the remaining parameter values automatically. The following example shows a layout identical to the one produced by typearea in Example 4-2-4 on page 204. Here a number of values have been explicitly set (e.g., those for the top and left margins), but the size of the page body has been automatically calculated from the paper size (a5paper), the values for top margin (tmargin) and left margin (lmargin), and a specified margin ratio of 1:2 (marginratio).

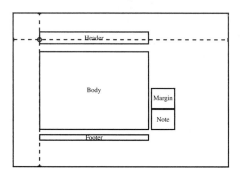

```
\usepackage[marginratio=1:2,
  paper=a5paper,landscape=true,
  tmargin=52pt,lmargin=74pt,
  headheight=30pt,marginparwidth=62pt,
  includehead,includemp]{geometry}
\usepackage{layouts}
% \showpage as previously defined
\showpage
```

4-2-7

The example also shows that with Boolean options it is permissible to leave out the value part (which then defaults to =true); with all other options the value part is mandatory.

The remainder of this section discusses the various page layout aspects that are supported by geometry. In most cases there is more than one way to achieve the same result because some of the parameters have to satisfy certain relations. If your specification violates such a relation, geometry will warn you and then ignore one or the other option setting.

Paper sizes   The paper size can be specified with the paper option, which accepts the values a0paper to a6paper, and b0paper to b6paper. Alternatively, the values letterpaper, legalpaper, and executivepaper can be used. For convenience you are allowed to denote the paper size by specifying the named paper as an option; for example, a5paper is equivalent to the specification paper=a5paper.

When formatting for a computer display you might want to try the option screen. To specify other nonstandard sizes you can use paperwidth and paperheight to define the appropriate dimensions explicitly.

With respect to general page characteristics, geometry supports the Boolean options twoside, landscape (switching paper height and width), and portrait. Obviously, portrait=false is just a different way of specifying landscape. *General page characteristics*

If a certain part of the page becomes invisible due to the binding method, you can specify this loss of white space with the option bindingoffset. It will add the specified value to the inner margin.

When the Boolean option twocolumn is specified, the text area will be set up to contain two columns. In this case the separation between columns can be specified through the option columnsep.

In Section 4.2.3 describing the typearea package, we stated that, depending on the nature of the document, it may be appropriate to consider the running header and/or footer (and in some cases even the part of the margin taken up by marginal notes) as being part of the text body. By default, geometry excludes the header, footer, and marginals. As these settings modify the relationship between body and margin sizes used for calculating missing values, they should be set appropriately. To change the defaults, a number of Boolean options[1] are available: includemp, to include the marginals, which is seldom necessary; includehead, to be used with heavy running headers; includefoot, which is rarely ever necessary, as the footer normally contains only a page number; and includeheadfoot and includeall, which are shorthand for combinations of the other options. *What constitutes the body area*

Footnotes are always considered to be part of the text area. With the option footnotesep you specify only the separation between the last text line and the footnotes; the calculation of the margins remains unaffected.

For specifying the text body size several methods are available; the choice of which to use is largely a matter of taste. You can explicitly specify the text area size by giving values for textwidth and textheight. In that case you should normally ensure that textheight holds an integral number of text lines to avoid underfull box messages for pages consisting only of text. A convenient way to achieve this goal is to use the lines option, which calculates the appropriate \textheight using the current values for \baselineskip and \topskip. *Text area*

Alternatively, you can set the Boolean option heightrounded, in which case geometry will adjust the \textheight appropriately. This Boolean option is especially useful if the body size is calculated automatically by the package—for example, if you specify the values for only some of the margins and let the package work out the rest.

As an alternative to specifying the text area and having the package calculate the body size by adding the sizes of the header, footer, and/or marginals as specified through the above options, you can give values for the whole body area and have the package calculate the text area by subtracting. This is done with the options width and height (this approach, of course, differs from the previ-

---

[1] The typearea package offers the same functionality, with similar (though in fact different) option names, such as headinclude instead of includehead.

ous approach only if you have included header and/or footer). If this method is used consider specifying `heightrounded` to let the package adjust the calculated `\textheight` as needed.

If you do not like specifying fixed values but prefer to set the body size relative to the page size, you can do so via the options `hscale` and `vscale`. They denote the fraction of the horizontal or vertical size of the page that should be occupied by the body area.

Margins   The size of the margins can be explicitly specified through the options `lmargin`, `rmargin`, `tmargin`, and `bmargin` (for the left, right, top, and bottom margins, respectively). If the Boolean option `twoside` is `true`, then `lmargin` and `rmargin` actually refer to the inner and outer margins, so the option names are slightly misleading. To account for this case, the package supports `inner` and `outer` as alternative names—but remember that they are merely aliases. Thus, if used with the `asymmetric` option (described below), they would be confusing as well. To give you even more freedom there exists another set of option names: `left`, `right`, `top`, and `bottom`. If you choose to specify only verso pages (the recto pages being automatically produced by selecting `twoside` or `asymmetric`), then the first or the last set of names is probably the best choice.

If none, or only some, of the margin sizes are specified, the missing ones are calculated. Given the equations

$$\text{paperwidth} \quad = \quad \text{left} + \text{width} + \text{right} \tag{4.1}$$

$$\text{paperheight} \quad = \quad \text{top} + \text{height} + \text{bottom} \tag{4.2}$$

then knowing two values from the righthand side allows the calculation of the third value (instead of `width` or `height` the body area might be specified through some of the other methods discussed above). If only one value from the righthand side is specified, the package employs two further equations to reduce the free variables:

$$\text{left/right} \quad = \quad \text{hmarginratio} \tag{4.3}$$

$$\text{top/bottom} \quad = \quad \text{vmarginratio} \tag{4.4}$$

The default value for the `hmarginratio` option is $2:3$ when `twoside` is `true`, and otherwise $1:1$. The default for `vmarginratio` is $2:3$ without exception.

The allowed values for these "ratio" options are restricted: both numbers have to be positive integers less than 100 separated with a colon. For example, you would use `4:5` instead of `1:1.25`.

If you wish to center the body area, use the option `centering`. It is a convenient shorthand for setting `hmarginratio` and `vmarginratio` both to $1:1$.

Asymmetrical and symmetrical layouts   In standard LaTeX classes the option `twoside` actually fulfills a dual purpose: beside setting up the running header and footer to contain different content on verso and recto pages, it automatically implements a symmetrical layout with left and right margins (including marginal notes) swapped on verso pages. This outcome is shown in the next example, which also highlights the fact that `geometry` by default selects a very large text area and does not leave sufficient space for marginal notes that fall outside the page.

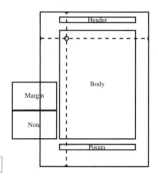 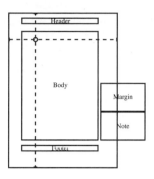

```
\usepackage[a6paper,twoside]
               {geometry}
\usepackage{layouts}
% \showpage as previously defined
\showpage \newpage \showpage
```

4-2-8

With the geometry package, however, asymmetrical page layouts are possible, simply by using the option asymmetric. The use of bindingoffset in the next example proves that an asymmetrical two-sided layout is indeed produced, as the offset is applied to the inner margins and not always to the left margin, even though the marginal notes always appear on the left. As we want the larger margin on the left, we have to change hmarginratio appropriately. At first glance the right margin on the verso page might appear incorrectly large given a marginal ratio of 2:1; this is due to the bindingoffset being added to it.

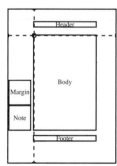 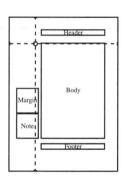

```
\usepackage[a6paper,asymmetric,
   bindingoffset=18pt,
   marginparwidth=.8in,reversemp,
   hmarginratio=2:1,vmarginratio=4:5,
   left=1in,top=1in]{geometry}
\usepackage{layouts}
% \showpage as previously defined
\showpage \newpage \showpage
```

4-2-9

The dimensions for the running header and its separation from the text area can be specified through the options headheight and headsep. The distance be- *Running header* tween the text area and the footer is available through footskip. There also exist *and footer* the Boolean options nohead, nofoot, and noheadfoot, which set these dimensions to zero. In most circumstances, however, it is better to use ignorehead, etc. as this will allow you to attach the header or footer on one or the other page without affecting the margin calculations.

As most documents do not contain many marginal notes, the space occupied by them by default does not count toward the margin calculations. This space can *Marginal notes* be specified with marginparwidth, and the separation from the text area can be set with `marginparsep`. Unless `includemp` is specified it is the user's responsibility to ensure that this area falls within the calculated or specified margin size.

By default, the marginal notes appear in the outer margin. By specifying the Boolean option `reversemp` this set-up can be reversed.

Miscellaneous features
Instead of using an external package, such as layouts, to visualize the results produced by geometry, one can use its built-in option `showframe`. By default, all settings, including any calculated values, are recorded in the transcript file of the current LaTeX run. Setting the Boolean option `verbose` ensures that these settings are also displayed on the terminal.

Some TeX extensions or device drivers such as pdfTeX or VTeX like to know about the dimensions of the paper that is being targeted. The geometry package accounts for this by providing the options `pdftex`, `vtex`, `dvipdfm`, and `dvips`. Naturally, at most one of them should be specified. If a document is processed with the pdfTeX program then the `pdftex` option is automatically selected (and the others are disabled).

Like most packages these days, geometry supports the extended syntax of the calc package if the latter is loaded before geometry.

To account for unusual behavior of the printing device, LaTeX maintains two dimension registers, `\hoffset` and `\voffset`, which will shift all output (on every page) horizontally to the right and vertically downward by the specified amount. The package supports the setting of these registers via the options `hoffset` and `voffset`. They have no effect on the calculation of other page dimensions.

Magnification
The TeX program offers a magnification feature that magnifies all specified dimensions and all used fonts by a specified factor. Standard LaTeX has disabled this feature, but with geometry it is again at the disposal of the user via the option `mag`. Its value should be an integer, where 1000 denotes no magnification. For example, `mag=1414` together with a5paper would result in printing on a4paper, as it enlarges all dimensions by $1.414(=\sqrt{2})$, the factor distinguishing two consecutive paper sizes of the ISO-A series. This ability can be useful, for example, if you later wish to photomechanically reduce the printed output to achieve a higher print resolution. As this option also scales fonts rather than using fonts designed for a particular size, it is usually not adequate if the resulting (magnified) size is your target size.

When magnification is used, you can direct TeX to leave certain dimensions unmagnified by prepending the string `true` to the unit. For example, `left=1truein` would leave a left margin of exactly one inch regardless of any magnification factor. Implicitly specified dimensions (such as the paper size values, when specifying a `paper` option) are normally subject to magnification unless the option `truedimen` is given.

Shortcuts
The previously described options allow you to specify individual values, but for the most common cases geometry also provides combination options. They allow you set several values in one pass by specifying either a single value (to be used repeatedly) or a comma-separated list of values (which must be surrounded by braces so that the commas are not mistaken for option delimiters).

The option `papersize` takes a list of two dimensions denoting the horizontal and vertical page dimensions.

The option `hmargin` sets the left and right margins, either to the same value if only a single value is given, or to a list of values. Similarly, `vmargin` sets the top and bottom margins. This operation can sometimes be shortened further by using the option `margin`, which passes its value (or list) to `hmargin` and `vmargin`. In the same way `marginratio` passes its value to `hmarginratio` and `vmarginratio` for further processing.

The text area dimensions can be specified using the body option, which takes one or two values setting `textwidth` and `textheight`. Alternatively, you can use the option `total`, which is a shortcut for setting `width` and `height`. You can also provide one or two scaling factors with the option `scale` that are then passed to `hscale` and `vscale`.

If the `geometry` package is used as part of a class you may wish to over-write some of its settings in the preamble of your document. In that case *Preamble usage* the `\usepackage` option interface is of little use because the package is already loaded. To account for such situations the package offers the command `\geometry`, which takes a comma-separated list of options as its argument. It can be called multiple times, each time overwriting the previous settings. In the next example its use is demonstrated by first loading the package and setting all margins to one inch and the header, footer, and marginals to be part of the body area, and then changing the right margin to two inches and excluding the marginals from the calculation.

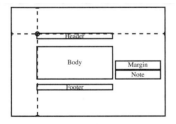

```
\usepackage[a6paper,landscape,
            margin=1in,includeall]{geometry}
% overwriting some values:
\geometry{right=2in,ignoremp}
\usepackage{layouts}
% \showpage as previously defined
\showpage
```

4-2-10

Two other options might be handy when using the `\geometry` interface. With `reset` you restore the package defaults and with `pass` you basically disable the package itself.

4.2.5 lscape—Typesetting individual pages in landscape mode

For most documents the longer side of the paper corresponds to the vertical direction (so-called *portrait* orientation). However, for some documents, such as slides and tables, it is better to use the other (*landscape*) orientation, where the longer side is horizontally oriented. Modern printers and `dvi` drivers usually allow printing in both orientations.

The landscape and portrait orientations require different page layouts, and with packages like geometry you have the tools at hand to design them as needed. But sometimes it is desirable to switch between portrait and landscape mode for only some pages. In that case the previously discussed packages do not help, as they set up the page design for the whole document.

For this case you can use the lscape package by David Carlisle that defines the environment landscape to typeset a selected set of pages in landscape orientation without affecting the running header and footer. It works by first ending the current page (with \clearpage, thereby typesetting any dangling floats). It then internally exchanges the values for \textheight and \textwidth and rotates every produced page body within its scope by 90 degrees. For the rotation it deploys the graphics package, so it works with any output device supported by that package capable of rotating material. When the environment ends it issues another \clearpage before returning to portrait mode.

For rotating individual floats, including or excluding their captions, a better alternative is provided by the rotating package, described in Section 6.3.3.

4.2.6 crop—Producing trimming marks

When producing camera-ready copy for publication, the final printing is normally done on "stock paper" having a larger size than the logical page size of the document. In that case the printed copy needs trimming before it is finally bound. For accurate trimming the printing house usually requires so-called crop marks on each page. Another reason for requiring crop marks is the task of mounting two or more logical pages onto a physical one, such as in color production where different colors are printed separately.

The crop package created by Melchior Franz supports these tasks by providing a simple interface for producing different kinds of crop marks. It also offers the ability to print only the text or only the graphics from a document, and the chance of inverting, mirroring, or rotating the output, among other things—all features useful during that part of the printing process.

Crop marks can be requested by using one of the following options:

cam Produces four marks that show the logical paper dimensions without touching them (see Example 4-2-11 on the next page). They are mainly intended for camera alignment.

cross Produces four large crosses at the corners of the logical page touching its edges.

frame Produces a frame around the logical page; mainly intended for clearly visualizing the page dimensions.

The package assumes that the \paperheight and \paperwidth dimensions correctly reflect the size of the *logical* page you you want to produce. The size of the *physical* page (the stock paper) you are actually printing on is then given as an option to the package. Options include a0, a1, a2, a3, a4, a5, a6, b0, b1, b2, b3, b3, b4, b5, b6, executive, legal, and executive. If you use the physical paper in landscape orientation (i.e., with the long side horizontally), you can also specify the option landscape. If none of these options matches your physical paper sizes, you can specify the exact sizes through the options width and height, both of which take dimensional values.

The following example sets up an artifically small logical page (to fit the example area of this book) using the geometry package and centers it on a physical page of A5 size. However, since all our examples are actually cropped to their "visible" size and since, for obvious reasons, we have not actually marked the borders of the A5 paper, you cannot see that it was properly centered at one stage—either believe us or try it yourself.

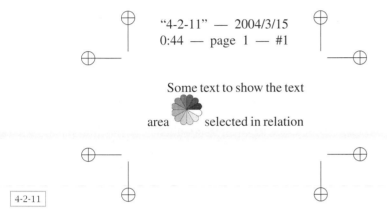

"4-2-11" — 2004/3/15
0:44 — page 1 — #1

Some text to show the text

area selected in relation

4-2-11

```
\usepackage{graphicx,geometry}
\geometry{paperwidth=2in,
          paperheight=1in,
          margin=5mm}
\usepackage[cam,a5,center]{crop}

Some text to show the text area
\includegraphics[width=8mm]
               {rosette.ps}
selected in relation to the crop
marks.
```

It should be clear from the description and the example that this package should be loaded *after* the document layout has been specified.

The informational text between the top crop marks is added by default. It can be suppressed by adding the option noinfo, though it is usually a good idea to keep it. The information contains both the page number (as known to LaTeX) and a page index, which starts with 1 and is incremented for every page being printed. Especially with large publications using several page numbering methods at once, this is a helpful device to ensure that pages are not misordered.

Several options of the crop package rely on support given by the printer driver. If no driver option is explicitly given, the package tries to determine the driver from installation settings for the graphics or color package. It is also possible to indicate the driver explicitly by using options such as dvips, pdflatex, or vtex. If one of these options is selected the paper size information is passed to the external driver program, which is important if you want to view the document using ghostview or similar programs.

If you want to print graphics separately—for example, because running the complete document through a color printer is infeasible—you can produce different versions of the same document: one containing only the text but no graphics (or, more precisely, without graphics included via \includegraphics) and one containing only the graphics (or, more precisely, with all text printed in the color "white"). These effects can be achieved using the options nographics and notext, respectively. Clearly, the latter option can be used only if the target device is capable of understanding color commands since internally the color package is being deployed. The next example[1] shows the use of the notext and cross options; compare it to the output of Example 4-2-11.

"4-2-12" — 2004/3/15
0:44 — page 1 — #1

Some text to show the text

area   selected in relation

```
\usepackage{graphicx,geometry}
\geometry{paperwidth=2in,
          paperheight=1in,
          margin=5mm}
\usepackage[cross,a5,nographics]
          {crop}
Some text to show the text area
\includegraphics[width=8mm]
          {rosette.ps}
selected in relation to the crop
marks.
```

4-2-12

Three other options require the output device to be able to obey the extended commands of the graphics and color packages for rotation, mirroring, and background coloring. With the option rotate the pages are turned through 180 degrees. The option mirror flips each page as shown in the next example. Finally, the option invert will invert white and black, so that the text appears in white on a black surface.

"4-2-13" — 2004/3/15
0:44 — page 1 — #1

Some text to show the text

area    selected in relation

```
\usepackage{graphicx,geometry}
\geometry{paperwidth=2in,
          paperheight=1in,
          margin=5mm}
\usepackage[frame,a5,mirror]{crop}
Some text to show the text area
\includegraphics[width=8mm]
          {rosette.ps}
selected in relation to the crop
marks.
```

4-2-13

---

[1]The cross crop marks look admittedly rather weird at this measure.

4.3 Dynamic page data: page numbers and marks

LaTeX's output routine, which produces the typeset pages, works asynchronously. That is, LaTeX assembles and prepares enough material to be sure that a page can be filled and then builds that page, usually leaving some residual material behind to be used on the next page(s). Thus, while preparing headings, paragraphs, and other page elements, it is usually not known on which page this material will eventually be placed because LaTeX might eventually decide that this material will not fit on the current page. (We have already discussed this problem in the section about page-wise footnote numbering.)

When the final page is typeset, we might want to repeat some information from its contents in the running header or footer (e.g., the current section head), to give the reader extra guidance. You cannot save this information in commands when the material is collected; during this phase LaTeX often reads too far ahead and your command would then contain data not appearing on the final page. LaTeX solves this problem by providing a mark mechanism through which you can identify data as being of interest for the assembled page. In the output routine all marks from the page are collected and the first and the last mark are made available. The detailed mechanism is explained in this section together with some useful extension packages.

4.3.1 LaTeX page numbers

The page number is controlled through a counter named page. This counter is automatically stepped by LaTeX whenever it has finished a page—that is, *after* it has been used. Thus, it has to be initialized to 1, whereas most other LaTeX counters require an initialization to 0 as they are stepped just before they get used.

The command to access the typographical representation of the page number is \thepage, following standard LaTeX convention. There is, however, another subtle difference compared to other LaTeX counters: the \thepage command is not defined by the LaTeX kernel but instead comes into existence only after the first execution of a \pagenumbering declaration, which typically happens in the document class file.

The best (though perhaps not the most convenient) way to get at the page number for the current page in the middle of the text is via a combination of the commands \label and \pageref, which should be put directly one following the other so that no page break can interfere.

We are now on page 6. This type of coding always gives correct results while "page 6", though okay	here, will be wrong at a later point in the paragraph, such as here: "page 6", because LaTeX decided to break
6	7

4-3-1

```
We are now on page~\label{p1}\pageref{p1}.
This type of coding always gives correct
results while ``page \thepage{}'', though
okay here, will be wrong at a later point
in the paragraph, such as here:  ``page
\thepage'', because \LaTeX{} decided to
break the paragraph over two pages.
```

Because of the asynchronous nature of the output routine you cannot safely use
\thepage within the document body. It is reliable only in declarations that influence the look and feel of the final page built by the output routine.

\pagenumbering{*style*}

The \pagenumbering command resets the page counter to 1 and redefines the
command \thepage to *style*{page}. Ready-to-use page counter styles include:
Alph, alph, Roman, roman, and arabic (see Section A.1.4).

For example, an often seen convention is to number the pages in the front
matter with roman numerals and then to restart the page numbers using arabic
numbers for the first chapter of the main matter. You can manually achieve this
effect by deploying the \pagenumbering command twice; the \frontmatter and
\mainmatter commands available with the book class implement this set-up implicitly behind the scenes.

4.3.2 lastpage—A way to reference it

Standard LaTeX has no way to refer to the number of pages in a document; that is,
you cannot write "this document consists of 6 pages" or generate "page 5 of 10"
without manually counting the pages yourself. The package lastpage by Jeffrey
Goldberg sets out to overcome this problem by automatically generating a label
with the name LastPage on the last page, so that you can refer to its page number
via \pageref{LastPage}. Example 4-4-5 on page 226 demonstrates its use.

The string produced by that call to \pageref is the content of \thepage as it
would appear on the last page. If your document restarts page numbering midway
through—for example, when the front matter has its own numbering—this string
will not reflect the absolute number of pages.

The package works by generating the label within the \AtEndDocument hook,
making sure that any pending floats are placed first. However, as this hook might
also be used by other packages to place textual material at the end of the document, there is a chance that the label may be placed too early. In that case you can
try to load lastpage after the package that generates this extra material.

4.3.3 chappg—Page numbers by chapters

For some publications it is required to restart numbering with every chapter and
to display the page number together with the chapter number on each page. This
can already be done with the commands at our disposal by simply putting

```
% Page numbers per chapter (repeat after each \chapter):
\pagenumbering{arabic} % first reset page numbering and then overwrite ...
\renewcommand\thepage{\thechapter--\arabic{page}} % ... the display style
```

after each \chapter command. But this technique is clumsy and requires us to put a lot of layout information in our document, something that is better avoided.

A better approach is to use the package chappg, originally written by Max Hailperin and later reimplemented and extended by Robin Fairbairns. It works with any document class that has a \chapter command and provides a new page numbering style bychapter to achieve the desired page numbering scheme. Furthermore, it extends the \pagenumbering command to accept an optional argument that enables you to put a prefix different from the chapter number before the page number. This ability is, for example, useful in the front matter where typically unnumbered headings are used.

<table>
<tr><td>. . . here we are in the middle of the front matter where

Preface-1</td><td>chapters are usually unnumbered.

Preface-2</td></tr>
</table>

```
\usepackage{chappg}
% \chapter*{Preface} % --- not shown
  \pagenumbering[Preface]{bychapter}
\ldots here we are in the middle of
the front matter where chapters are
usually unnumbered.
```

4-3-2

In fact, by exerting some care you can even use this package together with a class that does not define a chapter command. Suppose your highest heading level is \section and each section automatically starts a new page (the latter is an important requirement). Then the declaration

```
\makeatletter \@addtoreset{page}{section} \makeatother
\pagenumbering[\thesection]{bychapter}
```

will give you page numbers within sections. However, if sections do not start a new page this approach might fail, as LaTeX may have seen an upcoming section and incremented \thesection without actually putting that section onto the current page. If so, you will experience the same problem that we saw earlier with respect to \thepage.

Finally, the en dash between the prefix and the page number is also customizable, since it is produced by the command \chappgsep. Thus,

```
\renewcommand\chappgsep{/}
```

will give you pages like 3/1, 3/2, 3/3, 3/4, and so on, if "3" is the current chapter number.

4.3.4 LaTeX mark commands

The TeX primitive \mark, which you may encounter inside package code dealing with page layout or output routines, is ultimately responsible for associating some text (its argument) with a position on a page (i.e., the position where the \mark is executed). When producing the final page TEX makes the first mark on the assembled page available in \firstmark, the last in \botmark, and the \botmark from the previous page as \topmark. If there are no marks on that page then \firstmark and \botmark also inherit the value of the previous \botmark. Thus, if each heading command would internally issue a \mark with the heading text as its argument, then one could display the first or last heading text on a page in the running header or footer by using these commands.

*Low-level TEX marks cannot be used in LATEX*However, it is *not* possible to use these commands directly in LATEX, as LATEX uses a higher-level protocol to control marks, so please do not try this. We mention them here only to explain the underlying general mechanism. LATEX effectively structures the content of the \mark argument so that the direct use of this command will most likely result in strange error messages.

As a replacement for the \mark command, standard LATEX offers the following two commands to generate marks:

\markboth{*main-mark*}{*sub-mark*}   \markright{*sub-mark*}

The first command sets a pair of marker texts at the current point in the document. The second command also internally generates a pair of markers, but it changes only the *sub-mark* one, inheriting the *main-mark* text from a previous \markboth.

The original intention behind these commands was to provide somewhat independent marks—for example, chapter headings as *main-mark*s and section headings as *sub-mark*s. However, the choice of the command name \markright already indicates that Leslie Lamport had a specific marking scheme in mind when he designed those commands, which will become even more apparent when we look at the commands to retrieve the marker values in the output routine.

In the output routine \leftmark contains the *main-mark* argument of the last \markboth command before the end of the page. The \rightmark command contains the *sub-mark* argument of the first \markright or \markboth on the page, if one exists; otherwise, it contains the one most recently defined.

The marking commands work reasonably well for right markers "numbered within" left markers—hence the names (for example, when the left marker is changed by a \chapter command and the right marker is changed by a \section command). However, it produces somewhat anomalous results if a \markboth command is preceded by some other mark command on the same page—see the pages receiving L2 R1.1 and L5 R3.2 in Figure 4.2 on the next page. This figure shows schematically which left and right markers are generated for the pages being shipped out. For some type of running headers it would be better to display the first *main-mark* or the last *sub-mark*. For this purpose you could enlist the help of the extramarks package described below, as standard LATEX does not offer this possibility. Also notice that there is no way to set a *main-mark* without setting (and thus overwriting) the *sub-mark*.

In layouts that use running headers generated from heading texts it would be nice if these markers are automatically generated from the corresponding heading

galley material	marker pair	retrieved markers	
		\leftmark	\rightmark
\markboth{L1}{}	{L1}{}		
\newpage% ----page break ----		L1	
\markright{R1.1}	{L1}{R1.1}		
\markboth{L2}{}	{L2}{}		
\markright{R2.1}	{L2}{R2.1}		
\newpage% ----page break ---		L2	R1.1
\markright{R2.2}	{L2}{R2.2}		
\markright{R2.3}	{L2}{R2.3}		
\markright{R2.4}	{L2}{R2.4}		
\newpage% ----page break ----		L2	R2.2
\markboth{L3}{}	{L3}{}		
\markright{R3.1}	{L3}{R3.1}		
\newpage% ----page break ----		L3	
\newpage% ----page break ----		L3	R3.1
\markright{R3.2}	{L3}{R3.2}		
\markboth{L4}{}	{L4}{}		
\markboth{L5}{}	{L5}{}		
\newpage% ----page break ----		L5	R3.2
\markright{R5.1}	{L5}{R5.1}		
\end{document}		L5	R5.1

Figure 4.2: Schematic overview of how LaTeX's marker mechanism works

commands. Fortunately, there exists an interface that allows us to define which heading commands produce markers and what text is passed to the mark. This scheme works as follows: all standard heading commands internally invoke a command *name*mark, where *name* is the name of the heading command (e.g., \chaptermark, \sectionmark). These commands have one argument in which they receive the heading text or its short form from the optional argument of the heading command.

By default, they all do nothing. If redefined appropriately, however, they can produce a marker pair as needed by LaTeX. For instance, in the book class these commands are defined (approximately) as follows:

```
\renewcommand\chaptermark[1]{\markboth{\chaptername\ \thechapter. #1}{}}
\renewcommand\sectionmark[1]{\markright{\thesection. #1}}
```

In the case of a chapter, the word "Chapter" (or its equivalent in a given language; see Table 9.2 on page 547 in Section 9.1.3) followed by the sequence number of the chapter (stored in the counter chapter) and the contents of (a short version of) the chapter title will be placed in the *main-mark* argument of \markboth; at the same time the *sub-mark* will be cleared. For a section, the section number (stored in the counter section) followed by the contents of (a short version of) the section title will be passed to \markright, which generates a marker pair with a new *sub-mark*.

4.3.5 extramarks—**Providing new marks**

As we have seen so far, LaTeX's mark mechanism was built with a certain layout in mind and is, therefore, only partially usable for other applications. As a result a number of attempts have been made to extend or replace it with code that supports more complex marking mechanisms.

Part of the limitation is inherent in TeX itself, which provides only one type of marks and thus makes different independent marks difficult (though not impossible) to implement. This issue is resolved in eTeX, which provides independent mark classes. However, since this program is not yet in widespread use, there are no packages available that explore the new possibilities offered by the extension of the marking mechanism.

An extended mechanism within the main LaTeX model is provided by the extramarks package written by Piet van Oostrum (distributed as part of fancyhdr). It offers two additional (partially) independent marks, as well as further control over LaTeX standard marks by allowing one to retrieve the first or the last mark on a page for both *main-mark* and *sub-mark*.

To refer to the first or last *main-mark* on a given page, the package offers the commands \firstleftmark and \lastleftmark, respectively. Similarly, \firstrightmark and \lastrightmark allow you to access the first or last *sub-mark*.[1] An application is shown in Example 4-4-9 on page 229.

\extramarks{*left-xmark*}{*right-xmark*}

To add additional marks to the document the package provides the command \extramarks. It takes two mandatory arguments: the texts for two marks at the current point. To refer to the first *left-xmark* on a page \firstleftxmark is used; \lastleftxmark retrieves the last mark. In the same way \firstrightxmark and \lastrightxmark can be used in the output routine to access the *right-xmark*.

The next example shows these commands in action. With the help of fancyhdr (described in Section 4.4.2), a page layout is constructed in which the first *left-xmark* is shown at the top of a page and the last *right-xmark* is displayed at the bottom right of each page. Of particular interest in the example is the use of the \extramarks. We start with an \extramarks that contains "A story" in *left-xmark* and an empty *right-xmark*. It is immediately followed by a second set of marks, this time with the values "...continued" and "turn page to continue". As a result the first *left-xmark* on the first page will contain "A story" while on later pages it will contain "...continued". The last *right-xmark* on each page will always contain "turn page to continue". Thus, as long as our story continues, we will get proper

---

[1] As the reader will notice, \lastleftmark and \firstrightmark are simply aliases for LaTeX's \leftmark and \rightmark, with names providing a clearer indication of their functionalities.

continuation marks on the top and the bottom of each page. However, at the end of the story, there should be no "turn page to continue". To cancel that bottom mark, the example contains another \extramarks at the very end with an empty *right-xmark*. Its *left-xmark* still contains "…continued" to ensure that the last page displays the correct text at the top.

A story	…continued
Some text for our page that is reused over and over again. Some text for our page that is reused over and over	again. Some text for our page that is reused over and over again.
turn page to continue	

4-3-3

```
\usepackage{fancyhdr,extramarks}
\pagestyle{fancy}        \cfoot{}
\lhead{\firstleftxmark}
\rfoot{\lastrightxmark}
\newcommand\sample{ Some text for our
  page that is reused over and over again.}
\extramarks{A story}{}
\extramarks{\ldots continued}
        {turn page to continue}
\sample \sample \sample
\extramarks{\ldots continued}{}
```

    The extra marks can be mixed with LaTeX standard marks produced by the sectioning commands or through \markboth and \markright. Note, however, that the marks are not fully independent of each other: whenever \extramarks or one of the standard LaTeX mark commands is issued, LaTeX effectively generates all four marks (reusing the values for those not explicitly set). As a result the first mark of a particular kind may not be what you expect. For example, if your document starts with an \extramarks command, it implicitly generates an empty *main-mark* and *sub-mark*.

    A third type of primitive, \topmark, is also present in the mark model of TeX, which is normally not made available by LaTeX. It holds the value of the \botmark from the previous page, reflecting the "mark situation" at the very top of the page—hence its name. The reason that it is not made available by standard LaTeX is that it conflicts with LaTeX's float and \marginpar mechanism. In other words, each such object internally triggers the output routine, with the result that the \topmark value for the current page is clobbered.

    If, however, neither floats nor \marginpars are used, the \topmark information could be used, and for such situations extramarks offers an interface to it. People, who have an application for such a top mark can, therefore, access the *left-xmark* and *right-xmark* produced via \extramarks with the commands \topleftxmark and \toprightxmark, respectively.

4.4 Page styles

While the dimensions remain the same for almost all pages of a document, the format of the running headers and footers may change in the course of a document. In LaTeX terminology the formatting of running headers and footers is called a *page style*, with different formattings being given names like empty or plain to be easily selectable.

New page styles can be selected by using the command \pagestyle or the command \thispagestyle, both of which take the name of a page style as their mandatory argument. The first command sets the page style of the current and succeeding pages; the second applies to the current page only.

In small or medium-size documents sophisticated switching of page styles is normally not necessary. Instead, one can usually rely on the page styles automatically selected by the document class. For larger documents, such as books, typographic tradition, publisher requirements, or other reasons might force you to manually adjust the page style at certain places within the document.

LATEX's standard page styles   LATEX predefines four basic page styles, but additional ones might be provided by special packages or document classes.

empty   Both the header and the footer are empty.

plain   The header is empty and the footer contains the page number.

headings   The header contains information determined by the document class and the page number; the footer is empty.

myheadings   Similar to headings, but the header can be controlled by the user.

The first three page styles are used in the standard classes. Usually for the title page, a command \thispagestyle{empty} is issued internally. For the first page *Suppressing all* of major sectioning commands (like \part or \chapter, but also \maketitle), *page numbers* the standard LATEX class files issue a \thispagestyle{plain} command. This means that when you specify a \pagestyle{empty} command at the beginning of your document, you will still get page numbers on a page where a \chapter or \maketitle command is issued. Thus, to prohibit page numbers on all pages of your document, you must follow each such command with a \thispagestyle{empty} command or redefine the plain style to empty, by using \let\ps@plain=\ps@empty in your private customization package.

In the headings page style the sectioning commands set the page headers automatically by using \markboth and \markright, as shown in Table 4.3 on the facing page.

The standard page style myheadings is similar to headings, but it allows the user to customize a header by manually using the commands \markboth and \markright. It also provides a way to control the capture of titles from other sectional units like a table of contents, a list of figures, or an index. In fact, the commands (\tableofcontents, \listoffigures, and \listoftables) and the environments (thebibliography and theindex) use the \chapter* command, which does not invoke \chaptermark, but rather issues a \@mkboth command. The page style headings defines \@mkboth as \markboth, while the page style myheadings defines \@mkboth to do nothing and leaves the decision to the user.

	Command	*Document Class*	
		book, report	article
Two-sided Printing	\markboth[a]	\chapter	\section
	\markright	\section	\subsection
One-sided Printing	\markright	\chapter	\section

[a] *Specifies an empty right marker (see Figure 4.2 on page 219).*

Table 4.3: Page style defining commands in LaTeX

4.4.1 The low-level page style interface

Internally, the page style interface is implemented by the LaTeX kernel through four internal commands, of which two are called on any one page in order to format the running headers and footers. By redefining these commands different actions can be carried out.

\@oddhead   For two-sided printing, it generates the header for the odd-numbered pages; otherwise, it generates the header for all pages.

\@oddfoot   For two-sided printing, it generates the footer for the odd-numbered pages; otherwise, it generates the footer for all pages.

\@evenhead   For two-sided printing, it generates the header of the even-numbered pages; it is ignored in one-sided printing.

\@evenfoot   For two-sided printing, it generates the footer of the even-numbered pages; it is ignored in one-sided printing.

A named page style simply consists of suitable redefinitions for these commands stored in a macro with the name \ps@⟨*style*⟩; thus, to define the behavior of the page style *style*, one has to (re)define this command. As an example, the kernel definition of the plain page style, producing only a centered page number in the footer, is similar to the following code:

```
\newcommand\ps@plain{%
   \renewcommand\@oddhead{}%                          % empty recto header
   \let\@evenhead\@oddhead                            % empty verso header
   \renewcommand\@evenfoot
      {\hfil\normalfont\textrm{\thepage}\hfil}%       % centered
   \let\@oddfoot\@evenfoot                            %    page number
}
```

4.4.2 fancyhdr—**Customizing page styles**

Given that the page styles of standard LaTeX allow modification only via internal commands, it is not surprising that a number of packages have appeared that provide special page layouts—for example, rplain changes the plain page style so that the page number prints on the right instead of being centered. More elaborate packages exist as well. For example, the page style declaration features of the package titlesec (for defining heading commands, see Section 2.2.6) are worth exploring.

A well-established stand-alone package in this area is fancyhdr[1] by Piet van Oostrum, which allows easy customization of page headers and footers. The default page style provided by fancyhdr is named fancy. It should be activated via \pagestyle after any changes to \textwidth are made, as fancyhdr initializes the header and footer widths using the current value of this length.

Basic interface The look and feel of the fancy page style is determined by six declarations that define the material that will appear on the left, center, and right of the header and footer areas. For example, \lhead specifies what should show up on the left in the header area, while \cfoot defines what will appear in the center of the footer area. The results of all six declarations are shown in the next example.

LEFT   CENTER   RIGHT
```
\usepackage{fancyhdr}   \pagestyle{fancy}
\lhead{LEFT} \chead{CENTER} \rhead{RIGHT}
```
Some text for our page that might get reused over and over again.
Some text for our page that might get reused over and over again.
```
\lfoot{very-very-very-very-long-left} \cfoot{}
\rfoot{very-long-right}
\renewcommand\headrulewidth{2pt}
\renewcommand\footrulewidth{0.4pt}
\newcommand\sample{ Some text for our page
   that might get reused over and over again.}
\sample \par \sample
```

very-very-very-very-long-left-long-right

4-4-1

In many cases only one part of the footer and header areas receives material for typesetting. If you give more than one declaration with a non-empty argument, however, you have to ensure that the printed text does not get too wide. Otherwise, as the above example clearly shows, you will get partial overprints.

The thickness of the rules below the header and above the footer is controlled by the commands \headrulewidth (default 0.4pt) and \footrulewidth (default 0pt). A thickness of 0pt makes a rule invisible. Note that both are commands, not length parameters, and thus need changing via \renewcommand. More complicated changes are possible by redefining the \headrule and/or \footrule commands that produce the actual rules, as demonstrated in Example 4-4-6 on page 227. If you redefine these commands you may have to add negative vertical spaces be-

---

[1]In this book we describe version 2.0 of fancyhdr. Earlier versions were known under the name fancyheadings.

cause by default your material will appear at a distance of \baselineskip below the header text (or above the footer text).

Shown in the next example is the possibility of producing several lines of text in the running header or footer by using \\ in any of the declaration commands. If you take this tack, you usually have to enlarge \headheight (the height of the running header or footer box) because it is typically set to a value suitable only for holding a single line. If fancyhdr detects that \headheight is too small, it will issue a warning suggesting the smallest possible value that would be sufficient for the current document.

From: Frank   Page: 6
To: Michel   February 29, 2004
· ·

Some text for our page that might get reused over and over again.

Some text for our page that might get reused over and over again.

```
\usepackage{fancyhdr}   \pagestyle{fancy}
\setlength\headheight{23pt}
\lhead{From: Frank\\ To: Michel}
\rhead{Page: \thepage\\ \today}
\chead{}  \lfoot{} \cfoot{} \rfoot{}
\renewcommand\headrule{\vspace{-8pt}\dotfill}
% \sample defined as before
\sample \par \sample
```

4-4-2

Notice in the previous example that the use of \\ will result in stacked lines that are aligned according to the type of declaration in which they appear. For example, inside \lhead they align on the left and inside \rhead they align on the right. If this outcome is not what you want, consider using a simple tabular environment instead. Note the @{} in the column declaration for the tabular material, which acts to suppress the standard white space after the column. Without it the header material would not align properly at the border.

From: Frank   Page: 6
To: Michel   February 29, 2004

Some text for our page that might get reused over and over again.

Some text for our page that might get reused over and over again.

```
\usepackage{fancyhdr}   \pagestyle{fancy}
\setlength\headheight{23pt}
\lhead{From: Frank\\ To: Michel}
\rhead{\begin{tabular}[b]{l@{}}
           Page: \thepage\\ \today
        \end{tabular}}
\chead{}  \lfoot{} \cfoot{} \rfoot{}
% \sample defined as before
\sample \par \sample
```

4-4-3

The declarations we have seen so far do not allow you to change the page style depending on the type of the current page. This flexibility is offered by the more general declarations \fancyhead and \fancyfoot. They take an additional optional argument in which you specify to which type of page and to which field of the header/footer the declaration should apply. Page selectors are O or E denoting odd or even pages, respectively; the fields are selected with L, C, or R. If the page or field selector is missing the declaration applies to all page types or all fields.

Full control

Thus, LO means the left field on odd pages, while C would denote the center field on all pages. In other words, the declarations discussed earlier are shorthands for the more general form.

As the next example shows the selectors can even be sequenced. For example, RO,LE means apply this in the right field on odd pages and the left field on even pages.

```
6                    Memo
─────────────────────────

    Some  text  for  our
page  that  might  get
reused  over  and  over
again.

─────────────────────────
Author: Frank
```

```
Memo                      7
─────────────────────────

    Some  text  for  our
page  that  might  get
reused  over  and  over
again.

─────────────────────────
Author: Frank
```

```
\usepackage{fancyhdr}\pagestyle{fancy}
\fancyhead{} % clear header fields
\fancyhead[RO,LE]{\thepage}
\fancyhead[LO,RE]{Memo}
\fancyfoot{}  % clear footer fields
\fancyfoot[L]{Author: Frank}
\renewcommand\headrulewidth{0.4pt}
\renewcommand\footrulewidth{0.4pt}
% \sample defined as before
\sample \par \sample
```

4-4-4

In fact, \fancyhead and \fancyfoot are derived from an even more general declaration, \fancyhf. It has an identical syntax but supports one additional specifier type. In its optional argument you can use H or F to denote header or footer fields. Thus, \fancyfoot[LE] and \fancyhf[FLE] are equivalent, though the latter is perhaps less readable, which is why we stick with the former forms. The \fancyhf declaration is only an advantage if you want to clear all fields.

The next example shows an application of the lastpage package: in the footer we display the current and the total number of pages.

```
1  A TEST
─────────────────────────

1   A test

Some text for our page
that might get reused
over and over again.

    Page 6 of 7
```

```
        1    A TEST
─────────────────────────

    Some  text  for  our
page  that  might  get
reused  over  and  over
again.

    Page 7 of 7
```

```
\usepackage{fancyhdr,lastpage}
\pagestyle{fancy}
\fancyhf{} % --- clear all fields
\fancyhead[RO,LE]{\leftmark}
\fancyfoot[C]{Page \thepage\
             of \pageref{LastPage}}
% \sample defined as before
\section{A test}
\sample \par \sample
```

4-4-5

Width and position of header and footer

The headers and footers are typeset in a box that, by default, has the same width as \textwidth. The box can be made wider (or narrower) with the help of the command \fancyhfoffset.[1] It takes an optional argument to denote which box (header or footer) should be modified, at which side (left or right), and on what kind of page (even or odd)—the specification employs a combination

---

[1] This feature was added in version 2.1. Earlier releases used a different method.

of the letters HFLREO for this purpose. The mandatory argument then specifies the amount of extension (or reduction). In the same fashion as seen for other commands there also exist two useful shorthand forms: \fancyheadoffset and \fancyfootoffset are like \fancyhfoffset with H or F preset.

For example, to produce a running heading that spans marginal notes, use the sum of \marginparsep and \marginparwidth in the mandatory argument of \fancyheadoffset. With the calc package this can be specified elegantly with the declaration

```
\fancyheadoffset[RO,LE]{\marginparsep+\marginparwidth}
```

once these parameters have been assigned their correct values (this technique was, for example, used for the page styles used in this book).

In the next example the heading is extended into the outer margin while the page number is centered within the bounds of the text column. This result proves that the header and footer settings are, indeed, independent.

Within the header and footer fields the total width is available in the register \headwidth (recalculated for header and footer independently). It can be used to position objects in the fields. Below we redefine the \headrule command to produce a decorative heading line consisting of two blue rules spanning the whole head width.

```
\usepackage{color,fancyhdr}
\pagestyle{fancy} \fancyhf{}
\fancyheadoffset[RO,LE]{30pt}
\fancyhead[RO,LE]{TITLE}
\fancyhead[LO]{\rightmark}
\fancyhead[RE]{\leftmark}
\fancyfoot[C]{\thepage}
\renewcommand\headrule
  {{\color{blue}%
     \hrule height 2pt
          width\headwidth
     \vspace{1pt}%
     \hrule height 1pt
          width\headwidth
     \vspace{-4pt}}}
% \sample defined as before
\section{A-head}
\subsection{B-head}
\sample \sample
```

TITLE	1 A-HEAD
1 A-head	
1.1 B-head	
Some text for our page that might get reused over and over again.	
6	

1.1 B-head	TITLE
Some text for our page that might get reused over and over again.	
7	

4-4-6

You may have guessed one or the other default used by fancyhdr from the previous examples. The next example will show all of them (for ease of reference they are repeated as comments in the example code). By default, we have a thin rule below the header and no rule above the footer, the page number is centered

The fancyhdr *defaults*

in the footer, and the header displays both \leftmark and \rightmark with the order depending on the page type.

```
\usepackage{fancyhdr}
\pagestyle{fancy}
%\fancyhead[LE,RO]
%          {\slshape\rightmark}
%\fancyhead[LO,RE]
%          {\slshape\leftmark}
%\fancyfoot[C]{\thepage}
%\renewcommand\headrulewidth{0.4pt}
%\renewcommand\footrulewidth{0pt}

% \sample defined as before
\section{Test}
\subsection{B-head} \sample
\subsection{B-head2}\sample
```

1   TEST

1   Test

1.1   B-head

Some text for our page that might get reused over and over again.

6

---

1   TEST   1.2   B-head2

1.2   B-head2

Some text for our page that might get reused over and over again.

7

4-4-7

The separation between number and text in the running header is clearly too large but this is due to our extremely small measure in the example, so let us ignore this problem for the moment. How useful are these defaults otherwise? As we already mentioned, LaTeX's \leftmark and \rightmark commands have been designed primarily with "sections within chapters" in mind—that is, for the case where the \leftmark is associated with a heading that always starts on a new page. If this is not the case then you might end up with somewhat strange headers as exemplified below.

We put a section on page 5 (the page is not shown) that continues onto page 6. As a result we see the subsection 1.1 together with section 2 in the header of page 6, and a similar situation on page 7.

```
\usepackage{fancyhdr}
\pagestyle{fancy}
\newcommand\sample{ Some text
  for our page that we reuse.}

\setcounter{page}{5}
\section{A-head}    \newpage
% Above makes a section on
% page 5 (not displayed)
\subsection{B-head} \sample
\section{A-head2}    \sample
\subsection{B-head2}\sample
\section{A-head3}    \sample
```

1.1   B-head   2   A-HEAD2

1.1   B-head

Some text for our page that we reuse.

2   A-head2

Some text for our page that we reuse.

6

---

3   A-HEAD3   2.1   B-head2

2.1   B-head2

Some text for our page that we reuse.

3   A-head3

Some text for our page that we reuse.

7

4-4-8

To understand this behavior recall that \leftmark refers to the last mark produced by \markboth on that particular page, while \rightmark refers to the first mark produced from either \markright or \markboth.

If you are likely to produce pages like the above, such as in a document containing many short subsections, then the fancyhdr defaults are probably not suitable for you. In that case overwrite them in one way or another, as we did in most of the examples in this section. The question you have to ask yourself is this: what information do I want to present to the reader in such a heading? If the answer is, for example, the situation at the top of the page for even (left-hand) pages and the status on the bottom for odd pages, then a possible solution is given through the use of \firstleftmark and \lastrightmark from the extramarks package.

```
\usepackage{extramarks}
\usepackage{fancyhdr}
\pagestyle{fancy}
\fancyhead[RO]{\lastrightmark}
\fancyhead[RE]{\firstleftmark}
% \sample defined as before
\setcounter{page}{5}
\section{A-head}   \newpage
% Above makes a section on
% page 5 (not displayed)
\subsection{B-head} \sample
\section{A-head2}   \sample
\subsection{B-head2}\sample
\section{A-head3}   \sample
```

1.1 B-head	*1 A-HEAD*

1.1 B-head

Some text for our page that we reuse.

2 A-head2

Some text for our page that we reuse.

6

3 A-HEAD3	

2.1 B-head2

Some text for our page that we reuse.

3 A-head3

Some text for our page that we reuse.

7

4-4-9

To test your understanding explain why page 7 now shows only the A-head and try to guess what headers you would get if the first B-head (but not all of its section text) would have already been on page 5.

Despite the claim made earlier, there are two more defaults set by the fancy page style. Because they are somewhat hidden we have ignored them until now. We have not said how \leftmark and \rightmark receive their values; that they receive some data should be clear from the previous examples. As explained in Section 4.3.4 the sectioning commands pass their title argument to commands like \sectionmark, which may or may not be set up to produce page marks via \markboth or \markright. The fancy page style now sets up two such commands: \chaptermark and \sectionmark if the current class defines a \chapter command, or \sectionmark and \subsectionmark if it does not. Thus, if you want to provide a different marking mechanism or even if you just want to provide a somewhat different layout (for example, suppressing section numbers in the heading or not using \MakeUppercase for the mark text), you may have to define these commands yourself.

The next example repeats Example 4-4-7 on the preceding page, except that this time we provide our own \sectionmark and \subsectionmark that shorten the separation between number and text and avoid using \MakeUppercase.

<table>
<tr><td>

```
                          1 Test

1   Test

1.1   B-head
Some text for our page that
might get reused over and
over again.
                  6
```

</td><td>

```
1 Test              1.2 B-head2

1.2   B-head2
Some text for our page that
might get reused over and
over again.



                  7
```

</td><td>

```
\usepackage{fancyhdr}
\pagestyle{fancy}
\renewcommand\sectionmark[1]
 {\markboth{\thesection\ #1}{}}
\renewcommand\subsectionmark[1]
 {\markright{\thesubsection\ #1}}
% \sample defined as before
\section{Test}
\subsection{B-head} \sample
\subsection{B-head2}\sample
```

4-4-10
</td></tr>
</table>

So far, all of our examples have customized the fancy page style over and over again. However, the fancyhdr package also allows you to save your customizations under a name that can then be selected through the \pagestyle or \thispagestyle command. This is done with a \fancypagestyle declaration. It takes two arguments: the name of the page style and the customizations that should be applied when the page style is later called. Fields not set (or cleared) as well as the rule width settings are inherited from the fancyhdr defaults. This explains why we first use \fancyhf to clear all fields.

Defining "named" page styles

<table>
<tr><td>

```
6                    Memo

    Some text for our
page that might get
reused over and over
again.

              March 15, 2004
```

</td><td>

```
Memo                    7

    Some text for our
page that might get
reused over and over
again.

              March 15, 2004
```

</td><td>

```
\usepackage{fancyhdr}
\fancypagestyle{memo}{\fancyhf{}%
  \fancyhead[RO,LE]{\thepage}%
  \fancyhead[LO,RE]{Memo}%
  \fancyfoot[R]{\scriptsize\today}
  \renewcommand\headrulewidth{1pt}}
\pagestyle{memo}
% \sample defined as before
\sample \par \sample
```

4-4-11
</td></tr>
</table>

Some LaTeX commands, like \chapter and \maketitle, use \thispagestyle to automatically switch to the plain page style, thereby overriding the page style currently in effect. To customize page styles for such pages you can either modify the definitions of these commands (which could be painful) or change the meaning of the plain page style by providing a new definition with \fancypagestyle. This is, strictly speaking, not really the right approach—just assume that your new plain page style is now doing something fancy. But the fault really lies with LaTeX's standard classes,[1] which failed to use specially named page styles for these cases and instead directly referred to the most likely candidate. In practice, such

---

[1] The KOMA-Script classes, for example, use commands like \chapterpagestyle to refer to such special page styles, thus allowing easy customization.

a redefinition usually works very well for documents that need a `fancy` page style for most pages.

Sometimes it is desirable to modify the page style depending on the floating objects found on the current page. For this purpose `fancyhdr` provides a number of control commands. They can be applied in the page style declarations, thereby allowing the page style to react to the presence or absence of footnotes on the current page (`\iffootnote`), floats in the top area (`\iftopfloat`), or floats in the bottom area (`\ifbottomfloat`). Each takes two arguments: the first to typeset when the condition is satisfied, the second to execute otherwise. *Page styles depending on float objects*

In the next example we omit the head rule if there are top floats by redefining `\headrulewidth`. We also show the use of different heading texts on pages with or without top floats.

```
\usepackage{fancyhdr}
\pagestyle{fancy} \fancyhf{}
\chead{\iftopfloat{SPECIAL}{NORMAL}}
\cfoot{\thepage}
\renewcommand\headrulewidth
        {\iftopfloat{0pt}{0.4pt}}

% \sample defined as before
\sample
\begin{figure}[t]
  \centering
  \fbox{Sample t-figure}
\end{figure}
\sample
```

SPECIAL

Sample t-figure

Some text for our page that might get reused over and over again.   Some text

6

NORMAL

for our page that might get reused over and over again.

7

4-4-12

A similar control, `\iffloatpage`, is available to customize page styles for pages consisting only of floats—for example, to suppress running headers on such pages. If the page style is supposed to depend on several variables the controls can be nested, though that soon gets a little muddled. For example, to suppress head rules on all pages that contain either top or page floats, one would have to define `\headrulewidth` as follows: *Layout for float pages*

```
\renewcommand\headrulewidth
        {\iftopfloat{0pt}{\iffloatpage{0pt}{0.4pt}}}
```

In dictionaries and similar works the running header often shows the first and the last word explained on a page to allow easy access to the dictionary data. By defining a suitable command that emits a mark for each dictionary item, such a scheme can be easily implemented. In the example below we use LaTeX's *right-mark* to store such marks, retrieving them via `\firstrightmark` and `\lastrightmark` from the `extramarks` package. On pages devoted to only a single entry, we collapse the entry by testing whether both commands contain the same value via *Dictionary type headers* commands from the ifthen package. With a similar mechanism we prepared the index for this book.

```
\usepackage{ifthen,fancyhdr,extramarks}
\pagestyle{fancy} \fancyhf{}
\newcommand\combinemarks{\ifthenelse
   {\equal{\firstrightmark}{\lastrightmark}}%
   {\firstrightmark}% equal values
   {\firstrightmark---\lastrightmark}}
\chead{\combinemarks} \cfoot{\thepage}
\newcommand\idxitem[1]{\par\vspace{8pt}%
   \textbf{#1}\markright{#1}\quad\ignorespaces}
\idxitem{galley} Text formatted but not
   cut into pages.
\idxitem{OR} Output routine.
\idxitem{mark} An object in the galley
   used to communicate with the OR.
\idxitem{running header} page title
   changing with page contents.
```
4-4-13

---

galley—mark

galley Text formatted but not cut into pages.

OR Output routine.

mark An object in the galley used to communicate with the

6

---

running header

OR.

running header page title changing with page contents.

7

Problems in two-column mode   Dictionaries are often typeset in two or more columns per page. Unfortunately, LATEX's standard twocolumn mode is defective with respect to marks—the \leftmark always reflects the mark situation of the second column instead of containing the first mark from the first column. If this poses a problem use the reimplementation provided in the package fixltx2e. Alternatively, you can use the multicol package which also handles marks properly.

4.4.3 truncate—**Truncate text to a given length**

A potential problem when producing running headers or footers is the restricted space available: if the text is too long it will simply overprint. To help in this and similar situations you can deploy the package truncate written by Donald Arseneau. It provides a command to truncate a given text to a given width.

```
\truncate [marker] {width}{text}
```

If the argument *text* is too wide to fit the specified *width*, it will be truncated and a continuation *marker* placed at the end. If the optional *marker* argument is missing, a default marker stored in \TruncateMarker is used (its value, as provided by the package, is \,\dots).

By default, truncation is done at word boundaries and only if the words are not connected via an unbreakable space specified with a ~. For this reason the following example truncates the text after the word has. It also illustrates the use of a *marker* that requires an extra set of braces to hide the brackets that are supposed to appear as part of the text. To help you visualize the space occupied by the truncated text, | characters have been added to the left and right.

```
\usepackage{truncate}
|This text has been~truncated|

|\truncate{50pt}
        {This text has been~truncated}|

|\truncate[{\,[..]}]{100pt}
        {This text has been~truncated}|
```

|This text has been truncated|
|This text ... |
|This text has [..] |

4-4-14

Truncation within words can be achieved by specifying one of the options hyphenate, breakwords, or breakall to the package. The first two support truncation at hyphenation points, with the difference being that breakwords suppresses the hyphen character (the more common solution). The third option allows truncation anywhere within words. With these options the above example would have the following result:

This text has been trun-[..]   (hyphenate)

This text has been trun[..]   (breakwords)

This text has been trunc[..]   (breakall)

By default, the text (whether truncated or not) is printed flush left in a box of the specified *width*. Using the package option fit causes the printed text to have its natural width, up to a maximum of the specified *width*.

The next example combines the truncate package with fancyhdr. Notice the use of the fit option. Without it the header would always be flush left (the \headwidth was slightly reduced to better show its effect).

1   SECTION WITH...
1   Section with a long title
Some text for our page that might get reused over and over again.
6

1   SECTION WITH...
Some text for our page that might get reused over and over again.
7

```
\usepackage[fit]{truncate}
\usepackage{fancyhdr}
\pagestyle{fancy}
\fancyhf{} % --- clear all fields
\fancyhead[RO,LE]{\truncate
    {.95\headwidth}{\leftmark}}
\fancyfoot[C]{\thepage}
% \sample defined as before
\section{Section with a long title}
\sample \par \sample
```

4-4-15

4.5 Visual formatting

The final stage of the production of an important document often needs some hand-formatting to avoid bad page breaks. For this purpose, standard LaTeX offers the \pagebreak, \nopagebreak, \newpage, and \clearpage commands as well as the \samepage declaration, although the latter is considered obsolete in LaTeX 2$_\varepsilon$. A \samepage declaration together with a suitable number of \nobreak commands lets you request that a certain portion of your document be kept together. Unfortunately, the results are often not satisfactory; in particular, LaTeX will never make a page larger than its nominal height (\textheight) but rather moves everything in the scope of the \samepage declaration to the next page. The LaTeX 2$_\varepsilon$ command \enlargethispage* described below offers an alternative approach.

It is common in book production to "run" a certain number of pages (normally double spreads) short or long to avoid bad page breaks later on. This means that the nominal height of the pages is reduced or enlarged by a certain amount—for example, a \baselineskip. To support this practice, LaTeX 2$_\varepsilon$ offers the command \enlargethispage{*size*}.

\enlargethispage*{*size*}

If, for example, you want to enlarge or reduce the size of some pages by one (or more) additional lines of text, you could define

```
\newcommand\longpage[1][1]{\enlargethispage{#1\baselineskip}}
\newcommand\shortpage[1][1]{\enlargethispage{-#1\baselineskip}}
```

and use those commands between two paragraphs on the pages in question.[1] The \enlargethispage command enlarges the \textheight for the current page but otherwise does not change the formatting parameters. Thus, if \flushbottom is in force, the text will fill the \textheight for the page in question, if necessary by enlarging or shrinking vertical space within the page. In this way, the definitions add or remove exactly one line of text from a page while maintaining the positions of the other lines. This consideration is important to give a uniform appearance.

\enlargethispage*{*size*}

The companion command, \enlargethispage*, also enlarges or reduces the page height, but this time the resulting final page will be squeezed as much as possible (i.e., depending on the available white space on the page). This technique can be helpful if you wish to keep a certain portion of your document together

---

[1]Because this book contains so many examples, we had to use this trick a few times to avoid half-empty pages. For example, in this chapter all pages from 222 onward are run short by one line. This was necessary because of the many (large) examples in Section 4.4.2—all other formattings we tried ended in a half-empty page somewhere.

on one page, even if it makes the page slightly too long. (Otherwise, just use the `minipage` environment.) The trick is to request a large enough amount of extra space and then place an explicit page break where you want the page break to happen. For example:

```
\enlargethispage*{100cm}      % absurd request
\begin{center}
 \begin{tabular}{llll}        % slightly too long
  ....                        % tabular
 \end{tabular}
\end{center}
\pagebreak                    % forced page break
```

From the description above it is clear that both commands should be used only in the last stages of the production process, since any later alterations to the document (adding or removing a single word, if you are unlucky) can make your hand-formatting obsolete—resulting in ugly-looking pages.

To manually correct final page breaks, such as in a publication like this book (which poses some formidable challenges due to the many examples that cannot be broken across pages), it can be helpful to visualize TeX's reasons for breaking at a certain point and to find out how much flexibility is available on certain pages. Tools for this purpose are described in Appendix B.3.2.

4.5.1 nextpage—Extensions to \clearpage

In standard LaTeX the commands \clearpage and \cleardoublepage terminate the current paragraph and page after placing all dangling floats (if necessary, by producing a number of float pages). In two-sided printing \cleardoublepage also makes sure that the next page is a right-hand (odd-numbered) one by adding, if necessary, an extra page with an empty text body. However, this extra page will still get a page header and footer (as specified by the currently active page style), which may not be desirable.

4-5-1

```
\pagestyle{headings}
% right-hand page on the left in
% this example due to:
\setcounter{page}{1}

\section{A Test}
\subsection{A subsection}
Some text for our page.
\cleardoublepage
\section{Another Section}
This would appear on page 3.
```

The package nextpage by Peter Wilson extends this concept by providing the commands \cleartoevenpage and \cleartooddpage. Both commands accept an optional argument in which you can put text that should appear on the potentially generated page. In the next example we use this ability to provide a command \myclearpage that writes BLANK PAGE on such generated pages.

```
\usepackage{nextpage}\pagestyle{headings}
\newcommand\myclearpage{\cleartooddpage
    [\vspace*{\fill} \centering
     BLANK PAGE \vspace*{\fill}]}
\setcounter{page}{1} %right-hand page
\section{A Test}
\subsection{A subsection}
Some text for our page.
\myclearpage
\section{Another Section}
This would appear on page 3.
```
4-5-2

This code still results in a running header, but by now you surely know how to fix the example: just add a \thispagestyle{empty} to the above definition.

The nextpage package also provides two commands, \movetoevenpage and \movetooddpage, that offer the same functionality, except that they do not output dangling floats.

4.6 Doing layout with class

Page layout is normally defined by the document class, so it should come as no great surprise that the techniques and packages described in this chapter are usually applied behind the scenes (within a document class).

The standard classes use the LaTeX parameters and interfaces directly to define the page proportions, running headers, and other elements. More recently developed classes, however, often deploy packages like geometry to handle certain aspects of the page layout.

In this section we introduce two such implementations. By searching through the CTAN archive you might discover additional treasures.

4.6.1 KOMA-Script—A drop-in replacement for article et al.

The KOMA-Script classes, developed by Markus Kohm and based on earlier work by Frank Neukam, are drop-in replacements for the standard article/report/book classes that emphasize rules of typography laid down by Tschichold. The article class, for example, becomes scrartcl.

Page layout in the KOMA-Script classes is implemented by deploying the typearea package (see Section 4.2.3), with the classes offering the package options as class options. Extended page style design is done with the package scrpage (offering features similar to those provided by fancyhdr). Like typearea this package can also be used on a stand-alone basis with one of the standard classes. Layout specifications such as font control, caption layout, and so on have been extended by providing customization possibilities that allow manipulation in the preamble of a document.

Besides offering all features available in the standard classes, the KOMA-Script classes provide extra user control inside front and back matter as well as a number of other useful extensions.

The distribution is well documented. There exists both a German and an English guide explaining all features in detail. The German documentation is also available as a nicely typeset book [100], published by DANTE, the German TEX Users Group.

4.6.2 memoir—Producing complex publications

The memoir class written by Peter Wilson was originally developed as an alternative to the standard book class. It incorporates many features otherwise found only as add-on packages. The current version also works as an replacement for article and can, therefore, be used for all types of publications, from small memos to complex books.

Among other features it supports an extended set of document sizes (from 9pt to 14pt), configurable sectional headings, page headers and footers, and captions. Predefined layout styles are available for all such objects and it is possible to declare new ones as needed. The class supports declarative commands for all aspects of setting the page, text, and margin sizes, including support for trimming (crop) marks. Many components of the class are also available as stand-alone packages, for those users who wish to add a certain functionality to other classes (e.g., epigraphs, caption formatting).

Like the KOMA-Script classes, the memoir class is accompanied by an excellent manual of nearly 200 pages, discussing all topics related to document design and showing how to resolve potential problems with memoir.

## CHAPTER 5

Tabular Material

Data is often most efficiently presented in tabular form. TeX uses powerful primitives for arranging material in rows and columns. Because they implement only a low-level, formatting-oriented functionality, several macro packages have been developed that build on those primitives to provide a higher-level command language and a more user-friendly interface.

In LaTeX, two types of environments for constructing tables are provided. Most commonly the `tabular` environment or its math-mode equivalent, the `array` environment, is used. However, in some circumstances the `tabbing` environment might prove useful.

Tables typically form large units of the document that must be allowed to "float" so that the document may be paginated correctly. The environments described in this chapter are principally concerned with the table layout. To achieve correct pagination they will often be used within the `table` environment described in Chapter 6. An exception is the environments for multipage tables described in Section 5.4, which should never be used in conjunction with the LaTeX float mechanism. Be careful, however, not to confuse the `tabular` environment with the `table` environment. The former allows material to be aligned in columns, while the latter is a logical document element identifying its contents as belonging together and allowing the material to be floated jointly. In particular, one `table` environment can contain several `tabular` environments.

Tables contained within floating environments

After a taking a quick look at the `tabbing` environment, this chapter describes the extensions to LaTeX's basic `tabular` and `array` environments provided by the array package. This package offers increased functionality, especially in terms of a more flexible positioning of paragraph material, a better control of inter-column and inter-row spacing, and the possibility of defining new preamble specifiers. Several packages build on the primitives provided by the array package to provide specific extra functionality. By combining the features in these packages, you will be able to construct complex tables in a simple way. For example, the tabularx and tabulary packages provide extra column types that allow table column widths to be calculated automatically.

Standard LaTeX tabular environments do not produce tables that may be broken over a page. We give several examples of multipage tables using the supertabular and longtable environments provided by the similarly named packages.

We then briefly look at the use of color in tables and at several packages that give finer control over rules, and the spacing around rules, in tables. Next, we discuss table entries spanning multiple rows, created via the multirow package, and the dcolumn package, which provides a mechanism for aligning columns of figures on a decimal point.

We also discuss the use of footnotes in tables. The threeparttable package provides a convenient mechanism to have table notes and captions combined with a tabular layout.

The final section gives some practical advice on handling nested tables and large entries spanning multiple columns.

Mathematically oriented readers should consult the chapter on advanced mathematics, especially Section 8.2 on page 468, which discusses the alignment structures for equations. Further examples of table layouts may be found in the section on the graphics package, Section 10.3 on page 628.

5.1   Standard LaTeX environments

LaTeX has two families of environments that allow material to be lined up in columns—namely, the tabbing environment, and the tabular and array environments. The main differences between the two kinds of environments are:

- The tabbing environment is not as general as the tabular environment. It can be typeset only as a separate paragraph, whereas a tabular environment can be placed anywhere in the text or inside mathematics.

- The tabbing environment can be broken between pages, whereas the standard tabular environment cannot.

- With the tabbing environment the user must specify the position of each tab stop explicitly. With the tabular environment LaTeX can automatically determine the width of the columns.

- Multiple tabbing environments cannot be nested, whereas tabular environments can, thus allowing complex alignments to be realized.

5.1.1 Using the `tabbing` environment

This section deals with some of the lesser-known features of the `tabbing` environment. First, it must be realized that formatting is under the complete control of the user. Somewhat unexpectedly, when moving to a given tab stop, you will always end up at the exact horizontal position where it was defined, independently of where the current point is. As a consequence, the current point can move backward and overwrite previous text. The scope of commands in rows is usually limited to the region between tab stops.

Be aware that the usual LaTeX commands for making accents, `\'`, `\``, and `\=`, are redefined inside the `tabbing` environment. The accents are available by typing `\a'`, `\a``, and `\a=` instead. The `\-` command, which normally signals a possible hyphenation point, is also redefined, but this consideration is not so important because the lines in a `tabbing` environment are never broken.

Alternative names for accent commands

A style parameter `\tabbingsep`, used together with the `\'` command, allows text to be typeset at a given distance flush right from the following tab stop. Its default value is set equal to `\labelsep`, which in turn is usually 5 pt.

There exist a few common ways to define tab stops—that is, using a line to be typeset, or explicitly specifying a skip to the next tab stop. The next example shows a poor choice for the pattern on the first line, in which the first column on the second line is longer than the one specified. The last line redefines the tab position and shows the different uses of the backquote.

confused embrouillé *confused mind* esprit trouble
confusiondéconfiture

conjecture hypothèse   (from Greek)

5-1-1

```
\begin{tabbing}
\textbf{confused} \= embrouill\a'e \=
    \emph{confused mind} \= esprit trouble\kill
\textbf{confused} \> embrouill\a'e \>
    \emph{confused mind} \> esprit trouble \\
\textbf{confusion} \> d\a'econfiture  \\[3mm]
\textbf{conjecture} \=hypoth\a`ese
                \'(from Greek) \\
\end{tabbing}
```

If you use accents within the definition of a command that may be used inside a tabbing environment you must use the `\a...` forms because the standard accent commands such as `\'` will be interpreted as `tabbing` commands, as shown below. You may find it more convenient to use the `inputenc` package and enter the accented letters directly.

Tab one Tab two
7 bitcaf e
7 bit   café
8 bit   café

5-1-2

```
\usepackage[latin1]{inputenc}  \newcommand\acafe{caf\'e}
\newcommand\bcafe{caf\a'e}     \newcommand\ccafe{café}
\begin{tabbing}
Tab one \= Tab two \\
7 bit   \> \acafe  \\
7 bit   \> \bcafe  \\
8 bit   \> \ccafe \end{tabbing}
```

An alternative is provided by the Tabbing package (by Jean-Pierre Drucbert), which provides a Tabbing environment in which the accent commands are *not* redefined. Instead, the tabbing commands are named \TAB'....

Tab one Tab two
7 bit   café
7 bit   café
8 bit   café

```
\usepackage[latin1]{inputenc} \usepackage{Tabbing}
% definitions as before
\begin{Tabbing}Tab one \TAB= Tab two\\
7 bit    \TAB> \acafe \\
7 bit    \TAB> \bcafe \\
8 bit    \TAB> \ccafe \end{Tabbing}
```

5-1-3

The tabbing environment is most useful for aligning information into columns whose widths are constant and known. The following is from Table A.1 on page 855.

pc   Pica = 12pt
cc   Cicero = 12dd
cm   Centimeter = 10mm

```
\newcommand\lenrule[1]{\makebox[#1]{%
    \rule{.4pt}{4pt}\hrulefill\rule{.4pt}{4pt}}}
\begin{tabbing}
dd\quad \= \hspace{.55\linewidth} \= \kill
pc  \> Pica = 12pt \> \lenrule{1pc} \\
cc  \> Cicero  = 12dd \> \lenrule{1cc} \\
cm  \> Centimeter = 10mm \> \lenrule{1cm} \\
\end{tabbing}
```

5-1-4

5.1.2   Using the `tabular` **environment**

In general, when tables of any degree of complexity are required, it is usually easier to consider the tabular-like environments defined by LaTeX. These environments align material horizontally in rows (separated by \\) and vertically in columns (separated by &).

```
\begin{array}[pos]{cols}           rows \end{array}
\begin{tabular}[pos]{cols}         rows \end{tabular}
\begin{tabular*}{width}[pos]{cols} rows \end{tabular*}
```

The array environment is essentially the math mode equivalent of the tabular environment. The entries of the table are set in math mode, and the default inter-column space is different (as described below), but otherwise the functionality of the two environments is identical.

The tabular* environment has an additional width argument that specifies the required total width of the table. TeX may adjust the inter-column spacing to produce a table with this width, as described below.

Table 5.1 shows the various options available in the *cols* preamble declaration of the environments in the standard LaTeX tabular family. The array package introduced in the next section extends the list of preamble options.

l	Left-aligned column.
c	Center-aligned column.
r	Right-aligned column.
p{*width*}	Equivalent to `\parbox[t]{`*width*`}` .
|	Inserts a vertical line between two columns. The distance between the two columns is unaffected.
@{*decl*}	Suppresses inter-column space and inserts *decl* instead.
*{*num*}{*opts*}	Equivalent to *num* copies of *opts*.

Table 5.1: The preamble options in the standard LaTeX `tabular` environment

The visual appearance of the `tabular`-like environments can be controlled by various style parameters. These parameters can be changed by using the `\setlength` or `\addtolength` commands anywhere in the document. Their scope can be general or local. In the latter case the scope should be explicitly delimited by braces or another environment.

Style parameters

`\arraycolsep` Half the width of the horizontal space between columns in an `array` environment (default value 5pt).

`\tabcolsep` Half the width of the horizontal space between columns in a `tabular` environment (default value 6pt).

`\arrayrulewidth` The width of the vertical rule that separates columns (if a | is specified in the environment preamble) and the rules created by `\hline`, `\cline`, or `\vline` (default value 0.4pt).
    When using the array package, this width is taken into account when calculating the width of the table (standard LaTeX sets the rules in such a way that they do not affect the final width of the table).

`\doublerulesep` The width of the space between lines created by two successive | | characters in the environment preamble, or by two successive `\hline` commands (default value 2pt).

`\arraystretch` Fraction with which the normal inter-row space is multiplied. For example, a value of 1.5 would move the rows 50% farther apart. This value is set with `\renewcommand` (default value 1.0).

5.2 array—Extending the `tabular` environments

Over the years several extensions have been made to the `tabular` environment family, as described in the *LaTeX Manual*. This section explores the added functionality of the array package (developed by Frank Mittelbach, with contributions

Changed Option	
|	Inserts a vertical line. The distance between two columns will be enlarged by the width of the line, in contrast to the original definition of LaTeX.
New Options	
m{*width*}	Defines a column of width *width*. Every entry will be centered vertically in proportion to the rest of the line. It is somewhat like \parbox{*width*}.
b{*width*}	Coincides with \parbox[b]{*width*}.
>{*decl*}	Can be used before an l, r, c, p, m, or b option. It inserts *decl* directly in front of the entry of the column.
<{*decl*}	Can be used after an l, r, c, p{..}, m{..}, or b{..} option. It inserts *decl* immediately after the entry of the column.
!{*decl*}	Can be used anywhere and corresponds with the | option. The difference is that *decl* is inserted instead of a vertical line, so this option does not suppress the normally inserted space between columns, in contrast to @{...}.

Table 5.2: Additional preamble options in the array package

from David Carlisle). Many of the packages described later in the chapter build on the functionality of the array package so as to extend or adapt the tabular environment.

Table 5.2 shows the new options available in the *cols* preamble declaration of the environments in the tabular family.

5.2.1 Examples of preamble commands

If you would like to use a special font, such as \bfseries in a flush left column, you can write >{\bfseries}l. You no longer have to start every entry of the column with \bfseries.

A	**B**	*C*
100	**10**	*1*

```
\usepackage{array}
\begin{tabular}{|>{\large}c|>{\large\bfseries}l|>{\itshape}c|}
\hline A & B & C\\\hline 100 & 10 & 1 \\\hline
\end{tabular}
```

5-2-1

Extra space between rows   Notice the use of the \extrarowheight declaration in the second example below. It adds a vertical space of 4pt above each row. In fact, the effect of \extrarowheight will be visible only if the sum of its value, added to the product \baselineskip × \arraystretch, is larger than the actual height of the cell or, more precisely, in the case of p, m, or b, the height of the *first row* of the cell.

This consideration is important for tables with horizontal lines because it is often necessary to fine-tune the distance between those lines and the contents of the table. The default value of \extrarowheight is 0pt.

A	**B**	*C*
100	**10**	*1*

```
\usepackage{array}
\setlength\extrarowheight{4pt}
\begin{tabular}{|>{\large}c|>{\large\bfseries}l|>{\itshape}c|}
\hline A & B & C\\\hline 100 & 10 & 1 \\\hline
\end{tabular}
```

5-2-2

There are few restrictions on the declarations that may be used with the > preamble option. Nevertheless, for technical reasons beyond the scope of this book, it is not possible to change the font encoding for the table column. For example, if the current encoding is not T1, then >{\fontencoding{T1}\selectfont} does *not* work. No error message is generated but incorrect characters may be produced at the start of each cell in the column. If a column of text requires a special encoding then the encoding command should be placed explictly at the start of each cell in the column.

Font encoding changes not supported in a >{...} argument

The differences between the three paragraph-building options p (the paragraph box is aligned at the top), m (the paragraph box is aligned in the center), and b (the paragraph box is aligned at the bottom) are shown schematically in the following examples.

1 1 1 1	2 2 2 2	3 3 3 3
1 1 1 1	2 2 2 2	
1 1 1 1		

```
\usepackage{array}
\begin{tabular}{|p{1cm}|p{1cm}|p{1cm}|}
\hline 1 1 1 1 1 1 1 1 1 1 1 1 &
           2 2 2 2 2 2 2 2          & 3 3 3 3 \\ \hline
\end{tabular}
```

5-2-3

1 1 1 1		
1 1 1 1	2 2 2 2	
1 1 1 1	2 2 2 2	3 3 3 3

```
\usepackage{array}
\begin{tabular}{|m{1cm}|m{1cm}|m{1cm}|}
\hline 1 1 1 1 1 1 1 1 1 1 1 1 &
           2 2 2 2 2 2 2 2          & 3 3 3 3 \\ \hline
\end{tabular}
```

5-2-4

1 1 1 1		
1 1 1 1	2 2 2 2	
1 1 1 1	2 2 2 2	3 3 3 3

```
\usepackage{array}
\begin{tabular}{|b{1cm}|b{1cm}|b{1cm}|}
\hline 1 1 1 1 1 1 1 1 1 1 1 1 &
           2 2 2 2 2 2 2 2          & 3 3 3 3 \\ \hline
\end{tabular}
```

5-2-5

In columns that have been generated with p, m, or b, the default value of \parindent is 0pt. It can be changed with the \setlength command as shown in the next example where we indent the first column by 5 mm.

1 2 3 4 5 6	1 2 3 4 5 6 7 8
7 8 9 0 1 2 3 4	9 0 1 2 3 4 5 6
5 6 7 8 9 0	7 8 9 0

```
\usepackage{array}
\begin{tabular}
  {|>{\setlength\parindent{5mm}}p{2cm}|p{2cm}|}
\hline 1 2 3 4 5 6 7 8 9 0 1 2 3 4 5 6 7 8 9 0 &
  1 2 3 4 5 6 7 8 9 0 1 2 3 4 5 6 7 8 9 0 \\ \hline
\end{tabular}
```
5-2-6

The < preamble option was originally developed for the following application: >{$}c<{$} generates a column in math mode in a `tabular` environment. The use of this type of preamble in an `array` environment results in a column in LR mode because the additional $s cancel the existing $s.

$10!^{10!}$	a big number
10^{-999}	a small number

```
\usepackage{array}
\setlength\extrarowheight{4pt}
\begin{tabular}{|>{$}l<{$}|l|}   \hline
    10!^{10!}          & a big number    \\
    10^{-999}          & a small number  \\\hline
\end{tabular}
```
5-2-7

A major use of the ! and @ options is to add rubber length with the \extracolsep command so that TEX can stretch the table to the desired width in the `tabular*` environment. The use of \extracolsep in the array package environments is subjected to two restrictions: there can be at most one \extracolsep command per @ or ! expression, and the command must be directly entered into the @ expression, not as part of a macro definition. Thus, \newcommand\ef{\extracolsep{\fill}}, and then later @{\ef} in a `tabular` preamble, does not work, but \newcommand{e}{@{\extracolsep{\fill}}} could be used instead.

Typesetting narrow columns

TEX does not hyphenate the first word in a paragraph, so very narrow cells can produce overflows. This is corrected by starting the text with \hspace{0pt}.

Characteristics	Char- acteris- tics

```
\fbox{\parbox{11mm}{Characteristics}}%
\hfill
\fbox{\parbox{11mm}{\hspace{0pt}Characteristics}}
```
5-2-8

When you have a narrow column, you must not only make sure that the first word can be hyphenated, but also consider that short texts are easier to typeset in ragged-right mode (without being aligned at the right margin). This result is obtained by preceding the material with a \raggedright command (see Section 3.1.11). This command redefines the line-breaking command \\, so we must use the command \tabularnewline, which is defined in the array package, as in standard LATEX, to be the original definition of the row-ending \\ command of the `tabular` or `array` environment. Alternatively, we could have used the \arraybackslash command after the \raggedright in the third column. This locally redefines \\ to end the table row, as shown in Example 5-2-12 on page 249.

As shown in the example below, we can now typeset material inside a `tabular` environment ragged right, ragged left, or centered and still have control of the line breaks. The first word is now hyphenated correctly, although in the case of the Dutch text, we helped TEX a little by choosing the possible hyphenation points ourselves.

Super- con- scious- ness is a long word	Possibil- ités et es- pérances	Moge- lijkheden en hoop
Ragged left text in column one	Centered text in column two	Ragged right text in column three

```
\usepackage{array}
\begin{tabular}%
        [|>{\raggedleft\hspace{0pt}}p{14mm}%
        |>{\centering\hspace{0pt}}p{14mm}%
        |>{\raggedright\hspace{0pt}}p{14mm}|}
\hline
  Superconsciousness is a long word  &
  Possibilit\'es et esp\'erances     &
  Moge\-lijk\-heden en hoop   \tabularnewline
\hline
  Ragged left text in column one     &
  Centered text     in column two    &
  Ragged right text in  column three
                        \tabularnewline
\hline
\end{tabular}
```

5-2-9

Controlling the horizontal separation between columns

The default inter-column spacing is controlled by setting the length parameters \arraycolsep (for `array`) and \tabcolsep (for `tabular`). However, it is often desirable to alter the spacing between individual columns, or more commonly, before the first column and after the last column of the table.

onetwo	three–four	–	five		
1 2	3	– 4	–	5	

```
\usepackage{array}
\begin{tabular}{c@{}c!{}c@{--}c!{--}c}
  one&two&three&four&five\\
  1&2&3&4&5
\end{tabular}
```

5-2-10

In the example above, `@{}` has been used to remove the inter-column space between columns 1 and 2. An empty `!{}` has no effect, as demonstrated between columns 2 and 3. Note that a dash appears in place of the default inter-column space when specified using `@{--}` between columns 3 and 4, but is placed in the center of the default inter-column space when specified using `!{--}` between columns 4 and 5.

Using @{} *to remove*
space at the side of
the table A common use of @{} is to remove the space equal to the value of \tabcolsep (for tabular) that, by default, appears on each side of the table, as shown in the following example.

text text text text

one   two   **material following ...**

three   four

text text text text

text text text text

one   two **material following ...**

three   four

text text text text

```
\begin{flushleft} \textbf{text text text text}\\
\begin{tabular}{lr}
  one&two\\ three&four\\
\end{tabular}\textbf{material following \ldots}\\
\textbf{text text text text\\text text text text}\\
\begin{tabular}{@{}lr@{}}
  one&two\\ three&four\\
\end{tabular}\textbf{material following \ldots}\\
\textbf{text text text text}  \end{flushleft}
```

5-2-11

5.2.2 Defining new column specifiers

If you have a one-off column in a table, then you may use the > and < options to modify the style for that column:

> >{*some declarations*}c<{*some more decls*}

This code, however, becomes rather verbose if you often use columns of this form. Therefore, for repetitive use of a given type of column specifier, the following command has been defined:

> \newcolumntype{*col*}[*narg*]{*decl*}

Here, *col* is a one-letter specifier to identify the new type of column inside a preamble; *narg* is an optional parameter, giving the number of arguments this specifier takes; and *decl* are legal declarations. For example:

> \newcolumntype{x}{>{*some declarations*}c<{*some more decls*}}

The newly defined x column specifier can then be used in the preamble arguments of all array and tabular environments in which one needs columns of this form.

Quite often you may need math mode and LR mode columns inside a tabular or array environment. Thus, you can define the following column specifiers:

> \newcolumntype{C}{>{$}c<{$}}
> \newcolumntype{L}{>{$}l<{$}}
> \newcolumntype{R}{>{$}r<{$}}

From now on you can use C to get centered LR mode in an array environment, or centered math mode in a tabular environment.

The \newcolumntype command takes the same first optional argument as \newcommand, which declares the number of arguments of the column specifier being defined. However, \newcolumntype does not take the additional optional

argument forms of \newcommand; in the current implementation column specifiers
may have only mandatory arguments.

Super-con-scious-ness is a long word	Possibil-ités et es-pérances	Moge-lijkheden en hoop
Ragged left text in column one	Centered text in column two	Ragged right text in column three

```
\usepackage{array}
\newcolumntype{P}[1]
   {>{#1\hspace{0pt}\arraybackslash}p{14mm}|}
\begin{tabular}
     {|P{\raggedleft}P{\centering}P{\raggedright}}
\hline
  Superconsciousness is a long word    &
  Possibilit\'es et esp\'erances       &
  Moge\-lijk\-heden en hoop      \\\hline
  Ragged left text in column one        &
  Centered text    in column two        &
  Ragged right text in  column three \\\hline
\end{tabular}
```

5-2-12

A rather different use of the \newcolumntype command takes advantage of
the fact that the replacement text in \newcolumntype may refer to more than
one column. The following example shows the definition of a preamble option Z.
Modifying the definition in the document preamble would change the layout of all
tables in the document using this preamble option in a consistent manner.

one	two	three
1	2	3

```
\usepackage{array}  \newcolumntype{Z}{clr}
\begin{tabular}{Z} one&two&three\\1&2&3 \end{tabular}
```

5-2-13

The replacement text in a \newcolumntype command can be any of the primitives of array, or any new letter defined in another \newcolumntype command.

Any column specification in a tabular environment that uses one of these
newly defined column types is "expanded" to its primitive form during the first
stage of table processing. This means that in some circumstances error messages
generated when parsing the column specification refer to the preamble argument
after it has been rewritten by the \newcolumntype system, not to the preamble
entered by the user.

To display a list of all currently active \newcolumntype definitions on the
terminal, use the \showcols command in the preamble.

*Debugging column
type declarations*

5.3   Calculating column widths

As described in Appendix A.2, LATEX has two distinct modes for setting text: LR
mode, in which the text is set in a single line, and paragraph mode, in which text
is broken into lines of a specified length. This distinction strongly influences the
design of the LATEX table commands. The l, c, and r column types specify table
entries set in LR mode whereas p, and the array package m and t types, specify
table entries set in paragraph mode.

The need to specify the width of paragraph mode entries in advance sometimes causes difficulties when setting tables. We will describe several approaches
that calculate the required column widths based on the required total width of
the table and/or the table contents.

5.3.1 Explicit calculation of column widths

The environment `tabularc` can generate a table with a given number of equal-
width columns and a total width for the table equal to `\linewidth`. This approach
uses the calc package, discussed in Appendix A.3.1. It also uses the command
`\tabularnewline`, mentioned in Section 5.2.1. The environment takes the number of columns as its argument. This number (let us call it x) is used to calculate
the actual width of each column by subtracting two x times the column separation
and $(x + 1)$ times the width of the rules from the width of the line. The remaining
distance is divided by x to obtain the length of a single column. The contents of
the column are centered, and hyphenation of the first word is allowed.

```
\usepackage{array,calc}    \newlength\mylen
\newenvironment{tabularc}[1]
 {\setlength\mylen
          {\linewidth/(#1)-\tabcolsep*2-\arrayrulewidth*(#1+1)/(#1)}%
  \par\noindent                % new paragraph, flush left start
  \begin{tabular*}{\linewidth}%
    {*{#1}{|>{\centering\hspace{0pt}} p{\the\mylen}}|}}
 {\end{tabular*}\par}
\begin{tabularc}{3}
\hline
Material in column one & column two & This is column three
\tabularnewline\hline
... text omitted ...
```

5-3-1

Material in column one	column two	This is column three
Column one again	and column two	This is column three
Once more column one	column two	Last time column three

Calculating column widths in this way gives you full control over the amount
of space allocated to each column. Unfortunately, it is difficult to incorporate
information depending on the contents of the table into the calculation. For example, if some columns in the table use the c column type and so are set to their
natural width, you may wish to allocate the remaining space among the columns
using paragraph mode. As this width is not known until after the table has been
typeset, it is not possible to calculate all widths in advance. Two packages implement different algorithms that set the table multiple times so as to allocate widths
to certain columns. The first, tabularx, essentially tries to allocate space equally

between specified paragraph mode columns. The second, tabulary, tries to allocate more space to columns that contain "more data".

5.3.2   tabularx—**Automatic calculation of column widths**

The package tabularx (by David Carlisle) implements a version of the tabular* environment in which the widths of certain columns are calculated automatically depending on the total width of the table. The columns whose widths are automatically calculated are denoted in the preamble by the X qualifier. The latter column specification will be converted to p{*some value*} once the correct column width has been calculated.

```
\usepackage{tabularx}
\newcolumntype{Y}{>{\small\raggedright\arraybackslash}X}
```
5-3-2
```
\noindent\begin{tabularx}{100mm}{|Y|Y|Y|}
... text omitted ...
```

The Two Gentlemen of Verona	The Taming of the Shrew	The Comedy of Errors
Love's Labour's Lost	A Midsummer Night's Dream	The Merchant of Venice
The Merry Wives of Windsor	Much Ado About Nothing	As You Like It
Twelfth Night	Troilus and Cressida	Measure for Measure
All's Well That Ends Well	Pericles Prince of Tyre	The Winter's Tale
Cymbeline	The Tempest	

Changing the *width* argument to specify a width of \linewidth will produce the following table layout:

```
\usepackage{tabularx}
\newcolumntype{Y}{>{\small\raggedright\arraybackslash}X}
```
5-3-3
```
\noindent\begin{tabularx}{\linewidth}{|Y|Y|Y|}
... text omitted ...
```

The Two Gentlemen of Verona	The Taming of the Shrew	The Comedy of Errors
Love's Labour's Lost	A Midsummer Night's Dream	The Merchant of Venice
The Merry Wives of Windsor	Much Ado About Nothing	As You Like It
Twelfth Night	Troilus and Cressida	Measure for Measure
All's Well That Ends Well	Pericles Prince of Tyre	The Winter's Tale
Cymbeline	The Tempest	

Commands used to
typeset the X
columns
By default, the X specification is turned into p{*some value*}. Such narrow columns often require a special format, which may be achieved using the > syntax. Thus, you may give a specification like >{\small}X.

Another format that is useful in narrow columns is ragged right. As noted earlier, one must use the command \tabularnewline to end the table row if the last entry in row is being set ragged right. This specification may saved with \newcolumntype{Y}{>{\small\raggedright}X} (perhaps additionally adding \arraybackslash to make \\ denote the end of a row again). You may then use Y as a tabularx preamble argument.

The X columns are set using the p column, which corresponds to \parbox[t]. You may want to set the columns with, for example, an m column corresponding to \parbox[c]. It is impossible to change the column type using the > syntax, so another system is provided. The command \tabularxcolumn can be defined as a macro, with one argument, which expands to the tabular preamble specification to be used for X henceforth. When the command is executed, the supplied argument determines the actual column width.

The default definition is \newcommand\tabularxcolumn[1]{p{#1}}. A possible alternative definition is

```
\renewcommand\tabularxcolumn[1]{>{\small}m{#1}}
```

Column widths
Normally, all X columns in a single table are set to the same width. It is nevertheless possible to make tabularx set them to different widths. A preamble like the following

```
>{\setlength\hsize{.5\hsize}}X>{\setlength\hsize{1.5\hsize}}X
```

specifies two columns; the second column will be three times as wide as the first. However, when using this method two rules should be obeyed:

- The sum of the widths of all X columns should remain unchanged. In the above example, the new widths should add up to the width of two standard X columns.

- Any \multicolumn entries that cross any X column should not be used.

Superconsciousness is a long word	Mogelijkheden en hoop
Some text in column one	A somewhat longer text in column two

```
\usepackage{tabularx}    \tracingtabularx
\noindent
\begin{tabularx}{\linewidth}%
    {|>{\setlength\hsize{.85\hsize}}X|%
      >{\setlength\hsize{1.15\hsize}}X|}
Superconsciousness is a long word   &
Moge\-lijk\-heden en hoop                   \\
Some text in column one             &
A somewhat longer text in  column two \\
\end{tabularx}
```

5-3-4

If a \tracingtabularx declaration is made, say, in the document preamble, then all following tabularx environments will print information to the terminal and the log file about column widths as they repeatedly reset the tables to find the correct widths. For instance, the last example produced the following log:

Tracing tabularx calculations

```
Package tabularx Warning: Target width: \linewidth  = 207.0pt..

(tabularx)      Table Width    Column Width    X Columns
(tabularx)        439.19998pt    207.0pt         3
(tabularx)        206.99998pt     90.90001pt     2
(tabularx) Reached target.
```

5.3.3   tabulary—Column widths based on content

An alternative algorithm for determining column widths is provided by the tabulary package (also written by David Carlisle), which defines the tabulary environment. It is most suitable for cases in which the column widths must be calculated based on the content of the table. This often arises when you use LaTeX to typeset documents originating as SGML/XML or HTML, which typically employ a different table model in which multiple line material does not have a prespecified width and the layout is left more to the formatter.

The tabulary package provides the column types shown in Table 5.3 on the next page plus those provided by the array package in Table 5.2 on page 244, and any other preamble options defined via \newcolumntype.

> \begin{tabulary}{*width*}[*pos*]{*cols*} *rows* \end{tabulary}

The main feature of this package is its provision of versions of the p column specifier in which the width of the column is determined automatically depending on the table contents. The following example is rather artificial as the table only has one row. Nevertheless, it demonstrates that the aim of the column width allocation made by tabulary is to achieve equal row height. Normally, of course, the same row will not hold the largest entry of each column but in many cases of tabular material, the material in each cell of a given column has similar characteristics. In those situations the width allocation appears to provide reasonable results.

```
\usepackage{tabulary}
\setlength\tymin{10pt}
\setlength\tymax{\maxdimen}
```

a	b	c c c c	d d d d d d d d d d d d d
	b	c c c c	d d d d d d d d d d d d d
	b	c c c c	d d d d d d d d d d d d d
	b	c c c c	d d d d d d d d d d d d d
		c c	d d d d d d d

```
\begin{tabulary}{200pt}{|C|C|C|C|}
a & b b b b &
c c c c c c c c c c c c c c c c &
d d d d d d d d d d d d d d d d
... text omitted ...
```

J	Justified p column set to some width to be determined
L	Flush left p column set to some width to be determined
R	Flush right p column set to some width to be determined
C	Centered p column set to some width to be determined

Table 5.3: The preamble options in the tabulary package

Controlling the column width allocation

The tabulary package has two length parameters, \tymin and \tymax, which control the allocation of widths. By default, widths are allocated to each L, C, R, or J column in proportion to the natural width of the longest entry in each column. To determine this width tabulary always sets the table twice. In the first pass the data in L, C, R, and J columns is set in LR mode (similar to data in columns specified by the standard preamble options such as c). Typically, the paragraphs that are contained in these columns are set on a single line, and the length of this line is measured. The table is then typeset a second time to produce the final result, with the widths of the columns being set as if with a p preamble option and a width proportional to the natural lengths recorded on the first pass.

To stop very narrow columns from being too "squeezed" by this process, any columns that are narrower than \tymin are set to their natural widths. This length may be set with \setlength and is arbitrarily initialized to 10pt. If you know that a column will be narrow, it may be preferable to use, say, c rather than C so that the tabulary mechanism is never invoked on that column, and the column is set to its natural width.

Similarly, one very large entry can force its column to be too wide. To prevent this problem, all columns with natural length greater than \tymax (as measured when the entries are set in LR mode) are set to the same width (with the proportion being taken as if the natural length was *equal* to \tymax). This width is initially set to twice the text width.

The table in the above example is dominated by the large entry in the fourth column. By setting \tymin to 30pt we can prevent the first two columns from becoming too narrow, and by setting \tymax to 200pt we can limit the width of the fourth column and produce a more even spread of column widths.

a	b b b b	c c c c c c c c c c c c c c c c c c	d d d d d d d d d d d d d d d d d d d d d d d d d d d d d d d d d d d d d d d d d d d d d d d d d d d d d d d d d

```
\usepackage{tabulary}
\setlength\tymin{30pt}
\setlength\tymax{200pt}

\begin{tabulary}{200pt}{|C|C|C|C|}
... text omitted ...
```

5-3-6

Narrow p columns are sometimes quite challenging to set, and so you may redefine the command \tyformat to be any declarations made just after the

\centering or \ragged... declaration. By default, it redefines \everypar to in-sert a zero space at the start of every paragraph, so the first word may be hyphen-ated. (See Section 5.2.1 on page 246.)

Like tabularx, tabulary supports the optional alignment argument of tabular. Also because the whole environment is saved and evaluated twice, care should be taken with any LaTeX constructs that may have side effects such as writ-ing to files.

5.3.4 Differences between tabular*, tabularx, and tabulary

All three of these environments take the same arguments, with the goal of produc-ing a table of a specified width. The main differences between them are described here:

- tabularx and tabulary modify the widths of the *columns*, whereas tabular* modifies the widths of the inter-column *spaces*.

- The tabular and tabular* environments may be nested with no restrictions. However, if one tabularx or tabulary environment occurs inside another, then the inner one *must* be enclosed within { }.

- The bodies of tabularx and tabulary environments are, in fact, the argu-ments to commands, so certain restrictions apply. The commands \verb and \verb* may be used, but they may treat spaces incorrectly, and their argu-ments cannot contain a % or an unmatched { or }.

  \verb *only partially supported*

- tabular* uses a primitive capability of TeX to modify the inter-column space of an alignment. tabularx has to set the table several times as it searches for the best column widths, and is therefore much slower. tabulary always sets the table twice. For the latter two environments the fact that the body is expanded several times may break certain TeX constructs. Be especially wary of commands that write to external files, as the data may be written several times when the table is reset.

- tabularx attempts to distribute space equally among the X columns to achieve the desired width, whereas tabulary attempts to allocate greater widths to columns with larger entries.

5.4 Multipage tabular material

With Leslie Lamport's original implementation, a tabular environment must al-ways fit on one page. If it becomes too large, the text will overwrite the page's bottom margin, and you will get an Overfull \vbox message.

Two package files are available to construct tables longer than one page, supertabular and longtable. They share a similar functionality, but use rather dif-ferent syntax. The longtable package uses a more complicated mechanism, working with TEX's output routine to obtain optimal page breaks and to preserve the width of columns across all pages of a table. However, this mechanism may require the document to be processed several times before the correct table widths are calculated. The `supertabular` package essentially breaks the table into a sequence of page-sized `tabular` environments, and each page is then typeset separately. This approach does not require multiple passes and works in a larger range of circumstances. In particular, the `longtable` package does not support two-column or multicolumn mode.

Multipage tables in multicolumn typesetting

5.4.1   supertabular—**Making multipage tabulars**

\begin{supertabular}{*cols*}	*rows* \end{supertabular}
\begin{supertabular*}{*width*}{*cols*}	*rows* \end{supertabular*}
\begin{mpsupertabular}{*cols*}	*rows* \end{mpsupertabular}
\begin{mpsupertabular*}{*width*}{*cols*}	*rows* \end{mpsupertabular*}

The package `supertabular` (originally created by Theo Jurriens, and revised by Johannes Braams) defines the environment `supertabular`. It uses the `tabular` environment internally, but it evaluates the amount of used space every time it encounters a \\ command. When this amount reaches the value of \textheight, the package automatically inserts an \end{tabular} command, starts a new page, and inserts the table head on the new page, continuing the `tabular` environment. This means that the widths of the columns, and hence the width of the complete table, can vary across pages.

Three variant environments are also defined. The `supertabular*` environment uses `tabular*` internally, and takes a mandatory *width* argument to specify the width of the table. The `mpsupertabular` and `mpsupertabular*` environments have the same syntax as `supertabular` and `supertabular*`, respectively, but wrap the table portion on each page in a `minipage` environment. This allows the use of the \footnote command inside the tables, with the footnote text being printed at the end of the relevant page.

Inside a `supertabular` environment new lines are defined as usual by \\ commands. All column definition commands can be used, including @{...} and p{...}. If the `array` package is loaded along with `supertabular`, the additional tabular preamble options may be used. You cannot, however, use the optional positioning arguments, like t and b, that can be specified with \begin{tabular} and \begin{tabular*}.

Several new commands are available for use with `supertabular` as described below. Each of these commands should be used before the `supertabular` environment, as they affect all following `supertabular` environments.

\tablehead{*rows*}	\tablefirsthead{*rows*}

The argument to \tablehead contains the rows of the table to be repeated at the top of every page. If \tablefirsthead is also included, the first heading will use these rows in preference to the rows specified by \tablehead. The argument may contain full rows (ended by \\) as well as inter-row material like \hline.

\tabletail{*rows*}   \tablelasttail{*rows*}

These commands specify material to be inserted at the end of each page of the table. If \tablelasttail is used, these rows will appear at the end of the table in preference to the rows specified by \tabletail.

\topcaption[*lot caption*]{*caption*}   \bottoncaption[*lot caption*]{*caption*}
\tablecaption[*lot caption*]{*caption*}

These commands specify a caption for the supertabular, either at the top or at the bottom of the table. The optional argument has the same use as the optional argument in the standard \caption command—namely, it specifies the form of the caption to appear in the list of tables. When \tablecaption is used the caption will be placed at the default location, which is at the top. This default may be changed within a package or class file by using the declaration \@topcaptionfalse.

The format of the caption may be customized using the caption package, as shown in Example 5-4-4 on page 262.

\shrinkheight{*length*}

The supertabular environment maintains an estimate of the amount of space left on the current page. The \shrinkheight command, which must appear at the start of a table row, may be used to reduce this estimate. In this way it may be used to control the page-breaking decisions made by supertabular.

Example of the supertabular environment

```
\usepackage{supertabular}
\tablecaption{The ISOGRK3 entity set}
\tablehead
    {\bfseries Entity&\bfseries  Unicode Name&\bfseries Unicode\\ \hline}
\tabletail
    {\hline \multicolumn{3}{r}{\emph{Continued on next page}}\\}
\tablelasttail{\hline}
\begin{supertabular}{lll}
alpha              & GREEK SMALL LETTER ALPHA           & 03B1\\
beta               & GREEK SMALL LETTER BETA            & 03B2\\
chi                & GREEK SMALL LETTER CHI             & 03C7\\
Delta              & GREEK CAPITAL LETTER DELTA         & 0394\\
delta              & GREEK SMALL LETTER DELTA           & 03B4\\
epsi               & GREEK SMALL LETTER EPSILON         & 03B5\\
epsis              & GREEK LUNATE EPSILON SYMBOL        & 03F5\\
... text omitted ...
```

5-4-1

———— Page 1 ————　　　　　———— Page 2 ————

Table 1: The ISOGRK3 entity set

Entity	Unicode Name	Unicode
alpha	GREEK SMALL LETTER ALPHA	03B1
beta	GREEK SMALL LETTER BETA	03B2
chi	GREEK SMALL LETTER CHI	03C7
Delta	GREEK CAPITAL LETTER DELTA	0394
delta	GREEK SMALL LETTER DELTA	03B4
epsi	GREEK SMALL LETTER EPSILON	03B5
epsis	GREEK LUNATE EPSILON SYMBOL	03F5
epsiv	GREEK SMALL LETTER EPSILON	03B5
eta	GREEK SMALL LETTER ETA	03B7
Gamma	GREEK CAPITAL LETTER GAMMA	0393
gamma	GREEK SMALL LETTER GAMMA	03B3
gammad	GREEK SMALL LETTER DIGAMMA	03DD
iota	GREEK SMALL LETTER IOTA	03B9
kappa	GREEK SMALL LETTER KAPPA	03BA
kappav	GREEK KAPPA SYMBOL	03F0
Lambda	GREEK CAPITAL LETTER LAMDA	039B
lambda	GREEK SMALL LETTER LAMDA	03BB
mu	GREEK SMALL LETTER MU	03BC
nu	GREEK SMALL LETTER NU	03BD
Omega	GREEK CAPITAL LETTER OMEGA	03A9
omega	GREEK SMALL LETTER OMEGA	03C9
Phi	GREEK CAPITAL LETTER PHI	03A6

Continued on next page

Entity	Unicode Name	Unicode
phis	GREEK PHI SYMBOL	03D5
phiv	GREEK SMALL LETTER PHI	03C6
Pi	GREEK CAPITAL LETTER PI	03A0
pi	GREEK SMALL LETTER PI	03C0
piv	GREEK PI SYMBOL	03D6
Psi	GREEK CAPITAL LETTER PSI	03A8
psi	GREEK SMALL LETTER PSI	03C8
rho	GREEK SMALL LETTER RHO	03C1
rhov	GREEK RHO SYMBOL	03F1
Sigma	GREEK CAPITAL LETTER SIGMA	03A3
sigma	GREEK SMALL LETTER SIGMA	03C3
sigmav	GREEK SMALL LETTER FINAL SIGMA	03C2
tau	GREEK SMALL LETTER TAU	03C4
Theta	GREEK CAPITAL LETTER THETA	0398
thetas	GREEK SMALL LETTER THETA	03B8
thetav	GREEK THETA SYMBOL	03D1
Upsi	GREEK UPSILON WITH HOOK SYMBOL	03D2
upsi	GREEK SMALL LETTER UPSILON	03C5
Xi	GREEK CAPITAL LETTER XI	039E
xi	GREEK SMALL LETTER XI	03BE
zeta	GREEK SMALL LETTER ZETA	03B6

———— Page 1 ————　　　　　———— Page 2 ————

Example of the `supertabular*` environment

The width of a `supertabular` environment can be fixed to a given width, such as the width of the text, `\textwidth`. In the example below, in addition to specifying `supertabular*`, a rubber length has been introduced between the last two columns that allows the table to be stretched to the specified width. As usual with supertabular, each page of the table is typeset separately. The example demonstrates that the result may have different spacings between the columns on the first (left) and second (right) page.

```
\usepackage{array,supertabular}
\tablecaption{The ISOGRK3 entity set}
\tablefirsthead
      {\bfseries Entity&\bfseries Unicode Name&\bfseries Unicode\\ \hline}
\tablehead
      {\bfseries Entity&\bfseries Unicode Name&\bfseries Unicode\\ \hline}
\tabletail{\hline \multicolumn{3}{r}{\emph{Continued on next page}}\\}
\tablelasttail{\hline}
\centering
\begin{supertabular*}{\textwidth}{ll!{\extracolsep{\fill}}l}
alpha             & GREEK SMALL LETTER ALPHA        & 03B1\\
beta              & GREEK SMALL LETTER BETA         & 03B2\\
chi               & GREEK SMALL LETTER CHI          & 03C7\\
... text omitted ...
```

5-4-2

――――――――― Page 1 ―――――――――   ――――――――― Page 2 ―――――――――

Table 1: The ISOGRK3 entity set

Entity	Unicode Name	Unicode
alpha	GREEK SMALL LETTER ALPHA	03B1
beta	GREEK SMALL LETTER BETA	03B2
chi	GREEK SMALL LETTER CHI	03C7
Delta	GREEK CAPITAL LETTER DELTA	0394
delta	GREEK SMALL LETTER DELTA	03B4
epsi	GREEK SMALL LETTER EPSILON	03B5
epsis	GREEK LUNATE EPSILON SYMBOL	03F5
epsiv	GREEK SMALL LETTER EPSILON	03B5
eta	GREEK SMALL LETTER ETA	03B7
Gamma	GREEK CAPITAL LETTER GAMMA	0393
gamma	GREEK SMALL LETTER GAMMA	03B3
gammad	GREEK SMALL LETTER DIGAMMA	03DD
iota	GREEK SMALL LETTER IOTA	03B9
kappa	GREEK SMALL LETTER KAPPA	03BA
kappav	GREEK KAPPA SYMBOL	03F0
Lambda	GREEK CAPITAL LETTER LAMDA	039B
lambda	GREEK SMALL LETTER LAMDA	03BB
mu	GREEK SMALL LETTER MU	03BC
nu	GREEK SMALL LETTER NU	03BD
Omega	GREEK CAPITAL LETTER OMEGA	03A9
omega	GREEK SMALL LETTER OMEGA	03C9

Continued on next page

Entity	Unicode Name	Unicode
Phi	GREEK CAPITAL LETTER PHI	03A6
phis	GREEK PHI SYMBOL	03D5
phiv	GREEK SMALL LETTER PHI	03C6
Pi	GREEK CAPITAL LETTER PI	03A0
pi	GREEK SMALL LETTER PI	03C0
piv	GREEK PI SYMBOL	03D6
Psi	GREEK CAPITAL LETTER PSI	03A8
psi	GREEK SMALL LETTER PSI	03C8
rho	GREEK SMALL LETTER RHO	03C1
rhov	GREEK RHO SYMBOL	03F1
Sigma	GREEK CAPITAL LETTER SIGMA	03A3
sigma	GREEK SMALL LETTER SIGMA	03C3
sigmav	GREEK SMALL LETTER FINAL SIGMA	03C2
tau	GREEK SMALL LETTER TAU	03C4
Theta	GREEK CAPITAL LETTER THETA	0398
thetas	GREEK SMALL LETTER THETA	03B8
thetav	GREEK THETA SYMBOL	03D1
Upsi	GREEK UPSILON WITH HOOK SYMBOL	03D2
upsi	GREEK SMALL LETTER UPSILON	03C5
Xi	GREEK CAPITAL LETTER XI	039E
xi	GREEK SMALL LETTER XI	03BE
zeta	GREEK SMALL LETTER ZETA	03B6

――――――――― Page 1 ―――――――――   ――――――――― Page 2 ―――――――――

5.4.2 longtable—Alternative multipage tabulars

As pointed out at the beginning of this section, for more complex long tables, where you want to control the width of the table across page boundaries, the package longtable (by David Carlisle, with contributions from David Kastrup) should be considered. Like the supertabular environment, it shares some features with the table environment. In particular it uses the same counter, table, and has a similar \caption command. The \listoftables command lists tables produced by either the table or longtable environment.

The main difference between the supertabular and longtable environments is that the latter saves the information about the width of each longtable environment in the auxiliary .aux file. It then uses this information on a subsequent run to identify the widest column widths needed for the table in question. The use of the .aux file means that care should be taken when using the longtable in conjunction with the \nofiles command. One effect of \nofiles is to suppress the writing of the .aux file, so this command should not be used until after the final edits of that table have been made and the package has recorded the optimal column widths in the auxiliary file.

Use of the .aux *file*

To compare the two packages, Example 5-4-1 on page 257 is repeated here, but now uses longtable rather than supertabular. You can see that the width of the table is identical on both pages (the left and right parts of the picture). Note that in longtable, most of the table specification is *within* the longtable environment; in supertabular the specification of the table headings occurs via commands executed *before* the supertabular environment.

```
\usepackage{longtable}
\begin{longtable}{lll}
   \caption{The ISOGRK3 entity set}\\
      \bfseries Entity&\bfseries  Unicode Name&\bfseries  Unicode\\ \hline
\endfirsthead
      \bfseries Entity&\bfseries  Unicode Name&\bfseries  Unicode\\ \hline
\endhead
   \hline \multicolumn{3}{r}{\emph{Continued on next page}}
\endfoot
   \hline
\endlastfoot
alpha                & GREEK SMALL LETTER ALPHA              & 03B1\\
beta                 & GREEK SMALL LETTER BETA               & 03B2\\
chi                  & GREEK SMALL LETTER CHI                & 03C7\\
... text omitted ...
```

5-4-3

──── Page 1 ────

Table 1: The ISOGRK3 entity set

Entity	Unicode Name	Unicode
alpha	GREEK SMALL LETTER ALPHA	03B1
beta	GREEK SMALL LETTER BETA	03B2
chi	GREEK SMALL LETTER CHI	03C7
Delta	GREEK CAPITAL LETTER DELTA	0394
delta	GREEK SMALL LETTER DELTA	03B4
epsi	GREEK SMALL LETTER EPSILON	03B5
epsis	GREEK LUNATE EPSILON SYMBOL	03F5
epsiv	GREEK SMALL LETTER EPSILON	03B5
eta	GREEK SMALL LETTER ETA	03B7
Gamma	GREEK CAPITAL LETTER GAMMA	0393
gamma	GREEK SMALL LETTER GAMMA	03B3
gammad	GREEK SMALL LETTER DIGAMMA	03DD
iota	GREEK SMALL LETTER IOTA	03B9
kappa	GREEK SMALL LETTER KAPPA	03BA
kappav	GREEK KAPPA SYMBOL	03F0
Lambda	GREEK CAPITAL LETTER LAMDA	039B
lambda	GREEK SMALL LETTER LAMDA	03BB
mu	GREEK SMALL LETTER MU	03BC
nu	GREEK SMALL LETTER NU	03BD
Omega	GREEK CAPITAL LETTER OMEGA	03A9
omega	GREEK SMALL LETTER OMEGA	03C9
Phi	GREEK CAPITAL LETTER PHI	03A6
phis	GREEK PHI SYMBOL	03D5
phiv	GREEK SMALL LETTER PHI	03C6

Continued on next page

──── Page 1 ────

──── Page 2 ────

Entity	Unicode Name	Unicode
Pi	GREEK CAPITAL LETTER PI	03A0
pi	GREEK SMALL LETTER PI	03C0
piv	GREEK PI SYMBOL	03D6
Psi	GREEK CAPITAL LETTER PSI	03A8
psi	GREEK SMALL LETTER PSI	03C8
rho	GREEK SMALL LETTER RHO	03C1
rhov	GREEK RHO SYMBOL	03F1
Sigma	GREEK CAPITAL LETTER SIGMA	03A3
sigma	GREEK SMALL LETTER SIGMA	03C3
sigmav	GREEK SMALL LETTER FINAL SIGMA	03C2
tau	GREEK SMALL LETTER TAU	03C4
Theta	GREEK CAPITAL LETTER THETA	0398
thetas	GREEK SMALL LETTER THETA	03B8
thetav	GREEK THETA SYMBOL	03D1
Upsi	GREEK UPSILON WITH HOOK SYMBOL	03D2
upsi	GREEK SMALL LETTER UPSILON	03C5
Xi	GREEK CAPITAL LETTER XI	039E
xi	GREEK SMALL LETTER XI	03BE
zeta	GREEK SMALL LETTER ZETA	03B6

──── Page 2 ────

`\begin{longtable}[`*align*`]{`*cols*`}` *rows* `\end{longtable}`

The syntax of the longtable environment is modeled on that of the tabular environment. The main difference is that the optional *align* argument specifies *horizontal* alignment rather than vertical alignment as is the case with tabular.

The *align* argument may have the value [c], [l], or [r], to specify centering, left, or right alignment of the table, respectively. If this optional argument is omit- *Horizontal* ted then the alignment of the table is controlled by the two length parameters, *alignment* \LTleft and \LTright. They have default values of \fill, so by default tables will be centered.

Any length can be specified for these two parameters, but at least one of them should be a rubber length so that it fills up the width of the page, unless rubber lengths are added between the columns using the \extracolsep command. For instance, a table can be set flush left using the definitions

```
\setlength\LTleft{0pt}   \setlength\LTright{\fill}
```

or just by specifying \begin{longtable}[l].

You can, for example, use the \LTleft and \LTright parameters to typeset a multipage table filling the full width of the page. Example 5-4-2 on page 258, *Using parameters to* which used supertabular*, may be typeset using longtable and the declara- *control table width* tions shown below:

```
\setlength\LTleft{0pt}   \setlength\LTright{0pt}
\begin{longtable}{ll!{\extracolsep{\fill}}l}
```

In general, if \LTleft and \LTright are fixed lengths, the table will be set to the width of \textwidth − \LTleft − \LTright.

Before and after the table, longtable inserts vertical space controlled *Vertical space* by the length parameters \LTpre and \LTpost. Both default to the length *around table* \bigskipamount, but may be changed using \setlength.

Each row in the table is ended with the \\ command. As in the standard tabular environment, the command \tabularnewline is also available; it is use- *Table row* ful if \\ has been redefined by a command such as \raggedright. The star form *commands* * may also be used which inhibits a page break at this linebreak. In a tabular environment, this star form is accepted but has the same effect as \\. Conversely, a \\ command may be immediately followed by a \newpage command, which forces a page break at that point.

If a table row is terminated with \kill rather than \\, then the row will not be typeset. Instead, the entries will be used when determining the widths of the table columns. This action is similar to that of the \kill command in the tabbing environment.

The main syntactic difference between the longtable package and the supertabular package is that in longtable, rows to be repeated on each page *Rows used as the* as the table head or foot are declared *within* the environment body, rather than *table head and foot* before the environment as in supertabular. As shown in Example 5-4-3 on the preceding page, the table head and foot are specified by replacing the final \\ command by one of the commands listed below. Note that all of these commands, including those specifying the foot of the table, must come at the *start* of the environment. The command \endhead finishes the rows that will appear at the top of every page. The command \endfirsthead ends the declaration of rows for the start of the table. If this command is not used then the rows specified by \endhead will be used at the start of the table. Similarly, \endfoot finishes the rows that will appear at the bottom of every page, and \endlastfoot—if used—ends the rows to be displayed at the end of the table.

`\caption*`[*short title*]{*full title*}

The \caption command and its variant \caption* are essentially equivalent to writing a special \multicolumn entry

```
\multicolumn{n}{p{\LTcapwidth}}{...
```

where *n* is the number of columns of the table. The width of the caption can be controlled by redefining the parameter \LTcapwidth. That is, you can write \setlength\LTcapwidth{*width*} in the document preamble. The default value is 4 in. As with the \caption command in the figure and table environments, the optional argument specifies the text to appear in the list of tables if it is different from the text to appear in the caption.

When captions on later pages should differ from those on the first page, you should place the \caption command with the full text in the first heading, and put a subsidiary caption using \caption[ ] in the main heading, since (in this case) no entry is made in the list of tables. Alternatively, if the table number should not be repeated each time, you can use the \caption* command. As with the table environment, cross-referencing the table in the text is possible with the \label command.

By default, the caption is set in a style based on the caption style of the tables in standard LaTeX article class. If the caption package (described in Section 6.5.1) is used, then it is easy to customize longtable and table captions, keeping the style of captions consistent between these two environments.

Table 1: A standard table

1   2   3

Table 2: A longtable

1   2   3

Table 3: A supertabular

1   2   3

```
\usepackage{longtable,supertabular}
\usepackage[font=sl,labelfont=bf]{caption}
\begin{table}[t]\centering
 \caption{A standard table}
 \begin{tabular}{ccc}1&2&3\end{tabular}
\end{table}

\begin{longtable}{ccc}\caption{A longtable}\\
1&2&3\end{longtable}

\centering
\tablecaption{A supertabular}
\begin{supertabular}{ccc}1&2&3\\\end{supertabular}
```

5-4-4

You can use footnote commands inside the `longtable` environment. The footnote text appears at the bottom of each page. The footnote counter is not reset at
the beginning of the table, but uses the standard footnote numbering employed
in the rest of the document. If this result is not desired then you can set the
`footnote` counter to zero before the start of each table, and then reset it at the
end of the table if following footnotes must be numbered in the original sequence.

Footnotes in
`longtable`

To enable TEX to set very long multipage tables, it is necessary to break them
up into smaller chunks so that TEX does not have to keep everything in memory
at one time. By default, `longtable` uses a value of 20 rows per chunk, which can
be changed with a command such as `\setcounter{LTchunksize}{100}`. These
chunks do not affect page breaking. When TEX has a lot of memory available
LTchunksize can be set to a big number, which usually means that `longtable`
will be able to determine the final widths in fewer TEX runs. On most modern TEX
installations LTchunksize can safely be increased to accommodate several pages
of table in one chunk. Note that LTchunksize must be at least as large as the
number of rows in each of the head or foot sections.

Increase
LTchunksize *to*
reduce number of
LATEX runs required

Problems with multipage tables

When a float occurs on the same page as the start of a multipage table, unexpected results can occur. Both packages have code that attempts to deal with this
situation, but in some circumstances tables can float out of sequence. Placing a
`\clearpage` command before the table, thereby forcing a page break and flushing
out any floats, will usually correct the problem.

*Bad interaction
of floating
environments and
multipage tables*

Neither the `supertabular` nor the `longtable` environment will make a page
break after a line of text *within* a cell. Pages will be broken only between table
rows (or at `\hline` commands). If your table consists of large multiple line cells
set with the p preamble option, then LATEX may not be able to find a good page
break and may leave unwanted white space at the bottom of the page.

*p column entries
do not break*

The example below has room for six lines of text on each page but LATEX breaks
the page between the two table rows, leaving page 1 short.

```
\usepackage{longtable}
\begin{longtable}{llp{43mm}}
 entry 1.1 & entry 1.2 & entry 1.3, a long text entry taking several lines.\\
 entry 2.1 & entry 2.2 & entry 2.3, a long text entry taking several lines
                         when set in a narrow column.
\end{longtable}
```

5-4-5

Page 1 ———

entry 1.1   entry 1.2   entry 1.3, a long text
                        entry taking several
                        lines.

——— Page 1 ———

Page 2 ———

entry 2.1   entry 2.2   entry 2.3, a long text
                        entry taking several
                        lines when set in a
                        narrow column.

——— Page 2 ———

For some tables, the table rows form an important logical unit and the default behavior of not breaking within a row is desired. In other cases, it may be preferable to break the table manually to achieve a more pleasing page break. In the above example, we want to move the first two lines of page 2 to the bottom of page 1. Noting that TEX broke the third column entry after the word "several", we could end the table row at that point by using \\, insert blank entries in the first two columns of a new row, and place the remaining portion of the p entry in the final cell of this row. The first part of the split paragraph should be set with \parfillskip set to 0pt so that the final line appears full width, just as it would be if it were set as the first two lines of a larger paragraph.

```
\usepackage{longtable}
\begin{longtable}{llp{43mm}}
 entry 1.1 & entry 1.2 & entry 1.3, a long text entry taking several lines.\\
 entry 2.1 & entry 2.2 & \setlength{\parfillskip}{0pt}%
                         entry 2.3, a long text entry taking several\\
              &          & lines when set in a narrow column.
\end{longtable}
```

5-4-6

------------------ Page 1 ------------------   ------------------ Page 2 ------------------

entry 1.1   entry 1.2   entry 1.3, a long text   lines when set in a
                        entry taking several   narrow column.
                        lines.
entry 2.1   entry 2.2   entry 2.3, a long text
                        entry taking several

------------------ Page 1 ------------------   ------------------ Page 2 ------------------

5.5   Color in tables

The LATEX color commands provided by the color package are modeled on the font commands and may be used freely within tables. In particular, it is often convenient to use the array package preamble option > in order to apply a color to a whole column.

Day	Attendance
Monday	57
Tuesday	11
Wednesday	96
Thursday	122
Friday	210
Saturday	198
Sunday	40

```
\usepackage{array,color}
\begin{tabular}{>{\color{blue}\bfseries}lr}
Day & \textcolor{blue}{\bfseries Attendance}\\\hline
Monday&    57\\  Tuesday&    11\\
Wednesday& 96\\  Thursday& 122\\
Friday&    210\\ Saturday& 198\\
Sunday&    40
\end{tabular}
```

5-5-1

It is perhaps more common to use color as a background to highlight certain rows or columns. In this case using the \fcolorbox command from the color package does not give the desired result, as typically the background should cover the full extent of the table cell. The colortbl package (by David Carlisle) provides several commands to provide colored backgrounds and rules in tables.

Day	Attendance
Monday	57
Tuesday	11
Wednesday	96
Thursday	122
Friday	210
Saturday	198
Sunday	40
Total	724

```
\usepackage{colortbl}
\begin{tabular}
    {>{\columncolor{blue}\color{white}\bfseries}lr}
\rowcolor[gray]{0.8}
    \color{black} Day & \bfseries Attendance\\[2pt]
Monday&     57 \\   Tuesday&    11 \\
Wednesday& 96 \\   Thursday& 122 \\
Friday&    210 \\   Saturday& 198 \\
Sunday&     40 \\
\cellcolor[gray]{0.8}\color{black}Total& 724
\end{tabular}
```

5-5-2

5.6   Customizing table rules and spacing

In this section we look at a number of packages that extend the tabular functionality by providing commands for drawing special table rules and fine-tuning the row spacing.

5.6.1   Colored table rules

The colortbl package extends the style parameters for table rules, allowing colors to be specified for rules and for the space between double rules. The declarations \arrayrulecolor and \doublerulesepcolor take the same argument forms as the \color command of the standard LATEX color package.

Normally, these declarations would be used before a table, or in the document preamble, to set the color for all rules in a table. However, the rule color may be varied for individual rules using constructs very similar to the previous example.

```
\usepackage{colortbl} \setlength\arrayrulewidth{1pt}
\newcolumntype{B}{!{\color{blue}\vline}}
\newcommand\bhline
    {\arrayrulecolor{blue}\hline\arrayrulecolor{black}}
\newcommand\bcline[1]
    {\arrayrulecolor{blue}\cline{#1}\arrayrulecolor{black}}
\begin{tabular}{|cBc|c|}
\hline
  A  & B  & C   \\ \cline{1-1}\bcline{2-3}
  X  & Y  & Z   \\ \bhline
100 & 10 & 1   \\ \hline
\end{tabular}
```

A	B	C
X	Y	Z
100	10	1

5-6-1

5.6.2   Variable-width rules

Variable-width vertical rules may be constructed with the help of a !{*decl*} declaration and the basic TeX command \vrule with a width argument. This command
is used because it automatically fills the height of the column, whereas an explicit
height must be specified for LaTeX's \rule command. To construct variable-width
horizontal rules, it is again convenient to use a TeX command, \noalign, to set
the style parameter \arrayrulewidth so that it affects a single \hline, and then
reset the rule width for the rest of the table.

   In the example below, a new preamble option I is defined that produces a
wide vertical rule. Similarly, a \whline command is defined that produces a wide
horizontal rule.

```
\usepackage{array}
\newcolumntype{I}{!{\vrule width 3pt}}
\newlength\savedwidth
\newcommand\whline{\noalign{\global\savedwidth\arrayrulewidth
                           \global\arrayrulewidth 3pt}%
              \hline
              \noalign{\global\arrayrulewidth\savedwidth}}
\begin{tabular}{|cIc|c|} \hline
 A  & B  & C   \\ \hline
 X  & Y  & Z   \\ \whline
 100 & 10 & 1   \\ \hline \end{tabular}
```

A	B	C
X	Y	Z
100	10	1

5-6-2

5.6.3   hhline—**Combining horizontal and vertical lines**

The hhline package (by David Carlisle) introduces the command \hhline, which
behaves like \hline except for its interaction with vertical lines.

> \hhline{*decl*}

The declaration *decl* consists of a list of tokens with the following meanings:

=   A double \hline the width of a column.
–   A single \hline the width of a column.
~   A column without \hline; a space the width of a column.

| A \vline that "cuts" through a double (or single) \hline.
:   A \vline that is broken by a double \hline.

A double \hline segment between two \vlines.
t   The top rule of a double \hline segment.
b   The bottom rule of a double \hline segment.
*   *{3}{==#} expands to ==#==#==#, as in the * form for the preamble.

If a double \vline is specified (|| or ::), then the \hlines produced by \hhline are broken. To obtain the effect of an \hline "cutting through" the double \vline, use a #.

The tokens t and b can be used between two vertical rules. For instance, |tb| produces the same lines as #, but is much less efficient. The main uses for these are to make constructions like |t: (top left corner) and :b| (bottom right corner).

If \hhline is used to make a single \hline, then the argument should only contain the tokens "-", "~", and "|" (and * expressions).

An example using most of these features follows.

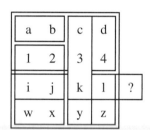

```
\usepackage{array,hhline}
\setlength\arrayrulewidth{.8pt}
\renewcommand\arraystretch{1.5}
\begin{tabular}{||cc||c|c||c}
              \hhline{|t:==:t:==:t|}
a & b & c & d \\ \hhline{|:==:|~|~||}
1 & 2 & 3 & 4 \\ \hhline{#==#~|=:b|-}
i & j & k & l & \multicolumn{1}{c|}{?}
              \\ \hhline{||--||---}
w & x & y & z \\ \hhline{|b:==:b:==:b|}
\end{tabular}
```

5-6-3

The lines produced by \hline consist of a single (TeX primitive) \hrule. The lines produced by \hhline are made up of lots of small line segments. TeX will place these very accurately in the .dvi file, but the dvi driver used to view or print the output might not line up the segments exactly. If this effect causes a problem, you can try increasing \arrayrulewidth to reduce the effect.

5.6.4 arydshln—Dashed rules

The arydshln package (by Hiroshi Nakashima) provides the ability to place dashed lines in tables. It is compatible with the array package, but must be loaded *after* array if both are used.

\hdashline[*dash/gap*]	\cdashline{*colspec*}[*dash/gap*]
\firsthdashline[*dash/gap*]	\lasthdashline[*dash/gap*]

The basic use of the package is very simple. A new preamble option ":" is introduced, together with two new commands \hdashline and \cdashline. These features may be used in the same way as the standard LaTeX "|" preamble option and \hline and \cline commands, except that dashed rather than solid lines are produced. If the array package is also loaded, then the commands \firsthdashline and \lasthdashline are defined. They are dashed analogues of the \firsthline and \lasthline commands defined in that package.

```
\usepackage{array,arydshln}
\setlength\extrarowheight{4pt}% extra space on row top
\begin{tabular}{|c::c|c|}
\hline
A    & B  & C  \\ \hline
X    & Y  & Z  \\ \hdashline
100  & 10 & 1  \\ \hline
\end{tabular}
```

5-6-4

Each of the commands takes an optional argument that may be used to specify the style of rule to be constructed. For example, an optional argument of [2pt/1pt] would specify that the rule should use 2pt dashes separated by 1pt spaces. The tabular preamble syntax does not allow for optional arguments on preamble options, so the ":" option does not have an optional argument in which to specify the dash style. Instead, an additional preamble option ";" is defined that takes a mandatory argument of the form *dash/gap*, as demonstrated in the example below.

The default size of the dashes and gaps is 4pt, which may be changed by setting the style parameters \dashlinedash and \dashlinegap via \setlength. This ability is shown in the example below.

```
\usepackage{array,arydshln}
\renewcommand\arraystretch{1.3333}% extra space evenly
                                  % distributed
\setlength\dashlinedash{1pt}
\setlength\dashlinegap{1pt}
\begin{tabular}{;{5pt/2pt}c::c;c;{5pt/2pt}}
\hdashline
A    & B  & C  \\ \hdashline
X    & Y  & Z  \\ \hdashline[5pt/2pt]
100  & 10 & 1  \\ \hdashline
\end{tabular}
```

5-6-5

Avoiding unsightly gaps The package may use any one of three methods for aligning the dashes within a table cell. The package may sometimes produce an overlarge gap at the edge of a table entry because there is not enough room to fit in the next "dash". If this happens you might try specifying an alternative placement algorithm using the command \ADLdrawingmode{m}, where m may be 1 (the default), 2, or 3.

The package documentation contains details of the placement algorithms used in each of these cases, but in practice you can just experiment with your particular table and dash styles to see which setting of \ADLdrawingmode gives the most pleasing result.

5.6.5   tabls—Controlling row spacing

One of the difficulties of using LATEX tables with irregular-sized entries is the challenge of obtaining a good spacing around large entries, especially in the presence of horizontal rules. The standard LATEX command \arraystretch or the \extrarowheight parameter introduced by the array package may help in this case. Both, however, affect all the rows in the table. It is sometimes desirable to have a finer-grained control, an ability that is provided by the tabls package (by Donald Arseneau). Note that tabls is incompatible with the array package and its derivatives. The package introduces three new parameters:

\tablinesep The minimum space between text on successive lines of a table. Negative values are treated as zero. The default is 1pt. If this parameter is set to 0pt, the code will not check the height of table entries to avoid touching text (which will emulate the default behavior of tabular).

\arraylinesep The equivalent to \tablinesep for the array environment.

\extrarulesep Extra space added above and below each \hline and \cline. There will be space of at least \extrarulesep + 0.5\tablinesep between an \hline and text in the following table row. Negative values will reduce the space below the line, until the line is touching the text. Larger negative values will *not* cause the line to overprint the text. The default value is 3pt.

In addition, the \hline command is extended with an optional argument like that of \\. This argument specifies additional space to insert below the rule.

A	B	C
100	10	1

```
\usepackage{tabls} \setlength\tablinesep{2pt}
\begin{tabular}{|c|c|c|} \hline
    \large A &\large B &\large C \\ \hline[5pt]
         100 &        10 &        1 \\[5pt] \hline
\end{tabular}
```

5-6-6

5.6.6   booktabs—Formal ruled tables

The vertical rules in a tabular environment are made up of a series of rule segments, one in each row of the table. Commands designed to improve vertical spacing between rows or around horizontal rules need to be carefully designed not to "break" any vertical rules by adding space between these rule segments. An alternative approach is taken by the booktabs package (by Simon Fear). It is designed to produce more formal tables according to a more traditional typographic style that uses horizontal rules of varying widths to separate table headings, but does not use any vertical rules. The | preamble option is not disabled when using this package, but its use is not supported and the extra commands for horizontal rules described below are not designed to work well in conjunction with vertical rules. Similarly, booktabs commands are not designed to support double rules as produced by the || or \hline\hline. *Do not use vertical rules* *Do not use double rules*

The booktabs commands may be used with the standard tabular environments, the extended versions provided by the array package, and in the longtable environment provided by the longtable package.

An example showing the most commonly used commands provided by the package is shown below.

```
\usepackage{booktabs}
\begin{tabular}{@{}llr@{}}
\toprule
   \multicolumn{2}{c}{Item} &\multicolumn{1}{c}{Price/lb} \\
\cmidrule(r){1-2}\cmidrule(l){3-3}
   Food & Category & \multicolumn{1}{c}{\$}\\
\midrule
   Apples & Fruit   & 1.50   \\
   Oranges & Fruit  & 2.00   \\
   Beef d & Meat    & 4.50   \\
\bottomrule
\end{tabular}
```

Item		Price/lb
Food	Category	$
Apples	Fruit	1.50
Oranges	Fruit	2.00
Beef d	Meat	4.50

5-6-7

\toprule [*width*]   \midrule [*width*]   \bottomrule [*width*]

The booktabs package provides the \toprule, \midrule, and \botrule commands. They are used in the same way as the standard \hline but have better vertical spacing, and widths specified by the length parameters \heavyrulewidth (for top and bottom rules) and \lightrulewidth (for mid-table rules). These parameters default to 0.08 em and 0.05 em, respectively (where the em is determined by the default document font at the point the package is loaded).

The spacing above and below the rules is determined by the length parameters: \abovetopsep (default 0 pt) is the space above top rules, \aboverulesep (default 0.4 ex) is the space above mid-table and bottom rules, \belowrulesep (default 0.65 ex) is the space below top and mid rules, and \belowbottomsep (default 0 pt) is the space below bottom rules.

If you need to control the widths of individual rules, all of these commands take an optional width argument. For example, \midrule[0.5pt] would produce a rule of width 0.5 pt.

When these commands are used inside a longtable environment, they may take an optional (*trim*) argument as described below for \cmidrule. This argument may be used to make the rules slightly less than the full width of the table.

\cmidrule [*width*] (*trim*) {*col1-col2*}

The \cmidrule command produces rules similar to those created with the standard LaTeX \cline command. The *col1-col2* argument specifies the columns over which the rule should be drawn. Unlike the rules created by \cline, these rules do not, by default, extend all the way to the edges of the column. Thus, one may use \cmidrule to produce rules on adjacent columns without them touching, as shown in the example above.

If the optional *width* argument is not specified, the rule will be of the width specified by the \cmidrulewidth length parameter (default 0.03 em).

By default, the rule extends all the way to the left, but is "trimmed" from the rightmost column by the length specified in the length parameter \cmidrulekern. The optional (*trim*) argument may contain one or more of the options l l*wd*, r r*wd*, where l and r indicate that the rule is to be trimmed from the left or right, respectively. Each l and r may optionally be followed by a width, in which case the rule is trimmed by this amount rather than by the default \cmidrulekern.

Normally, if one \cmidrule command immediately follows another, then the rules will be drawn across the specified columns on the same horizontal line. A command \morecmidrules is provided that may be used to terminate a row of mid-table rules. Following mid-table rules will then appear on a new line separated by the length \cmidrulesep, which by default is equal to \doublerulesep.

Each group of rules produced by \cmidrule is preceded and followed by a space of width \midrulesep, so this command generates the same spacing as \midrule. By default, however, the \cmidrule rules are lighter (thinner) than the rules produced by \midrule.

\addlinespace{*width*}

Extra space may be inserted between rows using \addlinespace. This command differs from using the optional argument to \\, as the former may also be used immediately before or after the rule commands.

If used in this position the command replaces the default spacing that would normally be produced by the rule. If the optional width argument is omitted it defaults to the length parameter \defaultaddspace (which defaults to 0.5 em).

\specialrule{*width*}{*abovespace*}{*belowspace*}

Finally, if none of the other commands produces a suitable rule then the command \specialrule may be used. It takes three mandatory arguments that specify the width of the rule, and the space above and below the rule.

As the intention of the package is to produce "formal" tables with well-spaced lines of consistent thickness, the package author warns against overuse of the optional arguments and special commands to produce lines with individual characteristics. Nevertheless, these features may be useful in special circumstances.

The example on the following page shows the effect of many of these options as well as demonstrating that overuse of the commands will produce a very unpleasing layout.

```
\usepackage{booktabs}
\begin{tabular}{@{}llr@{}}
\toprule
  \multicolumn{2}{c}{Item} &\multicolumn{1}{c}{Price/lb} \\
\cmidrule(r){1-2}\cmidrule(l){3-3}
  a & b & c \\
\cmidrule(l{2pt}r{2pt}){1-2}\cmidrule(l{2pt}r{2pt}){3-3}
\morecmidrules
\cmidrule(l{2pt}r{2pt}){2-3}
\addlinespace[5pt]
  Food& Category & \multicolumn{1}{c}{\$}\\
\midrule
  Apples & Fruit  & 1.50 \\
  Oranges & Fruit & 2.00 \\
\addlinespace
  Beef & Meat     & 4.50 \\
\specialrule{.5pt}{3pt}{3pt}
  x & y & z \\
\bottomrule
\end{tabular}
```

Item		Price/lb
a	b	c
Food	Category	$
Apples	Fruit	1.50
Oranges	Fruit	2.00
Beef	Meat	4.50
x	y	z

5-6-8

5.7   Further extensions

Two other package files extend the array package with additional functionality. The first provides for table entries spanning more than one row. The second makes it easier to align decimal numbers in a column.

You can simulate a cell spanning a few rows vertically by putting the material in a zero-height box and raising it.

100	qqq	
	A	B
20000000	10	10

```
\begin{tabular}{|c|c|c|}               \hline
        & \multicolumn{2}{c|}{qqq}\\\cline{2-3}
\raisebox{1.5ex}[0cm][0cm]{100}
        & A            & B            \\\hline
20000000 & 10          & 10           \\\hline
\end{tabular}
```

5-7-1

Similarly, you can use a standard tabular preamble of the form r@{.}l to create two table columns and produce the effect of a column aligned on a decimal point, but then the input looks rather strange. For an alternative solution, see Section 5.7.2 on page 274.

1.2
1.23
913.17

```
\begin{tabular}{r@{.}l}
  1 & 2 \\  1 & 23 \\ 913 & 17
\end{tabular}
```

5-7-2

This strategy is not always convenient, because you have to be aware that the "column" is really two columns of the table. This consideration becomes important when counting columns for the \multicolumn or \cline commands. Also, you need to locally set \extracolsep to 0pt if you use this construct in a tabular* environment, otherwise TeX may insert space after the decimal point to spread the table to the specified width.

5.7.1   multirow—**Vertical alignment in tables**

The multirow package (by Jerry Leichter) automates the procedure of constructing tables with columns spanning several rows by defining a \multirow command. Fine-tuning is possible by specifying optional arguments. This ability can be useful when any of the spanned rows are unusually large, when \strut commands are used asymmetrically about the centerline of spanned rows, or when descenders are not taken into account correctly. In these cases the vertical centering may not come out as desired, and the fixup argument *vmove* can then be used to introduce vertical shifts by hand.

> \multirow{*nrow*}[*njot*]{*width*}[*vmove*]{*contents*}

Inside an array, this command is somewhat less useful because the lines have an extra \jot of space (a length, by default equal to 3pt, that is used for opening up displays), which is not accounted for \multirow. Fixing this problem (in general) is almost impossible. Nevertheless, a semiautomatic fix is to set the length parameter \bigstrutjot to \jot, and then use the second argument *njot* of \multirow with a value equal to half the number of rows spanned.

You have some ability to control the formatting within cells. Just before the text to be typeset is expanded, the \multirowsetup macro is automatically executed to set up any special environment. Initially, \multirowsetup contains just \raggedright, but it can be redefined with \renewcommand.

The \multirow command works in one or more columns, as shown in the example below.

```
\usepackage{multirow}
\begin{tabular}{|l|l|l|l|l|}   \hline
\multirow{4}{14mm}{Text in column 1}
    & C2a & \multirow{4}{14mm}{Text in column 3}
              & C4a      \\
    & C2b &   & C4b      \\
    & C2c &   & C4c      \\
    & C2d &   & C4d      \\\hline
\end{tabular}
```

Text in column 1	C2a C2b C2c C2d	Text in column 3	C4a C4b C4c C4d

You are now in a position to typeset the small example shown at the beginning of this section without having to use the \raisebox command. First, you must change the alignment inside the \multirow paragraph to \centering. Next, you calculate the width of the text in the column, which is required by the \multirow command. If the column with the spanned rows has a fixed width, as in our other examples, this step is unnecessary.

```
\usepackage{multirow}

\renewcommand\multirowsetup{\centering}
\newlength\LL \settowidth\LL{100}
\begin{tabular}{|c|c|c|}          \hline
\multirow{2}{\LL}{100}&
        \multicolumn{2}{c|}{qqq}    \\\cline{2-3}
                       & A        & B    \\\hline
20000000               & 10       & 10   \\\hline
\end{tabular}
```

100	qqq	
	A	B
20000000	10	10

5-7-4

The effect of the optional vertical positioning parameter *vmove* can be seen below. Note the effect of the upward move by 3 mm of the lower third of the table.

Common text in column 1	Cell 1a
	Cell 1b
	Cell 1c
	Cell 1d
Common text in column 1	Cell 2a
	Cell 2b
	Cell 2c
	Cell 2d
Common text in column 1	Cell 3a
	Cell 3b
	Cell 3c
	Cell 3d

```
\usepackage{multirow}

\begin{tabular}{|l|l|}
\hline
\multirow{4}{25mm}{Common text in column 1}
& Cell 1a \\\cline{2-2} & Cell 1b\\\cline{2-2}
& Cell 1c \\\cline{2-2} & Cell 1d\\\hline
\multirow{4}{25mm}[-3mm]{Common text in column 1}
& Cell 2a \\\cline{2-2} & Cell 2b\\\cline{2-2}
& Cell 2c \\\cline{2-2} & Cell 2d\\\hline
\multirow{4}{25mm}[3mm]{Common text in column 1}
& Cell 3a \\\cline{2-2} & Cell 3b\\\cline{2-2}
& Cell 3c \\\cline{2-2} & Cell 3d\\\hline
\end{tabular}
```

5-7-5

5.7.2   dcolumn—**Decimal column alignments**

The dcolumn package (by David Carlisle) provides a system for defining columns of entries in array or tabular environments that are to be aligned on a "decimal point". Entries with no decimal part, those with no integer part, and blank entries are also dealt with correctly.

The package defines a "Decimal" tabular preamble option, D, that takes three arguments.

D{*inputsep*}{*outputsep*}{*decimal places*}

inputsep   A single character, used as separator (or "decimal point") in the source file (for example, "." or ",").

outputsep   The separator to be used in the output. It can be the same as the first argument, but may also be any math mode expression, such as `\cdot`.

decimal places   The maximum number of decimal places in the column. If this value is negative, any number of decimal places is allowed in the column, and all entries will be centered on the separator. Note that this choice can cause a column to be too wide (see the first two columns in the example below). Another possibility is to specify the number of digits *both* to the left and to the right of the decimal place, using an argument of the form *{left.right}* as described below.

If you do not want to use all three entries in the preamble, you can customize the preamble specifiers by using `\newcolumntype` as demonstrated below.

```
\newcolumntype{d}[1]{D{.}{\cdot}{#1}}
```

The newly defined "d" specifier takes a single argument specifying the number of decimal places. The decimal separator in the source file is the normal dot ".", while the output uses the math mode "·".

```
\newcolumntype{.}{D{.}{.}{-1}}
```

In this case the "." specifier has no arguments: the normal dot is used in both input and output. The typeset entries should be centered on the dot.

```
\newcolumntype{,}{D{,}{,}{2}}
```

The "," specifier defined here uses the comma "," as a decimal separator in both input and output, and the typeset column should have (at most) two decimal places after the comma.

These definitions are used in the following example, in which the first column, with its negative value for *decimal places* (signaling that the decimal point should be in the center of the column), is wider than the second column, even though they both contain the same input material.

1·2	1·2	1.2	1,2
1·23	1·23	12.5	300,2
1121·2	1121·2	861.20	674,29
184	184	10	69
·4	·4		,4
		.4	

```
\usepackage{dcolumn}
\newcolumntype{d}[1]{D{.}{\cdot}{#1}}
\newcolumntype{.}{D{.}{.}{-1}}
\newcolumntype{,}{D{,}{,}{2}}
\begin{tabular}{|d{-1}|d{2}|.|,|}
  1.2    & 1.2    &1.2     &1,2     \\
  1.23   & 1.23   &12.5    &300,2   \\
  1121.2 & 1121.2 &861.20  &674,29  \\
  184    & 184    &10      &69      \\
  .4     & .4     &        &,4      \\
         &        &.4      &        
\end{tabular}
```

If the table entries include only numerical data that must be aligned, the alignment forms shown in the above example should be sufficient. However, if the columns contain headings or other entries that will affect the width of the column, the positioning of the numbers within the column might not be as desired. In the example below, in the first column the numbers appear to be displaced toward the left of the column, although the decimal point is centered. In the second column the numbers are flush right under a centered heading, which is sometimes the desired effect but (especially if there are no table rules) can make the heading appear dissociated from the data. The final column shows the numbers aligned on the decimal point and centered as a block under the heading. This effect is achieved by using a third argument to the D preamble option of 4.2 specifying that at most four digits can appear to the left of the point, and two digits to the right of it.

wide heading	wide heading	wide heading
1000.20	1000.20	1000.20
123.45	123.45	123.45

```
\usepackage{dcolumn}
\begin{tabular}{|D..{-1}|D..{2}|D..{4.2}|}
\multicolumn{1}{|c|}{wide heading}&
\multicolumn{1}{c|}{wide heading}&
\multicolumn{1}{c|}{wide heading}\\[3pt]
  1000.20  & 1000.20  &1000.20 \\
  123.45   & 123.45   & 123.45
\end{tabular}
```

5-7-7

The following is a variant of an example in the *LATEX Manual* showing that D column alignments may be used for purposes other than aligning numerical data on a decimal point.

GG&A Hoofed Stock			
Year	Price low–high	Comments	Other
1971	97–245	Bad year for farmers in the West.	23,45
72	245–245	Light trading due to a heavy winter.	435,23
73	245–2001	No gnus was very good gnus this year.	387,56

```
\usepackage{dcolumn}
\newcolumntype{+}{D{/}{\mbox{--}}{4}}
\newcolumntype{,}{D{,}{,}{2}}
\begin{tabular}{|r||+|
      >{\raggedright}p{2.2cm}|,|}    \hline
\multicolumn{4}{|c|}{GG\&A Hoofed Stock}\\
\hline\hline
& \multicolumn{1}{c|}{Price}& &
\\ \cline{2-2} \multicolumn{1}{|c||}{Year}
& \mbox{low}/\mbox{high}
& \multicolumn{1}{c|}{Comments}
& \multicolumn{1}{c|}{Other}    \\ \hline
1971 & 97/245  &Bad year for farmers in
        the West. & 23,45        \\ \hline
  72 &245/245  &Light trading due to a
        heavy winter.  & 435,23\\ \hline
  73 &245/2001 &No gnus was very good
        gnus this year. & 387,56\\ \hline
\end{tabular}
```

5-7-8

5.8   Footnotes in tabular material

As stated in Section 3.2.2 on page 112, footnotes appearing inside tabular material are not typeset by standard LaTeX. Only the environments tabularx, longtable, mpsupertabular, and mpsupertabular* will automatically typeset footnotes.

As you generally want your "table notes" to appear just below the table, you will have to tackle the problem yourself by managing the note marks and, for instance, by using \multicolumn commands at the bottom of your tabular environment to contain your table notes.

5.8.1   Using minipage footnotes with tables

If a tabular or array environment is used inside a minipage environment, standard footnote commands may be used inside the table. In this case these footnotes will be typeset at the bottom of the minipage environment, as explained in Section 3.2.1 on page 110.

In the example below note the redefinition of \thefootnote that allows us to make use of the \footnotemark command inside the minipage environment. Without this redefinition \footnotemark would have generated a footnote mark in the style of the footnotes for the main page, as explained in Section 3.2.2.

PostScript Type 1 fonts

Courier[a]	cour, courb, courbi, couri
Charter[b]	bchb, bchbi, bchr, bchri
Nimbus[c]	unmr, unmrs
URW Antiqua[c]	uaqrrc
URW Grotesk[c]	ugqp
Utopia[d]	putb, putbi, putr, putri

---

[a]Donated by IBM.
[b]Donated by Bitstream.
[c]Donated by URW GmbH.
[d]Donated by Adobe.

5-8-1

```
\begin{minipage}{\linewidth}
\renewcommand\thefootnote{\thempfootnote}
\begin{tabular}{ll}
  \multicolumn{2}{c}{\bfseries PostScript
                      Type 1 fonts}              \\
  Courier\footnote{Donated by IBM.}
      & cour, courb, courbi, couri              \\
  Charter\footnote{Donated by Bitstream.}
      & bchb, bchbi, bchr, bchri                \\
  Nimbus\footnote{Donated by URW GmbH.}
      & unmr, unmrs                             \\
  URW Antiqua\footnotemark[\value{mpfootnote}]
      & uaqrrc                                  \\
  URW Grotesk\footnotemark[\value{mpfootnote}]
      & ugqp                                    \\
  Utopia\footnote{Donated by Adobe.}
      & putb, putbi, putr, putri
\end{tabular}
\end{minipage}
```

Of course, this approach does not automatically limit the width of the footnotes to the width of the table, so a little iteration with the minipage width argument might be necessary to achieve the desired effect.

5.8.2 threeparttable—Setting table and notes together

Another way to typeset table notes is with the package threeparttable, written by Donald Arseneau. This package has the advantage that it indicates unambiguously that you are dealing with notes inside tables. Moreover, it gives you full control of the actual reference marks and offers the possibility of having a caption for your tabular material. With this package the table notes are automatically set in a box with width set equal to the width of the table.

Table notes set to the width of the table

Normally, the threeparttable environment would be contained within a table environment so that the table would float. However, threeparttable may also be used directly, in which case it constructs a nonfloating table similar to the nonfloating table environment set-up described in Section 6-3-4 on page 295.

```
\usepackage{threeparttable}
\begin{threeparttable}
\caption[Example of a \texttt{threeparttable}
   environment]{\textbf{PostScript Type 1 fonts}}
\begin{tabular}{@{}ll@{}}
Courier\tnote{a} & cour, courb, courbi, couri  \\
Charter\tnote{b} & bchb, bchbi, bchr, bchri    \\
Nimbus\tnote{c}  & unmr, unmrs                 \\
URW Antiqua\tnote{c} & uaqrrc                  \\
URW Grotesk\tnote{c} & ugqp                    \\
Utopia\tnote{d}      & putb, putbi, putr, putri\\
\end{tabular}
\begin{tablenotes}
\item[a]Donated by IBM.
\item[b]Donated by Bitstream.
\item[c]Donated by URW GmbH.
\item[d]Donated by Adobe.
\end{tablenotes}

\begin{tablenotes}[flushleft,online]
\item[a]Donated by IBM.
\item[b]Donated by Bitstream.
\item[c]Donated by URW GmbH.
\item[d]Donated by Adobe.
\end{tablenotes}

\begin{tablenotes}[para]
\item[]Donated by:
\item[a]IBM, \item[b]Bitstream,
\item[c]URW GmbH,
\item[d]Adobe.
\end{tablenotes}
\end{threeparttable}
```

Table 1: **PostScript Type 1 fonts**

Courier[a]	cour, courb, courbi, couri
Charter[b]	bchb, bchbi, bchr, bchri
Nimbus[c]	unmr, unmrs
URW Antiqua[c]	uaqrrc
URW Grotesk[c]	ugqp
Utopia[d]	putb, putbi, putr, putri

  [a] Donated by IBM.
  [b] Donated by Bitstream.
  [c] Donated by URW GmbH.
  [d] Donated by Adobe.

a   Donated by IBM.
b   Donated by Bitstream.
c   Donated by URW GmbH.
d   Donated by Adobe.

  Donated by: [a] IBM,   [b] Bitstream, [c] URW GmbH,   [d] Adobe.

5-8-2

As its name suggests, the threeparttable environment consists of three parts. The **caption** consists of the usual \caption command (which may come before or after the table). The **table** may use one of the standard tabular or tabular* environments, the extended variants defined in the array package, or the tabularx environment defined in tabularx. Support for other tabular environments may be added in later releases, the package documentation lists the currently supported environments. The third part of a threeparttable is the text of the table **notes**, which consists of one or more tablenotes environments.

The threeparttable package offers several options to control the typesetting of the table notes:

para   Notes are set within a paragraph, without forced line beaks.

flushleft   No hanging indentation is applied to notes.

online   Note labels are printed normal size, not as superscripts.

normal   Normal default formatting is restored.

Each of these options may be used as a package option to set the default style for all such tables within the document. Alternatively, they may be used as shown in the example, on individual tablenotes environments.

In addition to these options the package has several commands that may be redefined to control the formatting in more specific ways than those provided by the package options. See the package documentation for details.

5.9   Applications

The following examples involve somewhat more complex placement requirements, allowing advanced functions such as the provision of nested tables. Here, we will put to work many of the features described in this chapter.

5.9.1   Managing tables with wide entries

Sometimes it is necessary to balance white space between narrow columns uniformly over the complete width of the table. For instance, the following table has a rather wide first row, followed by a series of narrow columns.

<table>
<tr><td colspan="3">this-is-a-rather-long-row</td><td></td></tr>
<tr><td>C1</td><td>C2</td><td>C3</td></tr>
<tr><td>2.1</td><td>2.2</td><td>2.3</td></tr>
<tr><td>3.1</td><td>3.2</td><td>3.3</td></tr>
</table>

```
\begin{tabular}{ccc}
\multicolumn{3}{c}{this-is-a-rather-long-row}\\
C1 &C2 &C3 \\ 2.1&2.2&2.3 \\ 3.1&3.2&3.3
\end{tabular}
```

5-9-1

You can put some rubber length in front of each column with the help of the \extracolsep command. The actual value of the rubber length is not important, as long as it can shrink enough to just fill the needed space. In this case you must, of course, specify a total width for the table. We could use \linewidth and make the table full width, but here we can obtain a better result by precalculating the width of the wide entry and specifying it as the total width of the `tabular*`.

```
\usepackage{array}
\newlength\Mylen

\settowidth\Mylen{this-is-a-rather-long-row}
\addtolength\Mylen{2\tabcolsep}
\begin{tabular*}{\Mylen}%
              {!{\extracolsep{4in minus 4in}}ccc}
\multicolumn{3}{c}{this-is-a-rather-long-row}\\
C1 &C2 &C3 \\ 2.1&2.2&2.3 \\ 3.1&3.2&3.3
\end{tabular*}
```

this-is-a-rather-long-row

C1	C2	C3
2.1	2.2	2.3
3.1	3.2	3.3

5-9-2

To achieve correct alignment, we needed to take into account the column separation (`\tabcolsep`) on both sides of an entry. Alternatively, we could have suppressed the inter-column spaces at the left and right of the `tabular*` by using `@{}` expressions.

5.9.2 Tables inside tables

The example below shows how, with a little bit of extra effort, you can construct complex table layouts with LaTeX.

`\firsthline`	`\lasthline`

The family of `tabular` environments allows vertical positioning with respect to the baseline of the text in which the environment appears. By default, the environment appears centered. This preference can be changed to align with the first or last line in the environment by supplying a `t` or `b` value to the optional position argument. Note that this approach does not work when the first or last element in the environment is an `\hline` command—in that case, the environment is aligned at the horizontal rule.

```
\usepackage{array}

Tables \begin{tabular}[t]{l}
  with no\\ hline \\ commands \\ used
\end{tabular}
versus tables
\begin{tabular}[t]{|l|}        \hline
  with some \\ hline \\ commands \\
\hline
\end{tabular} used.
```

Tables   with no   versus tables   used.
         hline
         commands
         used

| with some |
| hline |
| commands |

5-9-3

To achieve proper alignments you can use the two commands `\firsthline` and `\lasthline`, which are special versions of `\hline` defined in the array package. These commands enable you to align the information in the tables properly as long as their first or last lines do not contain extremely large objects.

5-9-4

Tables with no   versus tables   with some used.
        hline   hline
        commands   commands
        used

```
\usepackage{array}
Tables \begin{tabular}[t]{l}
 with no\\ hline \\ commands \\ used
\end{tabular}
versus tables
\begin{tabular}[t]{|l|} \firsthline
 with some \\ hline \\ commands \\
\lasthline
\end{tabular} used.
```

```
\setlength\extratabsurround{dim}
```

The implementation of the two commands contains an extra dimension, \extratabsurround, to add space at the top and the bottom of such an environment. It is helpful for properly aligning nested tabular material, as shown in the next example.

```
\usepackage{array}
\setlength\extratabsurround{5pt}
\begin{tabular}{|cc|}                                       \hline
\emph{name} & \emph{telephone}                        \\\hline\hline
    John & \begin{tabular}[t]{|cc|}                       \firsthline
          \emph{day} & \multicolumn{1}{c|}{\itshape telephone}
                                                        \\\hline\hline
          Wed & 5554434                                    \\\hline
          Mon &  \begin{tabular}[t]{|cc|}                 \firsthline
                 \emph{time} & \emph{telephone}         \\\hline\hline
                 8--10 & 5520104 \\ 1--5 & 2425588      \\\lasthline
                 \end{tabular}                          \\\lasthline
           \end{tabular}                                   \\\hline
Martin   & \begin{tabular}[t]{|cp{4.5cm}|}              \firsthline
          \emph{telephone} & \multicolumn{1}{c|}{\itshape instructions}
                                                        \\\hline\hline
          3356677 & Mary should answer forwarded message.   \\\lasthline
          \end{tabular}                                     \\\hline
 Peter   & \begin{tabular}[t]{|cl|}                      \firsthline
          \emph{month} &\multicolumn{1}{c|}{\itshape telephone}
                                                        \\\hline\hline
          Sep--May & 5554434  \\  Jun &  No telephone  \\
          Jul--Aug & 2211456  \\                           \lasthline
          \end{tabular}                                     \\\hline
\end{tabular}
```

name	telephone
John	day / telephone ...

(nested table structure)

		day	telephone
John		Wed	5554434
		Mon	time / telephone
			8–10 5520104
			1–5 2425588

Martin	telephone	instructions
	3356677	Mary should answer forwarded message.

Peter	month	telephone
	Sep–May	5554434
	Jun	No telephone
	Jul–Aug	2211456

5-9-5

A final example The LATEX code below shows how you can combine the various techniques and packages described earlier in this chapter. We used the package tabularx to generate a 12 column table in which columns 3 to 12 are of equal width. We used the package multirow to generate the stub head, "Prefix", which spans two rows in column 1. To position the stub head properly, we calculated the width of the title beforehand.

```
\usepackage{array,tabularx,multirow}
\newlength\Tl \settowidth{\Tl}{Prefix} \setlength\tabcolsep{1mm}
\newcommand\T[1]{$10^{#1}$}
\begin{tabularx}{\linewidth}{|l|l|*{10}{>{\small}X|}} \hline
\multicolumn{12}{|c|}{\textbf{Prefixes used in the SI system of units}}\\\hline
\multicolumn{2}{|c|}{Factor} &
\T{24}&\T{21}&\T{18}&\T{15}&\T{12}&\T{9}&\T{6}&\T{3}&\T{2}&\T{ }\\\cline{1-2}
\multirow{2}{\Tl}{Prefix}&Name   &
yotta &zetta &exa  &peta   &tera   &giga  &mega  &kilo  &hecto &deca \\
                        &Symbol &
... text omitted ...
```

5-9-6

Prefixes used in the SI system of units											
Factor		10^{24}	10^{21}	10^{18}	10^{15}	10^{12}	10^{9}	10^{6}	10^{3}	10^{2}	10
Prefix	Name	yotta	zetta	exa	peta	tera	giga	mega	kilo	hecto	deca
	Symbol	Y	Z	E	P	T	G	M	k	h	da
Prefix	Symbol	y	z	a	f	p	n	μ	m	c	d
	Name	yocto	zepto	atto	femto	pico	nano	micro	milli	centi	deci
Factor		10^{-24}	10^{-21}	10^{-18}	10^{-15}	10^{-12}	10^{-9}	10^{-6}	10^{-3}	10^{-2}	10^{-1}

## CHAPTER 6

Mastering Floats

Documents would be easier to read if all the material that belonged together was never split between pages. However, this is often technically impossible and TeX will, by default, split textual material between two pages to avoid partially filled pages. Nevertheless, when this outcome is not desired (as with figures and tables), the material must be "floated" to a convenient place, such as the bottom or the top of the current or next page, to prevent half-empty pages.

This chapter shows how "large chunks" of material can be kept conveniently on the same page by using a float object. We begin by introducing the parameters that define how LaTeX typesets its basic `figure` and `table` float environments, and we describe some of the packages that make it easy to control float placement (Section 6.2). We then continue by explaining how you can define and use your own floating environments, or, conversely, use LaTeX's `\caption` mechanism to enter information into the list of figures and tables for nonfloating material (Section 6.3.1).

It is often visually pleasing to include a "picture" inside a paragraph, with the text wrapping around it. Various packages have been written to achieve this goal more or less easily; in Section 6.4 we look at two of them in some detail.

The final section addresses the problem of customizing captions. There is a recognized need to be able to typeset the description of the contents of figures and tables in many different ways. This includes specifying sub-figures and sub-tables, each with its own caption and label, inside a larger float.

Many float-related packages have been developed over the years and we cannot hope to mention them all here. In fact, the packages that we describe often feature quite a few more commands than we are able to illustrate. Our aim is to enable you to make an educated choice and to show how a certain function can be obtained in a given framework. In each case consulting the original documentation will introduce you to the full possibilities of a given package.

6.1   Understanding float parameters

Floats are often problematic in the present version of LaTeX, because the system was developed at a time when documents contained considerably less graphical material than they do today. Placing floats (tables and figures) works relatively well as long as the space they occupy is not too large compared with the space taken up by the text. If a lot of floating material (pictures or tables) is present, however, then it is often the case that all material from a certain point onward floats to the end of the chapter or document. If this effect is not desired, you can periodically issue a `\clearpage` command, which will print all unprocessed floats. You can also try to fine-tune the float style parameters for a given document or use a package that allows you to always print a table or figure where it appears in the document. In the list below "float" stands for a table or a figure and a "float page" is a page that contains only floats and no text. Changes to most of the parameters will only take effect on the next page (not the current one).

`topnumber`   Counter specifying the maximum number of floats allowed at the top of the page (the default number is 2). This can be changed with the `\setcounter` command.

`bottomnumber`   Counter specifying the maximum number of floats allowed at the bottom of the page (the default number is 1). This can be changed with `\setcounter`.

`totalnumber`   Counter specifying the maximum number of floats allowed on a single page (the default number is 3). This can be changed with `\setcounter`.

`\topfraction`   Maximum fraction of the page that can be occupied by floats at the top of the page (e.g., 0.2 means 20% can be floats; the default value is 0.7). This can be changed with `\renewcommand`.

`\bottomfraction`   Maximum fraction of the page that can be occupied by floats at the bottom of the page (the default value is 0.3). This can be changed with `\renewcommand`.

`\textfraction`   Minimum fraction of a normal page that must be occupied by text (the default value is 0.2). This can be changed with `\renewcommand`.

`\floatpagefraction`   Minimum fraction of a float page that must be occupied by floats, thus limiting the amount of blank space allowed on a float page (the default value is 0.5). This can be changed with `\renewcommand`.

`dbltopnumber`   Analog of `topnumber` for double-column floats in two-column style (the default number is 2). This can be changed with `\setcounter`.

\dbltopfraction   Analog of \topfraction for double-column floats on a
    two-column page (the default value is 0.7). This can be changed with
    \renewcommand.

\dblfloatpagefraction   Analog of \floatpagefraction for a float page of
    double-column floats (the default value is 0.5). This can be changed with
    \renewcommand.

\floatsep   Rubber length specifying the vertical space added between floats ap-
    pearing at the top or the bottom of a page (the default is 12pt plus 2pt
    minus 2pt for 10pt and 11pt document sizes, and 14pt plus 2pt minus 4pt
    for 12pt document sizes). This can be changed with \setlength.

\textfloatsep   Rubber length specifying the vertical space added between
    floats, appearing at the top or the bottom of a page, and the text (the default
    is 20pt plus 2pt minus 4pt). This can be changed with \setlength.

\intextsep   Rubber length specifying the vertical space added below and above
    a float that is positioned in the middle of text when the h option is given (the
    default is similar to \floatsep). This can be changed with \setlength.

\dblfloatsep   Rubber length that is the analog of \floatsep for double-width
    floats on a two-column page (the default is like \floatsep). This can be
    changed with \setlength.

\dbltextfloatsep   Rubber length that is the analog of \textfloatsep for
    double-width floats on a two-column page (the default is like \textfloatsep
    on a text page, but is 8pt plus 2fil on a page that contains only floats). This
    can be changed with \setlength.

\topfigrule   Command to produce a separating item (by default, a rule) be-
    tween floats at the top of the page and the text. It is executed immediately
    before placing the \textfloatsep that separates the floats from the text.
    Like the \footnoterule, it must not occupy any vertical space.

\botfigrule   Same as \topfigrule, but put after the \textfloatsep skip sep-
    arating text from the floats at the bottom of the page.

\dblfigrule   Similar to \topfigrule, but for double-column floats.

Changing the values of these parameters lets you modify the behavior of
LaTeX's algorithm for placing floats. To obtain the optimal results, however, you
should be aware of the subtle dependencies that exist between these parameters.

If you use the default values in a document you will observe that, with many
floats, the formatted document will contain several float pages—that is, pages containing only floats. Often such pages contain a lot of white space. For example, you
may see a page with a single float on it, occupying only half of the possible space,

The problem of half-empty float pages so that it would look better if LaTeX had filled the remaining space with text. The reason for this behavior is that the algorithm is designed to try placing as many dangling floats as possible after the end of every page. The procedure creates as many float pages as it can until there are no more floats left to fill a float page. Float page production is controlled by the parameter \floatpagefraction, which specifies the minimum fraction of the page that must be occupied by float(s)—by default, half the page. In the standard settings every float is allowed to go on a float page (the default specifier is tbp), so this setting means that every float that is a tiny bit larger than half the page is allowed to go on a float page by itself. Thus, by enlarging its value, you can prevent half-empty float pages.

However, enlarging the value of \floatpagefraction makes it more difficult to produce float pages. As a result, some floats may be deferred, which in turn prevents other floats from being placed. For this reason it is often better to specify explicitly the allowed placements (for example, by saying \begin{figure}[tb]) for the float that creates the problem.

Another common reason for ending up with all floats at the end of your chapter is use of the bottom placement specifier, [b]. It indicates that the only acceptable place for a float is at the bottom of a page. If your float happens to be larger than \bottomfraction (which is by default quite small), then this float cannot be placed. This will also prevent all floats of the same type from being placed. The same problem arises if only [h] or [t] is specified and the float is too large for the remainder of the page or too large to fit \topfraction.

In calculating these fractions, LaTeX will take into account the separation (i.e., \textfloatsep) between floats and main text. By enlarging this value, you automatically reduce the maximum size a float is allowed to have to be considered as a candidate for placement at the top or bottom of the page.

In general, whenever a lot of your floats end up at the end of the chapter, look at the first ones to see whether their placement specifiers are preventing them from being properly placed.

6.2 Float placement control

Floats always after their call-out The float placement algorithm prefers to put floats at the top of the page, even if it means placing them before the actual reference. This outcome is not always acceptable but there is no easy cure for this problem short of substantially changing LaTeX's algorithm. The flafter package (by Frank Mittelbach) makes this change, thereby ensuring that floats are never placed before their references.

Sometimes, less drastic solutions might be preferred. For example, if the float belongs to a section that starts in the middle of a page but the float is positioned at the top of the page, the float will appear as if it belongs to the previous section. You might want to forbid this behavior while still allowing floats to be placed on the top of the page in other situations. For this purpose LaTeX offers you the following command.

```
\suppressfloats[placement]
```

The optional argument *placement* can be either t or b. If the command
\suppressfloats is placed somewhere in the document, then on the current
page any following floats for the areas specified by *placement* are deferred to
a later page. If no *placement* parameter is given, all remaining floats on the current page are deferred. For example, if you want to prevent floats from moving
backward over section boundaries, you can redefine your section commands in
the following way:

```
\renewcommand\section{\suppressfloats[t]%
                      \@startsection{section}{..}{..}{..} ...  }
```

Possible arguments to \@startsection are discussed in Section 2.2.2.

Another way to influence the placement of floats in LaTeX is to specify a ! in
conjunction with the placement specifiers h, t, and b. The placement of floats
on float pages is not affected by this approach. This means that for this float
alone, restrictions given by the settings of the parameters described earlier (e.g.,
\textfraction) are ignored. Thus, such a float can be placed in the designated
areas as long as neither of the following two restrictions is violated:

- The float fits on the current page; that is, its height plus the material already
  contributed to the page does not exceed \textheight.

- There are no deferred floats of the same type.

All other restrictions normally active (e.g., the number of floats allowed on a
page) are ignored. For example, if you specify [!b] this float can be placed on
the bottom of the page even if it is larger than the maximum size specified by
\bottomfraction. Also, any \suppressfloats commands are ignored while processing this float.

The order of the given specifiers is irrelevant, and all specifiers should be
given at most once. For example, [bt] is the same as [tb] and thus does *not*   *Algorithm to*
instruct LaTeX to try to place the float at the bottom and only then try to place it on   *determine allowed*
the top. LaTeX always uses the following order of tests until an allowed placement   *placement*
is found:

1. If ! is specified, ignore most restrictions as described above and continue.

2. If h is specified, try to place the float at the exact position. If this fails and
   no other position was specified, change the specifier to t (for a possible placement on the next page).

3. If t is specified, try to place it on the top of the current page.

4. If b is specified, try to place it on the bottom of the current page.

5. If p is specified, try to place it on a float page (or float column) when the
   current page (or column) has ended.

6. Steps 3 and 4 are repeated if necessary at the beginning of each subsequent
   page, followed by Step 5 at its end.

Sometimes you will find that LaTeX's float placement specifiers are too restric-

tive. You may want to place a float exactly at the spot where it occurs in the input file—that is, you do not want it to float at all. It is a common misunderstanding that specifying [h] means "here and nowhere else". Actually, that specifier merely directs LaTeX to *do its best* to place the float at the current position. If there is not enough room left on the page or if an inline placement is forbidden because of the settings of the style parameters (see Section 6.1), then LaTeX will ignore this request and try to place the float according to any other specifier given. Thus, if [ht] is specified, the float will appear on the top of some later page if it does not fit onto the current one. This situation can happen quite often if the floats you try to place in the middle of your text are moderately large and are thus likely to fall into positions where there is not enough space on the page for them. By ignoring an h and trying other placement specifiers, LaTeX avoids overly empty pages that would otherwise arise in such situations.

In some cases you might prefer to leave large gaps on your pages. For this reason the package float provides you with an [H] specifier that means "put the float here"—period. It is described in Section 6.3.1.

6.2.1   placeins—Preventing floats from crossing a barrier

Donald Arseneau wrote the package placeins to enable you to prevent floats from moving past a certain point in the output document by introducing a \FloatBarrier command. With the placeins package, when such a command is encountered, all floats that are not yet placed will be transferred to the output stream. This approach is useful if you want to ensure that all floats that belong to a section are placed before the next section starts.

For example, you could redefine the sectioning command and introduce the \FloatBarrier command in its definition inside the \@startsection command (see Section 2.2.2), as shown here:

```
\makeatletter              % needed if used in the preamble
\renewcommand\section{\@startsection
 {section}{1}{0mm}%              name, level, indent
 {-\baselineskip}%               beforeskip
 {0.5\baselineskip}%             afterskip
 {\FloatBarrier\normalfont\Large\bfseries}}% style
\makeatother               % needed if used in the preamble
```

The author of placeins anticipated that users might often want to output their floats before a new section starts, so his package provides the package option section, which automatically redefines \section to include the \FloatBarrier command. However, this option forces all floats to appear *before* the next section material is typeset. It prevents a float from a current section from appearing below the start of the new section, even if some material of the current section is present on the same page.

If you want to allow floats to pass the \FloatBarrier and appear at the bottom of a page (i.e., in a new section), specify the option below. To allow floats to pass it in the opposite direction and appear on the top of the page (i.e., in the previous section), specify the option above. *Turning the barrier into a membrane*

When using the option verbose the package shows processing information on the terminal and in the transcript file.

6.2.2   afterpage—Taking control at the page boundary

The afterpage package (by David Carlisle) implements a command \afterpage that causes the commands specified in its argument to be expanded after the current page is output. Although its author considers it "a hack that not even always works" (for example, \afterpage will fail in twocolumn mode), it has a number of useful applications.

Sometimes LaTeX's float positioning mechanism gets overloaded, and all floating figures and tables drift to the end of the document. You may flush out all the unprocessed floats by issuing a \clearpage command, but this tactic has the effect of making the current page end prematurely. The afterpage package allows you to issue the command \afterpage{\clearpage}. It will let the current page be filled with text (as usual), but then a \clearpage command will flush out all floats before the next text page begins. *Preventing floats at the end of the document*

With the multipage longtable environment (see Section 5.4.2), you can experience problems when typesetting the text surrounding the long table, and it may be useful to "float" the longtable. However, because such tables can be several pages long, it may prove impossible to hold them in memory and float them in the same way that the table environment is floated. Nevertheless, if the table markup is in a separate file (say ltfile.tex) you can use one of the following commands: *Floating multipage tables*

```
\afterpage{\clearpage\input{ltfile}}
\afterpage{\clearpage\input{ltfile}\newpage}
```

The first form lets text appear on the same page at the end of the longtable. The second ensures that the surrounding text starts again on a new page.

The \afterpage command can be combined with the float package and the [H] placement specifier, as explained at the end of Section 6.3.1.

6.2.3   endfloat—Placing figures and tables at the end

Some journals require figures and tables to be separated from the text and grouped at the end of a document. They may also want a list of figures and tables to precede them and potentially require markers indicating the original places occupied by the floats within the text. This can be achieved with the endfloat package (by James Darrell McCauley and Jeffrey Goldberg), which puts figures and tables by themselves at the end of an article into sections titled "Figures" and "Tables", respectively.

The endfloat package features a series of options to control the list of figures and tables, their section headings, and the markers left in the text. A list of available options follows.

figlist/nofiglist   Produce (default) or suppress the list of figures.

tablist/notablist   Produce (default) or suppress the list of tables.

lists/nolists   Produce or suppress the list of figures and the list of tables (shorthand for the combination of the previous two option sets).

fighead/nofighead   Produce or omit (default) a section heading before the collection of figures. The section headings text is given by \figuresection and defaults to the string "Figures".

tabhead/notabhead   Produce or omit (default) a section heading before the collection of tables. The section headings text is given by \tablesection and defaults to the string "Tables".

heads/noheads   Produce or omit a section heading before the collection of figures and before the collection of tables (shorthand for the combination of the previous two option sets).

markers/nomarkers   Place (default) or omit markers in text.

figuresfirst/tablesfirst   Put all figures before tables (default), or vice versa.

Hooks   The package offers the hooks \AtBeginFigures, \AtBeginTables, and \AtBeginDelayedFloats to control the processing of the collected floats. For instance, the instruction \AtBeginTables{\cleardoublepage} ensures that the delayed tables will start on a recto page.

When the floats are finally typeset, the command \efloatseparator is executed after each float. By default, it is defined to be \clearpage, which forces one float per page. If necessary, it can be redefined with \renewcommand.

Float markers in text   By default, the package indicates the original position of a float within the text by adding lines such as "[Figure 4 about here.]" at the approximate place. These notes can be turned off by specifying the nomarkers option when loading the package. The text and the formatting of the notes, which are defined via the commands \figureplace and \tableplace, can be changed with \renewcommand. For example, they might be adapted to a different language (the package does not support babel parameterization). A sample redefinition for French could look as follows:

```
\renewcommand\figureplace
  {\begin{center}[La figure~\thepostfig\ approx.\ ici.]\end{center}}
\renewcommand\tableplace
  {\begin{center}[La table~\theposttbl\ approx.\ ici.]\end{center}}
```

Within the replacement text \thepostfig and \theposttbl reference the current figure or table number, respectively. Such redefinitions can, for example, be put in the package configuration file `endfloat.cfg` that, if present, is loaded automatically by the package (with the usual caveat of nonportability).

By default, the delayed floats are processed when the end of the document is reached. However, in some cases one might wish to process them at an earlier *Premature output* point—for example, to display them at the end of each chapter. For this purpose endfloat offers the command `\processdelayedfloats`, which will process all delayed floats up to the current point. The float numbering will continue by default, so to restart numbering one has to reset the corresponding counters (details are given in the package documentation).

The endfloat package file creates two extra files with the extensions `.fff` and `.ttt` for storing the figure and table floats, respectively. As the environment *Caveats* bodies are written verbatim to these files, it is important that the `\end` command, (e.g., `\end{figure}`), always appears on a line by itself (without any white space) in the source document; otherwise, it will not be recognized. For the same reason the standard environment names (i.e., `figure`, `table`, and their starred forms) will be recognized only if they are directly used in the document. If they are hidden inside other environments recognition of the environment `\end` tag will fail.

By default, nonstandard float environments, such as the `sidewaysfigure` and `sidewaystable` environments of the rotating package, are not supported. It is possible, however, to extend the endfloat package to recognize such environments as well. As an example the distribution contains the file `efxmpl.cfg`, which extends endfloat to cover the environments of the rotating package. To become operational it should be included (copied) into `endfloat.cfg` so that its code is automatically loaded.

6.3   Extensions to LaTeX's float concept

By default, LaTeX offers two types of horizontally oriented float environments, `figure` and `table`. For many documents these prove to be sufficient; in other cases additional features are needed. In this section we now look at packages that extend this basic tool set to cover more complex cases.

The float package offers ways to define new float types and also provides one way to prevent individual floats from floating at all. A different approach to the latter problem is given by the caption package.

The last two packages described in this section, rotating and rotfloat, allow the rotation of the float content, something that might be necessary for unusually large float objects.

6.3.1   float—Creating new float types

The float package by Anselm Lingnau improves the interface for defining floating objects such as figures and tables in LaTeX. It adds the notion of a "float style" that governs the appearance of floats. New kinds of floats may be defined using the \newfloat command.

\newfloat{*type*}{*placement*}{*ext*}[*within*]

The \newfloat command takes four arguments, three mandatory and one optional, with the following meanings:

type   "Type" of the new class of floats, such as program. Issuing a \newfloat declaration will make the environments *type* and *type** available.

placement   Default placement parameters for the given class of floats (combination to LaTeX's t, b, p, and h specifiers or, alternatively, the H specifier).

ext   File name extension of an auxiliary file to collect the captions for the new float class being defined.

within   Optional argument specifying whether floats of this class will be numbered within some sectional unit of the document. For example, if the value of *within* is equal to chapter, the floats will be numbered within chapters (in standard LaTeX, this is the case for figures and tables in the report and book document classes).

The style of the float class   The \floatstyle declaration sets a default float style that will be used for all float types that are subsequently defined using \newfloat, until another \floatstyle command is specified. Its argument is the name of a float style, and should be one of the following predefined styles:

plain   The float style LaTeX usually applies to its floats—that is, nothing in particular. The only difference is that the caption is typeset below the body of the float, regardless of where it is given in the input markup.

plaintop   Same style as the plain float style except that the caption is placed at the top of the float.

boxed   The float body is surrounded by a box with the caption printed below.

ruled   The float style is patterned after the table style of *Concrete Mathematics* [59]. The caption is printed at the top of the float, surrounded by rules; another rule finishes off the float.

The float styles define the general layout of the floats, including the formatting of the caption. For example, the ruled style sets the caption flush left without a colon, while other styles center the caption and add a colon after the number. One has to be careful when mixing different float styles in one document so as not to produce typographic monsters.

Even though the package does not offer a user-level interface for defining new float styles, it is fairly easy to add new named styles. For details refer to the package documentation in `floats.dtx`.

The next example shows the declarations for two "nonstandard" new float types, `Series` and `XMLexa`. The former are numbered inside sections and use a "boxed" style, and the latter are numbered independently and use a "ruled" style (typographically this combination is more than questionable).

The introductory string used by LATEX in the captions of floats for a given *type* can by customized using the declaration `\floatname{type}{floatname}`. "XML Listing" is used for `XMLexa` floats in the example below. By default, a `\newfloat` command sets this string to its *type* argument if no other name is specified afterwards (shown with the `Series` float environment in the example). *Naming the float class*

---

1   New float environments

Some text for our page that might get reused over and over again.

XML Listing 1 A simple XML file

`<XMLphrase>Great fun!</XMLphrase>`

Some text for our page that might get reused over and over again.

XML Listing 2 Processing instruction

`<?xml version="1.0"?>`

Some text for our page that might get reused over and over again. Some text for our page that might get reused over and over again.

$$e = 1 + \sum_{k=1}^{\infty} \frac{1}{k!}$$

Series 1.1: Euler's constant

6-3-1

```
\usepackage{float}
\floatstyle{boxed}
\newfloat{Series}{b}{los}[section]
\floatstyle{ruled}
\newfloat{XMLexa}{H}{lox}
\floatname{XMLexa}{XML Listing}
\newcommand\xmlcode[1]{\ttfamily{#1}}
\newcommand\sample{Some text for our page
  that might get reused over and over again. }
\section{New float environments}
\sample
\begin{XMLexa} \caption{A simple XML file}
  \xmlcode{<XMLphrase>Great fun!</XMLphrase>}
\end{XMLexa}
\sample
\begin{XMLexa}
  \caption{Processing instruction}
  \xmlcode{<?xml version=''1.0''?>}
\end{XMLexa}
\sample
\begin{Series}
\caption{Euler's constant}
  \[e = 1 + \sum^\infty_{k=1} \frac{1}{k!}\]
\end{Series}
\sample
```

The command `\listof{type}{title}` produces a list of all floats of a given class. It is the equivalent of LATEX's built-in commands `\listoffigures` and `\listoftables`. The argument *type* specifies the type of the float as given in the `\newfloat` command. The argument *title* defines the text of the title to be used to head the list of the information associated with the float elements, as specified by the `\caption` commands. *Listing the captions of a float class*

The following example is a repetition of Example 6-3-1 on the preceding page (source only partially shown) with two \listof commands added.

XML Listings

List of Series

1   New float environments

Some text for our page which might get reused over and over again.

```
\usepackage{float}
% Float types ''Series'' and ''XMLexa'' and
% commands \xmlcode and \sample as defined
% in previous example
\listof{XMLexa}{XML Listings}
\listof{Series}{List of Series}
\section{New float environments}
\sample
\begin{XMLexa} \caption{A simple XML file}
 \xmlcode{<XMLphrase>Great fun!</XMLphrase>}
\end{XMLexa}
... text omitted ...
```

6-3-2

Customizing LATEX's standard float types

LATEX's two standard float types figure and table cannot be given a float style using \newfloat, as they already exist when the float package is loaded. To solve this problem the package offers the declaration \restylefloat{*type*}, which selects the current float style (specified previously with a \floatstyle declaration) for floats of this *type*.

For the same reason there exists the \floatplacement{*type*}{*placement*} declaration, which can be used to change the default placement specifier for a given float *type* (e.g., \floatplacement{table}{tp}). In the following example, both figure and table have been customized (not necessarily for the better) to exhibit the usage of these declarations.

Figure 1: Sample figure

1   Customizing standard floats

Some text for our page that might get reused over and over again. Some text for our page that might get reused over and over again.

Table 1 Sample table		
AAAA	BBBB	123
CCC	DDDD	45

```
\usepackage{graphicx,float}
\floatstyle{boxed} \restylefloat{figure}
\floatstyle{ruled} \restylefloat{table}
\floatplacement{table}{b}
% \sample as previously defined
\section{Customizing standard floats}
\sample
\begin{table}
 \begin{tabular}{@{}llr}
  AAAA&BBBB&123\\CCC&DDDD&45\end{tabular}
 \caption{Sample table}
\end{table}
\sample
\begin{figure} \centering
 \includegraphics[width=12mm]{rosette.ps}
 \caption{Sample figure}
\end{figure}
```

6-3-3

Place a float "here"

Modeled after David Carlisle's here package, the float package adds the [H] placement specifier which means "place the float Here regardless of any surrounding conditions". It is available for all float types, including LaTeX's standard `figure` and `table` environments. The [H] qualifier must always be used on a stand-alone basis; e.g., [Hbpt] is illegal.

If there is not enough space left on the current page, the float will be printed at the top of the next page together with whatever follows, even if there is still room left on the current page. It is the authors' responsibility to place their H floats in such a way that no large patches of white space remain at the bottom of a page. Moreover, one must carefully check the order of floats when mixing standard and [H] placement parameters. Indeed, a float with a [t] specifier, for example, appearing before one with an [H] specifier in the input file might be incorrectly positioned after the latter in the typeset output, so that, for instance, Figure 4 would precede Figure 3.

All float placement specifiers are shown together in the following example.	t Top of page b Bottom of page p Page of floats h Here, if possible H Here, always Table 1: Float placement specifiers With "h" instead of
6	7

6-3-4

```
\usepackage{float,array}
All float placement specifiers are
shown together in the following example.
\begin{table}[H]
\begin{tabular}{>{\ttfamily}cl}
  t & Top of page    \\ b & Bottom of page \\
  p & Page of floats \\
  h & Here, if possible \\ H & Here, always
\end{tabular}
\caption{Float placement specifiers}
\end{table}
With ``h'' instead of the ``H'' specifier
this text would have appeared before the
table in the current example.
```

In combination with the `placeins` and `afterpage` packages described in Sections 6.2.1 and 6.2.2, respectively, an even finer control on the placement of floats is possible. Indeed, in some cases, although you specify the placement parameter as [H], you do not really mean "at this point", but rather "somewhere close". This effect is achieved by using the \afterpage command:

```
\afterpage{\FloatBarrier\begin{figure}[H]...\end{figure}}
```

The \FloatBarrier command ensures that all dangling floats are placed first at a suitable point (due to \afterpage without producing a huge gap in the text), thereby solving the sequencing problem, described above. The [H] is then immediately placed afterwards. If you use \clearpage instead of \FloatBarrier, it would come out on top of the next page instead.

6.3.2   caption—For nonfloating figures and tables

An alternative to specifying the [H] option with the various float environments, as described in the previous section, is to define captioning commands that typeset and are entered into the "List of Figures" or "List of Tables" just like LaTeX's standard `figure` and `table` environments. This functionality is provided by the `caption` package (discussed in more detail in Section 6.5.1).

`\captionof{`*type*`}[`*short-text*`]{`*text*`}`   `\captionof*{`*type*`}{`*text*`}`

This command works analogously to LaTeX's `\caption` command, but takes an additional mandatory argument to denote the float *type* it should mimic. It can be used for any nonfloating material that should get a (numbered) caption whose text will also be added into the list of figures or list of tables. The starred form suppresses both the number and the "List of..." entry.

Watch out for incorrect numbering

The following example shows a normal figure and its nonfloating variant used together. In such a case there is always the danger that a floating figure will travel past its nonfloating counterparts. In the example we force this situation by pushing the floating figure to the bottom of the page. As a result, the numbering gets out of sync. One has to watch out for this problem when mixing floating and nonfloating objects.

List of Figures

1   Various kinds of figures

Here we mix standard and nonfloating figures.

Figure II

Figure 2: Nonfloating figure

As Figure 1 is forced to the bottom with an optional [b] argument it passes Figure 2 and the numbering

Figure I

Figure 1: Standard figure

```
\usepackage{caption}
\listoffigures
\section{Various kinds of figures}
Here we mix standard and nonfloating figures.
\begin{figure}[b]  \centering
 \fbox{Figure I}
 \caption{Standard figure}  \label{fig:I}
\end{figure}
\begin{center}
 \fbox{Figure II} \\
 \captionof{figure}[Fake LOF entry]
                {Nonfloating figure}
 \label{fig:II}
\end{center}
As Figure \ref{fig:I} is forced to
the bottom with an optional \texttt{[b]}
argument it passes Figure \ref{fig:II}
and the numbering gets out of sync.
```

6-3-5

6.3.3   rotating—**Rotating floats**

Sometimes it is desirable to turn the contents of a float sideways, by either 90 or 270 degrees. As TeX is not directly capable of performing such an operation, it needs support from an output device driver. To be as device independent as possible, LaTeX encapsulates the necessary operations in the packages graphics and graphicx (see Section 10.2). One of the earliest packages that used this interface was the rotating package written by Sebastian Rahtz and Leonor Barroca.[1]

---

[1] In fact, its original release predates the development of the graphics interface. It was later reimplemented as an extension of this interface.

The rotating package implements two environments, `sidewaysfigure` and `sidewaystable`, for turning whole floats sideways. These environments automatically produce page-sized floats, or more exactly column-sized floats (if used in `twocolumn` mode). Starred forms of these environments, which span both columns in `twocolumn` mode, exist as well.

By default, the floats are turned in such a way that they can be read from the outside margin, as you can see in the next example. If you prefer your floats to be always turned in the same way, you can specify one of the package options `figuresright` or `figuresleft`.

```
\usepackage{rotating}
\usepackage{fancyhdr}
\pagestyle{fancy}
\fancyhead[RO,LE]{Turned floats}

\begin{sidewaysfigure}
  \centering  \fbox{Figure Body}
  \caption{Caption}
\end{sidewaysfigure}
\begin{sidewaystable}
  \centering  \fbox{Table Body}
  \caption{Caption}
\end{sidewaystable}
```

6-3-6

The package also defines a number of environments for rotating arbitrary objects, such as `turn` or `rotate` (to rotate material with or without leaving space for it); see Section 10.3.4. Directly relevant to floats is the `sideways` environment, which enables you to turn the float body while leaving the caption untouched. It is used in the following example, which also exhibits the result of the `figuresright` option (which, despite its name, acts on `sidewaysfigure` and `sidewaystable`).

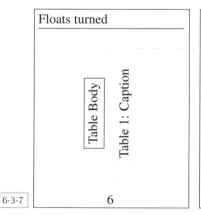

```
\usepackage[figuresright]{rotating}
\usepackage{fancyhdr}
\pagestyle{fancy}
\fancyhead[LE]{Floats turned}
\fancyhead[RO]{Floats partly turned}
\begin{sidewaystable} \centering
  \fbox{Table Body} \caption{Caption}
\end{sidewaystable}
\begin{table}  \centering
  \begin{sideways}
   \fbox{Table Body}
  \end{sideways}
  \caption{Caption}
\end{table}
```

6-3-7

Instead of turning the whole float or the float body, it is sometimes more appropriate to turn only the caption. This ability is supported by the rotating package through the `\rotcaption` command. Unfortunately, the layout produced by this command is hard-wired but can be customized through the caption package whose features are discussed in Section 6.5.1.

6.3.4 rotfloat—Combining float and rotating

To extend the new float styles, as introduced by the float package, with the `sidewaysfigure` and `sidewaystable` environments defined in the rotating package, you can use Axel Sommerfeldt's rotfloat package. It allows you to build new floats, which are rotated by 90 or 270 degrees.

The rotfloat package offers identical options to the rotating package. Internally, for every float *type*, rotfloat defines an additional environment with the name `sidewaystype` and its corresponding starred form. For instance, when you write

```
\newfloat{XMLexa}{lox}    \floatname{XMLexa}{XML Listing}
```

four environments become available: `XMLexa`, `XMLexa*`, `sidewaysXMLexa`, and `sidewaysXMLexa*`. Similarly, the commands for redefining the `table` or `figure` environments, for example,

```
\floatstyle{boxed}        \restylefloat{table}
```

will restyle not only the `table` and `table*` environments, but also the environments `sidewaystable` and `sidewaystable*`.

6.4 Inline floats

In TeX's typesetting model, text is first broken into paragraphs on a vertically oriented galley (or scroll). Once enough material is collected in this way TeX invokes its output routine, which chops off the first part of the galley, attaches running headers and footers as specified, and outputs the result in the `.dvi` file. It then restarts collecting text and breaking it into paragraphs to refill the galley.

As a consequence of this processing model, it is relatively easy to implement a float mechanism in which floats span the full width of the page or at least the full width of individual columns. Unfortunately, it is nearly impossible to have floats that occupy only parts of a text column and have the text flow around them. The reason being that when the paragraphs are broken into lines, their final positions are not yet known. It is therefore impossible to direct the paragraph builder to leave holes for the float objects if a later part of the process will decide on their final placement. In contrast, placing floats at the top or the bottom of a page (or column) only directs the output routine to chop off less material from the assembled galley without otherwise manipulating the galley content.

Because of this processing model, the production of inline floats with text flowing around the float object has to take place during the paragraph-generating phase. The best outcome that packages can currently achieve is to ensure that the inline floats do not fall off the page (by measuring the amount of material already assembled on the galley to decide whether there is enough space to fit in the inline float with its surrounding paragraph(s)).

Such an algorithm is, for example, implemented by the wrapfig package. Because the package's inline floats only "float" very little in comparison to standard floats, mixing both types can result in the float numbering getting out of sequence.[1] Most relevant packages leave the placement decisions completely to the user because the automatic solution comes out wrong in many cases, so that it not worth supplying it in the first place.

For this book we have chosen a total of three packages that are representative of what is available in this area. We have already discussed one such package (picinpar) in Section 3.1.14; two more are introduced here. The wrapfig package supports figures and tables and offers some support for automatic placement. The picins package allows precise control over the placement of inline figures and for this particular task can be quite interesting. Unlike other packages in this area, it does not support inline tables.

All packages have some problems so that it might be worthwhile to explore other possibilities such as floatflt by Mats Dahlgren (an extension of the floatfig package by Thomas Kneser), which works together with the multicol package. A good starting point to look for other packages is Graham Williams' *TEX online catalogue* [169].

6.4.1 wrapfig—**Wrapping text around a figure**

The package wrapfig (by Donald Arseneau) defines the `wrapfigure` and `wraptable` environments. These environments allow one to typeset a narrow float at the edge of some text, and then make the text wrap around it. Both produce captions with the standard caption layout for figures and tables. Although the environments have some limited ability to "float", no provision is made to synchronize them with regular floats. Thus, one must be aware that they may be printed out of sequence with standard floats.

```
\begin{wrapfigure}[nlines]{placement}[overhang]{width}
```

The `wrapfigure` and `wraptable` environments have two mandatory and two optional arguments with the following meanings:

nlines (optional) The number of narrow lines needed for the float (normally calculated automatically). Each display equation counts as three lines.

---

[1] In theory, one could do better and properly synchronize both types, although the coding would probably be quite difficult.

placement   Horizontal placement of the float, specified as *one* of the following letters: `r` or `R` (right side of the text), and `l` or `L` (left side of the text). There is no option for centering the float. For a two-sided document, the placement can alternatively be specified via `i` or `I` (inside edge) and `o` or `O` (outside edge). This refers to the inside and outside of the whole page, not to individual columns. In each case the uppercase variant allows the figure or table to float, while the lowercase variant puts it "exactly here".

overhang   (optional) Overhang of the float into the margin (default 0pt).

width   Width of the figure or table. Specifying `0pt` has a special meaning, such that the "natural width" will be used as the wrapping width. The caption is then typeset to the wrapping width. If the figure is wider than the space allotted, an "overfull box" will be generated and the figure or table contents can overwrite the wrapping text.

LaTeX will wrap surrounding text around the figure or table, leaving a gap of `\intextsep` at the top and bottom and `\columnsep` at the side, thereby producing a series of shortened text lines beside the figure. The size of the hole made in the text is the float width plus `\columnsep` minus the *overhang* value.

LaTeX calculates the number of short lines needed based on the height of the figure and the length `\intextsep`. This guess may be overridden by specifying the first optional argument (*nlines*), which is the desired number of shortened lines. It can be useful when the surrounding text contains extra vertical spacing that is not accounted for automatically.

Our first example shows a wrapped table, 4 cm wide and placed at the left side of the paragraph. The package calculated a wrapping of 5 lines, which would have left a lot of empty space below the caption, so we explicitly selected 4 lines of wrapping instead. The figure is referenced using LaTeX's standard `\label` and `\ref` commands.

> Wrapped Table
>
> Table 1: The Caption

Some text for our page that is reused over and over again. Some text for our page that is reused over and over again. Reference to Table 1. Some text for our page that is reused over and over again.

```
\usepackage{wrapfig}
% \sample as before
\begin{wraptable}[4]{l}{4cm}
  \centering\fbox{Wrapped Table}
  \caption{The Caption}\label{T}
\end{wraptable}
\sample \sample Reference to Table~\ref{T}.
\sample
```

6-4-1

The `wrapfigure` and `wraptable` environments should not be used inside another environment (e.g., *list*). They do work in `twocolumn` page layout (provided the column width is wide enough to allow inline floats).

Generally LaTeX will not be able to move `wrapfigure` and `wraptable` environments to their optimal places, so it is up to you to position them in the best fashion. It is best to wait to do so until just before printing your *final copy*, because any changes to the document can ruin their careful positioning. Information about float processing by wrapfig is written to the log file if you specify the verbose option. Here are some rules for good placement:

- The environments should be placed so as to not run over a page boundary and must not be placed in special places like lists.

- Only ordinary text should have to flow past the figure but not a section title or large equations. Small equations are acceptable if they fit.

- It is convenient to place \begin{wrapfigure} or \begin{wraptable} just after a paragraph has ended. If you want to start in the middle of a paragraph, the environment must be placed between two words where there is a natural line break.

Our second example displays a figure that is set to its natural width (last argument 0pt), but extends 20% into the left margin (specified by the optional argument). Instead of using the special unit \width, denoting the natural float width in this case, one can, of course, use some explicit dimension such as 30pt. The effect of this choice can be clearly seen by looking at the way the paragraph text is typeset below the picture when the text wrapping ends. As the example also shows, wrapping continues even across paragraph boundaries if necessary.

The formatting of the caption can be influenced by combining wrapfig with packages like caption, although an option like centerlast may not be the appropriate choice in narrow measures.

The starting place for the wrapfigure environment was manually determined in the current example by first setting the text without the figure to find the linebreaks.

This is a "wrapfigure".

Figure 1: An example of the wrapfigure environment

Some text for our page that is reused over and over again. Some text for our page that is reused over and over again. Some text for our page that is reused over and over again.

```
\usepackage{wrapfig}
\usepackage[labelfont={sf,bf},
   justification=centerlast]{caption}
% \sample as before
The starting place for the wrapfigure
environment was manually determined in
the current ex-
\begin{wrapfigure}[7]{l}[0.2\width]{0pt}
  \centering
  \fbox{This is a ``wrapfigure''.}
  \caption{An example of the
    \texttt{wrapfigure} environment}
\end{wrapfigure}
sample by first setting the text without
the figure to find the linebreaks.

\sample \sample \sample
```

6-4-2

In the preceding example we specified an *overhang* length explicitly. The overhang width can also be specified globally for all wrapfig environments by setting the \wrapoverhang length with LaTeX's \setlength command to a non-zero value. For example, to have all wrap figures and tables use the space reserved for marginal notes, you could write

```
\setlength  \wrapoverhang{\marginparwidth}
\addtolength\wrapoverhang{\marginparsep}
```

New "wrapping" environments for additional float types (as defined via the float package) with the same interface and behavior as `wrapfigure` or `wraptable` may be easily added, or directly invoked, using the `wrapfloat` environment:

```
\newfloat{XML}{lox}
\newenvironment{wrapXML}{\begin{wrapfloat}{XML}}{\end{wrapfloat}}
```

You can find other ways to fine-tune the behavior of wrapfig by reading the implementation notes at the end of the `wrapfig.sty` package file.

6.4.2 picins—**Placing pictures inside the text**

The picins package (by Joachim Bleser and Edmund Lang) defines the \parpic command, which allows you to place a "picture" at the left or right of one or more paragraphs with the paragraph text flowing around the picture.

> \parpic *(w,h)* *(x-o,y-o)* [*opt*] [*pos*] {*pict*}

w,h (optional) Width and height of the picture. The text lines that flow around the picture are set in a paragraph whose lines are shorter than the text width by an amount *w*. The height *h* is used to calculate the number of lines of text that will flow in this manner.

If the argument is not specified, the actual picture size ("bounding box") is used, if it can be calculated by LaTeX. Otherwise, an error results.

x-o,y-o (optional) The *x* and *y* offsets of the picture with respect to the upper-left corner of its bounding box (positive *x-o* yields a displacement to the right; positive *y-o* moves the picture downward). If the argument is absent, the picture is positioned using the *pos* specification.

opt (optional) Placement and box characteristics of picture, given as a pair of *one* positional and *one* frame specifier.

The *positional* specifiers are l (*left*) picture at left of paragraph and r (*right*) picture at right of paragraph.

The *frame* specifiers are d (*dash*) picture surrounded by dashed lines; f (*frame*) picture surrounded by full lines; o (*oval*) picture frame with rounded corners; s (*shadow*) picture surrounded by shadow box; and x (*box*) picture surrounded by "three-dimensional" box. When no option is specified, the picture is placed at the left of the paragraph.

pos (optional) Position of the picture inside its frame, given as one horizontal specifier, one vertical specifier, or a pair of horizontal and vertical specifiers. Possible *horizontal* specifiers are l (*left*) picture at left of frame and r (*right*) picture at right of frame. If no horizontal specifier is given, the picture is centered horizontally in its frame.

Possible *vertical* specifiers are t (*top*) picture at top of frame and b (*bottom*) picture at bottom of frame. If no vertical specifier is given, the picture is centered vertically in its frame.

If the offset argument *x-o,y-o* is present, the *pos* argument is ignored.

pict The source of the picture. It can be any LaTeX construct.

The following examples show various ways to place a picture inside a paragraph. We also introduce some other commands provided by the picins package to fine-tune the visual presentation of the typeset result.

We start by using picins's default setting, where the width and height of the contents are automatically calculated. In that case the "picture" is placed at the left of the paragraph. This paragraph has a normal indentation: if this effect is not desired, one has to start it with \noindent. The second part of the example pulls in an Encapsulated PostScript (EPS) picture and lets text flow around it. In this case the natural dimensions of the picture are read from the BoundingBox comment in the EPS source file. We added a dashed frame for more clarity.

Some text for our page that is reused over and over again. Some text for our page that is reused over and over again.

Some text for our page that is reused over and over again. Some text for our page that is reused over and over again. Some text for our page that is reused over and over again. Some text for our page that is reused over and over again. Some text for our page that is reused over and over again.

```
\usepackage{picins,graphicx}
\newcommand\sample{Some text for our page
             that is reused over and over again. }
\newcommand\FIG{\includegraphics
                [width=14mm]{cat}}
\parpic{\fbox{\Large\scshape Box}}
\sample\sample\par
\parpic[d]{\FIG}
\noindent\sample\sample\sample\sample
```

6-4-3

We can specify the dimensions of the picture ourselves, so that LaTeX will use these parameters in its typesetting calculations, and will not try to use the intrinsic information associated with the source. If no offsets or position parameters are given, the content is centered (first picture). On the second picture we shift the content 2mm to the right and 14mm down. There the "dr" argument produces a dashed frame and places the picture to the right.

A \picskip{*nlines*} command instructs LaTeX to continue to typeset the paragraph for *nlines* lines at the given indentation (as though the picture extended downward for that many lines). A zero value for *nlines* means that the following lines no longer need to be indented and that a new paragraph must start. The

Controlling the hole

horizontal space between the paragraph text and the picture can be controlled through the \pichskip command.

Some text for our page that is reused over and over again. Some text for our page that is reused over and over again.
    Here we prove that the "picture" can span more than a single paragraph.

Some text for our page that is reused over and over again. Some text for our page that is reused over and over again.
    Without the explicit request in the source this paragraph would have only one shortened line, like the one surrounding the previous "picture".

```
\usepackage{picins,graphicx}
% \sample as previously defined
\parpic(15mm,15mm)[f]{\FIG}\noindent
\sample\sample\par
Here we prove that the ``picture'' can
span more than a single paragraph.
\parpic(15mm,15mm)(2mm,14mm)[dr]{\FIG}%
\noindent\sample\sample\par
\picskip{2}
Without the explicit request in the source
this paragraph would have only one
shortened line, like the one surrounding
the previous  ``picture''.
```

6-4-4

Perhaps the results produced by the offset in the previous example were somewhat surprising. For this reason the next example studies its effects in some detail. If we specify an offset of 0mm,0mm the "picture" is placed with its reference point at the top-left corner of the area reserved for the picture. As most LaTeX constructs produce a box with the reference point at the left of the bottom baseline, the "picture" is effectively placed outside the intended area—that is, in a completely different place than it would be without any offset at all.

Some text for our page that is reused over and over again. Some text for our page that is reused over and over again.
    Some text for our page that is reused over and over again. Some text for our page that is reused over and over again.

Some text for our page that is reused over and over again. Some text for our page that is reused over and over again.
    Some text for our page that is reused over and over again. Some text for our page that is reused over and over again.

```
\usepackage{picins}
% \sample as previously defined
\parpic(15mm,10mm)(0mm,0mm)
       [dr]{\fbox{Box}}%
\sample\sample\par
\parpic(15mm,10mm)(2mm,5mm)
       [dr]{\fbox{Box}}%
\sample\sample\par
\parpic(15mm,10mm)(4mm,10mm)
       [dr]{\fbox{Box}}%
\sample\sample\par
\parpic(15mm,10mm)(6mm,15mm)
       [dr]{\fbox{Box}}%
\sample\sample\par
```

6-4-5

You can use the \parpic inside list environments at any depth. This is in contrast to other packages in this area, which often restrict the placement of pictures within lists. The following example features an itemize list with embedded \parpic commands. It also shows how line thickness (\linethickness), length of the dashes (\dashlength), and depth of the shade (\shadowthickness) and the 3-D effect (\boxlength) can all be controlled separately.

Some text for our page that is reused over and over again.

- Some text for our page that is reused over and over again. Some text for our page that is reused over and over again.

- Some text for our page that is reused over and over

again. Some text for our page that is reused over and over again.

- BOX Some text for our page that is reused over and over again. Some text for our page that is reused over and over again.

Some text for our page that is reused over and over again.

```
\usepackage{picins}
% \sample as previously defined
\sample
\begin{itemize} \item
  \dashlength{2mm}
  \linethickness{1mm}
  \parpic(15mm,10mm)[dr]{BOX}
  \sample\sample
\item
  \shadowthickness{3mm}
  \linethickness{.4pt}
  \parpic(15mm,10mm)[sr]{BOX}
  \sample\sample
\item
  \boxlength{2mm}
  \parpic(15mm,10mm)[x]{BOX}
  \sample\sample
\end{itemize} \sample
```

6-4-6

One can generate numbered captions for the pictures that will appear in LaTeX's "List of Figures". As the pictures do not float, one has to be careful when mixing them with ordinary floats to avoid out-of-sequence numbering. To specify a caption text you use the command \piccaption, which takes the same arguments as the standard \caption command but only stores them for use with the *next* \parpic.

For our first example we typeset the contents of a picture inside a framed shadow box, with the caption appearing outside the frame and below the picture. This corresponds to the default positioning for caption material. There is a space of 6 mm between picture and text as specified with the \pichskip command.

$$E = mc^2$$

Figure 1: Einstein's formula.

Some text for our page that is reused over and over again. Some text for our page that is reused over and over again.

```
\usepackage{picins}
\newcommand\FOR{\(\displaystyle E=mc^2\)}
% \sample as before
\pichskip{6mm}
\piccaption{Einstein's formula.}
\parpic(45mm,10mm)[s]{\FOR}
\sample\sample
```

6-4-7

The default caption placement can be explicitly requested with the declaration \piccaptionoutside. The package offers three other placement options that can be selected \piccaptioninside, \piccaptionside, and \piccaptiontopside. Their effects are shown in the next example. Even though *picins* uses its own command to specify the caption text, it is possible to influence the caption formatting by loading a package such as caption. We prove this by setting the caption label in bold sans serif font.

$$E = mc^2$$

Figure 1: Einstein's formula.

Some text for our page that is reused over and over again. Some text for our page that is reused over and over again. Some text for our page that is reused over and over again.

$$E = mc^2$$

Figure 2: Einstein's formula.

Some text for our page that is reused over and over again.

Figure 3: Einstein's formula.

$$E = mc^2$$

Some text for our page that is reused over and over again. Some text for our page that is reused over and over again.

```
\usepackage{picins}
\usepackage[labelfont={sf,bf}]{caption}
% \sample and \FOR as before
\piccaptioninside
\piccaption{Einstein's formula.}
\parpic(50mm,10mm)[s]{\FOR}
\sample\sample\sample

\piccaptionside
\piccaption{Einstein's formula.}
\parpic(30mm,10mm)[s]{\FOR}
\sample

\piccaptiontopside
\piccaption{Einstein's formula.}
\parpic(30mm,10mm)[sr]{\FOR}
\sample\sample
```

6-4-8

6.5   Controlling the float caption

When you want to explain what is shown in your floating environment (figure or table in standard LaTeX), you normally use a \caption command. After introducing the basic syntax and explaining the (low-level) interfaces available with standard LaTeX, this section describes the powerful caption package, which offers a large number of customization possibilities for adjusting the caption layout to your needs. As shown in the examples it can be combined with all other packages described in this chapter.

We then examine the subfig and subfloat packages, which introduce substructures for float objects. The section concludes with a discussion of the sidecap package (placing captions beside the float body) and the fltpage package (for generating full-page floats whose captions are placed on the opposite page).

```
\caption[short-text]{text}
```

This standard LaTeX command is only defined inside a float environment. It increments the counter associated with the float in question. If present, the optional argument *short-text* goes into the list of figures or tables. If only the mandatory argument *text* is specified, then it is used in those lists. If the caption is longer than one line, you are strongly advised to use the optional argument to provide a short and informative description of your float. Otherwise, the list of figures and tables may become unreadable and it may be difficult to locate the necessary information. In fact, LATEX allows multi-paragraph captions only if the *short-text* argument is present. Otherwise, you will get a "Runaway argument?" error.

The following example shows how standard LATEX typesets captions. Compare this layout to the customization provided by the various packages discussed in the next sections. Note how the optional argument of the second \caption command defines what text appears for that figure in the "List of Figures".

List of Figures

1   Caption

Figures 1 and 2 have captions.

A small Figure

Figure 1: Short caption text

A small Figure

Figure 2: Long caption text with some extra explanation that this figure is important even though it is small.

```
\listoffigures

\section{Caption}

Figures \ref{Fig1} and \ref{Fig2}
have captions.

\begin{figure}[ht]
\centerline{\fbox{\small A small Figure}}
\caption{Short caption text}\label{Fig1}
\end{figure}

\begin{figure}[ht]
\centerline{\fbox{\small A small Figure}}
\caption[Short entry in lof]
 {Long caption text with some extra
  explanation that this figure is important
  even though it is small.}\label{Fig2}
\end{figure}
```

6-5-1

Internally, \caption invokes the command \@makecaption{*label*}{*text*}. The *label* argument is the sequence number of the caption and some text like "Figure"; it is generated internally depending on the type of float. The *text* argument is passed on from the mandatory \caption argument; it is the text to be typeset. The default definition for the part responsible for the typesetting of a caption looks something like this:

```
\newcommand\@makecaption[2]{% #1 is e.g. Figure 1, #2 is caption text
  \vspace{\abovecaptionskip}%
  \sbox\@tempboxa{#1: #2}%
  \ifthenelse{\lengthtest{\wd\@tempboxa >\linewidth}}%    test size
     {\noindent #1: #2\par}%                              several lines
     {\centering
       \makebox[\linewidth][c]{\usebox\@tempboxa}\par}%   single line
     }%
  \vspace{\belowcaptionskip}%
}
```

After an initial vertical space of size \abovecaptionskip (default often 10 pt), the material is typeset in a temporary box \@tempboxa, and its width is compared to the line width. If the material fits on one line, the text is centered; if the material does not fit on a single line, it will be typeset as a paragraph with a width equal to the line width. Thereafter, a final vertical space of \belowcaptionskip (default typically 0 pt) is added, finishing the typesetting. The actual implementation that you find in the standard classes uses lower-level commands to speed up the processing so it looks somewhat different.

You can, of course, define other ways of formatting your captions. You can even supply different commands for making captions for each of the different types of floats. For example, the command \@makefigcaption can be used instead of \@makecaption to format the captions for a figure environment.

```
\newcommand\@makefigcaption[2]{....}
\renewenvironment{figure}
                 {\let\@makecaption\@makefigcaption \@float{figure}}
                 {\end@float}
```

This approach requires fairly low-level programming and is not very flexible, so it is normally better to use a package like caption (described below) to do this work for you.

Rather than force you to write your own code for customizing captions, we invite you to read the following pages, which describe a few packages that offer various styles to typeset captions.

6.5.1 caption—Customizing your captions

Axel Sommerfeldt developed the caption package[1] to customize the captions in floating environments. It not only supports LaTeX's standard figure and table environments, but also interfaces correctly with the \rotcaption command and the sidewaysfigure and sidewaystable environments of the rotating package. It works equally well with most of the other packages described in this chapter (see the original documentation for a complete compatibility matrix).

Like the geometry package, the caption package uses the extended option concept (based on the keyval package), in which options can take values separated from the option name by an equals sign. In most cases there exists a default value for an option; thus, you can specify the option without a value to produce this default behavior.

The customization possibilities of the caption package cover (nearly) all aspects of formatting and placing captions, and we will introduce them below. For those users who need even more customization, the package offers an interface to add additional option values (representing special formattings). One can even

---

[1]The caption package is, in fact, a completely rewritten version of Axel's caption2 package and makes the latter obsolete. Axel advises all users of caption2 to upgrade to caption as soon as possible and, if needed, to modify their LaTeX sources accordingly.

add additional options, a functionality used, for example, by the subfig package described in Section 6.5.2.

The first set of options we examine here are those that influence the overall shape of the caption: *Customizing the general shape*

singlelinecheck If the whole caption (including the label) fits on a single line, center[1] it (keyword true). With the keyword false, such captions are formatted identically to multiple-line captions.

format This option defines the overall shape of the caption (except when overwritten by the previous option). With the keyword default, you will get a typical "standard LaTeX" format that is, the label and the caption text are set as a single block. Absent any further customization by other options, the label and the text are separated by a colon and space, and the caption is set justified to full width.

As an alternative, the keyword hang specifies that the caption should be set with the label (and separation) to the left of the caption text. In other words, continuation lines are indented by the width of the label.

margin, width By default, the caption occupies the whole width of the column (or page). By specifying either a specific width or a margin, you can reduce the measure used for the caption. In either case the caption is centered in the remaining space. Thus, with the current implementation, it is not possible to specify different values for left and right (or inner and outer) margins.

indention If set to a given dimension, this option specifies an additional indention for continuation lines (e.g., on top of any indention already produced by the hang keyword).

Figure 1: Short caption

Figure 2: A caption that runs over more than one line

6-5-2

```
\usepackage{float,graphicx}
\usepackage[format=hang,margin=10pt]{caption}
\floatstyle{boxed} \restylefloat{figure}
\begin{figure}[ht]   \centering
   \includegraphics[width=8mm]{elephant}
   \includegraphics[width=10mm]{elephant}
   \caption{Short caption}
\end{figure}
\begin{figure}[ht]   \centering
   \includegraphics[width=15mm]{elephant}
   \caption{A caption that runs over more than one line}
\end{figure}
```

If you look at the previous example, you will notice that with this particular layout the space between box and caption appears very tight. Options for adjusting[2] such spaces are discussed on page 312. First, however, we look at options for *Customizing the fonts*

---

[1] Or do something else with it.

[2] However, in some float styles, such as "boxed", they are hard-wired and cannot be changed.

adjusting the fonts used within the caption, which are always working.

font   This option defines the font characteristics for the whole caption (label and text) unless overwritten. This option can take a comma-separated list of keyword values to specify the font family (rm, sf, or tt), font series (md or bf), font shape (up, it, sl, or sc), or font size (scriptsize, footnotesize, small, normalsize, large, or Large). If more than one keyword is used, then the list must be surrounded by braces to hide the inner comma from being misinterpreted as separating one option from the next (see the example below). Keywords for the same font attribute (e.g., the font shape) overwrite each other, but those for different attributes have the expected combined effect. To set the font attributes to their default settings use the keyword default.

labelfont   While the option font defines the overall font characteristics, this option specifies the (additional) attribute values to use for the caption label.

textfont   This option is like labelfont but is used for the caption text. In the next example we use it to reset the font series from boldface to medium.

Figure 1: Short caption

A B C D E F G H I J K L M

Table 1: A caption that runs over more than one line

```
\usepackage{float,graphicx}
\usepackage[font={sf,bf},textfont=md]{caption}
\floatstyle{boxed} \restylefloat{table}
\begin{figure}[ht] \centering
  \includegraphics[width=10mm]{Escher}
  \caption{Short caption}
\end{figure}
\begin{table}[ht] \centering A B C D E F G H I J K L M
  \caption{A caption that runs over more than one line}
\end{table}
```

6-5-3

Customizing the label further   Another frequent requirement is the customization of the layout for the caption label, such as by replacing the default colon after the label by something else, or omitting it altogether. Also, the separation between label and text may require adjustments. Both can be achieved with the following options and their keywords.

labelformat   With this option a format for the label can be selected. Out of the box the following keywords can be used: simple (label string, e.g., "Figure" and the number following each other and separated by a nonbreakable space), parens (number in parentheses), and empty (omit the label including the number altogether). The results of these keywords are shown in several examples in this chapter. Additional keywords for alternative formattings can be defined using the \DeclareCaptionLabelFormat declaration, as explained on page 313.

labelsep   This option specifies the separation between the label and the text. Available keywords are colon, period, space, and newline, which have the expected meanings. New keywords producing other kinds of separations can be defined using the declaration \DeclareCaptionLabelSeparator; see the package documentation for more details.

Figure 1

Figure 2.

6-5-4 A small elephant

```
\usepackage{float,graphicx}
\floatstyle{boxed} \restylefloat{figure}
\usepackage{caption}
\DeclareCaptionLabelSeparator{period-newline}{.\newline}
\captionsetup{aboveskip=3pt,singlelinecheck=false,
                labelsep=period-newline,labelfont={small,bf}}
\begin{figure}[ht] \centering
  \includegraphics[width=10mm]{Escher} \caption{}
\end{figure}
\begin{figure}[ht] \centering
  \includegraphics[width=10mm]{elephant}
  \caption{A small elephant}
\end{figure}
```

The actual formatting of the caption text within the general shape, such as the justification, can be customized using the following two options:

Paragraph-related customizations

justification This option specifies how the paragraph should be justified. The default is full justification (keyword `justified`). Using the keyword `centering` results in all lines being centered. The `raggedleft` and `raggedright` keywords produce unjustified settings with ragged margins at the indicated side.

If the `ragged2e` package is additionally loaded, you can use the keywords `Centering`, `RaggedLeft`, and `RaggedRight`, thereby employing the commands from that package that are described in Section 3.1.12.

Two other special justifications are available: `centerfirst` centers the first line and fully justifies the rest (with `\parfillskip` set to zero), whereas `centerlast` works the opposite way, centering the last line. Both shapes are sometimes requested for captions, but in most circumstances they produce questionable results.

Further specialized justification set-ups can be defined using the declaration `\DeclareCaptionJustification` as described in the documentation.

parskip This option controls the separation between paragraphs in multi-paragraph captions. It expects a dimension as its value. Recall that captions with several paragraphs are possible only if the optional caption argument is present!

Bild

Figure (1) *A caption that runs over more than one line to show*

6-5-5 *the effect of the centerfirst keyword.*

```
\usepackage[textfont={rm,it},labelfont={sf},
  labelformat=parens,labelsep=quad,
  justification=centerfirst,parskip=3pt]{caption}
\begin{figure}[ht] \centering
  {\fontfamily{put}\fontsize{60}{60}\bfseries Bild}
  \caption[A short caption text]
   {A caption that runs over more than one line
     to show the effect of the centerfirst keyword.}
\end{figure}
```

The final set of options deal with the position of the caption with respect to the float body. Note that none of these settings actually moves the caption in the particular place (you have to do that manually, or use a float style from the float package to do it for you). They only affect the space being inserted.

aboveskip   Space between the caption and float body—for example, "above" the caption if caption is the placed at the bottom. It typically defaults to 10pt.

belowskip   Space on the opposite side of the caption—that is, away from the float body. It is 0pt in most standard classes.

position   Specifies that the caption is placed above the float body (keyword top) or below the float body (keyword bottom). It does *not* place the caption there. That is still your task (or that of a package such as float).

Be careful with
the meanings of
the options
Note that the names aboveskip and belowskip give the wrong implications: they do *not* describe physical places, but rather are swapped if the caption is *marked* as being placed on the top. This is quite different from the parameters \abovecaptionskip and \belowcaptionskip in LaTeX's default implementation of the \caption command (see page 307) which *do* describe their physical place in relation to the caption! For some float package styles setting these options may have no effect.

An option list as specified in the previous example may not be to everyone's liking. In addition, it only allows us to customize the captions of all floats in the document regardless of their type. Sometimes, however, the captions for tables may need a different treatment than those for figures, for instance. In such a case the \captionsetup declaration will help.

\captionsetup[*type*]{*option-value-list*}

The \captionsetup declaration allows you to specify an *option-value-list* like the one possible when loading the package itself. The difference is that, if used with the optional *type* argument, this declaration specifies caption formatting for only this particular float type (e.g., figure) or any float type that has been set up with a \newfloat declaration from the float package.

\DeclareCaptionStyle{*name*}[*short-style*]{*long-style*}

Further assistance is available in the form of the \DeclareCaptionStyle declaration. It associates an option/value list with a name that can later be referred to as the value of a style option. The mandatory *long-style* argument is a list of option/value pairs that describe the formatting of a caption if the style *name* is selected. The optional *short-style* argument lists option/value pairs that are *also* executed whenever the caption is determined to be "short" (i.e., if it would fit on a single line).

It is possible to combine the style option with other options inside the argument of \captionsetup, as shown in the next example. There we select the style `default` (predefined) for all floats except `figures` but overwrite its setting for `labelfont`. Note that the example is intended to show possibilities of the package—not good taste.

Figure 1. *A long caption that runs over more than one line to show the effect of the style keyword.*

$$\boxed{\text{A B C D E F G H I J}}$$

Table 1: A long caption that runs over more than one line to show the effect of the style keyword.

```
\usepackage{caption,graphicx}
\DeclareCaptionStyle{italic}
  {labelfont={sf,bf},textfont={rm,it},indention=18pt,
   labelsep=period,justification=raggedright}
\captionsetup[figure]{style=italic}
\captionsetup{style=default,labelfont={sf,bf}}
\begin{figure}[ht]
  \centering  \includegraphics{cat}
  \caption{A long caption that runs over more
           than one line to show the effect of the
           style keyword.}
\end{figure}
\begin{table}[ht]
  \centering  \fbox{A B C D E F G H I J}
  \caption{A long caption that runs over more
           than one line to show the effect of the
           style keyword.}
\end{table}
```

6-5-6

> \DeclareCaptionLabelFormat{*name*}{*code*}

This declaration defines or redefines a `labelformat` keyword *name* to generate *code* to format the label, where *code* takes two arguments: #1 (a string like "Figure") and #2 (the float number). Thus, to produce parentheses around the whole label, you can define your own `parens` keyword as follows:

```
\DeclareCaptionLabelFormat{parens}{(#1\nobreakspace#2)}
```

While this approach would work well in all examples seen so far, the above definition nevertheless contains a potential pitfall: if #1 is empty for some reason (e.g., if you changed \figurename to produce nothing), the above definition would put a space in front of the number. To account for situations like this the caption package offers the \bothIfFirst command.

> \bothIfFirst{*first*}{*second*}   \bothIfSecond{*first*}{*second*}

The \bothIfFirst command tests whether *first* is non-empty and, if so, typesets both *first* and *second*. Otherwise, it typesets nothing. With its help the above declaration can be improved as follows:

```
\DeclareCaptionLabelFormat{parens}
                        {(\bothIfFirst{#1}{\nobreakspace}#2)}
```

As a second example, suppose you want your caption labels to look like this: "(4) Figure". You could set up a new format, named `parensfirst`, and later assign it to the `labelformat`:

```
\DeclareCaptionLabelFormat{parensfirst}
                          {(#2)\bothIfSecond{\nobreakspace}{#1}}
\captionsetup{labelformat=parensfirst}
```

In a similar fashion you can add new keywords for use with the `labelsep` using the `\DeclareCaptionLabelSeparator` declaration.

`\DeclareCaptionLabelSeparator{`*name*`}{`*code*`}`

After a `\DeclareCaptionLabelSeparator` the keyword *name* refers to *code* and can be used as the value to the `labelsep` option. For example, if you want to have a separation of one quad between the label and the text that should be allowed to stretch slightly, you can define

```
\DeclareCaptionLabelSeparator{widespace}{\hspace{1em plus .3em}}
```

and then use it as `labelsep=widespace` in the argument of `\captionsetup` or `\DeclareCaptionStyle`.

Providing new caption shapes and justifications
In addition to customizing the label format, you can define your own general caption shapes using `\DeclareCaptionFormat`, or specialized justification settings using `\DeclareCaptionJustification`. These are more specialized extensions and their internal coding is a bit more difficult, so we will not show an example here. If necessary, consult the package documentation.

External configuration files
Such declarations can be made in the preamble of your documents. Alternatively, if you are using the same settings over and over again, you can place them in a configuration file (e.g., `mycaption.cfg`) and then load this configuration as follows:

```
\usepackage[config=mycaption]{caption}
```

While it is possible to combine the `config` option with other options, it is probably clearer to specify additional modifications through a `\captionsetup` declaration in the preamble.

Continuing captions across floats
Sometimes figures or tables are so large that they will not fit on a single page. For such tables, the **longtable** or **supertabular** package may provide a solution. For multipage figures, however, no packages for automated splitting are available.

In the past a general solution to this problem was provided through the **captcont** package written by Steven Cochran, which supports the retention of a caption number across several float environments. Nowadays this functionality is readily available with the **caption** package. It provides the command `\ContinuedFloat`, to be used before issuing the `\caption` command if the current caption number should be retained.

If you prefer that the continued caption not to appear in the "List of..." list, use \caption with an empty optional argument (see Example 6-5-13 on page 321), or \caption*, which suppresses LOF entry and caption number.

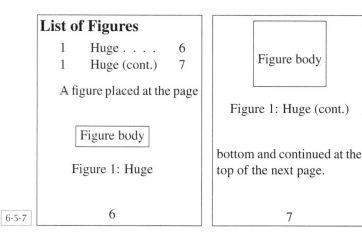

A figure placed at the page

Figure body

Figure 1: Huge

6

Figure body

Figure 1: Huge (cont.)

bottom and continued at the top of the next page.

7

```
\usepackage{caption}
\listoffigures  \medskip
\begin{figure}[!b]
  \centering \fbox{Figure body}
  \caption{Huge}
\end{figure}
A figure placed at the page bottom and
continued at the top of the next page.
\begin{figure}[!t]    \ContinuedFloat
  \centering
  \fbox{\rule[-.5cm]{0pt}{1.5cm}%
      Figure body}
  \caption{Huge (cont.)}
\end{figure}
```

6-5-7

The caption package collaborates smoothly with the other packages described in this chapter, as can be observed in the various examples. Note that in some cases this package has to be loaded *after* the packages whose captioning style one wants to modify.

6.5.2 subfig—Substructuring floats

The subfig package (by Steven Cochran) allows the manipulation and reference of small, "sub" figures and tables by simplifying the positioning, captioning, and labeling of such objects within a single float environment. If desired, sub-captions associated with these sub-floats can appear in the corresponding list of floats (e.g., the list of figures). In addition, a global caption can be present.

The package is based on the caption package, discussed in the previous section, and makes use of all its features for customizing the layout of captions.[1] The main user command to identify a sub-float object within a float is \subfloat.

\subfloat [*list-entry*] [*caption*] {*object*}

The mandatory *object* argument specifies the sub-float content, the optional *caption* argument denotes the caption text for this object, and, if necessary, the optional *list-entry* argument specifies an alternate form to be used in the list of figures (or tables). If no optional argument is provided, no caption (and no caption

---

[1]An earlier version of this package was known as subfigure. It had a number of customization possibilities in common with the caption2 package by Axel Sommerfeldt, but differed in some important details. When caption2 was upgraded, the author of this book persuaded Steven to base a new version of his code on the emerging caption package. The results are described in this section.

label) is produced. If you wish to get only an (alpha)numeric label, use an empty *caption* argument.

An empty *list-entry* signifies that for this instance the caption text should not be inserted in the "List of...". This special feature is relevant only if the sub-float captions should be listed there in the first place: see page 320 for information on creating this set-up.

Our first example shows a figure that features two \subfloat components. To reference them, you must associate labels with each of these \subfloat commands (be careful to put the \label commands *inside* the braces enclosing the contents of the \subfloat). We also place a \label following the \caption command to identify the enclosing figure environment, so that outside the environment we can refer to each of the components separately.

(a) Small   (b) Bigger

Figure 1: Two elephants

Figure 1 contains sub-figure 1a, which is smaller than sub-figure 1b.

```
\usepackage{subfig} \usepackage{graphicx}
\begin{figure} \centering
 \subfloat[Small]
   {\includegraphics[width=12mm]{elephant}\label{sf1}}
 \qquad
 \subfloat[Bigger]
   {\includegraphics[width=16mm]{elephant}\label{sf2}}
 \caption{Two elephants}\label{elephants}
\end{figure}
Figure~\ref{elephants} contains sub-figure~\ref{sf1},
which is smaller than sub-figure~\ref{sf2}.
```

6-5-8

Because the subfig package is based on caption, it is possible to influence the caption layouts for sub-floats using the options offered by the latter package. If it is not already loaded, subfig loads the caption package *without* any options. This means you have to either load caption first (as we did in the example below) or customize it after loading subfig by using a \captionsetup declaration.

(a) Short caption   (b) A longer caption
                         with more text

Figure 1: Default sub-figures

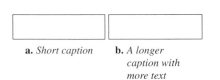

a. *Short caption*   **b.** *A longer*
                              caption with
                              more text

Figure 2: Customized sub-figures

```
\usepackage[font=sf]{caption}
\usepackage{subfig}
\newcommand\LCap{A longer caption with more text}
\newcommand\FIG{\fbox{\parbox{.4\textwidth}{\strut}}}
\begin{figure}[ht]  \centering
 \subfloat[Short caption]{\FIG} \subfloat[\LCap]{\FIG}
 \caption{Default sub-figures}
\end{figure}
\captionsetup[subfloat]{format=hang,textfont=it,
    labelfont={rm,bf},labelformat=simple,labelsep=period,
    margin=5pt,justification=raggedright}
\begin{figure}[ht] \centering
 \subfloat[Short caption]{\FIG} \subfloat[\LCap]{\FIG}
 \caption{Customized sub-figures}
\end{figure}
```

6-5-9

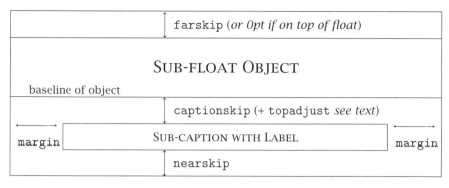

Figure 6.1: Spacing layout of the subfig package

As you can see, options for customizing the caption layouts can be set on various levels. Some default settings are already in place when the subfig package is loaded. Most noticeably, a setting of font=footnotesize for all sub-float captions accounts for the fact that our setting of sf when loading the caption package has no effect on the sub-captions. Another default that can be deduced is the use of parens with the labelformat option. But most other changes to the main caption layout are inherited by the sub-floats. *The default setting of the subfig package*

To overwrite such defaults, you can use any of the caption options when loading the subfig package, or you can specify them with a \captionsetup declaration using the *type* "subfloat" (as shown in the example). This will change all subsequent sub-float captions uniformly until they are overwritten by a further declaration. *Customizing all sub-captions*

Finally, if you want to customize sub-float captions just for a particular ⟨*type*⟩ of float (e.g., for all figures) you can do so by using sub⟨*type*⟩ instead of subfloat in the \captionsetup declaration. *Customizing sub-captions by type*

The subfig packages also offers a number of customization possibilities through a set of additional options (not available with the caption package) that expect a dimension as their value. They define the space produced around a sub-float. Assuming the default caption position below the object (i.e., position= bottom), we get a layout like that shown in Figure 6.1. *Spacing around sub-floats*

farskip   Specifies the space left on the side of the sub-float that is opposite the main float caption (e.g., on top if the main caption is at the bottom of the float). This space is ignored if it is the first object in the float body. The default value if not modified is 10pt.

nearskip   Specifies the space left on the side of the sub-float nearer the main caption to separate the sub-float object and its caption from surrounding material. It defaults to 0pt.

captionskip   Specifies the vertical space that separates the sub-float object and its caption (default 4pt). If there is no caption, this space is not added.

topadjust   Not applicable with position=bottom on the sub-float level. If the sub-caption is placed above the sub-float object (i.e., Figure 6.1 flipped upside down using position=top) this space is added to the captionskip used to separate caption and sub-float body.

The caption is set to the width of the sub-float object reduced on both sides by the value specified with the margin option already provided by caption package.

If the caption is placed above the sub-float object (i.e., using position=top for the sub-float), then captionskip is increased by topadjust to allow for adjusting the separation between the caption and the object in this case. Also, note that the position of farskip and nearskip depends on the placement of the main caption. When it comes first (i.e., position=top at the float-level) farskip and nearskip swap places.

Labeling the sub-captions   Internally, \subfloat uses a counter to keep track of the sub-floats within the current float and to produce a label for the caption from it. The counter name is sub⟨*type*⟩, where *type* is the current float type (e.g., the counter used for labeling sub-figures is called subfigure). Its representation is defined by \thesub⟨*type*⟩ and defaults to \alph{sub*type*}. These counters are incremented for each sub-float regardless of whether a caption was printed.

A somewhat more complex layout applying several of the above options has been used in the following example. It introduces three sub-tables, two on top of a third. Due to the option settings the table captions appear above the tables in small slanted type. Single-line captions are set flush left; multiple-line captions are set ragged right with hanging indentation. To show further customization possibilities, the \thesubtable command (which generates the "number" for a sub-float of type table) is redefined to produce two-level caption numbers on the sub-tables. Each of the \subfloat commands, as well as the enclosing table environment, is identified by a strategically positioned \label command. They allow us to address the components individually.

Table 1: Three sub-tables

(1.1) First   *(1.2) Second*

Table 1		Table 2

*(1.3) Third table with a much
longer caption*

Table 3

Table 1 contains sub-tables (1.1) to (1.3). But don't use now: 11.3 (see text).

```
\usepackage{subfig}
\captionsetup[table]    {position=top,aboveskip=5pt}
\captionsetup[subtable]{singlelinecheck=false,
                        format=hang,font={sl,small},
                        justification=raggedright}
\renewcommand\thesubtable{\thetable.\arabic{subtable}}
\newcommand\TAB[2]{\fbox{\parbox{#2\textwidth}{Table #1}}}

\begin{table}
\caption{Three sub-tables}\label{tbl}
\subfloat[First] {\TAB{1}{.4}\label{tbl1}}\hfill
\subfloat[Second]{\TAB{2}{.4}\label{tbl2}}\\
\subfloat[Third table with a much longer caption]
         {\TAB{3}{.8}\label{tbl3}}
\end{table}
Table \ref{tbl} contains sub-tables \subref{tbl1} to
\subref{tbl3}. But don't use now: \ref{tbl3} (see text).
```

6-5-10

The references to the individual sub-tables in the previous example were created using the `\subref` command, which returns the reference formatted according to the `listofformat` (see page 320). This avoids any problem created by our redefinition of the `\thetable`, which would cause the `\ref` command to produce numbers like "11.3", because it combines the table number "1" with the sub-table number (e.g., "1.3").

The starred version of this command, `\subref*`, returns only the plain sub-float number (e.g., the value of `\thesubtable`), if needed to construct more complex references, such as "Figure 1(a-c)".

Sometimes one wants to label sub-floats but omit textual captions. This is, for example, common practice when showing a set of pictures or photographs: *Captionless* the main caption explains the significance of individual sub-floats. It can easily *sub-floats* be achieved by using an empty optional argument on the `\subfloat` command, which results in a labeled sub-float. The next example shows this type of layout.

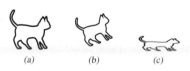

(a)   (b)   (c)

Figure 1: A group of cats: (a) the first cat, (b) a climbing one, and (c) one that is stretched.

6-5-11

```
\usepackage{graphicx}
\usepackage[font={scriptsize,sl},captionskip=3pt]{subfig}
\newcommand\FIG[1]{\includegraphics[#1]{cat}}

\begin{figure}   \centering
 \subfloat[]{\FIG{width=3pc}\label{a}}                \quad
 \subfloat[]{\FIG{angle=20,width=3pc}\label{b}}   \quad
 \subfloat[]{\FIG{height=1pc,width=3pc}\label{c}}
\caption[A group of cats]{A group of cats: \subref{a}
  the first cat, \subref{b} a climbing one,
   and \subref{c} one that is stretched.}
\end{figure}
```

It is also possible to fine-tune individual floats, if their sub-floats have unusual forms or excess white space. In Example 6-5-8 on page 316, we could, for example, *Manual fine-tuning* move the main caption closer to the sub-captions by adding the line

```
\captionsetup[subfloat]{nearskip=-3pt}
```

at the top of the float body. This command would apply to the current float only and cancel part of the `aboveskip` added above the main caption.

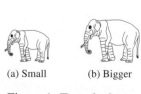

(a) Small   (b) Bigger

Figure 1: Two elephants

6-5-12

```
\usepackage{subfig} \usepackage{graphicx}
\begin{figure} \centering
 \captionsetup[subfloat]{nearskip=-3pt}
 \subfloat[Small]
    {\includegraphics[width=12mm]{elephant}\label{sf1}}
 \qquad
 \subfloat[Bigger]
    {\includegraphics[width=16mm]{elephant}\label{sf2}}
 \caption{Two elephants}\label{elephants}
\end{figure}
```

So far, we have discussed only sub-floats in `figure` or `table` environments. If you have added additional float types, you may want to be able to substructure them as well. This can be achieved with the `\newsubfloat` declaration.

> `\newsubfloat` [*option-value-list*] {*float-type*}

A prerequisite for using `\newsubfloat` is that there must already exist the environments to produce the given *float-type*—for example, environments declared with `\newfloat` from the float package. In that case `\newsubfloat` will set up `\subfloat` to be usable within their float bodies (e.g., by declaring the counter `\sub`⟨*float-type*⟩ to produce their labels). In the optional *option-value-list* argument, you can specify layout options that should apply only to this particular type of sub-float.

Producing list of ... entries
The sub-float captions are automatically entered into the external file holding the data for the corresponding "List of..." list. Such files have the extension `.lof` (a list of figures), `.lot` (list of tables), or the extension specified as the third argument to `\newfloat`.

The sub-float captions will not show up in these lists because only top-level float captions are typeset by default. To change this behavior, you have to set the counter's *ext*depth to 2 (where *ext* is the extension of the corresponding "List of..." file). For example, to make sub-figures captions appear you would use `\setcounter{lofdepth}{2}`, and for sub-tables you would change the value of `lotdepth`.

As explained in Section 2.3.2 the layout of such entries can be customized by redefining `\l@subfigure`, `\l@subtable`, and similar commands; the command name consists of float type prefixed by `l@sub`. However, subfig already offers three options that influence the entries in this list and they probably provide enough flexibility in most circumstances.

`listofindent`   The indentation for the sub-float caption inside the contents list. Its default value is `3.8em`.

`listofnumwidth`   The width reserved for the label in the contents list. Its default is `2.5em`.

`listofformat`   The format used for the label of the sub-float entry when displayed in the contents list. Possible keywords are `empty`, `simple`, `parens`, `subsimple`, and `subparens` (default). Additional formattings can be declared using the `\DeclareCaptionListOfFormat` command; for details, see the package documentation.
The typeset result is also used by the `\subref` command, so changing the value of this option will affect references created by this command.

The next example shows how the sub-floats appear in the contents listings. We set `lofdepth` to make them appear and extend `listofindent` to 5em so that they are slightly indented. We also use a continuation float to prove that sub-float numbering continues as well. To suppress the "List of..." entry for the continuation float we use an empty optional argument on the \caption command—the special feature provided by the caption package for such situations. Alternatively, we could have used \caption* to suppress both the caption number and the entry in the list of figures.

List of Figures

Figure I	Figure II
(a) First	(b) Second

Figure 1: Three figures

6-5-13

```
\usepackage[nearskip=-3pt,captionskip=5pt]{subfig}
\captionsetup[subfloat]{listofindent=4em,
                        listofformat=parens}
\setcounter{lofdepth}{2}
\listoffigures \medskip
\begin{figure}[!ht]\centering
  \subfloat[First]{\fbox{Figure I}}   \qquad
  \subfloat[Second]{\fbox{Figure II}}
  \caption{Three figures}
\end{figure}
\pagebreak        % <-- for illustration
\begin{figure}[!ht] \centering \ContinuedFloat
  \subfloat[Third]{\fbox{Figure III}}
  \caption[]{Three figures (cont.)}
\end{figure}
```

Like the caption package, subfig supports the use of external configuration files that contain your favorite settings using the option config. For example, *External configuration files*

```
\usepackage[config=xcaption]{subfig}
```

loads the file xcaption.cfg.

While it is possible to combine the config option with other options, a clearer approach is to to specify additional modifications through a \captionsetup declaration in the preamble.

6.5.3   subfloat—**Sub-numbering floats**

The subfloat package, developed by Harald Harders, can generate sub-numbers for figures or tables (analogous to the subequations environment of the amsmath package). While the subfig package sub-numbers objects inside one float, the subfloat package allows sub-numbering of the main captions of separate floats.

Figures (tables) for which sub-numbers are to be generated should be included inside a subfigures (subtables) environment. Alternatively, they can be placed between the commands \subfiguresbegin and \subfiguresend (\subtablesbegin and \subtablesend). While the environments must obey the basic nesting rules with respect to other environments, the commands can be placed anywhere. This flexibility can be helpful in unusual circumstances—for example, when sub-figures and sub-tables are intermixed.

The example that follows shows three figures. The first two are inside a subfigures environment, so they use sub-numbering ("1a" and "1b"). Both these labels are correctly handled by LaTeX's \listoffigures and \ref commands.

List of Figures

Figure I

Figure 1a: First figure

Figure II

Figure 1b: Second figure

Figures 1a and 1b in this

example are sub-numbered, while Figure 2 is not.

Figure III

Figure 2: Third figure

```
\usepackage{subfloat}
\listoffigures \medskip
\begin{subfigures}
 \begin{figure}[!ht]
  \centering\fbox{Figure I}
  \caption{First figure}\label{FI}
 \end{figure}
 \begin{figure}[!ht]
  \centering\fbox{Figure II}
  \caption{Second figure}\label{FII}
 \end{figure}
\end{subfigures}
Figures \ref{FI} and \ref{FII} in
this example are sub-numbered, while
Figure~\ref{FIII} is not.
\begin{figure}[!ht]
 \centering\fbox{Figure III}
 \caption{Third figure}\label{FIII}
\end{figure}
```

6-5-14

As in the previous example, the default caption label combines an Arabic numeral for the main figure with a lowercase letter to differentiate between the individual sub-figures. This label can be customized by redefining the command \thesubfloatfigure. Within its definition the command \themainfigure can be used to produce the main figure number[1] and the counter subfloatfigure to refer to the number of the sub-figure. Thus, to number sub-figures as "2.1", "2.2", and so on, one can define

```
\renewcommand\thesubfloatfigure{\themainfigure.\arabic{subfloatfigure}}
```

The same possibilities can be realized for tables by using the macros \thesubfloattable and \themaintable, and the counter subfloattable.

To enable users to automatically refer to the total number of sub-figures with the same main figure number, the package offers the option countmax. When it is used, the floats within a subfigures (subtables) environment are counted and the number is made available in the counter subfloatfiguremax (subfloattablemax). One could, for example, define

```
\renewcommand\thesubfloatfigure{\themainfigure
    (\arabic{subfloatfigure}/\arabic{subfloatfiguremax})}
```

to produce caption labels such as "2(1/3)", "2(2/3)", and "2(3/3)" when the second set of figures consists of three sub-figures. This counting is implemented as a two-

---

[1]For technical reasons the command \thefigure is not usable within sub-figures. The "alias" \themainfigure is provided for this purpose.

pass system that uses the \label and \ref mechanism internally—which means that it is expensive in terms of resources and time. For this reason the default is not to count.

6.5.4 sidecap—Place captions sideways

In their sidecap package Hubert Gäßlein and Rolf Niepraschk introduce two new environments, SCfigure and SCtable. They are analogous to LaTeX's figure and table, but typeset their captions at the side of the float in a minipage of a customizable width.

The package supports a number of options to influence the caption placement and formatting.

outercaption/innercaption   The caption is typeset on the outer (default) or inner side of the page, respectively, i.e., varying between verso and recto pages.

leftcaption/rightcaption   The caption is always typeset on the left or right side of the page, respectively.

wide   The caption or float may extend into the margin if necessary.

margincaption   The caption is set in the margin, with the float body appearing above the text. If this option is selected, the positioning of the float body with respect to the galley margins can be defined by using innerbody, outerbody, centerbody, leftbody, or rightbody.

raggedright/raggedleft/ragged   The caption text is not justified. With small measures, this option often leads to better results. With ragged the unjustified margin varies between verso and recto pages, so this is best used with innercaption, outercaption, or margincaption. Martin Schröder's ragged2e package is used, when available on the system.

If the sidecap package is combined with the caption package, you have the choice of specifying the justification with the above options or through the justification option of the caption package. Only ragged is unique, as caption offers no way to vary the justification between pages.

\begin{SCfigure}[rel-width] [float-spec] ⟨L-R material⟩ \end{SCfigure}
\begin{SCtable}[rel-width] [float-spec] ⟨L-R material⟩ \end{SCtable}

The environments SCfigure and SCtable (and their starred versions for spanning two columns) take two *optional* arguments. The *rel-width* argument defines the width of the caption relative to the width of the table or figure body (default 1.0). A large value (e.g., 20) reserves the maximal width available on the page. The second argument, *float-spec*, is LaTeX's standard float positional argument (e.g., [htb]). In contrast to standard LaTeX floats, the float body is assumed to be horizontal material (necessary to be able to measure it). If you require vertical material at this point, use a minipage environment inside the body.

The first example shows a table and a figure with their captions set beside them. For the table the defaults have been used, resulting in a caption that occupies the same amount of space as the table. The figure is set with the caption twice as wide as the figure body. With the defaults the caption would have been typeset on two lines even though ample space is available. Except for the justification, the actual caption layout has been customized using the caption package.

AAA	BBB
CCC	DDD
EEE	FFF

Table 1. *A small table with a rather long caption text*

Figure I

Figure 1. *A small figure*

Paragraph text showing how floats are horizontally aligned with respect to the galley.

```
\usepackage[ragged]{sidecap}
\usepackage[labelfont={sf,bf},textfont=it,
   labelsep=period]{caption}
Paragraph text showing how floats are
horizontally aligned with respect to the galley.
\begin{SCtable} \caption{A small table with a
                        rather long caption text}
   \begin{tabular}{|ll|}   AAA & BBB \\
            CCC & DDD \\ EEE & FFF \end{tabular}
\end{SCtable}
\begin{SCfigure}[2] \caption{A small figure}
   \framebox[.3\linewidth][c]{Figure I}
\end{SCfigure}
```

6-5-15

In addition to its options, the sidecap package offers some parameters to influence the formatting. The size of the separation between the body and the caption can be changed by redefining \sidecaptionsep (using \renewcommand). The default is to use the value of the parameter \marginparsep. Instead of repeatedly specifying an optional argument to the environments, you can set the (default) relation between the float body and the caption size by redefining \sidecaptionrelwidth. For tables, the caption is aligned at the top; for figures, it is aligned at the bottom. This default can be changed by using a declaration like \sidecaptionvpos{table}{b}, where the second argument should be any one of: t, c, or b.

Changing the default settings

The next example uses all three customization possibilities, and the floats are allowed to extend into the margin (option wide). In fact, because of the chosen value for \sidecaptionrelwidth, they are forced to use all space available.

AAA	BBB
CCC	DDD
EEE	FFF

Table 1: A small table with a rather long caption text

Text showing how the float is horizontally aligned with respect to the galley.

```
\usepackage[wide]{sidecap}
\renewcommand\sidecaptionsep{15pt}
\renewcommand\sidecaptionrelwidth{20}
\sidecaptionvpos{table}{c}
Text showing how the float is horizontally
aligned with respect to the galley.
\begin{SCtable} \caption{A small table with
                     a rather long caption text}
   \begin{tabular}{|ll|}   AAA & BBB \\
      CCC & DDD \\ EEE & FFF    \end{tabular}
\end{SCtable}
```

6-5-16

The package tries hard to produce a reasonable alignment between the float body and the caption text. In most cases, such as when the body consists of a `tabular` environment, it will produce satisfactory results. However, if the body contains straight text, perhaps as part of a `minipage` environment, you may have to help the alignment along by specifying a `\strut`, as shown in the next example. The second `\strut` on the last line is actually not necessary for a top-aligned caption but would be needed if the caption is bottom-aligned.

The example demonstrates the `ragged` option showing that it results in a ragged left setting if the caption appears in the left margin.

Table 1: A Some text for our page that misaligned is reused over and over again. caption Some text for our page that is reused over and over again.

Table 2: An Some text for our page that aligned is reused over and over again. caption Some text for our page that is reused over and over again.

6-5-17

```
\usepackage[margincaption,ragged]{sidecap}
% \sample as defined earlier
\begin{SCtable} \caption{A misaligned caption}
 \begin{minipage}{\linewidth}
  \sample \sample
\end{minipage}\end{SCtable}
\begin{SCtable} \caption{An aligned caption}
 \begin{minipage}{\linewidth}
 \strut \sample \sample \unskip\strut
\end{minipage}\end{SCtable}
```

6.5.5   fltpage—Captions on a separate page

When dealing with large figures or tables, sometimes insufficient room is left on the page to typeset the caption. Sebastian Gross's fltpage package addresses this problem by defining the environments FPfigure and FPtable. They are similar to `figure` and `table`, respectively, but typeset the caption for a full-page figure or table on the opposite page in `twoside` mode, or on the preceding or following page in `oneside` mode.

The package behavior is controlled by a number of options that specify the placement of the caption in relation to the float body (options in parentheses are alias option names):

closeFloats   The full-page floats are placed on the *next* possible page. In `twoside` mode the caption is placed on the bottom of the opposite page; in `oneside` mode it is always placed on the page before the float body.

rightFloats (CaptionBefore)   The float body always appears on a recto page and the caption on the previous page.

leftFloats (CaptionAfterwards)   The float body always appears on a verso page and the caption on the following page.

The "isolated" caption that refers to a full-page float is separated from the remaining text on the page by a horizontal rule. This rule can be suppressed by specifying the `noSeparatorLine` option. Moreover, to make the connection between the caption and the float, you can let the package add hints like "Table xx. (on the facing page)" by specifying the option `varioref`. In that case the `varioref` package is used to produce such texts in the document language.[1]

We next construct a simple example demonstrating the principles underlying the fltpage package. In the example we construct an artificial full-page table by putting a frame containing an invisible rule (of zero width) inside a box with dimensions that are a small fraction smaller than the page dimensions.[2] The figure caption is typeset at the bottom of the page opposite the float material. Because we load the `varioref` package and specify the `varioref` option, the text "*(on the next page)*" is inserted automatically by the fltpage package.

1   Full-page floats

Figure 1 is a full-page float whose caption and body are on separate pages.

Figure 1 *(on the next page)*: Caption for a full-page float for which there was no room on the same page

                         6

A full-page figure

                         7

```
\usepackage[twoside,varioref,
            closeFloats]{fltpage}
\listoffigures
\section{Full-page floats}
Figure~\ref{FP1} is a
full-page float whose caption
and body are on separate pages.
\begin{FPfigure}
 \setlength\fboxsep{0pt}
 \framebox[.97\linewidth][c]
    {\rule[-3cm]{0pt}
       {.97\textheight}%
     A full-page figure}
 \caption[A full-page figure]
    {Caption for a full-page float
     for which there was no room
     on the same page}\label{FP1}
\end{FPfigure}
```

6-5-18

Caveats   Unfortunately this package is no longer being developed. Thus, it is, for example, impossible to use it for float types other than `figure` and `table` (e.g., those that can be defined with the float package). Furthermore, problems may potentially arise if floats appear to close to each other in the source (the content of the second might overwrite the first). Nevertheless, if used with care, it provides a solution to the difficult problem of handling large floats that currently has no counterpart in any other package available.

---

[1] This feature may not work if the layout of the caption is customized by the caption package.
[2] This step is needed to avoid generating overfull boxes due to the width of the \framebox rules. The separation \fboxsep between the frame and the inner material is also set to zero points.

## CHAPTER 7

Fonts and Encodings

7.1 Introduction

Half of the job of (LA)TEX as a typesetting system is to process the source document and to calculate from it the characters' positions on the output page. But (LA)TEX has only a primitive knowledge about these characters, which it basically regards as black boxes having a width, height, and depth. For each font these dimensions are stored in a separate external file, the so-called TEX font metric or .tfm file.

The character shapes that correspond to such a .tfm file come into play at a later stage, after (LA)TEX has produced its .dvi file. Character placement information in the .dvi file and information about character shapes present in the .pk file or in outline descriptions (e.g., PostScript) are combined by a driver program that produces the character image on the output medium. Usually one driver program is needed for every output medium—for screen representation, a low-resolution laser printer, or other device. With TEX variants such as pdfTEX or VTEX that bypass the production of .dvi output and instead directly generate PDF or PostScript output, the situation is slightly different (but, as far as LATEX is concerned, similar). In that case the character shapes are "added" when the underlying formatter produces the final output format. That is, the driver program is internal, but the basic concepts are identical.

7.1.1 The history of LATEX's font selection scheme (NFSS)

When TEX was developed in 1979, only a dozen fonts were set up for use with the program: the "Almost Computer Modern" fonts, developed by Donald Knuth along with TEX. With only this restricted set of fonts being available, a straightforward approach for accessing them was used: a few control sequences were defined that changed from one external font to another.

This situation had not greatly changed five years later, when LATEX was first released. Only the names of the fonts supplied with (LA)TEX had changed, from Almost Computer Modern to Computer Modern, which was merely a slightly improved version of the former. So it was quite natural that LATEX's font selection scheme followed the plain TEX concept with the addition of size-changing commands that allowed typesetting in 10 predefined sizes.

As a result LATEX's font selection was far from general. For instance, when defining a heading command to produce a bolder font (by using a \bf command in its definition), the use of, say, \sf (for a sans serif font) inside that same heading did not produce a bold sans serif font but rather a medium-weight sans serif font (the bold attribute was ignored). Similarly, when, say, \bf was used inside emphasized text, the result was not a bold italic font, as normally desired, but rather a plain Roman bold font.

This behavior was caused by the fact that all the font-changing commands, such as \bf, referred to a fixed external font. As a consequence, rather than requesting an attribute change of the current font, they replaced the current font with another. Of course, LATEX enhanced the plain TEX mechanism to a certain extent by providing a set of size-changing commands. Nevertheless, the underlying concept of the original release had a major drawback: the correspondence tables were hard-wired into LATEX, so that changing the fonts was a difficult, if not impossible, task.

Since that time low-priced laser printers have become available and simultaneously a large number of font families from PostScript and other type formats have appeared. The number of fonts in METAFONT source format (freely available to every (LA)TEX installation) has also increased drastically. But, unfortunately, there was no easy and standard method for integrating these new fonts into LATEX—typesetting with LATEX meant typesetting in Computer Modern on almost all installations. Of course, individual fonts could be loaded using the \newfont command, but this capability cannot be called integration: it requires a great deal of user intervention, because the additional fonts do not change size under the control of size commands, and it was extremely complicated to typeset a whole document in a font family.

There have been a few efforts to integrate other fonts into LATEX. Typically, they involved exchanging one hard-wired font table with another. Thus, the resulting LATEX variant was as inflexible as the original one, as this approach merely forced the use of a different set of fonts.

This unsatisfactory situation was finally resolved in 1989 with the release of the New Font Selection Scheme (NFSS) [128, 130] written by Frank Mittelbach and Rainer Schöpf, which became widely known after it was successfully used in $\mathcal{A}_{\mathcal{M}}\mathcal{S}$-LATEX (see Chapter 8). This system contains a generic concept for varying font attributes individually and for integrating new font families easily into an existing LATEX system. The concept is based on five attributes that can be defined independently to access different fonts, font characteristics, or font families. To implement it, some of the LaTeX commands were redefined and some new commands were added.

Later, a prototype version for scalable fonts was coded by Mark Purtill. Starting from his work, Frank Mittelbach designed and implemented NFSS2 integrating work by Sebastian Rahtz (on PostScript fonts) and several others. This version became the standard LaTeX font selection scheme in 1994, when the current LaTeX version (LaTeX 2_ε) was released.

This font selection scheme has now been in worldwide use for more than a decade and the code has proven to be stable and successful, though some people feel that extensions would be useful. The LaTeX Project Team would welcome such experimental extensions in the form of external packages, which at a later stage might be consolidated into a successor of the base font selection mechanism.

7.1.2 Input and output encodings

As one of the side effects of being able to access more fonts, it became apparent that two related areas in TeX made hard-wired selections no longer appropriate: the areas of input and output (or font) encodings.

If we press a key on a keyboard (usually) some 8-bit number will be generated representing a certain character. An input encoding describes which character corresponds to which number. When using different national keyboards or different operating systems, the correspondence between character and number may vary widely. For example, on the German keyboard that the author used to write this text, the key labeled "ä" will generate the 8-bit number "228" when used with Linux or Windows, but it generates "132" when used with MS-DOS.

When your document is stored in a computer file, information that remains about the characters consists of only these 8-bit numbers; the information about the input encoding used is not explicitly stored. Thus, if you transfer a file to a different environment, such as, from the United States to the United Kingdom, you might find that the dollar signs in your document are suddenly interpreted as pound symbols when viewing your file with some program (editor) that makes the wrong assumption about the encoding used to write the file.

To help with input encoding problems, in 1994–1995 the LaTeX Project Team developed the inputenc package. It enables users to explicitly declare the input encoding used for documents or parts of documents. This mechanism allows you to safely transfer documents from one LaTeX installation to another and to achieve identical printed results.[1]

The inputenc package works by interpreting the 8-bit numbers present in the file (representing the characters) and mapping them to an "internal LaTeX representation", which uniquely (albeit on a somewhat ad hoc basis) covers all characters representable in LaTeX. For further processing, such as writing to some auxiliary

The input encoding concept

---

[1] Other solutions to this problem exist. For example, some people advertise the use of translation tables hard-wired into the program TeX itself. This works as long as all people exchanging documents use a TeX system with the same hard-wired tables but fails otherwise.

file, LaTeX exclusively uses this internal representation, thereby avoiding any possible misinterpretation.

However, at some point LaTeX has to associate these internal character representations with glyphs (i.e., character shapes in certain fonts) so another mapping must take place. TeX's fonts contain a maximum of 256 glyphs. These glyphs are not addressed by name, but rather by (8-bit) numbers representing the positions of the glyphs in the font (i.e., we have to map from a large unique naming space into several small ones). And it probably does not come as a large surprise to hear that these glyph positions again vary widely.

Thus, even after preserving the meaning of our dollar sign from the external file to the internals of LaTeX, we might still end up with the wrong shape on paper if we happen to select a font for printing that contains an unexpected glyph in the position (slot) we assumed was occupied by a dollar sign.[1] It is one of the tasks of NFSS to ensure either that any LaTeX internal character representation is properly rendered or, if that is impossible for some reason, that the user receives a proper error message.

Made-up accented characters prevent hyphenation
If fonts contain accented characters as individual glyphs, rather than only base characters plus accents (from which TeX then has to build up the accented glyphs internally), then it is preferable to use these glyphs because they typically have a better appearance. There is also a technical reason for this preference: the \accent primitive of TeX will suppress hyphenation. This defect might be acceptable if such words are occurring only infrequently, as when typesetting English. However, when dealing with, say, a French text in which all words with accents are never hyphenated, line breaking soon becomes a nightmare.

To cater to the different possibilities, a command such as \'e (LaTeX's internal representation for the character e-acute, é) sometimes has to initiate some complicated actions involving the \accent primitive. In other cases it merely informs the paragraph builder that it wants the glyph from a certain slot in the current font.

The output encoding concept
All this is achieved in LaTeX through the concept of output encodings, which map the LaTeX internal character representations to appropriate glyph positions or to glyph-building actions depending on the actual glyphs available in the font used for typesetting. Although the output encoding concept was fully introduced with NFSS2, it took several years to finally settle on its current implementation (the internals were rewritten several times while the developers were gaining more insight into the problems in this area).

∗   ∗   ∗

The following sections describe release 2 of NFSS, which was completed at the end of 1992 and became part of standard LaTeX in 1994. As far as the user interface is concerned, it is intended for integration into LaTeX3.

We start by discussing font characteristics in general and introduce the major attributes used in LaTeX for orthogonal font switching. We then describe the use of

---

[1]The example of the $ turning into a £ sign is not artificial: some of the original TeX fonts show this strangeness, and Knuth [82, p.339] even advocates typesetting a pound symbol using {\it\$}.

the high-level interface—that is, the commands a user normally has to deal with. This includes commands used in normal text (Section 7.3), special features for use in mathematical formulas (Section 7.4), and an overview of basic support packages for NFSS—those being distributed together with LaTeX (Section 7.5). It also covers the packages and commands provided to deal with the encoding issues mentioned earlier.

One of the important advantages of LaTeX's font selection scheme is the ease with which new fonts for use in the main text can be integrated. Besides the Computer Modern families, which are used by default, one can easily use other font families by adding the appropriate package in the preamble. Of course, for successful processing and printing the corresponding font files (e.g., the .tfm and .pk, Type 1, or TrueType files) must be installed on the system. The next three sections deal with major and minor font packages. Section 7.6 discusses PSNFSS, the standard PostScript support for LaTeX, which is part of the required set of packages available with any LaTeX distribution.

This is followed by a collection of other interesting packages for adjusting the document body fonts (Section 7.7) and by an introduction to the LaTeX world of symbols (Section 7.8). All packages described are available free of charge, and most (if not all) are part of a modern LaTeX distribution. Some pointers to commercial font support are given as well.

The final part of this chapter describes the low-level interfaces that are useful when defining complex new commands and that are important when new fonts are to be made available in LaTeX. Here you will find low-level commands for changing individual font attributes (Section 7.9), commands for setting up new fonts with LaTeX (Section 7.10), and a discussion of LaTeX's encoding models for text and math (Section 7.11). The chapter concludes with a section devoted to compatibility questions that arise with very old LaTeX documents.

7.2   Understanding font characteristics

There are many design principles that divide fonts into individual overlapping classes. Knowledge of these characteristics often proves helpful when deciding which font family to use in a special context (for further reading see, for example, the books [28, 41, 116] or the article [52]).

7.2.1   Monospaced and proportional fonts

Fonts can be either monospaced or proportionally spaced. In a monospaced font, each individual character takes up the same horizontal space regardless of its shape. In contrast, characters in a proportionally spaced font take up different amounts of space depending on their shape. In Figure 7.1 on the following page, you can see that the "i" of the monospaced font occupies the same space as the "m", while it is noticeably narrower in the proportional font. As a result, proportional fonts (also called typographical fonts) normally allow more words to be

iiiiiiiiii   iiiiiiiii
mmmmmmmmmm   mmmmmmmmmm

(monospaced)   (proportionally spaced)

Figure 7.1: Major font characteristics

placed on a page and are more readable than monospaced fonts. The extra spaces around individual characters of monospaced fonts make it more difficult for the eye to recognize word boundaries and thus make monospaced text less readable.

However, monospaced fonts do have their uses. Within the proper context, they enhance the quality of the printed document. For example, in tables or computer listings where proper alignment of information is important, a monospaced font is a natural choice. In computer science books, it is common practice to display computer programs in a monospaced font to make them easily distinguishable from surrounding explanations.

But the use of monospaced fonts goes beyond marking portions of a document as special. One can even consider choosing a monospaced font as the base font for a complete document. Such a font has the flavor of the manual or electric typewriter engine; it looks hand-made when used with unjustified paragraphs and therefore may be better suited to certain situations than a more professional-looking typographical font. Keep in mind, however, that monospaced fonts look very poor when lines are justified. (See Section 3.1.11 to learn how to turn off justification.)

7.2.2   Serifed and sans serif fonts

Another useful classification is based on the presence or absence of serifs. Serifs are the tiny horizontal strokes at the extremities of character shapes (see Figure 7.2). Originally they were produced by the chisel, when Roman capitals were engraved into stone. For this reason, serifed fonts are often referred to as "Roman" fonts.

Serifed fonts traditionally have been used for long texts because, it was argued, they are more readable. It was long thought that serifed letters give the eye more clues for identification. This is certainly true if only parts of the characters are visible, but for fully visible text recent research has shown that reading speed is not substantially affected by the absence of serifs [150].

Figure 7.2: Comparison of serifed and sans serif letters

$$
\begin{array}{ccccccccc}
A & B & C & a & b & c & x & y & z \\
A & B & C & a & b & c & x & y & z \\
A & B & C & a & b & c & x & y & z
\end{array}
$$

Figure 7.3: Comparison between upright and italic shapes

7.2.3   Font families and their attributes

Besides the crude classifications of serifed versus sans serif and monospaced versus proportional, fonts are grouped into font families. Members of a font family share common design principles and are distinguished by variations in size, weight, width, and shape.

Font shapes

An important attribute when classifying a member of a font family is its shape. Of course, sometimes it is a matter of personal judgment whether a set of fonts with different shapes constitutes one or several families. For example, Donald Knuth called his collection of 31 Computer Modern fonts a family [86], yet they form a meta-family of many families in the traditional sense.[1]

Although there is no uniform naming convention for font shapes, this is unimportant as long as one sticks to a particular scheme within LATEX.

Nearly every font family has one shape called the "upright" shape.[2] For example, in the font family used in this book (Lucida Bright), the font that you are now reading is in the upright shape. *The upright shape*

Another important shape that is present in most families is the "italic" shape, which looks *like this* in the Lucida Bright family. Italic characters are slanted to the right and the individual letters generally are drawn differently from their upright counterparts, as illustrated in Figure 7.3. The first line in that figure shows letters from the Computer Modern Serif family in upright shape, and the third line shows the same letters in italic shape. For better comparison, the second line gives the italic letters without the usual slant—that is, the letters are artificially shown in an upright position. *The italic shape*

Font families without serifs often lack a proper italic shape; instead, they have a "slanted" shape in which the characters slant to the right but are otherwise identical to their upright counterparts. The terms "sloped" and "oblique" are also commonly used for this shape. *The slanted or oblique shape*

---

[1]METAFONT, as a design tool, allows the production of completely different fonts from the same source description, so it is not surprising that in 1989 another family was created [92] based on the sources for the Computer Modern fonts. This family, Concrete Roman, was obtained merely by varying some METAFONT parameters in the source files; but since the result was so different, Knuth decided to give this family a different name.

[2]Sometimes you will also hear the term "Roman" shape. This is due to the fact that until recently typesetting was nearly always done using serifed fonts. Thus, "Roman" was considered to be the opposite of "italic" by many people. So be aware that in some books this term actually refers to the upright shape and not to a serifed font family.

EXAMPLE   Example   Example

(Normal Capitals)   (Small Caps)   (Faked Small Caps)

Figure 7.4: Comparison between caps and small caps

The small caps
shape

Faking small
capitals

Another common variant is the "small caps" shape, in which the lowercase letters are represented as capitals with a reduced height, as shown in Figure 7.4. If such a shape is not available for a specific family, typographers sometimes use upright capitals from smaller sizes,[1] but this practice does not produce the same quality as a well-designed small caps font. Real small caps have different widths and weight than capital letters from the same font that have been reduced to the height of designed small caps (you can clearly see that the strokes in the faked capitals in Figure 7.4 are much too thin).

It is an open argument whether one should consider "small caps" to be a shape or whether this would be better modeled as another independent axis. In the latter interpretation, fonts have a "case" attribute, which could be either mixed case (the normal case), all caps, small caps, or all lowercase. For certain font families this would certainly be the better solution, but currently the LaTeX font selection supports only four axes modeling small caps as a shape.[2]

There are a few other, less important shapes. Some families contain fonts in which the inner parts of the letters are drawn in a special fashion, most importantly perhaps the "outline" shapes, in which the inner parts of the letters are kept empty. For display purposes, some families also contain fonts that could be classified as "shaded"—that is, where the letters appear three-dimensional. Examples are shown in Figure 7.5 on the facing page.

Special variants of the Computer Modern meta-family have been produced by setting the METAFONT parameters to special values. For example, there is "upright italic", a shape in which the individual letters are drawn in italic fashion but without the usual slant (see the second line in Figure 7.3 on the previous page). This shape was devised for purposes of showing the abilities of METAFONT as a tool for meta-design, but some users might take a fancy to such an unusual shape.

Weight and width

Fonts of a certain shape within a family may differ in "weight". This characteristic refers to the thickness of the strokes used to draw the individual shapes. Once again, the commonly used names are not completely uniform, but it is relatively

---

[1] A good rule of thumb is to use capitals from a font that is about half a point larger than the x-height of the original font unless the x-height is very small. See discussion in Section 7.10.3 on page 428 for a way to determine the x-height of any font used with TeX.

[2] In some cases small caps fonts are in fact modeled as extra families to enable the combination of, say, small caps italic.

The LATEX Companion

Figure 7.5: Outline and shaded shapes

easy to arrive at a consistent classification. Some font manufacturers, for example, call the font weights intended to be used for normal text "book", while others call them "medium". For thin strokes the name "light" is commonplace, while thicker strokes are usually called "bold". In larger font families, finer distinctions are often necessary, so that we sometimes find a range starting with "ultra light", going through "extra light", "light", "semi light", and so on, and ending with "ultra bold" at the other end. Conversely, often only a few weights are present in some families. For example, the Computer Modern Roman family has only two weights, "medium" and "**bold**".

Another equally important attribute of a font is its "width"—the amount of expansion or contraction with respect to the normal or medium width in the family. Computer Modern Roman has bold fonts in "**medium width**" and "**extended width**". One application for condensed fonts is in titles and headings, where medium-width fonts, when used at large sizes, would consume too much space. Some typesetting systems can even condense fonts automatically to fit a given measure—for example, to exactly fill a particular line in a heading. This capability is not directly possible with (LA)TEX, but in any case the results are often aesthetically questionable.

Font sizes

Font sizes are traditionally measured in printer points (pt). There are 72.27 points to an inch.[1] The font size is not an absolute measure of any particular characteristic, but rather a value chosen by the font designer to guide the user. For example, in a 10pt font, letters of the alphabet are usually less than 10pt tall, and only characters such as parentheses have approximately this height.

Two fonts of the same size may not blend well with one another because the appearance of a font depends on many factors, such as the height of the lowercase letters (the x-height), the stroke width, and the depth of the descenders (the part of the letters below the baseline, as in the letter q).

In the (LA)TEX world, fonts are often available in sizes that are powers of 1.2— that is, in a geometric progression [82, p.17]. This arrangement was chosen because it makes it easy to produce an enlarged master copy that later can be photographically reduced, thereby effectively enlarging the final output resolution. For example, if an A5 brochure is to be produced, one could print it with magnifica-

---

[1] PostScript uses a slightly different measurement system in which 72 points equal an inch. These units, sometimes referred to as "big points", are available in TEX as bp.

Ten point type is different from ᴍᴀɢɴɪғɪᴇᴅ ғɪᴠᴇ ᴘᴏɪɴᴛ ᴛʏᴘᴇ

Figure 7.6: Scaled and designed fonts (Computer Modern)

tion of $1.44 \approx \sqrt{2}$ on A4 paper. Photographic reduction from the 300 dpi (dots per inch) output of a normal laser printer would produce an effective output resolution of 432 dpi and thus would give higher quality than is normally possible with such a laser printer.

However, this geometric ratio scheme used by (LA)TEX fonts produced with the METAFONT program is not common in the professional world, where usual point sizes are 7, 8, 9, 10, 11, 12, 14, 16, 18, 20, 24, 30, and 36. Yet not all fonts are available in all these sizes, and sometimes additional sizes are offered—such as display sizes for large headings and tiny sizes for subscripts and superscripts. The requirement for fixed sizes had its origin in the technology used. Fonts cast in metal had to exist (at a particular size) or you could not print in that size. In today's digitalized world, fonts are usually vectorized and thus can be scaled at will. As a result, many commercial font families nowadays are provided in only a single design size.

The use of magnified or reduced fonts instead of fonts designed for a specific size often gives somewhat less satisfactory results, because to the human eye fonts do not scale in a linear fashion. The characters in handcrafted fonts of larger sizes usually are narrower than fonts magnified from a smaller size of the same family. While it is acceptable to scale fonts within a small size range if necessary, one should use fonts designed for the desired size whenever possible. The difference between fonts scaled to a particular size and those designed for that size is shown in Figure 7.6, though admittedly the variations are often less noticeable.

7.2.4 Font encodings

As mentioned in the chapter introduction, TEX refers to the glyphs of a font by addressing them via 8-bit numbers. Such a mapping is called a font encoding. As far as LATEX is concerned, two fonts having the same font encoding are supposed to be interchangeable in the sense that given the same input they produce the "same" glyphs on the printed page. To illustrate what happens if we use a font with an encoding not suitable for our input, here is the first sentence of this section again (using the Zapf Dingbats font):

✿▲ ○❋■▼❖□■❉❉ ❉■ ▼❉❉ ❉❉●□▼❉□ ❉■▼□□❉◆❉▼❉□■✽ TEX
□❉❉❉□▲ ▼□ ▼❉❉ ❉●❏□❉▲ □❉ ❀ ❉□■▼ ○❉ ❀❉❉□❉▲▲❉■❉ ▼❉❉□
❖❉❀ ✗◿○❉▼ ■◆◆○○❉❉□▲✎

The result is an interesting puzzle, but nothing that we want to see in ordinary documents.

By classifying fonts according to their font encodings it is possible to modify other font characteristics, such as font family or font series, and still ensure that the typeset result will stay comprehensible.

The fonts that were originally distributed with TeX have only 128 glyphs per font and therefore do not include any accented characters as individual glyphs. *OT1 encoding* Instead, all such glyphs have to be constructed using the `\accent` primitive of TeX or by similar methods. As a result any word containing diacritics cannot be automatically hyphenated by LaTeX and kerning (correction of spacing between certain letters in the font) cannot be automatically applied. The encoding of these fonts is called `OT1`. Although it remains the default encoding for LaTeX, it is not advisable to use `OT1` for languages other than English.

As an alternative encoding, the TeX user community defined a 256-character encoding called `T1` that enables TeX to typeset correctly (with proper hyphenation *T1 encoding* and kerning) in more than 30 languages based on the Latin alphabet (see Section 7.5.1 on page 353 for further details). The use of the T1 encoding is, therefore, highly recommended. Nowadays nearly all font families amenable to use with LaTeX are available in this encoding; in fact, some are *only* available in the T1 encoding. Specifying `\usepackage[T1]{fontenc}` after the `\documentclass` command, makes T1 become the default encoding. Section 7.5.3 contains a more detailed discussion of the fontenc package. For more on font encodings refer to page 415 and Section 7.11 on page 440.

7.3 Using fonts in text

When you are writing a LaTeX document, appropriate fonts are normally chosen automatically by the (logical) markup tags used to structure the document. For example, the font attributes for a section heading, such as large size and bold weight, are defined by the document class and applied when a `\section` command is used, so that you seldom need to specify font attributes yourself.

However, occasionally it becomes necessary to specify font attributes directly. One common reason is the desire to change the overall font attributes, by choosing, for example, a different font family for the main text. This alteration often can be done by simply specifying an appropriate package (see Sections 7.6 and 7.7 for descriptions of such packages).

Another use for explicit font attributes can be to mark certain portions of the document as special—for example, to denote acronyms, example, or company names. For instance, in this book, names of packages are formatted in a sans serif font. This formatting could be achieved by surrounding the names with `\textsf{..}`, but it is much better practice to define a new command (say, `\LPack`) for this purpose so that additional information is included in the source document. By defining individual commands for logically different things—even those that are currently being typeset in the same way—it is easier to change the formatting later in a consistent way.

Last, but not least, in some cases you may want to override a decision taken by the document class. For example, you might want to typeset a table in a smaller size to make it fit on a page. This desire is legitimate, as document classes can format documents automatically only to a certain extent. Hand-formatting—like the insertion of page breaks—is thus often necessary to create the final version. Unfortunately, explicit formatting makes further use of the document (if changes are made) difficult and error prone. Therefore, as with all visual formatting commands, you should try to minimize the direct use of font-changing commands in a document.

7.3.1 Standard LaTeX font commands

The font used for the main text of a document is called the "main font", "body font", or "normal font". It is automatically selected at the beginning of the document and in certain constructs, such as footnotes, and figures. Certain logical markup tags, such as section headings, automatically switch to a different typeface or size, depending on the document class. These changes happen behind the scenes, and the only action required of the author is to introduce the correct logical markup in the document. However, sometimes it might be desirable to manually highlight individual parts of the text, by choosing an appropriate typeface; this is done with the commands described below.

Most font-changing commands come in two forms: a command with one argument, such as \textbf{...}, and a declarative form, such as \bfseries. The declarations do not take arguments but rather instruct LaTeX that from now on (up to the end of the current group of braces or environments) it should behave in a special way. Thus, you should not write something like \bfseries{...}, as this would make everything bold from this point until the end of the current environment.

To change the fonts for individual words or short phrases within your document you should make use of the font commands with one argument. The declarative forms are often better in the definition of new environments or commands. For longer passages in your document, you can also use the environment form of the declaration (the declarative name without the preceding backslash), as shown in the following example:

Some words in this sentence are **typeset in bold letters.**

The bold typeface continues here.

```
Some words in this sentence are
\begin{bfseries}typeset in bold letters.

The bold typeface\end{bfseries} continues here.
```

7-3-1

In fact, the font commands with one argument do not allow paragraph breaks in their arguments. Section 7.3.3 on page 344 contains a detailed comparison of the command declarative forms and their advantages and disadvantages in specific cases.

The main document font

To switch to the main document font you can use the command `\textnormal` or the declaration `\normalfont`. They are typically used only in the definition of commands or environments when it is important to define commands that always typeset in the same font regardless of the surrounding conditions. For example, the command to typeset the command names in this book is defined roughly as follows:

```
\newcommand\Lcs[1]{{\normalfont\ttfamily\textbackslash#1}%
                    \index{#1@{\normalfont\ttfamily\textbackslash#1}}}
```

Using `\normalfont` prevents the command names coming out *like \this in certain* places.

Standard font families

By default, LaTeX maintains three font families that can be selected with short command sequences. These families are a serifed text font, accessed with the command `\textrm`; a sans serif text font, accessed by `\textsf`; and a typewriter font (usually monospaced), accessed by `\texttt`. The declaration forms of these commands are `\rmfamily`, `\sffamily`, and `\ttfamily`, respectively.

The names of the external font families accessed by these commands depend on the document class but can be changed by packages or in the preamble (see Section 7.3.5). As an installation default, the serifed font family is Computer Modern Roman, the sans serif family is Computer Modern Sans, and the typewriter family is Computer Modern Typewriter. If you use a different set-up, take care to define these default families so that the fonts can be mixed freely without visual clashes. Also, make sure that the external fonts are available in the correct resolution for the targeted output device.

In this book, the serifed font family is Lucida Bright, the sans serif family is Lucida Sans, and the typewriter family is European Modern Typewriter. These have been chosen by simply[1] loading the package lucidabr and afterwards redefining `\ttdefault` to produce emtt; see Section 7.3.5 for more details on changing the default text fonts.

In most document classes, the serifed font, accessed by `\textrm`, is also the main font of the document, so the command `\textrm` is not used often. But if a document designer has chosen a sans serif font as the main typeface, then `\textrm` would be the alternative serifed font family.

---

[1] Somewhat more truthful: for the second edition of this book the Lucida fonts were scaled down slightly, while the European Modern Typewriter was scaled up to match the x-height of both families using specially designed `\DeclareFontShape` declarations.

Standard font series

Another attribute of a typeface that can be changed is the *series*. In LaTeX the series is a combination of two attributes: width and weight (boldness). LaTeX provides two commands for changing the series: `\textmd` and `\textbf`. The corresponding declarations are `\mdseries` and `\bfseries`, respectively. The first command selects a font with medium values for the width and the weight, while the latter switches to a bolder series. The actual values depend on the document class and its options or subsequent packages. As a default for the Computer Modern families, `\textbf` switches to a bold extended version of the current typeface, while `\textmd` returns to the medium width and medium weight version of the current typeface.

If finer control over the series attribute is desired, it is best to define additional high-level user commands with the help of the lower-level `\fontseries` declaration described in Section 7.9.1. Some packages that make large font families available for use with LaTeX provide such extra commands.

Standard font shapes

A third font attribute that may be changed independently of the others is the *shape* of the current typeface. The default shape for most documents is the upright shape. It can be accessed, if necessary, with the command `\textup` or the declaration `\upshape`.

Probably the most important commands for changing the shape are `\textit` and `\textsc`, which switch to an *italic* or CAPS AND SMALL CAPS font shape, respectively. The corresponding declarations are `\itshape` and `\scshape`.

An alternative to `\textit` is the `\textsl` command (its declaration form is `\slshape`), which switches to the slanted shape. A font family often contains only an italic or a slanted shape, yet Computer Modern Roman contains both.

At the point where one switches from slanted to upright, the characters usually come too close together, especially if the last slanted character has an ascender. The proper amount of extra white space that should be added at this boundary is called the "italic correction". The value of this adjustment depends on the individual character shape and is stored in the `.tfm` file. The italic correction is automatically added by the font commands with arguments but it must be inserted manually using `\/` when declarations are employed. For an upright font, the italic correction of the characters is usually zero or very small, but there are some exceptions. (In Computer Modern, to typeset a bold "f" in single quotes, you should say '`{\bfseries f\/}`' or '`\textbf{f}`', lest you get a bold 'f' in some fonts.) In slanted or italic fonts, the italic correction is usually positive, with the actual value depending on the shape of the character. The correct usage of shape-changing declarations that switch to slanted shapes is shown in the next example.

When switching back from *italic* or *slanted* shapes to an upright font one should add the *italic correction*, except when a small punctuation character follows.

```
\raggedright
When switching back from {\itshape italic\/} or
{\slshape slanted\/} shapes to an upright font
one should add the {\itshape italic correction},
except when a small punctuation character follows.
```

7-3-2

   If you use the command forms with one argument instead, the italic correction is added automatically. This topic is further discussed in Section 7.3.3.

   Small capitals are sometimes used in headings or to format names. For the latter case you can, for example, define the command \name with the definition

```
\newcommand\name[1]{\textsc{#1}}
```

or, using two declarations:

```
\newcommand\name[1]{{\normalfont\scshape #1}}
```

The first definition simply switches to the desired shape, while the second form initially resets all font attributes to their defaults. Which approach is preferable depends on the available fonts and the type of document. With Computer Modern only the Roman and typewriter families contain a small caps shape, so the second definition might be preferred in certain applications because it will use small caps (though serifed) even in a \sffamily context. The first command would result in a request for a medium series, small caps, shaped font in the Computer Modern Sans family. Because this font is not available, LaTeX would try to find a substitute by first changing the shape attribute to its default, with the result that you would not get small caps. (See Section 7.9.3 for further information about substitutions.)

   Another interesting use of the \scshape declaration is in the definition of an acronym tag:

```
\newcommand\acro[1]{{\scshape\MakeLowercase{#1}}}
```

This definition makes use of the LaTeX command \MakeLowercase, which changes all characters within its argument to lowercase (in contrast to the TeX primitive \lowercase, this command also changes characters referred to by commands, such as \OE to lowercase). As a result, all characters in the argument of \acro will be changed to lowercase and therefore typeset with small capitals.

   Another slightly special shape command available in LaTeX is the \emph command. This command denotes emphasis in normal text; the corresponding declaration is \em. Traditionally, emphasized words in text are set in italic; if emphasis is desired in an already italicized portion of the text, one usually returns to the upright font. The \emph command supports this convention by switching to the \itshape shape if the current font is upright, and to the \upshape shape if the current font is already slanted (i.e., if the shape is \itshape or \slshape). Thus,

`\tiny`	Size	`\normalsize`	Size	`\huge`	Size
`\scriptsize`	Size	`\large`	Size		Size
`\footnotesize`	Size	`\Large`	Size	`\Huge`	
`\small`	Size	`\LARGE`	Size		

Table 7.1: Standard size-changing commands

the user does not have to worry about the current state of the text when using the `\emph` command or the `\em` declaration.

Nevertheless, one has to be careful about the proper *use of italic corrections on both ends of the emphasized text.* It is therefore better to use the `\emph` command, which *automatically* takes care of the italic correction on both sides.

```
{\em Nevertheless, one has to be careful about
the\/ {\em proper\/} use of italic corrections
on both ends of the emphasized text}.  It is
therefore better to use the \verb=\emph= command,
which \emph{automatically} takes care of the
italic correction on both sides.
```

7-3-3

Using the upright shape for nested emphasis is not always very noticeable. A common typographic recommendation is, therefore, to use small capitals for the inner emphasis. This practice is not directly supported by standard LaTeX but can be achieved through the command `\eminnershape`, made available by the fixltx2e package.

Nevertheless, one has to be careful about the PROPER *use of italic corrections on both ends of the emphasized text.*

```
\usepackage{fixltx2e}
\renewcommand\eminnershape{\scshape}
{\em Nevertheless, one has to be careful about
the\/ {\em proper\/} use of italic corrections
on both ends of the emphasized text}.
```

7-3-4

Note that underlining for emphasis is considered bad practice in the publishing world. Underlining is used only when the output device can't do highlighting in another way—for example, when using a typewriter. Sections 3.1.6 and 3.1.7 discuss packages that change `\em` to produce underlining.

Standard font sizes

LaTeX has 10 size-changing commands (see Table 7.1). Since size changes are normally used only in the definition of commands, they have no corresponding command forms with one argument. The names of the commands have been retained from LaTeX 2.09 but in today's LaTeX their functionality has changed slightly. In LaTeX 2_ε such a command changes only the size of the current font, with all other attributes staying the same; in LaTeX 2.09 a size-changing command also automatically switched back to the main document font.

The size selected by these commands depends on the settings in the document class file and possibly on options (e.g., 11pt) specified with it. In general, \normalsize corresponds to the main size of the document, and the size-changing commands form an ordered sequence starting with \tiny as the smallest and going up to \Huge as the largest size. Sometimes more than one command refers to the same real size; for example, when a large \normalsize is chosen, \Huge can be the same as \huge. In any event, the order is always honored.

The size-related commands for the main text sizes (i.e., \normalsize, \small, and \footnotesize) typically influence the spacing around lists and displays as well. Thus, to change their behavior, one should not simply replace their definition by a call to \fontsize, but instead start from their original definitions, as documented in classes.dtx.

Unfortunately, there is currently no relative size-changing command in LaTeX—for example, there is no command for requesting a size 2 pt larger than the current one. This issue is partially resolved with the relsize package described in Section 3.1.4 on page 83.

7.3.2   Combining standard font commands

As already shown, the standard font-changing commands and declarations can be combined. The result is the selection of a typeface that matches the combination of all font attributes. For example:

One can typeset a text **in a large sans serif bold typeface** but note the unchanged leading! LaTeX uses the value in force at the *end* of the paragraph!

```
One can typeset a text
 {\sffamily\bfseries\large
  in a large sans serif bold typeface}
but note the unchanged leading!
\LaTeX{} uses the value in force at
the \emph{end} of the paragraph!
```

7-3-5

What happens behind the scenes is that the \sffamily command switches to the sans serif default family, then \bfseries switches to the default bold series in this family, and finally \large selects a large size but leaves all other font attributes unchanged (the leading appears to be unchanged because the scope of \large ends before the end of the paragraph). Font metric files (i.e., .tfm files) are loaded for all intermediate typefaces, even if these fonts are never used. In the preceding example, they would be "sans serif medium 10pt" after the \sffamily, then "sans serif bold extended 10pt" after the \bfseries, then "sans serif bold extended 14pt", which is the font that is finally used. Thus, such high-level commands can force LaTeX's font selection to unnecessarily load fonts that are never used. This normally does not matter, except for a small loss of processing speed when a given combination is used for the first time. However, if you have many different combinations of this type, you should consider defining them in terms of the primitive font-changing declarations (see Section 7.9).

Command	Corresponds to	Action
\textrm{...}	{\rmfamily...}	Typeset text in Roman family
\textsf{...}	{\sffamily...}	Typeset text in sans serif family
\texttt{...}	{\ttfamily...}	Typeset text in typewriter family
\textmd{...}	{\mdseries...}	Typeset text in medium series
\textbf{...}	{\bfseries...}	Typeset text in **bold** series
\textup{...}	{\upshape...}	Typeset text in upright shape
\textit{...}	{\itshape...}	Typeset text in *italic* shape
\textsl{...}	{\slshape...}	Typeset text in *slanted* shape
\textsc{...}	{\scshape...}	Typeset text in SMALL CAPS shape
\emph{...}	{\em...}	Typeset text *emphasized*
\textnormal{..}	{\normalfont..}	Typeset text in the document font

Table 7.2: Standard font-changing commands and declarations

7.3.3　Font commands versus declarations

We have already seen some examples of font commands that have arguments and change font attributes. These font-changing commands with arguments all start with \text... (except for the \emph command) to emphasize that they are intended for use in normal text and to make them easily memorizable. Using such commands instead of the declarative forms has the advantage of maintaining consistency with other LaTeX constructs. They are intended for typesetting short pieces of text in a specific family, series, or shape. Table 7.2 shows the effects of these commands.

A further advantage of these commands is that they automatically insert any necessary italic correction on either side of their argument. As a consequence, one no longer has to worry about forgetting the italic correction when changing fonts.

Only in a very few situations is this additional space wrong. For example, most typographers recommend omitting the italic correction if a small punctuation character, like a comma, directly follows the font change. As the amount of correction required is partly a matter of taste, you can define in which situations the italic correction should be suppressed. This is done by specifying the characters that should cancel a preceding italic correction in the list \nocorrlist.[1] The default definition for this command is

```
\newcommand{\nocorrlist}{,.}
```

It is best to declare the most often used characters first, as it will make the processing slightly faster.

---

[1] Any package that changes the \catcode of a character inside \nocorrlist must redeclare the list. Otherwise, the changed character will no longer be recognized by the suppression algorithm.

In addition to the global customization, it is possible to suppress the italic correction in individual instances. For this purpose, the command \nocorr is provided. Note that you have to put \nocorr on the left or right end inside the argument of the \text... commands, depending on which side of the text you wish to suppress the italic correction.

When using the LATEX high-level font commands, the proper *use of italic corrections is automatically taken care of.* Only *sometimes* one has to help LATEX by adding a \nocorr command.

```
\emph{When using the \LaTeX{} high-level font
commands, the \emph{proper} use of italic
corrections is automatically taken care of}
Only \emph{sometimes} one has to help \LaTeX{}
by adding a \verb=\nocorr= command.
```

7-3-6

In contrast, the use of the declaration forms is often more appropriate when you define your own commands or environments.

- **This environment produces boldface items.**
- **It is defined in terms of LATEX's itemize environment and NFSS declarations.**

```
\newenvironment{bfitemize}{\begin{itemize}%
  \normalfont\bfseries\raggedright}{\end{itemize}}
\begin{bfitemize}
\item This environment produces boldface items.
\item It is defined in terms of \LaTeX's
  \textttt{itemize} environment and NFSS declarations.
\end{bfitemize}
```

7-3-7

7.3.4 Accessing all characters of a font

Sometimes it is impossible to enter a character directly from the keyboard, even though the character exists in the font. Therefore, many useful characters are accessible via command names like \ss or \AE, which produce "ß" and "Æ", respectively. Some characters can also be implicitly generated from sequences of letters (this is a property of fonts) like ffi, which produces "ffi", and ---, which produces "—" in the standard TEX fonts.

In addition, the command \symbol allows you to access any character in a font by giving its number in the current encoding scheme as either a decimal, octal (preceded by '), or hexadecimal (preceded by ") number.

In the Cork font encoding (T1), characters like Þ, §, and ␣ are included and can be accessed with the \symbol command.

```
\fontencoding{T1}\selectfont
In the Cork font encoding (\textttt{T1}),
characters like \symbol{"DE}, \symbol{'237},
and \symbol{32} are included and can be
accessed with the \verb=\symbol= command.
```

7-3-8

The numbers corresponding to the characters in any font can be obtained by using the program nfssfont.tex, described in Section 7.5.7 on page 369.

Hook	Default value	Description
\encodingdefault	OT1	Encoding scheme for "main font"
\familydefault	\rmdefault	Family selected for "main font"
\seriesdefault	m	Series selected for "main font"
\shapedefault	n	Shape selected for "main font"
\rmdefault	cmr	Family selected by \rmfamily and \textrm
\sfdefault	cmss	Family selected by \sffamily and \textsf
\ttdefault	cmtt	Family selected by \ttfamily and \texttt
\bfdefault	bx	Series selected by \bfseries and \textbf
\mddefault	m	Series selected by \mdseries and \textmd
\itdefault	it	Shape selected by \itshape and \textit
\sldefault	sl	Shape selected by \slshape and \textsl
\scdefault	sc	Shape selected by \scshape and \textsc
\updefault	n	Shape selected by \upshape and \textup

Table 7.3: Font attribute defaults

7.3.5 Changing the default text fonts

To make it easier to modify the overall appearance of a document, LaTeX provides a set of built-in hooks that modify the behavior of the high-level font-changing commands discussed in the previous sections. These hooks are shown in Table 7.3. The values of these hooks can be set in package files or in the preamble of a document by using \renewcommand. Suitable values for these commands can be found by looking through the font tables in this chapter.

For example, by writing in the preamble

```
\renewcommand\familydefault{cmss}
```

a whole document would come out in Computer Modern Sans, because this re-definition changes the font family for the main font used by LaTeX. More exactly, the main document font is determined by the values of \encodingdefault, \familydefault, \seriesdefault, and \shapedefault. Thus, you have to make sure that these commands are defined in such a way that their combination points to an existing font shape in LaTeX's internal tables.

Suboptimal encoding default
The default value stored in \encodingdefault currently is OT1, which means that LaTeX assumes that most fonts use the original TeX encoding. This is actually a compatibility setting: in most circumstances it is better to use the T1 encoding because it contains many additional glyphs that are not available with OT1 and allows proper hyphenation for words with accented characters (see Section 7.5.1). Nowadays, some fonts are made available only in T1; that is, they do not support OT1 at all.

One also has to be aware that not every font encoding is suitable for use as a document-encoding default. A prerequisite is that the encoding must include most of the visible ASCII letters in their standard positions; see the discussion in Section 7.11 on page 440 for details. The \encodingdefault can be changed by loading the fontenc package with one or more options; see Section 7.5.3. For more information on font encodings refer to Section 7.9.1.

Another example, this time involving a series-changing command, would be to define \bfdefault to produce b so that the \bfseries command will use **bold** instead of **bold extended**, which is the default under Computer Modern. However, there is some risk in using such a setting since, for example, in Computer Modern only the Roman family has bold variants with a medium width. Computer Modern Typewriter and Computer Modern Sans have only bold extended variants. Thus, without further adjustments, a request for a bold sans serif font (i.e., \sffamily\bfseries), for example, might force LATEX to try font substitution, and finally select a medium-weight font. (This outcome can be avoided, as explained in Section 7.10.3, by specifying that the bold extended variants of the sans family should serve as substitutes for the bold medium ones.)

Wrong bold default can lead to problems

An example in which some default values are changed can be found in Section 7.10.8 on page 439, which covers setting up PostScript manually.

The initial setting of \familydefault means that changing \rmdefault will implicitly also change \familydefault to the new value, as long as no special setting for \familydefault is defined. However, if \familydefault is changed, \rmdefault is not affected.

7.3.6 LATEX 2.09 font commands

The two-letter font commands used in LATEX 2.09, such as \bf, are no longer defined by LATEX 2$_\varepsilon$ directly. Instead, they are defined (if at all) in the LATEX 2$_\varepsilon$ class files. For compatibility reasons the standard classes provide definitions for these commands that emulate their behavior in LATEX 2.09. However, it is legitimate for you to redefine them in a package or in the preamble according to your personal taste, something you should not do with basic font selection commands like \bfseries.

Because the old LATEX 2.09 font commands are now allowed to be defined freely in a document class or by the user, they are no longer used within the code for LATEX 2$_\varepsilon$. Instead, all internal references to fonts are created using either high- or low-level interfaces of LATEX's font selection scheme. This convention should be followed by package and class developers to ensure a consistent behavior throughout.

Do not use \bf and friends

7.4 Using fonts in math

Unlike the situation in text, automatic changes in font shapes are generally not desired in math formulas. For mathematicians, individual shapes convey specific information. For example, bold upright letters may represent vectors. If the characters in a formula were to change because of surrounding conditions, the result would be incorrect. For this reason handling of fonts in mathematical formulas is different than that in text.

Characters in a formula can be loosely put into two classes: symbols and alphabet characters (including digits). Internally, (LA)TEX distinguishes between eight types of math characters (to account for appropriate spacing), but for the discussion of fonts the division into two classes is generally adequate.

Some symbols, such as =, can be entered directly from the keyboard. The bulk of them, however, must be entered via a control sequence—for example, \leq stands for ≤. The other main group of characters in a formula, the alphabet characters, are entered directly from the keyboard.

More than 200 symbols are predefined in a standard (LA)TEX system, allowing the user to typeset almost any desired formula. These symbols are scattered over several fonts, but they are accessed in such a way that the user does not have to be aware of their internal representations. If necessary, additional symbol fonts can be made accessible in a similar way; see Section 7.10.7.

The most important difference between symbols and alphabet characters is that symbols always have the same graphical representation within one formula, while it is possible for the user to change the appearance of the alphabet characters. We will call the commands that change the appearance of alphabet characters in a formula "math alphabet identifiers" and the fonts associated with these commands "math alphabets". The alphabet identifiers are independent of surrounding font commands outside the formula, so a formula does not change if it is placed (for example) inside a theorem environment whose text is, by default, typeset in italics. This behavior is very important, because character shapes in a mathematical formula carry meanings that must not change because the formula is typeset in a different place in a document.

Some people who are familiar with the old method of font selection may be surprised by the fact that commands like \bfseries cannot be used in formulas. This is the price we must pay for the greater flexibility in choosing text font attributes—a flexibility that we do not want in a formula. We therefore need a different mechanism (math alphabet identifiers) for changing the typeface of certain alphabet characters in complicated formulas.

7.4.1 Special math alphabet identifiers

One alphabet and a huge number of symbols are not sufficient for scientists to express their thoughts. They tend to use every available typeface to denote special concepts. Besides the use of foreign alphabets such as Greek letters, which usually are accessed as symbols—\alpha, \beta, and so on—we find sans serif letters for matrices, bold serif letters for vectors, and Fraktur fonts for groups, ideals, or fields. Others use calligraphic shapes to denote sets. The conventions are endless, and—even more importantly—they differ from one discipline to another.

Command	*Example*	
\mathcal	$\mathcal{A}=a$	$\mathcal{A} = a$
\mathrm	max_i	max_i
\mathbf	$\sum x = \mathbf{v}$	$\sum x = \mathbf{v}$
\mathsf	G_1^2	G_1^2
\mathtt	$\mathtt{W}(a)$	$\mathtt{W}(a)$
\mathnormal	$\mathnormal{abc}=abc$	$abc = abc$
\mathit	$differ\neq\mathit{differ}$	$differ \neq \mathit{differ}$

Table 7.4: Predefined math alphabet identifiers in LaTeX

For this reason LaTeX makes it possible to declare new math alphabet identifiers and associate them with any desired font shape group instead of relying only on a predefined set that cannot be extended. These identifiers are special commands for use in a formula that typeset any alphabet character in their argument in a specific typeface. (Symbols cannot be changed in this way.) These identifiers may use different typefaces in different formulas, as we will see in Section 7.4.3, but within one formula they always select the same typeface regardless of the surrounding conditions.

Predefined alphabet identifiers

New math alphabet identifiers can be defined according to the user's needs, but LaTeX already has a few built in. These identifiers are shown in Table 7.4. As the last lines in the table show, the letters used in formulas are taken by default from the math alphabet \mathnormal. In contrast, the letters produced by \mathit have different spacing; thus this alphabet could be used to provide full-word variable names, which are common in some disciplines.

In LaTeX 2_ε math alphabet identifiers are commands with one argument, usually a single letter or a single word to be typeset in a special font.

Therefore, G can be computed as

$$G = \mathcal{A} + \sum_{i=1}^{n} \mathcal{B}_i \qquad (1)$$

7-4-1

```
Therefore, $\mathsf{G}$ can be computed as
\begin{equation}
    \mathsf{G} = \mathcal{A} +
        \sum_{i=1}^{n} \mathcal{B}_{i}
\end{equation}
```

This procedure differs from the way font commands were used in LaTeX 2.09, where commands, such as \rm would cause font changes (..{\rm A}..). (For the most important two-letter font-changing commands like \rm, \sf, \bf, \it, and \tt, the old syntax is still supported in the standard classes. For the others you can force the old behavior by specifying the package oldlfont; see Section 7.12.1. However, we suggest that you refrain from using such commands in new documents.)

As already mentioned, another difference between the old LaTeX 2.09 font selection scheme and NFSS is that text font declarations are no longer allowed in
formulas, as they merely change some characteristic of the current font rather
than switching to a specific font. Thus, if you write `{\bfseries..}` instead of
`\mathbf{..}` in a formula, LaTeX will produce an error message.

The command names for the math alphabet identifiers are chosen to be de-
scriptive rather than simple to type—they all start with `\math`. Therefore, if you
use the commands more than occasionally in your document, you should consider
defining some abbreviations in the preamble, such as the following:

```
\newcommand\mrm{\mathrm}
```

No default math
alphabet
You may wonder what the default math alphabet is—that is, from which alphabet the alphabet characters are selected if you do not specify an alphabet identifier
explicitly, as in the formula `$x  =  123$`. The answer is that no single default math
alphabet exists. The (LA)TeX system can be set up so that alphabetical characters
are fetched from different alphabets as long as the user has not explicitly asked
for a specific one, and this is normally the case, as the following example shows.

$$x = 12345 \qquad (1)$$
$$\mathrm{x} = 12345 \qquad (2)$$
$$x = 12345 \qquad (3)$$

```
\begin{eqnarray}
  x               &=& 12345                \\
  \mathrm{x}      &=& \mathrm{12345}        \\
  \mathnormal{x}  &=& \mathnormal{12345}
\end{eqnarray}
```

7-4-2

As you can see, `\mathrm` does not change the digits and `\mathnormal` does not
change the letters, so the default for digits in the normal set-up is the math alphabet associated with `\mathrm` and the default for letters is the one associated with
`\mathnormal`.[1] This behavior can be controlled with the `\DeclareMathSymbol`
command, which is explained in Section 7.10.7.

Defining new alphabet identifiers

New math alphabet identifiers are defined with the `\DeclareMathAlphabet` command. Suppose that you want to make a slanted sans serif typeface available as
a math alphabet. First you decide on a new command name, such as `\msfsl`, to
be used to select your math alphabet. Then you consult the font classification
tables in this chapter (starting on page 354) to find a suitable font shape group
to assign to this alphabet identifier. You will find that the Computer Modern
Sans family, for example, consists of a medium series with upright and slanted
shapes. If you decide to use the slanted shape of this family, you tell LaTeX using
`\DeclareMathAlphabet`.

---

[1] It is a strange fact that the math font that corresponds to the `\mathnormal` alphabet actually
contains old-style numerals. When the Computer Modern fonts were developed, space was a rare
commodity, so Donald Knuth squeezed a number of "nonmathematical" glyphs into these fonts
that are normally used only in text.

> `\DeclareMathAlphabet{`*cmd*`}{`*encoding*`}{`*family*`}{`*series*`}{`*shape*`}`

This declaration has four arguments besides the identifier: the encoding scheme, the family, the series, and the shape of the font to be used. The alphabet identifier defined in the example will always switch to Computer Modern Sans medium slanted.

We demonstrate this with the formula

$$\sum A_i = a \tan \beta \qquad (1)$$

```
\DeclareMathAlphabet{\msfsl}{OT1}{cmss}{m}{sl}
We demonstrate this with the formula
\begin{equation}
   \sum \msfsl{A}_{i} = a \tan \beta
\end{equation}
```

7-4-3

It is also possible to redefine an existing math alphabet identifier in a package file or in the preamble of your document. For example, the declaration

```
\DeclareMathAlphabet{\mathsf}{OT1}{pag}{m}{n}
```

will override the default settings for the `\mathsf` alphabet identifier. After that, `\mathsf` will switch to Adobe Avant Garde in your formulas. There is, however, a subtle point: if the math alphabet in question is part of a symbol font that is already loaded by LATEX for other reasons (e.g., `\mathcal`), it is better to use `\DeclareSymbolFontAlphabet` as it makes better use of TEX's somewhat limited resources for math; see page 435 for details.

7.4.2   Text font commands in math

As mentioned previously, text font declarations like `\rmfamily` cannot be used in math. However, the font-changing commands with arguments—for example, `\textrm`—can be used in both text and math. You can use these commands to temporarily exit the math context and typeset some text in the midst of your formula that logically belongs to the text the surrounding the formula. Note that the font used to typeset this text will depend on surrounding conditions—that is, it will pick up the current values of encoding, family, series, and shape, as in the next example.

The result will be

$$x = 10 \textbf{ and thus } y = 12$$

```
\sffamily The result will be
\[ x = 10 \textbf{ and thus } y = 12 \]
```

7-4-4

As you see, the Sans family was retained and the series was changed to bold. Perhaps more useful is the `\text` command, provided by the amstext package, which picks up the current values of encoding, family, series, and shape without changing any of them (see Section 8.6.1).

7.4.3 Mathematical formula versions

Besides allowing parts of a formula to be changed by using math alphabet identifiers, LaTeX lets you change the appearance of a formula as a whole. Formulas are typeset in a certain "math version", and you can switch between math versions outside of math mode by using the command \mathversion, thereby changing the overall layout of the following formulas.

LaTeX knows about two math versions called "normal" and "bold". Additional ones are sometimes provided in special packages. For example, the mathtime package (for the commercial MathTime fonts) sets up a math version called "heavy" to typeset formulas with ultra bold symbols as provided by the MathTime fonts.

As the name indicates, \mathversion{normal} is the default. In contrast, the bold version will produce bolder alphabet characters and symbols, though by default big operators, like \sum, are not changed. The following example shows the same formula first in the normal and then in the bold math version.[1]

$$\sum_{j=1}^{z} j = \frac{z(z+1)}{2} \tag{1}$$

$$\sum_{j=1}^{z} j = \frac{z(z+1)}{2} \tag{2}$$

```
\begin{equation}
  \sum_{j=1}^{z} j = \frac{z(z+1)}{2}
\end{equation}
\mathversion{bold}
\begin{equation}
  \sum_{j=1}^{z} j = \frac{z(z+1)}{2}
\end{equation}
```

7-4-5

Using \mathversion might be suitable in certain situations, such as in headings, but remember that changing the version means changing the appearance (and perhaps the meaning) of the entire formula. If you want to darken only some symbols or characters within one formula, you should not change the \mathversion. Instead, you should use the \mathbf alphabet identifier for characters and/or use the command \bm provided by the bm package; see Section 8.8.2.

If you change the math version with the \mathversion command, LaTeX looks in its internal tables to find where all the symbols for this new math version are located. It also may change all or some of the math alphabet identifiers and associate them with other font shapes in this version.

But what happens to math alphabet identifiers that you have defined yourself, such as the \msfsl from Example 7-4-3? As long as you declared them using only \DeclareMathAlphabet, they will stay the same in all math versions.

If the math alphabet identifier is to produce a different font in a special math version, you must inform LaTeX of that fact by using the \SetMathAlphabet command. For example, in the default set-up the \mathsf alphabet identifier is defined as follows:

```
\DeclareMathAlphabet{\mathsf}{OT1}{cmss}{m}{n}
\SetMathAlphabet{\mathsf}{bold}{OT1}{cmss}{bx}{n}
```

---

[1]For historical reasons LaTeX has two additional commands to switch to its standard math versions: \boldmath and \unboldmath.

The first line means that the default for \mathsf in all math versions is Computer Modern Sans medium. The second line states that the bold math version should use the font Computer Modern Sans bold extended instead.

\SetMathAlphabet{*cmd*}{*version*}{*encoding*}{*family*}{*series*}{*shape*}

From the previous example, you can see that \SetMathAlphabet takes six arguments: the first is the name of the math alphabet identifier, the second is the math version name for which you are defining a special set-up, and the other four are the encoding, family, series, and shape name with which you are associating it.

   As noted earlier, you can redefine an existing math alphabet identifier by using \DeclareMathAlphabet. If you do so, all previous \SetMathAlphabet declarations for this identifier are removed from the internal tables of LaTeX. Thus, the identifier will come out the same in all math versions unless you add new \SetMathAlphabet declarations for it.

7.5   Standard LaTeX font support

This section opens with a short introduction to the standard text fonts distributed together with LaTeX: Computer Modern and Extended Computer Modern. It is followed by a discussion of LaTeX's standard support packages for input and font encodings. The section concludes by describing a package for tracing LaTeX's font processing and another package for displaying glyph charts (a package the author used extensively while preparing the later parts of this chapter).

7.5.1   Computer Modern—The LaTeX standard fonts

Along with TeX, Donald Knuth developed a family of fonts called Computer Modern; see Table 7.5 on the next page. Until the early 1990s, essentially only these fonts were usable with TeX and, consequently, with LaTeX. Each of these text fonts contains 128 glyphs (TeX was working with 7 bits originally), which does not leave *Original TeX font* room for including accented characters as individual glyphs. Thus, using these *encoding* fonts means that accented characters have to be produced with the \accent primitive of TeX, which in turn means that automatic hyphenation of words with accented characters is impossible. While this restriction is acceptable with English documents that contain few foreign words, it is a major obstacle for other languages.

   Not surprisingly, these deficiencies were of great concern to the TeX users in Europe and eventually led to a reimplementation of TeX in 1989 to support 8-bit *T1 a.k.a. "Cork"* characters internally and externally. At the TeX Users conference in Cork (1990), *encoding* a standard 8-bit encoding for text fonts (T1) was developed that contains many diacritical characters (see Table 7.32 on page 449) and allows typesetting in more

Family	Series	Shape(s)	Example of Typeface
Computer Modern Roman (T1, OT1, TS1)			
cmr	m	n, it, sl, sc, ui	COMPUTER ROMAN SMALL CAPS
cmr	bx	n, it, sl	*Comp. Mod. Roman bold extended italic*
cmr	b	n	**Computer Modern Roman bold upright**
Computer Modern Sans (T1, OT1, TS1)			
cmss	m	n, sl	*Computer Modern Sans slanted*
cmss	bx	n	**Computer Modern Sans bold extended**
cmss	sbc	n	**Computer Modern Sans semibold condensed**
Computer Modern Typewriter (T1, OT1, TS1)			
cmtt	m	n, it, sl, sc	`Computer Modern Typewriter italic`
cmvtt	m	n, it	Proportional Computer Modern Typewriter
Computer Modern Fibonacci (T1, OT1)			
cmfib	m	n	Computer Modern Fibonacci
Computer Modern Funny Roman (T1, OT1)			
cmfr	m	n, it	Computer Modern Funny Roman
Computer Modern Dunhill (T1, OT1)			
cmdh	m	n	Computer Modern Dunhill

Table 7.5: Classification of the Computer Modern font families

than 30 languages based on the Latin alphabet. At the University of Bochum (under the direction of Norbert Schwarz) the Computer Modern font families were then reimplemented, and additional characters were designed, so that the resulting fonts completely conform to this encoding scheme. The first implementation of *EC fonts* these fonts was released under the name "DC fonts". Since then Jörg Knappen has finalized them and they are now distributed as "European Computer Modern Fonts", often shortened to "EC fonts".[1]

PostScript Type 1 instances Both Computer Modern and the EC fonts are considered standard in LaTeX and must be available at any installation. Although originally developed with META-FONT, there are now free Type 1 PostScript replacements as well. For Computer Modern these were produced by Blue Sky Research; Y&Y added the LaTeX, AMS, and Euler fonts. The EC fonts have been recently converted from METAFONT sources

CM-Super fonts

---

[1]Not to be confused with the European Modern Fonts™, a high-quality set of commercial fonts by Y&Y that are based on the Computer Modern design but have slightly different metrics [65].

to Type 1 PostScript by Vladimir Volovich. His implementation is called the CM-Super fonts package and, beside the EC fonts, it covers EC Concrete, EC Bright, and LH fonts (Cyrillic Computer Modern). In addition to the T1 encoding, the LaTeX standard encodings TS1, T2A, T2B, T2C, and X2 are supported by CM-Super. The CM-Super fonts have been automatically converted to the Type 1 format and although a sophisticated algorithm was used for this conversion, you cannot expect exactly the same quality as could be achieved by a manual conversion process.

Since the PostScript fonts have the same font metrics as their METAFONT counterparts they need no support package in the LaTeX document. Once installed they will be automatically used by the driver program (e.g., dvips) that converts the .dvi output to PostScript. The standard .fd files for Computer Modern provide only well-defined font sizes to avoid the generation of too many bit-mapped fonts. However, with PostScript the use of intermediate sizes (via \fontsize) is possible without any such side effect. The package fix-cm makes use of this feature.

Although the EC fonts were originally meant to be a drop-in extension (and replacement) for the 7-bit Computer Modern fonts, not all glyph shapes were kept in the end. For example, the German ß got a new design—a decision by the font designer that did not make everybody happy.

```
\fontencoding{OT1}\fontfamily{cmr}\selectfont
Computer Modern sharp s: \ss  \par
\fontencoding{T1}\fontfamily{cmr}\selectfont
EC Modern sharp s: \ss
```

Computer Modern sharp s: ß
EC Modern sharp s: ß

7-5-1

With the CM-Super fonts this is no longer a problem: if one prefers the original CM glyph over the EC glyph, on can simply exchange germandbls with germandbls.alt in the file cm-super-t1.enc.[1]

However, these are not the only differences between the original Computer Modern fonts and the new EC fonts. The latter have many more individual designs for larger font sizes (while CM fonts were scaled linearly) and in this respect the fact that both really are different font families is quite noticeable.[2] The particular example that follows is perhaps the most glaring difference of that kind.

The fox jumps
quickly over the fence!

The fox jumps
quickly over the fence!

```
\fontencoding{OT1}\sffamily\bfseries
\Huge     The fox jumps  \par
\normalsize quickly over the fence!\par
\fontencoding{T1}\sffamily\bfseries
\Huge     The fox jumps  \par
\normalsize quickly over the fence!\par
```

7-5-2

---

[1] An even better solution is to use a different name for the modified encoding file and then change the references in the (dvips) mapping file to use the new name.

[2] The historical mistake was to pretend to NFSS that both are the same families (e.g., cmr, cmss), just encoded according to different font encodings. Unfortunately, this cannot be rectified without huge backward compatibility problems.

This issue is no problem if one likes the EC designs and uses T1 throughout. Otherwise, a number of approaches can be taken to resolve this problem. One is to employ a different set of font definitions that do not make use of *all* individual EC font designs, and that are closer to those of the traditional CM fonts, but with improved typographical quality. Such a solution is provided by Walter Schmidt's package fix-cm, which is distributed as part of the core LaTeX distribution. Load this package directly after the document class declaration (or even before using \RequirePackage), as it takes effect only for fonts not already loaded by LaTeX— and the document class might load fonts.

The fox jumps
quickly over the fence!

The fox jumps
quickly over the fence!

```
\usepackage{fix-cm}
\fontencoding{OT1}\sffamily\bfseries
\Huge        The fox jumps  \par
\normalsize quickly over the fence!\par
\fontencoding{T1}\sffamily\bfseries
\Huge        The fox jumps  \par
\normalsize quickly over the fence!
```

7-5-3

Another possible solution is to use the Almost European fonts (by Lars Engebretsen) or the ZE-fonts (by Robert Fuster), both of which are sets of virtual fonts built upon the Computer Modern fonts. They implement the T1 encoding with the exception of a small number of glyphs that simply cannot be obtained from the CM font material.

Searching problems in .pdf documents

This approach has a number of disadvantages. For instance, these solutions do not support the companion symbol fonts, so the additional symbols provided by the textcomp package cannot be used at all. More importantly, the use of virtual fonts to build composite glyphs means that a resulting .pdf file would not be searchable for words containing diacritics, simply because instead of the accented character (as a single glyph) a complicated construction is placed in this file. In other words, the solutions help to make LaTeX believe that it deals with single glyphs (and thus allows proper hyphenation and kerning) but this information is lost again in the resulting output file, so further post-processing cannot be done properly.

However, as far as the selected fonts are concerned, the ae package shows the same result as fix-cm.

The fox jumps
quickly over the fence!

```
\usepackage{ae}
\fontencoding{T1}\sffamily\bfseries
\Huge        The fox jumps  \par
\normalsize quickly over the fence!
```

7-5-4

Latin Modern on the horizon

In 2002, three European TeX user groups (DANTE, GUTenberg, and NTG) initiated and funded a project to integrate all of the variants of the Computer Modern Roman typefaces into a single Latin Modern family of fonts. The project is being carried out by Bogusław Jackowski and Janusz Nowacki, and the first official version of the Latin Modern fonts was presented at the DANTE meeting in 2003.

The **Latin Modern** fonts are carefully handcrafted PostScript Type 1 fonts based on the designs of Knuth's *Computer Modern* families. They contain all the glyphs needed to typeset Latin-based European languages. At the moment the T1 and TS1 encodings are supported. In a later step the project will address glyphs needed for typesetting Native American, Vietnamese, and Transliteration. Also planned are 8-bit math encodings (based on earlier work by CLASEN/VIETH and ZIEGLER [40,175]).

```
\usepackage{lmodern} \usepackage[T1]{fontenc}
The \textbf{Latin Modern} fonts are carefully
handcrafted PostScript Type~1 fonts based on the
designs of Knuth's \emph{Computer Modern}
families. They contain all the glyphs needed to
typeset Latin-based European languages.  At the
moment the \texttt{T1} and \texttt{TS1} encodings
are supported.  In a later step the project will
address glyphs needed for typesetting Native
American, Vietnamese, and Transliteration. Also
planned are 8-bit math encodings (based on
earlier work by \textsc{Clasen/Vieth} and
\textsc{Ziegler}~[40,175]).
```

7-5-5

At the time of writing, the fonts were continuing to undergo further fine-tuning. For example, additional kerning pairs and language-dependent ligatures are being added. It is expected that a later version of the Latin Modern fonts will become the default fonts for LaTeX; for now, they can be used by loading the lmodern package and selecting the T1 encoding.

7.5.2   inputenc—Selecting the input encoding

If your computer allows you to write accented characters, either via single keystrokes or by some other input method (e.g., by pressing ` and then a to get à) and also displays them nicely in the editor...

```
Quand ils furent revenus un peu à eux, ils marchèrent vers
Lisbonne ; il leur restait quelque argent, avec lequel ils
espéraient se sauver de la faim après avoir échappé à la
tempête     (Voltaire)
```

...then ideally you would use such a text directly with LaTeX instead of having to type \'a, \^e, and so forth.

While with languages such as French and German the latter approach is still feasible, languages such as Russian and Greek really require the potential for direct input, as (nearly) every character in these languages has a command name as its internal LaTeX form. For example, the default Russian definition for \reftextafter contains the following text (meaning "on the next page"):

```
\cyrn\cyra\ \cyrs\cyrl\cyre\cyrd\cyru\cyryu\cyrshch\cyre\cyrishrt
\ \cyrs\cyrt\cyrr\cyra\cyrn\cyri\cyrc\cyre
```

Clearly, no one wants to type like this on a regular basis. Nevertheless, it has the advantage of being universally portable, meaning that it will be interpreted correctly on any LATEX installation. On the other hand, typing on an appropriate keyboard

на следующей странице

is clearly preferable, provided it is possible to make LATEX understand this kind of input. The problem is that what is stored in a file on a computer is not the characters we see in the above sequence, but rather octets (numbers) representing the characters. In different circumstances (using a different encoding), the same octets might represent different characters.

How does LATEX determine which interpretation it should use? As long as everything happens on a single computer and all programs interpret octets in files (when reading or writing) in the same manner, everything is usually fine. In such a situation it may make sense to activate an automatic translation mechanism that is built into several recent TEX implementations. If, however, any file produced on such a system is sent to a different computer, processing is likely to fail or, even worse, may appear to succeed, but will in fact produce wrong results by displaying incorrect characters.

To cope with this situation the inputenc package was created. Its main purpose is to tell LATEX the "encoding" used in the document or in a part of the document. This is done by loading the package with the encoding name as an option. For example:

```
\usepackage[cp1252]{inputenc}  % Windows 1252 (Western Europe) code page
```

From that point onward LATEX knows how to interpret the octets in the remainder of the document on any installation,[1] regardless of the encoding used for other purposes on that computer.

A typical example is shown below. It is a short text written in the koi8-r encoding popular in Russia. The right side shows what the text looks like on a computer using a Latin 1 encoding (e.g., in Germany). The left side shows that LATEX was nevertheless able to interpret the text correctly because it was told which input encoding was being used.

Русский язык (The Russian language)

```
\usepackage[russian]{babel}
\usepackage[koi8-r]{inputenc}
ÒÕÓÓËÉ ÑÚÙË  (The Russian language)
```

7-5-6

The list of currently supported encodings by inputenc is given below. The interface is well documented, and support for new encodings can be added easily. Thus, if the encoding used by your computer is not listed here, it is worth looking

---

[1] This statement is true only if the TEX installation has not been set up to make some hard-wired transformation when reading from a file. As mentioned in the introduction to this chapter, many TEX implementations have been extended to support such transformations, but if they are activated it is no longer possible to process documents in several languages in parallel.

into the inputenc package documentation[1] to see whether it was added recently. You can also search the Internet for encoding files for inputenc provided by other authors. For example, encodings related to the Cyrillic languages are distributed together with other font support packages for Cyrillic languages.

The ISO-8859 standard [67] defines a number of important single-byte encodings, of which those related to the Latin alphabet are supported by inputenc. For MS-DOS and Windows operating systems a number of single-byte encodings have been defined by IBM and Microsoft, of which a subset is currently supported. In addition, some encodings defined by other computer vendors are available. The perhaps somewhat ad hoc (and constantly growing) selection is mainly the result of contributions from the LaTeX user community.

latin1   This is the ISO-8859-1 encoding (also known as Latin 1). It can represent most Western European languages, including Albanian, Catalan, Danish, Dutch, English, Faroese, Finnish, French, Galician, German, Icelandic, Irish, Italian, Norwegian, Portuguese, Spanish, and Swedish.

latin2   The ISO Latin 2 encoding (ISO-8859-2) supports the Slavic languages of Central Europe that use the Latin alphabet. It can be used for the following languages: Croat, Czech, German, Hungarian, Polish, Romanian, Slovak, and Slovenian.

latin3   This character set (ISO-8859-3) is used for Esperanto, Galician, Maltese, and Turkish.

latin4   The ISO Latin 4 encoding (ISO-8859-4) can represent languages such as Estonian, Latvian, and Lithuanian.

latin5   The ISO Latin 5 encoding (ISO 8859-9) is closely related to Latin 1 and replaces the rarely used Icelandic letters from Latin 1 with Turkish letters.

latin9   Latin 9 (or ISO-8859-15) is another small variation on Latin 1 that adds the euro currency sign as well as a few other characters, such as the œ ligature, that were missing for French and Finnish. It is becoming increasingly popular as a replacement for Latin 1.

cp437   IBM 437 code page (MS-DOS Latin but containing many graphical characters to draw boxes).

cp437de   IBM 437 code page but with a "ß" (German sharp s) in place of a β (Greek beta) as used with German keyboards.

cp850   IBM 850 code page (MS-DOS multilingual ≈ latin1).

cp852   IBM 852 code page (MS-DOS multilingual ≈ latin2).

cp858   IBM 858 code page (IBM 850 with the euro symbol added).

cp865   IBM 865 code page (MS-DOS Norway).

---

[1] Process inputenc.dtx with LaTeX.

cp1250   Windows 1250 (Central and Eastern Europe) code page.

cp1252   Windows 1252 (Western Europe) code page.

cp1257   Windows 1257 (Baltic) code page.

ansinew   Windows 3.1 ANSI encoding; a synonym for cp1252.

decmulti   DEC Multinational Character Set encoding.

applemac   Macintosh (standard) encoding.

macce   Macintosh Central European code page.

next   Next Computer encoding.

utf8   Unicode's UTF8 encoding support.

Most TeX installations accept 8-bit characters by default. Nevertheless, without further adjustments, like those performed by inputenc, the results can be unpredictable: characters may vanish, or you might get whatever character is present in the current font at the octet location being referred to, which may or may not be the desired glyph. This behavior was the default for a long time, so it was not changed in LaTeX 2_ε because some people rely on it. However, to ensure that such mistakes can be caught, inputenc offers the option ascii, which makes any character outside the range 32–126 illegal.

\inputencoding{*encoding*}

Originally the inputenc package was written to describe the encoding used for a document as a whole—hence the use of options in the preamble. It is, however, possible to change the encoding in the middle of a document by using the command \inputencoding. This command takes the name of an encoding as its argument. Processing is rather computing intensive, as typically more than 120 characters are remapped each time. Nevertheless, we know of applications that change the encoding several times within a paragraph yet seem to work reasonably well.

UTF8 support   When inputenc was written, most LaTeX installations were on computers that used single-byte encodings like the ones discussed in this section. Today, however, another encoding is becoming popular as systems start to provide support for Unicode: UTF8. This variable-length encoding represents Unicode characters in one to four octets. Recently, some Linux distributions decided to use UTF8 as the default encoding for the operating system, leaving their LaTeX users baffled that files written using the keys on the keyboard were suddenly no longer accepted by LaTeX. For this reason encoding support for UTF8 was added to inputenc via the option utf8. Technically, it does not provide a full UTF8 implementation. Only Unicode characters that have some representation in standard LaTeX fonts are mapped (i.e., mainly Latin and Cyrillic character sets); all others will result in a suitable error message. In addition, Unicode combining characters are not supported, although that particular omission should not pose a problem in practice.

7-5-7

German umlauts in UTF-8: äöü
But interpreted as Latin 1: Ã¤Ã¶Ã¼

```
\usepackage[utf8]{inputenc}
\usepackage{textcomp} % for Latin interpretation
German umlauts in UTF-8:    ^^c3^^a4^^c3^^b6^^c3^^bc
\par\inputencoding{latin1}% switch to Latin 1
But interpreted as Latin 1: ^^c3^^a4^^c3^^b6^^c3^^bc
```

UTF8 has the property that ASCII characters represent themselves and most Latin characters are represented by two bytes. In the verbatim text of the example, the two-byte representations of the German umlauts in UTF8 are shown in TeX's hexadecimal notation, that is with each octet preceded by ^^. In an editor that does not understand UTF8, one would probably see them as similar to the output that is produced when they are interpreted as Latin 1 characters.

The UTF8 support offered by inputenc at the moment[1] is restricted to the character subset of Unicode directly supported by the inputenc mapping options (e.g., latin1, latin2) as described on page 359. A package with more comprehensive UTF8 support (including support for Chinese, Korean, and Japanese characters), though consequently more complex in its set-up, is the ucs package written by Dominique Unruh. You may want to give it a try if the inputenc solution does not cover your needs.

7.5.3   fontenc—Selecting font encodings

To be able to use a text font encoding with LaTeX, the encoding has to be loaded in the preamble or the document class. More precisely, the definitions to access the glyphs in fonts with a certain encoding have to be loaded. The canonical way to do this is via the fontenc package, which takes a comma-separated list of font encodings as a package option. The last of these encodings is automatically made the default document encoding. If Cyrillic encodings are loaded, the list of commands affected by \MakeUppercase and \MakeLowercase is automatically extended. For example,

```
\usepackage[T2A,T1]{fontenc}
```

will load all necessary definitions for the Cyrillic T2A and the T1 (Cork) encodings and set the latter to be the default document encoding.

In contrast to normal package behavior, one can load this package several times with different optional arguments to the \usepackage command. This is necessary to allow a document class to load a certain set of encodings and enable

Multiple uses of fontenc allowed

---

[1] This is more of a resource problem than a technical one and thus may change.

the user in the preamble to load still more encodings. Loading encodings more than once is possible without side effects (other than potentially changing the document default font encoding).

If language support packages (e.g., those coming with the babel system) are used in the document, it is often the case that the necessary font encodings are already loaded by the support package.

7.5.4 textcomp—Providing additional text symbols

When the T1 font encoding was defined in Cork, it was decided that this encoding should omit many standard text symbols such as † and instead include as many composite glyphs as possible. The rationale was that characters that are subject to hyphenation have to be present in the same font, while one can fetch other symbols without much penalty from additional fonts. These extra symbols have, therefore, been collected in a companion encoding.

In 1995, a first implementation of this encoding (TS1) was developed by Jörg Knappen [78, 79]. With the textcomp package, Sebastian Rahtz provided a LATEX interface to it.

Unfortunately, just as with the T1 encoding, the encoding design for TS1 was prepared based on glyph availability in the TEX world without considering that the majority of commercial fonts provide different sets of glyphs. As a result, the full implementation of this encoding is available for very few font families, among them EC and CM Bright fonts. For most PostScript fonts implementations of the encoding also exist, but half of the glyphs are missing and produce square blobs of ink.[1] Table 7.6 on pages 363–364 shows the glyphs made available by textcomp and the commands to access them. Commands colored in blue indicate that the corresponding glyph is most likely not available when PostScript fonts are used.

Subsets of the TS1 encoding   To help with these problems the textcomp package nowadays knows for many font families to what extent they implement the TS1 encoding. In addition, it offers a number of options that restrict the set of new commands for those font families it does not know about.

For any unknown font family, the option safe allows only commands available with the ISO-Adobe character set (except for \textcurrency but adding a fake \texteuro). The option euro replaces the fake euro symbol with a real glyph; hence if that glyph does not exist in the font, \texteuro will produce a nasty blob of ink.

The package option full enables all commands for fonts textcomp does not know about. This means in particular that the perfectly valid LATEX commands \textcircled and \t will stop working the moment a document font is selected that does not contain the necessary glyphs in its TS1 encoding. For this reason,

---

[1]The T1 encoding has the same problem when it comes to PostScript fonts, but fortunately only five (seldom used) glyphs are missing from most fonts; see Example 7-9-2 on page 417.

Accent symbols

Á	\capitalacute␣A	Ă	\capitalbreve␣A	Ǎ	\capitalcaron␣A
Ą	\capitalcedilla␣A	Â	\capitalcircumflex␣A	Ä	\capitaldieresis␣A
Ȧ	\capitaldotaccent␣A	À	\capitalgrave␣A	Ã	\capitalhungarumlaut␣A
Ā	\capitalmacron␣A	Â	\capitalnewtie␣A	Ų	\capitalogonek␣U
Å	\capitalring␣A	ÔO	\capitaltie␣OO	Ã	\capitaltilde␣A
ô	\newtie␣o	Ⓐ	\textcircled␣A	ôo	\t␣oo

Numerals (superior, fractions, old style)

¹	\textonesuperior	²	\texttwosuperior	³	\textthreesuperior
¼	\textonequarter	½	\textonehalf	¾	\textthreequarters
0	\textzerooldstyle	1	\textoneoldstyle	2	\texttwooldstyle
3	\textthreeoldstyle	4	\textfouroldstyle	5	\textfiveoldstyle
6	\textsixoldstyle	7	\textsevenoldstyle	8	\texteightoldstyle
9	\textnineoldstyle				

Pair symbols

⟨	\textlangle	⟩	\textrangle	⟦	\textlbrackdbl
⟧	\textrbrackdbl	↑	\textuparrow	↓	\textdownarrow
←	\textleftarrow	→	\textrightarrow	{	\textlquill
}	\textrquill				

Monetary and commercial symbols

฿	\textbaht	¢	\textcent	¢	\textcentoldstyle
₡	\textcolonmonetary	¤	\textcurrency	$	\textdollar
$	\textdollaroldstyle	đ	\textdong	€	\texteuro
ƒ	\textflorin	₲	\textguarani	£	\textlira
₦	\textnaira	₱	\textpeso	£	\textsterling
₩	\textwon	¥	\textyen		
℗	\textcircledP	☺	\textcopyleft	©	\textcopyright
℅	\textdiscount	℮	\textestimated	‰₀	\textpertenthousand
‰	\textperthousand	※	\textreferencemark	®	\textregistered
℠	\textservicemark	™	\texttrademark		

Footnote symbols

*	\textasteriskcentered	‖	\textbardbl	¦	\textbrokenbar
•	\textbullet	†	\textdagger	‡	\textdaggerdbl
○	\textopenbullet	¶	\textparagraph	·	\textperiodcentered
¶	\textpilcrow	§	\textsection		

Scientific symbols

°C	\textcelsius	°	\textdegree	÷	\textdiv
¬	\textlnot	℧	\textmho	−	\textminus
μ	\textmu	Ω	\textohm	ª	\textordfeminine
º	\textordmasculine	±	\textpm	√	\textsurd
×	\texttimes				

Blue indicates symbols unavailable in most PostScript fonts.

Table 7.6: Commands made available with **textcomp**

Various

″	\textacutedbl	´	\textasciiacute	˘	\textasciibreve
˘	\textasciicaron	¨	\textasciidieresis	`	\textasciigrave
¯	\textasciimacron	◯	\textbigcircle	ƀ	\textblank
⋆	\textborn	=	\textdblhyphen	=	\textdblhyphenchar
†	\textdied	o|o	\textdivorced	/	\textfractionsolidus
‶	\textgravedbl	‽	\textinterrobang	¿	\textinterrobangdown
✒	\textleaf	∞	\textmarried	♪	\textmusicalnote
№	\textnumero	'	\textquotesingle	‚	\textquotestraightbase
„	\textquotestraightdblbase	℞	\textrecipe	—	\textthreequartersemdash
~	\texttildelow	—	\texttwelveudash		

Blue indicates symbols unavailable in most PostScript fonts.

Table 7.6: Commands made available with **textcomp** (cont.)

the default option `almostfull` leaves these two commands untouched, to avoid the situation shown in the next example.

```
\usepackage[force,full]{textcomp}
```
CM fonts: ⓧ ŏo
Times fonts: ■ ■o
```
CM fonts: \textcircled{x}\quad \t oo \par    Times fonts:
\fontfamily{ptm}\selectfont\textcircled{x}\quad \t oo \par
```
7-5-8

Since Times Roman is a font that **textcomp** knows about, specifying `full` will still produce correct output; to get the ink blobs we also had to add `force` in the previous example. This option directs **textcomp** to ignore all knowledge about individual font families and use the subset denoted by the additional option in all cases.[1]

When **textcomp** gets loaded (with or without restricting options), a large number of new commands are made available to access the new symbols. In addition, a number of symbols that have been (historically) taken by LATEX from math fonts (e.g., \textbullet, or \textdagger) are now taken from the companion fonts; as a consequence, they now sometimes change their shapes when the font attributes (family, series, shape) are changed.

```
\usepackage[safe]{textcomp}
```
†¶• viz. †¶•
```
\textdagger\textparagraph\textbullet{} viz.\
\fontfamily{ptm}\selectfont\textdagger\textparagraph\textbullet
```
7-5-9

While this is usually the right solution, it may result in changes in unexpected places. For example, the `itemize` environment by default uses \textbullet to indicate first-level items. If the slightly bigger bullet is preferred, then we have to

---

[1] This option is best avoided, as it can produce incorrect output without any warning.

undo the change in the default setting by returning the default to the right math encoding (usually OMS[1]). Compare this to Example 7-5-9.

• now like •

```
\usepackage[safe]{textcomp}
\DeclareTextSymbolDefault{\textbullet}{OMS}
\textbullet{} now like \fontfamily{ptm}\selectfont\textbullet
```

Of course, a more sensible solution in this case may be to adjust the definition for \labelitemi (see Section 3.3.1). For example:

```
\renewcommand\labelitemi{\normalfont\UseTextSymbol{OMS}{\textbullet}}
```

Diacritical marks on uppercase letters are sometimes flattened in some font designs compared to their lowercase counterparts. The EC fonts follow this tradition. For example, the grave accents on ò and Ò are different (which is not the case with Lucida, the document font used in this book). This poses a problem if one needs an uncommon letter that is not available as a single glyph in the T1 encoding, but rather must be constructed by placing the diacritical mark over the base character. In that case the same diacritical mark is used, which can result in noticeable differences (see the X̀ in the next example). The \capital... accents shown in Table 7.6 on page 363 solve this problem by generating diacritical marks suitable for use with uppercase letters.

ÒX̀ ÒX̀ ÒX̀

```
\usepackage[T1]{fontenc}  \usepackage[safe]{textcomp}
\Huge \`o\`x  \`O\`X \capitalgrave O\capitalgrave X
```

LATEX offers a \textcompwordmark command, an invisible zero-width glyph that can, for example, be used to break up unwanted ligatures (at the cost of preventing hyphenation). When the textcomp package is loaded, this glyph has a height of 1ex, which makes it possible to use it as the argument to an accent command, thereby placing an accent between two letters. In the next example this command is used to produce the German -burg abbreviation. With the textcomp package two additional compound word marks become available: \textascendercompwordmark and \textcapitalcompwordmark that have the height of the ascender or capitals in the font, respectively.

b˘g (this fails)
b̆g   B̆G

```
\usepackage[T1]{fontenc}  \usepackage[safe]{textcomp}
b\u{}g (this fails) \par
b\u\textcompwordmark g \quad B\u\textcapitalcompwordmark G
```

The above example works only with T1-encoded fonts (textcomp is additionally needed for the \textcapitalcompwordmark). The default definition for \textcompwordmark in LATEX does not use a real zero-width character, but rather (lacking such a glyph) a zero-width space.

---

[1] One has to look for the default declaration in latex.ltx to find the right encoding.

As the $ sign is a glyph available in both the OT1 and T1 encodings, there is no point in removing its definition and forcing LaTeX to pick up the TS1 version if you are typesetting in this encoding. However, assume you want to use the variant dollar sign $, for your dollars automatically. In that case you have to get rid of the declarations in other encodings so that LaTeX will automatically switch to TS1.

```
\DeclareTextCommandDefault{\textdollar}
    {\UseTextSymbol{TS1}\textdollaroldstyle}   % set up new default
\UndeclareTextCommand{\textdollar}{OT1}        % do not use the defs in
\UndeclareTextCommand{\textdollar} {T1}        % OT1 or T1
```

Such redeclarations will, of course, work only if the document fonts contain the desired glyph in the TS1 encoding. In this book they would have failed, because Lucida Bright (the document font for this book) has only the restricted set of ISO-Adobe symbols available. So if you wonder where the $ and similar symbols shown in the book actually came from, the answer is simple: from the EC fonts.

What can you do if you want to use, say, \textborn, but the current font family you use does not implement it? One possible solution is to overwrite the default provided by the textcomp package using \DeclareTextCommandDefault. The idea is that the default switches to a font family that you know contains the desired symbol (for example, cmr if your main document font is a serifed font, or cmss if it is a sans serif one), and then you can use \UseTextSymbol to pick up the symbol from the TS1 encoding in that family.[1]

Burkhard and Holger
⋆8.11.1997

```
\usepackage[safe]{textcomp}
\DeclareTextCommandDefault{\textborn}
    {{\fontfamily{cmr}\selectfont\UseTextSymbol{TS1}{\textborn}}}
\fontfamily{ptm}\selectfont
                    Burkhard and Holger \textborn 8.11.1997
```

7-5-13

You can use this approach for any symbol defined by the textcomp package. In case of accents the definition is similar. This time we declare the default to have an argument and in the definition we use \UseTextAccent. For example:

```
\DeclareTextCommandDefault{\newtie}[1]
    {{\fontfamily{cmr}\selectfont\UseTextAccent{TS1}{\newtie}{#1}}}
```

In fact, for symbols (but not for accents), textcomp attempts to resolve the problem of missing glyphs by locally switching to a font family stored in \textcompsubstdefault (the default is Computer Modern Roman) and typesetting the symbol in this family, after having issued a suitable error message. Use the option warn to get only warnings instead of errors. Of course, such substitutions produce inferior results, especially for "textual symbols", if the current font

---

[1] For more abstract symbols this approach often gives an acceptable result; in case of accents your mileage may vary.

is visually incompatible with the substitution family. In the next example we use Computer Modern Sans as a substitute. Be careful to select a family that has full TS1 coverage; otherwise, your redefinition will produce endless errors!

Helvetica with №, Ω, ↺, ¶. Not perfect but better than nothing.

7-5-14

```
\usepackage[warn]{textcomp} \renewcommand\textcompsubstdefault{cmss}
\fontfamily{phv}\selectfont Helvetica with \textnumero, \textohm,
\textcopyleft, \textpilcrow. Not perfect but better than nothing.
```

According to the specifications the TS1 encoding contains old-style digits as well as the punctuations period and comma. It allows one to typeset dates and other (positive) numbers with old-style numerals by simply switching to the TS1 font encoding. Unfortunately, old-style numerals are usually unavailable in most PostScript fonts (you must buy the "expert" font set in most cases), so that this method works correctly for only a few font families.[1]

Arno ★■■.■■.■■■■, Burkhard and Holger ★8.11.1997

7-5-15

```
\usepackage[warn,safe]{textcomp}
\newcommand\born[1]{\textborn
                    {\fontencoding{TS1}\selectfont #1}}
\raggedright
\fontfamily{phv}\selectfont Arno \born{29.11.1984},
\fontfamily{ccr}\selectfont
                    Burkhard and Holger \born{8.11.1997}
```

The textcomp package solves this problem by redefining the \oldstylenums command to automatically use the old-style numerals in the TS1 encoding if the current font contains them. If not, it will issue a warning and produce lining numerals instead.

Arno ★29.11.1984, Burkhard and Holger ★8.11.1997

7-5-16

```
\usepackage[warn]{textcomp}
\newcommand\born[1]{\textborn\oldstylenums{#1}}
\raggedright
\fontfamily{phv}\selectfont Arno \born{29.11.1984},
\fontfamily{ccr}\selectfont
                    Burkhard and Holger \born{8.11.1997}
```

If you own fonts that textcomp does not know about (or for some reason assumes that they implement a smaller subset than they actually do), you can inform the package about the font family in question by using the configuration file textcomp.cfg. For example, the commercial Lucida Blackletter originally contained only the basic ISO-Adobe glyphs, so textcomp takes a conservative approach and allows only these symbols. But nowadays it also contains the

---

[1]If the glyphs are directly accessed by manually switching to the TS1 encoding, as is done in the example, a restricting option (e.g., safe) will have no effect.

\textohm symbol, so by using \DeclareEncodingSubset after loading the package (or in the configuration file) you can typeset it in this font family as well.

We can now typeset Ω, but then the ∎ will fail without warning.

```
\usepackage[T1]{fontenc} \usepackage{textcomp} \raggedright
\DeclareEncodingSubset{TS1}{hlcf}{3}
\fontfamily{hlcf}\selectfont  We can now typeset \textohm,
but then the \texteuro{} will fail without warning.
```

7-5-17

For details on the use of \DeclareEncodingSubset and the subset numbers used, see the documentation in ltoutenc.dtx in the standard LaTeX distribution.

7.5.5 exscale—Scaling large operators

Normally the font employed for large mathematical symbols is used in only one size. This set-up is usually sufficient, as the font includes most of the characters in several different sizes and (LA)TEX is specially equipped to automatically choose the symbol that fits best. However, when a document requires a lot of mathematics in large sizes—such as in headings—the selected symbols may come out too small. In this case, you can use the package exscale, which provides for math extension fonts in different sizes. The package only works for documents using Computer Modern math fonts. However, packages providing alternate math font set-ups often offer this functionality as a package option.

7.5.6 tracefnt—Tracing the font selection

The package tracefnt can be used to detect problems in the font selection system. This package supports several options that allow you to customize the amount of information displayed by NFSS on the screen and in the transcript file.

errorshow This option suppresses all warnings and information messages on the terminal; they will be written to the transcript file only. Only real errors will be shown. Because warnings about font substitutions and so on can mean that the final result will be incorrect, you should carefully study the transcript file before printing an important publication.

warningshow When this option is specified, warnings and errors are shown on the terminal. This setting gives you the same amount of information as LaTeX 2ε does without the tracefnt package loaded.

infoshow This option is the default when you load the tracefnt package. Extra information, which is normally only written to the transcript file, is now also displayed on your terminal.

debugshow This option additionally shows information about changes to the text font and the restoration of such fonts at the end of a brace group or the end of an environment. Be careful when you turn on this option because it can produce very large transcript files that can quickly fill up your disk space.

In addition to these "standard tracing" options,[1] the package tracefnt supports the following options:

pausing   This option turns all warning messages into errors to help in the detection of problems in important publications.

loading   This option shows the loading of external fonts. However, if the format or document class you use has already loaded some fonts, then these will not be shown by this option.

7.5.7   nfssfont.tex—Displaying font tables and samples

The LaTeX distribution comes with a file called nfssfont.tex that can be used to test new fonts, produce font tables showing all characters, and perform similar font-related operations. This file is an adaption of the program testfont.tex, which was originally written by Donald Knuth. When you run this file through LaTeX, you will be asked to enter the name of the font to test. You can answer either by giving the external font name without any extension—such as cmr10 (Computer Modern Roman 10pt)—if you know it, or by giving an empty font name. In the latter case you will be asked to provide a NFSS font specification, that is, an encoding name (default T1), a font family name (default cmr), a font series (default m), a font shape (default n), and a font size (default 10pt). The package then loads the external font corresponding to that classification.

Next, you will be requested to enter a command. Probably the most important one is \table, which produces a font chart like the one on page 434. Also interesting is \text, which produces a longer text sample. To switch to a new test font, type \init; to finish the test, type \bye or \stop; and to learn about all the other possible tests (at the moment basically still tailored for the OT1 encoding), type \help.

With a bit of care you can also use the program non-interactively, provided your LaTeX implementation supports input redirection. For example, if the file nfssfont.in contains

```
cmr10
\table \newpage \init

T1
cmss
bx
n
10
\text \bye
```

then a call like latex nfssfont < nfssfont.in (on UN*X implementations)

---

[1]It is suggested that package writers who support tracing of their packages use these four standard names if applicable.

would read all input from that particular file, first producing a glyph chart for the font cmr10 and then creating a text sample for T1/cmss/bx/n/10.

Two things are important here. First, the nfssfont.tex program issues an implicit \init command, so the first input line either should contain a font name or should be completely empty (to indicate that an NFSS classification follows). Second, the input to \init must appear on individual lines with nothing else (not even a comment, as that would mask the line ending), because the line ending indicates the end of the answer to a question like "Font encoding [T1]: \encoding=" that you would get if ran run the program interactively.

7.6 PSNFSS—PostScript fonts with LaTeX

The PSNFSS bundle, originally developed by Sebastian Rahtz, offers a complete working set-up of the LaTeX font selection scheme for use with common PostScript fonts, covering the "Base 35" fonts (which are built into any Level 2 PostScript printing device and the ghostscript interpreter) and the free Charter and Utopia fonts.[1] The current implementation of PSNFSS is maintained by Walter Schmidt and is part of the required set of support files for LaTeX that should be available with every LaTeX installation.

For normal use you will probably have to include only one (or more) of the packages listed in Table 7.7 on the next page to change the default Roman, sans serif, and/or typewriter typefaces. If you study this table you will notice that only two packages attempt to set up new fonts for math and that the first eight packages only change fonts in one of the three categories. Thus, to get Times as the Roman text font, Helvetica as the sans serif text font, and Courier as the typewriter text font, one would need to load mathptmx, helvet, and courier. So why is the times package, which does this all in one go, considered obsolete?

Scale Helvetica to blend with surrounding fonts

One reason is that Helvetica, if loaded at its nominal size, is actually too large to blend well with Times or Courier. That does not matter so much in a design where Helvetica is used only for headings, say. But if these fonts are going to be mixed in running text (something that is made easy by LaTeX commands such as \textsf), then using a package such as times will produce questionable results. The helvet package, on the other hand, offers the ability to scale the fonts by specifying the option scaled, which scales the fonts down to 95% of the requested size. This option is actually a keyword/value option, so that even finer control is possible—scaled=0.92 would load the fonts at 92% of their nominal size.

There is, however, one set of circumstances in which you might wish to use the times package after all: when you do not want to change the math font set-up, or you want to use some other set of fonts for math. In that case you can still load the helvet package afterwards to apply scaling.

---

[1] If the Utopia fonts are missing on your TeX installation they can be downloaded from the CTAN directory fonts/utopia. Consult the documentation of your TeX system on how to install them.

Package	Roman Font	Sans Serif Font	Typewriter Font	Formulas
(none)	CM Roman	CM Sans Serif	CM Typewriter	CM Math
mathptmx	Times			Times + Symbol
mathpazo	Palatino			Palatino + Pazo
charter	Charter			
utopia*	Utopia			
chancery	Zapf Chancery			
helvet		Helvetica		
avant		Avant Garde		
courier			Courier	
bookman	Bookman	Avant Garde	Courier	
newcent	New Century Schoolbook	Avant Garde	Courier	
Obsolete Packages				
times	Times	Helvetica	Courier	
palatino	Palatino	Helvetica	Courier	
mathptm	Times			Times + Symbol + CM
mathpple	Palatino			Palatino + Symbol + Euler

*An alternative package that includes math support is fourier, which is described in Section 7.7.7.

Table 7.7: Fonts used by PSNFSS packages

The PSNFSS bundle uses the Karl Berry naming scheme [19] throughout; the classification and the external font names are shown in Table 7.8 on the following page. Using this table, it is easy to access individual fonts without loading any package, such as via a call to \usefont. Because these fonts can be easily scaled to any size, this method offers attractive possibilities when designing headings or title pages, as it facilitates the use of sizes different from those created with the standard LaTeX font size commands.

Direct access to fonts

Utopia-Bold

```
\centering
\fontsize{20mm}{22mm}%    select size
\usefont{T1}{put}{b}{n}%  select font

Utopia-Bold
```

7-6-1

Family	Series	Shape(s)	External PostScript font names and examples
colspan			*Times* (OT1, T1, TS1)
ptm	m	n, sl, it, sc	Times-Roman (`ptmr`), Times-Italic (`ptmri`)
ptm	b, (bx)	n, sl, it, sc	Times-Bold (`ptmb`), Times-BoldItalic (`ptmbi`)
colspan			*Palatino* (OT1, T1, TS1)
ppl	m	n, sl, it, sc	Palatino-Roman (`pplr`), Palatino-Italic (`pplri`)
ppl	b, (bx)	n, sl, it, sc	Palatino-Bold (`pplb`), Palatino-BoldItalic (`pplbi`)
colspan			*New Century Schoolbook* (OT1, T1, TS1)
pnc	m	n, sl, it, sc	NewCenturySchlbk-Roman (`pncr`), NewCenturySchlbk-Italic (`pncri`)
pnc	b, (bx)	n, sl, it, sc	NewCenturySchlbk-Bold (`pncb`), NewCenturySchlbk-BoldItalic (`pncbi`)
colspan			*Bookman* (OT1, T1, TS1)
pbk	m	n, sl, it, sc	Bookman-Light (`pbkl`), Bookman-LightItalic (`pbkli`)
pbk	b, (bx)	n, sl, it, sc	Bookman-Demi (`pbkd`), Bookman-DemiItalic (`pbkdi`)
colspan			*Helvetica* (OT1, T1, TS1)
phv	m	n, sl, sc	Helvetica (`phvr`), Helvetica-Oblique (`phvro`)
phv	b, (bx)	n, sl, sc	Helvetica-Bold (`phvb`), Helvetica-BoldOblique (`phvbo`)
phv	mc	n, sl, sc	Helvetica-Narrow (`phvrrn`), Helvetica-Narrow-Oblique (`phvron`)
phv	bc	n, sl, sc	Helvetica-Narrow-Bold (`phvbrn`), Helvetica-Narrow-BoldOblique (`phvbon`)
colspan			*Avant Garde* (OT1, T1, TS1)
pag	m	n, sl, sc	AvantGarde-Book (`pagk`), AvantGarde-BookOblique (`pagko`)
pag	b, (bx)	n, sl, sc	AvantGarde-Demi (`pagd`), AvantGarde-DemiOblique (`pagdo`)
colspan			*Courier* (OT1, T1, TS1)
pcr	m	n, sl, sc	Courier (`pcrr`), CourierOblique (`pcrro`)
pcr	b, (bx)	n, sl, sc	Courier-Bold (`pcrb`), Courier-BoldOblique (`pcrbo`)
colspan			*Zapf Chancery* (OT1, T1, TS1)
pzc	m	it	ZapfChancery-MediumItalic (`pzcmi`)
colspan			*Utopia* (OT1, T1, TS1)
put	m	n, sl, it, sc	Utopia-Regular (`putr`), Utopia-Italic (`putri`)
put	b, (bx)	n, sl, it, sc	Utopia-Bold (`putb`), Utopia-BoldItalic (`putbi`)
colspan			*Charter* (OT1, T1, TS1)
bch	m	n, sl, it, sc	CharterBT-Roman (`bchr`), CharterBT-Italic (`bchri`)
bch	b, (bx)	n, sl, it, sc	CharterBT-Bold (`bchb`), CharterBT-BoldItalic (`bchbi`)
colspan			*Symbol and Zapf Dingbats* (U)
psy	m	n	Symbol (`psyr`): Σψμβολ
pzd	m	n	Zapf Dingbats (`pzdr`): ✳❂❒✼ ✣✸■✳☺❂▼▲

Table 7.8: Classification of font families in the PSNFSS distribution

The PSNFSS collection contains only two packages that modify the math set-up: mathptmx selects math fonts that blend with Times Roman (described in Section 7.6.2 on page 376) and mathpazo selects math fonts designed to work with Palatino (see Section 7.6.3 on page 377). The packages mathptm and mathpple are predecessors that are retained mainly for backward compatibility. Outside the PSNFSS collection a few other packages that change the math font set-up are available (in most cases involving commercial fonts). Some free packages are described in Section 7.7 on page 381, including one that uses Utopia for typesetting text and mathematics. A collection of sample pages with different text and math fonts appear in Section 8.8.3.

Most document classes designed for use with Computer Modern set up a leading (\baselineskip) of 10pt/12pt. This may appear to be too tight for several of the PostScript font families shown below, due to a larger x-height of the fonts. However, as this is a matter of document design and also depends on the chosen line width and other factors, the packages in the PSNFSS collection make no attempt to adjust the leading. For a given document class you can change the leading by a *factor* by issuing the declaration \linespread{*factor*} in the preamble. For example, \linespread{1.033} would change the leading from, say, 12pt to approximately 12.4pt. For best results, however, one needs to use a document class designed for the selected document fonts or, lacking such a class, to redefine the commands \normalsize, \footnotesize, and so on (see page 343 for details). Also remember that changing the leading might result in a noticeable number of "Underfull \vbox" warnings, if the \textheight is no longer an integral number of text lines (see page 930 for further details).

Adjusting the leading

By default, LaTeX selects a Roman typeface as the document font. Packages like helvet or avant change the default sans serif typeface (by changing \sfdefault) but do not change the default document font family. If such a typeface should be used as the document font, issue the line

Sans serif as document typeface

```
\renewcommand\familydefault{\sfdefault}
```

in the preamble of your document.

Besides supporting the common PostScript text fonts, the PSNFSS collection contains the interesting pifont package. It sets up various commands for use with the so-called Pi fonts (i.e., special symbol fonts like Zapf Dingbats and Symbol). It is described in Section 7.6.4 on page 378.

7.6.1 Font samples for fonts supported by PSNFSS

This section provides textual samples of the the fonts supported by the PSNFSS collection. The examples were generated by explicitly selecting the font size and leading via a call to \fontsize and then selecting the font with a \usefont command. For example, the first sample was generated with \fontsize{9}{13} \usefont{T1}{pag}{m}{n}.

ITC Avant Garde
Gothic
9pt/13pt (pag)

Avant Garde Gothic was designed by Herb Lubalin and Tom Carnase based on the distinctive logo designed for *Avant Garde* magazine. It is a geometric sans serif type with basic shapes built from circles and lines. Effective for headlines and short texts, but it needs generous leading. A (commercially available) condensed version that better retains legibility in lengthier texts was designed by Ed Benguiat.

For the price of £45, almost anything can be found floating in fields. ¡THE DAZED BROWN FOX QUICKLY GAVE 12345–67890 JUMPS! — ¿But aren't Kafka's Schloß and Æsop's Œuvres often naïve vis-à-vis the dœmonic phœnix's official rôle in fluffy soufflés?

ITC Bookman
10pt/12pt (pbk)

Bookman was originally design in 1860 by Alexander Phemister for the Miller & Richard foundry in Scotland (commercially available from Bitstream). The ITC revival by Ed Benguiat has a larger x-height and a moderate stroke contrast that is well suited for body text and display applications.

For the price of £45, almost anything can be found floating in fields. ¡THE DAZED BROWN FOX QUICKLY GAVE 12345–67890 JUMPS! — ¿But aren't Kafka's Schloß and Æsop's Œuvres often naïve vis-à-vis the dæmonic phœnix's official rôle in fluffy soufflés?

Bitstream Charter
10pt/12.4pt (bch)

Bitstream Charter is an original design by Matthew Carter intended to work well on low-resolution devices; hence, it contains squared serifs and avoids excessive use of curves and diagonals. It is useful for many applications, including books and manuals.

For the price of £45, almost anything can be found floating in fields. ¡THE DAZED BROWN FOX QUICKLY GAVE 12345–67890 JUMPS! — ¿But aren't Kafka's Schloß and Æsop's Œuvres often naïve vis-à-vis the dæmonic phœnix's official rôle in fluffy soufflés?

Courier
10pt/12pt (pcr)

Courier is a wide-running, thin-stroked monospaced font. It was designed by Howard Kettler of IBM and later redrawn by Adrian Frutiger. These days it is often used in combination with Times Roman, producing a striking contrast. One reason for the popularity of this combination is certainly its availability on any PostScript device. For alternatives see Section 7.7.4.

```
     For the price of £45, almost anything can be
     found floating in fields. ¡THE DAZED BROWN FOX
     QUICKLY GAVE 12345-67890 JUMPS! -- ¿But aren't
     Kafka's Schloß and Æsop's Œuvres often naïve
     vis-à-vis the dæmonic phœnix's official rôle in
     fluffy soufflés?
```

Helvetica was originally designed by Max Miedinger for the Haas foundry of *Helvetica*
Switzerland, hence the name. It was later extended by the Stempel foundry, with *10pt/13pt (phv)*
further refinements being made by Mergenthaler Linotype in the United States.
Helvetica is claimed to be the most popular typeface of all time.

> For the price of £45, almost anything can be found floating in fields.
> ¡THE DAZED BROWN FOX QUICKLY GAVE 12345–67890 JUMPS! —
> ¿But aren't Kafka's Schloß and Æsop's Œuvres often naïve vis-à-vis
> the dæmonic phœnix's official rôle in fluffy soufflés?

The New Century Schoolbook typeface was designed at the beginning of the *New Century*
20th century by Morris Benton of the American Type Founders. It was created *Schoolbook*
in response to a publisher's commission that sought a typeface with maximum *10pt/12.5pt (pnc)*
legibility for elementary schoolbooks.

> For the price of £45, almost anything can be found floating in
> fields. ¡THE DAZED BROWN FOX QUICKLY GAVE 12345–67890
> JUMPS! — ¿But aren't Kafka's Schloß and Æsop's Œuvres often
> naïve vis-à-vis the dæmonic phœnix's official rôle in fluffy soufflés?

Palatino, designed by Hermann Zapf, is one of the most widely used typefaces *Palatino*
today. You can feel the brush that created it, which gives it a lot of elegance. *10pt/11.5pt (ppl)*
Although originally designed as a display typeface, due to its legibility Palatino
soon gained popularity as a text face as well.

> For the price of £45, almost anything can be found floating in fields.
> ¡THE DAZED BROWN FOX QUICKLY GAVE 12345–67890 JUMPS! —
> ¿But aren't Kafka's Schloß and Æsop's Œuvres often naïve vis-à-vis the
> dæmonic phœnix's official rôle in fluffy soufflés?

Times Roman is Linotype's version of Monotype's Times New Roman, which *Times Roman*
was originally designed under the direction of Stanley Morison for the *London* *10pt/12pt (ptm)*
Times newspaper. The Adobe font that is built into many PostScript devices uses
Linotype's 12-point design.

> For the price of £45, almost anything can be found floating in fields. ¡THE
> DAZED BROWN FOX QUICKLY GAVE 12345–67890 JUMPS! — ¿But
> aren't Kafka's Schloß and Æsop's Œuvres often naïve vis-à-vis the dæmonic
> phœnix's official rôle in fluffy soufflés?

Utopia, designed by Robert Slimbach, combines the vertical stress and pro- *Utopia*
nounced stroke contrast of 18th-century Transitional types with contemporary *10pt/12.5pt (put)*
innovations in shape and stroke details.

For the price of £45, almost anything can be found floating in fields. ¡THE DAZED BROWN FOX QUICKLY GAVE 12345–67890 JUMPS! — ¿But aren't Kafka's Schloß and Æsop's Œuvres often naïve vis-à-vis the dæmonic phœnix's official rôle in fluffy soufflés?

ITC Zapf Chancery
10pt/12pt (pzc)

Zapf Chancery is a contemporary script based on chancery handwriting, developed during the Italian Renaissance for use by the scribes in the papal offices. Highly legible, it can be usefully applied for short texts and applications like invitations and awards.

For the price of £45, almost anything can be found floating in fields. ¡THE DAZED BROWN FOX QUICKLY GAVE 12345–67890 JUMPS! — ¿But aren't Kafka's Schloß and Æsop's Œuvres often naïve vis-à-vis the dæmonic phœnix's official rôle in fluffy soufflés?

7.6.2 mathptmx—Times Roman in math and text

The mathptmx package makes Times the document text font and implements a math font set-up for use with such documents. It builds on freely available Type 1 PostScript fonts and is, therefore, somewhat inferior to some of the commercially available solutions that offer fonts especially designed for this purpose. Nevertheless, it has the advantage of being (at least potentially) available in every TEX installation.[1]

The mathptmx package was co-authored by Alan Jeffrey, Sebastian Rahtz, and Ulrik Vieth. It was based upon earlier work by Alan Jeffrey [72], in particular the mathptm package (the predecessor to mathptmx) and, most importantly, the fontinst system [57, pp. 393–404], which provided the initial breakthrough in making PostScript fonts generally available with TEX.

Technically, the mathptmx package uses a collection of virtual fonts that implement the math fonts needed for TEX by drawing them from several font resources—Times Roman, Times Italic, Symbol, various Computer Modern fonts (mainly for delimiters, big operators, arrows, and the like), and Ralph Smith's Formal Script (RSFS). The RSFS fonts are a better solution for a script/calligraphic alphabet than Zapf Chancery, which is used in mathptm for this purpose.

An example showing a trigonometric function:

$$\sin\frac{\alpha}{2} = \pm\sqrt{\frac{1-\cos\alpha}{2}}$$

The script looks like this: $\mathcal{ABC}$.

```
\usepackage{mathptmx}

An example showing a trigonometric function:
\[ \sin \frac{\alpha}{2} =
      \pm \sqrt{\frac{1-\cos\alpha}{2}} \]
The script looks like this: $\mathcal{ABC}$.
```

7-6-2

It has some features in common with the mathpazo package. First, when loaded with the option slantedGreek, uppercase Greek letters are slanted instead

---

[1] The TEX installation must support virtual fonts, which is the case for nearly every distribution.

of being upright (the default). In either case the two extra commands \upDelta and \upOmega will print an upright Δ and Ω, respectively. Second, the functionality of the exscale package is automatically provided: thus big operators and delimiters scale with the current font size.

On the downside, the package disables \boldmath for the simple reason that no bold version of the Adobe Symbol font exists. You can get, of course, a bold math alphabet with \mathbf, but this gives you only upright Latin characters and digits. In particular, using the bm package to make individual symbols bold will produce questionable results, as the best the \bm command can do is to produce "poor man's bold" by overprinting the symbols with slight offsets.

Proper bold faces missing

```
\usepackage{mathptmx,bm}
Bold is difficult to achieve: {\boldmath$\alpha
  \neq A$} and at best looks questionable:
$A \neq \mathbf{A} = \bm\alpha - \bm\gamma$.
```

Bold is difficult to achieve: $\alpha \neq A$ and at best looks questionable: $A \neq \mathbf{A} = \boldsymbol{\alpha} - \boldsymbol{\gamma}$.

7-6-3

Another (small) potential problem is that the commands \jmath, \coprod, and \amalg are unavailable. If either issue turns out to be a real problem, then alternatives to consider are the TX fonts (Section 7.7.5) and the commercial solutions MathTime (Professional) by Michael Spivak and TM-Math by MicroPress.

7.6.3 mathpazo—Palatino in math and text

A package named mathpple supporting Adobe Palatino with matching math fonts was originally developed by Walter Schmidt based on earlier work by Aloysius Helminck. It used the same approach as mathptm; that is, it was built on the virtual font mechanism, combining symbols from Palatino, Symbol, Euler, and CM Math. As these fonts only partly match the style of Palatino, Diego Puga developed a set of Type 1 PostScript fonts (Pazo Math) intended to repair the defects apparent in the mathpple solution. The Pazo Math fonts contain glyphs that are unavailable in Palatino and for which Computer Modern or glyphs from Symbol look odd when combined with Palatino. These include a number of math glyphs, the uppercase Greek alphabet (upright and slanted), a blackboard bold alphabet, as well as several other glyphs (such as the euro symbol) in regular and bold weights and upright and slanted shapes.

The fonts are accessible with the mathpazo package developed by Diego Puga and Walter Schmidt as part of the PSNFSS collection. It makes Palatino the document text font and provides a math set-up that works by using virtual fonts accessing Palatino Italic, the Math Pazo fonts, and CM fonts (for the remaining symbols).

An example showing a trigonometric function:

$$\sin \frac{\alpha}{2} = \pm \sqrt{\frac{1 - \cos \alpha}{2}}$$

```
\usepackage{mathpazo}
An example showing a trigonometric function:
\[ \sin \frac{\alpha}{2} =
      \pm \sqrt{\frac{1-\cos\alpha}{2}}  \]
The script looks like this: $\mathcal{ABC}$.
```

7-6-4   The script looks like this: $\mathcal{ABC}$.

This package is very similar to the `mathptmx` package. In particular, it supports the option `slantedGreek` to make uppercase Greek letters slanted instead of upright (the default). In either case the two extra commands `\upDelta` and `\upOmega` will print an upright Δ and Ω, respectively. Also, it provides the functionality of the `exscale` package.

However, in contrast to the `mathptmx` package, which uses the Adobe Symbol font, for which no bold-weight variant exists, the `mathpazo` package provides full access to symbols in a bold weight.

Bold is easy to achieve: $\alpha \neq A$ and blends well: $A \neq \mathbf{A} = \alpha - \gamma$.

```
\usepackage{mathpazo,bm}
Bold is easy to achieve: {\boldmath$\alpha
 \neq A$} and blends well:
$A \neq \mathbf{A} = \bm\alpha - \bm\gamma$.
```

7-6-5

As mentioned above, the Pazo Math fonts contain a blackboard bold alphabet, which can be accessed through the math alphabet identifier `\mathbb`. The font contains the uppercase Latin letters and the digit "1". Be careful, however: all other digits are silently ignored!

ABCDEFGHIJK 1

```
\usepackage{mathpazo}
$\mathbb{ABCDEFGHIJK}$ $\mathbb{0123}$
```

7-6-6

If `\mathbb` should select a different alphabet, provided by some other package, it is best to suppress the Pazo Math one by using the option `noBBppl` when loading the package.

Commercial Palatino fonts

The package also offers two additional options that deal with the use of commercially available Palatino fonts[1] for the text font: `sc` selects Palatino with true small capitals (font family name `pplx`) and `osf` selects Palatino with small caps and old-style numerals (font family name `pplj`) instead of basic Palatino (`ppl`).

7.6.4 pifont—**Accessing Pi and Symbol fonts**

Fonts containing collections of special symbols, which are normally not found in a text font, are called Pi fonts. One such font, the PostScript font Zapf Dingbats, is available if you use the `pifont` package originally written by Sebastian Rahtz and now incorporated as part of PSNFSS.

Accessing glyphs from Zapf Dingbats

The directly accessible characters of the PostScript Zapf Dingbats font are shown in Table 7.9 on the next page. A given character can be chosen via the `\ding` command. The parameter for the `\ding` command is an integer that specifies the character to be typeset according to the table. For example, `\ding{'46}` gives ✆.

---

[1]These fonts are commercially available and are *not* part of the Base 35 fonts.

	´0	´1	´2	´3	´4	´5	´6	´7	
´04x		✁	✂	✃	✄	☎	✆	✇	˝2x
´05x	✈	✉	☛	☞	✌	✍	✎	✏	
´06x	✐	✑	✒	✓	✔	✕	✖	✗	˝3x
´07x	✘	✙	✚	✛	✜	✝	✞	✟	
´10x	✠	✡	✢	✣	✤	✥	✦	✧	˝4x
´11x	★	✩	✪	✫	✬	✭	✮	✯	
´12x	✰	✱	✲	✳	✴	✵	✶	✷	˝5x
´13x	✸	✹	✺	✻	✼	✽	✾	✿	
´14x	❀	❁	❂	❃	❄	❅	❆	❇	˝6x
´15x	❈	❉	❊	❋	●	○	■	❏	
´16x	❐	❑	❒	▲	▼	◆	❖	◗	˝7x
´17x	❘	❙	❚	❛	❜	❝	❞		
´24x		❡	❢	❣	❤	❥	❦	❧	˝Ax
´25x	♣	♦	♥	♠	①	②	③	④	
´26x	⑤	⑥	⑦	⑧	⑨	⑩	❶	❷	˝Bx
´27x	❸	❹	❺	❻	❼	❽	❾	❿	
´30x	①	②	③	④	⑤	⑥	⑦	⑧	˝Cx
´31x	⑨	⑩	❶	❷	❸	❹	❺	❻	
´32x	❼	❽	❾	❿	→	→	↔	↕	˝Dx
´33x	↘	→	↗	→	➡	→	→	⇛	
´34x	⇛	➠	➢	➣	➤	➥	➦	➧	˝Ex
´35x	➨	➩	➪	➫	➬	➭	➮	➯	
´36x		➱	➲	➳	➴	➵	➶	➷	˝Fx
´37x	➸	➹	➺	➻	➼	➽	⇒		
	˝8	˝9	˝A	˝B	˝C	˝D	˝E	˝F	

Table 7.9: Glyphs in the PostScript font Zapf Dingbats

The `dinglist` environment is a variation of the `itemize` list. The argument specifies the number of the character to be used at the beginning of each item.

➤ The first item.

➤ The second item in the list.

➤ A final item.

```
\usepackage{pifont}
\begin{dinglist}{"E4}
 \item The first item.    \item The second
   item in the list.      \item A final item.
\end{dinglist}
```

7-6-7

The environment `dingautolist` allows you to build an enumerated list from a sequence of Zapf Dingbats characters. In this case, the argument specifies the number of the first character of the sequence. Subsequent items will be numbered by incrementing this number by one. This makes some starting positions like 172, 182, 192, and 202 in Table 7.9 on the preceding page very attractive, as differently designed circled number sequences (1–10) start there.

① The first item in the list.

② The second item in the list.

③ The third item in the list.

References to list items work as expected: ①, ②, ③

```
\usepackage{pifont}
\begin{dingautolist}{'300}
 \item The first item in the list.\label{lst:a}
 \item The second item in the list.\label{lst:b}
 \item The third item in the list.\label{lst:c}
\end{dingautolist}
References to list items work as expected:
\ref{lst:a}, \ref{lst:b}, \ref{lst:c}
```
7-6-8

You can fill a complete line (with 0.5 inch space at left and right) with a given character using the command `\dingline`, where the argument indicates the desired character. For filling parts of a line, use the command `\dingfill`. This command works similar to LaTeX's `\dotfill` command, but uses the specified glyph instead of dots.

⇨ ⇨ ⇨   text text   ☙ ☙   text text   ☞ ☞

```
\usepackage{pifont}
\dingline{35}                    \par\medskip
\noindent\dingfill{233} text text
\dingfill{235} text text \dingfill{236}
```
7-6-9

Besides providing direct support for the Zapf Dingbats font, the pifont package includes a general mechanism for coping with any Pi font that conforms to the NFSS classification U/*family*/m/n—for example, the Symbol font with the family name psy.

Accessing individual glyphs from a Pi font

To access individual glyphs from such a Pi font, use the `\Pisymbol` command, which takes the *family* name as its first argument and the glyph position in the font as its second argument. Using this command one can readily access the characters in the Symbol font, shown in Table 7.10 on page 382. For example, `\Pisymbol{psy}{210}` gives ®. In fact, `\ding` (discussed earlier) is simply an abbreviation for `\Pisymbol` with the first argument set to pzd.

When only Greek letters are desired, you can use the `\Pifont` command and consult the correspondence in Table 7.10. Clearly, this solution is no match for a properly designed font for the Greek language but it might serve in an emergency—for example, to typeset the text above the entrance of Plato's Academy that states "Only geometers may enter":

ΜΗΔΕΙΣ ΑΓΕΩΜΕΤΠΗΤΟΣ ΕΙΣΙΤΩ.

```
\usepackage{pifont}
{\Pifont{psy}   MHDEIS\ AGEWMETPHTOS\ EISITW}.
```
7-6-10

You can also make itemized lists using `Pilist` or enumerated lists using the `Piautolist` environments as follows:

⇒ The first item.

⇒ The second.

★ The first item.

☆ The second.

✯ The third.

```
\usepackage{pifont}

\begin{Pilist}{psy}{'336}
   \item The first item. \item The second.
\end{Pilist}
\begin{Piautolist}{pzd}{'115}
   \item The first item. \item The second.
   \item The third.
\end{Piautolist}
```

7-6-11

The `\dingline` and `\dingfill` commands are also merely abbreviations for the more general commands `\Piline` and `\Pifill`, as shown below. The example reveals curious gaps in the last line. They are due to `\Piline` and `\Pifill` typesetting their symbols on an invisible grid so that symbols on different lines come out vertically aligned.

✄ ✄ ✄ ✄ ✄ ✄ ✄ ✄

⇒ ⇒ ⇒   text   ⇔ ⇔ ⇔   text   ⇐ ⇐ ⇐

7-6-12

```
\usepackage{pifont}

\Piline{pzd}{36}                \par\medskip
\noindent\Pifill{psy}{222} text
\Pifill{psy}{219}text\Pifill{psy}{220}
```

7.7   A collection of font packages

So far we have discussed font-related packages that belong to core LaTeX—that is, packages that are either part of the base distribution or, as for PSNFSS, are part of the "required" additions. There are, however, many other packages that provide font customization possibilities. Nowadays most of them are part of a LaTeX distribution. If they are not available on your local system, you can obtain them from an electronic archive or from a TeX organization; see Appendix C.

The packages described in the current section modify the document text fonts (and sometimes the math font set-up). As the section title indicates, they represent merely a selection of what is available. Further pointers can be found in the online package catalogue [169] or in one of the FAQ documents on LaTeX [46, 141].

7.7.1   eco—Old-style numerals with Computer Modern

The original Computer Modern fonts contain a set of old-style digits (e.g., 1982) as part of their math fonts, not because old-style numerals have anything to do with math, but because Donald Knuth tried to use the limited font space available in the most economical way, using some free slots in the math fonts to deposit the glyphs there. As the EC font implementation only concerned itself with a new

	´0	´1	´2	´3	´4	´5	´6	´7	
´04x		!	∀	#	∃	%	&	∍	˝2x
´05x	(	)	*	+	,	−	.	/	
´06x	0	1	2	3	4	5	6	7	˝3x
´07x	8	9	:	;	<	=	>	?	
´10x	≅	A	B	X	Δ	E	Φ	Γ	˝4x
´11x	H	I	ϑ	K	Λ	M	N	O	
´12x	Π	Θ	P	Σ	T	Y	ς	Ω	˝5x
´13x	Ξ	Ψ	Z	[	∴	]	⊥	_	
´14x	‾	α	β	χ	δ	ε	φ	γ	˝6x
´15x	η	ι	φ	κ	λ	μ	ν	o	
´16x	π	θ	ρ	σ	τ	υ	ϖ	ω	˝7x
´17x	ξ	ψ	ζ	{	|	}	~		
´24x		ϒ	′	≤	/	∞	ƒ	♣	˝Ax
´25x	♦	♥	♠	↔	←	↑	→	↓	
´26x	°	±	″	≥	×	∝	∂	•	˝Bx
´27x	÷	≠	≡	≈	…	|	—	↵	
´30x	ℵ	ℑ	ℜ	℘	⊗	⊕	∅	∩	˝Cx
´31x	∪	⊃	⊇	⊄	⊂	⊆	∈	∉	
´32x	∠	∇	®	©	™	∏	√	·	˝Dx
´33x	¬	∧	∨	⇔	⇐	⇑	⇒	⇓	
´34x	◊	⟨	®	©	™	Σ	⌠	|	˝Ex
´35x	⎝	⌈	|	⌊	⌈	⎰	⌊	|	
´36x		⟩	∫	⌈	|	⌋	⟩	|	˝Fx
´37x	⎠	⌉	|	⌋	⌉	⎱	⌋		
	˝8	˝9	˝A	˝B	˝C	˝D	˝E	˝F	

Table 7.10: Glyphs in the PostScript font Symbol

font encoding for text, this anomaly in the math fonts was unfortunately kept.[1]
Actually, the designers of the text companion encoding (TS1) added old-style numerals to that encoding, but so far this is of little practical relevance because too many font families implement only a subset of the TS1 encoding. See Section 7.5.4, page 367, for more information.

---

[1] Justin Ziegler together with the LATEX3 project team developed a rationalized font encoding design for 256-glyph math fonts [174]. Unfortunately, until now his theoretical work has not been implemented other than in a prototype using virtual fonts [40].

For easy access to old-style numerals hidden in the math fonts, LaTeX provides the command `\oldstylenums`, which can be used in text and within formulas. In its argument you should place the digits that you want to typeset as non-aligning digits. If the command is used in text, spaces in the argument are honored, but you should not try to put characters other than digits into it or the results will be unpredictable. One problem with the default definition of this command is that it will always generate old-style numerals from Computer Modern Roman, regardless of the surrounding fonts in use. For this reason the `textcomp` package contains a redefinition that produces the old-style numerals from the current font, provided they are available in the current font family; see Section 7.5.4 for details. *Basic LaTeX support for old-style numerals*

This approach for obtaining old-style numerals might be adequate if lining numerals are the norm and old-style numerals are required only once in a while. But in a document layout in which all text numerals are supposed to be presented in old-style it is not really acceptable to require the author to explicitly mark up every occurrence in this way. What is needed in such a case are text fonts that contain old-style instead of lining numerals in the standard slot positions.

The EC fonts contain both lining and old-style numerals (albeit in a somewhat inconvenient position), so it was just a matter of time until someone developed a series of virtual fonts that reencode the fonts to make old-style numerals be the default text numbers. The `eco` fonts by Sebastian Kirsch provide this reencoding and can be accessed by loading the `eco` package. Note that the package affects only the text numbers, so it is important to mark up mathematical digits properly. Otherwise, you will obtain a result like the one shown in the example.

In 1996 Sebastian developed fonts producing old-style numerals in text but lining numerals in math. So do not write "the value can be 1 or −1", as both numbers should be lining numerals. In text lining numerals can be obtained as well: 1996.

7-7-1

```
\usepackage{eco}

In 1996 Sebastian developed fonts producing
old-style numerals in text but lining numerals
in math. So do not write ``the value can be 1
or $-1$'', as both numbers should be lining
numerals. In text lining numerals can be
obtained as well: \newstylenums{1996}.
```

7.7.2 ccfonts, concmath—The Concrete fonts

For the text of his book *Concrete Mathematics* [59], Donald Knuth designed a new typeface [92] to go with the Euler mathematics fonts designed by Hermann Zapf [173]. This font family, called Concrete Roman, was created from the Computer Modern METAFONT sources by supplying different parameter settings.

Starting from the work done for the EC fonts, it was relatively easy to create Concrete Roman fonts in T1 and TS1 encodings (original work by Frank Mittelbach; current version by Walter Schmidt). The fonts available in these families are shown in Table 7.11 on the following page. Ulrik Vieth used the construction method outlined by Knuth [92] to develop a companion set of Concrete Math fonts including the full range of AMS symbols (as provided by the `amssymb` or `amsfonts` package).

Family	Series	Shape(s)	Example of the Typeface
Concrete Roman (T1, TS1,OT1)			
ccr	m	n, it, sl, sc	Concrete Roman medium
ccr	c	sl	*Concrete Roman condensed slanted (only* OT1 *and 9pt)*
Concrete Math (OML)			
ccm	m	it	*Concrete Math.* α Ω
Concrete Math (OMS)			
ccy	m, c	n	$\mathcal{C}$\⌡∇⌉⊔⌉ $\mathcal{M}$⊣⊔⟨¬ ⊘ ⊗

Table 7.11: Classification of the Concrete font families

The first package that provided access to these font families for normal text was beton (by Frank Jensen). The following example shows the combination of Concrete text and Euler math fonts (see also Section 7.7.10 on page 396):

Concrete Roman blends well with Euler Math, as can be seen with

$$\sum_{0 \leq k < n} k = \frac{n(n-1)}{2}$$

```
\usepackage{beton,euler}
Concrete Roman blends well with Euler Math,
as can be seen with
\[ \sum_{0\leq k<n} k = \frac{n(n-1)}{2} \]
```
7-7-2

A more recent development that also provides the use of Concrete fonts for math and supports the T1 and TS1 encodings is the ccfonts package (by Walter Schmidt). Both packages take care of small but important typographical details, such as increasing the value of \baselineskip slightly (see discussion on the facing page). As the Concrete fonts have no boldface series, the ccfonts package offers the option boldsans to use the semibold series of the Computer Modern Sans fonts as a replacement. As a result, without any further adjustments, headings in standard classes will be typeset using this font series.

1   Testing headings

An example showing a trigonometric function:

$$\sin \frac{\alpha}{2} = \pm \sqrt{\frac{1 - \cos \alpha}{2}}$$

The script looks like this: $\mathcal{ABC}$.
From textcomp: $ € ⋆ ∞ † ...

```
\usepackage[boldsans]{ccfonts}
\usepackage[full]{textcomp}
\usepackage{ragged2e} %small measure

\section{Testing headings}
An example showing a trigonometric function:
\[ \sin \frac{\alpha}{2} =
      \pm \sqrt{\frac{1-\cos\alpha}{2}}  \]
The script looks like this: $\mathcal{ABC}$.\\
From textcomp: \textdollaroldstyle\ \texteuro\
\textborn\ \textmarried\ \textdied\ \ldots
```
7-7-3

Family	Series	Shape(s)	Example of the Typeface
CM Bright (OT1, T1, TS1)			
cmbr	m	n, sl	CM Bright medium
cmbr	sb	n, sl	*CM Bright semibold slanted*
cmbr	bx	n	**CM Bright bold extended**
CM Typewriter Light (OT1, T1, TS1)			
cmtl	m	n, sl	Typewriter Light normal
CM Bright Math (OML)			
cmbrm	m, b	it	*Bright Math.* α Ω
CM Bright Math (OMS)			
cmbrs	m	n	$\mathcal{B}\nabla\rangle\}\langle\sqcup\;\mathcal{M}\dashv\sqcup\langle\neg\;\oslash\;\otimes$

Table 7.12: Classification of the Computer Modern Bright font families

Because the Concrete fonts are of considerably heavier weight than, say, Computer Modern, it is advisable to use them with a larger leading than most document classes provide by default. For this reason the package automatically enlarges the leading to 10/13 and similar ratios for other document sizes. If this adjustment is undesirable for some reason, it can be canceled with the option standard-baselineskips.

The feature provided by the exscale package is available as the package option exscale; see Section 7.5.5 on page 368 for details. The exscale package itself cannot be used because it is set up to work with only Computer Modern math fonts.

If the amssymb or amsfonts package is loaded, the ccfonts package automatically arranges to use the Concrete variants of the AMS symbol fonts.

Finally, the package offers the option slantedGreek to make uppercase Greek letters slanted instead of being upright (default). The two extra commands \upDelta and \upOmega will always typeset an upright Δ and Ω, respectively.

7.7.3   cmbright—The Computer Modern Bright fonts

Another font family whose design is based on the METAFONT sources of the CM fonts are the Computer Modern Bright (CM Bright) fonts by Walter Schmidt, shown in Table 7.12. This family of sans serif fonts is designed to serve as a legible body font. It comes with matching typewriter and math fonts, including the AMS symbols.

Loading the cmbright package in the preamble ensures that these families are selected throughout the document. It is recommended that you combine this package with fontenc, as shown in the next example, to achieve proper hyphenation with languages other than English. All CM Bright fonts have fully implemented T1 and TS1 encoding support.

1   A CM Bright document

The CM Bright family contains typewriter fonts and matching fonts for math formulas, e.g.,

$$\sum_{0 \leq k < n} k = \frac{n(n-1)}{2}$$

```
\usepackage[T1]{fontenc}
\usepackage{cmbright}
\section{A CM Bright document}
The CM Bright family contains
\texttt{typewriter} fonts and matching fonts
for math formulas, e.g.,
\[ \sum_{0\leq k<n} k = \frac{n(n-1)}{2} \]
```

7-7-4

By default, the package selects a slightly larger leading than the default classes to account for the use of sans serif fonts; this can be canceled by specifying the package option standard-baselineskips. Also in other respects, this package works similarly to other works by Walter Schmidt: the option slantedGreek produces slanted uppercase Greek letters, with \upDelta and \upOmega typesetting an upright Δ and Ω, respectively. When the amssymb or amsfonts package is loaded, the cmbright package automatically arranges to use the CM Bright variants of the AMS symbol fonts.

The METAFONT implementation of the fonts is freely available from CTAN archives; Type 1 format versions are commercially sold by MicroPress. Recently, a freely available Type 1 (although without manual hinting) was made available by Harald Harders under the name hfbright. Moreover, as mentioned in Section 7.5.1, the freely available CM-Super Type 1 fonts also cover parts of the CM Bright fonts.

7.7.4   luximono—A general-purpose typewriter font

The choice of monospaced (typewriter) fonts for use in program listings and other applications is not very wide. Of course, with the Computer Modern fonts a suitable typewriter family (cmtt) is included, but if the main document fonts are being replaced, freely available choices for typewriter fonts are few. Adobe Courier runs very wide and for that reason alone it is often a poor choice. While staying with cmtt might be an option, the font may not blend well with the chosen document font.

Recently, with the release of version 4.2 of XFree86, the free implementation of the X Windows system, a new, freely distributable, monospaced font family, called LuxiMono, has become available. This Type 1 encoded Postscript font comes with bold, oblique, and bold oblique versions (see Table 7.13 on the facing page). In that respect, it differs from other monospaced fonts, which are often offered only in medium series and more rarely in italic or oblique shapes.

Family	Series	Shape(s)	PostScript Font Names and Examples
			LuxiMono (T1, TS1)
ul9	m	n, sl	LuxiMono, *LuxiMono-Oblique*
ul9	b	n, sl	**LuxiMono-Bold**, ***LuxiMono-BoldOblique***

Table 7.13: Classification of the LuxiMono font family

These fonts are original designs by Kris Holmes and Charles Bigelow (Bigelow and Holmes, Inc.), for which hinting and kerning tables have been added by URW++ Design and Development GmbH. The LaTeX integration is provided through the luximono package written by Walter Schmidt.

The following example compares LuxiMono (scaled down to 85% using the option scaled), Computer Modern Typewriter, and Adobe Courier. LuxiMono still has the largest x-height (\fontdimen5) and, at the same time, the smallest width. Courier, running very wide, occupies the other end of the spectrum, with CM Typewriter being comfortably in between the two extremes.

```
The dazed brown fox quickly gave
12345-67890 jumps!  x-height=4.50502pt
(LuxiMono)
The dazed brown fox quickly gave
12345-67890 jumps!  x-height=4.3045pt
(CM Typewriter)
The dazed brown fox quickly gave
12345-67890 jumps!
x-height=4.25989pt (Adobe Courier)
```

7-7-5

```
\usepackage[T1]{fontenc}
\usepackage[scaled=0.85]{luximono}
\newcommand\allletters{The dazed brown
  fox quickly gave 12345--67890 jumps!
  x-height=\the\fontdimen5\font\ }
\raggedright
\textttt{\allletters (LuxiMono)}
\par \renewcommand\ttdefault{cmtt}
\textttt{\allletters (CM Typewriter)}
\par \renewcommand\ttdefault{pcr}
\textttt{\allletters (Adobe Courier)}
```

If the option scaled is given without a value, the fonts are scaled down to 87%, which gives them a running length approximately equal to that of Computer Modern Typewriter. To get exactly the same running length, 0.87478 should used for 10pt fonts, while for an 11pt document 0.86124 would be the correct value. This is due to the fact that LuxiMono scales linearly, while Computer Modern fonts have different designs for different sizes. Without scaling LuxiMono has the same running length as Adobe Courier.

```
\usepackage[T1]{fontenc}\usepackage[scaled]{luximono}
\usepackage[euro]{textcomp}

\textttt{This font contains a \texteuro{} symbol.}
\par \renewcommand\ttdefault{cmtt}
\textttt{This font contains a \texteuro{} symbol.}
```

```
This font contains a € symbol.
This font contains a € symbol.
```

7-7-6

Encoding	Family	Series	Shape(s)	Example of the Typeface
TX Roman				
OT1, T1, TS1, LY1	txr	m	n, it, sl, sc	TX Roman normal
OT1, T1, TS1, LY1	txr	bx, (b)	n, it, sl, sc	*TX Roman bold italic*
TX Sans				
OT1, T1, TS1, LY1	txss	m	n, (it), sl, sc	TX Sans normal
OT1, T1, TS1, LY1	txss	bx, (b)	n, (it), sl, sc	*TX Sans bold slanted*
TX Typewriter				
OT1, T1, TS1, LY1	txtt	m	n, (it), sl, sc	TX Typewriter normal
OT1, T1, TS1, LY1	txtt	bx, (b)	n, (it), sl, sc	TX Typewriter bold small caps
TX Math				
OML	txmi	m, bx	it	*TX Math.* α Ω
OMS	txms	m,bx	n	
U	txsya, txsyb	m, bx	n	

Table 7.14: Classification of the TX font families

Note that the LuxiMono fonts are supported only in the T1 encoding (see the use of fontenc in the examples). The subset of the textcomp symbols typically found in PostScript fonts is available—namely, those declared when loading textcomp with the option safe. However, since the euro symbol is available, it is best to load that package with the option euro.[1]

7.7.5 txfonts—Alternative support for Times Roman

With the mathptmx package, the PSNFSS bundle supports Times Roman as a document font for both text and math, primarily using Times Italic and the Adobe Symbol font for math characters (see Section 7.6.2). In 2000, Young Ryu released his own set of virtual fonts together with accompanying Type 1 fonts to provide math support for documents using Times Roman as the document font.

The extra fonts cover glyphs typically missing in PostScript fonts—for example, a full set of textcomp symbols, the full range of math symbols as implemented by AMS fonts (see Chapter 8), and others. Thus, these fonts are far more complete than their counterparts in the standard LaTeX PSNFSS package.

---

[1] To see the euro symbol in the various TeX fonts, it is important to have the newest version of the file 8r.enc installed.

The fonts are accessed by loading the package txfonts in the preamble. When the package is loaded, it sets up Times Roman as the main document font and Adobe Helvetica (scaled down to 95%) as the sans serif font. For the typewriter font a monospaced font developed by the package author is used.

Compare the next example with Example 7-6-2 on page 376. The extra line at the end shows a few symbols from textcomp that are unavailable with mathptmx.

An example showing a trigonometric function:

$$\sin\frac{\alpha}{2} = \pm\sqrt{\frac{1-\cos\alpha}{2}}$$

The script looks like this: $\mathcal{ABC}$.

From textcomp: $ € ★ ∞ † …

```
\usepackage{txfonts}\usepackage[full]{textcomp}
An example showing a trigonometric function:
\[ \sin \frac{\alpha}{2} =
      \pm \sqrt{\frac{1-\cos\alpha}{2}}  \]
The script looks like this: $\mathcal{ABC}$.\\
From textcomp: \textdollaroldstyle\ \texteuro\
\textborn\ \textmarried\ \textdied\ \ldots
```

7-7-7

The TX fonts (see Table 7.14 on the facing page) have support for the text font encodings OT1, T1, TS1, and LY1. However, the OT1 encoding is not faithfully implemented: some of the deficiencies in this encoding are (incorrectly) circumvented (for example, the fact that only either $ or £ is available in "real" OT1 fonts). Fixing these deficiencies means that the new definitions will not work with any other OT1-encoded font. As OT1 is still the default encoding with LATEX this change can lead to serious problems.[1]

The following example illustrates the use of the problematic definitions. In OT1-encoded Computer Modern, all glyphs are wrong: the $ turns into a £ sign and all others are simply dropped. On the other hand, there is no problem with T1, so one should always combine txfonts with \usepackage[T1]{fontenc}.[2]

```
\usepackage{txfonts}
\fontencoding{OT1}\selectfont     % LaTeX default encoding!
\L.\l.\textdollar.\textsterling.\r{A}.\r{a}\hfill (txfont)

\fontfamily{cmtt}\itshape         % italic CM Typewriter
\L.\l.\textdollar.\textsterling.\r{A}.\r{a}\hfill
                                            (all errors)
```

Ł.ł.$.£.Å.å   (txfont)
..£...   (all errors)

7-7-8   Ł.ł.$.£.Å.å   (okay)

```
\fontencoding{T1}\selectfont      % ... in T1
\L.\l.\textdollar.\textsterling.\r{A}.\r{a}\hfill (okay)
```

In addition, a more serious problem with the current release of the fonts is that the glyph side-bearings in math are extremely tight, up to the point that

---

[1] Strictly speaking, the fonts implement a new encoding that is similar to OT1 but not identical—and incorrectly call it OT1.

[2] As discussed in Section 7.3.5, T1 is the preferred encoding in any case.

characters actually touch if used in subscripts or superscripts.

A problematic example:

$$t[u_1, \ldots, u_n] = \sum_{k=1}^{n} \binom{n-1}{k-1}(1-t)^{n-k}t^{k-1}u_k$$

```
\usepackage{amsmath,txfonts}
A problematic example:
\[ t[u_1, \dots, u_n] = \sum_{k=1}^n
    \binom{n-1}{k-1} (1-t)^{n-k}t^{k-1}u_k \]
```
7-7-9

It is possible that these problems will be fixed in a future release of the fonts. For comparison, we show the previous example using mathptmx:

A problematic example:

$$t[u_1, \ldots, u_n] = \sum_{k=1}^{n} \binom{n-1}{k-1}(1-t)^{n-k}t^{k-1}u_k$$

```
\usepackage{amsmath,mathptmx}
A problematic example:
\[ t[u_1, \dots, u_n] = \sum_{k=1}^n
    \binom{n-1}{k-1} (1-t)^{n-k}t^{k-1}u_k \]
```
7-7-10

To summarize, the TX font families currently show some deficiencies in math typesetting, but offer a large range of symbols for math and text, including all symbols from the AMS math fonts and a full implementation of the textcomp symbols. If the focus is on having many symbols available in Type 1 fonts, such as when producing PDF documents, the fonts provide an interesting alternative.

7.7.6   pxfonts—**Alternative support for Palatino**

Young Ryu also developed a set of virtual fonts together with accompanying Type 1 fonts to provide math support for documents using Adobe Palatino as the main document font. The PX fonts (see Table 7.15 on the next page) are set up by loading the pxfonts package. For sans serif and typewriter fonts the package uses fonts from the txfonts set-up (scaled-down Helvetica and TX typewriter), so both font sets need to be installed.

The next example uses the same text as Example 7-7-7 on the preceding page but this time loads the pxfonts package.

An example showing a trigonometric function:

$$\sin \frac{\alpha}{2} = \pm \sqrt{\frac{1 - \cos \alpha}{2}}$$

The script looks like this: $\mathcal{ABC}$.
From textcomp: \$ € ★ ∞ † …

```
\usepackage{pxfonts}\usepackage[full]{textcomp}
An example showing a trigonometric function:
\[ \sin \frac{\alpha}{2} =
    \pm \sqrt{\frac{1-\cos\alpha}{2}}  \]
The script looks like this: $\mathcal{ABC}$.\\
From textcomp: \textdollaroldstyle\ \texteuro\
\textborn\ \textmarried\ \textdied\ \ldots
```
7-7-11

Since the PX fonts have the same font layout as the TX fonts, the OT1 problems shown in Example 7-7-8 on the previous page also arise with this family.

Encoding	Family	Series	Shape(s)	Example of the Typeface
PX Roman				
OT1, T1, TS1, LY1	pxr	m	n, it, sl, sc	PX Roman normal
OT1, T1, TS1, LY1	pxr	bx, (b)	n, it, sl, sc	*PX Roman bold italic*
PX Math				
OML	pxmi	m, bx	it	*PX Math.* α Ω
OMS	pxms	m,bx	n	$\mathcal{PX}$ ⌊⌈⌉ ⌉§⊔⌉\⌈⌉⌈ $\mathcal{M}$⊣⊔⟨¬ ⊘ ⊗
U	pxsya, pxsyb	m, bx	n	⋕√ △¬⋔⋏⋋⩵ ⇆ ⇌

Table 7.15: Classification of the PX font families

The typesetting in math is still very tight but not always so noticeable as in the TX fonts. Below, the Example 7-7-9 on the facing page is repeated for comparison.

A problematic example:

$$t[u_1, \dots, u_n] = \sum_{k=1}^{n} \binom{n-1}{k-1}(1-t)^{n-k}t^{k-1}u_k$$

7-7-12

```
\usepackage{amsmath,pxfonts}

A problematic example:
\[ t[u_1, \dots, u_n] = \sum_{k=1}^n
     \binom{n-1}{k-1} (1-t)^{n-k}t^{k-1}u_k \]
```

7.7.7   The Fourier-GUTenberg fonts

Adobe donated four fonts from the Utopia family (Utopia Regular, Utopia Italic, Utopia Bold, and Utopia BoldItalic) to the X-Consortium. Though not free software, these typefaces are available free of charge and basic support for them is available through the PSNFSS bundle (see Section 7.6).

The Fourier-GUTenberg bundle developed by Michel Bovani is a typesetting environment based on the Utopia typeface but complemented with the characters missing to provide a full T1 encoding (OT1 is *not* supported), a suitable set of math symbols, Greek sloped and upright letters, and a matching calligraphic and blackboard bold alphabet so that whole documents can be prepared without using any other typefaces. The font encoding is shown in Table 7.16 on the next page; a complete example page is given in Figure 8.4 on page 515.

An example showing a trigonometric function:

$$\sin \frac{\alpha}{2} = \pm\sqrt{\frac{1-\cos\alpha}{2}}$$

7-7-13   The alphabets are $\mathcal{ABC}$ and $\mathbb{ABC}$.

```
\usepackage{fourier}

An example showing a trigonometric function:
\[ \sin \frac{\alpha}{2} =
     \pm \sqrt{\frac{1-\cos\alpha}{2}}   \]
The alphabets are $\mathcal{ABC}$ and
$\mathbb{ABC}$.
```

Family	Series	Shape(s)	Examples
Utopia (T1, TS1)			
futs	m, b	(bx) n, sl, it, (sc)	Utopia-Regular **_Utopia-BoldItalic_**
Fourier math letters (FML)			
futm, futmi	m	it	$\Delta\Theta\Lambda$ $\alpha\beta\gamma$ $abcdef$ $\Delta\Theta\Lambda$ $\alpha\beta\gamma$
Fourier math symbols (FMS)			
futm	m	n	$\dashv\nleq\complement\|$ $\mathscr{ABCDEFGHIJKLM}$

Table 7.16: Classification of the Fourier-GUTenberg font families

The fourier package supports typesetting mathematics "à la French", with Greek letters and Roman uppercase letters in upright style, by specifying the option upright. Compare the next example to the output in Example 8-4-1 on page 490.

$$0 \xleftarrow{\zeta} F \times \Delta(n-1) \xrightarrow{\partial_0\alpha(b)} E^{\partial_0 b}$$

```
\usepackage{amsmath}\usepackage[upright]{fourier}
\[ 0 \xleftarrow [\zeta]{}  F \times \Delta (n - 1)
   \xrightarrow {\partial_0 \alpha(b)} E^{\partial_0 b} \]
```

7-7-14

If you require extended math support from the amsmath package as in the previous example, load this package first, so that certain aspects of the math formatting tuned for typesetting in Utopia will not be overwritten. For the same reason, you should load amssymb first, though you will find that fourier already contains several symbols normally available only with amssymb. In fact, the fourier package offers a small set of mathematical symbols not found elsewhere (e.g., certain integral signs, some delimiters, and other symbols). Some are shown in the next example.

$$\left[\!\left\|\times \# \times\right\|\!\right] \oiint \oiiint \slashint \widetilde{xxxxxx}$$

```
\usepackage{fourier}
\setlength\delimitershortfall{-2pt} % make delimiters grow
\[ \left\llbracket \left\VERT
    \xswordsup \nparallelslant \xswordsdown
 \right\VERT  \right\rrbracket
 \oiint \oiiint \slashint \widetilde{xxxxxx}   \]
```

7-7-15

Upright and slanted variants of the Greek letters can be used together in a single document by prefixing the command names with other. For example:

$$\Omega_\beta \neq \Omega_\beta$$

```
\usepackage[upright]{fourier}
\[ \Omega_\beta  \neq \otherOmega_\otherbeta \]
```

7-7-16

Without the upright option (or with the default option sloped), the letters are sloped according conventional typesetting of mathematics—that is, upright

Family	Series	Shape(s)	PostScript Font Names and Examples
URW Antiqua Condensed (OT1, T1, TS1)			
uaq	(m), mc	n, sl, (it),sc	URWAntiquaT-RegularCondensed
URW Grotesk Bold (OT1, T1, TS1)			
ugq	b, (bx), (m)	n, sl, (it), sc	**URWGroteskT-Bold**

Table 7.17: Classification of the URW Antiqua and Grotesk fonts

uppercase Greek and everything else slanted. The meaning of the \other... commands is swapped, accordingly.

7-7-17

$$\Omega_\beta \neq \Omega_\beta$$

```
\usepackage[sloped]{fourier}
\[ \Omega_\beta   \neq \otherOmega_\otherbeta \]
```

In the current implementation fourier does not support \boldmath. Consequently, using the bm package will most often lead to "poor man's bold"; see Section 8.8.2.

To complement the freely available fonts Adobe offers a commercial expert set containing old-style digits, real small capitals, a semibold series, and an extra *Support for the* bold series. To support these typefaces, the fourier package offers additional op- *commercial expert* tions: expert provides \textsb and \textblack to select the extra font series *fonts* and arranges to use real small capitals with \textsc. The oldstyle option provides the same support but additionally uses old-style numerals in text (\lining allows you to refer to lining numerals in that case). Finally, the fulloldstyle works like oldstyle but additionally arranges for old-style numerals to be used in formulas.

7.7.8   The URW Antiqua and Grotesk fonts

The German company URW made two PostScript fonts, URW Antiqua Condensed *URW's Antiqua* and URW Grotesk Bold, freely available. LaTeX support in the form of virtual *Condensed* fonts and .fd files is available. They are accessed using the classification given *10pt/12pt (uaq)* in Table 7.17. The sample below was typeset by specifying \fontfamily{uaq} \selectfont.

For the price of £45, almost anything can be found floating in fields. ¡THE DAZED BROWN FOX QUICKLY GAVE 12345-67890 JUMPS! — ¿But aren't Kafka's Schloß and Æsop's Œuvres often naïve vis-à-vis the dæmonic phœnix's official rôle in fluffy soufflés?

As its name indicates, the URW Grotesk Bold font is available only in a bold se- *URW's Grotesk Bold* ries (although within LaTeX selecting a medium series is supported for convenience *10pt/12pt (ugq)* but refers to the same bold font). As such, it is not suitable for general running text. Potential applications include headings and other display material.

For the price of £45, almost anything can be found floating in fields. ¡THE DAZED BROWN FOX QUICKLY GAVE 12345–67890 JUMPS! — ¿But aren't Kafka's Schloß and Æsop's Œuvres often naïve vis-à-vis the dæmonic phœnix's official rôle in fluffy souf- flés?

7.7.9 yfonts—Typesetting with Old German fonts

There exists a set of beautiful fonts for typesetting in Gothic, Schwabacher, and Fraktur designed in METAFONT[1] after traditional typefaces by Yannis Haralam- bous [62]. These days Type 1 versions of the fonts are available as well. To use the fonts, load the yfonts package written by Walter Schmidt. This package internally defines some local encodings that reflect the special features found in the fonts and integrates them fully with LaTeX's font management.

The commands `\gothfamily`, `\swabfamily`, and `\frakfamily` switch to Gothic, Schwabacher, and Fraktur, respectively. If one wants to typeset a whole document in such a typeface, the corresponding command should be used di- rectly *after* `\begin{document}`. Because of the nonstandard encodings of the fonts, redefining the document defaults (e.g., `\familydefault`) is not possible. In addition to the font switches, the usual `\text..` commands for typesetting short fragments are provided.

The package provides 𝔊otisch, also called Textur, Schwabacher, and Fraktur type- faces, also generally known as „gebroche- ne Schriften".

```
\usepackage{yfonts}\usepackage[document]{ragged2e}
The package provides \textgoth{Gotisch, also
called Textur}, \textswab{Schwabacher}, and
\textfrak{Fraktur} typefaces, also  generally
known as \textfrak{``ge\-bro\-che\-ne Schriften''}.
```

7-7-18

The fonts are available in the usual LaTeX sizes starting from 10pt, so that size- changing commands (e.g., `\normalsize` and larger) will work. There are, however, no further font series or shapes, so commands like `\emph`, `\textit`, and `\textbf` have no effect other than producing a warning. Following historical practice you can use Schwabacher to emphasize something inside text typeset in Fraktur.

For accents one can use the standard LaTeX representations (e.g., `\"a` for ä). To facilitate input, the fonts also contain ligatures that represent umlauts (e.g., `"a`). In Fraktur and Schwabacher there also exist alternate umlauts, which can be accessed with `*a` and similar ligatures. If the yfonts package is loaded with the option `varumlaut`, then `\"` produces the variant glyphs automatically.

---

[1]Compiling the fonts from the METAFONT sources sometimes produces error messages, but generally produces usable fonts when METAFONT is directed to ignore them. The collection also contains a font with baroque initials.

All three fonts contain a glyph for the "short s", accessed through the ligature
s:, and "sharp s", accessed by \ss, or through the ligature sz or "s.

Fraktur: ä ë ü ö ä ë ü ö ß ſ viz. s

Swab: ä ë ü ö ä ë ü ö ß ſ viz. s

Gothic: ä ë ü ö (unavail) ß ſ viz. s

```
\usepackage{yfonts}
\Large \frakfamily Fraktur: "a "e "u "o
\hfil *a *e *u *o \hfil sz \hfil s viz.\ s:
\par\swabfamily     Swab:    "a "e "u "o
\hfil *a *e *u *o \hfil sz \hfil s viz.\ s:
\par\gothfamily     Gothic:  "a "e "u "o
\hfil (unavail)    \hfil sz \hfil s viz.\ s:
```

7-7-19

The font selected with \gothfamily is not a copy of Gutenberg's font used for
his Bible (which had 288 glyphs altogether), but it follows Gutenberg's guidelines
on lowercase characters and implements as many ligatures as can be fit into a
7-bit font. For this reason many standard ASCII symbols are unavailable in this
font.

The two other fonts also implement only a subset of visible ASCII. Problematic
are the semicolon (which is missing in Schwabacher) and the characters +, =, ', [,
], /, *, @, &, and % (which are either missing or produce wrong or nonmatching
shapes). Their omission is seldom a problem since typically they are not needed
in documents using such fonts, but one needs to be aware that no warning or
error message is issued if they are used—the only indication is missing or wrong
glyphs in the printed output!

Symbols: + = ' [ ] / * $ % & ; @

Fraktur problems: + = ' [ ] / * $ % & ;

Swab problems: ſi ſt s ä ö ſli ſt $ ſſ ;

Gothic problems: + = ' [ ] / * $ %

```
\usepackage{yfonts}
\newcommand\test{+  =  ' [ ]  / * \$ \% \& ; @}
Symbols: \ttfamily                       \test
\par\frakfamily Fraktur problems:: \test
\par\gothfamily Swab    problems:: \test
\par\swabfamily Gothic  problems:: \test
```

7-7-20

The default line spacing of the standard classes is too large for the Old German fonts. For this reason the package implements the \fraklines command,
which selects a suitable \baselineskip for Fraktur or Schwabacher. It must be
repeated after every size-changing command.

The font collection also contains a font with decorative initials, as shown in
the next example.

ief ist ein Blindtext an dem sich ver-
schiedene Dinge ablesen lassen. Der
Grauwert der Schriftfläche wird sicht-
bar und man kann an ihm prüfen,
wie gut die Schrift zu lesen ist und wie sie auf
den Leser wirkt. Bei genauerem Hinsehen werden
die einzelnen Buchstaben und ihre Besonderheiten
erfennbar, ɛc

```
\usepackage[german]{babel}   \usepackage{color}
\usepackage[varumlaut]{yfonts}
\frakfamily\fraklines
\yinipar{\color{blue}D}ies ist ein Blindtext an dem
sich verschiedene Dinge ablesen lassen. Der Grauwert
der Schriftfl\"ache wird sichtbar und man kann an
ihm pr\"ufen, wie gut die Schrift zu lesen ist und
wie sie auf den Leser wirkt. Bei genauerem
Hinsehen werden die einzelnen Buchstaben und ihre
Besonderheiten erkennbar, \etc
```

7-7-21

The command `\yinipar` used above starts a new paragraph without indentation, producing a baroque dropped initial. For this command to work, a full paragraph (up to and including the next blank line or `\par`) must be typeset using `\fraklines`. Otherwise, the space left for the initial will be either too large or too small.

As an alternative, you can access these initials with the `\textinit` command or the font switch `\initfamily`, in which case initials aligned at the baseline are produced. The example also used the command `\etc`, which produces a once-popular symbol for "etc."; it is available in Fraktur only.

The font collection contains a second Fraktur font that has slightly wider glyphs with at the same time slightly thinner stems. It can be selected by redefining `\frakdefault` as shown in the next example. When compared to Example 7-7-21, the difference in running length can be clearly observed, resulting in an overfull box on the second line.

```
\usepackage[german]{babel}    \usepackage{color}
\usepackage[varumlaut]{yfonts}
\renewcommand\frakdefault{ysmfrak}

\frakfamily\fraklines
\yinipar{\color{blue}D}ies ist ein Blindtext an dem
sich verschiedene Dinge ablesen lassen. Der Grauwert
der Schriftfl\"ache wird sichtbar und man kann an ihm
pr\"ufen, wie gut die Schrift zu lesen ist und wie
sie auf den Leser wirkt. Bei genauerem Hinsehen
```

7-7-22

7.7.10 euler, eulervm—Accessing the Euler fonts

As mentioned earlier, Hermann Zapf designed a beautiful set of fonts for typesetting mathematics—upright characters with a handwritten flavor—named after the famous mathematician Leonhard Euler [99]. These fonts can be accessed as (math) alphabets of their own, or you can generally modify the math font set-up, thus making LaTeX use Euler math fonts (rather than Computer Modern) by default.

The Euler fonts contain three math alphabets: $\mathscr{SCRIPT}$, $\mathfrak{Euler\ Fraktur}$, and Euler Roman.[1] The script alphabet can be used via the eucal package, which makes this math alphabet available under the name `\mathcal` (obsolete alternate name `\EuScript`). If the package is loaded with the `mathscr` option, the math alphabet becomes available through the command `\mathscr`, with `\mathcal` retaining its original definition.

To access Euler Fraktur in formulas, you use the package eufrak, which defines the math alphabet `\mathfrak` (obsolete alternate name `\EuFrak`). There is no particular package to access the Euler Roman alphabet separately. The next ex-

---

[1]None of these alphabets is suitable for typesetting text as the individual glyphs have sidebearings specially tailored for use in math formulas.

Family	Series	Shape(s)	Example of the Typeface
Euler Roman (U)			
eur	m	n	Euler Roman medium
eur	b	n	**Euler Roman bold**
Euler Script (U)			
eus	m	n	$\mathscr{EULER\ SCRIPT}$
Euler Fraktur (U)			
euf	m	n	Euler Fraktur
Euler Extension (U)			
euex	m	n	$\sum\prod\int^{\infty}\{\}$

Table 7.18: Classification of the Euler math font families

ample shows Computer Modern Calligraphic, Euler Script, and Euler Fraktur side by side.

7-7-23

$$\mathcal{A} \neq \sum_{k<n} \mathscr{A}_k \neq \mathfrak{A}$$

```
\usepackage[mathscr]{eucal} \usepackage{eufrak}
\[ \mathcal{A} \neq \sum_{k<n} \mathscr{A}_k \neq \mathfrak{A} \]
```

The NFSS classification for the fonts in these families is shown in Table 7.18. The fonts in the current distribution of the Euler math families are available only in encoding schemes that differ from all other encoding schemes for mathematics. For this reason, the fonts are all assigned the encoding U (unknown).

The uncommon encoding makes it difficult to simply substitute the Euler math alphabets for the default CM math fonts. Yet the euler package, written by Frank Jensen, went exactly this way, redeclaring most of LaTeX's math font setup. In conjunction with the package beton, which sets up Concrete as the default text font family, it simulates the typography of Knuth's book *Concrete Mathematics* [59], as shown in Example 7-7-2.

One of the problems with extensive reencoding in macro packages, as done by the euler package, is that it is likely to break other packages that assume certain *Virtual Euler fonts* symbols in slot positions, as defined by more established font encodings. The eulervm package developed by Walter Schmidt attempts to avoid this problem by providing reencoded virtual fonts that follow as much as possible the standard math encodings OML, OMS, and OMX.

The eulervm package sets up a \mathnormal alphabet, which is based mainly on Euler Roman, and a \mathcal alphabet, which is based on Euler Script. It does not provide immediate support for the Euler Fraktur alphabet—to access this math alphabet one needs to additionally load the eufrak package. Also, the math symbols are taken from the Euler fonts, with a few exceptions coming from the Computer Modern math fonts. Compare the next example to Example 7-7-23 on the previous page and you will see that \mathcal has changed and that \sum and the indices are different, as they are now taken from the Euler fonts.

$$\mathcal{A} \neq \sum_{k<n} A_k \neq \mathfrak{A}$$

```
\usepackage{eulervm,eufrak}
\[ \mathcal{A} \neq \sum_{k<n} A_k \neq \mathfrak{A} \]
```
7-7-24

The option small causes eulervm to load all Euler fonts at 95% of their normal size, thereby enabling them to blend better with some document fonts (e.g., Adobe Minion). This option also affects the Euler Fraktur fonts if they are loaded with eufrak and the AMS symbol fonts.

Neither the standard \hbar command nor \hslash (from the amssymb package) is really usable with the Euler fonts if it is used without modification (i.e., with euler), because \hslash uses a Computer Modern style "h" and \hbar gets the slash in a strange position.

$$\hslash \neq \hbar$$

```
\usepackage{amssymb,euler}
\[ \hslash \neq \hbar \]
```
7-7-25

This issue restricts the usage of the euler package somewhat for physics and related fields. The eulervm package resolves this problem (partially) by providing a properly slashed "h" glyph built using the possibilities offered by the virtual font mechanism ([91] explains the concepts). It does, however, provide only a slashed version (\hslash); if \hbar is used, a warning is issued and the slashed glyph is used nevertheless.

$$\hslash \equiv \hbar$$

```
\usepackage{eulervm}
\[ \hslash \equiv \hbar \]
```
7-7-26

The functionality provided by the exscale package is automatically available. See Section 7.5.5 on page 368 for details.

In typical font set-ups the same digits are used in text and math formulas. The Euler fonts contain a set of digits that have a distinctive look and thus make digits in text and math look noticeably different.

By default, the digits of the main document font are used in formulas as well. To switch to the digits from Euler Roman, one has to explicitly request them by specifying the option euler-digits. It then becomes very important to distinguish between a number in a mathematical or a textual context. For example, one must watch out for omitted $ signs, as in the first line of the next example.

The value can be 1, 2, or −1 (wrong!)
The value can be 1, 2, or −1 (right!)

```
\usepackage{ccfonts}
\usepackage[euler-digits]{eulervm}
The value can be 1, 2, or $-1$      (wrong!)\par
The value can be $1$, $2$, or $-1$ (right!)
```
7-7-27

Normally, the math accent \hat is taken from the main document font, which might not be a good choice when text and math fonts are noticeably different. With the option euler-hat-accent, an alternative version from the Euler fonts is used instead. In the example we mimic that option and define the alternate accent under the name \varhat manually to enable comparison of the two (neither looks really perfect).

$\hat{x} \neq \hat{x}$ and $\hat{\mathfrak{K}} \neq \hat{\mathfrak{K}}$

7-7-28

```
\usepackage{palatino,eulervm,eufrak}
\DeclareMathAccent\varhat{\mathalpha}{symbols}{222}
\Large $ \hat x \neq \varhat x $ and
$ \hat \mathfrak{K} \neq \varhat \mathfrak{K} $
```

It is usually best to load the eulervm package after all the document fonts have been defined, because eulervm defines the math alphabets (e.g., \mathsf) by evaluating the document's default information that is current when the package is loaded. In the example below, the loading order is absolutely essential because the ccfonts package also tries to set up the math fonts and thus the one that comes last wins.

In the book *Concrete Mathematics* [59], where Euler and Concrete fonts were first used together, one can see that slanted $\leqslant$ and $\geqslant$ signs were once part of the Euler Math fonts. Somewhere along the way these two symbols got lost, though traces of their existence can be found in [92] and in macros that Donald Knuth developed for producing the book. With the help of the virtual font mechanism, Walter Schmidt brought them back in the eulervm package; compare the next example to Example 7-7-2 on page 384, which shows the straight $\leq$ sign.

Concrete Roman blends well with Euler Math, as can be seen with

$$\sum_{0 \leqslant k < n} k = \frac{n(n-1)}{2}$$

7-7-29

```
\usepackage{ccfonts,amssymb}
\usepackage[euler-digits]{eulervm}
Concrete Roman blends well with Euler Math,
as can be seen with
\[ \sum_{0\leq k<n} k = \frac{n(n-1)}{2} \]
```

7.8   The LaTeX world of symbols

Shortly after TeX and METAFONT came into existence, people started to develop new symbol fonts for use with the system. Over time the set of available symbols grew to a considerable number. The *Comprehensive LaTeX Symbol List* by Scott Pakin [134] lists 2590 symbols[1] and the corresponding LaTeX commands that produce them. For some symbols the necessary fonts and support packages may have to be obtained (e.g., from a CTAN host; see Appendix C) and installed by the user. They are usually accompanied by installation instructions and general documentation.

---

[1] Counted spring 2003.

	´0	´1	´2	´3	´4	´5	´6	´7	
´00x	△	◁	◁	▷	▷	∴	℘	☎	″0x
´01x	✓	⇨	♠	♪	♩	♩	∘	♫	
´02x	◄	►	⚡	♌	♋	⚲	⊛	♈	″1x
´03x	⌐	♀	♂	⚴	⊕	∝	⊰	∅	
´04x	●	↻	↺	○	☾	☽	♁	☿	″2x
´05x	‹	›	˰	ˬ	☺	☻	☼	☺	
´06x	♉	⋈	□	◇	⊠	⚷	✚	○	″3x
´07x	◯	○	∼	↝	⊏	⊐	≤	≥	
´10x	≈	✳	∗	✡	⬠	⋆	▽	◖	″4x
´11x	◗	◖	◗	▲	▼				
´12x	ɣ	ˊ	ˋ			ə	♂	♂	″5x
´13x	♃	♄	♅	♆	♇	♉	♊	♋	
´14x	♍	♎	♏	♐	♑	♒	♓	¢	″6x
´15x	‰	þ	Þ	ð	ɔ	◕	⊓	⊔	
´16x	⊟	⊟	∫	∬	∭	∮	∯	∫	″7x
´17x	∬	∭	∮	∯	¦	⌐	□	Ɐ	
	″8	″9	″A	″B	″C	″D	″E	″F	

Table 7.19: Glyphs in the wasy fonts

The fonts and packages described in this section form only a subset of what is available. If you cannot find a symbol here, the 70 pages of [134] are a valuable resource for locating what you need. We start by looking at a number of dingbat fonts, some of which contain quite unusual symbols. This examination is followed by an introduction to the TIPA system, which provides support for phonetic symbols. The section finishes with a discussion of ways to obtain a single (though in Europe not unimportant) symbol: the euro. Being a relatively new addition to the symbol world, it is missing in many fonts and thus needs alternative ways to produce it. All packages and fonts listed in this section and in [134] are freely available.

7.8.1 dingbat—A selection of hands

The dingbat package written by Scott Pakin provides access to two symbol fonts developed by Arthur Keller (ark10.mf) and Doug Henderson (dingbat.mf). The package makes a set of hands and a few other symbols available; the example shows most of them. Note that the \largepencil glyph is bigger than the space it officially occupies (shown by the \frame drawn around it).

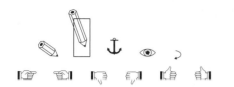

```
\usepackage{dingbat}

\smallpencil \quad \frame{\largepencil} \quad
\anchor \quad \eye  \quad \carriagereturn \\[5pt]
\leftpointright \quad \rightpointleft  \quad
\leftthumbsdown \quad \rightthumbsdown \quad
\leftthumbsup   \quad \rightthumbsup
```

7-8-1

These fonts exist only as a METAFONT implementation, so they are not really suitable when intending to produce PDF (e.g., with pdfTeX).

7.8.2   wasysym—Waldi's symbol font

The wasysym package developed by Axel Kielhorn provides access to the wasy fonts designed by Roland Waldi. These fonts first appeared in 1989 and are nowadays available both in METAFONT source and Type 1 outlines. They cover a wide range of symbols from different areas, including astronomical and astrological symbols, APL, musical notes, circles, and polygons and stars (see Table 7.19 on the facing page). The wasysym package defines command names like \phone to access each glyph. Alternatively, if you want only a few glyphs from the font, you can use the pifont interface and access the symbols directly under the name wasy.

7-8-2

☎ using wasysym
☎ using pifont

```
\usepackage{wasysym,pifont}
\phone\             using \textttt{wasysym} \par
\Pisymbol{wasy}{7} using \textttt{pifont}
```

7.8.3   marvosym—Interface to the MarVoSym font

The MarVoSym font designed by Martin Vogel is another Pi font containing symbols from various areas including quite uncommon ones, such as laundry signs (in case you are doing your own laundry lists ☺), astronomy and astrology symbols, and many others.

The LaTeX support package marvosym was written by Thomas Henlich, who also converted the font from TrueType format to PostScript Type 1. This package defines command names for all symbols, some of which are listed in the next example; the full set is given in marvodoc.pdf accompanying the distribution.

```
\usepackage{marvosym}

\Large   \Mobilefone\ \Faxmachine\ \Fixedbearing\ \Lineload\
\Coffeecup\ \Football\ \AtForty\ \IroningII\ \Cancer\ \Virgo\
\RewindToStart\ \ForwardToIndex\ \ComputerMouse\ \Keyboard\
\Female\ \FEMALE\ \Smiley\ \Frowny\ \Yingyang\ \Bicycle
```

7-8-3

	´0	´1	´2	´3	´4	´5	´6	´7	
´04x		🛑	⚌	△	⚠	🔺	ς	ϡ	"2x
´05x	(	)	×	+	,	-	.	/	
´06x	0	1	2	3	4	5	6	7	"3x
´07x	8	9	→	⇒	≤	≅	≥	⇔	
´10x	@	℧	⊠	C€	€	⚡	℔	⎯	"4x
´11x	📱	〽	⚠	☕	⥽		□	▫	
´12x	→	✂	---	✂	☎	⊘	☑	∢	"5x
´13x	🗵	☯	☞	∕	✗	≡	≢	∕	
´14x	ⓔ	☀	⚒	€	€	€	▥	⎯	"6x
´15x	☣	ⓘ	☢	⊠	↓	🌍	Ⓧ	⚽	
´16x	→	✂	---	✂	FAX	⎅FAX⎆	🖶	👨‍🦽	"7x
´17x	♟	⚲	⚡	○	♂	⚥	♀	⚤	
´20x	⚢	♀	⚥	⚣	⚨	⚩	†	☿	"8x
´21x	†	⊔	⊔	⊔	♡	@	℔	◻	
´22x	⊠	●	⬣	■	▮	●	━	□	"9x
´23x	⬚	L	I	O	T	L	I	T	
´24x	∅	β	♌	℔	€	✺	$	☹	"Ax
´25x	⊗	☺	Ⓐ	Ⓐ	Ⓟ	Ⓟ	🚲	🚞	
´26x	🚞	🚞	🖳	□	⏮	⏴	◀	▶	"Bx
´27x	⏭	⏩	▲	▼	⊼	⊻	Ⓕ	Ⓕ	
´30x	☉	☽	☿	♀	♂	♃	♄	♅	"Cx
´31x	♆	♀	♂	△	⟁	🖱	▦	⌨	
´32x	▭	▥	🖨	⊔95	⊔95	⊔60	⊔60	⊔50	"Dx
´33x	⊔40	⊔40	⊔40	⊔30	⊎	⊠	□	□	
´34x	♈	♉	♊	♋	♌	♍	♎	♏	"Ex
´35x	♐	♑	♒	♓	□	□	□	□	
´36x	A	p	□	□	□	□	□	·	"Fx
´37x	□	□	□	□	□	✈	👩	👨	
	"8	"9	"A	"B	"C	"D	"E	"F	

Table 7.20: Glyphs in the MarVoSym font

Assuming a recent distribution, one can also access the symbols directly by using Glyph Chart in Table 7.20 on the preceding page and the pifont interface with the Pi font name being mvs. In older distributions the file umvs.fd that makes this method work might be missing, but it can be easily added as shown below.

```
\begin{filecontents}{umvs.fd}
  \DeclareFontFamily{U}{mvs}{}
  \DeclareFontShape{U}{mvs}{m}{n}{<-> fmvr8x}{}
\end{filecontents}
\usepackage{pifont}

\Huge \Pisymbol{mvs}{73} \Pisymbol{mvs}{74} \Pisymbol{mvs}{98}
\Pisymbol{mvs}{120} \Pisymbol{mvs}{121} \Pisymbol{mvs}{234}
```

7-8-4

7.8.4 bbding—A METAFONT alternative to Zapf Dingbats

For those who cannot use PostScript Type 1 fonts, Karel Horak designed a font with METAFONT containing most of the symbols from Hermann Zapf's dingbat font. The package bbding by Peter Møller Neergaard provides an interface that defines command names for each symbol (using a naming convention modeled after WordPerfect's names for accessing the Zapf Dingbats font). The complete list can be found in the package documentation, a few examples are given below.

```
\usepackage{bbding}

\XSolid\ \XSolidBold\ \XSolidBrush\ \Plus\ \PlusOutline\ \DavidStar\
\DavidStarSolid\ \JackStar\ \JackStarBold\ \FourStar\ \FiveFlowerPetal\
\SixFlowerOpenCenter\ \PhoneHandset\ \Peace\ \OrnamentDiamondSolid
```

7-8-5

Alternatively, referring to the glyph chart in Table 7.21 on the following page, you can address individual symbols via the pifont interface, by accessing the font under the name ding (compare this to Table 7.9 on page 379 showing the original Zapf designs).

```
\usepackage{pifont}

\Pisymbol{ding}{13} \Pisymbol{ding}{15} \Pisymbol{ding}{8}
\Pisymbol{ding}{17} \Pisymbol{ding}{19} \Pisymbol{ding}{9}
```

7-8-6

7.8.5 ifsym—Clocks, clouds, mountains, and other symbols

The ifsym package written by Ingo Klöckl provides access to a set of symbol fonts designed in METAFONT. At present they are not available in Type 1 format. Depending on the chosen package option(s), different symbol sets are made available. We show only a small selection here. The full documentation (German only) is provided in the PostScript file ifsym.ps, which is part of the distribution. All available symbols are also listed in [134].

	´0	´1	´2	´3	´4	´5	´6	´7	
´00x									˝0x
´01x									
´02x									˝1x
´03x									
´04x									˝2x
´05x									
´06x									˝3x
´07x									
´10x									˝4x
´11x									
´12x									˝5x
´13x									
´14x									˝6x
´15x									
´16x									˝7x
´17x									
	˝8	˝9	˝A	˝B	˝C	˝D	˝E	˝F	

Table 7.21: Glyphs in the METAFONT font bbding

The option `clock` makes seven clock-related symbols available. It also provides the command `\showclock` to display an analog watch, with the hands showing the correct time. Its two arguments denote the hour (0–11) and minutes (0–59). The minutes displayed are rounded to the nearest 5-minute interval; using a value greater than 11 for the hour makes the symbol disappear without warning. All symbols are available in normal and bold extended series.

Normal: ⊘ rounded: ⊛
Problem:
Fixed symbols: ⊘ ⊛ ⊘ ◖

```
\usepackage[clock]{ifsym}
Normal: \showclock{3}{20} rounded: \textbf{\showclock{6}{17}}
\\ Problem: \showclock{16}{35}\\ Fixed symbols: \Taschenuhr{}
\StopWatchStart{} \StopWatchEnd{} \Interval{}
```

7-8-7

The option `weather` defines 22 weather symbols, a few of which are shown on the first line of the next example. The `\Thermo` command displays a different thermometer symbol depending on the number in its argument (0–6).

For alpinists and travelers the option `alpine` provides 17 symbols for use in route descriptions or maps. The option `misc` offers a set of unrelated symbols, some of which are also found in other fonts, and the option `geometry` provides commands for 30 geometric shapes, some of which are shown on the fourth line of the example.

```
\usepackage[weather,alpine,misc,geometry]{ifsym}
\Sun\ \Rain\ \Snow\ \Lightning\ \SunCloud\ \Thermo{1} \Thermo{4}\par
\Summit\ \Mountain\ \Joch\ \Hut\ \Flag\ \Tent\ \Village         \par
\Cube{5} \StrokeFive\ \Radiation\ \Fire\ \Telephone\ \Letter    \par
\TriangleUp\ \RightDiamond\ \SquareShadowC\ \SpinUp\ \SpinDown
```

7-8-8

The command `\textifsymbol` allows you to access symbols by their slot positions. Its optional argument defines the symbol font to use (default `ifsym`). Glyph charts of all `ifsym` fonts are part of the package documentation. Somewhat more interesting is the command `\textifsym`, which allows you to produce pulse diagrams. It can also be used to display digital digits (where b denotes an empty space of the right width).

```
\usepackage{ifsym}
\textifsymbol{3}  \textifsymbol[ifgeo]{113}     \par
\textifsym{LLL|H|L|h|l} \textifsym{MM<DD>m<d>M}\par
\textifsym{-31.458} \textit{\textifsym{-99.4b80}}
```

7-8-9

7.8.6 tipa—International Phonetic Alphabet symbols

The TIPA bundle [50] developed by Rei Fukui consists of a set of fonts and a corresponding package to enable typesetting of phonetic symbols with LaTeX. TIPA contains all the symbols, including diacritics, defined in the 1979, 1989, 1993, and 1996 versions of International Phonetic Alphabet (IPA). Besides IPA symbols, TIPA contains symbols that are useful for other areas of phonetics and linguistics including the following:

- Symbols used in American phonetics, for example, æ, ɛ, ɒ, and λ;
- Symbols used in the historical study of Indo-European languages, such as þ, ɸ, ƕ, ʐ, ь, ъ, and accents such as á and ĕ;
- Symbols used in the phonetic description of languages in East Asia, such as ɿ, ʅ, ɖ, ɳ, ƫ (needs option `extra`);
- Diacritics used in *extIPA Symbols for Disordered Speech* and *VoQS (Voice Quality Symbols)*, for example, n̥, f̬, and m̋ (needs option `extra`).

The IPA symbols are encoded in the standard LaTeX encoding T3, for which the package `tipa` provides additional support macros. The encoding is available for the font families Computer Modern Roman, Sans, and Typewriter (based on the

ASCII	:	;	"	|	0	1	2	3	4	5	6	7	8	9
TIPA	ː	ˑ	ˈ	|	ʉ	ɨ	ʌ	ɜ	ɥ	ʁ	ɒ	ɤ	θ	ə
ASCII	@	A	B	C	D	E	F	G	H	I	J	K	L	M
TIPA	ə	ɑ	β	ç	ð	ɛ	ɸ	ɣ	ɦ	ɪ	ɟ	ʁ	ʎ	ŋ
ASCII	N	O	P	Q	R	S	T	U	V	W	X	Y	Z	
TIPA	ŋ	ɔ	ʔ	ʕ	ɾ	ʃ	θ	ʊ	ʋ	ɯ	χ	ʏ	ʒ	

Table 7.22: TIPA shortcut characters

METAFONT designs for Computer Modern by Donald Knuth, as well as for Times Roman and Helvetica).

Strictly speaking, T3 is not a proper LaTeX text encoding, as it does not contain the visible ASCII characters in their standard positions. However, one can take the position that phonetic symbols form a language of their own and for this language, the TIPA system provides a highly optimized input interface in which digits and uppercase letters serve as convenient shortcuts (see Table 7.22) to input common phonetic symbols within the argument of \textipa or the environment IPA. All phonetic symbols are also available in long form; for example, to produce a ə one can use \textschwa. The following example shows the TIPA system in a Times and Helvetica environment.

In linguistics, fəʊ'nɛtɪk transcriptions are usually shown in square brackets, e.g., phonetics [fəʊ'nɛtɪks].

```
\usepackage{mathptmx,tipa}
In linguistics, f\textschwa\textupsilon
\textprimstress n\textepsilon t\i k transcriptions
are usually shown in square brackets, e.g.,
\textsf{phonetics \textipa{[f@U"nEtIks]}}.
```

7-8-10

TIPA defines *, \;, \:, \!, and \| as special macros with which to easily input phonetic symbols that do not have a shortcut input as explained above. In standard LaTeX all five are already defined for use in math mode, so loading tipa highjacks them for use by linguists. If that is not desirable, the option safe prevents these redefinitions. The long forms then have to be used—for example, the command \textroundcap instead of \|c. The following lines show a few more complicated examples with the output in Computer Modern Roman, Sans, and Typewriter.

ŋŎ̥ò̃ ŋŎâʔã

A) dɔg, B) kæt C) maʊs

*k̥m̩tóm *bhrâtēr

```
\usepackage{tipa}
\begin{IPA}
\textrm{N\!o\'{\~*o}\~o \r*N\!o\^aP\~a  } \par
\textsf{\*A) dOg, \*B) k\ae{}t \*C) maUs} \par
\texttt{*\|c{k}\r*mt\'om *bhr\'=at\=er}      \end{IPA}
```

7-8-11

If loaded with the option tone, TIPA provides a \tone command to produce "tone letters". The command takes one argument consisting of a string of numbers denoting pitch levels, 1 being the lowest and 5 the highest. Within this range, any combination is allowed and there is no limit on the length of the combination, as exemplified in the last line of the next example, which otherwise shows the usage of \tone to display the four tones of Chinese.

˥ma (mother) ˩˩˦ma (horse)
ˊma (hemp) ˥˩ma (scold)
∿∿

```
\usepackage[tone]{tipa}

\tone{55}ma (mother) \tone{214}ma (horse) \par
\tone{35}ma (hemp)    \tone{51}ma  (scold) \par
\tone{153325413}
```

7-8-12

The above examples merely scrape the surface of the possibilities offered by TIPA. To explore it in detail consult the tipaman manual, which is part of the TIPA distribution.

7.8.7   Typesetting the euro symbol (€)

On January 1, 2002, the euro (€) became the official currency in 12 countries of the European Union.[1] A long time before that event, the European Commission had a logo designed, to be used whenever one refers to the new European currency. The Commission now also encourages the use of symbols that are adjusted to the current font of a document. Meanwhile, most foundries have integrated specially designed euro symbols into their fonts, but there are still many fonts without euro in use. For instance, the PostScript standard fonts, which are hard-wired in most existing laser printers, cannot be assumed to have euro symbols.

The official LaTeX command to access a euro symbol is \texteuro, which is part of the textcomp package. However, many fonts simply do not contain a euro glyph. In such a case textcomp attempts to fake the symbol by putting two slashes through an uppercase C (e.g., in Times Roman €).

With popular fonts designed for use with TeX, the euro symbol usually available but, unfortunately, the euro sign designed by Jörg Knappen for the European Computer Modern fonts (i.e., LaTeX's default font families) is somewhat futuristic and considered acceptable by many people only in the sans serif family:

A normal €, *an italic €*, **a bold €**, ***a bold italic €***. Compare the sans serif € and typewriter € all in EC fonts.

```
\usepackage{textcomp}

A normal \texteuro{}, \textit{an italic \texteuro},
\textbf{a bold \texteuro},
\textbf{\itshape a bold italic \texteuro}.
Compare the \textsf{sans serif \texteuro}
and \texttt{typewriter \texteuro} all in EC fonts.
```

7-8-13

The situation is somewhat better with the Computer Modern Bright families. Although produced using the METAFONT designs of the European Computer

---

[1]More exactly, bank notes and coins were introduced on that day.

Modern fonts, the euro symbol comes out nicely, as nearly all serifs are dropped in these families.

A normal €, *a slanted €*, **a bold €**, **a bold slanted €**. Compare this to the `typewriter €` all in CM Bright.

```
\usepackage{cmbright,textcomp}
A normal \texteuro{}, \textsl{a slanted \texteuro},
\textbf{a bold \texteuro}, \textbf{\slshape a bold
slanted \texteuro}. Compare this to the
\texttt{typewriter \texteuro} all in CM Bright.
```

7-8-14

But what should be done if the fonts used in the document do not contain the symbol? In that case the solution is to use either separate symbol fonts that provide a generic euro symbol (with a neutral design, that can be combined with many font families) or symbol fonts specially designed to be used with certain text font families. In any event the symbol should be available in several weight (and width) series and sizes so that it can be effectively used in different typesetting situations (e.g., in a heading like the one of the current section).

eurosym—**euros for LaTeX**

The first set of fonts providing generic euro symbols for use with TeX were probably the EuroSym fonts designed by Henrik Theiling. They are available as META-FONT sources as well as PostScript Type 1 outlines and contain the euro symbol designed according to the official construction method. As a nice feature, the fonts contain a picture of the construction method in slot zero. So for those who always wanted to know how the symbol should be designed, the following example is illuminating:

```
\usepackage{eurosym}
\fontsize{40}{40}\usefont{U}{eurosym}{m}{n}\symbol{0}
```

7-8-15

Regular euros The eurosym package, which is used to access these fonts, defines the command `\euro`. By default, this command generates the official symbol to vary with the series and shape attributes of the current document font. See Table 7.23 on the next page for the set of possibilities.

Regular €, *a slanted €*, **a bold €**, and ***a bold italic €***.

```
\usepackage{eurosym}
Regular \euro{},  \textsl{a slanted \euro},
\textbf{a bold \euro}, and
\textbf{\itshape a bold italic \euro}.
```

7-8-16

Poor man's euros As an alternative, the package offers commands to construct a euro symbol from the letter "C" in the current font by combining it with horizontal bars (which exist in three widths). The next example shows that the results range from unacceptable to more or less adequate, depending on the shape of the "C" and the

Family	Series	Shape(s)	Example of the Typeface
EuroSym by Henrik Theiling (U)			
eurosym	m	n, (it), sl, ol	regular and outline: €, €
eurosym	(b), bx	n, (it), sl, ol	bold extended upright and slanted: €, €

Table 7.23: Classification of the EuroSym font family

chosen bar width. In any case a properly defined euro symbol for a font is preferable and should be used if available.

€, €, € (Times)
€, €, € (Helvetica)
€, €, € (Courier)

```
\usepackage{times,eurosym}
\rmfamily \geneuro, \geneuronarrow, \geneurowide\ (Times)\par
\sffamily \geneuro, \geneuronarrow, \geneurowide\ (Helvetica)\par
\ttfamily \geneuro, \geneuronarrow, \geneurowide\ (Courier)
```

7-8-17

With the package options `gen`, `gennarrow`, and `genwide`, one can change the `\euro` command so that it points to `\geneuro`, `\geneuronarrow`, or `\geneurowide`, respectively. In all cases you can access the official euro symbol using the command `\officialeuro`.

Finally, the package offers the convenient command `\EUR` to typeset an amount of money together with the euro symbol separated by a small space.[1] As different countries have different conventions about where to place the currency sign, the package recognizes the options `left` (default) and `right`.

7-8-18

Das Buch kostet 19,60 € im Handel.

```
\usepackage[right]{eurosym}

Das Buch kostet \EUR{19,60} im Handel.
```

Another way to format monetary amounts is provided by the `euro` package, which is documented on page 96.

The Adobe euro fonts

Adobe also offers a set of Type 1 fonts that contain the euro symbol. This font set contains serifed, sans serif (with a design close to the official logo), and typewriter variants. All are available in upright and italic shapes and in normal and bold weights. To exploit these fonts, one needs a PostScript printer or, more generally, a printer that can render such fonts (e.g., with the help of the `ghostscript` program).

While the fonts can be freely used for printing purposes, Adobe does not allow them to be generally distributed or included in a TeX distribution. For this reason you have to manually download them from the Adobe web site: `ftp://ftp.adobe.com/pub/adobe/type/win/all/eurofont.exe`. This is a self-extracting archive

---

[1] Some other packages use this command name to denote the euro symbol itself—an unfortunate inconsistency.

for Windows. On Unix platforms the fonts can be extracted from it using the program unzip.

After downloading the fonts, one has to rename them to conform to Karl Berry's font naming conventions [19] and, if necessary, get support files for LaTeX, such as .fd files, a mapping file for dvips, and a package to make them accessible in documents. Depending on the TeX installation (e.g., the TeXlive CD), these files might be already available. Otherwise, they can be downloaded from CTAN:fonts/euro.

eurosans—One way of getting euros from Adobe

Several LaTeX packages are available that provide access to the Adobe euro fonts, each using a different strategy. As its name indicates, the eurosans package developed by Walter Schmidt provides only access to Adobe's EuroSans fonts (see Table 7.24 on the next page). The reason being that the serifed variants seldom fit the body fonts of documents, while the more neutral sans serif designs blend well with most typefaces, except for typewriter fonts. As the EuroMono typefaces from Adobe are actually condensed versions of EuroSans, they have been integrated as a condensed series (NFSS classifications mc, bc and sbc) by the package. Weight (medium or boldface), shape (upright or oblique), and width (regular or condensed) vary according to surrounding conditions in the document.

An important aspect of this package (and one absent from other packages), is the ability to scale the fonts by a factor, using the option scaled. By default, it scales the fonts down to 95% of their nominal size. If a different scale factor is needed to match the size of the document font, an explicit value can be provided, as seen in the next example.

A regular € symbol, *an italic €*, **a bold €, and** *a bold italic €*.
A regular € symbol, *an italic €*, **a bold €,** and *a bold italic €*.

```
\usepackage{lucidabr} \usepackage[scaled=0.97]{eurosans}
A regular \euro{} symbol, \textit{an italic \euro},
\textbf{a bold \euro{}, and \textit{a bold italic \euro}}.
\par\sffamily
A regular \euro{} symbol, \textit{an italic \euro},
\textbf{a bold \euro{}, and \textit{a bold italic \euro}}.
```

7-8-19

Restricting variance The number of produced variations can be reduced (for example, varying the font series but always using normal shape) through a redefinition of the \euro command.

A regular € symbol, *not an italic €*, **a bold €,** and *not a bold italic €*.

```
\usepackage{lucidabr} \usepackage[scaled=0.97]{eurosans}
\DeclareRobustCommand{\euro}{{\fontencoding{U}%
   \fontfamily{eurosans}\fontshape{n}\selectfont E}}
A regular \euro{} symbol, \textit{not an italic \euro},
\textbf{a bold \euro{}, and \textit{not a bold italic \euro}}.
```

7-8-20

If there is no requirement for a serifed euro symbol, the eurosans package is usually preferable to other solutions, as it provides the most comprehensive set

Family	Series	Shape(s)	PostScript Font Names and Examples
			Adobe EuroSans (U)
eurosans	m	n, it, (sl)	EuroSans-Regular (zpeurs), EuroSans-Italic (zpeuris) €, €
eurosans	b, (bx)	n, it, (sl)	EuroSans-Bold (zpeubs), EuroSans-BoldItalic (zpeubis) **€**, **€**
eurosans	mc	n, it, (sl)	EuroMono-Regular (zpeurt), EuroMono-Italic (zpeurit) €, €
eurosans	(sbc), bc	n, it, (sl)	EuroMono-Bold (zpeubt), EuroMono-BoldItalic (zpeubit) **€**, **€**

Table 7.24: Classification of the Adobe euro font families (eurosans classification)

of font series and supports scaling of the fonts. The package documentation also describes how to install the fonts and the support files if necessary.

europs—Another way of getting euros from Adobe

A different approach was taken in the europs package developed by Jörn Clausen. It provides the command \EUR to access the symbols from the Adobe euro fonts. This command selects a different symbol depending on the font attributes of the surrounding text, as can be seen in the next example.

7-8-21

```
\usepackage{array,times,europs}
\begin{tabular}{rc>{\sffamily}c>{\ttfamily}c}
              & rm           & sf            & tt           \\
regular       &              \EUR &            \EUR &          \EUR \\
\itshape italic &\itshape\EUR & \itshape\EUR &\itshape\EUR \\
\bfseries\itshape bold italic & \bfseries\itshape\EUR &
                \bfseries\itshape\EUR &  \bfseries\itshape\EUR \\
(body font)   & C            & C             & C            \\
\end{tabular}
```

	rm	sf	tt
regular	€	€	€
italic	*€*	*€*	*€*
bold italic	**€**	**€**	**€**
(body font)	C	C	C

As this switch of shapes may not be desirable (e.g., the serifed euro may not blend well with the serifed document font), the package also offers the commands \EURtm (serifed symbol), \EURhv (sans serif symbol), and \EURcr (monospaced symbol)—the names being modeled after the three PostScript fonts Times, Helvetica, and Courier. These commands fix the font family, but react to requests for bold or oblique variants. However, as the last line in the previous example shows, none of the symbols blends particularly well with these fonts. Finally, the package offers \EURofc, which generates the official euro symbol (i.e., one from the sans serif regular font).

marvosym—Revisited for cash

Another free PostScript font that contains euro symbols as glyphs is the MarVoSym font, described in Section 7.8.3 on page 401. It is available in three shapes to blend with Times, Helvetica, and Courier. As this font is a Pi font, it comes in only one weight series, which somewhat limits its usefulness as a source for the euro symbol. The font contains two glyphs with the official euro design, which differ in their amounts of side-bearings. To better demonstrate this difference, the following example puts a frame around them. It also shows the other currency symbols available in this package.

```
\usepackage{times,marvosym}
```

Currencies: *ß*, *₰*, *Ẽ*, $, €
Comparisons: C €, C €, C €
Official logos: € or €

```
Currencies: \Shilling, \Denarius, \Pfund, \EyesDollar, \EURtm\par
Comparisons: C \EURtm, \textsf{C} \EURhv, \texttt{C} \EURcr  \par
Official logos: {\Large  \frame{\EUR} or \frame{\EURdig}}
```

7-8-22

7.9 The low-level interface

While the high-level font commands are intended for use in a document, the low-level commands are mainly for defining new commands in packages or in the preamble of a document; see also Section 7.9.4. To make the best use of such font commands, it is helpful to understand the internal organization of fonts in LaTeX's font selection scheme (NFSS).

One goal of LaTeX's font selection scheme is to allow rational font selection, with algorithms guided by the principles of generic markup. For this purpose, it would be desirable to allow independent changes for as many font attributes as possible. On the other hand, font families in real life normally contain only a subset of the myriad imaginable font attribute combinations. Therefore, allowing independent changes in too many attributes results in too many combinations for which no real (external) font is available and a default has to be substituted.

LaTeX internally keeps track of five independent font attributes: the "current encoding", the "current family", the "current series", the "current shape", and the "current size". The encoding attribute was introduced in NFSS release 2 after it became clear that real support of multiple languages would be possible only by maintaining the character-encoding scheme independently of the other font attributes.

The values of these attributes determine the font currently in use. LaTeX also maintains a large set of tables used to associate attribute combinations with external fonts (i.e., .tfm files that contain the information necessary for (LA)TEX to do its job). Font selection inside LaTeX is then done in two steps:

1. A number of font attributes are changed using the low-level commands \fontencoding, \fontfamily, \fontseries, \fontshape, and \fontsize.

2. The font corresponding to this new attribute setting is selected by calling the \selectfont command.

The second step comprises several actions. LaTeX first checks whether the font corresponding to the desired attribute settings is known to the system (i.e., the `.tfm` file is already loaded) and, if so, this font is selected. If not, the internal tables are searched to find the external font name associated with this setting. If such a font name can be found, the corresponding `.tfm` file is read into memory and afterwards the font is selected for typesetting. If this process is not successful, LaTeX tries to find an alternative font, as explained in Section 7.9.3.

7.9.1 Setting individual font attributes

Every font attribute has one command to change its current value. All of these commands will accept more or less any character string as an argument, but only a few values make sense. These values are not hard-wired into LaTeX's font selection scheme, but rather are conventions set up in the internal tables. The following sections introduce the naming conventions used in the standard set-up of LaTeX, but anyone can change this set-up by adding new font declarations to the internal tables. Obviously, anybody setting up new fonts for use with LaTeX should try to obey these conventions whenever possible, as only a consistent naming convention can guarantee that appropriate fonts are selected in a generically marked-up document.

If you want to select a specific font using this interface—say, Computer Modern Dunhill bold condensed italic 14 pt—a knowledge of the interface conventions alone is not enough, as no external font exists for every combination of attribute values. You could try your luck by specifying something like the following set of commands:

```
\fontencoding{OT1}\fontfamily{cmdh}\fontseries{bc}\fontshape{it}%
\fontsize{14}{16pt}\selectfont
```

This code would be correct according to the naming conventions, as we will see in the following sections. Because this attribute combination does not correspond to a real font, however, LaTeX would have to substitute a different font. The substitution mechanism may choose a font that is quite different from the one desired, so you should consult the font tables to see whether the desired combination is available. (Section 7.9.3 provides more details on the substitution process.) Every installation should have a local guide telling you exactly which fonts are available.

Choosing the font family

The font family is selected with the command `\fontfamily`. Its argument is a character string that refers to a font family declared in the internal tables. The character string was defined when these tables were set up and is usually a short letter sequence—for example, `cmr` for the Computer Modern Roman family. The family names should not be longer than five letters, because they will be combined with possibly three more letters to form a file name, which on some systems can have at most eight letters.

Weight Classes	
Ultra Light	ul
Extra Light	el
Light	l
Semi Light	sl
Medium (normal)	m
Semi Bold	sb
Bold	b
Extra Bold	eb
Ultra Bold	ub

Width Classes		
Ultra Condensed	50%	uc
Extra Condensed	62.5%	ec
Condensed	75%	c
Semi Condensed	87.5%	sc
Medium	100%	m
Semi Expanded	112.5%	sx
Expanded	125%	x
Extra Expanded	150%	ex
Ultra Expanded	200%	ux

Table 7.25: Weight and width classification of fonts

Choosing the font series

The series attribute is changed with the `\fontseries` command. The series combines a weight and a width in its argument; in other words, it is not possible to change the width of the current font independently of its weight. This arrangement was chosen because it is hardly ever necessary to change weight or width individually. On the contrary, a change in weight (say, to bold) often is accompanied by a change in width (say, to extended) in the designer's specification. This is not too surprising, given that weight changes alter the horizontal appearance of the letters and thus call for adjustment in the expansion (i.e., the width) to produce a well-balanced look.

In the naming conventions for the argument for the `\fontseries` command, the names for both the weight and the width are abbreviated so that each combination is unique. The conventions are shown in Table 7.25. These classifications are combined in the argument to `\fontseries`; however, any instance of m (standing for medium in weight or width) is dropped, except when both weight and width are medium. The latter case is abbreviated with a single m. For example, bold expanded would be bx, whereas medium expanded would be x and bold medium would be b.

Choosing the font shape

The `\fontshape` command is used to change the shape attribute. For the standard shapes, one- and two-letter abbreviations are used; these are shown in Table 7.26 on the facing page together with an example of the resulting shape in the Computer Modern Roman family.[1]

---

[1] The ol shape was produced using `\pcharpath` commands from the pst-char package, as Computer Modern does not contain such a shape. These types of graphical manipulations are discussed in [57].

Abbreviation	Description
n	upright (or normal) shape
it	*italic shape*
sl	*slanted or oblique shape*
sc	SMALL CAPS SHAPE
ui	*upright italic shape*
ol	OUTLINE shape

Table 7.26: Shape classification of fonts

Choosing the font size

The font size is changed with the \fontsize{⟨*size*⟩}{⟨*skip*⟩} command. This is the only font attribute command that takes two arguments: the ⟨*size*⟩ to switch to and the baseline ⟨*skip*⟩ (the distance from baseline to baseline for this size). Font sizes are normally measured in points, so by convention the unit is omitted. The same is true for the second argument. However, if the baseline skip should be a rubber length—that is, if it contains plus or minus—you have to specify a unit. Thus, a valid size change could be requested by

```
\fontsize{14.4}{17}\selectfont
```

Even if such a request is valid in principle, no corresponding external font may exist in this size. In this case, LATEX will try to find a nearby size if its internal tables allow for size correction or report an error otherwise.

If you use fonts existing in arbitrary sizes (for example, PostScript fonts), you can, of course, select any size you want. For example,

```
\fontsize{1in}{1.2in}\selectfont Happy Birthday
```

will produce a birthday poster line with letters in a one-inch size. However, there is one problem with using arbitrary sizes: if LATEX has to typeset a formula in this size (which might happen behind the scenes without your knowledge), it needs to set up all fonts used in formulas for the new size. For an arbitrary size, it usually has to calculate the font sizes for use in subscripts and sub-subscripts (at least 12 different fonts). In turn, it probably has to load a lot of new fonts—something you can tell by looking at the transcript file. For this reason you may finally hit some internal limit if you have too many different size requests in your document. If this happens, you should tell LATEX which sizes to load for formulas using the \DeclareMathSizes declaration, rather than letting it use its own algorithm. See Section 7.10.7 for more information on this issue.

Choosing the encoding

A change of encoding is performed with the command \fontencoding, where the argument is the internal name for the desired encoding. This name must be

Encoding	Description	Declared by
T1	LaTeX text encoding (Latin) a.k.a. "Cork" encoding	LaTeX
TS1	LaTeX symbol encoding (Latin)	LaTeX
T2A,B,C	LaTeX text encodings (Cyrillic)	Cyrillic support packages
T3	LaTeX Phonetic Alphabet encoding	tipa package
TS3	LaTeX phonetic alphabet encoding (extra symbols)	tipa package
T4	LaTeX text encoding (African languages)	—
T5	LaTeX text encoding (Vietnamese)	—
T7	LaTeX text encoding (reserved for Greek)	—
OT1	TeX text as defined by Donald Knuth	LaTeX
OT2	TeX text for Cyrillic languages (obsolete)	Cyrillic support packages
OT3	International phonetic alphabet encoding (obsolete)	—
OT4	TeX text with extensions for the Polish language	—
OT6	TeX text with extensions for the Armenian language	—
OML	TeX math text (italic) as defined by Donald Knuth	LaTeX
OMS	TeX math symbol as defined by Donald Knuth	LaTeX
OMX	TeX math extended symbol as defined by Donald Knuth	LaTeX
X2	Extended text encoding (Cyrillic)	Cyrillic support packages
U	Unknown encoding (for arbitrary rubbish)	LaTeX
L..	Local encoding (for private encodings)	—
LV1	Encoding used with some VTeX fonts	MicroPress
LY1	Alternative to T1 encoding	Y&Y

Table 7.27: Standard font encodings used with LaTeX

known to LaTeX, either as one of the predefined encodings (loaded by the kernel) or as declared with the \DeclareFontEncoding command (see Section 7.10.5). A set of standard encoding names are given in Table 7.27.

LaTeX's font selection scheme is based on the (idealistic) assumption that most (or, even better, all) fonts for text are available in the same encoding as long as they are used to typeset in the same language. In other words, encoding changes should become necessary only if one is switching from one language to another. In that case it is normally the task of the language support packages (e.g., those from the babel system) to arrange matters behind the scenes.

In the following example we change the encoding manually by defining an environment Cyr for typesetting in Cyrillic. In this environment both the font encoding and the input encoding are locally changed. That might sound strange but if you work with an editor or keyboard that can switch input encodings on the fly this might be exactly the way your text is stored. Of course, for proper language support, additional work would be necessary, such as changing the hyphenation rules. The encodings are declared to LaTeX by loading them with the fontenc pack-

age. T2A specifies one of the standard Cyrillic encodings; by loading T1 last, it
becomes the default encoding for the document.

<table>
<tr>
<td></td>
<td>

```
\usepackage[T2A,T1]{fontenc}\usepackage[koi8-r,latin1]{inputenc}
\newenvironment{Cyr}{\inputencoding{koi8-r}%
                     \fontencoding{T2A}\selectfont}{}
```
</td>
</tr>
</table>

Русский язык heißt auf
Deutsch: die russische
Sprache.

7-9-1

```
\raggedright \begin{Cyr}öÕÖÓËÉÊ ÑÚÙË\end{Cyr}
heißt auf Deutsch: die russische Sprache.
```

Unfortunately, T1 is not fully implementable for most PostScript fonts. The
following five characters are likely to show up as blobs of ink (indicating a missing
glyph in the font). Note that the per thousand and per ten thousand symbols are
actually formed by joining a percent sign and one or two additional small zeros;
only the latter glyph is missing.

Potential T1
encoding problems

7-9-2

ȷ ŋ Đ ‰ ‱
∎∎%∎%∎

```
\usepackage[T1]{fontenc}
\fontfamily{cmr}\selectfont
\j{} \ng{} \NG{} \textperthousand{} \textpertenthousand \par
\fontfamily{ptm}\selectfont
\j{} \ng{} \NG{} \textperthousand{} \textpertenthousand{}
```

As explained in Section 7.5.4 on page 362, the situation for TS1 is even worse,
as sometimes half the glyphs from that encoding are not available in a given
PostScript font.

7.9.2   Setting several font attributes

When designing page styles (see Section 4.4) or layout-oriented commands, you
often want to select a particular font—that is, you need to specify values for all
attributes. For this task LaTeX provides the command `\usefont`, which takes four
arguments: the encoding, family, series, and shape. The command updates those
attributes and then calls `\selectfont`. If you also want to specify the size and
baseline skip, place a `\fontsize` command in front of it. for example,

```
\fontsize{14}{16pt}\usefont{OT1}{cmdh}{bc}{it}
```

would produce the same result as the hypothetical example on page 413.

Besides `\usefont`, LaTeX provides the `\DeclareFixedFont` declaration, which
can be used to define new commands that switch to a completely fixed font. Such
commands are extremely fast because they do not have to look up any internal
tables. They are therefore very useful in command definitions that have to switch
back and forth between fixed fonts. For example, for the doc package (see Chapter 14), one could produce code-line numbers using the following definitions:

```
\DeclareFixedFont\CodelineFont{\encodingdefault}{\familydefault}
                     {\seriesdefault}{\shapedefault}{7pt}
\newcommand\theCodelineNo{\CodelineFont\arabic{CodelineNo}}
```

As you can see from the example, \DeclareFixedFont has six arguments: the name of the command to be defined followed by the five font attributes in the NFSS classification. Instead of supplying fixed values (except for the size), the built-in hooks that describe the main document font are used (see also Section 7.3.5). Thus, in the example above \CodelineFont still depends on the overall layout for the document (via the settings of \encodingdefault and other parameters). However, once the definition is carried out, its meaning is frozen, so later changes to the defaults will have no effect.

7.9.3 Automatic substitution of fonts

Whenever a font change request cannot be carried out because the combination is not known to LATEX, it tries to recover by using a font with similar attributes. Here is what happens: if the combination of encoding scheme, family, series, and shape is not declared (see Section 7.10.3), LATEX tries to find a known combination by first changing the shape attribute to a default. If the resulting combination is still unknown, it tries changing the series to a default. As a last resort, it changes the family to a default value. Finally, the internal table entry is looked up to find the requested size. For example, if you ask for \ttfamily\bfseries\itshape—a typewriter font in a bold series and italic shape (which usually does not exist)— then you will get a typewriter font in medium series and upright shape, because LATEX first resets the shape before changing the series. If, in such a situation, you prefer a typewriter font with italic shape, you have to announce your intention to LATEX using the sub function, which is explained on page 425.

The substitution process never changes the encoding scheme, because any alteration could produce wrong characters in the output. Recall that the encoding scheme defines how to interpret the input characters, while the other attributes define how the output should look. It would be catastrophic if, say, a £ sign were changed into a $ sign on an invoice just because the software tried to be clever.

Thus, every encoding scheme must have a default family, series, and shape, and at least the combination consisting of the encoding scheme together with the corresponding defaults must have a definition inside LATEX, as explained in Section 7.10.5.

7.9.4 Using low-level commands in the document

The low-level font commands described in the preceding sections are intended to be used in the definition of higher-level commands, either in class or package files or in the document preamble.

Whenever possible, you should avoid using the low-level commands directly in a document if you can use high-level font commands like \textsf instead. The reason is that the low-level commands are very precise instructions to switch to a particular font, whereas the high-level commands can be customized using packages or declarations in the preamble. Suppose, for example, that you have selected Computer Modern Sans in your document using `\fontfamily{cmss}\selectfont`. If you later decide to typeset the whole document with fonts from the PSNFSS bundle—say, Times—applying a package would change only those parts of the document that do not contain explicit `\fontfamily` commands.

7.10 Setting up new fonts

7.10.1 Overview

Setting up new fonts for use with LATEX basically means filling the internal font selection tables with information necessary for later associating a font request in a document with the external `.tfm` file containing character information used by (LA)TEX. Thus the tables are responsible for associating with

```
\fontencoding{OT1}\fontfamily{cmdh}\fontseries{m}\fontshape{n}%
\fontsize{10}{12pt}\selectfont
```

the external file `cmdunh10.tfm`. To add new fonts, you need to reverse this process. For every new external font you have to ask yourself five questions:

1. What is the font's encoding scheme—that is, which characters are in which positions?
2. What is its family name?
3. What is its series (weight and width)?
4. What is its shape?
5. What is its size?

The answers to these questions will provide the information necessary to classify your external font according to the LATEX conventions, as described in Section 7.9. The next few sections discuss how to enter new fonts into the NFSS tables so that they can be used in the main text. You normally need this information if you want to make use of new fonts—for example, if you want to write a short package file for accessing a new font family. Later sections discuss more complicated concepts that come into play if you want to use, for example, special fonts for math instead of the standard ones.

If new fonts from the non-TEX world are to be integrated into LATEX, it might be necessary to start even one step earlier: you may have to generate `.tfm` and probably virtual font files first. The tool normally used for this step is the fontinst program, written by Alan Jeffrey and further developed and now maintained by Lars Hellström. It is described in [57] and [64] and in the source documentation [74,75].

F	TT	W	[V.]	[N.]	[E]	[DD]
Foundry	Typeface Name	Weight	Variant	Encoding	Expansion	Design Size
e.g., p=Adobe	tm=Times	b=Bold	i=Italic	8t=T1	n=narrow	10=10 point

Table 7.28: Karl Berry's font file name classification scheme

7.10.2 Naming those thousands of fonts

A font naming scheme that can be used with TeX was proposed by Karl Berry [18], provoking some discussion [118]. The current version is described in [19] and has become the de facto standard in the TeX world. Berry tries to classify all font file names using eight alphanumeric characters, where case is not significant. This eight-character limit guarantees that the same file names can be used across all computer platforms and, more importantly, conforms to the ISO-9660 norm for CD-ROM. The principle of the scheme is described in Table 7.28, where the parts in brackets are omitted if they correspond to a default. For example, a design size is given only if the font is not linearly scaled. Table 7.8 on page 372 shows the classification of the 35 "basic" PostScript fonts according to LaTeX's font interface. For each font the full Adobe name and, in parentheses, the corresponding short (Karl Berry) file name is given (without the encoding part). For OT1, T1, or TS1 one would need to append 7t, 8t, or 8c, respectively, to obtain the full file name—for example, putr8t for Utopia Regular in T1 encoding.

The naming convention covers internal TeX names for fonts (i.e., those used in \DeclareFontShape declarations as described in the next section), names for virtual fonts and their components (e.g., particular reencodings of physical fonts) [91], and the names of physical fonts. In case of PostScript fonts, the physical font names are often different from those used internally by TeX.

A glimpse of the underworld In the latter case the mapping between internal font names and the external world has to happen when the result of a LaTeX run is viewed or printed. For example, the PostScript driver dvips uses mapping files (default extension .map) that contain lines such as

```
putr8r Utopia-Regular "TeXBase1Encoding ReEncodeFont " <8r.enc <putr8a.pfb
```

telling it that the font putr8r can be obtained from the external font putr8a.pfb by reencoding it via a special encoding vector (8r.enc in this case). However, when you look into t1put.fd (the file that contains the \DeclareFontShape declarations for the Utopia family in the T1 encoding), you will find that putr8r is not referenced. Instead, you will find names such as putr8t. The reason is that putr8t is a virtual font (built with the help of fontinst [74, 75]) that references putr8r. The latter link is difficult to find (other than through the naming convention itself) if you do not have access to the sources that were used to build the virtual fonts actually used by TeX. Fortunately, you seldom have to dig into that part of a TeX system; if you do, you will find more information in [57, Chapter 10] or in the references listed above.

7.10.3   Declaring new font families and font shape groups

Each family/encoding combination must be made known to LaTeX through the command \DeclareFontFamily. This command has three arguments. The first two arguments are the encoding scheme and the family name. The third is usually empty, but it may contain special options for font loading and is explained on page 426. Thus, if you want to introduce a new family—say, Computer Modern Dunhill with the old TeX encoding scheme—you would write

```
\DeclareFontFamily{OT1}{cmdh}{}
```

A font family normally consists of many individual fonts. Instead of announcing each family member individually to LaTeX, you have to combine fonts that differ only in size and declare them as a group.

Such a group is entered into the internal tables of LaTeX with the command \DeclareFontShape, which takes six arguments. The first four are the encoding scheme, the family name, the series name, and the shape name under which you want to access these fonts later on. The fifth argument is a list of sizes and external font names, given in a special format that we discuss below. The sixth argument is usually empty; its use is explained on page 426.

We will first show a few examples and introduce terminology; then we will discuss all the features in detail.

As an example, an NFSS table entry for Computer Modern Dunhill medium (series) upright (shape) in the encoding scheme "TeX text" could be entered as

```
\DeclareFontShape{OT1}{cmdh}{m}{n}{ <10> cmdunh10 }{}
```

assuming that only one external font for the size 10pt is available. If you also have this font available at 12pt (scaled from 10pt), the declaration would be

```
\DeclareFontShape{OT1}{cmdh}{m}{n}{ <10> <12>cmdunh10 }{}
```

If the external font is available in all possible sizes, the declaration becomes very simple. This is the case for Type 1 PostScript (outline) fonts, or when the driver program is able to generate fonts on demand by calling METAFONT.

For example, Times Roman bold (series) upright (shape) in the LaTeX T1 encoding scheme could be entered as

```
\DeclareFontShape{T1}{ptm}{b}{n}{ <-> ptmb8t }{}
```

This example declares a size range with two open ends (no sizes specified to the left and the right of the -). As a result, the same external .tfm file (ptmb8t) is used for all sizes and is scaled to the desired size. If you have more than one

.tfm file for a font—say, `emtt10` for text sizes and `emtt12` for display sizes (this is European Modern Typewriter)—the declaration could be

```
\DeclareFontShape{T1}{emtt}{m}{n}{<-12> emtt10 <12-> emtt12}{}
```

In this case, the `.tfm` file `emtt10` would be used for sizes smaller than 12pt, and `emtt12` for all sizes larger than or equal to 12pt.

The preceding examples show that the fifth argument of the command `\DeclareFontShape` consists of size specifications surrounded by angle brackets (i.e., `<...>`) intermixed with loading information for the individual sizes (e.g., font names). The part inside the angle brackets is called the "size info" and the part following the closing angle bracket is called the "font info". The font info is further structured into a "size function" (often empty) and its arguments; we discuss this case below. Within the arguments of `\DeclareFontShape`, blanks are ignored to help make the entries more readable.[1] In the unusual event that a real space has to be entered, you can use the command `\space`.

Simple sizes and size ranges

The size infos—the parts between the angle brackets in the fifth argument to `\DeclareFontShape`—can be divided into "simple sizes" and "size ranges". A simple size is given by a single (decimal) number, like `<10>` or `<14.4>`, and in principle can have any positive value. However, because the number represents a font size measured in points, you probably will not find values less than 4 or greater than 120. A size range is given by two simple sizes separated by a hyphen, to indicate a range of font sizes that share the same font info. The lower boundary (i.e., the size to the left of the hyphen) is included in the range, while the upper boundary is excluded. For example, `<5-10>` denotes sizes greater than or equal to 5pt and less than 10pt. You can omit the number on either side of the hyphen in a size range, with the obvious interpretation: `<->` stands for all possible sizes, `<-10>` stands for all sizes less than 10pt, and `<12->` stands for all sizes greater than or equal to 12pt.

Often several simple sizes have the same font info. In that case a convenient shorthand is to omit all but the last font infos:

```
\DeclareFontShape{OT1}{panr}{m}{n}{ <5> <6> <7> <8> <9> <10>
         <10.95> <12> <14.4> <17.28> <20.74> <24.88> pan10 }{}
```

This example declares the font Pandora medium Roman as being available in several sizes, all of them produced by scaling from the same design size.

---

[1]This is true only if the command is used at the top level. If such a declaration is used inside other constructs (e.g., the argument of `\AtBeginDocument`), blanks might survive and in that case entries will not be recognized.

Size functions

As noted earlier, the font info (the string after the closing angle bracket) is further structured into a size function and its argument. If an * appears in the font info string, everything to the left of it forms the function name and everything to the right is the argument. If there is no asterisk, as in all of the examples so far, the whole string is regarded as the argument and the function name is "empty".

Based on the size requested by the user and the information in the \DeclareFontShape command, size functions produce the specification necessary for LaTeX to find the external font and load it at the desired size. They are also responsible for informing the user about anything special that happens. For example, some functions differ only in terms of whether they issue a warning. This capability allows the system maintainer to set up LaTeX in the way best suited for the particular site.

The name of a size function consists of zero or more letters. Some of the size functions can take two arguments, one optional and one mandatory. Such an optional argument has to be enclosed in square brackets. For example, the specification

```
<-> s * [0.9] cmfib8
```

would select, for all possible sizes (we have the range 0 to ∞), the size function s with the optional argument 0.9 and the mandatory argument cmfib8.

The size specifications in \DeclareFontShape are inspected in the order in which they are given. When a size info matches the requested user size, the corresponding size function is executed. If this process yields a valid font, no further entries are inspected. Otherwise, the search continues with the next entry. The standard size functions are listed below. The document fntguide.tex [109], which is part of the LaTeX distribution, describes how to define additional functions should it ever become necessary.

The "empty" function   Because the empty function is used most often, it has the shortest possible name. (Every table entry takes up a small bit of internal memory, so the syntax chosen tries to find a balance between a perfect user interface and compactness of storage.) The empty function loads the font info exactly at the requested size if it is a simple size. If there is a size range and the size requested by the user falls within that range, it loads the font exactly at the user size.

For example, if the user requested 14.4, then the specification

```
<-> panr10
```

would load the .tfm file called panr10.tfm at 14.4pt. Because this font was designed for 10pt (it is the Pandora Roman font at 10pt), all the values in the .tfm file are scaled by a factor of 1.44.

Sometimes one wants to load a font at a slightly larger or smaller size than the one requested by the user. This adjustment may be necessary when fonts from one family appear to be too large compared to fonts from other families used in the same document. For this purpose the empty size function allows an optional argument to represent a scale factor that, if present, is multiplied by the requested size to yield the actual size to be loaded. Thus

```
<-> [0.95] phvr8t
```

would always load the `.tfm` file called `phvr8t.tfm` (Helvetica in T1 encoding) at 95% of the requested size. If the optional argument is used, the empty size function will issue a warning to alert the user that the font is not being loaded at its intended size.

The "s" function   The s function has the same functionality as the empty function, but does not produce warnings (the s means "silence"). Writing

```
\DeclareFontShape{T1}{phv}{m}{n}{ <-> s * [0.95] phvr8t }{}
```

avoids all the messages that would be generated on the terminal if the empty function were used. Messages are still written to the transcript file, so you can find out which fonts were used if something goes wrong. The helvet package is implemented in this way, except that the scaling factor is not hard-wired but rather passed via a package option to the \DeclareFontShape declaration.

The "gen" function   Often the external font names are built by appending the font size to a string that represents the typeface. For example, cmtt8, cmtt9, and cmtt10 are the external names for the fonts Computer Modern Typewriter at 8, 9, and 10pt, respectively. With font names organized according to such a scheme, you can make use of the gen function to shorten the entry. This function combines the font info and the requested size to generate (hence gen) the external font names. Thus, you can write

```
<8> <9> <10> gen * cmtt
```

as shorthand for

```
<8> cmtt8 <9> cmtt9 <10> cmtt10
```

thereby saving eight characters in the internal tables of NFSS. This function combines both parts literally, so you should not use it with decimal sizes like 14.4. Also, you must ensure that the digits in the external font name really represent the design size (for example, cmr17 is actually Computer Modern Roman at 17.28pt).

In all other respects, the gen function behaves like the empty function. That is, the optional argument, if given, represents a scale factor and, if used, generates an information message.

The "sgen" function The sgen function is the silent variant of the gen function. It writes any message only to the transcript file.

The "genb" function This size function is similar to gen, but is intended for fonts in which the size is encoded in the font name in centipoints, such as the EC fonts. As a consequence, a line such as

```
<9> <10> <10.95> <12> genb * ecrm
```

acts as shorthand for

```
<9> ecrm0900 <10> ecrm1000 <10.95> ecrm1095 <12> ecrm1200
```

An optional argument, if present, will have the same effect as it would with the empty function—it provides a scale factor and, if used, generates an information message.

The "sgenb" function The sgenb function is the silent variant of the genb function. It writes any message only to the transcript file.

The "sub" function The sub function is used to substitute a different font shape group if no external font exists for the current font shape group. In this case the argument is not an external font name but rather a different family, series, and shape combination separated by slashes (the encoding will not change for the reasons explained earlier). For example, the Computer Modern Sans family has no italic shape, only a slanted shape. Thus, it makes sense to declare the slanted shape as a substitute for the italic one:

```
\DeclareFontShape{OT1}{cmss}{m}{it}{ <-> sub * cmss/m/sl }{}
```

Without this declaration, LATEX's automatic substitution mechanism (see Section 7.9.3) would substitute the default shape, Computer Modern Sans upright.

Besides the substitution of complete font shape groups, there are other good uses for the sub function. Consider the following code:

```
\DeclareFontShape{OT1}{cmss}{m}{sl}{ <-8> sub * cmss/m/n
   <8> cmssi8  <9> cmssi9  <10><10.95> cmssi10  <12><14.4> cmssi12
   <17.28><20.74><24.88> cmssi17 }{}
```

This declaration states that for sizes smaller than 8pt LaTeX should look in the font shape declaration for OT1/cmss/m/n. Such substitutions can be chained. People familiar with the standard font distribution know that there is no Computer Modern Sans font smaller than 8pt, so the substituted font shape group will probably contain another substitution entry. Nevertheless, using this device has the advantage that when you get an additional font you have to change only one font shape group declaration—other declarations that use this the font will benefit automatically.

The "ssub" function   The ssub function has the same functionality as the sub function, but does not produces on-screen warnings (the first s means "silence").

The "subf" function   The subf function is a cross between the empty function and sub, in that it loads fonts in the same way as the empty function but produces a warning that this operation was done as a substitution because the requested font shape is not available. You can use this function to substitute some external fonts without having to declare a separate font shape group for them, as in the case of the sub function. For example,

```
\DeclareFontShape{OT1}{ptm}{bx}{n}{ <-> subf * ptmb7t }{}
```

would warn the user that the requested combination is not available and, therefore, that the font ptmb7t was loaded instead. As this is less informative than using the sub function, the latter should be preferred.

The "ssubf" function   The silent variant of subf, this function it writes its messages only to the transcript file.

The "fixed" function   This function disregards the requested size and instead loads the external font given as an argument. If present, the optional argument denotes the size (in points) at which the font will be loaded. Thus, this function allows you to specify size ranges for which one font in some fixed size will be loaded.

The "sfixed" function   The silent variant of fixed, this function is used, for example, to load the font containing the large math symbols, which is often available only in one size.

Font-loading options

As already mentioned, you need to declare each family using the command \DeclareFontFamily. The argument to this command, as well as the sixth argument to \DeclareFontShape, can be used to specify special operations that are carried out when a font is loaded. In this way, you can change parameters that are associated with a font as a whole.

For every external font, (LA)TEX maintains, besides the information about each character, a set of global dimensions and other values associated with the font. For example, every font has its own "hyphen character", the character that is inserted automatically when (LA)TEX hyphenates a word. Another example is the normal width and the stretchability of a blank space between words (the "interword space"); again a value is maintained for every font and changed whenever (LA)TEX switches to a new font. By changing these values when a font is loaded, special effects can be achieved.

Normally, changes apply to a whole family; for example, you may want to prohibit hyphenation for all words typeset in the typewriter family. In this case, the third argument of \DeclareFontFamily should be used. If the changes should apply only to a specific font shape group, you must use the sixth argument of \DeclareFontShape. In other words, when a font is loaded, NFSS first applies the argument of \DeclareFontFamily and then the sixth argument of \DeclareFontShape, so that it can override the load options specified for the whole family if necessary.

Below we study the information that can be set in this way (unfortunately, not everything is changeable) and discuss some useful examples. This part of the interface addresses very low-level commands of TEX. Because it is so specialized, no effort was made to make the interface more LATEX-like. As a consequence, the methods for assigning integers and dimensions to variables are somewhat unusual.

With \hyphenchar\font=⟨*number*⟩, (LA)TEX specifies the character that is inserted as the hyphen when a word is hyphenated. The ⟨*number*⟩ represents the position of this character within the encoding scheme. The default is the value of \defaulthyphenchar, which is 45, representing the position of the "-" character in most encoding schemes. If this number is set to –1, hyphenation is suppressed. Thus, by declaring

Changing the hyphenation character

```
\DeclareFontFamily{OT1}{cmtt}{\hyphenchar\font=-1}
```

you can suppress hyphenation for all fonts in the cmtt family with the encoding scheme OT1. Fonts with the T1 encoding have an alternate hyphen character in position 127, so that you can set, for example,

```
\DeclareFontFamily{T1}{cmr}{\hyphenchar\font=127}
```

This makes the hyphen character inserted by (LA)TEX different from the compound-word dash entered in words like "so-called". (LA)TEX does not hyphenate words that already contain explicit hyphen characters (except just after the hyphen), which can create a real problem in languages in which the average word length is much larger than in English. With the above setting this problem can be solved.

Every (LA)TEX font has an associated set of dimensions, which are changed by assignments of the form `\fontdimen`⟨*number*⟩`\font=`⟨*dimen*⟩, where ⟨*number*⟩ is the reference number for the dimension and ⟨*dimen*⟩ is the value to be assigned. The default values are taken from the `.tfm` file when the font is loaded. Each font has at least seven such dimensions:

`\fontdimen1`   Specifies the slant per point of the characters. If the value is zero, the font is upright.

`\fontdimen2`   Specifies the normal width of a space used between words (interword space).

`\fontdimen3`   Specifies the additional stretchability of the interword space—that is, the extra amount of white space that (LA)TEX is allowed to add to the space between words to produce justified lines in a paragraph. In an emergency (LA)TEX may add more space than this allowed value; in that case an "underfull box" will be reported.

`\fontdimen4`   Specifies the allowed shrinkability of the interword space—that is, the amount of space that (LA)TEX is allowed to subtract from the normal interword space (`\fontdimen2`) to produce justified lines in a paragraph. (LA)TEX will never shrink the interword space to less than this minimum.

`\fontdimen5`   Specifies the x-height. It defines the font-oriented dimension 1 ex.

`\fontdimen6`   Specified the quad width. It defines the font-oriented dimension 1 em.

`\fontdimen7`   Specifies the amount intended as extra space to be added after certain end-of-sentence punctuation characters when `\nonfrenchspacing` is in force. The exact rules for when TEX uses this dimension (all or some of the extra space) are somewhat complex; see *The TEXbook* [82] for details. It is always ignored or rather replaced by the value `\xspaceskip`, when that value is nonzero.

When changing the interword spacing associated with a font, you cannot use an absolute value because such a value must be usable for all sizes within one font shape group. You must, therefore, define the value by using some other parameter that depends on the font. You could say, for example,

```
\DeclareFontShape{OT1}{cmr}{m}{n}{...}
   {\fontdimen2\font=.7\fontdimen2\font}
```

This declaration reduces the normal interword space to 70% of its original value. In a similar manner, the stretchability and shrinkability could be changed.

Some fonts used in formulas need more than seven font dimensions—namely, the symbol fonts called "`symbols`" and "`largesymbols`" (see Section 7.10.7). TEX will not typeset a formula if these symbol fonts have fewer than 22 and 13

\fontdimen parameters, respectively. The values of these parameters are used to position the characters in a math formula. An explanation of the meaning of every such \fontdimen parameter is beyond the scope of this book; details can be found in Appendix G of *The TEXbook* [82].

One unfortunate optimization is built into the TEX system: TEX loads every .tfm file only once for a given size. It is, therefore, impossible to define one font shape group (with the \DeclareFontShape command) to load some external font—say, cmtt10—and to use another \DeclareFontShape command to load the same external font, this time changing some of the \fontdimen parameters or some other parameter associated with the font. Trying to do so changes the values for both font shape groups.

Suppose, for example, that you try to define a font shape with tight spacing by making the interword space smaller:

```
\DeclareFontShape{T1}{ptm}{m}{n}{ <-> ptmr8t }{}
\DeclareFontShape{T1}{ptm}{c}{n}{ <-> ptmr8t }
                {\fontdimen2\font=.7\fontdimen2\font}
```

This declaration will not work. The interword spacing for the medium shape will change when the tight shape is loaded to the values specified there, and this result is not what is wanted. The best way to solve this problem is to define a virtual font that contains the same characters as the original font, but differs in the settings of the font dimensions (see [73, 74, 91]). Another possible solution is to load the font at a slightly different size, as in the following declaration:

```
\DeclareFontShape{T1}{ptm}{c}{n}{ <-> [0.9999] ptmr8t }
                {\fontdimen2\font=.7\fontdimen2\font}
```

That strategy makes them different fonts for TEX with separate \fontdimen parameters. Alternatively, in this particular case you can control the interword space by setting \spaceskip, thereby overwriting the font values. See Section 3.1.12 for some discussion of that parameter.

7.10.4 Modifying font families and font shape groups

If you need a nonstandard font shape group declaration for a particular document, just place your private declaration in a package or the preamble of your document. It will then overwrite any existing declaration for the font shape combination. Note, however, that the use of \DeclareFontFamily prevents a later loading of the corresponding .fd file (see Section 7.10.6). Also, your new declaration has no effect on fonts that are already loaded.

Today's LATEX format preloads by default only a small number of fonts. However, by using the configuration file preload.cfg, more or fewer fonts can be loaded when the format is built. None of these preloaded fonts can be manipulated using font family or font shape declarations. Thus, if you want some special settings for the core fonts, you must ensure that none of these fonts is preloaded.

For additional information on ways to customize a LaTeX installation, refer to the document `cfgguide.tex` [110], which is part of the LaTeX distribution.

7.10.5 Declaring new font encoding schemes

Font changes that involve alterations in the encoding scheme require taking certain precautions. For example, in the T1 encoding, most accented letters have their own glyphs, whereas in the traditional TeX text encoding (OT1), accented letters must be generated from accents and letters using the `\accent` primitive. (It is desirable to use glyphs for accented letters rather than employing the `\accent` primitive because, among other things, the former approach allows for correct hyphenation.) If the two approaches have to be mixed, perhaps because a font is available only in one of the encodings, the definition of a command such as `\"` must behave differently depending on the current font encoding.

For this reason, each encoding scheme has to be formally introduced to LaTeX with a `\DeclareFontEncoding` command, which takes three arguments. The first argument is the name of the encoding under which you access it using the `\fontencoding` command. Table 7.27 on page 416 provides a list of standard encoding schemes and their internal NFSS names.

The second argument contains any code (such as definitions) to be executed every time LaTeX switches from one encoding to another using the `\fontencoding` command. The final argument contains code to be used whenever the font is accessed as a mathematical alphabet. Thus, these three arguments can be used to redefine commands that depend on the positions of characters in the encoding. To avoid spurious spaces in the output (coming from extra spaces in the arguments), the space character is ignored within them. In the unlikely event that you need spaces in a definition in one of the arguments, use the `\space` command.

The LaTeX3 project reserves the use of encodings starting with the following letters: T (standard text encodings with 256 characters), TS (symbols that are designed to extend the corresponding T encoding), X (text encodings that do not conform to the strict requirements for T encodings), M (standard math encodings with 256 characters), S (other symbol encodings), A (other special applications), OT (standard text encodings with 128 characters), and OM (standard math encodings with 128 characters). The letter O was chosen to emphasize that the 128-character encodings are old and *obsolete*. Ideally, these encodings will be superseded by standards defined by the TeX user groups so that in the future a change of encoding will be necessary only if one is switching from one language to another.

For your own private encodings, you should choose names starting with L for "local" or E for "experimental". Encodings starting with U are for "Unknown" or "Unclassified" encodings—that is, for fonts that do not fit a common encoding pattern. This naming convention ensures that files using official encodings are portable. New standard encodings will be added to the LaTeX documentation as they emerge. For example, the T2* and T5 encodings have appeared since the first edition of this book was published.

The \DeclareFontEncoding command stores the name of the newly declared encoding in the command \LastDeclaredEncoding. This feature is sometimes useful when you are declaring other related encoding information and is, for example, used in the encoding declaration files for the Cyrillic languages.

Also, as we saw in Section 7.9.3 on font substitution, the default values for the family, series, and shape may need to be different for different encodings. For this purpose, NFSS provides the command \DeclareFontSubstitution, which again takes the encoding as the first argument. The next three arguments are the default values (associated with this encoding) for family, series, and shape for use in the automatic substitution process, as explained in Section 7.9.3. It is important that these arguments form a valid font shape—in other words, that a \DeclareFontShape declaration exists for them. Otherwise, an error message will be issued when NFSS checks its internal tables at \begin{document}.

7.10.6 Internal file organization

Font families can be declared when a format file is generated, declared in the document preamble, or loaded on demand when a font change command in the document requests a combination that has not been used so far. The first option consumes internal memory in every LaTeX run, even if the font is not used. The second and third possibilities take a little more time during document formatting, because the font definitions have to be read during processing time. Nevertheless, it is preferable to use the latter solutions for most font shape groups, because it allows you to typeset a wide variety of documents with a single LaTeX format.

When the format is generated, LaTeX will read a file named fonttext.ltx, which contains the standard set of font family definitions and some other declarations related to text fonts. With some restrictions[1] this set can be altered by providing a configuration file fontdef.cfg; see the documentation cfgguide.tex.

All other font family definitions should be declared in external files loaded on request: either package files or font definition (.fd) files. If you place font family definitions in a package file, you must explicitly load this package after the \documentclass command. But there is a third possibility: whenever NFSS gets a request for a font family foo in an encoding scheme BAR, and it has no knowledge about this combination, it will try to load a file called barfoo.fd (all letters lowercase). If this file exists, it is supposed to contain font shape group definitions for the family foo in the encoding scheme BAR—that is, declarations of the form

```
\DeclareFontFamily{BAR}{foo}{..}
\DeclareFontShape{BAR}{foo}{..}{..}{..}{..}
  ...
\endinput
```

---

[1] Any such customization should not be undertaken lightly as it is unfortunately very easy to produce a LaTeX format that shows subtle or even glaring incompatibilities with other installations.

In this way it becomes possible to declare a huge number of font families for LaTeX without filling valuable internal memory with information that is almost never used.[1]

Each .fd file should contain all font definitions for one font family in one encoding scheme. It should consist of one or more \DeclareFontShape declarations and exactly one \DeclareFontFamily declaration. Other definitions should not appear in the file, except perhaps for a \ProvidesFile declaration or some \typeout statement informing the user about the font loading. As an alternative to the \typeout command, you can use the plain TeX command \wlog, which writes its argument only into the transcript file. Detailed information in the transcript file should be generated by all .fd files that are used in production, because looking at this transcript will help to locate errors by providing information about the files and their versions used in a particular job. If \typeout or \wlog commands are used, it is important to know that spaces and empty lines in a .fd file are ignored. Thus, you have to use the command \space in the argument to \typeout or \wlog to obtain a blank space on the screen and the transcript file.

New encoding schemes cannot be introduced via the .fd mechanism. NFSS will reject any request to switch to an encoding scheme that was not explicitly declared in the LaTeX format (i.e., fonttext.ltx), in a package file, or in the preamble of the document.

7.10.7 Declaring new fonts for use in math

Specifying font sizes

For every text size NFSS maintains three sizes that are used to typeset formulas (see also Section 8.7.1): the size in which to typeset most of the symbols (selected by \textstyle or \displaystyle); the size for first-order subscripts and superscripts (\scriptstyle); and the size for higher-order subscripts and superscripts (\scriptscriptstyle). If you switch to a new text size, for which the corresponding math sizes are not yet known, NFSS tries to calculate them as fractions of the text size. Instead of letting NFSS do the calculation, you might want to specify the correct values yourself via \DeclareMathSizes. This declaration takes four arguments: the outer text sizes and the three math sizes for this text size. For example, the class file for *The LaTeX Companion* contains settings like the following:

```
\DeclareMathSizes{14}{14}{10}{7}      \DeclareMathSizes{36}{}{}{}
```

The first declaration defines the math sizes for the 14 pt heading size to be 14 pt, 10 pt, and 7 pt, respectively. The second declaration (the size for the chapter head-

---

[1]Unfortunately, this feature is not fully available on (LA)TeX installations that use different search paths for the commands \input and \openin. On such systems the .fd feature can be activated at installation time by supplying NFSS with a full path denoting the directories containing all the .fd files. As a result, local .fd files—those stored in the current directory—may not be usable on such systems.

ings) informs NFSS that no math sizes are necessary for 36 pt text size. This avoids
the unnecessary loading of more than 30 additional fonts. For the first edition of
The LATEX Companion such declarations were very important to be able to process
the book with all its examples as a single document (the book loaded 228 fonts out
of a maximum of 255). Today, TEX installations are usually compiled with larger
internal tables (e.g., the laptop implementation used to write this chapter allows
1000 fonts), so conserving space is no longer a major concern. In any event you
should be careful about disabling math sizes, because if some formula is typeset
in such a size after all, it will be typeset in whatever math sizes are still in effect
from an earlier text size.

Adding new symbol fonts

We have already seen how to use math alphabet commands to produce letters
with special shapes in a formula. We now discuss how to add fonts containing
special symbols, called "symbol fonts", and how to make such symbols accessible
in formulas.

   The process of adding new symbol fonts is similar to the declaration of a new
math alphabet identifier: \DeclareSymbolFont defines the defaults for all math
versions, and \SetSymbolFont overrides the defaults for a particular version.

   The math symbol fonts are accessed via a symbolic name, which consists of a
string of letters. If, for example, you want to install the AMS fonts msbm10, shown
in Table 7.29 on the following page, you first have to make the typeface known to
NFSS using the declarations described in the previous sections. These instructions
would look like

```
\DeclareFontFamily{U}{msb}{}
\DeclareFontShape{U}{msb}{m}{n}{ <5> <6> <7> <8> <9> gen * msbm
        <10> <10.95> <12> <14.4> <17.28> <20.74> <24.88> msbm10}{}
```

And are usually placed in an .fd file. You then have to declare that symbol font
for all math versions by issuing the command

```
\DeclareSymbolFont{AMSb}{U}{msb}{m}{n}
```

It makes the font shape group U/msb/m/n available as a symbol font under the
symbolic name AMSb. If there were a bold series in this font family (unfortunately
there is not), you could subsequently change the set-up for the bold math version
by saying

```
\SetSymbolFont{AMSb}{bold}{U}{msb}{b}{n}
```

After taking care of the font declarations, you can make use of this symbol
font in math mode. But how do you tell NFSS that $a\lessdot b$ should produce

	´0	´1	´2	´3	´4	´5	´6	´7	
´00x	≨	≩	≰	≱	⊀	⊁	⋠	⋡	˝0x
´01x	≦̸	≧̸	⋦	⋧	≲	≳	⋨	⋩	
´02x	⋨	⋩	≾	≿	⋬	⋭	⊈	⊉	˝1x
´03x	⊊	⊋	⊈	⊉	≉	≇	╱	╲	
´04x	⊊	⊋	⊈	⊉	⊊	⊋	⊊	⊋	˝2x
´05x	⊊	⊋	⊄	⊅	∦	†	↿	↾	
´06x	↚	↛	↮	↬	⊬	⊮	⊭	⊯	˝3x
´07x	↤	↦	⇍	⇏	⇎	↮	＊	∅	
´10x	∄	A	B	C	D	E	F	G	˝4x
´11x	H	I	J	K	L	M	N	O	
´12x	P	Q	R	S	T	U	V	W	˝5x
´13x	X	Y	Z	⌢	⌢	⌢	⌢		
´14x	⊣	⊐					℧	ð	˝6x
´15x	≊	⊐	⌐	¬	⊏	⊐	⋉	⋊	
´16x	‖	‖	╲	∼	≈	≅	≋	≋	˝7x
´17x	⌢	⌢	F	ϰ	k	ℏ	ℏ	∍	
	˝8	˝9	˝A	˝B	˝C	˝D	˝E	˝F	

Table 7.29: Glyph chart for `msbm10` produced by the `nfssfont.tex` program

$a < b$, for example? To do so, you have to introduce your own symbol names to NFSS, using \DeclareMathSymbol.

\DeclareMathSymbol{*cmd*}{*type*}{*symbol-font*}{*slot*}

The first argument to \DeclareMathSymbol is your chosen command name. The second argument is one of the commands shown in Table 7.30 on the next page and describes the nature of the symbol—whether it is a binary operator, a relation, and so forth. (LA)TEX uses this information to leave the correct amount of space around the symbol when it is encountered in a formula. Incidentally, except for \mathalpha, these commands can be used directly in math formulas as functions with one argument, in which case they space their (possibly complex) argument as if it were of the corresponding type; see Section 8.9 on page 524.

   The third argument identifies the symbol font from which the symbol should be fetched—that is, the symbolic name introduced with the \DeclareSymbolFont command. The fourth argument gives the symbol's position in the font encoding, either as a decimal, octal, or hexadecimal value. Octal (base 8) and hexadecimal

Type	Meaning	Example	Type	Meaning	Example
\mathord	Ordinary	/	\mathopen	Opening	(
\mathop	Large operator	\sum	\mathclose	Closing	)
\mathbin	Binary operation	+	\mathpunct	Punctuation	,
\mathrel	Relation	=	\mathalpha	Alphabet character	A

Table 7.30: Math symbol type classification

(base 16) numbers are preceded by ' and ", respectively. If you look at Table 7.29 on the preceding page, you can easily determine the positions of all glyphs in this font. Such tables can be printed using the LATEX program **nfssfont.tex**, which is part of the LATEX distribution; see Section 7.5.7 on page 369. For example, \lessdot would be declared using

```
\DeclareMathSymbol{\lessdot}{\mathbin}{AMSb}{"6C}
```

Instead of a command name, you can use a single character in the first argument. For example, the eulervm package has several declarations of the form

```
\DeclareMathSymbol{0}{\mathalpha}{letters}{"30}
```

that specify where to fetch the digits from.

Because \DeclareMathSymbol is used to specify a position in some symbol font, it is important that all external fonts associated with this symbol font via the \DeclareSymbolFont and \SetSymbolFont commands have the same character in that position. The simplest way to ensure this uniformity is to use only fonts with the same encoding (unless it is the U, a.k.a. unknown, encoding, as two fonts with this encoding are not required to implement the same characters).

Besides \DeclareMathSymbol, LATEX knows about \DeclareMathAccent, \DeclareMathDelimiter, and \DeclareMathRadical for setting up math font support. Details about these slightly special declarations can be found in [109], which is part of every LATEX distribution.

If you look again at the glyph chart for msbm10 (Table 7.29 on the preceding page), you will notice that this font contains "blackboard bold" letters, such as 𝔸𝔹ℂ. If you want to use these letters as a math alphabet, you can define them using \DeclareMathAlphabet, but given that this symbol font is already loaded to access individual symbols, it is better to use a shortcut:

```
\DeclareSymbolFontAlphabet{\mathbb}{AMSb}
```

That is, you give the name of your math alphabet identifier and the symbolic name of the previously declared symbol font.

An important reason for not unnecessarily loading symbol fonts twice is that there is an upper limit of 16 math fonts that can be active at any given time in (LA)TEX. In calculating this limit, each symbol font counts; math alphabets count only if they are actually used in the document, and they count locally in each math version. Thus, if eight symbol fonts are declared, you can use a maximum of eight (possibly different) math alphabet identifiers within every version.

To summarize: to introduce new symbol fonts, you need to issue a small number of \DeclareSymbolFont and \SetSymbolFont declarations and a potentially large number of \DeclareMathSymbol declarations; hence, adding such fonts is best done in a package file.

Introducing new math versions

We have already mentioned that the standard set-up automatically declares two math versions, normal and bold. To introduce additional versions, you use the declaration \DeclareMathVersion, which takes one argument, the name of the new math version. All symbol fonts and all math alphabets previously declared are automatically available in this math version; the default fonts are assigned to them—that is, the fonts you have specified with \DeclareMathAlphabet or \DeclareSymbolFont.

You can then change the set-up for your new version by issuing appropriate \SetMathAlphabet and \SetSymbolFont commands, as shown in previous sections (pages 352 and 433) for the bold math version. Again, the introduction of a new math version is normally done in a package file.

Changing the symbol font set-up

Besides adding new symbol fonts to access more symbols, the commands we have just seen can be used to change an existing set-up. This capability is of interest if you choose to use special fonts in some or all math versions.

The default settings in LATEX are given here:

```
\DeclareMathVersion{normal}   \DeclareMathVersion{bold}

\DeclareSymbolFont{operators}       {OT1}{cmr}{m} {n}
\DeclareSymbolFont{letters}         {OML}{cmm}{m}{it}
\DeclareSymbolFont{symbols}         {OMS}{cmsy}{m}{n}
\DeclareSymbolFont{largesymbols}    {OMX}{cmex}{m}{n}

% Special bold fonts only for these:
\SetSymbolFont     {operators}{bold}{OT1}{cmr}{bx}{n}
\SetSymbolFont     {letters}  {bold}{OML}{cmm}{b}{it}
```

In the standard set-up, digits and text produced by "log-like operators" such as \log and \max are taken from the symbol font called operators. To change this situation so that these elements agree with the main text font—say, Computer

Modern Sans rather than Computer Modern Roman—you can issue the following commands:

```
\SetSymbolFont{operators}{normal}{OT1}{cmss}{m} {n}
\SetSymbolFont{operators}{bold}  {OT1}{cmss}{bx}{n}
```

Symbol fonts with the names `symbols` and `largesymbols` play a unique rôle in TEX, and for this reason they need a special number of `\fontdimen` parameters associated with them. Thus, only specially prepared fonts can be used for these two symbol fonts. In principle one can add such parameters to any font at load time by using the third parameter of `\DeclareFontFamily` or the sixth parameter of `\DeclareFontShape`. Information on the special parameters for these symbol fonts can be found in Appendix G of [82].

7.10.8   Example: Defining your own `.fd` files

If you want to set up new (PostScript) fonts and create the necessary `.fd` files, you should follow the procedure explained earlier in this section. If fontinst [74] is used to generate the necessary font metric files, then the corresponding `.fd` files are automatically generated as well. However, an `.fd` file for a single font family is also easy to write by hand, once you know which font encoding is used. As an example, let's study the declaration file `t1bch.fd` for Bitstream Charter in the T1 encoding:

```
\ProvidesFile{t1bch.fd}[2001/06/04 font definitions for T1/bch.]
% Primary declarations
\DeclareFontFamily{T1}{bch}{}
\DeclareFontShape{T1}{bch}{m}{n}{<-> bchr8t}{}
\DeclareFontShape{T1}{bch}{m}{sc}{<-> bchrc8t}{}
\DeclareFontShape{T1}{bch}{m}{sl}{<-> bchro8t}{}
\DeclareFontShape{T1}{bch}{m}{it}{<-> bchri8t}{}
\DeclareFontShape{T1}{bch}{b}{n}{<-> bchb8t}{}
\DeclareFontShape{T1}{bch}{b}{sc}{<-> bchbc8t}{}
\DeclareFontShape{T1}{bch}{b}{sl}{<-> bchbo8t}{}
\DeclareFontShape{T1}{bch}{b}{it}{<-> bchbi8t}{}
% Substitutions
\DeclareFontShape{T1}{bch}{bx}{n}{<->ssub * bch/b/n}{}
\DeclareFontShape{T1}{bch}{bx}{sc}{<->ssub * bch/b/sc}{}
\DeclareFontShape{T1}{bch}{bx}{sl}{<->ssub * bch/b/sl}{}
\DeclareFontShape{T1}{bch}{bx}{it}{<->ssub * bch/b/it}{}
\endinput
```

The file starts with an identification line and then declares the font family and encoding (i.e., bch in T1) using `\DeclareFontFamily`—the arguments of this command should correspond to the name of the `.fd` file, except that by convention the encoding is in lowercase there. Then each combination of series and shape is mapped to the name of a .tfm file. These fonts can and will be scaled to any desired size—hence the <-> declarations on the \DeclareFontShape commands. The second part of the file sets up some substitutions for combinations for which no font is available (i.e., replacing the bold extended series with the bold series).

Assuming you have bought the additional Charter fonts (Black and BlackItalic), which are *not* available for free, then you may want to add the related declarations to the .fd file. Of course, one would first need to provide the appropriate virtual fonts (using, for example, fontinst) to emulate the T1 character set; fortunately, for many fonts these can be downloaded from the Internet.[1]

Special license for .fd files   In contrast to most other files in the LATEX world, the usual license for .fd files allows their modification without renaming the files. However, you are normally not allowed to distribute such a modified file!

Another possible reason for producing your own .fd files might be the need to combine fonts from different font families and present them to LATEX as a single new font family. For example, in 1954 Hermann Zapf designed the Aldus font family as a companion to his Palatino typeface (which was originally designed as a display typeface). As Aldus has no bold series, Palatino is a natural choice to use as a bold substitute. In the example below we combine Aldus (with old-style numerals) in its medium series with Palatino bold, calling the resulting "font family" zasj. We present only a fragment of a complete .fd file that enables us to typeset Example 7-10-1 on the facing page.

```
\ProvidesFile{t1zasj.fd}
   [2003/10/12 font definitions for T1 Aldus/Palatino mix.]
\DeclareFontFamily{T1}{zasj}{}
% Medium series
\DeclareFontShape{T1}{zasj}{m}{n} {<->pasr9d}{}
\DeclareFontShape{T1}{zasj}{m}{sc}{<->pasrc9d}{}
\DeclareFontShape{T1}{zasj}{m}{it}{<->pasri9d}{}
\DeclareFontShape{T1}{zasj}{m}{sl}{<->ssub * pasj/m/it}{}
% Bold series
\DeclareFontShape{T1}{zasj}{b}{n}{<-> pplb8t}{}
\DeclareFontShape{T1}{zasj}{b}{sc}{<->pplbc8t}{}
\DeclareFontShape{T1}{zasj}{b}{sl}{<->pplbo8t}{}
\DeclareFontShape{T1}{zasj}{b}{it}{<->pplbi8t}{}
```

To access this "pseudo-family" we have to select zasj in the T1 encoding. We also have to ensure that \textbf switches to bold and not to bold extended, as our .fd file does not provide any substitutions. All that can be automatically provided by writing a tiny package (named fontmix.sty) like this:

```
\ProvidesPackage{fontmix}[2003/10/12 T1 Aldus/Palatino mix.]
\RequirePackage[T1]{fontenc}
\renewcommand\rmdefault{zasj} \renewcommand\bfdefault{b}
```

---

[1] A good resource is Walter Schmidt's home page: http://home.vr-web.de/~was/fonts.html.

Thus, by loading `fontmix`, we get Aldus with Palatino Bold for headlines. In many cases such a mixture does not enhance your text, so do not mistake this example as a suggestion to produce arbitrary combinations.

Zapf's Palatino and Aldus

This text is set in the typeface Aldus with matching *old-style* numerals '123456789'.

As a companion **bold face** Zapf's Palatino is selected.

```
\usepackage{fontmix}
% t1zasj.fd and fontmix.sty as defined above
\section*{Zapf's Palatino and Aldus}
This text is set in the typeface Aldus with
matching \emph{old-style} numerals '123456789'.

As a companion \textbf{bold face} Zapf's
Palatino is selected.
```

7-10-1

7.10.9   The order of declaration

NFSS forces you to give all declarations in a specific order so that it can check whether you have specified all necessary information. If you declare objects in the wrong order, it will complain. Here are the dependencies that you have to obey:

- `\DeclareFontFamily` checks that the encoding scheme was previously declared with `\DeclareFontEncoding`.

- `\DeclareFontShape` checks that the font family was declared to be available in the requested encoding (`\DeclareFontFamily`).

- `\DeclareSymbolFont` checks that the encoding scheme is valid.

- `\SetSymbolFont` additionally ensures that the requested math version was declared (`\DeclareMathVersion`) and that the requested symbol font was declared (`\DeclareSymbolFont`).

- `\DeclareSymbolFontAlphabet` checks that the command name for the alphabet identifier can be used and that the symbol font was declared.

- `\DeclareMathAlphabet` checks that the chosen command name can be used and that the encoding scheme was declared.

- `\SetMathAlphabet` checks that the alphabet identifier was previously declared with `\DeclareMathAlphabet` or `\DeclareSymbolFontAlphabet` and that the math version and the encoding scheme are known.

- `\DeclareMathSymbol` makes sure that the command name can be used (i.e., is undefined or was previously declared to be a math symbol) and that the symbol font was previously declared.

- When the `\begin{document}` command is reached, NFSS makes some additional checks—for example, verifying that substitution defaults for every encoding scheme point to known font shape group declarations.

7.11 LaTeX's encoding models

For most users it will probably be sufficient to know that there exist certain input and output encodings and to have some basic knowledge about how to use them, as described in the previous sections. However, sometimes it is helpful to know the whole story in some detail, so as either to set up a new encoding or to better understand packages or classes that implement special features. So here is everything you always wanted to know about encodings in LaTeX.

We start by describing the general character data flow within the LaTeX system, deriving from that the base requirements for various encodings and the mapping between them. We then have a closer look at the internal representation model for character data within LaTeX, followed by a discussion of the mechanisms used to map incoming data via input encodings into that internal representation.

Finally, we explain how the internal representation is translated, via the output encodings, into the form required for the actual task of typesetting.

7.11.1 Character data within the LaTeX system

Document processing with the LaTeX system starts by interpreting data present in one or more source files. This data, which represents the document content, is stored in these files in the form of octets representing characters. To correctly interpret these octets, LaTeX (or any other program used to process the file, such as an editor) must know the encoding that was used when the file was written. In other words, it must know the mapping between abstract characters and the octets representing them.

With an incorrect mapping, all further processing will be flawed to some extent unless the file contains only characters of a subset common in both encodings.[1]

LaTeX makes one fundamental assumption at this stage: that (nearly) all characters of visible ASCII (decimal 32–126) are represented by the number that they have in the ASCII code table; see Table 7.31 on the next page.

There is both a practical and a TeXnical reason for this assumption. The practical reason is that most 8-bit encodings in use today share a common 7-bit plane. The TeXnical reason is to effectively[2] use TeX, the majority of the visible portion of ASCII needs to be processed as characters of category "letter"—since only char-

---

[1] As most encodings in the Western world share as a common subset a large fraction of the ASCII code (i.e., most of the 7-bit plane), documents consisting mainly of unaccented Latin characters are still understandable if viewed or processed in an encoding different from the one in which they were originally written. However, the more characters outside visible ASCII are used, the less comprehensible the text will become. A text can become completely unintelligible when, for instance, Greek or Russian documents are reprocessed under the assumption that the text is encoded in, say, the encoding for U.S.-Windows.

[2] At least this was true when this interface was being designed. These days, with computers being much faster than before, it would be possible to radically change the input method of TeX by basically disabling it altogether and parsing the input data manually—that is, character by character.

Represented as Characters

Digits:	0 1 2 3 4 5 6 7 8 9
Lowercase letters:	a b c d e f g h i j k l m n o p q r s t u v w x y z
Uppercase letters:	A B C D E F G H I J K L M N O P Q R S T U V W X Y Z
Punctuation:	. , ; : ? ! ' '
Miscellaneous symbols:	* + - = ( ) [ ] / @

Not Represented as Characters

TEX syntax characters:	$ ^ _ { } # & % \ ~
Missing in (some) OT1 fonts	< > | "

Table 7.31: LICR objects represented with single characters

acters with this category can be used in multiple-character command names in TEX—or category "other"—since TEX will not, for example, recognize the decimal digits as being part of a number if they do not have this category code.

When a character—or more exactly an 8-bit number—is declared to be of category "letter" or "other" in TEX, then this 8-bit number will be transparently passed through TEX. This means that in the output TEX will typeset whatever symbol is in the font at the position addressed by that number.

A consequence of the assumption mentioned earlier is that fonts intended to be used for general text require that (most of) the visible ASCII characters are present in the font and are encoded according to the ASCII encoding. The exact list is given in Table 7.31.

All other 8-bit numbers (i.e., those outside visible ASCII) potentially being present in the input file are assigned a category code of "active", which makes them act like commands inside TEX. This allows LATEX to transform them via the input encodings to a form that we call the LATEX internal character representation (LICR).

LATEX internal character representation (LICR)

Unicode's UTF8 encoding is handled similarly: the ASCII characters represent themselves, and the starting octets for multiple-byte representations act as active characters that scan the input for the remaining octets. The result will be turned into an object in the LICR, if it is mapped, or it will generate an error, if the given Unicode character is not mapped.

The most important characteristic of objects in the LICR is that the representation is 7-bit ASCII so that it is invariant to any input encoding change, because all input encodings are supposed to be transparent with respect to visible ASCII. This enables LATEX, for example, to write auxiliary files (e.g., .toc files) using the LICR representation and to read them back in a different context (and possibly different encoding) without any misinterpretations.

The purpose of the output (or font) encoding is then to map the internal character representations to glyph positions in the current font used for typesetting or, in some cases, to initiate more complex actions. For example, it might place an accent (present in one position in the current font) over some glyph (in a different position in the current font) to achieve a printed image of the abstract character represented by the command(s) in the internal character encoding.

Because the LICR encodes all possible characters addressable within LaTeX, it is far larger than the number of characters that can be represented by a single TeX font (which can contain a maximum of 256 glyphs). In some cases a character in the internal encoding can be rendered with a font by combining glyphs, such as accented characters mentioned above. However, when the internal character requires a special shape (e.g., the currency symbol "¤"), there is no way to fake it if that glyph is not present in the font.

Nevertheless, the LaTeX model for character encoding supports automatic mechanisms for fetching glyphs from different fonts so that characters missing in the current font will get typeset—provided a suitable additional font containing them is available, of course.

7.11.2 LaTeX's internal character representation (LICR)

Technically speaking, text characters are represented internally by LaTeX in one of three ways, each of which will be discussed in the following sections.

Representation as characters

A small number of characters are represented by "themselves"; for example, the Latin A is represented as the character "A". Characters represented in this way are shown in Table 7.31 on the previous page. They form a subset of visible ASCII, and inside TeX all of them are given the category code of "letter" or "other". Some characters from the visible ASCII range are not represented in this way, either because they are part of the TeX syntax[1] or because they are not present in all fonts. If one uses, for example, "<" in text, the current font encoding determines whether one gets < (T1) or perhaps a ¡ (OT1) in the printout.[2]

Representation with character sequences

TeX's internal ligature mechanism supports the generation of new characters from a sequence of input characters. While this is actually a property of the font, some such sequences have been explicitly designed to serve as input shortcuts for characters that are otherwise difficult to address with most keyboards. Only a very few characters generated in this way are considered to belong to LaTeX's internal representation. These include the en dash and em dash, which are generated by

---

[1] The LaTeX syntax knows a few more characters, such as *[]. They play a dual rôle, also being used to represent the characters in straight text. sometimes problems arise trying to keep the two meanings apart. For example, a] within an optional argument is only possible when it is hidden by a set of braces; otherwise, LaTeX will think the optional argument has ended.

[2] This describes the situation in text. In math "<" has a well-defined meaning: "generate a less than relation symbol".

the ligatures -- and ---, and the opening and closing double quotes, which are generated by ` ` and ' ' (the latter can usually also be represented by the single character "). While most fonts also implement ! ` and ? ` to generate ¡ and ¿, this feature is not universally available in all fonts. For this reason *all* such characters have an alternative internal representation as a command (e.g., \textendash or \textexclamdown).

Representation as "font-encoding–specific" commands

The other way to represent characters internally in LATEX (and this covers the majority of characters) is with special LATEX commands (or command sequences) that remain unexpanded when written to a file or when placed into a moving argument. These special commands are sometimes referred to as "font-encoding–specific commands" because their meaning depends on the font encoding current when LATEX is ready to typeset them. Such commands are declared using special declarations, as discussed below. They usually require individual definitions for each font encoding. If no definition exists for the current encoding, either a default is used (if available) or an error message is presented to the user.

Technically, when the font encoding is changed at some point in the document, the definitions of the encoding-specific commands do not change immediately, as that would mean changing a large number of commands on the spot. Instead, these commands have been implemented in a such way that they notice, once they are used, if their current definition is no longer suitable for the font encoding in force. In such a case they call upon their counterparts in the current font encoding to do the actual work.

The set of "font-encoding–specific commands" is not fixed, but rather implicitly defined to be the union of all commands defined for individual font encodings. Thus, by adding new font encodings to LATEX, new "font-encoding–specific commands" might emerge.

7.11.3 Input encodings

Once the package inputenc is loaded (with or without options), the two declarations \DeclareInputText and \DeclareInputMath for mapping 8-bit input characters to LICR objects become available. Their usage should be confined to input encoding files (described below), packages, or, if necessary, to the preamble of documents.

These commands take an 8-bit number as their first argument, which can be given as a decimal number (e.g., 239), octal number (e.g., '357), or hexadecimal notation (e.g., "EF). It is advisable to use decimal notation given that the characters ' or " might get special meanings in a language support package, such as shortcuts for accents, thereby preventing octal or hexadecimal notation from working correctly if packages are loaded in the wrong order.

> \DeclareInputText{*number*}{*LICR-object*}

The \DeclareInputText command declares character mappings for use in text. Its second argument contains the encoding-specific command (or command sequence), that is the LICR object, to which the character number should be mapped. For instance,

```
\DeclareInputText{239}{\"\i}
```

maps the number 239 to the encoding-specific representation of ï, which is \"\i. Input characters declared in this way cannot be used inside mathematical formulas.

> \DeclareInputMath{*number*}{*math-object*}

If the number represents a character for use in mathematical formulas, then the declaration \DeclareInputMath must be used. For example, in the input encoding cp437de (German MS-DOS keyboard),

```
\DeclareInputMath{224}{\alpha}
```

associates the number 224 the command \alpha. Note that this declaration would make the key producing this number usable only in math-mode, as \alpha is not allowed elsewhere.

> \DeclareUnicodeCharacter{*hex-number*}{*LICR-object*}

This declaration is available only if the option utf8 is used. It maps Unicode numbers to LICR objects (i.e., characters usable in text). For example,

```
\DeclareUnicodeCharacter{00A3}{\textsterling}
\DeclareUnicodeCharacter{011A}{\v E}
\DeclareUnicodeCharacter{2031}{\textpertenthousand}
```

In theory, there should be only a single unique bidirectional mapping between the two name spaces, so that all such declarations could be already automatically made when the utf8 option is selected. In practice, the situation is a little more complicated. For one, it is not sensible to automatically provide the whole table, because that would require a huge amount of TeX's memory. Additionally, there are many Unicode characters for which no LICR object exists (so far), and conversely many LICR objects have no equivalents in Unicode.[1] The inputenc package solves that problem by loading only those Unicode mappings that correspond

---

[1] This is perhaps a surprising statement, but simply consider that, for example, accent commands like \" combined with some other character form a new LICR object, such as \"d (whether sensible or not). Many such combinations are not available in Unicode.

to the encodings used in a particular document (as far as they are known) and responds to any other request for a Unicode character with a suitable error message. It then becomes your task to either provide the right mapping information or, if necessary, load an additional font encoding.

As mentioned previously, the input encoding declarations can also be used in packages or in the preamble of a document. For this approach to work, it is important to load the inputenc package first, thereby selecting a suitable encoding. Subsequent input encoding declarations will act as a replacement for (or addition to) those being defined by the present input encoding.

There are two internal commands that you might see when using the inputenc package. The \IeC command is used internally by the \DeclareInputText declaration in certain circumstances. It ensures that when the encoding-specific command is written to a file, a space following it is not gobbled up when the file is read back in. This processing is handled automatically, so that a user never has to write this command. We mention it here because it might show up in .toc files or other auxiliary files.

The other command, \@tabacckludge, stands for "tabbing accent kludge". It is (unfortunately) needed because the current version of LATEX inherited an overloading of the commands \=, \`, and \', which normally denote certain accents (i.e., are encoding-specific commands, but have special meanings inside the tabbing environment). For this reason, mappings that involve any of these accents need to be encoded in a special way. If, for example, you want to map 232 to the character è which has the internal representation \`e, you should not write

```
\DeclareInputText{232}{\`e}
```

but rather

```
\DeclareInputText{232}{\@tabacckludge`e}
```

The latter form works everywhere, including inside a tabbing environment.

Mapping to text and/or math

For technical as well as conceptual reasons, TEX makes a very strong distinction between characters usable in text and those usable in math. Except for the visible ASCII characters, commands that produce characters can normally be used in either text or math mode but not in both modes.

Unfortunately, for some keyboard keys it is not clear whether they should be regarded as generating characters for use in math or text. For example, should the key generating the character ± be mapped to \textpm, which is an encoding-specific command and thus can be used only in text, or should it be mapped to \pm and therefore be available only in math?

The early releases of the inputenc package used the following strategy: all keyboard keys available in standard TEX fonts for text (i.e., those encoded in either

OT1 or T1) were mapped to encoding-specific text commands, while the remaining keys got mapped to available math commands. But using a strategy solely driven by the availability of glyphs has the disadvantage that only users with a good knowledge of TeX internals could tell immediately whether using a key labeled, say "¾" or "³" would be allowed only in text or only in math.[1]

What can be done to resolve this situation gracefully? The approach of checking for the current mode, as used in babel's \textormath command,

```
\ifmmode \ddots a\else \"a\fi
```

fails if such a construction is used in a math alignment structure (it selects the wrong part of the conditional and usually ends in an incomprehensible TeX error message). Fixing this problem by starting the above construction with \relax will prevent kerning and ligatures that may otherwise be present in a word. This is, in fact, a problem that is unsolvable in TeX. However, it can be solved if eTeX is used as the base formatter for LaTeX and as nowadays eTeX is available with nearly every TeX system, there are plans to make this program the basis for future maintenance releases of LaTeX.

At the time of this book's writing, work on an extension of inputenc (based on eTeX) was under way. This proposed extension will automatically support all accessible keyboard characters in text and formulas. Once it becomes officially available, you will be able to comfortably typeset your formulas by simply adding the option math when loading the inputenc package.

Input encoding files for 8-bit encodings

Input encodings are stored in files with the extension .def, where the base name is the name of the input encoding (e.g., latin1.def). Such files should contain only the commands described in the current section.

The file should start with a \ProvidesFile declaration describing the nature of the file. For example:

```
\ProvidesFile{latin1.def}[2000/07/01 v0.996 Input encoding file]
```

If there are mappings to encoding-specific commands that might not be available unless additional packages are loaded, one could declare defaults for them using \ProvideTextCommandDefault. For example:

```
\ProvideTextCommandDefault{\textonehalf}{\ensuremath{\frac12}}
\ProvideTextCommandDefault{\textcent}{\TextSymbolUnavailable\textcent}
```

The command \TextSymbolUnavailable, used above, issues a warning indicating that a certain character is not available with the currently used fonts. This can

---

[1] In the first releases of the inputenc package, "¾" was a text glyph but "³" a was math glyph— comprehensible?

be useful as a default—that is, when such characters are available only if special fonts are loaded and no suitable way exists to fake the characters with existing characters (as was possible for a default for \textonehalf above).

The remaining part of the file should consist only of input encoding declarations using \DeclareInputText or \DeclareInputMath. As mentioned earlier, the use of the latter command, though allowed, is discouraged. No other commands should be used inside an input encoding file; in particular, no commands that prevent reading the file several times (e.g., \newcommand), as the encoding files are often loaded several times in a single document!

Input mapping files for UTF8

As mentioned earlier, the mapping from Unicode to LICR objects is not done in a single large mapping file, but rather organized in a way that enables LATEX to load only those mappings that are relevant for the font encodings used in the current document. This is done by attempting to load for each encoding ⟨name⟩ a file ⟨name⟩enc.dfu that, if it exists, contains the mapping information for those Unicode characters provided by that particular encoding. Other than a number of \DeclareUnicodeCharacter declarations, such files should contain only a \ProvidesFile line.

As different font encodings often provide to a certain extent the same characters, it is quite common for declarations for the same Unicode character to be found in different .dfu files. It is, therefore, very important that these declarations in different files be identical (which in theory they should be anyway, but...). Otherwise, the declaration loaded last will survive, which may be a different one from document to document.

So anyone who wants to provide a new .dfu file for some encoding that was previously not covered should carefully check the existing definitions in .dfu files for related encodings. Standard files provided with inputenc are guaranteed to have uniform definition—they are, in fact, all generated from a single list that is suitably split up. A full list of currently existing mappings can be found in the file utf8enc.dfu.

7.11.4   Output encodings

As we learned earlier, output encodings define the mapping from the LICR to the glyphs (or constructs built from glyphs) available in the fonts used for typesetting. These mappings are referenced inside LATEX by two- or three-letter names (e.g., OT1 and T3). We say that a certain font is in a certain encoding if the mapping corresponds to the positions of the glyphs in the font in question. So what are the exact components of such a mapping?

Characters internally represented by ASCII characters are simply passed on to the font. In other words, TEX uses the ASCII code to select a glyph from the current font. For example, the character "A" with ASCII code 65 will result in typesetting

the glyph in position 65 in the current font. This is why LaTeX requires that fonts
for text contain all such ASCII letters in their ASCII code positions, as there is no
way to interact with this basic TeX mechanism (other than to disable it and do
everything "manually"). Thus, for visible ASCII, a one-to-one mapping is implicitly
present in all output encodings.

Characters internally represented as sequences of ASCII characters (e.g., "--"),
are handled as follows: when the current font is first loaded, TeX is informed that
the font contains a number of so-called ligature programs. These define certain
character sequences that are not to be typeset directly but rather to be replaced[1]
by some other glyphs from the font (the exact position of each replacement glyph
is font dependent and not important otherwise). For example, when TeX sees "--"
in the input (i.e., ASCII code 45 twice), a ligature program might direct it to use
the glyph in position 123 instead (which then would hold the glyph "–"). Again,
no interaction with this mechanism is possible. Some such ligatures are present
for purely aesthetic reasons and may or may not be available in certain fonts (e.g.,
ff generating "ff" rather than "ff"). Others are supposed to be implemented for a
certain encoding (e.g., "---" producing an \emdash).

Nevertheless, the bulk of the internal character representation consists of
"font-encoding–specific" commands. They are mapped using the declarations described below. All declarations have the same structure in their first two arguments: the font-encoding–specific command (or the first component of it, if it is a
command sequence), followed by the name of the encoding. Any remaining arguments will depend on the type of declaration.

Thus, an encoding XYZ is defined by a bunch of declarations all having the
name XYZ as their second argument. Of course, to be of any use, some fonts
must be encoded in that encoding. In fact, the development of font encodings is
normally done the other way around—namely, someone starts with an existing
font and then provides appropriate declarations for using it. This collection of
declarations is then given a suitable name, such as OT1. In the next section, we
will take the font ecrm1000, shown in Table 7.32 on the facing page, whose font
encoding is called T1 in LaTeX, and build appropriate declarations to access the
glyphs from a font encoded in this way. The blue characters in this table are those
that have to be present in the same positions in every text encoding, as they are
transparently passed through TeX.

Output encoding files

Like input encoding files, output encoding files are identified by the extension
.def. However, the base name of the file is slightly more structured: the name of
the encoding in lowercase letters, followed by the letters enc (e.g., t1enc.def for
the T1 encoding).

---

[1] The actions carried out by a font ligature program can, in fact, be far more complex, but for the
purpose of our discussion here this simplified view is appropriate. For an in-depth discussion, see
Knuth's paper on virtual fonts [91].

	´0	´1	´2	´3	´4	´5	´6	´7	
´00x	`	´	^	~	¨	˝	°	ˇ	˝0x
´01x	˘	¯	˙	¸	˛	‚	‹	›	
´02x	"	"	„	«	»	–	—		˝1x
´03x	0	1	J	ff	fi	fl	ffi	ffl	
´04x	␣	!	"	#	$	%	&	'	˝2x
´05x	(	)	*	+	,	-	.	/	
´06x	0	1	2	3	4	5	6	7	˝3x
´07x	8	9	:	;	<	=	>	?	
´10x	@	A	B	C	D	E	F	G	˝4x
´11x	H	I	J	K	L	M	N	O	
´12x	P	Q	R	S	T	U	V	W	˝5x
´13x	X	Y	Z	[	\	]	^	_	
´14x	`	a	b	c	d	e	f	g	˝6x
´15x	h	i	j	k	l	m	n	o	
´16x	p	q	r	s	t	u	v	w	˝7x
´17x	x	y	z	{	|	}	~	-	
´20x	Ă	Ą	Ć	Č	Ď	Ě	Ę	Ğ	˝8x
´21x	Ĺ	Ľ	Ł	Ń	Ň	Ŋ	Ő	Ŕ	
´22x	Ř	Ś	Š	Ş	Ť	Ţ	Ű	Ů	˝9x
´23x	Ÿ	Ź	Ž	Ż	IJ	İ	đ	§	
´24x	ă	ą	ć	č	ď	ě	ę	ğ	˝Ax
´25x	ĺ	ľ	ł	ń	ň	ŋ	ő	ŕ	
´26x	ř	ś	š	ş	ť	ţ	ű	ů	˝Bx
´27x	ÿ	ź	ž	ż	ij	¡	¿	£	
´30x	À	Á	Â	Ã	Ä	Å	Æ	Ç	˝Cx
´31x	È	É	Ê	Ë	Ì	Í	Î	Ï	
´32x	Đ	Ñ	Ò	Ó	Ô	Õ	Ö	Œ	˝Dx
´33x	Ø	Ù	Ú	Û	Ü	Ý	Þ	SS	
´34x	à	á	â	ã	ä	å	æ	ç	˝Ex
´35x	è	é	ê	ë	ì	í	î	ï	
´36x	ð	ñ	ò	ó	ô	õ	ö	œ	˝Fx
´37x	ø	ù	ú	û	ü	ý	þ	ß	
	˝8	˝9	˝A	˝B	˝C	˝D	˝E	˝F	

Characters marked in blue need to be present (in the same positions) in every text encoding, as they are transparently passed through TEX.

Table 7.32: Glyph chart for a T1-encoded font (ecrm1000)

Such files should contain only the declarations described in the current section. As output encoding files might be read several times by LaTeX, it is particularly important to adhere to this rule strictly and to refrain from using, for example, \newcommand, which prevents reading such a file multiple times!

For identification purposes an output encoding file should start with a \ProvidesFile declaration describing the nature of the file. For example:

```
\ProvidesFile{t1enc.def}[2001/06/05 v1.94 Standard LaTeX file]
```

To be able to declare any encoding-specific commands for a particular encoding, we first have to make this encoding known to LaTeX. This is achieved via the \DeclareFontEncoding declaration. At this point it is also useful to declare the default substitution rules for the encoding with the help of the command \DeclareFontSubstitution; both declarations are described in detail in Section 7.10.5 starting on page 430.

```
\DeclareFontEncoding{T1}{}{}
\DeclareFontSubstitution{T1}{cmr}{m}{n}
```

Having introduced the T1 encoding in this way to LaTeX, we can now proceed with declaring how font-encoding–specific commands should behave in that encoding.

\DeclareTextSymbol{*LICR-object*}{*encoding*}{*slot*}

Perhaps the simplest form of declaration is the one for text symbols, where the internal representation can be directly mapped to a single glyph in the target font. This is handled by the \DeclareTextSymbol declaration, whose third argument—the font position—can be given as a decimal, hexadecimal, or octal number. For example,

```
\DeclareTextSymbol{\ss}{T1}{255}
\DeclareTextSymbol{\AE}{T1}{'306}  % font position as octal number
\DeclareTextSymbol{\ae}{T1}{"E6}   % ... as hexadecimal number
```

declare that the font-encoding–specific commands \ss, \AE, and \ae should be mapped to the font (decimal) positions 255, 198, and 230, respectively, in a T1-encoded font. As mentioned earlier, it is safest to use decimal notation in such declarations, even though octal or hexadecimal values are often easier to identify in glyph charts like the one on the previous page. Mixing them like we did in the example above is certainly bad style. All in all, there are 49 such declarations for the T1 encoding.

\DeclareTextAccent{*LICR-accent*}{*encoding*}{*slot*}

Often fonts contain diacritical marks as individual glyphs to allow the production of accented characters by combining such a diacritical mark with some other glyph. Such accents (as long as they are to be placed on top of other glyphs) are declared using the `\DeclareTextAccent` command; the third argument *slot* is the position of the diacritical mark in the font. For example,

```
\DeclareTextAccent{\"}{T1}{4}
```

defines the "umlaut" accent. From that point onward, an internal representation such as \"a has the following meaning in the T1 output encoding: typeset "ä" by placing the accent in position 4 over the glyph in position 97 (the ASCII code of the character a). In fact, such a declaration implicitly defines a huge range of internal character presentations—that is, anything of the type \"⟨*base-glyph*⟩, where ⟨*base-glyph*⟩ is something defined via `\DeclareTextSymbol` or any ASCII character belonging to the LICR, such as "a".

Even those combinations that do not make much sense, such as \"\P (i.e., pilcrow sign with umlaut ¶) conceptually become members of the set of font-encoding–specific commands in this way. There are a total of 11 such declarations in the T1 encoding.

`\DeclareTextComposite`
            {*LICR-accent*}{*encoding*}{*simple-LICR-object*}{*slot*}

The glyph chart on page 449 contains a large number of accented characters as individual glyphs—for example, "ä" in position ′240 octal. Thus, in T1 the encoding-specific command \"a should not result in placing an accent over the character "a" but instead should directly access the glyph in that position of the font. This is achieved by the declaration

```
\DeclareTextComposite{\"}{T1}{a}{228}
```

which states that the encoding-specific command \"a results in typesetting the glyph 228, thereby disabling the accent declaration above. For all other encoding-specific commands starting with \", the accent declaration remains in place. For example, \"b will produce a "b̈" by placing an accent over the base character b.

The third argument, *simple-LICR-object*, should be a single letter, such as "a", or a single command, such as \j or \oe. There are 110 such composites declared for the T1 encoding.

`\DeclareTextCompositeCommand`
            {*LICR-object*}{*encoding*}{*simple-LICR-object*}{*code*}

Although not used for the T1 encoding, there also exists a more general variant of `\DeclareTextComposite` that allows arbitrary code in place of a slot position. This is, for example, used in the OT1 encoding to lower the ring accent over the

"A" compared to the way it would be typeset with TeX's \accent primitive. The accents over the "i" are also implemented using this form of declaration:

```
\DeclareTextCompositeCommand{\'}{OT1}{i}{\@tabacckludge'\i}
\DeclareTextCompositeCommand{\^}{OT1}{i}{\^\i}
```

What have we not covered for the T1 encoding? A number of diacritical marks are not placed on top of other characters but are placed somewhere below them. There is no special declaration form for such marks, as the actual placement usually involves low-level TeX code. Instead, the generic \DeclareTextCommand declaration can be used for this purpose.

\DeclareTextCommand{*LICR-object*}{*encoding*}[*num*][*default*]{*code*}

For example, the "underbar" accent \b in the T1 encoding is defined with the following wonderful piece of prose:

```
\DeclareTextCommand{\b}{T1}[1]
    {\hmode@bgroup\o@lign{\relax#1\crcr\hidewidth\sh@ft{29}%
    \vbox to.2ex{\hbox{\char9}\vss}\hidewidth}\egroup}
```

Without going into detail about what the code precisely means, we can see that the \DeclareTextCommand is similar in structure to \newcommand. That is, it has an optional *num* argument denoting the number of arguments (one here), a second optional *default* argument (not present here), and a final mandatory argument containing the code in which it is possible to refer to the argument(s) using #1, #2, and so on. T1 has four such declarations, for \b, \c, \d, and \k.

\DeclareTextCommand can also be used to build font-encoding–specific commands consisting of a single control sequence. In this case it is used without optional argument, thus defining a command with zero arguments. For example, in T1 there is no glyph for a ‰ sign, but there exists a strange little "₀" in position '30, which, if placed directly behind a %, will give the appropriate glyph. Thus, we can write

```
\DeclareTextCommand{\textperthousand}   {T1}{\%\char 24 }
\DeclareTextCommand{\textpertenthousand}{T1}{\%\char 24\char 24 }
```

This discussion has now covered all commands needed to declare the font-encoding–specific commands for a new encoding. As mentioned earlier, only these commands should appear in encoding definition files.

Output encoding defaults

What happens if an encoding-specific command is used for which there is no declaration in the current font encoding? In that case one of two things might happen: either LaTeX has a default definition for the LICR object, in which case this default is used, or the users gets an error message stating that the requested LICR object is unavailable in the current encoding. There are a number of ways to set up defaults for LICR objects.

`\DeclareTextCommandDefault{`*LICR-object*`}[`*num*`][`*default*`]{`*code*`}`

The `\DeclareTextCommandDefault` command provides the default definition for an *LICR-object* that is be used whenever there is no specific setting for the object in the current encoding. Such default definitions can, for example, fake a certain character. For instance, `\textregistered` has a default definition in which the character is built from two others, like this:

```
\DeclareTextCommandDefault{\textregistered}{\textcircled{\scshape r}}
```

Technically, the default definitions are stored as an encoding with the name "?". While you should not rely on this fact, as the implementation might change in the future, it means that you cannot declare an encoding with this name.

`\DeclareTextSymbolDefault{`*LICR-object*`}{`*encoding*`}`

In most cases, a default definition does not require coding but simply directs LaTeX to pick up the character from some encoding in which it is known to exist. The textcomp package, for example, consists of a large number of default declarations that all point to the TS1 encoding. Consider the following declaration:

```
\DeclareTextSymbolDefault{\texteuro}{TS1}
```

The `\DeclareTextSymbolDefault` command can, in fact, be used to define the default for any LICR object without arguments, not just those that have been declared with the `\DeclareTextSymbol` command in other encodings.

`\DeclareTextAccentDefault{`*LICR-accent*`}{`*encoding*`}`

A similar declaration exists for LICR objects that take one argument, such as accents (which gave this declaration its name). This form is again usable for any LICR object with one argument. The LaTeX kernel, for example, contains quite a number of declarations of the type:

```
\DeclareTextAccentDefault{\"}{OT1}
\DeclareTextAccentDefault{\t}{OML}
```

This means that if the `\"` is not defined in the current encoding, then use the one from an OT1-encoded font. Likewise, if you need a tie accent, pick up one from OML[1] if nothing better is available.

---

[1] OML is a math font encoding, but it contains this text accent mark.

`\ProvideTextCommandDefault{`*LICR-object*`}[`*num*`][`*default*`]{`*code*`}`

With the `\ProvideTextCommandDefault` declaration a different kind of default can be "provided". As the name suggests, it does the same job as the declaration `\DeclareTextCommandDefault`, except that the default is provided only if no default has been defined before. This is mainly used in input encoding files to provide some sort of trivial defaults for unusual LICR objects. For example:

```
\ProvideTextCommandDefault{\textonequarter}{\ensuremath{\frac14}}
\ProvideTextCommandDefault{\textcent}{\TextSymbolUnavailable\textcent}
```

Packages like textcomp can then replace such definitions with declarations pointing to real glyphs. Using `\Provide..` instead of `\Declare..` ensures that a better default is not accidentally overwritten if the input encoding file is read.

`\UndeclareTextCommand{`*LICR-object*`}{`*encoding*`}`

In some cases an existing declaration needs to be removed to ensure that a default declaration is used instead. This task can be carried out by the `\UndeclareTextCommand` command. For example, the textcomp package removes the definitions of `\textdollar` and `\textsterling` from the OT1 encoding because not every OT1-encoded font actually has these symbols.[1]

```
\UndeclareTextCommand{\textsterling}{OT1}
\UndeclareTextCommand{\textdollar}  {OT1}
```

Without this removal, the new default declarations to pick up the symbols from TS1 would not be used for fonts encoded with OT1.

`\UseTextSymbol{`*encoding*`}{`*LICR-object*`}`
`\UseTextAccent{`*encoding*`}{`*LICR-object*`}{`*simple-LICR-object*`}`

The action hidden behind the declarations `\DeclareTextSymbolDefault` and `\DeclareTextAccentDefault` is also available for direct use. Assume, for example, that the current encoding is U. In that case,

```
\UseTextSymbol{OT1}{\ss}
\UseTextAccent{OT1}{\'}{a}
```

has the same effect as entering the code below. Note in particular that the "a" is typeset in encoding U—only the accent is taken from the other encoding.

```
{\fontencoding{OT1}\selectfont\ss}
{\fontencoding{OT1}\selectfont\'{\fontencoding{U}\selectfont a}}
```

---

[1] This is one of the deficiencies of the old TeX encodings; besides missing accented glyphs, they are not even identical from one font to another.

A listing of standard LICR objects

Table 7.33 provides a comprehensive overview of the LATEX internal representations available with the three major encodings for Latin-based languages: OT1 (the original TEX text font encoding), T1 (the LATEX standard encoding, also known as Cork encoding), and LY1 (an alternate 8-bit encoding proposed by Y&Y). In addition, it shows all LICR objects declared by TS1 (the LATEX standard text symbol encoding) provided by loading the textcomp package.

The first column of the table shows the LICR object names alphabetically sorted, indicating which LICR objects act like accents. The second column shows a glyph representation of the object.

The third column describes whether the object has a default declaration. If an encoding is listed, it means that by default the glyph is being fetched from a suitable font in that encoding; constr. means that the default is produced from low-level TEX code; if the column is empty it means that no default is defined for this LICR object. In the last case a "Symbol unavailable" error is returned when you use it in an encoding for which it has no explicit definition. If the object is an alias for some other LCIR object, we list the alternative name in this column.

Columns four through seven show whether an object is available in the given encoding. Here ✗ means that the object is natively available (as a glyph) in fonts with that encoding, ○ means that it is available through the default for all encodings, and constr. means that it is generated from several glyphs, accent marks, or other elements. If the default is fetched from TS1, the LICR object is available only if the textcomp package is loaded.

Table 7.33: Standard LICR objects

LICR Object		Glyph	Default from	OT1	T1	LY1	TS1
ABC..XYZ	(Uppercase letters)	ABC..XYZ		✗	✗	✗	
abc..xyz	(Lowercase letters)	abc..xyz		✗	✗	✗	
0123..9	(Digits)	0123..9		✗	✗	✗	✗
.,/	(Punctuation)	.,/		✗	✗	✗	✗
;:?!"''	(Punctuation cont.)	;:?!"''		✗	✗	✗	
*+-=()[|]	(Misc)	*+-=()[|]		✗	✗	✗	
# & %		#&%		✗	✗	✗	
\"	(accent)	¨	OT1	✗	✗	✗	
\"A		Ä		constr.	✗	✗	
\"E		Ë		constr.	✗	✗	
\"I		Ï		constr.	✗	✗	
\"O		Ö		constr.	✗	✗	
\"U		Ü		constr.	✗	✗	
\"Y		Ÿ		constr.	✗	✗	
\"a		ä		constr.	✗	✗	
✗ defined in encoding　　○ defined via default							

LICR Object		Glyph	Default from	OT1	T1	LY1	TS1
\"e		ë		constr.	✘	✘	
\"\i		ï		constr.	✘	✘	
\"i	(alias)	ï	\"\i	constr.	✘	✘	
\"o		ö		constr.	✘	✘	
\"u		ü		constr.	✘	✘	
\"y		ÿ		constr.	✘	✘	
\$	(alias)	$	\textdollar	○	✘	✘	✘
\'	(accent)	´	OT1	✘	✘	✘	
\'A		Á		constr.	✘	✘	
\'C		Ć		constr.	✘	constr.	
\'E		É		constr.	✘	✘	
\'I		Í		constr.	✘	✘	
\'L		Ĺ		constr.	✘	constr.	
\'N		Ń		constr.	✘	constr.	
\'O		Ó		constr.	✘	✘	
\'R		Ŕ		constr.	✘	constr.	
\'S		Ś		constr.	✘	constr.	
\'U		Ú		constr.	✘	✘	
\'Y		Ý		constr.	✘	✘	
\'Z		Ź		constr.	✘	constr.	
\'a		á		constr.	✘	✘	
\'c		ć		constr.	✘	constr.	
\'e		é		constr.	✘	✘	
\'\i		í		constr.	✘	✘	
\'i	(alias)	í	\'\i	constr.	✘	✘	
\'l		ĺ		constr.	✘	constr.	
\'n		ń		constr.	✘	constr.	
\'o		ó		constr.	✘	✘	
\'r		ŕ		constr.	✘	constr.	
\'s		ś		constr.	✘	constr.	
\'u		ú		constr.	✘	✘	
\'y		ý		constr.	✘	✘	
\'z		ź		constr.	✘	constr.	
\.	(accent)	˙	OT1	✘	✘	✘	
\.I		İ		constr.	✘	constr.	
\.Z		Ż		constr.	✘	constr.	
\.\i		i		✘	✘	constr.	
\.i	(alias)	i	\.\i	✘	✘	constr.	
\.z		ż		constr.	✘	constr.	
\=	(accent)	¯	OT1	✘	✘	✘	
✘ defined in encoding ○ defined via default							

LICR Object		Glyph	Default from	OT1	T1	LY1	TS1
\AE		Æ	OT1	✗	✗	✗	
\DH		Đ			✗	✗	
\DJ		Đ			✗		
\H	(accent)	˝	OT1	✗	✗	✗	
\H O		Ő		constr.	✗	constr.	
\H U		Ű		constr.	✗	constr.	
\H o		ő		constr.	✗	constr.	
\H u		ű		constr.	✗	constr.	
\L		Ł	OT1	✗	✗	✗	
\NG		Ŋ			✗		
\OE		Œ	OT1	✗	✗	✗	
\O		Ø	OT1	✗	✗	✗	
\P	(alias)	¶	\textparagraph	○	○	✗	✗
\S	(alias)	§	\textsection	○	✗	✗	✗
\SS		SS	constr.	○	✗	○	
\TH		Þ			✗	✗	
\^	(accent)	ˆ	OT1	✗	✗	✗	
\^A		Â		constr.	✗	✗	
\^E		Ê		constr.	✗	✗	
\^I		Î		constr.	✗	✗	
\^O		Ô		constr.	✗	✗	
\^U		Û		constr.	✗	✗	
\^a		â		constr.	✗	✗	
\^e		ê		constr.	✗	✗	
\^\i		î		constr.	✗	✗	
\^i	(alias)	î	\^\i	constr.	✗	✗	
\^o		ö		constr.	✗	✗	
\^u		û		constr.	✗	✗	
_	(alias)	_	\textunderscore	○	✗	✗	
\`	(accent)	`	OT1	✗	✗	✗	
\`A		À		constr.	✗	✗	
\`E		È		constr.	✗	✗	
\`I		Ì		constr.	✗	✗	
\`O		Ò		constr.	✗	✗	
\`U		Ù		constr.	✗	✗	
\`a		à		constr.	✗	✗	
\`e		è		constr.	✗	✗	
\`\i		ì		constr.	✗	✗	
\`i	(avail)	ì	\`\i	constr.	✗	✗	
\`o		ò		constr.	✗	✗	

✗ defined in encoding   ○ defined via default

LICR Object		Glyph	Default from	OT1	T1	LY1	TS1
\'u		ù		constr.	✗	✗	
\ae		æ	OT1	✗	✗	✗	
\b	(accent)	‗	OT1	✗	✗	✗	
\c	(accent)	˛	OT1	✗	✗	✗	
\c C		Ç		constr.	✗	✗	
\c S		Ş		constr.	✗	constr.	
\c T		Ţ		constr.	✗	constr.	
\c c		ç		constr.	✗	✗	
\c s		ş		constr.	✗	constr.	
\c t		ţ		constr.	✗	constr.	
\capitalacute	(accent)	´	TS1	○	○	○	✗
\capitalcaron	(accent)	ˇ	TS1	○	○	○	✗
\capitaldieresis	(accent)	¨	TS1	○	○	○	✗
\capitalgrave	(accent)	`	TS1	○	○	○	✗
\capitalmacron	(accent)	¯	TS1	○	○	○	✗
\capitalogonek	(accent)	˛	TS1	○	○	○	✗
\capitalring	(accent)	°	TS1	○	○	○	✗
\capitaltilde	(accent)	~	TS1	○	○	○	✗
\copyright	(alias)	©	\textcopyright	○	○	○	✗
\d	(accent)	.	OT1	✗	✗	✗	
\dag	(alias)	†	\textdagger	○	○	✗	✗
\ddag	(alias)	‡	\textdaggerdbl	○	○	✗	✗
\dh		ð			✗	✗	
\dj		đ			✗		
\dots	(alias)	...	\textellipsis	○	○	✗	
\guillemotleft		«	OT1	✗	✗	✗	
\guillemotright		»	OT1	✗	✗	✗	
\guilsinglleft		‹	OT1	✗	✗	✗	
\guilsinglright		›	OT1	✗	✗	✗	
\i		ı	OT1	✗	✗	✗	
\j		ȷ	OT1	✗	✗	✗	
\k	(accent)	˛			✗	✗	
\k A		Ą			✗	constr.	
\k E		Ę			✗	constr.	
\k O		Ǫ			✗		
\k a		ą			✗	constr.	
\k e		ę			✗	constr.	
\k o		ǫ			✗		
\l		ł	OT1	✗	✗	✗	
\ng		ŋ			✗		

✗ defined in encoding   ○ defined via default

LICR Object		Glyph	Default from	OT1	T1	LY1	TS1
\o		ø	OT1	✘	✘	✘	
\oe		œ	OT1	✘	✘	✘	
\pounds	(alias)	£	\textsterling	○	✘	✘	✘
\quotedblbase		„			✘	✘	
\quotesinglbase		‚			✘	✘	
\r	(accent)	°	OT1	✘	✘	✘	
\r A		Å		✘	✘	✘	
\r U		Ů		constr.	✘	constr.	
\r a		å		constr.	✘	✘	
\r u		ů		constr.	✘	constr.	
\ss		ß	OT1	✘	✘	✘	
\t	(accent)	⁀	OML	✘	✘	○	
\textacutedbl		˝	TS1	○	○	○	✘
\textascendercompwordmark	invisible	TS1	○	○	○	✘
\textasciiacute		´	TS1	○	○	○	✘
\textasciibreve		˘	TS1	○	○	○	✘
\textasciicaron		ˇ	TS1	○	○	○	✘
\textasciicircum		^	constr.	○	✘	✘	
\textasciidieresis		¨	TS1	○	○	○	✘
\textasciigrave		`	TS1	○	○	○	✘
\textasciimacron		¯	TS1	○	○	○	✘
\textasciitilde		~	constr.	○	✘	✘	
\textasteriskcentered		∗	OMS/TS1	○	○	○	✘
\textbackslash		\	OMS	○	✘	✘	
\textbaht		฿	TS1	○	○	○	✘
\textbar				OMS	○	✘	✘	
\textbardbl		‖	TS1	○	○	○	✘
\textbigcircle		◯	TS1	○	○	○	✘
\textblank		␢	TS1	○	○	○	✘
\textborn		⋆	TS1	○	○	○	✘
\textbraceleft		{	OMS	○	✘	✘	
\textbraceright		}	OMS	○	✘	✘	
\textbrokenbar		¦	TS1	○	○	✘	✘
\textbullet		•	OMS/TS1	○	○	✘	✘
\textcapitalcompwordmark	invisible	TS1	○	○	○	✘
\textcelsius		℃	TS1	○	○	○	✘
\textcent		¢	TS1	○	○	✘	✘
\textcentoldstyle		¢	TS1	○	○	○	✘
\textcircled	(accent)	◯	OMS/TS1	○	○	○	✘
\textcircledP		Ⓟ	TS1	○	○	○	✘

✘ defined in encoding   ○ defined via default

LICR Object	Glyph	Default from	OT1	T1	LY1	TS1
\textcolonmonetary	₡	TS1	○	○	○	✗
\textcompwordmark	invisible	constr.	○	✗	○	
\textcopyleft	ↄ	TS1	○	○	○	✗
\textcopyright	©	constr./TS1	○	○	○	✗
\textcurrency	¤	TS1	○	○	✗	✗
\textdagger	†	OMS/TS1	○	○	✗	✗
\textdaggerdbl	‡	OMS/TS1	○	○	✗	✗
\textdblhyphenchar	⹀	TS1	○	○	○	✗
\textdblhyphen	=	TS1	○	○	○	✗
\textdegree	°	TS1	○	○	✗	✗
\textdied	✝	TS1	○	○	○	✗
\textdiscount	％	TS1	○	○	○	✗
\textdiv	÷	TS1	○	○	○	✗
\textdivorced	o|o	TS1	○	○	○	✗
\textdollar	$	OT1/TS1	○	✗	✗	✗
\textdollaroldstyle	$	TS1	○	○	○	✗
\textdong	đ	TS1	○	○	○	✗
\textdownarrow	↓	TS1	○	○	○	✗
\texteightoldstyle	8	TS1	○	○	○	✗
\textellipsis	...	constr.	○	○	✗	
\textemdash	—	OT1	✗	✗	✗	
\textendash	–	OT1	✗	✗	✗	
\textestimated	℮	TS1	○	○	○	✗
\texteuro	€	TS1	○	○	○	✗
\textexclamdown	¡	OT1	✗	✗	✗	
\textfiveoldstyle	5	TS1	○	○	○	✗
\textflorin	f	TS1	○	○	✗	✗
\textfouroldstyle	4	TS1	○	○	○	✗
\textfractionsolidus	/	TS1	○	○	○	✗
\textgravedbl	‶	TS1	○	○	○	✗
\textgreater	>	OML	○	✗	✗	
\textguarani	₲	TS1	○	○	○	✗
\textinterrobang	‽	TS1	○	○	○	✗
\textinterrobangdown	⸘	TS1	○	○	○	✗
\textlangle	⟨	TS1	○	○	○	✗
\textlbrackdbl	⟦	TS1	○	○	○	✗
\textleaf	☙	TS1	○	○	○	✗
\textleftarrow	←	TS1	○	○	○	✗
\textless	<	OML	○	✗	✗	
\textlira	₤	TS1	○	○	○	✗

✗ defined in encoding   ○ defined via default

LICR Object	Glyph	Default from	OT1	T1	LY1	TS1
\textlnot	¬	TS1	○	○	○	✗
\textlquill	{	TS1	○	○	○	✗
\textmarried	∞	TS1	○	○	○	✗
\textmho	℧	TS1	○	○	○	✗
\textminus	−	TS1	○	○	○	✗
\textmu	μ	TS1	○	○	✗	✗
\textmusicalnote	♪	TS1	○	○	○	✗
\textnaira	₦	TS1	○	○	○	✗
\textnineoldstyle	9	TS1	○	○	○	✗
\textnumero	№	TS1	○	○	○	✗
\textogonekcentered (accent)	˛			✗		
\textohm	Ω	TS1	○	○	○	✗
\textonehalf	½	TS1	○	○	✗	✗
\textoneoldstyle	1	TS1	○	○	○	✗
\textonequarter	¼	TS1	○	○	✗	✗
\textonesuperior	¹	TS1	○	○	○	✗
\textopenbullet	∘	TS1	○	○	○	✗
\textordfeminine	ª	constr./TS1	○	○	✗	✗
\textordmasculine	º	constr./TS1	○	○	✗	✗
\textparagraph	¶	OMS/TS1	○	○	✗	✗
\textperiodcentered	·	OMS/TS1	○	○	✗	✗
\textpertenthousand	‰₀	TS1	○	✗	○	✗
\textperthousand	‰	TS1	○	○	✗	✗
\textpeso	₱	TS1	○	○	○	✗
\textpilcrow	¶	TS1	○	○	○	✗
\textpm	±	TS1	○	○	○	✗
\textquestiondown	¿	OT1	✗	✗	✗	
\textquotedbl	"			✗	✗	
\textquotedblleft	"	OT1	✗	✗	✗	
\textquotedblright	"	OT1	✗	✗	✗	
\textquoteleft	'	OT1	✗	✗	✗	
\textquoteright	'	OT1	✗	✗	✗	
\textquotesingle	'	TS1	○	○	○	✗
\textquotestraightbase	ˌ	TS1	○	○	○	✗
\textquotestraightdblbase	ˌˌ	TS1	○	○	○	✗
\textrangle	⟩	TS1	○	○	○	✗
\textrbrackdbl	⟧	TS1	○	○	○	✗
\textrecipe	℞	TS1	○	○	○	✗
\textreferencemark	※	TS1	○	○	○	✗
\textregistered	®	constr./TS1	○	○	✗	✗

✗ defined in encoding   ○ defined via default

LICR Object		Glyph	Default from	OT1	T1	LY1	TS1
\textrightarrow		→	TS1	○	○	○	✗
\textrquill		⌠	TS1	○	○	○	✗
\textsection		§	OMS/TS1	○	✗	✗	✗
\textservicemark		℠	TS1	○	○	○	✗
\textsevenoldstyle		7	TS1	○	○	○	✗
\textsixoldstyle		6	TS1	○	○	○	✗
\textsterling		£	OT1/TS1	○	✗	✗	✗
\textsurd		√	TS1	○	○	○	✗
\textthreeoldstyle		3	TS1	○	○	○	✗
\textthreequartersemdash		—	TS1	○	○	○	✗
\textthreequarters		¾	TS1	○	○	✗	✗
\textthreesuperior		³	TS1	○	○	○	✗
\texttildelow		~	TS1	○	○	○	✗
\texttimes		×	TS1	○	○	○	✗
\texttrademark		™	constr./TS1	○	○	✗	✗
\texttwelveudash		—	TS1	○	○	○	✗
\texttwooldstyle		2	TS1	○	○	○	✗
\texttwosuperior		²	TS1	○	○	○	✗
\textunderscore		_	constr.	○	✗	✗	
\textuparrow		↑	TS1	○	○	○	✗
\textvisiblespace		␣	constr.	○	✗	○	
\textwon		₩	TS1	○	○	○	✗
\textyen		¥	TS1	○	○	✗	✗
\textzerooldstyle		0	TS1	○	○	○	✗
\th		þ			✗	✗	
\u	(accent)	˘	OT1	✗	✗	✗	
\u A		Ă		constr.	✗	constr.	
\u G		Ğ		constr.	✗	constr.	
\u a		ă		constr.	✗	constr.	
\u g		ğ		constr.	✗	constr.	
\v	(accent)	ˇ	OT1	✗	✗	✗	
\v C		Č		constr.	✗	constr.	
\v D		Ď		constr.	✗	constr.	
\v E		Ě		constr.	✗	constr.	
\v L		Ľ		constr.	✗	constr.	
\v N		Ň		constr.	✗	constr.	
\v R		Ř		constr.	✗	constr.	
\v S		Š		constr.	✗	✗	
\v T		Ť		constr.	✗	constr.	
\v Z		Ž		constr.	✗	✗	

✗ defined in encoding   ○ defined via default

LICR Object		Glyph	Default from	OT1	T1	LY1	TS1
\v c		č		constr.	✗	constr.	
\v d		ď		constr.	✗	constr.	
\v e		ě		constr.	✗	constr.	
\v l		ľ		constr.	✗	constr.	
\v n		ň		constr.	✗	constr.	
\v r		ř		constr.	✗	constr.	
\v s		š		constr.	✗	✗	
\v t		ť		constr.	✗	constr.	
\v z		ž		constr.	✗	✗	
\{	(alias)	{	\textbraceleft	○	✗	✗	
\}	(alias)	}	\textbraceright	○	✗	✗	
\~	(accent)	˜	OT1	✗	✗	✗	
\~A		Ã		constr.	✗	✗	
\~N		Ñ		constr.	✗	✗	
\~O		Õ		constr.	✗	✗	
\~a		ã		constr.	✗	✗	
\~n		ñ		constr.	✗	✗	
\~o		õ		constr.	✗	✗	

✗ defined in encoding   ○ defined via default

7.12   Compatibility packages for very old documents

The font interface in LaTeX changed from a fixed font structure (LaTeX 2.09 prior 1990) to a flexible system (LaTeX 2ε with NFSS version 2 integrated in 1993). During the years 1990–1993 NFSS version 1 was widely used in Europe. Although the differences between versions 1 and 2 have not been that enormous, they nevertheless make it impossible to run documents from that time successfully through today's LaTeX. For this reason a number of compatibility packages have been developed to help in processing documents written for LaTeX 2.09 with or without NFSS 1.

7.12.1   oldlfont, rawfonts, newlfont—Processing old documents

As we have seen, NFSS—and thus LaTeX 2ε—differs from LaTeX 2.09 in several ways in its treatment of font commands. This difference is most noticeable in math formulas, where commands like \bfseries are not supported. Nevertheless, it is a very simple matter to typeset older documents with NFSS.

Backward compatibility to 1993 and earlier

If you merely want to reprint a document, LaTeX will see the \documentstyle command and automatically switch to compatibility mode, thereby emulating the old font selection mechanism of LaTeX 2.09 as described in the first edition

of the *LaTeX Manual*. Alternatively, you can load the oldlfont package after the
\documentclass command. If you do so, all old font-selecting commands will be
defined, font-changing commands cancel each other, and all of these commands
can be used in mathematical formulas.

Some old documents refer to LaTeX 2.09 internal font commands such as
\twlrm or \nintt. These commands now generate error messages, because they
are no longer defined (not even in compatibility mode). One reason they are not
supported is that they were never available on all installations. To process a document containing such explicit font-changing commands, you have to define them
in the preamble using the commands described in Section 7.9. For example, for
the above commands, it would be sufficient to add the following definitions to the
preamble:

```
\newcommand\twlrm{\fontsize{12pt}{14pt}\normalfont\rmfamily}
\newcommand\nintt{\fontsize{9pt}{11pt}\normalfont\ttfamily}
```

A package exists to assist you in this task: if you load the rawfonts package with
the options only, twlrm, and nintt, it will make the above declarations for you.
If you load it without any option, it will define all LaTeX 2.09 hard-wired font commands for you.

Reusing parts of documents also is very simple: just paste them into the new
document and watch what happens. There is a good chance that LaTeX will happily
process the old document fragment and, if not, it will explicitly inform you about
the places where you have to change your source—for example, where you have
to change occurrences of \it, \sf, and similar commands in formulas to the
corresponding math alphabet identifier commands \mathit, \mathsf, and so on.

Backward
compatibility with
the first release of
NFSS
In the first release of NFSS, the two-letter font-changing commands were redefined to modify individual attributes only. For example, \sf and \it behaved
just like the NFSS2 commands \sffamily and \itshape, respectively. If you reprocess an old document that was written for this convention, load the package
newlfont in your document preamble to reinitiate it.

7.12.2 latexsym—**Providing symbols from LaTeX 2.09 lasy fonts**

Eleven math symbols provided by LaTeX 2.09 are no longer defined in the base
set-up of NFSS:

□ ◇ ⋈ ↝ ◁
℧ ▷ ⊏ ⊐ ⊴
⊵

```
\usepackage{latexsym}     \newcommand\Q[1]{$#1$ \quad}
\Q{\Box} \Q{\Diamond} \Q{\Join} \Q{\leadsto} \Q{\lhd} \Q{\mho}
\Q{\rhd} \Q{\sqsubset} \Q{\sqsupset} \Q{\unlhd} \Q{\unrhd}
```

7-12-1

If you want to use any of these symbols, load the latexsym package in your document. These symbols are also made available if you load the amsfonts or the
amssymb package; see Section 8.9.

CHAPTER **8**

Higher Mathematics

Basic LaTeX offers excellent mathematical typesetting capabilities for straightforward documents. However, when complex displayed equations or more advanced mathematical constructs are heavily used, something more is needed. Although it is possible to define new commands or environments to ease the burden of typing in formulas, this is not the best solution. The American Mathematical Society (AMS) provides a major package, amsmath, which makes the preparation of mathematical documents much less time-consuming and more consistent.[1] It forms the core of a collection of packages known as $\mathcal{A}_{\mathcal{M}}\mathcal{S}$-LaTeX [8] and is the major subject of this chapter. A useful book by George Grätzer [60] also covers these packages in detail.

This chapter describes briefly, and provides examples of, a substantial number of the many features of these packages as well as a few closely related packages; it also gives a few pointers to other relevant packages. In addition, it provides some essential background on mathematical typesetting with TeX. Thus, it covers some of standard LaTeX's features for mathematical typesetting and layout and contains some general hints on how to typeset mathematical formulas, though these are not the main aims of this chapter.

It is also definitely not a comprehensive manual of good practice for typesetting mathematics with LaTeX. Indeed, many of the examples are offered up purely for illustration purposes and, therefore, present neither good design, nor good mathematics, nor necessarily good LaTeX coding.

Advice on how to typeset mathematics according to late 20th-century U.S. practice can be found in Ellen Swanson's *Math into Type* [156]. Many details concerning how to implement this advice using TeX or, equally, standard LaTeX appear in Chapters 16–18 of Donald Knuth's *The TeXbook* [82].

---

[1]This package has its foundations in the macro-level extensions to TeX known as $\mathcal{A}_{\mathcal{M}}\mathcal{S}$-TeX.

To use the majority of the material described in this chapter, you need to load at least the amsmath package in the preamble of your document. If other packages are needed, they are clearly marked in the examples. Detailed installation and usage documentation is included with the individual packages.

8.1   Introduction to $\mathcal{A}_{\mathcal{M}}\mathcal{S}$-LATEX

The $\mathcal{A}_{\mathcal{M}}\mathcal{S}$-LATEX project commenced in 1987 and three years later $\mathcal{A}_{\mathcal{M}}\mathcal{S}$-LATEX version 1.0 was released. This was the original conversion to LATEX of the mathematical capabilities in Michael Spivak's $\mathcal{A}_{\mathcal{M}}\mathcal{S}$-TEX by Frank Mittelbach and Rainer Schöpf, working as consultants to the American Mathematical Society, with assistance from Michael Downes of the AMS technical staff. In 1994, further work was done with David M. Jones. This work was coordinated by Michael Downes and the packages have throughout been supported and much enhanced under his direction and the patronage of the AMS.[1]

Thanks to a great guy!   Michael, would have been the author of this chapter had he not died in spring 2003. Much of the chapter is based on the documentation he prepared for $\mathcal{A}_{\mathcal{M}}\mathcal{S}$-LATEX; thus, what you are reading is a particular and heartfelt tribute by its current authors to the life and work of our dearest friend and colleague with whom we shared many coding adventures in the uncharted backwaters of TEX.

Available package options   A few options are recognized by the amsmath package. Most of these affect only detailed positioning of the "limits" on various types of mathematical operators (Section 8.4.4) or that of equation tags (Section 8.2.4).

The following three options are often supplied as global document options, set on the \documentclass command. They are, however, also recognized when the amsmath package is loaded with the \usepackage command.

reqno   (**default**)   Place equation numbers (tags) on the right.

leqno   Place equation numbers (tags) on the left.[2]

fleqn   Position equations at a fixed indent from the left margin rather than centered in the text column.

Available sub-packages   The $\mathcal{A}_{\mathcal{M}}\mathcal{S}$-LATEX distribution also contains components that can be loaded independently by the \usepackage command. In particular, some features of the amsmath package are also available in these smaller packages:

amsopn   Provides \DeclareMathOperator for defining new operator names such as \Ker and \esssup.

---

[1]Some material in this chapter is reprinted from the documentation distributed with $\mathcal{A}_{\mathcal{M}}\mathcal{S}$-LATEX (with permission from the American Mathematical Society).

[2]When using the $\mathcal{A}_{\mathcal{M}}\mathcal{S}$-LATEX document classes, the default is leqno.

amstext   Provides the `\text` command for typesetting a fragment of text in the correct type size.

The following packages, providing functionality additional to that in amsmath, *Extension packages* must be loaded explicitly; they are listed here for completeness.

amscd   Defines some commands for easing the generation of commutative diagrams by introducing the CD environment (see Section 8.3.4 on page 488). There is no support for diagonal arrows.

amsthm   Provides a method to declare theorem-like structures and offers a `proof` environment. It is discussed in Section 3.3.3 on page 138.

amsxtra   Provides certain odds and ends that are needed for historical compatibility, such as `\fracwithdelims`, `\accentedsymbol`, and commands for placing accents as superscripts.

upref   Makes `\ref` print cross-reference numbers in an upright/Roman font regardless of context.

The principal documentation for these packages is the *User's Guide for the amsmath Package (Version 2.0)* [8].

The current $\mathcal{A}_{\mathcal{M}}$S-LATEX collection includes three document classes: amsart, amsproc, and amsbook, corresponding to LATEX's article, proc, and book, respectively. They are designed to be used in the preparation of manuscripts for submission to the AMS [6], but nothing prohibits their use for other purposes. With these class files the amsmath package is automatically loaded, so that you can start your document simply with `\documentclass{amsart}`. These classes are not covered in this book as they provide an interface similar to that provided by the LATEX standard classes; refer to [6] for details of their use. *The $\mathcal{A}_{\mathcal{M}}$S-LATEX document classes*

Some of the material in this chapter refers to another collection of packages from the American Mathematical Society, namely the AMSfonts distribution. These packages, listed below, set up various fonts and commands for use in mathematical formulas. *The AMSfonts collection*

amsfonts   Defines the `\mathfrak` and `\mathbb` commands and sets up the fonts msam (extra math symbols A), msbm (extra math symbols B and blackboard bold), eufm (Euler Fraktur), extra sizes of cmmib (bold math italic and bold lowercase Greek), and cmbsy (bold math symbols and bold script).

amssymb   Defines the names of the mathematical symbols available with the AMSfonts collection. These commands are discussed in Section 8.9. The package automatically loads the amsfonts package.

eufrak   Sets up the fonts for the Euler Fraktur letters (`\mathfrak`), as discussed in Section 7.7.10. This alphabet is also available from the amsfonts package.

eucal   Makes `\mathcal` use the Euler script instead of the usual Computer Modern script letters, see Section 7.7.10 for details.

All of these packages recognize the `psamsfonts` option, which will set up LaTeX to use the Y&Y/Blue Sky Research version of these fonts in the AMSfonts collection. This will be useful only if you have this version of the fonts installed on your system; they are available on CTAN and are often available as the default in modern distributions of LaTeX. The principal piece of documentation for these packages is the *User's Guide to AMSFonts Version 2.2d* [9].

A few important warnings

Watch out for fragile commands

Many of the commands described in this chapter are fragile and need to be `\protected` in moving arguments (see Appendix B.1 on page 892). Thus, when strange error messages appear, a missing `\protect` is a likely cause.

Do not abbreviate environments

It is never a good idea to use shortcut codes for LaTeX environments. With the `amsmath` display environments described in this chapter, such shortcuts are always disastrous—don't do it! For closely related reasons, you will also find that verbatim material cannot be used within these environments. Here are some examples of declarations for disaster:

```
\newenvironment{mlt}{\begin{multline}}{\end{multline}}
\newcommand\bga{\begin{gather}}  \newcommand\ega{\end{gather}}
```

Both will produce errors of the form "`\begin{...} ended by ...`". However, you can define synonyms and variant forms of these environments as follows:

```
\newenvironment{mlt}{\multline}{\endmultline}
\newenvironment{longgather}{\allowdisplaybreaks\gather}{\endgather}
```

Note that these must have the command form of an existing environment as the last command in the "begin-code", and the corresponding `\end...` command as the first thing in the "end-code". See also Section A.1.3, for more details.

8.2 Display and alignment structures for equations

The `amsmath` package defines several environments for creating displayed mathematics. These cover single- and multiple-line displays with single or multiple alignment points and various options for numbering equations within displays.

Throughout this section the term "equation" will be used in a very particular way: to refer to a *logical* distinct part of a mathematical display that is frequently numbered for reference purposes and is also labeled (commonly by its number in parentheses). Such labels are often called *tags*.

The complete list of all the display environments you will need for mathematical typesetting is given in Table 8.1 on the next page; the majority of these environments are covered in this section, along with examples of their use. Where

equation	equation*	One line, one equation
multline	multline*	One unaligned multiple-line equation, one equation number
gather	gather*	Several equations without alignment
align	align*	Several equations with multiple alignments
flalign	flalign*	Several equations: horizontally spread form of align
split		A simple alignment within a multiple-line equation
gathered		A "mini-page" with unaligned equations
aligned		A "mini-page" with multiple alignments

Table 8.1: Display environments in the amsmath package

appropriate they have starred forms in which there is no numbering or tagging of the equations.

In these examples of alignment environments, other commands from the amsmath package are also used. A detailed understanding of how these work is not necessary at this stage; an interested reader can turn to later sections for more information. The display width is the measure that defines the right and left margins (or extents) of a display; in the examples these extents are indicated by thin blue vertical rules at the right and left margins of the display.

Except where noted, all examples in this chapter are typeset with the mathematical material centered and the equation numbers, or tags, on the right (the default settings for the amsmath package). When the option leqno is specified for the amsmath package or the document class, the equation number tags will be printed at the left side of the equation.

8-2-1

$$(1) \qquad (a+b)^2 = a^2 + 2ab + b^2$$
$$\sin^2 \eta + \cos^2 \eta = 1$$

```
\usepackage[leqno]{amsmath}
\begin{equation} (a+b)^2 = a^2+2ab+b^2 \end{equation}
\[  \sin^2\eta+\cos^2\eta = 1  \]
```

To position the mathematics at a fixed indent from the left margin, rather than centered in the text column, you use the option fleqn. You will then normally need to set the size of the indent in the preamble. It is the value of the rubber length \mathindent, which gets its default value from the indentation of a first-level list—which is probably not the value you want! Observe the differences between the next example and the previous example. In this particular case, use of the reqno option is redundant (as it is the default), but it forces the equation number to the right side regardless of what the document class specifies.

8-2-2

$$(a+b)^2 = a^2 + 2ab + b^2 \qquad\qquad (1)$$
$$\sin^2 \eta + \cos^2 \eta = 1$$

```
\usepackage[fleqn,reqno]{amsmath}
\setlength\mathindent{1pc}
\begin{equation} (a+b)^2 = a^2+2ab+b^2 \end{equation}
\[  \sin^2\eta+\cos^2\eta = 1  \]
```

As later examples will show, as in standard LaTeX, & and \\ are used for column and line separation within displayed alignments. The details of their usage change in the amsmath environments, however (see the next section).

8.2.1   Comparison with standard LaTeX

Some of the multiple-line display environments allow you to align parts of the formula. In contrast to the original LaTeX environments eqnarray and eqnarray*, the structures implemented by the amsmath package use a slightly different and more straightforward method for marking the alignment points. Standard LaTeX's eqnarray* is similar to an array environment with {rcl} as the preamble and, therefore, requires two ampersand characters indicating the two alignment points. In the equivalent amsmath structures there is only a single alignment point (similar to a {rl} preamble), so only a single ampersand character should be used, placed to the left of the symbol (usually a relation) that should be aligned.

The amsmath structures give fixed spacing at the alignment points, whereas the eqnarray environment produces extra space depending on the parameter settings for array. The difference can be seen clearly in the next example, where the same equation is typeset using the equation, align, and eqnarray environments; the spaces in the eqnarray environment come out too wide for conventional standards of mathematical typesetting.

$$x^2 + y^2 = z^2 \tag{1}$$

$$x^2 + y^2 = z^2 \tag{2}$$
$$x^3 + y^3 < z^3 \tag{3}$$

$$x^2 + y^2 \quad = \quad z^2 \tag{4}$$
$$x^3 + y^3 \quad < \quad z^3 \tag{5}$$

```
\usepackage{amsmath}
\begin{equation}
  x^2 + y^2  =   z^2
\end{equation}
\begin{align}
   x^2 + y^2 &=   z^2 \\
   x^3 + y^3 &<   z^3
\end{align}
\begin{eqnarray}
   x^2 + y^2 &=& z^2 \\
   x^3 + y^3 &<& z^3
\end{eqnarray}
```

8-2-3

As in standard LaTeX, lines in an amsmath display are marked with \\ (or the end of the environment). Because line breaking in a mathematical display usually requires a thorough understanding of the structure of the formula, it is commonly considered to be beyond today's software capabilities. However, one of the last bigger projects undertaken by Michael Downes precisely tackled this problem; it resulted in the breqn package (see [42] for details).

Unlike eqnarray, the amsmath environments do not, by default, allow page breaks between lines (see Section 8.2.10).

Space after \\ not ignored   Another difference concerns the use of \\[*dimension*] or * within mathematical display environments. With amsmath, there must be no space between the \\ and the [or the *; otherwise, the optional argument or star will not be recognized. The reason is that brackets and stars are very common in mathematical formulas, so this restriction avoids the annoyance of having a genuine bracket belonging to the formula be mistaken for the start of the optional argument.

Finally, there is one less obvious change that is very unlikely to cause any problems for users: in standard LaTeX the parameter \mathindent is a non-rubber length, whereas in amsmath it becomes a rubber length. The reasons for, and consequences of, this change can are discussed in amsmath.dtx, the documented source of the amsmath package.

8.2.2   A single equation on one line

The equation environment produces a single equation with an automatically generated number or tag placed on the extreme left or right according to the option in use (see Section 8.2.11); equation* does the same but omits a tag.[1]

Note that the presence of the tag does not affect the positioning of the contents. If there is not enough room for it on the one line, the tag will be shifted up or down: to the previous line when equation numbers are on the left, and to the next line when numbers are on the right.

$$n^2 + m^2 = k^2$$

$$(1) \qquad n^p + m^p \neq k^p \qquad p > 2$$

```
\usepackage[leqno]{amsmath}

\begin{equation*}
  n^2 + m^2 = k^2
\end{equation*}
\begin{equation}
  n^p +m^p \neq k^p  \qquad p > 2
\end{equation}
```

8-2-4

8.2.3   A single equation on several lines: no alignment

The multline environment is a variation of the equation environment used only for equations that do not fit on a single line. In this environment \\ must be used to mark the line breaks, as they are not found automatically.

The first line of a multline will be aligned on an indentation from the left margin and the last line on the same indentation from the right margin.[2] The size of this indentation is the value of the length \multlinegap; thus, it can be changed using LaTeX's \setlength and \addtolength commands.

If a multline contains more than two lines, each line other than the first and last is centered individually within the display width (unless the option fleqn is used). It is, however, possible to force a single line to the left or the right by adding either \shoveleft or \shoveright within that line.

---

[1] Standard LaTeX also has equation, but not equation*, as the latter is similar to the standard displayed math environment.

[2] Never use multline for a single-line equation because the effect is unpredictable.

A `multline` environment is a single (logical) equation and thus has only a single tag, the `multline*` having none; thus, none of the individual lines can be changed by the use of `\tag` or `\notag`. The tag, if present, is placed flush right on the last line with the default `reqno` option or flush left on the first line when the `leqno` option is used.

First line of a multline

Centered Middle line

A right Middle

Another centered Middle

Yet another centered Middle

A left Middle

Last line of the multline   (1)

```
\usepackage{amsmath}
\begin{multline}
  \text{First line of a multline}      \\
  \text{Centered Middle line}          \\
  \shoveright{\text{A right Middle}} \\
  \text{Another centered Middle}       \\
  \text{Yet another centered Middle} \\
  \shoveleft{\text{A left Middle}}    \\
  \text{Last line of the multline}
\end{multline}
```

8-2-5

The next example shows the effect of `\multlinegap`. In the first setting, the "dy"s line up and make it appear that a tag is missing from the first line of the equation. When the parameter is set to zero, the space on the left of the second line does not change because of the tag, while the first line is pushed over to the left margin, thus making it clear that this is only one equation.

$$\sum_{t \in \mathbf{T}} \int_a^t \left\{ \int_a^t f(t-x)^2 \, g(y)^2 \, dx \right\} dy$$
$$= \sum_{t \notin \mathbf{T}} \int_t^a \left\{ g(y)^2 \int_t^a f(x)^2 \, dx \right\} dy \quad (2)$$

```
\usepackage{amsmath}
\begin{multline}  \tag{2}
  \sum_{t \in \mathbf{T}} \int_a^t
    \biggl\lbrace \int_a^t f(t - x)^2 \,
        g(y)^2 \,dx \biggr\rbrace \,dy \\
  = \sum_{t \notin \mathbf{T}} \int_t^a
    \biggl\lbrace g(y)^2 \int_t^a
        f(x)^2 \,dx \biggr\rbrace \,dy
\end{multline}
```

8-2-6

$$\sum_{t \in \mathbf{T}} \int_a^t \left\{ \int_a^t f(t-x)^2 \, g(y)^2 \, dx \right\} dy$$
$$= \sum_{t \notin \mathbf{T}} \int_t^a \left\{ g(y)^2 \int_t^a f(x)^2 \, dx \right\} dy \quad (2)$$

```
\setlength\multlinegap{0pt}
\begin{multline}  \tag{2}
  \sum_{t \in \mathbf{T}} \int_a^t
    \biggl\lbrace \int_a^t f(t - x)^2 \,
        g(y)^2 \,dx \biggr\rbrace \,dy \\
  = \sum_{t \notin \mathbf{T}} \int_t^a
    \biggl\lbrace g(y)^2 \int_t^a
        f(x)^2 \,dx \biggr\rbrace \,dy
\end{multline}
```

8.2.4   A single equation on several lines: with alignment

When a simple alignment is needed within a single multiple-line equation, the `split` environment is almost always the best choice. It uses a single ampersand (&) on each line to mark the alignment point.

8-2-7

$$(a+b)^4 = (a+b)^2(a+b)^2$$
$$= (a^2 + 2ab + b^2)(a^2 + 2ab + b^2) \quad (1)$$
$$= a^4 + 4a^3b + 6a^2b^2 + 4ab^3 + b^4$$

```
\usepackage{amsmath}
\begin{equation}
  \begin{split}
  (a + b)^4
    &= (a + b)^2 (a + b)^2         \\
    &= (a^2 + 2ab + b^2)
      (a^2 + 2ab + b^2)            \\
    &= a^4 + 4a^3b + 6a^2b^2 + 4ab^3 + b^4
  \end{split}
\end{equation}
```

Because it is always used as the content of a single (logical) equation, a `split` does not itself produce any numbering tag and hence there is no starred variant. If needed, the outer display environment will provide any needed tags.

Apart from commands such as `\label` or `\notag` that produce no visible material, a `split` structure should normally constitute the entire body of the equation being split. It can consist of either a whole `equation` or `equation*` environment or one whole line of a `gather` or `gather*` environment; see Section 8.2.5.

When the `centertags` option is in effect (the default), the tag (and any other material in the equation outside the `split`) is centered vertically on the total height of the material from the `split` environment. When the `tbtags` option is specified, the tag is aligned with the last line of the split when the tag is on the right, and with the first line of the split when the tag is on the left.

8-2-8

$$(a+b)^3 = (a+b)(a+b)^2$$
$$= (a+b)(a^2 + 2ab + b^2)$$
$$= a^3 + 3a^2b + 3ab^2 + b^3 \quad (1)$$

```
\usepackage[tbtags]{amsmath}
\begin{equation}
  \begin{split}
  (a + b)^3 &= (a + b) (a + b)^2         \\
    &= (a + b)(a^2 + 2ab + b^2) \\
    &= a^3 + 3a^2b + 3ab^2 + b^3
  \end{split}
\end{equation}
```

In the next example the command `\phantom` is used to adjust the horizontal positioning. It is first used in the preamble to define an "invisible relation symbol" of width equal to that of its argument (in this case, $=$). Within the example it is used to align certain lines by starting them with a "phantom, or invisible, sub-formula" (see Section 8.7.2 on page 503). The empty pair of braces {} is equivalent to \mathord{} and provides an invisible zero-width "letter" that is needed to achieve the correct spacing of $+\,h$ (without the {} it would look like this: $+h$).

```
\usepackage{amsmath}
\newcommand\relphantom[1]{\mathrel{\phantom{#1}}}
\newcommand\ve{\varepsilon}   \newcommand\tve{t_{\varepsilon}}
\newcommand\vf{\varphi}       \newcommand\yvf{y_{\varphi}}
\newcommand\bfE{\mathbf{E}}
\begin{equation} \begin{split}
  f_{h, \ve}(x, y)
    &= \ve \bfE_{x, y} \int_0^{\tve} L_{x, \yvf(\ve u)} \vf(x) \,du  \\
    &= h \int L_{x, z} \vf(x) \rho_x(dz)                            \\
    &\relphantom{=} {} + h \biggl[
       \frac{1}{\tve}
       \biggl( \bfE_{y} \int_0^{\tve}  L_{x, y^x(s)} \vf(x) \,ds
              - \tve \int L_{x, z} \vf(x) \rho_x(dz)        \biggr) + \\
    &\relphantom{=} \phantom{{} + h \biggl[ }
       \frac{1}{\tve}
       \biggl( \bfE_{y} \int_0^{\tve}  L_{x, y^x(s)} \vf(x) \,ds
              - \bfE_{x, y} \int_0^{\tve} L_{x, \yvf(\ve s)}
                                        \vf(x) \,ds     \biggr) \biggr]
\end{split} \end{equation}
```

Note that the equation number tag has been moved to the line below the displayed material. Although this does not seem to be a very wise decision, it is as far as the automated expertise built into the system at this stage can take us.

$$
\left|
\begin{aligned}
f_{h,\varepsilon}(x,y) &= \varepsilon \mathbf{E}_{x,y} \int_0^{t_\varepsilon} L_{x,y_\varphi(\varepsilon u)}\varphi(x)\,du \\
&= h \int L_{x,z}\varphi(x)\rho_x(dz) \\
&\quad + h\left[\frac{1}{t_\varepsilon}\left(\mathbf{E}_y \int_0^{t_\varepsilon} L_{x,y^x(s)}\varphi(x)\,ds - t_\varepsilon \int L_{x,z}\varphi(x)\rho_x(dz)\right) + \right. \\
&\qquad \left. \frac{1}{t_\varepsilon}\left(\mathbf{E}_y \int_0^{t_\varepsilon} L_{x,y^x(s)}\varphi(x)\,ds - \mathbf{E}_{x,y} \int_0^{t_\varepsilon} L_{x,y_\varphi(\varepsilon s)}\varphi(x)\,ds\right)\right]
\end{aligned}
\right|
$$

       8-2-9

$$\tag{1}$$

8.2.5   Equation groups without alignment

The gather environment is used to put two or more equations into a single display without alignment between the equations. Each equation is separately centered within the display width and has its individual number tag, if needed. Each line of a gather is a single (logical) equation.

8-2-10

$$(a+b)^2 = a^2 + 2ab + b^2 \tag{1}$$
$$(a+b) \cdot (a-b) = a^2 - b^2 \tag{2}$$

```
\usepackage{amsmath}

\begin{gather}
   (a + b)^2 = a^2 + 2ab + b^2        \\
   (a + b) \cdot (a - b) = a^2 - b^2
\end{gather}
```

Use \notag within the logical line to suppress the equation number for that line; or use gather* to suppress all equation numbers.

8-2-11

$$D(a,r) \equiv \{z \in \mathbf{C} \colon |z - a| < r\}$$
$$\operatorname{seg}(a,r) \equiv \{z \in \mathbf{C} \colon \Im z < \Im a, |z - a| < r\} \tag{1}$$
$$C(E,\theta,r) \equiv \bigcup_{e \in E} c(e,\theta,r) \tag{2}$$

```
\usepackage{amsmath}

\begin{gather}
  D(a,r) \equiv \{ z \in \mathbf{C}
        \colon |z - a| < r \}      \notag \\
  \operatorname{seg} (a, r) \equiv
        \{ z \in \mathbf{C} \colon
           \Im z < \Im a, \ |z - a| < r \}      \\
  C (E, \theta, r) \equiv
        \bigcup_{e \in E} c (e, \theta, r)
\end{gather}
```

8.2.6   Equation groups with simple alignment

The align environment should be used for two or more equations in a single display with vertical alignment. The simplest form uses a single ampersand (&) on each line to mark the alignment point (usually just before a Relation symbol).

8-2-12

$$(a+b)^3 = (a+b)(a+b)^2 \tag{1}$$
$$= (a+b)(a^2 + 2ab + b^2) \tag{2}$$
$$= a^3 + 3a^2b + 3ab^2 + b^3 \tag{3}$$

$$x^2 + y^2 = 1 \tag{4}$$
$$x = \sqrt{1 - y^2} \tag{5}$$

```
\usepackage{amsmath}

\begin{align}
   (a + b)^3  &= (a + b) (a + b)^2        \\
              &= (a + b)(a^2 + 2ab + b^2) \\
              &= a^3 + 3a^2b + 3ab^2 + b^3
\end{align}
\begin{align}
   x^2  + y^2 & = 1                    \\
   x          & = \sqrt{1-y^2}
\end{align}
```

8.2.7   Multiple alignments: align and flalign

An align environment can include more than one alignment point. The layout contains as many column-pairs as necessary and is similar to an array with preamble of the form {rlrl...}. If it consists of n such rl column-pairs, then the number of ampersands per line will be $2n - 1$: one ampersand for alignment within each column-pair giving n; and $n - 1$ ampersands to separate the column-pairs.

Within the `align` environment, the material is spread out evenly across the display width. All extra (or white) space within the line is distributed equally "between consecutive `rl` column-pairs" and the two display margins.

This example has two column-pairs.

$$\text{Compare } x^2 + y^2 = 1 \qquad x^3 + y^3 = 1 \qquad (1)$$
$$x = \sqrt{1 - y^2} \qquad x = \sqrt[3]{1 - y^3} \qquad (2)$$

This example has three column-pairs.

$$x = y \qquad X = Y \qquad a = b + c \qquad (3)$$
$$x' = y' \qquad X' = Y' \qquad a' = b \qquad (4)$$
$$x + x' = y + y' \quad X + X' = Y + Y' \quad a'b = c'b \qquad (5)$$

```
\usepackage{amsmath}

This example has two column-pairs.
\begin{align}    \text{Compare }
   x^2 + y^2 &= 1                     &
   x^3 + y^3 &= 1                     \\
   x         &= \sqrt   {1-y^2} &
   x         &= \sqrt[3]{1-y^3}
\end{align}
This example has three column-pairs.
\begin{align}
   x     &= y      & X   &= Y   &
     a   &= b+c                 \\
   x'    &= y'     & X'  &= Y'  &
     a'  &= b                   \\
   x + x' &= y + y'             &
   X + X' &= Y + Y' & a'b &= c'b
\end{align}
```

8-2-13

In the variant `flalign` the layout is similar except that there is no space at the margins. As a result, in the next example, Equation (3) now fits on a single line (while in Equation (2) this was still not possible).

This example has two column-pairs.

$$\text{Compare } x^2 + y^2 = 1 \qquad x^3 + y^3 = 1 \qquad (1)$$
$$x = \sqrt{1 - y^2} \qquad x = \sqrt[3]{1 - y^3} \qquad (2)$$

This example has three column-pairs.

$$x = y \qquad X = Y \qquad a = b + c \quad (3)$$
$$x' = y' \qquad X' = Y' \qquad a' = b \quad (4)$$
$$x + x' = y + y' \quad X + X' = Y + Y' \quad a'b = c'b \quad (5)$$

```
\usepackage{amsmath}

This example has two column-pairs.
\begin{flalign}  \text{Compare }
   x^2 + y^2 &= 1                     &
   x^3 + y^3 &= 1                     \\
   x         &= \sqrt   {1-y^2} &
   x         &= \sqrt[3]{1-y^3}
\end{flalign}
This example has three column-pairs.
\begin{flalign}
   x     &= y      & X   &= Y   &
     a   &= b+c                 \\
   x'    &= y'     & X'  &= Y'  &
     a'  &= b                   \\
   x + x' &= y + y'             &
   X + X' &= Y + Y' & a'b &= c'b
\end{flalign}
```

8-2-14

In both cases the minimum space between column-pairs can be set by changing \minalignsep. Its default value is 10pt but, misleadingly, it is *not* a length parameter. Thus, it must be changed by using \renewcommand. If we set it to zero for the first part of the example, Equation (2) gets squeezed onto a single line; if we set it to 15 pt later, the label (3) gets forced onto a line by itself.

Unfortunately, there is no such simple parametric method for controlling the spacing at the margins.

```
\usepackage{amsmath}
```

This example has two column-pairs.

Compare $x^2 + y^2 = 1$ $\qquad$ $x^3 + y^3 = 1$ $\qquad\qquad$ (1)

$$x = \sqrt{1 - y^2} \qquad x = \sqrt[3]{1 - y^3} \quad (2)$$

This example has three column-pairs.

8-2-15

$$x = y \qquad\qquad X = Y \qquad\qquad a = b + c$$
$$\qquad\qquad\qquad\qquad\qquad\qquad\qquad\qquad (3)$$
$$x' = y' \qquad\qquad X' = Y' \qquad\qquad a' = b \quad (4)$$
$$x + x' = y + y' \quad X + X' = Y + Y' \quad a'b = c'b \ (5)$$

```
\usepackage{amsmath}
This example has two column-pairs.
\renewcommand\minalignsep{0pt}
\begin{align}      \text{Compare }
  x^2 + y^2 &= 1                    &
  x^3 + y^3 &= 1                    \\
  x         &= \sqrt  {1-y^2} &
  x         &= \sqrt[3]{1-y^3}
\end{align}
This example has three column-pairs.
\renewcommand\minalignsep{15pt}
\begin{flalign}
  x   &= y     & X  &= Y  &
  a   &= b+c                   \\
  x'  &= y'    & X' &= Y' &
  a'  &= b                     \\
  x + x' &= y + y'             &
  X + X' &= Y + Y' & a'b &= c'b
\end{flalign}
```

The next example illustrates a very common use for align. Note the use of \text to produce normal text within the mathematical material.

8-2-16

$$x = y \qquad\qquad \text{by hypothesis} \quad (1)$$
$$x' = y' \qquad\qquad \text{by definition} \quad (2)$$
$$x + x' = y + y' \quad \text{by Axiom 1} \quad (3)$$

```
\usepackage{amsmath}
\renewcommand\minalignsep{2em}
\begin{align}
  x        &= y       && \text{by hypothesis} \\
  x'       &= y'      && \text{by definition} \\
  x + x'   &= y + y'  && \text{by Axiom 1}
\end{align}
```

8.2.8   Display environments as mini-pages

All the environments described so far produce material set to the full display width. A few of these environments have also been adapted to provide self-contained alignment structures, as if they were set as the only content of a minipage environment whose size, in both directions, is determined by its contents. The environment names are changed only slightly: to aligned and gathered. Note that an aligned environment avoids unnecessary space on the left and right; thus, it mostly resembles the flalign environment.

Like `minipage`, these environments take an optional argument that specifies the vertical positioning with respect to the material on either side. The default alignment of the box is centered (`[c]`). Of course, like `split` they are used only within equations and they never produce tags.

$$x^2 + y^2 = 1$$
$$x = \sqrt{1 - y^2}$$
$$\text{and also } y = \sqrt{1 - x^2}$$

$$(a + b)^2 = a^2 + 2ab + b^2$$
$$(a + b) \cdot (a - b) = a^2 - b^2 \qquad (1)$$

```
\usepackage{amsmath}

\begin{equation}
\begin{aligned}
  x^2 + y^2  &= 1                      \\
  x          &= \sqrt{1-y^2}     \\
  \text{and also }y &= \sqrt{1-x^2}
\end{aligned}                    \qquad
\begin{gathered}
  (a + b)^2 = a^2 + 2ab + b^2     \\
  (a + b) \cdot (a - b) = a^2 - b^2
\end{gathered}          \end{equation}
```

8-2-17

The same mathematics can also be typeset, albeit not very beautifully, using different vertical alignments for the environments.

$$x^2 + y^2 = 1$$
$$x = \sqrt{1 - y^2}$$
$$\text{and also } y = \sqrt{1 - x^2}$$

$$(a + b)^2 = a^2 + 2ab + b^2 \qquad (1)$$
$$(a + b) \cdot (a - b) = a^2 - b^2$$

```
\usepackage{amsmath}

\begin{equation}
\begin{aligned}[b]
  x^2 + y^2  &= 1                      \\
  x          &= \sqrt{1-y^2}     \\
  \text{and also }y &= \sqrt{1-x^2}
\end{aligned}                    \qquad
\begin{gathered}[t]
  (a + b)^2 = a^2 + 2ab + b^2     \\
  (a + b) \cdot (a - b) = a^2 - b^2
\end{gathered}
\end{equation}
```

8-2-18

They may be used in many ways—for example, to do some creative and useful grouping of famous equations. Incidentally, these mini-page display environments are among the very few from `amsmath` that are robust enough to be used inside other definitions, as in the following example.

$$\left.\begin{aligned} B' &= -\partial \times E \\ E' &= \partial \times B - 4\pi j \end{aligned}\right\} \quad \text{Maxwell's equations}$$

```
\usepackage{amsmath}
\newenvironment{rcase}
    {\left.\begin{aligned}}
    {\end{aligned}\right\rbrace}

\begin{equation*}
  \begin{rcase}
    B' &= -\partial\times E        \\
    E' &=  \partial\times B - 4\pi j \,,
  \end{rcase}
  \quad \text {Maxwell's equations}
\end{equation*}
```

8-2-19

You can also use the \minalignsep command to control the space between pairs of columns in an aligned environment, as shown in the next example.

8-2-20

$$
\left|\begin{array}{lll}
V_j = v_j & X_i = x_i - q_i x_j & = u_j + \sum_{i \ne j} q_i \\
V_i = v_i - q_i v_j & X_j = x_j & U_i = u_i
\end{array}\right| \quad (1)
$$

```
\usepackage{amsmath}

\renewcommand\minalignsep{5pt}
\begin{equation} \begin{aligned}
  V_j &= v_j                        &
  X_i &= x_i - q_i x_j              &
      &= u_j + \sum_{i\ne j} q_i \\
  V_i &= v_i                q_i v_j &
  X_j &= x_j                        &
  U_i &= u_i
\end{aligned} \end{equation}
```

8.2.9 Interrupting displays: \intertext

The \intertext command is used for a short passage of text (typically at most a few lines) that appears between the lines of a display alignment. Its importance stems from the fact that all the alignment properties are unaffected by the text, which itself is typeset as a normal paragraph set to the display width; this alignment would not be possible if you simply ended the display and then started a new display after the text. This command may appear only immediately after a \\ or * command.

Here the words "and finally" are outside the alignment, at the left margin, but all three equations are aligned.

8-2-21

$$
\begin{aligned}
A_1 &= N_0(\lambda; \Omega') - \phi(\lambda; \Omega') && (1) \\
A_2 &= \phi(\lambda; \Omega')\phi(\lambda; \Omega) && (2)
\end{aligned}
$$

and finally

$$
A_3 = \mathcal{N}(\lambda; \omega) \qquad (3)
$$

```
\usepackage{amsmath}
\begin{align}
  A_1 &= N_0 (\lambda ; \Omega')
      - \phi ( \lambda ; \Omega')   \\
  A_2 &= \phi (\lambda ; \Omega')
      \phi (\lambda ; \Omega)   \\
\intertext{and finally}
  A_3 &= \mathcal{N} (\lambda ; \omega)
\end{align}
```

8.2.10 Vertical space and page breaks in and around displays

As is usual in LaTeX, the optional argument \\[*dimension*] gives extra vertical space between two lines in all amsmath display environments (there must be no space between the \\ and the [character delimiting the optional argument). The vertical spaces before and after each display environment are controlled by the following rubber lengths, where the values in parentheses are those for \normalsize with the (default) 10pt option in the standard LaTeX classes:[1]

Space within the display…

…and around the display

\abovedisplayskip, \belowdisplayskip   The normal vertical space added above and below a mathematical display (default 10pt plus 2pt minus 5pt).

---

[1] These defaults are very much improved by the $\mathcal{A}_{\mathcal{M}}S$-LaTeX document classes.

`\abovedisplayshortskip, \belowdisplayshortskip`   The (usually smaller) vertical space added above and below a "short display" (`0pt plus 3pt` and `6pt plus 3pt minus 3pt`, respectively). A *short display* is one that starts to the right of where the preceding text line ends.

If you look closely, you can observe the results of these space parameters in the following example. The second equation is surrounded by less space because the text in front of it does not overlap with the formula.

We now have the following:

$$X = a \qquad a = c$$

and thus we have

$$X = c \tag{1}$$

And now we don't get much space around the display!

```
\usepackage{amsmath}
We now have the following:
\[  X = a \qquad  a = c \]
and thus we have
\begin{equation}  X = c \end{equation}
And now we don't get much space
around the display!
```

8-2-22

Since the four parameters `\abovedisplay..` and `\belowdisplay..` depend on the current font size, they cannot be modified in the preamble of the document using `\setlength`. Instead, they must be changed by modifying `\normalsize`, `\small`, and similar commands—a job usually done in a document class.

Page breaks around the display...   Automatic page breaking before and after each display environment is controlled by the penalty parameters `\predisplaypenalty` (for breaking before a display; default 10000, i.e., no break allowed) and `\postdisplaypenalty` (for breaking after a display, default 0; i.e., breaks allowed). The defaults are already set in standard LATEX and are not changed by amsmath.

...and within the display   Unlike standard LATEX, the amsmath display environments do not, by default, allow page breaks between lines of the display. The reason for this behavior is that correct page breaks in such locations depend heavily on the structure of the display, so they often require individual attention from the author.

With amsmath such individual control of page breaks is best achieved via the `\displaybreak` command, but it should be used only when absolutely necessary to allow a page break within a display. The command must go before the `\\` at which a break may be taken, and it applies only to that line and can be used only within an environment that produces a complete display. Somewhat like standard LATEX's `\pagebreak` (see Section 6.2.2 in [104]), `\displaybreak` takes an optional integer as its argument, with a value ranging from zero to four, denoting the desirability of the page break (there must be no space before the []): `\displaybreak[0]` means "it is permissible to break here" without encouraging a break; `\displaybreak` with no optional argument is the same as `\displaybreak[4]` and forces a break. This command cannot be used to discourage or prevent page breaks. Note that it makes no sense to break within a "minipage display", as those environments will never be split over two pages.

This kind of adjustment is fine-tuning, like the insertion of line breaks and page breaks in text. It should therefore be left until your document is nearly finalized. Otherwise, you may end up redoing the fine-tuning several times to keep up with changing document content.

The command `\allowdisplaybreaks`, which obeys the usual LaTeX scoping rules, is equivalent to putting `\displaybreak` before every line end in any display environment within its scope; it takes the same optional argument as `\displaybreak`. Within the scope of an `\allowdisplaybreaks` command, the `\\*` command can be used to prohibit a page break.

The effect of a `\displaybreak` command overrides both the default and the effect of an `\allowdisplaybreaks`.

Many authors wisely use empty lines between major structures in the document source to make it more readable. In most cases, such as before and after a heading, these empty lines do no harm. This is not universally true, however. Especially around and within mathematical display environments, one has to be quite careful: a blank line in front of such an environment will produce unexpected formatting because the empty line is in effect converted into a paragraph containing no text (and so containing just the invisible paragraph indentation box). The following display is consequently surrounded by spaces of size `\..displayshortskip`. Thus, the combined result is quite a lot of (possibly too much) space before the display (a whole empty line plus the `\abovedisplayshortskip`) and a very small amount of space after the display, as this example shows.

Be wary of empty lines around displays

Empty line before display:	`\usepackage{amsmath}` `Empty line before display:`
$$a \neq b$$	`\[  a \neq b   \]`
In both cases, too much space before! ...	`In both cases, too much space before! \ldots`
$$a \neq b \qquad (1)$$	`\begin{equation} a \neq b \end{equation}`
... and not a lot of space after!	`\ldots\ and not a lot of space after!`

8-2-23

With the amsmath package loaded, this behavior is exhibited by all the display math environments. Strangely enough, with standard LaTeX the `\[` case comes out looking more or less right.

Empty line before display:	`Empty line before display:`
$$a \neq b$$	`\[  a \neq b   \]`
Enough space now, but don't rely on it!	`Enough space now, but don't rely on it!`
$$a \neq b \qquad (1)$$	`\begin{equation} a \neq b \end{equation}`
Less space after in this case!	`Less space after in this case!`

8-2-24

To summarize, do not use empty lines around display environments!

8.2.11 Equation numbering and tags

In LaTeX the tags for equations are typically generated automatically and contain a printed representation of the LaTeX counter `equation`. This involves three processes: setting (normally by incrementing) the value of the `equation` counter; formatting the tag; and printing it in the correct position.

In practice, the first two processes are nearly always linked. Thus, the value of the `equation` counter is increased only when a tag containing its representation is automatically printed. For example, when a mathematical display environment has both starred and unstarred forms, the unstarred form automatically tags each logical equation while the starred form does not. Only in the unstarred form is the value of the `equation` counter changed.

Within the unstarred forms the setting of a tag (and the incrementing of the counter value) for any particular logical equation can be suppressed by putting `\notag` (or `\nonumber`[1]) *before* the `\\`. You can override the default automatic tag with one of your own design (or provide a new one) by using the command `\tag` *before* the `\\`. The argument of this command can be arbitrary normal text that is typeset (within the normal parentheses) as the tag for that equation.

Note that the use of `\tag` suppresses the incrementing of the counter value. Thus, the default tag setting is only visually the same as `\tag{\theequation}`; they are not equivalent forms. The starred form, `\tag*`, causes the text in its argument to be typeset without the parentheses (and without any other material that might otherwise be added with a particular document class).

$$x^2 + y^2 = z^2 \tag{1}$$
$$x^3 + y^3 = z^3$$
$$x^4 + y^4 = r^4 \tag{*}$$
$$x^5 + y^5 = r^5 \tag{*}$$
$$x^6 + y^6 = r^6 \tag{1'}$$
$$A_1 = N_0(\lambda; \Omega') - \phi(\lambda; \Omega') \tag{2}$$
$$A_2 = \phi(\lambda; \Omega')\,\phi(\lambda; \Omega) \tag{ALSO (2)}$$
$$A_3 = \mathcal{N}(\lambda; \omega) \tag{3}$$

```
\usepackage{amsmath}
\begin{align}
   x^2+y^2 &= z^2 \label{eq:A}          \\
   x^3+y^3 &= z^3 \notag                \\
   x^4+y^4 &= r^4 \tag{$*$}             \\
   x^5+y^5 &= r^5 \tag*{$*$}            \\
   x^6+y^6 &= r^6 \tag{\ref{eq:A}$'$}   \\
       A_1 &= N_0 (\lambda ; \Omega')
               - \phi ( \lambda ; \Omega') \\
       A_2 &= \phi (\lambda ; \Omega')
               \, \phi (\lambda ; \Omega)
               \tag*{ALSO (\theequation)}  \\
       A_3 &= \mathcal{N} (\lambda ; \omega)
\end{align}
```

8-2-25

Notice this example's use of the `\label` and `\ref` commands to provide some kinds of "relative numbering" of equations.

Referencing equations To facilitate the creation of cross-references to equations, the `\eqref` command (used in Example 8-2-29 on page 485), automatically adds the parentheses around the equation number, adding an italic correction if necessary. See also Section 2.4 on page 66 for more general solutions to managing references.

---

[1] The command `\notag` is interchangeable with `\nonumber`.

8.2.12 Fine-tuning tag placement

Optimal placement of equation number tags can be a rather complex problem in multiple-line displays. These display environments try hard to avoid overprinting an equation number on the equation contents; if necessary, the number tag is moved down or up, onto a separate line. The difficulty of accurately determining the layout of a display can occasionally result in a tag placement that needs further adjustment. Here is an example of the kind of thing that can happen, and a strategy for fixing it. The automatic tag placement is clearly not very good.

```
\usepackage{amsmath}
\begin{equation}  \begin{split}
  \lvert I_2 \rvert  &=     \left\lvert \int_{0}^T \psi(t)
     \left\{  u(a, t) - \int_{\gamma(t)}^a \frac{d\theta}{k}
       (\theta, t) \int_{a}^\theta c (\xi) u_t (\xi, t) \,d\xi
     \right\} dt \right\rvert                              \\
                &\le  C_6  \Biggl\lvert
     \left\lvert f \int_\Omega \left\lvert
        \widetilde{S}^{-1,0}_{a,-} W_2(\Omega, \Gamma_1)
       \right\rvert \ \right\rvert
     \left\lvert \lvert u \rvert
        \overset{\circ}{\to} W_2^{\widetilde{A}} (\Omega; \Gamma_r,T)
       \right\rvert              \Biggr\rvert
\end{split} \end{equation}
```

$$
\left|\,|I_2| = \left| \int_0^T \psi(t) \left\{ u(a,t) - \int_{\gamma(t)}^a \frac{d\theta}{k}(\theta, t) \int_a^\theta c(\xi)u_t(\xi, t)\, d\xi \right\} dt \right| \right.
$$

$$
\left. \le C_6 \left\| f \int_\Omega \left| \widetilde{S}_{a,-}^{-1,0} W_2(\Omega, \Gamma_l) \right| \right\| \left\| |u| \overset{\circ}{\to} W_2^{\widetilde{A}}(\Omega; \Gamma_r, T) \right\| \, \right|
$$

$$ \tag{1} $$

8-2-26

A fairly easy way to improve the appearance of such an equation is to use an align environment with a \notag on the first equation line:

```
\begin{align}
  \lvert I_2 \rvert  &= \left\lvert \int_{0}^T \psi(t)
                      ...
                 &\le  C_6  \Biggl\lvert            \notag \\
                      ...
\end{align}
```

This produces a good result but note that it misuses logical markup—it assumes the equation numbers to be on the right!

$$\left| I_2 \right| = \left| \int_0^T \psi(t) \left\{ u(a,t) - \int_{\gamma(t)}^a \frac{d\theta}{k}(\theta,t) \int_a^\theta c(\xi)u_t(\xi,t)\,d\xi \right\} dt \right|$$

$$\leq C_6 \left\| f \int_\Omega \left| \widetilde{S}_{a,-}^{-1,0} W_2(\Omega,\Gamma_l) \right| \right\| \left\| |u| \xrightarrow{\circ} W_2^{\widetilde{A}}(\Omega;\Gamma_r,T) \right\| \quad (1)$$

8-2-27

A \raisetag command is available that will further adjust the vertical position of the current equation number but *only* when it has been automatically moved from its "normal position". For example, to move such a tag upward[1] by 6pt, you could write \raisetag{6pt}. You can try adjusting the above equation with \raisetag but the correct value is not easy to divine: a value of 1.2\baselineskip looks about right!

A more sensible use is shown in the next example, where \raisetag with a negative argument is used to move the tag on the left down into the display.

$$(1)$$
$$\text{The sign function: } \mathcal{S}(x) = \begin{cases} -1 & x < 0 \\ 0 & x = 0 \\ 1 & x > 0 \end{cases}$$

```
\usepackage[leqno]{amsmath}
\begin{gather}   \raisetag{-10pt}
  \text{The sign function: \ }
    \mathcal{S}(x) =  \begin{cases}
            -1  &  x < 0 \\
             0  &  x = 0 \\
             1  &  x > 0
          \end{cases}
\end{gather}
```

8-2-28

Here we used a gather environment with a single line because the equation is (the only) one within which \raisetag unfortunately has no effect (it is coded using low-level TeX).

These kinds of adjustment constitute "fine-tuning", like line breaks and page breaks in text. They should therefore be left until your document is nearly finalized. Otherwise, you may end up redoing the fine-tuning several times to keep up with changing document content.

8.2.13   Subordinate numbering sequences

The amsmath package provides a subequations environment to support "equation sub-numbering" with tags of the form (2a), (2b), (2c), and so on. All the tagged equations within it use this sub-numbering scheme based on two normal LaTeX counters: parentequation and equation.

---

[1] The description in the file amsmath.dtx seems to indicate that a positive value should always move the tag toward the "normal position"—that is, downward for tags on the left, but the current implementation does not work in this way.

The next example demonstrates that the tag can be redefined to some extent, but note that the redefinition for \theequation must appear within the subequations environment! (Appendix A.1.4 discusses counter manipulations.)

$$f = g \qquad \text{(1a)}$$
$$f' = g' \qquad \text{(1b)}$$
$$\mathcal{L}f = \mathcal{L}g \qquad \text{(1c)}$$

$$f = g \qquad \text{(2i)}$$
$$f' = g' \qquad \text{(2ii)}$$
$$\mathcal{L}f = \mathcal{L}g + K \qquad \text{(2iii)}$$

Note the relationship between (1) and (2): only 1c and 2iii differ.

```
\usepackage{amsmath}

\begin{subequations}  \label{eq:1}
\begin{align}  f  &= g            \label{eq:1A} \\
               f' &= g'           \label{eq:1B} \\
     \mathcal{L}f  &= \mathcal{L}g \label{eq:1C}
\end{align}
\end{subequations}
\begin{subequations}  \label{eq:2}
\renewcommand\theequation{\theparentequation\roman{equation}}
\begin{align}  f  &= g            \label{eq:2A} \\
               f' &= g'           \label{eq:2B} \\
     \mathcal{L}f  &= \mathcal{L}g + K  \label{eq:2C}
\end{align}
\end{subequations}
Note the relationship between~\eqref{eq:1}
and~\eqref{eq:2}: only~\ref{eq:1C} and~\ref{eq:2C} differ.
```

8-2-29

The subequations environment must appear *outside* the displays that it affects. Also, it should not be nested within itself. Each use of this environment advances the "main" equation counter by one. A \label command within the subequations environment but outside any individual (logical) equation will produce a \ref to the parent number (e.g., to 2 rather than 2i).

8.2.14 Resetting the equation counter

It is fairly common practice to have equations numbered within sections or chapters, using tags such as (1.1), (1.2), ..., (2.1), (2.2), ... With amsmath this can easily be set up by using the declaration \numberwithin.[1]

For example, to get compound equation tags including the section number, with the equation counter being automatically reset for each section, put this declaration in the preamble: \numberwithin{equation}{section}.

8.3 Matrix-like environments

The amsmath package offers a number of matrix-like environments, all of which are similar to array in syntax and layout. Thinking of complex mathematical layouts in this way is a useful exercise, as quite a wide variety of two-dimensional mathematical structures and table-like layouts can be so described.

---

[1]As the name implies, \numberwithin can be applied to any pair of counters, but the results may not be satisfactory in all cases because of potential complications. See the discussion of the \@addtoreset command in Appendix A.1.4.

Three of these environments replace old commands that are kept well hidden
Old commands in standard LaTeX; cases (discussed in the next section) and matrix and pmatrix
disabled (discussed in the section after that). Because these old command forms use a
totally different notation, they are not truly part of LaTeX and they cannot be mixed
with the environment forms described here. Indeed, amsmath will produce an
explanatory error message if one of the old commands is used (see page 907).
If, contrariwise, you make the mistake of using the amsmath environment forms
without loading that package, then you will most probably get this error message:
"Misplaced alignment tab character &".

8.3.1   The cases **environment**

Constructions like the following, where a single equation has a few variants, are
very common in mathematics. To handle these constructions, amsmath provides
the cases environment. It produces a decorated array with two columns, both left
aligned.

$$P_{r-j} = \begin{cases} 0 & \text{if } r - j \text{ is odd,} \\ r!\,(-1)^{(r-j)/2} & \text{if } r - j \text{ is even.} \end{cases} \quad (1)$$

```
\usepackage{amsmath}
\begin{equation}     P_{r - j} =
\begin{cases}
   0   & \text{if $r - j$ is odd,} \\
   r! \, (-1)^{(r - j)/2}
       & \text{if $r - j$ is even.}
\end{cases}                \end{equation}
```

8-3-1

Notice the use of \text and the "embedded math mode" in the text strings. With
the help of the aligned environment, other environments similar to cases can be
defined, as in Example 8-2-19 on page 478.

8.3.2   The matrix environments

The matrix environments are similar to LaTeX's array, except that they do not have
an argument specifying the formats of the columns. Instead, a default format is
provided: up to 10 centered columns. Also, the spacing differs slightly from the
default in array. The example below illustrates the matrix environments matrix,
pmatrix, bmatrix, Bmatrix, vmatrix, and Vmatrix.[1]

$$\begin{matrix} 0 & 1 \\ 1 & 0 \end{matrix} \begin{pmatrix} 0 & -i \\ i & 0 \end{pmatrix}$$
$$\begin{bmatrix} 0 & -1 \\ 1 & 0 \end{bmatrix} \begin{Bmatrix} 1 & 0 \\ 0 & -1 \end{Bmatrix}$$
$$\begin{vmatrix} a & b \\ c & d \end{vmatrix} \begin{Vmatrix} i & 0 \\ 0 & -i \end{Vmatrix}$$

```
\usepackage{amsmath}
\begin{gather*}
   \begin{matrix} 0 & 1 \\ 1 & 0 \end{matrix}  \quad
   \begin{pmatrix} 0 & -i \\ i & 0 \end{pmatrix} \\
   \begin{bmatrix} 0 & -1 \\ 1 & 0 \end{bmatrix} \quad
   \begin{Bmatrix} 1 & 0 \\ 0 & -1 \end{Bmatrix} \\
   \begin{vmatrix} a & b \\ c & d \end{vmatrix} \quad
   \begin{Vmatrix} i & 0 \\ 0 & -i \end{Vmatrix}
\end{gather*}
```

8-3-2

---

[1]Note the warning above about possible problems when using matrix and pmatrix.

The maximum number of columns in a matrix environment is determined by the counter `MaxMatrixCols`, which you can change using LATEX's standard counter commands. As in standard `arrays`, the amount of space between the columns is given by the value of `\arraycolsep`, but no space is added on either side of the array. With more columns LATEX has to work a little harder and needs slightly more resources. However, with today's typical TEX implementations such limits are less important, so setting it to 20 or even higher is possible without a notice-able change in processing speed.

8-3-3

$$\begin{Vmatrix}
a & b & c & d & e & f & g & h & i & j & \cdots \\
& a & b & c & d & e & f & g & h & i & \cdots \\
& & a & b & c & d & e & f & g & h & \cdots \\
& & & a & b & c & d & e & f & g & \cdots \\
& & & & \ddots & \ddots & \cdots & \cdots & \cdots & \cdots & \cdots
\end{Vmatrix}$$

```
\usepackage{amsmath}
\setcounter{MaxMatrixCols}{20}
\[
 \begin{Vmatrix}
  \,a&b&c&d&e&f&g&h&i&j &\cdots\,{} \\
    &a&b&c&d&e&f&g&h&i &\cdots\,{} \\
    & &a&b&c&d&e&f&g&h &\cdots\,{} \\
    & & &a&b&c&d&e&f&g &\cdots\,{} \\
    & & & &\ddots&\ddots&\hdotsfor[2]{5}\,{}
 \end{Vmatrix} \]
```

This example also demonstrates use of the command `\hdotsfor` to produce a row of dots in a matrix, spanning a given number of columns (here 5). The spacing of the dots can be varied by using the optional parameter (here 2) to specify a multiplier for the default space between the dots; the default space between dots is 3 math units (see Appendix A.1.5). The thin space and the brace group `\,{}` at the end of each row simply make the layout look better; together they produce two thin spaces, about 6 mu or 1/3 em. (Spacing in formulas is discussed in more detail in Section 8.7.6 on page 507.)

To produce a small matrix suitable for use in text, use the `smallmatrix` environment. Note that the text lines are not spread apart even though the line before the small matrix contains words with descenders.

8-3-4

To show the effect of the matrix on surrounding lines inside a paragraph, we put it here: $\left(\begin{smallmatrix} 1 & 0 \\ 0 & -1 \end{smallmatrix}\right)$ and follow it with enough text to ensure that there is at least one full line below the matrix.

```
\usepackage{amsmath}
To show the effect of the matrix on surrounding
lines inside a paragraph, we put it here:
 $ \left( \begin{smallmatrix}
          1 & 0 \\ 0 & -1
      \end{smallmatrix}  \right) $
and follow it with enough text to ensure that
there is at least one full line below the matrix.
```

8.3.3   Stacking in subscripts and superscripts

The `\substack` command is most commonly used to typeset several lines within a subscript or superscript, using `\\` as the row delimiter.

A slightly more general structure is the `subarray` environment, which allows you to specify that the lines should be left or right aligned instead of centered.

Note that both environments need to be surrounded by braces when they appear as a subscript superscript.

$$\sum_{\substack{0 \le i \le m \\ 0 < j < n}} P(i,j) \qquad (1)$$

$$\sum_{\substack{i \in \Lambda \\ 0 \le i \le m \\ 0 < j < n}} P(i,j) \qquad (2)$$

```
\usepackage{amsmath}

\begin{gather}
  \sum_{\substack{0 \le i \le m \\ 0 < j < n}} P(i, j) \\
  \sum_{\begin{subarray}{l}  i \in \Lambda     \\
                            0 \le i \le m     \\
                            0 < j < n
        \end{subarray}}  P(i, j)
\end{gather}
```

8-3-5

8.3.4 Commutative diagrams

Some commands for producing simple commutative diagrams based on arrays are available in a separate package, amscd. It provides some useful shorthand forms for specifying the decorated arrows and other connectors. However, it is very limited—for example, these connectors can be only horizontal and vertical.

The picture environment could be used for more complex commutative diagrams but for most serious work in this area you will need one of the more comprehensive packages. These include Kristoffer Rose's XY-pic system (see [57, chapter 5]) and its extension [11] by Michael Barr; the diagram system [22, 23] by Francis Borceux; and the kuvio package [155] by Anders Svensson.

In the CD environment the notations @>>>, @<<<, @VVV, and @AAA give right, left, down, and up arrows, respectively.[1] The following examples also show the use of the command \DeclareMathOperator (see Section 8.6.2).

$$
\begin{array}{ccccc}
\mathrm{cov}(L) & \longrightarrow & \mathrm{non}(K) & \longrightarrow & \mathrm{cf}(K) \\
\downarrow & & \uparrow & & \uparrow \\
\mathrm{add}(L) & \longrightarrow & \mathrm{add}(K) & \longrightarrow & \mathrm{cov}(K)
\end{array}
$$

```
\usepackage{amsmath,amscd}
\DeclareMathOperator\add{add}
\DeclareMathOperator\cf {cf}
\DeclareMathOperator\cov{cov}
\DeclareMathOperator\non{non}

\[ \begin{CD}
   \cov (L) @>>> \non (K) @>>> \cf (K) \\
      @VVV           @AAA         @AAA       \\
   \add (L) @>>> \add (K) @>>> \cov (K) \\
\end{CD} \]
```

8-3-6

Decorations on the arrows are specified as follows. For the horizontal arrows, material between the first and second > or < symbols will be typeset as a super-script, and material between the second and third will be typeset as a subscript. Similarly, material between the first and second, or second and third, As or Vs of vertical arrows will be typeset as left or right "side-scripts"; this format is used in the next example to place the operator $\mathrm{End}\,P$ to the right of the arrow.

The notations @= and @| give horizontal and vertical double lines.

---

[1] For keyboards lacking the characters < and >, the notations @))) and @(((are alternatives.

A "null arrow" (produced by @.) can be used instead of a visible arrow to fill out an array where needed.

```
\usepackage{amsmath,amscd}
\DeclareMathOperator{\End}{End}
\[ \begin{CD}
    S^{W_\Lambda}\otimes T @>j>>       T            \\
      @VVV                           @VV{\End P}V \\
    (S \otimes T)/I              @=   (Z\otimes T)/J
\end{CD} \]
```

8-3-7

A similar layout, which does not look nearly as good, can be produced in standard LaTeX:

```
\[\begin{array}{ccc}
    S^{\mathcal{W}_\Lambda}\otimes T &
      \stackrel{j}{\longrightarrow}  &
    T                                                  \\
    \Big\downarrow                   & &
    \Big\downarrow\vcenter{%
      \rlap{$\scriptstyle{\mathrm{End}}\,,P$}} \\
    (S\otimes T)/I                   & = &
    (Z\otimes T)/J
\end{array}\]
```

8-3-8

This example shows clearly how much better the results are with the amscd package: the notation is enormously easier and, for example, the package produces longer horizontal arrows and much improved spacing between elements of the diagram. The more specialized packages will enable you to get even more beautiful results.

8.3.5 delarray—Delimiters surrounding an array

This section describes a useful general extension to the array package (see Section 5.2 on page 243) that allows the user to specify opening and closing extensible delimiters (see Section 8.5.3 to surround a mathematical array environment. The delarray package was written by David Carlisle, and its use is illustrated in the next, rather odd-looking, example (note that the delarray package is independent of amsmath but it automatically loads the array package if necessary).

```
\usepackage{delarray}
\[ \mathcal{Q} =
\begin{array}{t} ( {cc} ) X & Y \end{array}
\begin{array}{t} [ {cc} ] A & B \\ C & D   \end{array}
\begin{array}[b] \lgroup{cc}\rgroup L \\ M \end{array}
\]
```

8-3-9

The delimiters are placed on either side of the "preamble declaration" (here {cc}). They must be delimiters from Table 8.3 on page 498.

The most useful feature of this package is also illustrated in the preceding example: the use of the [t] and [b] optional arguments, which are not available with amsmath's matrix environments. These show that use of the delarray syntax is not equivalent to surrounding the array environment with \left and \right, since the delimiters are raised as well as the array itself.

8.4   Compound structures and decorations

This section presents some commands that produce a variety of medium-sized mathematical structures including decorated symbols and fraction-like objects.

8.4.1   Decorated arrows

The commands \xleftarrow and \xrightarrow produce horizontal relation arrows similar to those used for the commutative diagrams in Section 8.3.4; they are intended to have textual decorations above and/or below the arrow and the length of the arrow is chosen automatically to accommodate the text. These arrows are normally available in only one size. Thus, they will probably not be suited for use in fractions, subscripts, or superscripts, for example.

The textual decorations below and above the arrows are specified in an optional and a mandatory argument to the command.

$$0 \xleftarrow[\zeta]{} F \times \Delta(n-1) \xrightarrow{\partial_0 \alpha(b)} E^{\partial_0 b}$$

```
\usepackage{amsmath}
\[
  0 \xleftarrow [\zeta]{}  F \times \Delta (n - 1)
    \xrightarrow {\partial_0 \alpha(b)} E^{\partial_0 b}
\]
```

8-4-1

8.4.2   Continued fractions

The \cfrac command produces fraction arrays known as "continued fractions". By default, each numerator formula is centered; left or right alignment of a numerator is achieved by adding the optional argument [l] or [r].

$$\cfrac{1}{\sqrt{2} + \cfrac{1}{\sqrt{3} + \cfrac{1}{\sqrt{4} + \cfrac{1}{\sqrt{5} + \cfrac{1}{\sqrt{6} + \cdots}}}}}$$

```
\usepackage{amsmath}
\begin{equation*}
\cfrac {1}{\sqrt{2} +
 \cfrac {1}{\sqrt{3} +
  \cfrac {1}{\sqrt{4} +
   \cfrac[r] {1}{\sqrt{5} +
    \cfrac[l] {1}{\sqrt{6} + \dotsb }
   }}}}
\end{equation*}
```

8-4-2

8.4.3   Boxed formulas

The command \boxed puts a box around its argument; it works just like \fbox, except that the contents are in math mode. See also the commands described in Section 10.1.

8-4-3

$$\boxed{W_t - F \subseteq V(P_i) \subseteq W_t}$$ (1)

```
\usepackage{amsmath}

\begin{equation}
    \boxed { W_t - F \subseteq V(P_i) \subseteq W_t }
\end{equation}
```

8.4.4   Limiting positions

Subscripts and superscripts on integrals, sums, or other operators can be placed either above and below the mathematical operator or in the normal sub/super positions on the right of the operator. They are said to "take limits" if the superscript and subscript material is placed (in the "limit positions") above and below the symbol or operator name. Typically, no limits are used in text (to avoid spreading lines apart); in a display, the placement depends on the operator used. The default placements in LaTeX are illustrated in the following example.

8-4-4

$$\sum_{i=1}^{n} \qquad \int_0^\infty \qquad \lim_{n \to 0}$$

Text: $\sum_{i=1}^n$, $\int_0^\infty$, $\lim_{n\to 0}$.

```
\[
    \sum_{i=1}^n \qquad \int_0^\infty \qquad \lim_{n \to 0}
\]
Text: $\sum_{i=1}^n$, $\int_0^\infty$, $\lim_{n \to 0}$.
```

The placement of subscripts and superscripts on integrals, sums, and other operators is often dictated by the house-style of a journal. Recognizing this fact, amsmath offers a long list of options for controlling the positioning. In the following summary, *default* indicates what happens when the amsmath package is used with a standard LaTeX class but without any of these options.[1]

intlimits, nointlimits   In displayed equations only, place superscripts and subscripts of integration-type symbols above and below or at the side (default), respectively.

sumlimits, nosumlimits   In displayed equations only, place superscripts and subscripts of summation-type symbols (also called "large operators") above and below (default) or aside, respectively. This option also affects other big operators—$\prod$, $\coprod$, $\otimes$, $\oplus$, and so forth—but not integrals.

namelimits, nonamelimits   Like sumlimits or nosumlimits but for certain "operator names", such as $\det$, $\inf$, $\lim$, and $\max$, $\min$, that traditionally have subscripts placed underneath, at least when they occur in a displayed equation.

---

[1] But not necessarily when using the $\mathcal{A}_{\mathcal{M}}S$-LaTeX document classes.

The positioning on individual symbols/names can be controlled directly by placing one of the following TeX primitive commands immediately after the symbol or operator name: \limits, \nolimits, or \displaylimits. This last command, which specifies that the operator "takes limits" only when the mathematical style is a display style, is the default whenever a symbol of class Operator[1] appears or a \mathop construction is used. If an operator is to "take limits" outside a display, then this must be declared individually using the \limits command. Compare the next example to Example 8-4-4, noting that some commands show no effect as they merely reinforce the default.

$$\sum_{i=1}^{n} \qquad \int_{0}^{\infty} \qquad \lim_{n \to 0}$$

Text: $\sum_{i=1}^{n}, \int_{0}^{\infty}, \lim_{n\to 0}.$

```
\[
    \sum\nolimits_{i=1}^n \qquad \int\limits_0^\infty
    \qquad  \lim\displaylimits_{n \to 0}
\]
Text: $\sum\nolimits_{i=1}^n$, $\int\limits_0^\infty$,
$\lim\displaylimits_{n \to 0}$.
```

8-4-5

8.4.5   Multiple integral signs

The commands \iint, \iiint, and \iiiint give multiple integral signs with well-adjusted spaces between them, in both running text and displays. The command \idotsint gives two integral signs with ellipsis dots between them. The following example also shows the use of \limits to override the default for integral constructions and place the limit V underneath the symbol.

$$\iint_{V} \mu(v, w) \, du \, dv$$

$$\iiint_{V} \mu(u, v, w) \, du \, dv \, dw$$

$$\iiiint_{V} \mu(t, u, v, w) \, dt \, du \, dv \, dw$$

$$\int \cdots \int_{V} \mu(z_1, \ldots, z_k) \, \mathbf{dz}$$

```
\usepackage{amsmath}
\begin{gather*}
\iint      \limits _V \mu(v,w)
   \,du \,dv                                    \\
\iiint     \limits _V \mu(u,v,w)
   \,du \,dv \,dw                               \\
\iiiint    \limits _V \mu(t,u,v,w)
   \,dt \,du \,dv \,dw                          \\
\idotsint \limits _V \mu(z_1, \dots, z_k)
   \, \mathbf{dz}
\end{gather*}
```

8-4-6

8.4.6   Modular relations

The commands \mod, \bmod, \pmod, and \pod are provided by the amsmath package to deal with the special spacing conventions of the "mod" notation for equivalence classes of integers. Two of these commands, \mod and \pod, are variants of \pmod that are preferred by some authors; \mod omits the parentheses, whereas

---

[1] See Section 8.9.1 on page 524 for a discussion of the various mathematical classes of symbols.

\pod omits the "mod" and retains the parentheses. With amsmath the spacing of
\pmod is decreased within a non-display formula.

$$u \equiv v + 1 \quad \mathrm{mod}\ n^2$$
$$u \equiv v + 1 \bmod n^2$$
$$u = v + 1 \quad (\mathrm{mod}\ n^2)$$
$$u = v \mid 1 \quad (n^2)$$

8-4-7

The in-text layout: $u = v + 1 \ (\mathrm{mod}\ n^2)$

$$(m \bmod n) = k^2 ; \quad x \equiv y \quad (\mathrm{mod}\ b) ;$$
$$x \equiv y \quad \mathrm{mod}\ c ; \quad x \equiv y \quad (d) .$$

```
\usepackage{amsmath}
\begin{align*}
  u & \equiv v + 1 \mod{n^2}   \\
  u & \equiv v + 1 \bmod{n^2} \\
  u &   =     v + 1 \pmod{n^2} \\
  u &   =     v + 1 \pod{n^2}
\ond{align*}
The in-text layout: $ u = v + 1 \pmod{n^2} $
\begin{gather*}
  (m \bmod n) = k^2 \, ; \quad
  x \equiv y \pmod b \, ;         \\
  x \equiv y \mod c \, ;   \quad
  x \equiv y \pod d\, .
\end{gather*}
```

8.4.7   Fractions and generalizations

In addition to the common \frac, the amsmath package provides \dfrac
and \tfrac as convenient abbreviations for {\displaystyle\frac ...} and
{\textstyle\frac ...} (mathematical styles are discussed in more detail in Section 8.7.1 on page 502).

$$\frac{1}{k} \log_2 c(f) \quad \tfrac{1}{k} \log_2 c(f) \tag{1}$$

8-4-8

Text: $\sqrt{ \frac{1}{k} \log_2 c(f) } \quad \sqrt{ \frac{1}{k} \log_2 c(f) }$.

```
\usepackage{amsmath}
\begin{equation} \frac{1}{k} \log_2 c(f)
           \quad \tfrac{1}{k} \log_2 c(f) \end{equation}
Text: $ \sqrt{ \frac{1}{k} \log_2 c(f) } \quad
       \sqrt{ \dfrac{1}{k} \log_2 c(f) }\, $.
```

For binomial coefficients such as $\binom{n}{k}$, use the similar commands \binom,
\dbinom, and \tbinom.

$$\binom{k}{2} 2^{k-1} + \binom{k-1}{2} 2^{k-2} \tag{1}$$

8-4-9

Text: $\binom{k}{2} 2^{k-1} + \binom{k-1}{2} 2^{k-2}$.

```
\usepackage{amsmath}
\begin{equation} \binom{k}{2} 2^{k - 1}
           + \tbinom{k - 1}{2} 2^{k - 2} \end{equation}
Text: $ \binom{k}{2} 2^{k - 1}
       + \dbinom{k - 1}{2} 2^{k - 2} $.
```

All of these \binom and \frac commands are special cases of the generalized
fraction command \genfrac, which has six parameters.

\genfrac{*ldelim*}{*rdelim*}{*thick*}{*style*}{*num*}{*denom*}

The first two parameters, *ldelim* and *rdelim*, are the left and right delimiters, respectively. The third parameter, *thick*, is used to override the default thickness of

Style	Default Thickness (approximately)
text/display	0.40pt
script	0.34pt
scriptscript	0.24pt

Table 8.2: Default rule thickness in different math styles

the fraction rule; for instance, \binom uses 0pt for this argument so that the line is invisible. If it is left empty, the line thickness has the default value specified by the font set-up in use for mathematical typesetting. The examples in this chapter use the defaults listed in Table 8.2 in the various styles (see also Section 8.7.1).

The fourth parameter, *style*, provides a "mathematical style override" for the layout and font sizes used. It can take integer values in the range 0–3 denoting \displaystyle, \textstyle, \scriptstyle, and \scriptscriptstyle, respectively. If this argument is left empty, then the style is selected according to the normal rules for fractions (described in Table 8.5 on page 502). The last two arguments are simply the numerator (*num*) and denominator (*denom*).

To illustrate, here is how \frac, \tfrac, and \binom might be defined:

```
\newcommand\frac [2]{\genfrac      {}{}{}{}{#1}{#2}}
\newcommand\tfrac[2]{\genfrac      {}{}{}{1}{#1}{#2}}
\newcommand\binom[2]{\genfrac {(}{)}{0pt}{}{#1}{#2}}
```

Of course, if you want to use a particular complex notation (such as one implemented with \genfrac) repeatedly throughout your document, then you will do yourself (and your editor) a favor if you define a meaningful command name with \newcommand as an abbreviation for that notation, as in the examples above.

The old generalized fraction commands \over, \overwithdelims, \atop, \atopwithdelims, \above, and \abovewithdelims (inherited in standard LaTeX from primitive TeX) produce warning messages if they are used with the amsmath package.

8.4.8 Dottier accents

The \dot and \ddot mathematical accents are supplemented by \dddot and \ddddot, giving triple and quadruple dot accents, respectively.

$\dot{S}$ $\ddot{P}$ $\dddot{Q}$ $\ddddot{R}$

```
\usepackage{amsmath}
$ \dot{S} \quad \ddot{P} \quad \dddot{Q} \quad \ddddot{R} $
```

8-4-10

If you want to set up your own mathematical accents, then you should probably use the accents package developed by Javier Bezos. It provides methods of defining "faked" accents (see \accentset in the example) and general under-

accents (\underaccent, \undertilde), along with other features. It can be used
together with amsmath. For further details see [20].

8-4-11

$$\overset{*}{X} \quad \hat{\hat{h}} \quad \underset{\circ}{\mathcal{M}} \quad \underset{\sim}{C} \quad \underline{M} \quad \underaccent{\sim}{ABC}$$

```
\usepackage{accents}
\[ \accentset{\ast}{X}                      \quad
   \hat{\accentset{\star}{\hat h}}          \quad
   \underaccent{\diamond}{\mathcal{M}} \quad
   \undertilde{C}\quad\undertilde{M}\quad\undertilde{ABC} \]
```

8.4.9   amsxtra—Accents as superscripts

One feature available with this package is a collection of simple commands for
placing accents as superscripts to a sub-formula:

8-4-12

$$(xyz)^{\cdots} \quad (xyz)^{\cdot\cdot} \quad (xyz)^{\cdot}$$
$$(xyz)^{\smallsmile} \quad (xyz)^{\vee}$$
$$(xyz)^{\wedge} \quad (xyz)^{\sim}$$

```
\usepackage{amsxtra}
$(xyz)\spdddot$ \quad $(xyz)\spddot$ \quad $(xyz)\spdot$ \\
$(xyz)\spbreve$ \quad $(xyz)\spcheck$ \\
$(xyz)\sphat$   \quad $(xyz)\sptilde$
```

8.4.10   Extra decorations

Standard LATEX provides \stackrel for placing a superscript above a Relation symbol. The amsmath package makes the commands \overset and \underset available as well. They can be used to place material above or below any Ordinary symbol or Binary operator symbol, in addition to Relation symbols; they are typeset
just like the limits above and below a summation sign.

   The command \sideset serves a special purpose, complementary to the others: it adds decorations additional to the "normal" limits (which are set above and
below) to any Operator symbol such as $\sum$ or $\prod$. These are placed in the subscript
and superscript positions, on both the left and right of the Operator.

8-4-13

$$\overset{*}{X} > \underset{*}{X} \iff \underset{a,b\in\mathbf{R}^*}{\sideset{}{'}\sum}' \overset{a}{\underset{b}{X}} = X$$

```
\usepackage{amsmath}
\[ \overset{*}{X} > \underset{*}{X}
        \iff \sideset{}{'}\sum_{a,b \in \mathbf{R^*}}
               \overset{a}{\underset{b}{X}} = X \]
```

This more complex example shows how to fully decorate a product symbol.

8-4-14

$$\sideset{_{i=1}^{n}}{_{j=2}^{m}}\prod_{k>1} \mathcal{T}_{i,j}^{k}$$

```
\usepackage{amsmath}
\[ \sideset{_{i = 1}^n}{_{j = 2}^m}\prod_{k > 1}
                 \mathcal{T}_{i, j}^k \]
```

8.5   Variable symbol commands

Many LATEX commands are often thought of as producing a particular symbol when,
in fact, the exact form is not fixed (even when the font and size are fixed). Certain

features of TEX's mathematical typesetting can even be used to produce structures that can, in principle, grow to whatever size is required.

Such context-dependent variability is very important in mathematical typesetting, and this section discusses some aspects of it. With a few clearly noted exceptions, the commands covered in this section are available in standard LATEX.

A well-known, but not very exciting, example of such variability entails the mathematical operator symbols, such as \sum and \prod, which typically come in just two sizes: a smaller size that is used in running text and a larger size that is used in displayed formulas. Such symbols appear in Table 8.25 on page 536.

8.5.1 Ellipsis ...

Standard LATEX provides several types of mathematical ellipsis dots: \ldots, \cdots, and so on. When using amsmath, however, such ellipsis dots within math mode should almost always be marked up using simply \dots.[1]

The vertical position (on the baseline or centered) of the ellipsis, together with the space around it, are both automatically selected according to what kind of symbol follows \dots. For example, if the next symbol is a plus sign, the dots will be centered; if it is a comma, they will be on the baseline. In all cases, three dots are used but the spacing varies. These defaults from the amsmath package can be changed in a class file when different conventions are in use.

A series $H_1, H_2, \dots, H_n$, a sum $H_1 + H_2 + \dots + H_n$, an orthogonal product $H_1 \times H_2 \times \dots \times H_n$.

```
\usepackage{amsmath}

A series $H_1, H_2, \dots, H_n$, a sum
$H_1 + H_2 + \dots + H_n$, an orthogonal product
$H_1 \times H_2 \times \dots \times H_n$.
```

8-5-1

If the dots fall at the end of a mathematical formula, the next object will be something like \end or \) or $, which does not give any information about how to place the dots. In such a case, you must help by using \dotsc for "dots with commas", \dotsb for "dots with Binary operator/Relation symbols", \dotsm for "multiplication dots", \dotsi for "dots with integrals", or even \dotso for "none of the above". These commands should be used only in such special positions: otherwise you should just use \dots.

In this example, low dots are produced in the first instance and centered dots in the other cases, with the space around the dots being nicely adjusted.

A series $H_1, H_2, \dots$, a sum $H_1 + H_2 + \dots$, an orthogonal product $H_1 \times H_2 \times \dots$, and an infinite integral:

$$\int_{H_1} \int_{H_2} \dots -\Gamma\, d\Theta$$

```
\usepackage{amsmath}

A series $H_1, H_2, \dotsc\,$, a sum
$H_1 + H_2 + \dotsb\,$, an orthogonal product
$H_1 \times H_2 \times \dotsm\,$, and an infinite
integral:   \[ \int_{H_1} \int_{H_2} \dotsi \;
                {-\Gamma}\, d\Theta \]
```

8-5-2

---

[1]The commands \dots and \ldots can also be used in text mode, where both always produce a normal text ellipsis.

You can customize the symbols and spacing produced by the \dots command in various contexts by redefining the commands \dotsc, \dotsb, \dotsm, and \dotsi; this would normally be done in a class file. Thus, for example, you could decide to use only two dots in some cases.

8.5.2 Horizontal extensions

In principle, any mathematical accent command can be set up to produce the appropriate glyph from a range of widths whenever these are provided by the available fonts. However, in standard LaTeX there are only two such commands: \widehat and \widetilde.

This section describes a few commands that produce constructions similar to these extensible accents. They all produce compound symbols of mathematical class Ordinary (see Section 8.9.1 on page 524) and are illustrated in this example.

$$\widehat{\psi_\delta(t) E_t h} = \psi_\delta\widetilde{(t) E_t} h$$
$$\overline{\psi_\delta(t) E_t h} = \underline{\psi_\delta(t) E_t h}$$
$$\overbrace{\psi_\delta(t) E_t h} = \underbrace{\psi_\delta(t) E_t h} \quad \text{Do not change style}$$
$$\overrightarrow{\psi_\delta(t) E_t h} = \overleftarrow{\psi_\delta(t) E_t h} \quad \begin{array}{l}\text{Do not change style}\\\text{without amsmath}\end{array}$$
$$\underrightarrow{\psi_\delta(t) E_t h} = \underleftarrow{\psi_\delta(t) E_t h} \quad \text{Do need amsmath}$$
$$\underleftrightarrow{\psi_\delta(t) E_t h} = \overleftrightarrow{\psi_\delta(t) E_t h} \quad \text{Do need amsmath}$$

8-5-3

```
\usepackage{amsmath}
\begin{align*}
\widehat        {\psi_\delta(t) E_t h}
&= \widetilde   {\psi_\delta(t) E_t h}      \\
\overline       {\psi_\delta(t) E_t h}
&= \underline   {\psi_\delta(t) E_t h}      \\
\overbrace      {\psi_\delta(t) E_t h}
&= \underbrace  {\psi_\delta(t) E_t h}
& & \text{Do not change style}              \\
\overrightarrow {\psi_\delta(t) E_t h}
&= \overleftarrow {\psi_\delta(t) E_t h}
& &    \text{Do not change style}    \\[-3pt]
& & & \text{without \textsf{amsmath}}       \\
\underrightarrow  {\psi_\delta(t) E_t h}
&= \underleftarrow  {\psi_\delta(t) E_t h}
& & \text{Do need \textsf{amsmath}}         \\
\overleftrightarrow {\psi_\delta(t) E_t h}
&=\underleftrightarrow{\psi_\delta(t) E_t h}
& & \text{Do need \textsf{amsmath}}
\end{align*}
```

Further details of the availability and properties of these commands are unfortunately somewhat complex but they are summarized in the example. Here, "change style" means that the symbol employed is affected by the mathematical style in use so that they will look right when used, for example, in fractions or subscripts/superscripts (see Section 8.7.1 on page 502). Those that do not change style are suitable for use only at the top level of displayed mathematics.

Another horizontally extensible feature of LaTeX is the bar in a radical sign; it is described at the end of the next subsection.

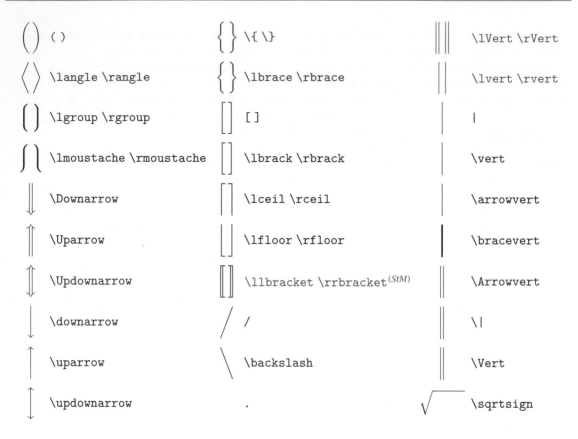

Symbols in blue require either the amsmath *package or, if additionally denoted with* (StM), *the* stmaryrd *package.*

A period (.) is not itself an extensible symbol but it can be used to produce an "invisible" delimiter.

The \sqrtsign symbol cannot be used with \left, \right, or \middle.

Synonyms: [\lbrack, [   ] \rbrack,]   { \lbrace, \{   } \rbrace, \} | \vert, | ‖ \Vert, \|

Table 8.3: Vertically extensible symbols

8.5.3 Vertical extensions

There is a much larger range available with vertical extensions. All of the symbols depicted in Table 8.26 on page 537 are potentially extensible, as are a few others. The full list is given in Table 8.3. These symbols become extensible only in certain usages; they must all be based on a construction of the following form:[1]

   \left ⟨*ext-Open*⟩ ⟨*sub-formula*⟩ \right ⟨*ext-Close*⟩

---

[1]If LaTeX is using the eTeX program, then you can also use these extensible symbols with \middle.

Here ⟨*ext-Open*⟩ and ⟨*ext-Close*⟩ can be any of the symbols (except `\sqrtsign`) listed in Table 8.3, or possibly others if additional packages are loaded. They must be symbols that have been set up to be extensible using the methods described in [109], which is part of every LaTeX distribution; thus, a symbol must be available to represent the absence of an actual glyph. This symbol, which is sometimes called the *null delimiter*, was chosen to be the period (.). The sizes of the actual glyphs used to typeset the extensible symbols are chosen to fit with the vertical size (height and depth) of the typeset *sub-formula* that lies in between them; the exact details of how this is done, and of the parameters that affect the process, can be found in Chapter 17 and Appendix G (Rule 19) of *The TeXbook* [82]. One can also request specific sizes for such symbols (see Section 8.7.3 on page 504).

The radical sign `\sqrtsign` is even more amazing—it grows both vertically and horizontally to fit the size of its argument. In LaTeX it is typically accessed via the `\sqrt` command, which is discussed further in Section 8.7.4 on page 504.

8-5-4

$$\sqrt{1 + \sqrt{1 + \sqrt{1 + \sqrt{1 + \sqrt{1 + \sqrt{1 + x}}}}}}$$

```
\[
  \sqrtsign{1 + \sqrtsign{1 + \sqrtsign{1 +
    \sqrtsign{1 + \sqrtsign{1 + \sqrtsign{1 + x}}}}}}
\]
```

8.6 Words in mathematics

8.6.1 The `\text` command

Math font-changing commands such as `\mathrm` are not intended for putting normal text inside mathematics; even for single words this task is often best carried out with the `\text` command, which is similar to the LaTeX command `\mbox` but is much better, ensuring that the text is set using the correct font size. The font will be the text font in use outside the current mathematical material.

8-6-1

Also, if $\Delta_{\text{max up}} = \Delta_{\text{min down}}$
(for all ups and downs) then
$$\Delta_{\text{sum of ups}} = \Delta_{\text{sum of downs}} \qquad (1)$$

```
\usepackage{amsmath}
\begin{gather}
  \text{Also, if } \Delta_{\text{max up}}
        = \Delta_{\text{min down}} \notag \\
  \text{(for all ups and downs) then} \notag \\
  \Delta_{\text{sum of ups}}
        = \Delta_{\text{sum of downs}}
\end{gather}
```

8.6.2 Operator names

The names of many well-known mathematical functions (such as log and sin) and operators (such as max and lim) are traditionally typeset as words (or abbreviations) in Roman type so as to visually distinguish them from shorter variable

arccos	`\arccos`	arcsin	`\arcsin`	arctan	`\arctan`
arg	`\arg`	cos	`\cos`	cosh	`\cosh`
cot	`\cot`	coth	`\coth`	csc	`\csc`
deg	`\deg`	det	`\det`$^{(\ell)}$	dim	`\dim`
exp	`\exp`	gcd	`\gcd`$^{(\ell)}$	hom	`\hom`
inf	`\inf`$^{(\ell)}$	inj lim	`\injlim`$^{(\ell)}$	ker	`\ker`
lg	`\lg`	lim	`\lim`$^{(\ell)}$	lim inf	`\liminf`$^{(\ell)}$
lim sup	`\limsup`$^{(\ell)}$	ln	`\ln`	log	`\log`
max	`\max`$^{(\ell)}$	min	`\min`$^{(\ell)}$	Pr	`\Pr`$^{(\ell)}$
proj lim	`\projlim`$^{(\ell)}$	sec	`\sec`	sin	`\sin`
sinh	`\sinh`	sup	`\sup`$^{(\ell)}$	tan	`\tan`
tanh	`\tanh`	$\varinjlim$	`\varinjlim`$^{(\ell)}$	$\varliminf$	`\varliminf`$^{(\ell)}$
$\varlimsup$	`\varlimsup`$^{(\ell)}$	$\varprojlim$	`\varprojlim`$^{(\ell)}$		

Blue functions require the amsmath *package.* (ℓ) *indicates that the operator takes limits in displays.*

Table 8.4: Predefined operators and functions

names that are set in "math italic". The most common function names have pre-defined commands to produce the correct typographical treatment; see Table 8.4. Most functions are available in standard LaTeX; those listed in blue in the table require loading amsmath. The functions marked with (ℓ) may "take limits" in display formulas (see Section 8.4.4).

$$\lim_{x \to 0} \frac{\sin^2(x)}{x^2} = 1$$

$$\varliminf_{n \to \infty} |a_{n+1}|/|a_n| = 0$$

$$\varinjlim (m_i^\lambda \cdot M)^* \le \varprojlim_{A/p \to \lambda(A)} A_p \le 0$$

```
\usepackage[fleqn]{amsmath}
\newcommand\abs[1]{\lvert#1\rvert}
\setlength\mathindent{0pt}
\begin{gather*}
  \lim_{x \rightarrow 0} \frac{ \sin^2(x) }{ x^2 } = 1 \\
  \varliminf_{n \rightarrow \infty}
    \abs{a_{n+1}} / \abs{a_n} = 0                    \\
  \varinjlim (m_i^\lambda \cdot M)^* \le
    \varprojlim_{A/p \rightarrow \lambda(A)}A_p \le 0
\end{gather*}
```

8-6-2

New functions of this type are needed frequently in mathematics, so the amsmath package provides a general mechanism for defining new "operator names".

| `\DeclareMathOperator*{`*cmd*`}{`*text*`}`   `\operatorname*{`*text*`}` |

The `\DeclareMathOperator` defines *cmd* to produce *text* in the appropriate font for "textual operators". If the new function being named is an operator that should, when used in displays, "take limits" (so that any subscripts and superscripts are placed in the "limits" positions, above and below, as with, for example, lim, sup, or min), then use the starred form \DeclareMathOperator*. In addition to using the proper font, \DeclareMathOperator sets up good spacing on either side of the function name when necessary. For example, it gives $A \operatorname{meas} B$ instead of $A meas B$. The *text* argument is processed using a "pseudo-text mode" in which

- The hyphen character – will print as a text hyphen (not as a minus sign); see \supminus in the next example.

- The asterisk character * will print as a raised text asterisk (not centered).

- Otherwise, the text is processed in math mode so that spaces are ignored and you can use subscripts, superscripts, and other elements.

The related command \operatorname (and its *-form) simply turns its argument into a function name, as in Example 8-2-11 on page 475. It is useful for "one-off" operators.

The next example shows how to provide the command \meas for the new function name "meas" (short for measure) and the operator functions \esssup and \supminus, both of which take limits.

$$\|f\|_\infty = \operatorname*{ess\,sup}_{x \in R^n} |f(x)|$$

$$\operatorname{meas}_1\{u \in R^1_+ : f^*(u) > \alpha\} =$$

$$\operatorname*{ess\,sup}_{x \in R^i} \ \operatorname{meas}_i\{u \in R^n : |f(u)| \geq \alpha\}$$

$$(\forall \alpha \in \operatorname*{sup\text{-}minus*}_{f^*} R_{*+})$$

8-6-3

```
\usepackage[fleqn]{amsmath}
\DeclareMathOperator \meas     {meas}
\DeclareMathOperator*\esssup  {ess \, sup}
\DeclareMathOperator*\supminus{sup - minus*}
\newcommand\abs [1]{\lvert#1\rvert}
\newcommand\norm[1]{\lVert#1\rVert}
\begin{gather*}
  \norm{f}_\infty = \esssup_{x \in R^n} \abs{f(x)}   \\
  \meas_1 \{ u \in R_+^1 \colon f^*(u)>\alpha \} =   \\
  \quad \esssup_{x \in R^i} \; \meas_i
      \{ u \in R^n \colon \abs{f(u)} \geq \alpha \}  \\
  \quad (\forall \alpha \in \supminus_{f^*} R_{*+})
\end{gather*}
```

Unfortunately, such declarations must appear in the preamble so it is not possible to change a declaration temporarily. In fact, \DeclareMathOperator works only for command names that have not been used previously, so it is not possible to overwrite an existing command directly. To do so, you must first remove the previous definition (in this case, of \csc) before redeclaring it; this removal is accomplished by using low-level TeX coding, as LaTeX provides no method for completing this task.

8-6-4

$$\varlimsup_{n \to \infty} \mathcal{Q}(u_n, u_n - u^\#) \geq \operatorname{cosec}(\mathcal{Q}'(u^\#))$$

```
\usepackage{amsmath}
%% Low-level TeX needed here to cancel
%% the old the definition of \csc:
\let \csc \relax
\DeclareMathOperator\csc{cosec}
\newcommand\calQ{\mathcal{Q}}
\[ \varlimsup_{n\to\infty} \calQ (u_n, u_n - u^{\#})
   \ge \csc (\calQ' (u^{\#}))                      \]
```

Style	Superscript	Subscript	Numerator	Denominator
D	S	S'	T	T'
D'	S'	S'	T'	T'
T	S	S'	S	S'
T'	S'	S'	S'	S'
S, SS	SS	SS'	SS	SS'
S', SS'	SS'	SS'	SS'	SS'

Table 8.5: Mathematical styles in sub-formulas

8.7   Fine-tuning the mathematical layout

Although LaTeX generally does a good job of laying out the elements of a formula, it is sometimes necessary to fine-tune the positioning. This section describes how to achieve some of the many detailed adjustments to the layout that are used to produce mathematical typography that is just a little bit better. Most of this section applies to all LaTeX mathematical material, but a few features are available only with the `amsmath` package; these will be clearly labeled.

8.7.1   Controlling the automatic sizing and spacing

Letters and mathematical symbols normally get smaller, and are more tightly spaced, when they appear in fractions, superscripts, or subscripts. In total, TeX has eight different styles in which it can lay out formulas:

D, D'	`\displaystyle`	Displayed on lines by themselves
T, T'	`\textstyle`	Embedded in text
S, S'	`\scriptstyle`	In superscripts or subscripts
SS, SS'	`\scriptscriptstyle`	In all higher-order superscripts or subscripts

The prime versions (D', T', etc.) represent the so-called *cramped* styles, which are similar to the normal styles except that superscripts are not raised so much.

TeX uses only three type sizes for mathematics in these styles: text size (also used in `\displaystyle`), script size, and scriptscript size. The size of each part of a formula can be determined according to the following scheme.

A symbol in style	Will be typeset in	And produces
D, D', T, T'	text size	(text size)
S, S'	script size	(script size)
SS, SS'	scriptscript size	(scriptscript size)

In LaTeX, the top-level part of a formula set in running text (within a $ pair or between \(...\)) is typeset using text style (style T). A displayed formula (e.g., one between \[...\]) will be typeset in display style (style *D*). The kind of style used in a sub-formula can then be determined from Table 8.5 on the facing page, where the last two columns describe the styles used in the numerator and the denominator of a fraction.

The various styles can be seen in this example:

8-7-1

$$b^0 + \frac{(k+p)_{j'} \pm \frac{(f+q)^{(pk)^y_{j'}}}{(h+y)}}{(l+q)^{(pk)}}$$

```
\normalsize                %% Style:
\[ b                       %% D
    ^0                     %% S
  +                        %% D
  \frac{(k + p)            %% T
      _{j'}                %% S'
  % \displaystyle
      \pm                  %% T    [D]
      \frac{(f + q)        %% S    [T]
            ^{(pk)         %% SS   [S]
              ^y           %% SS
              _{j'}}}      %% SS'
            {(h + y)}}     %% S'   [T']
    {(1 + q)               %% T'
      ^{(pk)}}             %% S'
\]
```

You can change the layout of this example by explicitly specifying the style to be used in each part. For example, if you remove the comment character in front of \displaystyle, then some of the styles will change to those shown in brackets. The result looks like this:

8-7-2

$$b^0 + \frac{(k+p)_{j'} \pm \frac{(f+q)^{(pk)^y_{j'}}}{(h+y)}}{(l+q)^{(pk)}}$$

Section 3.1.4 describes other ways to change the style of an individual symbol.

8.7.2 Sub-formulas

Whereas in text a pair of braces can simply indicate a group to which the effects of some declaration should be confined, within mathematics they do more than this. They delimit a sub-formula, which is always typeset as a separate entity that is added to the outer formula. As a side effect, sub-formulas are always typeset at their natural width and will not stretch or shrink horizontally when TeX tries to fit a formula in a paragraph line during line-breaking. As shown earlier, the sub-formula from a simple brace group is treated as if it was just a single symbol (of class Ordinary). An empty brace group, therefore, generates an invisible symbol that can affect the spacing. The exact details can be found in Chapters 17 and 18 and Appendix G of *The TeXbook* [82].

The contents of subscripts/superscripts and the arguments of many (but not all) commands, such as \frac and \mathrel, are also sub-formulas and get this same special treatment. Important examples of arguments that are not necessarily set as sub-formulas include those of \bm (see Section 8.8.2). If a group is needed only to limit the scope of a declaration (i.e., where a separately typeset sub-formula would be wrong), then \begingroup and \endgroup should be used. Note that specialized mathematical declarations such as style changes apply until the end of the current sub-formula, irrespective the presence of any other groups.

8.7.3 Big-g delimiters

To provide direct control of the sizes of extensible delimiters, LaTeX offers four commands: \big, \Big, \bigg, and \Bigg. These take a single parameter, which *must* be an extensible delimiter, and they produce ever-larger versions of the delimiter, from 1.2 to 3 times as big as the base size.

Three extra variants exist for each of the four commands, giving four sizes of Opening symbol (e.g., \bigl); four sizes of Relation symbol (e.g., \Bigm); and four sizes of Closing symbol (e.g., \Biggr).[1] All 16 of these commands can (and must) be used with any symbol that can come after either \left, \right, or (with eTeX) \middle (see Table 8.3 on page 498).

In standard LaTeX the sizes of these delimiters are fixed. With the amsmath package, however, the sizes adapt to the size of the surrounding material, according to the type size and mathematical style in use, as shown in the next example. The same is true when you load the exscale package (see Section 7.5.5), or when you use a font package that implements the exscale functionality as an option (e.g., most of the packages discussed in Sections 7.6 and 7.7).

$$\left(\mathbf{E}_y \int_0^{t_\varepsilon} L_{x,y^x(s)} \varphi(x)\, ds \right)$$

$$\left(\mathbf{E}_y \int_0^{t_\varepsilon} L_{x,y^x(s)} \varphi(x)\, ds \right)$$

```
\usepackage{amsmath}
\[ \biggl( \mathbf{E}_{y} \int_0^{t_\varepsilon}
     L_{x, y^x(s)} \varphi(x)\, ds \biggr) \]
\Large
\[ \biggl( \mathbf{E}_{y} \int_0^{t_\varepsilon}
     L_{x, y^x(s)} \varphi(x)\, ds \biggr) \]
```

8-7-3

8.7.4 Radical movements

In standard LaTeX, the placement of the index on a radical sign is sometimes not good. With amsmath, the commands \leftroot and \uproot can be used within the optional argument of the \sqrt command to adjust the positioning of this index. Positive integer arguments to these commands move the root index to the left and up, respectively, while negative arguments move it right and down. These

---

[1] See Section 8.9.1 on page 524 for the various mathematical classes of symbols.

arguments are given in terms of math units (see Section 8.7.6), which are quite small, so these commands are useful for fine adjustments.

8-7-4

$$\sqrt[\beta]{k} \qquad \sqrt[\beta]{k} \qquad \sqrt[\beta]{k}$$

```
\usepackage{amsmath}
\[
    \sqrt[\beta]{k} \qquad
    \sqrt[\leftroot{2}\uproot{4} \beta]{k} \qquad
    \sqrt[\leftroot{1}\uproot{3} \beta]{k}
\]
```

8.7.5 Ghostbusters™

To get math spacing and alignment "just right", it is often best to make creative use of some of primitive TeX's unique and sophisticated typesetting abilities. These features are accessed by a collection of commands related to \phantom and \smash; and they can be used in both mathematical and other text.

For instance, the large alignment example (Example 8-2-9 on page 474) uses lots of phantoms to get the alignment just right. Each of these phantoms produces an invisible "white box" whose size (width and total height plus depth) is determined by typesetting the text in its argument and measuring its size.

Conversely, the command \smash typesets its contents (in an LR-box) but then ignores both their height and depth, behaving as if they were both zero. The standard LaTeX command \hphantom is a combination of these, producing the equivalent of \smash{}: an invisible box with zero height and depth but the width of the phantom contents.

The \vphantom command makes the width of the phantom zero but preserves its total height plus depth. An example is the command \mathstrut, which is defined as "\vphantom(" so that it produces a zero-width box of height and depth equal to that of a parenthesis.

The amsmath package provides an optional argument for \smash, used as follows: \smash[t]{...} ignores the height of the box's contents, but retains the depth, while \smash[b]{...} ignores the depth and keeps the height. Compare these four lines, in which only the handling of $\sqrt{y}$ varies:

8-7-5

$$\sqrt{x} + \sqrt{y} + \sqrt{z}$$
$$\sqrt{x} + \sqrt{y} + \sqrt{z}$$
$$\sqrt{x} + \sqrt{y} + \sqrt{z}$$
$$\sqrt{x} + \sqrt{y} + \sqrt{z}$$

```
\usepackage{amsmath}
$\sqrt{x} + \sqrt{y}            + \sqrt{z}$ \\
$\sqrt{x} + \sqrt{\mathstrut y} + \sqrt{z}$ \\
$\sqrt{x} + \sqrt{\smash{y}}    + \sqrt{z}$ \\
$\sqrt{x} + \sqrt{\smash[b]{y}} + \sqrt{z}$
```

To get the three radical signs looking pleasantly similar, it seems that the thing to do may be to give the y some extra height with a strut—but that only makes things worse! The best solution turns out to be to smash the bottom of the y (but not the whole of it!).

In the next example, the top of the large fraction in the second line appears correctly at its normal height, while neither this height nor the depth of the p in the denominator on the first line affects the vertical space between the two lines. This, of course, would bring the two lines in this example confusingly close together. For this reason, another \strut was added. Nevertheless, more moderate use of smashing is often of benefit to such unbalanced displays.

$$f_p(x) = \begin{cases} \frac{1}{p} & x = p \\ \frac{(1-x)^{\frac{1}{2}}}{\frac{x-\sin(x-p)}{\sqrt{1-p}\,\cos(x-p)}} & x \neq p \end{cases}$$

```
\usepackage{amsmath}
\[
  f_p (x) =
  \begin{cases}
    \frac{1}{\smash[b]{p}}                        & x = p  \\
    \frac{\strut
      \smash[t]{\frac{(1 - x)^{\frac{1}{2}} }
                 { x - \sin (x - p)      } } }
     {\sqrt{1 - p} \, \cos (x - p)}    & x \neq p
  \end{cases}
\]
```

8-7-6

Another collection of examples illustrates a very common application of smashing: using a partial \smash to give fine control over the height of surrounding delimiters. It also shows that smashing can lead to problems because the real height of the line needs to be known; this is restored by \vphantom. In the following code, \Hmjd is the compound symbol defined by

```
\newcommand\Hmjd{\widetilde{\mathcal{H}^2}_{MJD}(\chi)}
```

To show the resulting vertical space we added some rules:

Appearance	Code	*Comment*
$\overline{\left(\widetilde{\mathcal{H}^2}_{MJD}(\chi)\right)}$	`\left(` `{\Hmjd } \right)`	*Outer brackets too large*
$\overline{(\widetilde{\mathcal{H}^2}_{MJD}(\chi))}$	`\left(` `\smash{\Hmjd } \right)`	*Outer brackets too small and rules too close*
$\overline{(\widetilde{\mathcal{H}^2}_{MJD}(\chi))}$	`\left( \smash[t]{\Hmjd } \right) \vphantom{\Hmjd}`	*Just right!*
$\overline{(\widetilde{\mathcal{H}^2}_{MJD}(\chi))}$	`\left( \smash[t]{\Hmjd } \right)`	*Both vphantom and partial smash are needed*

Smashes being ignored by TeX

A word of warning: in a few places, deficiencies in the very low-level TeX processing may cause errors in the fine details of typesetting. These possibilities are of particular concern in mathematical layouts where (1) a sub-formula (such as the numerator/denominator of a fraction or subscripts/superscripts) consists of exactly one LR-box, or a similarly constructed mathematical box, and also (2) that box does not have its natural size, as with the more complex forms of \makebox, smashes, and some phantoms. As an example look at the following:

8-7-7

$$\sqrt{\dfrac{a+b}{x_j}} \quad \sqrt{\dfrac{a+b}{x_j}} \quad \sqrt{\dfrac{a+b}{x_j}} \quad \sqrt{\dfrac{a+b}{x_j+b}}$$

```
\[
  \sqrt{ \frac{a+b}{x_j} }                \quad
  \sqrt{ \frac{a+b}{\smash{x_j}} }        \quad
  \sqrt{ \frac{a+b}{{}\smash{x_j}} }      \quad
  \sqrt{ \frac{a+b}{\smash{x_j+b}} }
\]
```

To shorten the depth of the radical, a \smash was added in the second radical, but without any effect. With an empty brace group (third radical), it suddenly worked. On the other hand, no workaround was needed for the forth radical.[1] For the same reason the \strut or an empty brace group was actually necessary in Example 8-7-6 on the facing page to see any effects from the \smash commands there. In summary, whenever you find that a \smash does not work, try adding an empty math sub-formula (from {}) before the lonely box, to keep it from being mistreated.

8.7.6   Horizontal spaces

Even finer, and more difficult, tuning requires the explicit spacing commands shown in Table 8.6 on the next page. Both the full and short forms of these commands are robust, and they can also be used outside math mode in normal text. They are related to the thin, medium, and thick spaces available on the machines used to typeset mathematics in the mid-20th century.

The amounts of space added by these \..space commands are, in fact, defined by the current values of the three parameters \thinmuskip, \medmuskip, and \thickmuskip; the table lists their default values with amsmath. These very low-level TeX parameters require values in "mu" (*math units*). They must therefore be set only via low-level TeX assignments (as shown in Example 8-9-2 on page 525) and not by \setlength or similar commands. Moreover, in normal circumstances their values should not be modified because they are used internally by TeX's mathematical typesetting (see Table 8.7 on page 525).

Do not change the parameter values

One math unit (1mu) is 1/18 of an em in the current mathematical font size (see also Table A.1 on page 855). Thus, the absolute value of a math unit varies with the mathematical style, giving consistent spacing whatever the style.

These math units can be used more generally to achieve even better control over space within mathematics. This is done via the amsmath command \mspace, which is like \hspace except that it can be used only within mathematics and its length argument must be given in math units (e.g., \mspace{0.5mu}). Thus, to get a negative \quad within a mathematical formula, you could write \mspace{-18.0mu}; this will, for example, normally give about half the space

---

[1] Technically this is due to the denominator being wider than the nominator in this case, so that it was not reboxed by TeX.

Positive Spaces			*Negative Spaces*			
Short	*Space*	*Full*	*Short*	*Space*	*Full*	*Amount*
\,	⇒⇐	\thinspace	\!	⇒⇐	\negthinspace	3 mu
\:	⇒⇐	\medspace		⇒⇐	\negmedspace	4 mu plus 2 mu minus 4 mu
\;	⇒⇐	\thickspace		⇒⇐	\negthickspace	5 mu plus 5 mu
	⇒ ⇐	\enskip				0.5 em
	⇒ ⇐	\quad				1 em
	⇒ ⇐	\qquad				2 em

Note: The "Amount" column is discussed in the text.

Table 8.6: Mathematical spacing commands

in a double subscript size as it does in the basic mathematical size. In contrast, \hspace{-1em} will produce the same amount of space whatever the mathematical font size (but \text{\hspace{-1em}} will produce variable-sized space).

8.8 Fonts in formulas

For most symbols in a formula, the font used for a glyph cannot be changed by a font declaration as it can be in text. Indeed, there is no concept of, for example, an italic plus sign or a small caps less than sign.

One exception involves the letters of the Latin alphabet, whose appearance can be altered by the use of math alphabet identifier commands such as \mathcal. The commands provided by standard LATEX for this purpose are discussed in Section 7.4; this section introduces a few more. Another exception relates to the use of bold versions of arbitrary symbols to produce distinct symbols with new meanings. This potentially doubles the number of symbols available, as boldness can be a recognizable attribute of a glyph for nearly every shape: depending on the font family, even "<" is noticeably different from "<". Although there is a \mathbf command, the concept of a math alphabet identifier cannot be extended to cover bold symbols; a better solution is discussed in Section 8.8.2.

To change the overall appearance of the mathematics in a document, the best approach is to replace all the fonts used to typeset formulas. This is usually done in the preamble of a document by loading a (set of) suitable packages, such as those discussed in Sections 7.6 and 7.7.

At the end of this section we showcase the effects of such extensive changes, made with but a few keystrokes, on a sample page of mathematics. Section 8.8.3 contains the same material typeset with both Computer Modern Math fonts (the default in LATEX) and 15 other font families for text and mathematics. All of the fonts used are readily available and about half of them are provided free of charge.

8.8.1   Additional math font commands

By loading the `amsfonts` (or `amssymb`) package, the Euler Fraktur alphabet
(`\mathfrak`) and a Blackboard Bold alphabet (`\mathbb`) become available.

<table>
<tr><td>8-8-1</td><td>$\forall n \in \mathbb{N} : \mathfrak{M}_n \leq \mathfrak{A}$</td><td>

```
\usepackage{amsfonts}
$ \forall n \in \mathbb{N} : \mathfrak{M}_n \leq \mathfrak{A} $
```
</td></tr>
</table>

As an example of small-scale changes to the mathematical typesetting, those
who prefer a visually distinct Blackboard Bold alphabet can load one from the
Math Pazo fonts. See Section 7.6.3 for more information on the Math Pazo fonts
and Section 7.4.1 for details on `\DeclareMathAlphabet`. In this example we first
load the amsfonts package and then overwrite its definition of `\mathbb`.

<table>
<tr><td>8-8-2</td><td>$\{n, m \in \mathbb{N} \mid \mathfrak{N}_{n,m}\}$</td><td>

```
\usepackage{amsfonts}
\DeclareMathAlphabet\mathbb{U}{fplmbb}{m}{n}
$ \lbrace n,m \in \mathbb{N} \mid  \mathfrak{N}_{n,m} \rbrace $
```
</td></tr>
</table>

This example shows how to include arbitrary alphabets from your LaTeX
distribution as math alphabets, with the crucial part being the arguments of
`\DeclareMathAlphabet`. Although getting these right may appear to be a tricky
matter, it is not so difficult once you know where to look. Fonts suitable for inclusion need to have an `.fd` file; that is, given a font family name in the Berry
naming convention (see Section 7.10.2), there should be a file ⟨*enc*⟩⟨*name*⟩`.fd`.
For example,

the (commercial) Lucida Handwriting font

has the family name `hlcw`. It is available in several encodings, including T1, so
one possible file to look at is `t1hlcw.fd`. In that file you will find the remaining
arguments for the declaration. The font is available only in series `m` and shape
`it`. All other font shapes contain substitutions (see Section 7.10.6 for details on
the file format for `.fd` files). Putting all this together enables us to provide a
`\mathscr` command. Another possibility is to use this alphabet as a replacement
for the standard `\mathcal` command.

<table>
<tr><td>8-8-3</td><td>$A_B \neq \mathscr{A}_\mathscr{B} \neq \mathcal{A}_\mathcal{B}$</td><td>

```
\DeclareMathAlphabet\mathscr{T1}{hlcw}{m}{it}
$A_B \neq \mathscr{A}_\mathscr{B} \neq \mathcal{A}_\mathcal{B}$
```
</td></tr>
</table>

Of course, the presence of the file `t1hlcw.fd` (and other support files) on
your system does not mean that the previous example will run there. To achieve
this goal, you must also install the corresponding commercial font. Most modern
LaTeX installations contain such support files for various commercial font sets, so
that you can use these fonts the moment you have bought them and added them
to your system. In this case you would need a file called `hlcriw8a.pfb`.

In truth, you probably do not need to buy any fonts, because the freely available fonts already include a huge choice. The `nfssfont.tex` program can provide

valuable help in choosing a font, by producing samples and character tables for the fonts available to your installation (see Section 7.5.7).

8.8.2 bm—Making bold

For bold Latin letters only, you can use the command `\mathbf`; for everything else, there is the bm package. Although amsmath provides `\boldsymbol` and `\pmb`, the rules about when to use which command, and many of the restrictions on when they work, can now be avoided: just load the bm package and use `\bm` to make any formula as bold and beautiful as the available fonts allow.

The example below shows many ways to use the `\bm` and `\mathbf` commands and a strategy for defining shorthand names for frequently occurring bold symbols, using both standard LaTeX's `\newcommand` and `\bmdefine`, which is provided by bm. Note that `\mathbf{xy}` is not identical to `\bm{xy}`: the former produces bold Roman "**xy**" and the latter produces "$\boldsymbol{xy}$" (i.e., bold math italic).

```
\usepackage{amsmath,amssymb,bm}
\newcommand\bfB{\mathbf{B}}   \newcommand\bfx{\mathbf{x}}
\bmdefine\bpi{\pi}            \bmdefine\binfty{\infty}
\section{The bold equivalence
  $\sum_{j < B} \prod_\lambda : \bm{\sum_{x_j} \prod_\lambda}$}
\begin{gather}
  B_\infty + \pi B_1 \sim  \bfB_{\binfty} \bm{+}\bpi \bfB_{\bm{1}}
    \bm {\sim B_\infty + \pi B_1}                                \\
  B_\binfty + \bpi B_{\bm{1}} \bm{\in} \bm{\biggl\lbrace}
    (\bfB, \bfx) : \frac {\partial \bfB}{\partial \bfx}
    \bm{\lnapprox} \bm{1} \bm{\biggr\rbrace}
\end{gather}
```

1   The bold equivalence $\sum_{j<B} \prod_\lambda : \boldsymbol{\sum_{x_j} \prod_\lambda}$

$$B_\infty + \pi B_1 \sim \mathbf{B_\infty} + \boldsymbol{\pi}\mathbf{B_1} \sim \boldsymbol{B_\infty + \pi B_1} \tag{1}$$

8-8-4

$$B_\infty + \boldsymbol{\pi} B_{\mathbf{1}} \boldsymbol{\in} \left\{ (\mathbf{B}, \mathbf{x}) : \frac{\partial \mathbf{B}}{\partial \mathbf{x}} \boldsymbol{\lessgtr} \mathbf{1} \right\} \tag{2}$$

In the above example bm tries its best to fulfill the requests for bold versions of individual symbols and letters, but if you look closely you will see that the results are not always optimal. For example, $\sum$, $\prod$, and $\lessgtr$ are all made bold by use of a technique known as *poor man's bold*, in which the symbol is overprinted three times with slight offsets. Also, the { is not made bold in any way. Such deficiencies are unavoidable because for some symbols there is simply no bold variant available when using the Computer Modern math fonts.

The situation changes when the txfonts are loaded by changing the first line of the previous example to `\usepackage{amsmath,amssymb,txfonts,bm}`. This family of fonts contains bold variants for *all* symbols from standard LaTeX and amssymb. It produces the following output:

1   The bold equivalence $\sum_{j<B}\prod_\lambda : \sum_{x_j}\prod_\lambda$

8-8-5

$$B_\infty + \pi B_1 \sim \mathbf{B_\infty} + \pi\mathbf{B_1} \sim \mathbf{B_\infty} + \pi\mathbf{B_1} \tag{1}$$

$$B_\infty + \pi B_1 \in \left\{ (\mathbf{B},\mathbf{x}) : \frac{\partial \mathbf{B}}{\partial \mathbf{x}} \gtrless 1 \right\} \tag{2}$$

What are the precise rules used by \bm to produce bold forms of the symbols in its argument? In a nutshell, it makes use of the fact that LaTeX includes a **bold** math version (accessible via \boldmath) for typesetting a whole formula in bold (provided suitable bold fonts are available and set up). For each symbol, the \bm command looks at this math version to see what would be done in that version. If the font selected for the symbol is different from the one selected in the normal math version, it then typesets the symbol in this bold font, obtaining a perfect result (assuming that the bold math version was set up properly). If the fonts in both versions are identical, it assumes that there is no bold variant available and applies poor man's bold (see above).

Load the bm *package after packages that change existing the math font set-up!*

With delimiters, such as \biggl\lbrace in the example, the situation is even more complex: a delimiter in TeX is typically typeset by a glyph chosen to match a requested height from a sequence of different sizes (see Section 8.5.3 on page 498). Moreover, these glyphs can live in different fonts and a particular size may or may not have bold variants, making it impossible for \bm to reliably work out whether it needs to apply poor man's bold. It therefore essentially typesets the delimiter using whatever fonts the bold math version offers. With the Computer Modern math fonts, only the smallest delimiter size is available in bold; all other sizes come from fonts that have no bold variants.

8-8-6

```
\usepackage{bm}
$\bm{\Biggl\lbrace\biggl\lbrace\Bigl\lbrace\bigl\lbrace \lbrace
     \mathcal{Q}
     \rangle \bigr\rangle\Bigr\rangle\biggr\rangle\Biggr\rangle}$
```

This situation can be improved by use of the txfonts (as in Example 8-8-5) or use of another font set with full bold variants, such as the pxfonts shown here:

8-8-7

```
\usepackage{pxfonts,bm}
$\bm{\Biggl\lbrace\biggl\lbrace\Bigl\lbrace\bigl\lbrace \lbrace
     \mathcal{Q}
     \rangle \bigr\rangle\Bigr\rangle\biggr\rangle\Biggr\rangle}$
```

Normally, \bm requires that if a command that itself takes arguments is within its argument, then that command must be fully included (i.e., both the command and its arguments must appear) in the argument of \bm; as a result, all parts of the typeset material will be in bold. If you really need the output of a command with arguments to be only partially bold, then you have to work harder. You should place the symbol(s) that should not be bold in an `\mbox` and explicitly reset the math version within the box contents using `\unboldmath`. TEX considers an `\mbox` to be a symbol of class Ordinary (see Section 8.9.1); hence, to get the spacing right, you may have to surround it by a `\mathbin`, `\mathrel`, or `\mathop`.

$\sqrt[2]{x \times \alpha}$ but $\sqrt[2]{x \times \alpha}$
or the similar $\sqrt{x \times \alpha}$

```
\usepackage{amsmath,bm}

$ \bm{\sqrt[2]{x \times \alpha}} $  but
$ \bm{\sqrt[2]{x \mathbin{\mbox{\unboldmath$\times$}}} \alpha}} $    8-8-8
   or the similar
$ \bm{\sqrtsign}{\bm{x} \times \bm{\alpha}} $
```

Fortunately, such gymnastics are seldom needed. In most cases involving commands with arguments, only parts of the arguments need to be made bold, which can be achieved by using `\bm` inside those arguments. As with `\sqrtsign` in the example above, for the common case of bold accents `\bm` is specially programmed to allow the accent's argument to be outside its own argument. However, if you need such accents regularly, it is wise to define your own abbreviation using `\bmdefine`, as in the next example.

Speeding up the processing Although `\bmdefine\bpi{\pi}` appears to be simply shorthand for `\newcommand\bpi{\bm{\pi}}`, in fact almost the opposite is true: `\bm` defines a new hidden temporary command using `\bmdefine` and then immediately uses this temporary command to produce the bold symbol. In other words, `\bmdefine` does all the hard work! If you frequently use, for example, something that is defined via `\bm{\alpha}}`, then a new `\bmdefine` is executed at every use. If you set things up by doing `\bmdefine\balpha{\alpha}`, then `\bmdefine` does its time-consuming work only once, however many times `\balpha` is used.

$\hat{a} \neq \hat{a} \neq \hat{a} = \hat{a} \neq \widehat{a}$

```
\usepackage{bm}   \bmdefine\bhat{\hat}
                                                                        8-8-9
$\hat a \neq \bm{\hat a} \neq \bm\hat a = \bhat a \neq \bm\widehat a$
```

This example also shows that the variable-width accents (e.g., `\widehat`) share a deficiency with the delimiters: in the Computer Modern math set-up they come from a font for which no bold variant is available.

Dealing with strange errors The `bm` package tries very hard to produce the correct spacing between symbols (both inside and outside the argument of `\bm`). For this effort to work, `\bm` has to "investigate" the definitions of the commands in its argument to determine the correct mathematical class to which each of the resulting symbols belongs (see Section 8.9.1 on page 524). It is possible that some strange constructions could confuse this investigation. If this happens then LATEX will almost certainly stop with a strange error. Ideally, this problem should not arise with constructs from standard LATEX or the $\mathcal{A}_{\mathcal{M}}\mathcal{S}$-LATEX distributions, but proper parsing in TEX is extremely difficult and the odd overlooked case might still be present. For instance, the author got trapped when writing this section by the fact that `\bm` was trying to process the argument of \hspace instead of producing the desired space (this problem is fixed in version 1.1a).

If some command does produce an error when used inside \bm, you can always surround it *and all its arguments* with an extra level of braces—for example, writing \bm{..{\cmd..}..} rather than simply \bm{..\cmd..}. The \bm command will not attempt to parse material surrounded by braces but will use the \boldmath version to typeset the whole of the formula within the braces. The resulting bold sub-formula is then inserted as if it were a "symbol" of class Ordinary. Thus, to obtain the right spacing around it, you may have to explicitly set its class; for instance, for a relation you would use \bm{..\mathrel{\cmd..}..} (see Section 8.9.1 on page 524).

8.8.3   A collection of math font set-ups

In this section show a sample text typeset with different font set-ups for math and text. Figure 8.1 shows the sample text typeset in Computer Modern text and math fonts—the default font set-up in LaTeX. Figures 8.2 to 8.16 on pages 514–523 (with blue captions to visually separate caption and sample) have also been generated by typesetting this sample text, each time loading different support packages for text and math fonts. These packages do all the work required to modify LaTeX's internal tables. For other set-ups and additional information see [24].

---

1   Sample page of mathematical typesetting

First some large operators both in text: $\iiint_Q f(x,y,z)\,dx\,dy\,dz$ and $\prod_{\gamma \in \Gamma_{\widetilde{C}}} \partial(\widetilde{X}_\gamma)$; and also on display:

$$\iiiint_Q f(w,x,y,z)\,dw\,dx\,dy\,dz \leq \oint_{\partial Q} f'\left(\max\left\{\frac{\|w\|}{|w^2+x^2|};\frac{\|z\|}{|y^2+z^2|};\frac{\|w\oplus z\|}{\|x\oplus y\|}\right\}\right)$$

8-8-10

$$\approx \biguplus_{Q \in \bar{Q}}\left[f^*\left(\frac{\int \mathbb{Q}(t)}{\sqrt{1-t^2}}\right)\right]_{t=\alpha}^{t=\vartheta} \tag{1}$$

For x in the open interval $]-1,1[$ the infinite sum in Equation (2) is convergent; however, this does not hold throughout the closed interval $[-1,1]$.

$$(1-x)^{-k} = 1 + \sum_{j=1}^{\infty}(-1)^j\left\{{k \atop j}\right\}x^j \quad \text{for } k \in \mathbb{N}; k \neq 0. \tag{2}$$

Figure 8.1: Sample page typeset with Computer Modern fonts

1   Sample page of mathematical typesetting

First some large operators both in text: $\iiint_Q f(x,y,z)\,dx\,dy\,dz$ and $\prod_{\gamma \in \Gamma_{\widetilde{C}}} \partial(\widetilde{X}_\gamma)$;
and also on display:

$$\iiiint_Q f(w,x,y,z)\,dw\,dx\,dy\,dz \leq \oint_{\partial Q} f'\left(\max\left\{ \frac{\|w\|}{|w^2+x^2|}; \frac{\|z\|}{|y^2+z^2|}; \frac{\|w \oplus z\|}{\|x \oplus y\|} \right\} \right)$$

$$\lessapprox \biguplus_{Q \in \bar{Q}} \left[f^* \left(\frac{\int Q(t)}{\sqrt{1-t^2}} \right) \right]_{t=\alpha}^{t=\vartheta} \tag{1}$$

8-8-11

For x in the open interval $]{-}1,1[$ the infinite sum in Equation (2) is convergent; however, this does not hold throughout the closed interval $[-1,1]$.

$$(1-x)^{-k} = 1 + \sum_{j=1}^{\infty} (-1)^j \left\{ \begin{matrix} k \\ j \end{matrix} \right\} x^j \quad \text{for } k \in \mathbb{N};\ k \neq 0. \tag{2}$$

Figure 8.2: Sample page typeset with Concrete fonts

1   Sample page of mathematical typesetting

First some large operators both in text: $\iiint_Q f(x,y,z)\,dx\,dy\,dz$ and $\prod_{\gamma \in \Gamma_{\widetilde{C}}} \partial(\widetilde{X}_\gamma)$;
and also on display:

$$\iiiint_Q f(w,x,y,z)\,dw\,dx\,dy\,dz \leqslant \oint_{\partial Q} f'\left(\max\left\{ \frac{\|w\|}{|w^2+x^2|}; \frac{\|z\|}{|y^2+z^2|}; \frac{\|w \oplus z\|}{\|x \oplus y\|} \right\} \right)$$

$$\lessapprox \biguplus_{Q \in \bar{Q}} \left[f^* \left(\frac{\int Q(t)}{\sqrt{1-t^2}} \right) \right]_{t=\alpha}^{t=\vartheta} \tag{1}$$

8-8-12

For x in the open interval $]{-}1,1[$ the infinite sum in Equation (2) is convergent; however, this does not hold throughout the closed interval $[-1,1]$.

$$(1-x)^{-k} = 1 + \sum_{j=1}^{\infty} (-1)^j \left\{ \begin{matrix} k \\ j \end{matrix} \right\} x^j \quad \text{for } k \in \mathbb{N};\ k \neq 0. \tag{2}$$

Figure 8.3: Sample page typeset with Concrete and Euler fonts

1 Sample page of mathematical typesetting

First some large operators both in text: $\iiint_{\mathcal{Q}} f(x, y, z)\, dx\, dy\, dz$ and $\prod_{\gamma \in \Gamma_{\widehat{C}}} \partial(\widetilde{X}_\gamma)$; and also on display:

$$\iiiint_{\mathbf{Q}} f(w, x, y, z)\, dw\, dx\, dy\, dz \leq \oint_{\partial \mathbf{Q}} f' \left(\max \left\{ \frac{\|w\|}{|w^2 + x^2|}; \frac{\|z\|}{|y^2 + z^2|}; \frac{\|w \oplus z\|}{\|x \oplus y\|} \right\} \right) \tag{1}$$

$$\approx \biguplus_{\mathbb{Q} \in \bar{\mathbb{Q}}} \left[f^* \left(\frac{\int \mathbb{Q}(t)}{\sqrt{1 - t^2}} \right) \right]_{t=\alpha}^{t=\vartheta}$$

For x in the open interval $]-1, 1[$ the infinite sum in Equation (2) is convergent; however, this does not hold throughout the closed interval $[-1, 1]$.

$$(1 - x)^{-k} = 1 + \sum_{j=1}^{\infty} (-1)^j \left\{ \begin{matrix} k \\ j \end{matrix} \right\} x^j \quad \text{for } k \in \mathbb{N}; \ k \neq 0. \tag{2}$$

Figure 8.4: Sample page typeset with Fourier fonts

8-8-13

The Concrete Roman text fonts were designed by Donald Knuth, matching math fonts were designed by Ulrik Vieth; see Section 7.7.2. They are shown in Figure 8.3, which was produced by adding \usepackage[boldsans]{ccfonts} to the preamble of the sample document. Note that Concrete fonts have no boldface, so that the ∂Q subscript on the integral comes out in poor man's bold.

Figure 8.3 combines Concrete Roman with Euler Math (designed by Hermann Zapf). This combination was produced with

```
\usepackage{ccfonts}    \usepackage[euler-digits]{eulervm}
```

and shows no deficiencies with bold symbols in math; see also Section 7.7.10. You will probably want to design different headings, as the default (Computer Modern boldface extended) does not blend very well with Concrete Roman.

In Figure 8.4 we see Utopia combined with Fourier Math fonts (designed by Michel Bovani). This combination has been discussed in Section 7.7.7 and was produced by adding \usepackage{fourier} to the preamble. Again, the boldface subscript shows deficiencies, but these are expected to be addressed in a future release of the fonts.

The METAFONT versions of Concrete Roman and Math are freely available. Scalable outlines can be purchased from MicroPress.[1] The Fourier set-up is freely available in Type 1 format.

---

[1]http://www.micropress-inc.com

1   Sample page of mathematical typesetting

First some large operators both in text: $\underset{\mathscr{Q}}{\iiint} f(x,y,z)\,dx\,dy\,dz$ and $\prod_{\gamma\in\Gamma_{\widetilde{C}}}\partial(\widetilde{X}_\gamma)$; and also on display:

$$\iiiint_{\mathbf{Q}} f(w,x,y,z)\,dw\,dx\,dy\,dz \leq \oint_{\partial\mathbf{Q}} f'\left(\max\left\{\frac{\|w\|}{|w^2+x^2|};\frac{\|z\|}{|y^2+z^2|};\frac{\|w\oplus z\|}{\|x\oplus y\|}\right\}\right) \tag{1}$$

$$\gtrapprox \biguplus_{Q\in\bar{\mathbf{Q}}}\left[f^*\left(\frac{\int\mathbb{Q}(t)\}}{\sqrt{1-t^2}}\right)\right]_{t=\alpha}^{t=\vartheta}$$

8-8-14

For x in the open interval $]-1,1[$ the infinite sum in Equation (2) is convergent; however, this does not hold throughout the closed interval $[-1,1]$.

$$(1-x)^{-k} = 1 + \sum_{j=1}^{\infty}(-1)^j\left\{{k\atop j}\right\}x^j \quad \text{for } k\in\mathbb{N};\, k\neq 0. \tag{2}$$

Figure 8.5: Sample page typeset with Times and Symbol

1   Sample page of mathematical typesetting

First some large operators both in text: $\underset{Q}{\iiint} f(x,y,z)\,dx\,dy\,dz$ and $\prod_{\gamma\in\Gamma_{\widetilde{C}}}\partial(\widetilde{X}_\gamma)$; and also on display:

$$\iiiint_{\mathbf{Q}} f(w,x,y,z)\,dw\,dx\,dy\,dz \leq \oint_{\partial\mathbf{Q}} f'\left(\max\left\{\frac{\|w\|}{|w^2+x^2|};\frac{\|z\|}{|y^2+z^2|};\frac{\|w\oplus z\|}{\|x\oplus y\|}\right\}\right) \tag{1}$$

$$\gtrapprox \biguplus_{Q\in\bar{\mathbf{Q}}}\left[f^*\left(\frac{\int\mathbb{Q}(t)\}}{\sqrt{1-t^2}}\right)\right]_{t=\alpha}^{t=\vartheta}$$

8-8-15

For x in the open interval $]-1,1[$ the infinite sum in Equation (2) is convergent; however, this does not hold throughout the closed interval $[-1,1]$.

$$(1-x)^{-k} = 1 + \sum_{j=1}^{\infty}(-1)^j\left\{{k\atop j}\right\}x^j \quad \text{for } k\in\mathbb{N};\, k\neq 0. \tag{2}$$

Figure 8.6: Sample page typeset with Times and TX fonts

1 Sample page of mathematical typesetting

First some large operators both in text: $\iiint_Q f(x, y, z)\, dx\, dy\, dz$ and $\prod_{\gamma \in \Gamma_{\widetilde{C}}} \partial(\widetilde{X}_\gamma)$; and also on display:

$$\iiiint_{\mathbf{Q}} f(w, x, y, z)\, dw\, dx\, dy\, dz \leq \oint_{\partial Q} f' \left(\max \left\{ \frac{\|w\|}{|w^2 + x^2|}; \frac{\|z\|}{|y^2 + z^2|}; \frac{\|w \oplus z\|}{\|x \oplus y\|} \right\} \right)$$

$$\lessapprox \biguplus_{\mathbb{Q} \in \bar{\mathbb{Q}}} \left[f^* \left(\frac{\int \mathbb{Q}(t)}{\sqrt{1 - t^2}} \right) \right]_{t=\alpha}^{t=\vartheta} \tag{1}$$

For x in the open interval $]-1, 1[$ the infinite sum in Equation (2) is convergent; however, this does not hold throughout the closed interval $[-1, 1]$.

$$(1 - x)^{-k} = 1 + \sum_{j=1}^{\infty} (-1)^j \left\{ \begin{matrix} k \\ j \end{matrix} \right\} x^j \quad \text{for } k \in \mathbb{N}; k \neq 0. \tag{2}$$

Figure 8.7: Sample page typeset with Times and TM Math fonts

This page spread shows three math font set-ups for use with Times Roman as a body font. With Times Roman being one of the predominant fonts in use today, several solutions have been developed to provide support for it.

Figure 8.5 shows a free solution devised by Alan Jeffrey and others (discussed in Section 7.6.2), which was produced by adding \usepackage{mathptmx} to the preamble. It deploys Adobe's Symbol font for most mathematical symbols and due to a missing set of bold symbols for math, shows the typical deficiencies in this respect. In contrast to other font solutions it does not offer its own shapes for the extended AMS symbol set but uses the standard Computer Modern shapes.

Figure 8.6 also shows a freely available implementation deploying the TX fonts (designed by Young Ryu). It offers the full range of mathematical symbols including boldface variants, but uses exceptionally tight spacing so that sometimes symbols in formulas touch each other; see Section 7.7.5 for details. It can be activated by adding \usepackage{txfonts} in the preamble.

In Figure 8.7 we see the commercially available TM Math solution by Micro-Press,[1] which uses considerably wider spacing in formulas. It comprises bold symbols and offers its own shapes for the AMS extended symbol set. It can be activated through \usepackage{tmmath,tmams} in the preamble.

Other commercial Math fonts in Type 1 format for use with Times Roman are MathTime and MathTime Professional (designed by Michael Spivak), available through Y&Y[2] and PcTeX,[3] respectively.

[1]http://www.micropress-inc.com   [2]http://www.YandY.com   [3]http://www.pctex.com

1   Sample page of mathematical typesetting

First some large operators both in text: $\iiint_Q f(x,y,z)\,dx\,dy\,dz$ and $\prod_{\gamma \in \Gamma_{\widetilde{C}}} \partial(\widetilde{X}_\gamma)$; and also on display:

$$\iiiint_Q f(w,x,y,z)\,dw\,dx\,dy\,dz \leq \oint_{\partial Q} f'\left(\max\left\{\frac{\|w\|}{|w^2 + x^2|}; \frac{\|z\|}{|y^2 + z^2|}; \frac{\|w \oplus z\|}{\|x \oplus y\|}\right\}\right)$$

$$\gtrapprox \biguplus_{Q \in \bar{Q}}\left[f^*\left(\frac{\int Q(t)\}}{\sqrt{1 - t^2}}\right)\right]_{t=\alpha}^{t=\vartheta}$$

8-8-17

(1)

For x in the open interval $]{-}1, 1[$ the infinite sum in Equation (2) is convergent; however, this does not hold throughout the closed interval $[-1, 1]$.

$$(1-x)^{-k} = 1 + \sum_{j=1}^{\infty} (-1)^j \begin{Bmatrix} k \\ j \end{Bmatrix} x^j \quad \text{for } k \in \mathbb{N}; k \neq 0. \tag{2}$$

Figure 8.8: Sample page typeset with Palatino and Math Pazo

1   Sample page of mathematical typesetting

First some large operators both in text: $\iiint_Q f(x,y,z)\,dx\,dy\,dz$ and $\prod_{\gamma \in \Gamma_{\widetilde{C}}} \partial(\widetilde{X}_\gamma)$; and also on display:

$$\iiiint_Q f(w,x,y,z)\,dw\,dx\,dy\,dz \leq \oint_{\partial Q} f'\left(\max\left\{\frac{\|w\|}{|w^2 + x^2|}; \frac{\|z\|}{|y^2 + z^2|}; \frac{\|w \oplus z\|}{\|x \oplus y\|}\right\}\right)$$

(1)

$$\gtrapprox \biguplus_{Q \in \bar{Q}}\left[f^*\left(\frac{\int Q(t)\}}{\sqrt{1 - t^2}}\right)\right]_{t=\alpha}^{t=\vartheta}$$

8-8-18

For x in the open interval $]{-}1, 1[$ the infinite sum in Equation (2) is convergent; however, this does not hold throughout the closed interval $[-1, 1]$.

$$(1-x)^{-k} = 1 + \sum_{j=1}^{\infty} (-1)^j \begin{Bmatrix} k \\ j \end{Bmatrix} x^j \quad \text{for } k \in \mathbb{N}; k \neq 0. \tag{2}$$

Figure 8.9: Sample page typeset with Palatino and PX fonts

1 Sample page of mathematical typesetting

First some large operators both in text: $\iiint_Q f(x, y, z)\, dx\, dy\, dz$ and $\prod_{\gamma \in \Gamma_{\hat{C}}} \partial(\tilde{X}_\gamma)$; and also on display:

$$\iiiint_Q f(w, x, y, z)\, dw\, dx\, dy\, dz \le \oint_{\partial Q} f' \left(\max \left\{ \frac{\|w\|}{|w^2 + x^2|}, \frac{\|z\|}{|y^2 + z^2|}, \frac{\|w \oplus z\|}{\|x \oplus y\|} \right\} \right)$$

$$\widetilde{\approx} \biguplus_{\mathbb{Q} \in \bar{Q}} \left[f^* \left(\frac{\int \mathbb{Q}(t)\, \}}{\sqrt{1 - t^2}} \right) \right]_{t=\alpha}^{t=\vartheta}$$

$$(1)$$

For x in the open interval $]{-}1, 1[$ the infinite sum in Equation (2) is convergent; however, this does not hold throughout the closed interval $[-1, 1]$.

$$(1 - x)^{-k} = 1 + \sum_{j=1}^{\infty} (-1)^j \left\{ {k \atop j} \right\} x^j \quad \text{for } k \in \mathbb{N}; k \ne 0. \qquad (2)$$

Figure 8.10: Sample page typeset with Palatino and PA Math fonts

The typeface Palatino was designed by Hermann Zapf for the Stempel foundry in 1948 based on lettering from the Italian Renaissance. Since then it has become one of the most widely used typefaces, and probably the most popular Old Style revival in existence. A number of math font set-ups are available for use with Palatino as the text font.

Figure 8.8 shows the freely available Math Pazo fonts (designed by Diego Puga), which can be activated with \usepackage{mathpazo}. It offers boldface symbols and a matching blackboard bold alphabet, but does not contain specially designed shapes for the AMS symbol set; see also Section 7.6.3.

In contrast, the free PX fonts (designed by Young Ryu) comprise the complete symbol set. They are shown in Figure 8.9. Just like the TX fonts, they are very tightly spaced; see Section 7.7.6 for details. This set-up can be activated with \usepackage{pxfonts}.

Figure 8.10 shows the commercial solution offered by MicroPress.[1] It provides a similar range of symbols as the Math Pazo solution with roughly the same running length, though with noticeably different shapes. This set-up can be activated with \usepackage{pamath}.

---

[1] http://www.micropress-inc.com

1 Sample page of mathematical typesetting

First some large operators both in text: $\iiint_Q f(x,y,z)\,dx\,dy\,dz$ and $\prod_{\gamma\in\Gamma_{\widetilde{C}}}\partial(\widetilde{X}_\gamma)$;
and also on display:

$$\iiiint_Q f(w,x,y,z)\,dw\,dx\,dy\,dz \le \oint_{\partial Q} f'\left(\max\left\{\frac{\|w\|}{|w^2+x^2|}; \frac{\|z\|}{|y^2+z^2|}; \frac{\|w\oplus z\|}{\|x\oplus y\|}\right\}\right)$$

$$\gtrsim \biguplus_{Q\in\bar{Q}}\left[f^*\left(\frac{\int Q(t)}{\sqrt{1-t^2}}\right)\right]_{t=\alpha}^{t=\vartheta}$$

(1)

8-8-20

For x in the open interval $]-1,1[$ the infinite sum in Equation (2) is convergent; however, this does not hold throughout the closed interval $[-1,1]$.

$$(1-x)^{-k} = 1 + \sum_{j=1}^{\infty}(-1)^j\left\{{k\atop j}\right\}x^j \quad \text{for } k\in\mathbb{N};\, k\neq 0. \tag{2}$$

Figure 8.11: Sample page typeset with Baskerville fonts

1 Sample page of mathematical typesetting

First some large operators both in text: $\iiint_Q f(x,y,z)\,dx\,dy\,dz$ and $\prod_{\gamma\in\Gamma_{\widetilde{C}}}\partial(\widetilde{X}_\gamma)$;
and also on display:

$$\iiiint_Q f(w,x,y,z)\,dw\,dx\,dy\,dz \le \oint_{\partial Q} f'\left(\max\left\{\frac{\|w\|}{|w^2+x^2|}; \frac{\|z\|}{|y^2+z^2|}; \frac{\|w\oplus z\|}{\|x\oplus y\|}\right\}\right)$$

$$\gtrsim \biguplus_{Q\in\bar{Q}}\left[f^*\left(\frac{\int Q(t)}{\sqrt{1-t^2}}\right)\right]_{t=\alpha}^{t=\vartheta}$$

(1)

8-8-21

For x in the open interval $]-1,1[$ the infinite sum in Equation (2) is convergent; however, this does not hold throughout the closed interval $[-1,1]$.

$$(1-x)^{-k} = 1 + \sum_{j=1}^{\infty}(-1)^j\left\{{k\atop j}\right\}x^j \quad \text{for } k\in\mathbb{N};\, k\neq 0. \tag{2}$$

Figure 8.12: Sample page typeset with Charter fonts

1 Sample page of mathematical typesetting

First some large operators both in text: $\iiint\limits_{Q} f(x,y,z)\,dx\,dy\,dz$ and $\prod_{y\in\Gamma_{\widetilde{C}}} \partial(\widetilde{X}_y)$; and also on display:

$$\iiiint\limits_{\mathbf{Q}} f(w,x,y,z)\,dw\,dx\,dy\,dz \le \oint_{\partial Q} f' \left(\max\left\{ \frac{\|w\|}{|w^2 + x^2|}; \frac{\|z\|}{|y^2 + z^2|}; \frac{\|w \oplus z\|}{\|x \oplus y\|} \right\} \right)$$

$$\lesssim \biguplus_{Q \in \bar{Q}} \left[f^{\star} \left(\frac{\int \mathfrak{Q}(t)\,|}{\sqrt{1 - t^2}} \right) \right]_{t=\alpha}^{t=\vartheta} \tag{1}$$

For x in the open interval $]-1,1[$ the infinite sum in Equation (2) is convergent; however, this does not hold throughout the closed interval $[-1,1]$.

$$(1 - x)^{-k} = 1 + \sum_{j=1}^{\infty} (-1)^j \begin{Bmatrix} k \\ j \end{Bmatrix} x^j \quad \text{for } k \in \mathbb{N}; \, k \neq 0. \tag{2}$$

Figure 8.13: Sample page typeset with Lucida Bright

Figure 8.11 deploys the Baskerville typeface as a text font. This "transitional" typeface was originally designed by John Baskerville (1706–1775) and can be obtained from many font vendors. The math fonts are BA Math from MicroPress[1]—their distribution also contains a variant of the Baskerville text fonts used here. The BA Math fonts include bold weights but do not contain shapes for the AMS symbol set. Note that although the individual symbols do not look very large, the display formulas take more vertical space than in other examples. The font set-up is activated with \usepackage{ba}.

Figure 8.12 shows the use of the commercial CH Math fonts (also from MicroPress[1]). Their distribution has been designed to work with the freely available Charter fonts; see Section 7.6.1. The CH Math fonts comprise the full set of mathematical symbols including the AMS additions and are activated by adding the preamble line \usepackage{chmath,chams}.

The Lucida Bright and Lucida New Math fonts are displayed in Figure 8.13. This set of commercial text and math fonts has been designed by Charles Bigelow and Kris Holmes and can be obtained from Y&Y.[2] The font set-up covers all standard mathematical symbols including AMS additions and is activated by loading the lucidabr package. As you will notice, the formulas run very wide, which enhances legibility at the cost of space. The body font in this book is Lucida Bright. However, for the examples, we usually used Computer Modern to make them come out as in standard LaTeX.

---

[1]http://www.micropress-inc.com   [2]http://www.YandY.com

1 Sample page of mathematical typesetting

First some large operators both in text: $\iiint_Q f(x, y, z)\, dx\, dy\, dz$ and $\prod_{\gamma \in \Gamma_{\widetilde{c}}} \partial(\widetilde{X}_\gamma)$; and also on display:

$$
\iiiint_Q f(w, x, y, z)\, dw\, dx\, dy\, dz \leq \oint_{\partial Q} f' \left(\max \left\{ \frac{\|w\|}{|w^2 + x^2|}; \frac{\|z\|}{|y^2 + z^2|}; \frac{\|w \oplus z\|}{\|x \oplus y\|} \right\} \right)
$$

$$
\gtrsim \biguplus_{Q \in \bar{Q}} \left[f^* \left(\frac{\int Q(t)\,\big\rangle}{\sqrt{1 - t^2}} \right) \right]_{t=\alpha}^{t=\vartheta}
\tag{1}
$$

For x in the open interval $]-1, 1[$ the infinite sum in Equation (2) is convergent; however, this does not hold throughout the closed interval $[-1, 1]$.

$$
(1 - x)^{-k} = 1 + \sum_{j=1}^{\infty} (-1)^j \left\{ \begin{matrix} k \\ j \end{matrix} \right\} x^j \quad \text{for } k \in \mathbb{N}; \ k \neq 0.
\tag{2}
$$

8-8-23

Figure 8.14: Sample page typeset with CM Bright fonts

---

1 Sample page of mathematical typesetting

First some large operators both in text: $\iiint_Q f(x, y, z)\, dx\, dy\, dz$ and $\prod_{\gamma \in \Gamma_{\widetilde{c}}} \partial(\widetilde{X}_\gamma)$; and also on display:

$$
\iiiint_\mathbf{Q} f(w, x, y, z)\, dw\, dx\, dy\, dz \leq \oint_{\partial \mathbf{Q}} f' \left(\max \left\{ \frac{\|w\|}{|w^2 + x^2|}; \frac{\|z\|}{|y^2 + z^2|}; \frac{\|w \oplus z\|}{\|x \oplus y\|} \right\} \right)
$$

$$
\gtrsim \biguplus_{Q \in \bar{\mathbf{Q}}} \left[f^* \left(\frac{\int \mathbf{Q}(t)\,\big\rangle}{\sqrt{1 - t^2}} \right) \right]_{t=\alpha}^{t=\vartheta}
\tag{1}
$$

For x in the open interval $]-1, 1[$ the infinite sum in Equation (2) is convergent; however, this does not hold throughout the closed interval $[-1, 1]$.

$$
(1 - x)^{-k} = 1 + \sum_{j=1}^{\infty} (-1)^j \left\{ \begin{matrix} k \\ j \end{matrix} \right\} x^j \quad \text{for } k \in \mathbb{N}; \ k \neq 0.
\tag{2}
$$

8-8-24

Figure 8.15: Sample page typeset with Helvetica Math fonts

---

1   Sample page of mathematical typesetting

First some large operators both in text: $\iiint_Q f(x, y, z)\, dx\, dy\, dz$ and $\prod_{\gamma \in \Gamma_{\hat{c}}} \partial(\tilde{X}_\gamma)$; and also on display:

$$\iiiint_Q f(w, x, y, z)\, dw\, dx\, dy\, dz \leq \oint_{\partial Q} f' \left(\max \left\{ \frac{\|w\|}{|w^2 + x^2|}; \frac{\|z\|}{|y^2 + z^2|}; \frac{\|w \oplus z\|}{\|x \oplus y\|} \right\} \right)$$

$$\lessapprox \biguplus_{Q \in \bar{Q}} \left[f^* \left(\frac{\|\mathbb{Q}(t_i)\|}{\sqrt{1 - t^2}} \right) \right]_{t=a}^{t=\emptyset} \tag{1}$$

8-8-25

For x in the open interval $]{-1}, 1[$ the infinite sum in Equation (2) is convergent; however, this does not hold throughout the closed interval $[-1, 1]$.

$$(1 - x)^{-k} = 1 + \sum_{j=1}^{\infty} (-1)^j \left\{ \begin{matrix} k \\ j \end{matrix} \right\} x^j \quad \text{for } k \in \mathbb{N};\ k \neq 0. \tag{2}$$

Figure 8.16: Sample page typeset with Info Math fonts

This page spread shows two sans serif set-ups and an "informal" math font set-up. The solutions involving sans serif fonts can be usefully deployed in many circumstances, such as conventional articles, presentations (e.g., slides, reports), online documentation, or magazines. On the other hand, the Informal Math solution should probably be confined to announcements, fliers, and similar material.

Figure 8.14 shows the Computer Modern Bright set of fonts (designed by Walter Schmidt), which are based on the Computer Modern font design. The solution offers the full range of math symbols in normal and bold weights and is activated by loading the cmbright package; see Section 7.7.3. The fonts are freely available in METAFONT format, and the Type 1 versions are commercially available from MicroPress.[1]

Figure 8.15 shows a math font set-up for use with Helvetica (originally designed by Max Miedinger). The HV math fonts are designed at MicroPress[1] and comprise the full set of mathematical symbols. The set-up is activated by loading the packages hvmath and hvams (for the AMS symbol set). While the Type 1 fonts are only commercially available, you can obtain 300 dpi bitmapped fonts free of charge from MicroPress.

Finally, Figure 8.16 shows the Informal Math solution also offered by Micro-Press.[1] The font design is loosely based on Adobe's Tekton family of fonts. The set-up is activated by loading the infomath package. Note that the text fonts are only available in OT1 and that the AMS symbol set is not supported.

---

[1] http://www.micropress-inc.com

8.9   Symbols in formulas

The tables at the end of this section advertise the large range of mathematical symbols provided by the $\mathcal{A}_{\mathcal{M}}\mathcal{S}$ fonts packages, including the command to use for each symbol. They also include the supplementary symbols from the St Mary Road Font, which was designed by Alan Jeffrey and Jeremy Gibbons. This package extends the Computer Modern and $\mathcal{A}_{\mathcal{M}}\mathcal{S}$ symbol font collections and should normally be loaded in addition to amssymb, but always after it. It provides extra symbols for fields such as functional programming, process algebra, domain theory, linear logic, and many more. For a wealth of information about an even wider variety of symbols, see the *Comprehensive LaTeX Symbol List* by Scott Pakin [134].

The tables indicate which extra packages need to be loaded to use each symbol command. They are organized as follows: symbols with command names in black are available in standard LaTeX without loading further packages; symbols in blue require loading either amsmath, amssymb, or stmaryrd, as explained in the table notes. If necessary, further classification is given by markings: $^{(StM)}$ signals a symbol from stmaryrd when the table also contains symbols from other packages; $^{(kernel)}$ identifies symbols that are available in standard LaTeX but only by combining two or more glyphs, whereas a single glyph exists in the indicated package; and $^{(var)}$ marks "Alphabetic symbols" (of type \mathalpha; see Table 7.30 on page 435) that change appearance when used within the scope of a math alphabet identifier (see Section 7.4).

8.9.1   Mathematical symbol classes

The symbols are classified primarily by their "mathematical class", occasionally called their "math symbol type". This classification is related to their "meaning" in standard technical usage, but its importance for mathematical typography is that it influences the layout of a formula. For example, TeX's mathematical formatter adjusts the horizontal space on either side of each symbol according to its mathematical class. There are also some finer distinctions made, for example, between accents and simple symbols and in breaking up the enormous list of Relation symbols into several tables.

The set-up for mathematics puts each symbol into one of these classes: Ordinary (Ord), Operator (Op), Binary (Bin), Relation (Rel), Opening (Open), Closing (Close), or Punctuation (Punct). This classification can be explicitly changed by using the commands \mathord, \mathop, \mathbin, \mathrel, \mathopen, \mathclose, and \mathpunct, thereby altering the surrounding spacing. In this example, \# and \top (both Ord by default) are changed into a Rel and an Op.

$$a\#\top_x^\alpha x_b^\alpha$$

$$a \# \underset{x}{\top} x_b^\alpha$$

```
\usepackage[fleqn]{amsmath}

\[ a            \#            \top _x^\alpha x^\alpha_b \]
\[ a \mathrel{\#} \mathop{\top}_x^\alpha x^\alpha_b \]
```

8-9-1

Right Object

		Ord	Op	Bin	Rel	Open	Close	Punct	Inner
	Ord	0	1	(2)	(3)	0	0	0	(1)
	Op	1	1	*	(3)	0	0	0	(1)
	Bin	(2)	(2)	*	*	(2)	*	*	(2)
Left	Rel	(3)	(3)	*	0	(3)	0	0	(3)
Object	Open	0	0	*	0	0	0	0	0
	Close	0	1	(2)	(3)	0	0	0	(1)
	Punct	(1)	(1)	*	(1)	(1)	(1)	(1)	(1)
	Inner	(1)	1	(2)	(3)	(1)	0	(1)	(1)

*0 = no space,   1 = \thinmuskip,   2 = \medmuskip,   3 = \thickmuskip,   * = impossible*

Entries in (blue) are not added when in the mathematical "script styles" (see also Sections 8.7.1 and 8.7.6).

Table 8.7: Space between symbols

A symbol can be declared to belong to one of the above classes using the mechanism described in Section 7.10.7. In addition, certain sub-formulas—most importantly fractions, and those produced by \left and \right—form a class called Inner; it is explicitly available through the \mathinner command.

In TEX, spacing within formulas is done simply by identifying the class of each object in a formula and then adding space between each pair of adjacent objects as defined in Table 8.7; this table is unfortunately hard-wired into TEX's mathematical typesetting routines and so cannot be changed by macro packages.[1] In this table 0, 1, 2, and 3 stand for no space, a thin space ($\,$), a medium space ($\:$), and a thick space ($\;$), respectively. The exact amounts of space used are listed in Section 8.7.6 on page 507.

A Binary symbol is turned into an Ordinary symbol whenever it is not preceded and followed by symbols of a nature compatible with a binary operation; for this reason, some entries in the table are marked with a star to indicate that they are not possible. For example, `$+x$` gives $+x$ (a "unary plus") and not $+x$; the latter can be produced by `${}+x$`.

Finally, an entry in (blue) in Table 8.7 indicates that the corresponding space is not inserted when the style is script or scriptscript.

As an example of applying these rules, consider the following formula (the default values are deliberately changed to show the added spaces more clearly):

8-9-2

$$a - b = - \max\{x, y\}$$

```
\thinmuskip=10mu \medmuskip=17mu \thickmuskip=30mu
\[
  a - b = -\max \{ x , y \}
\]
```

---

[1] Although a few of the entries in the table are questionable, on the whole it gives pleasing results.

$$A\,B\,C\,D\,E\,F\,G\,H\,I\,J\,K\,L\,M\,N\,O\,P\,Q\,R\,S\,T\,U\,V\,W\,X\,Y\,Z$$
$$a\,b\,c\,d\,e\,f\,g\,h\,i\,j\,k\,l\,m\,n\,o\,p\,q\,r\,s\,t\,u\,v\,w\,x\,y\,z$$
$$0\,1\,2\,3\,4\,5\,6\,7\,8\,9$$

Table 8.8: Latin letters and Arabic numerals

TEX identifies the objects as Ord, Bin, Ord, and so on, and then inserts spaces as follows:

```
a      -      b      =      -    \max \{   x    ,       y   \}
Ord \: Bin \: Ord \; Rel \; Ord \, Op  Open Ord Punct \, Ord Close
```

The minus in front of `\max` is turned into an Ordinary because a Binary cannot follow a Relation.

Table 8.7 reveals a difference[1] between a "`\left...\right`" construction, in which the entire sub-formula delimited by the construction becomes a single object of class Inner (see Section 8.5.3 on page 498), and commands like `\Bigl` and `\Bigr` that produce individual symbols of the classes Opening and Closing, respectively. Although they may result in typesetting delimiters of equal vertical size, spacing differences can arise depending on adjacent objects in the formula. For example, Ordinary followed by Opening gets no space, whereas Ordinary followed by Inner is separated by a thin space. The spaces inside the sub-formula within a "`\left...\right`" construction are as expected, beginning with an Opening symbol and ending with a Closing symbol. In this example we again use larger spaces to highlight the difference.

$$a\!\left(\sum x\right) \quad \neq \quad a\left(\sum x\right)$$

```
\thinmuskip=10mu \medmuskip=17mu \thickmuskip=30mu
\[ a \Bigl( \sum x \Bigr) \neq  a \left( \sum x \right) \]
```

8-9-3

In summary, it is not enough to look up a symbol in the tables that follow; rather, it is also advisable to check that the symbol has the desired mathematical class to ensure that it is properly spaced when used. Example 8-9-4 on page 528 shows how to define new symbols that differ only in their mathematical class from existing symbols.

8.9.2   Letters, numerals, and other Ordinary symbols

The unaccented ASCII Latin letters and Arabic numeral digits (see Table 8.8) all referred to as "Alphabetic symbols". The font used for them can vary: in mathematical formulas, the default font for Latin letters is italic whereas for the Arabic digits it is upright/Roman. Alphabetical symbols are all of class Ordinary.

---

[1]Another important distinction is that the material within a "`\left...\right`" construction is processed separately as a sub-formula (see Section 8.7.2 on page 503).

Δ	`\Delta`$^{(var)}$	Γ	`\Gamma`$^{(var)}$	Λ	`\Lambda`$^{(var)}$	Ω	`\Omega`$^{(var)}$	Φ	`\Phi`$^{(var)}$
Π	`\Pi`$^{(var)}$	Ψ	`\Psi`$^{(var)}$	Σ	`\Sigma`$^{(var)}$	Θ	`\Theta`$^{(var)}$	Υ	`\Upsilon`$^{(var)}$
Ξ	`\Xi`$^{(var)}$	α	`\alpha`	β	`\beta`	χ	`\chi`	δ	`\delta`
F	`\digamma`	ϵ	`\epsilon`	η	`\eta`	γ	`\gamma`	ι	`\iota`
κ	`\kappa`	λ	`\lambda`	μ	`\mu`	ν	`\nu`	ω	`\omega`
ϕ	`\phi`	π	`\pi`	ψ	`\psi`	ρ	`\rho`	σ	`\sigma`
τ	`\tau`	θ	`\theta`	υ	`\upsilon`	ε	`\varepsilon`	$\varkappa$	`\varkappa`
φ	`\varphi`	ϖ	`\varpi`	ϱ	`\varrho`	ς	`\varsigma`	ϑ	`\vartheta`
ξ	`\xi`	ζ	`\zeta`						

Symbols in blue require the amssymb package $^{(var)}$ indicates a variable Alphabetic symbol.

Table 8.9: Symbols of class `\mathord` (Greek)

Unlike the Latin letters, the mathematical Greek letters are no longer closely related to the glyphs used for typesetting normal Greek text. Due to an interesting 18th-century happenstance, in the major European tradition of mathematical typography the default font for lowercase Greek letters in mathematical formulas is italic whereas for uppercase Greek letters it is upright/Roman. (In other fields, such as physics and chemistry, the typographical traditions are slightly different.)

The capital Greek letters in the first columns of Table 8.9 are also Alphabetic symbols whose font varies, with the default being upright/Roman. Those capital Greek letters not present in this table are the letters that have the same appearance as some Latin letter (e.g., *A* and *Alpha*, *B* and *Beta*, *K* and *Kappa*, *O* and *Omicron*). Similarly, the list of lowercase Greek letters there is no omicron because it would be identical in appearance to the Latin *o*. Thus, in practice, the Greek letters that have Latin look-alikes are not used in mathematical formulas.

Table 8.10 lists other letter-shaped symbols of class Ordinary. The first four are Hebrew letters. Table 8.11 lists the remaining symbols in the Ordinary class,

$\$$	`\$`	$\Im$	`\Im`	$\Re$	`\Re`	$\aleph$	`\aleph`
$\Bbbk$	`\Bbbk`	$\beth$	`\beth`	$\circledS$	`\circledS`	$\complement$	`\complement`
$\daleth$	`\daleth`	ℓ	`\ell`	$\eth$	`\eth`	$\Finv$	`\Finv`
$\Game$	`\Game`	$\gimel$	`\gimel`	$\hbar$	`\hbar`$^{(ker)}$	$\hslash$	`\hslash`
$\imath$	`\imath`	$\jmath$	`\jmath`	$\$$	`\mathdollar`	$\P$	`\mathparagraph`
$\S$	`\mathsection`	$\pounds$	`\mathsterling`	$\mho$	`\mho`	$\P$	`\P`
∂	`\partial`	$\pounds$	`\pounds`	$\S$	`\S`	$\wp$	`\wp`

Symbols in blue require the amssymb *package.*

Synonyms: $\$$ `\mathdollar`, `\$` $\P$ `\mathparagraph`, `\P` $\S$ `\mathsection`, `\S` $\pounds$ `\mathsterling`, `\pounds`

Table 8.10: Symbols of class `\mathord` (letter-shaped)

!	!	.	.	/	/
?	?	@	@	|	|
#	\#	%	\%	&	\&
_	_	‖	|	∠	\angle^(ker)
‖	\Arrowvert	|	\arrowvert	`	\backprime
\	\backslash	⁝	\bracevert	★	\bigstar
◆	\blacklozenge	■	\blacksquare	▼	\blacktriangledown
▲	\blacktriangle	⊥	\bot	♣	\clubsuit
©	\copyright	╲	\diagdown	╱	\diagup
◇	\diamondsuit	∅	\emptyset	∃	\exists
♭	\flat	∀	\forall	♡	\heartsuit
∞	\infty	↯	\lightning^(StM)	¬	\lnot
◊	\lozenge	∡	\measuredangle	∇	\nabla
♮	\natural	¬	\neg	∄	\nexists
′	\prime	♯	\sharp	♠	\spadesuit
◁	\sphericalangle	□	\square	√	\surd
⊤	\top	▽	\triangledown	△	\triangle
©	\varcopyright^(StM)	∅	\varnothing	‖	\Vert
|	\vert				

Symbols in blue require either the amssymb *package or, if flagged with* ^(StM), *the* stmaryrd *package.*

Note that the exclamation sign, period, and question mark are not treated as punctuation in formulas.

Synonyms: ¬ \lnot, \neg | \vert, | ‖ \Vert, \|

Table 8.11: Symbols of class \mathord (miscellaneous)

including some common punctuation. These behave like letters and digits, so they never get any extra space around them.

A common mistake is to use the symbols from Table 8.11 directly as Binary operator or Relation symbols, without using a properly defined math symbol command for that type. Thus, if you use commands such as \#, \square, or \&, check carefully that you get the correct inter-symbol spaces or, even better, define your own symbol command.

$a\neg b$ $x\square y + z$

$a \neg b$ $x\ \square\ y + z$

$a\neg b$ $x\ \square\ y + z$

```
\usepackage[fleqn]{amsmath}   \usepackage{amssymb}
\DeclareMathSymbol\bneg   {\mathbin}{symbols}{"3A}
\DeclareMathSymbol\rsquare{\mathrel}{AMSa}{"03}
\[ a \neg b               \qquad  x \square           y + z \]
\[ a \mathbin{\neg} b \qquad  x \mathrel{\square} y + z \]
\[ a \bneg            b      \qquad  x \rsquare           y + z \]
```

8-9-4

The \DeclareMathSymbol declaration is explained in Section 7.10.7. The correct values for its arguments are most easily found by looking at the definitions

$\acute{x}$	\acute{x}	$\bar{x}$	\bar{x}	$\breve{x}$	\breve{x}	$\check{x}$	\check{x}
$\ddddot{x}$	\ddddot{x}	$\dddot{x}$	\dddot{x}	$\ddot{x}$	\ddot{x}	$\dot{x}$	\dot{x}
$\grave{x}$	\grave{x}	$\hat{x}$	\hat{x}	x	\mathring{x}	$\tilde{x}$	\tilde{x}
$\vec{x}$	\vec{x}	$\widehat{xyz}$	\widehat{xyz}	$\widetilde{xyz}$	\widetilde{xyz}		

Accents in blue require the amsmath *package.*

The last two accents are available in a range of widths, the largest suitable one being automatically used.

Table 8.12: Mathematical accents, giving sub-formulas of class \mathord

in the file `amssymb.sty` or `fontmath.ltx` (for the core symbols). For example, we looked up \neq and \square, replaced the \mathord in each case, and finally gave the resulting symbol a new name.

8.9.3 Mathematical accents

The accent commands available for use in formulas are listed in Table 8.12. Most of them are already defined in standard LaTeX. See Section 8.4.8 for ways to define additional accent commands and Section 8.5.2 for information about extensible accents. Adding a mathematical accent to a symbol always produces a symbol of class Ordinary. Thus, without additional help, one cannot use the accents to produce new Binary or Relation symbols.

8-9-5

$a = b$ but $a \tilde{=} b$ which is not $a \mathrel{\tilde{=}} b$

```
\usepackage{amstext}
\[  a = b  \text{ but }  a \tilde{=} b
     \text{ which is not } a \mathrel{\tilde{=}} b  \]
```

Other ways to place symbols over Relation symbols are shown in Section 8.4.10. When adding an accent to an i or j in mathematics, it is best to use the dotless variants \imath and \jmath; for example, use \hat{\jmath} to get $\hat{\jmath}$.

8.9.4 Binary operator symbols

There are more than 100 symbols of class Binary operators from which to choose. Most of these Binary symbols are shown in Table 8.13 on the next page. Some of them are also available, under different names, as Relation symbols.

The amssymb package offers a few box symbols for use as Binary operators; many more are added by stmaryrd. These are shown in Table 8.14.

The stmaryrd package can be loaded with the option `heavycircles`. It causes each circle symbol command in Table 8.15 on page 531 that starts with \var to swap its definition with the corresponding command without the "var"; for example, the symbol \varodot becomes \odot, and vice versa.

∗	*	+	+	−	-
⨿	\amalg	∗	\ast	⦶	\baro[(StM)]
⊼	\barwedge	⫽	\bbslash[(StM)]	▽	\bigtriangledown
△	\bigtriangleup	⋒	\Cap	∩	\cap
⋓	\Cup	∪	\cup	⋎	\curlyvee
⋏	\curlywedge	†	\dag	†	\dagger
‡	\ddag	‡	\ddagger	⋄	\diamond
⊛	\divideontimes	÷	\div	∔	\dotplus
⋒	\doublecap	⋓	\doublecup	⍀	\fatbslash[(StM)]
⨟	\fatsemi[(StM)]	⫻	\fatslash[(StM)]	⋗	\gtrdot
⊺	\intercal	⫼	\interleave[(StM)]	∧	\land
⟭	\lbag[(StM)]	⊲	\leftslice[(StM)]	⋋	\leftthreetimes
⋖	\lessdot	∨	\lor	⋉	\ltimes
⋀	\merge[(StM)]	⊖	\minuso[(StM)]	⋢	\moo[(StM)]
∓	\mp	⊞	\nplus[(StM)]	±	\pm
⟮	\rbag[(StM)]	⊳	\rightslice[(StM)]	⋌	\rightthreetimes
⋊	\rtimes	∖	\setminus	∖	\smallsetminus
⊓	\sqcap	⊔	\sqcup	⫽	\sslash[(StM)]
⋆	\star	⫾	\talloblong[(StM)]	×	\times
◁	\triangleleft	▷	\triangleright	⊎	\uplus
▽	\varbigtriangledown[(StM)]	△	\varbigtriangleup[(StM)]	⋎	\varcurlyvee[(StM)]
⋏	\varcurlywedge[(StM)]	⋇	\vartimes[(StM)]	⊻	\veebar
∨	\vee	∧	\wedge	≀	\wr
⅄	\Ydown[(StM)]	⋊	\Yleft[(StM)]	⋋	\Yright[(StM)]
⅄	\Yup[(StM)]				

Symbols in *blue* require either the amssymb *package or, if flagged with* [(StM)], *the* stmaryrd *package.*

The left and right triangles are also available as Relation symbols.

The stmaryrd *package confusingly changes the Binary symbols* \bigtriangleup *and* \bigtriangledown *into Operators, leaving only the synonyms* \varbigtriangleup *and* \varbigtriangledown *for the Binary operator forms.*

Synonyms:　∧ \land, \wedge　　∨ \lor, \vee　　⋓ \doublecup, \Cup　　⋒ \doublecap, \Cap

　　　　　　∗ \ast, *　　† \dag, \dagger　　‡ \ddag, \ddagger

Table 8.13: Symbols of class \mathbin (miscellaneous)

⊛	\boxast[(StM)]	⊟	\boxbar[(StM)]	⊡	\boxbox[(StM)]	⧅	\boxbslash[(StM)]
⊙	\boxcircle[(StM)]	⊡	\boxdot	□	\boxempty[(StM)]	⊟	\boxminus
⊞	\boxplus	⧄	\boxslash[(StM)]	⊠	\boxtimes	□	\oblong[(StM)]

All symbols require either the amssymb *package or, if flagged with* [(StM)], *the* stmaryrd *package.*

Table 8.14: Symbols of class \mathbin (boxes)

●	\bullet	·	\cdot	.	\centerdot
◯	\bigcirc	⊛	\circledast	◉	\circledcirc
⊖	\circleddash	○	\circ	⊛	\oast$^{(StM)}$
⊕	\obar$^{(StM)}$	◎	\ocircle$^{(StM)}$	⊕	\obar$^{(StM)}$
⊙	\odot	⊘	\ogreaterthan$^{(StM)}$	⊘	\olessthan$^{(StM)}$
⊖	\ominus	⊕	\oplus	⊘	\oslash
⊗	\otimes	⊗	\ovee$^{(StM)}$	⊘	\owedge$^{(StM)}$
◯	\varbigcirc$^{(StM)}$	⊛	\varoast$^{(StM)}$	⊕	\varobar$^{(StM)}$
⊘	\varobslash$^{(StM)}$	◎	\varocircle$^{(StM)}$	⊙	\varodot$^{(StM)}$
⊘	\varogreaterthan$^{(StM)}$	⊘	\varolessthan$^{(StM)}$	⊖	\varominus$^{(StM)}$
⊕	\varoplus$^{(StM)}$	⊘	\varoslash$^{(StM)}$	⊗	\varotimes$^{(StM)}$
⊗	\varovee$^{(StM)}$	⊘	\varowedge$^{(StM)}$		

Symbols in blue require either the amssymb *package or, if flagged with* $^{(StM)}$, *the* stmaryrd *package.*

Option heavycircles *of the* stmaryrd *package affects all commands starting with* \var *and their normal variants.*

Synonyms: ⊛ \oast, \circledast   ◎ \ocircle, \circledcirc

Table 8.15: Symbols of class \mathbin (circles)

8.9.5   Relation symbols

The class of binary Relation symbols forms a collection even larger than that of the Binary operators. The lists start with symbols for equality and order (Table 8.16 on the next page). You can put a slash through any Relation symbol by preceding it with the \not command; this negated symbol represents the complement (or negation) of the relation.

<table>
<tr><td>8-9-6</td><td>$u \not< v$ or $a \notin \mathbf{A}$</td><td>$ u \not< v$ or $a \not\in \mathbf{A} $</td></tr>
</table>

Especially with larger symbols, this generic method of negating a Relation symbol does not always give good results because the slash will always be of the same size, position, and slope. Therefore, some specially designed "negated symbols" are also available (see Table 8.17 on the following page). If a choice is available, the designed glyphs are usually preferable. To see why, compare the symbols in this example.

<table>
<tr><td>8-9-7</td><td>≰ ⋡ ≁
≰ ⋡ ≁</td><td>\usepackage{amssymb}
$ \not\leq \ \not\succeq \ \not\sim $ \par
$ \nleq \quad \ \nsucceq \quad \ \nsim \quad $</td></tr>
</table>

Next come the Relation symbols for sets and inclusions, and their negations (see Tables 8.18 and 8.19).

<	`<`	=	`=`	>	`>`	≊	`\approxeq`
≈	`\approx`	≍	`\asymp`	⋍	`\backsimeq`	∽	`\backsim`
≏	`\Bumpeq`	≎	`\bumpeq`	≗	`\circeq`	≅	`\cong`
⋞	`\curlyeqprec`	⋟	`\curlyeqsucc`	≑	`\Doteq`	≒	`\doteqdot`
≐	`\doteq`	≖	`\eqcirc`	≂	`\eqsim`	⪀	`\eqslantgtr`
⪇	`\eqslantless`	≡	`\equiv`	≒	`\fallingdotseq`	≧	`\geqq`
⩾	`\geqslant`	≥	`\geq`	≥	`\ge`	⋙	`\gggtr`
⋙	`\ggg`	≫	`\gg`	⪆	`\gtrapprox`	⋛	`\gtreqless`
⪌	`\gtreqqless`	≷	`\gtrless`	≳	`\gtrsim`	⇆	`\leftrightarroweq`(StM)
≦	`\leqq`	⩽	`\leqslant`	≤	`\leq`	⪅	`\lessapprox`
≶	`\lesseqgtr`	⪋	`\lesseqqgtr`	≶	`\lessgtr`	≲	`\lesssim`
≤	`\le`	⋘	`\llless`	⋘	`\lll`	≪	`\ll`
⪷	`\precapprox`	≼	`\preccurlyeq`	≼	`\preceq`	≺	`\prec`
≓	`\risingdotseq`	≃	`\simeq`	∼	`\sim`	⪸	`\succapprox`
≽	`\succcurlyeq`	≽	`\succeq`	≿	`\succsim`	≻	`\succ`
≈	`\thickapprox`	∼	`\thicksim`	≜	`\triangleq`		

Symbols in blue require either the amssymb package or, if flagged with (StM), the stmaryrd package.

Synonyms: ≤ \le, \leq   ≥ \ge, \geq   ≒ \Doteq, \doteqdot   ⋘ \llless, \lll   ⋙ \gggtr, \ggg

Table 8.16: Symbols of class `\mathrel` (equality and order)

⪊	`\gnapprox`	≩	`\gneqq`	⪈	`\gneq`	⋧	`\gnsim`
⪈	`\gvertneqq`	⪉	`\lnapprox`	≨	`\lneqq`	⪇	`\lneq`
⋦	`\lnsim`	⪇	`\lvertneqq`	≇	`\ncong`	≠	`\neq`
≠	`\ne`	≱	`\ngeqq`	⋛̸	`\ngeqslant`	≱	`\ngeq`
≯	`\ngtr`	≰	`\nleqq`	≰	`\nleqslant`	≰	`\nleq`
≮	`\nless`	⋠	`\npreceq`	⊀	`\nprec`	≁	`\nsim`
⋡	`\nsucceq`	⊁	`\nsucc`	⪹	`\precnapprox`	⪵	`\precneqq`
⋨	`\precnsim`	⋨	`\precsim`	⪺	`\succnapprox`	⪶	`\succneqq`
⋩	`\succnsim`						

Symbols in blue require either the amssymb package or, flagged with (StM), the stmaryrd package.

Synonyms: ≠ \ne, \neq

Table 8.17: Symbols of class `\mathrel` (equality and order—negated)

◄	`\blacktriangleleft`	▶	`\blacktriangleright`	∈	`\inplus`(StM)
∈	`\in`	∋	`\niplus`(StM)	∋	`\ni`
⋬	`\ntrianglelefteqslant`(StM)	⋭	`\ntrianglerighteqslant`(StM)	∋	`\owns`
⊑	`\sqsubseteq`	⊏	`\sqsubset`	⊒	`\sqsupseteq`
⊐	`\sqsupset`	⋐	`\Subset`	⋑	`\Supset`
⊆	`\subseteqq`	⊆	`\subseteq`	⊑	`\subsetpluseq`(StM)
⊕	`\subsetplus`(StM)	⊂	`\subset`	⊇	`\supseteqq`
⊇	`\supseteq`	⊞	`\supsetpluseq`(StM)	⊞	`\supsetplus`(StM)
⊃	`\supset`	◁	`\trianglelefteq`	▷	`\trianglerighteq`
▷	`\trianglerighteqslant`(StM)	⊴	`\trianglelefteqslant`(StM)	◁	`\vartriangleleft`
▷	`\vartriangleright`	△	`\vartriangle`		

Symbols in blue *require either the* amssymb *package or, if flagged with* (StM)*, the* stmaryrd *package.*

Synonyms: ∋ `\owns`, `\ni`

Table 8.18: Symbols of class `\mathrel` (sets and inclusion)

∉	`\notin`	⊊	`\nsubseteqq`	⊄	`\nsubseteq`
⊉	`\nsupseteqq`	⊉	`\nsupseteq`	⋬	`\ntrianglelefteq`
⋪	`\ntriangleleft`	⋫	`\ntrianglerighteq`	⋭	`\ntriangleright`
⊊	`\subsetneqq`	⊊	`\subsetneq`	⊋	`\supsetneqq`
⊋	`\supsetneq`	⊊	`\varsubsetneqq`	⊊	`\varsubsetneq`
⊋	`\varsupsetneqq`	⊋	`\varsupsetneq`		

Symbols in blue *require the* amssymb *package.*

Table 8.19: Symbols of class `\mathrel` (sets and inclusion—negated)

They are followed by Relation symbols that are arrow-shaped (see Tables 8.20 and 8.21). Some extensible arrow constructions that produce compound Relation symbols are described in Section 8.5.2 on page 497.

In addition to `\not`, used to negate general Relation symbols, other building blocks have been especially designed to negate or extend arrow-like symbols; these are collected in Table 8.22.

8-9-8   ←/→   ↚

```
\usepackage{stmaryrd}
$\Longarrownot\longleftrightarrow \qquad  \arrownot\hookleftarrow$
```

Finally, in Table 8.23 on page 535 you will find a miscellaneous collection of Relation symbols.

↺ \circlearrowleft	↻ \circlearrowright	⋎ \curlyveedownarrow[StM]
⋎ \curlyveeuparrow[StM]	⋏ \curlywedgedownarrow[StM]	⋏ \curlywedgeuparrow[StM]
↷ \curvearrowleft	↶ \curvearrowright	--→ \dasharrow
←-- \dashleftarrow	--→ \dashrightarrow	⇓ \Downarrow
↓ \downarrow	⇊ \downdownarrows	⇂ \downharpoonright
← \gets	↩ \hookleftarrow	↪ \hookleftarrow
↪ \hookrightarrow	⇐ \Leftarrow	← \leftarrow
↢ \leftarrowtail	⇽ \leftarrowtriangle[StM]	⇿ \leftrightarrowtriangle[StM]
↼ \leftharpoondown	↼ \leftharpoonup	⇇ \leftleftarrows
⇔ \Leftrightarrow	⇆ \leftrightarrows	↔ \leftrightarrow
⇋ \leftrightharpoons	↭ \leftrightsquigarrow	⇚ \Lleftarrow
⟸ \Longleftarrow	⟵ \longleftarrow	⟺ \Longleftrightarrow
⟷ \longleftrightarrow	⇚ \Longmapsfrom[StM]	⟻ \longmapsfrom[StM]
⟼ \Longmapsto[StM]	⟼ \longmapsto	⟹ \Longrightarrow
⟶ \longrightarrow	↫ \looparrowleft	↬ \looparrowright
↰ \Lsh	⇐ \Mapsfrom[StM]	↤ \mapsfrom[StM]
⇒ \Mapsto[StM]	↦ \mapsto	⊸ \multimap
↗ \nearrow	↗ \nnearrow[StM]	↖ \nnwarrow[StM]
↖ \nwarrow	↾ \restriction	↣ \rightarrowtail
↦ \rightarrowtriangle[StM]	⇒ \Rightarrow	→ \rightarrow
⇁ \rightharpoondown	⇀ \rightharpoonup	⇄ \rightleftarrows
⇌ \rightleftharpoons	⇉ \rightrightarrows	↝ \rightsquigarrow
⇛ \Rrightarrow	↱ \Rsh	↘ \searrow
↓ \shortdownarrow[StM]	← \shortleftarrow[StM]	→ \shortrightarrow[StM]
↑ \shortuparrow[StM]	↘ \ssearrow[StM]	↙ \sswarrow[StM]
↙ \swarrow	→ \to	↞ \twoheadleftarrow
↠ \twoheadrightarrow	⇑ \Uparrow	↑ \uparrow
↿ \upharpoonleft	↾ \upharpoonright	⇕ \Updownarrow
↕ \updownarrow	⇈ \upuparrows	

Symbols in blue require either the amssymb *package or, if flagged with* [StM], *the* stmaryrd *package.*

Synonyms: ← \gets, \leftarrow   → \to, \rightarrow   ↾ \restriction, \upharpoonright

--→ \dashrightarrow, \dasharrow

Table 8.20: Symbols of class \mathrel (arrows)

⇍ \nLeftarrow	⇎ \nLeftrightarrow	⇏ \nRightarrow
↚ \nleftarrow	↮ \nleftrightarrow	↛ \nrightarrow

Symbols in blue require the amssymb *package.*

Table 8.21: Symbols of class \mathrel (arrows—negated)

/	\Arrownot[StM]	/	\Longarrownot[StM]	⊢	\Mapsfromchar[StM]	⊣	\Mapstochar[StM]
/	\arrownot[StM]	/	\longarrownot[StM]	⊢	\mapsfromchar[StM]	⊣	\mapstochar
⸖	\lhook	/	\not	⸲	\rhook		

Symbols in blue require the stmaryrd *package.*

These symbols are for combining, mostly with arrows; e.g., \longarrownot\longleftarrow *gives* ←—.

Use \joinrel *to "glue" relational symbols together, e.g.,* \lhook\joinrel\longrightarrow *gives* ↪—→.

The dimensions of these symbols make them unsuitable for other uses.

Table 8.22: Symbols of class \mathrel (negation and arrow extensions)

:	:	∋	\backepsilon	∵	\because	⚬	\between
⋈	\bowtie	⊣	\dashv	⌢	\frown	⋈	\Join
∣	\mid	⊨	\models	∤	\nmid	∦	\nparallel
∤	\nshortmid	∦	\nshortparallel	⊯	\nVDash	⊮	\nvDash
⊮	\nVdash	⊯	\nvdash	‖	\parallel	⊥	\perp
⋔	\pitchfork	∝	\propto	∣	\shortmid	‖	\shortparallel
⌢	\smallfrown	⌣	\smallsmile	⌣	\smile	∴	\therefore
∝	\varpropto	⊩	\Vdash	⊨	\vDash	⊢	\vdash
⊪	\Vvdash						

Relation symbols in blue require the amssymb *package.*

\therefore *is a Relation symbol, so its spacing may not be as expected in common uses.*

Table 8.23: Symbols of class \mathrel (miscellaneous)

8.9.6 Punctuation

The symbols of class Punctuation appear in Table 8.24, together with some other punctuation-like symbols. Note that some of the typical punctuation characters (i.e., ". ! ?") are not set up as mathematical punctuation but rather as symbols of class Ordinary. This can cause unexpected results for common uses of these symbols, especially in the cases of ! and ?. Some of the dots symbols listed here are of class Inner; Section 8.5.1 on page 496 provides information about using dots for mathematical ellipsis.

The : character produces a colon with class Relation—not a Punctuation symbol. As an alternative, standard LaTeX offers the command \colon as the Punctuation symbol. However, the amsmath package makes unfortunate major changes to the spacing produced by the command \colon, so that it is useful only for a particular layout in constructions such as f\colon A\to B where it produces $f\colon A \to B$. It is therefore wise to always use \mathpunct{:} for the simple punctuation colon in mathematics.

, ,		$\cdots$	\cdots	...	\hdots	...	\ldots	...	\mathellipsis
; ;		:	\colon	$\ddots$	\ddots	$\vdots$	\vdots

Punctuation symbols in blue require the amsmath *package.*

The logical amsmath *commands normally used to access* \cdots *and* \ldots *are described in Section 8.5.1.*

The \colon *command is redefined in amsmath, making it unsuitable for use as a general punctuation character.*

Synonyms: ... \hdots, \ldots   ... \mathellipsis, \ldots

Table 8.24: Symbols of class \mathpunct, \mathord, \mathinner (punctuation)

$\int$	\int		$\oint$	\oint		$\Box\Box$	\bigbox(StM)
$\bigcap$	\bigcap		$\bigcup$	\bigcup		$\curlyvee\curlyvee$	\bigcurlyvee(StM)
$\curlywedge\curlywedge$	\bigcurlywedge(StM)		$\interleave\interleave$	\biginterleave(StM)		$\nplus\nplus$	\bignplus(StM)
$\odot\odot$	\bigodot		$\oplus\oplus$	\bigoplus		$\otimes\otimes$	\bigotimes
$\parallel\parallel$	\bigparallel(StM)		$\sqcap\sqcap$	\bigsqcap(StM)		$\sqcup\sqcup$	\bigsqcup
$\triangledown\triangledown$	\bigtriangledown(StM)		$\triangle\triangle$	\bigtriangleup(StM)		$\uplus\uplus$	\biguplus
$\bigvee\bigvee$	\bigvee		$\bigwedge\bigwedge$	\bigwedge		$\coprod\coprod$	\coprod
$\prod\prod$	\prod		$\smallint\smallint$	\smallint		$\sum\sum$	\sum

Operator symbols in blue require the stmaryrd *package.*

The stmaryrd *package confusingly changes the Binary symbols* \bigtriangleup *and* \bigtriangledown *into Operators, but there are alternative commands for the Binary operator forms.*

Note that \smallint *does not change size.*

Table 8.25: Symbols of class \mathop

8.9.7 Operator symbols

The Operator symbols typically come in two sizes, for text and display uses; most of them are related to similar Binary operator symbols. Whether an Operator symbol takes limits in displays depends on a variety of factors (see Section 8.4.4). The available collection is shown in Table 8.25.

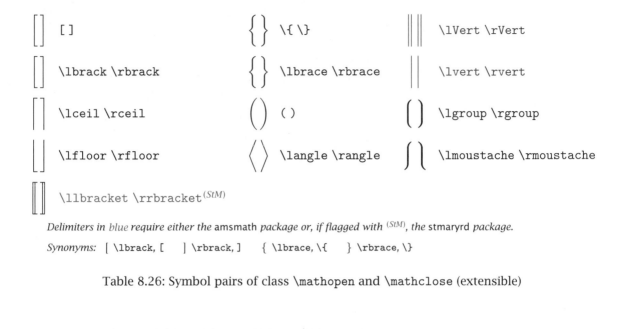

Delimiters in *blue* require either the amsmath *package or, if flagged with* (StM)*, the* stmaryrd *package.*

Synonyms: [\lbrack, [   ] \rbrack,]   { \lbrace, \{   } \rbrace, \}

Table 8.26: Symbol pairs of class \mathopen and \mathclose (extensible)

⎡⎤ \llceil \rrceil (StM)   & ⅋ \binampersand \bindnasrepma (StM)   ⦃ ⦄ \Lbag \Rbag (StM)

⎣⎦ \llfloor \rrfloor (StM)   ⦇ ⦈ \llparenthesis \rrparenthesis (StM)

All these pairs of symbols require the stmaryrd *package and are not extensible.*

Table 8.27: Symbol pairs of class \mathopen and \mathclose (non-extensible)

8.9.8 Opening and Closing symbols

The paired extensible delimiters, when used on their own (i.e., without a preceding \left, \right, or \middle), produce symbols of class Opening or Closing; these pairs are listed in Table 8.26. See Section 8.5.3 on page 498 for further information about the extensible symbols.

To improve the flexibility of the vertical bar notation, amsmath defines some new pairs of paired extensible delimiter commands: \lvert, \rvert, \lVert, and \rVert. These commands are comparable to standard LaTeX's \langle and \rangle commands.

The stmaryrd package adds a collection of non-extensible paired symbols of class Opening and Closing, which are listed in Table 8.27.

## CHAPTER 9

LaTeX in a Multilingual Environment

This chapter starts with a short introduction to the technical problems that must be solved if you want to use (LA)TeX with a non-English language. Most of the remaining part of the chapter discusses the babel system, which provides a convenient way of generating documents in different languages. We look in particular how we can typeset documents in French, German, Russian, Greek, and Hebrew, as the typesetting of those languages illustrates various aspects of the things one has to deal with in a non-English environment. Section 9.5 explains the structure of babel's language definition files for the various language options. Finally, we say a few words about how to handle other languages, such as Arabic and Chinese, that are not supported by babel.

9.1 TeX and non-English languages

Due to its popularity in the academic world, TeX spread rapidly throughout the world and is now used not only with the languages based on the Latin alphabet, but also with languages using non-Latin alphabetic scripts, such as Russian, Greek, Arabic, Persian, Hebrew, Thai, Vietnamese, and several Indian languages. Implementations also exist for Chinese, Japanese, and Korean, which use Kanji-based ideographic scripts.

With the introduction of 8-bit TeX and METAFONT, which were officially released by Donald Knuth in March 1990, problems of multilingual support could be more easily addressed for the first time. Nevertheless, by themselves, these versions do not solve all the problems associated with providing a convenient environment for using LaTeX with multiple and/or non-English languages.

To achieve this goal, TeX and its companion programs should be made truly international, and the following points should be addressed:

1. Adjust all programs to the particular language(s):

   - Support typesetting in different directions, this ability is offered by several programs (e.g., eTeX, Omega) [27, 97],
   - Create proper fonts containing national symbols [137],
   - Define standard character set encodings, and
   - Generate patterns for the hyphenation algorithm.

2. Provide a translation for the language-dependent strings, create national layouts for the standard documents, and provide TeX code to treat the language-dependent typesetting rules automatically [120].

3. Support processing of multilingual documents (more than one language in the same document) and work in international environments (one language per document, but a choice between several possibilities). For instance, the sorting of indexes and bibliographic references should be performed in accordance with a given language's alphabet and collating sequence; see the discussion on xindy in Section 11.3.

At the same time, you should be able to conveniently edit, view, and print your documents using any given character set, and LaTeX should be able to successfully process files created in this way. There exist, however, almost as many different character encoding schemes as there are languages (for example, IBM PC personal computers have dozens of code pages). In addition, several national and international standards exist, such as the series ISO-8859-x [67]. Therefore, some thought should be given to the question of compatibility and portability. If a document is to be reproducible in multiple environments, issues of standardization become important. In particular, sending 8-bit encoded documents via electronic mail generated problems at one time, because some mail gateways dropped the higher-order bit, rendering the document unprocessable. The e-mail problem is more or less solved now that almost all mailers adhere to the Multipart Internet Mail Extensions (MIME) standard, in which the use of a particular encoding standard (e.g., ISO-8859-x) is explicitly declared in the e-mail's header. The fact remains, however, that it is necessary to know the encoding in which a document was produced. For this purpose LaTeX offers the inputenc package, described in Section 7.11.3 on page 443.

Document encoding problems will ultimately be solved when new standards that can encode not only the alphabetic languages, but also ideographic scripts like Chinese, Japanese, and Korean are introduced. Clearly, 8 bits is not sufficient to represent even a fraction of the "characters" in those scripts. Multi-byte electronic coding standards have been developed to serve this need—in particular, "16-bit" Unicode [165], which is a subset of the multi-byte ISO-10646 [69,70]. Unicode will likely become the base encoding of most operating systems in the near future. Moreover, Unicode lies at the very heart of the XML [26] meta-language, on which all recently developed markup languages of the Internet are based. Thus, the integrity of electronic documents and data—structural as well as content-wise—can be fully guaranteed. LATEX supports a restricted version of Unicode's UTF8 representation through the inputenc option utf8 discussed in Section 7.5.2.

At its Portland, Oregon, meeting in July 1992, TUG's Technical Council set up the Technical Working Group on Multiple Language Coordination (TWGMLC), chaired by Yannis Haralambous. This group was charged with promoting and coordinating the standardization and development of TEX-related software adapted to different languages. Its aim was to produce for each language or group of languages a package that would facilitate typesetting. Such a package should contain details about fonts, input conventions, hyphenation patterns, a LATEX option file compatible with the babel concept (see Section 9.1.3), possibly a preprocessor, and, of course, documentation in English and the target language.

9.1.1   Language-related aspects of typesetting

When thinking about supporting typesetting documents in languages other than English, a number of aspects that need to be dealt with come to mind.

First and foremost is the fact that other languages have different rules for hyphenation, something that TEX accommodates through its support for multiple hyphenation patterns. In some languages, however, certain letter combinations change when they appear at a hyphenation point. TEX does not support this capability "out of the box".

Some languages need different sets of characters to be properly typeset. This issue can vary from the need for additional "accented letters" (as is the case with many European languages) to the need for a completely different alphabet (as is the case with languages using the Cyrillic or Greek alphabet). When non-European languages need to be supported, the typesetting direction might be different as well (such as right to left for Arabic and Hebrew texts) or so many characters might be needed (as is the case with the Kanji script, for instance) that TEX's standard mechanisms cannot deal with them.

A more "subtle" problem turns up when we look at the standard document classes that each LATEX distribution supplies. They were designed for the Anglo-American situation. A specific example where this preference interferes with supporting other languages is the start of a chapter. For some languages it is not enough to just translate the word "Chapter"; the order of the word and the denomination of the chapter needs to be changed as well, solely on the basis of grammatical rules. Where the English reader expects to see "Chapter 1", the French reader expects to see "1er Chapitre".

9.1.2   Culture-related aspects of typesetting

An even more thorny problem when faced with the need to support typesetting of many languages is the fact that typesetting rules differ, even between countries that use the same language. For instance, hyphenation rules differ between British English and American English. Translations of English words might vary between countries, just as they do for the German spoken in Germany and the German spoken (and written) in Austria.

Typographic rules may differ between countries, too. No worldwide standard tells us how nested lists should be typeset; on the contrary, their appearance may differ for different languages, or countries, or even printing houses. With these aspects we enter the somewhat fuzzy area comprising the boundary between language aspects of typesetting and cultural aspects of typesetting. It is not clear where that boundary lies. When implementing support for typesetting documents written in a specific language, this difference needs to be taken into account. The language-related aspects can be supported on a general level, but the cultural aspects are more often than not better (or more easily) handled by creating specific document classes.

9.1.3   Babel—LATEX speaks multiple languages

The LATEX distribution contains a few standard document classes that are used by most users. These classes (article, report, book, and letter) have a certain American look and feel, which not everyone likes. Moreover, the language-dependent strings, such as "Chapter" and "Table of Contents" (see Table 9.2 on page 547 for a list of commands holding language-dependent strings), come out in English by default.

The babel package developed by Johannes Braams [25] provides a set of options that allow the user to choose the language(s) in which the document will be typeset. It has the following characteristics:

- Multiple languages can be used simultaneously.

- The hyphenation patterns, which are loaded when INITEX is run to produce the LATEX format, can be defined dynamically via an external file.

- Translations for the language-dependent strings and commands for facilitating text input are provided for more than 20 languages (see Table 9.1 on the facing page).

In the next section we describe the user interface of the babel system. We then discuss the additional commands for various languages and describe the support for typesetting languages using non-Latin alphabets. Finally, we discuss ways to tailor babel to your needs and go into some detail about the structure of the *language definition files* (.ldf) that implement the language-specific commands in babel. Throughout the sections, examples illustrate the use of various languages supported by babel.

Language	Option	Language	Option
Bahasa	bahasa	Icelandic	icelandic
Basque	basque	Interlingua	interlingua
Breton	breton	Irish Gaelic	irish
Bulgarian	bulgarian	Italian	italian
Catalan	catalan	Latin	latin
Croatian	croatian	Lower Sorbian	lowersorbian
Czech	czech	North Sami	samin
Danish	danish	Norwegian	norsk, nynorsk
Dutch	dutch, afrikaans	Polish	polish
English	english (*USenglish*, *american*, *canadian*), UKenglish (*british*), australian (*newzealand*)	Portuguese	portuges (*portuguese*), brazilian (*brazil*)
		Romanian	romanian
Esperanto	esperanto	Russian	russian
Estonian	estonian	Scottish Gaelic	scottish
Finnish	finnish	Serbian	serbian
French	french (*frenchb*, *francais*, *acadian*, *canadien*)	Slovakian	slovak
		Slovenian	slovene
Galician	galician	Spanish	spanish
German	german (*germanb*), ngerman, austrian, naustrian	Swedish	swedish
		Turkish	turkish
Greek	greek, polutonikogreek	Ukrainian	ukrainian
Hebrew	hebrew	Upper Sorbian	uppersorbian
Hungarian	magyar (*hungarian*)	Welsh	welsh

Options typeset in parentheses are alias names for the preceding option.

Other options for a single language typically differ in hyphenation rules, date handling, or language-dependent strings.

Table 9.1: Language options supported by the babel system

9.2   The babel user interface

Any language that you use in your document should be declared as an option when loading the babel package. Alternatively, because the language(s) in which a document is written constitute a global characteristic of the document, the languages can be indicated as *global options* on the \documentclass command. This strategy makes them available to any package that changes behavior depending on the language settings of the document. Currently supported options are enumerated in Table 9.1. For example, the following declaration prepares for typesetting in the languages German (option `ngerman` for new hyphenation rules) and Italian (option `italian`):

```
\usepackage[ngerman,italian]{babel}
```

The last language appearing on the `\usepackage` command line will be the default language used at the beginning of the document. In the above example, the language-dependent strings, the hyphenation patterns (if they were loaded for the given language when the LATEX format was generated with INITEX; see the discussion on page 580), and possibly the interpretation of certain language-dependent commands (such as the date) will be for Italian from the beginning of the document up to the point where you choose a different language.

If one decides to make `ngerman` and `italian` global options, then other packages can also detect their presence. For example, the following code lets the package varioref (described in Section 2.4.2 on page 68) detect and use the options specified on the `\documentclass` command:

```
\documentclass[ngerman,italian]{article}
\usepackage{babel}
\usepackage{varioref}
```

If you use more than one language in your document and you want to define your own language-dependent strings for the varioref commands, you should use the methods described in Section 9.5 on page 579 and not those discussed in Section 2.4.2.

9.2.1 Setting or getting the current language

Within a document it is possible to change the current language in several ways. For example, you can change all language-related settings including translations for strings like "Chapter", the typesetting conventions, and the set-up for shorthand commands. Alternatively, you can keep the translations unchanged but modify everything else (e.g., when typesetting short texts in a foreign language within the main text). Finally, you can change only the hyphenation rules.

`\selectlanguage{`*language*`}`   `\begin{otherlanguage}{`*language*`}`

A change to all language-related settings is implemented via the command `\selectlanguage`. For instance, if you want to switch to German, you would use the command `\selectlanguage{german}`. The process is similar for switching to other languages. Each language must have been declared previously as a language option in the preamble as explained earlier. The `\selectlanguage` command calls the macros defined in the language definition file (see Section 9.5) and activates the special definitions for the language in question. It also updates the setting of TEX's `\language` primitive used for hyphenation.

The environment otherlanguage provides the same functionality as the \selectlanguage declaration, except that the language change is local to the environment. For mixing left-to-right typesetting with right-to-left typesetting, the use of this environment is a prerequisite. The argument *language* is the language one wants to switch to.

\foreignlanguage{*language*}{*phrase*}   \begin{otherlanguage*}{*language*}

The command \foreignlanguage typesets *phrase* according to the rules of *language*. It switches only the extra definitions and the hyphenation rules for the language, *not* the names and dates. Its environment equivalent is otherlanguage*.

The expansion of fixed document element names depends on the language, e.g., in English we have "References" or "Chapter". Auf Deutsch ergibt sich "Literatur" oder "Kapitel".
Voici en français : "Références" ou "Chapitre".
But in short phrases "Références" does not change!

```
\usepackage[german,french,english]{babel}
\raggedright

The expansion of fixed document element names
depends on the language, e.g., in English
we have ''\refname'' or ''\chaptername''.  \par
\selectlanguage{german} Auf Deutsch ergibt sich
''\refname'' oder ''\chaptername''.          \par
\begin{otherlanguage}{french} Voici en
 fran\c cais: ''\refname'' ou ''\chaptername''.
 \par\foreignlanguage{english}{But in short
 phrases ''\refname'' does not change!}
\end{otherlanguage}
```

9-2-1

\begin{hyphenrules}{*language*}

For the contents of the environment hyphenrules, *only* the hyphenation rules of *language* to be used are changed; \languagename and all other settings remain unchanged. When no hyphenation rules for *language* are loaded into the format, the environment has no effect.

As a special application, this environment can be used to prevent hyphenation altogether, provided that in language.dat the "language" nohyphenation is defined (by loading zerohyph.tex, as explained in Section 9.5.1 on page 580).

This text shows the effect of hyphenation.
This text shows the effect of hyphenation.

```
\usepackage[english]{babel}
\begin{minipage}{5cm}
 This text shows the effect of hyphenation.\par
 \begin{hyphenrules}{nohyphenation}
 This text shows the effect of hyphenation.
 \end{hyphenrules}
\end{minipage}
```

9-2-2

Note that this approach works even if the "language" nohyphenation is not specified as an option to the babel package.

If more than one language is used, it might be necessary to know which language is active at a specific point in the document. This can be checked by a call to \iflanguage:

\iflanguage{*language*}{*true-clause*}{*false-clause*}

The first argument in this syntax, *language*, is the name of a language, which is first checked to see whether it corresponds to a language declared to babel. If the *language* is known, the command compares it with the current language. If they are the same, the commands specified in the *true-clause* are executed; otherwise, the commands specified in the third argument, *false-clause*, are executed.

This step is actually carried out by comparing the \l@⟨*language*⟩ commands that point to the hyphenation patterns used for the two languages (see Section 9.5.1 on page 580). Thus, two "languages" are considered identical if they share the same pattern (e.g., dialects[1] of a language such as austrian), especially with languages for which no patterns are loaded.

English and Austrian use different while German and Austrian use the same hyphenation patterns.

```
\usepackage[german,english]{babel}
English and Austrian use \iflanguage{austrian}{the same}{different}
\foreignlanguage{german}{while German
    and Austrian use \iflanguage{austrian}{the same}{different}}
hyphenation patterns.
```

9-2-3

\languagename

The control sequence \languagename contains the name of the current language.

(1) The language is english.
(2) The language is german.
(3) The language is french.
(4) The language is english.
(5) Pas en français.
(6) The language is german.

```
\usepackage[german,french,english]{babel}
\par(1) The language is \languagename.
\par(2) \selectlanguage{german}%
        The language is \languagename.
\par(3) \begin{otherlanguage}{french}
            The language is \languagename.
        \end{otherlanguage}
\par(4) \foreignlanguage{english}{%
            The language is \languagename.}
\par(5) \iflanguage{french}{En fran\c cais.}
                          {Pas en fran\c cais.}
\par(6) The language is \languagename.
```

9-2-4

Language-dependent strings

Most document classes available in a LaTeX installation define a number of commands that are used to store the various language-dependent strings. Table 9.2 on the facing page presents an overview of these commands, together with their default text strings.

---

[1] Only in the implementation in babel! Some languages are implemented as "dialects" of the others for TeXnical reasons; no discrimination is intended.

Command	English String	Command	English String
\abstractname	Abstract	\indexname	Index
\alsoname	see also	\listfigurename	List of Figures
\appendixname	Appendix	\listtablename	List of Tables
\bibname	Bibliography	\pagename	Page
\ccname	cc	\partname	Part
\chaptername	Chapter	\prefacename	Preface
\contentsname	Contents	\proofname	Proof
\enclname	encl	\refname	References
\figurename	Figure	\seename	see
\glossaryname	Glossary	\tablename	Table
\headtoname	To (letter class)		

Table 9.2: Language-dependent strings in babel (English defaults)

9.2.2   Handling shorthands

For authors who write in languages other than English, it is sometimes awkward to type the input needed to produce the letters of their languages in the final document. More often than not, they need letters with accents above or below—sometimes even more than one accent. When you need to produce such glyphs and do not have the ability to use 8-bit input, but rather have to rely on 7-bit input encodings, an easier way to type those instructions would be welcome. For this reason (among others, as will be discussed later), babel supports the concept of "shorthands". A "shorthand" is a one- or two-character sequence, the first character of which introduces the shorthand and is called the "shorthand character". For a two-character shorthand, the second character specifies the behavior of the shorthand.

Babel knows about three kinds of shorthands—those defined by "the system", "the language", and "the user". A system-defined shorthand sequence can be overridden by a shorthand sequence defined as part of the support for a specific language; a language-defined shorthand sequence can be overridden by a user-defined one.

Document-level commands for shorthands

This section describes the shorthand commands that can be used in the document and various aspects of the shorthand concept. Language-level or system-level shorthands are declared in language definition files; see Section 9.5 on page 579.

```
\useshorthands{char}
```

The command \useshorthands initiates the definition of user-defined shorthand sequences. The argument *char* is the character that starts these shorthands.

> `\defineshorthand{`*charseq*`}{`*expansion*`}`

The command `\defineshorthand` defines a shorthand. Its first argument, *charseq*, is a one- or two-character sequence; the second argument, *expansion*, is the code to which the shorthand should expand.

> `\aliasshorthand{`*char1*`}{`*char2*`}`

The command `\aliasshorthand` lets you use another character, *char2*, to perform the same functions as the default shorthand character, *char1*. For instance, if you prefer to use the character | instead of ", you can enter `\aliasshorthand{"}{/}`.

This shows the use and effect of "a: ä and "i: ï.

This shows the use and effect of |a: ä and |i: ï.

```
\usepackage[english]{babel}    \useshorthands{"}
\defineshorthand{"a}{\"{a}}    \defineshorthand{"i}{\"{\i}}
\aliasshorthand{"}{|}
This shows the use and effect of \verb="a=: "a and \verb="i=: "i.

This shows the use and effect of \verb=|a=: |a and \verb=|i=: |i.
```
9-2-5

> `\languageshorthands{`*language*`}`

The command `\languageshorthands` is used to switch between shorthands for the *language* specified as an argument. The *language* must have been declared to babel for the current document. When switching languages, the language definition files usually issue this command for the language in question. For example, the file `frenchb.ldf` contains the following command:

```
\languageshorthands{french}
```

Sometimes it is necessary to temporarily switch off the shorthand action of a given character because it needs to be used in a different way.

> `\shorthandon{`*chars*`}` `\shorthandoff{`*chars*`}`

The command `\shorthandoff` sets the `\catcode` for each of the characters in its argument *chars* to "other" (12). Conversely, the command `\shorthandon` sets the `\catcode` to "active" (13) for its argument *chars*. Both commands only act on "known" shorthand characters. If a character is not known to be a shorthand character, its category code will be left unchanged.

For instance, the language definition file `german.ldf` defines two commands, `\mdqoff` and `\mdqon`, that turn the shorthand action of the character " off and on, respectively. They are defined as follows:

```
\newcommand\mdqon{\shorthandon{"}}
\newcommand\mdqoff{\shorthandoff{"}}
```

The language definition file for French (`frenchb.ldf`) makes the "double" punctuation characters "?", "!", ":", and ";" active. One can eliminate this behavior by specifying each as an argument to a `\shorthandoff` command. This step is necessary with certain packages, where the same characters have a special meaning. Below is an example with the xy package, where the use of ";" and "?" as shorthand characters is turned off inside xy's xy environment [57, Chapter 5], because these characters have a functional meaning there.

Voici un exemple avec *xypic* :

$$\bullet \longrightarrow x$$

Quelle belle flèche !

```
\usepackage{xy}    \usepackage[french]{babel}
Voici un exemple avec \emph{xypic}:
\[ \shorthandoff{;?}
\begin{xy}  (0,0)*{\bullet}, (0,0) ; (10,0),
   **\dir {-} ?>* \dir {>}, (12,0)*{x},  \end{xy}
\]
Quelle belle fl\'eche !
```

9-2-6

9.2.3 Language attributes

Sometimes the support for language-dependent typesetting needs to be tailored for different situations. In such a case it is possible to define attributes for the particular language. Two examples of the use of attributes can be found in the support for typesetting of Latin texts. When the attribute medieval is selected, certain document element names are spelled differently; also, the letters "u" and "V" are defined to be a lowercase and uppercase pair. The attribute withprosodicmarks can be used when typesetting grammars, dictionaries, teaching texts, and the like, where prosodic marks are important for providing complete information on the words or the verses. This attribute makes special shorthands available for breve and macron accents that may interfere with other packages.

`\languageattribute{`*language*`}{`*langattrs*`}`

The command `\languageattribute` declares which attributes are to be used for a given language. It must be used in the preamble of the document following the command `\usepackage[...]{babel}` that loads the babel package. The command takes two arguments: *language* is the name of a language, and *langattrs* is a comma-separated list of attributes to be used for that language. The command checks whether the *language* is known in the current document and whether the attribute(s) are known for this language.

For instance, babel has two variants for the Greek language: monotoniko (one-accent), the default, and polutoniko (multi-accent). To select the polutoniko variant, one must specify it in the document preamble, using the command `\languageattribute`. The following two examples illustrate the difference.

The Greek word for 'Index' is Ευρετήριο.

```
\usepackage[greek,english]{babel}

The Greek word for 'Index' is \selectlanguage{greek}\indexname.
```

9-2-7

With the polutoniko attribute we get a different result:

The Greek word for 'Index'
is Εὑρετήριο.

```
\usepackage[greek,english]{babel}
\languageattribute{greek}{polutoniko}
The Greek word for 'Index' is \selectlanguage{greek}\indexname.
```

9-2-8

9.3   User commands provided by language options

This section gives a general overview of the features typically offered by the various language options. It includes translations of language-dependent strings and a survey of typical shorthands intended to ease language-specific document content or to solve language-specific typesetting requirements. Some language options define additional commands to produce special date formats or numbers in a certain style. Also discussed are layout modifications as undertaken for French and Hebrew as well as the interfaces for dealing with different scripts (e.g., Latin and Cyrillic) in the same document.

9.3.1   Translations

As discussed earlier, babel provides translations for document element names that LATEX uses in its document classes. The English versions of these strings are shown in Table 9.2 on page 547. Table 9.3 on page 551 shows the translations for a number of languages, some of them not using the normal Latin script.

Apart from the translated strings in Table 9.3, the language definition files supply alternative versions of the command \today, as shown in the following example.

In England the date is
'29th February 2004', while in
Bulgaria it is '29 февруари
2004 г.'. In Catalonia they write
'29 de febrer de 2004'.

```
\usepackage[catalan,bulgarian,british]{babel}
\raggedright
In England the date is '\today', while in Bulgaria
it is '{\selectlanguage{bulgarian}\today}'. In Catalonia
they write '{\selectlanguage{catalan}\today}'.
```

9-3-2

9.3.2   Available shorthands

Many of the language definition files provide shorthands. Some are meant to ease typing, wheras others provide quite extensive trickery to achieve special effects. You might not be aware of it, but LATEX itself defines a shorthand (although it is not called by that name) that you probably use quite often: the character tilde (~), which is used to enter a "nonbreakable" space.

A number of shorthand definitions deal with "accented characters". They were invented in the days when TEX did not yet support 8-bit input or 8-bit hyphenation

Command	French	Greek	Polish	Russian
\abstractname	Résumé	Περίληψη	Streszczenie	Аннотация
\alsoname	*voir aussi*	βλέπε επίσης	Porównaj także	см. также
\appendixname	Annexe	Παράρτημα	Dodatek	Приложение
\bibname	Bibliographie	Βιβλιογραφία	Bibliografia	Литература
\ccname	Copie à	Κοινοποίηση	Kopie:	исх.
\chaptername	Chapitre	Κεφάλαιο	Rozdział	Глава
\contentsname	Table des matières	Περιεχόμενα	Spis treści	Содержание
\enclname	P. J.	Συνημμένα	Załącznik	вкл.
\figurename	Fig.	Σχήμα	Rysunek	Рис.
\glossaryname	Glossaire	Γλωσσάρι	Glossary	Glossary
\headtoname		Προς	Do	вх.
\indexname	Index	Ευρετήριο	Indeks	Предметный указатель
\listfigurename	Table des figures	Κατάλογος Σχημάτων	Spis rysunków	Список иллюстраций
\listtablename	Liste des tableaux	Κατάλογος Πινάκων	Spis tablic	Список таблиц
\pagename	page	Σελίδα	Strona	с.
\partname	Deuxième partie	Μέρος	Część	Часть
\prefacename	Préface	Πρόλογος	Przedmowa	Предисловие
\proofname	Démonstration	Απόδειξη	Dowód	Доказательство
\refname	Références	Αναφορές	Literatura	Список литературы
\seename	*voir*	βλέπε	Porównaj	см.
\tablename	Tab.	Πίνακας	Tablica	Таблица

9-3-1   *In French* \partname *also generates the part number as a word, e.g., "Première, Deuxième, ... "*

Table 9.3: Language-dependent strings in babel (French, Greek, Polish, and Russian)

patterns. When proper 8-bit hyphenation patterns are available, it is normally better to apply those and to use the inputenc package to select the proper input encoding (see Section 7.1.2 on page 329). However, if special processing needs to take place when an accented character appears next to a hyphenation point (as is the case for the Dutch hyphenation rules), the use of shorthands cannot be circumvented.[1]

The double quote

The most popular character to be used as a shorthand character is the double quote character ("). This character is used in this way for Basque, Bulgarian, Catalan, Danish, Dutch, Estonian, Finnish, Galician, German, Icelandic, Italian, Latin, Norwegian, Polish, Portuguese, Russian, Serbian, Slovenian, Spanish, Swedish, Ukrainian, and Upper Sorbian. To describe all uses of the double quote

---

[1]This statement is true only if the underlying formatter is TEX. Omega, for example, provides additional functionality so that such cases can be handled automatically.

character as a shorthand character would go too far. Instead, it is recommended that you check the documentation that comes with the babel package for each language if you want to know the details. What can be said here is that its uses fall into a number of categories, each of which deserves a description and a few examples.

Insert accented letters For a number of languages shorthands have been created to facilitate typing accented characters. With the availability of 8-bit input and output encodings this usage might seem to have become obsolete, but this is not true for all cases. For the Dutch language, for instance, an accent needs to be removed when the hyphenation point is next to the accented letter.

Den Koning van Hispaniën heb ik altijd ge-eerd! Den Koning van Hispaniën heb ik altijd geëerd!

```
\usepackage[dutch]{babel}
Den Koning van Hispani"en heb ik altijd ge"eerd!
Den Koning van Hispani"en heb ik altijd ge"eerd!
```
9-3-3

Insert special characters In the Catalan language a special glyph, the "geminated l", is needed for proper typesetting [167].

The "geminated l" appears in words such as intel·ligència, il·lusio.

```
\usepackage[catalan,english]{babel}
The ``geminated~l'' appears in words such as
\foreignlanguage{catalan}{inte"lig\'{e}ncia, i"llusio}.
```
9-3-4

This character can also be typeset by using the commands \lgem and \Lgem or through the combinations "\l." and "\L." once catalan is selected.

Insert special quoting characters By default, LATEX supports single and double quotes: 'quoted text' and "quoted text". This support is not desirable in European languages. Many have their own conventions and more often than not require different characters for this purpose. For example, in Dutch traditional typesetting the opening quote should be placed on the baseline, in German typesetting the closing quote is reversed, and French typesetting requires guillemets. For Icelandic typesetting the guillemets are used as well, but the other way around—that is, pointing "inward" instead of "outward" (a convention also sometimes used in German typography).

English "quoted text" has quotes different from Dutch „quoted text" or German „quoted text" or French « quoted text ».

```
\usepackage[dutch,ngerman,french,english]{babel}
English ``quoted text'' has quotes different from
\selectlanguage{dutch}Dutch "`quoted text"' or
\selectlanguage{ngerman}German "`quoted text"' or
\selectlanguage{french}French \og quoted text\fg.
```
9-3-5

The T1 font encoding provides the guillemets (see Table 7.32 on page 449), but its support for French typesetting relies on the commands \og and \fg. These commands not only produce the guillemets, but also provide proper spacing between them and the text they surround.

Insert special hyphenation rules   A number of languages have specific rules about what happens to characters at a line break. For instance, in older German spelling `..ck..` is hyphenated as `..k-k..` and a triple `f` in a compound word is normally typeset as `ff`—except when hyphenated, in which case the third `f` reappears as shown in the example.

<table>
<tr>
<td>Brote bak-
ken</td>
<td>Farbstoff-
fabrik</td>
<td>

```
\usepackage[german]{babel}
\fbox{\parbox[t]{1,5cm}{Brote ba"cken}}    \quad
\fbox{\parbox[t]{1,5cm}{Farbsto"ffabrik}}
```
</td>
</tr>
</table>

9-3-6

Insert special hyphenation indications   A number of shorthands are used to inform LATEX about special situations with regard to hyphenation. For instance, in a number of languages it is sometimes necessary to prevent LATEX from typesetting a ligature—for example, in a compound word. This goal can be achieved by inserting a small kern between the two letters that would normally form a ligature. The shorthand `"|` is available for this purpose in many language definitions.

<table>
<tr>
<td>Das deutsche Wort „Auflage" sollte nicht so, sondern als »Auflage« gesetzt werden.</td>
<td>

```
\usepackage[german]{babel}
Das deutsche Wort "'Auflage"' sollte nicht so,
sondern als ">Auf"|lage"< gesetzt werden.
```
</td>
</tr>
</table>

9-3-7

Another popular shorthand is `"-`, which inserts an explicit hyphen sign but allows hyphenation in the rest of the word:

<table>
<tr>
<td>minister-
president</td>
<td>minister-
presi-
dent</td>
<td>

```
\usepackage[dutch]{babel}
\fbox{\parbox[t]{1cm}{minister-president}} \quad
\fbox{\parbox[t]{1cm}{minister"-president}}
```
</td>
</tr>
</table>

9-3-8

There is also `""` (similar to `"-`, but does not print the `-`), `"=` (inserts an explicit hyphen with a breakpoint, allowing hyphenation in the combined words separately), and `"~` (inserts an explicit hyphen without a breakpoint). The following example shows the effects of these shorthands, using the same word.

<table>
<tr>
<td>Minister-Präsident</td>
<td>Minister-
Präsident</td>
<td rowspan="5">

```
\usepackage[german]{babel}
\newcommand\present[1]{%
    \fbox{\parbox[t]{30mm}{#1}}
    \fbox{\parbox[t]{13,5mm}{#1}}\par}
\present{Minister-Pr"asident}
\present{Minister"-Pr"asident}
\present{Minister""Pr"asident}
\present{Minister"=Pr"asident}
\present{Minister"~Pr"asident}
```
</td>
</tr>
<tr>
<td>MinisterPräsident</td>
<td>Minister-
Präsident</td>
</tr>
<tr>
<td>MinisterPräsident</td>
<td>Minister
Präsident</td>
</tr>
<tr>
<td>Minister-Präsident</td>
<td>Minister-
Präsident</td>
</tr>
<tr>
<td>Minister-Präsident</td>
<td>Minister-Präsident</td>
</tr>
</table>

9-3-9

The tilde

For the languages Basque, Estonian, Galician, Greek, and Spanish, the tilde character is used for a different purpose than inserting an unbreakable space.

- For Estonian typography, the tilde-accent needs to be set somewhat lower than LATEX's normal positioning.

- For Greek multi-accented typesetting, LATEX needs to see the tilde as if it were a normal letter. This behavior is needed to make the ligatures in the Greek fonts work correctly.

- For Basque, Galician, and Spanish, the tilde is used in the shorthands ~n~⟨letter⟩ (ñ), ~N~⟨letter⟩ (Ñ), and ~-. The construction ~- (as well as ~-- and ~---) produces a dash that disallows a linebreak after it. When the tilde is followed by any other character, it retains its original function as an "unbreakable space" (producing the overfull first line in the example). If such a space is needed before an "n", this can be achieved by inserting an empty group (the second line in the example).

La eñe está presente en \alph y \Alph. Como en castellano no se usan números romanos en minúscula, \roman se redefine para que los dé en versalitas.

```
\usepackage[spanish,activeacute]{babel}
La e~ne est'a presente en \verb|\alph|~y~\verb|\Alph|.
Como en castellano~{}no se usan n'umeros romanos
en min'uscula, \verb|\roman| se redefine para que
los d'e en versalitas.
```

9-3-10

The colon, semicolon, exclamation mark, and question mark

For the languages Breton, French, Russian, and Ukrainian, these four characters are used as shorthands to facilitate the use of correct typographic conventions. For Turkish typography, this ability is needed only for the colon and semicolon. The convention is that a little white space should precede these characters.

En français on doit mêtre un petit bout de « white space » devant le ponctuation : comme ça ! For English this is not done: as shown here!

```
\usepackage[english,french]{babel}
En fran\c{c}ais on doit m\^{e}tre un petit bout de \og
white space \fg\ devant le ponctuation: comme \c{c}a!
\selectlanguage{english}
For English this is not done: as shown here!
```

9-3-11

This white space is added automatically by default, but this setting can be changed in a configuration file. The use of the colon as a shorthand character can lead to problems with other packages or when including PostScript files in a document. In such cases it may be necessary to disable this shorthand (temporarily) by using \shorthandoff, as explained in Example 9-2-6 on page 549.

The grave accent

The support for the languages Catalan and Hungarian makes it possible to use the grave accent (`) as a shorthand character.

- For Catalan this use of the grave accent character is not supported by default; one has to specify the option `activegrave` when loading babel. The purpose of this shorthand is to facilitate the entering of accented characters while retaining hyphenation. The shorthand can be used together with the letters a, e, o and A, E, O.

"Pàgina, Apèndix, Pròleg" are Catalan translations for "Page, Appendix, and Preface".

```
\usepackage[english,catalan,activegrave]{babel}
``P`agina, Ap`endix, Pr`oleg'' \selectlanguage{english}
are Catalan translations for ``Page, Appendix, and Preface''.
```

9-3-12

- For Hungarian this shorthand can be used with both uppercase and lowercase version of the characters c, d, g, l, n, s, t, and z. Its purpose is to insert discretionaries to invoke the correct behavior at hyphenation points.

loccsan	locs-csan
eddzünk	edz-dzünk
poggyász	pogy-gyász
Kodállya	Kodály-lya
mennyei	meny-nyei
vissza	visz-sza
pottyan	poty-tyan
rizzsel	rizs-zsel

```
\usepackage[hungarian]{babel}
\newcommand\present[1]{\fbox{\parbox[t]{20mm}{#1}}
                       \fbox{\parbox[t]{8,5mm}{#1}}\par}
\present{lo`ccsan}
\present{e`ddz\"unk}
\present{po`ggy\'asz}
\present{Kod\'a`llya}
\present{me`nnyei}
\present{vi`ssza}
\present{po`ttyan}
\present{ri`zzsel}
```

9-3-13

The acute accent

The support for the languages Catalan, Galician, and Spanish makes it possible to use the acute accent (') as a shorthand character.

- For the support of Catalan typesetting, this shorthand can be used together with the vowels (a, e, i, o, u), both uppercase and lowercase. Its effect is to add the accent and to retain hyphenation.

- For the support of Galician typesetting, this shorthand offers the same functionality as for Catalan with the addition that entering 'n will produce ñ.

"Páxina, Capítulo, Apéndice" are Galician translations for "Page, Chapter, and Appendix".

```
\usepackage[english,galician,activeacute]{babel}
''P'axina, Cap'itulo, Ap'endice''
\selectlanguage{english}  are Galician translations
for ''Page, Chapter, and Appendix''.
```

9-3-14

- For the support of Spanish typesetting, this shorthand offers similar functionality as for Catalan and Galician, with the addition that also 'u and 'U are made available.

The described functionality is made available when the `activeacute` option is used. This support is made optional becasue the acute accent has other uses in LaTeX, which will fail when this character is turned into a shorthand.

The caret

The support for the languages Esperanto and Latin makes it possible to use the caret accent (^) as a shorthand character.

- For typesetting the Esperanto language, two accents are needed: the caret and the breve accent. The caret appears on the letters c, g, h, j, and s; the breve appears on the character u. Both accents can appear on lowercase *and* uppercase letters. The caret is defined as a shorthand that retains hyphenation and sets the caret accent somewhat lower on the character "h" (ĥ). Used together with the letter u, this shorthand typesets the breve accent (^u results in ŭ); used together with the vertical bar, it inserts an explicit hyphen sign, allowing hyphenation in the rest of the word.

"Paĝo, Ĉapitro, Citaĵoj" are Esperanto translations for "Page, Chapter, and References".

```
\usepackage[english,esperanto]{babel}
''Pa^go, ^Capitro, Cita^joj'' \selectlanguage{english}
are Esperanto translations for ''Page, Chapter, and
References''.
```

9-3-15

- When a Latin text is being typeset and the attribute withprosodicmarks has been selected, the caret is defined to be a shorthand for adding a breve accent to the lowercase vowels (except the medieval ligatures æ and œ). This is done while retaining hyphenation points.

ă ĕ ĭ ŏ ŭ

```
\usepackage[latin]{babel} \languageattribute{latin}{withprosodicmarks}
\ProsodicMarksOn ^a ^e ^i ^o ^u
```

9-3-16

The equals sign

The support for the languages Latin (with the attribute withprosodicmarks selected) and Turkish makes it possible to use the equals sign (=) as a shorthand character.

- When a Latin text is being typeset and the attribute withprosodicmarks has been selected, the equals sign is defined to be a shorthand for adding a macron accent to the lowercase vowels (except the medieval ligatures æ and œ). This is done while retaining hyphenation points.

9-3-17

```
                        \usepackage[latin]{babel} \languageattribute{latin}{withprosodicmarks}
ā ē ī ō ū                \ProsodicMarksOn =a =e =i =o =u
```

- When Turkish typesetting rules are to be followed, the equals sign needs to be preceded by a little white space. This is achieved automatically by turning the equals sign into a shorthand that replaces a preceding space character with a tiny amount of white space.

9-3-18

```
a =b                    \usepackage[english,turkish]{babel}
a=b                     \selectlanguage{english} a =b \par \selectlanguage{turkish} a =b
```

The disadvantage of having the equals sign turn into a space character is that it may cause many other packages to fail, including the usage of PostScript files for graphics inclusions. Make sure that the shorthand is turned off with \shorthandoff.

The greater than and less than signs

The support for the Spanish language makes it possible to use the greater than and less than signs (< and >) as shorthand characters for inserting a special quoting environment. This environment inserts different quoting characters when it is nested within itself. It supports a maximum of three levels of nested quotations. It also automatically inserts the closing quote signs when a new paragraph is started *within* a quote.

9-3-19

Some text with «quoted text with a "nested quote" within it.
    »A second paragraph in the quotation.»

```
\usepackage[spanish]{babel}
Some text with <<quoted text with a <<nested quote>>
within it.

A second paragraph in the quotation.>>
```

Note that when characters are turned into shorthands, the ligature mechanism in the fonts no longer works for them. In the T1 font encoding, for instance, a ligature is defined for two consecutive "less than" signs that normally results in typesetting guillemets. In the example above, the nested quote shows clearly that this does not happen.

The period

The support for the Spanish language also allows the use of the period (.) as a shorthand character in math mode. Its purpose is to control whether decimal numbers are written with the comma (`\decimalcomma`) or the period (`\decimalpoint`) as the decimal character.

```
1000,10          \usepackage[spanish]{babel}
1000.10          \decimalcomma $1000.10$ \par \decimalpoint $1000.10$
```
9-3-20

9.3.3   Language-specific commands

Apart from the translations and shorthands discussed above, some language definition files provide extra commands. Some of these are meant to facilitate the production of documents that conform to the appropriate typesetting rules. Others provide extra functionality not available by default in LATEX. A number of these commands are described in this section.

Formatting dates

For some languages more than one format is used for representing dates. In these cases extra commands are provided to produce a date in different formats. In the Bulgarian tradition months are indicated using uppercase Roman numerals; for such dates the command `\todayRoman` is available.

```
29 февруари 2004 г.      \usepackage[bulgarian]{babel}
29. II. 2004 г.          \today  \par \todayRoman
```
9-3-21

When writing in the Esperanto language two slightly different ways of representing the date are provided by the commands `\hodiau` and `\hodiaun`.

```
29–a de februaro, 2004
la 29–a de februaro, 2004      \usepackage[esperanto]{babel}
la 29–an de februaro,  2004    \today \par \hodiau \par \hodiaun
```
9-3-22

When producing a document in the Greek language the date can also be represented with Greek numerals instead of Arabic numerals. For this purpose the command `\Grtoday` is made available.

```
29 Φεβρουαρίου 2004      \usepackage[greek]{babel}
ΚΘ′ Φεβρουαρίου ‚ΒΔ′     \today \par \Grtoday
```
9-3-23

The support for typesetting Hebrew texts offers the command `\hebdate` to translate any Gregorian date, given as "day, month year", into a Gregorian date in Hebrew. The command `\hebday` replaces LATEX's normal `\today`. When you want to produce "normal" Hebrew dates, you need to use the package hebcal, which provides the command \Hebrewtoday. When it is used *outside* the Hebrew environment it produces the Hebrew date in English.

<table>
<tr><td>29 בפברואר 2004
ז' באדר, תשס"ד
29th February 2004: Adar 7, 5764
8 בנובמבר 1997</td><td>\usepackage[english,hebrew]{babel}
\usepackage{hebcal}

\hebday \par   \Hebrewtoday \par
\selectlanguage{english} \today: \Hebrewtoday
\selectlanguage{hebrew} \hebdate{8}{11}{1997}</td></tr>
</table>

9-3-24

The support for the Hungarian language provides the command \ontoday to produce a date format used in expressions such as "on February 10th".

For the Upper and Lower Sorbian languages two different sets of month names are employed. By default, the support for these languages produces "new-style" dates, but "old-style" dates can be produced as well. The "old-style" date format for the Lower Sorbian language can be selected with the command \olddatelsorbian; \newdatelsorbian switches (back) to the modern form. For Upper Sorbian similar commands are available, as shown in the example.

<table>
<tr><td>29. februara 2004
29. małego rožka 2004
29. februara 2004
29. małeho róžka 2004</td><td>\usepackage[usorbian,lsorbian]{babel}
\newdatelsorbian \today \par
\olddatelsorbian \today \par
\newdateusorbian \today \par
\olddateusorbian \today</td></tr>
</table>

9-3-25

In Swedish documents it is customary to represent dates with just numbers. Such dates can occur in two forms: YYYY-MM-DD and DD/MM YYYY. The command \datesymd changes the definition of the command \today to produce dates in the first numerical form; the command \datesdmy changes the definition of the command \today to produce dates in the second numerical format.

<table>
<tr><td>Default date format: 29 februari 2004
\datesymd gives: 2004-02-29
\datesdmy gives: 29/2 2004</td><td>\usepackage[swedish]{babel}
Default date format: \today\\
\verb|\datesymd| gives: \datesymd \today \\
\verb|\datesdmy| gives: \datesdmy \today</td></tr>
</table>

9-3-26

Numbering

The support for certain languages provides additional commands for representing numbers by letters. LaTeX provides the commands \alph and \Alph for this purpose. For the Esperanto language the commands \esper and \Esper are provided. The support for the Greek language changes the definition of \alph and \Alph to produce Greek letters while the support for the Bulgarian language changes them to produce Cyrillic letters. The support for the Russian and Ukrainian languages provides the commands \asbuk and \Asbuk as alternatives to the LaTeX commands.

Value	default \alph	\Alph	Esperanto \esper	\Esper	Greek \alph	\Alph	Russian \asbuk	\Asbuk	Bulgarian \alph	\Alph	Hebrew \alph	\Alph	\Alphfinal
1	a	A	a	A	α′	Α′	а	А	а	А	א	א׳	א׳
2	b	B	b	B	β′	Β′	б	Б	б	Б	ב	ב׳	ב׳
3	c	C	c	C	γ′	Γ′	в	В	в	В	ג	ג׳	ג׳
4	d	D	ĉ	Ĉ	δ′	Δ′	г	Г	г	Г	ד	ד׳	ד׳
5	e	E	d	D	ε′	Ε′	д	Д	д	Д	ה	ה׳	ה׳
6	f	F	e	E	ϛ′	ϛ′	е	Е	е	Е	ו	ו׳	ו׳
7	g	G	f	F	ζ′	Ζ′	ж	Ж	ж	Ж	ז	ז׳	ז׳
8	h	H	g	G	η′	Η′	з	З	з	З	ח	ח׳	ח׳
9	i	I	ĝ	Ĝ	ϑ′	Θ′	и	И	и	И	ט	ט׳	ט׳
10	j	J	h	H	ι′	Ι′	к	К	к	К	י	י׳	י׳
11	k	K	ĥ	Ĥ	ια′	ΙΑ′	л	Л	л	Л	יא	י״א	י״א
12	l	L	i	I	ιβ′	ΙΒ′	м	М	м	М	יב	י״ב	י״ב
13	m	M	j	J	ιγ′	ΙΓ′	н	Н	н	Н	יג	י״ג	י״ג
14	n	N	ĵ	Ĵ	ιδ′	ΙΔ′	о	О	о	О	יד	י״ד	י״ד
15	o	O	k	K	ιε′	ΙΕ′	п	П	п	П	טו	ט״ו	ט״ו
16	p	P	l	L	ιϛ′	Ιϛ′	р	Р	р	Р	טז	ט״ז	ט״ז
17	q	Q	m	M	ιζ′	ΙΖ′	с	С	с	С	יז	י״ז	י״ז
18	r	R	n	N	ιη′	ΙΗ′	т	Т	т	Т	יח	י״ח	י״ח
19	s	S	o	O	ιϑ′	ΙΘ′	у	У	у	У	יט	י״ט	י״ט
20	t	T	p	P	κ′	Κ′	ф	Ф	ф	Ф	כ	כ׳	ך׳
21	u	U	s	S	κα′	ΚΑ′	х	Х	х	Х	כא	כ״א	כ״א
22	v	V	ŝ	Ŝ	κβ′	ΚΒ′	ц	Ц	ц	Ц	כב	כ״ב	כ״ב
23	w	W	t	T	κγ′	ΚΓ′	ч	Ч	ч	Ч	כג	כ״ג	כ״ג
24	x	X	u	U	κδ′	ΚΔ′	ш	Ш	ш	Ш	כד	כ״ד	כ״ד
25	y	Y	ŭ	Ŭ	κε′	ΚΕ′	щ	Щ	щ	Щ	כה	כ״ה	כ״ה
26	z	Z	v	V	κϛ′	Κϛ′	э	Э	ю	Ю	כו	כ״ו	כ״ו
27	-	-	z	Z	κζ′	ΚΖ′	ю	Ю	я	Я	כז	כ״ז	כ״ז
28	-	-	-	-	κη′	ΚΗ′	я	Я	-	-	כח	כ״ח	כ״ח
29	-	-	-	-	κϑ′	ΚΘ′	-	-	-	-	כט	כ״ט	כ״ט
30	-	-	-	-	λ′	Λ′	-	-	-	-	ל	ל׳	ל׳
40	-	-	-	-	μ′	Μ′	-	-	-	-	מ	מ׳	ם׳
50	-	-	-	-	ν′	Ν′	-	-	-	-	נ	נ׳	ן׳
100	-	-	-	-	ρ′	Ρ′	-	-	-	-	ק	ק׳	ק׳
250	-	-	-	-	σν′	Σ″Ν′	-	-	-	-	רנ	ר״נ	ר״ן
500	-	-	-	-	φ′	Φ′	-	-	-	-	תק	ת״ק	ת״ק

Table 9.4: Different methods for representing numbers by letters

9-3-27

For Hebrew typesetting the \alph command is changed to produce Hebrew letter sequences using the "Gimatria" scheme. As there are no uppercase letters \Alph produces the same letter sequences but adds apostrophes. In addition, an extra command, \Alphfinal, generates Hebrew letters with apostrophes and final letter forms, a variant needed for Hebrew year designators. Table 9.4 compares the various numbering schemes.

In French typesetting, numbers should be typeset following different rules than those employed in English typesetting. Namely, instead of separating thousands with a comma, a space should be used. The command \nombre is provided for this purpose. It can also be used *outside* the French language environment, where it will typeset numbers according to the English rules. The command \nombre takes an optional argument, which can be used to replace the default decimal separator (stored in \decimalsep). This feature can be useful in combination with the package dcolumn (see Section 5.7.2), in which you have to use the optional argument to achieve correct alignment.

```
\usepackage[english,french]{babel}  \usepackage{dcolumn}
\newcolumntype{d}{D{,}{\decimalsep}{-1}} % align at explicit ','
                                         % but output \decimalsep
```

```
                                  12,34567
12,345 67
                                  12,345 67
9 876 543,21
```

```
\begin{tabular}{|d|}  \hline
            12,34567  \\ % recognized but not correctly formatted
    \nombre{12,34567} \\ % not recognized but correctly formatted
 \nombre[,]{12,34567} \\
 \nombre[,]{9876543,21} \\ \hline
\end{tabular}
\par\vspace{1cm}    \selectlanguage{english} % change language
\begin{tabular}{|d|}       \hline
  \nombre[,]{12,34567} \\ \nombre[,]{9876543,21} \\ \hline
\end{tabular}
```

```
                              12.345,67
9,876,543.21
```

9-3-28

In Greece an alternative way of writing numbers exists. It is based on using letters to denote number ranges. This system was used in official publications at the end of the 19th century and the beginning of the 20th century. At present most Greeks use it for small numbers. The knowledge of how to write numbers larger than 20 or 30 is not very widespread, being primarily used by the Eastern Orthodox Church and scholars. They employ this approach to denote numbers up to 999.999. This system works as follows:

- Only numbers greater than 0 can be expressed.

- For the units 1 through 9 (inclusive), the letters alpha, beta, gamma, delta, epsilon, stigma, zeta, eta, and theta are used, followed by a mark similar to the mathematical symbol "prime", called the "numeric mark". Because the letter stigma is not always part of the available font, it is often replaced by the first two letters of its name as an alternative. In the babel implementation the letter stigma is produced, rather than the digraph sigma tau.

- For the tens 10 through 90 (inclusive), the letters iota, kappa, lambda, mu, nu, xi, omikron, pi, and qoppa are used, again followed by the numeric mark. The qoppa that appears in Greek numerals has a distinct zig-zag form that is quite different from the normal qoppa, which resembles the Latin "q".

- For the hundreds 100 through 900 (inclusive), the letters rho, sigma, tau, upsilon, phi, chi, psi, omega, and sampi are used, also followed by the numeric mark.

- Using these rules any number between 1 and 999 can be expressed by a group of letters denoting the hundreds, tens, and units, followed by *one* numeric mark.

- For the number range 1.000 through 999.000 (inclusive), the digits before the decimal point are expressed by the same letters as above, this time with a numeric mark in front of this letter group. This mark is rotated 180 degrees and placed *under* the baseline. As can be seen in the example below, when two letter-groups are combined, *both* numeric marks are used.

123456 in Greek notation: ͵ρκ͵γυνϛ´

987654 in Greek notation: ͵ϠΠΖΧΝΔ´

```
\usepackage[english,greek]{babel}
\newcommand\eng[1]{\foreignlanguage{english}{#1}}

123456 \eng{in Greek notation:} \greeknumeral{123456} \par
987654 \eng{in Greek notation:} \Greeknumeral{987654}
```

9-3-29

In ancient Greece yet another numbering system was used, which closely resembles the Roman one in that it employs letters to denote important numbers. Multiple occurrences of a letter denote a multiple of the "important" number; for example, the letter I denotes 1, so III denotes 3. Here are the basic digits used in the Athenian numbering system:

- I denotes the number one (1).
- Π denotes the number five (5).
- Δ denotes the number ten (10).
- H denotes the number one hundred (100).
- X denotes the number one thousand (1000).
- M denotes the number ten thousand (10000).

Moreover, the letters Δ, H, X, and M, when placed under the letter Π, denote five times their original value; for example, the symbol 𐅆 denotes the number 5000, and the symbol 𐅄 denotes the number 50. Note that the numbering system does not provide negative numerals or a symbol for zero.

The Athenian numbering system, among others, is described in an article in Encyclopedia Δομή, Volume 2, seventh edition, page 280, Athens, October 2, 1975. This numbering system is supported by the package athnum, which comes with the babel system. It implements the command \athnum.

6284 in Athenian notation: 𐅆XHH𐅄ΔΔΔIIII

```
\usepackage[english,greek]{babel}
\usepackage{athnum}
\newcommand\eng[1]{\foreignlanguage{english}{#1}}

6284 \eng{in Athenian notation:} \\ \athnum{6284}
```

9-3-30

In Icelandic documents, numbers need to be typeset according to Icelandic rules. For this purpose the command \tala is provided. Like \nombre it takes an optional argument, which can be used to replace the decimal separator used, such as for use with the dcolumn package.

3 141,592 653 3,141.592,653	``` \usepackage[english,icelandic]{babel} \usepackage{dcolumn} \newcolumntype{d}{D{,}{\decimalsep}{-1}} \tala{3141,592653} \par \foreignlanguage{english}{\tala{3141,592653}}\par \bigskip \begin{tabular}{|d|} \hline ```

<table>
<tr><td align="center">3,14</td><td rowspan="3">```
                3,14   \\
  \tala[,]{123,4567} \\ \tala[,]{9876,543} \\ \hline
\end{tabular}
```</td></tr>
<tr><td align="center">123,456 7</td></tr>
<tr><td align="center">9 876,543</td></tr>
</table>

9-3-31

Miscellaneous extras

In French typesetting it is customary to print family names in small capitals, *without* hyphenating a name. For this purpose the command \bsc (boxed small caps) ... *for French* is provided. Abbreviations of the French word "numéro" should be typeset according to specific rules; these have been implemented in the commands \no and \No. Finally, for certain enumerated lists the commands \primo, \secundo, \tertio, and \quarto are available when typesetting in French.

	``` \usepackage[french]{babel} ```
9-3-32 Leslie LAMPORT Nº 9 1º 3º	``` Leslie~\bsc{Lamport} \quad \No9 \ \primo \ \tertio ```

In the Italian language it is customary to write together the article and the following noun—for example, "nell'altezza". To carry out the hyphenation of such ... *for Italian* constructs the character ' is made to behave as a normal letter.

In the Hungarian language the definite article can be either "a" or "az", depending on the context. Especially with references and citations, it is not always ... *for Hungarian* known beforehand which form should be used. The support for the Hungarian language contains commands that know the rules dictating when a "z" should be added to the article. These commands all take an argument that determines which form of the definite article should be typeset together with that argument.

\az{*text*}   \Az{*text*}

These commands produce the article and the argument. The argument can be a star (as in \az*), in which case just the article will be typeset. The form \Az is intended for the start of a sentence.

\aref{*text*}   \Aref{*text*}   \apageref{*text*}   \Apageref{*text*}

The first two commands should be used instead of a(z)~\ref{*label*}. When an equation is being referenced, the argument may be enclosed in parentheses instead of braces. For page references use \apageref (or \Apageref) to allow LaTeX to automatically produce the correct definite article.

LATEX		Serbian		Russian	
\tan	tan	\tg	tg	\tg	tg
\cot	cot	\ctg	ctg	\ctg	ctg
\sinh	sinh	\sh	sh	\sh	sh
\cosh	cosh	\ch	ch	\ch	ch
\tanh	tanh	\th	th	\th	th
\coth	coth	\cth	cth	\cth	cth
\csc	csc			\cosec	cosec
\arcsin	arcsin	\sh	sh		
\arccos	arccos	\arch	arch		
\arctan	arctan	\arctg	arctg	\arctg	arctg
		\arcctg	arcctg	\arcctg	arcctg *(extra)*

Table 9.5: Alternative mathematical operators for Eastern European languages

---

> \acite{*text*} \Acite{*text*}

For citations the command \acite should be used. Its argument may be a list of citations, in which case the first element of the list determines which form of the article should be typeset.

… specials for math In Eastern Europe a number of mathematical operators have a different appearance in equations than they do in "the Western world". Table 9.5 shows the relevant commands for different languages. The Russian commands are also valid for Bulgarian and Ukrainian language support. The package grmath, which comes as part of the babel distribution, changes the definitions of these operators to produce abbreviations of their Greek names. The package can only be used in conjunction with the greek option of babel.

9.3.4 Layout considerations

Some of the language support files in the babel package provide commands for automatically changing the layout of the document. Some simply change the way LATEX handles spaces after punctuation characters or ensure that the first paragraph that follows a section heading is indented. Others go much further.

Spaces after In *The TEXbook* [82, pp.72–74], the concept of extra white space after punc-
punctuation tuation characters is discussed. Good typesetting practice mandates that inter-
characters sentence spaces behave a little differently than interword spaces with respect to shrinkage and expansion (during justification). However, this practice is not considered helpfull in all cases, so for a number of languages (Breton, Bulgarian, Czech, Danish, Estonian, Finnish, French, German, Norwegian, Russian, Spanish, Turkish, and Ukrainian) this feature is switched off by calling the command \frenchspacing.

9-3-33

Anotherlayout concept that is built into most LATEX classes is the suppression
of the paragraph indentation for the first paragraph that follows a section heading. *Paragraph*
Again, for some languages this behavior is wrong; the support for French, Serbo- *indention after*
Croatian, and Spanish changes it to have *all* paragraphs indented. In fact, you can *heading*
request this behavior for any document by loading the package indentfirst.

The support for French (and Breton, for which support is derived from the
support for the French language) takes this somewhat further to accomodate the
typesetting rules used in France. It changes the general way lists are typeset by
LATEX by reducing the amount of vertical white space in them. For the itemize *Layout of lists*
environment, it removes all vertical white space between the items and changes
the appearance of the items by replacing " • " with "–".

```
\usepackage[french,english]{babel}
\begin{minipage}[t]{4cm}
  Some text with a list.
  \begin{itemize} \item item 1
    \item item 2  \end{itemize}
  And some text following.
\end{minipage}
\quad \selectlanguage{french}
\begin{minipage}[t]{4cm}
  Some text with a list.
  \begin{itemize} \item item 1
    \item item 2  \end{itemize}
  And some text following.
\end{minipage}
```

9-3-34

Some text with a list.

- item 1

- item 2

And some text following.

Some text with a list.
– item 1
– item 2
And some text following.

┌───┐
│ \FrenchLayout   \StandardLayout   │
└───┘

For documents that are typeset in more than one language, the support for French
provides a way to ensure that lists have a uniform layout throughout the document, either the "French layout" or the "LATEX layout". This result can be achieved
by using the command \FrenchLayout or \StandardLayout in the preamble of
the document. Unfortunately, when your document is being typeset with something other than one of the document classes provided by standard LATEX, or
when you use extension packages such as paralist, such layout changes may
have surprising and unwanted effects. In such cases it might be safest to use
\StandardLayout.

┌───┐
│ \AddThinSpaceBeforeFootnotes   \FrenchFootnotes   │
└───┘

In the French typesetting tradition, footnotes are handled differently than they are
in the Anglo-American tradition. In the running text, a little white space should *Layout of footnotes*
be added before the number or symbol that calls the footnote. This behavior is
optional and can be selected by using the \AddThinSpaceBeforeFootnotes command in the preamble of your document. The text of the footnote can also be

typeset according to French typesetting rules; this result is achieved by using the command \FrenchFootnotes.

Some text[a].   Some text[a].

────────   ────────
[a]with a footnote   [a.] with a footnote

```
\usepackage[french,english]{babel}
\AddThinSpaceBeforeFootnotes

\begin{minipage}{70pt} Some text\footnote{with a footnote}.
\end{minipage}
\selectlanguage{french}\FrenchFootnotes
\begin{minipage}{70pt} Some text\footnote{with a footnote}.
\end{minipage}
```

9-3-35

Layout of captions   The final layout change performed by the babel support for the French language is that the colon in captions for tables and figures is replaced with an en dash when one of the document classes of standard LATEX is used.

Internal commands redefined for magyar   The support for typesetting Hungarian documents goes even further: it redefines a number of internal LATEX commands to produce correct captions for figures and tables. Using the same means, it changes the layout of section headings. The definition of the theorem environment is changed as well. As explained above, such changes may lead to unexpected and even unwanted behavior, so be careful.

Right to left typesetting   To support typesetting Hebrew documents, even more drastic changes are needed because the Hebrew language has to be typeset from right to left. This requires the usage of a TEX extension (i.e., eTEX with a LATEX format) to correctly typeset a Hebrew document.

9.3.5 Languages and font encoding

As shown in some of the earlier examples, some languages cannot be supported by, for instance, simply translating some texts and providing extra support for special hyphenation needs. Many languages require characters that are not present in LATEX's T1 encoding. For some, just a few characters are missing and can be constructed from the available glyphs; other languages are not normally written using the Latin script. Some of these are supported by the babel system.

Extensions to the OT1 and T1 encodings

For some languages just a few characters are missing in the OT1 encoding and sometimes even in the T1 encoding. When the missing characters can be constructed from the available glyphs, it is relatively easy to rectify this situation. Such is the case for the Old Icelandic language. It needs a number of characters that can be represented by adding the "ogonek" to available glyphs. To access these you should use the shorthands in the next example. Note that each of these shorthands is composed of " and an 8-bit character, so use of the inputenc package is required.

```
\usepackage[icelandic]{babel}
\usepackage[T1]{fontenc}   \usepackage[latin1]{inputenc}
```

ǫ Q ǫ́ Q́ ę Ę ę́ Ę́ but: "é "É   `"o "O "ó "Ó "e "E "é "É     but:  "\'e "\'E`

Old Icelandic may not be a language in daily use, but the Polish language certainly is. For this language the OT1 encoding is missing a few characters (note that they are all included in T1). Again the missing characters *can* be constructed, and their entry is supported with shorthands. The support for entering the letters "pointed z" and "accented z" comes in two forms, as illustrated below. The reason for this duality is historical.

ą Ą ć Ć ę Ę ł ń Ń ó Ó ś Ś
ż Ż ź Ź "x "X
"r "R ż Ż ź Ź

```
\usepackage[polish]{babel}
"a "A "c "C "e "E "l "n  "N "o "O  "s "S \par
\polishrz "r "R "z "Z "x "X               \par
\polishzx "r "R "z "Z "x "X               \par
```

All such shorthands were devised when 7-bit font encodings were the norm and producing a glyph such as "Ą" required some internal macro processing (if it was possible at all). With today's 8-bit fonts there is no requirement to use the shorthands. For example, with T1-encoded fonts, standard input methods may be used instead.

ą Ą ć Ć ę Ę ł ń Ń ó Ó ś Ś
ż Ż ź Ź

```
\usepackage[T1]{fontenc}
\k a \k A \'c \'C \k e \k E \l{} \'n \'N \'o \'O \'s \'S\par
\.z \.Z \'z \'Z
```

Basic support for switching font encodings

In the situation where simply constructing a few extra characters to support the correct typesetting of a language does not offer a sufficient solution, switching from one font encoding to another becomes necessary. This section describes the commands provided by babel and its language support files for this task. Note that these commands are normally "hidden" by babel's user interface.

`\latinencoding`	`\cyrillicencoding`	`\hebrewencoding`

The babel package uses `\latinencoding` to record the Latin encoding (OT1 or T1) used in the document. To determine which encoding is used, babel tests whether the encoding current at `\begin{document}` is T1; if it is not, it (perhaps wrongly) assumes OT1.

The languages that are typeset using the Cyrillic alphabet define the command `\cyrillicencoding` to store the name for the Cyrillic encoding. The command `\hebrewencoding` serves the same purpose for the Hebrew font encoding. At the time of writing no `\greekencoding` command was available, because babel supported only a single encoding (LGR) for Greek.

> `\textlatin{text}`

This command typesets its argument in a font with the Latin encoding, independent of the encoding of the surrounding text.

> `\textcyrillic{text}`

This command is (only) defined when one of the options `bulgarian`, `russian`, or `ukrainian` is used. It typesets its argument using a font in the Cyrillic encoding stored in `\cyrillicencoding`.

> `\textgreek{text}`   `\textol{text}`

These commands are defined by the `greek` language option. Both typeset their arguments in a font with the Greek encoding; the command `\textol` uses an outline font.

Declarative forms for these `\text...` commands are also available; they are called `\latintext`, `\greektext`, `\outlfamily`, and `\cyrillictext`.

Basic support for switching typesetting directions

To support the typesetting of Hebrew texts, the direction of typesetting also needs to be changed. Several commands with different names have been defined for this purpose.

> `\sethebrew`   `\unsethebrew`

The command `\sethebrew` switches the typesetting direction to "right to left", switches the font encoding to a Hebrew encoding, *and* shifts the "point of typesetting" to start from the right margin. The command `\unsethebrew` switches the typesetting direction to "left to right", switches the font encoding to the one in use when `\sethebrew` was called, *and* shifts the "point of typesetting" to start from the left margin.

> `\R{text}`   `\L{text}`

The commands `\R` and `\L` should be used when a small piece of Hebrew text needs to appear in the same location relative to the surrounding text. The use of these commands is illustrated in the following example. Note the location of the second text typeset with Hebrew characters.

```
\usepackage[X2,T1]{fontenc} \usepackage[greek,russian,hebrew,english]{babel}
Some English text, \R{hebrew text}, \textgreek{Greek text},
\textcyrillic{Cyrillic text}
\sethebrew more Hebrew text\unsethebrew{}, more English text.
```

9-3-39

Some English text, טוגעוק פורפ, Γρεεχ τεξτ, Ћӝтім-
мій тіе̨ъ̨ті , more English text.   סןעו וגעוק פורפ

9.4 Support for non-Latin alphabets

The babel distribution contains support for three non-Latin alphabets: the Cyrillic
alphabet, the Greek alphabet, and the Hebrew alphabet. They are discussed in the
following sections.

9.4.1 The Cyrillic alphabet

The Cyrillic alphabet is used by several of the Slavic languages in Eastern Europe,
as well as for writing tens of languages used in the territory encompassed by the
former Soviet Union. Vladimir Volovich and Werner Lemberg, together with the
LaTeX team, have integrated basic support for the Cyrillic language into LaTeX. This
section addresses the issues of Cyrillic fonts, the encoding interface, and their
integration with babel.

Historically, support for Russian in TeX has been available from the American
Mathematical Society [14]. The AMS system uses the wncyr fonts and is based on
a transliteration table originally designed for Russian journal names and article
titles in the journal *Mathematical Reviews*. In this journal the AMS prefers that
the same character sequence in the electronic files produce either the Russian
text with Russian characters or its transliteration with English characters, without
any ambiguities.

However, with the spread of TeX in Russia, proper support for typesetting Russian (and later other languages written in the Cyrillic alphabet) became necessary.
Over the years several 7- and 8-bit input encodings were developed, as well as
many font encodings. The Cyrillic system is designed to work for any 8-bit input
encoding and is able to map all of them onto a few Cyrillic font encodings, each
supporting a number of languages.

Fonts and font encodings

For compatibility reasons, only the upper 128 characters in an 8-bit TeX font are
available for new glyphs. As the number of glyphs in use in Cyrillic-based languages during the 20th century far exceeds 128, four "Cyrillic font encodings"
have been defined [17]. Three of them—T2A, T2B, and T2C—satisfy the basic structural requirements of LaTeX's T* encodings and, therefore, can be used in multilingual documents with other languages being based on standard font encodings.[1]

The work on the T2* encodings was performed by Alexander Berdnikov in
collaboration with Mikhail Kolodin and Andrew Janishewsky. Vladimir Volovich
provided the integration with LaTeX.

---

[1] The fourth Cyrillic encoding, X2, contains Cyrillic glyphs spread over the 256 character positions,
and is thus suitable only for specific, Cyrillic-only applications. It is not discussed here.

Two other LATEX Cyrillic font encodings exist: the 7-bit OT2 encoding developed by the American Mathematical Society, which is useful for short texts in Cyrillic, and the 8-bit LCY encoding, which is incompatible with the LATEX's T* encodings and, therefore, unsuitable for typesetting multilingual documents. The OT2 encoding was designed in such a way that the same source could be used to produce text either in the Cyrillic alphabet or in a transliteration.

Cyrillic Computer Modern fonts

The default font family with LATEX is Knuth's Computer Modern, in its 7-bit (OT1-encoded CM fonts) or 8-bit (T1-encoded EC fonts) incarnation. Olga Lapko and Andrey Khodulev developed the LH fonts, which provide glyph designs compatible with the Computer Modern font family and covering all Cyrillic font encodings. They provide the same font shapes and sizes as those available for its Latin equivalent, the EC family. These fonts are found on CTAN in the directory fonts/cyrillic/lh. Installation instructions appear in the file INSTALL in that distribution.[1]

A collection of hyphenation patterns for the Russian language that support the T2* encodings, as well as other popular font encodings used for Russian typesetting (including the Omega internal encoding), are available in the ruhyphen distribution on CTAN (language/hyphenation/ruhyphen). The patterns for other Cyrillic languages should be adapted to work with the T2* encodings.

Using Cyrillic in your documents

Support for Cyrillic in LATEX is based on the standard fontenc and inputenc packages, as well as on the babel package. For instance, one can write the following in the preamble of the document:

```
\usepackage[T2A]{fontenc}     \usepackage[koi8-r]{inputenc}
\usepackage[russian]{babel}
```

The input encoding koi8-r (KOI8 optimized for Russian) can be replaced by any of the following Cyrillic input encodings:

cp855   Standard MS-DOS Cyrillic code page.

cp866   Standard MS-DOS Russian code page. Several variants, distinguished by differences in the code positions 242–254, exist: cp866av (Cyrillic Alternative), cp866mav (Modified Alternative Variant), cp866nav (New Alternative Variant), and cp866tat (for Tatar).

cp1251   Standard MS Windows Cyrillic code page.

---

[1]Other fonts, including Type 1 fonts, can also be used, provided that their TEX font encoding is compatible with the T2* encodings. In particular, the CM-Super fonts cover the whole range of Cyrillic encodings; see Section 7.5.1 on page 353 for details.

koi8-r   Standard Cyrillic code page that is widely used on UNIX-like systems for Russian language support. Variants for Ukrainian are koi8-u and koi8-ru. An ECMA variant (ISO-IR-111 ECMA) is isoir111.

iso88595   ISO standard ISO 8859-5 (also called ISO-IR-144).

maccyr   Apple Macintosh Cyrillic code page (also known as Microsoft cp10007) and maccukr, the Apple Macintosh Ukrainian code page.

ctt, dbk, mnk, mnk, mos, ncc   Mongolian code pages.

Not all of these code pages are part of the standard inputenc distribution, so some may have to be obtained separately.

When more than one input encoding is used within a document, you can use the \inputencoding command to switch between them. To define the case of text, two standard LaTeX commands, \MakeUppercase and \MakeLowercase, can produce uppercase or lowercase, respectively. The low-level TeX \uppercase and \lowercase should never be used in LaTeX and will not work for Cyrillic.

In the previous example of a preamble, the font encoding to be used was explicitly declared. For multilingual documents *all* encodings needed should be enumerated via the \usepackage[...]{fontenc} command. Changing from one font encoding to another can be accomplished by using the \fontencoding command, but it is advisable that such changes be performed by a higher-level interface such as the \selectlanguage command. In particular, when using babel, you can write

```
\usepackage[koi8-r]{inputenc}  \usepackage[russian]{babel}
```

where babel will automatically choose the default font encoding for Russian, which is T2A, when it is available. Table 9.6 on the following page shows the layout of the T2A encoding.

Font encodings for Cyrillic languages

The Cyrillic font encodings support the languages listed below. Note that some languages, such as Bulgarian and Russian, can be properly typeset with more than one encoding.

T2A: Abaza, Avar, Agul, Adyghei, Azerbaijani, Altai, Balkar, Bashkir, Bulgarian, Buryat, Byelorussian, Gagauz, Dargin, Dungan, Ingush, Kabardino-Cherkess, Kazakh, Kalmyk, Karakalpak, Karachaevskii, Karelian, Kirghiz, Komi-Zyrian, Komi-Permyak, Kumyk, Lak, Lezghin, Macedonian, Mari-Mountain, Mari-Valley, Moldavian, Mongolian, Mordvin-Moksha, Mordvin-Erzya, Nogai, Oroch, Osetin, Russian, Rutul, Serbian, Tabasaran, Tadzhik, Tatar, Tati, Teleut, Tofalar, Tuva, Turkmen, Udmurt, Uzbek, Ukrainian, Hanty-Obskii, Hanty-Surgut, Gipsi, Chechen, Chuvash, Crimean-Tatar

	´0	´1	´2	´3	´4	´5	´6	´7	
´00x	`	´	^	~	¨	˝	°	˘	˝0x
´01x	˘	¯	˙	¸	˛	I	⟨	⟩	
´02x	``	''	^	˷	˘	–	—		˝1x
´03x	₀	₁	J	ff	fi	fl	ffi	ffl	
´04x	␣	!	"	#	$	%	&	'	˝2x
´05x	(	)	*	+	,	-	.	/	
´06x	0	1	2	3	4	5	6	7	˝3x
´07x	8	9	:	;	<	=	>	?	
´10x	@	A	B	C	D	E	F	G	˝4x
´11x	H	I	J	K	L	M	N	O	
´12x	P	Q	R	S	T	U	V	W	˝5x
´13x	X	Y	Z	[	\	]	^	_	
´14x	`	a	b	c	d	e	f	g	˝6x
´15x	h	i	j	k	l	m	n	o	
´16x	p	q	r	s	t	u	v	w	˝7x
´17x	x	y	z	{	|	}	~	-	
´20x	Ѓ	Ғ	Ђ	Ћ	ħ	Ж	З	Љ	˝8x
´21x	Ї	Қ	Ќ	Қ	Æ	Ң	Ӈ	S	
´22x	Ө	Ҫ	Ў	Ү	Ұ	Ҳ	Ц	Ч	˝9x
´23x	Ч	Є	Ә	Њ	Ё	№	¤	§	
´24x	ѓ	ғ	ђ	ħ	h	ж	з	љ	˝Ax
´25x	ï	қ	ќ	к	æ	ң	ӈ	s	
´26x	ө	ҫ	ў	ү	ұ	х	ц	ч	˝Bx
´27x	ч	є	ә	њ	ё	„	«	»	
´30x	А	Б	В	Г	Д	Е	Ж	З	˝Cx
´31x	И	Й	К	Л	М	Н	О	П	
´32x	Р	С	Т	У	Ф	Х	Ц	Ч	˝Dx
´33x	Ш	Щ	Ъ	Ы	Ь	Э	Ю	Я	
´34x	а	б	в	г	д	е	ж	з	˝Ex
´35x	и	й	к	л	м	н	о	п	
´36x	р	с	т	у	ф	х	ц	ч	˝Fx
´37x	ш	щ	ъ	ы	ь	э	ю	я	
	˝8	˝9	˝A	˝B	˝C	˝D	˝E	˝F	

Characters marked in blue need to be present (in their specified positions) in every text encoding, as they are transparently passed through TEX.

Table 9.6: Glyph chart for a T2A-encoded font (`larm1000`)

T2B: Abaza, Avar, Agul, Adyghei, Aleut, Altai, Balkar, Byelorussian, Bulgarian,
Buryat, Gagauz, Dargin, Dolgan, Dungan, Ingush, Itelmen,
Kabardino-Cherkess, Kalmyk, Karakalpak, Karachaevskii, Karelian, Ketskii,
Kirghiz, Komi-Zyrian, Komi-Permyak, Koryak, Kumyk, Kurdian, Lak,
Lezghin, Mansi, Mari-Valley, Moldavian, Mongolian, Mordvin-Moksha,
Mordvin-Erzya, Nanai, Nganasan, Negidal, Nenets, Nivh, Nogai, Oroch,
Russian, Rutul, Selkup, Tabasaran, Tadzhik, Tatar, Tati, Teleut, Tofalar,
Tuva, Turkmen, Udyghei, Uigur, Ulch, Khakass, Hanty-Vahovskii,
Hanty Kazymskii, Hanty Obskii, Hanty Surgut, Hanty Shurysharskii, Gipsi,
Chechen, Chukcha, Shor, Evenk, Even, Enets, Eskimo, Yukagir, Crimean
Tatar, Yakut

T2C: Abkhazian, Bulgarian, Gagauz, Karelian, Komi-Zyrian, Komi-Permyak,
Kumyk, Mansi, Moldavian, Mordvin-Moksha, Mordvin-Erzya, Nanai, Orok
(Uilta), Negidal, Nogai, Oroch, Russian, Saam, Old-Bulgarian, Old-Russian,
Tati, Teleut, Hanty-Obskii, Hanty-Surgut, Evenk, Crimean Tatar

The basic LATEX distribution comes with all the encoding and font definition
files for handling Cyrillic. The babel package includes support for Bulgarian, Russian, and Ukrainian. Together with the font files (to be installed separately), LATEX
can use this pacakge to provide complete support for typesetting languages based
on the Cyrillic alphabet.

Running *MakeIndex* and BiBTEX

Recognizing that standard *MakeIndex* and BiBTEX programs cannot handle 8-bit
input encodings natively, the T2 bundle comes with utilities to allow Cyrillic 8-bit
input to be handled correctly by those programs.

For indexes, rumakeindex is a wrapper for *MakeIndex* that creates a properly
sorted index when Cyrillic letters are used in the entries. Use of the rumakeindex
utility also requires the sed program.[1] The utility should be run instead of standard *MakeIndex* when you are creating an index containing Cyrillic characters.
Note that the rumakeindex script on UN*X uses the koi8-r encoding, whereas
the corresponding batch file on MS-DOS, rumkidxd.bat, uses the cp866 encoding,
and the batch file on MS Windows, rumkidxw.bat, uses the cp1251 encoding. If a
different encoding is needed, changes have to be introduced in the relevant files.
Alternatively, you might consider using xindy, a newer index preparation program,
which is described in Section 11.3.

For bibliographic references, rubibtex is a wrapper for BiBTEX that produces
Cyrillic letters in item names, which correspond to the reference keys when a
BiBTEX bibliographic database is used. You should also install the citehack package
from the T2 bundle in that case. Moreover, the installed version of the BiBTEX
program should be able to handle 8-bit input (e.g., the BiBTEX8 program described

---

[1] Available on any UN*X and for Microsoft operating systems on PC distributed by GNU (e.g., at
http://www.simtel.net).

in Section 13.1.1). As in the case of *MakeIndex* described above, the rubibtex script
and batch files also require the sed program.

Note that the rubibtex script on UN*X uses the koi8-r encoding, whereas the
corresponding batch file on MS-DOS, rubibtex.bat, uses the cp866 encoding. When
another encoding is needed, changes should be introduced in the relevant files.

9.4.2   The Greek alphabet

Greek support in babel comes in two variants: the one-accent monotoniko (the
default), which is used in most cases in everyday communications in Greece today,
and the multi-accent polutoniko, which has to be specified as an attribute, as
explained in Section 9.2.3.

The first family of Greek fonts for TeX was created during the mid-1980s by
Silvio Levy [114]. Other developers improved or extended these fonts, or developed their own Greek fonts.

In babel the Greek language support is based on the work of Claudio Beccari in collaboration with Apostolos Syropoulos, who developed the Greek cb font
family [12]. In their paper these authors discuss in some detail previous efforts to
support the Greek language with TeX. The sources of the cb fonts are available on
CTAN in the directory languages/greek/cb or on the TeXlive CD in the directory
texmf/fonts/source/public/cbgreek. Hyphenation patterns corresponding to
this font family are found in the file grhyph.tex or grphyph.tex in the same
directory on CTAN and in texmf/tex/generic/hyphen on TeXlive.

The cb font uses the LGR font encoding. At the time of this book's writing,
work was under way to design a font encoding that is compatible with LaTeX's
standards. When it is ready, it will become the T7 encoding. Table 9.7 on the next
page shows the layout of the complete LGR encoding.

It is possible to use Latin alphabetic characters for inputting Greek according
to the translation scheme shown in Table 9.8 on page 576. This table shows that
the Latin "v" character has no direct equivalent in the Greek transcription. In
fact, it is used to indicate that one *does not* want a final sigma. For example, "sv"
generates a median form sigma although it occurs in a final position.

By default, the greek option of babel will use monotoniko Greek. Multi-
accented mode is requested by specifying the language attribute polutoniko for
the greek option:

```
\usepackage[greek]{babel}
\languageattribute{greek}{polutoniko}
```

For both modes, some seldom-used characters have been defined to behave like
letters (\catcode 11). For monotoniko Greek, this is the case for the characters '
and ". In the polutoniko variant, the characters <, >, ~, ', and | also behave like
letters. The reason for this behavior is that the LGR encoding contains many ligatures with these characters to produce the right glyphs; see Table 9.9 on page 576.
Table 9.10 shows the available composite accent and spiritus combinations.

	'0	'1	'2	'3	'4	'5	'6	'7	
'00x	–		Δ	H	X	M	ϛ	ϟ	"0x
'01x	ι	Aι	Hι	Ωι					
'02x			ʮ	ϙ					"1x
'03x	€	‰		ϡ	'	,	˘	¯	
'04x	˜	!	,	ˬ	˭	%	·	′	"2x
'05x	(	)	*	+	,	-	·	/	
'06x	0	1	2	3	4	5	6	7	"3x
'07x	8	9	:	·	<	=	>	;	
'10x	˘	A	B	^	Δ	E	Φ	Γ	"4x
'11x	H	I	Θ	K	Λ	M	N	O	
'12x	Π	X	P	Σ	T	Υ	˝	Ω	"5x
'13x	Ξ	Ψ	Z	[	˘	]	˘	^	
'14x	`	α	β	ς	δ	ε	φ	γ	"6x
'15x	η	ι	ϑ	χ	λ	μ	ν	ο	
'16x	π	χ	ρ	ς	τ	υ		ω	"7x
'17x	ξ	ψ	ζ	«	‚	»	~	—	
'20x	ὰ	ά	ᾶ	ᾰ	ᾳ	ᾴ	ᾲ	ᾷ	"8x
'21x	ἀ	ἂ	ἄ	ἆ	ᾀ	ᾂ	ᾄ	ᾆ	
'22x	ἁ	ἃ	ἅ	Ϝ	ᾁ	ᾃ	ᾅ		"9x
'23x	ὴ	ή	ῆ		ῂ	ῄ	ῇ		
'24x	ἠ	ἢ	ἤ	ἦ	ᾐ	ᾒ	ᾔ	ᾖ	"Ax
'25x	ἡ	ἣ	ἥ	ἧ	ᾑ	ᾓ	ᾕ	ᾗ	
'26x	ὼ	ώ	ῶ	ῳ	ῲ	ῴ	ῷ	ῷ	"Bx
'27x	ὤ	ὢ	ὦ	ὧ	ᾠ	ᾢ	ᾤ	ᾦ	
'30x	ὥ	ὣ	ὧ	Ϝ	ᾡ	ᾣ	ᾥ		"Cx
'31x	ὶ	ί	ῖ	ῗ	ὺ	ύ	ῦ	ῧ	
'32x	ἰ	ἲ	ἴ	ἶ	ὐ	ὒ	ὔ	ὖ	"Dx
'33x	ῐ	ῑ	ΐ	Ϊ	ῠ	ῡ	ΰ	Ϋ	
'34x	ὲ	έ	ἐ	ἒ	ὸ	ό	ὀ	ὂ	"Ex
'35x	ἑ	ἓ	ἔ	ἕ	ὁ	ὃ	ὄ	ὅ	
'36x	ϊ	ἵ	ἱ	ῒ	ϋ	ὕ	ὑ	ὓ	"Fx
'37x	ᾳ	η	ῳ	ῥ	ῤ		'	‚	
	"8	"9	"A	"B	"C	"D	"E	"F	

Characters marked in blue should be ASCII characters in every LATEX text encoding (compare Table 9.6 on page 572), as they are transparently passed through TEX. In LGR this is not the case for A–Z and a–z, which can produce problems in multilingual documents.

Table 9.7: Glyph chart for an LGR-encoded font (grmn1000)

a	b	c	d	e	f	g	h	i	j	k	l	m	n	o	p	q	r	s	t	u	v	w	x	y	z
α	β	ς	δ	ε	φ	γ	η	ι	ϑ	κ	λ	μ	ν	ο	π	χ	ρ	ς	τ	υ		ω	ξ	ψ	ζ
A	B	C	D	E	F	G	H	I	J	K	L	M	N	O	P	Q	R	S	T	U	V	W	X	Y	Z
Α	Β	῾	Δ	Ε	Φ	Γ	Η	Ι	Θ	Κ	Λ	Μ	Ν	Ο	Π	Χ	Ρ	Σ	Τ	Υ		Ω	Ξ	Ψ	Z

9-4-1

Table 9.8: Greek transliteration with Latin letters for the LGR encoding

	Input	*Result*	*Example*
Acute	'a 'e 'h 'i 'o 'u 'w	ά έ ή ί ό ύ ώ	g'ata	γάτα
Diaresis	"i "u "I "U	ϊ ϋ Ϊ Ϋ	qa"ide'uh|c	χαϊδεύης
Rough breathing	<a <e <h <i <o <r <u <w	ἁ ἑ ἡ ἱ ὁ ῥ ὑ ὡ	<'otan	ὅιταν
Smooth breathing	>a >e >h >i >o >r >u >w	ἀ ἐ ἠ ἰ ὀ ῤ ὐ ὠ	>'aneu	ἄνευ
Grave	\`a \`e \`h \`i \`o    \`u \`w	ὰ ὲ ὴ ὶ ὸ ὺ ὼ	dad\`i	δαδὶ
Circumflex	~a ~h ~i ~u ~w	ᾶ ῆ ῖ ῦ ῶ	ful~hc	φυλῆς
Diacritic below	a| h| w|	ᾳ ῃ ῳ		
	\`w| 'w| >\`w| >'w| <\`w| <'w|	ῲ ῴ ῷ ῷ ῷ ῷ		

9-4-2

Table 9.9: LGR ligatures producing single-accented glyphs

Input	*Result*	*Input*	*Result*
'"i '"i '"u '"u	ῗ ῗ ῧ ῧ	'"I '"I '"U '"U	Ϊ͂ Ϊ͂ Ϋ͂ Ϋ͂
>\`a >\`e >\`h >\`i >\`o >\`u >\`w	ἂ ἒ ἢ ἲ ὂ ὒ ὢ	>\`A >\`E >\`H >\`I >\`O >\`U >\`W	Ἂ Ἒ Ἢ Ἲ Ὂ Υ̓̀ Ὢ
>'a >'e >'h >'i >'o >'u >'w	ἄ ἔ ἤ ἴ ὄ ὔ ὤ	>'A >'E >'H >'I >'O >'U >'W	Ἄ Ἔ Ἤ Ἴ Ὄ Υ̓́ Ὤ
<\`a <\`e <\`h <\`i <\`o <\`u <\`w	ἃ ἓ ἣ ἳ ὃ ὓ ὣ	<\`A <\`E <\`H <\`I <\`O <\`U <\`W	Ἃ Ἓ Ἣ Ἳ Ὃ Ὓ Ὣ
<'a <'e <'h <'i <'o <'u <'w	ἅ ἕ ἥ ἵ ὅ ὕ ὥ	<'A <'E <'H <'I <'O <'U <'W	Ἅ Ἕ Ἥ Ἵ Ὅ Ὕ Ὥ
>\~a >\~h >\~i >\~u >\~w	ἆ ἦ ἶ ὖ ὦ	>\~A >\~H >\~I >\~U >\~W	Ἆ Ἦ Ἶ Ὗ Ὦ
<\~a <\~h <\~i <\~u <\~w	ἇ ἧ ἷ ὗ ὧ	<\~A <\~H <\~I <\~U <\~W	Ἇ Ἧ Ἷ Ὗ Ὧ

9-4-3

Table 9.10: Available composite spiritus and accent combinations

9.4.3 The Hebrew alphabet

The first support for Hebrew that became part of the babel distribution was developed by Boris Lavva and Alon Ziv, based on earlier work that offered support for typesetting Hebrew texts with LᴬTEX 2.09 and TEX--XᴇT. This support was developed further by these two authors and Rama Porrat. At the time of writing Tzafrir Cohen has started a sourceforge project called "ivritex" (http://ivritex.sf.net) to extend the work even more.

כותרת של מאמר שנכתב באמצעות LaTeX
בעברית

רמה פורת

2 בפברואר 2002

1   זאת ההתחלה

אפשר להתחיל בעברית ואחר כך לעבור ללועזית and continue with English text
אפשר גם לכלול נוסחאות $102 = 83 + a^2$ ולחזור לעברית.

1.1   תת סעיף בעבודה

* המצב לא טוב אבל יש תקווה לעתיד.

* יש לפניך שולחן עם המון מטבעות. לכל מטבע צד לבן וצד שחור. עייניך
קשורות. אתה יודע ש 10 מטבעות הן עם הצד הלבן למעלה, והשאר עם
הצד השחור למעלה. עליך לחלק את המטבעות לשתי קבוצות, כך שבכל
קבוצה יהיה אותו מספר של לבנים (כלומר צד לבן למעלה).
לא מצאת את הפיתרון? rama@huji.ac.il

2   Last section

אפשר להשתמש בכל האפשרויות של התוכנה בגירסתה הלועזית.

9-4-4

Figure 9.1: A Hebrew document

The current support for typesetting Hebrew is based on fonts from the Hebrew University of Jerusalem. These fonts have a particular 7-bit encoding for which the Local Hebrew encoding (LHE) has been developed. Figure 9.1 used the Jerusalem font; in Table 9.11 on the following page the encoding of these fonts is shown. The support in babel uses the Jerusalem font as the regular font, Old Jaffa for a font with an italic shape, and the Dead Sea font for typesetting bold letters. When a sans serif font is needed, the Tel Aviv font is used; it is also deployed as a replacement for a typewriter font.

As an alternative to these fonts, two other (copyrighted, but freely available on CTAN) fonts are supported: Hclassic is a "modernized Classical Hebrew" font; Hcaption is a slanted version of it. Furthermore, three shalom fonts are available: ShalomScript10 contains handwritten Hebrew letters; ShalomStick10 contains sans serif letters; and ShalomOldStyle10 contains old-style letters. Yet an-

	´0	´1	´2	´3	´4	´5	´6	´7	
´02x	אַ	אָ	וו	וי	ֽ	״	ֻ	שׁ	˝1x
´03x	שׂ	־	–	—	–				
´04x		!	„					֬	˝2x
´05x	(	)			֗		֗	/	
´06x	֗	֔	֖	֑	֘	֪	֙	֮	˝3x
´07x	֒	֓	:	׃	׀	֗	׀	?	
´10x	…	֑	֓	֖	ֵ	֘	֔	֙	˝4x
´11x	֙	֔	֓	֗	֚	֖	ֵ	֘	
´12x	֭	֗	֓	֖	֙	֕	֕	֗	˝5x
´13x	֗	֗	״	׳	\				
´14x	א	ב	ג	ד	ה	ו	ז	ח	˝6x
´15x	ט	י	ך	כ	ל	ם	מ	ן	
´16x	נ	ס	ע	ף	פ	ץ	צ	ק	˝7x
´17x	ר	ש	ת						
	˝8	˝9	˝A	˝B	˝C	˝D	˝E	˝F	

Table 9.11: Glyph chart for an LHE-encoded font (shold10)

other available family of fonts are the Frank Ruehl fonts, which come in regular, bold extended, and slanted shapes. The Carmel font family offers regular and slanted shapes and was designed for headers and emphasized text. The Redis family comes with regular, slanted, and bold extended shapes. For all supported font families, the package hebfont defines commands to select them. These commands are shown in Table 9.12 on the next page.

A few input encodings are available as part of the support for Hebrew. They are not automatically provided with the inputenc distribution.

si960   This 7-bit Hebrew encoding uses ASCII character positions 32–127. Also known as "oldcode", it is defined by Israeli standard SI-960.

8859-8   This 8-bit mixed Hebrew and Latin encoding is also known as "newcode". It is defined by the standard ISO 8859-8.

cp862   This IBM code page is commonly used by MS-DOS on IBM-compatible personal computers. It is also known as "pccode".

cp1255   The MS Windows 1255 (Hebrew) code page resembles ISO 8859-8. In addition to Hebrew letters, this encoding contains vowels and dots (nikud).

Command	Corresponds to Declaration	Font Family	Example
\textjm	\rmfamily	Jerusalem font	ומפומפף
\textds	\bfseries	Dead Sea font	ומפומפף
\textoj	\itshape	Old Jaffa font	ומפומפף
\textta	\sffamily	Tel Aviv font	ומפומפף
	\ttfamily		
\textcrml	\fontfamily{crml}	Carmel fonts	ומפומפף
\textfr	\fontfamily{fr}}	Frank Ruehl fonts	ומפומפף
\textredis	\fontfamily{redis}	Redis fonts	ומפומפף
\textclas	\fontfamily{clas}	Classic fonts	ומפומפף
\textshold	\fontfamily{shold}	Shalom Old Style font	ומפומפף
\textshscr	\fontfamily{shscr}	Shalom Script font	ומפומפף
\textshstk	\fontfamily{schstk}	Shalom Stick font	ומפומפף

Table 9.12: Hebrew font-changing commands

9-4-5

9.5   Tailoring babel

This section explains some of the commands that are made available by the core
babel package to construct language definition files (which are usually loaded
when a language option is requested). Section 9.5.3 then looks in some detail at
the template file language.skeleton, which can be used as a basis to provide
support for additional languages.

   Language definition files (file extension .ldf) have to conform to a number of
conventions, since they complement the common shared code of babel provided
in the file babel.def for producing language-dependent text strings. Similarly,
to allow for language switching like the capability built into babel, certain rules
apply. The basic working assumptions follow.

- Each language definition file ⟨lang⟩.ldf must define five macros, which
  are subsequently used to activate and deactivate the language-specific definitions. These macros are \⟨language⟩hyphenmins, \captions⟨language⟩,
  \date⟨language⟩, \extras⟨language⟩, and \noextras⟨language⟩, where
  ⟨language⟩ is either the name of the language definition file or the name of a
  babel package option. These macros and their functions are discussed below.

- When a language definition file is loaded, it can define \l@⟨language⟩ to be a
  variant (*dialect*) of \language0 when \l@⟨language⟩ is undefined.

- The language definition files must be written in a way that they can be read
  not just in the preamble of the document, but also in the middle of document
  processing.

9.5.1 Hyphenating in several languages

Since TEX version 3.0, hyphenation patterns for multiple languages can be used together. These patterns have to be administered somehow. In particular, the plainTEX user has to know for which languages patterns have been loaded, and to what values of the command sequence \language they correspond. The babel package abstracts from this low-level interface and manages this information by using an external file, language.dat, in which one records which languages have hyphenation patterns *and* in which files these patterns are stored. This configuration file is then processed[1] when INITEX is run to generate a new LATEX format. An example of this file is shown here:

```
%%% Filename    : language.dat
%%% Description : Instruct iniTeX which pattern files to load.

english        ushyph.tex                    % American English
=usenglish
=american
russian        ruhyph.tex                    % Russian
french         frhyph.tex     frhyphx.tex % French
=patois
=francais
ukenglish      gbhyph.tex                    % UK English
=british
german         dehypht.tex                   % Traditional German
%ngerman       dehyphn.tex                   % New German (not loaded)
%dutch         nehyph96.tex                  % Dutch (not loaded)

dumylang       dumyhyph.tex                  % For testing new language
nohyphenation  zerohyph.tex                  % Language with no patterns
```

This configuration file language.dat can contain empty lines and comments, as well as lines that start with an equals (=) sign. Such a line will instruct LATEX that the hyphenation patterns just processed will be known under an alternative name. The first element on each line specifies the name of the language; it is followed by the name of the file containing the hyphenation patterns. An optional third entry can specify a hyphenation exception file in case the exceptions are stored in a separate file (e.g., frhyphx.tex in the previous example).

For each language in language.dat, the command \l@⟨*language*⟩ is defined in the LATEX format (i.e., \l@english and so on). When the document is processed with such a format, babel checks for each language whether the command \l@⟨*language*⟩ is defined and, if so, it loads the corresponding hyphenation pat-

---

[1]Make sure that you do not have several such files in your TEX installation, because it is not always clear which of them will be examined during the format generation. The authors nearly got bitten during the book production when INITEX picked up the system configuration file and not the specially prepared one containing all the patterns for the examples.

terns; otherwise, it loads the patterns for the default language 0 (the one loaded first by INITEX; English in the example above).

```
initex latex.ltx
This is TeX, Version 3.14159 (Web2C 7.3.3.1) (INITEX)
(/tex/texmf/tex/latex/base/latex.ltx
(/tex/texmf/tex/latex/base/texsys.cfg)
   ....
24 hyphenation exceptions
Hyphenation trie of length 33878 has 835 ops out of 1501
   2 for language 5
   207 for language 4
   224 for language 3
   86 for language 2
   135 for language 1
   181 for language 0
No pages of output.
```

Six "languages" are loaded into the format, as defined in the language.dat file: english (0), russian (1), french (2), ukenglish (3), german (4), dumylang (5), and nohyphenation (6; implicitly defined with no hyphenation tries). Babel uses these text strings (or their equivalents, specified preceeded by an = sign in language.dat) to identify a language.

If language.dat cannot be opened for reading during the INITEX run, babel will attempt to use the default hyphenation file hyphen.tex instead. It informs the user in this event.

9.5.2 The package file

To help make use of the features of LaTeX, the babel package contains a package file called babel.sty. This file is loaded by the \usepackage command and defines all the language options supported by babel (see Table 9.1 on page 543). It also takes care of a number of compatibility issues with other packages. Local customization for babel can be entered in the configuration file bblopts.cfg, which is read at the end of babel.sty.

Apart from the language options listed in Table 9.1 on page 543, babel pre-declares a few options that can influence the behavior of language definition files. For instance, activeacute and activegrave by default do nothing, but they are used with, for instance, Catalan (catalan.ldf) to activate the acute and grave accents when the relevant options are specified.

A third option, KeepShorthandsActive, instructs babel to keep shorthand characters active when processing of the package file ends. Note that this is *not* the default as it can cause problems with other packages. Nevertheless, in some cases, such as when you need to use shorthand characters in the preamble of a document, this option can be useful.

9.5.3 The structure of the babel language definition file

The babel distribution comes with the file language.skeleton, which provides a convenient skeleton for developing one's own language file to support a new language. It serves as a convenient model to understand how the babel core commands are used. The file is shown here, and the commands used in it are described as they occur.

Throughout language.skeleton, you will find the string "⟨language⟩"; it should be replaced by the name of the language for which you are providing support. If this language is known to have a dialect that needs a slightly different support, you can arrange for this support as well. In such a case, the strings "⟨dialect⟩" should be replaced by the name of the dialect. If your language does not need support for a dialect, you should remove the corresponding lines of code.

Copyright and introduction The file starts with copyright and license information.

```
 1   % \iffalse meta-comment
 2   %
 3   % Copyright 1989-2003 Johannes L. Braams and any individual authors
 4   % listed elsewhere in this file.  All rights reserved.
 5   %
 6   % This file is part of the Babel system release 3.7.
 7   % --------------------------------------------------
 8   %
 9   % This work may be distributed and/or modified under the
10   % conditions of the LaTeX Project Public License, either version 1.3
11   % of this license or (at your option) any later version.
12   % The latest version of this license is in
13   %    http://www.latex-project.org/lppl.txt
14   % and version 1.3 or later is part of all distributions of LaTeX
15   % version 2003/12/01 or later.
16   %
17   % This work has the LPPL maintenance status "maintained".
18   %
19   % This Current Maintainer of this work is Johannes Braams.
20   %
21   % \fi
22   % \CheckSum{0}
23   %%%     docstring          = " This file can act as a template for
24   %%%                          people who want to provide extra
25   %%%                          languages to be included in the babel
26   %%%                          distribution.
27   %
```

Identification of the language This is followed by information identifying the file and language.

```
28   %<*dtx>
29   % \iffalse
30   %    Tell the \LaTeX\ system who we are and write an entry in the
31   %    transcript file.
32   \ProvidesFile{<language>.dtx}
33   %</dtx>
34   %<code>\ProvidesLanguage{<language>}
35   %\fi
36   %\ProvidesFile{<language>.dtx}
37          [2003/03/18 v1.5 <Language> support from the babel system]
```

\ProvidesLanguage{*name*}[*release-information*]

The command \ProvidesLanguage (line 32) identifies the language definition file. It uses the same syntax as LaTeX's \ProvidesPackage. For instance, the file welsh.sty contains the following declaration:

\ProvidesLanguage{welsh}

The *release-information* can be used to indicate that at least this version of babel is required.

The next section then sets up a documentation driver to allow for typesetting the file itself using the doc package. See Chapter 14 for details.   *A documentation driver*

```
38   %\iffalse
39   %% Babel package for LaTeX version 2e
40   %% Copyright (C) 1989 -- 2003
41   %%          by Johannes Braams, TeXniek
42   %
43   %% Please report errors to: J.L. Braams
44   %%                    babel@braams.cistron.nl
45   %
46   %    This file is part of the babel system, it provides the source code for
47   %    the <Language> language definition file.
48   %<*filedriver>
49   \documentclass{ltxdoc}
50   \newcommand*{\TeXhax}{\TeX hax}
51   \newcommand*{\babel}{\textsf{babel}}
52   \newcommand*{\langvar}{$\langle \mathit lang \rangle$}
53   \newcommand*{\note}[1]{}
54   \newcommand*{\Lopt}[1]{\textsf{#1}}
55   \newcommand*{\file}[1]{\texttt{#1}}
56   \begin{document}
57    \DocInput{<language>.dtx}
58   \end{document}
59   %</filedriver>
60   %\fi
61   %% \GetFileInfo{<language>.dtx}
62   %
```

The following part starts with the documentation of the features provided by the language definition file. Use the methods described in Chapter 14 for documenting code and providing a short user manual.   *Documentation and initialization*

```
63   % \changes{v1.1}{1994/02/27}{Rearranged the file a little}
64   % \changes{v1.2}{1994/06/04}{Update for \LaTeXe}
65   % \changes{v1.3}{1995/05/13}{Update for \babel\ release 3.5}
66   % \changes{v1.4}{1996/10/30}{Update for \babel\ release 3.6}
67   % \changes{v1.5}{1997/03/18}{Update for \babel\ release 3.7}
68   %
69   % \section{The <Language> language}
70   %
71   %    The file \file{\filename}\footnote{The file described in this
72   %    section has version number \fileversion\ and was last revised on
73   %    \filedate.}  defines all the language definition macros for the
74   %    <Language> language.
75   %
76   % \StopEventually{}
```

```
77    %
78    %        The macro |\LdfInit| takes care of preventing that this file is
79    %        loaded more than once, checking the category code of the
80    %        \textttt{@} sign, etc.
81    %        \begin{macrocode}
82    %<*code>
83    \LdfInit{<language>}{captions<language>}
84    %        \end{macrocode}
85    %
```

\LdfInit

The macro \LdfInit (line 83) performs a couple of standard checks that have
to be made at the beginning of a language definition file, such as checking the
category code of the @ sign and preventing the .ldf file from being processed
twice.

Defining language
and dialects

```
86    %        When this file is read as an option, i.e. by the |\usepackage|
87    %        command, \textttt{<language>} could be an 'unknown' language in
88    %        which case we have to make it known.  So we check for the
89    %        existence of |\l@<language>| to see whether we have to do
90    %        something here.
91    %
92    %        \begin{macrocode}
93    \ifx\undefined\l@<language>
94      \@nopatterns{<Language>}
95      \adddialect\l@<language>0\fi
96    %        \end{macrocode}
97    %        For the <Dialect> version of these definitions we just add a
98    %        ''dialect''. Also, the macros |\captions<dialect>| and
99    %        |\extras<dialect>| are |\let| to their \textttt{<language>}
100   %        counterparts when these parts are defined.
101   %        \begin{macrocode}
102   \adddialect\l@<dialect>\l@<language>
103   %        \end{macrocode}
104   %        The next step consists of defining commands to switch to (and
105   %        from) the <Language> language.
106   %
```

\adddialect{\l@*variant*}{\l@*lang*}

The command \adddialect adds the name of a variant (dialect) language
\l@*variant*, for which already defined hyphenation patterns can be used (the ones
for language *lang*).[1] If a language has more than one variant, you can repeat this
section as often as necessary.

"Dialect" is somewhat of a historical misnomer, as *lang* and *variant* are at the
same level as far as babel is concerned, without co-notation indicating whether
one or the other is the main language. The "dialect" paradigm comes in handy
if you want to share hyphenation patterns between various languages. Moreover,
if no hyphenation patterns are preloaded in the format for the language *lang*,
babel's default behavior is to define this language as a "dialect" of the default
language (\language0).

---

[1]When loading hyphenation patterns with INITEX babel uses the \addlanguage command to declare the various languages specified in language.dat; see Section 9.5.1.

For instance, the first line below indicates that for Austrian one can use the hyphenation patterns for German (defined in `german.ldf`). The second line tells us that Nynorsk shares the hyphenation patterns of Norsk (in `norsk.ldf`).

```
\adddialect{austrian}{german}
\adddialect{nynorsk}{norsk}
```

The following example shows how language variants can be obtained using the dialect mechanism, where there can be differences in the names of sectioning elements or for the date.

Dialectical variants:
Norsk: Bibliografi
Nynorsk: Litteratur
Dutch: 29 februari 2004

9-5-1 Afrikaans: 29 Februarie 2004

```
\usepackage[dutch,afrikaans,norsk,nynorsk,english]{babel}
Dialectical variants:                                    \par
\selectlanguage{norsk}    Norsk:    \bibname  \par
\selectlanguage{nynorsk}  Nynorsk:  \bibname  \par
\selectlanguage{dutch}    Dutch:    \today    \par
\selectlanguage{afrikaans} Afrikaans: \today
```

The next part deals with the set-up for language attributes, if necessary.

Defining language attributes

```
107  %      Now we declare the |<attrib>| language attribute.
108  %      \begin{macrocode}
109  \bbl@declare@ttribute{<language>}{<attrib>}{%
110  %      \end{macrocode}
111  %      This code adds the expansion of |\extras<attrib><language>| to
112  %      |\extras<language>|.
113  %      \begin{macrocode}
114      \expandafter\addto\expandafter\extras<language>
115      \expandafter{\extras<attrib><language>}%
116      \let\captions<language>\captions<attrib><language>
117      }
118  %      \end{macrocode}
119  %
```

> `\bbl@declare@ttribute{`*lang*`}{`*attr*`}{`*exec*`}`

This command (used on line 109) declares that for the attribute *attr* in the language *lang*, the code *exec* should be executed. For instance, the file `greek.ldf` defines an attribute polutoniko for the Greek language:

```
\bbl@declare@ttribute{greek}{polutoniko}{...}
```

When you load the Greek language with the `polutonikogreek` option (which is equivalent to setting the attribute polutoniko), Greek will then be typeset with multiple accents (according to the code specified in the third argument).

If you want to define more than one attribute for the current language, repeat this section as often as necessary.

Adjusting Now we deal with the minimum number of characters required to the left and
hyphenation right of hyphenation points.
patterns

```
120  %  \begin{macro}{\<language>hyphenmins}
121  %     This macro is used to store the correct values of the hyphenation
122  %     parameters |\lefthyphenmin| and |\righthyphenmin|.
123  %     \begin{macrocode}
124  \providehyphenmins{<language>}{\tw@\thr@@}
125  %     \end{macrocode}
126  %  \end{macro}
127  %
```

`\providehyphenmins{`*lang*`}{`*hyphenmins*`}`   `\⟨`*language*`⟩hyphenmins`

The command `\providehyphenmins` (line 124) provides a *default* setting for the
hyphenation parameters `\lefthyphenmin` (minimum number of characters on the
left before the first hyphen point) and `\righthyphenmin` (minimum numbers on
the right) for the language *lang*, by defining `\⟨`*language*`⟩hyphenmins` unless it is
already defined for some reason. The babel package detects whether the hyphenation file explicitly sets `\lefthyphenmin` and `\righthyphenmin` and automatically defines `\⟨`*language*`⟩hyphenmins`, in which case the `\providehyphenmins`
declaration has no effect.

The syntax inside babel is storage optimized, dating back to the days when
every token counted. Thus, the argument *hyphenmins* contains the values for both
parameters simply as two digits, making the assumption that you will never want
a minimum larger than 9. If this assumption is wrong, you must surround the
values with braces within *hyphenmins*. For example,

```
\providehyphenmins{german}{{10}{5}}
```

would request to leave at least 10 characters before a hyphen and at least 5 characters after it (thus essentially never hyphenate).

If you want to explicitly overwrite the settings regardless of any existing specification, you can do so by providing a value for `\⟨`*language*`⟩hyphenmins` yourself.
For instance,

```
\def\germanhyphenmins}{43}
```

never considers hyphenation points with less than four letters before and three
letters after the hyphen. Thus, it will never hyphenate a word with less than seven
characters.

Hyphenation patterns are built with a certain setting of these parameters in
mind. Setting their values lower than the values used in the pattern generation
will merely result in incorrect hyphenation. It is possible, however, to use higher
values in which case the potential hyphenation points are simply reduced.

Translations for The translations for language-dependent strings are set up next.
language-dependent
strings

```
128  %  \begin{macro}{\captions<language>}
129  %     The macro |\captions<language>| defines all strings used in the
130  %     four standard documentclasses provided with \LaTeX.
131  %     \begin{macrocode}
```

```
132  \def\captions<language>{}
133  %    \end{macrocode}
134  % \end{macro}
135  %
136  % \begin{macro}{\captions<dialect>}
137  %    \begin{macrocode}
138  \let\captions<dialect>\captions<language>
139  %    \end{macrocode}
140  % \end{macro}
141  %
```

> \captions⟨*language*⟩{*replacement text definitions*}

The macro \captions⟨*language*⟩ (line 132) defines the macros that hold the translations for the language-dependent strings used in LATEX for the language ⟨*language*⟩. It must also be provided for each dialect being set up. If the dialect uses the same translation, \let can be used (as shown in line 138). Otherwise, you have to provide a full definition.

```
142  % \begin{macro}{\date<language>}
143  %    The macro |\date<language>| redefines the command |\today| to
144  %    produce <Language> dates.
145  %    \begin{macrocode}
146  \def\date<language>{%
147  }
148  %    \end{macrocode}
149  % \end{macro}
150  %
151  % \begin{macro}{\date<dialect>}
152  %    The macro |\date<dialect>| redefines the command |\today| to
153  %    produce <Dialect> dates.
154  %    \begin{macrocode}
155  \def\date<dialect>{%
156  }
157  %    \end{macrocode}
158  % \end{macro}
159  %
```

> \date⟨*language*⟩{*definition of date*}

The macro \date⟨*language*⟩ (line 146) defines the text string for the \today command for the language ⟨*language*⟩ being defined in a .ldf file.

For some languages (or dialects), extra definitions have to be provided. This is done in the next section.

Providing extra features

```
160  % \begin{macro}{\extras<language>}
161  % \begin{macro}{\noextras<language>}
162  %    The macro |\extras<language>| will perform all the extra
163  %    definitions needed for the <Language> language. The macro
164  %    |\noextras<language>| is used to cancel the actions of
165  %    |\extras<language>|.  For the moment these macros are empty but
166  %    they are defined for compatibility with the other
167  %    language definition files.
168  %
169  %    \begin{macrocode}
170  \addto\extras<language>{}
171  \addto\noextras<language>{}
172  %    \end{macrocode}
```

```
173   %  \end{macro}
174   %  \end{macro}
175   %
176   %  \begin{macro}{\extras<dialect>}
177   %  \begin{macro}{\noextras<dialect>}
178   %     Also for the ''<dialect>'' variant no extra definitions are
179   %     needed at the moment.
180   %     \begin{macrocode}
181   \let\extras<dialect>\extras<language>
182   \let\noextras<dialect>\noextras<language>
183   %     \end{macrocode}
184   %  \end{macro}
185   %  \end{macro}
186   %
```

$\boxed{\texttt{\textbackslash extras}\langle\textit{language}\rangle\{\textit{extra definitions}\}}$

The macro \extras⟨language⟩ (line 170) contains all extra definitions needed for the language ⟨language⟩ being defined in a .ldf file. Such extras can be commands to turn shorthands on or off, to make certain characters active, to initiate French spacing, to position umlauts, and so on.

$\boxed{\texttt{\textbackslash noextras}\langle\textit{language}\rangle\{\textit{reverse extra definitions}\}}$

To allow switching between any two languages, it is necessary to return to a known state for the TeX engine—in particular, with respect to the definitions initiated by the command \extras⟨language⟩. The macro \noextras⟨language⟩ (line 171) must contain code to revert all such definitions so as to bring TeX back to a known state.

Clean up and finish The file finishes with the following lines of code.

```
187   %     The macro |\ldf@finish| takes care of looking for a
188   %     configuration file, setting the main language to be switched on
189   %     at |\begin{document}| and resetting the category code of
190   %     \texttt{@} to its original value.
191   %     \begin{macrocode}
192   \ldf@finish{<language>}
193   %</code>
194   %     \end{macrocode}
195   %
196   % \Finale
197   %\endinput
```

$\boxed{\texttt{\textbackslash ldf@finish}\{\textit{lang}\}}$

The macro \ldf@finish (line 192) performs a couple of tasks that are necessary at the end of each .ldf file. The argument *lang* is the name of the language as it is defined in the language definition file. The macro starts by verifying whether the system contains a file *lang*.cfg—that is, a file with the same name as the language definition file, but with the extension .cfg. This file can be used to add site-specific actions to a language definition file, such as adding strings to \captions⟨language⟩ to support local document classes, or activating or deactivating shorthands for acute or grave accents. In particular, the babel distribution

for French written by Daniel Flipo comes with a file `frenchb.cfg` that contains
a few (commented-out) supplementary definitions for typesetting French that can
be activated (uncommented) by the user if they appear to be useful. Other tasks
performed by the macro include resetting the category code of the @ sign, and
preparing the language to be activated at the beginning of the document.

Adding definitions to babel's data structures

On various lines (114, 170, 171), the command `\addto` was used to extend one of
the babel data structures holding translations or code for a certain language.

> `\addto\`*csname*`[`*code*`]`

This command extends the definition of the control sequence *csname* with the
TEX code specified in *code*. The control sequence *csname* does not have to have
been defined previously. As an example, the following lines are taken from the
file `russianb.ldf`, where code is added to the commands `\captionsrussian`,
`\extrasrussian`, and `\noextrasrussian`.

```
\addto\captionsrussian{%
  \def\prefacename{%
    {\cyr\CYRP\cyrr\cyre\cyrd\cyri\cyrs\cyrl\cyro\cyrv\cyri\cyre}}%
  ...
  }
\addto\extrasrussian{\cyrillictext}
\addto\noextrasrussian{\latintext}
\initiate@active@char{"}
\addto\extrasrussian{\languageshorthands{russian}}
\addto\extrasrussian{\bbl@activate{"}}
\addto\noextrasrussian{\bbl@deactivate{"}}
```

Language-level commands for shorthands

Shorthands on the language or system level are set up in the language definition
files. An incomplete example of this process was given in the previous section. In
this section we describe all commands and declarations that can be used for this
purpose.

> `\initiate@active@char{`*char*`}`

This macro can be used in language definition files to turn the character *char* into
a "shorthand character". When the character is already defined to be a shorthand
character, this macro does nothing. Otherwise, it defines the control sequence
`\normal@char`⟨*char*⟩ to expand to the character *char* in its "normal state" and it

defines the active character to expand to \normal@char⟨*char*⟩ by default. Subsequently, its definition can be changed to expand to \active@char⟨*char*⟩ by calling \bbl@activate⟨*char*⟩. When a character has been made active, it will remain active until deactivated or until the end of the document is reached. Its definition can be changed at any time during the typesetting stage of the document.

For example, several language definition files make the double quote character active with the following statement:

    \initiate@active@char{"}

For French the configuration file frenchb.cfg defines two-character shorthands:

    \initiate@active@char{<<}   \initiate@active@char{>>}

| \bbl@activate{*char*}   \bbl@deactivate{*char*} |

The command \bbl@activate "switches on" the active behavior of the character *char* by changing its definition to expand to \active@char⟨*char*⟩ (instead of \normal@char⟨*char*⟩). Conversely, the command \bbl@deactivate lets the active character *char* expand to \normal@char⟨*char*⟩. This command does not change the \catcode of the character, which stays active.

| \textormath{*text-code*}{*math-code*} |

Recognizing that some shorthands declared in the language definition files have to be usable in both text and math modes, this macro allows you to specify the code to execute when in text mode (*text-code*) or when in math mode (*math-code*). As explained on page 446, providing commands for use in text and math can have unwanted side effects, so this macro should be used with great care.

| \allowhyphens   \bbl@allowhyphens |

When LATEX cannot hyphenate a word properly by itself—for instance, because it is a compound word or because the word contains accented letters constructed using the \accent primitive—it needs a little help. This help involves making LATEX think it is dealing with two words, which appear as one word on the page. For this purpose babel provides the command \allowhyphens, which inserts an invisible horizontal skip, unless the current font encoding is T1.[1] In some cases one wants to insert this "help" unconditionally; for these cases \bbl@allowhyphens is available. This invisible skip has the effect of making LATEX think it is dealing with two words that can be hyphenated separately.

---

[1]In contrast to the OT1 encoding, the T1 encoding contains most accented characters as real glyphs so that the \accent primitive is almost never used.

```
\declare@shorthand{name}{charseq}{exec}
```

The macro `\declare@shorthand` defines shorthands to facilitate entering text in the given language. The first argument, *name*, specifies the name of the collection of shorthands to which the definition belongs. The second argument, *charseq*, consists of one or more characters that correspond to the shorthand being defined. The third argument, *excec*, contains the code to be executed when the shorthand is encountered in the document. A few examples from various language definition files follow.

```
\declare@shorthand{dutch}{"y}{\textormath{\ij{}}{\ddot y}}
\declare@shorthand{german}{"a}{\textormath{\"{a}\allowhyphens}{\ddot a}}
\declare@shorthand{french}{;}{...}
\declare@shorthand{system}{;}{\string;}
```

The latter two instructions are found in the file `frenchb.ldf`, where the first handles the case where the ; character is active and the third argument provides code for ensuring that a thin space is inserted before "high" punctuation (;, :, !, and ?). The last command deals with the case where these French punctuation rules are inactivated (note that these four punctuation characters are made active in `frenchb.ldf`).

9.6 Other approaches

In general, the babel package does a good job of translating document element names and making text input somewhat more convenient. However, for several languages, individuals or local user groups have developed packages and versions of TeX that cope with a given language on a deeper level—in particular, by better integrating the typographic traditions of the target language.

An example of such a package is french [51, 66], which was developed by Bernard Gaulle. Special customized versions of (LA)TeX exist (e.g., Polish and Czech, distributed by the TeX user groups GUST and C$_S$TUG, respectively).

9.6.1 More complex languages

In the world of non-Latin alphabets, one more level of complexity is added when one wants to treat the Arabic or Hebrew [140] languages. Not only are they typeset from right to left, but, in the case of Arabic, the letter shapes change according to their positions in a word.

Several systems to handle Hebrew are available on CTAN (`language/hebrew`). In particular, babel offers an interface for Hebrew written by Boris Lavva. For

Arabic there is the ArabTEX system [102], developed by Klaus Lagally. This package extends the capabilities of (LA)TEX to generate Arabic writing using an ASCII transliteration (CTAN `nonfree/language/arabtex`).

Serguei Dachian, Arnak Dalalyan, and Vardan Hakobian provide Armenian support (CTAN `language/armtex`).

For the languages of the Indian subcontinent, most of the support is based on the work of Frans Velthuis. In particular, recently Anshuman Panday developed packages for Bengali (`bang` package and associated fonts on CTAN `language/bengali`), Sanskrit (Anshuman Panday's `denag` package on CTAN `language/devanagari`), and Gurmukhi (CTAN `language/gurmukhi/pandey`).

Oliver Corff and Dorjpalam Dorj's `manjutex` package can be used for typesetting languages using the Manju (Mongolian) scripts (CTAN `language/manju/manjutex`).

Ehitopian language support, compatible with `babel`, is available through Berhanu Beyene, Manfred Kudlek, Olaf Kummer, and Jochen Metzinger's `ethiop` package and fonts (CTAN `language/ethiopia/ethiop`).

For Chinese, Japanese, and Korean (the so-called CJK scripts), one can use Werner Lemberg's `cjk` package [113], which contains fonts and utilities (CTAN `language/chinese/CJK`).

9.6.2 Omega

No discussion of multilingual typesetting would be complete without mentioning Omega [137], an extension of TEX developed by Yannis Haralambous and John Plaice. Omega's declared aim is to improve on TEX's multilingual typesetting abilities by making significant changes to the executable *TEX, the Program*. It potentially provides far simpler solutions in many of the areas addressed by `babel` by offering the following features:

- Omega can be used to read text files in any encoding (8-bit, 16-bit, or more).

- Omega handles shorthands internally by applying specified transformations to recognized sequences of input characters.

- Omega has an internal structure that is far more flexible than that of TEX for handling large sets of characters and large fonts.

- Omega supports many different types of script and all writing directions used for present-day scripts.

These enhancements to the TEX typesetting paradigm will make it easier to typeset a range of languages: Arabic, Bantu, Basque, Georgian, Hindi, Khmer, Chinese, Cree, or Mongolian—and all within the same document! It is also hoped (at end 2003) that enhancements to LATEX will soon appear to support these new facilities, thus providing a fully multilingual LATEX system.

## CHAPTER 10

Graphics Generation and Manipulation

TEX probably has the best algorithm for formatting paragraphs and building pages from them. But in this era of ever-increasing information exchange, most publications do not limit themselves to text—the importance of graphical material has grown tremendously. TEX by itself does not address this issue, as it deals only with positioning (black) boxes on a page. Knuth, however, provided a hook for implementing "features" that are not available in the basic language, via the `\special` command. The latter command does not affect the output page being formatted, but TEX will put the material, specified as an argument in the `\special` command, literally at the current point in the .dvi file.[1] The dvi driver then has to interpret the received information and produce the output image accordingly (see also [144]).

The *LATEX Graphics Companion* [57, Chapter 1] describes in detail various approaches that can be used to produce graphics with TEX. The following list gives a short overview. Interested readers are referred to that book for more details.

1. ASCII drawing, such as PICTEX, which provides a complete plotting language where most graphical elements are implemented by combining a very large number of small dots.

2. Picture-element fonts, such as LATEX's `picture` environment. Kristoffer Rose's `xypic` system [57, Chapter 5] uses special fonts to typeset diagrams.

---

[1]In certain situations the `\special` command may change the formatting because it can produce an additional breakpoint and it might prevent LATEX from noticing spaces.

3. Picture macro packages, mainly based on the `picture` environment or on TeX's raw line-drawing commands. Among others, packages exist for drawing chemical formulae [57, Section 6.2], trees, and bar charts (see Section 10.1.6).

4. Picture fonts, where each character to be typeset is one, possibly enormous, "letter" in a font. One can use METAFONT or MetaPost for generating the pictures [57, Chapter 3], or else use already existing bitmaps and transform them into a `.pk` file directly [57, Section 1.3].

5. Half-tone fonts—blocks consisting of various levels of grey, which can be combined in the normal TeX way to generate pictures [39, 93].

6. Graphics material included via the `\special` command. This approach is by definition device dependent, as it relies on the possibilities of the `dvi` driver and the output device. The `graphics` package, described in Section 10.2, offers a higher-level support layer on top of TeX's `\special` command. This approach has become very common because of the wide availability of low-cost PostScript printers and previewers. Other high-level systems allowing one to use PostScript together with LaTeX are `psfrag` and `pstricks` [57, Chapter 4].

In this chapter we look at techniques for producing portable graphics (mainly based on item 3) and at the high-level interface to device-dependent graphics support (item 6).

In particular, the first section discusses LaTeX's built-in graphics tools. We look at how to build ornaments, which can be useful for making important material stand out. Then we turn our attention to two packages, `epic` and `eepic`, that extend the `picture` environment by introducing a set of new commands. They are described in detail and examples show how they are used in practice.

LaTeX 2_ε provides a generalized driver-independent interface to include external graphic material and to scale and rotate LaTeX boxes.[1] Section 10.2 deals with graphics file inclusion. For this LaTeX offers both a simple interface (`graphics`; see Section 10.2.2), which can be combined with the separate rotation and scaling commands, and a more complex interface (`graphicx`; see Section 10.2.3), which has its own powerful set of image manipulation options. Free-standing scaling and rotation is the subject of Section 10.3.

In the final section we say a few words about important display languages (PostScript, PDF, SVG). We also briefly discuss `dvips`, an often-used `dvi` to PostScript translation program, and describe `pspicture`, an extension of LaTeX's `picture` environment that uses PostScript drawing primitives interfaced to the `dvips` driver.

---

[1]A generalized package for color is also available; see the *LaTeX Manual* [104] for more details.

10.1 Producing portable graphics and ornaments

Portable graphics in LaTeX essentially mean graphics built from boxes, lines, and characters. LaTeX boxes are reviewed briefly in Appendix A.2. Here, we first present packages that provide extensions to the usual LaTeX boxes. Later, this section deals with line graphics.

10.1.1 boxedminipage—Boxes with frames

The `boxedminipage` environment, defined in the `boxedminipage` package (by Mario Wolczko), behaves like the standard `minipage` environment, but the result is surrounded by a frame, as if it was placed inside an `\fbox`. The thickness and separation of the rules are controlled by the `\fboxrule` and `\fboxsep` parameters, respectively. However, in contrast to a construction involving `\fbox`, one can use verbatim commands inside the environment body.

> This is an example of a small boxed minipage sporting a footnote[a] and a \verb command.
>
> ───────────
> [a] Very simple example

```
\usepackage{boxedminipage}
\begin{boxedminipage}[t]{5cm}
 This is an example of a small boxed  minipage
 sporting a footnote\footnote{Very simple example}
 and a \verb=\verb= command.
\end{boxedminipage}
```

10-1-1

10.1.2 shadow—Boxes with shadows

The `shadow` package (by Mauro Orlandini) defines the `\shabox` command. It is similar to the LaTeX command `\fbox`, except that a "shadow" is added to the bottom and the right side of the box.

Three parameters control the visual appearance of the box (defaults are given in parentheses): `\sboxrule` defines the width of the lines for the frame (0.4pt); `\sboxsep` defines the separation between the frame and the text (10pt); and `\sdim` specifies the dimension of the shadow (4pt).

> A complete paragraph can be highlighted by putting it in a parbox, nested inside a shabox.

```
\usepackage{shadow}
\setlength\sdim{10pt}
\shabox{\parbox{6cm}{A complete
 paragraph can be highlighted by
 putting it in a parbox,
 nested inside a \texttt{shabox}.}}
```

10-1-2

10.1.3 `fancybox`—**Ornamental boxes**

Timothy Van Zandt, in the framework of his `seminar` package for producing slides,
developed the `fancybox` package. It introduces various new commands for boxing
and framing data in LaTeX. In this section we review only a few of the more basic
commands. More information can be found in the documentation accompanying
the `seminar` package.

The package introduces four variants for the `\fbox` command. As with the
`\fbox` command, the distance between the box and the frame is given by the
length parameter `\fboxsep` (LaTeX's default is 3pt). Other parameters governing
these boxes are described below.

The `\shadowbox` command adds a shadow with width `\shadowsize` (default
4pt). The box is aligned at the base of the shadow, which makes it probably less
suitable for inline usage than the `\shabox` command described earlier. Notice the
different spacing defaults.

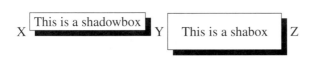

```
\usepackage{fancybox}
\usepackage{shadow}
X \shadowbox{This is a shadowbox}
Y \shabox{This is a shabox} Z
```

10-1-3

The `\ovalbox` command generates a frame with rounded corners. The width
of the frame is the same as those produced by standard picture elements when
the `\thinlines` declaration is in effect. The `\Ovalbox` command is similar but has
a frame width corresponding to the size produced by a `\thicklines` declaration.
The diameter of the corner arcs is set with a `\cornersize` declaration. The form
`\cornersize{`*num*`}` sets the diameter to *num* × minimum (width of box, height
of box); the form `\cornersize*{`*len*`}` sets the diameter to the length *len*. The
default is `\cornersize{0.5}`.

```
\usepackage{fancybox}
\centering
                \ovalbox{This is an ovalbox}
\cornersize{1} \ovalbox{This is an ovalbox}
\\[8pt]
\setlength\fboxsep{6pt} \cornersize*{7mm}
\Ovalbox{\shortstack{This is an\\Ovalbox}}
```

10-1-4

The package also provides `\fancyoval` as an alternative to LaTeX's `\oval` picture command. While `\oval` always makes the diameter of the corner arcs as large
as possible, `\fancyoval` uses the `\cornersize` declaration to set the diameter.

```
\usepackage{fancybox,color}
\cornersize{0.7}
\begin{picture}(110,40)
  \put(25,20){\oval(50,40)}
\color{blue}
  \put(85,20){\makebox(0,0){Test}}
  \put(85,20){\fancyoval(50,40)}
\end{picture}
```

Finally, the package offers the \doublebox command, which generates two square frames. Their widths and relations to each other and the text are fractions of the \fboxrule parameter value: the width of the inner frame is 0.75 of \fboxrule and that of the outer frame is 1.5 of \fboxrule. The distance between the two frames is 1.5 of \fboxrule plus 0.5 pt.

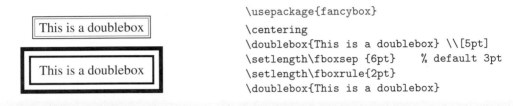

```
\usepackage{fancybox}
\centering
\doublebox{This is a doublebox} \\[5pt]
\setlength\fboxsep {6pt}    % default 3pt
\setlength\fboxrule{2pt}
\doublebox{This is a doublebox}
```

None of the above commands have optional arguments, unlike \framebox and \makebox. You can get exactly the same functionality by using \makebox in the argument of these framing commands.

```
\usepackage{fancybox}
\centering
\cornersize{0.8}
\ovalbox{\makebox[6cm][l]
         {This is an ovalbox}}  \\[8pt]
\shadowbox{\makebox[5cm]
         {This is a shadowbox}}
```

For some types of documents, such as slides, it would be nice to allow for framed pages—that is, to apply commands like those introduced in this section as part of the page style. This capability is supported by the fancybox package through the declaration \fancypage{*inner*}{*outer*}. The completed page, before headers and footers are added, is boxed (so it has width \textwidth and height \textheight) and then passed to the code specified in *inner* as an argument. Next the headers and footers are added using the new width of the page, in case they are changed by *inner*. The result is passed as an argument to the code in *outer*, which again that expects one argument. Thus, in the simplest case, you could specify one of the boxing commands from this section, or even leave one of the arguments empty. The next example shows an application where the arguments also contain some parameter settings to influence the form of the added frames.

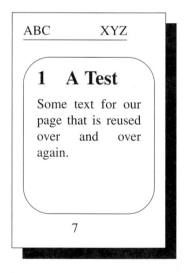

```
\setlength\textwidth{180pt}
\setlength\textheight{7\baselineskip}
\pagestyle{headings}

\usepackage{fancybox}

\newcommand\sample{ Some text for our
 page that is reused over and over again.}
\fancypage
  {\setlength\fboxsep{10pt}\ovalbox}
  {\setlength{\fboxsep}{8pt}%
   \setlength{\shadowsize}{8pt}%
   \shadowbox}
\sample \section{A Test}
\sample\sample
```

10-1-8

*Incorrect running
headers or footers*

Notice that the position of the running header was automatically corrected to fit the extended text width covering the frame. However, this correction works only for standard page styles. If, for example, fancyhdr is used, then the resulting headers and footers will be too small, as this package uses its own method of producing these objects.

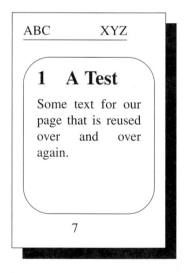

```
\usepackage{fancyhdr}
\pagestyle{fancy}
\cfoot{\thepage}
\lhead{ABC} \rhead{XYZ}
% Uncomment next line for
% proper header alignment:
%  \fancyhfoffset[R]{20.8pt}
\usepackage{fancybox}
% \sample as before
\fancypage
 {\setlength\fboxsep{10pt}%
  \ovalbox}
 {\setlength{\fboxsep}{8pt}%
  \setlength{\shadowsize}{8pt}%
  \shadowbox}
\sample\sample
\section{A Test} \sample
```

10-1-9

In the case of fancyhdr, the problem can be corrected by adding an extra offset with `\fancyhfoffset`. The value of `20.8pt` was manually calculated as twice the separation between text and frame (`10pt`) and the width of the frame line (`0.4pt`).

The \fancypage declaration is applied to all pages starting with the current one until another \fancypage declaration appears within the document. If you want to add frames only to the current page, use \thisfancypage instead. "Current" in this context means the page under construction when the declaration is first seen by LaTeX, even if that point in the document later ends up on a different page. Thus, it behaves like \pagestyle in this respect. If problems arise, you either have to move the declaration to some earlier or later point in the document or stop LaTeX from looking too far ahead by adding a \pagebreak command somewhere before the declaration. *Caveats*

The other potential problem with the commands \thisfancypage and \fancypage is that they change LaTeX's output routine and, therefore, may not work with other packages that do the same (fancyhdr is an example, though, with some care, both packages can coexist). Also, bad arguments can cause serious errors, which generate uninformative error messages.

\fancyput*(*x*,*y*)[*horizontal-material*]

A somewhat more powerful way to add material to every page in fixed locations is provided by the \fancyput declaration. It has a syntax similar to LaTeX's \put command, but requires the specification of dimensions for the *x* and *y* coordinates. The origin (0pt,0pt) is one inch from the top and left of the paper. Thus, to put something two inches from the left and three inches from the top, you would specify (1in,-2in).

Some text for our page that is reused over and over again. Some text for our page that is reused over and over again. **DRAFT**

1   A Test

Some text for our page that is reused over and over again.   Some text for our page that is

```
\usepackage{color,fancybox}
\fancyput(2in,-1.2in)
  {\Huge\bfseries
   \textcolor{blue}{DRAFT}}
% \sample as before
\sample\sample
\section{A Test} \sample \sample
```

10-1-10

The variant form \thisfancyput affects only the current page, analogous to \thisfancypage. If the starred form is used (for either command), then, instead of replacing it, the new material is added to existing material previously inserted with \fancyput or \thisfancyput.

The package also predefines boxed versions of the standard LaTeX display environments. The size of the resulting box is determined by the longest line. All environments support an optional argument for positioning the box in relation to the objects on the line; it can be t for top alignment or b for bottom alignment, but the default is to center the box. *Boxed display environments*

The environments Bcenter, Bflushleft, and Bflushright generate a box with the contents centered, flushleft, and flushright, respectively. The example shows all of them in action. Note the use of \vspace to ensure that the outer Bflushleft box is bottom aligned. Compare this to the examples discussed in Section A.2.2 on page 862.

```
\usepackage{fancybox}
\newcommand\HR{\rule{.5em}{0.4pt}}

\HR\begin{Bflushleft}[b]
  \begin{Bflushleft}[t] A A A\\ A A A\\ A A
  \end{Bflushleft}    \HR
  \begin{Bflushright}[t] B\\ B B B\\ B B B\\ B B
  \end{Bflushright}    \par\vspace{0pt}
\end{Bflushleft}    \HR
\begin{Bcenter} C C C\\ C\\ C C\end{Bcenter} \HR
```

A A A _   B
A A A B B B
A A   B B B   C C C
_   B B _ C _
       C C

10-1-11

Bitemize, Benumerate, and Bdescription implement boxed versions of the itemize, enumerate, and description environments, respectively. The internal implementation uses LATEX's tabular environment, which means that vertical-mode material such as \vspace don't work. Instead, the \item command takes an optional argument (using parentheses!) to specify extra white space in front of the item. Its usage is shown in the next example.

For math applications, Beqnarray produces a boxed environment similar to that created by eqnarray, but the equation number always comes out on the right. Beqnarray* is like eqnarray*, but the generated box is just large enough to hold all the equations.

- First item
- A second one
  on two lines
Test: - A third with extra space

```
\usepackage{fancybox}
Test: \fbox{\begin{Bitemize}[b]
    \item First item
    \item A second one\\ on two lines
    \item(2pt) A third with extra space
  \end{Bitemize}}
  \par\bigskip
Test: \fbox{\begin{Beqnarray}[t]
            y & = & x^2           \\
    a^2 + 2ab + b^2 & = & (a + b)^2 \\
  \int_0^\infty e^{-ax} dx & = & \frac{1}{a}
  \end{Beqnarray}}
```

$$
\begin{aligned}
[t]y &= x^2 & (1)\\
a^2 + 2ab + b^2 &= (a+b)^2 & (2)\\
\int_0^\infty e^{-ax}dx &= \frac{1}{a} & (3)
\end{aligned}
$$

Test:

10-1-12

The package also reimplements several commands to typeset verbatim texts. For such applications, however, the fancyvrb package by the same author provides superior interfaces (see Section 3.4.3).

10.1.4 epic—An enhanced picture environment

Standard LATEX provides a picture environment that allows you to generate line-style graphics of arbitrary complexity through basic commands for drawing lines, vectors, quarter-circles, and Bézier curves. Thus, creating complex graphics, although possible, requires a lot of manual effort. Most of these picture-drawing commands require explicit specification of coordinates for every *object*. Using higher-level commands can reduce the number of coordinates that need to be manually calculated. Basically, two approaches can be taken to the design of such commands:

- A set of objects can be selected so that the entire set can be plotted by specifying one or two coordinate pairs—the \shortstack command falls under this approach.

- Commands are provided that will do most of the computations internally and require only simple coordinate pairs to be specified—the \multiput command is an example of this approach.

The obvious advantage of using commands that implement these approaches is not only that they are easier to specify initially, but any subsequent modification to the layout requires minimal recalculations.

The frequently used primitive command \line has severe limitations and drawbacks. Its arguments are very nonintuitive and require extensive calculations. Often the thought process in writing a \line command involves several steps:

1. Calculating the coordinates of the two end points

2. Calculating the horizontal and vertical

3. Translating these distances into an (x, y) pair for specifying a slope and a horizontal distance for specifying the length of the line

4. Determining whether the desired slope is available and, if not, repeating steps 1 through 3 until a satisfactory slope is achieved

This mechanism is very cumbersome. Moreover, the length of the shortest available line at different slopes is not the same due to the way that the \line command is implemented. To overcome these difficulties, the epic package (by Sunil Podar) provides a powerful high-level user interface to the picture environment [139]. Its main aim is to reduce the amount of manual calculations required to specify the layout of *objects*. In this way, the epic package makes it possible to produce sophisticated pictures with less effort than before.

High-level line commands

The package introduces a number of powerful line-drawing commands, while at the same time providing a simpler syntax. In particular, these commands take only the coordinates of the end points, thus eliminating the other steps involved in specifying a line.

$$\boxed{\texttt{\textbackslash dottedline}\,[\textit{dotchar}]\,\{\textit{dotgap}\}(x_1, y_1)(x_2, y_2)...(x_n, y_n)}$$

The \dottedline command connects the specified points by drawing a dotted line between each pair of coordinates. At least two points must be defined. The dotted line is drawn with an inter-dot gap as specified in the mandatory argument *dotgap* (in \unitlength). Because the number of dots to be plotted must be an integer, the inter-dot gap may not come out exactly as specified.

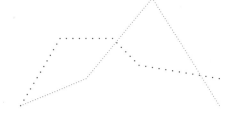

```
\usepackage{epic}\setlength{\unitlength}{1pt}
\begin{picture}(150,80)(0,0)
 \dottedline{2}(0,00)(50,20)(100,80)(150,0)
 \thicklines
 \dottedline{5}(0,0)(30,50)(70,50)(90,30)(150,20)
\end{picture}
```

10-1-13

By default (i.e., if no optional *dotchar* argument is used), \dottedline plots tiny squares, produced internally by the \picsquare command. The size of the squares depends on the current setting of the \thinlines, \thicklines, or \linethickness command. In fact, most of the epic commands internally use \picsquare for plotting lines.

By using the optional *dotchar* argument, you can plot any object along the line specified by the coordinates. Note that some characters like "*" in the Roman font do not come out centered, although most other characters and objects do.

```
\usepackage{epic}
\setlength{\unitlength}{1pt}    \thicklines
\begin{picture}(140,110)(0,0)
  \dottedline              {2}(0,110)(140,110)
  \dottedline[$\diamond$]{10}(0,110)(140,110)
  \dottedline     {2}(20,0)(40,0)(50,40)(120,0)
  \dottedline[*]{10}(20,0)(40,0)(50,40)(120,0)
  \dottedline              {2}(0,0)(30,90)(70,50)(140,0)
  \dottedline[\LaTeX]{20}(0,0)(30,90)(70,50)(140,0)
\end{picture}
```

10-1-14

$$\boxed{\texttt{\textbackslash dashline}\,[\textit{stretch}]\,\{\textit{dashlength}\}\,[\textit{dashdotgap}]\,(x_1, y_1)(x_2, y_2)...(x_n, y_n)}$$

The \dashline command connects the specified points by drawing a dashed line between each pair of coordinates. At least two points must be specified. Internally, each dash is constructed using the \dottedline command. The mandatory parameter *dashlength* determines the length of each dash, and the optional argument *dashdotgap* gives the gap between the dots that are used to construct the dash, both in \unitlength terms. By default, a solid-looking dash is constructed.

```
\usepackage{epic}
\setlength{\unitlength}{1mm}
\begin{picture}(70,22)(0,-2)
\dashline{3}[0.7](0,20)(63,20)
\thicklines
\dashline{3}(0,16)(63,16)
\dashline[-30]{3}(0,12)(63,12)
\dashline[+15]{3}(0,8)(63,8)
\dashline[+30]{3}(0,4)(63,4)
\dashline[+30]{3}[0.7](0,0)(63,0)
\end{picture}
```

10-1-15

In the definition of the \dashline command, the optional *stretch* parameter must be an integer between -100 and ∞. It indicates the percentage by which the number of dashes is "stretched" or increased (*stretch* > 0) or is "shrunk" or reduced (*stretch* < 0). If *stretch* is zero, the minimum number of dashes compatible with an approximately equal spacing relative to the empty space between the dashes is used. The idea behind the *stretch* percentage parameter is that if several dashed lines of different lengths are being drawn, then all dashed lines with identical *stretch* values will have a similar visual appearance. The default settings for the *stretch* percentage can be changed by redefining the command \dashlinestretch:

```
\renewcommand\dashlinestretch{-50} % Only integers permitted
```

Its value defines the increase or reduction that will be applied to all subsequent \dashline commands except for those where the *stretch* parameter is explicitly specified as the first optional argument.

> \drawline [*stretch*] $(x_1, y_1)(x_2, y_2)...(x_n, y_n)$

The \drawline command connects the given points by drawing a line between each pair of coordinates using line segments of the closest slope available in the line fonts of LaTeX. A minimum of two points must be specified. Only a finite number of slopes are available in the line segment fonts, so unavailable slopes are *Unwanted jagged* produced by repeatedly using very short line segments of a nearby slope. As a *lines* consequence, some lines may appear jagged (in the next example all sloped lines show this effect). This is the price you must pay for being allowed to implicitly specify lines of any slope. However, the problem vanishes if the eepic package is used in addition to epic.

A \drawline command can generate thick or thin lines depending on the setting of the \thinlines or \thicklines parameters in effect. These are the only two thicknesses available for such lines.

The optional *stretch* parameter is similar to the one described for the \dashline command. If *stretch* is zero, the result is the minimum number of dashes required to make the line appear solid, with each dash being "connected" at the ends. If *stretch* is greater than zero, more dashes are used in constructing the line, giving a less jagged appearance (compare the two houses in the example).

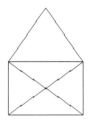
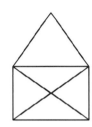

```
\usepackage{epic} \setlength{\unitlength}{2mm}
\begin{picture}(25,14)
  \drawline(0,0)(0,7)(5,14)(10,7)
            (0,7)(10,0)(0,0)(10,7)(10,0)

  \thicklines
  \drawline[70](15,0)(15,7)(20,14)(25,7)
              (15,7)(25,0)(15,0)(25,7)(25,0)
\end{picture}
```

10-1-16

As with the \dashlinestretch parameter and the \dashline command, the parameter \drawlinestretch allows you to set the default value for the *stretch* percentage parameter of the \drawline command.

Plotting scientific data

When presenting scientific data, it is often desirable to produce graphs that show obtained (two-dimensional) data sets in relation to each other. One representation strategy is to plot one set of experimentally obtained data points using a certain type of graphical representation (e.g., filled circles) and another using some different symbol (e.g., diamonds). For further clarification you might want to join the individual data points with some kind of line, perhaps using different types of "lines" to help the reader distinguish between the resulting curves.

One way to achieve this result is to plot the experimental results using a sequence of basic \put statements, followed by a \dottedline, \dashline, or \drawline command, that connects the data points. In other words, you specify the coordinates twice. To facilitate this process, epic offers the three environments dottedjoin, dashjoin, and drawjoin corresponding to the above commands and accepting the same optional and mandatory arguments. These environments use the new command \jput (join and put), which is identical to the regular \put command of LATEX except that it can be used inside these three environments only. All objects put within the scope of any of the three environments via a \jput command are, in addition to being plotted, joined by lines of their respective type. It is up to the user to center the objects at the plotted points.

An instance of any of the three join environments defines a separate "curve"; hence, every set of points belonging to a different "curve" should be enclosed in a separate join environment. The prime motivation for designing the join environments was to allow for plotting graphs that use different types of curves and dissimilar lines.

```
\usepackage{epic} \setlength{\unitlength}{1pt}
\newcommand\cb{\makebox(0,0){$\bullet$}}
\newcommand\cd{\makebox(0,0){$\diamond$}}

\begin{picture}(80,80)
  \begin{dashjoin}[30]{10}
    \jput(0,0)[\cb]\jput(30,70)[\cb]\jput(70,50)[\cb]\jput(80,60)[\cb]
  \end{dashjoin}
  \begin{dottedjoin}{5}
    \jput(0,30){\cd}\jput(20,30){\cd}\jput(45,0){\cd}\jput(60,80){\cd}
    \jput(80,50){\cd}
  \end{dottedjoin}
\end{picture}
```

10-1-17

Another way to produce graphs that is offered by the epic package is through the \putfile{*file*}{*object*} command. It is similar to LATEX's \put command, except that the *x* and *y* coordinates required by the \put command are read from an external file and the same *object* is plotted at each of those coordinates. This command is provided because TEX lacks the capability of doing floating-point arithmetic, which is required if you wish to plot a parametric curve different from a straight line. The coordinates of points on such curves can easily be generated by a program in some computer language and subsequently read in by TEX. The external file must contain the (x, y) coordinate pairs, one pair per line, with a space between the two coordinates. The % is available as a comment character, but you should leave at least one space following the *y* entry if a comment appears on the same line as data because a % masks the newline character.

Loading externally generated graphic data

For example, to plot a smooth curve along a set of coordinates, you can use the following procedure:

1. Create a file with the x, y coordinates of the data points, which you might call plot.data, for example.

2. If you wish, smooth the data.

3. Place the following code inside a picture environment in your LATEX file: \putfile{*plot.data*}{\picsquare}

As the command name indicates, \putfile uses \put and not \jput. This choice is unfortunate, as it means that using \putfile inside one of the ..join environments will plot objects at the coordinates but not connect them, even though there is technically nothing to prevent this connection. There is, however, a small trick you can use if you are interested in creating such linkage: ensure that \put always executes \jput inside your pictures. Because \jput behaves exactly like LATEX's \put command if used outside the ..join environments, there is no harm in making this a global substitution. This approach is used in the next example.

```
\usepackage{epic}    \renewcommand\put{\jput} % <- always use \jput
\begin{filecontents}{test.put}
0 0                                     % sample data in external file
30 70                                   % note that coordinates are
70 50                                   % separated by a space
80 60
\end{filecontents}
\newcommand\cd{\makebox(0,0){$\diamond$}}
\begin{picture}(80,80)
 \begin{dashjoin}{6}[2] \putfile{test.put}{\cd} \end{dashjoin}
 \put(30,75){\makebox(0,0)[b]{\scriptsize maximum}}
\end{picture}
```

maximum

10-1-18

Placing objects at regular intervals

What is missing in the example graphs so far are labeled axes. The epic doesn't offer off-the-shelf commands to do the full job, but with \multiputlist and \grid it offers tools that can help you with the more tedious tasks.

\multiputlist(*x,y*)(Δ*x,*Δ*y*)[*pos*]{*item1,item2,item3,...,itemN*}

This command, which is a variant of LaTeX's \multiput command, allows the *same* object to be placed at regularly spaced coordinates. The \multiputlist command is similar, but permits the objects to be *different*. When the \multiputlist command is executed, the objects to be "put" are picked up from the *list of items*, as the coordinates are incremented. (The first item goes in position 1, the second item in position 2, and so on.) For example, you can plot numbers along the x-axis in a graph by specifying

```
\multiputlist(0,0)(10,0){1.00,1.25,1.50,1.75,2.00}
```

The objects in the list can be virtually anything, including \makebox, \framebox, or math characters. This command enforces a certain regularity and symmetry on the layout of the various objects in a picture.

\grid(*width,height*)(Δ*width,*Δ*height*)[*initial-X-int,initial-Y-int*]

The \grid command makes a grid of dimensions *width* units by *height* units. Vertical lines are drawn at intervals of Δ*width* and horizontal lines at intervals of Δ*height*. When the third (optional) argument is specified, the borders of the grid will be labeled with numbers whose starting values are the integer numbers *initial-X-int* and *initial-Y-int*, respectively. They will be incremented by Δ*width* and Δ*height* along the axes.

The `\grid` command produces a box. Therefore, it must be `\put` at the required coordinates. For example:

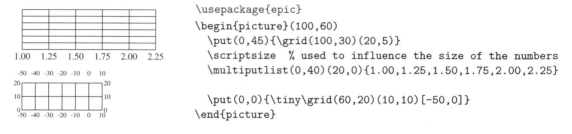

```
\usepackage{epic}
\begin{picture}(100,60)
  \put(0,45){\grid(100,30)(20,5)}
  \scriptsize  % used to influence the size of the numbers
  \multiputlist(0,40)(20,0){1.00,1.25,1.50,1.75,2.00,2.25}

  \put(0,0){\tiny\grid(60,20)(10,10)[-50,0]}
\end{picture}
```

10-1-19

If you need more flexibility than that offered by `\grid` for producing a regular two-dimensional structure, then `\matrixput` might offer the answer.

> `\matrixput(x, y)(Δx₁, Δy₁){n₁}(Δx₂, Δy₂){n₂}{object}`

$\matrixput(x, y)(\Delta x_1, \Delta y_1)\{n_1\}(\Delta x_2, \Delta y_2)\{n_2\}\{object\}$

This command is the two-dimensional equivalent of the primitive LaTeX command `\multiput`. It is more efficient, however, to use `\matrixput` than multiple `\multiput` statements. This command is especially useful for drawing pictures where a pattern is repeated at regular intervals in two dimensions.

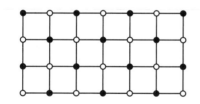

```
\usepackage{epic} \setlength{\unitlength}{2pt}
\begin{picture}(62,32)   \thicklines
  \matrixput(0,0)(10,0){7}(0,10){4}{\circle{2}}
  \matrixput(10,0)(20,0){3}(0,20){2}{\circle*{2}}
  \matrixput(0,10)(20,0){4}(0,20){2}{\circle*{2}}
  \matrixput(1,0)(10,0){6}(0,10){4}{\line(1,0){8}}
  \matrixput(0,1)(10,0){7}(0,10){3}{\line(0,1){8}}
\end{picture}
```

10-1-20

10.1.5 eepic—Extending the epic package

LaTeX provides a basic but limited picture-drawing capability, which is extended by commands for drawing solid lines, dotted lines, dashed lines, and new environments suitable for plotting graphs of the epic package (described in the previous section). However, epic inherits many of LaTeX's limitations in picture drawing. As a result, some of the functions take a long time to accomplish or the output is not of very high quality. In LaTeX, special fonts are used to draw lines and circles. For this reason only lines with certain slopes are supported and only a limited set of diameters is available when drawing circles, ovals, or disks.

The following example shows some of these limitations. Here, the circle and disk on the left are too small (without producing any warning) and the `\line` commands produce errors because the required slope is not available. Loading epic does not help in this case.

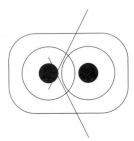

```
\usepackage{epic}
\begin{picture}(0,0)
  \put(0,0) {\circle{80}} \put(0,0) {\circle*{24}}
  \put(30,0){\circle{40}} \put(30,0){\circle*{16}}
  \put(15,0){\oval(90,60)}
  \put(0,12){\line(15,-2){30}}\put(0,-12){\line(15,2){30}}
\end{picture}
```

10-1-21

Compare this result to Example 10-1-22 on the next page, which shows the correct output—it is strikingly different.

At the end of the 1980s, the pic programming language was developed to provide a "natural language" method of describing simple pictures and graphs (see [77]). A preprocessor, like GNU's gpic, can translate these graphics commands into output that the UN*X formatter, troff, understands. More interestingly for us, it can also generate TEX \special commands, which many dvi driver programs support. For instance, the dvips dvi-to-PostScript translator, described in Section 10.4.2, can interpret these commands.

The eepic package, written by Conrad Kwok, is an extension of both LATEX and epic that overcomes some of the limitations in LATEX, epic, and gpic by generating gpic \specials using TEX commands. Because eepic is a superset of epic, you can use it to process any picture that relies on epic commands and get better-looking output.

eepic's reimplementation of LATEX commands

The extensions in eepic allow users to draw lines having any slope and to draw circles of any size. However, the limitation of slopes for vectors remains the same. Thus, the only slopes that can be handled are of the form x/y, where x and y are integers in the range $[-4, 4]$.

\line(x,y){*length*}

The syntax of the \line command is the same in eepic as in LATEX. Now, however, x and y can be any integers acceptable to TEX. Furthermore, there is no longer a lower limit for the *length* parameter (about 3.5 mm in standard LATEX).

\circle{*diameter*}   \circle*{*diameter*}   \oval(x,y)[*part*]

The syntax for drawing hollow and filled circles, \circle and \circle*, is the same as that in LATEX. Now, however, the *diameter* parameter can be any number acceptable to TEX, and a circle with a diameter of (exactly) the specified value will be drawn. The \oval command has been modified so that the maximum diameter of the quarter-circles at the corners can be set to any value by setting the variable \maxovaldiam to the desired TEX dimension (default 40pt).

The following example repeats Example 10-1-21 on the facing page, except that now eepic has been loaded and \maxovaldiam has been used. All elements appear as specified in the revised example.

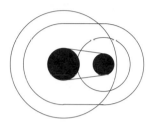

```
\usepackage{eepic} \setlength\maxovaldiam{60pt}
\begin{picture}(0,0)
  \put(0,0) {\circle{80}} \put(0,0) {\circle*{24}}
  \put(30,0){\circle{40}} \put(30,0){\circle*{16}}
  \put(15,0){\oval(90,60)}
  \put(0,12){\line(15,-2){30}}\put(0,-12){\line(15,2){30}}
\end{picture}
```

10-1-22

eepic's reimplementation of epic commands

The epic package generates standard dvi files and requires the presence of only the standard LATEX fonts. The eepic package, as an extension to epic, offers better line-drawing output, provides faster operation, and requires less memory. It reimplements the \drawline, \dashline, and \dottedline commands (see page 601) and the corresponding join environments, dashjoin, dottedjoin, and drawjoin (see page 604).

Compare the diagonal lines in the following example with those in Example 10-1-16 on page 604. Note that when eepic is loaded in conjunction with epic it smoothes the result of any line-drawing command. Both packages must be loaded in the right order.

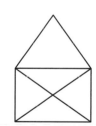

```
\usepackage{epic,eepic} \setlength{\unitlength}{2mm}
\begin{picture}(25,14)
  \drawline(0,0)(0,7)(5,14)(10,7)
           (0,7)(10,0)(0,0)(10,7)(10,0)
  \thicklines
  \drawline[70](15,0)(15,7)(20,14)(25,7)
              (15,7)(25,0)(15,0)(25,7)(25,0)
\end{picture}
```

10-1-23

The eepic package also introduces a number of new commands. Apart from the \path command, these commands do not have equivalents in LATEX and epic. The end of this section discusses portability issues as they relate to these packages.

\allinethickness{*dimension*}	\Thicklines

The \allinethickness command sets the line thickness of all line-drawing commands, including lines in slopes, circles, ellipses, arcs, ovals, and splines.

After issuing `\Thicklines`, the thickness of all subsequently drawn lines will be about 1.5 times greater than that with `\thicklines`.

`\path(`x_1, y_1`)(`x_2, y_2`)...(`x_n, y_n`)`

The `\path` command is a fast version of the `\drawline` command. The optional *stretch* argument of the latter command is not allowed, so `\path` draws only solid lines. This command is mainly used for drawing complex paths.

`\spline(`x_1, y_1`)(`x_2, y_2`)...(`x_n, y_n`)`

The `\spline` command draws a Chaikin's curve that passes through only the first and last points. All other points act as control points only.

`\ellipse{`*x-diameter*`}{`*y-diameter*`}`   `\ellipse*{`*x-diameter*`}{`*y-diameter*`}`

In analogy to the `\circle` and `\circle*` commands, the `\ellipse` and `\ellipse*` commands draw a hollow or filled ellipse using the specified *x-diameter* and *y-diameter* parameters.

`\arc{`*diameter*`}{`*start-angle*`}{`*end-angle*`}`

The `\arc` command draws a circular arc. The first parameter, *diameter*, is given in `\unitlength` terms. Both *start-angle* and *end-angle* are in radians; *start-angle* must lie within the interval $[0, \frac{\pi}{2}]$, and *end-angle* can be any value between *start-angle* and *start-angle* $+ 2\pi$. Arcs are drawn clockwise, with the angle 0 pointing to the right on the paper.

`\filltype{`*area-fill-type*`}`

The `\filltype` command specifies the type of area fill for the `\circle*` and `\ellipse*` commands. The instruction itself does not draw anything, but merely changes the interpretation of * in the two commands specified above. Possible values for *area-fill-type* are `black` (default), `white`, and `shade`. For example, you can change the area fill type to white with `\filltype{white}`.

Portability issues   The `eepic` package is not necessarily available at all LaTeX sites or, even if it is available, it may not be supported by the chosen output device. To avoid the portability problems that can arise from its use, and at the same time take advantage of `eepic`'s more precise printout, take the following precautions:

- Do not use `\line` commands, but use `\drawline` instead. The `\line` command in LaTeX supports only a limited set of slopes.

- Do not use the `\arc` command. Use the command `\spline` if a complex curve is really necessary.

- Avoid using solid or small inter-dot gaps in drawing long dashed lines, as these need a lot of TeX memory in the original epic implementation. Use the \drawline command with negative stretch to draw dashed lines.

If your installation does not support eepic but you have to print your document, then you should use the eepic emulation macros defined with the eepicmu package. The extended commands are emulated in the following ways: *Emulating the* eepic *commands*

- Circles larger than 40pt are drawn using \oval.
- Ellipses are drawn using \oval.
- Arcs generate a warning but are ignored otherwise.
- Splines are approximated with \drawline.
- \path is substituted by \drawline.
- \Thicklines is substituted by \thicklines.
- \allinethickness is substituted by \thicklines and \linethickness.

Because the eepic package redefines several commands of the epic package, the eepic package declaration must follow the epic package declaration. Although not strictly necessary, it is good practice to always include epic when using eepic commands. In any case, the eepic emulation package eepicmu will work only when both are specified.

10.1.6   Special-purpose languages

Building on LaTeX's picture environment, possibly extended with the epic and eepic packages, several package authors have implemented high-level user interfaces intended to make entering graphical information more straightforward and less error prone by adopting a syntax that is more familiar to the end user in a particular application domain. Some of the systems are quite complex (*The Graphics Companion* [57] describes several of them in detail). In this section we merely give a flavor of what is possible in this area by showing a few short examples.

If you do not have access to a drawing package but need to include a few continuously sloping curves, the curves package written by I. L. Maclaine-cross offers some intriguing features. It allows you to vary curve thickness over a large range, to control end slopes, and to specify closed curves with continuous slopes. It can also build large circles and circular arcs with \arc, providing independent scaling of curve abscissa and ordinates to fit graphs. Furthermore, it offers affine scaling for making arcs or circles become elliptical and it supports symbols and dash patterns. In the simple example that follows, \curve draws a curve through the specified coordinate pairs, \closecurve draws a closed curve with continuous tangents at all points, and \tagcurve generally acts like \curve except that the first and last segments are not drawn.

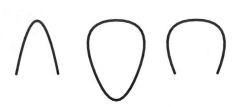

```
\usepackage{curves}
\setlength{\unitlength}{0.4pt}
\linethickness{0.7mm}
\begin{picture}(400,110)(-10,0)
   \curve(0,0, 40,100, 80,0)
   \closecurve(150,0, 190,100, 230,0)
   \tagcurve(380,0, 300,0, 340,100, 380,0, 300,0)
\end{picture}
```

10-1-24

Hideki Isozaki's ecltree package allows you to draw simple tree structures. It offers a bundle environment for labeling a top node, which can contain one or more down nodes defined by \chunk commands, whose optional argument can be used to add comments on a line. The \drawwith command allows you to control the line style by specifying as an argument one of epic's line-drawing commands (described in Section 10.1.4). The bundle environment and \chunk commands can be nested, as shown in the following LaTeX code.

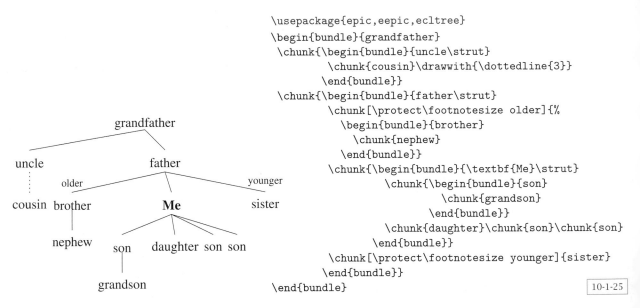

```
\usepackage{epic,eepic,ecltree}
\begin{bundle}{grandfather}
 \chunk{\begin{bundle}{uncle\strut}
        \chunk{cousin}\drawwith{\dottedline{3}}
     \end{bundle}}
 \chunk{\begin{bundle}{father\strut}
     \chunk[\protect\footnotesize older]{%
       \begin{bundle}{brother}
        \chunk{nephew}
       \end{bundle}}
     \chunk{\begin{bundle}{\textbf{Me}\strut}
        \chunk{\begin{bundle}{son}
              \chunk{grandson}
            \end{bundle}}
        \chunk{daughter}\chunk{son}\chunk{son}
        \end{bundle}}
     \chunk[\protect\footnotesize younger]{sister}
   \end{bundle}}
\end{bundle}
```

10-1-25

The bar package was written by Joachim Bleser and Edmund Lang to produce bar charts. A barenv environment encloses the data defining a bar chart. Each data point is specified using a \bar command, whose two mandatory arguments give the ordinate of the entry and the hatching type. The package also offers quite a few \set... commands to fine-tune the presentation of the information, as shown in the example that follows.

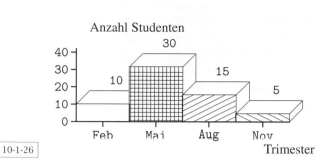

```
\usepackage{epic,eepic,bar}
\begin{barenv}
\setdepth{10}% 3-D effect
\setstretch{1.4}% stretch y-dimension
\setnumberpos{up}% numbers above bars
\setxvaluetyp{month}% (German) months on x-axis
\setxaxis{2}{12}{3}\setxname{Trimester}
\setyaxis{0}{40}{10}\setyname{Anzahl Studenten}
\bar{10}{1} \bar{30}{4}
\bar{15}{6} \bar{5}{7}
\end{barenv}
```

10-1-26

As already stated, much more complex structural data can be entered in a convenient way by using a dedicated package. One example is Shinsaku Fujita's XΥMT$_E$X bundle [48, 49] or [57, Chapter 6] for drawing chemical diagrams. By using command names inspired by standard nomenclature known to practitioners in the field, complex formulas can be entered simply. In the following example, we use the hetarom subpackage, designed for specifying the structure of vertical heterocyclic compounds.

```
\usepackage{eepic,hetarom}
\decaheterov[af]{4==O}
  {1==CH$_3$;6==H$_3$C;9A==H;%
   {{10}A}==\lmoiety{HOCH$_2$}}
\hspace*{-15mm}
\nonaheterov[bjge]{1==S;2==N}{3==Cl}
```

10-1-27

10.2 LaTeX's device-dependent graphics support

Since the introduction of LaTeX2_ε in 1994, LaTeX has offered a uniform syntax for including every kind of graphics file that can be handled by the different drivers. In addition, all kinds of graphic operations (such as resizing and rotating) as well as color support are available.

These features are not part of the LaTeX2_ε kernel, but rather are loaded by the standard, fully supported color, graphics, and graphicx extension packages. As the TeX program does not have any direct methods for graphic manipulation, the packages have to rely on features supplied by the "driver" used to print the dvi file. Unfortunately, not all drivers support the same features, and even the internal method of accessing these extensions varies among drivers. Consequently, all of these packages take options such as dvips to specify which external driver is being used. Through this method, unavoidable device-dependent information is localized in a single place, the preamble of the document.

The packages graphics and graphicx can both be used to scale, rotate, and reflect LaTeX material, or to include graphics files prepared with other programs. The difference between the two is that graphics uses a combination of macros with a "standard" or TeX-like syntax, while the "extended or "enhanced" graphicx package presents a key/value type of interface for specifying optional parameters to the \includegraphics and \rotatebox commands.

10.2.1 Options for graphics and graphicx

When using LaTeX's graphics packages, the necessary space for the typeset material after performing a file inclusion or applying some geometric transformation is reserved on the output page. It is, however, the task of the *device driver* (e.g., dvips, xdvi, dvipsone) to perform the actual inclusion or transformation in question and to show the correct result. As different drivers require different code to carry out an action like rotation, one has to specify the target driver as an option to the graphics packages—for example, option dvips if you use one of the graphics packages with Tom Rokicki's dvips program, or option textures if you use one of the graphics packages and work on a Macintosh using Blue Sky's Textures program.

Some drivers, such as previewers, are incapable of performing certain of the desired functions. Hence, they may display the typeset material so that it overlaps with the surrounding text. Table 10.1 on the facing page shows the drivers currently supported and their possible limitations. Support for other drivers is added occasionally, so it is worth checking the online documentation of the package for a driver not listed in this table.

The driver-specific code is stored in files with the extension .def—for example, dvips.def for the PostScript driver dvips. As most of these files are maintained by third parties, the standard LaTeX distribution contains only a subset of the available files and not necessarily the latest versions. While there is usually no problem if LaTeX is installed as part of a full TeX installation, you should watch out for incompatibilities if you update the LaTeX graphics packages manually.

Setting a default driver It is also possible to specify a default driver using the \ExecuteOptions declaration in the *configuration* file graphics.cfg. For example, the declaration \ExecuteOptions{emtex} makes the emTeX drivers become the default. In this case the graphics packages pick up the driver code for the emTeX TeX system on a PC if the package is called without a driver option. These days most TeX installations are distributed with a ready-to-use graphics.cfg file.

In addition to the driver options, the packages support some options controlling which features are enabled (or disabled):

draft   Suppress all "special" features, such as including external graphics files in the final output. The layout of the page will not be affected, because LaTeX still reads the size information concerning the bounding box of the external material. This option is of particular interest when a document is under development and you do not want to download the (often huge)

Option	Author of Driver	Features
dvips	T. Rokicki	All functions
dvialw	N. Beebe	File inclusion with scaling only
dvipdf	S. Lesenko	All functions
dvilaser	Arbortext	File inclusion with scaling only
dvipsone	Y&Y	All functions
dvitops	J. Clark	All functions, but no nested rotations
dviwin	H. Sendoukas	File inclusion
dviwindo	Y&Y	All functions
dvi2ps	original	File inclusion with scaling only
emtex	E. Mattes	File inclusion only, but no scaling
ln	B. H Kelly	File inclusion for DEC's LN03 printer
oztex	A. Trevorrow	File inclusion, color, rotation
pdftex	Hán Thế Thánh	All functions
pctexps	PCTeX	File inclusion, color, rotation
pctexwin	PCTeX	File inclusion, color, rotation
pctex32	PCTeX	All functions
pctexhp	PCTeX	File inclusion only
psprint	A. Trevorrow	File inclusion only
pubps	Arbortext	Rotation, file inclusion
truetex	Kinch	Graphics inclusion and some color
tcidvi	Kinch	TrueTeX with extra support for Scientific Word
textures	Blue Sky	All functions for Textures

Table 10.1: Overview of color and graphics capabilities of device drivers

graphics files each time you work on it. When draft mode is activated, the picture is replaced by a box of the correct size containing the name of the external file.

final   The opposite of draft. This option can be useful when, for instance, "draft" mode was specified as a global option with the \documentclass command (e.g., for showing overfull boxes), but you do not want to suppress the graphics as well.

hiresbb In PostScript files look for bounding box comments that are of the form %%HiResBoundingBox (which typically have real values) instead of the standard %%BoundingBox (which should have integer values). With the graphicx package, this and the previous options are also available locally for individual \includegraphics commands.

hiderotate Do not show the rotated material (for instance, when the previewer cannot rotate material and produces error messages).

hidescale Do not show the scaled material (for instance, when the previewer does not support scaling).

```
%!PS-Adobe-2.0
%%BoundingBox:100 100 150 150
100 100      translate % put origin at 100 100
  0   0      moveto    % define current point
 50  50      rlineto   % trace diagonal line
 50 neg 0    rlineto   % trace horizontal line
 50  50 neg  rlineto   % trace other diagonal line
stroke                 % draw (stroke) the lines
  0   0      moveto    % redefine current point
/Times-Roman findfont  % get Times-Roman font
 50          scalefont % scale it to 50 big points
             setfont   % make it the current font
(W) show               % draw an uppercase W
```

Figure 10.1: The contents of the file w.eps

10.2.2 The \includegraphics syntax in the graphics package

With the graphics package, an image file can be included by using the following command:

\includegraphics*[*llx,lly*] [*urx,ury*] {*file*}

If the [*urx,ury*] argument is present, it specifies the coordinates of upper-right corner of the image as a pair of TEX dimensions. The default units are big (PostScript) points; thus, [1in,1in] and [72,72] are equivalent. If only one optional argument is given, the lower-left corner of the image is assumed to be located at [0,0]. Otherwise, [*llx,lly*] specifies the coordinates of that point. Without optional arguments, the size of the graphic is determined by reading the external *file* (containing the graphics itself or a description thereof; see below).

The starred form of the \includegraphics command "clips" the graphics image to the size of the specified bounding box. In the normal form (without the *), any part of the graphics image that falls outside the specified bounding box overprints the surrounding text.

The examples in the current and next sections use a small PostScript program (in a file w.eps) that paints a large uppercase letter "W", and a few lines. Its source is shown in Figure 10.1. Note the BoundingBox declaration, which stipulates that the image starts at the point 100, 100 (in big points), and goes up to 150, 150; that is, its natural size is 50 big points by 50 big points.

In the examples we always embed the \includegraphics command in an \fbox (with a blue frame and zero \fboxsep) to show the space that LATEX reserves for the included image. In addition, the baseline is indicated by the horizontal rules produced by the \HR command, defined as an abbreviation for \rule{1em}{0.4pt}.

The first example shows the inclusion of the `w.eps` graphic at its natural size. Here the picture and its bounding box coincide nicely.

```
\usepackage{graphics,color}
\newcommand\HR{\rule{1em}{0.4pt}}
\newcommand\bluefbox[1]{\textcolor{blue}{%
    \setlength\fboxsep{0pt}\fbox{\textcolor{black}{#1}}}}
left\HR \bluefbox{\includegraphics{w.eps}}\HR right
```

10-2-1

Next, we specify a box that corresponds to a part of the picture (and an area outside it) so that some parts fall outside its boundaries, overlaying the material surrounding the picture. If the starred form of the command is used, then the picture is clipped to the box, as shown on the right.

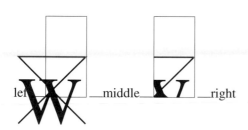

```
\usepackage{graphics,color}
% \bluefbox and \HR as before
left\HR
  \bluefbox{\includegraphics
            [120,120][150,180]{w.eps}}
\HR middle\HR
  \bluefbox{\includegraphics*
            [120,120][150,180]{w.eps}}
\HR right
```

10-2-2

In the remaining examples we combine the `\includegraphics` command with other commands of the graphics package to show various methods of manipulating an included image. (Their exact syntax is discussed in detail in Section 10.3.) We start with the `\scalebox` and `\resizebox` commands. In both cases we can either specify a change in one dimension and have the other scale proportionally, or specify both dimensions to distort the image.

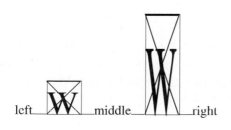

```
\usepackage{graphics,color}
% \bluefbox and \HR as before
left\HR
  \bluefbox{\scalebox{.5}{%
    \includegraphics{w.eps}}}%
\HR middle\HR
  \bluefbox{\scalebox{.5}[1.5]{%
    \includegraphics{w.eps}}}%
\HR right
```

10-2-3

```
\usepackage{graphics,color}
% \bluefbox and \HR as before
left\HR
  \bluefbox{\resizebox{10mm}{!}{%
    \includegraphics{w.eps}}}%
\HR middle\HR
  \bluefbox{\resizebox{20mm}{10mm}{%
    \includegraphics{w.eps}}}%
\HR right
```

10-2-4

Adding rotations makes things even more interesting. Note that in comparison to Example 10-2-1 on the preceding page the space reserved by LATEX is far bigger. LATEX "thinks" in rectangular boxes, so it selects the smallest size that can hold the rotated image.

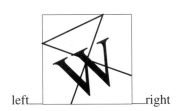

```
\usepackage{graphics,color}
% \bluefbox and \HR as before
left\HR
  \bluefbox{\rotatebox{25}{%
    \includegraphics{w.eps}}}%
\HR right
```

10-2-5

10.2.3 The \includegraphics **syntax in the** graphicx **package**

The extended graphics package graphicx also implements \includegraphics but offers a syntax for including external graphics files that is somewhat more transparent and user-friendly. With today's TEX implementations, the resultant processing overhead is negligible, so we suggest using this interface.

\includegraphics*[*key val list*]{*file*}

The starred form of the command exists only for compatibility with the standard version of \includegraphics, as described in Section 10.2.2. It is equivalent to specifying the clip key.

The *key val list* is a comma-separated list of *key=value* pairs for keys that take a value. For Boolean keys, specifying just the key is equivalent to *key*=true; not specifying the key is equivalent to *key*=false. Possible keys are listed below:

bb   The bounding box of the graphics image. Its value field must contain four dimensions, separated by spaces.

bbllx,bblly,bburx,bbury The lower-left and upper-right x and y coordinates (obsolete[1]).

hiresbb Makes LATEX search for %%HiResBoundingBox comments instead of the normal %%BoundingBox. Some applications use this key to specify more precise bounding boxes, because the numbers can normally have only integer values. It is a Boolean, either "true" or "false".

viewport Takes four arguments (like bb), but in this case the origin is identified with respect to the bounding box specified in the file. To view a 20bp square at the lower-left corner of the picture, for example, you would specify viewport=0 0 20 20.

trim Similar to the viewport key, but the four dimensions correspond to the amount of space to be trimmed (cut off) at the left-hand side, bottom, right-hand side, and top of the included graphics.

natheight,natwidth The natural height and width of figure.[2]

angle The rotation angle (in degrees, counterclockwise).

origin The origin for the rotation, similar to the origin parameter of the \rotatebox command described on page 632 and in Figure 10.2 on page 632.

width The required width (the width of the image is scaled to that value).

height The required height (the height of the image is scaled to that value).

totalheight The required total height (height + depth of the image is scaled to that value). This key should be used instead of height if images are rotated more than 90 degrees, because the height can disappear (and become the depth) and LATEX may have difficulties satisfying the user's request.

keepaspectratio A Boolean variable that can have the value "true" or "false" (see above for defaults). When it is true, specifying both the width and height parameters does not distort the picture, but the image is scaled so that neither the width nor height *exceeds* the given dimensions.

scale The scale factor.

clip Clip the graphic to the bounding box. It is a Boolean, either "true" or "false".

---

[1]Kept for backward compatibility only. [bbllx=a, bblly=b, bburx=c, bbury=d] is equivalent to [bb = a b c d], so the latter form should be used.

[2]These arguments can be used for setting the lower-left coordinate to (0 0) and the upper-right coordinate to (natwidth natheight) and are thus equivalent to bb=0 0 w h, where w and h are the values specified for these two parameters.

draft   Locally switch to draft mode. A Boolean-value key, like `clip`.

type   The graphics type; see Section 10.2.5.

ext   The file extension of the file containing the image data.

read   The file extension of the file "read" by LATEX to determine the image size, if necessary.

command   Any command to be applied to the file.

If the size is given without units for the first seven keys (`bb` through `trim`), then TEX's "big points" (equal to PostScript points) are assumed.

The first nine keys (`bb` through `natwidth`) specify the size of the image. This information needs to be given in case TEX cannot read the file, the file contains incorrect size information, or you wish to clip the image to a certain rectangle.

The next seven keys (`angle` through `scale`) have to do with scaling or rotation of the included material. Similar effects can be obtained with the **graphics** package and the \includegraphics command by placing the latter inside the argument of a \resizebox, \rotatebox, or \scalebox command (see the examples in Section 10.2.2 and the in-depth discussion of these commands in Section 10.3).

It is important to note that keys are read from left to right, so that [`angle=90`, `totalheight=2cm`] means rotate by 90 degrees and then scale to a height of 2 cm, whereas [`totalheight=2cm`, `angle=90`] would result in a final *width* of 2 cm.

By default, LATEX reserves for the image the space specified either in the file or in the optional arguments. If any part of the image falls outside this area, it will overprint the surrounding text. If the starred form is used or the `clip` option is specified, any part of the image outside this area is not printed.

The last four keys (`type`, `ext`, `read`, `command`) suppress the parsing of the file name. When they are used, the main *file* argument should have no file extension (see the description of the \DeclareGraphicsRule command below).

Below we repeat some of the examples from Section 10.2.2 using the syntax of the **graphicx** package, showing extra facilities offered by the extended package. In most cases the new form is easier to understand than the earlier version. In the simplest case without any optional arguments, the syntax for the \includegraphics command is the same in both packages.

If we use the `draft` key, we get just a frame showing the bounding box. This feature is not offered by the **graphics** package on the level of individual graphics.

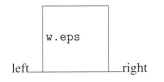

```
\usepackage{graphicx}
% \HR as before
left\HR
 \includegraphics[draft]{w.eps}%
\HR right
```

10-2-6

The effects of the `bb`, `clip`, `viewport`, and `trim` keys are seen in the following examples. Compare them with Example 10-2-2 on page 617.

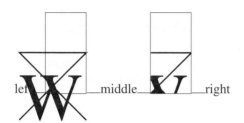

```
\usepackage{graphicx,color}
% \bluefbox and \HR as before
left\HR\bluefbox{\includegraphics
     [bb=120 120 150 180]{w.eps}}%
\HR middle\HR
 \bluefbox{\includegraphics
     [bb=120 120 150 180,clip]{w.eps}}%
\HR right
```

10-2-7

Using `viewport` or `trim` allows us to specify the desired result in yet another way. Notice that we actually trim a negative amount, effectively enlarging the space reserved for the picture.

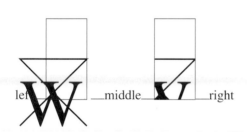

```
\usepackage{graphicx,color}
% \bluefbox and \HR as before
left\HR\bluefbox{\includegraphics
     [viewport=20 20 50 80]%
     {w.eps}}
\HR middle\HR
\bluefbox{\includegraphics
     [trim= 20 20 0 -30,clip]{w.eps}}%
\HR right
```

10-2-8

If you want to apply a scale factor to the image, use the `scale` key. With this key, however, you can only scale the picture equally in both directions.

10-2-9

```
\usepackage{graphicx,color}
% \bluefbox and \HR as before
left\HR \bluefbox{\includegraphics[scale=.5]{w.eps}}\HR right
```

To make the dimensions of an image equal to a given value, use the `width` or `height` key (the other dimension is then scaled accordingly). If you use both keys simultaneously, you can distort the image to fit a specified rectangle, as shown in the following example:

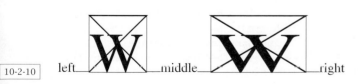

```
\usepackage{graphicx,color}
% \bluefbox and \HR as before
left\HR \bluefbox{\includegraphics
    [width=15mm]{w.eps}}%
\HR middle\HR
 \bluefbox{\includegraphics
    [height=15mm,width=25mm]{w.eps}}%
\HR right
```

10-2-10

You can make sure that the aspect ratio of the image itself remains intact by specifying the `keepaspectratio` key. LaTeX then fits the image as best it can to the rectangle you specify.

```
\usepackage{graphicx,color}
% \bluefbox and \HR as before
left\HR \bluefbox{\includegraphics
     [height=15mm,width=25mm]{w.eps}}%
\HR middle\HR
 \bluefbox{\includegraphics[height=15mm,
    width=25mm,keepaspectratio]{w.eps}}%
\HR right
```

10-2-11

Rotations using the `angle` key add another level of complexity. The reference point for the rotation is the reference point of the original graphic—normally the lower-left corner if the graphic has no depth. By rotating around that point, the height and depth change so that the graphic moves up and down with respect to the baseline, as can be seen in the next examples.

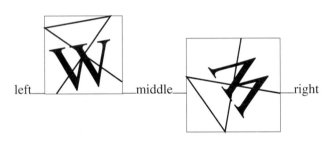

```
\usepackage{graphicx,color}
% \bluefbox and \HR as before
left\HR
  \bluefbox{\includegraphics
              [angle=10]{w.eps}}%
\HR middle\HR
  \bluefbox{\includegraphics
              [angle=125]{w.eps}}%
\HR right
```

10-2-12

The real fun starts when you specify both a dimension and a rotation angle for an image, since the order in which they are given matters. The graphicx package interprets the keys *from left to right*. You should pay special attention if you plan to rotate images and want to set them to a certain height. The next examples show the difference between specifying an angle of rotation before and after a scale command. In the first case, the picture is rotated and then the result is scaled. In the second case, the picture is scaled and then rotated.

```
\usepackage{graphicx,color}
% \bluefbox and \HR as before
left\HR\bluefbox{\includegraphics
     [angle=45,width=10mm]{w.eps}}%
\HR middle\HR
\bluefbox{\includegraphics
     [width=10mm,angle=45]{w.eps}}%
\HR right
```

10-2-13

LATEX considers the height and the depth of the rotated bounding box separately. The `height` key refers only to the height; that is, it does not include the depth. In general, the total height of a (rotated) image should fit in a given space, so you should use the `totalheight` key (see Figure 10.2 on page 632 for a description of the various dimensions defining a LATEX box). Of course, to obtain special effects you can manipulate rotations and combinations of the `height` and `width` parameters at will. Here we show some of key combinations and their results.

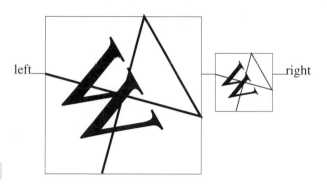

```
\usepackage{graphicx,color}
% \bluefbox and \HR as before
left\HR\bluefbox{%
  \includegraphics[angle=-60,%
                   height=15mm]%
    {w.eps}}\HR
\bluefbox{%
  \includegraphics[angle=-60,%
                   totalheight=15mm]%
    {w.eps}}\HR right
```

10-2-14

```
\usepackage{graphicx,color}
% \bluefbox and \HR as before
left\HR\bluefbox{\includegraphics
        [angle=-60,totalheight=20mm,%
         width=30mm]{w.eps}}\HR
\bluefbox{\includegraphics
        [angle=-60,totalheight=20mm,%
         width=30mm,keepaspectratio]%
    {w.eps}}\HR right
```

10-2-15

10.2.4 Setting default key values for the graphicx package

Instead of specifying the same set of key/value pairs over and over again on individual \includegraphics commands, you can specify global default values for keys associated with such commands. To do so, you use the \setkeys declaration provided by the keyval package, which is automatically included when graphicx is used.

\setkeys{*identifier*}{*key val list*}

The *identifier* is an arbitrary string defined by the macro designer. For example, for \includegraphics the string Gin was chosen. The *key val list* is a comma-separated list of key/value pairs.

As an example, consider the case where graphicx is used and all figures are to be scaled to the width of the line. Then you would specify the following:

```
\setkeys{Gin}{width=\linewidth}
```

All images included with the \includegraphics command will then be automatically scaled to the current line width. (Using \linewidth in such a case is usually preferable to using \columnwidth, as the former changes its value depending on the surrounding environment, such as quote.)

You can specify defaults in a similar way for any key used with the \rotatebox command (the other command that has a key/value syntax when graphicx is used). It has the *identifier* Grot; thus,

```
\setkeys{Grot}{origin=ct}
```

specifies that ct should be used for the origin key on all \rotatebox commands unless locally overwritten.

10.2.5 Declarations guiding the inclusion of images

While key/value pairs can be set only when the graphicx package is used, the declarations described in this section can be used with both the graphics and the graphicx packages.

Where to find image files

By default, LATEX looks for graphics files in the same directories where it looks for other files. But for larger projects it might be preferable to keep the image files together in a single directory or in a set of directories. A list of directories where LATEX should search for graphics files can be specified through the command \graphicspath, whose argument is a list of directories, each inside a pair of braces {} (even if the list contains only one directory). For example,

```
\graphicspath{{./eps/}{./tiff/}}
```

causes LATEX to look in the subdirectories eps and tiff of the current directory.

Defining the file extension search order

The \DeclareGraphicsExtensions command lets you specify the behavior of the system when no file extension is given in the argument of the \includegraphics command. Its argument {*ext-list*} is a comma-separated list of file extensions. Full file names are constructed by appending each extension of the list *ext-list* in turn until a file corresponding to the generated full file name is found.

Because the algorithm tests for the existence of a file to determine which extension to use, when the \includegraphics command is specified without an extension, the graphics file must exist at the time LATEX is run. However, if a file extension *is* specified, such as \includegraphics{gr.eps} instead of \includegraphics{gr}, then the graphics file need not exist at the time of the

LaTeX run.[1] LaTeX needs to know the size of the image, however, so it must be specified in the arguments of the \includegraphics command or in a file actually read by LaTeX. (This file can be either the graphics file itself or another file specified with the read key or constructed from the list of file extensions. In the latter case the file must exist at the time LaTeX is run.)

With the declaration shown below, the \includegraphics command will first look for the file file.ps and, if no such file exists, for the file file.ps.gz:

```
\DeclareGraphicsExtensions{.ps,.ps.gz}
  \includegraphics{file}
```

If you want to make sure that a full file name must always be specified, then you should use the following declaration. In the cases shown below, the size of the (bitmap) image is specified explicitly on the \includegraphics command each time.

```
\DeclareGraphicsExtensions{{}}
  \includegraphics[1in,1in]{file.pcx}
  \includegraphics[75pt,545pt][50pt,530pt]{file.pcx}
  \includegraphics[bb=75 545 50 530]{file.pcx}
```

The action that has to take place when a file with a given extension is encountered is controlled by the following command:

\DeclareGraphicsRule{*ext*}{*type*}{*read-file*}{*cmd*}

Any number of these declarations is allowed. The meanings of the arguments are described below.

ext   The extension of the image file. It can be specified explicitly or, if the argument to \includegraphics does not have an extension, can be determined from the list of extensions specified in the argument *ext-list* of the \DeclareGraphicsExtensions command. A star (*) can be used to specify the default behavior for all extensions that are not explicitly declared. For example,

```
\DeclareGraphicsRule{*}{eps}{*}{}
```

causes all undeclared extensions to be treated as EPS files, and the respective graphics files are read to search for a %%BoundingBox comment.

type   The "type" of the file involved. All files of the same type are input with the same internal command (which must be defined in the corresponding driver file). For example, files with an extension of .ps, .eps, or .ps.gz should all be classified as being of type eps.

---

[1] For instance, it can be created on the fly with a suitable \DeclareGraphicsRule declaration.

	ext	type	read-file	cmd
Basic PostScript	.ps	eps	.ps	
	.eps	eps	.eps	
Dynamic Decompression	.pz	eps	.bb	`gunzip -c #1
	.ps.gz	eps	.ps.bb	`gunzip -c #1
	.eps.gz	eps	.eps.bb	`gunzip -c #1
MS-DOS-related Formats	.tif	tiff		
	.pcx	bmp		
	.bmp	bmp		
	.msp	bmp		
Mac-related Formats	.pict	pict		
	.pntg	pntg		

Table 10.2: Arguments of \DeclareGraphicsRule

read-file The extension of the file that should be read to determine the size of the graphics image. It can be identical to *ext*, but, in the case of compressed or binary images, which cannot be interpreted easily by LaTeX, the size information (the bounding box) is normally put in a separate file. For example, for compressed gzipped PostScript files characterized by the extension .ps.gz, the corresponding readable files could have extension .ps.bb. If the *read-file* argument is empty (i.e., {}), then the system does not look for an external file to determine the size, and the size must be specified in the arguments of the command \includegraphics. If the driver file specifies a procedure for reading size files for *type*, then that procedure is used; otherwise, the procedure for reading .eps files is used. Therefore, in the absence of any other specific format, you can select the size of a bitmap picture by using the syntax for PostScript images (i.e., with a %%BoundingBox line).

cmd The command to be inserted in the \special argument instead of the file name. In general *cmd* is empty, but for compressed files you might want to uncompress the image file before including it in the file to be printed if the driver supports such an operation. For instance, with the dvips driver, you could use

```
\DeclareGraphicsRule{.ps.gz}{eps}{.ps.bb}{`gunzip #1}
```

where the argument #1 denotes the full file name. In this case the final argument causes dvips to use the gunzip command to uncompress the file before inserting it into the PostScript output.

Various possibilities for the arguments of the \DeclareGraphicsRule command are shown in Table 10.2.

The system described so far can give some problems if the extension *ext* does not correspond to the *type* argument. One could, for instance, have a series of PostScript files called `file.1`, `file.2`, ... Neither the `graphics` nor the `graphicx` package can automatically detect that these are PostScript files. With the `graphicx` package, this determination can be handled by using a `type=eps` key setting on each `\includegraphics` command. To handle this situation more generally, you can define a default type by using a `\DeclareGraphicsRule` declaration for a type * as explained above.

10.2.6   A caveat: Encapsulation is important

We will describe PostScript in more detail in Section 10.4, but it is already important at this point to emphasize that PostScript is a page description language that deals with the appearance of a *complete printed page*. This makes it difficult for authors to include smaller PostScript pictures created by external tools into their electronic (LATEX) documents. To solve this problem Adobe has defined the *Encapsulated PostScript* file format (EPS or EPSF), which complies with the *PostScript Document Structuring Conventions Specification* [2] and the *Encapsulated PostScript File Format Specification* [3].

The EPS format defines standard rules for importing PostScript language files into different environments. In particular, so as not to interfere destructively with the PostScript page being built, EPS files should be "well behaved". For instance, they must not contain certain PostScript operators, such as those manipulating the graphics state, interpreter stack, and global dictionaries.

Most modern graphics applications generate an EPS-compliant file that can be used without difficulty by LATEX. Sometimes, however, you may be confronted with a bare PostScript file that does not contain the necessary information. For use with LATEX, a PostScript file does not have to conform strictly to the structuring conventions mentioned previously. If the file is "well behaved" (see above), it is enough that the PostScript file contains the dimensions of the box occupied by the picture. These dimensions are provided to LATEX via the PostScript comment line %%BoundingBox, as shown below:

```
%!
%%BoundingBox: LLx LLy URx URy
```

The first line indicates that we are dealing with a nonconforming EPS file. Note that the %! characters *must* occupy the first two columns of the line. The second line, which is the more important one for our purpose, specifies the size of the included picture in PostScript "big" points, of which there are 72 to an inch (see Table A.1 on page 855). Its four parameters are the x and y coordinates of the lower-left corner (LLx and LLy) and the upper-right corner (URx and URy) of the picture. For instance, a full A4 page (210 mm by 297 mm) with zero at the lower-left corner would need the following declaration:

```
%!
%%BoundingBox: 0 0 595 842
```

If your picture starts at $(100, 200)$ and is enclosed in a square of 4 inches (288 points), the statement would be

```
%!
%%BoundingBox: 100 200 388 488
```

A PostScript display program, such as ghostview, lets you easily determine the bounding box of a picture by moving the cursor on its extremities and reading off the corresponding coordinates. In general, it is good practice to add one or two points to make sure that the complete picture will be included, because of the potential for rounding errors during the computations done in the interpreter.

10.3   Manipulating graphical objects in LaTeX

In addition to the \includegraphics command, the graphics and graphicx packages implement a number of graphical manipulation commands.

With the exception of the \rotatebox command, which also supports a key/value pair syntax in the graphicx package, the syntax for these commands is identical in both packages.

10.3.1   Scaling a LaTeX box

The \scalebox command lets you magnify or reduce text or other LaTeX material by a scale factor.

> \scalebox{*h-scale*} [*v-scale*] {*material*}

The first of its arguments specifies the factor by which both dimensions of the *material* are to be scaled. The following example shows how this works.

This text is normal.
This text is large.
This text is tiny.

```
\usepackage{graphics} % or graphicx
\noindent This text is normal.   \\
\scalebox{2}{This text is large.}\\
\scalebox{0.5}{This text is tiny.}
```

10-3-1

A supplementary optional argument, if present, specifies a separate vertical scaling factor. It is demonstrated in the following examples, which also show how multiple lines can be scaled by using the standard LaTeX \parbox command.

```
\usepackage{graphics} % or graphicx
\fbox{\scalebox{1.5}{%
  \parbox{.5in}{America \&\\Europe}}}
\fbox{\scalebox{1.5}[1]{%
  \parbox{.5in}{America \&\\Europe}}}
```

10-3-2

\reflectbox{*material*}

This command is a convenient abbreviation for \scalebox{-1}[1]{*material*}, as seen in the following example:

```
\usepackage{graphics} % or graphicx
\noindent America?\reflectbox{America?}    \\
          America?\scalebox{-1}[1]{America?}
```

10-3-3

More interesting special effects can also be obtained. Note in particular the use of the zero-width \makebox commands, which hide their contents from LaTeX and thus offer the possibility of fine-tuning the positioning of the typeset material.

```
\usepackage{graphics} % or graphicx
\noindent America?\scalebox{-1}{America?}    \\
          America?\scalebox{1}[-1]{America?}\\
          America?\makebox[0mm][r]{%
              \scalebox{-1}{America?}}\\
          \makebox[0mm][l]{America?}%
              \scalebox{1}[-1]{America?}
```

10-3-4

10.3.2 Resizing to a given size

It is possible to specify that LaTeX material should be typeset to a fixed horizontal or vertical dimension:

\resizebox*{*h-dim*}{*v-dim*}{*material*}

When the aspect ratio of the material should be maintained, then it is enough to specify one of the dimensions, replacing the other dimension with a "!" sign.

```
\usepackage{graphics} % or graphicx
\fbox{\resizebox{5mm}{!}{%
  \parbox{14mm}{London,\\ Berlin \&\\ Paris}}}
\fbox{\resizebox{!}{10mm}{%
  \parbox{14mm}{London,\\ Berlin \&\\ Paris}}}
```

10-3-5

When explicit dimensions for both *h-dim* and *v-dim* are supplied, then the contents can be distorted. In the following example the baseline is indicated by a horizontal rule drawn with the \HR command.

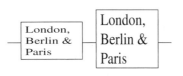

```
\usepackage{graphics} % or graphicx
\HR\begin{tabular}{lll}
        K\"oln & Lyon   & Oxford \\
        Rhein  & Rh\^one & Thames
   \end{tabular}\HR\par\bigskip
\HR\resizebox{2cm}{.5cm}{%
   \begin{tabular}{lll}
        K\"oln & Lyon    & Oxford \\
        Rhein  & Rh\^one & Thames
   \end{tabular}}\HR
```

10-3-6

As usual with LaTeX commands involving box dimensions, you can refer to the natural lengths \depth, \height, \totalheight, and \width as dimensional parameters:

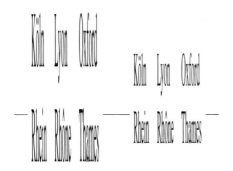

```
\usepackage{graphics} % or graphicx
\HR\fbox{\resizebox{\width}{.7\height}{%
   \parbox{14mm}{London,\\ Berlin \&\\Paris}}}\HR
\fbox{\resizebox{\width}{.7\totalheight}{%
   \parbox{14mm}{London,\\ Berlin \&\\Paris}}}\HR
```

10-3-7

The unstarred form \resizebox bases its calculations on the height of the LaTeX material, while the starred \resizebox* command takes into account the total height (the depth plus the height) of the LaTeX box. The next \parbox examples, which have a large depth, show the difference.

```
\usepackage{graphicx}
\HR\resizebox{20mm}{30mm}{%
        \begin{tabular}{lll}
        K\"oln & Lyon    & Oxford \\
        Rhein  & Rh\^one & Thames
        \end{tabular}}\HR
\HR\resizebox*{20mm}{30mm}{%
        \begin{tabular}{lll}
        K\"oln & Lyon    & Oxford \\
        Rhein  & Rh\^one & Thames
        \end{tabular}}\HR
```

10-3-8

10.3.3   Rotating a LaTeX box

LaTeX material can be rotated through an angle with the \rotatebox command. An alternative technique useful with environments is described in Section 10.3.4.

```
\rotatebox{angle}{material}
```

The *material* argument is typeset inside a LaTeX box and rotated through *angle* degrees counterclockwise around the reference point.

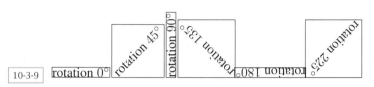

```
\usepackage{graphics} % or graphicx
\newcommand\MyRot[1]{\frame
        {\rotatebox{#1}{rotation
                      $#1^\circ$}}}
\MyRot{0}  \MyRot{45} \MyRot{90}
\MyRot{135}\MyRot{180}\MyRot{225}
```

10-3-9

To understand where the rotated material is placed on the page, we need to look at the algorithm employed. Below we show the individual steps carried out when rotating \fbox{text} by 75 degrees. Step 1 shows the unrotated text; the horizontal line at the left marks the baseline. First the *material* (in this case, \fbox{text}) is placed into a box. This box has a reference point around which, by default, the rotation is carried out. This point is shown in step 2 (the original position of the unrotated material is shown as well for reference purposes). Then the algorithm calculates a new bounding box (i.e., the space reserved for the rotated material), as shown in step 3. Next the material is moved horizontally so that the left edges of the new and the old bounding boxes are in the same position (step 4). TeX's typesetting position is then advanced so that additional material is typeset to the right of the bounding box in its new position, as shown by the line denoting the baseline in step 5. Step 6 shows the final result, again with the baseline on both sides of the rotated material.

The rotation algorithm

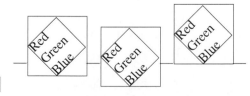

For more complex material it is important to keep in mind the location of the reference point of the resulting box. The following example shows how it can be shifted by using the placement parameter of the \parbox command.

```
\usepackage{color,graphics} % or graphicx
\HR\bluefbox{\rotatebox{45}{%
    \fbox{\parbox{3em}{Red\\Green\\Blue}}}}%
\HR\bluefbox{\rotatebox{45}{%
    \fbox{\parbox[t]{3em}{Red\\Green\\Blue}}}}%
\HR\bluefbox{\rotatebox{45}{%
    \fbox{\parbox[b]{3em}{Red\\Green\\Blue}}}}\HR
```

10-3-10

The extended graphics package graphicx offers more flexibility in specifying the point around which the rotation is to take place by using *key val* pairs.

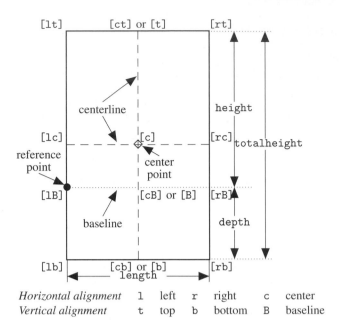

Horizontal alignment	l	left	r	right	c	center
Vertical alignment			t	top	b	bottom	B	baseline

10-3-11

Figure 10.2: A LaTeX box and possible `origin` reference points

> \rotatebox[*key val list*]{*angle*}{*material*}

The four possible keys in this case are `origin`, `x`, `y`, and `units`. The possible values for the `origin` key are shown in Figure 10.2 (one value each for the horizontal and vertical alignments can be chosen), as are the actual positions of these combinations with respect to the LaTeX box produced from *material*.

The effect of these possible combinations for the `origin` key on an actual LaTeX box can be studied below, where two matrices of the results are shown for 90-degree and 45-degree rotated boxes. To better appreciate the effects, the unrotated text is shown against a grey background.

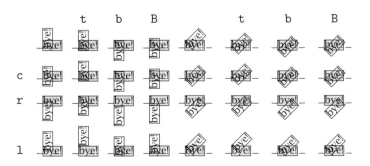

If the specification of the `origin` is not enough, you also can supply the *x* and *y* coordinates (relative to the reference point) for the point around which the rotation is to take place. For this purpose, use the keys x and y and the format x=*dim*, y=*dim*. A matrix showing some sample values and their effect on a box rotated by 90 degrees appear below.

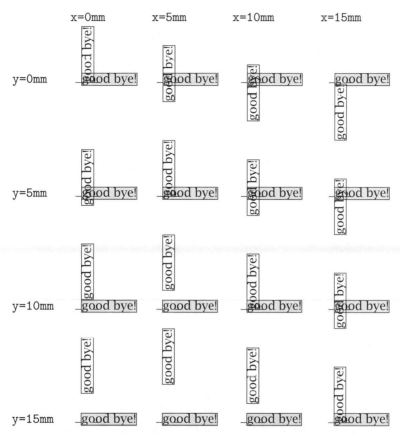

The interpretation of the *angle* argument of `\rotatebox` can be controlled by the `units` keyword, which specifies the number of units counterclockwise in a full circle. The default is 360, so using `units=-360` would mean that angles are specified clockwise. Similarly, a setting of `units=6.283185` changes the degree specification to radians. Rather than changing the `units` key on individual `\rotatebox` commands, you should probably set up a default interpretation using the `\setkeys` declaration as described in Section 10.2.4.

10.3.4 rotating—Revisited

The material in the section can be compared to Sebastian Rahtz's rotating package, which was introduced in Section 6.3.3 on page 296. The functionality of rotating is

implemented in this package through the environments turn and rotate; the latter environment generates an object that occupies no space. Using environments
has the advantage that the rotated material can contain \verb commands. However, the extended syntax of the \rotatebox command is not supported, so in
most cases the latter command is preferable.

Turning  a bit.

```
\usepackage{rotating}
Turning \begin{rotate}{-20}\Large\LaTeX\end{rotate}%
        \begin{turn}{20}\verb=\LaTeX=\end{turn} a bit.
```

10-3-12

10.4   Display languages: PostScript, PDF, and SVG

After typesetting an electronic document, one usually would like to view the generated output "page"—on paper via a printing device, on a PC screen, with a dedicated program or inside a browser, or (why not?) on a portable phone.

Several display languages have been developed over the years. For printing
devices PostScript, which is essentially a language for describing a static output
page, has become the most important player. In the early 1990s, Adobe developed
a light-weight version of PostScript, called the Portable Document Format (PDF) [5].
PDF implements a similar imaging model as PostScript but introduces a more
structured format to improve performance for interactive viewing. It also adds
links and annotations for navigation.

The increasing affordability of the personal computer has drastically reduced
the production cost of electronic documents. The World Wide Web makes distributing these documents worldwide cheap, easy, and fast. The development of
the XML family of standards has made it possible to apply a unified approach to
handle the huge amount of information stored electronically and to transform it
into various customizable presentation forms.

Various techniques are now available to transform LaTeX documents into PDF,
HTML (XHTML), or XML so that the information can be made available on the web
(several chapters of *The Web Companion* [56] are dedicated to explaining such
techniques). A particularly interesting approach, described below, involves transforming LaTeX-encoded information into a Scalable Vector Graphics (SVG) format.

Thus, LaTeX can continue to play a major role in the integrated worldwide
cyberspace. Especially in the area of scientific documents, it will remain an important (intermediate) format for generating high-quality printable PDF or browsable
SVG output.

This section gives a short introduction to these three display languages—
PostScript, PDF, and SVG. It briefly describes dvips, a dvi-to-PostScript translator,
and discusses pspicture, an enhancement of LaTeX's picture environment using
PostScript.

10.4.1   The PostScript language

PostScript [4] is a page description language. It provides a method for expressing the appearance of a printed page, including text, lines, and graphics.

A device- and resolution-independent, general-purpose, programming language, PostScript describes a complete "output page". The language is stack oriented and uses "reverse Polish" or postfix notation. It includes looping constructs, procedures, and comparison operators, and it supports many data types, including reals, Booleans, arrays, strings, and complex objects such as dictionaries.

PostScript programs are generally written in the form of ASCII source text, which is easy to create, understand, transmit, and manipulate. Because PostScript is resolution and device independent, the same ASCII file can be viewed on a computer display with a previewer, such as ghostscript/ghostview, and printed on a small laser printer or a high-resolution phototypesetter.

The PostScript language lets you mix the following features in any number of combinations:

- Arbitrary shapes can be constructed from lines, arcs, and cubic curves. The shapes may self-intersect and contain disconnected sections and holes.

- The painting primitives permit shapes to be outlined with lines of any thickness, filled with any color, or used as a clipping path to crop any other graphic.

- Text is fully integrated with graphics. In PostScript, text characters are treated as graphical shapes that may be operated on by any of the language's graphics operators. This is fully true for Type 3 fonts, where character shapes are defined as ordinary PostScript language procedures. In contrast, Adobe's Type 1 format defines a special smaller language where character shapes are defined by using specially encoded procedures (see below). For complex languages with many thousands of characters (e.g., Chinese and Japanese), composite Type 0 fonts can be used.

- Images (such as photographs or synthetically generated images) can be sampled at any resolution and with a variety of dynamic ranges. PostScript provides facilities to control the rendering of images on the output device.

- Several color models (device based: RGB, HSB, CMYK; standard based: CIE) are available, and conversion from one model to another is possible.

- A general coordinate system facility supports all combinations of linear transformations, including scaling, rotation, reflection, and skewing. These transformations apply uniformly to all page elements, including text, graphical images, and sampled images.

- Dictionaries for color spaces, fonts, forms, images, half-tones, and patterns are available.

- Compression filters, such as JPEG and LZW, are available.

Type 1 and OpenType font outlines

As a complement to the PostScript language, Adobe has defined its Type 1 font format [1]. A Type 1 font program consists of a clear text (ASCII) portion, plus an encoded and encrypted portion. The PostScript language commands used in a Type 1 font program conform to a much stricter syntax than do normal PostScript language programs.

Adobe's Type 1 model is, like PostScript, fully device and resolution independent. It uses mathematical expressions—in particular, Bézier curves—to define character outlines, thereby guaranteeing flexibility and rendering accuracy. Characters are defined at a size of 1 point in a 1000 by 1000 coordinate system, which can then be scaled, rotated, and skewed at will. Hints can be included to make the representation as exact as possible on a wide variety of devices and pixel densities.

Recently, Adobe and Microsoft jointly developed OpenType,[1] a new cross-platform font file format. This extension of the TrueType font outline format can also support Type 1 font data. OpenType adds new typographic features as well.

You can move OpenType font files back and forth between platforms (Macintosh and Windows), improving cross-platform portability for any documents that use these types. The bitmap, outline, and metric data are combined into a single, cross-platform OpenType font file, simplifying font management.

OpenType fonts are based on Unicode, an international multi-byte character encoding that covers virtually all of the world's languages. OpenType thus makes multilingual typography easier by including multiple language character sets in one font. The basic OpenType fonts contain the standard range of Latin characters used in the Western world, as well as several international characters (e.g., the euro symbol). Pro versions add a full range of accented characters to support Central and Eastern European languages, such as Turkish and Polish, and many contain Cyrillic and Greek character extensions in the same font.

Given that OpenType fonts may contain more than 65,000 glyphs, they provide far more typographic capabilities by combining base character sets, expert sets, and extensive additional glyphs into one file. For instance, a single font file may contain many nonstandard glyphs, such as old-style figures, true small capitals, fractions, swashes, superiors, inferiors, titling letters, contextual and stylistic alternates, and a full range of ligatures.

OpenType manages the mapping between characters and glyphs. In particular, its layout features can be used to position or substitute glyphs. For any character, there is a default glyph and positioning behavior. The application of layout features to one or more characters may change the positioning, or substitute a different glyph.

Over the years, thousands of typefaces, including those of the world's major typesetting companies, such as Linotype, Agfa-Compugraphic, Monotype, Autologic, and Varityper, have become available in PostScript Type 1 format. More

---

[1] See http://partners.adobe.com/asn/developer/opentype/main.html.

recently, Adobe has converted the entire Adobe Type Library (thousands of fonts) into OpenType, and other type foundries are following Adobe's example.

In the TeX world, the Ω (Omega) program (`http://omega.cse.unsw.edu.au`), an extension of TeX developed by Yannis Haralambous and John Plaice that features multi-byte data structures and is based on Unicode for its internal character representation, can take advantage of OpenType fonts.

10.4.2   The dvips PostScript driver

Tom Rokicki's dvips program[1] is undoubtedly the most widely used dvi-to-PostScript driver. It is a very mature product, with many important and useful features. The \special support in dvips is extensive; in particular, it supports the pic commands of the eepic package mentioned in Section 10.1.5.

The dvips program will automatically generate missing fonts if METAFONT exists on the system. If a font cannot be generated, a scaled version of the same font at a different size will be used instead (although dvips will complain about the poor aesthetics of the resulting output). Moreover, this facility is configurable and is not limited simply to running METAFONT.

The output from dvips can be controlled in two ways: by command-line switches for a particular job and by commands in one or more configuration files. Using configuration files, you can set parameters globally for the whole system, on a per-printer basis, and on a per-user basis.

When dvips starts up, a global `config.ps` file is searched for.[2]

The dvips driver has a plethora of command-line options. Table 10.3 on the following page presents a summary of those options.

With the help of the -d option for dvips, you can track down errors and understand what is going on. You must supply an integer specifying the class of information to be displayed. To get several types of information, simply add the numbers together for the types in which you are interested. Choose from the following:

1	specials	4	fonts	16	headers	64	files
2	paths	8	pages	32	font compression	128	memory

For example, calling dvips with the -d 4 option yields information about which fonts are being called and where they are loaded from. An option of -d -1 (all flags are activated) displays a very detailed log of everything dvips does. It will, however, generate an enormous volume of data, so this facility should be used only as a last resort, if a more refined approach fails.

---

[1] The manual is at `http://www.ctan.org/tex-archive/dviware/dvips/dvips_man.pdf`. See also [57, Chapter 11] for a detailed description.

[2] This file must exist on the search path of dvips which is usually something like `texmf/dvips/config` below the root of the TeX installation tree.

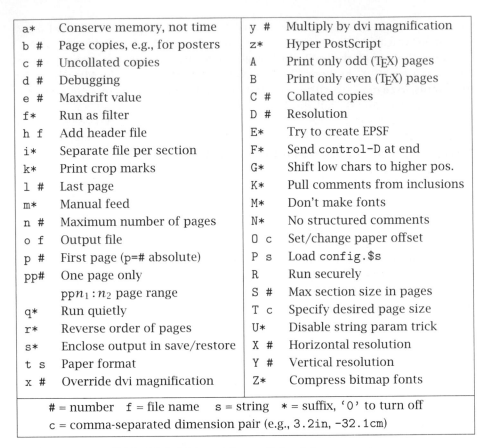

a*	Conserve memory, not time	y #	Multiply by dvi magnification
b #	Page copies, e.g., for posters	z*	Hyper PostScript
c #	Uncollated copies	A	Print only odd (TeX) pages
d #	Debugging	B	Print only even (TeX) pages
e #	Maxdrift value	C #	Collated copies
f*	Run as filter	D #	Resolution
h f	Add header file	E*	Try to create EPSF
i*	Separate file per section	F*	Send control-D at end
k*	Print crop marks	G*	Shift low chars to higher pos.
l #	Last page	K*	Pull comments from inclusions
m*	Manual feed	M*	Don't make fonts
n #	Maximum number of pages	N*	No structured comments
o f	Output file	O c	Set/change paper offset
p #	First page (p=# absolute)	P s	Load `config.$s`
pp#	One page only	R	Run securely
	ppn_1:n_2 page range	S #	Max section size in pages
q*	Run quietly	T c	Specify desired page size
r*	Reverse order of pages	U*	Disable string param trick
s*	Enclose output in save/restore	X #	Horizontal resolution
t s	Paper format	Y #	Vertical resolution
x #	Override dvi magnification	Z*	Compress bitmap fonts

# = number   f = file name   s = string   * = suffix, '0' to turn off
c = comma-separated dimension pair (e.g., `3.2in`, `-32.1cm`)

Table 10.3: Major options of the dvips program

10.4.3   pspicture—An enhanced picture environment for dvips

David Carlisle's pspicture package reimplements, and extends, LaTeX's picture environment with the help of PostScript commands that are placed in TeX \special commands. It eliminates limitations in standard LaTeX where picture offers only a discrete range of slopes and thicknesses for lines and a limited range of diameters for circles.

There exists a certain amount of overlap between this package and the eepic package, described earlier. Moreover, the pspicture package can be considered as a sort of "stand-in" for the pict2e package that was announced by Leslie Lamport in 1994 in the second edition of the LaTeX book, but which was never written.[1]

However, pspicture has the disadvantage that a picture can no longer be

---

[1]For the next LaTeX release a first implementation of the pict2e package (by Hubert Gäßlein and Rolf Niepraschk) is being considered for inclusion in LaTeX.

viewed with a dvi program that has no facility to interpret and display PostScript commands.[1] A "poor man's" workaround is the companion package texpicture. It uses the standard picture commands as much as possible, but silently omits any picture object that cannot be drawn with standard LaTeX. Of course, the visual result in this case will probably not conform to the finally envisaged version—but at least the document will compile.

The dvi file produced with pspicture contains embedded \special commands that are set up to be recognized by Rokicki's dvips driver. Thus, the driver file pspicture.ps, which contains the PostScript code referenced in the \special commands for use by the downstream PostScript interpreter, must be present on the TeX installation in the relevant dvips directory, so that it can be found and included by dvips when needed.

Extended or changed commands

The pspicture package extends the functionality of several commands that are available inside LaTeX's picture environment.

The \circle and \circle* commands are similar to their counterparts in standard LaTeX but have no limit on their diameters. The thickness of the circle is altered by the \linethickness command. The size of the circle produced by \circle* is not affected by \linethickness.

\circle extensions

| \oval[*radius*](*x,y*)[*part*] |

The \oval command acts as described in the LaTeX book, but there is no maximum diameter for the circular arcs, so the oval (in the absence of the optional parameter [*part*]) always consists of two semicircular arcs joined by a pair of parallel lines. To obtain a "rectangle with rounded corners", a second optional argument *radius* was added at the beginning of the \oval command. If this option is used, \oval works with circular arcs of radius min(*radius*, $x/2, y/2$). The following example shows the difference.

\oval extensions

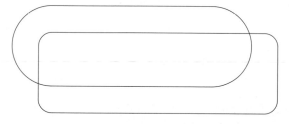

10-4-1

```
\usepackage{pspicture}
\begin{picture}(200,120)
  \put(90,40) {\oval    (180,60)}
  \put(110,20){\oval[10](180,60)}
\end{picture}
```

The \vector and \line commands are as described in the LaTeX book but no longer have any restrictions on their slopes. The thickness of a sloping line is altered by the \linethickness command. The arrowheads drawn by the vector

\line and \vector extensions

---

[1]If you use pdftex to generate PDF directly, you will encounter the same problem. In this case pspicture should not be used.

command are of triangular shape, and by default, are larger than LaTeX's defaults. The size can be controlled with the `\arrowlength` command described below.

The `\thinlines`, `\thicklines`, and `\linethickness` commands alter the thickness of *all* lines, including slanted lines and circular arcs.

All other commands of LaTeX's picture environment, such as `\dashbox`, `\framebox`, `\makebox`, `\multiput`, `\put`, and `\shortstack`, are unaltered and act as described in the LaTeX book.

The next example shows how the pspicture package uses PostScript to extend LaTeX's picture environment. To allow a better understanding of what is going on, we also use the graphpap's `\graphpaper` command to draw a coordinate grid at a specified position with a given range (first line in the picture environment). Here is what pspicture produces.

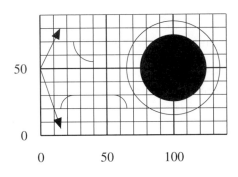

```
\usepackage{pspicture}\usepackage{graphpap}
\begin{picture}(140,90)
\graphpaper(0,0)(140,90)
\put(0,50){\vector(1,2){15}}
\put(0,50){\vector(2,-6){15}}
\put(40,20){\oval(50,20)[t]}
\put(40,70){\oval(30,30)[bl]}
\put(100,50){\circle{70}}
\put(100,50){\circle*{50}}
\end{picture}
```

10-4-2

To clearly see the effects of the extensions implemented by pspicture, we would like to compare how LaTeX's standard picture environment would display the above code. However, these commands cannot be run with LaTeX's picture environment, because we have used unsupported arguments for the `\vector`, `\circle`, and `\circle*` commands. Therefore, we must specify the texpicture package instead of pspicture, as shown below. Thanks to the overlayed coordinate grid, the limitations with respect to the pspicture case are clearly visible. Indeed, the second `\vector` is truncated, while the diameters of the two circles no longer correspond to what is required.

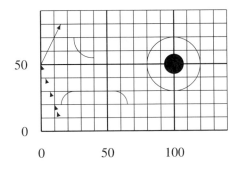

```
\usepackage{texpicture}\usepackage{graphpap}
\begin{picture}(140,90)
\graphpaper(0,0)(140,90)
\put(0,50){\vector(1,2){15}}
\put(0,50){\vector(2,-6){15}}
\put(40,20){\oval(50,20)[t]}
\put(40,70){\oval(30,30)[bl]}
\put(100,50){\circle{70}}
\put(100,50){\circle*{50}}
\end{picture}
```

10-4-3

New commands

The pspicture package also introduces a set of new commands. The \Line and \Vector commands make it easier to draw a line by allowing you to specify "relative coordinates".

```
\put(x1,y1){\Line(x2,y2)}      \put(x1,y1){\Vector(x2,y2)}
```

The above syntax will result in drawing a line (or a vector) between points (x1,y2) and (x1+x2,y1+y2).

```
\put(x1,y1){\Curve(x2,y2){m}}
```

The \Curve commands is similar to \Line, but generates a line whose curvature is controlled by m (try 1 or −1 first). The value of m does not have to be an integer. Negative numbers curve the line in the opposite way to positive numbers.

```
\arrowlength{size}
```

The \arrowlength command specifies the size of the triangular arrowhead drawn by the \vector and \Vector commands. Like \linethickness, it is an absolute value in points (i.e., not affected by \unitlength) with the unit omitted.

Some of the extra features that are not available with the picture environment in standard LaTeX are shown below. The possibilities of arbitrary slopes for the \line and \vector commands were mentioned previously. The more friendly user interface (allowing for relative coordinates) of the \Vector, \Line, and \Curve commands is appreciated. The first \oval command draws a normal ellipse with a thick line (using the \thicklines command), while the second \oval command draws a rectangle with rounded corners and thin-line borders (using the \thinlines command). Finally, we set the line width to 3pt with the \linethickness command and show the effect on circles and lines.

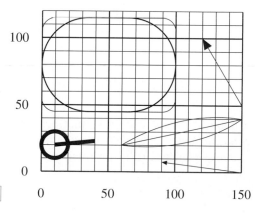

```
\usepackage{pspicture}\usepackage{graphpap}
\begin{picture}(150,120)
\graphpaper(0,0)(150,120)
\arrowlength{4pt} \put(150,00){\vector(-8,1){60}}
\arrowlength{8pt} \put(150,50){\Vector(-30,50)}
\put(60,20){\Line(90,20)}
\put(60,20){\Curve(90,20){2}}
\put(60,20){\Curve(90,20){-2}}
\thicklines \put(50,80){\oval(100,70)}
\thinlines  \put(50,80){\oval[10](100,70)}
\linethickness{3pt}
        \put(10,20){\circle{20}}
        \put(10,20){\line(10,1){30}}
\end{picture}
```

10-4-4

10.4.4 The Portable Document Format

Adobe's Portable Document Format (PDF) [5] is a direct descendant of the PostScript language. Whereas PostScript is a full-blown programming language, PDF is a second-generation, more light-weight graphics language optimized for faster download and display. Most of the advantages of PostScript remain: PDF guarantees page fidelity, down to the smallest glyph or piece of white space, while being portable across different computer platforms. For these reasons, PDF is being used ever more frequently in the professional printing world as a replacement for PostScript. Moreover, all present-day browsers will embed or display PDF material, alongside HTML, using plug-in technology.

The main differences between PostScript and PDF are the following:

- There are no built-in programming language functions: for example, PDF in general cannot calculate values.

- PDF guarantees full page independence by clearly separating resources from page objects.

- PDF files are compact and fully searchable.

- Interactive hyperlinks make PDF files easy to navigate.

- PDF's security features allow PDF documents to have special access rights and digital signatures applied.

- Font outlines need not be included in the file, because PDF files carry sufficient font information information to allow PDF-enabled applications (e.g., Adobe's Acrobat Reader) to mimic the appearance of a font.

- PDF has advanced compression features to keep the size of PDF files small. Moreover, .png, .jpeg, and .gif images can be inserted directly.

- PDF 1.4 and later versions support a transparent imaging model (PostScript uses an opaque model) and feature multimedia support.

- PDF 1.4 and later versions introduce tagged PDF, a stylized form of PDF that contains information on content and structure. Tagged PDF lets applications extract and reuse page data (text, graphics, images). For instance, tagged PDF allows text to reflow for display on handheld devices, such as Palm OS or Pocket PC systems.

- PDF 1.5, released at the end of 2003, includes features for further optimizing multimedia delivery.

PDF can be viewed and printed on many different computer platforms by downloading and installing Adobe's Acrobat Reader.[1] Other PDF viewers exist as well. The best-known free ones are ghostscript,[2] which can also produce PDF from PostScript, and Xpdf.[3]

---

[1] Freely downloadable from http://www.adobe.com/products/acrobat/readermain.html.

[2] See http://www.cs.wisc.edu/~ghost/.

[3] See http://www.foolabs.com/xpdf/home.html.

Generating PDF directly from TeX

If you have a PostScript file generated from a LaTeX source, you can convert it to PDF by using a "distiller" program. Adobe's Acrobat Distiller is the best known and most sophisticated of these programs, but ghostscript (and ImageMagick's convert, which is built on it) also performs well.

To generate PDF directly without going through the dvi-generating step, we have pdfTeX (see below) and MicroPress's VTeX,[1] which has its own direct PDF-generating TeX engine. If you already have a dvi file, you can use Mark Wicks's dvipdfm dvi driver.[2]

Hán Thế Thánh's pdfTeX is an extension of TeX that creates PDF directly from TeX source files [161]. It also enhances the typesetting capabilities of TeX in some interesting areas [158, 159]. Since 2002 pdfTeX has been part of the standard TeX distributions.

The pdfTeX program lets you include annotations, hyperlinks, and bookmarks in the generated PDF output file. It can work with TrueType fonts and supports the inclusion of pictures in .png, .jpeg, and .gif formats. The most common technique, the inclusion of Encapsulated PostScript figures, has been replaced by PDF inclusion in this program. EPS files can be converted to PDF by ImageMagick's convert utility (which calls ghostscript internally), Acrobat Distiller, or other PostScript-to-PDF converters.

Navigation is an important aspect of PDF documents. The hyperref package [56, Chapter 2] developed by Sebastian Rahtz and Heiko Oberdiek extends the functionality of the LaTeX cross-referencing commands (including the table of contents, bibliographies, and so on) to produce \special commands that a dvi driver or pdfTeX can turn into hypertext links. The hyperref package also provides new commands to allow the user to write ad hoc hypertext links, including those to external documents and URLs.

Because PDF lacks programming language commands, it cannot deal with general raw PostScript commands, such as those used by the pstricks package [57, Chapter 4]. Thus, these commands are not supported.[3]

The standard LaTeX graphics and color packages have a pdftex option, which allow you to use normal color, text rotation, and graphics inclusion commands. The implementation of graphics inclusion makes sure that however often a graphic is used (even if it is used at different scales or transformed in different ways), it is embedded only once.

Producing correct PostScript or PDF

Getting correct PostScript or PDF output from LaTeX systems can sometimes be quite difficult. Michael Shell, in the context of the IEEEtran document class files, but independent of them, has developed the "testflow" diagnostic suite. A test file

---

[1] See http://www.micropress-inc.com/.

[2] See http://gaspra.kettering.edu/dvipdfm/.

[3] General PostScript commands *can* be used with MicroPress's VTeX, which has a built-in PostScript interpreter.

`testflow.tex` is first compiled on the user's system. Next, a PostScript version, `testflow.ps`, and a PDF version, `testflow.pdf`, for the output are produced and printed on the output device for comparison to reference files. The input test file is designed to test the various components of LaTeX's "print work flow". Its purpose is to provide helpful information to assist users in getting their LaTeX system configured correctly so as to produce good PostScript and PDF output.[1]

10.4.5 Scalable Vector Graphics

Since the mid-1990s, the World Wide Web and the general availability of the personal computer have made the generation, maintenance, and dissemination of electronic documents worldwide cheap, easy, and fast. Moreover, the development of the XML family of standards and the ubiquity of platform-independent scripting languages allow one to save and handle huge amounts of electronically stored information and to transform it into various customizable presentation forms.

For LaTeX documents, a variety of techniques are available to transform them into PDF, XHTML, or XML so that the information can be made available on the web. Thus, LaTeX can continue to play a major role in the integrated worldwide cyberspace, in particular for scientific documents, and especially in areas where fine typesetting is a must.

After a short introduction to Scalable Vector Graphics (SVG), we explain succinctly how LaTeX-encoded information can be encoded into an SVG-format (see [58] for more detail).

SVG for portable graphics on the web

As the web has grown in popularity and complexity, users and content providers have sought ever better, more precise, and more scalable graphical rendering—not just the low-resolution `.gif` or `.png` images that are commonly used in today's web pages. To address this need, the World Wide Web Consortium published the SVG Recommendation, whose current version is 1.1.[2]

SVG is an open-standard vector graphics language for describing two-dimensional graphics using XML syntax. It lets you produce web pages containing high-resolution computer graphics.

As an XML instance, SVG consists of Unicode text. It features the usual vector graphics functions. Its fundamental primitive is the *graphics object*, whose model contains the following:

- Graphics paths consisting of polylines, Bézier curves, and other elements:
  - Simple or compound, closed or open
  - (Gradient) filled, (gradient) stroked

---

[1] Detailed instructions and a detailed explanation available at CTAN: `macros/latex/contrib/IEEEtran/testflow/testflow_doc.txt`.

[2] *Scalable Vector Graphics (SVG) 1.1 Specification*, available at `http://www.w3.org/TR/SVG11/`, was published on January 14, 2003.

- – Can be used for clipping
- – Can be used for building common geometric shapes

- Patterns and markers

- Templates and symbol libraries

- Transformations:

   - – Default coordinate system: x is right, y is down,[1] the unit is one pixel
   - – Viewport maps an area in world coordinates to an area on screen
   - – Transformations alter the coordinate system (2×3 transformation matrix for computers; translate, rotate, scale, skew for humans)
   - – Can be nested

- Inclusion of bitmap or raster images

- Clipping, filter, and raster effects; alpha masks

- Animations, scripts, and extensions

- Groupings and styles

- SVG fonts (independent from fonts installed on the system)

The W3C SVG web site (`http://www.w3.org/Graphics/SVG`) is a good first source of information and has a lot of pointers to other sites.

Transforming a LATEX document into an SVG document

If one has a pure LATEX source document (i.e., one that includes no EPS files, nor uses any extensions that need TEX `\special` commands), the `dvi` file can be translated into SVG with Adrian Frischauf's `dvi2svg`.[2]

We interacted with the `dvi2svg` Java library via a small UNIX script called `dvi2svg.sh`, whose use is as follows:

```
> dvi2svg.sh
Usage: dvi2svg.sh [options] [DVIFILE]
Options:
 -o [FILENAME] : Specify an output filename prefix. If not
                 set, dvi2svg will take the input filename.
 -d : set the debug mode to on(1)/off(0 default)
```

An example of the use of the `dvi2svg` program is the translation of two examples in this chapter into SVG. We compile the LATEX file `svgexa.tex` and then run

---

[1] The reference point of the display area is the upper-left corner. For PostScript, where y runs upward, the reference point of the page is the lower-left corner.

[2] See `http://www.activemath.org/~adrianf/dvi2svg/`. The dvi2svg program includes SVG font outlines for the characters referenced in the `dvi` file. SVG font instances were generated for all standard Computer Modern and LATEX fonts and come with the dvi2svg distribution.

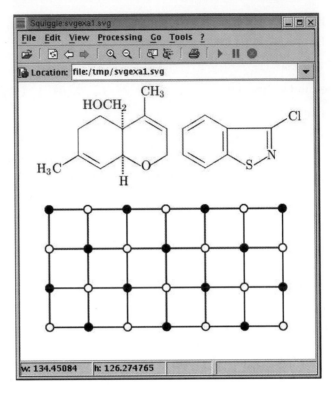

Figure 10.3: SVG generated from a `dvi` file

`dvi2svg.sh` on the generated `dvi` file to obtain the SVG file svgexa1.

```
> dvi2svg.sh svgexa.dvi -o svgexa
DEBUG from converter.DviToSvg => Converting file: svgexa.dvi
DEBUG from converter.DviToSvg => Writing result to: svgexa
DEBUG from converter.DviToSvg => Reader has been created
DEBUG from converter.DviToSvg => Writer has been created
Converting ...............FINISHED
> ls -l svgexa*.svg
-rw-rw-r--   1 goossens     23792 Jun 25 19:44 svgexa1.svg
```

Figure 10.3 shows the generated SVG file as viewed with the squiggle program.[1] For more complex LaTeX files (in particular, those with EPS or PDF inclusions) you can first generate a PostScript file with dvips, and then use Wolfgang Glunz's pstoedit program (see [58] for an explanation of how it works).

---

[1]The squiggle SVG browser is part of the Apache Batik distribution (`http://xml.apache.org/batik`). SVG can also be viewed with Adobe's browser plugin svgview (`http://www.adobe.com/svg`).

CHAPTER 11

Index Generation

To find a topic of interest in a large document, book, or reference work, you usually turn to the table of contents or, more often, to the index. Therefore, an index is a very important part of a document, and most users' entry point to a source of information is precisely through a pointer in the index. You should, therefore, plan an index and develop it along with the main text [38]. For reasons of consistency, it is beneficial, with the technique discussed below, to use special commands in the text to always print a given keyword in the same way in the text and the index throughout the whole document.

This chapter first reviews the basic indexing commands provided by standard LaTeX, and explains which tools are available to help you build a well-thought-out index. The LaTeX Manual itself does not contain a lot of information about the syntax of the \index entries. However, several articles in *TUGboat* deal with the question of generating an index with TeX or LaTeX [47,162,163]. The syntax described in Section 11.1 is the one recognized by *MakeIndex* [37,103] and xindy [71,76,152], the most widely used index preparation programs.

Section 11.2 describes how the *MakeIndex* processor is used. The interpretation of the input file and the format of the output file are controlled by style parameters. Section 11.2.4 lists these parameters and gives several simple examples to show how changing them influences the typeset result.

Section 11.3 presents xindy, an alternative to *MakeIndex*. It's preferable to use this program whenever you have non-English documents or other special demands, such as production of technical indexes. The xindy program provides total flexibility for merging and sorting index entries, and for arbitrary formatting of references.

The final section describes several LaTeX packages to enhance the index and to create multiple indexes, which will be discussed with the help of an example.

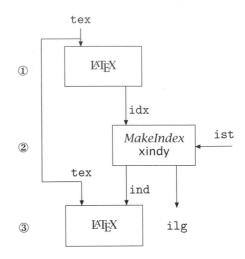

① A raw index (`.idx` file) is generated by running LaTeX.

② The raw index, together with some optional style information (`.ist` file), is used as input to the index processor, which creates an alphabetized index (`.ind` file) and a transcript (`.ilg` file).

③ The index (`.ind` file) is read by LaTeX to give the final typeset result.

Figure 11.1: The sequential flow of index processing and the various auxiliary files used by LaTeX and external index processors

The process of generating an index is shown schematically in Figure 11.1. The steps for generating an index with LaTeX and either *MakeIndex* or xindy are illustrated in this figure.

Figure 11.2 on the next page shows, with an example, the various steps involved in transforming an input file into a typeset index. It also shows, in somewhat more detail, which files are involved in the index-generating process. Figure 11.2(a) shows some occurrences of index commands (`\index`) in the document source, with corresponding pages listed on the left. Figure 11.2(b) shows a raw index `.idx` file generated by LaTeX. File extensions may differ when using multiple indexes or glossaries. After running the `.idx` file through the index processor, it becomes an alphabetized index `.ind` file with LaTeX commands specifying a particular output format [Figure 11.2(c)]. The typeset result after formatting with LaTeX is shown in Figure 11.2(d).

LaTeX and *MakeIndex*, when employed together, use several markup conventions to help you control the precise format of the output. The xindy program has a *MakeIndex* compatibility mode that supports the same format. In Section 11.1, which describes the format of the `\index` command, we always use the default settings.

11.1 Syntax of the index entries

This section describes the default syntax used to generate index entries with LaTeX and either *MakeIndex* or xindy. Different levels of complexity are introduced progressively, showing, for each case, the input file and the generated typeset output.

```
Page vi:    \index{animal}                          \indexentry{animal}{vi}
Page 5:     \index{animal}                          \indexentry{animal}{5}
Page 6:     \index{animal}                          \indexentry{animal}{6}
Page 7:     \index{animal}                          \indexentry{animal}{7}
Page 11:    \index{animalism|see{animal}}           \indexentry{animalism|see{animal}}{11}
Page 17:    \index{animal@\emph{animal}}            \indexentry{animal@\emph{animal}}{17}
            \index{mammal|textbf}                   \indexentry{mammal|textbf}{17}
Page 26:    \index{animal!mammal!cat}               \indexentry{animal!mammal!cat}{26}
Page 32:    \index{animal!insect}                   \indexentry{animal!insect}{32}
```

           (a) The input file   *(b) The* `.idx` *file*

```
\begin{theindex}
  \item animal, vi, 5-7
    \subitem insect, 32
    \subitem mammal
      \subsubitem cat, 26
  \item \emph{animal}, 17
  \item animalism, \see{animal}{11}
  \indexspace
  \item mammal, \textbf{17}
\end{theindex}
```

animal, vi, 5–7
   insect, 32
   mammal
      cat, 26
animal, 17
animalism, *see* animal

mammal, **17**

           (c) The `.ind` *file*   *(d) The typeset output*

Figure 11.2: Stepwise development of index processing

Figures 11.3 and 11.4 on page 656 show the input and generated output of a small LATEX document, where various simple possibilities of the \index command are shown, together with the result of including the showidx package (see Section 11.4.2). To make the index entries consistent in these figures (see Section 11.1.7), the commands \Com and \Prog were defined and used. The index-generating environment theindex has been redefined to get the output on one page (Section 11.4.1 explains how this can be done).

After introducing the necessary \index commands in the document, we want to generate the index to be included once again in the LATEX document on a subsequent run. If the main file of a document is main.tex, for example, then the following changes should be made to that file: *Generating the raw index*

- Include the makeidx package with a \usepackage command.

- Put a \makeindex command in the document preamble.

- Put a \printindex command where the index is to appear—usually at the end, right before the \end{document} command.

You then run LATEX on the entire document, causing it to generate the file main.idx, which we shall call the .idx file.

11.1.1 Simple index entries

Each \index command causes LATEX to write an entry in the .idx file. The following example shows some simple \index commands, together with the index entries that they produce. The page number refers to the page containing the text where the \index command appears. As shown in the example below, duplicate commands on the same page (such as \index{stylistic} on page 23) produce only one "23" in the index.

style, 14	Page iii: \index{style}
style , 16	Page xi: \index{Stylist}
style, iii, 12	Page 12: \index{style}
style , 15	\index{styles}
style file, 34	Page 14: \index{ style}
styles, 12	Page 15: \index{style }
Stylist, xi	Page 16: \index{ style }
stylist, 34	Page 23: \index{stylistic}
stylistic, 23	\index{stylistic}
	Page 34: \index{style file}
	\index{stylist}

Spaces can be harmful Pay particular attention to the way spaces are handled in this example. Spaces inside \index commands are written literally to the output .idx file and, by default, are treated as ordinary characters by *MakeIndex*, which places them in front of all letters. In the example above, look at the style entries on pages 14 and 16. The leading spaces are placed at the beginning of the index and on two different lines because the trailing blank on page 16 lengthens the string by one character. We end up with four different entries for the same term, an effect that was probably not desired. It is therefore important to eliminate such spurious spaces from the \index commands when you use *MakeIndex*. Alternatively, you can specify the -c option when running the index processor. This option suppresses the effect of leading and trailing blanks (see Sections 11.2.2 and 11.3.1). Another frequently encountered error occurs when the same English word is spelled inconsistently with initial lowercase and uppercase letters (as with Stylist on page xi), leading to two different index entries. Of course, this behavior is wanted in languages like German, where "Arm" (arm) and "arm" (poor) are really two completely different words. In English, such spurious double entries should normally be eliminated.

If you use xindy, space compression is done automatically. Furthermore, xindy supports international indexing and thus correctly and automatically handles case sensitivity in a language-specific way. Therefore, with xindy you won't encounter the problems mentioned above.

11.1.2 Generating subentries

A maximum of three levels of index entries (main, sub, and subsub entries) are available. To produce such entries, the argument of the \index command should contain both the main entries and subentries, separated by a ! character. This character can be redefined in the *MakeIndex* style file (see Table 11.1 on page 660).

box, 21
    dimensions of, 33
    parameters, 5
dimensions
    figure, 12
    rule
      height, 12
      width, 3
    table, 9

```
Page 3:    \index{dimensions!rule!width}
Page 5:    \index{box!parameters}
Page 9 :   \index{dimensions!table}
Page 12:   \index{dimensions!rule!height}
           \index{dimensions!figure}
Page 21:   \index{box}
Page 33:   \index{box!dimensions of}
```

11.1.3 Page ranges and cross-references

You can specify a page range by putting the command \index{...|(} at the beginning of the range and the command \index{...|)} at the end of the range. Page ranges should span a homogeneous numbering scheme (e.g., Roman and Arabic page numbers cannot fall within the same range). Note that *MakeIndex* and xindy do the right thing when both ends of a page range fall on the same page, or when an entry falls inside an active range.

You can also generate cross-reference index entries without page numbers by using the see encapsulator. Because the "see" entry does not print any page number, the commands \index{...|see{...}} can be placed anywhere in the input file *after* the \begin{document} command. For practical reasons, it is convenient to group all such cross-referencing commands in one place.

fonts
    Computer Modern, 13–25
    math, *see* math, fonts
    PostScript, 5
table, ii–xi, 14

```
Page ii:   \index{table|(}
Page xi:   \index{table|)}
Page 5:    \index{fonts!PostScript|(}
           \index{fonts!PostScript|)}
Page 13:   \index{fonts!Computer Modern|(}
Page 14:   \index{table}
Page 17:   \index{fonts!math|see{math, fonts}}
Page 21:   \index{fonts!Computer Modern}
Page 25:   \index{fonts!Computer Modern|)}
```

11.1.4 Controlling the presentation form

Sometimes you may want to sort an entry according to a key, while using a different visual representation for the typesetting, such as Greek letters, mathematical symbols, or specific typographic forms. This function is available with the syntax *key@visual*, where *key* determines the alphabetical position and the string *visual* produces the typeset text of the entry.

delta, 14
δ, 23
delta wing, 16
flower, 19
ninety, 26
xc, 28
ninety-five, 5
tabular environment, 23

Page 5:   `\index{ninety-five}`
Page 14:   `\index{delta}`
Page 16:   `\index{delta wing}`
Page 19:   `\index{flower@\textbf{flower}}`
Page 23:   `\index{delta@$\delta$}`
              `\index{tabular@\texttt{tabular} environment}`
Page 26:   `\index{ninety}`
Page 28:   `\index{ninety@xc}`

For some indexes, certain page numbers should be formatted specially. For example, an italic page number might indicate a primary reference, or an *n* after a page number might denote that the item appears in a footnote on that page. *MakeIndex* allows you to format an individual page number in any way you want by using the encapsulator syntax specified by the | character. What follows the | sign will "encapsulate" or enclose the page number associated with the index entry. For instance, the command `\index{keyword|xxx}` will produce a page number of the form `\xxx{n}`, where *n* is the page number in question. Similarly, the commands `\index{keyword|(xxx}` and `\index{keyword|)xxx}` will generate a page range of the form `\xxx{n-m}`.

Preexisting commands (like `\textit` in the example below) or user commands can be used to encapsulate the page numbers. As an example, a document containing the command definition

    `\newcommand\nn[1]{#1n}`

would yield something like this:

tabular, **ii**, *21*, 22n
tabbing, 7, *34–37*

Page ii: `\index{tabular|textbf}`
Page 7:   `\index{tabbing}`
Page 21:   `\index{tabular|textit}`
Page 22:   `\index{tabular|nn}`
Page 34:   `\index{tabbing|(textit}`
Page 37:   `\index{tabbing|)textit}`

The `see` encapsulator is a special case of this facility, where the `\see` command is predefined by the `makeidx` package.

11.1.5   Printing special characters

To typeset one of the characters having a special meaning to *MakeIndex* or xindy (!, ", @, or |)[1] in the index, precede it with a " character. More precisely, any character is said to be quoted if it follows an unquoted " that is not part of a \" command. The latter case is for allows for umlaut characters. Quoted !, @, ", and | characters are treated like ordinary characters, losing their special meaning. The " preceding a quoted character is deleted before the entries are alphabetized.

---

[1] As noted earlier, in *MakeIndex* other characters can be substituted for the default ones and carry a special meaning. This behavior is explained on page 662.

@ sign, 2		`\index{bar@\texttt{"|}|see{vertical bar}}`
|, *see* vertical bar	Page 1:	`\index{quote (\verb+""+)}`
exclamation (!), 4		`\index{quote@\texttt{""} sign}`
Ah!, 5	Page 2:	`\index{atsign@\texttt{"@} sign}`
Mädchen, 3	Page 3:	`\index{maedchen@M\"{a}dchen}`
quote ("), 1	Page 4:	`\index{exclamation ("!)}`
" sign, 1	Page 5:	`\index{exclamation ("!)!Ah"!}`

11.1.6   Creating a glossary

LaTeX also has a `\glossary` command for making a glossary. The `\makeglossary` command produces a file with an extension of `.glo`, which is similar to the `.idx` file for the `\index` commands. LaTeX transforms the `\glossary` commands into `\glossaryentry` entries, just as it translates any `\index` commands into `\indexentry` entries.

MakeIndex can also handle these glossary commands, but you must change the value for some of the style file keywords, as shown in the style file `myglossary.ist`.

```
% MakeIndex style file myglossary.ist
keyword   "\\glossaryentry"           % keyword for glossary entry
preamble  "\n \\begin{theglossary}\n"  % Begin glossary entries
postamble "\n\n \\end{theglossary}\n"  % End   glossary entries
```

In addition, you have to define a suitable `theglossary` environment.

11.1.7   Defining your own index commands

As was pointed out in the introduction, it is very important to use the same visual representation for identical names or commands throughout a complete document, including the index. You therefore can define user commands, which always introduce similar constructs in the same way into the text and the index.

For example, you can define the command `\Index`, whose argument is entered at the same time in the text and in the index.

```
\newcommand\Index[1]{#1\index{#1}}
```

As explained in more detail below, you must be careful that the argument of such a command does not contain expandable material (typically control sequences) or spurious blanks. In general, for simple terms like single words, there is no problem and this technique can be used. You can even go one step further and give a certain visual representation to the entry—for instance, typesetting it in a typewriter font.

```
\newcommand\Indextt[1]{\texttt{#1}\index{#1@\texttt{#1}}}
```

Finally, you can group certain terms by defining commands that have a generic meaning. For instance, LATEX commands and program names could be treated with special commands, as in the following examples:

```
\newcommand\bs{\symbol{'134}} % print backslash in typewriter OT1/T1
\newcommand\Com[1]{\texttt{\bs#1}\index{#1@\texttt{\bs#1}}}
\newcommand\Prog[1]{\texttt{#1}\index{#1@\texttt{#1} program}}
```

The `\Com` command adds a backslash to the command's name in both text and index, simplifying the work of the typist. The `\bs` command definition is necessary, because `\textbackslash` would be substituted in an `OT1` font encoding context, as explained in Section 7.3.5 on page 346. At the same time, commands will be ordered in the index by their names, with the \-character being ignored during sorting. Similarly, the `\Prog` command does not include the `\texttt` command in the alphabetization process, because entries like `\index{\texttt{`*key*`}` and `\index{`*key*`}` would then result in different entries in the index.

11.1.8   Special considerations

When an `\index` command is used directly in the text, its argument is expanded only when the index is typeset, not when the `.idx` file is written. However, when the `\index` command is contained in the argument of another command, characters with a special meaning to TEX, such as \, must be properly protected against expansion. This problem is likely to arise when indexing items in a footnote, or when using commands that put their argument in the text and enter it at the same time in the index (see the discussion in Section 11.1.7). Even in this case, robust commands can be placed in the "@" part of an entry, as in `\index{rose@\textit{rose}}`, but fragile commands must be protected with the `\protect` command.

As with every argument of a command you need to have a matching number of braces. However, because `\index` allows special characters like % or \ in its argument if the command is used in main text, the brace matching has an anomaly: braces in the commands `\{` and `\}` take part in the matching. Thus, you cannot write `\index{\{}` or something similar.

11.2   makeindex—A program to format and sort indexes

In the previous section we showed examples where we ran the *MakeIndex* program using its default settings. In this section we will first take a closer look at the *MakeIndex* program, and then discuss ways of changing its behavior.

11.2.1   Generating the formatted index

To generate the formatted index, you should run the *MakeIndex* program by typing the following command (where `main` is the name of the input file):

```
makeindex main.idx
```

This produces the file `main.ind`, which will be called the `.ind` file here. If *MakeIndex* generated no error messages, you can now rerun LATEX on the document and the index will appear. (You can remove the `\makeindex` command if you do not want to regenerate the index.) Page 658 describes what happens at this point if there are error messages.

In reading the index, you may discover additional mistakes. These should be corrected by changing the appropriate `\index` commands in the document and regenerating the `.ind` file (rerunning LATEX *before* and *after* the last step).

An example of running *MakeIndex* is shown below. The `.idx` file, `main.idx`, is generated by a first LATEX run on the input shown in Figure 11.3 on the next page. You can clearly see that two files are written—namely, the ordered `.ind` index file for use with LATEX, called `main.ind`, and the index `.ilg` log file, called `main.ilg`, which (in this case) will contain the same text as the output on the terminal. If errors are encountered, then the latter file will contain the line number and error message for each error in the input stream. Figure 11.4 on the following page shows the result of the subsequent LATEX run. The example uses the `showidx` package for controlling the index (see Section 11.4.2).

```
> makeindex main
This is makeindex, version 2.13 [07-Mar-1997] (using kpathsea).
Scanning input file main.idx....done (8 entries accepted, 0 rejected).
Sorting entries....done (24 comparisons).
Generating output file main.ind....done (19 lines written, 0 warnings).
Output written in main.ind.
Transcript written in main.ilg.
```

11.2.2   Detailed options of the *MakeIndex* program

The syntax of the options of the *MakeIndex* program are described below:

```
makeindex [-ciglqr] [-o ind] [-p no] [-s sty] [-t log] [idx0 idx1 ...]
```

-c   Enable blank compression. By default, every blank counts in the index key. The -c option ignores leading and trailing blanks and tabs and compresses intermediate ones to a single space.

-i   Use standard input (`stdin`) as the input file. When this option is specified and -o is not, output is written to standard output (`stdout`, the default output stream).

```
\documentclass{article}
\usepackage{makeidx,showidx}
\newcommand\bs{\symbol{'134}}% print backslash
\newcommand\Com[1]{\texttt{\bs#1}%
        \index{#1@\texttt{\bs#1}%
        \index{#1@\texttt{#1} program}}
\makeindex
\begin{document}
\section{Generating an Index}
Using the \textsf{showidx} package users can
see where they define index entries.
\par Entries are entered into the index by the
\Com{index} command. More precisely, the argument
of the \Com{index} command is written literally into
the auxiliary file \texttt{idx}. Note, however, that
information is actually written into that file only
when the \Com{makeindex} command was given in the
document preamble.

\section{Preparing the Index}
To prepare the index for printing, the
\texttt{idx} file has to be transformed by an external
program, such as \Prog{makeindex}.
This program writes the \texttt{ind} file.
\begin{verbatim}
makeindex filename
\end{verbatim}

\section{Printing the Index}
During the final production run of a document the
index can be included by putting a \Com{printindex}
command at the position in the text where you want
the index to appear (normally at the end).
This command will input the \texttt{ind} file
prepared by the index processor and \LaTeX{} will
typeset the information.
\printindex
\end{document}
```

Figure 11.3: Example of \index commands and the showidx package. This file is run through LaTeX once, then the index processor is executed and LaTeX is run a second time.

---

1 Generating an Index

Using the showidx package users can see where they define index entries.

Entries are entered into the index by the \index command. More precisely, the argument of the \index command is written literally into the auxiliary file idx. Note, however, that information is actually written into that file only when the \makeindex command was given in the document preamble.

Margin: index@\index index@\index makeindex@ \makeindex

2 Preparing the Index

In order to prepare the index for printing, the idx file has to be transformed by an external program, like makeindex. This program writes the ind file.

```
makeindex filename
```

3 Printing the Index

During the final production run of a document the index can be included by putting a \printindex command at the position in the text where you want the index to appear (normally at the end). This command will input the ind file prepared by makeindex and LaTeX will typeset the information.

Margin: include index Final production run printindex@ \printindex makeindex@makeindex program

Index Entries

Final production run, 1
include index, 1
\index, 1

\makeindex, 1
makeindex program, 1
\printindex, 1

1

Figure 11.4: This figure shows the index generated by the example input of Figure 11.3. All index entries are shown in the margin, so it is easy to check for errors or duplications.

-g   Employ German word ordering in the index, following the rules given in German standard DIN 5007. In this case the normal precedence rule of *MakeIndex* for word ordering (symbols, numbers, uppercase letters, lowercase letters) is replaced by the German word ordering (symbols, lowercase letters, uppercase letters, numbers). Additionally, this option enables *MakeIndex* to recognize the German TeX commands "a, "o, "u, and "s as ae, oe, ue, and ss, respectively, for sorting purposes. The quote character must be redefined in a style file (see page 662); otherwise, you will get an error message and *MakeIndex* will abort. Note that not all versions of *MakeIndex* recognize this option.

-l   Use letter ordering. The default is word ordering. In word ordering, a space comes before any letter in the alphabet. In letter ordering, spaces are ignored. For example, the index terms "point in space" and "pointing" will be alphabetized differently in letter and word ordering.

-q   Operate in quiet mode. No messages are sent to the error output stream (`stderr`). By default, progress and error messages are sent to `stderr` as well as the transcript file. The -q option disables the `stderr` messages.

-r   Disable implicit page range formation. By default, three or more successive pages are automatically abbreviated as a range (e.g., 1–5). The −r option disables this default, making explicit range operators the only way to create page ranges.

-o *ind*   Take *ind* as the output index file. By default, the file name base of the first input file *idx0* concatenated with the extension `.ind` is used as the output file name.

-p *no*   Set the starting page number of the output index file to *no*. This option is useful when the index file is to be formatted separately. Other than pure numbers, three special cases are allowed for *no*: any, odd, and even. In these special cases, the starting page number is determined by retrieving the last page number from the `.log` file of the last LaTeX run. The `.log` file name is determined by concatenating the file name base of the first raw index file (*idx0*) with the extension `.log`. The last source page is obtained by searching backward in the log file for the first instance of a number included in square brackets. If a page number is missing or if the `.log` file is not found, no attempt will be made to set the starting page number. The meaning of each of the three cases follows:

any The starting page is the last source page number plus one.

odd The starting page is the first odd page following the last source page number.

even The starting page is the first even page following the last source page number.

-s *sty*   Take *sty* as the style file. There is no default for the style file name. The environment variable INDEXSTYLE defines where the style file resides.

-t *log*   Take *log* as the transcript file. By default, the file name base of the first input file *idx0* concatenated with the extension .ilg is used as the transcript file name.

11.2.3   Error messages

MakeIndex displays on the terminal how many lines were read and written and how many errors were found. Messages that identify errors are written in the transcript file, which, by default, has the extension .ilg. *MakeIndex* can produce error messages when it is reading the .idx file or when it is writing the .ind file. Each error message identifies the nature of the error and the number of the line where the error occurred in the file.

Errors in the reading phase   In the reading phase, the line numbers in the error messages refer to the positions in the .idx file being read.

Extra '!' at position ...
> The \index command's argument has more than two unquoted ! characters. Perhaps some of them should be quoted.

Extra '@' at position ...
> The \index command argument has two or more unquoted @ characters with no intervening !. Perhaps one of the @ characters should be quoted.

Extra '|' at position ...
> The \index command's argument has more than one unquoted | character. Perhaps the extras should be quoted.

Illegal null field
> The \index command argument does not make sense because some string is null that shouldn't be. The command \index{!funny} will produce this error, since it specifies a subentry "funny" with no entry. Similarly, the command \index{@funny} is incorrect, because it specifies a null string for sorting.

Argument ... too long (max 1024)
> The document contained an \index command with a very long argument. You probably forgot the right brace that should delimit the argument.

Errors in the writing phase   In the writing phase, line numbers in the error messages refer to the positions in the .ind file being written.

Unmatched range opening operator
> An \index{...|(} command has no matching \index{...|)} command following it. The "..." in the two commands must be completely identical.

Unmatched range closing operator
> An \index{...|)} command has no matching \index{...|(} command preceding it.

Extra range opening operator
  Two \index{...|(} commands appear in the document with no intervening
  command \index{...|)}.

Inconsistent page encapsulator ... within range
  MakeIndex has been instructed to include a page range for an entry and
  a single page number within that range is formatted differently—for ex-
  ample, by having an \index{cat|see{animals}} command between an
  \index{cat|(} command and an \index{cat|)} command.

Conflicting entries
  MakeIndex thinks it has been instructed to print the same page number twice in two different ways. For example, the command sequences
  \index{lion|see{...}} and \index{lion} appear on the same page.

MakeIndex can produce a variety of other error messages indicating that something is seriously wrong with the .idx file. If you get such an error, it probably
means that the .idx file was corrupted in some way. If LaTeX did not generate any
errors when it created the .idx file, then it is highly unlikely to have produced a
bad .idx file. If, nevertheles, this does happen, you should examine the .idx file
to establish what went wrong.

11.2.4   Customizing the index with *MakeIndex*

MakeIndex ensures that the formats of the input and output files do not have to
be fixed, but they can be adapted to the needs of a specific application. To achieve
this format independence, the *MakeIndex* program is driven by a style file, usually characterized with a file extension of .ist (see also Figure 11.1 on page 648).
This file consists of a series of keyword/value pairs. These keywords can be divided into input and output style parameters. Table 11.1 on the following page
describes the various keywords and their default values for the programming of
the input file. This table shows, for instance, how to modify the index level separator (level, with ! as default character value). Table 11.2 on page 661 describes
the various keywords and their default values for steering the translation of the
input information into LaTeX commands. This table explains how to define the way
the various levels are formatted (using the item series of keywords). Examples will
show in more detail how these input and output keywords can be used in practice.
MakeIndex style files use UN*X string syntax, so you must enter \\ to get a single
\ in the output.

   In the following sections we show how, by making just a few changes to the
values of the default settings of the parameters controlling the index, you can
customize the index.

A stand-alone index

The example style mybook.ist (shown below) defines a stand-alone index for a
book, where "stand-alone" means that it can be formatted independently of the

Keyword	Default Value	Description
keyword (s)	"\\indexentry"	Command telling *MakeIndex* that its argument is an index entry
arg_open (c)	'{'	Argument opening delimiter
arg_close (c)	'}'	Argument closing delimiter
range_open (c)	'('	Opening delimiter indicating the beginning of an explicit page range
range_close (c)	')'	Closing delimiter indicating the end of an explicit page range
level (c)	'!'	Delimiter denoting a new level of subitem
actual (c)	'@'	Symbol indicating that the next entry is to appear in the actual index file
encap (c)	'|'	Symbol indicating that rest of argument list is to be used as an encapsulating command for the page number
quote (c)	'"'	Symbol that escapes the character following it
escape (c)	'\\'	Symbol without any special meaning unless it is followed by the quote character, in which case that character loses its special function and both characters will be printed. This is included because \" is the umlaut character in TeX. The two symbols quote and escape must be distinct.
page_compositor (s)	"-"	Composite page delimiter

(s) attribute of type string, (c) attribute of type char (enclose in single or double quotes, respectively)

Table 11.1: Input style parameters for *MakeIndex*

main source. Such a stand-alone index can be useful if the input text of the book is frozen (the page numbers will no longer change), and you only want to reformat the index.

```
% MakeIndex style file mybook.ist
preamble
  "\\documentclass[12pt]{book} \n\n \\begin{document} \n
   \\begin{theindex}\n"
postamble
  "\n\n\\end{theindex} \n \\end{document}\n"
```

Assuming that the raw index commands are in the file mybook.idx, then you can call *MakeIndex* specifying the style file's name:

```
makeindex  -s mybook.ist -o mybookind.tex mybook
```

A nondefault output file name is used to avoid clobbering the source output (presumably mybook.dvi). If the index is in file mybook.ind, then its typeset output will also be in mybook.dvi, thus overwriting the .dvi file for the main document.

Keyword	Default Value	Description
Context		
preamble (s)	"\\begin{theindex}\n"	Preamble command preceding the index
postamble (s)	"\n\n\\end{theindex}\n"	Postamble command following the index
Starting Page		
setpage_prefix (s)	"\n\\setcounter{page}{"	Prefix for the command setting the page
setpage_suffix (s)	"}\n"	Suffix for the command setting the page
New Group/Letter		
group_skip (s)	"\n\n\\indexspace\n"	Vertical space inserted before a new group
heading_prefix (s)	""	Prefix for heading of a new letter group
heading_suffix (s)	""	Suffix for heading of a new letter group
headings flag (n)	0	A value flag=0 inserts nothing between the different letter groups; a value flag>0 (<0) includes an uppercase (lowercase) instance of the symbol characterizing the new letter group, prefixed with heading_prefix and appending heading_suffix
Entry Separators		
item_0 (s)	"\n\\item "	Command to be inserted in front of a level 0 entry
item_1 (s)	"\n \\subitem "	Ditto for a level 1 entry starting at level ≥ 1
item_2 (s)	"\n \\subsubitem "	Ditto for a level 2 entry starting at level ≥ 2
item_01 (s)	"\n \\subitem "	Command before a level 1 entry starting at level 0
item_12 (s)	"\n \\subsubitem "	Ditto for a level 2 entry starting at level 1
item_x1 (s)	"\n \\subitem "	Command to be inserted in front of a level 1 entry when the parent level has no page numbers
item_x2 (s)	"\n \\subsubitem "	Ditto for a level 2 entry
Page Delimiters		
delim_0 (s)	", "	Delimiter between an entry and the first page number at level 0
delim_1 (s)	", "	Ditto at level 1
delim_2 (s)	", "	Ditto at level 2
delim_n (s)	", "	Delimiter between different page numbers
delim_r (s)	"-"	Designator for a page range
Page Encapsulators		
encap_prefix (s)	"\\"	Prefix to be used in front of a page encapsulator
encap_infix (s)	"{"	Infix to be used for a page encapsulator
encap_suffix (s)	"}"	Suffix to be used for a page encapsulator
Page Precedence		
page_precedence (s)	"rnaRA"	Page number precedence: a, A are lower-, uppercase alphabetic; n is numeric; r and R are lower- and uppercase Roman
Line Wrapping		
line_max (n)	72	Maximum length of an output line
indent_space (s)	"\t\t"	Indentation commands for wrapped lines
indent_length (n)	16	Length of indentation for wrapped lines

"\n" and "\t" are a new line and a tab; (s) attribute of type string; (n) attribute of type number

Table 11.2: Output style parameters for *MakeIndex*

Moreover, if you want the page numbers for the index to come out correctly, then you can specify the page number where the index has to start (e.g., 181 in the example below).

```
makeindex  -s mybook.ist  -o mybookind.tex -p 181  mybook
```

MakeIndex can also read the LaTeX log file mybook.log to find the page number to be used for the index (see the -p option described on page 655).

Changing the "special characters"

The next example shows how you can change the interpretation of special characters in the input file. To do so, you must specify the new special characters in a style file (for instance, myinchar.ist shown below). Using Table 11.1 on page 660, in the following example we change the @ character (see page 651) to =, the sublevel indicator ! (see page 650) to >, and the quotation character " (see page 652) to ! (the default sublevel indicator).

```
% MakeIndex style file myinchar.ist
actual '='       % = instead of default @
quote '!'        % !                      "
level '>'        % >                      !
```

In Figure 11.5 on the next page, which should be used in conjunction with the german option of the babel package, the double quote character (") is used as a shortcut for the umlaut construct \". This shows another feature of the ordering of *MakeIndex*: namely, the constructs " and \" are considered to be different entries (Br"ucke and Br\"ucke, M"adchen and M\"adchen, although in the latter case the key entry was identical, Maedchen). Therefore, it is important to use the same input convention throughout a complete document.

Changing the output format of the index

You can also personalize the output format of the index. The first thing that we could try is to build an index with a nice, big letter between each letter group. This is achieved with the style myhead.ist, as shown below (see Table 11.2 on the preceding page for more details) and gives the result shown in Figure 11.6.

```
% MakeIndex style file myhead.ist
heading_prefix "{\\bfseries\\hfil "      % Insert in front of letter
heading_suffix "\\hfil}\\nopagebreak\n" % Append after letter
headings_flag      1                     % Turn on headings (uppercase)
```

```
" sign, 1                   Page 1:    \index{\texttt{"} sign}
= sign, 2                   Page 2:    \index{\texttt{@} sign}
@ sign, 2                   Page 2:    \index{\texttt{!=} sign}
Brücke, 5                   Page 3:    \index{Maedchen=M\"{a}dchen}
Brücke, V                   Page c:    \index{Maedchen=M"adchen}
Brücke, v                   Page v:    \index{Bruecke=Br"ucke}
dimensions                  Page 5:    \index{Br"ucke}
    rule                    Page V:    \index{Br\"ucke}
        width, 3            Page 3:    \index{dimensions>rule>width}
exclamation (!), 4          Page 4:    \index{exclamation (!!)}
    Ah!, 5                  Page 5:    \index{exclamation (!!)>Ah!!}
Mädchen, c
Mädchen, 3
```

Figure 11.5: Example of the use of special characters with *MakeIndex*

```
        Symbols             Page 2:    \index{\texttt{"@} sign}
@ sign, 2                   Page 3:    \index{dimensions!rule!width}
        B                   Page 5:    \index{box!parameters}
box, 21                                \index{fonts!PostScript}
    dimensions of, 33       Page 9:    \index{dimensions!table}
    parameters, 5           Page 12:   \index{dimensions!rule!height}
        D                   Page 17:   \index{dimensions!figure}
dimensions                  Page 21:   \index{box}
    figure, 17                         \index{fonts!Computer Modern}
    rule                    Page 33:   \index{box!dimensions of}
        height, 12                     \index{rule!depth}
        width, 3            Page 41:   \index{rule!width}
    table, 9               Page 48:   \index{rule!depth}
        F
fonts
    Computer Modern, 21
    PostScript, 5
        R
rule
    depth, 33, 48
    width, 41
```

Figure 11.6: Example of customizing the output format of an index

```
Page 2:     \index{\texttt{"@} sign}
Page 3:     \index{dimensions!rule!width}
Page 5:     \index{box!parameters}
            \index{fonts!PostScript}
Page 9:     \index{dimensions!table}
Page 12:    \index{dimensions!rule!height}
Page 17:    \index{dimensions!figure}
Page 21:    \index{box}
            \index{fonts!Computer Modern}
Page 33:    \index{box!dimensions of}
            \index{rule!depth}
Page 41:    \index{rule!width}
Page 48:    \index{rule!depth}
```

Figure 11.7: Adding leaders to an index

You could go a bit further and right-adjust the page numbers, putting in dots between the entry and the page number to guide the eye, as shown in Figure 11.7. This effect can be achieved by adding the following commands:

```
% MakeIndex style file myright.ist
delim_0    "\\dotfill "
delim_1    "\\dotfill "
delim_2    "\\dotfill "
```

The LaTeX command \dotfill can be replaced by fancier commands, but the underlying principle remains the same.

Treating funny page numbers

As described earlier, *MakeIndex* accepts five basic kinds of page numbers: digits, uppercase and lowercase alphabetic, and uppercase and lowercase Roman numerals. You can also build composed page numbers. The separator character for composed page numbers is controlled by the *MakeIndex* keyword page_compositor; the default is the hyphen character (–), as noted in Table 11.1 on page 660. The precedence of ordering for the various kinds of page numbers is given by the keyword page_precedence; the default is rRnaA, as noted in Table 11.2 on page 661.

    Let us start with an example involving simple page numbers. Assume the pages with numbers ii, iv, 1, 2, 5, a, c, A, C, II, and IV contain an \index command with the word style. With the default page_precedence of rnaRA this would be typeset in the index as shown below. The c and C entries are considered to be Roman numerals, rather than alphabetic characters:

style, ii, iv, c, 1, 2, 5, a, II, IV, C, A

This order can be changed by using the `page_precedence` keyword, as shown in the style file `mypages.ist`.

```
% MakeIndex style file mypages.ist
page_precedence "rRnaA"
```

Running *MakeIndex* on the same index entries now yields:

style, ii, iv, c, II, IV, C, 1, 2, 5, a, A

The next step you can take is to use composed page numbers in your document. As noted earlier, the default input separator is the hyphen. Suppose you have a reference to the word `style` on the following (unsorted) series of pages: `C-3`, `1-1`, `D-1-1`, `B-7`, `F-3-5`, `2-2`, `D-2-3`, `A-1`, `B-5`, and `A-2`. After running *MakeIndex*, the following sorted output is obtained:

style, 1-1, 2-2, A-1, A-2, B-5, B-7, C-3, D-1-1, D-2-3, F-3-5

The separator can be changed to, for example, a dot, by using the `page_compositor` keyword, shown in the style file `mypagsep.ist`.

```
% MakeIndex style file mypagsep.ist
page_compositor "."
```

Running *MakeIndex* on the same index entries with the "-" replaced by "." now yields the following results:

style, 1.1, 2.2, A.1, A.2, B.5, B.7, C.3, D.1.1, D.2.3, F.3.5

11.2.5 *MakeIndex* pitfalls

The `\index` command tries to write its argument unmodified to the `.idx` file whenever possible.[1] This behavior has a number of different consequences. If the index text contains commands, as in `\index{\Prog}`, the entry is likely wrongly sorted because in main text this entry is sorted under the sort key `\Prog` (with the special character `\` as the starting sort character) regardless of the definition of the `\Prog` command. On the other hand, if it is used in some argument of another command, `\Prog` will expand before it is written to the `.idx` file; the placement in the index will then depend on the expansion of `\Prog`. The same thing happens

---

[1]The way LaTeX deals with the problem of preventing expansion is not always successful. The index package (see Section 11.4.3) uses a different approach that prevents expansion in *all* cases.

when you use \index inside your own definitions. That is, all commands inside the index argument are expanded (except when they are robust or preceded by \protect).

For sorting, *MakeIndex* assumes that pages numbered with Roman numerals precede those numbered with Arabic numerals, which in turn precede those numbered with alphabetic numbers. This precedence order can be changed (see the entry page_precedence in Table 11.2 on page 661).

MakeIndex will place symbols (i.e., patterns starting with a non-alphanumeric character) before numbers, and before alphabetic entries in the output. Symbols are sorted according to their ASCII values. For word sorting, uppercase and lowercase are considered the same, but for identical words, the uppercase variant will precede the lowercase one. Numbers are sorted in numeric order.

Spaces are treated as ordinary characters when alphabetizing the entries and for deciding whether two entries are the same (see also the example on page 650). Thus, if "␣" denotes a space character, the commands \index{cat}, \index{␣cat}, and \index{cat␣} will produce three separate entries. All three entries look similar when printed. Likewise, \index{a␣space} and \index{a␣space} produce two different entries that look the same on output. For this reason it is important to check for spurious spaces by being careful when splitting the argument of an \index command across lines in the input file. The *MakeIndex* option -c turns off that behavior and trims leading and trailing white space, compressing all white space within to one blank. We recommend that you use it all the time.

11.3   xindy—An alternative to *MakeIndex*

The xindy program by Roger Kehr and Joachim Schrod is a flexible indexing system that represents an alternative to *MakeIndex*. It avoids several limits, especially for generating indexes in non-English languages. Usage of xindy is recommended in the following cases:

- You have an **index with non-English words** and you want to use a drop-in replacement.
  Migration from *MakeIndex* is easy because xindy can be used without changing the index entries in your document. A compatibility style file will produce results corresponding to *MakeIndex*'s default set-up. The main difference will be that sorting index entries will work out of the box.

- You want to ensure that the index is **more consistent** than that created with *MakeIndex*.
  Because *MakeIndex* takes every indexed term literally, you need to specify index visualization explicitly, as explained in Section 11.1.4 on page 651. In particular, this step is needed if your visualization needs LaTeX commands. If you forget your special visualization in one place, you will get an inconsistent

index. The xindy program takes common LaTeX representations and computes
the index key from them—therefore you do not have to specify the difference between the index key and the visualization, every time. (For example,
you no longer need the different definitions of \Index and \Indextt from
Section 11.1.7 on page 653.) Of course, you can still provide specific visualiza-
tions in your index entry.

- You want more **checks for correctness**.
  If you have an index cross-reference with see, as explained in Section 11.1.3
  on page 651, xindy checks that the referenced index entry really exists. This
  way you can avoid dangling references in your indexes.

- You want to create a **technical index in an efficient way**.
  Many technical indexes involve heavy LaTeX markup in the index keys. The
  xindy program allows user-defined construction of the index keys from this
  markup. This gives you the ability to emit index entries automatically from
  your LaTeX commands, so as to get every usage of a technical term into the
  index. However, you will have to invest the time to define your index key
  construction rules.

- You want to create an **index with "unusual" terms**.
  For certain terms, special sorting rules exist due to historical reasons. For
  example, village and people's names are sometimes sorted differently than
  they're spelled—"St. Martin" is sorted as "Martin" or as "Saint Martin" dependent on context, "van Beethoven" is sorted as "Beethoven", and so on. Symbol
  indexes are another example where sort order is more or less arbitrarily defined, but should be consistent over a series of work.

The xindy program offers these advantages because it has dropped many
of *MakeIndex*'s hard-wired assumptions that are not valid in international documents with arbitrary location reference structures. Instead, xindy provides a flexible framework for configuring index creation, together with a simple *MakeIndex*-
like script for standard tasks.

The power of xindy is largely derived from five key features:

Internationalization   xindy can be easily configured for languages with different
letter sets and/or different sorting rules. You can define extra letters or complete alphabets, and you can provide a set of rules to sort and group them. At
the moment, about 50 predefined language sets are available.

Modular configuration   xindy is configured with declarations that can be combined and reused. For standard indexing tasks, LaTeX users do not have to do
much except grab available modules.

Markup normalization   A tedious problem related to technical or multilanguage
indexes concerns markup and nontext material. The xindy program allows
you to ignore different encodings for the same subject, or to easily strip
markup items such as math mode.

User-definable location references   An index entry points to locations. Fancy indexes may use not only page numbers, but also book names, law paragraphs, and structured article numbers (e.g., "I-20", "Genesis 1, 31"). The xindy program enables you to sort and group your location references arbitrarily.

Highly configurable markup   xindy provides total markup control. This feature is usually not of importance for LATEX users, but comes in handy for indexing non-TEX material.

Availability   If the xindy program is not part of your TEX distribution, its web site (www. xindy.org) offers distributions for many operating systems and more reference documentation. Note that its Windows support is not as good as its UN*X or Linux support. CTAN holds xindy distribution files as well.

11.3.1   Generating the formatted index with xindy

The xindy program comes with a command texindy that allows it to be used in a simple, *MakeIndex*-like way for standard tasks. Options equivalent to those of *MakeIndex* are not described here in detail again; refer to Section 11.2.2 instead. The options -M and -L are described in more detail in the following sections.

```
texindy [-gilqr] [-o ind] [-t log] [-L language] [-M module] [idx1 idx2 ...]
```

-i   Use standard input (stdin) as the input file.

-o *ind*   Take *ind* as the output index file.

-t *log*   Take *log* as the transcript file.

-q   Operate in quiet mode.

-g   Use German mode (equivalent to -L german-din -M german-sty).

-l   Use letter ordering; the default is word ordering (equivalent to -M letter-order).

-r   Disable implicit page range formation (equivalent to -M no-ranges).

-M *module*   Use the xindy module *module* to configure processing.

-L *language*   Take *language* as the language configuration for word ordering.

The files *idx1*, *idx2*, and so on contain raw index entries. If you specify more than one input file, you might want to use -o to name the output file, as the default output file name is always computed from *idx1*.

When you use option -c, -p, or -s, you will be warned that these *MakeIndex* options are not supported. In fact, xindy style files are self-written modules and are specified with option -M; Section 11.3.4 explains their creation in more detail.

The `texindy` command compresses blanks by default, since the authors think that this is the behavior you would expect from an index processor. In fact, the whole TeX program suite works by default under the assumption that sequences of white space are essentially one blank. If you insist on *MakeIndex*-compatible behavior, you can use the module `keep-blanks`, as explained in Section 11.3.3.

MakeIndex has the `-p` option to output a LaTeX command to the `.ind` file that sets the page counter. It may even try to parse the LaTeX log file for that purpose. The xindy program has no such option, and this omission is by design. The xindy authors believe that having a separate LaTeX document for an index is too prone to error and that the ability to include a LaTeX file with the `\printindex` command into the main document is a much better approach.

If the index text contains commands, as in `\index{\Prog}`, it is likely that the entry is sorted incorrectly as `texindy` ignores unknown TeX macros by default *Indexing LaTeX* under the assumption that they do not produce text. You will need either to spec- *commands* ify an explicit sort key in your index entry, as in `\index{prog@\Prog}`, or to write a xindy style file with a merge rule, as explained in Section 11.3.4. On the other hand, if it is used in some argument of another command, `\Prog` will expand before it is written to the `.idx` file. The placement in the index will then depend on the expansion of `\Prog`.

11.3.2 International indexing with xindy

Most non-English languages present additional challenges for index processing. They have accented characters or language-specific characters that obey special rules on how to sort them. It is usually not enough to ignore the accents, and, of course, one must not use the binary encoding of national characters for sorting. In fact, it would be very hard to use binary encoding for sorting even if one wants to— most implementations of LaTeX output many non-ASCII characters as `^^xy`, where xy is the hex code of the respective character.

The reality is different: either foreign characters are input with macros, or the inputenc package is used. For example, a LaTeX user in Western Europe on a Linux system is likely to add `\usepackage[latin1]{inputenc}` to all her documents, while a Windows user would use the inputenc option `ansinew` or `utf8`. Then, the raw index file suddenly has lots of LaTeX commands in it, since all national and accented characters are output as commands. In *MakeIndex*, the author needs to separately specify sort and print keys for such index entries. This specification may be managed for some entries, but matters become very error prone if it must be done for all entries that have national characters. In addition, creating index entries automatically by LaTeX commands (as recommended in Section 11.1.7) is no longer possible.

The xindy program deals with this problem. It knows about LaTeX macros for national characters and handles them as needed. It allows you to define new alphabets and their sort order as well as more complex multiphase sort rules to

Base Alphabet	Argument to xindy −L Option		
Latin scripts	albanian	gypsy[3]	portuguese
	croatian	hausa	romanian
	czech	hungarian	russian-iso[2]
	danish	icelandic	slovak-small
	english	italian	slovak-large
	esperanto	kurdish-bedirxan	slovenian
	estonian	kurdish-turkish	spanish-modern
	finnish	latin	spanish-traditional
	french	latvian	swedish
	general[1]	lithuanian	turkish
	german-din	lower-sorbian	upper-sorbian
	german-duden	norwegian	vietnamese
	greek-iso[2]	polish	
Cyrillic scripts	belarusian	mongolian	serbian
	bulgarian	russian	ukrainian
	macedonian		
Other scripts	greek	klingon	

[1] general *is the default language option and provides definitions approximately well suited for Western European languages, without support for any national characters.*
[2] *-iso *language options assume that the raw index entries are in the ISO 8859-9 encoding.*
[3] gypsy *is a northern Russian dialect.*

Table 11.3: Languages supported by xindy

describe the appropriate sorting scheme. You can then address typical real-world requirements, such as the following:

German German recognizes two different sorting schemes to handle umlauts: normally, *ä* is sorted like *ae*, but in phone books or dictionaries, it is sorted like *a*. The first scheme is known as *DIN order*, the second as *Duden order* [44].

Spanish In Spanish, the ligature *ll* is a separate letter group, appearing after *l* and before *m*.

French In French, the first phase of sorting ignores the diacritics, so that *cote*, *côte*, *coté* and *côté* are all sorted alike. In the next phase, within words that differ only in accents, the accented letters are looked at from right to left. Letters with diacritics then follow letters without them. Thus, *cote* and *côte* come first (no accent on the *e*), and then words with *o* come before words with *ô*.

The xindy program provides *language modules* for a growing number of languages. Such a language module defines the alphabet with all national characters, their sort rules, and letter group definitions adapted to that language. In addition, accented characters commonly used within that language are handled correctly. The predefined language modules cover Western and Eastern European languages. Currently, there is no support available for Asian languages.

There are about 50 predefined languages available, as listed in Table 11.3 on the facing page. You select one of these languages with the texindy option -L.

You can also build your own xindy language module. The xindy utility make-rules simplifies this procedure if your language fulfills the following criteria:

- Its script system uses an alphabet with letters.

- It has a sort order based on these letters (and on accents).

- No special context backtracking is required for sorting; accents influence only the sort order of the accented letters.

The xindy web site (www.xindy.org) has more information about language module creation with or without make-rules. If you create a new one, please contribute it to the xindy project.

11.3.3   Modules for common tasks

Like *MakeIndex*, xindy may be configured by creating a personal style file, as explained in Section 11.3.4. Most users, however, do not need the full power of xindy configuration. They merely want to solve common problems with a predefined set of possible solutions.

To simplify the completion of common tasks, xindy is distributed with a set of modules, listed in Table 11.4 on the next page. They provide standard solutions for sorting, page range building, and layout requirements. If you have no further demands, you can build your international index without a personal style file; you just specify a language option and the modules you want on the texindy command line. If you use the texindy command, you will deal with three categories of modules:

Automatic modules   These modules establish a behavior that is conformant to *MakeIndex*. You cannot turn them off as long as you use the texindy command. If you do not want their behavior, you have to use xindy directly as described in Section 11.3.4.

Default modules   Some modules are activated by default and can be turned off with texindy options.

Add-on modules   You can select one or more additional modules with the xindy option -M.

The automatic module latex-loc-fmts indicates a difference between xindy and *MakeIndex*. In *MakeIndex*, you can use a general encapsulation notation to enclose your page number with an arbitrary command (see Section 11.1.4). In xindy,

xindy Module	Category	Description
Sorting		
word-order	Default	A space comes before any letter in the alphabet: "index style" is listed before "indexing". Turn it off with -l.
		Prefix words are sorted first: "index style" is listed before "indexing" since *index* is a prefix of *indexing*. Turn it off with -l.
letter-order	Add-on	Spaces are ignored: "index style" is sorted after "indexing".
keep-blanks	Add-on	Leading and trailing white space (blanks and tabs) are not ignored; intermediate white space is not changed.
ignore-hyphen	Add-on	Hyphens are ignored: "ad-hoc" is sorted as "adhoc".
ignore-punctuation	Add-on	All kinds of punctuation characters are ignored: hyphens, periods, commas, slashes, parentheses, and so on.
numeric-sort	Auto	Numbers are sorted numerically, not like characters: "V64" appears before "V128".
Page Numbers		
page-ranges	Default	Appearances on more than two consecutive pages are listed as a range: "1–4". Turn it off with -r.
ff-ranges	Add-on	Uses implicit "ff" notation for ranges of three pages, and explicit ranges thereafter: 2f, 2ff, 2–6.
ff-ranges-only	Add-on	Uses only implicit ranges: 2f, 2ff.
book-order	Add-on	Sorts page numbers with common book numbering scheme correctly—Roman numerals first, then Arabic numbers, then others: i, 1, A-1.
Markup and Layout		
tex	Auto	Handles basic TeX conventions.
latex-loc-fmts	Auto	Provides LaTeX formatting commands for page number encapsulation.
latex	Auto	Handles LaTeX conventions, both in raw index entries and output markup; implies tex.
makeindex	Auto	Emulates the default *MakeIndex* input syntax and quoting behavior.
latin-lettergroups	Auto	Layout contains a single Latin letter above each group of words starting with the same letter.
german-sty	Add-on	Handles umlaut markup of babel's german and ngerman options.

Table 11.4: xindy standard modules

you have to define a location reference class with a corresponding markup definition for each command (see page 678). The latex-loc-fmts module provides such definitions for the most common encapsulations, textbf and textit.

11.3.4   Style files for individual solutions

The xindy program is a highly configurable tool. The chosen functionality is specified in a style file. The texindy command provides convenient access for most purposes, by building a virtual style file from existing modules. If you want to extend the features provided, change functionality, or build your own indexing scheme, you have to use xindy directly and write your own style file, which is just another module. The available xindy modules may be reused.

This section demonstrates how to use xindy with your own style file. It describes the basic concepts underlying the xindy program and gives examples for typical extensions.

The xindy style files are also the means by which you create indexes for non-LaTeX documents (e.g., XML documents, other Unicode-based markup systems). Features used for that purpose are not described in this section as they are beyond the scope of this book. If you're interested, you'll find more material at the xindy web site. To understand xindy style files, we need to present more detail on the basic model that xindy uses. Figure 11.8 on the following page shows the processing steps. A xindy style file contains merge rules, sort rules, location specifications, and markup specifications. Using these declarations, it defines how the raw index from the .idx file is transformed into the tagged index in the .ind file.

The xindy process model

- Merge rules specify how a sort key is computed from a raw key. The sort key identifies an index entry uniquely—there are no special characters in it. Some index entries come with an explicit sort key, when the \index{*sort-key*@*raw-key*} notation is used. Remember that raw keys may have LaTeX commands in them, or the same index entry may be input in different ways. While some of these differences are created on the author level and are therefore document-specific, most differences are due to expansion of LaTeX commands and thus computation of a sort key can be automated.

- Sort rules declare alphabets, and order within alphabets. The alphabet may not only consist of single characters, but sometimes multiple may characters form a unit for sorting (e.g., ll in Spanish). Such new characters must be ordered relative to other characters. A xindy language module consists of alphabet declarations, sort rules, and letter group definitions.

- After sorting, index entries with the same sort key are combined into a consolidated index entry with several locations and a print key. From the raw keys, the first one that appeared in the document is selected as the print key. Ordering, grouping, mixing, and omitting locations to get the final list of locations is a complex task that may be influenced in many ways by location specifications.

- Markup specifications describe which LaTeX commands are added to the consolidated index entries, thus producing a tagged index that can be used as input for LaTeX.

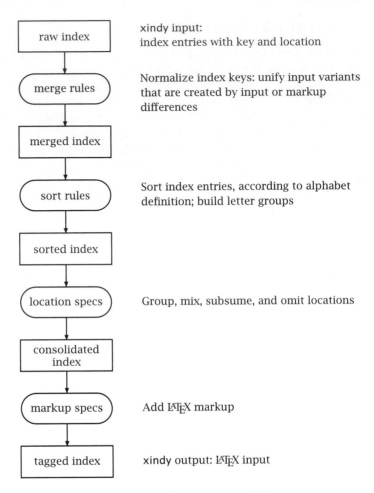

Figure 11.8: xindy process model

Calling **xindy** directly

The xindy options are very similar to those of available with texindy. You specify
your style file like any other module.

```
xindy [-qvV] [-o ind] [-d magic] [-t log] [-L lang] [-M module] [idx0 idx1 ...]
```

-o *ind* Take *ind* as the output index file.

-M *module* Use the xindy module *module* to configure processing.

-L *lang* Take *lang* as the language configuration for word ordering.

-q Operate in quiet mode.

-v   Operate in verbose mode.

-V   Output the version number and terminate.

-d *magic* Produce debugging messages; *magic* decides which xindy component
will output them.

Building a xindy style file

A xindy style file will usually start with loading predefined modules that provide
much of the desired functionality. Recall that you also have to name explicitly
those modules listed as *automatic* (auto) in Table 11.4 on page 672. Afterwards,
you can provide definitions of your own that extend or override the already loaded
modules.

```
;;; xindy example style file

;; use tex automatic modules
(require "latex.xdy")
(require "makeindex.xdy")

;; useful add-on modules
(require "ff-ranges-only.xdy")

;;; provide own definitions
;;;

;; separate page list entries by newline instead of comma
;; (please ignore paper waste :-)
(markup-location-list :sep "~n")

;; sort ö after normal o
(sort-rule "ö" "o~e")

;; End
```

The previous example of a xindy style file showed some of the syntax ele- *Style file syntax*
ments that are available. We now give more precise definitions:

- Basically, a style file consists of a list of declarative clauses in parentheses,
starting with a declaration name and followed by several parameters.

- A parameter may be either a string or an option. An option has a keyword,
written as :opt, and may have an argument, usually a string but also a number
or a fixed value like none. As the name indicates, options are optional; which
options are valid depends on the function. A parameter may also comprise a
list of parameters in parentheses, as shown in some examples below.

- Comments start with a semicolon and go until the end of line. The examples
show a typical way to use different numbers of semicolons: one for inline

comments (after xindy clauses), two for block comments in front of code, and three for comments with "section headers" for the style file. But this is merely a convention—in all places the first semicolon starts the comment.

- Strings are enclosed in double quotes. Newlines are allowed in strings. Within strings, the tilde is an escape character that makes the following letter do something special. For example, ~n specifies a newline.

Merge and sort rules

Merge rules help to normalize raw index entries before sorting and grouping take place. They can be used to unify different notations and to strip the entry from markup material that is irrelevant to sorting. If you merge different index entries, they will appear as one entry and consequently have the same printed representation; that is, all of them will look like the first one that appears in your document. Note that you can only merge single words, not whole phrases.

A merge rule takes two parameters, and declares that occurrences of the first parameter within a word are substituted by the second parameter. Within the second parameter, the virtual characters ~b and ~e may be used: ~b is ordered in front of all other characters, whereas ~e comes after all characters. These two virtual characters are not output, as merge rules are used to construct the sort key from the raw key—and sort keys are internal entry identificators.

Unify index entries   For example, in a city index, places with St in their name may also be written with Saint. Those different spellings should be unified to one index entry nevertheless. In other words, indexing St Barth and Saint Barth shall result in only one index entry.

```
( merge-rule "St"  "Saint" )
```

Unify using regular   In a merge rule, you can also specify a pattern (regular expression) and a *expressions*   replacement string. So-called *extended regexps* are the default and are defined in the POSIX 1003.2 standard. On UN*X systems, you will find their description in the man page of egrep. You can also use *basic regular expressions*, with the option :bregexp in the merge rule. The replacement string may refer to subexpressions, which leads to powerful specifications that are often hard to create and debug. Note also that usage of regular expressions will slow processing down. To index XML tags without angles, you can write:

```
( merge-rule "<(.*)>" "\1" )
```

This will cause \index{<HTML>} and \index{HTML} to be unified as one entry, which may not be the desired effect. To list them separately, but next to each other, you could modify <HTML> to HTML~e as follows:

```
( merge-rule "<(.*)>" "\1~e" )
```

Sort rules specify how characters or character sequences are sorted (i.e., at which position in the alphabet they should be placed). A sort rule consists of two strings. The first string is sorted like the second one. The second string may use ~b and ~e to specify the sort order, as explained above.

Letter groups

The xindy program checks for each letter group to see whether it matches a prefix of the entries' sort key. The longest match assigns the index entry to this letter group. If no match is found, the index entry is put into the group default.

The following definitions add all entries with the given prefixes to the same letter group *ABC*: *Combine letter groups*

```
( define-letter-group "ABC" :prefixes ("a") )
( define-letter-group "ABC" :prefixes ("b") )
( define-letter-group "ABC" :prefixes ("c") )
```

With indexes that are a bit unbalanced on, say, the letter *X*, you may want to build an extra letter group named *xsl* that contains all entries that start with xsl:. These entries will be sorted before all other entries that start with x. *Extra letter groups*

```
( define-letter-group "xsl" :before "x" :prefixes ("xsl:") )
```

Locations

The list of references behind an index entry may contain several groups that have a nonobvious but required order—perhaps Roman numbers, then Arabic numbers, then letters-Arabic numbers combined. We associate this scheme with a typical book having preface matter, normal content, and appendices. In xindy, each such group is called a location class. Within each location class, references are ordered as well. References may be combined to ranges like *10–15* or *5ff*. As you see, xindy allows you to manipulate sorting and range building in various ways.

As an example, to change the minimal length of page ranges, just modify your location class for pages: *Page range length*

```
( define-location-class "pages"
                 ("arabic-numbers")
                 :min-range-length 4 )
```

To suppress ranges for Roman numbers, change the :min-range-length option as follows: *Suppress page ranges*

```
( define-location-class "pages"
                 ("roman-numerals-lowercase")
                 :min-range-length none )
```

Nonstandard
locations
If your raw index contains references with non-numeric components and an unusual syntax (e.g., `Pasta::II.4`), you have to define a special alphabet so that xindy knows how to sort. Use it to define a location class that describes the reference syntax, including separators:

```
( define-alphabet "my-chapters" ("Starters" "Pasta" "Meat" "Sweets") )
( define-location-class "my-index"
                        ("my-chapters" :sep "::"
                         "roman-numerals-uppercase" :sep "."
                         "arabic-numbers") )
```

Location formatting

The xindy program has a very flexible mechanism for formatting, sorting, and grouping locations with special meanings. In your document, you mark up index entries for special formatting, such as \index{*keyword*|*definition*}. In xindy, you define an attribute with a corresponding markup definition.

You can also configure how your different index entry categories should interact: mix them or list them separately, allow subsuming ranges between them or not, omit entries once part of a range or not.

The following examples illustrate different variations of handling references with special formatting.

Input:	1 4 5 6 7 **7** 9 10
Example 1: mix, subsume, omit	1 4-7 **9** 10
Example 2: mix, subsume	1 4-7 **7** **9** 10
Example 3: don't mix, definitions first	**7** **9** 1 4-7 10

Example 1: Mix, subsume, and omit locations.

```
;; mix definition and default
   (define-attributes (("definition" "default")))

;; allow subsuming ranges, omit definition references within ranges
   (merge-to "definition" "default" :drop)

;; define markup
   (markup-location :attr "definition" :open "\textbf{" :close "}" )
```

Example 2: Mix and subsume locations.

```
;; mix definition and default
   (define-attributes (("definition" "default")))

;; allow subsuming ranges, keep definition references within ranges
   (merge-to "definition" "default")
```

```
;; define markup
   (markup-location :attr "definition" :open "\textbf{" :close "}" )
```

Example 3: Do not mix locations, list definitions first.

```
;; separate definition and default, definitions come first
   (define-attributes (("definition") ("default")))

;; define markup
   (markup-location :attr "definition" :open "\textbf{" :close "}" )
```

Note that :define-attributes has one parameter in parentheses. It consists of either one list of attribute names enclosed in parentheses or a list of strings, each string enclosed in parentheses. All attributes that are together in one brace are mixed. If you have several attributes, an expression like

```
(("definition" "important") ("default"))
```

would indicate that definitions may be mixed with the group of important references, but not with default references.

11.4   Enhancing the index with LaTeX features

This section describes LaTeX's support for index creation. It presents possibilities to modify the index layout and to produce multiple indexes.

11.4.1   Modifying the layout

You can redefine the environment theindex, which by default is used to print the index. The layout of the theindex environment and the definition of the \item, \subitem, and \subsubitem commands are defined in the class files article, book, and report. In the book class you can find the following definitions:

```
\newenvironment{theindex}
   {\@restonecoltrue\if@twocolumn\@restonecolfalse\fi
    \twocolumn[\@makeschapterhead{\indexname}]%
    \@mkboth{\MakeUppercase\indexname}{\MakeUppercase\indexname}%
    \thispagestyle{plain}\parindent\z@  \parskip\z@ \@plus .3\p@\relax
    \columnseprule \z@  \columnsep 35\p@   \let\item\@idxitem}
   {\if@restonecol\onecolumn\else\clearpage\fi}
\newcommand\@idxitem   {\par\hangindent 40\p@}
\newcommand\subitem    {\par\hangindent 40\p@ \hspace*{20\p@}}
\newcommand\subsubitem{\par\hangindent 40\p@ \hspace*{30\p@}}
```

Although this is programmed in a fairly low-level internal language, you can probably decipher what it sets up. First it tests for two-column mode and saves the result. Then it sets some spacing parameters, resets the page style to plain, and calls \twocolumn. Finally it changes \item to execute \@idxitem, which produces a paragraph with a hanging indention of 40 points. A higher-level reimplementation (using ifthen) might perhaps look as follows:

```
\renewenvironment{theindex}
   {\ifthenelse{\boolean{@twocolumn}}{\setboolean{@restonecol}{false}}%
                                     {\setboolean{@restonecol}{true}}%
    \twocolumn[\chapter*{\indexname}]%
    \markkboth{\MakeUppercase\indexname}{\MakeUppercase\indexname}%
    \setlength\parindent{0pt}\setlength\parskip{0pt plus 0.3pt}%
    \setlength\columnseprule{0pt}\setlength\columnsep{35pt}%
    \thispagestyle{plain}\let\item\@idxitem }
   {\ifthenelse{\boolean{@restonecol}}{\onecolumn}{\clearpage}}
```

Adjusting this definition allows you to make smaller modifications, such as changing the page style or the column separation.

You can also make an index in three rather than two columns. To do so, you can use the multicol package and the multicols environment:

```
\renewenvironment{theindex}{%
   \begin{multicols}{3}[\chapter*{\indexname}][10\baselineskip]%
   \addcontentsline{toc}{chapter}{\indexname}%
   \setlength\parindent{0pt}\pagestyle{plain}\let\item\@idxitem}
   {\end{multicols}}
```

We require at least 10 lines of free space on the current page; otherwise, we want the index to start on a new page. In addition to generating a title at the top, we enter the heading as a "Chapter" in the table of contents (.toc) and change the page style to plain. Then the \item command is redefined to cope with index entries (see above), and the entries themselves are typeset in three columns using the multicols environment.

11.4.2 showidx, repeatindex, tocbibind, indxcite—Little helpers

Several useful little LATEX packages exist to support index creation. A selection is listed in this section, but by browsing through the on-line catalogue [169] you will probably find additional ones.

Show index entries in margin The package showidx (by Leslie Lamport) can help you improve the entries in the index and locate possible problems. It shows all \index commands in the margin of the printed page. Figure 11.4 on page 656 shows the result of including the showidx package.

Handle page breaks gracefully The package repeatindex (by Harald Harders) repeats the main item of an index if a page or column break occurs within a list of subitems. This helps the reader correctly identify to which main item a subitem belongs.

The package tocbibind (by Peter Wilson) can be used to add the table of con- *Table of contents*
tents itself, the bibliography, and the index to the *Table of Contents* listing. See *support*
page 48 for more information on this package.

The package indxcite (by James Ashton) automatically generates an author *Automatic author*
index based on citations made using BIBTEX. This type of functionality is also *index*
available with the bibliography packages natbib and jurabib, both of which are
described in detail in Chapter 12.

11.4.3   index—Producing multiple indexes

The index package (written by David Jones and distributed as part of the camel
package) augments the LaTeX's indexing mechanism in several areas:

- Multiple indexes are supported.

- A two-stage process is used for creating the raw index files (such as the default
  `.idx` file) similar to that used to create the `.toc` file. First the index entries
  are written to the `.aux` file, and then they are copied to the `.idx` file at the
  end of the run. With this approach, if you have a large document consisting
  of several included files (using the `\include` command), you no longer lose
  the index if you format only part of the document with `\includeonly`. Note,
  however, that this makes the creation of a chapter index more difficult.

- A starred form of the `\index` command is introduced. In addition to entering
  its argument in the index, it typesets the argument in the running text.

- To simplify typing, the `\shortindexingon` command activates a shorthand notation. Now you can type `^{foo}` for `\index{foo}` and `_{foo}`
  for `\index*{foo}`. These shorthand notations are turned off with the
  `\shortindexingoff` command. Because the underscore and circumflex characters have special meanings inside math mode, this shorthand notation is
  unavailable there.

- The package includes the functionality of the showidx package. The command
  `\proofmodetrue` enables the printing of index entries in the margins. You
  can customize the size and style of the font used in the margin with the
  `\indexproofstyle` command, which takes a font definition as its argument
  (e.g., `\indexproofstyle{\footnotesize\itshape}`).

- The argument of `\index` is never expanded when the index package is used.
  In standard LaTeX, using `\index{\command}` will sometimes write the expansion of `\command` to the `.idx` file (see Section 11.2.5 on page 665). With the
  index package, `\command` itself is always written to the `.idx` file. While this
  is helpful in most cases, macro authors can be bitten by this behavior. In Section 11.1.7, we recommended that you define commands that automatically
  add index entries. Such commands often expect that `\index` will expand its
  parameter and they may not work when you use the index package. Be careful
  and check the results of the automatic indexing—this is best practice, anyhow.

You can declare new indexes with the \newindex command. The command \renewindex, which has an identical syntax, is used to redefine existing indexes.

\newindex{*tag*}{*raw-ext*}{*proc-ext*}{*indextitle*}

The first argument, *tag*, is a short identifier used to refer to the index. In particular, the commands \index and \printindex are redefined to take an optional argument—namely, the tag of the index to which you are referring. If this optional argument is absent, the index with the tag "default" is used, which corresponds to the usual index. The second argument, *raw-ext*, is the extension of the raw index file to which LaTeX should write the unprocessed entries for this index (for the default index it is .idx). The third argument, *proc-ext*, is the extension of the index file in which LaTeX expects to find the processed index (for the default index it is .ind). The fourth argument, *indextitle*, is the title that LaTeX will print at the beginning of the index.

As an example we show the set-up used to produce this book. The preamble included the following setting:

```
\RequirePackage{index}
\proofmodetrue                    % while proofing the index entries
\newindex{xauthor}{adx}{and}{People}
\newindex{xcmds}{cdx}{cnd}{Index of Commands and Concepts}
```

In the backmatter, printing of the index was done with the following lines:

```
\printindex[xcmds] \printindex[xauthor]
```

For each generated raw index file (e.g., tlc2.adx for the list of authors) we ran *MakeIndex* to produce the corresponding formatted index file for LaTeX:

```
makeindex -o tlc2.and -t tlc2.alg tlc2.adx
```

While all of these tools help to get the correct page numbers in the index, the real difficulty persists: choosing useful index entries for your readers. This problem you still have to solve (if you are lucky, with help).

In fact, the index of this book was created by a professional indexer, Richard Evans of Infodex Indexing Services in Raleigh, North Carolina. Dick worked closely with Frank to produce a comprehensive index that helps you, the reader, find not only the names of things (packages, programs, commands, and so on) but also the tasks, concepts, and ideas described in the book. But let him tell you (from the Infodex FAQ at http://www.mindspring.com/~infodex):

Question: Why do I need an indexer? Can't the computer create an index?

Answer: To exactly the same degree that a word processor can write the book. Indexes are creative works, requiring human intellect and analysis.

LaTeX can process the indexing markup, but only a human indexer can decide what needs to be marked up. Our sincere thanks to Dick for his excellent work.

CHAPTER 12

Managing Citations

12.1 Introduction

Citations are cross-references to bibliographical information outside the current document, such as to publications containing further information on a subject and source information about used quotations. It is certainly not necessary to back everything by a reference, but background information for controversial statements, acknowledgments of other work, and source information for used material should be given.

There are numerous ways to compile bibliographies and reference lists. They can be prepared manually, if necessary, but usually they are automatically generated from a database containing bibliographic information (see Chapter 13). This chapter introduces some of the many presentation forms of bibliographical sources and it reviews different traditions regarding how such sources are referred to in a document.

The chapter begins a short introduction to the major citation schemes in common use. This is followed by a description of LaTeX's standard markup for bibliography lists and its interface to the BibTeX program that can be used to produce such lists automatically from a (suitably prepared) document source. More detailed information on BibTeX is then given in Chapter 13. In the current chapter we are only interested in how BibTeX can be used to produce a bibliography list.

Armed with this knowledge we plunge into a detailed discussion of how LaTeX supports the different citation schemes. At the time we wrote the first edition of this book, LaTeX basically supported the "number-only" system. A decade later, the situation has changed radically. Today, most major citation schemes are well supported by extension packages.

We end this chapter by discussing packages that can deal with multiple bibli-ographies in one document. This is not difficult if the reference lists are prepared manually, but it poses some challenges if you want to interact with BibTeX, as well.

12.1.1 Bibliographical reference schemes

There are four common methods of referring to sources: the "short-title", "author-date", "author-number", and "number-only" systems. The first of these is often used in books on humanities; the second appears mainly in science and social science works. The other two are less often used, although the last is quite com-mon within the LaTeX world, as it has been actively promoted by Leslie Lamport and originally was the only form of citation supported by LaTeX. Outside the LaTeX world a variation of it, called "numeric by first citation", is quite popular as well.

The short-title system In the short-title system, the reference to a source is given directly in the text, either inline or as a footnote, often in the form "Hart, *Hart's Rules*, p. 52". In the context of the publication, if abbreviations for the title are established, the form "Goossens et al., *LGC*" may appear as an alternative. Many variations exist. For instance, the first time a work is cited it might be presented with a lot of detail; later references might then use a shorter form—citing only the author's name and a short title or the year. In case of repeated citations to the same work in direct succession, you might find *Ibid.* instead of a repeated reference. An implementa-tion of the short-title system that allows all kinds of customizations is provided by the jurabib package (see Section 12.5.1).

Because in the short-title system a full reference is usually given the first time a work is cited, you can omit a list of references or a bibliography that contains all cited works in a single place.

The author-date system In the author-date system (often referred to as the Harvard system after one of its better known typographical variants), references to sources are also given directly in the text. This time, however, they show the author's name (or names) and the year of the publication. The full citation is given in a list of references or a bibliography. If the author published more than one work in a given year, that year is suffixed with lowercase letters (e.g., 2001a, 2001b).

There have been many attempts over the years to provide author-date citation support for LaTeX. With the natbib package (discussed in Section 12.3.2) there is now a very flexible and general solution available.

In all citation schemes that use author names, a work by three or more authors is usually referred to by using the name of the first author followed by *et al.* Especially with the author-date system, this may lead to ambiguous citations if different groups containing the same main author published in the same year. This problem can be seen in the following example.

```
\usepackage{chicago} \bibliographystyle{chicago}
```
```
Multiple authors can be problematical, e.g., \shortcite{LGC97} and
\shortcite{test97} or worse \shortcite{LGC97,test97}.   \bibliography{tex}
```

Multiple authors can be problematical, e.g., (Goossens et al. 1997) and (Goossens et al. 1997) or worse (Goossens et al. 1997; Goossens et al. 1997).

References

Goossens, M., S. Rahtz, and F. Mittelbach (1997). *The LaTeX Graphics Companion: Illustrating Documents with TeX and PostScript*. Tools and Techniques for Computer Typesetting. Reading, MA, USA: Addison-Wesley Longman.

Goossens, M., B. User, and J. Doe (1997). Ambiguous citations. Submitted to the IBM Journal of Research and Development.

12-1-1

In the above example the bibliography is produced from the sample BibTeX database `tex.bib` shown in Figure 12.2 on page 690. This database is used in most examples in this chapter. Above we applied the BibTeX style `chicago` to it, a style that aims to implement a bibliography and reference layout as suggested by *The Chicago Manual of Style* [38].

One way to resolve such ambiguous citations is to use all author names in such a case, although that approach will lead to lengthy citations and is not feasible if the number of authors exceeds a certain limit. Another solution is to append a, b, and so on, to the year, even though the citations are actually for different author groups. This strategy is, for example, advocated in [29]. If the bibliography is compiled manually, as outlined in Section 12.1.2, this result can be easily achieved. When using BibTeX, you have to use a BibTeX style file that recognizes these cases and provides the right data automatically. For example, the style `chicago` cannot be used in this case, but all BibTeX styles produced with `makebst` (see Section 13.5.2) offer this feature:

Multiple authors might be problematical, e.g., Goossens et al. [1997a] and Goossens et al. [1997b] or even Goossens et al. [1997a,b]. But then it might not.

References

M. Goossens, S. Rahtz, and F. Mittelbach. *The LaTeX Graphics Companion: Illustrating Documents with TeX and PostScript*. Tools and Techniques for Computer Typesetting. Addison-Wesley Longman, Reading, MA, USA, 1997a. ISBN 0-201-85469-4.

M. Goossens, B. User, and J. Doe. Ambiguous citations. Submitted to the IBM J. Res. Dev., 1997b.

12-1-2

```
\usepackage{natbib}
\bibliographystyle
            {abbrvnat}
Multiple authors might
be problematical,
e.g., \cite{LGC97} and
\cite{test97} or even
\cite{LGC97,test97}.
But then it might not.

\bibliography{tex}
```

The author-number system

In the author-number system, the references to the sources are given in the form of the author's name (or names) followed by a number, usually in parentheses or brackets, indicating which publication of the author is cited. In the corresponding bibliography all publications are numbered on a per-author (or author group) basis. In the LaTeX world this system is fairly uncommon as it is difficult to produce manually. As far as we know, there is currently no BibTeX support

available for it, though this situation might change in the future. A variation of
the above is to number all publications sequentially. For this case suitable B<small>IB</small>T_EX
styles exist.

The number-only system

Finally, in the number-only system, publications are sequentially numbered
in the bibliography. Citations in the text refer to these numbers, which are usually surrounded by brackets or parentheses. Sometimes raised numbers are used
instead. In a slight variation, known as "alpha" style, citations comprise the author's name and the year of the publication. Thus, the bibliographic label and the
citation may look like "[Knu86]".

One argument against this system—put forward, for example, in *The Chicago
Manual of Style* [38]—is that it raises the costs of publication since a late addition
or deletion of a reference may require renumbering and consequently costly (and
error-prone) changes to many pages throughout the manuscript. With automatic
cross-referencing facilities as provided by LaTeX, this argument no longer holds
true. In fact, the number-only system is the default system provided with LaTeX.

Numerical by first citation

A fairly popular form of the number-only system numbers the publications
sequentially by their first citation in the text (and presents them in that order in
the bibliography). This is fairly easy to provide with LaTeX. The next two sections
and Section 12.2.3 explain how to avoid references in the table of contents that
might mess up the expected order.

12.1.2 Markup structure for citations and bibliography

The standard LaTeX environment for generating a list of references or a bibliography is called `thebibliography`. In its default implementation it automatically
generates an appropriate heading and implements a vertical list structure in which
every publication is represented as a separate item.

```
\begin{thebibliography}{widest-label}
\bibitem[label1]{cite-key1}  bibliographic information
\bibitem[label2]{cite-key2}  bibliographic information
      . . .
\end{thebibliography}
```

The *widest-label* argument is used to determine the right amount of indentation for individual items. If the works are numbered sequentially, for example,
it should contain the number of items.

Individual publications are introduced with a `\bibitem` command. Its mandatory argument is a unique cross-reference *key* that refers to this publication in
the text. The optional argument defines the textual representation that is used
in the citation and as the *label* in the list. If this argument is not specified, the
publications are numbered with Arabic numerals by default. Within a publication
the command `\newblock` may be used to separate major blocks of information.

Depending on the layout produced by the class, it may result in some extra space or in starting a new line.

References

[1] Goossens, M., S. Rahtz, and F. Mittelbach (1997). *The LaTeX Graphics Companion: Illustrating Documents with TeX and PostScript.* Reading, MA, USA: Addison-Wesley Longman.

[2] Goossens, M., B. User, and J. Doe (1997). Ambiguous citations.

```
\begin{thebibliography}{2}
\bibitem{LGC97} Goossens, M., S.~Rahtz,
   and F.~Mittelbach (1997).
  \newblock \emph{The \LaTeX{} Graphics Companion:
  Illustrating Documents with \TeX{} and
  PostScript}. \newblock Reading, MA, USA:
  Ad\-di\-son-Wes\-ley Longman.
\bibitem{test97} Goossens, M., B.~User, and J.~Doe
   (1997). \newblock Ambiguous citations.
\end{thebibliography}
```

12-1-3

Producing a large bibliography manually in this way is clearly a tedious and difficult task and the result is normally not reusable, as nearly all journals and publishers have their own house styles with different formatting requirements. For this reason it is generally better to use BibTeX, a program that generates ready-to-use LaTeX input from a database of bibliographical information. This is discussed in the next section.

Note that without the optional argument to \bibitem the references are numbered in the order in which they appear in the bibliography. Thus, if you produce the bibliography manually, numbering and sorting them by order of first citation becomes your task. In contrast, when using BibTeX, this result can be achieved automatically.

Order by first citation done manually

Inside a document, publications are cited by referring to the *cite-key* arguments of the \bibitem commands. For this purpose LaTeX offers the \cite command, which takes such a key as its argument. It can, in fact, take a comma-separated list of such keys and offers an optional argument to specify additional information such as page or chapter numbers. The precise syntax is described in Section 12.2.1. For short-title or author-date citation schemes, additional citation commands are available once the supporting packages are loaded.

12.1.3 Using BibTeX to produce the bibliography input

The BibTeX program gathers all citation keys used in a document, looks them up in a bibliographical database, and generates a complete thebibliography environment that can be loaded by LaTeX in a subsequent run. Depending on the BibTeX style used, it can either sort the entries according to some scheme (e.g., author names, year of publication) or produce a bibliography with entries in the order in which they appear in the .aux file. Note that using such a "nonsorting" style automatically generates a bibliography by order of first citation as required by the house styles of many publishers. An example of such a BibTeX style is unsrt.

Order by first citation produced with BibTeX

The procedure for running LaTeX and BibTeX is shown schematically in Figure 12.1 on the next page. At least three LaTeX runs are necessary—first to produce

① Run LaTeX, which generates a list of \cite references in its auxiliary file, .aux.

② Run BibTeX, which reads the auxiliary file, looks up the references in a database (one or more .bib files), and then writes a file (the .bbl file) containing the formatted references according to the format specified in the style file (the .bst file). Warning and error messages are written to the log file (the .blg file). Note that BibTeX never reads the original LaTeX source file.

③ Run LaTeX again, which now reads the .bbl file containing the bibliographic information.

④ Run LaTeX a third time, resolving all references.

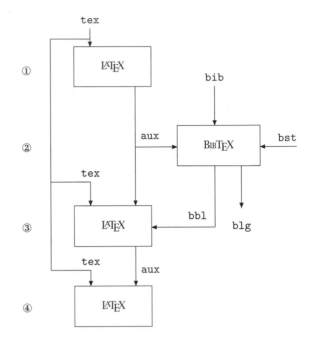

Figure 12.1: Data flow when running BibTeX and LaTeX

data for BibTeX, then to load the result from the BibTeX run, and finally to resolve the cross-references to the bibliographical list added by the previous run.

\bibliography{*file-list*}   \bibliographystyle{*style*}

To inform BibTeX which databases are to be searched to resolve citations, you should specify their names, separated by commas (and without the extension .bib), as an argument to the command \bibliography. This command should be placed at the point where the bibliography should finally appear. In addition, you have to tell BibTeX how the bibliographic entries should be formatted. This is done by using the command \bibliographystyle in the preamble with a suitable BibTeX style as its argument. It is, of course, important that the *cite-keys* used in the document uniquely identify an entry in the database file(s), so that the citation reference can be resolved when the document is processed.

To enable BibTeX to access the information without the need to parse the LaTeX source files, these commands write two lines to the .aux file. For a similar reason the \cite command, as well as any variant of it, writes its *key* to this file. For example, in Example 12-1-2 the .aux file would contain (beside other entries):

```
\bibstyle{abbrvnat}
\citation{LGC97}
```

```
\citation{test97}
\bibdata{tex}
```

Do not confuse these commands with those intended for use in the document. They exist solely to facilitate internal communication between LaTeX and BibTeX. If you mistakenly use `\bibdata` instead of `\bibliography`, then LaTeX will process your document without failure, but BibTeX will complain that it does not find any database information in the `.aux` file.

The precise format of a BibTeX entry will be described in detail in Chapter 13. To be able to understand the examples in the next sections more easily, you should nonetheless know that the basic structure of a BibTeX entry consists of three parts:

1. A publication *entry type* (e.g., "`book`", "`article`", "`inproceedings`", "`phdthesis`").

2. A *user-chosen keyword* identifying the publication. If you want to reference the entry in your document, then the argument *cite-key* of the `\cite` command should be identical (also in case) to this keyword.

3. A *series of fields* consisting of a field identifier with its data between quotes or curly braces (e.g., "`author`", "`journal`", and "`title`").

A sample database is shown in Figure 12.2 on the following page. This database is used in most examples throughout the chapter to show how applying different BibTeX style files to it results in different presentation forms.

Various schemes exist for conveniently associating bibliography keywords with their entries in a database. A popular one is the so-called Harvard system, where you take the author's surname (converted to lowercase) and the year of publication, and combine them using a colon (e.g., `smith:1987`).

BibTeX entries are read by BibTeX in the bibliography database (the `.bib` file), and the formatting of the entries is controlled by an associated bibliography style (the `.bst` file), which contains a set of instructions written in a stack-based language. The latter is interpreted by the BibTeX program (see Section 13.6).

BibTeX knows which fields are required, optional, and ignored for any given entry type (see Table 13.1 on page 763). It will issue warnings, such as "`author name required`", if something is missing. The style file can control the typesetting of both the citation string in the main text and the actual bibliography entry inside the `thebibliography` environment.

It is important to remember that BibTeX is not required for managing citations (except for the package jurabib and those packages intended for producing multiple bibliographies). You can produce a bibliography without BibTeX by providing the bibliographic entries yourself using the syntax described in Section 12.1.2. It is also a simple matter to manually edit the output from BibTeX to cope with special cases. Moreover, if your LaTeX document has to be self-contained, you can include the contents of the `.bbl` file in your document.

```
@String{ttct       = "Tools and Techniques for Computer
                     Typesetting"   }

@Book{LGC97,
  author =         "Michel Goossens and Sebastian Rahtz
                    and Frank Mittelbach",
  title =          "The {\LaTeX} Graphics Companion:
                    Illustrating Documents with {\TeX}
                    and {PostScript}",
  publisher =      "Ad{\-d}i{\-s}on-Wes{\-l}ey Longman",
  address =        "Reading, MA, USA",
  pages =          "xxi + 554",
  year =           "1997",
  ISBN =           "0-201-85469-4",
  series =         ttct
}
@UNPUBLISHED{test97,
  author = "Michel Goossens and Ben User
              and Joe Doe",
  title  = "Ambiguous citations",
  year   = "1997",
  note   = "Submitted to the " # ibmjrd
}
@Book{LWC99,
  author =         "Michel Goossens and Sebastian Rahtz",
  title =          "The {\LaTeX} {Web} companion:
                    integrating {\TeX}, {HTML},
                    and {XML}",
  publisher =      "Ad{\-d}i{\-s}on-Wes{\-l}ey Longman",
  address =        "Reading, MA, USA",
  pages =          "xxii + 522",
  year =           "1999",
  ISBN =           "0-201-43311-7",
  note =           "With Eitan M. Gurari and Ross Moore
                    and Robert S. Sutor",
  series =         ttct
}
@Book{Knuth-CT-a,
  Author         = "Donald E. Knuth",
  Title          = "The {\TeX}book",
  Publisher      = "Ad{\-d}i{\-s}on-Wes{\-l}ey",
  Address        = "Reading, MA, USA",
  Volume         = "A",
  Series         = "Computers and Typesetting",
  pages          = "ix + 483",
  year           = 1986,
  isbn           = "0-201-13447-0",
}
@Article{Knuth:TB10-1-31,
  Author         = "Donald E. Knuth",
  Title          = "{Typesetting  Concrete
                    Mathematics}",
  Journal        = "TUGboat",
  Volume         = "10",
  Number         = "1",
  Pages          = "31--36",
  year           = 1989,
  month          = apr,
  issn           = "0896-3207"
}
```

```
@Book{vLeunen:92,
  author         = "Mary-Claire van Leunen",
  gender         = "sf",
  title          = "A handbook for scholars",
  publisher      = "Oxford University Press",
  address        = "Walton Street, Oxford OX2 6DP, UK",
  pages          = "xi + 348",
  year           = "92"
}

@manual{GNUMake,      key = {make},
  title = {{GNU Make}, A Program for Directing
Recompilation},   organization= "Free
Software Foundation",address = "Boston,
Massachusetts",ISBN={1-882114-80-9},year = 2000}

@book{G-G,
  TITLE     = {{Gutenberg Jahrbuch}},
  EDITOR    = {Hans-Joachim Koppitz},
  PUBLISHER = {Gutenberg-Gesellschaft, Internationale
                Vereinigung f\"ur Geschichte und
                Gegenwart der Druckkunst e.V.},
  ADDRESS   = {Mainz, Germany},
  NOTE      = {Contains results on the past and present
                history of the art of printing. Founded
                by Aloys Ruppel. Published since 1926.}
}
@misc{oddity,
  title         = "{{TUGboat} The Communications of the
                  {\TeX} User Group}",
  howpublished = "Quarterly published.",
  year          = {1980ff}
}
@InProceedings{MR-PQ,
  author       = "Frank Mittelbach and Chris Rowley",
  title        = "The Pursuit of Quality: How can
                  Automated Typesetting achieve the
                  Highest Standards of Craft
                  Typography?",
  pages        = "261--273",
  crossref     = "EP92"}
@InProceedings{Southall,
  Author       = "Richard Southall",
  Title        = "Presentation Rules and Rules of
                  Composition in the Formatting of
                  Complex Text",
  Pages        = "275--290",
  crossref     = "EP92"}
@Proceedings{EP92,
  title        = "{EP92}---Proceedings of Electronic
                  Publishing, '92",
  shorttitle   = "{EP92}",
  editor       = "Christine Vanoirbeek and Giovanni Coray",
  publisher    = "Cambridge University Press",
  address      = "Cambridge",
  year         = 1992,
  booktitle    = "{EP92}---Proceedings of Electronic
                  Publishing, '92"
}
```

Figure 12.2: Sample BIBTEX database `tex.bib`

This database uses different conventions in individual entries (e.g., lower-, upper-, or mixed-case field names, different indentations) to show some features and problems in later examples. By applying one of the tools from Section 13.4 it could be normalized.

12.2   The number-only system

12.2.1   Standard LaTeX—Reference by number

As mentioned earlier in this chapter, the number-only system is the default citation method directly supported by standard LaTeX. That is, without loading any additional packages, it is the only method supported by the provided markup commands. Bibliographic citations inside the text of a LaTeX document are then flagged with the command \cite.

`\cite[`*text*`]{`*key*`}      \cite[`*text*`]{`*key1,key2,...*`}      \nocite{`*key-list*`}`

The \cite command associates each keyword in the list in its mandatory argument with the argument of a \bibitem command from the thebibliography environment to produce the citation reference. As with other LaTeX identifiers, these keys are case-sensitive.

The citation numbers generated are defined by the order in which the keys appear on the \bibitem commands inside the thebibliography environment or, if an optional argument is used with \bibitem, by the data provided in that argument.

The optional parameter *text* is an additional note, which will be printed together with the text generated by the \cite command as shown in the following example. For comparison we have used an unbreakable space (~) in the first citation and a small space (\,) in the second. Of course, such typographical details should be handled uniformly throughout a publication.

Color support for LaTeX is described in [2, chap. 9] and the hyperref package in [1, pp. 35–67].

```
\bibliographystyle{plain}
Color support for \LaTeX{} is described in
\cite[chap.~9]{LGC97} and the \texttt{hyperref}
package in \cite[pp.\,35--67]{LWC99}.
```

12-2-1

To save space, the examples in this chapter often omit the bibliography list. They are generated by placing \bibliography{tex} at the end of the example document when automatically generating the example output for the book. Thus, you should read examples such as 12-2-1 as follows: the result is produced by generating the bibliography with BibTeX, applying the style plain (shown), and using the database tex.bib (not shown; see Figure 12.2). Thus, the actual document that produced the example contained \bibliography{tex} near the end.

A note on the examples in this chapter

In conjunction with BibTeX, you can use the \nocite variant of the \cite command. Its sole purpose is to write the keys from the *key-list* argument into the .aux file, so that the associated bibliography information will appear in the bibliography even if the publication is otherwise not cited. For technical reasons it has to appear *after* \begin{document}, even though it does not produce any output and would logically be best placed in the preamble. It can be used as often as necessary. As a special case \nocite{*} includes all entries of the chosen BıʙTᴇX data in the list of references.

As stated above, the association between a \cite command and one or more bibliography entries is made via the *key-list* argument. The citation text, which will actually appear in the typeset text, depends on the chosen bibliographic style.

Customizing citation references and the bibliography

Unfortunately, standard LaTeX is not equipped with an easily customizable interface through which you can adjust the formatting of the citation references. Thus, to change the default brackets around the numbers into parentheses, for example, we need to redefine the internal LaTeX command \@cite.

Even worse, the user-level \cite command sets the internal temporary switch @tempswa to indicate whether an optional argument was present. Thus, if we want to handle that optional argument, we need to evaluate the value of that switch. The \@cite command receives two arguments: the list of obtained references and the note (if present). In the following example we typeset (#1 and, if @tempswa is true, follow it by a comma and ␣#2. This is then followed by the closing parenthesis. The \nolinebreak[3] ensures that a break after the comma is taken only reluctantly.

```
\bibliographystyle{plain}    \usepackage{ifthen}
\makeatletter
\renewcommand\@cite[2]{(({#1\ifthenelse{\boolean{@tempswa}}
                                  {,\nolinebreak[3] #2}{}})}
\makeatother
```

Color support for LaTeX is described in (2) and the hyperref package in (1, pp. 35–67).

```
Color support for \LaTeX{} is described in \cite{LGC97} and
the \textttt{hyperref} package in \cite[pp.\,35--67]{LWC99}.
```
12-2-2

The redefinition of \@cite for purposes like the above can be avoided by loading the cite package; see Section 12.2.2.

For the thebibliography environment, which holds the list of the actual references, the situation is unfortunately not much better—the default implementation offers few customization possibilities. To modify the layout of the labels in front of each publication (e.g., to omit the brackets), you have to change the internal LaTeX command \@biblabel.

References

1. D. E. Knuth. *The TEXbook*, volume A of *Computers and Typesetting*. Addison-Wesley, Reading, MA, USA, 1986.

2. D. E. Knuth. Typesetting Concrete Mathematics. *TUGboat*, 10(1):31–36, Apr. 1989.

```
\bibliographystyle{abbrv}
\makeatletter
\renewcommand\@biblabel[1]{#1.}
\makeatother
\nocite{Knuth-CT-a,Knuth:TB10-1-31}
\bibliography{tex}
```
12-2-3

Packages that implement a variation of the author-date system (e.g., the apalike, chicago, or natbib package), typically unconditionally redefine \@biblabel to simply swallow its argument and typeset nothing. After all, such a bibliography is used by looking up the author name, so a label is unnecessary. The natbib package is somewhat more careful: if it detects that \@biblabel was changed, then it honors the redefinition.

As mentioned earlier, different blocks of information, such as the authors or the title, are separated inside one \bibitem in the bibliography by \newblock commands, which are also automatically inserted by most BibTeX styles. Normally, bibliographic entries are typeset together in one paragraph. If, however, you want your bibliography to be "open", with each block starting on a new line with succeeding lines inside a block indented by a length \bibindent (default 1.5em), then the class option openbib should be specified. This option is supported by all standard classes. The result is shown in the next example; we also redefine \@biblabel to get raised labels.

References

[1] M. Goossens and S. Rahtz.
The LaTeX Web companion: integrating TeX, HTML, and XML.
Tools and Techniques for Computer Typesetting. Addison-Wesley Longman, Reading, MA, USA, 1999.
With Eitan M. Gurari and Ross Moore and Robert S. Sutor.

[2] D. E. Knuth.
Typesetting Concrete Mathematics.
TUGboat, 10(1):31–36, Apr. 1989.

12-2-4

```
\documentclass[openbib]{article}
\bibliographystyle{abbrv}
\setlength\bibindent{24pt}

\makeatletter
\renewcommand\@biblabel[1]
            {\textsuperscript{#1}}
\makeatother
\nocite{LWC99,Knuth:TB10-1-31}
\bibliography{tex}
```

12.2.2 cite—Enhanced references by number

One shortcoming that becomes readily apparent when you use LaTeX's default method of citing publications is the fact that it faithfully keeps the order of citations as given in the *key-list* argument of the \cite command. The following example therefore shows a very strangely ordered list of numbers (the unresolved reference was added deliberately):

Good information about TeX and LaTeX can be found in [2, 1, 3, ?, 4].

12-2-5

```
\bibliographystyle{plain}
Good information about \TeX{} and \LaTeX{} can be found in
\cite{LGC97,LWC99,Knuth-CT-a,Knuth:ct-b,Knuth:TB10-1-31}.
```

This situation can be easily improved by simply loading the cite package (by Donald Arseneau), as in the following example:

Good information about TeX and LaTeX can be found in [?,1–4].

12-2-6

```
\usepackage{cite}    \bibliographystyle{plain}
Good information about \TeX{} and \LaTeX{} can be found in
\cite{LGC97,LWC99,Knuth-CT-a,Knuth:ct-b,Knuth:TB10-1-31}.
```

By default, the cite package sorts citation numbers into ascending order, representing three or more consecutive numbers as a number range. Any non-numeric label is moved to the front (in the above example the "?" generated by the unresolved reference). If sorting is not desired you can globally prevent it by loading the package with the option nosort. Compression into ranges can be suppressed by using the option nocompress.

Customizing the
citation layout

To customize the typeset reference the cite package offers a number of commands. For example, \citeleft and \citeright determine the material placed on the left and right sides of the citation string, respectively. These commands can be used to typeset parentheses instead of brackets as seen in the following example, which should be compared to Example 12-2-2 on page 692. We can also redefine \citemid, the separation between citation and optional note, to produce a semicolon and a space.

Color support for LaTeX is described in (2) and the hyperref package in (1; pp. 35–67).

```
\usepackage{cite}      \bibliographystyle{plain}
\renewcommand\citeleft{(} \renewcommand\citeright{)}
\renewcommand\citemid{;\nolinebreak[3] }
Color support for \LaTeX{} is described in \cite{LGC97} and
the \textttt{hyperref} package in \cite[pp.\,35--67]{LWC99}.
```
12-2-7

Customizing breaks
within citations

Another important aspect of citation management is controlling the behavior near the end of a line. Consider the string "see [2–3,713]". Besides not allowing any kind of line break within this string, one could allow breaking after the "see", after the commas, or after the en dash in a range.

By default, the cite package discourages line breaks before the citation with \nolinebreak[3], discourages line breaks after a comma separating the optional note with \nolinebreak[2], and very strongly discourages line breaks after en dashes in a range and after commas separating individual citation numbers. You can control the last three cases by redefining \citemid, \citedash, and \citepunct. For example, to prevent breaks after the en dashes while allowing breaks after commas without much penalty, you could specify

```
\renewcommand\citedash{\mbox{--}\nolinebreak}
\renewcommand\citemid{,\nolinebreak[1] }
\renewcommand\citepunct{,\nolinebreak[1]\hspace{.13em plus .1em minus .1em}}
```

There are several interesting points to note here. All three definitions are responsible not only for controlling any line breaks but also for adding the necessary punctuation: a dash for the range, a comma and a full blank before the optional note, or a comma and a tiny space between individual citations. For instance, if you want no space at all between citations, you can redefine \citepunct to contain only a comma. The other important and probably surprising aspect is the \mbox surrounding the en dash. This box is absolutely necessary if you want to control LaTeX's ability to break at this point. TeX automatically adds a break point after an explicit hyphen or dash, so without hiding it in a box, the \nolinebreak command would never have any effect—the internally added break point would still allow a line break at this point. Finally, the \hspace command allows for some stretching or shrinking; if you prefer a fixed space instead, remove the `plus` and `minus` components.

The high penalty that is added before a citation is hard-wired in the code. It is, however, inserted only if you have not explicitly specified a penalty in your document. For instance, "see~\cite{..}" will be honored and no break will happen between "see" and the citation.

One more customization command, \citeform, allows you to manipulate the individual reference numbers. By default, it does nothing, so the labels are typeset unchanged. In the following example we colored them. Other kinds of manipulation are possible, too (e.g., adding parentheses in Example 12-2-9). *Customizing citation numbers*

Color support for LaTeX is described in [2] and the hyperref package in [1, pp. 35–67].

```
\usepackage{cite,color}  \bibliographystyle{plain}
\renewcommand\citeform[1]{\textcolor{blue}{#1}}
Color support for \LaTeX{} is described in \cite{LGC97} and
the \texttt{hyperref} package in \cite[pp.\,35--67]{LWC99}.
```

12-2-8

```
\citen{key-list}
```

The package offers an additional command, \citen (its aliases are \citenum and \citeonline), that can be used to get a list of numbers without the surrounding \citeleft and \citeright (e.g., the default brackets). Other formatting is still done. In the next example we surround individual references to citations with parentheses, something that admittedly looks a little strange when used together with the default bracketing of the whole citation.

(1)–(3),(5) but [(4), §5]

```
\usepackage[nospace]{cite}  \bibliographystyle{plain}
\renewcommand\citeform[1]{(#1)}
\citen{LGC97,LWC99,test97,vLeunen:92} but \cite[\S5]{Knuth-CT-a}
```

12-2-9

The package offers a number of options to handle standard configuration requests or to influence the package behavior in other ways. Some of them have already been discussed, but here is the full list:

adjust/noadjust   Enables (default) or disables "smart" handling of space before a \cite or \citen command. By default, spaces before such commands are normalized to an interword space. If you write see\cite{..}, a space is inserted automatically.

compress/nocompress   Enables (default) or disables compression of consecutive numbers into ranges.

sort/nosort   Enables (default) or prevents sorting of the numbers.

space   A full interword space is used after commas, and breaking at this point is not actively discouraged. The default (option not specified) is to use a small space and to discourage, but allow, breaking.

nospace   Eliminates the spaces after commas in the list of numbers, but retains the space after the comma separating the optional note. The result of this option shown in Example 12-2-9 on the previous page. It is not the opposite of the space option!

verbose By default, cite warns only once per reference for undefined citations. When this option is specified, the warning is repeated each time an undefined reference is cited.

The latest release of the cite package can also display citation references as superscript numbers if the package is loaded with the option superscript (or super). In the past this ability was provided by the separate package overcite (developed by the same author), which is still available for compatibility reasons.

Citations with superscript numbers

If the \cite command is used with an optional argument, then the whole list of citations will be typeset as though the cite package was loaded without the superscript option.

With the superscript or super option in effect, the customization commands \citeleft, \citeright, and \citemid affect only citations with an optional argument, while \citedash, \citepunct, and \citeform affect all citations. For details of their use, see the discussion on pages 694–695.

Good information about TeX and LaTeX can be found in.[2,1–4] For hyperref see (1, pp. 35–67).

```
\usepackage[superscript]{cite}  \bibliographystyle{plain}
\usepackage{color}
\renewcommand\citeform[1]{\textcolor{blue}{#1}}
\renewcommand\citeleft{(} \renewcommand\citeright{)}
Good information about \TeX{} and \LaTeX{} can be found in
\cite{LGC97,LWC99,Knuth-CT-a,Knuth:ct-b,Knuth:TB10-1-31}.
For \textttt{hyperref} see \cite[pp.\,35--67]{LWC99}.
```

12-2-10

You will probably not need to change your source document, regardless of whether the superscript option is used. In particular, a space before the citation command will be ignored if the citations are raised. In principle, you can add this option without having to adjust your document sources, provided your writing style does not use the numerical citation as part of the sentence structure, as in the above example.

If superscript numbers are used for citation labels, special care is needed when punctuation characters surround the citation. By default, the cite package automatically moves a punctuation character following a citation in front of the superscript. Punctuation characters that will migrate in this way are stored in the command \CiteMoveChars, with ".,;:" being the default (! and ? are not included, but can be added). A problem that can result from this process is doubling of periods. This case is detected by the package and one punctuation character is suppressed; see the second citation in the next example.

... book;[2] see also
Goossens et al.[1]

```
\usepackage[superscript]{cite}     \bibliographystyle{plain}
\ldots\ book~\cite{Knuth-CT-a}; see also Goossens et al.~\cite{LGC97}.
```

12-2-11

Unfortunately, with capitalized abbreviations or the use of \@ *after* a period, the suppression of double periods fails. Possible workarounds are shown in the

next example. Note, however, that the solution with `U.S.A\@.` only works together
with the cite package, but it gives the wrong spacing if no citation is present (you
are effectively claiming that the sentence ends after the abbreviation)!

et al..[1]	et al.[1]	`\usepackage[super]{cite}` `\bibliographystyle{plain}`
U.S.A..[?]	U.S.A.[?]	`et al.\@ \cite{LGC97}.  \hfil  et al.\ \cite{LGC97}.\par` `U.S.A. \cite{unknown}.  \hfil  U.S.A\@. \cite{unknown}.`

12-2-12

There is yet another pitfall that you may encounter: the final punctuation
character does not migrate inside a preceding quotation—a style, for example, advocated by *The Chicago Manual of Style* [38]. In this case you may have to rewrite
part of your source text accordingly.

	`\usepackage[super]{cite}     \bibliographystyle{plain}`
For details see "The TEXbook".[1] But	`For details see ``The \TeX book'' \cite{Knuth-CT-a}.`
wanted is "The TEXbook."[1]	`But wanted is ``The \TeX book.'' \cite{Knuth-CT-a}`

12-2-13

The main options of the cite package were discussed on page 695. Three more
options related to raising the reference numbers exist. With the option `nomove`
specified, punctuation characters are not migrated before the superscript citation.
With the option `ref` specified, citations with an optional argument have the word
"Ref". prepended. This is internally implemented by changing `\citeleft`, so if
you want a different string or want to change from brackets to, say, parentheses,
you have to redefine the customization commands instead of using this option.

	`\usepackage[super,ref]{cite}  \bibliographystyle{plain}`
Color support is described in "LGC"[2] and the hyperref pack-age in "LWC" [Ref. 1, pp. 35–67].	`Color support is described in ``LGC'' \cite{LGC97} and the` `\texttt{hyperref} package in ``LWC'' \cite[pp.\,35--67]{LWC99}.`

12-2-14

Finally, the `biblabel` option raises the labels in the bibliography. (By default, they retain their default layout regardless of whether you use the option
`superscript` or its alias `super`.)

12.2.3   notoccite—**Solving a problem with unsorted citations**

If you want the publications in the bibliography to appear in exactly the order in
which they are cited in the document, then you should use unsorted citation styles
(e.g., the BIBTEX style `unsrt`). This approach will not work, however, if citations are
present inside headings or float captions. In that case, these citations will also
appear in the table of contents or list of figures, and so on. As a result they will be
moved to the beginning of the bibliography even though they appear much later
in the text.

You can circumvent this problem by specifying an optional argument for
`\caption`, `\section`, or similar commands without the citation, so that no citations will be written into such tables. If you have to use citations in these places,

then a "manual" solution is to first delete any auxiliary files left over from previous LaTeX runs, then run LaTeX once, and then run BibTeX. In that case BibTeX will pick up only citations from the main document. Clearly, this approach is prone to error and you may find that your citation order got mangled after all when you finally see your article in print.

Donald Arseneau developed the small package notoccite to take care of this problem by redefining the internal command `\@starttoc` in such a way that citations do not generate `\citation` commands for BibTeX within the table of contents and similar lists. Simply loading that package will take care of the problem in all cases—provided you have not used some other package that redefines `\@starttoc` (for example, notoccite cannot be combined with hyperref or the AMS document classes).

12.3   The author-date system

Depending on the structure of the sentence, the author-date system normally uses one of two different forms for references: if the author's name appears naturally in the sentence, it is not repeated within the parentheses or brackets; otherwise, both the author's name and the year of publication are used. This style poses an unsolvable problem when LaTeX's standard syntax should be used, as only one command (`\cite`) is available.

Consequently, anyone developing support for the author-date system has had to extend the LaTeX syntax for citing publications. The following example shows the two forms and their implementation (with two new commands) as provided by the natbib system.

Knuth (1989) shows ... This is explained in the authoritative manual on TeX (Knuth, 1986).

```
\usepackage{natbib}
\citet{Knuth:TB10-1-31} shows \ldots\ This is explained
in the authoritative manual on \TeX{}~\citep{Knuth-CT-a}.
```

12-3-1

Extending the LaTeX syntax for citing publications does not solve the problem completely. In order to produce the different forms of citation references needed in the author-date system, the information that is passed back from the bibliography through the optional argument of the `\bibitem` command needs to be structured. Without a special structure it is impossible to pick up the data needed for the textual references (e.g., producing just the year in parentheses). That is, a bibliographical entry like

```
\bibitem[Donald~E. Knuth 1986]{Knuth-CT-a}    Donald~E. Knuth.
  \newblock \emph{The {\TeX}book}, volume~A of \emph{Computers and
    Typesetting}. \newblock Addison-Wesley, Reading, MA, USA, 1986.
```

will allow the `\cite` command to produce "(Donald E. Knuth 1986)" but not "Donald E. Knuth (1986)" or just "Knuth" or just "1986" as well. You also have to ensure that \bibitem does not display the label, but that outcome can be fairly easily arranged.

The solution used by all implementations for author-date support is to introduce a special syntax within the optional argument of \bibitem. In some implementations this structure is fairly simple. For instance, chicago requires only

```
\bibitem[\protect\citeauthoryear{Goossens, Rahtz, and Mittelbach}
                     {Goossens et~al.}{1997}]{LGC97}
```

This information can still be produced manually, if needed. Other packages go much further and encode a lot of information explicitly. For example, jurabib asks for the following kind of argument structure (same publication):

```
\bibitem[{Goossens\jbbfsasep Rahtz\jbbstasep Mittelbach\jbdy {1997}}%
   {}{{0}{}{book}{1997}{}{}{}{xxi + 554}{Reading, MA, USA\bpubaddr {}
   Ad{\-d}i{\-s}on-Wes{\-l}ey Longman\bibbdsep {} 1997}}{{The {\LaTeX}
   Graphics Companion: Illustrating Documents with {\TeX} and {PostScript}}%
   {}{}{}{}{}{}{}{}}]{LGC97}
```

As we shall see (Section 12.5.1), this approach gives a lot of flexibility when referring to the publication, but it is clear that no one wants to produce a bibliography environment with such a structure manually. Hence, the only usable solution in this case is to use an external tool like BibTeX to generate the entries automatically.

12.3.1 Early attempts

Over the years several independent add-on packages have been developed to support the author-date system. Unfortunately, each one introduced a different set of user-level commands. Typically, the add-ons consist of a LaTeX package providing the user commands and one or more BibTeX styles to generate the thebibliography environment with a matching syntax in the optional argument of the \bibitem command.

For example, the chicago package, which aimed to implement the recommendations of *The Chicago Manual of Style* [38], offers the following list of commands (plus variants all ending in NP to omit the parentheses—for example, \citeNP):

(Goossens, Rahtz, and Mittelbach 1997)

(Goossens, Rahtz, and Mittelbach)

Goossens, Rahtz, and Mittelbach (1997)

(Goossens and Rahtz 1999)

(Goossens and Rahtz)

Goossens and Rahtz (1999)

(1999), 1999

```
\usepackage{chicago} \bibliographystyle{chicago}
\cite{LGC97}                        \\
\citeA{LGC97}                       \\
\citeN{LGC97}                       \\
\shortcite{LWC99}                   \\
\shortciteA{LWC99}                  \\
\shortciteN{LWC99}                  \\
\citeyear{LWC99}, \citeyearNP{LWC99}
```

12-3-2

Several BibTeX styles (chicago, chicagoa, jas99, named, and newapa) are compatible with the chicago package. All of them are still in use, even though the package itself is rarely included in LaTeX distributions these days (natbib can be used instead to provide the user-level syntax).

In contrast, only two commands are provided by David Rhead's authordate1–4 package, the original support package for the BibTeX styles authordate1 to authordate4. It implements recommendations by the Cambridge and Oxford University Presses and various British standards.

(Goossens *et al.* , 1997) or (1997)

```
\usepackage{authordate1-4}
\bibliographystyle{authordate2}
\cite{LGC97}  or  \shortcite{LGC97}
```

12-3-3

As a final example we look briefly at the harvard package by Peter Williams and Thorsten Schnier. In contrast to the two previously described packages, harvard has been further developed and updated for LaTeX 2_ε. It implements a number of interesting features. For example, a first citation gives a full author list, whereas a later citation uses an abbreviated list (unless explicitly requested otherwise). The user-level commands are shown in the next example.

(Goossens, Rahtz & Mittelbach 1997)
(Goossens et al. 1997)   second citation
(Goossens, Rahtz & Mittelbach 1997) long names forced
Goossens et al. (1997)
(e.g., Goossens et al. 1997)
Goossens et al.
Knuth's (1986)

```
\usepackage{harvard}
\bibliographystyle{agsm}
\cite{LGC97}                                  \\
\cite{LGC97} \hfill second citation  \\
\cite*{LGC97}\hfill long names forced\\
\citeasnoun{LGC97}                       \\
\citeaffixed{LGC97}{e.g.,}             \\
\citename{LGC97}                          \\
\possessivecite{Knuth-CT-a}
```

12-3-4

The harvard package requires a specially prepared bibliography environment in which \bibitem is replaced by \harvarditem, a command with a special syntax used to carry the information needed for author-date citations. A few BibTeX styles (including agsm, dcu, kluwer, and nederlands) implement this special syntax.

Many of these packages support the author-date system quite well. Nevertheless, with different packages using their own syntax and supporting only half a dozen BibTeX styles each, the situation stayed unsatisfactory for a long time. Matters changed for the better when Patrick Daly published his natbib support package, described in the next section.

12.3.2 natbib—Customizable author-date references

Although most publishers will indicate which bibliographic style they prefer, it is not always evident how to change from one system to the other if one has to prepare source texts adhering to multiple styles.

To solve the problem of incompatible syntaxes described in the previous section, Patrick Daly developed the natbib package (for "NATural sciences BIBliography"). This package can accept several \bibitem variants (including \harvarditem) as produced by the different BibTeX styles. Thus, for the first time, (nearly) all of the author-date BibTeX styles could be used with a single user-level syntax for the citation commands.

The natbib package is compatible with packages like babel, chapterbib, hyperref, index, and showkeys, and with various document classes including the standard LaTeX classes, amsbook and amsart, classes from the KOMA-Script bundle, and memoir. It cannot be used together with the cite package, but provides similar sorting and compressing functions via options.

The natbib package therefore acts as a single, flexible interface for most of the available bibliographic styles when the author-date system is required. It can also be used to produce numerical references, as we will see in Section 12.4.1.

The basic syntax

The two central commands of natbib are \citet (for textual citation) and \citep (for parenthetical citation).

```
\citet[post-note]{key-list}     \citet[pre-note][post-note]{key-list}
\citep[post-note]{key-list}     \citep[pre-note][post-note]{key-list}
```

Both commands take one mandatory argument (the *key-list* that refers to one or more publications) and one or two optional arguments to add text before and after the citation. LaTeX's standard \cite command can take only a single optional argument denoting a *post-note*. For this reason the commands implement the following syntax: with only one optional argument specified, this argument denotes the *post note* (i.e., a note placed after the citation); with two optional arguments specified, the first denotes a *pre-note* and the second a *post-note*. To get only a *pre-note* you have to add an empty second argument, as seen in lines 4 and 8 in the next example. Also note that natbib redefines \cite to act like \citet.[1]

Goossens et al. (1997)	`\usepackage{natbib}`
Goossens et al. (1997, chap. 2)	`\citet{LGC97}` \\
Goossens et al. (see 1997, chap. 2)	`\citet[chap.~2]{LGC97}` \\
pre-note only: Goossens et al. (see 1997)	`\citet[see][chap.~2]{LGC97}` \\
	`pre-note only: \citet[see][]{LGC97}` \\[5pt]
(Goossens et al., 1997)	`\citep{LGC97}` \\
(Goossens et al., 1997, chap. 2)	`\citep[chap.~2]{LGC97}` \\
(see Goossens et al., 1997, chap. 2)	`\citep[see][chap.~2]{LGC97}` \\
pre-note only: (see Goossens et al., 1997)	`pre-note only: \citep[see][]{LGC97}`

12-3-5

---

[1] To be precise, \cite is redefined to act like \citet if natbib is used in author-date mode as discussed in this section. If used in author-number mode (see Section 12.4.1), it works like \citep.

Both commands have starred versions, \citet* and \citep* (with otherwise identical syntax), that will print the full list of authors if it is known.[1] These versions will work only when this feature is supported by the used BibTeX style file. In other words, the information must be made available through the optional argument of \bibitem; if it is missing, the abbreviated list is always printed.

Goossens, Rahtz, and Mittelbach (1997)
(see Goossens, Rahtz, and Mittelbach, 1997)

```
\usepackage{natbib}
\citet*{LGC97}                       \\
\citep*[see][]{LGC97}
```

12-3-6

Two other variant forms exist: \citealt works like \citet but does not generate parentheses, and \citealp is \citep without parentheses. Evidently, some of the typeset results come out almost identically.

Goossens et al. 1997
Goossens et al., 1997
Goossens, Rahtz, and Mittelbach 1997
Goossens, Rahtz, and Mittelbach, 1997
Goossens and Rahtz, 1999, p. 236 etc.

```
\usepackage{natbib}
\citealt{LGC97}                      \\
\citealp{LGC97}                      \\
\citealt*{LGC97}                     \\
\citealp*{LGC97}                     \\
\citealp[p.~236]{LWC99} etc.
```

12-3-7

When using the author-date system it is sometimes desirable to just cite the author(s) or the year. For this purpose natbib provides the following additional commands (\citeauthor* is the same as \citeauthor when the full author information is unavailable):

Goossens et al.
Goossens, Rahtz, and Mittelbach
1997 or (1997)

```
\usepackage{natbib}
\citeauthor{LGC97}                      \\
\citeauthor*{LGC97}                     \\
\citeyear{LGC97}  or  \citeyearpar{LGC97}
```

12-3-8

Even more complex mixtures of text and citation information can be handled with the command \citetext. It takes one mandatory argument and surrounds it with the parentheses used by other citation commands. By combining this command with \citealp or other commands that do not produce parentheses, all sorts of combinations become possible.

(see Goossens et al., 1997 or Knuth, 1986)

```
\usepackage{natbib}
\citetext{see \citealp{LGC97} or \citealp{Knuth-CT-a}}
```

12-3-9

Forcing names to upper case

Sometimes a sentence starts with a citation, but the (first) author of the cited publication has a name that starts with a lowercase letter. In that case the commands discussed so far cannot be used. The natbib package solves this problem by providing for all commands variants that capitalize the first letter. They are

---

[1] If you plan to also use the jurabib package (see Section 12.5.1), then avoid the starred forms as they are not supported by that package.

easy to remember: just capitalize the first letter of the corresponding original command. For example, instead of \citet*, use \Citet*. Here are some additional examples.

Normal citation: van Leunen (92)
Van Leunen (92) or Van Leunen 92
(Van Leunen, 92) or Van Leunen, 92
Van Leunen

```
\usepackage{natbib}

Normal citation: \citet{vLeunen:92}        \\
\Citet{vLeunen:92} or \Citealt{vLeunen:92}  \\
\Citep{vLeunen:92} or \Citealp{vLeunen:92}  \\
\Citeauthor{vLeunen:92}
```

12-3-10

As a final goody, natbib lets you define alternative text for a citation that can be used instead of the usual author-date combination. For the definition use \defcitealias (usually in the preamble), and for the retrieval use \citetalias or \citepalias.

Goossens et al. (1997) = Dogbook II
(Goossens et al., 1997) = (Dogbook II)
Alias changed: (see Dogbook II 2ed)

```
\usepackage{natbib} \defcitealias{LGC97}{Dogbook~II}

\citet{LGC97} = \citetalias{LGC97}    \\
\citep{LGC97} = \citepalias{LGC97}   \par
\defcitealias{LGC97}{Dogbook~II~2ed}
Alias changed: \citepalias[see][]{LGC97}
```

12-3-11

With the commands introduced in this section, natbib offers the same features (with minor differences) as other support packages for the author-date system (e.g., the packages described in Section 12.3.1). In addition, it provides features not found elsewhere. On the other hand, in a few cases natbib does not offer directly equivalent commands. For example, harvard's \possessivecite command (shown in Example 12-3-4) has no direct correspondence in natbib, but it can be easily built manually. To emulate it, you can either directly use \citeauthor and \citeyearpar, as is done in the first line of the next example, or define your own command if this type of construction is used more often.

Knuth's (1986)
Knuth's (1986)

```
\usepackage{natbib} \bibliographystyle{agsm}
\newcommand\possessivecite[1]{\citeauthor{#1}'s \citeyearpar{#1}}
\citeauthor{Knuth-CT-a}'s \citeyearpar{Knuth-CT-a} \\
\possessivecite{Knuth-CT-a}
```

12-3-12

Multiple citations

In standard LaTeX, multiple citations can be made by including more than one citation *key-list* argument to the \cite command. The same is possible for the citation commands \citet and \citep (as well as their variant forms). The natbib package then automatically checks whether adjacent citations in the *key-list* have the same author designation. If so, it prints the author names only once. This feature requires that the author names be spelled identically. For instance, natbib will consider "D. Knuth" and "Donald Knuth" to be two different authors.

Goossens et al. (1997); Goossens and Rahtz (1999)
(Goossens et al., 1997; Goossens and Rahtz, 1999)
(Knuth, 1989, 1986)

```
\usepackage{natbib}
\citet{LGC97,LWC99}        \\
\citep{LGC97,LWC99}        \\
\citep{Knuth:TB10-1-31,Knuth-CT-a}
```

12-3-13

The last line in the previous example exhibits a potential problem when using several keys in one citation command: the references are typeset in the order of the *key-list*. If you specify the option sort, then the citations are sorted into the order in which they appear in the bibliography, usually alphabetical by author and then by year.

(Knuth, 1986, 1989)

```
\usepackage[sort]{natbib}
\citep{Knuth:TB10-1-31,Knuth-CT-a}
```

12-3-14

While all the citation commands support *key-lists* with more than one citation key, they are best confined to \citep; already \citet gives questionable results. The situation gets worse when you use optional arguments: with \citet any *prenote* is added before each year (which could be considered a defect in the package). More generally, it is not at all clear what these notes are supposed to refer to. Hence, if you want to add notes it is better to separate your citations.

(see van Leunen, 92; Knuth, 1986, p. 55)
(see Knuth, 1986, 1989, p. 55)
van Leunen (see 92); Knuth (see 1986, p. 55)
Knuth (see 1986, 1989, p. 55)

```
\usepackage{natbib}
\citep[see][p.~55]{vLeunen:92,Knuth-CT-a}  \\
\citep[see][p.~55]{Knuth-CT-a,Knuth:TB10-1-31} \\
\citet[see][p.~55]{vLeunen:92,Knuth-CT-a}  \\
\citet[see][p.~55]{Knuth-CT-a,Knuth:TB10-1-31}
```

12-3-15

Full author list only with the first citation

The harvard package automatically typesets the first citation of a publication with the full list of authors and subsequent citations with an abbreviated list. This style of citation is quite popular in some disciplines, and natbib supports it if you load it with the option longnamesfirst. Compare the next example to Example 12-3-4 on page 700.

(Goossens, Rahtz & Mittelbach 1997)   first citation
(Goossens et al. 1997)   second
(Goossens, Rahtz & Mittelbach 1997) names forced
Goossens et al. (1997)
(e.g., Goossens et al. 1997)
Goossens et al.

```
\usepackage[longnamesfirst]{natbib}
\bibliographystyle{agsm}
\citep{LGC97} \hfill first citation  \\
\citep{LGC97} \hfill         second  \\
\citep*{LGC97}\hfill    names forced  \\
\citet{LGC97}                         \\
\citep[e.g.,][]{LGC97}                \\
\citeauthor{LGC97}
```

12-3-16

Some BibTeX style files are quite cleverly programmed. For example, when the agsm BibTeX style, used in the previous example, detects that shortening a list of authors leads to ambiguous citations, it will refuse to produce an abbreviated list. Thus, after adding the `test97` citation to the example, all citations suddenly come out in long form.[1] BibTeX styles produced with `makebst` avoid such ambiguous citations by adding a suffix to the year, but other BibTeX styles (e.g., `chicago`) happily produce them; see Example 12-3-18 below.

```
                                                      \usepackage[longnamesfirst]{natbib}
                                                      \bibliographystyle{agsm}
(Goossens, Rahtz & Mittelbach 1997)   first citation  \citep{LGC97} \hfill  first citation  \\
(Goossens, Rahtz & Mittelbach 1997)        second      \citep{LGC97} \hfill           second  \\
(Goossens, User & Doe 1997)          first citation    \citep{test97}\hfill  first citation  \\
(Goossens, User & Doe 1997)         second citation    \citep{test97}\hfill second citation
```

12-3-17

Some publications have so many authors that you may want to always cite them using their abbreviated name list, even the first time. You can achieve this effect by listing their keys, separated by commas, in the argument of the `\shortcites` declaration. This example also shows that use of the `chicago` style can lead to ambiguous citations (lines 1 and 2 versus line 5).

```
                                                        \usepackage[longnamesfirst]{natbib}
                                                        \bibliographystyle{chicago}
                                                        \shortcites{LGC97}
(Goossens et al., 1997)                 first citation  \citep{LGC97} \hfill  first citation \\
(Goossens et al., 1997)                second citation  \citep{LGC97} \hfill second citation \\
(Goossens, Rahtz, and Mittelbach, 1997)        forced   \citep*{LGC97}\hfill          forced \\
(Goossens, User, and Doe, 1997)         first citation  \citep{test97}\hfill  first citation \\
(Goossens et al., 1997)                second citation  \citep{test97}\hfill second citation
```

12-3-18

Customizing the citation reference layout

So far, all of the examples have shown round parentheses around the citations, but this is by no means the only possibility offered by natbib. The package internally knows about more than 20 BibTeX styles. If any such style is chosen with a `\bibliographystyle` command, then a layout appropriate for this style is selected as well. For example, when using the agu style (American Geophysics Union) we get:

```
Goossens et al. [1997]                  \usepackage{natbib} \bibliographystyle{agu}
[Knuth, 1986; Goossens and Rahtz, 1999] \citet{LGC97}  \\  \citep{Knuth-CT-a,LWC99} \\
[see Knuth, 1986, chap. 2]              \citep[see][chap.~2]{Knuth-CT-a}
```

12-3-19

By default, the citation layout is determined by the chosen BibTeX style (or natbib's defaults if a given style is unknown to natbib). By including a `\citestyle` declaration you can request to use the citation style associated with a BibTeX style that is different from the one used to format the bibliography. In the next example

---

[1] Something that puzzled the author when he first encountered it while preparing the examples.

we use the `agsm` style for the citations while the overall style remains `agu`. If you compare this example to Example 12-3-19 you see that the textual formatting is unchanged (e.g., italic for author names), but the parentheses and the separation between authors and year have both changed.

Goossens et al. (1997)	`\usepackage{natbib} \bibliographystyle{agu}`
(*Knuth* 1986, *Goossens and Rahtz* 1999)	`\citestyle{agsm}`
(see *Knuth* 1986, chap. 2)	`\citet{LGC97}  \\  \citep{Knuth-CT-a,LWC99} \\`
	`\citep[see][chap.~2]{Knuth-CT-a}`

12-3-20

It is also possible to influence the layout by supplying options: `round` (default for most styles), `square`, `curly`, or `angle` will change the type of parentheses used, while `colon`[1] (default for most styles) and `comma` will change the separation between multiple citations. In the next example, we overwrite the defaults set by the `agu` style, by loading `natbib` with two options.

Goossens et al. {1997}	`\usepackage[curly,comma]{natbib}`
{*Knuth*, 1986, *Goossens and Rahtz*, 1999}	`\bibliographystyle{agu}`
{see *Knuth*, 1986, chap. 2}	`\citet{LGC97}  \\  \citep{Knuth-CT-a,LWC99} \\`
	`\citep[see][chap.~2]{Knuth-CT-a}`

12-3-21

Yet another method to customize the layout is mainly intended for package and/or class file writers: the `\bibpunct` declaration. It takes seven arguments (the first optional) that define various aspects of the citation format. It is typically used to define the default citation format for a particular BibTeX style. For example, the `natbib` package contains many definitions like this:

```
\newcommand\bibstyle@chicago{\bibpunct{(}{)}{;}{a}{,}{,}}
```

That definition will be selected when you choose `chicago` as your BibTeX style or when you specify it as the argument to `\citestyle`. Similar declarations can be added for BibTeX styles that `natbib` does not directly support. This effect is most readily realized by grouping such declarations in the local configuration file `natbib.cfg`. For details on the meanings of the arguments, see the documentation accompanying the `natbib` package.

If there are conflicting specifications, then the following rules apply: the lowest priority is given to internal `\bibstyle@`⟨*name*⟩ declarations, followed by the options specified in the `\usepackage` declarations. Both are overwritten by an explicit `\bibpunct` or `\citestyle` declaration in the document preamble.

Forcing all author names on a single line

Normally, `natbib` does not prevent a line break within the author list of a citation. By specifying the option `nonamebreak`, you can ensure that all author names in one citation will be kept on a single line. In normal circumstances this is seldom a good idea as it is likely to cause overfull hboxes, but it helps with some `hyperref` problems.

---

[1]Despite its name this option will produce a ";" semicolon.

Customizing the bibliography layout

The thebibliography environment, as implemented by natbib, automatically adds a heading before the list of publications. By default, natbib selects an unnumbered heading of the highest level, such as \chapter* for a book type class or \section* for the article class or a variant thereof. The actual heading inserted is stored in the command \bibsection. Thus, to modify the default, you have to change its definition. For instance, you can suppress the heading altogether or choose a numbered heading.

For one particular situation natbib offers direct support: if you specify the option sectionbib, you instruct the package to use \section*, even if the highest sectional unit is \chapter. This option is useful if natbib and chapterbib are used together (see Section 12.6.1).

Between \bibsection and the start of the list, natbib executes the hook \bibpreamble, if defined. It allows you to place some text between the heading and the start of the actual reference list. It is also possible to influence the font used for the bibliography by defining the command \bibfont. This hook can also be used to influence the list in other ways, such as setting it unjustified by adding \raggedright. Note that both \bibpreamble and \bibfont are undefined by default (and thus need \newcommand), while \bibsection needs redefining with \renewcommand.

Finally, two length parameters are available for customization. The first line in each reference is set flush left, and all following lines are indented by the value stored in \bibhang (default 1em). The vertical space between the references is stored in the rubber length \bibsep (the default value is usually equal to \itemsep as defined in other lists).

To show the various possibilities available we repeat Example 12-1-2 on page 685 but apply all kinds of customization features (not necessarily for the better!). Note the presence of \par at the end of \bibpreamble. Without it the settings in \bibfont would affect the inserted text!

Multiple authors might be problematical, e.g., Goossens et al. [1997a] and Goossens et al. [1997b] or even Goossens et al. [1997a,b]. But then it might not.

1 References

Some material inserted between heading and list.

M. Goossens, S. Rahtz, and F. Mittelbach. *The LATEX Graphics Companion: Illustrating Documents with TEX and PostScript.* Tools and Techniques for Computer Typesetting. Addison-Wesley Longman, Reading, MA, USA, 1997a. ISBN 0-201-85469-4.

M. Goossens, B. User, and J. Doe. Ambiguous citations. Submitted to the IBM J. Res. Dev., 1997b.

```
\usepackage{natbib}
\bibliographystyle{abbrvnat}
\renewcommand\bibsection{\section{\refname}}
\newcommand\bibpreamble{Some material
        inserted between heading and list.\par}
\newcommand\bibfont
                  {\footnotesize\raggedright}
\setlength\bibhang{30pt}
\setlength\bibsep{1pt plus 1pt}

Multiple authors might be problematical,
e.g., \cite{LGC97} and \cite{test97} or even
\cite{LGC97,test97}. But then it might not.

\bibliography{tex}
```

12-3-22

Publications without author or year information

To use the author-date citation system, the entries in your list of publications need to contain the necessary information. If some information is missing, citations with \citet or its variants may produce strange results.

If the publication has no author but an editor, then most BibTeX styles will use the latter. However, if both are missing, the solutions implemented differ greatly. BibTeX files in "Harvard" style (e.g., agsm) use the first three letters from the key field if present; otherwise, they use the first three letters from the organization field (omitting "The␣" if necessary); otherwise, they use the full title. If an entry has no year, then "n.d." is used. This will result in usable entries except in the case where part of the key field is selected:

Koppitz (n.d.) / *TUGboat The Communications of the TeX User Group* (1980ff) / mak (2000)

```
\usepackage{natbib} \bibliographystyle{agsm}
\citet{G-G} / \citet{oddity} / \citet{GNUMake}
```
12-3-23

With the same entries, BibTeX styles produced with makebst (e.g., unsrtnat) use the following strategy: if a key field is present, the whole field is used as an "author"; otherwise, if an organization field is specified, its first three letters are used (omitting "The␣" if necessary); otherwise, the first three letters of the citation label are used. A missing year is completely omitted. In case of textual citations, this means that only the author name is printed. In that situatiuin, or when the key field is used, it is probably best to avoid \citet and always use \citep to make it clear to the reader that you are actually referring to a publication and not just mentioning some person in passing.

Koppitz / odd [1980ff] / make
[Koppitz] / [odd, 1980ff] / [make]

```
\usepackage{natbib} \bibliographystyle{unsrtnat}
\citet{G-G} / \citet{oddity} / \citet{GNUMake} \\
\citep{G-G} / \citep{oddity} / \citep{GNUMake}
```
12-3-24

As a final example we show the results when using chicago. Here the GNU manual comes out fine (the full organization name is used), but the entry with the date missing looks odd.

Koppitz (Koppitz) / odd (80ff) / Free Software Foundation (2000)
(Koppitz, Koppitz) / (odd, 80ff) / (Free Software Foundation, 2000)

```
\usepackage{natbib} \bibliographystyle{chicago}
\citet{G-G} / \citet{oddity} / \citet{GNUMake} \\
\citep{G-G} / \citep{oddity} / \citep{GNUMake}
```
12-3-25

Forcing author-date style

The natbib package produces author-date citations by default, when used together with most BibTeX styles. You can also explicitly request the author-date system by loading the package with the option authoryear.

However, for this approach to work, it is important that the BibTeX style passes author-date information back to the document. Hence, .bst files, such as LaTeX's plain, which have been developed for numerical citation systems only, are unable to transfer this information. In that case natbib will ignore the authoryear option and, if you use \citet or one of its variants, you get warnings about missing author information and output similar to the following:

```
\usepackage{natbib} \bibliographystyle{plain}
```

| 12-3-26 |

(author?) [3] / **(author?)** [1] / **(author?)** [2]   `\citet{G-G} / \citet{oddity} / \citet{GNUMake}`

Here it is best to switch to a BIBTEX style that supports the author-date system, such as plainnat instead of plain.

Indexing citations automatically

Citations can be entered in the index by inserting a \citeindextrue command at any point in the document. From that point onward, and until the next \citeindexfalse (or the end of the current group) is encountered, all variants of the \citet and \citep commands will generate entries in the index file (if one is written). With \citeindextrue in effect, the \bibitem commands in the thebibliography environment will also generate index entries. If this result is not desired, issue a \citeindexfalse command before entering the environment (e.g., before calling \bibliography).

The index format is controlled by the internal command \NAT@idxtxt. It has the following default definition:

```
\newcommand\NAT@idxtxt{\NAT@name\ \NAT@open\NAT@date\NAT@close}
```

Thus, it produces entries like "Knuth (1986)". For citations without author or year information the results will most likely come out strangely. The citations in Example 12-3-24 will generate the following entries:

```
\indexentry{{Koppitz}\ []}{6}
\indexentry{{odd}\ [1980ff]}{6}
\indexentry{{make}\ []}{6}
```

If you want to redefine the command, for example, to just generate the author's name, you can do so in the file natbib.cfg or in the preamble of your document. In the latter case, do not forget \makeatletter and \makeatother!

It is also possible to produce a separate index of citations by using David Jones's index package (see Section 11.4.3). It allows you to generate multiple index lists using the \newindex command. For this to work you must first declare the list and then associate automatic citation indexing with this list in the preamble:

```
\usepackage{index}
\newindex{default}{idx}{ind}{Index}                    % the main index
\newindex{cite}{cdx}{cnd}{Index of Citations}
\renewcommand\citeindextype{cite}
```

Later on use \printindex[cite] to indicate where the citation index should appear in the document.

BⅰʙTᴇX styles for natbib

As mentioned in the introduction, natbib was developed to work with various BⅰʙTᴇX styles that implement some form of author-date scheme. In addition to those third-party styles, natbib works with all styles that can be produced with the custom-bib bundle (see Section 13.5.2 on page 798). It is distributed with three styles—abbrvnat, plainnat, and unsrtnat—that are extensions of the corresponding standard styles. They have been adapted to work better with natbib, allowing you to use some of its features that would be otherwise unavailable. These styles also implement a number of extra fields useful in the days of electronic publications:

doi   For use with electronic journals and related material. The Digital Object Identifier (DOI) is a system for identifying and exchanging intellectual property in the digital environment, and is supposedly more robust than URLs (see http://www.doi.org for details). The field is optional.

eid   As electronic journals usually have no page numbers, they use a sequence identifier (EID) to locate the printed version. The field is optional and will be used in place of the page number if present.

isbn   The International Standard Book Number (ISBN), a 10-digit unique identification number (see www.isbn.org). The ISBN is defined in ISO Standard 2108 and has been in use for more than 30 years. The field is optional.

issn   The International Standard Serial Number (ISSN), an 8-digit number that identifies periodical publications (see www.issn.org). The field is optional.

url   The Uniform Resource Locator (URL) for identifying resources on the web. The field is optional. As URL addresses are typically quite long and are set in a typewriter font, line-breaking problems may occur. They are therefore automatically surrounded with a \url command, which is given a simple default definition if undefined. Thus, by using the url package (see Section 3.1.8), you can drastically improve the line-breaking situation as then URLs can be broken at punctuation marks.

12.3.3   bibentry—Full bibliographic entries in running text

Instead of grouping all cited publications in a bibliography, it is sometimes required to directly typeset the full information the first time a publication is referenced. To help with this task Patrick Daly developed the bibentry package as a companion to the natbib package.

```
\nobibliography{BIBTEX-database-list}      \bibentry{key}
```

This command works as follows: instead of the usual `\bibliography` command, which loads the `.bbl` file written by BIBTEX and typesets the bibliography, you use `\nobibliography` with the same list of BIBTEX database files. This command will read the `.bbl` and process the information, so that references to entries can be made elsewhere in the document. To typeset a citation with the full bibliographical information, use `\bibentry`. The usual author-date citation can be produced with any of the natbib commands. Here is an example:

```
\usepackage{bibentry,natbib}
\bibliographystyle{agu}
```

For details see Knuth, D. E., Typesetting Concrete Mathematics, *TUGboat*, *10*, 31–36, 1989. General information can be found in Knuth, D. E., *The TEXbook*, vol. A of *Computers and Typesetting*, Addison-Wesley, Reading, MA, USA, 1986.

As shown by *Knuth* [1989] ...

```
\raggedright \setlength\parindent{12pt}
\nobibliography{tex}
For details see \bibentry{Knuth:TB10-1-31}.
General information can be found in
\bibentry{Knuth-CT-a}.

As shown by \citet{Knuth:TB10-1-31} \ldots
```

12-3-27

There are a number of points to be noted here: the `\nobibliography` command must be placed inside the body of the document but before the first use of a `\bibentry` command. In the preamble a `\nobibliography` will be silently ignored, and any `\bibentry` command used before it will produce no output. Such a command is therefore best placed directly after `\begin{document}`.

Potential pitfalls

Another potential problem relates to the choice of BIBTEX style. The bibentry package requires the entries in the `.bbl` file to be of a certain form: they must be separated by a blank line, and the `\bibitem` command must be separated from the actual entry text by either a space or a newline character. This format is automatically enforced for BIBTEX styles produced with makebst but other BIBTEX styles may fail, including some that work with natbib.

The `\bibentry` command automatically removes a final period in the entry so that the reference can be used in mid-sentence. However, if the entry contains other punctuation, such as a period as part of a note field, the resulting text might still read strangely. In that case the only remedy might be to use an adjusted BIBTEX database entry.

One can simultaneously have a bibliography and use the `\bibentry` command to produce full citations in the text. In that case, place the `\bibliography` command to produce the bibliography list at the point where it should appear. Directly following `\begin{document}`, add the command `\nobibliography*`. This variant takes no argument, because the BIBTEX database files are already specified on the `\bibliography` command. As a consequence, all publications cited with `\bibentry` will also automatically appear in the bibliography, because a single `.bbl` file is used.

12.4 The author-number system

As mentioned in the introduction, currently there exists no BibTeX style file that implements the author-number system for documents in which the publications should be numbered individually for each author. If, however, the publications are numbered sequentially throughout the whole bibliography, then ample support is provided by BibTeX and by the natbib package already encountered in conjunction with the author-date system.

12.4.1 natbib—Revisited

Although originally designed to support the author-date system, natbib is also capable of producing author-number and number-only references. Both types of references are provided with the help of BibTeX styles specially designed for numbered bibliographies, similar to the BibTeX styles normally used for the author-date style of citations.

By default, natbib produces author-date citations. If you are primarily interested in citing references according to the number-only or author-number system, load natbib with the numbers option.

For comparison, we repeat Example 12-3-5 on page 701 with the numbers option loaded. This option automatically implies the options square and comma; thus, if you prefer round parentheses, use the option round and overwrite the default choice.

```
                                       \usepackage[numbers]{natbib}
Goossens et al. [1]                    \citet{LGC97}                        \\
Goossens et al. [1, chap. 2]           \citet[chap.~2]{LGC97}               \\
Goossens et al. [see 1, chap. 2]       \citet[see][chap.~2]{LGC97}          \\
pre-note only: Goossens et al. [see 1] pre-note only: \citet[see][]{LGC97}  \\[5pt]
[1]                                    \citep{LGC97}                        \\
[1, chap. 2]                           \citep[chap.~2]{LGC97}               \\
[see 1, chap. 2]                       \citep[see][chap.~2]{LGC97}          \\
pre-note only: [see 1]                 pre-note only: \citep[see][]{LGC97}
```

12-4-1

As you can see, the \citet command now generates citations according to the author-number system, while \citep produces number-only citations. In fact, if natbib is set up to produce numerical citations, LaTeX's \cite command behaves like \citep. In author-date mode, natbib makes this command act as short form for the command \citet.

All variant forms of \citet and \citep, as discussed in Section 12.3.2, are also available in numerical mode, though only a few make sense. For example, \citep* gives the same output as \citep, because there are no authors inside the parentheses.

Goossens, Rahtz, and Mittelbach [1]
Goossens et al.
Goossens, Rahtz, and Mittelbach
1997 or [1997]

```
\usepackage[numbers]{natbib}
\citet*{LGC97}                      \\
\citeauthor{LGC97}                  \\
\citeauthor*{LGC97}                 \\
\citeyear{LGC97}   or   \citeyearpar{LGC97}
```

12-4-2

The commands \citealt and \citealt* should probably not be used, as without the parentheses the citation number is likely to be misinterpreted. However, in certain situations \citep might be useful to obtain that number on its own and then perhaps use it together with \citetext.

Goossens et al. 1
Goossens, Rahtz, and Mittelbach 1
1
1, p. 236 etc.

```
\usepackage[numbers]{natbib}
\citealt{LGC97}                     \\
\citealt*{LGC97}                    \\
\citealp{LGC97}                     \\
\citealp[p.~236]{LGC97} etc.
```

12-4-3

Some journals use numerical citations with the numbers raised as superscripts. If loaded with the option super, the natbib package supports this type of citation. In that case our standard example (compare with Example 12-4-1) will produce the following:

Goossens et al.[1]
Goossens et al.[1], chap. 2
Goossens et al. see[1], chap. 2
pre-note only: Goossens et al. see[1]

[1]

[1] (chap. 2)
[1] (chap. 2)
pre-note only:[1]

```
\usepackage[super]{natbib}
\citet{LGC97}                                  \\
\citet[chap.~2]{LGC97}                         \\
\citet[see][chap.~2]{LGC97}                    \\
pre-note only: \citet[see][]{LGC97}   \\[5pt]
\citep{LGC97}                                  \\
\citep[chap.~2]{LGC97}                         \\
\citep[see][chap.~2]{LGC97}                    \\
pre-note only: \citep[see][]{LGC97}
```

12-4-4

As you will observe, the use of the optional arguments produces somewhat questionable results; in the case of \citep the *pre-note* will not appear at all. Thus, with this style of citation, it is usually best to stick to the basic forms of any such commands.

For superscript citations natbib removes possible spaces in front of the citation commands so as to attach the number to the preceding word. However, in contrast to the results produced with the cite package, punctuation characters will not migrate in front of the citation, nor is there any check for double periods. To illustrate this we repeat Example 12-2-11 from page 696.

...Knuth's book[2]; see also
Goossens et al.[1].
...Knuth's book;[2] see also
Goossens et al.[1]

```
\usepackage[super]{natbib}
\ldots Knuth's book~\citep{Knuth-CT-a}; see also \citet{LGC97}.
\par %%% Manually corrected in two places:
\ldots Knuth's book;\citep{Knuth-CT-a}  see also \citet{LGC97}
```

12-4-5

The packages natbib and cite are unfortunately incompatible (both modify LaTeX's internal citation mechanism), so in cases like Example 12-4-5 you have to change the input if natbib is to be used.

Sorting and compressing numerical citations

As seen in Section 12.2.2 the cite package sorts multiple citations and optionally compresses them into ranges. This feature is also implemented by natbib and can be activated through the options sort and sort&compress.

We have already encountered sort in connection with author-date citations. With numerical citations (i.e., the options numbers and super), the numbers are sorted. To show the effect we repeat Example 12-2-5 from page 693, except that we omit the undefined citation.

Good information about TeX and LaTeX can be found in [1, 2, 3, 4].

```
\usepackage[sort]{natbib} \bibliographystyle{plain}
Good information about \TeX{} and \LaTeX{} can be found in
\citep{LGC97,LWC99,Knuth-CT-a,Knuth:TB10-1-31}.
```

12-4-6

With the option sort&compress, the numbers are not only sorted but also compressed into ranges if possible. In author-date citation mode, this option has the same effect as sort.

Good information about TeX and LaTeX can be found in [1–4].

```
\usepackage[sort&compress]{natbib}\bibliographystyle{plain}
Good information about \TeX{} and \LaTeX{} can be found in
\citep{LGC97,LWC99,Knuth-CT-a,Knuth:TB10-1-31}.
```

12-4-7

The rules for selecting numerical mode

As mentioned previously, natbib, by default, works in author-date mode. However, for the previous two examples, natbib selected numerical mode without being explicitly told to do so (via the numbers or super option). This result occurs because the plain BibTeX style does not carry author-date information in the \bibitem commands it generates. Whenever there is a single \bibitem without the relevant information, natbib automatically switches to numerical mode. Even specifying the option authoryear will not work in that case.

If a BibTeX style supports author-date mode, then switching to numerical mode can be achieved by one of the following methods, which are listed here in increasing order of priority:

1. By selecting a \bibliographystyle with a predefined numerical citation style (e.g., defined in a local configuration file, or in a class or package file).

2. By specifying the option numbers or super, as shown in most examples in this section.

3. By explicitly using \bibpunct with the fourth mandatory argument set to n or s (for details, see the package documentation).

4. By explicitly using \citestyle with the name of a predefined numerical bibliography style.

Customizing natbib in numerical mode

The majority of options and parameters to customize natbib have already been discussed on pages 705–707, but in numerical mode there are two more commands available to modify the produced layout. By default, citation numbers are typeset in the main body font. However, if you define \citenumfont (as a command with one argument), it will format the citation number according to its specification.

Similarly, you can manipulate the format of the number as typeset within the bibliography by redefining \bibnumfmt using \renewcommand.[1] The default definition for this command usually produces square brackets around the number.

Images are discussed elsewhere, see (**1**, **2**).

References

1. M. Goossens, S. Rahtz, and F. Mittelbach. *The LaTeX Graphics Companion: Illustrating Documents with TeX and PostScript.* Tools and Techniques for Computer Typesetting. Addison-Wesley Longman, Reading, MA, USA, 1997. ISBN 0-201-85469-4.

2. D. E. Knuth. *The TeXbook*, volume A of *Computers and Typesetting*. Addison-Wesley, Reading, MA, USA, 1986. ISBN 0-201-13447-0.

```
\usepackage[numbers,round]{natbib}
\bibliographystyle{abbrvnat}
\newcommand\bibfont{\small\raggedright}
\setlength\bibhang{30pt}        % ignored!
\setlength\bibsep{1pt plus 1pt}
\newcommand\citenumfont[1]{\textbf{#1}}
\renewcommand\bibnumfmt[1]{\textbf{#1.}}
```

Images are discussed elsewhere,
see \citep{LGC97,Knuth-CT-a}.

```
\bibliography{tex}
```

12-4-8

While \bibsection, \bibpreamble, \bibfont, and \bibsep work as before, the parameter \bibhang has no effect, since in a numbered bibliography the indentation is defined by the width of the largest number.

12.5 The short-title system

12.5.1 jurabib—Customizable short-title references

Classifying the jurabib package developed by Jens Berger as a package implementing the short-title system is not really doing it justice (no pun intended), as in fact it actually supports other citation systems as well.

Besides short-title citations it offers support for author-date citations (by providing the natbib command interface), various options to handle specific requirements from the humanities, and special support for citing juridical works such as commentaries (hence the name jurabib).

---

[1]The package is unfortunately somewhat inconsistent in providing or not providing defaults for the customization hooks. This means that you have to use either \newcommand or \renewcommand depending on the context.

The package uses an extended option concept where options are specified with a "*key=value*" syntax. The package supports more than 30 options, each of which may be set to a number of values, covering various aspects of presenting the citation layout in the text and the references in the bibliography. In this book we can show only a small selection of these possibilities. For further information refer to the package documentation, which is available in English and German.

Default used for all examples in this section!
It is inconvenient to handle so many options as part of the \usepackage declaration, so jurabib offers the \jurabibsetup command as an alternative. It can be used in the preamble or in the package configuration file jurabib.cfg (to set the defaults for all documents). Settings established when loading the package or via \jurabibsetup in the preamble will overwrite such global defaults. For the examples in this section we will use the following defaults

```
\jurabibsetup{titleformat=colonsep,commabeforerest=true}
```

and extend or overwrite them as necessary. Their meaning is explained below.

In contrast to natbib, the jurabib package requires the use of specially designed BibTeX style files. It expects a \bibitem command with a specially structured optional argument to pass all kinds of information back to the user-level citation commands (see page 699). These BibTeX styles also implement a number of additional fields useful in conjunction with jurabib.

To show the particular features of jurabib, we use the small BibTeX database shown in Figure 12.3 on the facing page together with the database used previously (Figure 12.2 on page 690). If not explicitly documented otherwise, all examples in this section have the line

```
\newpage\bibliography{tex,jura}
```

implicitly appended at the end when processed.

The basic syntax

Like the natbib package, the jurabib package extends the standard LaTeX citation command \cite with a second optional argument.

\cite[*post-note*]{*key(s)*}   \cite[*annotator*][*post-note*]{*key(s)*}

If two optional arguments are present, then the *post-note* argument moves to the second position, the same behavior found with the natbib syntax. But in the default set-up there is a big difference in that we do not have a *pre-note* argument but rather an *annotator* argument provided for a citation method used in legal works.[1] In that discipline, works often have an original author (under which the work is listed in the bibliography) as well as annotators who provide commentaries in the particular edition. These annotators are mentioned in the citation

---

[1] See page 721 if you want it to be a *pre-note* instead.

```
@BOOK{zpo,                                    @BOOK{bschur,
   author      = {Adolf Baumbach and Wolfgang Lauterbach     author      = {Hans Brox and Wolf-Dietrich Walker},
                 and Jan Albers and Peter Hartmann},         title       = {Besonderes Schuldrecht},
   title       = {Zivilproze\ss ordnung mit                 shorttitle  = {BSchuR},
                 Gerichtsverfassungsgesetz und anderen       language    = {ngerman},
                 Nebengesetzen},                            edition     = {27.},
   shorttitle  = {ZPO},                                     year        = 2002,
   language    = {ngerman},                                 address     = {M\"unchen}
   edition     = {59. neubearb.},                        }
   year        = 2002,                                   @BOOK{bgb,
   address     = {M\"unchen}                                author      = {Otto Palandt},
}                                                           shortauthor= {Otto Palandt},
@BOOK{aschur,                                               title       = {B\"urgerliches Gesetzbuch},
   author      = {Hans Brox and Wolf-Dietrich Walker},      shorttitle  = {BGB},
   title       = {Allgemeines Schuldrecht},                 language    = {ngerman},
   language    = {ngerman},                                 edition     = {62.},
   edition     = {29.},                                     year        = 2003,
   year        = 2003,                                      publisher   = {Beck Juristischer Verlag},
   address     = {M\"unchen}                                address     = {M\"unchen}
}                                                        }
```

Figure 12.3: Sample BibTeX database `jura.bib`

but not in the bibliography. Without further adjustments a citation will list only the author surnames (separated by slashes if there are several authors), followed by the *annotator* if present, followed by a possible *post-note*. If the BibTeX entry contains a `shortauthor` field, then it is used instead of the surnames. If you want to specify an *annotator*, use an empty *post-note*. By default, a title or short title is shown only if the author is cited with different works in the same document.

Brox/Walker
Brox/Walker, § 123
Otto Palandt/Heinrichs
Otto Palandt/Heinrichs, § 26

```
\usepackage{jurabib} \bibliographystyle{jurabib}
\cite{aschur}                            \\
\cite[\S\,123]{aschur}                   \\
\cite[Heinrichs][]{bgb}                  \\
\cite[Heinrichs][\S\,26]{bgb}
```

12-5-1

As you see, there is no way to determine from the typeset result that "Walker" is a co-author but "Heinrichs" is an annotator. To make this distinction immediately visible, jurabib offers a number of options implementing common citation styles. You can, for example, change the font used for the annotator, or change the separator between author and annotator. Both of these changes have been specified in the first part of the next example. You can also move the annotator before the author, a solution shown in two variants in the second part of the example.

Brox/Walker
Otto Palandt–*Heinrichs*, § 26
Heinrichs, Otto Palandt, § 26
Heinrichs in: Otto Palandt, § 26

```
\usepackage{jurabib} \bibliographystyle{jurabib}
\jurabibsetup{annotatorformat=italic,annotatorlastsep=divis}
\cite{aschur}  \\ \cite[Heinrichs][\S\,26]{bgb} \\
\jurabibsetup{annotatorfirstsep=comma}
\cite[Heinrichs][\S\,26]{bgb} \\
\jurabibsetup{annotatorfirstsep=in,annotatorformat=normal}
\cite[Heinrichs][\S\,26]{bgb}
```

12-5-2

Another way to clearly distinguish authors and annotators is to use the option `authorformat` with the keyword and (which replaces slashes with commas and "and"), the keyword `dynamic` (in which case different fonts are used depending on whether an *annotator* is present), or the keyword `year` (which moves the publication year directly after the author). The `authorformat` option can also be used to influence other aspects of the formatting of author names. Some examples are shown below. A complete list of allowed keywords is given in the package documentation. Note that if you use several keywords together (as done below), you need an additional set of braces to indicate to jurabib where the keyword list ends and the next option starts.

BROX and WALKER
OTTO PALANDT/HEINRICHS, § 26

```
\usepackage{jurabib} \bibliographystyle{jurabib}
\jurabibsetup{authorformat={and,smallcaps}}
\cite{aschur}  \\ \cite[Heinrichs][\S\,26]{bgb} \par
```

12-5-3

If the keyword `dynamic` is used, the annotator's name is set in italics while the original author's name is set in the body font.[1] For works without an annotator, author names are set in italics. One can think of this style as labeling those people who have actually worked on the particular edition.

Brox/Walker
Otto Palandt/*Heinrichs*, § 26

```
\usepackage{jurabib} \bibliographystyle{jurabib}
\jurabibsetup{authorformat=dynamic}
\cite{aschur}  \\ \cite[Heinrichs][\S\,26]{bgb} \par
```

12-5-4

The keywords `and`, `dynamic`, and `year` can be combined, while `smallcaps` and `italic` contradict each other with the last specification winning:

Brox and *Walker* (2003)
Otto Palandt (2003)/*Heinrichs*, § 26

```
\usepackage{jurabib} \bibliographystyle{jurabib}
\jurabibsetup{authorformat={and,smallcaps,year,italic}}
\cite{aschur}  \\ \cite[Heinrichs][\S\,26]{bgb} \par
```

12-5-5

The information passed back by BIBTEX is very detailed and structured into individual fields whose contents can be accessed using the `\citefield` command.

`\citefield`[*post-note*]{*field*}{*key(s)*}

The *field* argument is one of the following fields from the BIBTEX database entry referenced by the *key* argument: author, shortauthor, title, shorttitle, url, or year. It can also be apy (address-publisher-year combination).

---

[1]The fonts used can be customized by redefining the commands `\jbactualauthorfont` and `\jbactualauthorfontifannotator`.

Whether more than a single *key* is useful is questionable for most fields. Indeed, even with \cite multiple keys are seldom useful unless no optional arguments are present.

BROX, HANS/WALKER, WOLF-DIETRICH
BSchuR, § 53
Reading, MA, USA: Addison-Wesley Longman, 1997
Allgemeines Schuldrecht; Besonderes Schuldrecht

```
\usepackage{jurabib} \bibliographystyle{jurabib}
\jurabibsetup{authorformat=smallcaps}
\citefield{author}{aschur}              \\
\citefield[\S\,53]{shorttitle}{bschur} \\
\citefield{apy}{LGC97}                  \\
\citefield{title}{aschur,bschur}
```

12-5-6

If you are familiar with the German language, you will notice that the hyphenation of "Schul-drecht" is incorrect: it should have been "Schuld-recht". How to achieve this hyphenation automatically is explained on page 733.

Citations with short and full titles

As mentioned before, by default jurabib does not include a title in the citation text. The exception occurs when there are several works cited by the same author, so that a title is necessary to distinguish between them. This behavior can be changed in several ways, but first we have a look at the "title" that will be used:

Brox/Walker: Allgemeines Schuldrecht
Brox/Walker: BSchuR
Knuth: The TEXbook
Knuth: TUGboat 10 [1989]

```
\usepackage{jurabib} \bibliographystyle{jurabib}
\cite{aschur}      \\   \cite{bschur}      \\[2pt]
\cite{Knuth-CT-a} \\   \cite{Knuth:TB10-1-31}
```

12-5-7

If you compare the first two lines of the previous example with the BIBTEX database files listed in Figure 12.3 on page 717, you see that the shorttitle field was used if available; otherwise, the title field was used. In fact, you will get a warning from jurabib for this adjustment: "shorttitle for aschur is missing – replacing with title". A different approach is taken for entries of type article or periodical; there, a missing shorttitle is replaced by the the journal name and year of publication, which is why we got "TUGboat 1989".

```
\citetitle[post-note][annotator]{key(s)}
\cite*[post-note][annotator]{key(s)}
```

To force the production of a title in the citation, you can use \citetitle instead of \cite. To leave out the title, you can use \cite*. You should, however, be aware that the latter command can easily lead to ambiguous citations, as shown in the next example.

Baumbach et al.: ZPO, Brox/Walker, and Brox/Walker are three different books, or not?

```
\usepackage{jurabib} \bibliographystyle{jurabib}
\citetitle{zpo}, \cite*{aschur}, and \cite*{bschur}
are three different books, or not?
```

12-5-8

Also note that this meaning of \cite* is quite different from its use in natbib (where it denotes using a full list of authors). If you switch between both packages depending on the circumstances, it might be better to avoid it altogether.

> \citetitleonly[*post-note*]{*key*}

It is also possible to refer to only the title, including a *post-note* if desired.

ZPO, § 13

```
\usepackage{jurabib} \bibliographystyle{jurabib}
\citetitleonly[\S\,13]{zpo}
```

12-5-9

Getting short-title citations automatically

Short-title citations can be generated by default by specifying the option titleformat and the keyword all. Like authorformat, this option can take several keywords. We already know about colonsep, which we used as a default setting for all the examples. In the next example we overwrite it with commasep and print the titles in *italic*.

Brox/Walker, *Allgemeines Schuldrecht*, § 123
Brox/Walker, *BSchuR*
Otto Palandt/Heinrichs, *BGB*
Knuth, *TUGboat 10 [1989]*

```
\usepackage{jurabib} \bibliographystyle{jurabib}
\jurabibsetup{titleformat={all,commasep,italic}}
\cite[\S\,123]{aschur}  \\  \cite{bschur}     \\
\cite[Heinrichs][]{bgb} \\ \cite{Knuth:TB10-1-31}
```

12-5-10

> \citetitlefortype{*BIBTEX-type-list*}   \citenotitlefortype{*BIBTEX-type-list*}

Instead of citing all works with titles you can select short-title citations based on a particular BIBTEX type. For example,

```
\citetitlefortype{article,book,manual}
```

would reference these three types with the title and all other publication types without it, unless the author is cited with several works. Since such a list can grow quite large, alternatively you can select automatic title citations for all works (with titleformat) and then specify those types that should have no titles when referenced. This is done in the next example for the type book. Nevertheless, the book by Knuth is cited with its title, since we also cite an article by him.

Brox/Walker
Goossens/Rahtz
Knuth: The TEXbook
Knuth: TUGboat 10 [1989]

```
\usepackage{jurabib} \bibliographystyle{jurabib}
\jurabibsetup{titleformat=all} \citenotitlefortype{book}
\cite{bschur}      \\   \cite{LWC99}           \\
\cite{Knuth-CT-a} \\  \cite{Knuth:TB10-1-31}
```

12-5-11

Indexing citations automatically

The author names in citations can be entered in the index by using the option authorformat with the keyword indexed. By default, this is done only for citations inside the text; authors referred to only in the bibliography are not listed. This behavior can be changed by setting `\jbindexbib` in the preamble or in a configuration file. For formatting the index entries, `\jbauthorindexfont` is available. For example,

```
\renewcommand\jbauthorindexfont[1]{\textit{#1}}
```

means that the author names will appear in italic in the index.

Instead of placing the author names in the main index, you can produce a separate author index by loading the index package (see Section 11.4.3) and then using a construction like

```
\usepackage{index}
\newindex{default}{idx}{ind}{Index}            % the main index
\newindex{authors}{adx}{and}{Index of Authors}
\renewcommand\jbindextype{authors}
```

in the preamble, and later on `\printindex[authors]` to indicate where the author index should appear in the document.

No support is available for more elaborate indexes as required for some types of law books (e.g., "Table of Cases" or "Table of Statutes"). If this is required, consider using the camel package instead of jurabib.

Using natbib citation semantics

The optional *annotator* argument is useful only in legal studies. In other disciplines, it is more common to require a *pre-note* (e.g., "compare..."). To account for this, the meanings of the optional arguments can be modified by loading the package with the option see.

| `\cite[`*pre-note*`][`*post-note*`]{`*key(s)*`}`   (with option see) |

The see option replaces the default *annotator* optional argument with a *pre-note* argument in case two optional arguments are used. The `\cite` command then has the same syntax and semantics as it does with the natbib package.

(Goossens/Rahtz/Mittelbach)
(Goossens/Rahtz/Mittelbach, chap. 2)

(compare Goossens/Rahtz/Mittelbach)
(see Goossens/Rahtz/Mittelbach, chap. 2)

```
\usepackage[see,round]{jurabib}
\bibliographystyle{jurabib}
\cite{LGC97}                    \\
\cite[chap.~2]{LGC97}           \\[3pt]
\cite[compare][]{LGC97}         \\
\cite[see][chap.~2]{LGC97}
```

12-5-12

This work was cited as ...

When using a short-title system for citations (e.g., by setting titleformat to all), it can be helpful to present the reader with a mapping between the full entry and the short title. This is commonly done by displaying the short title in parentheses at the end of the corresponding entry in the bibliography. The jurabib package supports this convention with the option howcited. It can take a number of keywords that configure the mechanism in slightly different ways. For example, the keyword all instructs the package to add "how cited" information to all entries in the bibliography. Thus, if we add to Example 12-5-10 on page 720 the line

```
\jurabibsetup{howcited=all}
```

we will get the following bibliography listing. Note that the short title is formatted in exactly the same way as it will appear in the citation.

Brox, Hans/Walker, Wolf-Dietrich: Besonderes Schuldrecht. 27th edition. München, 2002 (cited: Brox/Walker, *BSchuR*)

Brox, Hans/Walker, Wolf-Dietrich: Allgemeines Schuldrecht. 29th edition. München, 2003 (cited: Brox/Walker, *Allgemeines Schuldrecht*)

Knuth, Donald E.: Typesetting Concrete Mathematics. TUGboat, 10 April 1989, Nr. 1, 31–36, ISSN 0896–3207 (cited: Knuth, *TUGboat 10 [1989]*)

Palandt, Otto: Bürgerliches Gesetzbuch. 62th edition. München: Beck Juristischer Verlag, 2003 (cited: Otto Palandt, *BGB*)

12-5-13

However, it is usually not necessary to display for all entries how they are cited. For articles, the short-title citation is always "author name, journal, and year". If a work is cited with its full title (i.e., if there is no shorttitle field) or if only a single publication is cited for a certain author, then the reader will generally be able to identify the corresponding entry without any further help. To allow for such a restricted type of "back-references", jurabib offers the keywords compare, multiple, and normal.

If you use compare, then a back-reference is created only if the entry contains a shorttitle field and the title and shorttitle fields differ. With respect to Example 12-5-13 this means that only the first and last entries would show the back-references.

If you use multiple instead, then back-references are generated whenever an author is cited with several works except for citations of articles. In the above example, the first two entries would get back-references. If we also had a citation to Knuth-CT-a, then it would also show a back-reference, while Knuth's article in *TUGboat* would be still without one.

Both keywords can be used together. In that case back-references are added to entries for authors with several publications as well as to entries whose short titles differ from their main titles.

Finally, there is the keyword normal (it is also used if you specify the option without a value). This keyword works slightly differently from the others in that it needs support to be present in the BIBT_EX database. If it is used, an entry gets a back-reference if and only if the BIBT_EX field `howcited` is present. The field can have two kinds of values. If it has a value of "1", the back-reference lists exactly what is shown in the citation in text. With any other value, the actual contents of the `howcited` field are used for the back-reference, including any formatting directives contained therein.

The text surrounding the back-reference can be customized by redefining the commands `\howcitedprefix` and `\howcitedsuffix`. In addition, you can specify what should happen with entries that have been added via `\nocite` by changing `\bibnotcited` (empty by default). Because these commands may contain text that should differ depending on the main language of the document, they are redefined using a special mechanism (`\AddTo`) that is explained on page 733.

... Brox/Walker: BSchuR ... Knuth ...

References

Brox, Hans/Walker, Wolf-Dietrich: Besonderes Schuldrecht. 27th edition. München, 2002 (cited as Brox/Walker: BSchuR).

Brox,   Hans/Walker,   Wolf-Dietrich: Allgemeines Schuldrecht. 29th edition. München, 2003 (not cited).

Knuth, Donald E.: Typesetting Concrete Mathematics. TUGboat, 10 April 1989, Nr. 1, 31–36, ISSN 0896–3207 (cited as Knuth).

```
\usepackage{jurabib}
\bibliographystyle{jurabib}
\jurabibsetup{howcited=all}
\AddTo\bibsall{%
   \renewcommand\howcitedprefix
                  { (cited as }%
   \renewcommand\howcitedsuffix{).}%
   \renewcommand\bibnotcited
                  { (not cited).}}
\nocite{aschur}
\ldots \cite{bschur} \ldots
\cite{Knuth:TB10-1-31} \ldots
\bibliography{jura,tex}
```

12-5-14

Full citations inside the text

While producing full citations inside the text with natbib requires a separate package and some initial preparation, this citation method is fully integrated in jurabib. The complete entry can be shown for one or more individual citations, for all citations, or automatically for only the first citation of a work. This citation method is most often used in footnotes; see page 726 for information on how to automatically arrange footnote citations.

> `\fullcite[`*post-note*`] [`*annotator*`]{`*key(s)*`}`

This command works like `\cite` but displays the full bibliographical data. The *annotator*, if present, will be placed in front of the citation just as if `annotatorfirstsep=in` had been specified.

Compare the next example with Example 12-3-27 from page 711. The keyword `citationreversed` arranges for the author name to appear with surname last (in the bibliography the surname comes first). Related keywords are `allreversed` (surname last in text and bibliography) and `firstnotreversed` (surname first for first author, last for all others in multiple-author works).

For details see Donald E. Knuth: Typesetting Concrete Mathematics. TUGboat, 10 April 1989, Nr. 1, ISSN 0896–3207. General information can be found in Donald E. Knuth: The TEXbook. Volume A, Computers and Typesetting. Reading, MA, USA: Addison-Wesley, 1986, ISBN 0–201–13447–0.
As shown by Knuth (1989) ...

```
\usepackage{jurabib}
\bibliographystyle{jurabib}
\jurabibsetup{authorformat=citationreversed}

\raggedright \setlength\parindent{12pt}
For details see \fullcite{Knuth:TB10-1-31}.
General information can be found in
\fullcite{Knuth-CT-a}.

As shown by \citet{Knuth:TB10-1-31} \ldots
```

12-5-15

Getting full citations automatically   The `\cite` command automatically generates full citations if the `citefull` option is specified together with one of the following keywords: `all` (all references are full citations), `first` (first citation is full, subsequent ones are abbreviated), `chapter` (same as `first` but restarts with each chapter), and `section` (like `chapter` but restarts at the `\section` level). All settings imply `annotatorfirstsep=in`, as can be seen in the second citation in the example. If one of the above settings has been included in the configuration file and you want to turn it off for the current document, use the keyword `false`.

See Baumbach, Adolf et al.: Zivilprozeßordnung mit Gerichtsverfassungsgesetz und anderen Nebengesetzen. 59th edition. München, 2002 ...
As shown by Heinrichs in: Baumbach et al., § 216 the interpretation ...

```
\usepackage{jurabib}
\bibliographystyle{jurabib}
\jurabibsetup{citefull=first}
See \cite{zpo} \ldots

As shown by \cite[Heinrichs][\S\,216]{zpo}
the interpretation \ldots
```

12-5-16

```
\citefullfirstfortype{BIBTEX-type-list}
```

Further control is possible by specifying the BIBTEX entry types for which a full citation should be generated on the first occurrence. In the example below (otherwise similar to Example 12-5-15), we request that only entries of type `article` should be subject to this process.

For details see Knuth, Donald E.: Typesetting Concrete Mathematics. TUGboat, 10 April 1989, Nr. 1, ISSN 0896–3207. General information can be found in Knuth: The TEXbook.
As shown by Knuth: TUGboat 10 [1989]

```
\usepackage{jurabib} \bibliographystyle{jurabib}
\jurabibsetup{citefull=first}
\citefullfirstfortype{article}
For details see \cite{Knuth:TB10-1-31}. General
information can be found in \cite{Knuth-CT-a}.

As shown by \cite{Knuth:TB10-1-31}
```

12-5-17

```
\nextciteshort{key-list} \nextcitefull{key-list}
\nextcitereset{key-list} \nextcitenotitle{key-list}
```

Sometimes it is not correct to make the first citation to a work be the full entry, such as in an abstract or preface. On the other hand, you may want to have a certain citation show the full entry again, even though it appeared earlier. For this purpose four commands are available that modify how individual citations are presented from the given point onward.[1]

If you use \nextciteshort, all citations specified in the *key-list* will be typeset as short-title citations from then on (e.g., lines A, B, D in the example). If you use \nextcitereset, the citations will (again) be typeset in the normal way; thus, the next citation will be a full citation if there has not been one yet (lines C and F) and otherwise citations will be set as short-title citations (line E). With \nextcitefull, you force full entries from then on (line G). With \nextcitenotitle, you get only the author name(s), even if it results in ambiguous citations.

A) Knuth: The TEXbook

B) Knuth: TUGboat 10 [1989]

C) Knuth, Donald E.: The TEXbook. Volume A, Computers and Typesetting. Reading, MA, USA: Addison-Wesley, 1986, ISBN 0–201–13447–0

D) Knuth: TUGboat 10 [1989]

E) Knuth: The TEXbook

F) Knuth, Donald E.: Typesetting Concrete Mathematics. TUGboat, 10 April 1989, Nr. 1, ISSN 0896–3207

G) Knuth, Donald E.: The TEXbook. Volume A, Computers and Typesetting. Reading, MA, USA: Addison-Wesley, 1986, ISBN 0–201–13447–0

H) Knuth

```
\usepackage[citefull=first]{jurabib}
\bibliographystyle{jurabib}
\nextciteshort{Knuth-CT-a,Knuth:TB10-1-31}
A) \cite{Knuth-CT-a}                    \\
B) \cite{Knuth:TB10-1-31}               \\
\nextcitereset{Knuth-CT-a}
C) \cite{Knuth-CT-a}                    \\
D) \cite{Knuth:TB10-1-31}               \\
\nextcitereset{Knuth-CT-a,Knuth:TB10-1-31}
E) \cite{Knuth-CT-a}                    \\
F) \cite{Knuth:TB10-1-31}               \\
\nextcitefull{Knuth-CT-a}
\nextcitenotitle{Knuth:TB10-1-31}
G) \cite{Knuth-CT-a}                    \\
H) \cite{Knuth:TB10-1-31}
```

12-5-18

If full citations are used within the main document it is not absolutely necessary to assemble them in a bibliography or reference list. You may, for example, have all citations inline and use a bibliography for suggested further reading or other secondary material.

```
\citeswithoutentry{key-list}
```

This declaration lists those keys that should not appear in the bibliography even though they are cited in the text. The *key-list* is a list of comma-separated keys without any white space. You can repeat this command as often as necessary.

---

[1]The command names seem to indicate that they change the "next" citation, but in fact they change all further citations until they are overwritten.

Think of it as the opposite of \nocite. Both commands are used in the next example.

This is explained in Brox, Hans/Walker, Wolf-Dietrich: Allgemeines Schuldrecht. 29th edition. München, 2003. As shown in Brox/Walker...

Selected further reading

Baumbach, Adolf et al.: Zivilprozeßordnung mit Gerichtsverfassungsgesetz und anderen Nebengesetzen. 59th edition. München, 2002

```
\usepackage{jurabib}
\renewcommand\refname
        {Selected further reading}
\bibliographystyle{jurabib}
\citeswithoutentry{aschur}
\jurabibsetup{citefull=first}
This is explained in \cite{aschur}.
\par As shown in \cite{aschur}\ldots
\nocite{zpo}
\bibliography{jura}
```
12-5-19

Suppressing the bibliography altogether While \citeswithoutentry prevents individual works from appearing in the bibliography it is not possible to use it to suppress all entries, as you would get an empty list consisting of just the heading. If you want to omit the bibliography altogether, use \nobibliography in place of the usual \bibliography command. This command will read the .bbl file produced by BibTeX to enable citation references, but without producing a typeset result. You still need to specify jurabib as the BibTeX style and run BibTeX in the normal way.

Citations as footnotes or endnotes

All citation commands introduced so far have variants that generate footnote citations or, when used together, with the endnotes package, generate endnotes. Simply prepend foot to the command name (e.g., \footcite instead of \cite, \footcitetitle instead of \citetitle, and so forth). This allows you to mix footnote and other citations freely, if needed.

The footnote citations produced by jurabib are ordinary footnotes, so you can influence their layout by loading the footmisc package, if desired.

...to use LaTeX on the web.* Also discussed by Goossens/Rahtz is generating PDF and HTML.

---

*Goossens, Michel/Rahtz, Sebastian: The LaTeX Web companion: integrating TeX, HTML, and XML. Reading, MA, USA: Addison-Wesley Longman, 1999, Tools and Techniques for Computer Typesetting, ISBN 0–201–43311–7.

```
\usepackage[ragged,symbol]{footmisc}
\usepackage{jurabib}
\bibliographystyle{jurabib}
\ldots to use \LaTeX{} on the
web.\footfullcite{LWC99}
Also discussed by \cite{LWC99}
is generating PDF and HTML.
```
12-5-20

Getting footnote citations automatically If all your citations should be automatically typeset as footnotes, use the super option. In that case jurabib will automatically choose the \foot.. variants, so \cite will produce \footcite, and so forth. This is shown in the next example. There we also use citefull=first so that the first footnote looks like the one in the previous example (to save space we show only the second page, where due to the ridiculously small height of the example page the last line of that footnote is carried over). The other two citations are then automatically shortened, with the third being shortened even further because of the `ibidem` option (explained on the following page).

We also use the option `lookat`, which is responsible for the back-reference to the earlier note containing the full citation. This option is allowed only if you simultaneously use the `citefull` option and have all your initial citations in footnotes, as it requires a "number" to refer to.

You have to be careful to use a footnote style that produces unique numbers. If footnotes are numbered by chapter or by page, for example, then such references are ambiguous. This problem can be solved by loading the `varioref` package, in which case these back-references will also show page numbers. If `varioref` is loaded for other reasons and you do not want page references in this place, use `\jbnovarioref` to suppress them. If footnotes are numbered by chapter, then an alternative solution is to use the `\labelformat` declaration as provided by `varioref` to indicate to which chapter the footnote belongs:

```
\labelformat{footnote}{\thechapter--#1}
```

The `lookat` option is particularly useful in combination with command `\nobibliography`, so that all your bibliographical information is placed in footnotes without a summary bibliography.

Also discussed is generating PDF[2] and HTML.[3]

43311–7.
  [2]Goossens/Rahtz (as in n. 1), chap. 2.
  [3]Ibid., chap. 3–4.

12-5-21

```
\usepackage{jurabib} \bibliographystyle{jurabib}
\jurabibsetup{super,citefull=first,ibidem,lookat}

\ldots to use \LaTeX{} on the web.\cite{LWC99}
    \newpage % Next page shown on the left:
Also discussed is generating PDF\cite[chap.~2]
{LWC99} and HTML.\cite[chap.~3--4]{LWC99}
```

It is possible to customize the appearance of the back-references by using the commands `\lookatprefix` and `\lookatsuffix`. Both are language dependent, which is the reason for using the `\AddTo` declaration (see page 733). The example sets up a style commonly seen in law citations [21].

Also discussed is generating PDF[2] and HTML.[3]

43311–7.
  [2]Goossens/Rahtz, *supra* note 1, chap. 2.
  [3]Goossens/Rahtz, *supra* note 1, chap. 3–4.

12-5-22

```
\usepackage{jurabib} \bibliographystyle{jurabib}
\jurabibsetup{super,citefull=first,lookat}
\AddTo\bibsall{\renewcommand\lookatprefix
       {, \emph{supra} note }
      \renewcommand\lookatsuffix{}}

\ldots to use \LaTeX{} on the web.\cite{LWC99}
    \newpage % Next page shown on the left:
Also discussed is generating PDF\cite[chap.~2]
{LWC99} and HTML.\cite[chap.~3--4]{LWC99}
```

By loading the `endnotes` package in a set-up similar to the one from the previous example, you can turn all your citations into endnotes. As you can see, the endnotes do not have a final period added by default. If you prefer a period, add the option `dotafter` with the keyword value `endnote`.

. . . to typeset with graphics.[1] Also discussed is typesetting music[2] and games.[3]

Notes

[1]Goossens, Michel/Rahtz, Sebastian/Mittelbach, Frank: The LaTeX Graphics Companion: Illustrating Documents with TeX and PostScript. Reading, MA, USA: Addison-Wesley Longman, 1997, Tools and Techniques for Computer Typesetting, ISBN 0–201–85469–4

[2]Goossens/Rahtz/Mittelbach (as in n. 1), chap. 7

[3]Goossens/Rahtz/Mittelbach (as in n. 1), chap. 8

```
\usepackage{jurabib,endnotes}
\bibliographystyle{jurabib}
\jurabibsetup{citefull=first,%
              super,lookat}
\ldots to typeset with
graphics.\cite{LGC97} Also
discussed is typesetting
music\cite[chap.~7]{LGC97} and
games.\cite[chap.~8]{LGC97}
\theendnotes
```

12-5-23

Ibidem—In the same place

In some disciplines it is customary to use the Latin word "ibidem" (abbreviated as "ibid." or "ib.") if you repeat a reference to the immediately preceding citation. The jurabib package supports this convention in several variants if the option `ibidem` is specified. This option must be used with footnote-style citations (e.g., when using `\footcite` or with the option `super` activated).

If `ibidem` is used without a value (which is the same as using it with the keyword `strict`), then the following happens: if a citation refers to the same publication as the immediately preceding citation on the *current* page, then it is replaced by "Ibid.", if necessary keeping a *post-note*. You can see this situation in the next example: the first citation is a short-title citation; the second citation is identical so we get "Ibid." with the *post-note* dropped; and the third and forth citations refer to different parts of the same publication so we get the *post-note* as well. The fifth citation refers to a different publication by the same authors, so another short-title citation is produced. The sixth citation refers to the same publication, but the short-title citation is repeated because it is on a new page. The seventh and eighth citations are again to the other publication, so we get first a short-title citation and then "Ibid." with a *post-note*.

text[1] text[2,3] text[4,5]

text[6,7] text[8]

---
[1] Brox/Walker: BSchuR, § 7.
[2] Ibid.
[3] Ibid., § 16.
[4] Ibid., § 7.
[5] Brox/Walker: Allgemeines Schuldrecht.

---
[6] Brox/Walker: Allgemeines Schuldrecht, § 3.
[7] Brox/Walker: BSchuR.
[8] Ibid., § 15.

```
\usepackage[marginal,multiple]{footmisc}
\usepackage[super,ibidem]{jurabib}
\bibliographystyle{jurabib}
text \cite[\S\,7]{bschur}
text \cite[\S\,7]{bschur}
     \cite[\S\,16]{bschur}
text \cite[\S\,7]{bschur}
\cite{aschur}    \newpage % <---
text \cite[\S\,3]{aschur}
     \cite{bschur}
text \cite[\S\,15]{bschur}
```

12-5-24

If you typeset your document with the class option `twoside`, then you can use the keyword `strictdoublepage`. It means that "Ibid." will also be used across page boundaries as long as the preceding citation is still visible (i.e., on the same spread). Repeating Example 12-5-24 with this setting will change the sixth citation to "Ibid.".

The `ibidem` option usually generates a lot of very short footnotes, so it might be economical to use it together with the `para` option of `footmisc`. We also add the `perpage` option so that the footnote numbers remain small. Note, however, that this makes it impossible to use the `lookat` option because the footnote numbers are no longer unique.

```
\usepackage[para,multiple,perpage]{footmisc}
\usepackage{jurabib}
\bibliographystyle{jurabib}
\jurabibsetup{super,ibidem=strictdoublepage}
text \cite[\S\,7]{bschur} text
\cite[\S\,7]{bschur} \cite[\S\,16]{bschur}
text \cite[\S\,7]{bschur} \cite{aschur}
\newpage          text \cite[\S\,3]{aschur}
\cite{bschur} text \cite[\S\,15]{bschur}
```

text[1] text[2,3] text[4,5]

[1] Brox/Walker: BSchuR, §7.   [2] Ibid.   [3] Ibid., §16.   [4] Ibid., §7.   [5] Brox/Walker: Allgemeines Schuldrecht.

text[1,2] text[3]

[1] Ibid., §3.   [2] Brox/Walker: BSchuR.   [3] Ibid., §15.

12-5-25

It is even possible to ignore all page boundaries by using the `nostrict` keyword. The reader might find it difficult to decipher the references, however, because "Ibid." and the citation to which it refers may be moved arbitrarily far apart. If necessary, you can disable the `ibidem` mechanism for the next citation by preceding it with `\noibidem`.

```
\usepackage{jurabib} \bibliographystyle{jurabib}
\jurabibsetup{super,ibidem=nostrict}
  \ldots \fullcite{bschur} \ldots
\newpage % page above not shown on the left
         A page without a citation.
\newpage This page has references.\cite{bschur}
         Or like this?   \noibidem\cite{bschur}
```

A page without a citation.

This page has references.[2] Or like this?[3]

[2] Ibid.
[3] Brox/Walker.

12-5-26

The use of "Ibid." without any further qualification allows you to reference just the immediately preceding citation. Thus, if citations are frequently mixed, the mechanism will insert short-title references most of the time. This situation will change if you use the `ibidem` option with the keyword `name` (which automatically implies `citefull=first`). In that case "Ibid." will be used with the full name of the author, thus allowing a reference to an earlier—not directly preceding—citation. If only the surnames of the authors are required, add the `authorformat` option with the keyword `reducedifibidem`. Its effect is seen in the next example, where citations to `bschur` and `zpo` alternate. A variant is to always use name and short title except for the first citation of a publication; this format can be requested with the keyword `name&title`.

If the same author is cited with more than one publication, then using the `ibidem` option with the `name` keyword is likely to produce ambiguous references. For those citations the jurabib package automatically switches to the `name&title&auto` method described below.

text[1] text[2,3] text[4,5] text[6]

---

[1] Brox, Hans/Walker, Wolf-Dietrich: Besonderes Schuldrecht. 27th edition. München, 2002, § 7.

[2] Brox/Walker, ibid., § 8.

[3] Baumbach, Adolf et al.: Zivilprozeßordnung mit Gerichtsverfassungsgesetz und anderen Nebengesetzen. 59th edition. München, 2002, § 16.

[4] Brox/Walker, ibid., § 7.

[5] Baumbach et al., ibid.

[6] Baumbach et al., ibid., § 3.

```
\usepackage[marginal,ragged,multiple]{footmisc}
\usepackage{jurabib} \bibliographystyle{jurabib}
\jurabibsetup{super,ibidem=name}
\jurabibsetup{authorformat=reducedifibidem}
text \cite[\S\,7]{bschur} text
\cite[\S\,8]{bschur} \cite[\S\,16]{zpo}
text \cite[\S\,7]{bschur} \cite{zpo}
text \cite[\S\,3]{zpo}
```

12-5-27

If `name&title&auto` was selected (either implicitly or explicitly), then the following happens: the first citation of a publication automatically displays the full entry (citation 5 in the next example). Immediately following citations to the same work will show only the name of the author(s) (citations 4 and 8). If there are intervening citations, then the name(s) and short titles are shown (citations 3, 6, and 7).

text[3] text[4,5] text[6,7] text[8]

---

[3] Brox, Hans/Walker, Wolf-Dietrich: Allgemeines Schuldrecht, ibid., § 7.

[4] Brox, Hans/Walker, Wolf-Dietrich, ibid., § 8.

[5] Baumbach, Adolf et al.: Zivilprozeßordnung mit Gerichtsverfassungsgesetz und anderen Nebengesetzen. 59th edition. München, 2002, § 16.

[6] Brox, Hans/Walker, Wolf-Dietrich: BSchuR, ibid., § 7.

[7] Baumbach, Adolf et al., ibid.

[8] Baumbach, Adolf et al., ibid., § 3.

```
\usepackage[marginal,ragged,multiple]{footmisc}
\usepackage{jurabib} \bibliographystyle{jurabib}
\jurabibsetup{super,ibidem=name&title&auto}
  Full citations: \cite{aschur} \cite{bschur}
  not shown on the left!
\newpage
  text \cite[\S\,7]{aschur} text
  \cite[\S\,8]{aschur} \cite[\S\,16]{zpo}
  text \cite[\S\,7]{bschur} \cite{zpo}
  text \cite[\S\,3]{zpo}
```

12-5-28

Another convention in certain disciplines is to replace the author's name with the Latin word "Idem" (meaning "the same") if the author of successive citations is identical. This is catered for by the option `idem`, which accepts the keywords `strict`, `strictdoublepage`, and `nostrict` with the same semantics as used with the `ibidem` option. Both options can be combined as shown in the next example. Due to the keywords used we get different citations: some use "Idem, ibid."; after the page break "Idem" is suppressed, because of the option `strict`; and in the last three citations it is used again (even with the full citation) because they all refer to different publications of Donald Knuth.

```
\usepackage[flushmargin,%
            multiple]{footmisc}
\usepackage[super,idem=strict,%
            ibidem=name]{jurabib}
\bibliographystyle{jurabib}

\ldots text \cite{Knuth-CT-a}
text \cite[p.~22]{Knuth-CT-a}
text \cite{vLeunen:92}
\cite{vLeunen:92}\ldots
\newpage % <--
\ldots text \cite{vLeunen:92}
text \cite[p.~16]{vLeunen:92}
text \cite[p.~308]{Knuth-CT-a}
text \cite{Knuth:TB10-1-31}
\cite[p.~80]{Knuth-CT-a}\ldots
```

…text[1] text[2] text[3,4]…

…text[5] text[6] text[7] text[8,9]…

---

[1] Knuth, Donald E.: The TEXbook. Volume A, Computers and Typesetting. Reading, MA, USA: Addison-Wesley, 1986, ISBN 0–201–13447–0.
[2] Idem, ibid., p. 22.
[3] Leunen, Mary-Claire van: A handbook for scholars Walton Street, Oxford OX2 6DP, UK: Oxford University Press, 92.
[4] Idem, ibid.

---

[5] Leunen, Mary-Claire van, ibid.
[6] Idem, ibid., p. 16.
[7] Knuth, Donald E.: The TEXbook, ibid., p. 308.
[8] Idem: Typesetting Concrete Mathematics. TUGboat, 10 April 1989, Nr. 1, ISSN 0896–3207.
[9] Idem: The TEXbook, ibid., p. 80.

12-5-29

You have to ask yourself whether this type of citation is actually helpful to your readers. Butcher [29], for example, argues against it. Of course, you may not have a choice in the matter—it might be required. You should, however, note that the sixth citation in the previous example is actually wrong: van Leunen is a female author, so the correct Latin form would be "Eadem" and not "Idem" (though some style manuals do not make that distinction). If necessary, jurabib offers possibilities for adjusting your citations even on that level of detail; see page 734.

There is another convention related to recurring citations, though it is becoming less common: to signal that a citation refers to an earlier reference, it is flagged with *op. cit.* (*opere citato*, "in the work cited"). This practice is supported with the option opcit. The citation should be "close by" so that the reader has a chance to find it. For this reason jurabib offers the keywords chapter and section in analogy to the citefull option.

…text[1] text[2] text[3] some more text[4,5]

---

[1] Knuth, Donald E.: The TEXbook. Volume A, Computers and Typesetting. Reading, MA, USA: Addison-Wesley, 1986, ISBN 0–201–13447–0.
[2] Idem, *op. cit.*, p. 22.
[3] Free Software Foundation: GNU Make, A Program for Directing Recompilation. 2000.
[4] Knuth, *op. cit.*
[5] Free Software Foundation, *op. cit.*

```
\usepackage[multiple]{footmisc}
\usepackage[super,idem=strict,%
    citefull=first,opcit]{jurabib}
\bibliographystyle{jurabib}

\ldots text \cite{Knuth-CT-a} text
\cite[p.~22]{Knuth-CT-a} text
\cite{GNUMake} some more text
\cite{Knuth-CT-a}\cite{GNUMake}
```

12-5-30

In law citations [21], it is common to use the word "*supra*" to indicate a reference to a previous citation. This can be accomplished by changing the \opcit command, which holds the generated string, as follows:

```
\renewcommand\opcit{\textit{supra}}
```

Alternatively, you can use the method shown in Example 12-5-22 on page 727.

Cross-referencing citations

BIBTEX supports the notion of cross-references between bibliographical entries via
the `crossref` field. For example, an entry of type `inproceedings` can reference
the proceedings issue in which it appears. Depending on the number of references
to such an issue, BIBTEX then decides whether to produce a separate entry for
the issue or to include information about it in each `inproceedings` entry. See
Section 13.2.5 for details.

If BIBTEX decides to produce separate entries for the cross-referenced citations,
a question arises about what should happen if they are referenced in a `\fullcite`
or `\footfullcite` command in the text. To handle this situation jurabib offers
three keywords applicable to the `crossref` option: with the keyword `normal` (the
default), cross-references are typeset as an `author/editor`, `title` combination
(or `shortauthor`, `shorttitle` if available); with the keyword `short`, only the
`author` or `editor` is used as long as there are no ambiguities; and with the keyword `long`, cross-references are listed in full. The default behavior is shown below
(where the editors and the short title were selected by jurabib).

Mittelbach, Frank/Rowley, Chris: The Pursuit of Quality: How
can Automated Typesetting achieve the Highest Standards of Craft Typography? In Vanoirbeek/Coray: EP92
Southall, Richard: Presentation Rules and Rules of Composition
in the Formatting of Complex Text. In Vanoirbeek/Coray: EP92
Mittelbach/Rowley

```
\usepackage{jurabib}
\jurabibsetup{citefull=first,
              crossref=normal}
\bibliographystyle{jurabib}
\cite{MR-PQ}      \par
\cite{Southall}   \par
\cite{MR-PQ}
```

12-5-31

You can combine any of the three keywords with the keyword `dynamic`, in
which case the first cross-reference is given in a longer form when cited the first
time and in the shorter form on all later occasions. Here we combine it with the
keyword `long` so that we get a full citation to Vanoirbeek/Coray in the first citation and a short title citation in the second.

Frank Mittelbach/Chris Rowley: The Pursuit of Quality: How can
Automated Typesetting achieve the Highest Standards of Craft Typog-
raphy? In Christine Vanoirbeek/Giovanni Coray, editors: EP92—
Proceedings of Electronic Publishing, '92. Cambridge: Cambridge
University Press, 1992
Richard Southall: Presentation Rules and Rules of Composition in
the Formatting of Complex Text. In Vanoirbeek/Coray: EP92

```
\usepackage{jurabib}
\jurabibsetup{citefull=first,
    authorformat=
          citationreversed,
    crossref={dynamic,long}}
\bibliographystyle{jurabib}
\cite{MR-PQ}      \par
\cite{Southall}
```

12-5-32

Author-date citation support

As mentioned earlier, jurabib supports the commands `\citet` and `\citep` as introduced by natbib. It also offers `\citealt`, `\citealp`, `\citeauthor`, `\citeyear`,
and `\citeyearpar`. Those forms for which it makes sense are also available as

footnote citations by prefixing the command name with foot (e.g., \footcitet).
Not provided are the starred forms available with natbib.

Goossens/Rahtz (1999)	`\usepackage{jurabib}`
Goossens/Rahtz (1999, chap. 2)	`\bibliographystyle{jurabib}`
see Goossens/Rahtz (1999, chap. 2)	`\citet{LWC99}` `\\`
pre-note only: see Goossens/Rahtz (1999)	`\citet[chap.~2]{LWC99}` `\\`
	`\citet[see][chap.~2]{LWC99}` `\\`
(Goossens/Rahtz, 1999)	`pre-note only: \citet[see][]{LWC99}` `\\[5pt]`
(Goossens/Rahtz, 1999, chap. 2)	`\citep{LWC99}` `\\`
(see Goossens/Rahtz, 1999, chap. 2)	`\citep[chap.~2]{LWC99}` `\\`
pre-note only: (see Goossens/Rahtz, 1999)	`\citep[see][chap.~2]{LWC99}` `\\`
	`pre-note only: \citep[see][]{LWC99}` `\\[5pt]`
Knuth, 1986	`\citealp{Knuth-CT-a}` `\\`
Knuth	`\citeauthor{Knuth-CT-a}` `\\`
(1986)	`\citeyearpar{Knuth-CT-a}`

12-5-33

A combination of author-date and short-title citations is achieved by setting
authorformat=year, as already introduced in Example 12-5-5. The formatting of
the year can be influenced with \jbcitationyearformat, and the position of the
date can be moved after the title (if present) by specifying \jbyearaftertitle.

	`\usepackage{jurabib} \bibliographystyle{jurabib}`
	`\jurabibsetup{authorformat=year,annotatorformat=italic}`
	`\renewcommand\jbcitationyearformat[1]{\oldstylenums{#1}}`
Brox/Walker 2003	`\jbyearaftertitle`
Otto Palandt/*Heinrichs* 2003, § 26	`\cite{aschur}  \\  \cite[Heinrichs][\S\,26]{bgb}`

12-5-34

Language support

Most strings that are generated automatically in a bibliography entry or as part
of a full citation, are language dependent; they depend on the main language of
the document. The jurabib package supports this by collaborating with the babel
package. Depending on the main language of the document (determined by the
last option to the babel package), jurabib loads a special language definition file
(extension .ldf) that contains definitions for all kinds of commands that produce
textual material within citations and bibliography entries. At the moment approximately 10 languages are supported. These language files (e.g., enjbbib.ldf for
English) are a good source for finding out details about customization possibilities. To modify such a command from such files for a particular language (or for
all languages), jurabib offers the \AddTo declaration.

`\AddTo\bibsall{`*code*`}`   `\AddTo\bibs`⟨*language*⟩`{`*code*`}`

The declaration \AddTo takes two arguments: a command name that holds all
language-related definitions for one language and the *code* that should be added

to this storage place.[1] The first argument is either \bibsall, in which case *code* is used for all languages, or \bibs⟨*language*⟩ (e.g., \bibgerman), in which case *code* is applied for that particular *language*.[2] In Example 12-5-14 on page 723 and Example 12-5-22 on page 727 we used \AddTo to change the presentation of back-references for all languages, by adding the redefinitions to \bibsall. Below we shorten the "Ibid." string when typesetting in the English language. The default for other languages is left unchanged in this case.

Some text[1] and[2] or[3] and more text.[4]

```
\usepackage[super,ibidem,titleformat=all]{jurabib}
\AddTo\bibsenglish{\renewcommand\ibidemname{Ib.}%
                  \renewcommand\ibidemmidname{ib.}}
\bibliographystyle{jurabib}
Some text\cite{vLeunen:92} and\cite{vLeunen:92}
\jurabibsetup{ibidem=name} % <-- change convention
or\cite{Knuth-CT-a} and more text.\cite{Knuth-CT-a}
```

12-5-35

---

[1]van Leunen: A handbook for scholars.

[2]Ib.

[3]Knuth, Donald E.: The TEXbook. Volume A, Computers and Typesetting. Reading, MA, USA: Addison-Wesley, 1986, ISBN 0–201–13447–0.

[4]Knuth, Donald E., ib.

While certain strings—calling an editor (\editorname) "(Hrsg.)", for example—should clearly be consistent throughout the whole bibliography, certain other aspects—most importantly, hyphenation—depend on the language used in the actual entry. For instance, a book with a German title should be hyphenated with German hyphenation patterns, regardless of the main language of the document. This is supported by jurabib through an extra field (language) in the BibTEX database file. If that field is specified in a given entry, then jurabib assumes that the title should be set in that particular language. Thus, if hyphenation patterns for that language are available (i.e., loaded in the format), they will be applied. For instance, if we repeat the last part of Example 12-5-6 from page 719 with babel loaded, we get the correction hyphenation:

Allgemeines Schuldrecht; Besonderes Schuldrecht

```
\usepackage[ngerman,english]{babel}
\usepackage{jurabib} \bibliographystyle{jurabib}
\citefield{title}{aschur,bschur}
```

12-5-36

Distinguishing the author's gender

Earlier, we mentioned that the female form of "Idem" is "Eadem". In the German language, we have "Derselbe" (male), "Dieselbe" (female), "Dasselbe" (neuter), and "Dieselben" (plural). To be able to distinguish the gender of the author, jurabib offers the BibTEX field gender, which takes a two-letter abbreviation for the gender as its value.

---

[1]The babel package uses a similar mechanism with the \addto declaration.

[2]Unfortunately, jurabib does not use exactly the same concept as babel. If you specify ngerman with babel to get German with new hyphenation patterns, then this is mapped to german, so you have to update \bibsgerman. If you use any of the dialects (e.g., austrian), then jurabib will not recognize those and will use english after issuing a warning. In that case use \bibsall for changing definitions.

gender	Meaning	In Citation	In Bibliography
sf	single female	\idemSfname, \idemsfname	\bibidemSfname, \bibidemsfname
sm	single male	\idemSmname, \idemsmname	\bibidemSmname, \bibidemsmname
pf	plural female	\idemPfname, \idempfname	\bibidemPfname, \bibidempfname
pm	plural male	\idemPmname, \idempmname	\bibidemPmname, \bibidempmname
sn	single neuter	\idemSnname, \idemsnname	\bibidemSnname, \bibidemsnname
pn	plural neuter	\idemPnname, \idempnname	\bibidemPnname, \bibidempnname

Table 12.1: Gender specification in jurabib

Possible values and the commands that contain the "Idem" strings, if specified, are given in Table 12.1. The commands with an uppercase letter in their name are used at the beginning of a sentence, the others in mid-sentence. Those starting with \bibidem.. are used in the bibliography if the option bibformat with the keyword ibidem is specified. Since the feature is computing intensive, it is not activated by default but has to be requested explicitly. Thus, to change to "Eadem" in case of female authors, we have to specify values for \idemSfname and \idemsfname and use the option lookforgender.

Some text[1] and[2] or[3] and more text.[4]

---

[1]van Leunen: A handbook for scholars.
[2]Eadem: A handbook for scholars.
[3]Knuth: The TEXbook.
12-5-37 [4]Idem: The TEXbook.

```
\usepackage[super,idem=strict,titleformat=all,
       lookforgender=true]{jurabib}
\AddTo\bibsenglish{\renewcommand\idemSfname{Eadem}%
       \renewcommand\idemsfname{eadem}}
\bibliographystyle{jurabib}

Some text\cite{vLeunen:92} and\cite{vLeunen:92}
or\cite{Knuth-CT-a} and more text.\cite{Knuth-CT-a}
```

Customizing the in-text citation layout further

Most of the author and title formatting is handled by the options authorformat and titleformat, which were discussed earlier. There also exist a few more options and commands that we have not mentioned so far.

If the whole citation should be surrounded by parentheses, simply specify the option round or square.

To place information about the edition as a superscript after the short title, specify the option superscriptedition. With a value of all this will be applied to all short-title citations, with the keyword commented applying only to publications of type commented, and with the keyword multiple applying only to publications that are cited with several different editions. The last two options are primarily intended for juridical works.

[Baumbach et al.: ZPO[59]]
[Brox/Walker[27], § 3]
12-5-38 [Otto Palandt/Heinrichs[62]]

```
\usepackage{jurabib} \bibliographystyle{jurabib}
\jurabibsetup{square,superscriptedition={all}}
\citetitle{zpo}\\ \cite[\S\,3]{bschur}\\ \cite[Heinrichs][]{bgb}
```

Alternatively, you can explicitly specify in the BibTeX database for each entry whether the edition should be shown as a superscript by setting the special field `ssedition` to the value 1 and by using the option `superscriptedition` with the keyword `switch`.

By specifying `authorformat=and` you will get author names separated by commas and "and" (actually by `\andname`, a command that has different values in different languages). But you cannot have the second and third author names separated by ", and" in this way. For adjustments on such a fine level, you can redefine `\jbbtasep` (**b**etween **t**wo **a**uthors **sep**aration), `\jbbfsasep` (**b**etween **f**irst and **s**econd **a**uthors **sep**aration), and `\jbbstasep` (**b**etween **s**econd and **t**hird **a**uthors **sep**aration).[1]

(Brox and Walker)
(Goossens, Rahtz, and Mittelbach)

```
\usepackage[round]{jurabib}
\renewcommand\jbbtasep{ and }    \renewcommand\jbbfsasep{, }
\renewcommand\jbbstasep{, and } \bibliographystyle{jurabib}
\cite{aschur} \\ \cite{LGC97}
```

12-5-39

You may also want to manually specify the fonts used for the author names and the short title, instead of relying on the possibilities offered by the supplied options. For this you have `\jbauthorfont`, `\jbannotatorfont`, `\jbactualauthorfont`, `\jbauthorfontifannotator`, and `\jbtitlefont` at your disposal, all of which are commands with one argument.

Customizing the bibliography layout

The formatting of the bibliography in standard LaTeX or with natbib is largely controlled by the used BibTeX style file or, if the bibliography entries are manually produced, by the formatting directives entered by the user. For example, a citation to the entry Knuth-CT-a from our sample database would be formatted by natbib's plainnat as follows:

```
Donald~E. Knuth.
\newblock {\em The {\TeX}book}, volume~A of {\em Computers and Typesetting}.
\newblock Ad{\-d}i{\-s}on-Wes{\-l}ey, Reading, MA, USA, 1986.
```

This means that formatting decisions, such as using emphasis for the title of the book and the series, and the presentation of the "volume" field, have all been made by the BibTeX style file.

In contrast, the BibTeX styles that come with the jurabib package use a drastically different approach: their output is highly structured, consisting of a large number of LaTeX commands, so that the final formatting (as well as the order of elements to some extent) can still be tweaked on the LaTeX level. In fact, they have to be adjusted on that level if you are not satisfied with the formatting produced

---

[1]No other possibilities are needed, since jurabib always uses "et al." whenever there are four or more authors.

from their default definitions. For example, the same citation as above processed
with the jurabib BᴵⱯTₑX style results in the following entry:

```
\jbbibargs {\bibnf {Knuth} {Donald~E.} {D.~E.} {} {}} {Donald~E. Knuth} {au}
{\bibtfont {The {\TeX}book}\bibatsep\ \volumeformat {A} Computers and
Typesetting\bibatsep\  \apyformat {Reading, MA, USA\bpubaddr {}
Ad{\-d}i{\-s}on-Wes{\-l}ey\bibbdsep {} 1986} \jbPages{ix + 483}\jbisbn {
0--201--13447--0}} {\bibhowcited} \jbdoitem \bibAnnoteFile {Knuth-CT-a}
```

Most of the above commands are further structured. The \bibnf command takes
five arguments (the different parts of the author's name) and, depending on which
are nonempty, passes them on to commands like \jbnfIndNoVonNoJr (name without "von" and "Junior" parts) for further processing. Consequently, it is possible
to interact with this process at many levels so that all kinds of requirements can
be catered for, although this somewhat complicates the customization of the layout. For this reason we restrict ourselves to showing just the most important
customization possibilities. For further control strategies, consult the package
documentation.

In the default set-up, the formatting of the bibliography is fairly independent
of that used for the citations. If you specify authorformat=italic, author names
are typeset in italics in the text but there is no change in the bibliography. The
easiest way to change that is to use the option biblikecite; then formatting
decisions for the citations will also be used in the bibliography as far as possible.
If that is not desired or not sufficient, explicit formatting directives are available;
they are discussed below.

The fonts used in a bibliographical entry are controlled by the following set of
commands: \biblnfont and \bibfnfont for formatting the last and first names
of the author, and \bibelnfont and \bibefnfont for the last and first names
of the editor, if present. The command \bibtfont is used for titles of books,
\bibbtfont for titles of essays (i.e., entries involving a BᴵⱯTₑX booktitle field),
and \bibjtfont for titles, or rather names, of journals. The font for article titles
within such a journal is customized with \bibapifont. The commands all receive
the text they act upon as an argument, so any redefinition must also use an argument or \text.. font commands as shown in the next example (picking the
argument up implicitly).

KNUTH, DONALD E.: The TₑXbook. Volume A,
Computers and Typesetting. Reading, MA,
USA: Addison-Wesley, 1986, ix + 483, ISBN
0–201–13447–0

KNUTH, DONALD E.: *"Typesetting Concrete
Mathematics"*. TUGboat, 10 April 1989,
Nr. 1, 31–36, ISSN 0896–3207

```
\usepackage{jurabib}
\bibliographystyle{jurabib}
\renewcommand\biblnfont{\MakeUppercase}
\renewcommand\bibfnfont{\textsc}
\renewcommand\bibtfont {\textsf}
\renewcommand\bibapifont[1]{\textit{``#1''}}
\nocite{Knuth-CT-a,Knuth:TB10-1-31}
\bibliography{tex}
```

12-5-40

The punctuation separating different parts in the entry can be customized by another set of commands: `\bibansep` sets the punctuation and space after the author name, `\bibeansep` does the same after the editor name, `\bibatsep` produces punctuation after the title (the space is already supplied!), and `\bibbdsep` is the punctuation *before* the date. With `\bibjtsep` the journal title separation is set. There are similar commands for adjusting other parts.[1] In the next example we use these commands to remove the default colon after the author's name and then typeset a semicolon after the title, no comma before the year, and the word "in" before the journal name. We also use the `dotafter` option with the keyword `bibentry` to add a final period after each entry.

Knuth, Donald E. Typesetting Concrete Mathematics; in TUGboat, 10 April 1989, Nr. 1, 31–36, ISSN 0896–3207.

Mittelbach, Frank/Rowley, Chris The Pursuit of Quality: How can Automated Typesetting achieve the Highest Standards of Craft Typography? In **Vanoirbeek/Coray** EP92, 261–273.

Vanoirbeek, Christine/Coray, Giovanni, editors EP92— Proceedings of Electronic Publishing, '92; Cambridge: Cambridge University Press 1992.

```
\usepackage[dotafter=bibentry]
            {jurabib}
\bibliographystyle{jurabib}
\renewcommand\bibjtsep{in }
\renewcommand\bibansep{ }
\renewcommand\bibatsep{;}
\renewcommand\bibbdsep{}
\nocite{Knuth:TB10-1-31,MR-PQ}
\bibliography{tex}
```

12-5-41

We already saw that the separation between different author names in a citation can be adjusted by means of the `authorformat` option and various keywords. However, except for the keyword `allreversed`, this has no effect on the entries in the bibliography. To modify the formatting there, you have to redefine the commands `\bibbtasep`, `\bibbfsasep`, and `\bibbstasep`. The naming convention is the same as for the corresponding citation commands. A similar set of commands, `\bibbtesep`, `\bibbfsesep`, and `\bibbstesep`, is available to specify the separation between editor names in an entry.

Hans Brox and **Wolf-Dietrich Walker:** Allgemeines Schuldrecht. 29th edition. München, 2003

Michel Goossens, **Sebastian Rahtz**, and **Frank Mittelbach:** The LATEX Graphics Companion: Illustrating Documents with TEX and PostScript. Reading, MA, USA: Addison-Wesley Longman, 1997, Tools and Techniques for Computer Typesetting, xxi + 554, ISBN 0–201–85469–4

```
\usepackage[authorformat=allreversed]
            {jurabib}
\bibliographystyle{jurabib}
\renewcommand\bibbtasep{ and }
\renewcommand\bibbfsasep{, }
\renewcommand\bibbstasep{, and }
\nocite{aschur,LGC97}
\bibliography{tex,jura}
```

12-5-42

Adjusting the general layout of the bibliography The main option for influencing the general layout of the bibliography list is `bibformat`, which can take a number of keywords as its value. If you specify the keyword `nohang`, then the default indentation (of `2.5em`) for the second and

---

[1] This area of jurabib is somewhat inconsistent in its naming conventions and command behavior. Perhaps this will change one day.

subsequent lines of a bibliographical entry is suppressed. Alternatively, you can explicitly set the indentation by changing the dimension parameter \jbbibhang, as in the next example. There we also use the keywords compress (using less space around entries) and raggedright (typesetting entries unjustified). For improved quality, especially when typesetting to a small measure, you may want to load the package ragged2e. Note the use of the newcommands option to overload the standard \raggedright (as used by jurabib) with \RaggedRight.

Brox, Hans/Walker, Wolf-Dietrich: Allgemeines Schuldrecht. 29th edition. München, 2003

Baumbach, Adolf et al.: Zivilprozeßordnung mit Gerichtsverfassungsgesetz und anderen Nebengesetzen. 59th edition. München, 2002

Brox, Hans/Walker, Wolf-Dietrich: Besonderes Schuldrecht. 27th edition. München, 2002

```
\usepackage[newcommands]{ragged2e}
\usepackage[bibformat={compress,%
                       raggedright}]
          {jurabib}
\bibliographystyle{jurunsrt}
\setlength\jbbibhang{1pc}

\nocite{aschur,zpo,bschur}
\bibliography{jura}
```

12-5-43

If you use the keyword tabular, then the bibliography is set in a two-column table with the left column containing the author(s) and the right column the remainder of the entry. By default, the first column is one third of \textwidth and both columns are set ragged. The defaults can be changed by redefining a number of commands, as shown in the next example. The width of the right column is specified by

```
\renewcommand\bibrightcolumn{\textwidth-\bibleftcolumn-\bibcolumnsep}
```

Normally it is enough to change \bibleftcolumn and/or \bibcolumnsep. The calc package is automatically loaded by jurabib, so we can make use of it when specifying dimensions.

Brox, Hans/ Walker, Wolf-Dietrich	Allgemeines Schuldrecht. 29th edition. München, 2003
Knuth, Donald E.	Typesetting Concrete Mathematics. TUGboat, 10 April 1989, Nr. 1, 31–36, ISSN 0896–3207
Free Software Foundation	GNU Make, A Program for Directing Recompilation. 2000

```
\usepackage[bibformat=tabular]{jurabib}
\bibliographystyle{jurabib}
\renewcommand\bibleftcolumn{6.5pc}
\renewcommand\bibcolumnsep{1pc}
\renewcommand\bibleftcolumnadjust
             {\raggedright}
\renewcommand\bibrightcolumnadjust{}
\nocite{aschur,Knuth:TB10-1-31}
\nocite{GNUmake}
\bibliography{tex,jura}
```

12-5-44

If you use the keyword numbered, the bibliography will be numbered even though the actual citations in the text use the author-date or short-title scheme. Currently, it is impossible to refer to those numbers.

Some publishers' house styles omit the author's name (or replace it by a dash or other character) if that author is cited with several works. This is supported through the keyword `ibidem`, which by default generates "Idem" or, more precisely, the result from executing `\bibidemSmname`. To get a (predefined) rule instead, use `\jbuseidemhrule`. If you want something else, redefine `\bibauthormultiple`. Both possibilities are shown in the next example. The jurabib package automatically detects if an entry appears on the top of a page and will use the author name in that case. Because of this mechanism it may take several (extra) LATEX runs before the document compiles without "Rerun to get..."

Brox, Hans/Walker, Wolf-Dietrich: Besonderes Schuldrecht. 27th edition. München, 2002

—— Allgemeines Schuldrecht. 29th edition. München, 2003

Knuth, Donald E.: The TEXbook. Volume A, Computers and Typesetting. Reading, MA, USA: Addison-Wesley, 1986, ix + 483, ISBN 0–201–13447–0

—— Typesetting Concrete Mathematics. TUGboat, 10 April 1989, Nr. 1, 31–36, ISSN 0896–3207

```
\usepackage[bibformat=ibidem]
                {jurabib}
\bibliographystyle{jurabib}
\jbuseidemhrule  % use default rule
% Alternative generic redefinition
% instead of the default rule:
%\renewcommand\bibauthormultiple
%              {[same name symbol]}
\nocite{aschur,bschur}
\nocite{Knuth-CT-a,Knuth:TB10-1-31}
\bibliography{tex,jura}
```

12-5-45

A variant bibliography layout collecting works under the author names is available through the keyword `ibidemalt`. This keyword automatically implies the keyword `compress`.

Baumbach, Adolf et al.:
  ▷ Zivilprozeßordnung mit Gerichtsverfassungsgesetz und anderen Nebengesetzen. 59th edition. München, 2002

Brox, Hans/Walker, Wolf-Dietrich:
  ▷ Besonderes Schuldrecht. 27th edition. München, 2002
  ▷ Allgemeines Schuldrecht. 29th edition. München, 2003

Palandt, Otto:
  ▷ Bürgerliches Gesetzbuch. 62th edition. München: Beck Juristischer Verlag, 2003

```
\usepackage{jurabib}
\jurabibsetup{bibformat=ibidemalt}
\bibliographystyle{jurabib}
\nocite{aschur,bschur,zpo,bgb}
\bibliography{jura}
```

12-5-46

Annotated bibliographies If you want to produce an annotated bibliography, use the option `annote`. If the current BIBTEX entry has an `annote` field, it will be typeset after the entry using `\jbannoteformat` to format it (the default is to typeset it in `\small`). If there is no `annote` field, then jurabib searches for a file with the extension `.tex` and the key of the entry as its base name. If this file exists, its contents will be used as the annotation text.

Knuth, Donald E.: The TEXbook. Volume A, Computers and Typesetting. Reading, MA, USA: Addison-Wesley, 1986, ix + 483, ISBN 0–201–13447–0

The authoritative user manual on the program TEX by its creator.

12-5-47

```
\begin{filecontents}{Knuth-CT-a.tex}
   The authoritative user manual on the program \TeX{}
   by its creator.
\end{filecontents}
\usepackage[annote]{jurabib}\bibliographystyle{jurabib}
\renewcommand\jbannoteformat[1]
   {{\footnotesize\begin{quote}#1\end{quote}}}
\nocite{Knuth-CT-a}
\bibliography{tex}
```

Since it is a nuisance to have many files (one for each annotation) cluttering your current directory, jurabib offers a search path declaration in analogy to the \graphicspath command provided by the graphics package. Thus, after

```
\bibAnnotePath{{./books}{./articles}}
```

annotation files are searched for in the subdirectories books and articles of the current directory.

Using external configuration files

Customization of jurabib is possible on two levels: by specifying options or, for finer control, by redefining certain declarations or executing commands. In the previous sections we have already encountered a number of package options together with the keywords they accept but they represented less than a third of what is available. In the default configuration file jurabib.cfg, you will find a \jurabibsetup declaration listing *all* options together with all their keyword values—nearly 100 possibilities in total. They are all commented out so that you can produce your own configuration file by copying the default one and uncommenting those options you want to execute normally. If you save this configuration in a file with extension .cfg, you can load it instead of the default configuration by using the config option. For example,

```
\usepackage[config=law]{jurabib}
```

will load the option file law.cfg, which should contain a \jurabibsetup declaration and possibly some additional customization commands. For example, such a file might contain

```
\jurabibsetup{lookat,opcit,commabeforerest,titleformat=colonsep}
\renewcommand\opcit{\textit{supra}
```

and perhaps some other initializations to implement citations for juridical publications. As mentioned earlier, such defaults stored in a file can be overwritten by using additional options during loading or with a \jurabibsetup declaration in the preamble.

BıBTEX styles for jurabib

The jurabib package is distributed together with four BıBTEX style files: jurabib, jureco, jurunsrt, and jox. They differ only in minor details: jureco produces a slightly more compact bibliography, leaving out some data, while jurunsrt is the same as jurabib without sorting, so that the references appear in order of their citation in the document. The jox style produces references in "Oxford style". Since jurabib requires very specially formatted \bibitem commands, the above styles are currently the only ones that can be used together with the package.

All four styles provide a number of additional BıBTEX entries as well as a number of additional fields for existing entries. Having additional fields in a BıBTEX database is usually not a problem, since BıBTEX ignores any field it doesn't know about. Thus, such a database can be used with other BıBTEX styles that do not provide these fields. Additional entries are slightly different, since using them means you have to use jurabib to be able to refer to them.

Additional BıBTEX types   The additional entries are www for citing a URL, periodical for periodicals that are not cited by year but by volume number, and commented for commentaries in juridical works.

The standard BıBTEX fields are described in Table 13.2 on page 765. The following additional fields are available when using one of the jurabib BıBTEX styles:

annote   An annotation that is typeset if jurabib is used with the option annote; see page 740 for details.

booktitleaddon   Extra information to be typeset after a booktitle text of a collection.

dissyear   Year of a dissertation, habilitation, or other source if that work is also being published as a book (perhaps with a different year).

editortype   Position of the person mentioned in the editor field (if not really an "editor").

flanguage   Foreign language, in case of a translated work.

founder   In juridical works, the original founder of a publication (in contrast to the editor). The name is shown followed by the replacement text of \foundername, which defaults to "␣(Begr.)".

gender   Gender of the author or authors. The jurabib package uses this information to select the right kind of words for "Idem" in the current language; see page 734.

howcited   Text to use for back-reference information, or 1 to indicate that a normal back-reference should be generated. This field is evaluated by the option howcited if used together with the keyword normal; see page 721.

oaddress/opublisher/oyear   Information about the first edition of a work.

`shortauthor` Text to use as the author information in a short-title citation. By default, jurabib automatically selects the last name (or names) from the author or editor field.

`shorttitle` Text to use as the title information in a short-title citation. If it is not specified the whole `title` is used.

`sortkey` String to be used for sorting in unusual situations. To sort "von Bismarck, Otto" under B, you can use `sortkey"Bismarck, Otto von"`.

`ssedition` Flag to indicate that this entry should be typeset with the edition shown as a superscript. It requires the use of the `superscriptedition` option together with the keyword switch; see page 735.

`titleaddon` Extra information to be placed after a title but not used, for example, when generating a short title.

`totalpages` Total number of pages in a publication. If present, it will be shown followed by the replacement text of the command `\bibtotalpagesname`, which is language dependent.

`translator` Translator of the publication.

`updated` Date of the last update in a loose-leaf edition or a similar work. The field is only available for the BibTeX type `commented`. By default, "last update *date*" is generated. This can be customized through the commands `\updatename` and `\updatesep`.

`urldate` Date when a URL was known to be current. By default, jurabib produces the string "visited on *date*" when this field is used. It can be changed by redefining the command `\urldatecomment`.

`url` A URL related to the current publication. In case of the entry type `www`, it is required; otherwise, it is optional.

`volumetitle` A volume title that follows the volume number in the presentation. This field is available for the types `book`, `commented`, `incollection`, and `inbook`.

12.5.2 camel—Dedicated law support

Anyone who needs to comply with the conventions used in (Anglo-American) legal works may also be interested in the camel "bibliography engine" [15, 16] written by Frank Bennett, Jr., in 1997. It implements citation conventions as specified in the *Blue Book* [21] (though for an earlier edition) and offers features such as classified citations. It can be used to generate table of cases, statutes, and much more. However, as camel is currently not being developed any further (volunteers welcome), one has to take some rough edges in the software as features.

In contrast to the packages described so far, camel uses its own set of commands to specify citations (\source instead of \cite), bibliographical databases (\citationdata instead of \bibliography), citation conventions (\citationstyle instead of \bibliographystyle), and printed bibliographies (\printbibliography as the second part of the functionality of \bibliography).

The next example shows these commands in action. The \source command takes an optional first argument in which one can specify what kind of citation should be given (e.g., "f" for full reference, "t" for title omitted, "a" for author name omitted). A second optional argument after the *key* can be used to specify page numbers in the reference.

An interesting feature is that the package recognizes so-called interword connectors between citations (e.g., "see-also" and "cited-in" in our example). As a result those citations are considered to belong together and are automatically placed into the same footnote.

…text [1] … somewhat later … [2]

References

D. E. KNUTH, THE TEXBOOK (Computers and Typesetting, 1986).

---

[1] D. E. KNUTH, (Computers and Typesetting, 1986); *see also* Knuth, TUGBOAT, V. 10, N. 1, p. 31 (1989).

[2] H. BROX AND W.-D. WALKER, BESONDERES SCHULDRECHT 24, 130, 216 (27. ed. 2002) *cited in* ZIVILPROZESSORDNUNG MIT GERICHTSVERFASSUNGSGESETZ UND ANDEREN NEBENGESETZEN (59. neubearb. ed. 2002).

```
\usepackage{camel}
\forcefootnotes
\citationstyle{law}
\citationdata{jura,tex}

\ldots text \source[t]{Knuth-CT-a}
see-also \source[f]{Knuth:TB10-1-31}
\ldots\ somewhat later \ldots
\source[f]{bschur}[24,130,216]
cited-in \source[a]{zpo}

\printbibliography[labels=false]{all}
```

12-5-48

Another feature that can be of interest is the ability to produce subject bibliographies using the \citationsubject declaration.

…text [1] …later… [2]

Law

[1] H. BROX AND W.-D. WALKER, BESONDERES SCHULDRECHT (27. ed. 2002)

TEX literature

[1] D. E. KNUTH, THE TEXBOOK (Computers and Typesetting, 1986)

[2] Knuth, *Typesetting Concrete Mathematics*, TUGBOAT, V. 10, N. 1, p. 31 (1989)

---

[1] THE TEXBOOK (Computers and Typesetting, 1986); *see also Typesetting Concrete Mathematics*, TUGBOAT, V. 10, N. 1, p. 31 (1989).

[2] H. BROX AND W.-D. WALKER, (27. ed. 2002).

```
\usepackage{camel}
\citationsubject[o=tts,i=ttb]
        {tex}{\TeX{} literature}
\citationsubject[o=lts,i=ltb]
            {jur}{Law}
\forcefootnotes
\citationstyle{law}
\citationdata{jura,tex}

\ldots text
\source[a,s=tex]{Knuth-CT-a}
see-also \source[f,s=tex]
        {Knuth:TB10-1-31}
\ldots later\ldots
\source[t,s=jur]{bschur}
\printbibliography{jur}
\printbibliography{tex}
```

12-5-49

The citation data are written to external files (extension specified with o= on the \citationsubject declaration). Such files have to be processed by *MakeIndex*:

```
makeindex -s camel.ist -o ⟨jobname⟩.ttb jobname.tts
makeindex -s camel.ist -o ⟨jobname⟩.ltb jobname.lts
```

The results are then read back in (i= argument) on the next LaTeX run.

12.6   Multiple bibliographies in one document

In large documents that contain several independent sections, such as conference proceedings with many different articles, or in a book with separate parts written by different authors, it is sometimes necessary to have separate bibliographies for each of the units. In such a scenario citations are confined to a certain part of the document, the one to which the bibliography list belongs.

A complementary request is to have several bibliographies in parallel, such as one for primary sources and one for secondary literature. In that case one has to be able to reference works in different bibliographies from any point in the document.

Both requests can be automatically resolved if none of the bibliographies contain the same publication[1] and you are prepared to produce the bibliographies manually, by means of several thebibliography environments without using BibTeX. In that case the \bibitem commands within the environment provide the right cross-referencing information for the \cite commands (or their variants) to pick up from anywhere in the document. Having the same publication in several bibliographies (or more exactly the same reference key) is not possible, since that would lead to a "multiply defined labels" warning (see page 928) and to incorrect references. Of course, this could be manually corrected by choosing a different key for such problematical citations.

Being deprived of using BibTeX has a number of consequences. First, it will be more difficult to impose a uniform format on the bibliographical entries (something that BibTeX automatically handles for you). Second, using an author-date or short-title citation scheme will be difficult (since natbib requires a special structure within the optional argument of \bibitem) to downright impossible (since the structure required by jurabib is not suitable for manual production); see Section 12.3 for a discussion of the required \bibitem structures in both cases.

To be able to use BibTeX for this task people had to find a way to generate several .bbl files from one source document. As discussed in Section 12.1.3, the interaction with BibTeX normally works as follows: each citation command (e.g., \cite) writes its *key-list* as a \citation command into the .aux file. Similarly, \bibliography and \bibliographystyle commands simply copy their arguments to the .aux file. BibTeX then reads the master .aux file (and, if necessary,

---

[1] This could happen, for example, if you compile the proceedings of a conference and each article therein has its own bibliography.

	_____Bibliographies per Unit_____			
	chapterbib	bibunits	bibtopic	multibib
Bibliography per chapter	X	X	X	n/a
Bibliography per other unit	Restrictions	X	X	n/a
Deal with escaping citations	X	Restrictions	Error	n/a
Additional global bibliography	Labor	X	no	n/a
Above typeset together somewhere	X	No	No	n/a
Multiple global bibliographies	No	No	X	X
Multiple bibliographies per unit	No	No	X	no
cite compatible	X	X	X	X
jurabib compatible	X	X	**Restrictions**	X
natbib compatible	X	X	X	X
Support for unsorted BibTeX styles	X	X	No	X
Requires tailored .bib files	No	No	Yes	**No**
	chapterbib	bibunits	bibtopic	multibib
			_____Per Topic_____	

Blue entries indicate features (or missing features) that may force a selection.

Table 12.2: Comparison of packages for multiple bibliographies

those from \included files) searching for occurrences of the above commands. From the provided information it produces a single .bbl file. To make BibTeX work for the above scenarios, four problems have to be solved:

1. Generate one .aux file for every bibliography in the document that can be used as input for BibTeX.

2. Ensure that each citation command writes its information to the correct .aux file, so that BibTeX, when it processes a given .aux file, will add the corresponding bibliographical data in the .bbl file but not in the others.

3. Ensure that the resulting .bbl files are read back into LaTeX at the right place.

4. Handle the problem of escaping citations due to their placement in sectioning or \caption commands. A citation in such a place would later appear in the table of contents or list of figures, and there (in a different context) LaTeX would have problems in resolving it.

The packages chapterbib, bibunits, bibtopic, and multibib, which are described in this section, solve the above problems in different ways. They all have their own advantages and disadvantages. A short comparison of these packages appears in Table 12.2, where blue entries indicate features (or missing features) that may force a selection when one is looking for a solution for bibliographies per unit or with bibliographies per topic, or a combination of both.

12.6.1   chapterbib—**Bibliographies per included file**

The chapterbib package (developed by Donald Arseneau based on original work by Niel Kempson) allows multiple bibliographies in a LaTeX document, including the same cited items occurring in more than one bibliography.

It solves the problem of producing several .aux files for BibTeX, by relying on the \include mechanism of LaTeX; you can have one bibliography per \included file. This package can be used, for example, to produce a document with bibliographies per chapter (hence the name), where each chapter is stored in a separate file that is included with the \include command. This approach has the following restrictions:

- Each \include file needs to have its own \bibliography command. The database files that are listed in the argument can, of course, be different in each file. What is not so obvious is that each file must also contain a \bibliographystyle command, though for reasons of uniformity *preferably with the same style argument* (Example 12-6-1 on the next page shows that different styles can be applied).

- An \include file not containing a \bibliography command cannot contain citation commands, as they would not get resolved.

- Citation commands outside of \include files (with the exception of those appearing in the table of contents; see below) will not be resolved, unless you include a thebibliography environment on that level. Without special precautions, this environment has to be entered manually. If you use BibTeX on the document's .aux file you will encounter errors, because BibTeX sees multiple \bibdata and \bibstyle commands (when processing the included .aux files). In addition, you will get *all* citations from *all* \include files added, and that is perhaps not desirable. If you do want a cohesive bibliography for the whole document, there is a rootbib option to help with this task. However, it requires adding and removing the option at different stages in the process; see the package documentation for details.

- Units containing a local bibliography will always start a new page (because of the \include command). For cases where this is not appropriate, chapterbib offers some support through a \cbinput command and cbunit environment; see the package documentation for details. Unless you need the gather option, it might be better to use the bibunits package in such situations.

By default, the thebibliography environment generates a numberless heading corresponding to the highest sectioning level available in the document class (e.g., \chapter* with the book class). However, if bibliographies are to be generated for individual parts of the document this may not be the right level. In that case you can use the option sectionbib[1] to enforce \section* headings for the bibliographies.

---

[1] If both chapterbib and natbib are used, use the sectionbib option of natbib instead!

In the following example, we present the `\include` files `article-1.tex` and `article-2.tex` in `filecontents` environments, which allows us to process this example automatically for the book. In real life these would be different files on your computer file system. We also use `\stepcounter` to change the `chapter` counter rather than using `\chapter` to avoid getting huge chapter headings in the example. Note that both included files refer to a publication with the key `Knuth-CT-a`. These are actually treated as different keys in the sense that one refers to the publication from `article-1.bbl` and the other refers to that from `article-2.bbl`.

... see [Knu86] ...	... see [2] and [1] ...
Bibliography	**Bibliography**
[Knu86] Donald E. Knuth. *The TeXbook*, volume A of *Computers and Typesetting*. Addison-Wesley, Reading, MA, USA, 1986.	[1] Hans Brox and Wolf-Dietrich Walker. *Besonderes Schuldrecht*. München, 27. edition, 2002.
	[2] Donald E. Knuth. *The TeXbook*, volume A of *Computers and Typesetting*. Addison-Wesley, Reading, MA, USA, 1986.

```
\begin{filecontents}{article-1.tex}
 \stepcounter{chapter}
 \ldots\ see \cite{Knuth-CT-a} \ldots
 \bibliographystyle{alpha}
 \bibliography{tex}
\end{filecontents}
\begin{filecontents}{article-2.tex}
 \stepcounter{chapter}
 \ldots see \cite{Knuth-CT-a}
  and \cite{bschur} \ldots
 \bibliographystyle{plain}
 \bibliography{tex,jura}
\end{filecontents}

\usepackage[sectionbib]{chapterbib}
\include{article-1}
\include{article-2}
```

12-6-1

If you wish to group all the bibliographies together (for example, at the end of the document), use the option `gather` and place a `\bibliography` command at the point where the combined bibliography should appear. The argument to that command can be left empty as it is not used to communicate with BibTeX.

Instead of `gather`, you may want to use the option `duplicate`. It will produce "chapter bibliographies", plus the combined listing. Both options work only in document classes that have a `\chapter` command. The headings generated by either option can be customized by redefining the command `\StartFinalBibs`, which is executed at the point where the top-level `\bibliography` command is encountered. In the following example it generates an unnumbered `\chapter` heading, sets up the running head via `\chaptermark`, and then redefines `\bibname`, which provides the text used in the heading for each sub-bibliography. As you can see `\thechapter` is used to number the sub-bibliographies, so this mechanism works only if all chapters have bibliographies; otherwise, the numbering will be wrong.

If you do not place the combined bibliography at the end of the document, make sure that `\bibname` is properly reset afterwards. Otherwise, any subsequent bibliography in an `\include` file will inherit the modified definition.

If the highest heading unit in your document is `\section`, the redefinition of `\StartFinalBibs` can be done in a similar way. You then have to use `\refname` instead of `\bibname`, since that is the command used in classes derived from the article document class.

References by article

Article 1

[Knu86] Donald E. Knuth. *The TEXbook*, volume A of *Computers and Typesetting*. Addison-Wesley, Reading, MA, USA, 1986.

Article 2

[1] Hans Brox and Wolf-Dietrich Walker. *Besonderes Schuldrecht*. München, 27. edition, 2002.

[2] Donald E. Knuth. *The TEXbook*, volume A of *Computers and Typesetting*. Addison-Wesley, Reading, MA, USA, 1986.

```
% included files as in
% previous example
\usepackage
    [gather,sectionbib]
    {chapterbib}
\renewcommand\StartFinalBibs
    {\chapter*
    {References by article}%
    \chaptermark
    {References by article}%
    \renewcommand\bibname
    {Article~\thechapter}}
\include{article-1}
\include{article-2}
\bibliography{}
```

12-6-2

If citations are placed into sectioning or `\caption` commands they will appear eventually in some table of contents list (i.e., at the top level). Nevertheless, chapterbib will properly resolve them, by inserting extra code into `.toc`, `.lof`, and `.lot` files so that a `\cite` command is able to determine to which local bibliography it belongs. If you have additional table of contents lists set up, as explained in Section 2.3.4, you have to be careful to avoid citations that may end up in these new contents lists, as chapterbib is unaware of them.

Some BibTEX styles unfortunately use `\newcommand` declarations instead of `\providecommand` in the generated `.bbl` files, which makes such files unsuitable for repeated loading. If you get "Command ⟨*name*⟩ already defined" errors for this reason, surround the `\bibliography` commands and their arguments in braces. For example, write

Command already defined error

```
{\bibliography{tex,jura}}
```

The chapterbib package is compatible with most other packages, including the citation packages discussed earlier in this chapter. If you plan to use it together with babel, load the chapterbib package first.

12.6.2 bibunits—**Bibliographies for arbitrary units**

The bibunits package developed by Thorsten Hansen (from original work by Jose Alberto Fernandez) generates separate bibliographies for different units (parts) of the text (chapters, sections, or `bibunit` environments). The package will separate the citations of each unit of text into a separate file to be processed by BibTEX. A global bibliography can also appear in the document, and citations can be placed in both at the same time.

One way to denote the units that should have a separate bibliography is by enclosing them in a `bibunit` environment.

> `\begin{bibunit}[`*style*`]` ... `\putbib[`*file-list*`]` ... `\end{bibunit}`

Setting up defaults The optional parameter *style* specifies a style for the bibliography different from a default that may have been set up (see below). Instead of `\bibliography` you use a `\putbib` command to place the bibliography. It can appear anywhere within the unit as proven by the example. The optional argument *file-list* specifies a comma-separated list of BibTeX database files; again a default can be set up. A default BibTeX style can be set with `\defaultbibliographystyle`; without it, `plain` is used as the default. Similarly, `\defaultbibliography` can be used to define a default list of BibTeX databases. In its absence `\jobname.bib` is tried. To be effective the default declarations have to appear after `\begin{document}`.

1   First one

[1] was used to produce [2].

References

[1] Free Software Foundation, Boston, Massachusetts. *GNU Make, A Program for Directing Recompilation*, 2000.

[2] Donald E. Knuth. Typesetting Concrete Mathemat-

ics. *TUGboat*, 10(1):31–36, April 1989.

2   Another one

References

[1] Hans Brox and Wolf-Dietrich Walker. *Allgemeines Schuldrecht*. München, 29. edition, 2003.

As described by [1] ...

```
\usepackage{bibunits}
\defaultbibliographystyle{plain}
\section{First one}
\begin{bibunit}[plain]
 \cite{GNUMake} was used to
 produce \cite{Knuth:TB10-1-31}.
 \putbib[tex]
\end{bibunit}
\section{Another one}
\begin{bibunit}[plain]
 \putbib[jura]
 As described by \cite{aschur}
 \ldots
\end{bibunit}
```

12-6-3

For each unit `bibunits` writes the `\citation` commands (used to communicate with BibTeX) into the file bu⟨*num*⟩.aux, where ⟨*num*⟩ is an integer starting with 1. Thus, to generate the necessary bibliographies, you have to run BibTeX on the files bu1, bu2, and so forth. As a consequence, with the default settings you cannot process more than one document that uses bibunits in the same directory, as the the auxiliary files would be overwritten.[1]

After generating the bibliographies you have to rerun LaTeX at least twice to resolve the new cross-references. Be aware that older versions of the package do *not* warn you about the need for a further rerun.

A global bibliography, in addition to the bibliographies for the individual units, can be generated by using `\bibliography` and `\bibliographystyle` as usual. Outside of a `bibunit` environment, the standard commands should be used

---

[1] If necessary, you can direct the package to use different names; see the package documentation.

to generate a citation for the global bibliography. Inside `bibunit`, use `\cite*` and `\nocite*` instead of `\cite` and `\nocite` to generate a citation for both the local and the global bibliography. There are, however, a number of restrictions. If the `natbib` package is also loaded, then `\cite*` has the meaning defined by `natbib` and cannot be used for generating a global citation (use `\nocite` outside the unit in that case). In addition, refrain from using numerical citation labels, since they are likely to produce ambiguous labels in the global bibliography, as shown in the next example. A better choice would be a BibTeX style such as `alpha`.

1   First one

[1] was used to produce [2].

References

[1] Free Software Foundation, Boston, Massachusetts. *GNU Make, A Program for Directing Recompilation*, 2000.

[2] Donald E. Knuth. Typesetting Concrete Mathematics. *TUGboat*, 10(1):31–36, April 1989.

2   Another one

As described by [1] ...

References

[1] Donald E. Knuth. Typesetting Concrete Mathematics. *TUGboat*, 10(1):31–36, April 1989.

Global References

[1] Donald E. Knuth. Typesetting Concrete Mathematics. *TUGboat*, 10(1):31–36, April 1989.

```
\usepackage{bibunits}
\section{First one}
\begin{bibunit}[plain]
 \cite{GNUMake} was used to
 produce \cite*{Knuth:TB10-1-31}.
 \putbib[tex]
\end{bibunit}
\section{Another one}
\begin{bibunit}[plain]
 As described by
 \cite*{Knuth:TB10-1-31}
 \ldots   \putbib[tex]
\end{bibunit}
\renewcommand\refname
    {Global References}
\bibliographystyle{plain}
\bibliography{tex}
```

12-6-4

Rather than using `\cite*` everywhere in your document, you can specify the package option `globalcitecopy`. All local citations are then automatically copied to the global bibliography as well.

Instead of specifying the bibliography units with `bibunit` environments explicitly, you can specify the sectioning unit for which bibliography units should be generated automatically.

`\bibliographyunit[`*unit*`]`

This command specifies for which document unit references must be generated, such as *unit*=`\chapter` (for each chapter) or *unit*=`\section` (for each section). If the optional argument is not given, the command `\bibliographyunit` deactivates further bibliography units. When `\bibliographyunit` is active, the `\bibliographystyle` and `\bibliography` commands specify the BibTeX files and the style to be used by default for a global bibliography, as well as in the local units. If you wish to specify information for local bibliographies only, use `\bibliography*` and `\bibliographystyle*` instead. These declarations *cannot* be used in the preamble but must be placed after `\begin{document}`.

Getting unresolved references There is, however, a catch with the approach: the normal definition of the `thebibliography` environment, which surrounds the reference lists, generates a heading of the highest sectioning level. Hence, if you use `\chapter` units in a report, the heading generated by that environment will prematurely end the unit and consequently you will end up with undefined references, as shown in the example (using `\section` units in an `\article` class).

---

1 First one

[**?**] was used to produce [**?**].

References

[1] Free Software Foundation, Boston, Massachusetts. *GNU Make, A Program for Directing Recompilation*, 2000.

[2] Donald E. Knuth. Typesetting Concrete Mathemat-

ics. *TUGboat*, 10(1):31–36, April 1989.

2 Another one

As described by [**?**] …

References

[1] Hans Brox and Wolf-Dietrich Walker. *Allgemeines Schuldrecht*.

```
\usepackage{bibunits}
\bibliographyunit[\section]
\bibliographystyle*{plain}
\bibliography*{tex,jura}
\section{First one}
  \cite{GNUMake} was
used  to produce
  \cite{Knuth:TB10-1-31}.
  \putbib
\section{Another one}
  As described by
  \cite{aschur} \ldots
  \putbib
```

12-6-5

To resolve this problem, you can provide your own definition for the `thebibliography` environment, so that it uses a different sectioning level than the one specified on the `\bibliographyunit` declaration. Alternatively, you can use the option `sectionbib` (use `\section*` as a heading in `thebibliography`) or `subsectionbib` (use `\subsection*`) to change the `thebibliography` environment for you.

---

1 First one

[1] was used to produce [2].

References

[1] Free Software Foundation, Boston, Massachusetts. *GNU Make, A Program for Directing Recompilation*, 2000.

[2] Donald E. Knuth. Typesetting Concrete Mathemat-

ics. *TUGboat*, 10(1):31–36, April 1989.

2 Another one

As described by [1] …

References

[1] Hans Brox and Wolf-Dietrich Walker. *Allgemeines Schuldrecht*. München, 29. edition, 2003.

```
\usepackage[subsectionbib]
          {bibunits}
\bibliographyunit[\section]
\bibliographystyle*{plain}
\bibliography*{tex,jura}
\section{First one}
  \cite{GNUMake} was
used  to produce
  \cite{Knuth:TB10-1-31}.
  \putbib
\section{Another one}
  As described by
  \cite{aschur} \ldots
  \putbib
```

12-6-6

Note that the unit specified on the `\bibliographyunit` command has to be different from the one referred to in the option. In the above example the unit was `\section`, so we used the `subsectionbib` option.

To resolve the problem of escaping citations (see page 746), the package offers the option `labelstoglobalaux`. However, this has the side effects that such citations will appear in the global bibliography and that numerical reference schemes are likely to produce incorrect labels; see the package documentation for details.

12.6.3 bibtopic—Combining references by topic

In contrast to chapterbib and bibunits, which collect citations for individual units of a document, the package bibtopic written by Stefan Ulrich (based on earlier work by Pierre Basso) combines reference listings by topic. You can, for example, provide a primary reference listing separate from a reference list for further reading, or put all references to books separate from those to articles.

Within the document all citations are produced with \cite, \nocite, or variants thereof (if natbib or similar packages are also loaded). Thus, separation into topics is handled at a later stage. To produce separate bibliographies by topic you have to group the bibliographical entries that belong to one topic in a separate BibTeX database file (e.g., one for primary sources and one for secondary literature). The bibliographies are then generated by using several `btSect` environments. Ways to generate separate database files are described in Chapter 13. You can, for example, use the program bibtool to extract reference entries according to some criteria from larger BibTeX database collections.

```
\begin{btSect}[style]{file-list}
```

The `btSect` environment generates a bibliography for all citations from the whole document that have entries in the BibTeX database files listed in the comma-separated *file-list* argument. If the optional *style* argument is present, it specifies the BibTeX style to use for the current bibliography. Otherwise, the style specified by a previous \bibliography declaration is used. If no such declaration was given, the BibTeX style plain is used as a default.

Unless the package was loaded with the option `printheadings` the environment produces no heading. Normally, you have to provide your own heading using \section* or a similar command.

```
\btPrintCited     \btPrintNotCited     \btPrintAll
```

Within a `btSect` environment one of the above commands can be used to define which bibliographical entries are included among those from the specified *file-list* databases. The \btPrintCited command prints all references from *file-list* that have been somewhere cited in the document, \btPrintNotCited prints those that have not been cited, and \btPrintAll prints all entries in the BibTeX database files.

The following example shows the basic concepts using two topics: "TeX related" and "Juridical" literature. The first bibliography uses the default plain style; for the second bibliography we explicitly specified the BibTeX style abbrv (this is meant as an illustration—mixing styles is usually a bad idea). As you can see, if you specify numerical BibTeX styles, bibtopic automatically uses consecutive numbers throughout all bibliographies, to ensure that the references in the document are unique.

We saw the citations [3], [2], and [1].

Juridical literature

[1] Hans Brox and Wolf-Dietrich Walker. *Besonderes Schuldrecht*. München, 27. edition, 2002.

[2] Hans Brox and Wolf-Dietrich Walker. *Allgemeines Schuldrecht*. München, 29. edition, 2003.

TeX literature

[3] D. E. Knuth. *The TeXbook*, volume A of *Computers and Typesetting*. Addison-Wesley, Reading, MA, USA, 1986.

```
\usepackage{bibtopic}
We saw the citations \cite{Knuth-CT-a},
\cite{aschur}, and \cite{bschur}.
\begin{btSect}{jura}
  \section*{Juridical literature}
  \btPrintCited
\end{btSect}
\begin{btSect}[abbrv]{tex}
  \section*{\TeX{} literature}
  \btPrintCited
\end{btSect}
```

12-6-7

For every `btSect` environment, the bibtopic package generates a separate `.aux` file that by default is constructed from the base name of the source document (`\jobname`) and a sequence number. You can change this naming scheme by redefining `\thebtauxfile` using the counter `btauxfile` to automatically obtain a sequence number. For the book examples we used the following redefinition:

```
\renewcommand\thebtauxfile{\jobname+\arabic{btauxfile}}
```

Bibliographic topics per logical unit

The bibtopic package is incompatible with chapterbib and bibunits. However, it provides the environment `btUnit` to confine the citations to logical units. Within such units the `btSect` environment can be used in the normal way, allowing for topic bibliographies by chapter or other unit. In that case *all* citations have to appear within such units (escaping citations, discussed on page 746, are not handled so you have to ensure that they do not happen). By default, numerical styles restart their numbering per unit (e.g., per article in a proceedings issue). If you want continuous numbering use the option `unitcntnoreset`.

Problem with nonsorting BibTeX styles

While bibtopic works with most BibTeX styles, there are some exceptions. The most important one is that it does not work as expected with "unsorted" styles (e.g., `unsrt`). If such a style is used, then the order in the bibliography is determined by the order in the BibTeX database file and *not* by the order of citation in the document. If the latter order is required, you should use the multibib package described in the next section.

The bibtopic package is compatible with most other packages that provide extensions to the citation mechanism, including cite, natbib, and jurabib. There are some restrictions with respect to the production of the bibliography lists. For example, hooks to influence the layout as provided by natbib or jurabib may not be functional. Details are given in the package documentation.

We saw the citations Knuth: The TEXbook and Brox/ Walker: Allgemeines Schuldrecht.

TEX literature

Knuth, Donald E.: The TEXbook. Volume A, Computers and Typesetting. Reading, MA, USA: Addison-Wesley, 1986, ix + 483, ISBN 0–201–13447–0

Juridical literature

Brox, Hans/Walker, Wolf-Dietrich: Allgemeines Schuldrecht. 29th edition. München, 2003

```
\usepackage{bibtopic,jurabib}
\bibliographystyle{jurabib}
We saw the citations \cite{Knuth-CT-a}
and \cite{aschur}.
\begin{btSect}{tex}
  \section*{\TeX{} literature}
  \btPrintCited
\end{btSect}
\begin{btSect}{jura}
  \section*{Juridical literature}
  \btPrintCited
\end{btSect}
```

12-6-8

12.6.4   multibib—Separate global bibliographies

Like bibtopic, the multibib package written by Thorsten Hansen provides separate global bibliographies. While the former package separates the bibliographies by using separate BibTEX database files, multibib works by providing separate citation commands to distinguish citations in different bibliographies.

There are advantages and disadvantages with either method. With multibib, different types of citations are clearly marked already in the source document. As a consequence, however, moving a citation from one bibliography to a different one in a consistent manner requires changes to the document in various places. In contrast, with bibtopic it merely requires moving the corresponding database entry from one file to another. On the other hand, bibtopic often requires tailored .bib files for each new document, while with multibib one can use generally available collections of BibTEX database files. A final difference is that multibib allows variants of the \cite command, as provided by natbib and other packages, to be used only for the main bibliography; bibliographies for secondary topics must use \cite and \nocite.

```
\newcites{type}{title}
```

The \newcites declaration defines an additional set of citation commands for a new *type* of citations. The heading for the additional bibliography listing is *title*. Once this declaration is given the four additional commands are available for use. The command \cite⟨type⟩, like \cite, generates a citation within the text and its corresponding reference appears in the bibliography listing for the new *type*. Similarly, \nocite⟨type⟩ adds a citation to the *type* bibliography without appearing in the text. The corresponding bibliography appears at the point where the \bibliography⟨type⟩ command is given, and the BibTEX style used for this bibliography is defined with \bibliographystyle⟨*type*⟩. An example is shown below.

A book on graphics in LaTeX is [1]; suggestions on citations can be found in [vL92].

LaTeX references

[1] Michel Goossens, Sebastian Rahtz, and Frank Mittelbach. *The LaTeX Graphics Companion: Illustrating Documents with TeX and PostScript*. Tools and Techniques for Computer Typesetting. Addison-Wesley Longman, Reading, MA, USA, 1997.

General references

[vL92] Mary-Claire van Leunen. *A handbook for scholars*. Oxford University Press, Walton Street, Oxford OX2 6DP, UK, 92.

```
\usepackage{multibib}
\newcites{latex}
           {\LaTeX{} references}
A book on graphics in \LaTeX{} is
\citelatex{LGC97}; suggestions on
citations can be found in
\cite{vLeunen:92}.

\bibliographystylelatex{plain}
\bibliographylatex{tex}

\renewcommand\refname
           {General references}
\bibliographystyle{alpha}
\bibliography{tex}
```
12-6-9

The \newcites declaration can be used several times, thereby creating additional citation types. It is limited only by the number of output files that can be used simultaneously by TeX. The .aux file written for communication with BibTeX has the name ⟨*type*⟩.aux. For this reason one has to be a bit careful when selecting the *type* in the first argument to \newcites, to avoid overwriting other .aux files.

For numerical citation styles the references are by default numbered sequentially over all bibliographies to avoid ambiguous references. When using the option resetlabels, each bibliography restarts the numbering.

LaTeX offers an interface to include graphics.[1] LaTeX's default citation scheme is number-only.[2]

LaTeX references

[1] Michel Goossens, Sebastian Rahtz, and Frank Mittelbach. *The LaTeX Graphics Companion: Illustrating Documents with TeX and PostScript*. Tools and Techniques for Computer Typesetting. Addison-Wesley Longman, Reading, MA, USA, 1997.

General references

[2] Mary-Claire van Leunen. *A handbook for scholars*. Oxford University Press, Walton Street, Oxford OX2 6DP, UK, 92.

```
\usepackage[super]{cite}
\usepackage{multibib}
\newcites{latex}{\LaTeX{} references}
\LaTeX{} offers an interface to include
graphics.\citelatex{LGC97} \LaTeX's
default citation scheme is
number-only.\cite{vLeunen:92}.

\bibliographystylelatex{plain}
\bibliographylatex{tex}

\renewcommand\refname
           {General references}
\bibliographystyle{plain}
\bibliography{tex}
```
12-6-10

## CHAPTER 13

Bibliography Generation

While a table of contents (see Section 2.3) and an index (discussed in Chapter 11) make it easier to navigate through a book, the presence of bibliographic references should allow you to verify the used sources and to probe further subjects you consider interesting. To make this possible, the references should be precise and lead to the relevant work with a minimum of effort.

There exist many ways for formatting bibliographies, and different fields of scholarly activities have developed very precise rules in this area. An interesting overview of Anglo-Saxon practices can be found in the chapter on bibliographies in *The Chicago Manual of Style* [38]. Normally, authors must follow the rules laid out by their publisher. Therefore, one of the more important tasks when submitting a book or an article for publication is to generate the bibliographic reference list according to those rules.

Traditional ways of composing such lists by hand, without the systematic help of computers, are plagued with the following problems:

- Citations, particularly in a document with contributions from many authors, are hard to make consistent. Difficulties arise, such as variations in the use of full forenames versus abbreviations (with or without periods); italicization or quoting of titles; spelling "ed.", "Ed.", or "Editor"; and the various forms of journal volume number.

- A bibliography laid out in one style (e.g., alphabetic by author and year) is extremely hard to convert to another (e.g., numeric citation order) if requested by a publisher.

- It is difficult to maintain one large database of bibliographic references that can be reused in different documents.

In Chapter 12 we were mainly concerned with the citation of sources within the text. In the present chapter we concentrate on the formatting of reference lists and bibliographies, and we discuss possibilities for managing collections of citations in databases. The chapter is heavily based on the BibTeX program, written by Oren Patashnik, which integrates well with LaTeX.

We start by introducing the program and variants of it, touching on recent developments geared toward creating a successor. This is followed by a detailed introduction to the BibTeX database format, which collects information on how to specify bibliographical data in a suitable form to be processed by BibTeX. Instead of collecting your own bibliographical data, there is also the possibility of drawing information from various on-line sources that offer such data in BibTeX format. Some of them are introduced in Section 13.3.

Having collected data for BibTeX databases, the next natural step is to look for management tools that help in managing such databases. Section 13.4 offers tools of various flavors for this task, ranging from command-line utilities to GUI-based tools for various platforms.

Once everything is under control, we return to the task of typesetting and look at how different BibTeX styles can be used to produce different bibliography layouts from the same input. As there may not be a suitable style for a particular set of layout requirements available, Section 13.5 discusses how to generate customized styles using the **custom-bib** package without the need for any BibTeX style programming.

For those readers who really want to (or have to) dig into the mysteries of BibTeX style programming, the final section gives more details about the format of such style files, including a short overview of the commands and intrinsic functions available. The global structure of the generic style documentation file btxbst.doc is explained, and it is shown how to adapt an existing style file to the needs of a particular house style or foreign language.

13.1   The BibTeX program and some variants

The BibTeX program was designed by Oren Patashnik to provide a flexible solution to the problem of automatically generating bibliography lists conforming to different layout styles. It automatically detects the citation requests in a LaTeX document (by scanning its .aux file or files), selects the needed bibliographical information from one or more specified databases, and formats it according to a specified layout style. Its output is a file containing the bibliography listing as LaTeX code that will be automatically loaded and used by LaTeX on the following run. Section 12.1.3 on page 687 discussed the interface between the two programs in some detail.

At the time of this book's writing BibTeX was available as version 0.99c, but if you look into the first edition of this book (a decade back), you will find that it also talks about version 0.99c. The version 0.99a probably dates back to 1986. In other words, the program has been kept stable for a very long period of time. As a consequence, the BibTeX database format is very well established in the LaTeX world, with many people having numerous citation entries collected over the years. Thus, it comes as no surprise that all development that happened in the last decade is based on that format as a standard.

In this section we briefly survey a number of developments in this arena. Some new projects have surfaced especially in recent years, but there are also some projects that date back a few years.

13.1.1   bibtex8—An 8-bit reimplementation of BibTeX

Due to its age and origins BibTeX is 7-bit, ASCII based. Although it is able to handle foreign characters, its functionality in this respect is rather limited. The BibTeX8 program written by Niel Kempson and Alejandro Aguilar-Sierra is an 8-bit reimplementation of BibTeX with the ability to specify sorting order information. This allows you to store your BibTeX database entries in your favorite 8-bit code page, and to use the inputenc package in your LaTeX document (see Sections 7.5.2 and 7.11.3). Sorting order information related to a specific encoding can be specified on the command line—for example,

```
bibtex8 -c 88591lat tlc2
```

on the author's machine. The sorting order is stored in files with the extension .csf (e.g., in the above example in the file 88591lat.csf). The distribution comes with a number of such files for the most popular encodings. The format is well documented so that it should be possible to provide your own .csf file if necessary. Related command-line options are -7 and -8 to force 7-bit or 8-bit processing, respectively, without a special sorting order.

The BibTeX8 program offers a second set of command-line options that allows you to enlarge its internal tables. In 1995, when the first release of the program was written, standard BibTeX had only small, hard-wired internal tables, making it impossible to typeset, say, a bibliography listing with several hundred citations. These days most installations use higher compile defaults (e.g., 5000 citations) so that the flexibility of BibTeX8 in this respect is seldom needed. But in case a particular job hits one of the limits and emits a message like "Sorry—you've exceeded BibTeX's..." you can use BibTeX8 with a suitable command-line setting to get around the problem. You can find out about the possible options by calling the program without any input or with the option -h or --help.

13.1.2   Recent developments

Besides BibTeX and BibTeX8, both of which have been available for a long time, there have been some more recent developments that target bibliography generation. In this section we briefly introduce three projects that might be of interest to the reader. It is quite possible that one or the other project merge together in the future, so this list should be viewed as a snapshot of the situation in 2003 and as proof that there is a renewed interest in further development.

bibulus—Bibliographies with XML and perl

The program bibulus by Thomas Widmann is a BIBTEX replacement written in perl.[1] It does not use BIBTEX's database file format but rather works with bibliographical entries stored in XML format and provides its own document type definition (`bibulus.dtd`). This way bibliographical entries can be manipulated and processed with any application that understands XML. To enable the reuse of existing `.bib` files, the program provides a tool to convert your BIBTEX databases to XML format.

The bibulus program uses Unicode internally and thus is truly multilingual; at the same time it is able to read and write output in other encodings. The textual strings generated by the program have been translated into a large number of languages. The current implementation of bibulus provides support for more than a dozen languages.

From the program's point of view LATEX is only one of the different possible target output formats. Alternatives range from plain text output, to HTML, to input formats for other programs dealing with citations.

Like the other two programs described below, bibulus is work in progress. It is available from `http://www.nongnu.org/bibulus`, where you will also find further information on the project.

BIBTEX++—A BIBTEX successor in Java

The BIBTEX++ project is a Java-based implementation of a citation manager written by Emmanuel Donin de Rosière in the course of a master thesis [146] supervised by Ronan Keryell. Being intended to serve as a BIBTEX successor, it can, of course, be used in the LATEX world, but it also accepts other bibliography formats and different style languages and can produce output for several typesetting systems. The program is integrated in a web-based environment, so it can retrieve lacking information from various Internet sources. BIBTEX++ uses a plug-in concept that allows you to dynamically extend its functionalities, perhaps to support special formatting conventions or to generate output for other formatters.

Existing BIBTEX style files can be converted to a BIBTEX++ style using a translation program that was developed as part of the project. The result can be further customized by using the BIBTEX++ concepts, thus easing the initial development of a new style.

The project's home is at `http://bibtex.enstb.org`, where you will find a CVS repository as well as compiled binaries and further information.

---

[1]For installation and use it needs a recent perl implementation (5.8+).

MIBibTeX—A multilingual successor of BibTeX

The program MIBibTeX, developed by Jean-Michel Hufflen, is a reimplementation and extension of BibTeX with particular focus on multilingual features. A first release became available in 2001. However, the author found that the approach taken back then was not really suitable for the typographical conventions used in some languages. At that stage of the project he developed a questionnaire to obtain more insight into the problems and conventions with bibliographic data in different European countries. In response, a new implementation was started; its first results were presented at various conferences in 2003.

The current release (v1.3) implements a style language named nbst, for specifying layout and formatting directives. This language is close, but not identical, to XSLT, the language for manipulating and processing XML documents.

The project's home is at `http://lifc.univ-fcomte.fr/~hufflen/texts/mlbibtex/mlbibtex/mlbibtex.html`, where further information can be found.

13.2   The BibTeX database format

A BibTeX database is a plain text (ASCII) file that contains bibliographical entries internally structured as keyword/value pairs. A typical database file was shown in Figure 12.2 on page 690. In this section we study the allowed syntax of its entries in some detail; see also [135].

Each entry in a BibTeX database consists of three main parts: a *type* specifier, followed by a *key*, and finally the *data* for the entry itself. The *type* describes the general nature of the entry (e.g., whether it is an article, book, or some other publication). The *key* is used in the interface to LaTeX; it is the string that you have to place in the argument of a \cite command when referencing that particular entry. The *data* part consists of a series of *field entries* (depending on the *type*), which can have one of two forms as seen in the following generic format and example:

```
@type_specifier{key_identifier,      @book{lamport86,
  field_name_1 = "field_text_1",       author = "Leslie Lamport",
  field_name_2 = {field_text_2},       title  = "{\LaTeX{}} A Document
        .   .   .                                 Preparation system",
  field_name_n = {field_text_n}        publisher = {Addison-Wesley},
}                                      year   = 1986               }
```

The comma is the field separator. Spaces surrounding the equals sign or the comma are ignored. Inside the text part of a field (enclosed in a pair of double quotes or a pair of braces) you can have any string of characters, but braces must be matched. The quotes or braces can be omitted for text consisting entirely of numbers (like the year field in the example above). Note that LaTeX's comment character % is not a comment character inside .bib database files. Instead, any-thing outside an entry is considered a comment as long as it does not contain an @ sign (which would be misinterpreted as the start of a new entry).

BIBTEX *ignores* the case of the letters for the entry type, key, and field names. You must, however, be careful with the key. LaTeX honors the case of the keys spec-ified as the argument of a \cite command, so the key for a given bibliographic entry must match the one specified in the LaTeX file (see Section 12.2.1).

13.2.1   Entry types and fields

As discussed above, you must describe each bibliographic entry as belonging to a certain class, with the information itself tagged by certain fields.

The first thing you have to decide is what type of entry you are dealing with. Although no fixed classification scheme can be complete, with a little creativity you can make BIBTEX cope reasonably well with even the more bizarre types of publications. For nonstandard types, it is probably wise not to attach too much importance to BIBTEX's warning messages (see below).

Most BIBTEX styles have at least the 13 standard entry types, which are shown in Table 13.1 on the facing page. These different types of publications demand different kinds of information; a reference to a journal article might include the volume and number of the journal, which is usually not meaningful for a book. Therefore, different database types have different fields. In fact, for each type of entry, the fields are divided into three classes:

Required   Omission of the field will produce a warning message and, possibly, a badly formatted bibliography entry. If the required information is not mean-ingful, you are using the wrong entry type. If the required information is meaningful but, say, already included in some other field, simply ignore the warning.

Optional   The field's information will be used if present, but you can omit it without causing formatting problems. Include the optional field if it can help the reader.

Ignored   The field is ignored. BIBTEX ignores any field that is not required or op-tional, so you can include any fields in a .bib file entry. It is a good idea to put all relevant information about a reference in its .bib file entry, even informa-tion that may never appear in the bibliography. For example, the abstract of a paper can be entered into an abstract field in its .bib file entry. The .bib file is probably as good a place as any for the abstract, and there exist bibli-ography styles for printing selected abstracts (see the abstract bibliography style mentioned in Table 13.4 on page 791).

Table 13.1 on the facing page describes the standard entry types, along with their required and optional fields, as used by the standard bibliography styles.

article	An article from a journal or magazine. *Required*: author, title, journal, year. *Optional*: volume, number, pages, month, note.
book	A book with an explicit publisher. *Required*: author or editor, title, publisher, year. *Optional*: volume or number, series, address, edition, month, note.
booklet	A work that is printed and bound, but without a named publisher or sponsoring institution. *Required*: title. *Optional*: author, howpublished, address, month, year, note.
inbook	A part of a book, e.g., a chapter, section, or whatever and/or a range of pages. *Required*: author or editor, title, chapter and/or pages, publisher, year. *Optional*: volume or number, series, type, address, edition, month, note.
incollection	A part of a book having its own title. *Required*: author, title, booktitle, publisher, year. *Optional*: editor, volume or number, series, type, chapter, pages, address, edition, month, note.
inproceedings	An article in a conference proceedings. *Required*: author, title, booktitle, year. *Optional*: editor, volume or number, series, pages, address, month, organization, publisher, note.
manual	Technical documentation. *Required*: title. *Optional*: author, organization, address, edition, month, year, note.
mastersthesis	A master's thesis. *Required*: author, title, school, year. *Optional*: type, address, month, note.
misc	Use this type when nothing else fits. A warning will be issued if all optional fields are empty (i.e., the entire field is empty). *Required*: none. *Optional*: author, title, howpublished, month, year, note.
phdthesis	A Ph.D. thesis. *Required*: author, title, school, year. *Optional*: type, address, month, note.
proceedings	Conference proceedings. *Required*: title, year. *Optional*: editor, volume or number, series, address, publisher, note, month, organization.
techreport	A report published by a school or other institution, usually numbered within a series. *Required*: author, title, institution, year. *Optional*: type, number, address, month, note.
unpublished	A document having an author and title, but not formally published. *Required*: author, title, note. *Optional*: month, year.

Table 13.1: BIBTEX's entry types as defined in most styles

The fields within each class (required or optional) are listed in the typical order of occurrence in the output. A few entry types, however, may perturb the alphabetic ordering slightly, depending on which fields are missing. The meaning of the individual fields is explained in Table 13.2 on the next page. Nonstandard bibliography styles may ignore some optional fields or use additional ones like `isbn` when creating the reference (see also the examples starting on page 793). Remember that, when used in a `.bib` file, the entry-type name is preceded by an `@` character.

Sorting of entries Most BibTeX style files sort the bibliographical entries. This is done by internally generating a sort key from the author's/editor's name, the date of the publication, the title, and other information. Entries with identical sort keys will appear in citation order.

The author information is usually the `author` field, but some styles use the `editor` or `organization` field. In addition to the fields listed in Table 13.1, each entry type has an optional `key` field, used in some styles for alphabetizing, for cross-referencing, or for forming a `\bibitem` label. You should therefore include a `key` field for any entry whose author information is missing. Depending on the style the `key` field can also be used to overwrite the automatically generated internal key for sorting.[1] A situation where a `key` field is useful is the following:

```
organization = "The Association for Computing Machinery",
key = "ACM"
```

Without the `key` field, the `alpha` style would construct a label from the first three letters of the information in the `organization` field. Although the style file will strip off the article "The", you would still get a rather uninformative label like "[Ass86]". The `key` field above yields a more acceptable "[ACM86]".

We now turn our attention to the fields recognized by the standard bibliography styles. These "standard" fields are shown in Table 13.2 on the facing page. Other fields, like `abstract`, can be required if you use one of the extended nonstandard styles shown in Table 13.4 on page 791. As nonrecognized fields are ignored by the BibTeX styles, you can use this feature to include "comments" inside an entry: it is enough to put the information to be ignored inside braces following a field that is not recognized by the BibTeX style.

As with the names of the entry types in Table 13.1 on the preceding page, the names of the fields should be interpreted in their widest sense to make them applicable in a maximum number of situations. And you should never forget that a judicious use of the `note` field can solve even the more complicated cases.

13.2.2   The text part of a field explained

The text part of a field in a BibTeX entry is enclosed in a pair of double quotes or curly braces. Part of the text itself is said to be *enclosed in braces* if it lies inside a matching pair of braces other than the ones enclosing the entire entry.

---

[1]Some BibTeX styles (e.g., `jurabib`) use the `sortkey` field instead.

`address`	Usually the address of the `publisher` or other institution. For major publishing houses, just give the city. For small publishers, specifying the complete address might help the reader.
`annote`	An annotation. Not used by the standard bibliography styles, but used by others that produce an annotated bibliography (e.g., `annote`). The field starts a new sentence and hence the first word should be capitalized.
`author`	The name(s) of the author(s), in BibTeX name format (Section 13.2.2).
`booktitle`	Title of a book, part of which is being cited (Section 13.2.2). For book entries use the `title` field.
`chapter`	A chapter (or section or whatever) number.
`crossref`	The database key of the entry being cross-referenced (Section 13.2.5).
`edition`	The edition of a book (e.g., "Second"). This should be an ordinal, and should have the first letter capitalized, as shown above; the standard styles convert to lowercase when necessary.
`editor`	Name(s) of editor(s), in BibTeX name format. If there is also an `author` field, then the `editor` field gives the editor of the book or collection in which the reference appears.
`howpublished`	How something strange has been published.
`institution`	Institution sponsoring a technical report.
`journal`	Journal name. Abbreviations are provided for many journals (Section 13.2.3).
`key`	Used for alphabetizing, cross-referencing, and creating a label when the `author` and `editor` information is missing. This field should not be confused with the key that appears in the `\cite` command and at the beginning of the database entry.
`month`	The month in which the work was published or, for an unpublished work, in which it was written. For reasons of consistency the standard three-letter abbreviations (`jan`, `feb`, `mar`, etc.) should be used (Section 13.2.3).
`note`	Any additional information that can help the reader.
`number`	The number of a journal, magazine, technical report, or work in a series. An issue of a journal or magazine is usually identified by its volume and number; a technical report normally has a number; and sometimes books in a named series carry numbers.
`organization`	The organization that sponsors a conference or that publishes a `manual`.
`pages`	One or more page numbers or range of numbers (e.g., 42–111 or 7,41,73–97 or 43+, where the '+' indicates pages that do not form a simple range).
`publisher`	The publisher's name.
`school`	The name of the school where the thesis was written.
`series`	The name of a series or set of books. When citing an entire book, the `title` field gives its title and an optional `series` field gives the name of a series or multivolume set in which the book is published.
`title`	The work's title, typed as explained in Section 13.2.2.
`type`	The type of a technical report (e.g., "Research Note"). This name is used instead of the default "Technical Report". For the type `phdthesis` you could use the term "Ph.D. dissertation" by specifying: `type = "{Ph.D.} dissertation."` Similarly, for the `inbook` and `incollection` entry types you can get "section 1.2" instead of the default "chapter 1.2" with `chapter = "1.2,"` `type = "Section."`
`volume`	The volume of a journal or multivolume book.
`year`	The year of publication or, for an unpublished work, the year it was written. Generally, it should consist of four numerals, such as 1984, although the standard styles can handle any `year` whose last four nonpunctuation characters are numerals, such as "about 1984".

Table 13.2: BibTeX's standard entry fields

The structure of a name

The `author` and `editor` fields contain a list of names. The exact format in which these names are typeset is decided by the bibliography style. The entry in the `.bib` database tells BibTeX what the name is. You should always type names exactly as they appear in the cited work, even when they have slightly different forms in two works. For example:

```
author = "Donald E. Knuth"              author = "D. E. Knuth"
```

If you are sure that both authors are the same person, then you could list both in the form that the author prefers (say, Donald E. Knuth), but you should always indicate (e.g., in our second case) that the original publication had a different form.

```
author = "D[onald] E. Knuth"
```

BibTeX alphabetizes this as if the brackets were not there, so that no ambiguity arises as to the identity of the author.

Most names can be entered in the following two equivalent forms:

```
"John Chris Smith"              "Smith, John Chris"
"Thomas von Neumann"            "von Neumann, Thomas"
```

The second form, with a comma, should always be used for people who have multiple last names that are capitalized. For example,

```
"Lopez Fernandez, Miguel"
```

If you enter `"Miguel Lopez Fernandez,"` BibTeX will take `"Lopez"` as the middle name, which is wrong in this case. When the other parts are not capitalized, no such problem occurs (e.g., `Johann von Bergen` or `Pierre de la Porte`).

If several words of a name have to be grouped, they should be enclosed in braces. BibTeX treats everything inside braces as a single name, as shown below.

```
{{Boss and Friends, Inc.} and {Snoozy and Boys, Ltd.}}
```

In this case, `Inc.` and `Ltd.` are not mistakenly considered as first names.

In general, BibTeX names can have four distinct parts, denoted as `First`, `von`, `Last`, and `Jr`. Each part consists of a list of name tokens, and any list but `Last` can be empty. Thus, the two entries below are different:

```
"von der Schmidt, Alex"        "{von der Schmidt}, Alex"
```

The first has `von`, `Last`, and `First` parts, while the second has only `First` and `Last` parts (`von der Schmidt`), resulting possibly in a different sorting order.

A "Junior" part can pose a special problem. Most people with "Jr." in their name precede it with a comma, thus entering it as follows:

```
"Smith, Jr., Robert"
```

Certain people do not use the comma, and these cases are handled by considering the "Jr." as part of the last name:

```
"{Lincoln Jr.}, John P."          "John P. {Lincoln Jr.}"
```

Recall that in the case of "Miguel Lopez Fernandez", you should specify

```
"Lopez Fernandez, Miguel"
```

The First part of his name has the single token "Miguel"; the Last part has two tokens, "Lopez" and "Fernandez"; and the von and Jr parts are empty.
   A complex example is

```
"Johannes Martinus Albertus van de Groene Heide"
```

This name has three tokens in the First part, two in the von part, and two in the Last part. BibTeX knows where one part ends and the other begins because the tokens in the von part begin with lowercase letters (van de in this example).
   In general, von tokens have the first letter at brace-level 0 in lowercase. Technically speaking, everything in a "special character" is at brace-level 0 (see page 768), so you can decide how BibTeX treats a token by inserting a dummy special character whose first letter past the TeX control sequence is in the desired case, upper or lower. For example, in

```
Maria {\MakeUppercase{d}e La} Cruz
```

BibTeX will take the uppercase "De La" as the von part, since the first character following the control sequence is lowercase. With the abbrv style you will get the correct abbreviation M. De La Cruz, instead of the incorrect M. D. L. Cruz if you did not use this trick.
   BibTeX handles hyphenated names correctly. For example, an entry like

```
author = "Maria-Victoria Delgrande",
```

with the abbrv style, results in "M.-V. Delgrande".
   When multiple authors are present, their names should be separated with the word "and", where the "and" must not be enclosed in braces.

```
author = "Frank Mittelbach and Rowley, Chris"
editor = "{Lion and Noble, Ltd.}"
```

There are two authors, Frank Mittelbach and Chris Rowley, but only one editor, since the "and" is enclosed in braces. If the number of authors or editors is too large to be typed *in extenso*, then the list of names can be ended with the string "and others", which is converted by the standard styles into the familiar *"et al."*

To summarize, you can specify names in BibTeX using three possible forms (the double quotes and curly braces can be used in all cases):

```
"First von Last"          e.g. {Johan van der Winden}
"von Last, First"         e.g. "von der Schmidt, Alexander"
"von Last, Jr, First"     e.g. {de la Porte, Fils, {\'Emile}}
```

The first form can almost always be used. It is, however, not suitable when there is a Jr part, or when the Last part has multiple tokens and there is no von part.

The format of the title

The bibliography style decides whether a title is capitalized. Usually, titles of books are capitalized, but those for articles are not. A title should always be typed as it appears in the original work. For example:

```
TITLE = "A Manual of Style"
TITLE = "Hyphenation patterns for ancient Greek and Latin"
```

Different languages and styles have their own capitalization rules. If you want to override the decisions of the bibliography style, then you should enclose the parts that should remain unchanged inside braces. Note that this will not be sufficient when the first character after the left brace is a backslash (see Section 13.2.2). It is usually best to enclose whole words in braces, because otherwise LaTeX may lose kerning or ligatures when typesetting the word. In the following example, the first version is preferable over the second:

```
TITLE = "The Towns and Villages of {Belgium}"
TITLE = "The Towns and Villages of {B}elgium"
```

Accented and special characters

BibTeX accepts accented characters. If you have an entry with two fields

```
author = "Kurt G{\"o}del",
year = 1931,
```

then the alpha bibliography style will yield the label [Göd31], which is probably what you want. As shown in the example above, the entire accented character must be placed in braces; in this case either {\"o} or {\"{o}} will work. These braces must not themselves be enclosed in braces (other than the ones that might delimit the entire field or the entire entry); also, a backslash must be the very first character inside the braces. Thus, neither `{G{\"{o}}del}` nor `{G\"{o}del}` works here.

This feature handles accented characters and foreign symbols used with L<small>A</small>T_EX. It also allows user-defined "accents". For purposes of counting letters in labels, B<small>IB</small>T_EX considers everything inside the braces to be a single letter. To B<small>IB</small>T_EX, an accented character is a special case of a "special character", which consists of everything from a left brace at the topmost level, immediately followed by a backslash, up through the matching right brace. For example, the field

```
author = "\OE{le} {\'{E}mile} {Ren\'{e}} van R{\i\j}den"
```

has two special characters: "`{\'{E}mile}`" and "`{\i\j}`".

In general, B<small>IB</small>T_EX does not process T_EX or L<small>A</small>T_EX control sequences inside a special character, but it will process other characters. Thus, a style that converts all titles to lowercase transforms

```
"The {\TeX BOOK\NOOP} Saga" into "The {\TeX book\NOOP} saga"
```

The article "The" remains capitalized because it is the first word in the title.

The special character scheme has its uses for handling accented characters (although the introduction of additional braces may upset the generation of ligatures and kerns). It may help to make B<small>IB</small>T_EX's alphabetizing do what you want, but again with some caveats; see the discussion of the `\SortNoop` command on page 771. Also, since B<small>IB</small>T_EX counts an entire special character as just one letter, you can force extra characters inside labels.

13.2.3   Abbreviations in B<small>IB</small>T_EX

B<small>IB</small>T_EX text fields can be abbreviated. An abbreviation is a string of ASCII characters starting with a letter and not containing a space or any of the following 10 characters:

```
"   #   %   '   (   )   ,   =   {   }
```

You can define your own abbreviations with the `@string` command in a `.bib` file, as shown below.

```
@string{AW        = "Addison--Wesley Publishing Company"}
@STRING{cacm      = "Communications of the ACM"}
@String{pub-AW    = {{Ad\-di\-son-Wes\-ley}}}
@String{pub-AW:adr = "Reading, MA, USA"}
@String{TUG       = "\TeX{} Users Group"}
@String{TUG:adr   = {Providence, RI, USA}}
```

Abbreviations can be used in the text field of B<small>IB</small>T<small>E</small>X entries, but they should not be enclosed in braces or quotation marks. With the above string definitions, the following two ways of specifying the journal field are equivalent:

```
journal = "Communications of the ACM"
journal = cacm
```

The case of the name for an abbreviation is not important, so CACM and cacm are considered identical, but B<small>IB</small>T<small>E</small>X produces a warning if you mix different cases. Also, the @string command itself can be spelled as all lowercase, all uppercase, or a mixture of the two cases.

@string commands can appear anywhere in the .bib file, but an abbreviation must be defined before it is used. It is good practice to group all @string commands at the beginning of a .bib file, or to place them in a dedicated .bib file containing only a list of abbreviations. The @string commands defined in the .bib file take precedence over definitions in the style files.

You can concatenate several strings (or @string definitions) using the concatenation operator #. Given the definition

```
@STRING{TUB = {TUGboat }}
```

you can easily construct nearly identical journal fields for different entries:

```
@article(tub-98,    journal = TUB # 1998,  ...
@article(tub-99,    journal = TUB # 1999,  ...
@article(tub-00,    journal = TUB # 2000,  ...
```

Most bibliography styles contain a series of predefined abbreviations. As a convention, there should always be three-letter abbreviations for the months: jan, feb, mar, and so forth. In your B<small>IB</small>T<small>E</small>X database files you should always use these three-letter abbreviations for the months, rather than spelling them explicitly. This assures consistency inside your bibliography. Information about the day of the month is usually best included in the month field. You might, for example, make use of the possibility of concatenation:

```
month = apr # "~1,"
```

Names of popular journals in a given application field are also made available as abbreviations in most styles. To identify them you should consult the documentation associated with the bibliographic style in question. The set of journals listed in Table 13.3 on the facing page should be available in all styles. You can easily define your own set of journal abbreviations by putting them in @string commands in their own database file and listing this database file as an argument to L<small>A</small>T<small>E</small>X's \bibliography command.

acmcs	ACM Computing Surveys	jcss	Journal of Computer and System Sciences
acta	Acta Informatica	scp	Science of Computer Programming
cacm	Communications of the ACM	sicomp	SIAM Journal on Computing
ibmjrd	IBM Journal of Research and Development	tocs	ACM Transactions on Computer Systems
ibmsj	IBM Systems Journal	tods	ACM Transactions on Database Systems
ieeese	IEEE Transactions on Software Engineering	tog	ACM Transactions on Graphics
ieeetc	IEEE Transactions on Computers	toms	ACM Transactions on Mathematical Software
ieeetcad	IEEE Transactions on Computer Aided Design of Integrated Circuits	toois	ACM Transactions on Office Information Systems
ipl	Information Processing Letters	toplas	ACM Transactions on Programming Languages and Systems
jacm	Journal of the ACM	tcs	Theoretical Computer Science

Table 13.3: Predefined journal strings in BibTeX styles

13.2.4   The BibTeX preamble

BibTeX offers a @preamble command with a syntax similar to that of the @string command except that there is no name or equals sign, just the string. For example:

```
@preamble{ "\providecommand\url[1]{\texttt{#1}}"   #
           "\providecommand\SortNoop[1]{}"                 }
```

You can see how the different command definitions inside the @preamble are concatenated using the # symbol. The standard styles output the argument of the @preamble literally to the .bbl file, so that the command definitions are available when LaTeX reads the file. If you add LaTeX commands in this way, you must ensure that they are added using \providecommand and not \newcommand. There are two reasons for this requirement. First, you deprive yourself of the ability to change the definition in the document (e.g., the bibliography might add a simple definition for the command \url that you may want to replace by the definition from the url package). Second, sometimes the bibliography is read in several times (e.g., with the chapterbib package), an operation that would fail if \newcommand is used.

   The other example command used above (\SortNoop) was suggested by Oren Patashnik to guide BibTeX's sorting algorithm in difficult cases. This algorithm normally does an acceptable job, but sometimes you might want to override BibTeX's decision by specifying your own sorting key. This trick can be used with foreign languages, which have different sorting rules from English, or when you want to order the various volumes of a book in a way given by their original date of publication and independently of their re-edition dates.

Suppose that the first volume of a book was originally published in 1986, with a second edition appearing in 1991, and the second volume was published in 1990. Then you could write

```
@book{ ...  volume=1,  year = "{\SortNoop{86}}1991"  ...
@book{ ...  volume=2,  year = "{\SortNoop{90}}1990"  ...
```

According to the definition of \SortNoop, LaTeX throws away its argument and ends up printing only the true year for these fields. For BibTeX \SortNoop is an "accent"; thus, it will sort the works according to the numbers 861991 and 901990, placing volume 1 before volume 2, just as you want.

Be aware that the above trick may not function with newer BibTeX styles (for example, those generated with custom-bib) and that some styles have added a sortkey field that solves such problems in a far cleaner fashion.

13.2.5 Cross-referencing entries

BibTeX entries can be cross-referenced. Suppose you specify \cite{Wood:color} in your document, and you have the following two entries in the database file:

```
@Inbook{Wood:color, author = {Pat Wood}, crossref={Roth:postscript},
        title = {PostScript Color Separation}, pages={201--225}}
@Book{Roth:postscript, editor = {Stephen E. Roth}, title =
        {{Real World PostScript}}, booktitle = {{Real World PostScript}},
        publisher=AW, address=AW:adr, year=1988, ISBN={0-201-06663-7}}
```

The special crossref field tells BibTeX that the Wood:color entry should inherit missing fields from the entry it cross-references—Roth:postscript. BibTeX automatically puts the Roth:postscript entry into the reference list if it is cross-referenced by a certain number of entries (default 2) on a \cite or \nocite command, even if the Roth:postscript entry itself is never the argument of a \cite or \nocite command. Thus, with the default settings, Roth:postscript will automatically appear on the reference list if one other entry besides Wood:color cross-references it.

The default is compiled into the BibTeX program, but on modern installations[1] it can be changed on the command-line by specifying --min-crossrefs together with the desired value:

```
bibtex --min-crossrefs=1 12-5-41
```

For instance, the bibliography for Example 12-5-41 from page 738 was produced with the above setting to ensure that the proceedings entry was typeset as a separate reference even though there was only one cross-reference to it. On the other hand, if you want to avoid a separate entry for the whole proceedings regardless

---

[1]In BibTeX8 this option is named -min_crossrefs or -M.

of the number of entries referencing it, set the `--min-crossrefs` option to a suitably large value (e.g., 500).

A cross-referenced entry must occur later in the database files than every entry that cross-references it. Thus, all cross-referenced entries could be put at the end of the database. Cross-referenced entries cannot themselves cross-reference another entry.

You can also use LaTeX's `\cite` command inside the fields of your BibTeX entries. This can be useful if you want to reference some other relevant material inside a note field:

```
note = "See Eijkhout~\cite{Eijkhout:1991} for more details"
```

However, such usage may mean that you need additional LaTeX and BibTeX runs to compile your document properly. This will happen if the citation put from BibTeX into the `.bbl` file refers to a key that was not used in a citation in the main document. Thus, LaTeX will be unable to resolve this reference in the following run and will need an additional BibTeX and an additional LaTeX run thereafter.

13.3   On-line bibliographies

If you search the Internet you will find a large number of bibliography entries for both primary and secondary publications in free as well as commercial databases. In this section we mention a few free resources on scientific publications that offer bibliographic data in BibTeX and some other formats.

Nelson Beebe maintains nearly 400 BibTeX databases related to scientific journals and particular scientific topics.[1] These range from "Acta Informatica" and "Ada User Journal" to "X Journal" and "X Resource [journal]". All are available as `.bib` source file, `.html`, `.pdf`, and `.ps` listings.

Nelson Beebe's most interesting `.bib` databases, as far as TeX is concerned, are the files `texbook2.bib` and `texbook3.bib` (books about TeX, METAFONT, and friends), `type.bib` (a list of articles and book about typography), `gut.bib` (the contents of the French *Cahiers Gutenberg* journal), `komoedie.bib` (the contents of the German *Die TeXnische Komödie* journal), `texgraph.bib` (sources explaining how to make TeX and graphics work together), `texjourn.bib` (a list of journals accepting TeX as input), `tugboat.bib` (all the articles in *TUGboat*), and `standard.bib` (software standards). The web resources provided by Nelson Beebe also include a series of BibTeX styles and many command-line tools for manipulating bibliography data (discussed in Section 13.4.3).

The Collection of Computer Science Bibliographies by Alf-Christian Achilles, containing more than 1.2 million references, can be found at `http://liinwww.ira.uka.de/bibliography/index.html` and at several mirror sites. The data

---

[1] The bibliographic databases and support programs for maintaining and manipulating them can be found at `http://www.math.utah.edu:8080/pub/tex/bib/index-table.html`.

included comes from external bibliographical collections like those created by Nelson Beebe. One added-value feature is the search functionality, which allows you to research authors, particular subjects, topics, and other categories. Nearly all of the reference data is available in BibTeX format.

Another interesting source is CiteSeer, Scientific Literature Digital Library, developed by Steve Lawrence, which can be found at `http://citeseer.nj.nec.com`. Helpful features include extensive search possibilities, context information on publications (e.g., related publications), citations to the document from other publications, statistical information about citations to a citation, and much more.

These examples represent merely a small selection of the vast amount of material found on the Internet. They might prove useful if you are interested in research papers on mathematics, computer science, and similar subjects.

13.4 Bibliography database management tools

As BibTeX databases are plain text files, they can be generated and manipulated with any editor that is able to write ASCII files. However, with large collections of BibTeX entries, this method can get quite cumbersome and finding information becomes more and more difficult. For this reason people started to develop tools to help with these tasks. Many of them can be found at `http://www.tug.org/tex-archive/biblio/bibtex/utils/`.

A selection of such tools is described in this section. They range from command-line tools for specific tasks to programs with a graphical user interface for general database maintenance. New products of both types are emerging, so it is probably worthwhile to check out available Internet resources (e.g., `http://bibliographic.openoffice.org/biblio-sw.html`).

13.4.1 biblist—Printing BibTeX database files

A sorted listing of all entries in a BibTeX database is often useful for easy reference. Various tools, with more or less the same functionality, are available, and choosing one or the other is mostly a question of taste. In this section we discuss one representative tool, the biblist package written by Joachim Schrod. It can create a typeset listing of (possibly large) BibTeX databases. Later sections show some more possibilities.

To use biblist you must prepare a LaTeX document using the article class. Options and packages like twoside, german, or geometry can be added. Given that entries are never broken across columns, it may not be advisable to typeset them in several columns using multicol, however.

The argument of the \bibliography command must contain the names of all BibTeX databases you want to print. With a \bibliographystyle command you can choose a specific bibliography style. By default, all bibliography entries in the database will be output. However, if you issue explicit \nocite commands (as we did in the example), only the selected entries from the databases will be printed. Internal cross-references via the `crossref` field or explicit `\cite` commands are marked using boxes around the *key* instead of resolving the latter.

13-4-1 | (March 16, 2004)   `tex.bib`

References

MR-PQ ....
    Frank Mittelbach and Chris Rowley.
    The pursuit of quality: How can automated typesetting achieve the highest standards of craft typography?
    In Vanoirbeek and Coray EP92 , pages 261–273.

EP92 ....
    Christine Vanoirbeek and Giovanni Coray, editors.
    EP92—Proceedings of Electronic Publishing, '92, Cambridge, 1992. Cambridge University Press.

```
\usepackage{biblist}
\bibliographystyle
          {alpha}
\nocite{MR-PQ}
\footnotesize
\bibliography{tex}
```

You must run LaTeX, BibTeX, and LaTeX. No additional LaTeX run is necessary, since the cross-references are not resolved to conserve space. For this reason you will always see warnings about unresolved citations.

13.4.2   `bibtools`—A collection of command-line tools

Several sets of interesting BibTeX tools are widely available. The first set was written (mostly) by David Kotz. His tools are collectively available for UN*X systems (or `cygwin` under Windows). You may have to adjust the library path names at the top of the scripts to make them work in your environment.

aux2bib Given an `.aux` file, this `perl` script creates a portable `.bib` file containing only the entries needed for the particular document. This ability is useful when LaTeX files need to be shipped elsewhere. The script works by using a special BibTeX style file (`subset`) to extract the necessary entries, which means that only standard fields are supported.

bibkey This C-shell script uses the `sed`, `egrep`, and `awk` utilities to prepare the list of all entries having a given string as (part of) their citation key.

    Usage: `bibkey` *string file*

    Characters in the `string` parameter above that have a special meaning in regular expressions used by either `sed` or `egrep` must be escaped with a \ (e.g., \\ for the backslash). Case is ignored in the search. Any valid `egrep` expression is allowed, including, for example, a search for multiple keys:

```
bibkey 'bgb|zpo' jura.bib
```

looktex Entries containing a given string in a BibTeX database are listed when this C-shell script is run. It is a generalization of the `bibkey` script, and all comments about that script also apply in this case.

Bibliography files
../EX/jura
July 13, 2003

References

[aschur]   Hans Brox and Wolf-Dietrich Walker. *Allgemeines Schuldrecht*. München, 29. edition, 2003.

[bgb]   Otto Palandt. *Bürgerliches Gesetzbuch*. Beck Juristischer Verlag, München, 62. edition, 2003.

[bschur]   Hans Brox and Wolf-Dietrich Walker. *Besonderes Schuldrecht*. München, 27. edition, 2002.

[zpo]   Adolf Baumbach, Wolfgang Lauterbach, Jan Albers, and Peter Hartmann. *Zivilprozeßordnung mit Gerichtsverfassungsgesetz und anderen Nebengesetzen*. München, 59. neubearb. edition, 2002.

Figure 13.1: Output of the program printbib

makebib This C-shell script makes an exportable .bib file from a given set of .bib files and an optional list of citations.

Usage: makebib *bibfile(s) [citekey(s)]*

The output is written to subset.bib. If *citekey(s)* is not given, then all references in the *bibfile(s)* are included.

printbib This C-shell script makes a .dvi file from a .bib file for handy reference. It is sorted by cite key and includes keyword and abstract fields.

Usage: printbib *bibfile(s)*

The file abstract.dvi is generated and can be run through a dvi driver to be printed. Figure 13.1 shows the output when running this shell script on the database jura.bib from page 717.

bib2html This perl script produces an HTML version of one or more BibTEX database files.

Usage: bib2html *style* [-o *outputfile*] *bibfile(s)*

There are several *styles* from which to choose; Figure 13.2 on the facing page was produced using the style alpha on the jura.bib database. If no *outputfile* is given, the file bib.html is used as a default. Instead of generating a listing of a complete database you can use the option -a and specify an .aux file, in which case a bibliography containing only references from this document is created.

Usage: bib2html *style* [-o *outputfile*] -a *auxfile*

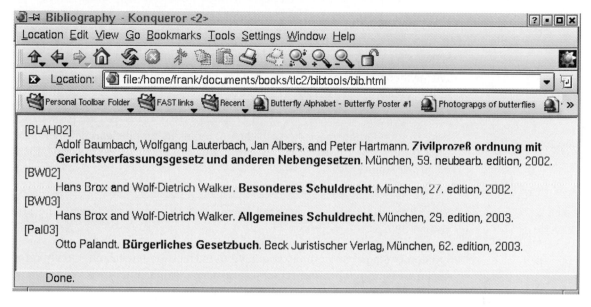

Figure 13.2: Output of the program bib2html

13.4.3   `bibclean`, etc.—A second set of command-line tools

A second set of tools to handle BIBTEX databases were developed by Nelson Beebe.
We give a brief description of each of them.

bibclean   This C program is a pretty-printer, syntax checker, and lexical analyzer
for BIBTEX bibliography database files [13]. The program, which runs on UN*X,
Vax/VMS, and Windows platforms, has many options, but in general you can
just type

```
bibclean < bibfile(s) > outfile
```

For example, when used on the database file `tex.bib`, the bibclean program
reports the following problem:

```
%% "EX/tex.bib", line 99: Unexpected value in ''year = "1980ff"''.
```

bibextract   This program extracts from a list of BIBTEX files those bibliography
entries that match a pair of specified regular expressions, sending them to
stdout, together with all `@preamble` and `@string` declarations. Two regular
expressions must be specified: the first to select `keyword` values (if this string
is empty then all entries are examined), and the second to further select from
the value part of the entries which bibliography entries must be output. Regular expressions should contain only lowercase strings.

For example, the following command will extract all entries containing "PostScript" in any of the fields:

```
bibextract "" "postscript" bibfile(s) > new-bibfile
```

The next command will extract only those entries containing the string Adobe in the author or organization field:

```
bibextract "author|organization" "adobe" bibfile(s) > new-bibfile
```

Note that one might have to clean the .bib files using bibclean before bibextract finds correct entries. For example, the two entries with author "Mittelbach" are found with

```
bibclean tex.bib | bibextract "author" "mittelbach"
```

Using bibextract alone would fail because of the entry containing the line year=1980ff.

citefind and citetags   Sometimes you have to extract the entries effectively referenced in your publication from several large BibTeX databases. The Bourne shell scripts citefind and citetags use the awk and sed tools to accomplish that task. First, citetags extracts the BibTeX citation tags from the LaTeX source or .aux files and sends them to the standard output *stdout*. There, citefind picks them up and tries to find the given keys in the .bib files specified. It then writes the resulting new bibliography file to *stdout*. For instance,

```
citetags *.aux | citefind - bibfile(s) > outfile
```

Nelson Beebe also developed the showtags package, which adds the citation key to a bibliography listing. In other words, it does a similar job to biblist as shown in Example 13-4-1 on page 775 or the program printbib as shown in Figure 13.1 on page 776.

References

MR-PQ

[MR92] Frank Mittelbach and Chris Rowley. The pursuit of quality: How can automated typesetting achieve the highest standards of craft typography? In Vanoirbeek and Coray [VC92], pages 261–273.

EP92

[VC92] Christine Vanoirbeek and Giovanni Coray, editors. *EP92—Proceedings of Electronic Publishing, '92*, Cambridge, 1992. Cambridge University Press.

```
\usepackage
  {showtags}
\bibliographystyle
  {is-alpha}
\nocite{MR-PQ}
\footnotesize
\bibliography{tex}
```

13-4-2

13.4.4   bibtool—A multipurpose command-line tool

The program bibtool was developed by Gerd Neugebauer for manipulating BibTeX databases. It combines many of the features from the programs and scripts discussed earlier and adds several new features under the hood of a single program. It is distributed as a C source file, though you may find precompiled binaries—for example, in the Debian distribution. It has been successfully compiled on many architectures, provided a suitable C compiler is available.

In this section we show some of the features provided by the program. Many more are described in the user manual [132] accompanying it.

Pretty-printing, merging, and sorting

In its simplest invocation you can call the program with one or more BibTeX databases as its argument, in which case the program acts as a pretty-printer and writes the result to *stdout*.[1] If the option -o *file* is used, then the result is written to the specified *file*. For example, to use it on the database shown in Figure 12.2 on page 690, we could write

```
bibtool tex.bib -o new-tex.bib
```

This would produce a pretty-printed version of that database in `new-tex.bib`. All entries will be nicely indented, with every field on a separate line, and all the equals signs will be lined up. For instance, the worst-looking entry in `tex.bib`

```
@manual{GNUMake,     key = {make},
  title = {{GNU Make}, A Program for Directing
  Recompilation},   organization= "Free
  Software Foundation",address = "Boston,
  Massachusetts",ISBN={1-882114-80-9},year = 2000}
```

has now been reformatted as follows:

```
@Manual{          gnumake,
  key           = {make},
  title         = {{GNU Make}, A Program for Directing Recompilation},
  organization  = "Free Software Foundation",
  address       = "Boston, Massachusetts",
  isbn          = {1-882114-80-9},
  year          = 2000
}
```

If you specify several database files, then all are merged together in the output.   *Merging and sorting* If desired, you can sort them according to the reference keys (using the option -s or -S for reverse sort). Alternatively, you can specify your own sort key using the resource[2] `sort.format`:

```
bibtool -- 'sort.format="%N(author)"'  tex.bib jura.bib
```

---

[1]If no input files are specified bibtool reads from *stdin*. Thus, you can also use it as a filter in a UN*X pipe construction, which can be handy sometimes.

[2]Resources are program directives that you assign values. This is often done in external files (explained later); on the command line they can be specified after the - option.

Be aware that sorting may produce an invalid bibliography file if the file contains internal cross-references, since the entries referenced via a BIBTEX `crossref` field have to appear *later* in the database and this may not be the case after sorting. The manual explains how to define sort keys that take this problem into account.

Removing duplicate keys Merging databases together may also result in duplicate entries or, more precisely, in entries that have the same reference keys for use with LATEX. A database containing such duplicates will produce errors if processed by BIBTEX. If you specify the option `-d`, then the duplicates are written out as comments rather than as real entries, which keeps BIBTEX happy. However, it might mean that different entries are actually collapsed into a single one (if they happened to have identical keys), so you need to use this option with some care.

Normalization and rewriting of entries

BIBTEX supports both double quotes and braces as field delimiters, so the mixture used in the GNUmake entry is perfectly legal though perhaps not advisable. A better approach is to stick to one scheme, always using braces or always using double quotes. The rewriting rule

```
bibtool -- 'rewrite.rule {"^\"\([^#]*\)\"$" "{\1}"}'  tex.bib
```

changes the field delimiters to brace groups, except in cases where strings are concatenated. It produces the following result for the sample entry:

```
@Manual{          gnumake,
  key           = {make},
  title         = {{GNU Make}, A Program for Directing Recompilation},
  organization  = {Free Software Foundation},
  address       = {Boston, Massachusetts},
  isbn          = {1-882114-80-9},
  year          = 2000
}
```

Readers who are familiar with regular expressions will probably be able to understand the rather complex field rewriting rule above without further explanation. If not, the manual discusses these features at great length.

External resource files Rewriting rules (and, in fact, any other resource definitions) can also be placed in a separate file (default extension `.rsc`) and loaded using the option `-r`. For example, to remove double-quote delimiters you can use

```
bibtool -r braces  tex.bib
```

which loads the distribution file `braces.rsc` containing three rewriting rules similar to the one above covering additional cases.

Rewriting rules can be restricted to work only on certain fields by specifying those fields followed by a # sign before the regular expression pattern. For example, the following rule will rewrite the year field if it contains only two digits potentially surrounded by double quotes or braces and the first digit is not zero (since we do not know if 02 refers to 2002 or 1902):

```
rewrite.rule {year # "^[\"{]?\([1-9][0-9]\)[\"}]?$" "19\1"}
```

Instead of rewriting you can do semantic checks using the `check.rule` re-   *Semantic*
source. For instance,   *checks*

```
check.rule {year # "^[\"{]?\([0-9][0-9]\)[\"}]?$" "\@ \$: year = \1\n"}
```

will generate a warning that a year field with suspicious contents was found if the field contains only two digits (in the message part \@ is replaced by the entry type and \$ by the reference key). Applying it to our sample database, we get

```
*** BibTool: Book vleunen:92: year = 92
```

More elaborate semantic checks are discussed in the user manual.

BibTeX databases may also contain @string declarations used as abbreviations   *Removing* @string
in the entries. In certain cases you may want those to be replaced by the strings   *declarations*
themselves. This can be done as follows:

```
bibtool -- 'expand.macros=ON' tex.bib
```

This has the result that the series field for the entries lgc97 and lwc99 changes from

```
series = ttct
```

to the expanded form

```
series      = {Tools and Techniques for Computer Typesetting}
```

The bibtool program expands strings whose definitions are found in the database files themselves—abbreviations that are part of the BibTeX style file are left untouched. If they should also get expanded, you have to additionally load a .bib file that contains them explicitly as @string declarations.

Extracting entries

For selecting a subset of entries from a database a number of possibilities exist. The option −x *aux-file* will check in the specified *aux-file* for \citation requests and generate from them a new .bib file containing only entries required for the particular document. For example:

```
bibtool -x 12-1-1.aux -o 12-1-1.bib
```

There is no need to specify any source database(s), since this information is also picked up from the .aux file. Any cross-referenced entries will automatically be included as necessary.

Another possibility is provided with the option -X *regexp*, which extracts all entries whose reference key matches the regular expression *regexp*. For example,

```
bibtool -X '^mr-\|^so-' tex.bib
```

will select the two entries with the reference keys MR-PQ and Southall. Details on regular expressions can be found in the manual. Using regular expressions will select only entries that are explicitly matched. Thus, cross-referenced entries such as EP92 in this example will not be included automatically, though this outcome can be forced by setting the resource select.crossrefs to ON.

In addition, several resources can be set to guide selection. For example, to select all entries with Knuth or Lamport as the author or editor, you could say

```
bibtool -- 'select={author editor "Knuth\|Lamport"}' tex.bib
```

To find all entries of type book or article, you could say

```
bibtool -- 'select={@book @article}' tex.bib
```

To find all entries that do not have a year field, you could say

```
bibtool -- 'select.non={year ".+"}' tex.bib
```

By combining such resource definitions in a resource file and by passing the results of one invocation of bibtool to another, it is possible to provide arbitrarily complicated rewriting and searching methods.

Reference key generation

As we learned in Chapter 12 the reference key, the string used as an argument in the \cite command to refer to a bibliography entry, can be freely chosen (with a few restrictions). Nevertheless, it is often a good idea to stick to a certain scheme since that helps you remember the keys and makes duplicate keys less likely. The bibtool program can help here by changing the keys in a database to conform to such a scheme. Of course, that makes sense only for databases not already in use; otherwise, BibTeX would be unable to find the key specified in your documents.

Two predefined schemes are available through the options -k and -K. They both generate keys consisting of author names and the first relevant word of the title in lowercase (excluding "The" and similar words) and ignoring commands and braces. Thus, when running bibtool on the database from Figure 12.3 on page 717, and then searching for lines containing an @ sign (to limit the listing),

```
bibtool -k jura.bib | grep @
```

we get the following output:

```
@Book{            baumbach.lauterbach.ea:zivilproze,
@Book{            brox.walker:allgemeines,
@Book{            brox.walker:besonderes,
@Book{            palandt:burgerliches,
```

The slightly strange key ending in :zivilproze is due to the fact that the entry contains Zivilproze\ss␣ordnung, making the program believe the word ends after \ss, which itself is discarded because it is a command. Similarly, \"u is represented as "u" in the fourth key. You can dramatically improve the situation by additionally loading the resource file tex_def.rsc. This file uses the tex.define resource to provide translation for common LaTeX commands, so that

```
bibtool -r tex_def -k jura.bib | grep @
```

produces the keys

```
@Book{            baumbach.lauterbach.ea:zivilprozessordnung,
@Book{            brox.walker:allgemeines,
@Book{            brox.walker:besonderes,
@Book{            palandt:buergerliches,
```

Other BibTeX database-manipulating programs have similar problems in parsing blank-delimited commands, so it is usually better to use \ss{} or {\ss} in such places. For example, in Figure 13.2 on page 777 you can see that bib2html was also fooled by the notation and added an incorrect extra space in the first entry.

The other key-generating option (-K) is similar. It adds the initials of the author(s) after the name:

```
@Book{            baumbach.a.lauterbach.w.ea:zivilproze,
@Book{            brox.h.walker.w:allgemeines,
```

Other schemes can be specified using the powerful configuration options documented in the user manual.

13.4.5   pybliographer—An extensible bibliography manager

The pybliographer scripting environment developed by Frédéric Gobry is a tool for managing bibliographic databases. In the current version it supports the following formats: BIBTEX, ISI (web of knowledge), Medline, Ovid, and Refer/EndNote. It can convert from one format to another. It is written in Python, which means that it is readily available on UN*X platforms; usage on Windows systems may prove to be difficult, even though there are Python implementations for this platform as well. The home of Progpybliographer is `http://pybliographer.org`.

The graphical front end for pybliographer, which builds on the Gnome libraries, is called pybliographic. Upon invocation you can specify a database to work with, usually a local file, though it can be a remote database specified as a URL. For example,

```
pybliographic http://www.math.utah.edu:8080/pub/tex/bib/tugboat.bib
```

will bring up a work space similar to the one shown in Figure 13.3 on the facing page. It will be similar, but not identical, because the graphical user interface is highly customizable. For instance, in the version used by the author an "editor" column was added between "author" and date columns in the main window. If you wish to see other fields use the preference dialog (Settings → Preferences → Gnome). On UN*X systems the preferences are stored in the file `.pybrc.conf`. Although this file is not user editable, you can remove it to restore the default configuration if necessary.

Figure 13.3 shows several other interesting features. On the bottom of the main window you see that the loaded database (`tugboat.bib`) contains 2446 entries, 3 of which are currently displayed. This is due to the fact that we searched *Hierarchical* it for entries matching the regular expression pattern `Mittelbach` in the `author` *searching* field (30 entries found), within the results searched for entries containing `LaTeX3` or `class design` in the `title` field (5 entries found), and within these results restricted the search to publications from the years 1995 to 1999. The search dialog window shows the currently defined hierarchical views available. By clicking on either of them you can jump between the different views; by right-clicking you can delete views no longer of interest. The fields available for searching are customizable. The initial settings offer only a few fields.

To edit an existing entry you can double-click it in the main window. Alternatively, you can use the Edit menu from the toolbar, or you can right-click an entry, which pops up a context menu. The latter two possibilities can also be used to delete entries or add new ones. The edit dialog window shows the entry in a format for manipulation opened at the "Mandatory" tab holding the fields that are mandatory for the current entry type. In addition, there are the optional fields in the "Optional" tab and possibly other fields in the "Extra" tab. This classification is done according to the current settings and can be easily adjusted according to your own preference. While pybliographic is capable of correctly loading databases with arbitrary field names, they will all appear in the Extra tab, which may not be

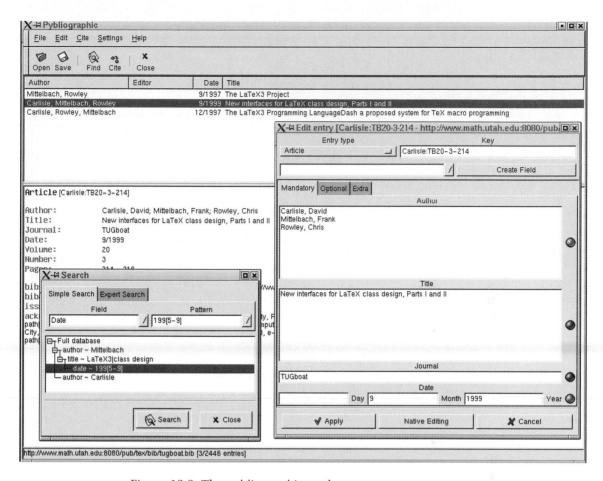

Figure 13.3: The pybliographic work space

convenient if you work with extended BibTeX styles such as jurabib that consider additional fields to be either required or optional. In such cases it pays to adjust the default settings (Settings → Entries, Fields).

To the right of the fields you can see round buttons that are either green or red. With the red buttons pybliographic signals that the field content contains some data that the program was unable to parse correctly and that editing the text is likely to result in loss of data. For example, in the title field it was unable to interpret the command \LaTeX{} correctly and so displayed LaTeX instead. The journal field is flagged because the database actually contains

Signaling dangerous contents

```
Journal      = j-tugboat,
```

This reference to an abbreviation would get lost the moment you modify that

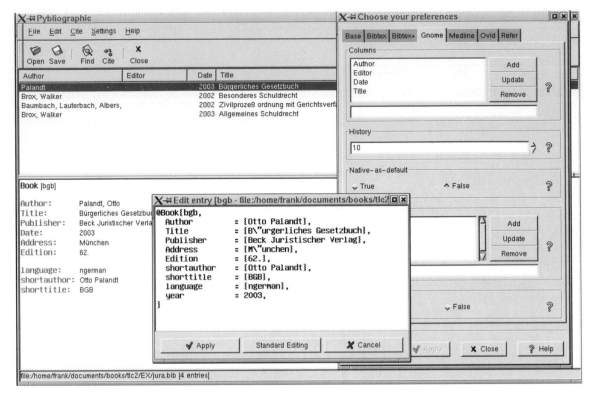

Figure 13.4: Native editing in pybliographic

particular field. To modify such entries you have to change to "Native Editing", as shown in Figure 13.4. This can be done by clicking the "Native Editing" button in the editing dialog window. The window then changes to the format shown in the middle window of Figure 13.4, offering a standard BIBTEX entry format that you can manipulate at will. It is then your responsibility to ensure that the BIBTEX syntax is obeyed. As seen in the right window in that figure, there is the possibility to make the native editing mode serve as the default.

Default
capitalization
rules
While loading a database pybliographic does some capitalization normalization on a number of fields (e.g., `title`). As this is better done by BIBTEX when formatting for a particular journal you should consider disabling this feature (Settings → Preferences → Bibtex+ → Capitalize). In fact, with languages other than English you have to disable it to avoid proper nouns being incorrectly changed to lowercase.

The distribution also contains a number of command-line scripts. The documentation describes how to provide additional ones. For example, to convert files between different formats you can use pybconvert. The script

```
pybconvert bibtex..refer tex.bib
```

converts the BibTeX database tex.bib to the Refer format, resulting in output such as the following:

```
%T A handbook for scholars
%P xi + 348
%I Oxford University Press
%F vLeunen:92
%D 92
%C Walton Street, Oxford OX2 6DP, UK
%A van Leunen, Mary-Claire
```

Depending on the contents of individual fields you may receive warnings, such as "warning: unable to convert '\textsl'", since pybliographer has no idea how to convert such commands to a non-TeX format such as Refer. In that case you should manually correct the results as necessary.

The script pycompact is similar to the aux2bib perl script or the -x option of bibtool discussed earlier. However, unlike the latter option, it does not include cross-referenced entries, so it is safer to use bibtool if available.

An interesting script is pybcheck, which expects a list of BibTeX database files or a directory name as its argument. It then checks all databases for correct syntax, duplicate keys, and other issues. For example, running "pybcheck EX" results in

```
file 'EX/jura.bib' is ok [4 entries]
file 'EX/tex.bib' is ok [12 entries]
```

This script simply verifies the individual databases, so duplicate entries across different files are not detected.

Emacs users can run the command directly from a compile buffer via M-x compile followed by pybcheck *file(s)*. From the output window you can then jump directly to any error detected using the middle mouse button.

13.4.6   JBibtexManager—A BibTeX database manager in Java

The JBibtexManager program developped by Nizar Batada is a BibTeX database manager written in Java; see Figure 13.5 on the following page. Due to the choice of programming language it works on all platforms for which Java 1.4 or higher is available (e.g., Windows, UN*X flavors, Mac).

This program offers searching on the author, editor, title, and keyword values; sorting on the type, reference key, author, year, title, journal, editor, and keywords; and, of course, standard editing functions, including adding, deleting, copying, and pasting between different bibliographies. It automatically detects duplicate reference keys if bibliographies are merged. In addition, it offers the possibility

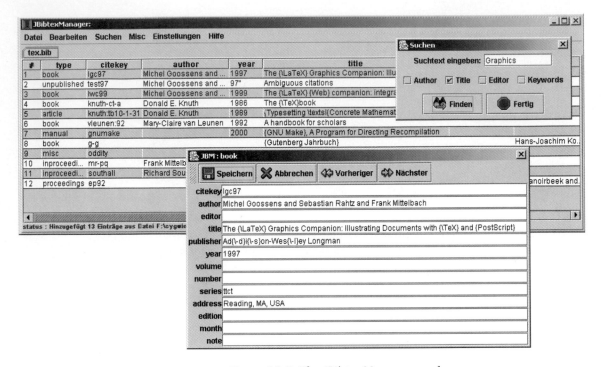

Figure 13.5: The JBibtexManager work space

to search a bibliography for duplicate entries (i.e., entries that differ only in their reference keys, if at all).

Like pybliographic, this program can import data in several bibliography formats: BIBTEX, INSPEC, ISI (web of knowledge), Medline (XML), Ovid, and Scifinder. Export formats of HTML and plain text are available. With formats that do not contain any reference key information, the program automatically generates suitable keys provided the author information is structured in a way the program understands.

Although JBibtexManager is intended to work primarily with BIBTEX databases, importing such files for the first time can pose some problems as not all syntax variations of the BIBTEX format are supported. In particular, there should be at most one field per line. Thus, the GNUmake entry in our sample tex.bib database would not be parsed correctly. In addition, entries are recognized only if the entry type (starting with the @ sign) starts in the first column. If not, the entry is misinterpreted as a comment and dropped.[1]

Of course, these types of problems happen only the first time an externally generated bibliography is loaded; once the data is accepted by the system, it will

---

[1] There are plans to lift these restrictions in a future version.

be saved in a way that enables it to be reloaded again. One way to circumvent the problems during the initial loading is to preprocess the external database with a tool like bibtool or bibclean, since after validation and pretty-printing the entries are in an acceptable format.

Unknown fields in a database entry are kept unchanged but they are neither visible nor modifiable from within the program. It is, however, possible to customize the recognized fields on a per-type basis so that the program is suitable for use with extended BibTeX styles such as those used by jurabib or natbib.

The program is available on CTAN. Its current home is http://csb. stanford.edu/nbatada/JBibtexManager, but there are plans to merge it with a similar project called BibKeeper under the new name JabRef.

13.4.7   BibTexMng—A BibTeX database manager for Windows

The BibTexMng program developed by Petr and Nikolay Vabishchevich implements a BibTeX database manager on Windows; see Figure 13.6 on the next page. It supports all typical management tasks—editing, searching, sorting, moving, or copying entries from one file to another.

In contrast to pybliographic or JBibtexManager, the BibTexMng program deals solely with BibTeX databases; it has no import or export functions to other bibliographical formats. The only "foreign" export formats supported are .bbl files (i.e., processing a selection of entries with BibTeX or BibTeX8 from within the program) and producing HTML from a selection of entries.

In the current release the program unfortunately knows about only the standard BibTeX entry types (see Table 13.1 on page 763), the standard BibTeX fields (Table 13.2), and the following fields:

```
abstract, affiliation, contents, copyright, isbn, issn, keywords,
language, lccn, location, mrnumber, price, size, and url
```

Any other field is silently discarded the first time a BibTeX database is loaded; the same thing happens to entry types if they do not belong to the standard set. This means that the program is not usable if you intend to work with BibTeX styles, such *Not usable with* as jurabib, that introduce additional fields or types, as neither can be represented jurabib *et al.* by the program. It does, however, work for most styles available, including those intended for natbib (e.g., styles generated with custom-bib).

Another limitation to keep in mind is that the BibTexMng program does not support @string declarations. If those are used in an externally generated BibTeX database, you have to first remove them before using the database with BibTexMng. Otherwise, the entries will be incorrectly parsed. To help with this task the program offers to clean an external database for you (via File → Cleaning of BibTeX database). This operation replaces all strings by their definitions and removes all unknown fields, if any exist.

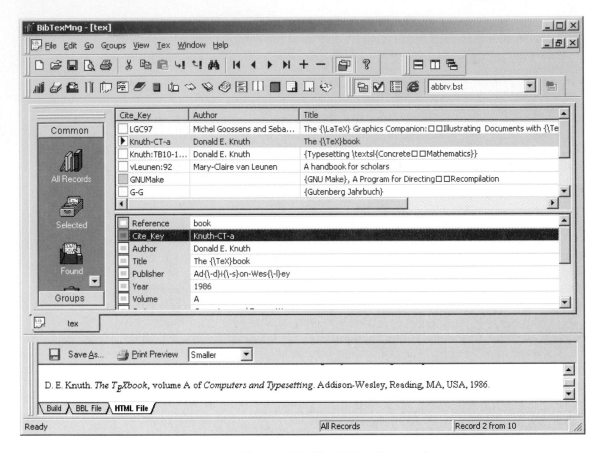

Figure 13.6: The BibTexMng work space

13.5   Formatting the bibliography with BibTEX styles

Now that we know how to produce BibTEX database entries and manipulate them
using various management tools, it is time to discuss the main purpose of the
BibTEX program. This is to generate a bibliography containing a certain set of entries (determined from the document contents) in a format conforming to a set of
conventions.

We first discuss the use of existing styles and present example results produced by a number of standard and nonstandard styles. We then show how the
custom-bib package makes it possible to produce customized styles for nearly
every requirement with ease.

13.5.1   A collection of BibTeX style files

Various organizations and individuals have developed style files for BibTeX that correspond to the house style of particular journals or editing houses. Nelson Beebe has collected a large number of BibTeX styles. For each style he provides an example file, which allows you to see the effect of using the given style.[1] Some of the BibTeX styles—for instance, authordate⟨*i*⟩, jmb, and named—must be used in conjunction with their accompanying LaTeX packages (as indicated in Table 13.4) to obtain the desired effect.

You can also customize a bibliography style, by making small changes to one of those in the table (see Section 13.6.3 for a description of how this is done). Alternatively, you can generate your own style by using the custom-bib program (as explained in Section 13.5.2 on page 798).

Table 13.4: Selected BibTeX style files

Style Name	Description
abbrv.bst	Standard BibTeX style
abbrvnat.bst	natbib variant of abbrv style
abstract.bst	Modified alpha style with abstract keyword
acm.bst	Association for Computing Machinery BibTeX style
agsm.bst	Australian government publications BibTeX style
alpha.bst	Standard BibTeX style
amsalpha.bst	alpha-like BibTeX style for $\mathcal{A}_{\mathcal{M}}S$-TeX
amsplain.bst	plain-like BibTeX style for $\mathcal{A}_{\mathcal{M}}S$-TeX (numeric labels)
annotate.bst	Modified alpha BibTeX style with annote keyword
annotation.bst	Modified plain BibTeX style with annote keyword
apa.bst	American Psychology Association
apalike.bst	Variant of apa BibTeX style
apalike	LaTeX package for use with apalike.bst
apalike2.bst	Variant of apalike BibTeX style
astron.bst	Astronomy BibTeX style
authordate*i*.bst	*i*=[1,4]; series of BibTeX styles producing author-date reference list
authordate*1-4*	LaTeX package to be used together with authordate*i*.bst
bbs.bst	Behavioral and Brain Sciences BibTeX style
cbe.bst	Council of Biology Editors BibTeX style (includes such journals as *American Naturalist* and *Evolution*)
cell.bst	Small modifications to jmb BibTeX style
	continued on next page

[1] See Appendix C to find out how you can obtain these files from one of the TeX archives if they are not already on your system.

continued from previous page

Style name	Description
harvard	LaTeX package for use with Harvard styles (e.g., agsm)
humanbio.bst	Human Biology BibTeX style
humannat.bst	*Human Nature* and *American Anthropologist* journals
ieeetr.bst	*Transactions of the Institute of Electrical and Electronic Engineers* BibTeX style
is-abbrv.bst	abbrv BibTeX style with ISSN and ISBN keyword added
is-alpha.bst	alpha BibTeX style with ISSN and ISBN keyword added
is-plain.bst	plain BibTeX style with ISSN and ISBN keyword added
is-unsrt.bst	unsrt BibTeX style with ISSN and ISBN keyword added
jmb.bst	*Journal of Molecular Biology* style
jmb	LaTeX package for use with jmb.bst
jox.bst	Style for use with jurabib (Oxford style)
jtb.bst	*Journal of Theoretical Biology* BibTeX style
jurabib.bst	Style for use with jurabib
jureco.bst	Style for use with jurabib (compact)
jurunsrt.bst	Style for use with jurabib (unsorted)
kluwer.bst	Kluwer Academic Publishers BibTeX style
named.bst	BibTeX style with [author(s), year] type of citation
named	LaTeX package for use with named.bst
namunsrt.bst	Named variant of unsrt BibTeX style
nar.bst	*Nucleic Acid Research* BibTeX style
nar	LaTeX package for use with nar.bst
nature.bst	*Nature* BibTeX style
nature	LaTeX package for use with nature.bst
newapa.bst	Modification of apalike.bst
newapa	LaTeX package for use with newapa.bst
phaip.bst	American Institute of Physics journals BibTeX style
phapalik.bst	American Psychology Association BibTeX style
phcpc.bst	*Computer Physics Communications* BibTeX style
phiaea.bst	Conferences of the International Atomic Energy Agency BibTeX style
phjcp.bst	*Journal of Computational Physics* BibTeX style
phnf.bst	*Nuclear Fusion* BibTeX style
phnflet.bst	*Nuclear Fusion Letters* BibTeX style
phpf.bst	*Physics of Fluids* BibTeX style
phppcf.bst	Physics version of apalike BibTeX style
phreport.bst	Internal physics reports BibTeX style
phrmp.bst	*Reviews of Modern Physics* BibTeX style

continued on next page

continued from previous page	
Style name	*Description*
plain.bst	Standard BibTEX style
plainnat.bst	natbib variant of plain style
plainyr.bst	plain BibTEX style with primary sort by year
siam.bst	Society of Industrial and Applied Mathematics BibTEX style
unsrt.bst	Standard BibTEX style
unsrtnat.bst	natbib variant of unsrt style

In theory, it is possible to change the appearance of a bibliography by simply using another the BibTEX style. In practice, there are a few restrictions due to the fact that the BibTEX style interface was augmented by some authors so that their styles need additional support from within LATEX. We saw several such examples in Chapter 12. For instance, all the author-date styles need a special LATEX package such as natbib or harvard to function, and the BibTEX styles for jurabib will work only if that package is loaded.

On the whole the scheme works quite well, and we prove it in this section by showing the results of applying different BibTEX styles (plus their support packages if necessary) without otherwise altering the sample document. For this we use the by now familiar database from Figure 12.2 on page 690 and cite five publications from it: an article and a book by Donald Knuth, which will show us, how different publications by the same author are handled; the manual from the Free Software Foundation, which is an entry without an author name; the unpublished entry with many authors and the special BibTEX string "and others"; and a publication that is part of a proceeding, so that BibTEX has to include additional data from a different entry.

In our first example we use the standard plain BibTEX style, which means we use the following input:

```
\bibliographystyle{plain}
\nocite{Knuth:TB10-1-31,GNUMake,MR-PQ,Knuth-CT-a,test97}
\bibliography{tex}
```

To produce the final document, the example LATEX file has to be run through LATEX once to get the citation references written to the .aux file. Next, BibTEX processes the generated .aux file, reading the relevant entries from the BibTEX database tex.bib. The actual bibliography style in which the database entries are to be output to the .bbl file for later treatment by LATEX is specified with the command \bibliographystyle in the LATEX source. Finally, LATEX is run twice more—first to load the .bbl file and again to resolve all references.[1] A detailed explanation of this procedure was given in Section 12.1.3 on page 687, where you will also find a graphical representation of the data flow (Figure 12.1).

---

[1]In fact, for this example only one run is necessary—there are no cross-references to resolve because we used \nocite throughout.

The `plain` style has numeric labels (in brackets) and the entries are alphabetically sorted by author, year, and title. In case of the GNU manual the organization was used for sorting. This will give the following output:

References

[1] Free Software Foundation, Boston, Massachusetts. *GNU Make, A Program for Directing Recompilation*, 2000.

[2] Michel Goossens, Ben User, and Joe Doe. Ambiguous citations. Submitted to the IBM Journal of Research and Development, 1997.

[3] Donald E. Knuth. *The TEXbook*, volume A of *Computers and Typesetting*. Addison-Wesley, Reading, MA, USA, 1986.

[4] Donald E. Knuth. Typesetting Concrete Mathematics. *TUGboat*, 10(1):31–36, April 1989.

[5] Frank Mittelbach and Chris Rowley. The pursuit of quality: How can automated typesetting achieve the highest standards of craft typography? In Christine Vanoirbeek and Giovanni Coray, editors, *EP92—Proceedings of Electronic Publishing, '92*, pages 261–273, Cambridge, 1992. Cambridge University Press.

13-5-1

By replacing `plain` with `abbrv` we get a similar result. Now, however, the entries are more compact, since first names, month, and predefined journal names (Table 13.3 on page 771) are abbreviated. For instance, `ibmjrd` in the second reference now gives "IBM J. Res. Dev." instead of "IBM Journal of Research and Development".

[1] Free Software Foundation, Boston, Massachusetts. *GNU Make, A Program for Directing Recompilation*, 2000.

[2] M. Goossens, B. User, and J. Doe. Ambiguous citations. Submitted to the IBM J. Res. Dev., 1997.

[3] D. E. Knuth. *The TEXbook*, volume A of *Computers and Typesetting*. Addison-Wesley, Reading, MA, USA, 1986.

[4] D. E. Knuth. Typesetting Concrete Mathematics. *TUGboat*, 10(1):31–36, Apr. 1989.

[5] F. Mittelbach and C. Rowley. The pursuit of quality: How can automated typesetting achieve the highest standards of craft typography? In C. Vanoirbeek and G. Coray, editors, *EP92—Proceedings of Electronic Publishing, '92*, pages 261–273, Cambridge, 1992. Cambridge University Press.

13-5-2

With the standard BibTeX style `unsrt` we get the same result as with the `plain` style, except that the entries are printed in order of first citation, rather than being sorted. The standard sets of styles do not contain a combination of `unsrt` and `abbrv`, but if necessary it would be easy to integrate the differences between `plain` and `abbrv` into `unsrt` to form a new style.

[1] Donald E. Knuth. Typesetting Concrete Mathematics. *TUGboat*, 10(1):31–36, April 1989.

[2] Free Software Foundation, Boston, Massachusetts. *GNU Make, A Program for Directing Recompilation*, 2000.

[3] Frank Mittelbach and Chris Rowley. The pursuit of quality: How can automated typesetting achieve the highest standards of craft typography? In Christine Vanoirbeek and Giovanni Coray, editors, *EP92—Proceedings of Electronic Publishing, '92*, pages 261–273, Cambridge, 1992. Cambridge University Press.

[4] Donald E. Knuth. *The TeXbook*, volume A of *Computers and Typesetting*. Addison-Wesley, Reading, MA, USA, 1986.

[5] Michel Goossens, Ben User, and Joe Doe. Ambiguous citations. Submitted to the IBM Journal of Research and Development, 1997.

13-5-3

The standard style `alpha` is again similar to `plain`, but the labels of the entries are formed from the author's name and the year of publication. The slightly strange label for the GNU manual is due to the fact that the entry contains a `key` field from which the first three letters are used to form part of the label. Also note the interesting label produced for the reference with more than three authors. The publications are sorted, with the label being used as a sort key, so that now the GNU manual moves to fourth place.

[GUD97] Michel Goossens, Ben User, and Joe Doe. Ambiguous citations. Submitted to the IBM Journal of Research and Development, 1997.

[Knu86] Donald E. Knuth. *The TeXbook*, volume A of *Computers and Typesetting*. Addison-Wesley, Reading, MA, USA, 1986.

[Knu89] Donald E. Knuth. Typesetting Concrete Mathematics. *TUGboat*, 10(1):31–36, April 1989.

[mak00] Free Software Foundation, Boston, Massachusetts. *GNU Make, A Program for Directing Recompilation*, 2000.

[MR92] Frank Mittelbach and Chris Rowley. The pursuit of quality: How can automated typesetting achieve the highest standards of craft typography? In Christine Vanoirbeek and Giovanni Coray, editors, *EP92—Proceedings of Electronic Publishing, '92*, pages 261–273, Cambridge, 1992. Cambridge University Press.

13-5-4

Many BIBTEX styles implement smaller or larger variations of the layouts produced with the standard styles. For example, the `phaip` style for American Institute of Physics journals implements an unsorted layout (i.e., by order of citation), but omits article titles, uses abbreviated author names, and uses a different structure for denoting editors in proceedings. Note that the entry with more than three authors has now been collapsed, showing only the first one.

[1] D. E. Knuth, TUGboat **10**, 31 (1989).

[2] Free Software Foundation, Boston, Massachusetts, *GNU Make, A Program for Directing Recompilation*, 2000.

[3] F. Mittelbach and C. Rowley, The pursuit of quality: How can automated typesetting achieve the highest standards of craft typography?, in *EP92—Proceedings of Electronic Publishing, '92*, edited by C. Vanoirbeek and G. Coray, pages 261–273, Cambridge, 1992, Cambridge University Press.

[4] D. E. Knuth, *The TEXbook*, volume A of *Computers and Typesetting*, Addison-Wesley, Reading, MA, USA, 1986.

[5] M. Goossens, B. User, and J. Doe, Ambiguous citations, Submitted to the IBM J. Res. Dev., 1997.

13-5-5

If we turn to styles implementing an author-date scheme, the layout usually changes more drastically. For instance, labels are normally suppressed (after all, the lookup process is by author). The `chicago` style, for example, displays the author name or names in abbreviated form (first name reversed), followed by the date in parentheses. In addition, we see yet another way to handle the editors in proceedings and instead of the word "pages" we get "pp." For this example we loaded the `natbib` package to enable author-date support.

Free Software Foundation (2000). *GNU Make, A Program for Directing Recompilation*. Boston, Massachusetts: Free Software Foundation.

Goossens, M., B. User, and J. Doe (1997). Ambiguous citations. Submitted to the IBM Journal of Research and Development.

Knuth, D. E. (1986). *The TEXbook*, Volume A of *Computers and Typesetting*. Reading, MA, USA: Addison-Wesley.

Knuth, D. E. (1989, April). Typesetting Concrete Mathematics. *TUGboat 10*(1), 31–36.

Mittelbach, F. and C. Rowley (1992). The pursuit of quality: How can automated typesetting achieve the highest standards of craft typography? In C. Vanoirbeek and G. Coray (Eds.), *EP92—Proceedings of Electronic Publishing, '92*, Cambridge, pp. 261–273. Cambridge University Press.

13-5-6

As a final example we present another type of layout that is implemented with the help of the jurabib package. Since more customizing is necessary we show the input used once more. The trick used to suppress the heading is *not* suitable for use in real documents as the space around the heading would be retained!

```
\usepackage[bibformat=ibidem]{jurabib}
\bibliographystyle{jurabib}    \jbuseidemhrule    % use default rule
\renewcommand\refname{}        % suppress heading for the example
\nocite{Knuth:TB10-1-31,GNUMake,MR-PQ,Knuth-CT-a,tost97,LCC97}
\bibliography{tex}
```

This will produce a layout in which the author name is replaced by a rule if it has been listed previously. In case of multiple authors the complete list has to be identical (see first two entries). Also, for the first time ISBN and ISSN numbers are shown when present in the entry. If you look closely, you will see many other smaller and larger differences. For example, this is the first style that does not translate titles of articles and proceeding entries to lowercase but rather keeps them as specified in the database (see page 809 for a discussion of how BibTeX styles can be modified to achieve this effect).

As the original application field for jurabib was law citations, it is one of the BibTeX styles that does not provide default strings for the journals listed in Table 13.3 on page 771; as a result, we get an incomplete first entry. BibTeX will warn you about the missing string in this case. You can then provide a definition for it in the database file or, if you prefer, in a separate database file that is loaded only if necessary.

Goossens, Michel/Rahtz, Sebastian/Mittelbach, Frank: The LaTeX Graphics Companion: Illustrating Documents with TeX and PostScript. Reading, MA, USA: Addison-Wesley Longman, 1997, Tools and Techniques for Computer Typesetting, xxi + 554, ISBN 0–201–85469–4

Goossens, Michel/User, Ben/Doe, Joe: Ambiguous citations. 1997, Submitted to the

Knuth, Donald E.: The TeXbook. Volume A, Computers and Typesetting. Reading, MA, USA: Addison-Wesley, 1986, ix + 483, ISBN 0–201–13447–0

—— Typesetting Concrete Mathematics. TUGboat, 10 April 1989, Nr. 1, 31–36, ISSN 0896–3207

Free Software Foundation: GNU Make, A Program for Directing Recompilation. 2000

Mittelbach, Frank/Rowley, Chris: The Pursuit of Quality: How can Automated Typesetting achieve the Highest Standards of Craft Typography? In **Vanoirbeek, Christine/Coray, Giovanni, editors:** EP92—Proceedings of Electronic Publishing, '92. Cambridge: Cambridge University Press, 1992, 261–273

13-5-7

13.5.2 `custom-bib`—Generate BibTeX styles with ease

So far, we have discussed how to influence the layout of the bibliography by using different bibliography styles. If a particular BibTeX style is recommended for the journal or publisher you are writing for, then it is all that it is necessary. However, a more likely scenario is that you have been equipped with a detailed set of instructions that tell you how references should be formatted, but without pointing you to any specific BibTeX style—a program that may not even be known at the publishing house.

Hunting for an existing style that fits the bill or can be adjusted slightly to do so (see Section 13.6.3) is an option, of course, but given that there are usually several variations in use for each typographical detail, the possibilities are enormous and thus the chances of finding a suitable style are remote. Consider the following nine common requirements for presenting author names:

Requirement	*Example*
Full name surname last	Donald Erwin Knuth/Michael Frederick Plass
Full name surname first	Knuth, Donald Erwin/Plass, Michael Frederick
Initials and surname	D. E. Knuth/M. F. Plass
Surname and initials	Knuth, D. E./Plass, M. F.
Surname and dotless initials	Knuth D E/Plass M F
Surname and concatenated initials	Knuth DE/Plass MF
Surname and spaceless initials	Knuth D.E./Plass M.F.
Only first author reversed with initials	Knuth, D. E./M. F. Plass
Only first author reversed with full names	Knuth, Donald Ervin/Michael Frederick Plass

Table 13.5: Requirements for formatting names

Combining these with a specification for the separation symbol to use (e.g., comma, semicolon, slash), the fonts to use for author names (i.e., Roman, bold, small caps, italic, other), and perhaps a requirement for different fonts for surname and first names, you will get more than 500 different styles for presenting author names in the bibliography. Clearly, this combinatorial explosion cannot be managed by providing predefined styles for every combination.

Faced with this problem, Patrick Daly, the author of `natbib`, started in 1993 to develop a system that is capable of providing customized BibTeX styles by collecting answers to questions like the above (more than 70!) and then building a customized `.bst` file corresponding to the answers.

The system works in two phases: (1) a collection phase in which questions are interactively asked and (2) a generation phase in which the answers are used to build the BibTeX style. Both phases are entirely done by using LaTeX and thus can be carried out on any platform without requiring any additional helper program.

The collection is started by running the program `makebst.tex` through LaTeX and answering the questions posed to you. Most of the questions are presented in

the form of menus that offer several answers. The default answer is marked with
a * and can be selected by simply pressing ⟨*return*⟩. Other choices can be selected
by typing the letter in parentheses in front of the option. Selecting a letter not
present produces the default choice.

Initializing the system

We now walk you through the first questions, which are somewhat special because
they are used to initialize the system. Each time we indicate the suggested answer.

```
Do you want a description of the usage? (NO)
```

Replying with y will produce a description of the procedure (as explained above);
otherwise, the question has no effect.

```
Enter the name of the MASTER file (default=merlin.mbs)
```

Here the correct answer is ⟨*return*⟩. The default `merlin.mbs` is currently the only
production master file available, though this might change one day.

```
Name of the final OUTPUT .bst file? (default extension=bst)
```

Specify the name for your new BιBTEX style file, without an extension—for example, `ttct` (Tools and Techniques for Computer Typesetting series). As a result of
completing the first phase you will then receive a file called `ttct.dbj` from which
the BιBTEX style file `ttct.bst` is produced in the second phase.

```
Give a comment line to include in the style file.
Something like for which journals it is applicable.
```

Enter any free-form text you like, but note that a ⟨*return*⟩ ends the comment. It
is carried over into the resulting files and can help you at a later stage to identify
the purpose of this BιBTEX style.

```
Do you want verbose comments? (NO)
```

If you enter y to this question the context of later questions will be shown in the
following form:

```
<<STYLE OF CITATIONS:
   ...
>>STYLE OF CITATIONS:
```

Whether this provides any additional help is something you have to decide for
yourself. The default is not to provide this extra information.

```
Name of language definition file (default=merlin.mbs)
```

catalan	Language support for Catalan	italian	Language support for Italian
dansk	Language support for Danish	norsk	Language support for Norwegian
dutch	Language support for Dutch	polski	Language support for Polish
esperant	Language support for Esperanto	portuges	Language support for Portuguese
finnish	Language support for Finnish	slovene	Language support for Slovene
french	Language support for French	spanish	Language support for Spanish
german	Language support for German		

Table 13.6: Language support in `custom-bib` (summer 2003)

If you are generating a B\textsc{ib}T\textsc{e}X style for a language other than English you can enter the name of the language here. Table 13.6 lists currently supported languages. Otherwise, reply with ⟨*return*⟩.

```
Include file(s) for extra journal names? (NO)
```

By answering y you can load predefined journal names for certain disciplines into the B\textsc{ib}T\textsc{e}X style. You are then asked to specify the files containing these predefined names (with suitable defaults given).

   This concludes the first set of questions for initializing the system. What follows are many questions that offer choices concerning layout and functional details. These can be classified into three categories:

Citation scheme   The choice made here influences later questions. If you choose author-date support, for example, you will get different questions then if you choose a numerical scheme.

Extensions   These questions are related to extending the set of supported B\textsc{ib}T\textsc{e}X fields, such as whether to include a `url` field.

Typographical details   You are asked to make choices about how to format specific parts of the bibliographical entries. Several of the choices depend on the citation scheme used.

While it is possible to change your selections in the second phase of the processing (or to start all over again), it is best to have a clear idea about which citation scheme and which extensions are desired before beginning the interactive session. The typographical details can be adjusted far more easily in the second phase if that becomes necessary. We therefore discuss these main choices in some detail.

Selecting the citation scheme

The citation scheme is selected by answering the following question:

```
STYLE OF CITATIONS:
(*) Numerical as in standard LaTeX
```

```
(a) Author-year with some non-standard interface
(b) Alpha style, Jon90 or JWB90 for single or multiple authors
(o) Alpha style, Jon90 even for multiple authors
(f) Alpha style, Jones90 (full name of first author)
(c) Cite key (special for listing contents of bib file)
```

The default choice is "numerical". If you want to produce a style for the author-date scheme, select a (and disregard the mentioning of "nonstandard interface"). For alpha-style citations, use either b, o, or f depending on the label style you prefer. Choice c is of interest only if you want to produce a style for displaying BibTEX databases, so do not select it for production styles.

If the default (i.e., a numerical citation scheme) was selected, the follow-up question reads:

```
HTML OUTPUT (if non author-year citations)
(*) Normal LaTeX output
(h) Hypertext output, in HTML code, in paragraphs
(n) Hypertext list with sequence numbers
(k) Hypertext with keys for viewing databases
```

Select the default. All other choices generate BibTEX styles that produce some sort of HTML output (which needs further manipulation before it can be viewed in browsers). This feature is considered experimental.

If you have selected an author-date citation scheme (i.e., a), you will be rewarded with a follow-up question for deciding on the support interface from within LaTEX:

```
AUTHOR--YEAR SUPPORT SYSTEM (if author-year citations)
(*) Natbib for use with natbib v5.3 or later
(o) Older Natbib without full authors citations
(l) Apalike for use with apalike.sty
(h) Harvard system with harvard.sty
(a) Astronomy system with astron.sty
(c) Chicago system with chicago.sty
(n) Named system with named.sty
(d) Author-date system with authordate1-4.sty
```

The default choice, natbib, is usually the best, offering all the possibilities described in Sections 12.3.2 and 12.4.1. The option o should *not* be selected. If you have documents using citation commands from, say, the harvard package (see Example 12-3-4 on page 700), the option h would be suitable. For the same reason, the other options might be the right choice in certain circumstances. However, for document portability, natbib should be the preferred choice. Note in particular that some of the other packages mentioned in the options are no longer distributed in the mainstream LaTEX installation.

Determining the extensions supported

Besides supporting the standard BɪʙTₑX entry types (Table 13.1 on page 763) and fields (Table 13.2), `makebst.tex` can be directed to support additional fields as optional fields in the databases, so that they will be used if present. Some of these extensions are turned off by default, even though it makes sense to include them in nearly every BɪʙTₑX style file.

```
LANGUAGE FIELD
(*) No language field
(1) Add language field to switch hyphenation patterns temporarily
```

Replying with 1 will greatly help in presenting foreign titles properly. Example 12-5-6 on page 719 shows the problems that can arise and explains how they can be resolved when a `language` field is present (see Example 12-5-36 on page 734). So a derivation from the default is suggested.

```
ANNOTATIONS:
(*) No annotations will be recognized
(a) Annotations in annote field or in .tex file of citekey name
```

Choosing a will integrate support for an `annote` field in the `.bst` file as well as support for including annotations stored in files of the form ⟨*citekey*⟩`.tex`. However, in contrast to jurabib, which also offers this feature, the inclusion cannot be suppressed or activated using a package option. Since you are quite likely to want this feature turned on and off depending on the document, you might be better served by using two separate BɪʙTₑX styles differing only in this respect.

The nonstandard field `eid` (electronic identifier) is automatically supported by all generated styles. The fields `doi`, `isbn`, and `issn` are included by default but can be deselected. Especially for supporting the REVTₑX package from the American Physical Society, a number of other fields can be added.

Finally, support for URLs can be added by answering the following question with something different from the default.

```
URL ADDRESS: (without REVTeX fields)
(*) No URL for electronic (Internet) documents
(u) Include URL as regular item block
(n) URL as note
(1) URL on new line after rest of reference
```

We suggest including support for URLs as references to electronic resources become more and more common. In the bibliography the URL is tagged with `\urlprefix\url[`*field-value*`]`, with default definitions for both commands. By loading the url package, better line breaking can be achieved.

As one of the last questions you are offered the following choice:

```
COMPATIBILITY WITH PLAIN TEX:
(*) Use LaTeX commands which may not work with Plain TeX
(t) Use only Plain TeX commands for fonts and testing
```

We strongly recommend retaining the default! LaTeX 2_ε is nearly a decade old, and NFSS should have found its way into every living room. Besides, the plain TeX commands (\rm, \bf, and so on) are no longer officially part of LaTeX. They may be defined by a document class (for compatibility reasons with LaTeX 2.09)—but then they may not. Thus, choosing the obsolete syntax may result in the BibTeX style not functioning properly in all circumstances.[1]

Note that the questions about the extensions are mixed with those about typographical details and do not necessarily appear in the order presented here.

Specifying the typographical details

The remaining questions (of which there are plenty) concern typographical details, such as formatting author names, presenting journal information, and many more topics. As an example we show the question block that deals with the formatting of article titles:

```
TITLE OF ARTICLE:
(*) Title plain with no special font
(i) Title italic (\em)
(q) Title and punctuation in single quotes ('Title,' ..)
(d) Title and punctuation in double quotes (''Title,'' ..)
(g) Title and punctuation in guillemets (<<Title,>> ..)
(x) Title in single quotes ('Title', ..)
(y) Title in double quotes (''Title'', ..)
(z) Title in guillemets (<<Title>>, ..)
```

If you make the wrong choice with any of them, do not despair. You can correct your mistake in the second phase of the formatting as explained below.

Generating the BibTeX style from the collected answers

The result of running makebst.tex through LaTeX and answering all these questions is a new file with the extension .dbj. It contains all your selections in a special form suitable to be processed by DOCSTRIP, which in turn produces the final BibTeX style (see Section 14.2 for a description of the DOCSTRIP program). Technically speaking, a BibTeX bibliographic style file master (merlin.mbs by default) contains alternative coding that depends on DOCSTRIP options. By choosing

---

[1]Warning: in older versions the question was "NEW FONT SELECTION SCHEME" and the default was to use the obsolete commands. So be careful.

entries from the interactive menus discussed above, some of this code is activated, thereby providing the necessary customization.

If you specified `ttct` in response to the question for the new `.bst` file, for example, you would now have a file `ttct.dbj` at your disposal. Hence, all that is necessary to generate the final BibTeX style `ttct.bst` is to run

```
latex ttct.dbj
```

The content of the `.dbj` files generated from the first phase is well documented and presented in a form that makes further adjustments quite simple. Suppose you have answered `y` in response to the question about the title of articles on the previous page (i.e., use double quotes around the title) but you really should have replied with `d` (use double quotes around title and punctuation). Then all you have to do is open the `.dbj` file with a text editor and search for the block that deals with article titles:

```
%--------------------
%TITLE OF ARTICLE:
%    %: (def) Title plain
% tit-it,%: Title italic
% tit-qq,qt-s,%: Title and punctuation in single quotes
% tit-qq,%: Title and punctuation in double quotes
% tit-qq,qt-g,%: Title and punctuation in guillemets
% tit-qq,qt-s,qx,%: Title in single quotes
  tit-qq,qx,%: Title in double quotes
% tit-qq,qt-g,qx,%: Title in guillemets
%--------------------
```

Changing the behavior then entails nothing more than uncommenting the line you want and commenting out the line currently selected:

```
%--------------------
%TITLE OF ARTICLE:
%    %: (def) Title plain
% tit-it,%: Title italic
% tit-qq,qt-s,%: Title and punctuation in single quotes
  tit-qq,%: Title and punctuation in double quotes
% tit-qq,qt-g,%: Title and punctuation in guillemets
% tit-qq,qt-s,qx,%: Title in single quotes
% tit-qq,qx,%: Title in double quotes
% tit-qq,qt-g,qx,%: Title in guillemets
%--------------------
```

After that, rerun the file through LaTeX to obtain an updated BibTeX style.

13.6 The BIBTEX style language

This section presents a condensed introduction to the language used in BIBTEX style files. The information should suffice if you want to slightly modify an existing style file. For more details, consult Oren Patashnik's original article, "Designing BIBTEX Styles" [136].

BIBTEX styles use a postfix stack language (like PostScript) to tell BIBTEX how to format the entries in the reference list. The language has 10 commands, described in Table 13.7 on page 807, to manipulate the language's objects: constants, variables, functions, the stack, and the entry list.

BIBTEX knows two types of functions: built-in functions, provided by BIBTEX itself (see Table 13.8 on page 808), and user functions, which are defined using either the MACRO or FUNCTION command.

You can use all printing characters inside the pair of double quotes delimiting string constants. Although BIBTEX, in general, ignores case differences, it honors the case inside a string. Spaces are significant inside string constants, and a string constant cannot be split across lines.

Variable and function names cannot begin with a numeral and may not contain any of the 10 restricted characters shown on page 769. BIBTEX ignores case differences in the names of variables, functions, and macros.

Constants and variables can be of type integer or string (Boolean true and false are represented by the integers 1 and 0, respectively).

There are three kinds of variables:

Global variables These are either integer- or string-valued variables, which are declared using an INTEGERS or STRINGS command.

Entry variables These are integer- or string-valued variables, which are declared using the ENTRY command. Each of these variables will have a value for each entry on the list read in a BIBTEX database.

Fields These are string-valued, read-only variables that store the information from the database file. Their values are set by the READ command. As with entry variables there is a value for each entry.

13.6.1 The BIBTEX style file commands and built-in functions

Table 13.7 on page 807 gives a short description of the 10 BIBTEX commands. Although the command names appear in uppercase, BIBTEX ignores case differences.

It is recommended (but not required) to leave at least one blank line between commands and to leave no blank lines within a command. This convention helps BIBTEX recover from syntax errors.

Table 13.8 on page 808 gives a short overview of BIBTEX's 37 built-in functions (for more details, see [136]). Every built-in function with a letter in its name ends with a $ sign.

13.6.2   The documentation style `btxbst.doc`

Oren Patashnik based the standard BibTeX style files `abbrv`, `alpha`, `plain`, and `unsrt` on a generic file, `btxbst.doc`, which is well documented and should be consulted for gaining a detailed insight into the inner workings of BibTeX styles.

In the standard styles, labels have two basic formatting modes: *alphabetic*, like [Lam84], and *Numeric*, like [34]. References can be ordered in three ways:

Sorted, alphabetic labels   Alphabetically ordered, first by citation label, then by author(s) (or its replacement field), then by year and title.

Sorted, numeric labels   Alphabetically ordered, first by author(s) (or its replacement field), then by year and title.

Unsorted   Printed in the order in which thee references are cited in the text.

The basic flow of a style file is controlled by the following command-lines, which are found at the end of the `btxbst.doc` file:

```
EXECUTE {begin.bib}          % Preamble and \begin{thebibliography}
EXECUTE {init.state.consts}  % Initialize the state constants
ITERATE {call.type$}         % Loop over entries producing output
EXECUTE {end.bib}            % Write \end{thebibliography} command
```

These commands are explained in Tables 13.7 and 13.8.

The code of a style file starts with the declaration of the available fields with the ENTRY declaration and the string variables to be used for the construction of the citation label.

Each entry function starts by calling `output.bibitem` to write `\bibitem` and its arguments to the `.bbl` file. Then the various fields are formatted and printed by the function `output` or `output.check`, which handles the writing of separators (commas, periods, `\newblock`'s) as needed. Finally, `fin.entry` is called to add the final period and finish the entry.

Next come some functions for formatting chunks of an entry. There are functions for each of the basic fields. The `format.names` function parses names into their "First von Last, Junior" parts, separates them by commas, and puts an "and" before the last name (but ending with "et al." if the last of multiple authors is `"others"`). The `format.authors` function applies to authors, and `format.editors` operates on editors (it appends the appropriate title: ", editor" or ", editors").

The next part of the file contains all the functions defining the different types accepted in a `.bib` file (i.e., functions like `article` and `book`). These functions actually generate the output written to the `.bbl` file for a given entry. They must precede the READ command. In addition, a style designer should provide a function `default.type` for unknown types.

ENTRY   {*field-list*}   {*integer-variable-list*}   {*string-variable-list*}

Declares the fields and entry variables. BibTeX declares automatically one supplementary field `crossref`, used for cross-referencing, and an additional string entry variable `sort.key$`, used by the SORT command. There should be only one ENTRY command per style file. For instance, for the styles `alpha` and `plain` you have, respectively,

```
ENTRY   { address author booktitle ... } {} { label extra.label sort.label }
ENTRY   { address author booktitle ... } {} { label }
```

EXECUTE   {*function-name*}

Executes a single function.

```
EXECUTE {begin.bib}
```

FUNCTION   {*function-name*}   {*definition*}

Defines a new function. You cannot change the definition of a FUNCTION outside a style file.

```
FUNCTION {end.bib}
{ newline$  "\end{thebibliography}" write$ newline$ }
```

MACRO   {*macro-name*}   {*definition*}

Defines a string macro. You can change the definition of a MACRO outside a style file.

```
MACRO {feb} {"February"}
```

INTEGERS   {*global-integer-variable-list*}

Declares global integer variables.

```
INTEGERS { longest.label.width last.extra.num }
```

STRINGS   {*global-string-variable-list*}

Declares global string variables.

```
STRINGS { longest.label last.sort.label next.extra }
```

ITERATE   {*function-name*}

Executes a single function, once for each entry in the list, in the list's current order.

```
ITERATE {longest.label.pass}
```

REVERSE   {*function-name*}

Executes a single function, once for each entry in the list, in reverse order.

```
REVERSE {reverse.pass}
```

READ

Extracts from the database file the field values for each entry in the list. There should be only one READ command per style file. The ENTRY and MACRO commands must precede READ.

SORT

Sorts the entry list using the values of the string entry variable `sort.key$`.

Table 13.7: BibTeX style file commands

$\mathcal{I}_1$ $\mathcal{I}_2$ >	($\mathcal{I}$)	1 (if $\mathcal{I}_1 > \mathcal{I}_2$) or 0 (otherwise)	
$\mathcal{I}_1$ $\mathcal{I}_2$ <	($\mathcal{I}$)	1 (if $\mathcal{I}_1 < \mathcal{I}_2$) or 0 (otherwise)	
$\mathcal{I}_1$ $\mathcal{I}_2$ =	($\mathcal{I}$)	1 (if $\mathcal{I}_1 = \mathcal{I}_2$) or 0 (otherwise)	
S_1 S_2 =	($\mathcal{I}$)	1 (if $S_1 = S_2$) or 0 (otherwise)	
$\mathcal{I}_1$ $\mathcal{I}_2$ +	($\mathcal{I}_1 + \mathcal{I}_2$)	Add two integers	
$\mathcal{I}_1$ $\mathcal{I}_2$ −	($\mathcal{I}_1 - \mathcal{I}_2$)	Subtract two integers	
S_1 S_2 *	($S_1 S_2$)	Concatenate two strings	
$\mathcal{L}$ $\mathcal{V}$:=		Assign to $\mathcal{V}$ the value of $\mathcal{L}$	
S add.period$	($S.$)	Add dot to string unless that string ends with '.', '?', or '!'	
call.type$		Execute function whose name is the type of an entry (e.g., book)	
S "t" change.case$	(S)	Convert S to lowercase except at beginning	
S "l" change.case$	(S)	Convert S completely to lowercase	
S "u" change.case$	(S)	Convert S completely to uppercase	
S chr.to.int$	($\mathcal{I}$)	Translate single string character to ASCII equivalent	
cite$	(cite-string)	Push \cite command argument	
$\mathcal{L}$ duplicate$	($\mathcal{L}$ $\mathcal{L}$)	Duplicate entry	
$\mathcal{L}$ empty$	($\mathcal{I}$)	1 (if $\mathcal{L}$ missing field or blank string) or 0 (otherwise)	
S_1 $\mathcal{I}$ S_2 format.name$	(S)	Format $\mathcal{I}$ names S_1 according to name specifications S_2	
$\mathcal{I}$ $\mathcal{F}_1$ $\mathcal{F}_2$ if$		Execute $\mathcal{F}_1$ if $\mathcal{I} > 0$, else execute $\mathcal{F}_2$	
$\mathcal{I}$ int.to.chr$	(S)	Translate integer into one ASCII character table	
$\mathcal{I}$ int.to.str$	(S)	Push string equivalent of integer	
$\mathcal{L}$ missing$	($\mathcal{I}$)	1 (if $\mathcal{L}$ missing field) or 0 (otherwise)	
newline$		Start a new line in the .bbl file	
S num.names$	($\mathcal{I}$)	Number of names in S	
$\mathcal{L}$ pop$		Throw away top element on stack	
preamble$	(S)	Push concatenation of all @preamble strings read in database files	
S purify$	(S)	Remove non-alphanumeric characters	
quote$	(S)	Push double-quote character string	
skip$		Do nothing	
stack$		Pop and print whole stack	
S $\mathcal{I}_1$ $\mathcal{I}_2$ substring$	(S)	Substring of S starting at $\mathcal{I}_1$ and with a length of $\mathcal{I}_2$	
$\mathcal{L}_1$ $\mathcal{L}_2$ swap$	($\mathcal{L}_2$ $\mathcal{L}_1$)	Swap the literals	
S text.length$	($\mathcal{I}$)	Number of "text" characters	
S $\mathcal{I}$ text.prefix$	(S)	Front $\mathcal{I}$ characters of S	
$\mathcal{L}$ top$		Pop and print top of stack	
type$	(S)	Push current entry's type (e.g., book or "" if unknown)	
S warning$		Pop and print top (string) literal and a warning message	
$\mathcal{F}_1$ $\mathcal{F}_2$ $\mathcal{I}$ while$		Execute $\mathcal{F}_2$ while function value $\mathcal{I}$ of $\mathcal{F}_1$ has $\mathcal{I} > 0$	
S width$	($\mathcal{I}$)	Push width of S (TeX units)	
S write$		Write S to output buffer	

Table 13.8: BibTeX style file built-in functions

The built-in functions are preceded by the variable they consume on the stack. If they leave a result on the stack, it is shown in parentheses. A "literal" $\mathcal{L}$ is an element on the stack. It can be an integer $\mathcal{I}$, a string S, a variable $\mathcal{V}$, a function $\mathcal{F}$, or a special value denoting a missing field. If the popped literal has an incorrect type, BibTeX complains and pushes the integer 0 or the null string, depending on the function's resulting type.

The next section of the `btxbst.doc` file contains definitions for the names of the months and for certain common journals. Depending on the style, full or abbreviated names may be used. These definitions are followed by the READ command, which inputs the entries in the `.bib` file.

Then the labels for the bibliographic entries are constructed. Exactly which fields are used for the primary part of the label depends on the entry type.

The labels are next prepared for sorting. When sorting, the sort key is computed by executing the `presort` function on each entry. For alphabetic labels you might have to append additional letters (a, b, …) to create a unique sorting order, which requires two more sorting passes. For numeric labels, either the sorted or the original order can be used. In both cases, you need to keep track of the longest label for use with the `thebibliography` environment.

Finally, the `.bbl` file is written by looping over the entries and executing the `call.type$` function for each one.

13.6.3   Introducing small changes in a style file

Often it is necessary to make slight changes to an existing style file to suit the particular needs of a publisher.

As a first example, we show you how to eliminate the (sometimes unpleasant) standard BibTeX style feature that transforms titles to lowercase. In most cases, you will want the titles to remain in the same case as they are typed. A variant of the style `unsrt` can be created for this purpose. We will call it `myunsrt`, since it is different from the original style. Similar methods can be used for other styles.

Looking at Table 13.8 on the facing page, you will probably have guessed that function `change.case$` is responsible for case changes. With the help of an editor and looking for the above string, you will find that function `format.title` must be changed. Below we show that function before and after the modification:

```
FUNCTION {format.title}              FUNCTION {format.title}
{                                    {
  title empty$                         title empty$
    { "" }                               { "" }
    { title "t" change.case$ }           { title } % <== modified
  if$                                  if$
}                                    }
```

      Before Modification   *After Modification*

With the help of Table 13.8 on the preceding page, you can follow the logic of the function and the substitution performed.

Another function that must be changed in a similar way is `format.edition`. Here we can omit the inner if statement since there would be no difference in the branches.

```
FUNCTION {format.edition}          FUNCTION {format.edition}
{ edition empty$                   { edition empty$
   { "" }                             { "" }
   { output.state mid.sentence =      { edition  " edition" * }
      { edition "l" change.case$    if$
                   " edition" * }   }
      { edition "t" change.case$
                   " edition" * }
    if$
   }
 if$
}
```

Before Modification   *After Modification*

In `format.chapter.pages`, `format.thesis.type`, and `format.tr.number`, similar changes must be made.

Adding a new field

Sometimes you may want to add a new field. As an example, let's add an `annote` field. Two approaches can be taken: the one adopted in the style `annotate` or the one used in the style `annotation`. Let us look at the simpler solution first. The style `annotation`, based on `plain`, first adds the field `annote` to the ENTRY definition list; the `fin.entry` function is changed then to treat the supplementary field. As seen in the example of the function `book`, the function `fin.entry` is called at the end of each function defining an entry type.

```
FUNCTION {fin.entry}   FUNCTION {fin.entry}
{ add.period$          { add.period$
  write$                 write$
  newline$               newline$
}                        "\begin{quotation}\noindent{\sc Key:\ }" cite$ * write$
                          annote missing$
                          'skip$
                          { "\\{\sc Annotation:\ }" write$  annote  write$ }
                        if$
                        "\end{quotation}" write$  newline$
                       }
```

Before Modification   *After Modification*

After outputting the citation string inside a quotation environment, the annotation text is written following the text "Annotation", which starts a separate line. If the field is absent, nothing is written (the test, `annote missing$`, takes the `skip$` branch of the `if$` command).

The other style, `annotate`, based on `alpha`, takes a more complicated approach. After adding the element `annotate` to the ENTRY definition list, the function `format.annotate` is created to format that supplementary field. The function has a decision flow similar to the code shown above.

```
FUNCTION {format.annotate}
{ annotate empty$
    { "" }
    { " \begin{quotation}\noindent " annotate * " \end{quotation} " *  }
  if$
}
```

The formatting routine for each of the entry types of Table 13.1 on page 763 has a supplementary line `format.annotate write$` just following the call to `fin.entry`.

Foreign language support

If you want to adapt a BibTeX style to languages other than English, you will, at the very least, have to translate the hard-coded English strings in the BibTeX style files, like "edition" in the example at the beginning of this section.

First you should edit a style file and introduce the new terms in the necessary places. As you are working with only one language, it is possible to introduce the proper language-specific typographic conventions at the same time. An example of this approach is the `nederlands` style developed by Werenfried Spit. This `harvard`-based style has been adapted to Dutch following the recommendations of Van Dale (1982). We will now look at some examples of functions that were adapted by this style.

In Dutch, one does not distinguish between one or more editors. The generic Dutch word `redactie` replaces the two possibilities.

```
FUNCTION {format.editors}              FUNCTION {format.editors}
{ editor empty$                        { editor empty$
    { "" }                                 { "" }
    { editor format.names                  {  editor format.names
      editor num.names$ #1 >                  ", redactie" *
        { " (eds)" * }                     }
        { " (ed.)" * }                   if$
      if$                              }
    }
  if$
}
```
Before Modification   *After Modification*

The following examples show how, for one particular language, you can go relatively far in the customization (in form and translation) of an entry—in this case, the format of the edition field. In this example, up to the third edition, Dutch-specific strings are used. Starting with the fourth edition, the generic string i^e is used, where i is the number of the edition. You can also see the nesting of the `if$` statements and the use of the case-changing command `change.case$`.

```
FUNCTION {format.edition}              FUNCTION {format.edition}
{ edition empty$                       { edition empty$
  { "" }                                 { "" }
  { output.state mid.sentence =          { edition "1" =
    { edition "l" change.case$ " edition" * }      { "Eerste" }
    { edition "t" change.case$ " edition" * }      { edition "2" =
    if$                                      { "Tweede" }
  }                                          { edition "3" =
  if$                                          { "Derde" }
}                                              { edition "\textsuperscript{e} " * }
                                               if$
                                             }
                                             if$
                                           }
                                           if$
                                           output.state mid.sentence =
                                             { "l" change.case$ " druk" * }
                                             { "t" change.case$ " druk" * }
                                           if$
                                         }
                                         if$
                                       }
```

Before Modification   After Modification

Of course, the strings for the names of the months should be changed and some other language-specific strings can be defined.

```
MACRO {jan} {"januari"}     MACRO {feb} {"februari"}
MACRO {mar} {"maart"}         ...
```

In addition, the sorting routine for the names, sort.format.names, must know about the language-dependent rules for showing names in the right order.

Also, most languages have articles or other short words that should be ignored for sorting titles.

```
FUNCTION {sort.format.title}           FUNCTION {sort.format.title}
{ 't :=                                { 't :=
  "A " #2                                "De " #3
    "An " #3                               "Een " #4 t chop.word
      "The " #4 t chop.word            chop.word
    chop.word                          sortify
  chop.word                            #1 global.max$ substring$
  sortify                            }
  #1 global.max$ substring$
}
```

Before Modification   After Modification

Here the chop.word function chops the word specified from the string presented on the stack—in this case, the definite (De) and indefinite (Een) articles.

LaTeX Package Documentation Tools

In this chapter we describe the doc system, a method to document LaTeX macros and environments. A large proportion of the LaTeX code available is documented using its conventions and support tools. The underlying principle is that LaTeX code and comments are mixed in the same file and that the documentation or the stripped package file(s) are obtained from the latter in a standard way. In this chapter we explain the structure that these files should have, and show how, together with the program DOCSTRIP, you can build self-installing procedures for distributing your LaTeX package(s) and generating the associated documentation. This chapter will also help you understand the code written by others, install it with ease, and produce the documentation for it (not necessarily in that order).

We end the chapter with a few words about how version control works and how RCS/CVS information can be extracted with LaTeX. Applying version control methods can be useful for any larger documentation project.

14.1   doc—Documenting LaTeX and other code

The idea of integrated documentation was first employed by Donald Knuth when he developed the TeX program using the WEB system, which combines Pascal-like meta source code and documentation. Thanks to his approach, it was particularly easy to port TeX and its companion programs to practically any computer platform in the world.

Subsequently, authors of LᴬTEX packages started to realize the importance of documenting their LᴬTEX code. Many now distribute their LᴬTEX macros using the framework defined with the **doc** package (by Frank Mittelbach) and its associated DOCSTRIP utility (originally by Frank Mittelbach with later contributions by Johannes Braams, Denys Duchier, Marcin Woliński, and Mark Wooding). We should mention at this point that there exists an experimental reimplementation with new features and a cleaner and streamlined interface written by Lars Hellström. It is currently distributed as xdoc2, indicating that this is a frozen (and therefore usable) snapshot of work in progress; the final version will be called xdoc.

Both systems allow LᴬTEX code and documentation to be held in one and the same TEX source file. The obvious advantage is that a sequence of complex TEX instructions becomes easier to understand with the help of comments inside the file. In addition, updates are more straightforward because only a single source file needs to be changed.

The **doc** package provides a set of commands and establishes some conventions that allow specially prepared sources files to contain both code and its documentation intermixed with each other.

To produce the documentation you need a driver (file) that loads the **doc** package and then interprets the source file. To produce a ready-to-run version of your code you need to first process the source package with DOCSTRIP (see Section 14.2). This step is usually implicitly done by providing an `.ins` file that is run through LᴬTEX.

In its simplest form the driver for the documentation is an external file. However, these days the driver is more commonly made part of the source file, so that all you have to do to produce the documentation is to run the source file through LᴬTEX. The possibilities are discussed in detail in Section 14.1.4.

The most important important commands and concepts are discussed in the next sections. Table 14.1 on page 820 gives an overview of all **doc** user commands. Further details on any of them can be found in the documented source `doc.dtx` of the **doc** package, which can also serve as a prime (though somewhat aged) example of the **doc** system. You may additionally want to refer to the tutorial "How to Package Your LᴬTEX Package" by Scott Pakin, which describes various aspects of the **doc** package and DOCSTRIP. It is available on CTAN at `http://www.ctan.org/tex-archive/info/dtxtut`.

14.1.1 General conventions for the source file

A LᴬTEX file to be used with the **doc** system consists of *documentation parts* intermixed with *code parts*. Every line of a documentation part starts with a percent sign (%) in the first column. It can contain arbitrary TEX or LᴬTEX commands, but the % character cannot be used as a comment character. User comments are created by using the `^^A` character instead. Longer text blocks can be turned into comments by surrounding them with `%␣\iffalse ... % \fi`. All other parts of the file are called code parts. They contain the code described in the documentation parts.

Depending on how the code parts are structured it is possible to use such a file directly with LATEX, although these days this is seldom done. Instead, DOCSTRIP is typically used to produce the production files. If the former approach is taken LATEX bypasses the documentation parts at high speed and pastes the macro definitions together, even if they are split into several code parts.

On the other hand, if you want to produce the documentation of the macros, then the code parts should be typeset verbatim. This is achieved by surrounding these parts by the `macrocode` environment.

```
%␣␣␣␣\begin{macrocode}
   ⟨code lines⟩
%␣␣␣␣\end{macrocode}
```

It is mandatory that you put *exactly* four spaces between the % character and `\end{macrocode}`. The reason being that when LATEX is processing the `macrocode` environment, it is actually looking for that particular string and not for the command `\end` with the argument `macrocode`.

Inside a code part all TEX commands are allowed. Even the percent sign can be used to suppress unwanted spaces at the ends of lines.

If you prefer, instead of the `macrocode` environment, you can use the `macrocode*` environment. It produces the same results except that spaces are displayed as ␣ characters when the documentation is printed.

14.1.2   Describing new macros and environments

Most packages contain commands and environments to be employed by users in their documents. To provide a short manual describing their features, a number of constructs are offered by the **doc** package.

```
\DescribeMacro{macro name}      \DescribeEnv{environment name}
```

The `\DescribeMacro` command takes one argument, which will be shown in the margin and produces a special index entry, for example,

```
% \DescribeMacro{\DocInput} \DescribeMacro{\IndexInput}
% Finally the \meta{input commands} part ...
```

A similar macro, `\DescribeEnv`, can be used to indicate that at this point a LATEX environment is being explained.

```
\begin{macro}{name}      \begin{environment}{name}
```

To describe the definition of a new macro, you use the `macro` environment. It takes one argument: the name of the new macro. This argument is also used to print the name in the margin and to produce an index entry. Actually, the index entries for usage and for definition are different, which allows for easy reference. Here is an example taken from the sources of the **doc** package itself:

```
% \begin{macro}{\MacroTopsep}
%    Here is the default value for the \verb+\MacroTopsep+
%    parameter used above.
%    \begin{macrocode}
\newlength\MacroTopsep
\setlength\MacroTopsep{7pt plus 2pt minus 2pt}
%    \end{macrocode}
% \end{macro}
```

Another environment, with the unimaginative name `environment`, documents the code of environments. It works like the `macro` environment but expects the name of an environment as its argument.

`\MakeShortVerb{\`*c*`}`   `\MakeShortVerb*{\`*c*`}`   `\DeleteShortVerb{\`*c*`}`

When you have to quote a lot of material verbatim, such as command names, it is awkward to always have to type `\verb+...+`. Therefore, the **doc** package provides an abbreviation mechanism that allows you to pick a character *c*, which you plan to use only very rarely inside your document, to delimit your verbatim text (the character " is often chosen, but if that character is already used for another purpose, such as for generating umlauts, then you may prefer "|"). Then, after including the command `\MakeShortVerb{\`*c*`}`, the sequence *c*text*c* becomes the equivalent of `\verb`*c*text*c*.

The variant form `\MakeShortVerb*` does the same but uses `\verb*`. If you later want to use *c* with its original meaning, just type `\DeleteShortVerb {\`*c*`}`. You can repeat this sequence using *c* as a shorthand for `\verb` and reverting to its original meaning as many times as needed.[1] Note that the abbreviated *c*-form, like `\verb` itself, cannot appear in the argument of another command, but it may be used freely inside `verbatim` and `macrocode` environments.

You can divide your documented package file into two parts, the first typically containing a general description and the second giving a detailed description of the implementation of the macros. When generating the document the user will be able to suppress this latter part if you place the command `\StopEventually` at the division point between the two parts.

`\StopEventually{`*final text*`}`   `\Finale`

The `\StopEventually` macro takes one argument in which you put all the information that you want to see printed if the user decides to stop typesetting the document at that point (for example, a bibliography, which is usually printed at

---

[1] This feature has also been made available as a stand-alone package, **shortvrb**; it was discussed in Section 3.4. See Example 3-4-2 on page 152.

the end of the document). When the driver file contains an `\OnlyDescription`
declaration, LaTeX will process the argument of `\StopEventually` and then stop
reading the file.[1] Otherwise, the `\StopEventually` macro saves its argument in a
macro called `\Finale`, which can later be used to get things back (usually at the
very end). This scheme makes changes in two places unnecessary.[2]

To document the change history, the `\changes` command can be placed
within the description part of the changed code.

```
\changes{version}{date}{text}
```

The information in the `\changes` command may be used to produce an auxiliary file (LaTeX's `\glossary` mechanism is used for this purpose), which can be
printed after suitable formatting. To cause the change information to be written,
include `\RecordChanges` in the driver file. To read and print the sorted change
history, put the `\PrintChanges` command at a suitable point, typically after the
`\PrintIndex` command in the driver.

To generate the sorted file containing the changes, you should run the raw
glossary file through *MakeIndex* using an adequate style (like `gglo.ist`, supplied
with the doc distribution; see Section 11.1.6 on page 653 for more information
about how *MakeIndex* treats glossaries).

14.1.3 Cross-referencing all macros used

Inside a `macrocode` or `macrocode*` environment, index entries are produced for
every command name. In this way you can easily find out where a specific macro
is used. Since TeX works considerably more slowly when it has to produce such an
array of index entries you can turn off this feature by using `\DisableCrossrefs`
in the driver file. To turn it on again, use `\EnableCrossrefs`.

Finer control is provided with the `\DoNotIndex` command, which takes one
argument containing a comma-separated list of commands that are *not* to be entered in the index. More than one `\DoNotIndex` command can be present, and
their contents will be combined. A frequent use of this macro is to exclude native
LaTeX commands from the index.

Production (or not) of index entries is controlled by using or omitting the
following declarations in the driver file preamble (if no declaration is provided, no
index is produced). Using `\PageIndex` makes all index entries refer to their page
number. With `\CodelineIndex`, index entries produced by `\DescribeMacro` and
`\DescribeEnv` refer to the relevant page numbers, but those produced by the
`macro` and `macrocode` environments refer to the code lines, which are numbered
automatically.

---

[1] The slightly strange command name is due to a misunderstanding by the package author: the
German word for "perhaps" is "eventuell" and when he found out it had been in use for years.

[2] The default is to typeset the whole document. This default can also be explicitly set by using the
`\AlsoImplementation` macro.

If index entries are produced they have to be sorted by an external program, such as *MakeIndex* (see Chapter 11). The doc package uses special conventions for the index entries, so you need to run *MakeIndex* with the -s switch (see Section 11.2.4 on page 659) to specify a suitable style—for example, gind.ist, which is distributed with the doc system.

To read and print the sorted index, you must put the \PrintIndex command near the end of your driver file, possibly preceded by bibliography commands, as needed for your citations.

14.1.4   The documentation driver

To get the documentation for a set of macros with the doc system, you have to prepare a driver (file) with the following characteristics:

```
\documentclass[⟨options⟩]{⟨document-class⟩}
\usepackage{doc}
⟨preamble⟩
\begin{document}
    ⟨input-commands⟩
\end{document}
```

The ⟨*document-class*⟩ may be any legal class, such as article or ltxdoc (described in Section 14.3); in the latter case the doc package is already loaded by the class. In the ⟨*preamble*⟩, you should place declarations that manipulate the behavior of the doc system, such as \DisableCrossrefs, \OnlyDescription, and \CodelineIndex.

| \DocInput{*file name*}   \IndexInput{*file name*} |

Finally, the ⟨*input-commands*⟩ part should contain one or more \DocInput and/or \IndexInput commands. The \DocInput command is used for files prepared for the doc system, whereas \IndexInput can be used for macro files that do not obey the conventions of the doc system. The latter command takes a file name as its argument and produces a verbatim listing of the file, indexing every command as it goes along. This functionality can be handy if you want to learn something about macros without enough documentation.

It is also possible to use the \PrintIndex and \PrintChanges (if the changes are recorded by \RecordChanges) commands. Some people put them directly into the source file, but it is better practice to place them into the driver. You can then combine several packages in one document and produce a combined index.

As mentioned in the introduction, most often the driver is included directly in the source file instead of being a separate file of its own. How this works is explained in the next section.

14.1.5   Conditional code in the source

The features discussed so far can be used to produce a LaTeX source in literate programming style that can be directly used by loading it as a package (where TeX bypasses the comments) or printed by processing it with a driver file as explained in the previous section. But this requires the structure of such a file to be linear; in other words, TeX will see *all* code exactly in the order in which it is present in the file.

Experiences with the doc system soon suggested that it would be a valuable extension to be able to conditionally produce the ready-to-run files—by building them from several source files or extracting them from parts of one or more source files, for example. For this reason the doc system was extended in two directions:

- A syntax was developed to label parts of the code so that the components could be referred to separately.

- The DOCSTRIP program (see Section 14.2), which was originally used only to strip the comments from doc files, was extended to offer a scripting language in which it became possible to specify how a ready-to-run file is generated from labeled code parts of one or more source files.

Of course, a source containing such conditional code can usually no longer be used directly and requires the DOCSTRIP program before it can be turned into a ready-to-run file. However, the additional possibilities offered by this approach outweigh the inconvenience of an extra production step during installation so much that these days nearly all usages of doc take advantage of it.

Code fragments for conditional inclusion are marked in the source file with "tags". The simplest format is a <*name> and </name> pair surrounding some part of the code. This enables us to include or exclude that part by referring to its *name* in a DOCSTRIP script. The tags must be placed at the beginning of the line preceded by a %. For example:

```
%<*style>
     some lines of code
%</style>
```

It is possible to attach more than one tag to a part by combining several *names* with the Boolean operators | for logical or, & for logical and, and ! for negation (using lazy evaluation from the left). For example,

```
%<*Aname|Bname&!Cname>
     some lines of code
%</Aname|Bname&!Cname>
```

means that this block should be included when either Aname is asked for, or Bname is requested but Cname is not.

There are two other forms of directives for including or excluding single lines of code. A line starting with %<+*name*> will be included (without its tag) if *name* is requested. A line starting with %<-*name*> will be included if *name* is *not* requested in a DOCSTRIP run.

The above directives can be nested in each other. If this is done the inner tags are evaluated only if the outer tags are true (i.e., if the whole block is requested for inclusion).

```
%<*Aname>
            code line 1
%<+Bname> code line 2
%<-Bname> code line 3
            code line 4
%</Aname>
```

Here nothing is included if Aname is not requested. If it is requested, we get code lines 1, 2, and 3 if Bname is also asked for, and lines 1, 2, and 4 otherwise.

You may have wondered how the conditional coding allows us to include the driver in the main source file. For this you have to place the code for the driver as the first code block and surround it by some tag (e.g., driver). If the user now runs the source file through LʌTEX, the driver code is the first code that is not behind % signs so it will be executed. Since it ends in \end{document}, the LʌTEX run will not execute any later code in the file. Thus, the documentation is typeset assuming that the driver loads the whole file using \DocInput. To generate the actual package file(s), you use a DOCSTRIP script (see Section 14.2 on page 824) that ignores the driver code by not requesting code from a block tagged driver.

Table 14.1: Overview of **doc** package commands

Preamble and input commands
\AlsoImplementation
Typeset complete file marked up according to **doc** conventions, including code part (default).
\CharacterTable{*character table*}
User interface to character table checking.
\CheckSum{*checksum*}
User interface to set the checksum of the document (number of backslashes in the code).
\CheckModules
Format module directives of DOCSTRIP specially (default).
\CodelineIndex
Index commands using code line numbers.
\CodelineNumbered
Number code lines but don't index commands.
continued on next page

continued from previous page

`\DisableCrossrefs`

    Don't produce index entries for commands within the code.

`\DocInput{`*file*`}`

    Read in *file* assuming doc conventions.

`\DontCheckModules`

    Don't format module directives of DOCSTRIP specially.

`\EnableCrossrefs`

    Produce index entries for commands within the code.

`\IndexInput{`*file*`}`

    Read in *file*, print it verbatim, and produce a command cross-reference index.

`\OnlyDescription`

    Don't format code; stop at `\StopEventually`.

`\PageIndex`

    Index commands using page numbers.

`\PrintChanges`

    Print the history listing here.

`\PrintIndex`

    Print the index listing here.

`\RecordChanges`

    Produce a history listing.

Document structure commands

`\bslash`

    Print a backslash (\). Only useful in typewriter fonts!

`\DeleteShortVerb{\`*char*`}`

    Undo the previous definition of `\MakeshortVerb` or `\MakeshortVerb*` for *char*.

`\DescribeEnv{`*env*`}`

    Flags point in text where environment *env* is described.

`\DescribeMacro{`*cmd*`}`

    Flags point in text where macro *cmd* is described.

`\begin{environment}{`*env*`}`

    Environment surrounding description of environment *env*.

`\Finale`

    Command executed at very end of document (see also `\StopEventually`).

`\begin{macro}{`*cmd*`}`

    Environment surrounding description of macro *cmd*.

`\begin{macrocode}`

    Environment surrounding the TeX code.

`\begin{macrocode*}`

    Same as the `macrocode` environment, but spaces are printed as ␣ characters.

`\MakeShortVerb{\`*char*`}`

    Define abbreviation character *char* for `\verb`.

continued on next page

continued from previous page

`\MakeShortVerb*{\char}`

> Define abbreviation character *char* for `\verb*`.

`\meta{arg}`

> Print its argument as a meta sentence (default ⟨*arg*⟩).

`\SpecialEscapechar{char}`

> Specify new single escape character to be used instead of \.

`\StopEventually{cmds}`

> In the argument *cmds*, specify which commands should be executed at the end of the document (they are stored in `\Finale`).

`\begin{verbatim}`

> Slightly altered version of LATEX's standard `verbatim` environment to surround verbatim text ignoring percent characters in column 1.

`\begin{verbatim*}`

> Same as the `verbatim` environment, but spaces are printed as ␣ characters.

Index commands

`\*`

> Symbol used in index entries to refer to a higher-level entry (default ~).

`\actualchar`

> Character used to separate "key" and actual index in an index entry (default =).

`\DoNotIndex{cmd_1,...,cmd_n}`

> Names of commands that should not show up in the index.

`\encapchar`

> Character used to separate the actual index and the command to format the page number in an index entry (default |).

`\IndexMin`

> Length parameter (default 80pt) defining the minimal amount of space that should be left on a page to start an index.

`\IndexParms`

> Macro controlling the formatting of the index columns.

`\IndexPrologue{text}`

> Overwrite default text to be placed on top of index.

`\levelchar`

> Character used to separate different index levels in an index entry (default >).

`\main{number}`

> Define the formatting style for page numbers or code line numbers of index entries for major references (default underlined digits).

`\quotechar`

> Character used to suppress the special meaning of the following character in an index entry (default *).

`\SortIndex{key}{entry}`

> Produce an index entry for *entry*, sorting it by *key*.

continued on next page

continued from previous page
\SpecialEnvIndex{*entry*}
Produce an index entry for usage of environment *entry*.
\SpecialIndex{*cmd*}
Produce a command index (printing the argument verbatim in the index).
\SpecialMainEnvIndex{*env*}
Produce a main index entry for an environment (\main page encapsulator).
\SpecialMainIndex{*cmd*}
Produce a main index entry for a macro (\main page encapsulator).
\SpecialUsageIndex{*cmd*}
Produce an index entry for a macro (\usage page encapsulator).
\usage{*number*}
Define the formatting style for page numbers of index entries for usage descriptions (default italic digits).
\verbatimchar
Character used to delimit \verb constructs within an index entry (default +).
History information
\changes{*version*}{*date*}{*reason*}
Record history information for use in a history listing.
\docdate
By convention holds the date of the most recent documentation update.
\filedate
By convention holds the date of the most recent code update.
\filename
By convention holds the name of the source file.
\fileversion
By convention holds the version number of the source file.
\GlossaryMin
Length parameter (default 80pt) defining the minimal amount of space that should be left on a page to start the change history.
\GlossaryParms
Macro controlling the formatting of the change history columns.
\GlossaryPrologue{*text*}
Overwrite default text placed on top of history listing.
Layout and typesetting parameters
\@idxitem
Macro specifying how index items should be typeset (by default, they are set as a paragraph with a hanging indentation of 30pt for items requiring more than one line).
\AltMacroFont
Font used to typeset DOCSTRIP module code (default \small\ttfamily\slshape).
\DocstyleParms
Macro controlling the formatting of the TEX code.
continued on next page

continued on next page

continued from previous page

`\generalname`
    String placed before change entries on the top level.

`\MacrocodeTopsep`
    Vertical space above and below each `macrocode` environment.

`\MacroFont`
    Font used to typeset the main part of the code (default `\small\ttfamily`).

`\MacroIndent`
    Width of the indentation for every code line.

`\MacroTopsep`
    Vertical space above and below each `macro` environment.

`\MakePercentCommand`
    Activate "%" as TeX's comment initiator character.

`\MakePercentIgnore`
    Deactivate "%" as TeX's comment initiator character.

`\MakePrivateLetters`
    Macro specifying symbols to be considered as letters (default @).

`\Module`
    Macro with one argument defining the formatting of DOCSTRIP module directives.

`\PrintDescribeEnv`
    Macro with one argument defining the formatting of `\DescribeEnv`.

`\PrintDescribeMacro`
    Macro with one argument defining the formatting of `\DescribeMacro`.

`\PrintEnvName`
    Like `\PrintDescribeEnv` but for the argument of the `environment` environment.

`\PrintMacroName`
    Like `\PrintDescribeMacro` but for the argument of the `macro` environment.

`\ps@titlepage`
    Macro specifying page style for the title page of articles bundled in a journal (default `\ps@plain`).

`StandardModuleDepth`
    Counter holding the highest level of DOCSTRIP directives, which are still formatted using `\MacroFont`. Deeper-nested directives are formatted using `\AltMacroFont`.

`\theCodelineNo`
    Control the typesetting of line numbers (default script-size Arabic numerals).

14.2   docstrip.tex—**Producing ready-to-run code**

When doc was originally written in the late 1980s, the intention was to provide a "literate programming" environment [81] for LATEX, in which LATEX code and documentation were intermixed in the same source file. As it soon turned out, making TeX parse (and then ignore) all the documentation when reading a file added a heavy time penalty.[1] To avoid this problem Frank Mittelbach looked for ways to automatically strip all comments from files written for the **doc** system.

The problem with any external program developed for such a purpose is that it may or may not be available for the user's operating system and even if available may not be installed. But one program is always available on a system that can run LaTeX: the TeX program itself. To achieve widest portability, the DOCSTRIP program was therefore written in low-level TeX language. Since those early days the program has undergone many revisions that changed its purpose from being a simple stripping device to serving as a fully customizable installation tool—one that is even able to distribute files to the right directories on a target machine. Johannes Braams, Denys Duchier, Marcin Woliński, Mark Wooding, David Carlisle, and others contributed to this metamorphosis; details of the program's evolution can be found in the documented source (which uses literate programming, of course). Here are today's main applications of the DOCSTRIP program:

- Strip a literate programming source of most of its documentation (i.e., the lines that start with a single % sign in the first column).

- Build ready-to-run code files by using code from one or more source files and including parts of it according to options specified.

- Automatically install the produced files in the right directories on the target if desired, thereby enormously easing the installation of updates or additions to a LaTeX installation.

The last possibility in particular is not very widely known but deserves the attention of a wider audience as it can be set up with relatively little effort.

14.2.1   Invocation of the DOCSTRIP utility

From its first days of existence DOCSTRIP could be run interactively by processing docstrip.tex with LaTeX:

```
latex docstrip.tex
```

LaTeX then asks a few questions about how to process a given file. When the user has answered these questions, DOCSTRIP does its job and strips the comments from the source.

However, this method of processing was intended to do nothing more than stripping off comments. With today's sources, which contain conditional code and are intended to be combined to form the final "executable", it is usually no longer appropriate. Instead, the developers of packages typically provide an installation file (by convention having the extension .ins) that is used to invoke DOCSTRIP behind the scenes. In this case the user simply says

```
latex name.ins
```

---

[1] In those days producing a single page with TeX could easily take half a minute or longer.

This results in the generation of all "executables" from the source distribution and optionally installs them in the right places. All standard LaTeX distributions (e.g., `base`, `graphics`, and `tools`) are distributed in this form and so are most contributed packages that are described in this book.

In the next section we discuss how to construct your own installation scripts for DOCSTRIP. Section 14.2.3 then shows how to set up DOCSTRIP for automatically installing the generated files in the right places.

14.2.2 DOCSTRIP script commands

A DOCSTRIP installation script has the following general form:

```
\input docstrip
⟨other DOCSTRIP commands⟩
\endbatchfile
```

It starts by loading the DOCSTRIP code using the TeX primitive `\input` (without braces around the file name), which makes it possible to process such a script with TeX formats other than LaTeX. This is followed by the DOCSTRIP commands that actually do the work of building new files, communicating with the user, and carrying out other necessary tasks. At the very end the script contains `\endbatchfile`. Without that statement DOCSTRIP would display a * prompt while waiting for further input from the user.

Generating new files

The main reason for constructing a DOCSTRIP script is to describe which files should be generated, from which sources, and which optional (tagged) pieces of code should be included. This is done by using `\generate` declarations.

```
\generate{\file{result-file}{\from{source-file₁}{tag-list₁}
                            \from{source-file₂}{tag-list₂}
                                       ...
                            \from{source-fileₙ}{tag-listₙ}}}
```

Within the argument to `\generate` you specify the *result-file* you want to produce by using a `\file` declaration. The second argument to `\file` contains one or more `\from` commands listing the *source-files* that should be used to build the *result-file*. With each `\from` declaration the second argument specifies the *tag-list* to use with the particular *source-file*. Then only the code piece tagged with the appropriate tags and all the untagged source pieces from that file are included (see Section 14.1.5 on page 819).

The *source-files* are used in the order specified: first the code from *source-file₁* is included (according to the tag specification), then the code from *source-file₂*, and so on. The *tag-lists* in each \from command are comma-separated lists and indicate that code with these tags should be included.

With the syntax specification for \generate as given above, you can produce one *result-file* from one or more *source-files*. By using \generate as often as needed, this is general enough to produce any kind of distribution. It is, however, not very efficient. Suppose you have one large source file from which you want to produce many small files—for example, suppose the source for the doc package, doc.dtx, is used to generate doc.sty, shortvrb.sty, gind.ist, and gglo.ist. The file is nearly 5000 lines long, so by using four \generate declarations, DOC STRIP would have to process 20000 lines. To speed up this process, \generate allows you to specify several \file commands within its argument. These files are processed in parallel, meaning that the source files are opened only once and distribution of source code to *result-files* is done in parallel.

```
\generate{\file{doc.sty}{\from{doc.dtx}{package}}
          \file{shortvrb.sty}{\from{doc.dtx}{shortvrb}}
          \usepostamble\istpost
          \file{gind.ist}{\from{doc.dtx}{gind}}
          \file{gglo.ist}{\from{doc.dtx}{gglo}}
         }
```

As you can see, certain other commands (\usepostamble, for example) are allowed within the argument of the \generate command. In the above example this has the effect of replacing the standard postamble with a different one (since the standard postamble will add an \endinput to the end of the generated file, something not desirable in a style file for *MakeIndex*).

There are some restrictions with this approach. For instance, DOCSTRIP will complain if the order of source files in one \file command conflicts with the order in a different one; the precise rules are discussed in the DOCSTRIP documentation [125]. If that happens, the simplest solution is to use two separate \generate declarations.

Restrictions on parallel extraction

Communicating with the user

The DOCSTRIP scripting language offers some limited possibilities for communication with the user. Keep in mind that interactive questions, though sometimes useful, can make an installation process quite cumbersome, so these tools should be used with care.

\Msg{*message*}   \Ask{*cmd*}{*question*}

The \Msg command can be used to present a *message* on the terminal; thus, it offers a similar functionality as LaTeX's \typeout command. \Ask is similar to LaTeX's \typein command, with the difference that no trailing space is generated from pressing return in reply to a *question*. This way simple questions can be asked (using a bit of low-level programming). For example:

```
\Ask\answer{Should we continue? (y/n)}
\ifx\answer\y
  % code for ''y'' as answer
\else
  % otherwise
\fi
```

`\ifToplevel{code}`

You may want to give certain information, or run certain code, only if a DOCSTRIP script is executed on its own, but not if it is called as part of a larger installation (see below). Such information or code can be placed in the argument of an `\ifToplevel` command. For example, all the individual installation scripts from the L*A*T*E*X base distribution say what to do with the generated files. But if you use the master installation script `unpack.ins`, the messages in the sub-scripts are suppressed to avoid repeating the same information over and over again.

`\askforoverwritetrue`   `\askforoverwritefalse`

Before DOCSTRIP writes its output to a file, it checks whether that operation will overwrite some existing version of this file. If so, case the default behavior is to ask the user if overwriting is acceptable. This check can explicitly be turned off (or on if it was turned off) by using the command `\askforoverwritefalse` or `\askforoverwritetrue`, respectively, in the DOCSTRIP script.

`\askonceonly`

Setting `\askforoverwritefalse` in a distribution script may not be the right thing to do, as it essentially means that it is okay to overwrite other people's files, no matter what. However, for large installations, such as the base L*A*T*E*X distribution, being asked individually about hundreds of files is not very helpful either. For this reason DOCSTRIP offers the declaration `\askonceonly`. This means that after the first time the script asks the user a question, the user is given an option to have DOCSTRIP assume that all future questions will get a "yes" as the answer. This applies to *all* future questions (manually produced by `\Ask` or generated through a file overwrite).

`\showprogress`   `\keepsilent`

For amusement and because in the original implementation everything was so slow, there was a way to direct DOCSTRIP to show its progress when stripping comments and building new files. These days most scripts run in silent mode.

Master installation scripts

In large distributions, such as the LaTeX base distribution, it is convenient to provide individual DOCSTRIP scripts for processing individual parts. For example, `format.ins` generates the main format file `latex.ltx` and its customization files such as `fonttext.cfg`, and `classes.ins` generates the standard classes, such as the files `article.cls` and `report.cls`.

Nevertheless, you do not want to force the user to process a dozen or more installation scripts (30 in case of the LaTeX base distribution). Therefore, DOCSTRIP offers the command `\batchinput`, which enables you to include installation scripts in some master installation script. Do not use `\input` for this purpose, because this command is exclusively reserved for loading the DOCSTRIP code once, as explained above, and is ignored otherwise. Except for the fact that it contains some special handcrafted code at the beginning so that it can be processed using `initex`, the file `unpack.ins` from the base LaTeX distribution is a good example for such a master installation script.

Setting up preambles and postambles

As mentioned earlier DOCSTRIP not only writes selected lines of code to the output files, but also precedes them with a *preamble* and finishes each file with a *postamble*. There are default texts for both operations, but usually a DOCSTRIP script explicitly defines what should be used in these places, such as a copyright notice or your standard disclaimer (see also [108]).

```
\preamble  ⟨text lines⟩ \endpreamble
\postamble ⟨text lines⟩ \endpostamble
```

The information you want to add to the start of DOCSTRIP's output file should be listed between the `\preamble` and `\endpreamble` commands. Lines that you want to add at the end should be listed between the `\postamble` and `\endpostamble` commands. Everything that DOCSTRIP finds for both the preamble and postamble is written to the output file, but preceded with two % characters (or, more exactly, with the current definition of the command `\MetaPrefix`). In general, only straight text should be used, and literal command names should be of the form `\string\foo`. In addition to the user preamble, DOCSTRIP also includes some information about the current file (i.e., its name and the sources from which it was generated). This information is always added unless you use `\nopreamble` (see below) or you sidestep the standard preamble generation (explained in DOCSTRIP package documentation [125]).

It is also possible to define a number of "named" preambles or postambles and later refer to them when generating files. In fact, this is the usual way to produce the preambles in larger projects.

```
\declarepreamble\cmd ⟨text⟩ \endpreamble          \usepreamble\cmd
\declarepostamble\cmd ⟨text⟩ \endpostamble        \usepostamble\cmd
```

The \declarepreamble declaration works like \preamble except that it stores the preamble text for later use in \cmd. To activate such a preamble, \usepreamble is called in a DOCSTRIP script. For postambles, the declarations \declarepostamble and \usepostamble are provided. Examples of them can be found in all DOCSTRIP installation scripts in the distributions of the standard LATEX components.

```
\nopreamble     \nopostamble
```

To fully suppress the writing of a preamble or a postamble, you can use the declarations \nopreamble and \nopostamble, respectively.

14.2.3 Installation support and configuration

A number of years ago the TEX users community decided on a standard directory structure for TEX installations (TDS), designed to be usable on all platforms for which TEX and LATEX are available [164]. Since then this standard has further evolved to the point that it is now in use on most major TEX distributions.

To make it easier to integrate new packages into a TDS-conforming installation or to install package upgrades, the DOCSTRIP program was extended so that under certain circumstances it can be directed to automatically install the generated files in the right places in this structure. For this operation to work, the DOCSTRIP scripts must contain certain directives. In addition, the user has configured the DOCSTRIP program by providing a docstrip.cfg file suitable for the installation on the current machine.

```
\usedir{relative-directory-path}
```

For the developer of a DOCSTRIP script there is minimal extra work involved: for each generated file its position in the TDS directory tree needs to be known, but this is usually clear for all such files. This place is then specified with \usedir as a directory path relative to the TDS root directory in the DOCSTRIP just before calling the \generate command or within the argument to \generate before the next \file declaration. For most packages, one such \usedir declaration is sufficient. For example, the file format.ins in the standard LATEX distribution states

```
\usedir{tex/latex/base}
\generate{\file{latex.ltx}{\from{ltdirchk.dtx}{initex,2ekernel,dircheck}
                 \from{ltplain.dtx}{2ekernel}
                 ...}
     \file{tracefnt.sty}{\from{ltfsstrc.dtx}{package,trace}}
     \file{flafter.sty}{\from{ltoutput.dtx}{flafter}}
     ...}
```

to place the LaTeX format file (and others) in the correct directory. In more complex bundles, files may need to be distributed to different directories depending on their type. For example, the installation script for the jurabib package states

```
\generate{
   \usedir{tex/latex/jurabib}
     \file{jurabib.sty}{\from{jurabib.dtx}{package}}
     \file{dejbbib.ldf}{\from{jurabib.dtx}{german}}
     ...
   \usedir{tex/bibtex/bst/jurabib}
     \file{jurabib.bst}{\from{jurabib.dtx}{jurabst}}
     ...
   \usedir{tex/doc/latex/jurabib}
     \file{jbtest.tex}{\from{jurabib.dtx}{test}}
     ...
   }
```

to generate the files needed by LaTeX in `tex/latex/jurabib`, the BibTeX styles in `tex/bibtex/bst/jurabib`, test documents in `tex/doc/latex/jurabib`, and so on. By itself, the \usedir declaration has no effect: DOCSTRIP still generates files only in the current directory.

   To allow DOCSTRIP to make use of such \usedir declarations, you have to provide it with a configuration file (`docstrip.cfg`) that contains a declaration for the root directory of your installation and a set of translations to local directories for the paths used in the argument to \usedir.

\BaseDirectory{*directory*}
\DeclareDirectory{*usedir-path*}{*local-translation*}

The \BaseDirectory declaration specifies the absolute path to the root directory of your TeX installation; other paths are then given relative to this starting directory. In addition, you have to provide for each *relative-directory-path* used in the argument of \usedir a translation to a local directory. For example, to teach DOC-STRIP the directory structure used by the emTeX distribution, you might have a set of declarations like this:

```
\BaseDirectory{c:/emtex}
\DeclareDirectory{tex/latex/base}{texinputs/latex}
\DeclareDirectory{tex/latex/jurabib}{texinputs/latex}
```

Once DOCSTRIP knows about a \BaseDirectory, it will attempt to interpret all \usedir declarations in its scripts. If it finds one for which it doesn't know a translation to a local directory (through \DeclareDirectory), it will complain and generate the file in the current directory instead. You should then add an appropriate declaration to the `.cfg` file.

Sometimes it is necessary to put some files outside of the base directory, such as when your BibTEX program is on a different disc. In that case use the starred form of \DeclareDirectory, which expects an absolute path name in the second argument. For example:

```
\DeclareDirectory{tex/bibtex/bst/jurabib}{d:/bibtex/bst}
```

Installation
directories
must exist
Since TEX is unable to create new directories, it is a prerequisite that all local directories specified with \DeclareDirectory actually exist. If one of them is not available when you run a DOCSTRIP script, you will receive a TEX error message stating that it cannot write to some file, and asking you to specify a different one.

On a fully TDS-conforming installation, all translations to local directory names are trivial. For example,

```
\BaseDirectory{/usr/local/lib/texmf-local}
\DeclareDirectory{tex/latex/base}{text/latex/base}
\DeclareDirectory{tex/latex/jurabib}{tex/latex/jurabib}
\DeclareDirectory{tex/bibtex/bst/jurabib}{tex/bibtex/bst/jurabib}
```

directs DOCSTRIP to install into a local TDS tree (i.e., texmf-local) and not into the main installation tree. You have then to make sure that your local tree is searched first.

\UseTDS

To ease the configuration work necessary to describe a TDS-conforming installation, DOCSTRIP offers the declaration \UseTDS. It directs the program to use the \usedir specifications literally if no explicit \DeclareDirectory declaration is specified. Thus, on most installations, a single \UseTDS in the .cfg file is all that is needed.

Security
considerations
By default, DOCSTRIP will generate files only in the current working directory. Even with a configuration file containing a \BaseDirectory declaration, it will always write to directories explicitly specified with \DeclareDirectory or, if you use \UseTDS, to the appropriate TDS directories below your base directory. It will not overwrite files in other places, though (in these days of *viruses* and other nasty creatures) you should be aware that TEX, as such, is capable of doing so and therefore might pose some security threat. In fact, some implementations (for example, those on the TEXlive CD) will not let TEX write to files specified with absolute path names or to files starting with a period in their name, unless explicitly authorized. For example, on the author's system one has to specify

```
openout_any=r latex jurabib.ins
```

to take advantage of the automatic installation features of DOCSTRIP.

\maxfiles{*number*}   \maxoutfiles{*number*}

There are two other declarations that you may wish to add to a DOCSTRIP configuration file. On some operating systems there is a limit on the number of files that can be opened by a program. If that is the case you can limit the total number of open files with a \maxfiles declaration and the total number of concurrently opened output files with \maxoutfiles (TeX itself has a limit of 16). Use these declarations only when necessary.

14.2.4   Using DOCSTRIP with other languages

With some restrictions it is possible to use the DOCSTRIP mechanism to distribute and generate files not intended for a TeX installation. What you have to bear in mind is that DOCSTRIP operates on a line-by-line basis when reading source files. As a result, doing something like unpacking binary files with it is bound to produce unusable files.

Furthermore, the use of preambles and postambles is likely to conflict with the syntax requirements of the language for which the file is intended. For example, generating a shell script with a number of lines starting with %% is probably not a good idea. This problem can be circumvented by changing the \MetaPrefix (which by default produces \DoubleperCent). For a shell script, where you probably want a # sign as the comment character, this modification can be a little tricky as TeX regards the # as special. Try

Changing the comment character

```
\renewcommand\MetaPrefix{\string##}
```

to produce a single hash sign as a \MetaPrefix. To return to the default setting, use the following definition:

```
\renewcommand\MetaPrefix{\DoubleperCent}
```

Another potential problem to watch out for is DOCSTRIP's standard behavior of stripping away all lines starting with a single percent sign. If your code contains such lines you may want to retain them. This can be achieved by surrounding that block with two special lines as follows:

Verbatim copying

```
%<<tag-name
    ⟨code lines to be copied verbatim⟩
%tag-name
```

You can use any *tag-name*. The important point is that this "verbatim" block ends when DOCSTRIP encounters a single line just containing a percent sign followed by *tag-name*. The other important point to note is that the *tag-name* is not used for conditional exclusion or inclusion but only for specifying the block to be copied verbatim. If such a block should be written only in some circumstances, as controlled through the second argument of \from, you have to additionally surround it by a set of conditional tags (see Section 14.1.5).

14.3 ltxdoc—A simple LᴬTEX documentation class

The ltxdoc class was designed for documenting the core LᴬTEX source files, which are used to build the LᴬTEX format and all packages distributed as part of the core distribution. This class is built on the article class, but extends it slightly with a few commands helpful for documenting LᴬTEX code. It also includes some layout settings specially tailored to accommodate the typical requirements of a source file in doc style (e.g., a line width to hold 72 characters in typewriter fonts and a wider left margin to allow for long macro names to be placed into it).

A special feature is that the class can be used to produce a single document from a larger number of source files in doc style. This has the advantage that one can produce a full index of macro usage across all source files. For example, the driver file source2e.tex generates the documented source listing of the 40 files that make up the LᴬTEX kernel. It generates a document with nearly 600 pages including an index and a change history (reaching back to the early 1990s).

14.3.1 Extensions provided by ltxdoc

As extensions, the class offers a small set of commands to describe LᴬTEX commands and their arguments. These command really should have been in the doc package, but due to some historical accident have never been added there.

\cmd{\name} \cs{name}   \marg{arg} \oarg{arg} \parg{arg}

The command \cmd prints a command *name* in typewriter font; for example, writing \cmd{\foo} typesets \foo. In contrast to \verb+\foo+ (which is otherwise similar), it can be used anywhere—even in the arguments of other commands. The command \cs offers the same functionality for those who prefer the syntax without the backslash. In fact, it is slightly more powerful because it can also typeset commands that are made \outer—a plain TEX concept normally not used in LᴬTEX. Furthermore, ltxdoc makes "|" an abbreviation for \verb so that you can type |\foo| in the documentation. If this is not desired for some reason, you have to cancel it in the source (after \begin{document}) via \DeleteShortVerb{\|}.

The commands \marg, \oarg, and \parg produce the LᴬTEX syntax for mandatory, optional, and picture arguments, respectively. Thus, writing

    \cs{makebox}\parg{x-dimen,y-dimen}\oarg{pos}\marg{text}

produces the (probably less-known) syntax diagram for `\makebox` in `picture` environments: `\makebox(`⟨*x-dimen,y-dimen*⟩`)[`⟨*pos*⟩`]{`⟨*text*⟩`}`.

> `\DocInclude{`*file*`}`

The `\DocInclude` command is similar to `\include` except that it uses `\DocInput` on *file* (with the implicit extension `.dtx` or `.fdd`) instead of using `\input` on a *file* (with the implicit extension `.tex`). This command is used in `source2e.tex` to "include" all `.dtx` files that form the LaTeX kernel.

14.3.2   Customizing the output of documents that use ltxdoc

To customize documents using the ltxdoc class you can create a configuration file (`ltxdoc.cfg`). This configuration file will be read whenever the ltxdoc class is used, so it can be used to customize the typesetting of all the source files, without having to edit lots of small driver files, which would be the manual alternative.

If `ltxdoc.cfg` is installed in a directory always searched by LaTeX, it is applied to all documentation files using the ltxdoc class. If it is placed in the current directory, it applies only to documents processed in this directory.

The simplest form of customization is to pass one or more options to the article class upon which ltxdoc is based. For instance, if you wish all your documentation to be formatted for A4 paper, add the line

```
\PassOptionsToClass{a4paper}{article}
```

to `ltxdoc.cfg` and install it in a place searched by LaTeX.

As discussed in Section 14.1.2, the `\StopEventually` command separates the source files into a "user" documentation and a "implementation" part. To be able to produce only the user manual, the doc package provides the command `\OnlyDescription`, which suppresses the implementation part. This command may also be used in the configuration file, but as the doc package loaded after the configuration file is read, you must delay the execution of `\OnlyDescription`. The simplest way is to use `\AtBeginDocument`:

```
\AtBeginDocument{\OnlyDescription}
```

For example, the documented source of the fixltx2e package, the file `fixltx2e.dtx`, generates 30 pages of documented code listings if you run

```
latex fixltx2e.dtx
```

and no configuration file. However, most people are not interested in *how* certain macros from the LaTeX kernel are patched in this package, but rather which problems are solved when loading it. With the above configuration line the output is reduced to a 10-page user manual, listing only the problems that are solved.

When the driver `source2e.tex` for the kernel documentation is processed, an index and a change history are produced by default; however, indexes are not normally produced for individual files. If you are really interested in the source listings in detail, you will probably want to have an index as well. Again the index commands provided by the doc package may be used, and again their execution must be delayed. Thus, the addition to the configuration file could look as follows:

```
\AtBeginDocument{\AlsoImplementation  % force processing everything
                 \CodelineIndex       % select index per code line
                 \EnableCrossrefs }   % enable it
\AtEndDocument{\PrintIndex}
```

Similar lines would be necessary if you want to produce a change history listing. Recall that the doc package generates `.idx` and `.glo` files with a special syntax that require adequate style files for processing with *MakeIndex* (see Section 14.1.3 on page 817).

14.4   Making use of version control tools

When developing a program or writing a large document, such as a user manual or a book (like this one), version control—the task of keeping a software system consisting of many versions and configurations well organized—is an important issue. The *Revision Control System* (RCS) is a software tool that can assist you with that task. RCS manages revisions of text documents—in particular, source programs, documentation, and test data. It automates storage, retrieval, logging, and identification of revisions, and it provides selection mechanisms for composing configurations. In addition, it is able to insert management information in the text document, in so-called *RCS fields*.

The *Concurrent Versions System* (CVS; see `http://www.cvshome.org`), originally developed as a front end to RCS, extends the notion of revision control from a collection of files in a single directory to a hierarchical collection of directories consisting of revision-controlled files. These directories and files can be combined to form a software release. CVS provides the functions necessary to manage these software releases and to control the concurrent editing of source files among multiple software developers.

RCS and CVS offer a keyword substitution interface in which fields with a certain structure are updated with management information whenever a file is checked into the system. The most important keywords are $Author$ (account of the person doing the check-in), $Date$ (date and time of check-in in UTC), Id (combination field, with file name, revision, date, time, author, state, and optional locked by), $RCSfile$ (archive file without path name), $Revision$ (revision number assigned to the revision), and $Source$ (full path name of archive file). Initially, one simply adds one or more of these keywords (e.g., Id) to the source.

Upon first check-in, they are replaced by the structure $\langle keyword\rangle$:␣$\langle value\rangle$␣\$, as can be seen in the next example. Later check-ins then update the $\langle value\rangle$ as appropriate.

If you put LaTeX documents under source control, you will often want to have access to the data of the RCS fields within your document—perhaps to place the date of the last check-in and the revision number into the running heading. Because of the syntax using dollar signs (which indicate formulas in LaTeX), you cannot use the keywords directly in your text, but there exist packages that provide LaTeX tags to give you access to this information in a way suitable for typesetting.

14.4.1   rcs—Accessing individual keywords

The rcs package written by Joachim Schrod lets you extract RCS information from any keyword field and places the data into command names for later use.

\RCS $keyword$	\RCS $keyword:␣value␣$
\RCSdef $keyword$	\RCSdef $keyword:␣value␣$

The \RCS command parses a dollar-delimited string for a *keyword* and its corresponding *value*; it is able to recognize the two variants shown above. From the *keyword*, it constructs a command name \RCS*keyword* that can be used to later retrieve the *value*. The *keyword* can be any string containing only letters that are usable in a command name; thus, you are not limited to the RCS keyword names mentioned above (though only these keywords are automatically updated by a standard RCS/CVS system). The \RCSdef command works like \RCS but additionally prints the keyword and value on the terminal.

In the next example we retrieve four typical keys and typeset their values later in the text. As all examples in this book are automatically generated from the book sources (see page 162), the values that you see after the keywords are those corresponding to the file for this chapter.

<table>
<tr><td>

The file ch-ldoc.tex,v has the revision number 1.59. Last check-in was done by frank on March 14, 2004 at 23:11:59 UTC.

</td><td>

```
\usepackage{rcs}
\RCS $Date: 2004/03/14 23:11:59 $ \RCS $Author: frank $
\RCS $RCSfile: ch-ldoc.tex,v $    \RCS $Revision: 1.59 $
The file \RCSRCSfile{} has the revision number
\RCSRevision.  Last check-in was done by \RCSAuthor{}
on \RCSDate{} at \RCSTime\,\textsc{utc}.
```

</td></tr>
</table>

14-4-1

If you look closely at the previous example, you will notice that \RCSDate does not reproduce the value of $Date$ (which is a numeric date format and the time) but instead produces a date string that looks suspiciously like those being produced by \today. This is, in fact, what happens: the value is internally parsed and the check-out date in the format used by \today is stored in \RCSDate. In this way language-specific packages (e.g., from the babel system) may supply their own methods of presenting a date.

For keywords whose values are further manipulated, the original value is automatically made available in the command \RCSRaw*keyword* (e.g., \RCSRawDate). It is possible to provide your own manipulation routines for other keywords; how this is done is explained in the package documentation (rcs-user.tex).

For convenience, the package defines a couple of additional commands. To parse the $Date$, you can use the command \RCSdate (lowercase "d") instead of the \RCS command used above. This is equivalent to writing

```
\RCS $Date: 2004/03/14 23:11:59 $      \date{\RCSDate}
```

The last check-in date is now automatically used as the date in the document title.[1] Of course, the \RCSDate command is still available for other uses.

Another alternative to \RCS is to use the command \RCSID for parsing a keyword. Besides setting up the corresponding \RCS*keyword* command to hold the value, it typesets the keyword and value literally in the running footer. This command can be used at most once (since each invocation overwrites the footer line) and is best combined with the keyword Id or $Header$. As the rcs package more or less bypasses LATEX's page style interface, the command does not work if you use \pagestyle commands in your source that update the running footer. In that case use \RCS and manually place the relevant information in the page style using the methods and packages described in Section 4.4.

The package also contains some code to typeset RCS revision history logs that can be produced with the Log keyword. However, this is most likely of no use to the majority of our readers, as it requires a special RCS version and does not work with CVS. If you are interested consult the package documentation.

14.4.2   rcsinfo—Parsing the Id keyword

In contrast to the rcs package, which deals with any string that conforms to the RCS/CVS keyword syntax, the rcsinfo package by Jürgen Vollmer concentrates on a single keyword: Id.

```
\rcsInfo $Id$      \rcsInfo $Id:␣value␣$
```

If present, the \rcsInfo command parses the *value* and stores all information obtained in a set of commands for later retrieval. Otherwise, it places default values in the retrieval commands—in case of date information, the current date as known to LATEX and for all other data strings like --owner--.

The following example shows all commands set up by the package and their respective output. As you can see, the \rcsInfoLongDate depends on the current language. Here we get a date in Italian format.

---

[1] You often see \date{\today} in documents, but this is seldom a good idea because it produces the date of the last formatting run and not the date of the last modification.

```
                                   \usepackage[italian]{babel} \usepackage{rcsinfo}
                                   \rcsInfo $Id: ch-ldoc.tex,v 1.59 2004/03/14 23:11:59 frank Exp $
ch-ldoc.tex    1.59                \rcsInfoFile  \quad  \rcsInfoRevision                        \par
2004/03/14   23:11:59              \rcsInfoDate  \quad  \rcsInfoTime                            \par
14 marzo 2004                       \rcsInfoLongDate                                            \par
2004, 3, 14    frank               \rcsInfoYear, \rcsInfoMonth, \rcsInfoDay \quad \rcsInfoOwner\par
Exp   –not-locked–                 \rcsInfoStatus \quad \rcsInfoLocker
```

14-4-2

To influence its behavior the package offers a few options:

today/nottoday   By default, \rcsinfo changes LaTeX's internal date information
     to the check-in information obtained. The \today command will then gener-
     ate a date string based on this information. If nottoday is used, \today will
     produce a date string showing the date of the LaTeX run.

fancyhdr/nofancy   When specifying fancyhdr the rcsinfo package issues a num-
     ber of fancyhdr declarations to set up a running footer. You still have to
     provide your own running header definitions and activate everything with
     \pagestyle[fancy], so it is probably better to keep full control and do the
     full set-up yourself.

long/short   This option works only if the fancyhdr option is used. It then de-
     cides whether a long (default) or a short date string is used in the footer line.

For those who want to convert their LaTeX documents to HTML using the la-
tex2html program [56, Chapter 3], rcsinfo offers direct support in the form of a
perl file, rcsinfo.perl; this file must be placed in the appropriate directory in
the latex2html installation. Refer to the rcsinfo manual for more information.

A LaTeX Overview for Preamble, Package, and Class Writers

This appendix gives an overview of the basic programming concepts underlying the LaTeX formatter. We explain how to define new commands and environments, including those with an optional argument. We discuss how LaTeX handles counters and their representation; we also introduce horizontal and vertical space parameters and explain how they are handled. The second section reviews the important subject of (LA)TeX boxes and their use. A good understanding of this topic is very important to fully appreciate and exploit the information presented in this book. The third section is devoted to two package files, calc and ifthen, that make calculations and building control structures with LaTeX easier. They have been used in many examples of LaTeX code throughout this book. Finally, we describe in detail the LaTeX 2ε interface that allows you to define your own options for packages and class files.

A.1 Linking markup and formatting

This section reviews the syntax for defining commands and environments with LaTeX. It is important that you exclusively use the LaTeX constructs described below, rather than the lower-level TeX commands. Then, not only will you be able to take advantage of LATEX's consistency checking, but your commands will also be portable, (probably) without modification, to future versions of LATEX.

A.1.1 Command and environment names

In the current LATEX incarnation, it is possible to enter accented characters and other non-ASCII symbols directly into the source, so it would seem reasonable to expect that such characters could also be used in command and environment names (e.g., \größer). However, this is not the case—LATEX multi-character command names must be built from basic ASCII letters (i.e., a...z and A...Z) in case of command names prefixed with a backslash.[1] This means that \vspace* is actually not a command by itself; rather, it is the command \vspace followed by the modifier *. Technically, you could write \vspace␣* or even put the * on the next line of your document.[2]

Environment and counter names On the other hand, names of environments and counters are different. In this case the * is part of the name. Thus, when writing \begin{figure␣*}, the space would become part of the name. This is due to implementation details and seems to indicate that with environment names some additional ASCII characters work. For example:

```
\newenvironment{foo.bar:baz␣with␣space}{}{}
```

However, this is not true in general because, depending on additional packages being loaded, such environment names may no longer be recognized or may produce strange errors. Thus, it is best not to explore that implementation (mis)feature and instead to rely on officially supported names—those containing only lowercase and uppercase letters and the star character.

Citation and label keys Strictly speaking, \cite and \label keys have the same kind of restriction. Nevertheless, it has become common practice to use keys containing colons (e.g., sec:cmds), so that most packages provide extra support to allow for at least the colon character in such keys. Characters outside the ASCII range and characters used in LATEX's syntax (e.g., _ or #) can never be used in names, whether they are keys, counters, environments, or multi-character command names.

With single-character command names, the situation is different again: any (single) character can be used. For example, \$ is a perfectly valid LATEX command, but \foo$bar would be interpreted as the command \foo followed by the start of a math formula (signaled by $) followed by the (math) characters b, a, and r. Any following text will also be typeset in math mode.

LATEX commands (i.e., those constructs starting with a backslash) are classified into three basic categories: document-level commands, package and class writer commands, and internal "kernel" commands.

---

[1] Strictly speaking this is not true, as TEX can be configured to support other configurations. There are, however, valid reasons why this is not being done for standard LATEX. Some of these reasons are discussed in Section 7.11 describing LATEX's encoding model.

[2] It is bad style to use this in your documents but there is unfortunately no way to prevent it.

Document-level commands, such as \section, \emph, and \sum, usually have (reasonably) short names, all in lowercase.

Document-level commands

Class and package writer commands, by convention, have longer mixed-case names, such as \InputIfFileExists and \RequirePackage. Some of them can be usefully applied in the document source, but many will stop working after \begin{document} has been processed.

Class and package writer commands

Most of the internal commands used in the LaTeX implementation, such as \@tempcnta, \@ifnextchar, and \z@ contain @ their name. This effectively prevents these names from being used in documents for user-defined commands. However, it also means that they cannot appear in a document, even in the preamble, without taking special precautions.

Internal LaTeX commands

As a few of the examples in this book demonstrate, it is sometimes necessary to have such bits of "internal code" in the preamble. The commands \makeatletter and \makeatother make this easy to do: the difficult bit is to remember to add them, failure to do so can result in some strange errors. For an example of their use, see page 852. Note that package and class files should never contain these commands: \makeatletter is not needed as this is always set up when reading such files; and the use of \makeatother would prematurely stop this behavior, causing all kinds of havoc.

Careful with internal commands!

Unfortunately, for historical reasons the distinction between these categories is often blurred. For example, \hbox is an internal command that should preferably be used only in the LaTeX kernel, whereas \m@ne is the constant −1 and could have been \MinusOne.

Nevertheless, this rule of thumb is still useful: if a command has @ in its name, then it is not part of the supported LaTeX language—and its behavior may change in future releases! Any such command should be used with great care. On the other hand, mixed-case commands or those described in the *LaTeX Manual* [104] are guaranteed to be supported in future releases of LaTeX 2_ε.

A.1.2 Defining new commands

It is often advantageous to define new commands (e.g., for representing repetitive input strings or recurring combinations of commands). A new command is defined using the \newcommand command sequence, which can have one optional argument, defining the number of arguments taken by the new command.

```
\newcommand{cmd}[narg]{command definition}
```

The number of arguments is in the range $0 \le narg \le 9$. If your new command has no arguments, then the [0] can be omitted. Inside the *command definition* part, the arguments are referenced as #1 to #*narg*.

PostScript and its variant Encapsulated PostScript are often used for including graphics in LaTeX documents ...

A-1-1

```
\newcommand{\PS}{Post\-Script}
\newcommand{\EPS}{Encapsulated \PS}

\PS{} and its variant \EPS{} are often used for
including graphics in \LaTeX{} documents \ldots
```

The *cmd* argument always has to contain a single "token" (the name of the
Omitting argument command to be defined), so one can omit the braces around this argument. While
braces we do not recommend the use of this TEX syntax feature in other places, it is
commonly used with \newcommand and similar declarations. In fact, we have often
used this more concise syntax in this book:

```
\newcommand\PS {Post\-Script}
\newcommand\EPS{Encapsulated \PS}
```

Note, however, that this is only possible with arguments that are single tokens to
TEX (i.e., names starting with a backslash). Trying to do the same with, for instance,
environment or counter names will fail. For example,

```
\setcounter mycount {5}
\newenvironment myenv{...}{...}
```

is invalid LATEX syntax.

If a command should work both in math mode and in text mode, special care
should be taken in its definition. One could, for example, use \mbox but this has
a number of drawbacks.

The series of $x_1, \ldots, x_n$ or $x_1, \ldots, x_n +$
$G x_1, \ldots, x_n$

```
\newcommand\xvec{\mbox{$x_1,\ldots,x_n$}}
The series of \xvec\ or $\xvec+G_{\xvec}$
```

A-1-2

A better solution is offered by the LATEX 2_ε command \ensuremath. As the
name implies, \ensuremath ensures that its argument is always typeset in math
mode by surrounding it, if necessary, with $ signs. Thus, the above example could
be shortened to

The series of $x_1, \ldots, x_n$ or $x_1, \ldots, x_n +$
$G_{x_1, \ldots, x_n}$

```
\newcommand\xvec{\ensuremath{x_1,\ldots,x_n}}
The series of \xvec\ or $\xvec+G_{\xvec}$
```

A-1-3

This has the additional advantage of producing correctly sized symbols in subscripts or superscripts, which is not the case if an \mbox is used in the definition.

Existing commands must be *redefined* with the command \renewcommand,
which otherwise has the same syntax as \newcommand. Note that you can redefine a command with a different number of arguments than the original one has.
Therefore, you could redefine the \xvec command of the above example, so that
it now takes one argument:

The series of $x_1, \ldots, x_n$ or $x_1, \ldots, x_n +$
$G_{x_1, \ldots, x_n}$
The series of $x_1, \ldots, x_n$ or $x_1, \ldots, x_k +$
$G_{x_1, \ldots, x_k}$

```
\newcommand\xvec{\ensuremath{x_1,\ldots,x_n}}
The series of \xvec\ or $\xvec+G_{\xvec}$ \par
\renewcommand\xvec[1]{\ensuremath{x_1,\ldots,x_{#1}}}
The series of \xvec{n} or $\xvec{k}+G_{\xvec{k}}$
```

A-1-4

When redefining a command (or an environment—see below), you must, of
course, be cautious. Commands that you are planning to redefine might be used in

the class or packages you have loaded (try redefining \uppercase in a document that is formatted with the class book).

Commands with one optional argument

In LaTeX, you can also define commands so that their first argument is optional. The syntax is

> \newcommand{*cmd*}[*narg*] [*default*] {*command definition*}

An example of such a command definition is shown below:

> \newcommand\LB[1][3]{\linebreak[#1]}

The default for the optional argument is given between the second pair of square brackets—the string "3" in this case. Inside the command definition, the optional argument has the number #1, while the mandatory arguments (when present) are addressed #2 to #*narg*. Thus, typing \LB is a short way of saying \linebreak[3], while \LB[2] uses the actual specified value. That is, you will obtain the same effect as when typing \linebreak[2].

In the next example we define the command \lvec, which can be used inside or outside of formulas (due to \ensuremath). Under the assumption that the upper subscript is usually n we made it optional, while the vector variable has to be given explicitly.

For the series $x_1 + \cdots + x_n$ we have

$$x_1 + \cdots + x_n = \sum_{k=1}^{n} G_{y_1 + \cdots + y_k}$$

```
\newcommand\lvec[2][n]
  {\ensuremath{#2_1+\cdots + #2_{#1}}}
For the series \lvec{x}  we have
\[ \lvec{x} = \sum_{k=1}^{n} G_{\lvec[k]{y}} \]
```

A-1-5

In general, it is most practical to associate the case that occurs most often with the form of the command without parameters and to represent the cases that are used less often with longer command strings with an optional argument.

Argument restrictions

As explained above, user-defined commands can have one optional argument and up to nine arguments in total. If defined with \newcommand, each of the arguments can receive arbitrary text with a small number of restrictions:

- Braces must be properly balanced because otherwise LaTeX will be unable to determine where the argument ends.

- The \verb command, the verbatim environment, and related commands or environments are not supported within arguments.

- In an optional argument a closing bracket "]" is allowed only if hidden inside braces (e.g., `\item[{a}]` is allowed) without the braces the first] would be misinterpreted as the end of the optional argument.

Deliberately restricting argument contents The allowed content of arguments can be deliberately further restricted by using the `\newcommand*` variant of the declaration.

> `\newcommand*{`*cmd*`}[`*narg*`][`*default*`]{`*command definition*`}`

The starred form works like `\newcommand` but defines a *cmd* that is not, in TeX terms, long. This means that the newly defined command does not accept empty lines or `\par` commands in its argument(s). This restriction can be useful for commands whose arguments are not intended to contain whole paragraphs of text.

Relation to TeX primitives Commands that have been defined with the low-level TeX primitive `\def` do not accept `\par` in their argument. Thus, they are equivalent to being defined with `\newcommand*`. The low-level TeX equivalent to `\newcommand` is `\long\def`.

Nesting new commands in each other

Sometimes it is necessary to nest command definitions, most commonly in the combination of commands being defined as part of the definition of some new environment. If the inner command (or environment) has arguments there is a problem referring to them. Clearly we cannot use #1, #2, and so on, since this notation already denotes the argument(s) of the outer command or environment. The TeX solution is to double the hash marks; thus, ##1 would refer to the first argument of the inner definition and in case of three nested definitions we would need ####1.

To make this abstract concept a bit clearer, we define a command `\DEFlvec` that (re)defines the `\lvec` command from Example A-1-5 on the preceding page over and over again. As a first argument to `\DEFlvec` we pass the vector name that is being hard-wired into the redefinition of `\lvec`. As the second argument we pass the upper index that will become the default value for the optional argument of `\lvec`. Thus, since the vector name is now part of the definition, `\lvec` has only an optional argument.

Default: $x_1 + \cdots + x_n \neq x_1 + \cdots + x_k$
Now: $y_1 + \cdots + y_i \neq y_1 + \cdots + y_k$

```
\newcommand\lvec{}
\newcommand\DEFlvec[2]{\renewcommand\lvec[1][#2]%
            {\ensuremath{#1_1+\cdots + #1_{##1}}}}
\DEFlvec{x}{n}   % initial definition
Default: $\lvec \neq \lvec[k]$ \par
\DEFlvec{y}{i} Now: $\lvec \neq \lvec[k]$
```

A-1-6

The technique used in the above example is worth studying. Try to visualize the actual definitions being carried out, for example, when the "initial definition" is executed. Also note the need for a top-level definition for `\lvec`: the actual

definition is irrelevant but without it we would be unable to "redefine" it inside
\DEF1vec command.

Special declarations for use in packages and classes

Beside \newcommand and \renewcommand, which were originally provided as user
commands (e.g., for the document preamble), LaTeX offers some extra methods of
(re)defining commands that are intended for use in class and package files.

\providecommand*{*cmd*}[*narg*][*default*]{*command definition*}

This declaration works exactly like \newcommand and \newcommand*, except that
it is ignored if the command to be defined already exists. Such a feature is useful
in sources that may get used in several documents, such as bibliography entries.
For example, instead of using \newcommand in the @preamble of BibTeX for logos
and other constructs used in the BibTeX entries, you can use \providecommand to
avoid error messages if such commands are already defined in the document.

\DeclareRobustCommand*{*cmd*}[*narg*][*default*]{*command definition*}

This command takes the same arguments as \newcommand and \newcommand* but
declares a robust command, even if some code within the *command definition* is
fragile. You can use this command to define new robust commands, or to redefine existing commands and make them robust. Information is placed into the
transcript file if *cmd* is redefined, so it does not produce an error in this case.

\CheckCommand*{*cmd*}[*narg*][*default*]{*command definition*}

This command takes the same arguments as \newcommand and \newcommand* but,
rather than defining ⟨*cmd*⟩, checks that the current definition of ⟨*cmd*⟩ is exactly
as given by ⟨*command definition*⟩. An error is raised if the definitions differ, or if
one accepts \par in its arguments and the other does not (i.e., was defined using a
starred form). This command is useful for checking the state of the system before
a package starts altering the definitions of commands. It allows you to check, in
particular, that no other package has redefined the same command.

A.1.3   Defining new environments

You can define and redefine an environment with the \newenvironment and
\renewenvironment commands, respectively. You must specify, in each case,
which actions should take place when you enter and leave an environment. For
an environment called "myenv" this is signaled by the commands \begin{myenv}
and \end{myenv} inside your document.

```
\newenvironment{name}[narg]{begdef}{enddef}
\renewenvironment{name}[narg]{begdef}{enddef}
```

As with the \newcommand declaration, the number of arguments is in the range $0 \le narg \le 9$. In the case of no parameters, you can omit [0]. Inside the definition part, *begdef*, these parameters are referenced as #1 to #*narg*. If arguments are present, then they are defined when *entering* the environment by specifying them on the command \begin{myenv}, as shown below:

```
\begin{myenv}{arg_1}...{arg_k}
```

Arguments not available in end-tag

When *exiting* an environment with the command \end{myenv} no parameters can be specified. Moreover, the parameters specified with the \begin{myenv} command when entering the environment (see above) are no longer available in the definition part *enddef*, where you define the actions that should take place when leaving the *myenv* environment. This means that it is your responsibility to store information needed at the end of an environment (see the Citation environment defined below).

Technically, a \newenvironment declaration for the environment *myenv* defines a command *myenv* that is called during the \begin{*myenv*} processing and a command \end*myenv* that is executed (besides other things) by \end{*myenv*}. You may find that it is sometimes these commands rather than the environment tags that are used inside packages and classes to define related environments or commands. An example where this might be useful is given on page 468. In other situations, it is not advisable to follow this practice without a thorough understanding of LATEX's kernel implementation.

Our first example defines an environment of type "Abstract", which is often used to give a short summary of the contents of an article or a book. It starts by typesetting a boldfaced and centered title, followed by the text of the abstract inside a quote environment. The final \par command ensures that any following text starts a new paragraph.

Abstract

This abstract explains the approach used to solve the problems at hand.

Some text following the abstract. Some text following the abstract. And some more.

```
\newenvironment{Abstract}
  {\begin{center}\normalfont\bfseries Abstract%
   \end{center}\begin{quote}}{\end{quote}\par}
\begin{Abstract}
 This abstract explains the approach used
 to solve the problems at hand.
\end{Abstract}
Some text following the abstract. Some text
following the abstract. And some more.
```

A-1-7

Our second example is somewhat more complex. It shows you how a Citation environment can be defined for quoting citations by famous people.

The LaTeX code shown below defines the counter `Citctr`, for numbering the citations, and a box `\Citname`, for storing the name of the person whom we are citing so that we can typeset it at the end of the citation, when the `\end{Citation}` command is encountered (remember that the value of the argument specified on the `\begin{Citation}` command is no longer available at that stage). When entering the environment, we save the value of the argument, typeset in italic, in the box `\Citname` and increment our counter. We then start a `description` environment. This environment will have a single `\item` containing the counter value preceded by the word "Citation". When exiting the `Citation` environment, we twice issue a stretchable horizontal space separated by an allowed—but discouraged—line break. It is important that this space survives if a line break happens before or after it, so `\hspace*` is used. We also throw in a `\quad` of space that ensures a proper separation between the citation and the name if they appear on the same line, but will vanish if a break is taken between them. Then we typeset the contents of the box `\Citname` before leaving the `description` environment. This will put the author's name flush right and the last line of the citation flush left, regardless of whether they end up on separate lines, as you can see in the next example. Without this adjustment the text of the citation would always be fully justified, often with a lot of white space between the words. For a discussion of the counter and box commands used in this example, see Sections A.1.4 and A.2.

```
\newcounter{Citctr} \newsavebox{\Citname}
\newenvironment{Citation}[1]
   {\sbox\Citname{\emph{#1}}%
    \stepcounter{Citctr}\begin{description}
     \item[Citation \arabic{Citctr}]}
   {\hspace*{\fill}\nolinebreak[1]%
    \quad\hspace*{\fill}%
%% \finalhyphendemerits=0 %% see text below
    \usebox{\Citname}\end{description}}
```

Citation 1 Man is the measure of all things.

Protagoras

This is some regular text in between two Citation environments.

Citation 2 On mourra seul.   *Blaise Pascal*

More regular text ...

Citation 3 Necessity is the plea for every infringement of human freedom.

William Pitt

```
\begin{Citation}{Protagoras} Man is the
 measure of all things.    \end{Citation}
This is some regular text in between two
Citation environments.
\begin{Citation}{Blaise Pascal}
 On mourra seul.           \end{Citation}
More regular text \ldots
\begin{Citation}{William Pitt} Necessity
 is the plea for every infringement of
 human freedom.           \end{Citation}
```

A-1-8

Surprisingly, the name in the last citation is typeset on a line of its own, even though there is clearly enough space to place it alongside with the citation. The reason is that TeX's paragraph-breaking algorithm prefers solutions that do not have the second-to-last line ending in a hyphen and therefore selects a three-line paragraph breaking at the `\nolinebreak`.

A hyphen on the second-to-last line of a paragraph

There are two ways to correct this behavior. First, we can discourage breaking at this point by using an optional argument of [3] instead of [1], which would work in that particular example but may not work always. Second, we can tell TEX's algorithm not to take that hyphen into account by setting the low-level TEX integer parameter \finalhyphendemerits to zero. This requires a somewhat unusual syntax, as shown in the example code above (though commented out there to display the behavior without it).

As with \newcommand one can make the first argument of an environment optional:

\newenvironment{*name*}[*narg*] [*default*]{*begdef*}{*enddef*}

The *default* value for the optional argument is given between the second pair of square brackets. Inside the *begdef* part, which is executed when the environment *name* is entered, the optional argument can be accessed with #1. The mandatory arguments (when present) are addressed as #2 to #*narg*. When the *name* environment is used without an optional parameter, #1 will contain the string specified as *default*.

As an example, we reimplement the altDescription environment from Example 3-3-27 on page 149, this time with an optional argument instead of a mandatory argument specifying the width of the indentation. Another difference from the earlier definition is that the list labels will be placed flush right if possible (by placing \hfil at the left in \makelabel). When used without an optional argument the indentation will be 1em (i.e., a \quad). By specifying the widest entry as an optional argument, you make sure that the description parts of all your entries line up nicely.

The example first shows the (default) behavior of the altDescription list, then displays what it looks like when using the optional argument.

```
\usepackage{calc}
\newenvironment{altDescription}[1][\quad]%
  {\begin{list}{}{%
    \renewcommand\makelabel[1]{\hfil\textsf{##1}}%
    \settowidth\labelwidth{\makelabel{#1}}%
    \setlength\leftmargin{\labelwidth+\labelsep}}}
  {\end{list}}
```

First   This is a short term with text that wraps.

Long term   This is a long term.

Even longer term   A very long term.

```
\begin{altDescription}
\item[First] This is a short term with text that wraps.
\item[Long term] This is a long term.
\item[Even longer term] A very long term.
\end{altDescription}
\begin{altDescription}[Even longer term]
\item[First] This is a short term with text that wraps.
\item[Long term] This is a long term.
\item[Even longer term] A very long term.
\end{altDescription}
```

     First   This is a short term with text that wraps.

     Long term   This is a long term.

Even longer term   A very long term.

A-1-9

A.1.4   Defining and changing counters

Every number internally generated by LaTeX has a *counter* (register) associated with it. The name of the counter is usually identical to the name of the environment or the command that generates the number except that it does not start with \. The following is the list of all counters used in LaTeX's standard document classes:

part	paragraph	figure	enumi
chapter	subparagraph	table	enumii
section	page	footnote	enumiii
subsection	equation	mpfootnote	enumiv
subsubsection			

An environment declared by \newtheorem can also have a counter with the same name associated with it, unless the optional argument indicates that it is to be numbered together with another environment.

The value of a counter is a single integer. Several counters can be combined into a number, as is usually the case for numbering section headings. For example, in the book or report classes, 7.4.5 identifies the fifth subsection of the fourth section in the seventh chapter.

Below we describe all the basic LaTeX commands that define counters and modify or display their values. These commands are much more powerful if used in conjunction with the calc package, which is discussed in Section A.3.1.

\newcounter{*newctr*}[*oldctr*]

This command globally defines a new counter, *newctr*, and initializes it to zero. If a counter with the name *newctr* is already defined, an error message is printed. When you specify the name of another counter as the optional argument, *oldctr*, then the newly defined *newctr* is reset when the counter *oldctr* is incremented with the \stepcounter or \refstepcounter command. It also defines \the*newctr* to expand to \arabic{*newctr*}.

\@addtoreset{*reset-ctr*}{*ctr*}   \@removefromreset{*reset-ctr*}{*ctr*}

The operation that defines that one counter is reset whenever another counter is stepped is also available as the kernel command \@addtoreset.[1] Unfortunately, the opposite declaration is not available in the kernel, but only when loading the package remreset. If this small package is loaded, then counters can be unraveled if necessary. For example, the report class defines that the footnote counter is to be reset whenever a new chapter starts. If you want your footnotes nevertheless

Warning:
\@removefromreset
needs a package!

---

[1] See also the \numberwithin declaration provided by the amsmath package. It is discussed in Section 8.2.14 on page 485.

to be numbered sequentially throughout a document, then specifying

```
\usepackage{remreset}
\makeatletter \@removefromreset{footnote}{chapter} \makeatletter
```

in the preamble, or the equivalent code[1] in a package or class, will do the job.

\setcounter{*ctr*}{*val*}   \addtocounter{*ctr*}{*val*}

With \setcounter the value of counter *ctr* is globally set equal to the value *val*. With \addtocounter it is globally incremented by *val*.

\stepcounter{*ctr*}   \refstepcounter{*ctr*}

Both commands globally increment the counter *ctr* and reset all subsidiary counters—that is, those declared with the optional argument *oldctr* on the \newcounter command or with the first argument of \@addtoreset. The \refstepcounter command additionally defines the current \ref value to be the text generated by the command \the*ctr*. Note that whereas stepping a counter is a global operation, setting the current \ref value is done locally and thus is only valid inside the current group. For that reason the next example does not produce the desired result but instead picks up the section number. The correct solution would be to move \refstepcounter before the \textbf command.

5   A Failure

Exercise 5.a: A test.

Exercise 5.b: Another test.

Referencing exercises: 5 and 5.

```
\newcounter{ex} \renewcommand\theex{\thesection.\alph{ex}}
\newenvironment{EX}{\begin{flushleft}%
   \textbf{\refstepcounter{ex}Exercise~\theex:}}
   {\end{flushleft}}
\setcounter{section}{4} % for testing
\section{A Failure}
\begin{EX} \label{A} A test.          \end{EX}
\begin{EX} \label{B} Another test. \end{EX}
Referencing exercises: \ref{A} and \ref{B}.
```

A-1-10

\value{*ctr*}   \arabic{*ctr*}   \roman{*ctr*}   \Roman{*ctr*}
\alph{*ctr*}   \Alph{*ctr*}   \fnsymbol{*ctr*}

The \value command produces the current value of a counter to be used in places where LATEX expects to see a number, such as in the *val* argument of the \setcounter or \addtocounter command or when comparing numbers using the \ifthenelse command from the ifthen package. It is *not* suitable to print that number! For that reason a set of presentation commands are available, all of which take a counter name as argument.

---

[1] In that case use \RequirePackage and *omit* \makeatletter and \makeatother!

With `\arabic` the counter value is represented as an Arabic numeral. With `\roman` and `\Roman` lowercase and uppercase Roman numerals are produced, respectively.

The remaining commands can be used only if the counter value is within a certain range. The `\alph` command displays the value as a lowercase letter: a, b, c,..., z. Thus, the value should lie in the range 1,...,26; otherwise, an error is signaled. The `\Alph` command is similar but produces uppercase letters. Finally, `\fnsymbol` represents the counter value as a traditional footnote symbol (e.g., $*$, $\dagger$). In that case the value must not be greater than 9, unless an extension package, like footmisc, is used. The next example shows all of these commands in action.

Counter presentations with restricted ranges

A-1-11

```
\newcounter{exa}\setcounter{exa}{8}
\arabic{exa}, \roman{exa}, \Roman{exa}, \alph{exa},
\Alph{exa}, \fnsymbol{exa} \par
\setcounter{exa}{1994} Anno Domini \scshape{\roman{exa}}
```

8, viii, VIII, h, H, ††
Anno Domini MCMXCIV

`\the⟨ctr⟩`

A shorthand to produce the default visual representation for a counter *ctr* is provided by the command `\the⟨ctr⟩` (e.g., `\thesection` for the section counter). As mentioned earlier this command is initialized by the `\newcounter` declaration to produce `\arabic{ctr}`. However, in LaTeX such a visual representation often involves more than a single number. For example, with sectioning counters one usually displays the value of the current section as well as the value of the current subsection, and so on. For this reason `\the⟨ctr⟩` is typically (re)defined to produce a more complex representation. This practice becomes even more important when you consider that `\refstepcounter` not only increments a certain counter and resets lower-level counters but also defines the "current" label (as picked up by `\label`) to be the result of `\the⟨ctr⟩` for the counter being stepped.

As an example, inside the standard article class, we find definitions for sectioning equivalent to the following:

```
\newcounter{part}           \newcounter{subsection}[section]
\newcounter{section}        \newcounter{subsubsection}[subsection]
\renewcommand\thepart         {\Roman{part}}
\renewcommand\thesection      {\arabic{section}}
\renewcommand\thesubsection   {\thesection.\arabic{subsection}}
\renewcommand\thesubsubsection{\thesubsection.\arabic{subsubsection}}
```

You see how lower-level counters are reset when upper-level counters are stepped, as well as how the representation of the counters (the `\the...` commands) are constructed from the current counter and the counters at a higher level. Note how the part counter does not influence any of the lower levels.

As another example, we look at Table 3.6 on page 130, which shows the structure of the enumeration list counters. In fact, these counters are defined inside the file `latex.ltx`, which contains the kernel code for LATEX. Only the representation and label field commands are defined in the standard class files as follows:

```
\renewcommand\theenumi   {\arabic{enumi}}   \newcommand\labelenumi   {\theenumi.}
\renewcommand\theenumii  {\alph{enumii}}    \newcommand\labelenumii  {(\theenumii)}
\renewcommand\theenumiii {\roman{enumiii}}  \newcommand\labelenumiii {\theenumiii.}
\renewcommand\theenumiv  {\Alph{enumiv}}     \newcommand\labelenumiv  {\theenumiv.}
```

Finally, we show how the standard classes handle the `equation` counter. Like the enumeration counters, this counter is declared inside `latex.ltx`. In the article class the counter is never reset:

```
\renewcommand\theequation{\arabic{equation}}
```

In the report and book classes the equation number is reset for each chapter with the `\@addtoreset` command:

```
\@addtoreset{equation}{chapter}
\renewcommand\theequation{\thechapter.\arabic{equation}}
```

Also, the representation differs in both cases.[1]

A.1.5 Defining and changing space parameters

In (LA)TEX two kinds of space parameters (lengths) exist: "rigid" lengths (called `<dimen>` in *The TEXbook* [82]), which are fixed, and "rubber" lengths (called `<skip>` in *The TEXbook*), which have a natural length and a degree of positive and negative elasticity. New lengths in LATEX are allocated as type `<skip>`, so that you always have the choice of initializing them as rigid or rubber lengths (by specifying `plus` and `minus` parts). On the other hand, all standard lengths in LATEX are of type rigid, unless specifically declared in Appendix C of the *LATEX Manual* to be rubber. Here we discuss the commands provided by LATEX for dealing with lengths.

`\newlength{`*cmd*`}`

The declaration `\newlength` allocates a new (rubber) length register and associates the command name *cmd* with it. If a command *cmd* already exists, you will get an error message. The new length is preset to zero. Just like with `\newcommand` you will find that the braces around *cmd* are often omitted in actual code since the argument must consist of a single command name.

---

[1]The actual definition is somewhat more complex, since some low-level code is used to suppress the chapter number if it is zero.

sp	Scaled point (65536 sp = 1 pt) TEX's smallest unit
pt	Point = $\frac{1}{72.27}$ in = 0.351 mm
bp	Big point = $\frac{1}{72}$ in = 0.353 mm, also known as PostScript point
dd	Didôt point = $\frac{1}{72}$ of a French inch, = 0.376 mm
mm	Millimeter = 2.845 pt
pc	Pica = 12 pt = 4.218 mm
cc	Cicero = 12 dd = 4.531 mm
cm	Centimeter = 10 mm = 2.371 pc
in	Inch = 25.4 mm = 72.27 pt = 6.022 pc
ex	Height of a small "x" in the current font
em	Width of capital "M" in current font
mu	Math unit (18 mu = 1 em) for positioning in math mode

Table A.1: LATEX's units of length

> \setlength{*cmd*}{*length*}   \addtolength{*cmd*}{*length*}

This sets the value of the length command *cmd* equal to the length *length* or, in case of \addtolength, adds the specified amount to the existing value. In the examples below, the TEX command \the is used to typeset the actual contents of the length variable. It requires the register command name *without* braces!

<table>
<tr><td></td><td></td><td>\newlength\Mylen</td></tr>
<tr><td></td><td>Mylen = 28.45274pt</td><td>\setlength \Mylen{10mm} Mylen = \the\Mylen
\addtolength\Mylen{0pt plus 4pt minus 2pt}</td></tr>
<tr><td>A-1-12</td><td>Mylen = 28.45274pt plus 4.0pt minus 2.0pt</td><td>\par Mylen = \the\Mylen</td></tr>
</table>

Lengths can be specified in various units, as shown in Table A.1. Notice the difference between the typographic point (pt), which is normally used in TEX, and the (big) point used by PostScript, for example. Thus, when reserving space for an EPS picture you need to specify the bounding box dimension in bp to get the correct space.

> \settowidth{*cmd*}{*text*}
> \settoheight{*cmd*}{*text*}   \settodepth{*cmd*}{*text*}

Instead of specifying a length value explicitly, three commands are available that allow you to measure a given text and assign the result. With \settowidth the value of the length command *cmd* is set equal to the natural width of the typeset version of *text*. This command is very useful for defining lengths that vary with the string contents or the type size. The other two commands work similarly but

\hspace{*len*}	Horizonal space of width *len* that can be a rigid or a rubber length
\enspace	Horizonal space equal to half a quad
\quad	Horizonal space equal to the em value of the font
\qquad	Twice a \quad
\hfill	Horizontal rubber space that can stretch between 0 and ∞
\hrulefill	Similar to \hfill, but draws a horizontal line
\dotfill	Similar to \hfill, but draws a dotted line

Table A.2: Predefined horizontal spaces

measure the height and the depth rather than the width of the typeset *text*.

```
                                   \newlength\Mylen    \raggedright% to make example nicer
width = 48.03pt                    \settowidth \Mylen{Typography} width  = \the\Mylen \\
height = 6.7799pt                  \settoheight\Mylen{Typography} height = \the\Mylen \\
depth = 2.16492pt                  \settodepth \Mylen{Typography} depth  = \the\Mylen \par
Use larger font and recalculate:   Use larger font and recalculate: \\
width = 57.63602pt                 \settowidth\Mylen{\large Typography} width = \the\Mylen
```

A-1-13

```
\fill    \stretch{dec-num}
```

These two rubber lengths are intended to be used in the argument of \vspace and similar commands. The \fill rubber length is preset with a natural length of zero but can stretch to any positive value. Do not change its value! It is used in various places in the kernel and a change would produce strange effects.

An often more useful rubber length is provided by the \stretch command—in fact, \fill is equivalent to \stretch{1}. More generally, \stretch{*dec-num*} has a stretchability of *dec-num* times \fill. It can be used to fine-tune the positioning of text horizontally or vertically—for instance, to provide spaces that have a certain relation to each other. Example A-1-15 demonstrates its application.

Horizontal space

Table A.2 shows horizontal space commands known to LᴬTᴇX. A flexible horizontal space of any desired width is produced by the \hspace command. The command \hspace* is the same as \hspace, but the space is never removed—not even at a line boundary.

A space in front of or following an \hspace or \hspace* command is significant, as the following example shows:

```
This is a    0.5 in wide space.    \par This is a\hspace{0.5in}0.5~in wide space.
This is a    0.5 in wide space.    \par This is a \hspace{0.5in}0.5~in wide space.
This is a    0.5 in wide space.    \par This is a \hspace{0.5in} 0.5~in wide space.
```

A-1-14

The next example shows how rubber lengths can be used to fine-tune the positioning of information on a line. Note that the \hfill command is, in fact,

\smallskip	Vertical skip of \smallskipamount (default about one quarter of \baselineskip)
\medskip	Vertical skip of \medskipamount (default about one half of \baselineskip)
\bigskip	Vertical skip of \bigskipamount (default about one \baselineskip)
\vfill	Vertical rubber length that can stretch between 0 and ∞

Table A.3: Predefined vertical spaces

an abbreviation for \hspace{\fill}. To save typing, we also defined a command with an optional argument, \HS, which behaves like \hfill when used without an argument, but can be made less or more flexible than that command by specifying the stretchability (a value of 1 has the same effect as \hfill).

left   right
left $\frac{2}{5}$ right
left   middle   right
left ——— middle ——— right
left .... right
left .... right
left .... right
left .... right

```
\newcommand{\HS}[1][1.]{\hspace{\stretch{#1}}}
\begin{center}
left \hfill                          right\\
left \HS[2]\fbox{$\frac{2}{5}$}\HS[5] right\\
left \HS           middle \hfill      right\\
left \hrulefill\ middle \hrulefill\   right\\
left \dotfill\                        right\\
left \dotfill\ \HS[.5] \dotfill\      right\\
left \dotfill\ \HS     \dotfill\      right\\
left \dotfill\ \HS[2.] \dotfill\      right
\end{center}
```

A-1-15

Vertical space

A vertical space is produced with the \vspace command, which works similarly to \hspace. In particular, a \vspace* command will generate vertical space that will never be eliminated, even when it falls on a page break where a \vspace command will be ignored at this point. Table A.3 shows vertical space commands known to LaTeX that are common to all standard classes.

    LaTeX users are often confused about the behavior of the \vspace command. When used inside a paragraph, the vertical space is added after the end of the line with \vspace; between paragraphs it behaves as you would expect.

    The use of a \vspace command inside

a paragraph is considered somewhat odd. It could perhaps be used with a negative space value to get rid of redundant space.

    Between paragraphs, adjusting the spacing is somewhat more useful, and it allows control of the white space before and after displayed material.

A-1-16

```
The \vspace{3mm}use of a \verb!\vspace! command
inside a paragraph is considered somewhat odd.
It could perhaps be used with a negative space
value to get rid of redundant space.

\vspace{\baselineskip}

Between paragraphs, adjusting the spacing is
somewhat more useful, and it allows control
of the white space before and after displayed
material.
```

Stretchable space as introduced on page 856 can also be used for vertical material. The \vfill command is, in fact, an abbreviation for a blank line followed by \vspace{\fill}. More generally, you can use the \stretch command in combination with \vspace to control the layout of a complete page. This could be useful for designing a title page: if the title should be placed one third of the way down the page, one simply has to place \vspace*{\stretch{1}} before it and \vspace*{\stretch{2}} after it.

```
\newcommand\HRule{\noindent\rule{\linewidth}{1.5pt}}
\begin{titlepage}
  \vspace*{\stretch{1}}
  \HRule
  \begin{flushright}
    \LARGE   Geoffrey Chaucer \\
             The Canterbury Tales
  \end{flushright}
  \HRule
  \vspace*{\stretch{2}}
  \begin{center}
    \textsc{London 1400}
  \end{center}
\end{titlepage}
```

A-1-17

\addvspace{*space*}

While LATEX's user command \vspace unconditionally adds a vertical space (which is removed only at page boundaries, while its starred form even suppresses this action), there exists another command for adding vertical space that is often used in the kernel and in some package files. The \addvspace command has somewhat different semantics, and although it appears to be a user-level command judging from its name, in fact it is not.

Use with care—if at all

In contrast to \vspace the command \addvspace is allowed only in vertical mode (i.e., between paragraphs). If used in horizontal mode, it issues the famous "Something's wrong-perhaps a missing \item" error, which most LATEX users know and love. Most of the time this error has nothing to do with a misplaced \item but simply signals a misplaced \addvspace command. But it shows some of the history of this command: originally, it was developed and used solely for spacing items in list environments.

The other important semantic difference between \vspace and \addvspace is that the latter adds a space whose size depends on any directly preceding space. The precise rules are inherited from LATEX 2.09 and show some strange discontinuities that nobody these days seems to be able to explain fully, though for backward compatibility the command is retained in this form. If s is the space to be added by \addvspace and ℓ is the size of the vertical space (if any) before the current point, then the following rules apply:

If	$s < 0pt < \ell$	do	backup by s
elseif	$\ell = 0pt$	do	add an additional space of s
		else	make a space of $\max(\ell, s)$ out of the two

If we ignore for the moment the special cases in the first two lines of the rules, then the idea behind \addvspace can be described as follows: if we have two vertically oriented constructs, such as a list and a heading, and both want to surround themselves with some vertical spacing before and after, it is probably not a good idea if both such spaces are applied if the objects directly follow each other. In that case using the maximum of both spaces is usually a better solution. This is why lists, headings, and other typeset elements use \addvspace rather than \vspace.

This has some rather surprising effects. If you have two such display objects following each other, then only the maximum of the space surrounding them is used. But if you try to enlarge that space slightly, such as by placing \vspace{4pt} between them, then suddenly the space will be far larger. This result occurs because in a sequence like

Surprising space size changes

```
\addvspace{10pt} \vspace{4pt} \addvspace{8pt}
```

the second \addvspace will be unable to see the first and will add all of its space (with the result that the total space is 22pt); without the \vspace in the middle you would get 10pt total. The \vspace does not interact with the following \addvspace because it actually generates a space of 4pt followed by a space of 0pt, so that the second rule applies.

If you notice that your space got too large and you reduce your correction to, say, \vspace{2pt}, nothing will change substantially (you still get 20pt). Even more surprisingly, if you try to make the original space smaller by using, say, \vspace{-3pt}, you will end up with 15pt total space—still more than before.

To actually get a space of 7pt in that place, you would need to back up by 11pt. Unfortunately, there is no way to determine the size of the necessary space other than by experimenting or looking into the definitions of the objects above and below, to find out what \addvspace values are used at a given point.

The same problem arrises if some other invisible object separates two consecutive \addvspace commands. For example, a color-changing command or a \label will effectively hide a previous \addvspace, with the result that suddenly not the maximum, but the sum of both spaces, appears.

| \addpenalty{*penalty*} |

Although \addpenalty is not a spacing command it is described here because it is intended to work together with \addvspace. A penalty is TEX's way of assigning a "badness" to break points. A high penalty means that this is a bad place to break, while a negative penalty indicates to TEX that this is a rather good place to start a new line or a new page. Details of this mechanism can be found in Chapters 14 and 15 of [82].

The \addpenalty command requires a TEX penalty value as an argument (useful values are between -10000 and 10000). For example, \@startsection discussed in Chapter 2 uses \addpenalty to make the space before a heading become a good place to break (default value -300). If \addpenalty and \addvspace are mixed, then this has two effects:

- LATEX will still use the maximum of the spaces even if \addpenalty appears between two \addvspace commands.

- LaTeX moves the potential break "visually" to the beginning of the white space, even if there is an \addvspace before the \addpenalty.

The second feature is important to avoid white space remaining at the bottom of pages. See page 937 for a discussion of how this is achieved.

A.2 Page markup—Boxes and rules

The theory of composing pages out of boxes lies at the very heart of TeX, and several LaTeX constructs are available to take advantage of this method of composition. A *box* is a rectangular object with a height, depth, and width. Its contents can be arbitrarily complex, involving other boxes, characters, spaces, and so forth. Once built it is used by LaTeX as a single, fixed object that behaves similarly to a (potentially huge) character. A box cannot be split and broken across lines or pages. Boxes can be moved up, down, left, and right. LaTeX has three types of boxes:

LR (left–right) The contents of this box are typeset from left to right. Line breaking is impossible and commands like \\ and \newline are ignored or produce error messages.

Par (paragraphs) This kind of box can contain several lines, which will be typeset in paragraph mode just like normal text. Paragraphs are put one on top of the other. Their widths are controlled by a user-specified value.

Rule This (thin or thick) line is often used to separate various logical elements on the output page, such as table rows and columns, and running titles and the main text.

LaTeX's boxes all start a paragraph (just like characters) if used in vertical mode, while TeX's primitive box commands (e.g., \hbox) behave differently depending on where they are used. There are a number of reasons to avoid using the TeX primitives directly; see the discussion in Section A.2.5. The situation with rules is slightly different; we therefore will discuss TeX's primitive rule commands below.

A.2.1 LR boxes

```
\mbox{text}                    \fbox{text}
\makebox[width][pos]{text}    \framebox[width][pos]{text}
```

The first line considers the *text* inside the curly braces as a box, without or with a frame drawn around it. For example, \fbox{some words} gives | some words |. The two commands on the second line are a generalization of these commands. They allow the user to specify the width of the box and the positioning of the text inside.

some words

| some words |

```
\makebox[5cm]{some words}         \par
\framebox[5cm][r]{some words}
```

A-2-1

In addition to centering the text with the positional argument [c] (the default), you can position the text flush left ([l]) or flush right ([r]). There is also an [s] specifier that will stretch your *text* from the left margin to the right margin of the box provided it contains some stretchable space (e.g., some \hspace or the predefined spaces given in Table A.2 on page 856). Interword spaces are also stretchable (and shrinkable to a certain extent), as explained on page 428. The appearance of frameboxes can be controlled by two style parameters:

\fboxrule   The width of the lines for the box produced with the command \fbox or \framebox. The default value in all standard classes is 0.4pt.

\fboxsep   The space left between the edge of the box and its contents by \fbox or \framebox. The default value in all standard classes is 3pt.

Any changes to these parameters obey the normal scoping rules and affect all frameboxes within the scope. The change to \fboxsep in the next example, for instance, applies only to the second box.

A-2-2

| Boxed Text | Boxed Text | Boxed Text |

```
\fbox{Boxed Text} \hfill
\setlength\fboxrule{2pt}%
{\setlength\fboxsep{2mm}\fbox{Boxed Text}}
\hfill \fbox{Boxed Text}
```

The box commands with arguments for specifying the dimensions of the box allow you to make use of four special length parameters: \width, \height, \depth, and \totalheight. They specify the natural size of the *text*, where \totalheight is the sum of \height and \depth.

A-2-3

| A few words of advice |
| A few words of advice |
| A few words of advice |

```
\usepackage{calc}
\framebox{ A few words of advice }                    \par
\framebox[\width + 8mm][s]{ A few words of advice }
\par  \framebox[1.5\width]{ A few words of advice }
```

Zero-width boxes are very handy if you want to put a marker on the page (e.g., for placement of figures) or to allow text to be put into the margins. The principle of operation is shown below, where a zero-width box is used to tag text, without influencing the centering. Note that the optional parameter [l] ([r]) makes the material stick out to the right (left).

A-2-4

A sentence.[123]
Some more text in the middle.
[321]A sentence.

```
\centering
A sentence.\makebox[0pt][l]{\textsuperscript{123}}\\
Some more text in the middle.                        \\
\makebox[0cm][r]{\textsuperscript{321}}A sentence.
```

⟺As seen in the margin of the current line, boxes with a vanishing width can be used to make text stick out into the margin. This effect was produced by beginning the current paragraph in the following way:

```
\noindent\makebox[0cm][r]{$\Longleftrightarrow$}%
As seen in the margin ...
```

An interesting possibility is to raise or lower boxes. This can be achieved by the very powerful \raisebox command, which has two mandatory arguments and two optional arguments:

> \raisebox{*lift*}[*height*][*depth*]{*contents*}

To raise or lower the box produced from the *contents*, one specifies the amount of *lift* as a dimension, with negative values lowering the box. As with other boxes, one can make use of the special commands \height, \depth, \totalheight, or even \width to refer to the natural dimensions of the box produced from *contents*. This is used in the next example to raise the word "upward" so that the descender of the "p" aligns with the baseline and to lower the word "downward" so that it is placed completely below the baseline.

x111x upward x222x   downward   x333x

```
x111x \raisebox{\depth}{upward} x222x
      \raisebox{-\height}{downward} x333x
```

A-2-5

Normally, LATEX takes the added height and depth into account when calculating the distance between the lines, so that a raised or lowered box can result in spreading lines apart. This can be manipulated by specifying a *height* and a *depth* that the user wants LATEX to actually use when placing its material on the page. The second pair of lines below shows that LATEX does not realize that text has been moved upward and downward; thus, it composes the lines as though all the text was on the baseline.

x111x downward x222x
x333x upward x444x

x111x downward x222x
x333x upward x444x

```
\begin{flushleft}
x111x \raisebox{-1ex}{downward} x222x        \\
x333x \raisebox{1ex}{upward} x444x           \\[4mm]
x111x \raisebox{-1ex}[0cm][0cm]{downward} x222x\\
x333x \raisebox{1ex}[0cm]{upward} x444x
\end{flushleft}
```

A-2-6

A somewhat more useful application is discussed in Section 5.7 on page 272, which addresses the subject of columns spanning multiple rows in tabular material.

A.2.2 Paragraph boxes

Paragraph boxes are constructed using the \parbox command or minipage environment. The *text* material is typeset in paragraph mode inside a box of width

width. The vertical positioning of the box with respect to the text baseline is controlled by the one-letter optional parameter *pos* ([c], [t], or [b]).

\parbox[*pos*]{*width*}{*text*}	\begin{minipage}[*pos*]{*width*} *text* \end{minipage}

The center position is the default, as shown in the next example. Note that LaTeX might produce wide interword spaces if justification is requested (default) and the measure is incredibly small.

This is the contents of the left-most parbox.   CURRENT LINE

This is the right-most parbox. Note that the typeset text looks sloppy because LaTeX cannot nicely balance the material in these narrow columns.

```
\parbox{.3\linewidth}{This is
   the contents of the left-most
   parbox.}
\hfill CURRENT LINE \hfill
\parbox{.3\linewidth}{This is
   the right-most parbox.
   Note that the typeset text
   looks sloppy because \LaTeX{}
   cannot nicely balance the
   material in these narrow
   columns.}
```

A-2-7

The minipage environment is very useful for the placement of material on the page. In effect, it is a complete miniversion of a page and can contain its own footnotes, paragraphs, and array, tabular, multicols, and other environments. Note, however, that it cannot contain floats or \marginpar commands, but it can appear inside figure or table environments, where it is often used for constructing a pleasing layout of the material inside the float. A simple example of a minipage environment at work is given below. The baseline is shown with an en dash generated by the command \HR. Note the use of the *pos* placement parameter ([c], [t], or [b]) on the three minipage environments.

```
\newcommand\HR{\rule{.5em}{0.4pt}}
\HR
\begin{minipage}[b]{12mm}
         A A A A A A A A A A A A A A
\end{minipage}\HR
\begin{minipage}[c]{12mm}
         B B B B B B B B B B B B B B B B B B B B B B B
\end{minipage}\HR
\begin{minipage}[t]{12mm}
         C C C C C C
\end{minipage}\HR
```

A-2-8

If you desire more complicated alignments, then you might have to stack the different minipage environments. Compare the behavior of the next examples.

Below, we try to align the two leftmost blocks at their top and align the resulting block at the bottom with a third block by adding another level of minipages.

```
                    C C C C
_A A A xx B B B B_C C C _
 A A A    B B B B
 A A A    B B B B
 A A A    B B B B
 A A A    B B B B
          B B B B
```

```
\newcommand\HR{\rule{.5em}{0.4pt}}
\HR\begin{minipage}[b]{30mm}
    \begin{minipage}[t]{12mm}
        A A A A A A A A A A A A A A
    \end{minipage} xx  \begin{minipage}[t]{12mm}
        B B B B B B B B B B B B B B B B B B B B B B
    \end{minipage}
\end{minipage}\HR
\begin{minipage}[b]{12mm}  C C C C C C C \end{minipage}\HR
```
A-2-9

However, we do not get the expected result. Instead, the two top-aligned minipages inside the bottom-aligned minipage form a paragraph with a single line (the minipages are considered to be large units in the line containing xx). Thus, the bottom line of the outer minipage is still the one containing the xx characters. To prevent this we need to add some invisible space after the paragraph, as shown next.

```
A A A xx B B B B
A A A    B B B B
A A A    B B B B
A A A    B B B B
A A A    B B B B  C C C C
_        B B B B_C C C _
```

```
\newcommand\HR{\rule{.5em}{0.4pt}}
\HR\begin{minipage}[b]{30mm}
    \begin{minipage}[t]{12mm}
        A A A A A A A A A A A A A A
    \end{minipage} xx  \begin{minipage}[t]{12mm}
        B B B B B B B B B B B B B B B B B B B B B B
    \end{minipage}
    \par\vspace{0mm}
\end{minipage}\HR
\begin{minipage}[b]{12mm}  C C C C C C C \end{minipage}\HR
```
A-2-10

In the case below, the two rightmost environments are aligned at their top inside another enclosing environment, which is aligned at its bottom with the first one. If you compare it with the previous example, then you see that you obtain a quite different result, although the sequence of alignment parameters is the same. Only the stacking order of the minipage environments is different.

```
          B B B B xx C C C C
A A A B B B B    C C C
A A A B B B B
A A A B B B B
A A A B B B B
_A A A _B B B B          _
```

```
\newcommand\HR{\rule{.5em}{0.4pt}}
\HR\begin{minipage}[b]{12mm}
    A A A A A A A A A A A A A A A A \end{minipage}\HR
\begin{minipage}[b]{30mm}   \begin{minipage}[t]{12mm}
        B B B B B B B B B B B B B B B B B B B B B B
    \end{minipage} xx
    \begin{minipage}[t]{12mm}  C C C C C C C  \end{minipage}
    \par\vspace{0mm}
\end{minipage}\HR
```
A-2-11

Again, we had to add some vertical space to achieve alignment. This does not, however, always produce the desired result. If, for instance, a letter with a descender appears in the last line of the stacked `minipage`, as in the example below, then the alignment of the baselines is not perfect.

```
B B B B xx C C C C
B B B B    C C C
A A A B B B B
A A A B B B B
A A A B B B B
A A A B B B B
_A A A _gg jj          _
```
```
\newcommand\HR{\rule{.5em}{0.4pt}}
\HR\begin{minipage}[b]{12mm}
      A A A A A A A A A A A A A A \end{minipage}\HR
\begin{minipage}[b]{30mm}  \begin{minipage}[t]{12mm}
      B B B B B B B B B B B B B B B B B B B B B B gg jj
\end{minipage} xx
\begin{minipage}[t]{12mm}  C C C C C C  \end{minipage}
\par\vspace{0mm}
\end{minipage}\HR
```

A-2-12

To correct this problem, you have to add (negative) vertical space that compensates for the depth of the letters.

Perhaps the easiest way (albeit the most dangerous) is to use the TeX primitive `\prevdepth`. This dimension register can be used only in vertical mode (i.e., after a paragraph has ended), and contains the depth of the previous line. In the next example this primitive is used to back up by this amount, thereby pretending that the bottom of the box is located at the baseline of the last line.

When using `\prevdepth` in this way one has to be careful. As already mentioned, it gives an error if used outside vertical mode. Furthermore, TeX overloads this primitive by setting it to -1000pt at the beginning of a vertical box and after a horizontal rule.[1] Thus, using `\vspace*` instead of `\vspace` in the example would give a nasty surprise, because `\vspace*` actually puts in an invisible rule to ensure that the space will survive at a page break. As a result the value of `\prevdepth` inside would be -1000pt and we would effectively be adding a space of 1000 points at the bottom of the box.

Surprising effects of `\prevdepth`

```
B B B B xx C C C C
B B B B    C C C
A A A B B B B
A A A B B B B
A A A B B B B
A A A B B B B
_A A A _gg jj          _
```
```
\newcommand\HR{\rule{.5em}{0.4pt}}
\HR\begin{minipage}[b]{12mm}
      A A A A A A A A A A A A A A \end{minipage}\HR
\begin{minipage}[b]{30mm}  \begin{minipage}[t]{12mm}
      B B B B B B B B B B B B B B B B B B B B B B gg jj
\par\vspace{-\prevdepth}
\end{minipage} xx
\begin{minipage}[t]{12mm}  C C C C C C  \end{minipage}
\par\vspace{0pt}
\end{minipage}\HR
```

A-2-13

Sometimes it is helpful to predefine the vertical dimension of a paragraph box. For this purpose today's LaTeX offers additional optional arguments for `\parbox` and the `minipage` environment.

---

[1] TeX uses `\prevdepth` to calculate the interline space needed and -1000pt indicates that this space should be suppressed.

```
\parbox[pos][height][inner-pos]{width}{text}
\begin{minipage}[pos][height][inner-pos]{width}  text  \end{minipage}
```

The *inner-pos* argument determines the position of the *text* within the box. It can be t, c, b, or s. If not specified, the value of *pos* will be used. You can think of *height* and *inner-pos* as the vertical equivalent of the *width* and *pos* arguments of a \makebox. If you use the s position, the *text* will be vertically stretched to fill the given *height*. Thus, in this case you are responsible for providing vertically stretchable space if necessary, using, for example, the \vspace command.

As with the other box commands you can use \height, \totalheight, and so on to refer to the natural dimensions of the box when specifying the optional argument.

| Some text on top. | This time a few lines on the top of the box. But only |
| And a few lines on the bottom of the | one line |
| xx box. | down here. | xx

```
\usepackage{calc}
xx \fbox{\parbox[b][\height+\baselineskip][s]
           {20mm}{Some text on top. \par\vfill
                  And a few lines on the
                  bottom of the box.}}
     \fbox{\parbox[b][\height+\baselineskip][s]
           {20mm}{This time a few lines on the
                  top of the box. But only one
                  line \par\vfill down here.}} xx
```

A-2-14

A.2.3　Rule boxes

LATEX's rule boxes are drawn with the \rule command:

```
\rule[lift]{width}{height}
```

If we write \rule[4pt]{2cm}{1mm} then we get a 2 cm long rule that is 1 mm thick and raised 4 pt above the baseline: ▬▬▬▬▬▬. The \rule command can also be used to construct rule boxes with zero width, that is invisible rules (also called *struts*). These struts are useful if you need to control the height or width of a given box (for example, to increase the height of a framed box with \fbox or \framebox, or to adjust locally the distance between rows in a table). Compare the following:

x111x [some text] x222x | more text | x333x

```
x111x
  \fbox{some text}
x222x
  \fbox{\rule[-5mm]{0cm}{15mm}more text}
x333x
```

A-2-15

As mentioned earlier, LATEX makes boxes (including rules) behave like characters. For example, if used outside a paragraph they automatically start a new paragraph. With rules this is not always the desired behavior. To get a rule between two paragraphs, for instance, we have to use \noindent to suppress a paragraph indentation; otherwise, the line would be indented and stick out to the right.

> ... Some text for our page that might get reused over and over again.
>
> ---
>
> A following paragraph.   Some text for our page that might get reused over and over again.

A-2-16

```
\newcommand\sample{ Some text for our page
    that might get reused over and over again.}
\ldots \sample                            \par
\noindent\rule{\linewidth}{0.4pt} \par
A following paragraph. \sample
```

Due to this behavior the rule sits on the baseline of a one-line paragraph and is therefore visually much closer to the following paragraph. To place it at equal distance between the two lines, one could use the optional *lift* argument, but determining the right value (roughly 2.5 pt in this particular case) remains a matter of trial and error.

One solution is to suppress the generation of interline space, using the low-level TeX command \nointerlineskip, and to add the necessary spaces explicitly as shown in the next example. This time we omit \noindent so that the rule is indented by \parindent, and we use calc to calculate the rule width such that it leaves a space of size \parindent on the right as well.

> ... Some text for our page that might get reused over and over again.
>
> ---
>
> A following paragraph.   Some text for our page that might get reused over and over again.

A-2-17

```
\usepackage{calc}    % \sample as before
\ldots \sample                            \par
\nointerlineskip \vspace{5.3pt}
\rule{\linewidth-2\parindent}{0.4pt}\par
\nointerlineskip \vspace{5.3pt}
A following paragraph. \sample
```

The sum of the vertical spaces used plus the height of the rule amounts to 12 points (i.e., \baselineskip). However, this does not make the baselines of the two paragraphs 12 points apart; rather, it makes the distance from the bottom of the last line in the first paragraph (i.e., as produced by the "g" in "again") to the top of the first line in the next paragraph (i.e., as produced by the "A") be 12 points. Thus, if the text baselines should preferably fall onto a grid, a variant of Example A-2-16 using the optional *lift* argument is more appropriate.

Instead of using \rule together with \nointerlineskip, package or class writers often use the primitive TeX rule commands. They have the advantage of automatically suppressing interline space and do not require you to specify all dimensions. On the downside, they have an unusual syntax and cannot be used if the rule needs horizontal or vertical shifting, as in the previous example.

```
\hrule height height depth depth width width \relax
\vrule height height depth depth width width \relax
```

The \hrule primitive can only be used between paragraphs, while the \vrule primitive has to appear within paragraphs. If encountered in the wrong place,

	width	height	depth
\hrule	*	0.4pt	0.4pt
\vrule	0.4pt	*	*

Table A.4: Default values for TeX's rule primitives

the commands stop or start a paragraph as necessary. The commands can be followed by one or more of the keywords `height`, `depth`, and `width` together with a dimension value. Any order is allowed, and missing keywords get the defaults shown in Table A.4. An asterisk in that table means that the rule will extend to the boundary of the outer box. The `\relax` command at the end is not required but ensures that TeX knows that the rule specification has ended and will not misinterpret words in the text as keywords.

    In the next example we use the default value for `\hrule`, resulting in a rule of 0.4pt height running through the whole galley width (since this is effectively the next outer box).

... Some text for our page that might get reused over and over again.

A following paragraph. Some text for our page that might get reused over and over again.

```
% \sample as before
\ldots \sample                        \par
\vspace{3pt}\hrule\relax\vspace{3pt}
A following paragraph. \sample        \par
```

A-2-18

A.2.4   Manipulating boxed material

Material can be typeset once and then stored inside a named box, whose contents can later be retrieved.

`\newsavebox{`*cmd*`}`	Declare box
`\sbox{`*cmd*`}{`*text*`}`	Fill box
`\savebox{`*cmd*`}[`*width*`][`*pos*`]{`*text*`}`	Fill box
`\usebox{`*cmd*`}`	Use contents

The command `\newsavebox` globally declares a command *cmd* (for example, `\mybox`), which can be thought of as a named bin. Typeset material can be stored there for later (multiple) retrieval.

    The `\sbox` and `\savebox` commands are similar to `\mbox` and `\makebox`, except that they save the constructed box in the named bin (previously allocated with `\newsavebox`) instead of directly typesetting it. The `\usebox` command then allows the nondestructive use of the material stored inside such named bins. You can reuse the same bin (e.g., `\mybox`) several times within the scope of the current environment or brace group. It will always contain what was last stored in it.

    Be careful not to use the command name `\mybox` directly, since it contains only the TeX number of the box in question. As a consequence, `\mybox` on its own will merely typeset the character at the position corresponding to the box number in the current font. Thus, you should manipulate boxes exclusively using the commands described above.

```
\newsavebox{\myboxa}\newsavebox{\myboxb}
\sbox{\myboxa}{inside box a}
\savebox{\myboxb}[2cm][l]{inside box b}
  x1x \usebox{\myboxa} x2x \usebox{\myboxb} x3x
\savebox{\myboxb}[2cm][r]{inside box b}
  \par
  x1x \usebox{\myboxa} x2x \usebox{\myboxb} x3x
```

x1x inside box a x2x inside box b   x3x

A-2-19

x1x inside box a x2x   inside box b x3x

In addition to the above commands, there exists the lrbox environment with the following syntax:

```
\begin{lrbox}{cmd}    text    \end{lrbox}
```

Here *cmd* should be a box register previously allocated with \newsavebox. The environment lrbox will save the *text* in this box for later use with \usebox. Leading and trailing spaces are ignored. Thus, lrbox is basically the environment form of \sbox. You can make good use of this environment if you want to save the body of some environment in a box for further processing. For example, the following code defines the environment fcolumn, which works like a column-wide minipage but surrounds its body with a frame.

```
\usepackage{calc}
\newsavebox{\fcolbox} \newlength{\fcolwidth}
\newenvironment{fcolumn}[1][\linewidth]
  {\setlength{\fcolwidth}{#1-2\fboxsep-2\fboxrule}%
   \begin{lrbox}{\fcolbox}\begin{minipage}{\fcolwidth}}
  {\end{minipage}\end{lrbox}\noindent\fbox{\usebox{\fcolbox}}}}
```

In this environment verbatim text like \fcolbox can be used.

A-2-20

```
\begin{fcolumn}    In this environment verbatim text like
  \verb=\fcolbox= can be used.                        \end{fcolumn}
```

The above definition is interesting in several respects. The environment is defined with one optional argument denoting the width of the resulting box (default \linewidth). On the next line we calculate (using the calc package) the internal line length that we have to pass to the minipage environment. Here we have to subtract the extra space added by the \fbox command on both sides. Then the lrbox and minipage environments are started to typeset the body of the fcolumn environment into the box \fcolbox. When the end of the environment is reached those environments are closed. Then the \fcolbox is typeset inside an \fbox command. The \noindent in front suppresses any indentation in case the environment is used at the beginning of a paragraph or forms a paragraph by itself.

The boxedminipage described in Section 10.1.1 on page 595 can be implemented in a similar fashion. The only essential difference from the previous code is that we omit `\noindent` and pass the width as a mandatory argument and the position as an optional argument.

```
\usepackage{calc}
\newsavebox{\fcolbox} \newlength{\fcolwidth}
\newenvironment{boxedminipage}[2][c]
  {\setlength{\fcolwidth}{#2-2\fboxsep-2\fboxrule}%
   \begin{lrbox}{\fcolbox}%
   \begin{minipage}[#1]{\fcolwidth}}
  {\end{minipage}\end{lrbox}\fbox{\usebox{\fcolbox}}}
left \begin{boxedminipage}[b]{4cm}
     In this environment verbatim text like
        \verb=\fcolbox= can be used.
     \end{boxedminipage}
right
```

left | In this environment verbatim text like \fcolbox can be used. | right

A-2-21

If you compare this definition with the actual code in the package (which originates in LATEX 2.09), it will be apparent that the coding features offered with the current version of LATEX have their advantages.

A.2.5   Box commands and color

Even if you do not intend to use color in your own documents, by taking note of the points in this section you can ensure that your class or package is compatible with the color package. This may benefit people who choose to use your class or package together with the color package extensions.

The simplest way to ensure "color safety" is to always use LATEX box commands rather than TEX primitives—that is, to use `\sbox` rather than `\setbox`, `\mbox` rather than `\hbox`, and `\parbox` or the minipage environment rather than `\vbox`. The LATEX box commands have new options that make them as powerful as the TEX primitives.

As an example of what can go wrong, consider that in {\ttfamily *text*} the font is restored just *before* the }, whereas in the similar-looking construct {\color{green} *text*} the color is restored just *after* the final }. Normally, this distinction does not matter. But consider a primitive TEX box assignment such as

```
\setbox0=\hbox{\color{green} some text}
```

Now the color-restore operation occurs after the } and so is *not* stored in the box. Exactly which bad effects this introduces will depend on how color is implemented: the problems can range from getting the wrong colors in the rest of the document to causing errors in the dvi driver used to print the document.

Also of interest is the command `\normalcolor`. This is normally just `\relax` (i.e., does nothing), but you can use it like `\normalfont` to set regions of the page, such as captions or section headings, to the "main document color".

A.3   Control structure extensions

A.3.1   calc—Arithmetic calculations

The package calc (by Kresten Thorup and Frank Jensen) contains a set of macros for enhanced arithmetic in LaTeX. Usual arithmetic in TeX is done by simple low-level operations like \advance and \multiply. This package defines an infix notation arithmetic for LaTeX. In fact, it reimplements the LaTeX commands \setcounter, \addtocounter, \setlength, and \addtolength so that they can accept integer and length expressions rather than simple numbers and lengths.

An integer expression can contain integer numbers, TeX's integer registers, LaTeX's counters (e.g., \value{ctr}), parentheses, and binary operators (, , ,). For instance, to advance a counter by five:

```
\usepackage{calc}      \newcounter{local}
\setcounter{local}{2} % initial setting for the example
The value is currently ''\thelocal''.\\
\setcounter{local}{\value{local}+5}
The value has now changed to ''\thelocal''.
```

A-3-1
The value is currently "2".
The value has now changed to "7".

An example is the definition of a command to print the time (note that the TeX register \time contains the number of minutes since midnight):

```
\usepackage{calc}
\newcounter{hours}\newcounter{minutes}
\newcommand\printtime{\setcounter{hours}{\time/60}%
            \setcounter{minutes}{\time-\value{hours}*60}%
            \thehours h \theminutes min}
```

A-3-2
The time is 18h 53min.   The time is \printtime.

When dealing with lengths, the subexpressions that are added or subtracted must be of the same type. That is, you cannot have "2cm+4", but an expression like "2cm+4pt" is legal because both subexpressions have dimensions. You can only divide or multiply by integers, so "2cm*4" is a legal subexpression but "2cm*4pt" is forbidden. Also, the length part must come first in an expression; thus, "4*2cm" is not allowed.

The commands described above allow you to calculate the width of one column in an n-column layout using the following single command (supposing that the variable n is stored as the first argument of a LaTeX macro):

```
\setlength\linewidth{(\textwidth-\columnsep*(#1-1))/#1}
```

The restriction that you can only multiply and divide by integers has been relaxed for calculations on lengths (dimensions). Those operations are allowed with real numbers.

> \real{*decimal constant*}   \ratio{*length expression*}{*length expression*}

A real number can be represented in two forms: the first command converts the *decimal constant* into a form that can be used in a calc formula. The second form denotes the real number obtained by dividing the value of the first expression by the value of the second expression.

As an example, assume you want to scale a figure so that it occupies the full width of the page (\textwidth). If the original dimensions of the figure are given by the length variables \Xsize and \Ysize, then the height of the figure after scaling will be:

```
\setlength\newYsize{\Ysize*\ratio{\textwidth}{\Xsize}}
```

The calc package is used in many examples in this book. If you do not want to apply it, you need to express the code given in the examples in the form of primitive (LA)TEX constructs. For example, the setting of \fcolwidth on page 869 has to be translated from

```
\setlength\fcolwidth{#1-2\fboxsep-2\fboxrule}%
```

to the following statements:

```
\setlength\fcolwidth{#1}%
\addtolength\fcolwidth{-2\fboxsep}%
\addtolength\fcolwidth{-2\fboxrule}
```

Besides the fact that the infix notation provided by the calc package is certainly more readable (and much easier to modify), it contains constructs for division and multiplication that cannot be expressed with standard LATEX constructs. For example, to express the \topmargin calculation from page 198, the following code is necessary:

```
\setlength\topmargin{297mm}
\addtolength\topmargin{-\textheight}
\divide\topmargin by 3                    % TeX calculation
\addtolength\topmargin{-1in}
\addtolength\topmargin{-\headheight}
\addtolength\topmargin{-\headsep}
```

A.3.2   ifthen—Advanced control structures

Sometimes you may want to typeset different material depending on the value of a logical expression. This is possible with the standard package ifthen (written by Leslie Lamport, and reimplemented for the current LATEX version by David Carlisle), which defines commands for building control structures with LATEX.

\ifthenelse{*test*}{*then-code*}{*else-code*}

If the condition *test* is true, the commands in the *then-code* part are executed. Otherwise, the commands in the *else-code* part are executed.

A simple form of a condition is the comparison of two integers. For example, if you want to translate a counter value into English:

```
\usepackage{ifthen}
\newcommand\toEng[1]{\arabic{#1}\textsuperscript{%
 \ifthenelse{\value{#1}=1}{st}{%
  \ifthenelse{\value{#1}=2}{nd}{%
   \ifthenelse{\value{#1}=3}{rd}{%
    \ifthenelse{\value{#1}<20}{th}}%
                              {\typeout{Value too high}}}}}}
```

This is the 3rd section in the 1st appendix.

| A-3-3 |

```
This is the \toEng{section} section in the \toEng{chapter}
appendix.
```

The following example defines a command to print the time in short form. It shows how complex operations (using the calc package) can be combined with conditional control statements.

```
\usepackage{ifthen,calc}
\newcounter{hours}\newcounter{minutes}

\newcommand{\Printtime}{\setcounter{hours}{\time/60}%
        \setcounter{minutes}{\time-\value{hours}*60}%
        \ifthenelse{\value{hours}<10}{0}{}\thehours:%
        \ifthenelse{\value{minutes}<10}{0}{}\theminutes}
```

| A-3-4 | The current time is "18:53".

```
The current time is ``\Printtime''.
```

\equal{*string1*}{*string2*}

The \equal command evaluates to *true* if the two strings *string1* and *string2* are equal after they have been completely expanded. You should be careful when using fragile commands in one of the strings; they need protection with the \protect command.

```
\usepackage{ifthen,shortvrb}  \MakeShortVerb\|
\newcommand\BB{\CC}\newcommand\CC{\DD}
\newcommand\DD{AA}  \newcommand\EE{EE}
|\BB|=|\EE|?  \ifthenelse{\equal{\BB}{\EE}}{True}{False}.\par
|\BB|=|\CC|?  \ifthenelse{\equal{\BB}{\CC}}{True}{False}.\par
|\DD|=|\BB|?  \ifthenelse{\equal{\DD}{\BB}}{True}{False}.
```

\BB=\EE? False.
\BB=\CC? True.

| A-3-5 | \DD=\BB? True.

One application for the preceding command could be in the definition of a command for printing an item and for entering it in the index. In the case where it is defined, the index entry will be typeset in boldface; otherwise, it will appear in a normal face. We use an optional argument for the least frequently occurring situation of the definition.

```
\usepackage{ifthen}
\newcommand{\IX}[2][R]{\texttt{#2}%
  \ifthenelse{\equal{#1}{D}}%
    {\index{#2|textbf}}{\index{#2}}}
we define item \IX[D]{AAAA}
\ldots{}    we reference item \IX{AAAA}
```

we define item AAAA ... we reference item AAAA

A-3-6

This gives the required visual representation in the .idx file by specifying entries of the following type:

```
\indexentry{AAAA|textbf}{874}    \indexentry{AAAA}{874}
```

A more complicated example, where you have complete control of what goes or does not go into the index or in the text, involves the extended index command \IXE, defined in the following example. Its default optional argument "!*!,!" contains a string that you will probably never want to use in the text (we hope). If you use the command \IXE with only one (normal) argument, then you will enter the same information into the index and the text. By specifying an optional argument, you can enter something in the index that is different from what is printed in the text. All possible combinations are shown below. The vertical bars around the commands show that no unwanted spaces are generated.

```
\usepackage{ifthen}
\newcommand\IXE[2][!*!,!]{%
 \ifthenelse{\equal{#1}{!*!,!}}%
   {\ifthenelse{\equal{#2}{}}{}{\textbf{#2}\index{#2}}}%
   {\ifthenelse{\equal{#1}{}}{}{\index{#1}}%
    \ifthenelse{\equal{#2}{}}{}{\textbf{#2}}}}
```

Identical in text and index |**both**|.
Different in text and index |**text**|.
Only to index ||.
In text only |**textonly**|.
Nothing in text or index ||.

```
\par Identical in text and index |\IXE{both}|.
\par Different in text and index |\IXE[index]{text}|.
\par Only to index |\IXE[indexonly]{}|.
\par In text only |\IXE[]{textonly}|.
\par Nothing in text or index |\IXE[]{}|.
```

A-3-7

The .idx file contains only three entries, since the case with the empty optional argument "[]" does not generate an index entry:

```
\indexentry{both}{874}
\indexentry{index}{874}
\indexentry{indexonly}{874}
```

TeX switches	
hmode	true, if typesetting is done in a horizontal direction (e.g., inside a paragraph or an LR box).
vmode	true, if typesetting is done vertically (e.g., if TeX is between paragraphs).
mmode	true, if TeX is typesetting a formula.
LaTeX switches	
@twoside	true, if LaTeX is typesetting for double-sided printing.
@twocolumn	true, if LaTeX is typesetting in standard two-column mode (false inside multicols environments).
@firstcolumn	true, if @twocolumn is true and LaTeX is typesetting the first column.
@newlist	true, if LaTeX is at the beginning of a list environment (will be set to false when text *after* the first \item command is encountered).
@inlabel	true, after an \item command until the text following it is encountered.
@noskipsec	true, after a run-in heading until the text following it is encountered.
@tempswa	Temporary switch used internally by many LaTeX commands to communicate with each other.

Table A.5: LaTeX's internal \boolean switches

> \boolean{*string*}   \newboolean{*string*}   \setboolean{*string*}{*value*}

Basic TeX knows about some switches that can have the value true or false.[1] To define your own switch, use \newboolean where *string* is a sequence of letters. This switch is initially set to false. To change its value, use \setboolean where the *value* argument is either the string true or false. You can then test the value by using \boolean in the first argument of \ifthenelse. It is also possible to test all such internal flags of LaTeX with this command (the most common ones are shown in Table A.5). An example could be a test to see whether a document is using a one- or two-sided layout.

\usepackage{ifthen}

| A-3-8 | Two-sided printing. | \ifthenelse{\boolean{@twoside}}{Two-sided}{One-sided} printing. |

> \lengthtest{*test*}

To compare dimensions, use \lengthtest. In its *test* argument you can compare two dimensions (either explicit values like 20cm or names defined by \newlength) using one of the operators <, =, or >.

As an example, let us consider a figure characterized by its dimensions \Xsize and \Ysize. It should be made to fit into a rectangular area with dimen-

---

[1] In the LaTeX kernel they are normally built using the more primitive \newif command.

sions \Xarea and \Yarea, but without changing the aspect ratio of the figure. The following code calculates the new dimensions of the figure (\newX and \newY). The trick is to first calculate and compare the aspect ratios of both the rectangle and the figure, and then to use the result to obtain the magnification factor.

```
\newlength{\sizetmp}\newlength{\areatmp}
\setlength\sizetmp{1pt*\ratio{\Xsize}{\Ysize}}
\setlength\areatmp{1pt*\ratio{\Xarea}{\Yarea}}
\ifthenelse{\lengthtest{\sizetmp > \areatmp}}%
  {\setlength\newX{\Xarea}\setlength\newY{\newX*\ratio{\Ysize}{\Xsize}}}
  {\setlength\newY{\Yarea}\setlength\newX{\newY*\ratio{\Xsize}{\Ysize}}}
```

> \isodd{*number*}

With the \isodd command you can test whether a given *number* is odd. If, for example, the string generated by a \pageref command is a valid number (as it normally is), then you can use the command in the following way:

This is an even-numbered page.	This is an odd-numbered page.
6	7

```
\usepackage{ifthen} \newcounter{pl}
\newcommand\pcheck{\stepcounter{pl}\label{pl-\thepl}%
  \ifthenelse{\isodd{\pageref{pl-\thepl}}}{odd}{even}}
This is an \pcheck-numbered page.  \newpage
This is an \pcheck-numbered page.
```

A-3-9

The \isodd command is specially tailored to support the above application even though the result of \pageref might be undefined in the first LᴬTEX run. Note that you cannot omit the \label and \pageref and instead simply use \thepage. The reason is that pages are built asynchronously. As a consequence, your code might get evaluated while a page is being built, and later on LᴬTEX's output routine might decide to move that bit of the text to the next page, making the evaluation invalid if \thepage were used.

> \whiledo{*test*}{*do-clause*}

The \whiledo command is valuable for executing certain repetitive command sequences. The following simple example shows how the command works:

I should not talk during seminar (1). I should not talk during seminar (2). I should not talk during seminar (3). I should not talk during seminar (4).

```
\usepackage{ifthen}  \newcounter{howoften}
\setcounter{howoften}{1}
\whiledo{\value{howoften}<5}{I should not talk
    during seminar (\thehowoften).
    \stepcounter{howoften}}
```

A-3-10

```
\and    \or    \not    \(    \)
```

Multiple conditions can be combined into logical expressions via the logical operators (\or, \and, and \not), using the commands \(and \) as parentheses. A simple example is seen below.

```
\usepackage{ifthen}
\newcommand{\QU}[2]{%
 \ifthenelse{\(\(\equal{#1}{ENG}\and\equal{#2}{yes}\)
     \or     \(\equal{#1}{FRE}\and\equal{#2}{oui}\)\)}%
        {``OK''}{``not OK''}}
```

A-3-11

You agree "OK" or don't "not OK".
D'accord "OK" ou pas "not OK"?

```
You agree \QU{ENG}{yes} or don't \QU{ENG}{no}. \par
D'accord  \QU{FRE}{oui} ou pas   \QU{FRE}{non}?
```

A.4 Package and class file structure

In this section we discuss what commands are available for the authors of package or class files. Even if you do not intend to write your own package, this section will help you understand the structure and content of class and package files like book or varioref, and thus help you to make better use of them.

The general structure of class and package files is identical and consists of the following parts:

⟨*identification*⟩
⟨*initial code*⟩
⟨*declaration of options*⟩
⟨*execution of options*⟩
⟨*package loading*⟩
⟨*main code*⟩

All these parts are optional. We discuss the commands available in each of the individual parts below. Table A.6 on page 879 gives a short overview.

A.4.1 The identification part

This part of a class or package file is used to define the nature of the file and may also state the LaTeX 2ε distribution release minimally required.

```
\ProvidesClass{name}[release information]
```

A class file identifies itself with a \ProvidesClass command. The argument *name* corresponds to the name of the class as it will be used in the mandatory argument of the \documentclass command (i.e., the file name without an extension). The optional argument *release information*, if present, should begin with a date in the form YYYY/MM/DD, separated with a space from the version number or identification, followed optionally by some text describing the class. For example, the class report contains something like

```
\ProvidesClass{report}[2001/04/21 v1.4e Standard LaTeX document class]
```

In a document you can make use of the *release information* by specifying the date as a second optional argument to the \documentclass command as follows:

```
\documentclass[twocolumn]{report}[2001/04/21]
```

This enables LATEX to check that the report class used has at least a release date of 2001/04/21 or is newer. If the class file is older, a warning is issued. Thus, if you make use of a new release of a class file and send your document to another site, the people there will be informed if their LATEX distribution is out of date.

> \ProvidesPackage{*name*}[*release information*]

This command identifies a package file. The structure is the same as for the \ProvidesClass command. Again, the date in the *release information* can be used in a second optional argument to \usepackage to ensure that an up-to-date version of the package file is loaded. For example:

```
\usepackage[german]{varioref}[2001/09/0]
```

> \ProvidesFile{*filename*}[*release information*]

This command identifies any other type of file. For this reason *filename* must contain the full file name including the extension.

> \NeedsTeXFormat{*format*}[*release*]

In addition to one of the above commands, the ⟨*identification*⟩ part usually contains a \NeedsTeXFormat declaration. The *format* must be the string LaTeX2e. If the optional *release* argument is specified, it should contain the release date of the required LATEX 2_ε distribution in the form YYYY/MM/DD. For example,

```
\NeedsTeXFormat{LaTeX2e}[2001/06/01]
```

would require at least the LATEX 2_ε release distributed on June 1, 2001. If this command is present, anyone who tries to use your code together with an older LATEX release will receive a warning message that something might fail. A newer release date is accepted without a warning.

All four declarations are optional. Nevertheless, their use in distributed class and package files will ease the maintenance of these files.

Identification part
`\NeedsTeXFormat{`*format*`}[`*release*`]`
Needs to run under *format* (LaTeX2e) with a release date not older than *release*
`\ProvidesClass{`*name*`}[`*release info*`]`   `\ProvidesPackage{`*name*`}[`*release info*`]`
Identifies class or package *name* and specifies *release information*
`\ProvidesFile{`*name*`}[`*release info*`]`
Identifies other file *name* (with extension) and specifies *release information*
Declaration of options
`\DeclareOption{`*option*`}{`*code*`}`
Declares *code* to be executed for *option*
`\PassOptionsToPackage{`*option list*`}{`*package-name*`}`
Passes *option-list* to *package-name*
`\DeclareOption*{`*code*`}`
Declares *code* to be executed for any unknown option
`\CurrentOption`
Refers to current option for use in `\DeclareOption*`
Execution of options
`\ExecuteOptions{`*option-list*`}`
Executes code for every option listed in *option-list*
`\ProcessOptions`   `\ProcessOptions*`
Processes specified options for current class or package; starred form obeys the specified order
Package loading
`\RequirePackage[`*option-list*`]{`*package*`}[`*release*`]`
Loads *package* with given *option-list* and a release date not older than *release*
Special commands for package and class files
`\AtEndOfPackage{`*code*`}`   `\AtEndOfClass{`*code*`}`
Defers execution of *code* to end of current package or class
`\AtBeginDocument{`*code*`}`   `\AtEndDocument{`*code*`}`
Executes *code* at `\begin{document}` or `\end{document}`
`\IfFileExists{`*file*`}{`*then-code*`}{`*else-code*`}`
Executes *then-code* if *file* exists, *else-code* otherwise
`\InputIfFileExists{`*file*`}{`*then-code*`}{`*else-code*`}`
If *file* exists, executes *then-code* and then inputs *file*; otherwise executes *else-code*
Special class file commands
`\LoadClass[`*option-list*`]{`*class*`}[`*release*`]`
Like `\RequirePackage` for class files, but does not see global options if not explicitly passed to it
`\PassOptionsToClass{`*option-list*`}{`*class*`}`
Passes *option-list* to *class*
`\OptionNotUsed`
For use in `\DeclareOption*` if necessary

Table A.6: Commands for package and class files

A.4.2   The initial code part

You can specify any valid LATEX code in the ⟨*initial code*⟩ part, including code that loads packages with the \RequirePackage command (see Section A.4.5) if their code is required in one of the option declarations. For example, you might want to load the calc package at this point, if you plan to use it later. However, normally this part is empty.

A.4.3   The declaration of options

In this part all options known to the package or class are declared using the \DeclareOption command. It is forbidden to load packages in this part.

\DeclareOption{*option*}{*code*}

The argument *option* is the name of the option being declared and *code* is the code that will execute if this option is requested. For example, the paper size option a4paper normally has a definition of the following form:

```
\DeclareOption{a4paper}{\setlength\paperheight{297mm}%
                       \setlength\paperwidth{210mm}}
```

In principle, any action—from setting a flag to complex programming instructions—is possible in the *code* argument of \DeclareOption.

    An important function for use in \DeclareOption is the command \PassOptionsToPackage. It can pass one or more options to some other package that is loaded later.

\PassOptionsToPackage{*option-list*}{*package-name*}

The argument *option-list* is a comma-separated list of options that should be passed to the package with name *package-name* when it is loaded in the ⟨*package loading*⟩ part.[1] Suppose, for example, that you want to define a class file that makes use of two packages, say, A and B, both supporting the option infoshow. To support such an option in the class file as well, you could declare

```
\DeclareOption{infoshow}{%
    \PassOptionsToPackage{infoshow}{A}%
    \PassOptionsToPackage{infoshow}{B}%
    ⟨code to support infoshow in the class⟩}
```

    If a package or class file is loaded with an option that it does not recognize, it will issue a warning (in case of a package file) or silently ignore the option (in case of a class file), assuming that it is a global option to be passed to other packages

---

[1]It is the responsibility of the package writer to actually load such packages. LATEX does not check that packages receiving options via \PassOptionsToPackage are actually loaded later on.

subsequently loaded with \usepackage. However, this behavior is not hard-wired and can be modified using a \DeclareOption* declaration.

\DeclareOption*{*code*}

The argument *code* specifies the action to take if an unknown option is specified on the \usepackage or \RequirePackage command. Within this argument \CurrentOption refers to the name of the option in question. For example, to write a package that extends the functionality of some other package, you could use the following declaration:

Command does not act on global options!

```
\DeclareOption*{\PassOptionsToPackage{\CurrentOption}{A}}
```

This would pass all options not declared by your package to package A. If no \DeclareOption* declaration is given, the default action, described above, will be used.

By combining \DeclareOption* with \InputIfFileExists (see below), you can even implement conditional option handling. For example, the following code tries to find files whose names are built up from the option name:

```
\DeclareOption*{\InputIfFileExists{g-\CurrentOption.xyz}{}%
      {\PackageWarning{somename}{Option \CurrentOption\space
                                      not recognized}}}
```

If the file g-*option*.xyz can be found, it will be loaded; otherwise, the option is ignored with a warning.

A.4.4 The execution of options

Two types of actions are normally carried out after all options are declared. You might want to set some defaults, such as the default paper size. Then the list of options specified needs to be examined and the code for each such option needs to be executed.

\ExecuteOptions{*option-list*}

The \ExecuteOptions command executes the code for every option listed in *option-list* in the order specified. It is just a convenient shorthand to set up defaults by executing code specified earlier with a \DeclareOption command. For example, the standard class **book** issues something similar to

```
\ExecuteOptions{letterpaper,twoside,10pt}
```

to set up the defaults. You can also use \ExecuteOptions when declaring other options, such as a definition of an option that automatically implies others. The \ExecuteOptions command can be used only prior to executing the

\ProcessOptions command because, as one of its last actions, the latter command reclaims all of the memory taken up by the code for the declared options.

```
\ProcessOptions
```

When the \ProcessOptions command is encountered, it examines the list of options specified for this class or package and executes the corresponding code. More precisely, when dealing with a package the global options (as specified on the \documentclass command) and the directly specified options (the optional argument to the \usepackage or \RequirePackage command) are tested. For every option declared by the package, the corresponding code is executed. This execution occurs in the same order in which the options were specified by the \DeclareOption declarations in the package, not in the order in which they appear on the \usepackage command. Global options that are not recognized are ignored. For all other unrecognized options the code specified by \DeclareOption* is executed or, if this declaration is missing, an error is issued.

Thus, packages that use only \DeclareOption* when declaring options will not act upon global options specified on the \documentclass, but rather will accept only those that are explicitly given on the \usepackage or \RequirePackage declaration.

In the case of a class file, the action of \ProcessOptions is the same without the added complexity of the global options.

There is one potential problem when using \ProcessOptions: the command *Preventing* searches for a following star (even on subsequent lines) and thereby may incor-*unwanted expansion* rectly expand upcoming commands following it. To avoid this danger use \relax at the end to stop the search immediately and start the execution of the options.

```
\ProcessOptions*
```

For some packages it may be more appropriate if they process their options in the order specified on the \usepackage command rather than using the order given through the sequence of \DeclareOption commands. For example, in the babel package, the last language option specified is supposed to determine the main document language. Such a package can execute the options in the order specified by using \ProcessOptions* instead of \ProcessOptions.

A.4.5 The package loading part

Once the options are dealt with, it might be time to load one or more additional packages—for example, those to which you have passed options using \PassOptionsToPackage.

```
\RequirePackage [option-list] {package} [release]
```

This command is the package/class counterpart to the document command \usepackage. If *package* was not loaded before, it will be loaded now with the options specified in *option-list*, the global options from the \documentclass command, and all options passed to this package via \PassOptionsToPackage.

LATEX loads a package only once because in many cases it is dangerous to execute the code of a package several times. Thus, if you require a package with a certain set of options, but this package was previously loaded with a different set not including all options requested at this time, then the user of your package has a problem. In this situation LATEX issues an error message informing users of your package about the conflict and suggesting that they load the package with a \usepackage command and all necessary options.

The optional *release* argument can be used to request a package version not older than a certain date. For this scheme to work, the required package must contain a \ProvidesPackage declaration specifying a release date.

\RequirePackageWithOptions{*package*}[*release*]

This command works like \RequirePackage except that the options passed to it are exactly those specified for the calling package or class. This facilitates the generation of variant packages that take exactly the same set of options as the original. See also the discussion of \LoadClassWithOptions on page 887.

A.4.6 The main code part

This final part of the file defines the characteristics and implements the functions provided by the given class or package. It can contain any valid LATEX construct and usually defines new commands and structures. It is good style to use standard LATEX commands, as described in this appendix, such as \newlength, \newcommand, \CheckCommand, and so on, rather than relying on primitive TEX commands, as the latter do not test for possible conflicts with other packages.

A.4.7 Special commands for package and class files

\AtEndOfPackage{*code*}   \AtEndOfClass{*code*}

Sometimes it is necessary to defer the execution of some code to the end of the current package or class file. The above declarations save the *code* argument and execute it when the end of the package or class is reached. If more than one such declaration is present in a file, the *code* is accumulated and finally executed in the order in which the declarations were given.

\AtBeginDocument{*code*}   \AtEndDocument{*code*}

Other important points at which you might want to execute deferred code are the beginning and the end of the document or, more exactly, the points where the \begin{document} and \end{document} are processed. The above commands allow packages to add code to this environment without creating any conflicts with other packages trying to do the same.

Note, however, that code in the `\AtBeginDocument` hook is part of the preamble. Thus, restrictions limit what can be put there; in particular, no typesetting can be done.

`\IfFileExists{`*file*`}{`*then-code*`}{`*else-code*`}`
`\InputIfFileExists{`*file*`}{`*then-code*`}{`*else-code*`}`

If your package or class tries to `\input` a file that does not exist, the user ends up in TeX's file-error loop. It can be exited only by supplying a valid file name. Your package or class can avoid this problem by using `\IfFileExists`. The argument *file* is the file whose existence you want to check. If this *file* is found by LATEX, the commands in *then-code* are executed; otherwise, those in *else-code* are executed. The command `\InputIfFileExists` not only tests whether *file* exists, but also inputs it immediately after executing *then-code*. The name *file* is then added to the list of files to be displayed by `\listfiles`.

`\PackageWarning{`*name*`}{`*warning-text*`}`
`\PackageWarningNoLine{`*name*`}{`*warning-text*`}`
`\PackageInfo{`*name*`}{`*info-text*`}`

When a package detects a problem it can alert the user by printing a warning message on the terminal. For example, when the multicol package detects that `multicols*` (which normally generates unbalanced columns) is used inside a box, it issues the following warning:[1]

```
\PackageWarning{multicol}{multicols* inside a box does
  not make sense.\MessageBreak  Going to balance anyway}
```

This will produce a warning message, which is explicitly broken into two lines via the `\MessageBreak` command:

```
Package multicol Warning: multicols* inside a box does not make sense.
(multicol)                Going to balance anyway on input line 6.
```

The current line number is automatically appended. Sometimes it would be nice to display the current file name as well, but unfortunately this information is not available on the macro level.

Depending on the nature of the problem, it might be important to tell the user the source line on which the problem was encountered. In other cases this information is irrelevant, such as when the problem happens while the package is being loaded. In this situation `\PackageWarningNoLine` should be used; it produces the same result as `\PackageWarning` but omits the phrase "on input line *num*".

---

[1] In a box, balancing is essential since a box can grow arbitrarily in vertical direction, so all material would otherwise end up in the first column.

If the information is of lower importance and should appear just in the transcript file, then one can use `\PackageInfo`. For example, after loading the shortvrb package and issuing the declaration `\MakeShortVerb\=`, the transcript file will show the following:

```
Package shortvrb Info: Made = a short reference for \verb on input line 3.
```

A `\PackageInfoNoLine` command is not provided. If you really want to suppress the line number in an informational message, use `\@gobblo` as the last token in the second argument of `\PackageInfo`.

`\PackageError{`*name*`}{`*short-text*`}{`*long-text*`}`

If the problem detected is severe enough to require user intervention, one can signal an error instead of a warning. If the error is encountered, the *short-text* is displayed immediately and processing stops. For example, if inputenc encounters an 8-bit character it does not recognize, it will produce the following error:

```
! Package inputenc Error: Keyboard character used is undefined
(inputenc)                 in inputencoding 'latin1'.

See the inputenc package documentation for explanation.
Type  H <return>  for immediate help.
 ...

l.5 abc^^G
?
```

If the user then presses "h" or "H", the *long-text* is offered. In this case it is:

```
You need to provide a definition with \DeclareInputText
or \DeclareInputMath before using this key.
```

As before, you can explicitly determine the line breaks in the error and help texts by using `\MessageBreak`.

`\ClassWarning{`*name*`}{`*warning-text*`}`
`\ClassWarningNoLine{`*name*`}{`*warning-text*`}`
`\ClassInfo{`*name*`}{`*info-text*`}`
`\ClassError{`*name*`}{`*short-text*`}{`*long-text*`}`

Information, warning, and error commands are not only available for packages—similar commands are provided for document classes. They differ only in the produced texts: the latter commands print "Class" instead of "Package" in the appropriate places.

```
% ----------------------------- identification -----------------------
\NeedsTeXFormat{LaTeX2e}
\ProvidesClass{myart}[1994/01/01]
% ---------------------------- initial code ------------------------
\RequirePackage{ifthen}      \newboolean{cropmarks}
% ------------------------- declaration of options --
\DeclareOption{cropmarks}{\setboolean{cropmarks}{true}}
\DeclareOption{bind}     {\AtEndOfClass{\addtolength\oddsidemargin{.5in}%
                         \addtolength\evensidemargin{-.5in}}}
\DeclareOption*          {\PassOptionsToClass{\CurrentOption}{article}}
% ------------------------- execution of options ---------------------
\ProcessOptions
% -----------------------------package loading ---------------------
\LoadClass{article}                        % the real code
% ---------------------------- main code ------------------------
\newenvironment{Notes}{...}{...}           % the new environment
\ifthenelse{\boolean{cropmarks}}           % support for cropmarks
   {\renewcommand{\ps@plain}{...} ...}{}
```

Figure A.1: An example of a class file extending article

A.4.8   Special commands for class files

It is sometimes helpful to build a class file as a customization of a given general class. To support this concept two commands are provided.

> \LoadClass [*option-list*] {*class*} [*release*]

The \LoadClass command works like the \RequirePackage command with the following three exceptions:

- The command can be used only in class files.

- There can be at most one \LoadClass command per class.

- The global options are not seen by the *class* unless explicitly passed to it via \PassOptionsToClass or specified in the *option-list*.

> \PassOptionsToClass{*option-list*}{*class*}

The command \PassOptionsToClass can be used to pass options to such a general class. An example of such a class file augmentation is shown in Figure A.1. It defines a class file myart that accepts two extra options, cropmarks (making crop marks for trimming the pages) and bind (shifting the printed pages slightly to the outside to get a larger binding margin), as well as one additional environment, Notes.

The `cropmarks` option is implemented by setting a Boolean switch and re-defining various `\pagestyles` if this switch is `true`. The `bind` option modifies the values of `\oddsidemargin` and `\evensidemargin`. These length registers do not have their final values at the time the `bind` option is encountered (they are set later, when the article class is loaded by `\LoadClass`), so the modification is deferred until the end of the `myart` class file using the `\AtEndOfClass` command.

`\OptionNotUsed`

If your *code* for `\DeclareOption*` inside a class file is more complex (e.g., trying to handle some options but rejecting others), you might need to explicitly inform LATEX that the option was not accepted with the help of the `\OptionNotUsed` command. Otherwise, LATEX will think that the option was used and will not produce a warning if the option is not picked up by a later package.

`\LoadClassWithOptions{`*class*`}[`*release*`]`

This command is similar to `\LoadClass`, but it always calls the *class* with exactly the same option list that is being used by the current class, rather than the options explicitly supplied or passed on by `\PassOptionsToClass`. It is mainly intended to allow one class to build on another. For example:

```
\LoadClassWithOptions{article}
```

This should be contrasted with the following slightly different construction:

```
\DeclareOption*{\PassOptionsToClass{\CurrentOption}{article}}
\ProcessOptions                    \LoadClass{article}
```

As used here, the effects are more or less the same, but the version using `\LoadClassWithOptions` is slightly quicker (and less onerous to type). If, however, the class declares options of its own, then the two constructions are different. Compare, for example,

```
\DeclareOption{landscape}{...}
\ProcessOptions                    \LoadClassWithOptions{article}
```

with:

```
\DeclareOption{landscape}{...}
\DeclareOption*{\PassOptionsToClass{\CurrentOption}{article}}
\ProcessOptions                    \LoadClass{article}
```

In the first example, the article class will be called with the option `landscape` only when the current class is called with this option. In the second example, however, the option `landscape` will never be passed to the article class, because the default option handler only passes options that are *not* explicitly declared.

```
\@ifpackageloaded{package}{true-code}{false-code}
\@ifpackagelater{package}{date}{true-code}{false-code}
\@ifpackagewith{package}{options}{true-code}{false-code}
```

Sometimes it is useful to be able to find out if a package was already loaded, and if so, how. For this purpose, three commands are made available to class (and package) writers. To find out if a *package* has already been loaded, use `\@ifpackageloaded`. If it was loaded, the *true-code* is executed; otherwise, the *false-code* is executed. To find out if a *package* has been loaded with a version more recent than *date*, use `\@ifpackagelater`. Finally, to find out if a *package* has been loaded with at least the options in the (comma-separated) list *options*, use `\@ifpackagewith`.

The `fontenc` package cannot be tested with the above commands. That's because it pretends that it was never loaded to allow for repeated reloading with different options (see the file `ltoutenc.dtx` in the LaTeX distribution for details).

A.4.9   A minimal class file

Every class file *must* contain four things: a definition of `\normalsize`, values for `\textwidth` and `\textheight`, and a specification for page numbering. Thus, a minimal document class file[1] looks like this:

```
\NeedsTeXFormat{LaTeX2e}
\ProvidesClass{minimal}[1995/10/30 Standard LaTeX minimal class]
\renewcommand\normalsize{\fontsize{10pt}{12pt}\selectfont}
\setlength\textwidth{6.5in}
\setlength\textheight{8in}
\pagenumbering{arabic}        % needed even though this class will
                             % not show page numbers
```

This class file will, however, not support footnotes, marginals, floats, or other features. Naturally, most classes will contain more than this minimum!

---

[1] This class is in the standard distribution, as `minimal.cls`.

Tracing and Resolving Problems

In an ideal world all documents you produced would compile without problems and give high-quality output as intended. If you are that lucky, there will be no need for you to consult this appendix, ever. However, if you run into a problem of some kind, the material in this appendix should help you to resolve your problem easily.

We start with an alphabetical list of all error messages, those after which LaTeX stops and asks for advice. "All" in this context means all LaTeX kernel errors (their text starts with LaTeX Error:), practically all TeX errors (i.e., those directly produced by the underlying engine), and errors from the packages amsmath, babel, docstrip, calc, color, graphics, graphicx, inputenc, fontenc, and textcomp. Errors reported by other packages—those that identify themselves as

    ! Package ⟨*package*⟩ Error: ⟨*error text*⟩

where ⟨*package*⟩ is not one of the above—are not included. For such errors you should refer to the package description elsewhere in the book or consult the original package documentation.

But even if there are no real errors that stop the processing, warning and information messages might be shown on the terminal or in the transcript file. They are treated in Section B.2, where you will find all LaTeX core messages and all relevant TeX messages that may need your attention, together with an explanation of their possible causes and suggestions on how to deal with them.

The final section deals with tools for tracing problems in case the error or warning information itself is not sufficient or does not exist. We will explore ways to display command definitions and register values, then take a look at diagnosing and solving page-breaking problems. This is followed by suggestions for identifying and solving paragraph-breaking problems. We finish with a description of the trace package, which helps in thoroughly tracing command execution, in case your own definitions or those of others produce unexpected results.

Some of the material in this appendix can be considered "low-level" TEX, something that, to the authors' knowledge, has never been described in a "LATEX" book. It is, however, often important information. Directing the reader to books like *The TEXbook* does not really help, since most of the advice given in books about plain TEX is not applicable to LATEX or produces subtle errors when used. We therefore try to be as self-contained as possible by offering all relevant information about the underlying TEX engine as far as it makes sense within the LATEX context.

B.1   Error messages

When LATEX stops to display an error message, it also shows a line number indicating how far it got in the document source. However, because of memory considerations in the design of TEX itself, it does not directly show to which file this source line number belongs. For simple documents this is not a problem, but if your document is split over many files you may have to carefully look at the terminal output or the transcript file to identify the file LATEX is currently working on when the error occurs.

Finding the source Whenever LATEX starts reading a file, it displays a "(" character that is immedi-
line of an error ately followed by the file name. Once LATEX has finished reading the file, it displays the matching ")" character. In addition, whenever it starts preparing to output a page, it displays a "[" character followed by the current page number. Thus, if you see something like

```
(./trial.tex [1] (./ch-1.tex [2] [3] (./table-1.tex [4] [5]) [6]
! Undefined control sequence.
<argument> A \textss
                         {Test}
l.235 \section{A \textss{Test}}
                                  \label{sec:test}

?
```

you can deduce that the error happened inside an argument of some command (<argument>) and was detected when LATEX gathered material for page 7. It got as far as reading most of line 235 in the file ch-1.tex. In this example the error is readily visible in the source line: \textsf was misspelled as \textss inside the argument to the \section command. In some cases, however, the relationship between error and source line is blurred or even nonexistent.

For example, if you define `\renewcommand\thepart{\Alp{part}}`, then the typo will appear only when you use the `\part` command that executes your definition. In that case you get

```
! Undefined control sequence.
\thepart ->\Alp
                {part}
l.167 \par{Test}
```

In this particular case the actual error is not on line 167 and most likely not even in the current file—the `\part` command merely happens to call the faulty definition of `\thepart`.

Sometimes an error is detected by LATEX while it is preparing a new page. Since this is an asynchronous operation, the source line listed in the error message is of no value whatsoever. So if you do not understand how the error should be related to the source line, you may well be right—there is, indeed, no relationship. Here is an example:

```
! Undefined control sequence.
\thepage ->\romen
                  {page}
l.33 T
       his is a sample text to fill the page.
```

One way to obtain additional information about an error (or information about how LATEX intends to deal with it) is to reply ⟨*h*⟩ in response to the ? that follows the error message. If used with a TEX error such as the one above, we get

```
? h
The control sequence at the end of the top line
of your error message was never \def'ed. If you have
misspelled it (e.g., '\hobx'), type 'I' and the correct
spelling (e.g., 'I\hbox'). Otherwise just continue,
and I'll forget about whatever was undefined.
```

You probably already see the problem with advice coming directly from the TEX engine: you may have to translate it, because it often talks about commands that are not necessarily adequate for LATEX documents (e.g., for `\def` you should read `\newcommand` or `\renewcommand`). With real LATEX errors this is not the case, though here you sometimes get advice that is also not really helpful:

```
You're in trouble here.  Try typing  <return>  to proceed.
If that doesn't work, type  X <return>  to quit.
```

Well, thank you very much, we already knew that! It is, however, worth a try, since there are many messages with more detailed advice.

Displaying the stack of partially expanded macros

Another way to get additional information about an encountered error is to set the counter `errorcontextlines` to a large positive value. In that case LATEX will list the stack of the current macro executions:

```
1   ! Undefined control sequence.
2   \thepage ->\romen
3                        {page}
4   \@oddfoot ->\reset@font \hfil \thepage
5                                        \hfil
6   \@outputpage ...lor \hb@xt@ \textwidth {\@thefoot
7                                         }\color@endbox }}\globa...
8
9   \@opcol ...lumn \@outputdblcol \else \@outputpage
10                                        \fi \global \@mparbotto...
11  <output> ...specialoutput \else \@makecol \@opcol
12                                        \@startcolumn \@whilesw...
13  <to be read again>
14                       T
15  l.33 T
16        his is a sample text to fill the page.
```

You read this bottom up: LATEX has seen the T (lines 15 and 16) but wants to read it again later (`<to be read again>`, lines 13 and 14) because it switched to the output routine (`<output>`). There it got as far as executing the command `\@opcol` (lines 11 and 12), which in turn got as far as calling `\@outputpage` (lines 9 and 10), which was executing `\@thefoot` (lines 6 and 7). Line 4 is a bit curious since it refers to `\@oddfoot` rather than `\@thefoot` as one would expect (`\@thefoot` expands to `\@oddfoot`, so it is immediately fully expanded and not put onto the stack of partially expanded macros). Inside `\@oddfoot` we got as far as calling `\thepage`, which in turn expanded to `\romen` (lines 1 and 2), which is finally flagged as an undefined command (line 1).

Fortunately, in most cases it is sufficient only to display the error message and the source line. This is why LATEX's default value for `errorcontextlines` is `-1`, which means not showing any intermediate context.

Persistent errors

Errors can also occur when LATEX is processing an intermediate file used to transfer information between two runs (e.g., `.aux` or `.toc` files). Data in such files can be corrupted due to an error that happened in a previous run. Even if you have corrected that error in your source, traces of it may still be present in such external files. Therefore, in some cases you may have to delete those files before running LATEX again, although often the problem vanishes after another run.

Errors due to fragile commands

Common sources for such nasty errors in LATEX are so-called *fragile* commands used unprotected in *moving arguments*. Technically, a moving argument is an argument that is internally expanded by LATEX without typesetting it directly, by using the internal LATEX construct `\protected@edef`.[1] But as a rule of thumb you

---

[1] Some people have heard that the TEX primitive `\edef` exists for this purpose. It is not advisable to use it in your own commands, however, unless you know that it will never receive arbitrary document input. You should use `\protected@edef` instead, since that command prevents fragile commands from breaking apart if they are prefixed by `\protect`!

can think of it as an argument that is moved somewhere else before typesetting—for example, the arguments of sectioning commands, such as \section (sent to the table of contents), the argument of \caption (sent to the list of figures or tables), and the arguments of \markboth and \markright.

The best, though not very helpful, definition of a fragile command is that it is a command that produces errors if it is not preceded with a \protect command when used in a moving argument. Today, most common LaTeX commands have been made robust, so that such protection is not necessary. However, if you get strange errors from a command used in a moving argument, try preceding it with \protect. Typically, core LaTeX commands with optional arguments are fragile, but \sqrt[3]{-1} is robust and so are *all* user-defined commands with an optional argument. On the other hand, \cong is fragile in standard LaTeX, yet it becomes robust once the amsmath package is loaded. In other words, there are no precise rules defining which commands belong to which category. User-defined commands with only mandatory arguments are fragile if they contain any fragile commands in their definition. For example, the definition

```
\newcommand\frail{\ifthenelse{\value{section}<10 \and
                  \value{subsection}=1}%
                 {\typeout{Yes}}{\typeout{No}}}
```

is fragile because the comparison argument of \ifthenelse is fragile. If you used \frail in the @ expression of a tabular (not that this makes much sense),

```
\nonstopmode        \begin{tabular}{@{\frail}l} x \end{tabular}
```

you would see the following 134 errors before LaTeX finally gives up (the left column displays the number of occurrences):

```
 1 ! Argument of \@array has an extra }.
 2 ! Argument of \@firstoftwo has an extra }.
 1 ! Extra }, or forgotten $.
 4 ! Extra }, or forgotten \endgroup.
 1 ! LaTeX Error:  Illegal character in array arg.
 1 ! LaTeX Error: Can be used only in preamble.
51 ! Misplaced \cr.
 2 ! Missing # inserted in alignment preamble.
 1 ! Missing = inserted for \ifnum.
49 ! Missing \cr inserted.
 2 ! Missing control sequence inserted.
 2 ! Missing number, treated as zero.
 1 ! Missing { inserted.
 2 ! Missing } inserted.
 1 ! Paragraph ended before \renew@command was complete.
 2 ! Paragraph ended before \reserved@b was complete.
 1 ! Paragraph ended before \reserved@c was complete.
```

```
2 ! Undefined control sequence.
1 ! Use of \@argtabularcr doesn't match its definition.
7 ! Use of \@array doesn't match its definition.
```

In fact, in this particular example TeX gets into a loop in which it tries to insert a \cr command, immediately rejects its own idea, and then repeats this process.

All TeX errors ⬙ What we can learn from this example is the following: whenever you encounter
can be caused by a strange TeX error that has no simple explanation (e.g., a misspelled command
a fragile command name), it is possibly due to a fragile command that got broken in a moving
in a moving argument—so try protecting it with \protect at the point where the error oc-
argument! curs. Since this can be the reason behind every TeX error, we shall not repeat this
possible cause for every one of them (after all, more than 60 TeX error messages
are explained below).

Errors ⬙ As discussed in Section A.1.1, a few restrictions are placed on the charac-
produced by ters that can be used in reference key arguments of \label and \bibitem. In a
cross-reference keys nutshell, such keys sometimes act like moving arguments and, depending on the
combination characters used and the packages loaded, all kinds of dreadful TeX
errors may show up. In that case protection with using the \protect command
will *not* work; instead, you have to use a simpler key conforming to the syntax
restrictions for such keys.

Alphabetical listing of TeX and LaTeX errors

In the list of errors below, all TeX and all package errors are flagged with a boxed
reference at the end of the error message. Unflagged error messages are LaTeX
errors with the prefix "LaTeX Error:" omitted.

* If LaTeX stops by just displaying a star, then it has reached the end of
  your source document without seeing a request to finish the job (i.e.,
  \end{document} or \stop) and is now waiting for input from the terminal.
  While this is in itself not an error, in most circumstances it means that something went seriously wrong. If there have been no previous errors and your
  document finishes with \end{document}, then you might have forgotten to
  close a verbatim environment so that the remainder of the document was
  processed "verbatim". To find the source of this problem in a large document,
  reply \end{foo}, which either should give you an "Environment ... ended
  by..." error (indicating what environment LaTeX thinks is still open) will be
  swallowed without any reaction, in which case you know that you are indeed
  in some "verbatim" context. In the latter event, try to interrupt LaTeX (by pressing Control-C or whatever your installation requires) and reply with "x" to
  the "Interruption" error to quit the job. Looking afterwards at the last page
  in the typeset document usually gives some hint about where things started
  to go wrong.

`'⟨character⟩' invalid at this point` `calc`

> You loaded the calc package and one of the formulas in `\setcounter`, `\setlength`, `\addtocounter`, or `\addtolength` used a syntax not supported by calc. See Section A.3.1 for details.

`⟨command⟩ allowed only in math mode` `amsmath`

> This command or environment can be used only in math mode. Check carefully to see what is missing from your document.

`⟨name⟩ undefined`

> This error is triggered when you use `\renewcommand` for a ⟨name⟩ that is unknown to LATEX. Either ⟨name⟩ was misspelled or you should have used `\newcommand` instead.

`\< in mid line`

> The `\<`, defined within a tabbing environment, was encountered in the middle of a line. It can be used only at the beginning of a line (e.g., after `\\`).

`A <Box> was supposed to be here` `TEX`

> This error is the result of using a box command, such as `\sbox`, with an invalid first argument (i.e., one not declared with `\newsavebox`). Usually, you first get the error "Missing number, treated as zero" indicating that TEX uses box register zero.

`Accent ⟨command⟩ not provided by font family ⟨name⟩` `textcomp`

> The textcomp package implements the TS1 encoding, which is unfortunately implemented fully by just a minority of the font families usable with LATEX. No accent will be printed. See Section 7.5.4 for information on how to provide an alternative representation for it.

`Argument of ⟨command⟩ has an extra }` `TEX`

> A right brace was used in place of a mandatory command argument (e.g., `\mbox}`). Fragile commands, when used without `\protect` in a moving argument, often break in a way that generates this or one of the other "extra" errors discussed below.

`Bad \line or \vector argument`

> LATEX issues this error if you specified a negative length or used an illegal slope with either `\line` or `\vector`. In the latter case, see Chapter 10 for alternatives.

`Bad math environment delimiter`

> This error is triggered when a `\(` or `\[` command is encountered inside a formula, or when `\)` or `\]` is found in normal text. Check whether these commands are properly matched in your document.

`\begin{⟨env⟩} allowed only in paragraph mode` `amsmath`

> There are many places, such as within LR-mode text or math mode, where it

does not make sense to have a math display. With amsmath the whole display ⟨*env*⟩ will simply be ignored.

`\begin{split}` won't work here [amsmath]

Either this `split` environment is not within an equation or perhaps you need to use `aligned` here.

`\begin{`⟨*env*⟩`}` on input line ⟨*line number*⟩ ended by `\end{`⟨*other env*⟩`}`

You receive this error when LaTeX detects that the environment ⟨*env*⟩ was incorrectly terminated with the end-tag for the environment ⟨*other env*⟩. The most likely case is that you, indeed, forgot to close the environment ⟨*env*⟩.

Another possible source of this error is trying to use verbatim-like environments or an amsmath display environment inside the definition of your own environments, which is often impossible. See Section 3.4.3 on page 164 for solutions involving verbatim-like environments.

If neither is the case and you are absolutely sure that all environments are properly nested, then somewhere between the start of ⟨*env*⟩ and the point where the error was found there must be a command that issues an `\endgroup` without a prior matching `\begingroup` so that LaTeX is fooled into believing that the ⟨*env*⟩ environment ended at this point. One way to find that problem is to move the end-tag closer to the begin-tag, until the problem disappears.

`Can be used only in preamble`

LaTeX has encountered a command or environment that should be used only inside a package or the preamble (i.e., before `\begin{document}`). This error can also be caused by a second `\begin{document}`.

`Cannot include graphics of type:` ⟨*ext*⟩ [graphics/graphicx]

You will get this error if you have specified a graphics type in the second argument of `\DeclareGraphicsRule` or used the `type` keyword of `\includegraphics` for which the loaded graphics driver has no support.

`Cannot be used in preamble`

Some commands—for example, `\nocite`—are allowed only in the document body (i.e., after `\begin{document}`). Move the declaration to that point.

`Cannot define Unicode char value < 00A0` [inputenc]

Values less than "00A0 (decimal 160) are either invalid as Unicode values for text characters or must not be redefined in LaTeX.

`Cannot determine size of graphic in` ⟨*file*⟩ [graphics/graphicx]

You did not specify an explicit image size on the `\includegraphics` command and LaTeX was unable to determine the image size from the graphics ⟨*file*⟩ directly. It does this automatically, for example, for `.eps` files reading the bounding box information, but is unable to extract this information from binary bitmap images such as `.jpg`, `.gif`, and `.png` files.

`\caption outside float`

> A `\caption` command was found outside a float environment, such as a `figure` or `table`. This error message is disabled by some of the extension packages described in Chapter 6.

`Command ⟨name⟩ already defined`

> You try to declare a command, an environment, a new savebox, a length, or a counter with a ⟨*name*⟩ that already has a meaning in LaTeX. Your declaration is ignored and you have to choose a different name. This error is also triggered if you use `\newcommand` with a ⟨*name*⟩ starting in `\end...`, even if `\renewcommand` claims the ⟨*name*⟩ is unused. It will also be issued if you try to define an environment ⟨*name*⟩ but the command `\end⟨name⟩` already has a definition. For instance, you cannot define an environment `graf` because TeX has a low-level command called `\endgraf`.

`Command ⟨name⟩ invalid in math mode`

> This is either a warning or an error message indicating that you have used a command in math mode that should be used only in normal text. In case of an error message, use h to get further help.

`Command ⟨name⟩ not defined as a math alphabet`

> This error is issued when you try to use `\SetMathAlphabet` on a ⟨*name*⟩ that was not previously declared with `\DeclareMathAlphabet` or `\DeclareSymbolFontAlphabet` to be a math alphabet identifier.

`Counter too large`

> This error is produced if you try to display a counter value with `\fnsymbol`, `\alph`, or `\Alph` and the value is outside the available range for the chosen display form.

`Corrupted NFSS tables`

> LaTeX tried some font substitution and detected an inconsistency in its internal tables. This error happens if font substitution was triggered and the substitution rules contain a loop (i.e., some circular `sub` declarations exist) or when the default substitution arguments for the current encoding point to a nonexistent font shape group.

`Dimension too large` `TeX`

> TeX can only deal with absolute sizes that are less than `16383.99998pt` (about 226 inches). Even on a huge page this range should be enough.

`\displaybreak cannot be applied here` `amsmath`

> An enclosing environment such as `split`, `aligned`, or `gathered` has created an unbreakable block.

`Division by 0` `graphics/graphicx`

> Usually, you will get this error when you scale a graphic that has a height of zero. This can happen unintentionally—for example, if you specify

`angle=-90,height=3cm` on `\includegraphics`. The rotation turns the image sideways, making the height zero, a value difficult to scale. In such a case use `totalheight` instead.

Double subscript `TEX`

Two subscripts appear in a row (e.g., `x_i_2`) and LaTeX does not know whether you mean x_{i2} or x_{i_2}. Add braces to indicate the subscripts: `x_{i_2}`.

Double superscript `TEX`

LaTeX found two superscripts in a row. See the explanation above.

Encoding file '⟨*name*⟩' not found `fontenc`

If you ask for encoding ⟨*enc*⟩, LaTeX tries to load the definitions for this encoding from the file ⟨*enc*⟩`enc.def` (after converting ⟨*enc*⟩ to lowercase letters). If this encoding file does not exist or cannot be found by LaTeX, you will get this error message.

Encoding scheme ⟨*name*⟩ unknown

The encoding scheme ⟨*name*⟩ you have specified in a declaration or in `\fontencoding` is not known to the system. Either you forgot to declare it using `\DeclareFontEncoding` or you misspelled its name.

Environment ⟨*name*⟩ undefined

You get this error if you use `\renewenvironment` on an environment name that is unknown to LaTeX. Either the ⟨*name*⟩ was misspelled or you should have used `\newenvironment` instead.

Erroneous nesting of equation structures; `amsmath`
trying to recover with 'aligned'

Only certain `amsmath` display structures can be nested; `aligned` is one of these, so the system replaces a wrongly nested environment with it. This is probably not what you intended, so you should change the wrongly nested environment.

Extra & on this line `amsmath`

This error occurs only when you are using old `amsmath` environments that are not described in this book. If it does occur, then it is disastrous and you need to check very carefully the environment where it occurred.

Extra alignment tab has been changed to \cr `TEX`

If you use an alignment structure, such as `tabular` or one of the display math environments (e.g., `eqnarray` or `split` from the `amsmath` package), then each row is divided into a defined number of columns separated by & signs. The error means that there are too many such characters, probably because you forgot a `\\` indicating the end of the row (`\cr` is TeX's name for the row end, but it is not a fully functional equivalent to `\\`).

Extra \endgroup `TEX`

TeX has seen an `\endgroup` without a preceding matching `\begingroup`.

`Extra \or` [TeX]

> TeX encountered an `\or` primitive that has no matching low-level `\ifcase` conditional.

`Extra \right` [TeX]

> This error is issued by TeX if it finds a `\right` command without a matching `\left` in a formula. Recall that `\left`/`\right` pairs must be part of the same "sub-formula". They cannot, for example, be separated by & in an alignment or appear on different grouping levels.

`Extra }, or forgotten $` [TeX]

> This error is triggered when math formula delimiters (e.g., `$...$`, `\[...\]`) and brace groups are not properly nested. TeX thinks it has found a superfluous `}`, as in `$x}$`, and is going to ignore it. While in this example the deletion of the closing brace is the right choice, it would be wrong in `\mbox{\(a}`. There a closing `\)` is missing, so deleting the `}` will produce additional errors.

`Extra }, or forgotten \endgroup` [TeX]

> The current group was started with `\begingroup` (used, for example, by `\begin{..}`) but TeX found a closing `}` instead of the corresponding `\endgroup`. You will get this error if you leave a stray `}` inside a body of an environment.

`File '⟨name⟩' not found`

> LaTeX is trying to load the file ⟨name⟩ but cannot find it, either because it does not exist or because the underlying TeX program is looking in the wrong place. If the file exists but LaTeX claims it is not available, it is possible that your TeX installation uses a hashing mechanism to speed up file access, and you may have to run a special program to make your installation aware of newly installed files (e.g., mktexlsr with the TeX live distribution on the CD-ROM).
>
> The error is issued by commands like `\input` and `\usepackage` if they cannot find the requested file. You can suggest an alternate file in response to the error. If the new name is specified without an extension, the old extension is reused if known to LaTeX. If you want to omit loading the file, press ⟨*Enter*⟩; to quit the run, type x or X. In some cases you might receive a similar low-level TeX error "! I can't find file '⟨name⟩'" that is slightly more difficult to quit; see the entry on page 901.
>
> If a graphics file requested with `\includegraphics` is missing, it may help to press h to learn which extensions have been tried when looking for the file.

`File ended while scanning ⟨something⟩` [TeX]

> This error is part of a "Runaway..." error; check the explanations on page 909.

`Float(s) lost`

> One or more floats (e.g., `figure` or `table`) or `\marginpar` commands have not been typeset. The most likely reason is that you placed a float environment or marginal note inside a box by mistake—inside another float or `\marginpar`,

or inside a `minipage` environment, a `\parbox`, or a `\footnote`. LaTeX might detect this problem very late, such as when finishing the document. This can make it very difficult to find the offending place in the source. The best solution in this case is to half your document repeatedly (for example, by using the primitive `\endinput`), until the fraction producing the error is small enough that you spot it.

If incorrect nesting is not the root cause, then you may have encountered a serious coding problem in the float algorithm, probably caused by some extra packages you loaded.

`Font family` ⟨*cdp*⟩+⟨*family*⟩ `unknown`
> You tried to declare a font shape group with `\DeclareFontShape` without first declaring the font ⟨*family*⟩ as being available in the encoding ⟨*cdp*⟩ using `\DeclareFontFamily`.

`Font` ⟨*name*⟩ `not found`
> LaTeX's internal font tables contain wrong information, so LaTeX was unable to find the external font ⟨*name*⟩. Either this font was never installed, its `.tfm` file cannot be found by TeX for some reason, or the `\DeclareFontShape` declaration referring to it contains a spelling error.

`Font` ⟨*internal-name*⟩=⟨*external-name*⟩ `not loadable:` ⟨*reason*⟩ [TeX]
> TeX was unable to load a font with the LaTeX name ⟨*internal-name*⟩ having the structure `\`⟨*encoding*⟩`/`⟨*family*⟩`/`⟨*series*⟩`/`⟨*shape*⟩`/`⟨*size*⟩ in NFSS notation.[1] For example, it might say `\T1/cmr/m/it/10` (Computer Modern medium italic 10 points in T1 encoding). This should give you a good hint as to which font has a problem, even if you are not able to do much about it. There are two possible ⟨*reason*⟩s:
>
> `Bad metric (TFM) file` [TeX]
> > The TeX metric file for the font (i.e., ⟨*external-name*⟩`.tfm`) is corrupted. Your installation may have some utility programs to check `.tfm` files in detail, although this usually requires expert help.
>
> `Metric (TFM) file not found` [TeX]
> > The TeX metric file for the font (i.e., ⟨*external-name*⟩`.tfm`) was not found. Your installation may have a package (e.g., cmbright) to support a certain font family but the corresponding fonts are not available or are not properly installed.

`Font` ⟨*internal-name*⟩=⟨*external*⟩ `not loaded: Not enough room left` [TeX]
> TeX can load only a certain number of fonts and there was no space left to load ⟨*internal-name*⟩. To find out which fonts are loaded, use the package tracefnt described in Section 7.5.6. One possible reason for excessive loading of fonts is the use of unusual font sizes for which LaTeX has to calculate and load the corresponding math fonts; see Section 7.10.7 for details.

---

[1]This is, in fact, a single command name, but due to the slashes in the name you cannot enter it directly in your document.

`Font shape ⟨font shape⟩ not found`

This error message is issued when there is something very wrong with a `\DeclareFontShape` declaration—perhaps if it does not contain any size specifications. Check the set-up for the font shape group in question.

`I can't find file '⟨name⟩'` ⌈TₑX⌉

A low-level TₑX error raised when TₑX cannot find a file that was requested to load. This error can be bypassed only by providing TₑX with a file that it can find, or by stopping the run altogether (if your operating system allows that). To get past this error, many installations offer a file `null.tex` so that you can reply `null` in response. LᴬTₑX normally uses the error message "File '⟨name⟩' not found", which supports various user actions. However, depending on the package coding, you may get the current error instead.

`I can't write on file '⟨name⟩'` ⌈TₑX⌉

TₑX is not allowed to write data to the file ⟨name⟩. It is probably read-only or you may not have writing permission for its directory. On some TₑX implementations (e.g., those on the TₑXlive CD), the error may be preceded by a line like the following:

```
tex: Not writing to /texmf/tex/latex/base/latex.ltx (openout_any = p).
```

These TₑX installations are by default configured to be "paranoid" (hence, "p" above) when writing to files. They allow you to write only to files below the current directory and *not* to any files specified with an absolute path name or starting with a dot in their name. To change that behavior you have to modify the settings in the file `texmf.cnf`.

`Illegal character in array arg`

You will get this error if the column specification for a `tabular` or `array` environment or a `\multicolumn` command contains characters that are not defined as column specifiers to LᴬTₑX. A likely cause is that you used the extended syntax of the `array` package, described in Chapter 5, but forgot to load the package in the preamble (e.g., after you have copied a table from one document to another).

`Illegal parameter number in definition of ⟨command⟩` ⌈TₑX⌉

This error occurs when a (re)defined command or environment uses #⟨*digit*⟩ in the replacement text, with a digit higher than the declared number of parameters. This error can be implicitly caused by nesting declaration commands, such as `\newcommand`, and forgetting that inner commands refer to their arguments by doubling the # characters; see page 846 for details. Another possible cause is referring to environment arguments in the second mandatory argument of `\newenvironment` or `\renewenvironment`.

`Illegal unit of measure (pt inserted)` ⌈TₑX⌉

You will get this error if you misspell or forget the unit when specifying the value for a length parameter; see Section A.1.5.

`Improper argument for math accent:`   amsmath
`Extra braces must be added to prevent wrong output`
> The whole of the "accented sub-formula" must be surrounded by braces.

`Improper discretionary list` TEX
> This error is produced by TeX if it encounters a `\disretionary` command whose arguments contain anything other than characters, boxes, or kerns, after expansion.

`Improper \hyphenation` TEX
> If you want to specify a hyphenation exception with `\hyphenation`, then you have to ensure that the argument contains only letters and – characters to indicate the hyphenation points. The problem is that, for example, accented characters in some font encodings are individual glyphs (allowed) but in other font encodings produce complicated constructs requiring the `\accent` primitive. For example, if the T1 encoding is used, then `\"u` refers to a single glyph. Thus,
>
> `\usepackage[T1]{fontenc} \hyphenation{T\"ur-stop-per}`
>
> is valid. The same hyphenation exception used with the default OT1 encoding would produce this error. See page 455 for an explanation of character differences in the major encodings.

`Improper \prevdepth` TEX
> You used `\the\prevdepth` or `\showthe\prevdepth` outside of vertical mode, which is not allowed. This error will also show up if you mistakenly placed a float (e.g., a `figure` or `table`) inside a math display environment.

`Improper \spacefactor` TEX
> You used `\the\spacefactor` or `\showthe\spacefactor` outside of horizontal mode, which is not allowed.

`\include cannot be nested`
> LaTeX encountered an `\include` command inside a file loaded with `\include`. Because of implementation constraints this is impossible. Either change the inner `\include` into `\input` or rearrange your document file structure so that all `\include` statements are in the main document file.

`Incompatible list can't be unboxed` TEX
> TeX was asked to unpack a box with horizontal material while trying to build a vertical list, or vice versa. Either you encountered a serious programming error in a package or you used some commands in a way explicitly not supported. For example, the commands from the soul package will produce this error when they are nested into each other.

`Incomplete ⟨conditional⟩; all text was ignored after line ⟨number⟩` TEX
> A low-level TeX conditional was unfinished (no matching `\fi`) when LaTeX reached the end of the current input file.

`Infinite glue shrinkage found` ⟨*somewhere*⟩ [TeX]

To break paragraphs into lines or the galley into pages, TeX assumes that there is no rubber length that can arbitrarily shrink, since that would mean that any amount of material can be placed into a single line or onto a single page. Thus, `\hspace{0pt minus 1fil}` in a paragraph, or `\vspace{0pt minus 1fil}` between paragraphs is not allowed and will raise this error (⟨*somewhere*⟩ gives some indication about where the offending material was found).

`Interruption` [TeX]

You will get this error after interrupting the LaTeX run (with Control-C or whatever your installation offers), so you should not be surprised by it. To finish the run prematurely, press x followed by ⟨*Return*⟩. Just pressing ⟨*Return*⟩ will continue the run.

`Invalid use of` ⟨*command*⟩ [amsmath]

You have used an amsmath command in a place where it does not make sense. Look up the correct use of this command.

`Keyboard character used is undefined in input encoding` ⟨*name*⟩ [inputenc]

The 8-bit number encountered in the document is not mapped by the input encoding ⟨*name*⟩ to some LICR object (see Sections 7.5.2 and 7.11.3). Check whether the document is really stored in the specified encoding.

`Language definition file` ⟨*language*⟩`.ldf not found` [babel]

When LaTeX processes the option list for babel and encounters an unknown option ⟨*language*⟩, it tries to load a file by the name of ⟨*language*⟩.ldf. This message is displayed when LaTeX fails to find it. This error can be caused by a simple typing mistake, or the file might not be stored on LaTeX's search path.

`Limit controls must follow a math operator` [TeX]

You can use `\limits` or `\nolimits` only following math operators such as `\sum`. See Table 8.4 for a list of common operator commands.

`\LoadClass in package file`

The `\LoadClass` command is only allowed in class files; see Section A.4.

`Lonely \item—perhaps a missing list environment`

The `\item` command is only allowed within list structures but LaTeX believes that this one was found outside a list.[1]

`Math alphabet identifier` ⟨*id*⟩ `is undefined in math version` ⟨*name*⟩

The math alphabet identifier ⟨*id*⟩ was used in a math version (⟨*name*⟩) for which it was not set up. An additional `\SetMathAlphabet` declaration should be added to the preamble of the document to assign a font shape group for this alphabet identifier.

---

[1] In contrast to the "...perhaps a missing `\item`" error, LaTeX's diagnosis in this case is usually correct.

`Math version ⟨name⟩ is not defined`

A math alphabet or a symbol font was assigned to a math version that is unknown to LaTeX. Either you misspelled its name or you forgot to declare this version (perhaps you have to add some package file). It is also possible that the math version you selected with `\mathversion` is not known to the system.

`Misplaced alignment tab character & `TeX

LaTeX found an & character outside of `tabular`, `align`, or one of the other alignment environments. If you want to typeset &, use `\&` instead. A possible cause is use of the amsmath environment `cases` or `matrix` without loading the package.

`Misplaced \cr`   or   `Misplaced \crcr` TeX

A `\cr` is the TeX low-level command for ending a row in an alignment structure (`\crcr` is a variation thereof); the corresponding LaTeX command is `\\`. TeX believes it came across such a command outside of an alignment structure.

`Misplaced \noalign` TeX

The TeX primitive `\noalign` is internally used to place "nonaligned" material between rows of alignment displays. It is therefore allowed only directly following the command that finishes a row. For example, you get this error when you use `\hline` outside of `array` or `tabular`, or not directly after `\\` within these environments.

`Misplaced \omit` TeX

The TeX primitive `\omit` is internally used to change the column specifications in an alignment display (e.g., to span rows with `\multicolumn` inside a `tabular`). The `\omit` command (and thus the commands calling it) is allowed only at the very beginning of an alignment cell (i.e., following `\\` or &).

`Missing \begin{document}`

This error occurs if typesetting is attempted while still within the document preamble.[1] It is most likely due to a declaration error that is misinterpreted by LaTeX. The error is also produced by text following `\begin{filecontents}` on the same line.

`Missing control sequence inserted` TeX

You used `\newcommand` or `\renewcommand` without providing a command name (starting with a backslash) as the first argument.

`Missing \cr inserted` TeX

TeX thinks it is about time to end the row in an alignment structure and inserted its low-level command for this purpose. In a LaTeX document, this guess is usually wrong, so TeX's recovery attempt usually fails in such a case.

---

[1] Typesetting inside an `\sbox` or `\savebox` declaration is accepted, but it is usually wise to move such declarations after `\begin{document}`, since some packages may delay their final set-up until that point.

`Missing delimiter (. inserted)` [TeX]

A \left, \right, or one of the \big.. commands was not followed by a delimiter. As corrective action the empty delimiter "." was inserted. See Section 8.5.3 on page 498 for details.

`Missing \endcsname inserted` [TeX]

This error can arise from using commands as part of the name of a counter or environment (e.g., \newenvironment{Bl\"ode}).

`Missing number, treated as zero` [TeX]

This error occurs when TeX is looking for a number or a dimension but finds something else. For example, using \value{page} instead of \thepage would produce this error, since an isolated \value makes TeX expect a low-level counter assignment. In general, using a length register without a proper mutator function like \setlength can trigger this error. You also get this message when \usebox is not followed by a box bin defined with \newsavebox, since internally such bins are represented by numbers.

`Missing p-arg in array arg`

There is a p column specifier not followed by an expression in braces (containing the width) in the argument to tabular, array, or \multicolumn.

`Missing @-exp in array arg`

There is an @ column specifier not followed by an expression in braces (containing the inter-column material) in the argument to tabular, array, or \multicolumn.

`Missing # inserted in alignment preamble` [LaTeX]

An alignment preamble specifies the layout of the columns in an alignment structure. Internally, TeX uses # to denote the part of the column that should receive input. In LaTeX this is unlikely to appear as a first error.

`Missing = inserted for \ifnum` [TeX]

TeX complains that the low-level \ifnum conditional is not followed by two numbers separated by <, =, or >. This error can occur when you forget the comparison operator in \ifthenelse.

`Missing = inserted for \ifdim` [TeX]

The low-level \ifdim conditional is not followed by a comparison between two lengths.

`Missing $ inserted` [TeX]

TeX has encountered something in normal text that is allowed only in math mode (e.g., \sum, \alpha, ^), or something that is not allowed inside math (e.g., \par) while processing a formula. It has therefore inserted a $ to switch to math mode or to leave it. If, for example, you tried to get an underscore by simply using _ instead of _, LaTeX would typeset the rest of the paragraph as a formula, most likely producing more errors along the way.

`Missing \endgroup inserted` TEX

This error indicates that a grouping structure in the document is incorrectly nested. Environments internally use `\begingroup` and `\endgroup` and for some reason TEX thinks that such a group was not properly closed. If you cannot determine why the group structure is faulty, try using the `\showgroups` or `\tracinggroups` feature of eTEX, as explained on page 917.

`Missing \right. inserted` TEX

Your formula contains a `\left` without a matching `\right`. Recall that `\left`/`\right` delimiter pairs must be part of the same "sub-formula"; they cannot, for example, be separated by `&` in an alignment or appear on different grouping levels.

`Missing { inserted` TEX

TEX thinks there is an open brace missing and inserted one. This error is, for example, caused by a stray `}` inside a `tabular` cell.

`Missing } inserted` TEX

Something is wrong in the grouping structure of the document and TEX tries to recover by inserting a closing brace. This attempt either gets it onto the right track again or causes you to receive more errors. Usually, the problem becomes apparent if you look at the typeset output. If you cannot determine why the group structure is faulty, try using the `\showgroups` or `\tracinggroups` feature of eTEX, as explained on page 917.

`Multiple \label's: label ⟨`*label*`⟩ will be lost` amsmath

Within the `amsmath` display environments, you can have only one `\label` per equation. It is usually best to remove all but the last, as it is the only one that will be effective.

`Multiple \tag` amsmath

Within the `amsmath` display environments, you can have only one `\tag` command per equation. All but the first will be ignored.

`No counter '⟨`*name*`⟩' defined`

The counter ⟨*name*⟩ referenced in either `\setcounter`, `\addtocounter`, or the optional argument of `\newcounter` or `\newtheorem` is unknown to LATEX. It must first be declared with `\newcounter`.

`No Cyrillic encoding definition files were found` babel

The language definition files for the supported "Cyrillic languages" check whether any of the known Cyrillic font encoding files (e.g., T2A, T2B) can be found. If not, this error message is displayed and you need to install Cyrillic support for LATEX first.

`No declaration for shape ⟨`*font shape*`⟩`

The `sub` or `ssub` size function used in a `\DeclareFontShape` command refers to a substitution shape that is unknown to LATEX's font selection scheme.

No driver specified `color/graphics/graphicx`

The package graphics, graphicx, or color was loaded without specifying a target device option. On most installations this is done using the configuration files graphics.cfg and color.cfg.

No \title given

A LaTeX class has executed \maketitle without seeing a \title declaration. Only \date is optional when this command is used.

Not a letter `TeX`

You specified a hyphenation exception with \hyphenation but the argument to this command contained some characters that TeX does not consider to be letters. For example, \hyphenation{la-ryn-gol-o-gist's} would produce such an error since ' is not a "letter" in TeX's categorization.

Not in outer par mode

This error is issued when a \marginpar or a float environment, such as table or figure, encountered inside a box-producing command or environment. For instance, you cannot use a \marginpar in a footnote, a float, a tabular, or a similar place (since all of them produce boxes). Move the offending object to the main galley.

Number too big `TeX`

You assigned or used a number in \setcounter or \addtocounter that is larger than the largest number that TeX can handle (2147483647, hexadecimal 7FFFFFFF). This error can also happen when modifying a length register with \setlength or \addtolength.

OK `TeX`

You used a TeX tracing command, like \show or \showthe; after displaying the data LaTeX stopped with this message to allow for some interaction on the command line (e.g., entering i\show.. to view some other values). This message is also shown if \tracingonline is positive and commands are used that normally only write to the transcript file; see the next message.

OK (see the transcript file) `TeX`

You used a TeX tracing command, like \showbox or \showlists, without also directing LaTeX to display the result on the terminal.

Old form ⟨command⟩ should be \begin{⟨envname⟩} `amsmath`

You have used cases, matrix, or pmatrix in its non-amsmath command form (probably with its old internal syntax). Change to the amsmath environment form with standard internal syntax.

Only one # is allowed per tab `TeX`

This error indicates a broken alignment template. In LaTeX it should not occur, unless caused by a fragile command in a moving argument.

`Option clash for package` ⟨*name*⟩

The package ⟨*name*⟩ was requested twice with a conflicting set of options. When you press H in response to this error, LATEX will show you the sets of conflicting options. As LATEX loads a package only once,[1] the best solution is to specify all options on the first occasion. If this is not possible, because the package is already loaded as part of the class or another package, you can try to specify the required options as global options to the \documentclass command. In an emergency you can even load a package before \documentclass by using \RequirePackage. See Section 2.1.1 for details.

`Page height already too large`

You used \enlargethispage on a page whose vertical size is already larger than 8191.99998pt, or roughly 113 inches. LATEX thinks that this is dangerously large and will not extend the page size as requested.

`Paragraph ended before` ⟨*command*⟩ `was complete` TEX

As discussed in Section A.1.2, commands defined with \newcommand* or \renewcommand* are not allowed to contain \par or an empty line. If they do, you will get a Runaway argument together with this error. The ⟨*command*⟩ listed may not be the one used in your document. For example, \emph{..\par..} will list \text@command in the error message (i.e., the internal command called by \emph).

`(Please type a command or say '\end')` TEX

You have replied with ⟨*Return*⟩ in response to *. See the very first entry in this list of errors.

`\pushtabs and \poptabs don't match`

You issued a \poptabs command in a tabbing environment, but there was no previous \pushtabs command issued.

`\RequirePackage or \LoadClass in Options Section`

A \RequirePackage or \LoadClass was found inside a package or class file between the \DeclareOption commands and \ProcessOptions. Loading packages or classes in this part is not allowed as it would clobber the data structure holding the current set of options; see Section A.4 for details. If you want to load a package when a certain option is specified, use a flag to indicate that the option was selected and load it after the \ProcessOptions command has done its job.

`Rotation not supported` graphics/graphicx

You have requested rotation with \rotatebox or a similar command but the selected graphics driver does not support rotation of objects. LATEX will leave the right amount of space but the printed document might show the image in the wrong position.

---

[1] The only exception is the fontenc package, which can be loaded as often as needed with different options; see Section 7.5.3 on page 361.

Runaway ⟨*something*⟩ TEX

TEX thinks it has scanned too far while looking for the end of ⟨*something*⟩, where ⟨*something*⟩ can be either `argument`, `definition`, `preamble`, or `text`. Unless low-level TEX code is at fault, the most likely cause is `argument`. For example, you forgot the closing brace of an argument, it might cause TEX to scan until it reaches the end of the file or until its memory is filled—whichever comes first. Incomplete definitions done with `\newcommand`, `\newenvironment`, and so forth also claim that the `argument` has run away. Only low-level definitions, involving TEX primitives like `\def`, produce a `Runaway definition`.

A `Runaway preamble` means that an alignment structure has problems (that should not occur in normal LATEX documents) and `Runaway text` usually refers to a token register assignment (this should never happen unless there is a serious package implementation error).

In contrast to the situation with normal error messages, you will not get a line number that indicates where the error was detected (since TEX often has reached the end of the file). Instead, you will see the beginning of the material that was being absorbed. For example, if you have a definition without the final closing brace,

```
\newcommand\foo{bar
\begin{document} Some text \end{document}
```

you will get

```
Runaway argument?
{bar \begin {document} Some text \end {document}
! File ended while scanning use of \@argdef.
<inserted text>
                \par
<*> samplefile.tex

?
```

The fact that TEX in that case inserted `\par` as a recovery action is of little help, since the complete document was already swallowed. Instead of "`File ended while...`", you might see some other message at this point, such as "`Paragraph ended before...`".

Scaling not supported graphics/graphicx

You have requested scaling with `\resizebox` or a similar command but the selected graphics driver does not support scaling of objects. LATEX will leave the right amount of space but the printed document will show the image at the original (unscaled) size.

Something's wrong-perhaps a missing \item

This error message is produced by an `\addvspace` command when encountered in horizontal mode. The follow-up remark about "perhaps a missing

`\item`" is unfortunately seldom correct. For example, forgetting the closing brace on `\mbox` as in `\mbox{...\section{..}...` would produce this error, since the `\section` command that executes `\addvspace` internally is now used in horizontal mode.

Identify which command issued the `\addvspace` causing the error, and check whether that command was used incorrectly. Refer to page 858 for an in-depth discussion of the `\addvspace` command.

`Sorry, I can't find` ⟨*format*⟩ `...`   [TeX]

If you get this message, then LaTeX never started because TeX did not find the ⟨*format*⟩ containing the basic LaTeX definitions. There is a problem with your TeX installation and you have to consult the installation documentation.

`Suggested extra height (`⟨*value*⟩`) dangerously large`

Using the ⟨*value*⟩ with `\enlargethispage` would make the resulting page too large (more than 113 inches) for LaTeX's liking.

`Symbol font` ⟨*name*⟩ `is not defined`

You tried to make use of the symbol font ⟨*name*⟩—for example, within a `\DeclareMathSymbol` command—without declaring it first with a `\DeclareSymbolFont` declaration.

`Symbol` ⟨*command*⟩ `not provided by font family` ⟨*name*⟩   [textcomp]

The `textcomp` package implements the TS1 encoding, which is unfortunately implemented fully by just a minority of the font families usable with LaTeX. The package will typeset the symbol using a default family stored in `\textcompsubstdefault`. You can turn the error into a warning by loading `textcomp` with the option `warn`. See Section 7.5.4 for more details.

`Tab overflow`

LaTeX supports up to 13 tabulator positions (`\=`) inside a `tabbing` environment, and you have used a larger number. If not all of them are needed at the same time, you can try solving the problem by using `\pushtabs` and/or providing template lines with `\kill`.

`\tag not allowed here`   [amsmath]

The `\tag` command is allowed only within the top level of a mathematical display. It is usually best to move it to the end of the logical equation in which it occurs.

`TeX capacity exceeded,` ⟨*explanation*⟩   [TeX]

TeX ran out of some sort of memory and died. This error is discussed in detail in Section B.1.1 on page 915.

`Text line contains an invalid character`   [TeX]

The input file contains a strange, nonprinting character that is rejected by TeX. This may happen if you used a word processor to create the file and did not save it as "text".

The attribute ⟨*attrib*⟩ is unknown for language ⟨*lang*⟩ `babel`

You tried to activate an attribute for a language ⟨*lang*⟩ that is not defined in the language definition file for this language. Check the documentation of babel with respect to this language.

The character '⟨*char*⟩' is not a shorthand character in ⟨*language*⟩ `babel`

When a user uses the command \shorthandon and passes it a ⟨*char*⟩ that is not defined to be a shorthand for the current ⟨*language*⟩, this error message is displayed and the instruction is ignored.

The font size command \normalsize is not defined...

A class file needs to provide a minimal set-up, including a definition for \normalsize; see Section A.4.9 on page 888 for details.

There's no line here to end

This error is triggered if \newline or \\ is found outside a paragraph (i.e., after a \par or an empty line). If the intention was to produce extra vertical space, use \vspace or any of the other commands described on page 857.

This may be a LaTeX bug

To the author's knowledge, until now this message never actually signaled a LaTeX bug. It means, however, that LaTeX got thoroughly confused by previous errors and lost track of the state of its float data structure. It is best to stop and correct previous errors first.

This NFSS system isn't set up properly

This error occurs when LaTeX detects a mistake while trying to verify the font substitution tables at \begin{document}. It means that either a \DeclareFontSubstitution or \DeclareErrorFont[1] declaration is corrupted. These declarations need to point to valid font shapes (declared with \DeclareFontShape). Type h for additional information and inform your system maintainer. If you are the system maintainer, read the end of Section 7.10.5.

Too deeply nested

Standard LaTeX supports a total of six levels of lists nested in each other. Those levels can include up to four lists of type itemize or enumerate. This error signals that your document has overflowed one of these limits. You probably have forgotten to end some list environments properly. If you really need additional levels, you need to copy the base definitions for list, itemize, and/or enumerate into a private package and modify their hard-wired constants.

Too many columns in eqnarray environment

The eqnarray environment supports a maximum of three columns (i.e., two & signs per row). For serious math, consider the amsmath package described in Chapter 8, which allows for more complex display structures.

---

[1] The declaration \DeclareErrorFont is used during installation and points to a font (font shape + size) that should be used when everything else fails. Its default is Computer Modern Roman 10pt, which should be available with any TeX installation. See [109] for further details.

`Too many math alphabets used in version` ⟨*name*⟩

You used too many different math alphabet identifiers in your formulas. If this error occurs after adding the bm package, define `\newcommand\bmmax{0}` before loading bm and try again; this prevents the package from preallocating math alphabets.

`Too many unprocessed floats`

Floats that cannot be placed immediately are deferred by LaTeX, possibly causing subsequent floats to be deferred as well. LaTeX can defer up to 18 floats, then you will receive this error message. Using the package morefloats will increase this limit to 36 but if there is a float that cannot be placed for some reason this change will merely delay receiving the above error. See Chapter 6 for ways to deal with this situation.

This error can also be triggered if you have too many `\marginpar` commands within a single paragraph. A `\marginpar` temporarily uses two storage bins for deferred floats as long as the current paragraph has not been typeset (this allows a maximum of nine marginal notes per paragraph, or fewer if there are already some deferred floats).

`Two \documentclass or \documentstyle commands`

Only one such command is allowed per document. Your document includes more than one, perhaps as the result of combining two originally separate documents.

`Two \LoadClass commands`

A class can load at most one other class to do the bulk of processing. See Section A.4 for a detailed discussion of how classes are built.

`Undefined color` ⟨*name*⟩ `color`

You have requested a color with `\color` or a similar command from the color package without previously defining it with `\definecolor`. See [57] or the color package documentation for details.

`Undefined control sequence` TEX

This is perhaps the most common of all LaTeX errors, though it shows up as a TeX error message: you have used a command name that was not previously defined. Often you may have simply mistyped the name in your document (e.g., `\bmox` instead of `\mbox`). To carry on in such a case, you can respond with `i\mbox`, inserting the correct name. Later on you can correct your source document. It is also possible to get this error as a result of using a fragile command in a moving argument.

`Undefined font size function` ⟨*name*⟩

A size function used in `\DeclareFontShape` was misspelled. Check the entry or tell your system maintainer.

`Undefined tab position`

This error is raised if you try to advance in a tabbing environment with `\>`, `\+`, `\-`, or `\<` to a tabulator position that was not previously set up with `\=`.

Either the \= is actually missing or perhaps you have used \+ or \pushtabs and got confused when specifying the tabular position to which you actually want to move.

UTF-8 string \u8:⟨*8-bit-sequence*⟩ not set up for LaTeX use `inputenc`

The Unicode character denoted by the UTF8 ⟨*8-bit-sequence*⟩ is not known to LaTeX. Under the precondition that it is available in a font encoding used in the document, it has to be set up using the \DeclareUnicodeCharacter declaration; see Section 7.11.3 on page 443.

Unknown graphics extension: ⟨*ext*⟩ `graphics/graphicx`

You will get this error if you try to load a fully specified graphics file (with extension ⟨*ext*⟩) and the graphics driver does not know the particular extension and there is no default rule set up. The dvips program, for example, interprets every unknown extension as EPS, so with this driver you will never see this error but probably others.

Unknown option '⟨*option*⟩' for package '⟨*name*⟩'

You specified an ⟨*option*⟩ for package ⟨*name*⟩ that is not declared by that package. Consult the package documentation on the available options.

Use of ⟨*command*⟩ doesn't match its definition `TeX`

Low-level macro definitions made with \def, instead of \newcommand and friends, sometimes require special argument delimiters (e.g., the (..) of the picture commands). If ⟨*command*⟩ is a LaTeX command, check its syntax. Otherwise, this is most likely a spurious error due to using a fragile command in a moving argument without \protect.

\usepackage before \documentclass

The \usepackage declaration can be used only after the main class was loaded with \documentclass. Inside a class file you instead have to use \RequirePackage.[1]

\verb ended by end of line

To better detect errors, the argument of \verb must be placed on a single line. Thus, this error signals that you either forgot the final delimiter for the argument or the argument was broken over several lines in the source. In case of very long arguments, it may help to split them over several \verb commands or, if necessary, masking a line break in the source with a % sign.

\verb illegal in command argument

Except in very special situations (explicitly documented in this book), it is not possible to use \verb (or verbatim) in the argument of other commands. If you need verbatim text in such a place, use, for example, \SaveVerb and \UseVerb from the fancyvrb package described in Section 3.4.3.

You already have nine parameters `TeX`

LaTeX supports command or environment definitions with a maximum of

---

[1] It is technically possible to load a package before a class by using \RequirePackage, but this should be avoided unless you know what you are doing.

nine parameters, but your \newcommand or \newenvironment specified 10 or more.

You can't use 'macro parameter #' in ⟨some⟩ mode `TEX`

TeX found a stray # character somewhere that does not seem to be a reference to an argument of some command. If you wanted to typeset this symbol, use \# instead.

You can't use '\spacefactor' in vertical mode `TEX`

TeX lets you refer to the \spacefactor only when you are building a horizontal list. You will get this error when you use the LaTeX command \@ outside of a paragraph. Since many internal commands start with an @ in their names, you might also get this error if you use code containing such internal commands (e.g., \@startsection) in the preamble of your document without surrounding it with \makeatletter and \makeatother. In that case TeX sees \@ followed by the letters startsection, and a later use of this code then executes \@ that in turn produces this error message.

You can't use '\prevdepth' in horizontal mode `TEX`

The \prevdepth dimension can be used only while in vertical mode (i.e., between paragraphs).

You can't use '\end' in internal vertical mode `TEX`

This is one of the more misleading TeX error messages, since it refers to the TeX primitive \end (ending a TeX run) that was redefined by LaTeX to become the end-tag of environments. The error means that LaTeX's \end{document} or the \stop command was encountered while LaTeX was building a box. For example, \begin{figure}...\stop would generate it.

You can't use '⟨command⟩' in ⟨some⟩ mode `TEX`

TeX complains that ⟨command⟩ is not allowed in one of its modes. Some specific variations of this theme have already been discussed. If you haven't used ⟨command⟩ directly, then the most likely cause for this error is a broken fragile command in a moving argument.

You haven't defined output directory for '⟨path⟩' `docstrip`

The configuration file docstrip.cfg contains a declaration for \BaseDirectory but the internal ⟨path⟩ in the DOCSTRIP script has no translation to a local directory. Use \DeclareDirectory or \UseTDS in docstrip.cfg to specify a translation as described in Section 14.2.3 on page 830.

You haven't defined the language ⟨language⟩ yet `babel`

Various user interface commands of babel check whether their argument is a language that was specified in the option list when babel was loaded. If the ⟨language⟩ was *not* specified, processing is stopped and this error message is displayed.

You haven't specified a language option `babel`

This message is shown when no known languages have been specified for babel—that is, neither in the option list to babel nor in the global option list (this is likely to be due to a typo). You should expect that processing your document will nevertheless produce many more errors.

B.1.1   Dying with memory exceeded

The TeX program contains a number of internal tables of fixed size used for storing away different kinds of information needed at run time. Whenever any of these tables overflows, LaTeX will abort with a "TeX capacity exceeded" error.

Until the mid-1990s, memory problems could, in fact, be due to the size of the document. In some cases it was impossible to process a document as a whole.[1] These days such limitations are gone or are at least less severe. For one, the average TeX implementation is already equipped with huge internal tables. In addition, most implementations allow you to modify the table sizes via configuration files instead of requiring you to manually recompile TeX. In some cases you may have to generate a new LaTeX format; for more details, consult the documentation of your TeX distribution.[2]

Nevertheless, people experience this dreadful error once in a while, usually as the result of a faulty command definition. Below are four candidates reduced to the bare bones of the problem we want to discuss—in reality, such problems usually lurk in more complex definitions.

```
\newcommand\FAILa{.\FAILa}           \newcommand\FAILb{\FAILb x}
\newcommand\FAILc{\typeout{.}\FAILc} \newcommand\FAILd{.\par\FAILd}
```

If you execute \FAILa as defined above, you will receive the following output (the reported memory size possibly differs) after a short while:

```
! TeX capacity exceeded, sorry [main memory size=1500001].
\FAILa ->.
            \FAILa
```

The main memory is the part of TeX in which macro definitions and the material for the current page are stored. Looking at the above recursive definition, it is clear that it generates a never-ending sequence of periods. Since paragraph breaking is deferred until TeX sees a \par command or a blank line to globally optimize the line breaks, TeX waits in vain for a chance to break the paragraph material into lines.

---

[1] The first edition of this book required a specially compiled version of the TeX program with all such tables enlarged by a factor of 10 and could be processed only on a large UN*X workstation.

[2] The TeX live distribution, which comes with this book, lets you specify the size of most tables through the configuration file `texmf.cnf`. See the TeX live manual for details.

Exceeding main memory because of too many macro definitions is less likely these days. Nevertheless, even that can happen (in theory) if the size of this memory is small and you load many packages, have a large number of huge deferred floats, or use macro packages[1] that produce new macros on the fly.

If you get this error only with larger documents and LATEX actually produces pages before giving up, you can try to find out whether the memory is gradually filling up (which suggests a table size problem) by setting \tracingstats=2 in the preamble of your document. TEX will then report the main memory status after finishing each page, producing output like the following:

```
[765]
Memory usage before: 4262&161788; after: 1286&157691; still untouched: 1323176
[766]
Memory usage before: 3825&160983; after: 636&156520; still untouched: 1323176
[767]
Memory usage before: 3652&160222; after: 771&156307; still untouched: 1323176
```

The number reported to the left of the & is the memory devoted to large objects such as boxes; the number on the right is the amount of memory used by macro definitions and character data. Thus, one can expect a reduction in both values whenever a page has finished (i.e., the after: value). If the right-hand value is slowly increasing, however, then something is probably adding more and more definitions.

If we use \FAILb, we overflow a different table. Here the recursion happens before LATEX actually reaches the end on the macro expansion and thus needs to store away the unprocessed part of the expansion.

```
! TeX capacity exceeded, sorry [input stack size=1500].
\FAILb ->\FAILb
                x
```

With today's size for the input stack, this message usually appears only if a recursion like the one above makes that stack grow at a frightening speed. In a normal LATEX document you will seldom find nested definitions that make this stack grow beyond a value of 50 (for this book the maximum value was 35).

What happens if you execute either \FAILc or \FAILd? Both are similar to \FAILa but neither overflows any internal TEX table. Instead, both will simply fill your hard disk. The only action of \FAILc is to show periods on your screen and in the transcript file, thereby very slowly filling up the disk with a huge transcript. \FAILd, on the other hand, contains a \par in its definition and therefore is able to typeset paragraphs (each consisting of a single dot); as a result it produces pages in rapid succession. Such an experiment ended on the author's machine with a document containing 22279 pages and the following message:

```
tex: fwrite: No space left on device
```

---

[1]For example, varioref defines two labels internally for every use of \vref, which can result in a noticeable amount of memory consumption in large documents.

On your private machine, this is merely a nuisance, easily rectified. On systems with shared resources, however, you should be careful when letting LaTeX run unattended. This type of error once hit a student very badly; this individual processed such a document on a mainframe in batch mode without a time or size limit and was presented a bill for computer processing time of several thousand dollars.

Several other internal tables can overflow in principle. Below is the complete list of those not already discussed, along with an explanation for the most likely reason for the overflow. Some additional information can be found in [82, p. 300].

`buffer size` The characters in the lines being read from a file. Since the default size is usually quite large, the most likely cause for an overflow is lost line breaks due to a faulty conversion of a file during transfer from one operating system to another. A buffer overflow can also be caused by some PC word processing programs, which internally put an entire paragraph on a single line even though the text appears to be broken into several lines on the screen.

`exception dictionary` The number of hyphenation exceptions as specified by `\hyphenation`. LaTeX has some exceptions specified for the English language, and some language packages specify additional exceptions. However, if this table overflows, you must have been doing a very thorough job.

`font memory` The font metric data loaded by LaTeX. These days an overflow is unlikely. If it happens, LaTeX has loaded too many fonts—probably because you used many different font sizes and LaTeX calculated and loaded math fonts for all the sizes. Increase the table size, if possible, or refer to Chapter 7 for information on how to reduce the number of fonts.

`grouping levels` The number of unfinished groups that delimit the scope for setting parameters, definitions, and other items—for instance, braces, the start of environments, or math mode delimiters. An overflow usually indicates a programming error (e.g., a definition that opens more groups than it closes). That type of error is sometimes difficult to identify. Good help is available with the eTeX program,[1] which offers the command `\showgroups` to produce a listing of stacked groups starting with the innermost one. For example, placing it into the footnote on the current page will yield

```
### semi simple group (level 3) entered at line 2955 (\begingroup)
### insert group (level 2) entered at line 2955 (\insert0{)
### semi simple group (level 1) entered at line 2921 (\begingroup)
### bottom level
```

The semi simple group on level 1 is due to the fact that this text is typeset in a `description` environment (the `\begin` command issues internally a `\begingroup` command). The `\footnote` command is implemented with the TeX primitive `\insert`, which contributes level 2. In fact, another semi simple group is started by `\footnote`, which ensures that color changes remain local.

---

[1] On many installations you can call `elatex` instead of `latex` when processing a document.

What we can deduce from this example is that the relationships among top-level document commands and internal groups are far from obvious or simple. However, the line numbers that show when a group was entered do help, since there are usually no long-ranging groups in normal documents.

As an alternative, the eTeX program offers the internal tracing counter \tracinggroups. If it is set to a positive number, the entry and exit of groups is recorded in the transcript file; with \tracingonline having a positive value, this information also appears on screen.

hash size   The number of command names known to TeX. Most packages contribute a fixed number of new command names. Each \label or \bibitem command in the document generates one new internal command name. Thus, packages that internally use the \label command (e.g., varioref) may significantly contribute to filling that table in large documents.

number of strings   The number of strings—command names, file names, and built-in error messages—remembered by TeX. In some cases TeX is able to free unused space but usually such strings survive even if they are used only locally. One possible reason for overflowing this table is the use of many files in an application. Each opening for reading or writing of a file contributes, even when the same file is used many times over.

For historical reasons, TeX has a somewhat unusual string-handling concept involving several tables, each of which can overflow. Thus, if you change the hash size to allow for more commands, you may need to adjust the number of strings and quite likely the pool size, and vice versa.

parameter stack size   The total number of command parameters of nested commands being expanded but not yet fully processed. For example, suppose a command with 4 arguments calls a command with 5 arguments, which in turn calls a command with 3 arguments thereby, using up 12 slots in this table. The moment TeX reaches the end of a macro replacement text it will free the stack. Thus, with today's implementations it is quite difficult to hit that limit, unless you use a flaky recursive definition with arguments, for example:

```
\newcommand\FAIL[3]{\typeout{Got #1, #2 and #3 but \FAIL is a mess}\DO}
```

Do you see the problem? Since the \typeout contains \FAIL by mistake, it gets called again, before its replacement text has been fully processed (picking up the characters i, s, and a as arguments). As a result, \DO is never executed and we finally get

```
! TeX capacity exceeded, sorry [parameter stack size=1500].
\FAIL #1#2#3->
                 \typeout {Got #1, #2 and #3 but \FAIL is a mess}\DO
l.18 \FAIL 123
```

This is similar to the \FAILb example from page 916, except that because of the number of arguments the `parameter stack` overflowed first.

`pattern memory` The memory available to store hyphenation patterns. This table cannot overflow during normal document processing, since such patterns are loaded only during format generation. If you receive this error during that process, reduce the number of languages for which you load hyphenation patterns into your format. These days pattern loading is normally defined in the file `language.dat`.

`pool size` The characters in strings—command names and file names (including the full path on some implementations). If this table overflows, the most likely cause is the use of too many files, especially if they have long absolute path names. This can, for example, happen if a document includes many graphics and one uses \graphicspath to make LaTeX search for the images in several directories—every attempt to open a file contributes to this string pool.

`save size` The set of values to restore when a group ends. With today's default limits, this is again difficult to overflow. The most likely cause is the use of both local and global assignments to the same object, something that can happen only through the use of low-level TeX programming, since LaTeX assignments are either always local (for most types) or always global (e.g., counter assignments).

 To avoid unnecessary growth of the `save stack`, the `document` environment has a special implementation[1] so that it does not produce a group (as normal environments do). Without it every new definition would automatically push an unnecessary "undefined" value onto the `save stack`—unnecessary, because by the time that group would end all processing would stop anyhow.

`semantic nest size` The number of token lists being worked on simultaneously. Boxes, math formulas, and other elements start a new list, suspending work on the current structure. Once they are finished TeX has to continue constructing the suspended object, so all such unfinished objects are remembered in the `semantic nest` stack. With a default size of several hundred objects, it is very difficult to get even close to this limit with normal documents.[2] In an emergency, TeX offers \showlists, which displays all unfinished lists that TeX is currently working on.

`text input levels` The number of simultaneously open input sources (e.g., files opened by \include, \input, or \usepackage). On the author's implementation of TeX one would need to nest 1500 files to reach this limit.

---

[1] As a side effect it is impossible to use \begin{document} inside another environment since the grouping structure is not obeyed.

[2] The author could not think of any problematic definition that would not hit any of the other limits first.

B.2   Warnings and informational messages

While error messages make LaTeX stop and wait for user input, warning messages
are simply displayed on the terminal and in the transcript file and processing
continues. If applicable, LaTeX also shows the source line number that triggered
the warning. The warnings are prefixed by "LaTeX Warning:" or "LaTeX Font
Warning:" if they are issued by the core LaTeX code. Otherwise, they identify the
issuing package or class by starting with "Package ⟨*name*⟩ Warning:" or "Class
⟨*name*⟩ Warning:", respectively. TeX warnings, such as "Overfull...", have no
standard prefix string.

In addition to warnings, LaTeX writes informational messages to the transcript
file without displaying this information on the terminal. To better distinguish between informational and warning messages, warnings are shown in blue in the
following alphabetical listing.

Calculating math sizes for size ⟨*text size*⟩
   LaTeX has to guess the correct font sizes for subscripts and superscripts because it could not find the information for the current ⟨*text size*⟩ in its internal tables. This message usually is followed by several font size correction
   warnings because LaTeX's initial guess is seldom successful. This situation can
   arise when you select an uncommon size using the \fontsize command; see
   Section 7.10.7 if the math formulas look strange.

Citation '⟨*key*⟩' on page ⟨*number*⟩ undefined
   The ⟨*key*⟩ specified as an argument to \cite or \nocite is not defined by a
   \bibitem command or you need another run of LaTeX (and perhaps BibTeX) to
   make it known to LaTeX. The latter case is indicated by an additional warning,
   "Label(s) may have changed...", as discussed on page 924. The page number
   is omitted if the warning is emitted by \nocite.

Checking defaults for ⟨*cdp*⟩/⟨*font shape*⟩
   This message is written in the transcript file at \begin{document} while LaTeX
   is verifying that the substitution defaults for the encoding ⟨*cdp*⟩ are sensible.
   It is followed either by ...okay or by an error message that is generated when
   the ⟨*font shape*⟩ group specified with \DeclareFontEncoding is unknown
   to LaTeX.

Command ⟨*name*⟩ invalid in math mode
   This is either a warning or an error message indicating that you have used a
   command in math mode that should be used only in normal text. A warning
   will be generated when an obsolete, yet still valid, construction is used.

Document Class: ⟨*name*⟩ ⟨*date*⟩ ⟨*additional-info*⟩
   This line is produced by a \ProvidesClass command in the document class
   code. Although not a warning, it appears both on the terminal and in the
   transcript file. If a document produces different output on different installa-

tions, you should compare the "Document Class:", "File:", and "Package:" messages to identify any release differences.

Encoding ⟨name⟩ has changed to ⟨new name⟩ for ...
This warning is issued when in the declaration of a symbol font different encoding schemes in different math versions have been used. It may mean that the \DeclareMathSymbol commands for this symbol font are not valid in all math versions.

(\end occurred ⟨when⟩ ᴛᴇX
You receive this warning at the very end of your run whenever TeX finds the \end{document} or \stop command to be premature. As a warning the message is unfortunately misleading, because it refers to a TeX primitive \end that was reused by LaTeX to become the environment end-tag. The ⟨when⟩ can be one of two cases:

inside a group at level ⟨number⟩) ᴛᴇX
In this case the LaTeX run ended while there were still some open groups. Such groups include explicit braces that are not closed (e.g., {\itshape..), use of \bgroup and \begingroup in macro code without their counterparts, and unclosed environments in the source. The latter normally triggers a suitable LaTeX error first (i.e., "\begin{⟨env⟩} on...") unless you ended the run with \stop, since in that case no check for mismatched environments is made.

when ⟨condition⟩ on line ⟨line number⟩ was incomplete) ᴛᴇX
In this case LaTeX completed the run while a low-level TeX conditional remained unfinished. With LaTeX documents using only standard commands, this problem should not occur unless you ended the document inside a file loaded with \include. In other cases it probably means there is a bug in a package. Try to identify the source of the conditional (by looking at the ⟨line number⟩) to see in which command it was used. Note that the ⟨line number⟩ may not be in the current file—unfortunately, TeX does not divulge the file name. In very difficult situations you can try to use eTeX's advanced tracing options to pinpoint the problem: if \tracingifs is set to 1, you will get detailed trace information about nested conditionals as they are executed.

Empty 'thebibliography' environment
This warning is issued if a thebibliography environment has no \bibitem commands. It often indicates a problem with a BibTeX run. For example, the BibTeX program may have been unable to resolve a single citation.

External font ⟨name⟩ loaded for size ⟨size⟩
LaTeX has ignored your request to load some font shape at size ⟨size⟩ and has loaded the external font ⟨name⟩ instead. (This message is generated by the size function fixed.)

`Faking` ⟨*command*⟩ `for font family` ⟨*name*⟩ `in TS1 encoding` textcomp
The glyph ⟨*command*⟩ is not available in the TS1 encoding of the current font
family. LATEX has responded by "faking" it in some way. This is, for example,
done for the `\texteuro` glyph (€), if unavailable. Section 7.8.7 describes ways
to get a real euro symbol.

`File '`⟨*name*⟩`' already exists on the system.`
`Not generating it from this source`
This warning is generated by a `filecontents` environment when the file
⟨*name*⟩ already exists somewhere in the search path of LATEX. If you want to
unpack the file nevertheless, either delete (or rename) the version found by
LATEX or extract the file manually with the help of an editor.

`File:` ⟨*name*⟩ ⟨*date*⟩ ⟨*additional-info*⟩
This line is produced from the `\ProvidesFile` command used to identify a
file and its last modification date. By convention, the ⟨*additional-info*⟩ starts
with a version number, though it is not required. Although of the same importance as `\ProvidesClass`, this information is written only to the transcript file to avoid cluttering the terminal with messages. If a document produces different output on different installations, you should compare the
"Document Class:", "File:", and "Package:" messages to identify any release differences.

`File:` ⟨*encoding*⟩⟨*family*⟩`.fd` ⟨*date*⟩ ⟨*additional-info*⟩
This important special case of the previous informational message indicates
that a font definition file for some ⟨*encoding*⟩ (usually displayed in lowercase)
and ⟨*family*⟩ combination was loaded. Such files contain font shape group
declarations and are described in Section 7.10.6.

`Float too large for page by` ⟨*value*⟩
A float is too tall by ⟨*value*⟩ to fit in the current `\textheight`. It will be printed
on a page by itself (if permitted), thereby possibly overflowing into the bottom
margin. If the float is not allowed to go on a float page, it will prevent all
further floats in its class from being placed.

`Font shape` ⟨*font shape*⟩ `in size` ⟨*size*⟩ `not available`
LATEX issues this message when it tries to select a font for which the requested
font attribute combination is not available and a substitution is defined in
the internal tables. Depending on the contents of these tables, one of the
following additional messages will be issued:

`external font` ⟨*name*⟩ `used`
LATEX has selected the external font ⟨*name*⟩ in that particular situation
and does not know to which font shape group it belongs. (This message
is generated by the size function `subf`.)

`size` ⟨*size*⟩ `substituted`
LATEX has selected the correct shape, but since the requested size is not

available LATEX has chosen the nearby size ⟨*size*⟩. This action is taken automatically if none of the simple sizes or size ranges in the ⟨*font shape*⟩ group declaration matches.

shape ⟨*font shape*⟩ tried
> LATEX has selected a different ⟨*font shape*⟩ group because the requested one is not available for the requested ⟨*size*⟩. (This message is generated by the size function sub.)

Font shape ⟨*font shape*⟩ will be scaled to size ⟨*size*⟩
> LATEX has loaded the requested font by scaling it to the desired size. To print a document containing scaled fonts, your printer driver must have these fonts in the correct size or must be able to scale them automatically.

Font shape ⟨*font shape*⟩ undefined. Using '⟨*other shape*⟩' instead
> This warning is given when a combination of font attributes is specified for which LATEX has no font shape definition. For example, requesting \fontseries{b}\ttfamily would normally trigger this warning, since Computer Modern fonts have neither bold typewriter nor bold extended typewriter. However, when the latter combination is requested, you will not receive this warning but only some information in the transcript file because for \textbf{\texttt{..}} the .fd files contain an explicit substitution rule.
>
> If LATEX identifies a particular symbol that it cannot typeset in the requested shape, the above warning is followed by "for symbol ⟨*name*⟩".

Foreign command ⟨*command*⟩;   amsmath
\frac or \genfrac should be used instead
> Although the use of ⟨*command*⟩ is not an error, you are strongly discouraged from using this old form for your (generalized) fractions in LATEX. Use the amsmath commands instead.

Form feed has been converted to Blank Line
> The filecontents environment detected a "form feed" character (^^L) in the source and will write it as an empty line (\par command if interpreted by LATEX) into the external file. As filecontents was designed to distribute textual data, it cannot be used for handling arbitrary binary files.

'h' float specifier changed to 'ht'   or
'!h' float specifier changed to '!ht'
> You specified h or !h as a float placement without giving any other options. LATEX requires some alternative in case "here" leads to an impossible placement because not enough room is left on the current page. If you really want to prevent floats from floating, consider using the float package described in Section 6.3.1.

Ignoring text '⟨*text*⟩' after \end{⟨*env*⟩}
> This warning is issued by filecontents or filecontents* when textual material is detected following the \end tag.

Label '⟨*key*⟩' multiply defined
> The document contains two or more \label commands with the same ⟨*key*⟩. References to this ⟨*key*⟩ will always refer to the last \label defined. Ensure that all ⟨*key*⟩s are different.

Label(s) may have changed. Rerun to get cross-references right
> LaTeX has detected that the label definitions, as compared to those in the previous run, have been modified and that (at least) one additional LaTeX run is necessary to resolve cross-references properly.
>
> In theory it is possible, through unlikely, that this message will persist regardless of the number of processing runs.[1] If this is the case, compare the .aux files of different runs to determine which label alternates between different states and resolve the problem manually.

Loose \hbox (badness ⟨*number*⟩) ⟨*somewhere*⟩ TeX
> TeX produced a horizontal box with a badness of 13 or greater (which corresponds to using 50% or more of the available stretchability). This warning can be safely ignored unless you are a perfectionist; in fact, it will not be produced unless you change the default for \hbadness. See the message "Underfull \hbox…" on page 928 for more details.

Loose \vbox (badness ⟨*number*⟩) ⟨*somewhere*⟩ TeX
> TeX produced a vertical box with a badness of 13 or greater (which corresponds to using 50% or more of the available stretchability). The warning is produced only if \vbadness was set to a value below 100. See the message "Underfull \vbox…" on page 930 for more details.

Making ⟨*char*⟩ an active character babel
> For each character that is turned into a shorthand character, this information message will be written to the transcript file. When a document shows unexpected results, this information might help if the problems are caused by inadvertent use of a shorthand character.

Marginpar on page ⟨*number*⟩ moved
> A \marginpar could not be aligned with the text line to which it was originally attached, because a preceeding \marginpar already occupies the space.

Missing character: There is no ⟨*char*⟩ in font ⟨*name*⟩! TeX
> Although this message usually indicates a serious problem, unfortunately it is only written to the transcript file (unless \tracingonline is positive). It means that somewhere in the source a request for a symbol ⟨*char*⟩ was made for which the current font (⟨*name*⟩ is the external name) has no glyph in the corresponding position. The displayed ⟨*char*⟩ may differ on different

Watch out for
this message in
the transcript!

---

[1]For example, if the \label is near the page boundary between pages "iii" and "iv", the use of \pageref before the \label might result in a situation where the \label will be moved to page "iv" if the textual reference "iii" is used, and vice versa.

TeX installations.[1] For example, using the command\ `\symbol` can produce this warning because you can ask for any font slot with this command. However, standard font-encoding–specific commands, as discussed in Section 7.11.4 on page 455, should never produce this warning.

No `\author` given
: You used `\maketitle` without specifying an author first. In contrast to a missing `\title` this omission generates a warning.

No auxiliary output files
: This information is displayed when you use a `\nofiles` declaration in the document preamble.

No characters defined by input encoding change to ⟨*name*⟩
: The input encoding file ⟨*name*⟩`.def` does not seem to contain any input encoding declarations. For the `ascii` encoding, this is the expected behavior; for all other encodings, it indicates a problem.

No file ⟨*name*⟩
: LaTeX displays this information whenever it tries to read from an auxiliary file (e.g., `.aux` or `.toc`) but cannot find the file. This is not considered an error since such files are created only after the first run. However, the same routine is also used by `\include`, so that, unfortunately, a missing "include file" will trigger this unsuspicious warning too.

No input encoding specified for ⟨*language*⟩ language `babel`
: This message can appear when no specific input encoding was specified in the document and one of the supported languages needs the Cyrillic alphabet for typesetting. For these languages several input encodings are popular; therefore, the language definition insists that the one used *must* be explicitly mentioned.

No hyphenation patterns were loaded for the language '⟨*language*⟩' `babel`
: All language definition files check whether hyphenation patterns for the language selected were loaded into the LaTeX format. If this is not the case, this message is displayed and a default set of hyphenation patterns will be used. The default patterns are the those loaded into pattern register 0 (typically American English).

No positions in optional float specifier. Default added ...
: A float environment (e.g., `figure` or `table`) was used with its optional placement argument, but it did not contain any suitable information. Hence, LaTeX used its default placement rules.

---

[1] Sometimes you see something like `^^G`, sometimes real characters are displayed. Unfortunately, there is no guarantee that they correspond to your input: some translation that depends on the operating system may happen when the characters are written to the transcript file.

`Oldstyle digits unavailable for family` ⟨*name*⟩ `textcomp`
> You used `\oldstylenums` with a font family that does not contain old-style digits. As an emergency measure LaTeX produced lining digits (from the current font family) instead. See Section 7.5.4 for details.

`Optional argument of \twocolumn too tall on page` ⟨*number*⟩
> The material in the optional argument to `\twocolumn` was so tall, that fewer than three lines remain on the page. LaTeX will not start two-column mode on the current page and will start a new page instead.

`\oval, \circle, or \line size unavailable`
> The requested size for the mentioned commands is unavailable. LaTeX will choose the closest available size. See, for example, Section 10.4.3 for ways to avoid this problem.

`Overfull \hbox (badness` ⟨*number*⟩`)` ⟨*somewhere*⟩ `TeX`
> TeX was forced to build a horizontal box (e.g., the line of a paragraph or a `\makebox`) of a certain width and was unable to squeeze the material into the given width, even after shrinking any available space as much as possible. As a result, the material will stick out to the right. In most cases this is quite noticeable, even if the total amount is small. You have to correct this problem manually, since TeX was unable to resolve it (Sections 3.1.11 and B.3.3 give some advice). For a list and explanation of the possible origins (i.e., the ⟨*somewhere*⟩), see the warning "Underfull `\hbox`..." on page 928.

`Overfull \vbox (badness` ⟨*number*⟩`)` ⟨*somewhere*⟩ `TeX`
> TeX was asked to built a vertical box of a fixed size (e.g., a `\parbox` or a `minipage` with a second optional argument; see Appendix A.2.2 on page 866) and found more material than it could squeeze in. The excess material will stick out at the bottom. Whether this result poses a problem depends on the circumstances. For a list and explanation of the possible origins (i.e., the ⟨*somewhere*⟩), see the warning "Underfull `\vbox`..." on page 930.

`Overwriting encoding scheme` ⟨*something*⟩ `defaults`
> This warning is issued by `\DeclareFontEncodingDefaults` when it overwrites previously declared defaults for "text" or "math".

`Overwriting` ⟨*something*⟩ `in version` ⟨*name*⟩ `...`
> A declaration, such as `\SetSymbolFont` or `\DeclareMathAlphabet`, changed the assignment of font shapes to ⟨*something*⟩ (a symbol font or a math alphabet) in math version ⟨*name*⟩.

`Package:` ⟨*name*⟩ ⟨*date*⟩ ⟨*additional-info*⟩
> This line is produced by the `\ProvidesPackage` command, which is used to identify a package and its last modification date. By convention, the ⟨*additional-info*⟩ starts with a version number, though it is not required. Although of the same importance as `\ProvidesClass`, this information is written to just the transcript file to avoid cluttering the terminal with messages. If

a document produces different output on different installations, you should compare the "Document Class:", "File:", and "Package:" messages to identify any release differences.

Redeclaring font encoding ⟨*name*⟩
> This warning is issued if \DeclareFontEncoding is used for an encoding that is already defined (thereby potentially changing its defaults).

Redeclaring math accent ⟨*name*⟩
> This warning is issued if \DeclareMathAccent is used for a math accent that was previously declared. If the command to be declared is known but not an accent, you get an error message instead.

Redeclaring math alphabet ⟨*name*⟩
> A \DeclareMathAlphabet or \DeclareSymbolFontAlphabet command was issued to declare ⟨*name*⟩, which was already defined to be a math alphabet identifier. The new declaration overrides all previous settings for ⟨*name*⟩.

Redeclaring math symbol ⟨*name*⟩
> The command ⟨*name*⟩ was already declared as a math symbol and your declaration overrides the old definition.

Redeclaring math version ⟨*name*⟩
> You issued a \DeclareMathVersion command for a version that was already declared. The new declaration overrides all previous settings for this version with the default values.

Redeclaring symbol font ⟨*name*⟩
> You issued a \DeclareSymbolFont command for a symbol font that was previously declared. The new declaration overrides the symbol font in all known math versions.

Reference '⟨*key*⟩' on page ⟨*number*⟩ undefined
> A reference created with \ref, \pageref, or one of the other cross-reference commands discussed in Chapter 2 used a ⟨*key*⟩ for which LaTeX has not seen a corresponding \label command. If the \label is somewhere in the document, you simply need another LaTeX run to make it known to LaTeX. This situation is indicated by the additional warning "Label(s) may have changed..." discussed on page 924.

Size substitutions with differences up to ⟨*size*⟩ have occurred
> This message will appear at the end of the run if LaTeX selected at least one significantly different font size because a requested size was not available. The ⟨*size*⟩ is the maximum deviation that was needed.

Some font shapes were not available, defaults substituted
> This message will appear at the end of the run if LaTeX had to use automatic font substitution for some font shapes.

`Tab has been converted to Blank Space`

The `filecontents` environment detected a "tab" character (`^^I`) in the source and will write it as a space into the external file.

`Text page ⟨number⟩ contains only floats`

One or more floats processed as "top" or "bottom" floats are together so tall that very little space (less than two lines) is left for normal text on the current page. Therefore, LaTeX decided to place only floats on the page in question (even if some or all of the floats do not explicitly allow for this placement). This message can appear only when the placement parameters for floats were changed drastically from their default values; see the beginning of Chapter 6 for details.

`There were multiply-defined labels`

This warning appears at the end of a LaTeX run when LaTeX detected at least one pair of `\label` or `\bibitem` commands with the same key. Check the transcript file and make sure that all keys used are different.

`There were undefined references`

This warning appears at the end of a LaTeX run when LaTeX detected references to unknown keys and concluded that rerunning the document would not resolve them. You should check the transcript file for all occurrences of "Reference ⟨key⟩ undefined" and "Citation ⟨key⟩ undefined" and correct them, either by fixing a misprint or by adding the necessary `\label` or `\bibitem` commands. In case of missing citation ⟨keys⟩, all you may have to do is rerun BibTeX and then LaTeX.

`Tight \hbox (badness ⟨number⟩) ⟨somewhere⟩` TeX

TeX produced a horizontal box and had to shrink the interior spaces. You will see this message only if `\hbadness` is set to a value less than 100. See the message "Underfull \hbox..." below for more details.

`Tight \hbox (badness ⟨number⟩) ⟨somewhere⟩` TeX

TeX produced a vertical box and had to shrink the interior spaces. You will see this message only if `\vbadness` is set to a value less than 100. See the message "Underfull \vbox..." on page 930 for more details.

`Try loading font information for ⟨cdp⟩+⟨family⟩`

You will find such a message in the transcript file whenever LaTeX tries to load a `.fd` file for the encoding/family combination ⟨cdp⟩/⟨family⟩.

`Unable to redefine math accent ⟨accent⟩` amsmath

This warning is rare but it may be issued when loading the amsmath package with nonstandard mathematical fonts.

`Underfull \hbox (badness ⟨number⟩) ⟨somewhere⟩` TeX

TeX was forced to build a horizontal box (e.g., the line of a paragraph or a `\makebox`) of a certain width, and the white space within that box had to stretch more than it was designed to do (i.e., stretched more than 100% of the available `plus` parts in stretchable spaces). Internally, this situation is expressed by a badness value greater than 100; a value of 800 means that twice the total stretchability was used to produce the required width.[1]

Whether such an underfull box actually presents a noticeable problem is something that you may have to check visually in the produced output. If the badness is 10000 the box can be arbitrarily bad. Since TEX's value for infinity is quite low, it might mean that TEX has favored one very bad line over several bad but still acceptable lines that appear in succession. In that case using `\emergencystretch` can help you; see Section 3.1.11.

The limit of badness values above which such warnings are shown is controlled by the integer parameter `\hbadness`. LATEX's default is 1000, so warnings appear only for really bad boxes. If you want to produce an important document try a more challenging value, such as `\hbadness=10`, to find out how many lines TEX really considers imperfect.

Note that the warning always talks about `\hbox`, regardless of the actual box construct used in the source, since it is directly generated by TEX. The location where the problem occurred is indicated by ⟨*somewhere*⟩, which is one of the following four possibilities:

detected at line ⟨*line number*⟩ TEX
> An explicitly constructed box (construction ending at line ⟨*line number*⟩ in the source) has the problem—for example, a `\makebox` with an explicit width argument or some other LATEX construct that builds boxes.

has occurred while \output is active TEX
> TEX was in the process of building a page and encountered the problem while attaching running headers and footers and the like. Since this is an asynchronous operation, no line number is given. Look at the page generated closest to where the warning was issued to determine whether it warrants manual correction.

in alignment at lines ⟨*line numbers*⟩ TEX
> The box is part of a `tabular` or some math alignment environment. The ⟨*line numbers*⟩ give you the source position of the whole alignment structure, since by the time TEX encounters the problem it no longer has a way to relate it back to the source in more detail.

in paragraph at lines ⟨*line numbers*⟩ TEX
> The underfull box is due to a badly spaced line in the paragraph (source line numbers given as ⟨*line numbers*⟩). The additional symbolic display of the line in question should help you to pinpoint the problem.

---

[1] The exact formula is $\min(100r^3, 10000)$ where r is the ratio of "stretch used" to "stretch available", unless there is infinite stretch present (e.g., introduced by a command like `\hfill`), in which case the badness will be zero.

`Underfull \vbox (badness ⟨number⟩) ⟨somewhere⟩` TEX

TEX was forced to build a vertical box (e.g., a `\parbox` or a `minipage`) of a certain height, and the vertical space in that box had to stretch more than it was supposed to; see the discussion of badness and stretchability in the description of the "Underfull `\hbox`..." warning. You can suppress all warnings for badness values below a certain limit by setting `\vbadness=⟨value⟩`. Then LATEX issues warnings only for boxes with a badness larger than ⟨value⟩ (the default is 1000). The ⟨somewhere⟩ indicates the origin of the problem and can be one of the following cases:

`detected at line ⟨line number⟩` TEX

The box was explicitly constructed (the ⟨line number⟩ points to the end of the box construction) and there is not enough stretchable space available. For example,

`\parbox[c][2in][s]{4cm}{test test}`

would produce this warning because the box should be 2 inches high and the contents should fill this height (argument `[s]`), but there is nothing stretchable available. For instance, something like `\par\vfill` between the two words. See Appendix A.2.2 for details on paragraph boxes.

`has occurred while \output is active` TEX

In the most frequent case, the space on the current page needed stretching beyond acceptable limits in TEX's eyes. Whether this is visually a real problem depends on many factors, such as the type of spaces on the page. For example, a large stretch in front of a heading is usually less severe than a spaced-out list. Thus, the best advice is to check such pages manually. Often, `\enlargethispage` or `\pagebreak` will help.

If the problem appears surprisingly often, then the spacing parameters for lists, paragraphs, and headings should be examined to see whether they are too rigid (see Chapters 2 to 4). Also check whether the `\textheight` corresponds to an integral number of text lines; see the discussion on page 197.

`in alignment at lines ⟨line-numbers⟩` TEX

This warning should not arise with standard LATEX but can occur in some specialized applications. In such a case use ⟨line-numbers⟩ to itentify the source lines in your document.

`Unused global option(s): [⟨option-list⟩]`

Some of the options specified on `\documentclass` have been used by neither the class nor any package in the preamble. A likely reason is that the names of the options have been misspelled. Also note that some packages do not react to global options, but only to those explicitly specified when loading the package. See Appendix A.4 for details.

```
Writing file '⟨name⟩'
```
This informational message is produced by both `filecontents` and `filecontents*` when they write their body to an external file ⟨name⟩.

```
Writing text '⟨text⟩' before \end{⟨env⟩} as last line of ⟨file⟩
```
This warning is issued by the `filecontents` or `filecontents*` environment when it detects textual material directly preceeding the `\end` tag.

```
You have more than once selected the attribute '⟨attrib⟩'  babel
for language ⟨language⟩
```
This message is displayed if the same attribute is entered more than once in the second argument of `\languageattribute`; only the first occurrence will trigger the activation of the attribute.

```
You have requested ⟨package-or-class⟩ '⟨name⟩',
but the ⟨package-or-class⟩ provides '⟨alternate-name⟩'
```
You requested loading of ⟨name⟩ via `\usepackage` or `\RequirePackage` (in case of a package) or via `\documentclass` or `\LoadClass` (in case of a class), but the package or class provides a variant of the original with the internal name ⟨alternate-name⟩. Unless this was a typo by the package or class provider, it means that your installation has a package or class variant that is likely to behave differently from the original. Thus, your document may be formatted differently when processed on another installation. Whether this is the correct behavior is something you need to investigate by looking at the package in question.

```
You have requested release '⟨date⟩' of LaTeX,
but only release '⟨old-date⟩' is available
```
A `\NeedsTeXFormat` command has requested a LATEX release of at least ⟨date⟩ but the date of your format is ⟨old-date⟩. Usually, such a request is made to ensure that a certain feature of the LATEX format is available, so it is likely that your document will produce additional errors or strange formatting later. Update to a more recent version of LATEX.

```
You have requested, on line ⟨num⟩, version '⟨date⟩' of ⟨name⟩,
but only version '⟨old-date⟩' is available
```
A class or package was required to have a date not older than ⟨date⟩ but the version on your installation is from the date ⟨old-date⟩. Update the class or package in question.

B.3   TEX and LATEX commands for tracing

In this section we discuss tools and techniques for tracing and for displaying status information—for example, finding out why something is strangely spaced on the page or why your own command definition does the wrong thing.

B.3.1   Displaying command definitions and register values

In many situations it is useful to get some information about LATEX's current internals, the precise definitions of commands, the values of registers, and so on. For example, if the use of \newcommand reports that the command to be defined is already defined, you may want to know its current definition, to ensure that you do not redefine an important command.

Displaying command definitions

For this purpose TeX offers the command \show, which displays the definition of the token following it and then stops and displays a question mark while waiting for user intervention. For example, after defining \xvec as in Example A-1-4 on page 844, we can display its definition as follows:

```
\newcommand\xvec[1]{\ensuremath{x_1,\ldots,x_{#1}}}
\show\xvec
```

This will produce the following output on the terminal and in the transcript file:

```
> \xvec=\long macro:
#1->\ensuremath {x_1,\ldots ,x_{#1}}.
l.6 \show\xvec

?
```

The first line, twhich starts with >, shows the token being displayed (\xvec) and gives its type (\long macro), indicating that \xvec is a macro that accepts \par commands in its argument; in other words, this macro was defined with \newcommand rather than \newcommand*. The second line shows the argument structure for the command (up to ->), revealing that the command has one argument (#1). Note that while the argument on the \newcommand declaration was indicated with [1], it is now shown differently. The rest of the line—and possibly further lines, if necessary—shows the definition part. The code is terminated with a period that is not part of the definition but helps to identify stray spaces at the end of the definition, if any. Note that the code display is normalized. Thus, after a command that would swallow subsequent spaces, you will see a space regardless of whether a space was coded in the original definition.

Following the display of the definition, the source line (including the line number in the input file) is shown. Then LATEX stops with a question mark. To continue you can press enter. Alternatively, you can type h to see what other possibilities are available.

Not all commands produce such easily understandable output. Assume that you try to display a command that was defined to have an optional argument, such as \lvec as defined in Example A-1-5 on page 845:

```
\newcommand\lvec[2][n]
  {\ensuremath{#2_1+\cdots + #2_{#1}}}
\show\lvec
```

In that case you will get this result:

```
> \lvec=macro:
->\@protected@testopt \lvec \\lvec {n}.
```

Apparently, the \lvec command has no arguments whatsoever (they are picked
up later in the processing). And something else is strange in this output: what
is \\lvec? Is it the command \\ followed by the letters lvec, or is it a strange
command \\lvec that has two backslashes as part of its name? It is actually the
latter, though there is no way to determine this fact from looking at the output
of the \show command. Such strange command names, which cannot be generated easily by the user, are sometimes used by LATEX internally to produce new
command names from existing ones using \csname and \endcsname and other
low-level mechanisms of TEX.

So what should you do, if you want to see the definition of \\lvec? It should be clear   *Displaying internal*
that writing \show in front of such a command will not work, as in normal situations TEX   *commands with*
will see \\ and think that it is the command to "show". For that reason, you have to use   *strange names*
the same low-level mechanisms first to generate the command name in a way that it is
considered a single token by TEX and then to feed this token to \show:

```
\expandafter\show\csname \string\lvec \endcsname
```

Technically, what happens is that a command name is generated from the tokens between \csname and \endcsname. Inside that construct, the \string command turns the
command \lvec into a sequence of characters starting with a backslash that no longer
denotes the start of a command. This is why the resulting command name contains two
backslashes at the beginning. The \expandafter command delays the evaluation of the
following \show command so that \csname can perform all of its work before \show is
allowed to look at the result.

That's quite a mouthful of low-level TEX, but after typing it in, we are rewarded with
the following output:

```
> \\lvec=\long macro:
[#1]#2->\ensuremath {#2_1+\cdots + #2_{#1}}.
<recently read> \\lvec
```

This time we do not see a source file line after the command display, but the words
<recently read>. They indicate that TEX has assembled the token \\lvec somewhere in
memory rather than reading it directly from a file.

What would happen if we forgot the initial \expandafter in the previous input? We
would get the following result:

```
> \csname=\csname.
l.5 \show\csname
                 \string\lvec \endcsname
?
! Extra \endcsname.
l.5 \show\csname \string\lvec \endcsname

?
```

Detecting a primitive command
First we are told that \csname is a \csname, which seems like totally useless information but, in fact, indicates that \csname is a primitive command or register already built into the TeX program—in contrast to, say, \lvec, which was a macro defined via \newcommand. LaTeX also shows how far it has read the input line by placing the unread tokens (\string and friends) into the next line. Since we carry on, TeX will stop again shortly (after having consumed the whole line) to complain about a spurious \endcsname because the matching \csname was shown but not executed.

Displaying register values
The \show command is useful for learning about commands and their definitions or finding out if something is a primitive of TeX. But it does not help in finding the current values of length or counter registers. For example,

```
\show\parskip \show\topmargin \show\topsep
```

will give us the following information:

```
> \parskip=\parskip.
1.5 \show\parskip
                      \show\topmargin \show\topsep
?
> \topmargin=\dimen73.
1.5 \show\parskip \show\topmargin
                                  \show\topsep
?
> \topsep=\skip23.
1.5 \show\parskip \show\topmargin \show\topsep
```

From the above we can deduce that \parskip is a TeX primitive (the fact that it is a rubber length is not revealed), that \topmargin is actually the \dimen register (rigid length) with register number 73, and that \topsep is the \skip register (rubber length) with number 23.

If we want to know the value of any such register, we need to deploy a different TeX primitive, called \showthe instead of \show, which gives us the following output on the terminal and also proves that \parskip is, indeed, a rubber length:

```
> 0.0pt plus 1.0pt.
1.5 \showthe\parskip
```

Using \showthe in this way allows us to display the values of the length registers allocated with \newlength and of internal TeX registers such as \baselineskip and \tolerance. What we cannot display directly with it are the values of LaTeX counters allocated with \newcounter. For this we have to additionally deploy a \value command that turns a LaTeX counter name into a form that is accepted by \showthe. For example,

```
\showthe\value{footnote}
```

would show the current value of the footnote counter on the terminal.

Instead of displaying the meaning of a macro or the value of a register on the terminal, you can alternatively typeset this kind of data by using \meaning instead of \show and \the instead of \showthe. The output is slightly different: the name and the type of a token are not shown by \meaning; instead, only its "meaning" is presented. Compare the next example with the output shown earlier in this section. *Typesetting command definitions or register values*

B-3-1

```
\long macro:#1->\ensuremath
{x_1,\ldots ,x_{#1}}
0.0pt plus 1.0pt
16.0pt
8.0pt plus 2.0pt minus 4.0pt
footnote=0
```

```
\newcommand\xvec[1]{\ensuremath{x_1,\ldots,x_{#1}}}
\ttfamily     % use typewriter
\raggedright
\meaning\xvec    \par \the\parskip\par
\the\topmargin  \par \the\topsep \par
footnote=\the\value{footnote}
```

If displaying command definitions or register values is insufficient for determining a problem, you can alternatively trace the behavior of the commands in action; see Section B.3.5 on page 945.

B.3.2   Diagnosing page-breaking problems

Once in a while LaTeX produces unexpected page breaks or shows some strange vertical spaces and you would like to understand where they are coming from or what precise dimensions are involved. For these tasks TeX offers a few low-level tracing tools.

Symbolic display of the page contents

If you specify \showoutput somewhere in your document, TeX will display (starting with the current page) symbolic representations of complete pages on the terminal and the transcript file. This will generate a large amount of output, of which we will show some extracts that have been produced by compiling the first paragraph of this section separately.

Every page output will start with the string Completed box being shipped out followed by the current page number in brackets. Then you get many lines showing the boxes that make up the page, starting with a \vbox (vertical box) and its sizes in pt containing the whole page. To indicate that something is the contents of a box, everything inside is recursively indented using periods instead of blanks. Spaces, even if they are rigid, are indicated by the keyword \glue (see line 3 or 6); stretchable space has some plus and/or minus components in its value, as we will see later. Whether it is a horizontal or a vertical space is determined by the box in which this space is placed. For example, the \glue of 16.0pt on line 3 is a vertical space that came from \topmargin; see also Example B-3-1. In the extract you also see an empty \vbox of height 12pt (lines 5 to 7), which is the empty running header, followed in line 8 by the space from \headsep (25pt), followed by the box containing the text area of the page starting at line 10. Lines 15 and following show how individual characters are displayed; here \T1/cmr/m/n/10 indicates the font for each character. The \glue in between (e.g., line 19, marks an interword space with its stretch and shrink components).

```
 1   Completed box being shipped out [1]
 2   \vbox(633.0+0.0)x407.0
 3   .\glue 16.0
 4   .\vbox(617.0+0.0)x345.0, shifted 62.0
 5   ..\vbox(12.0+0.0)x345.0, glue set 12.0fil
 6   ...\glue 0.0 plus 1.0fil
 7   ...\hbox(0.0+0.0)x345.0
 8   ..\glue 25.0
 9   ..\glue(\lineskip) 0.0
10   ..\vbox(550.0+0.0)x345.0, glue set 502.00241fil
11   ...\write-{}
12   ...\glue(\topskip) 3.1128
13   ...\hbox(6.8872+2.15225)x345.0, glue set - 0.17497
14   ....\hbox(0.0+0.0)x15.0
15   ....\T1/cmr/m/n/10 O
16   ....\T1/cmr/m/n/10 n
17   ....\T1/cmr/m/n/10 c
18   ....\T1/cmr/m/n/10 e
19   ....\glue 3.33252 plus 1.66626 minus 1.11084
20   ....\T1/cmr/m/n/10 i
21   ....\T1/cmr/m/n/10 n
22   ....\glue 3.33252 plus 1.66626 minus 1.11084
23   ....\T1/cmr/m/n/10 a
```

As a second example from a page trace, we show the symbolic display of the structures near a line break. You see the space added by TeX at the right end of a text line (\rightskip on line 5) and the box containing the line. Thus, line 6 is outdented again. It contains a symbolic representation for the costs to TeX to break after this line, indicated by the command \penalty. The actual value here is due to the value of the \clubpenalty parameter.[1] This is followed in line 7 by the vertical space added between the lines, computed by TeX by taking the value of \baselineskip and subtracting the depth of the previous line box and the height of the following line box, which starts at line 8.

```
 1   ....\T1/cmr/m/n/10 s
 2   ....\T1/cmr/m/n/10 o
 3   ....\T1/cmr/m/n/10 m
 4   ....\T1/cmr/m/n/10 e
 5   ....\glue(\rightskip) 0.0
```

---

[1]The penalty to break after the first line in a paragraph is given by the integer parameter \clubpenalty; the cost for breaking before the last line by \widowpenalty. Both default to 150, that is, they slightly discourage a break.

```
6   ...\penalty 150
7   ...\glue(\baselineskip) 2.96054
8   ...\hbox(6.8872+1.94397)x345.0, glue set 0.55421
9   ....\T1/cmr/m/n/10 s
10  ....\T1/cmr/m/n/10 t
```

As a final example, we look at some part of the symbolic page output produced from a line like this:

```
\begin{itemize} \item test \end{itemize}  \section{Test}
```

The particular part of interest is the one generated from \end{itemize} and \section{Test}. What we see here (lines 1 to 7) is a curious collection of \glue statements, most of which cancel each other, intermixed with a number of \penalty points:

```
1   ...\penalty -51
2   ...\glue 10.0 plus 3.0 minus 5.0
3   ...\glue -10.0 plus -3.0 minus -5.0
4   ...\penalty -300
5   ...\glue 10.0 plus 3.0 minus 5.0
6   ...\glue -10.0 plus -3.0 minus -5.0
7   ...\glue 15.0694 plus 4.30554 minus 0.86108
8   ...\glue(\parskip) 0.0 plus 1.0
9   ...\glue(\baselineskip) 8.12001
10  ...\hbox(9.87999+0.0)x345.0, glue set 290.70172fil
```

These lines are generated from various \addpenalty and \addvspace commands issued; for example, lines 1 and 2 are the penalty and the rubber space added by \end{itemize}. The \section command then adds a breakpoint to indicate that the place before the section is a good place to break a page (using \@secpenalty with a value of -300). In fact, the break should be taken before the \glue from line 2, or else there would be a strange space at the bottom of that page. As it is technically impossible to remove material from the vertical galley, \addpenalty uses the trick to back up by adding a negative space (line 3), add the penalty (line 4), and then reissue the \glue (line 5). In lines 6 and 7, the same method is used by \addvspace to add the vertical space before the heading.

Lines 8 and 9 are added by TEX when placing the actual heading text (line 10) into the galley. Note that technically the heading is considered a "paragraph", so \parskip is added. This is the reason why enlarging this parameter requires careful planning. The same care should be taken when adjusting other parameters (like the one added on line 7).

The \showoutput command will also produce symbolic displays of overfull *Side effect of* boxes. Tracing ends at the next closing brace or environment. Thus, to see the \showoutput output for full pages, you have to ensure that the page break happens before the next group ends.

Tracing page-break decisions

If you want to trace page-breaking decisions, TeX offers symbolic information that you can turn on by setting the internal counter \tracingpages to a positive integer value:

```
\tracingonline=1 \tracingpages=1
```

Setting \tracingonline to a positive value will ensure that the tracing information will appear not only in the transcript file (default), but also on the terminal.

Processing the previous paragraph starting with "If you want to..." as a separate document, we get the following lines of tracing information:

```
1   %% goal height=522.0, max depth=4.0
2   % t=10.0 g=522.0 b=10000 p=150 c=100000#
3   % t=22.0 g=522.0 b=10000 p=150 c=100000#
4   % t=55.0 plus 4.0 g=522.0 b=10000 p=-51 c=100000#
5   % t=77.0 plus 8.0 g=522.0 b=10000 p=300 c=100000#
6   % t=89.0 plus 8.0 g=522.0 b=10000 p=0 c=100000#
7   % t=90.94397 plus 8.0 plus 1.0fil g=522.0 b=0 p=-10000 c=-10000#
```

The first line starting with two percent signs shows the target height for the page (i.e., 522pt in this case), which means 43 lines at a \baselineskip of 12pt with 2pt missing since the skip to position the first base line, \topskip, has a value of 10pt. If the goal height does not result in an integral number of lines, problems like underfull \vboxes are likely to happen.

Target size of a break The remaining lines, starting with one percent sign, indicate a new potential page-break position that TeX has considered. You can interpret such lines as follows: t= shows the length of the galley so far and, if the galley contains vertical rubber spaces, their total amount of stretch and shrink. Line 4, for example, shows that in the layout of this book verbatim displays have an extra space of 10pt plus a stretch of 4pt (the verbatim lines are typeset in a smaller font with only 11pt of \baselineskip) and the same amount is added between lines 4 and 5.

Page goal height The g= specifies the goal height at this point. This value changes only if objects like floats have reduced the available space for the galley in the meantime.

Page badness With b=, TeX indicates the badness of the page if a break would be taken at this point. The badness is calculated from the factor by which the available stretch or shrink in t= must be multiplied to reach the goal height given in g=. In the example the page is barely filled, so it is always 10000 (infinitely bad), except for line 7, where, due to the added fil stretch, the page is suddenly considered optimal (b=0).

Break penalty With each breakpoint TeX associates a numerical \penalty as the cost to break at this point. Its value is given by p=. For example, it is not allowed to break directly before the verbatim display, which is why there is a large addition to t= between lines 3 and 4. On the other hand, a break after the display is given a bonus (p=-51). Line 5 shows that breaking after the first line of the two-line paragraph fragment following the verbatim text is considered bad (p=300), as it would result in both a club and a widow line (\clubpenalty and \widowpenalty each have a value of 150 and their values are added together).

Finally, c= describes the calculated cost to break at this breakpoint, which *Costs of* is derived from a formula taking the badness of the resulting page (b=) and the *a page break* penalty to break here (p=) into account. TEX looks at these cost values and will eventually break at the point with minimal cost. If the line ends in #, then TEX thinks that it would be the best place to break the page after evaluating all break-points seen so far. In the example, all lines show this #—not surprising, given that TEX considers all but the last breakpoint to be equally bad.

If the pages would become too full if a break is taken at a particular break-point, then TEX indicates fact this with b=*. At this point TEX stops looking for other breakpoints and instead breaks the page at the best breakpoint seen so far.

For additional details on the output produced by these low-level display de-vices, consult [82, p.112].

B.3.3   Diagnosing and solving paragraph-breaking problems

If TEX is unable to find a suitable set of points at which to break a paragraph into lines, it will, as a last resort, produce one or more lines that are "overfull". For each of them you will get a warning on the screen and in the transcript file, such as

```
Overfull \hbox (17.57108pt too wide) in paragraph at lines 3778--3793
/hlhr8t@8.80005pt/showing you a sym-bolic dis-play of the text line and the
line num-ber(s) of the paragraph|
```

showing you a symbolic display of the text line and the line number(s) of the paragraph▉ containing it. If you look at the symbolic display, you can easily diagnose that the problem is TEX's inability[1] to hyphenate the word "paragraph". To explicitly flag such lines in your document, you can set the parameter \overfullrule to a positive value. For the present paragraph it was set to 5pt, producing the blob of ink clearly marking the line that is overfull. The standard document classes enable this behavior with the option draft. On the other hand, you may not mind lines being only slightly overfull. In that case you can change the parameter \hfuzz (default 0.1pt); only lines protruding by more than the value of \hfuzz into the margin will then be reported.

If TEX is unable to break a paragraph in a satisfying manner, the reasons are often hyphenation problems (unbreakable words, as in the above example), prob-lems with the parameter settings for the paragraph algorithm, or simply failure of the text to fit the boundary conditions posed by the column measure or other

---

[1] TEX is, in fact, perfectly capable of hyphenating para-graph; for the example, we explicitly pre-vented it from doing so. The paragraph would have been perfect otherwise.

parameters, together with aesthetic requirements like the allowed looseness of individual lines. In the latter case the only remedy is usually a partial rewrite.

Dealing with hyphenation problems

With the relevant hyphenation patterns loaded, TeX is able to do a fairly good job for many languages [115]. However, it usually will not find all potential hyphenation points, so that sometimes one has to assist TeX in this task. To find out which hyphenation points in words like "laryngologist" are found by TeX, you can place such words or phrases in the argument of the command \showhyphens:

```
\showhyphens{laryngologist laryngopharyngeal}
```

Running this statement through LaTeX will give you some tracing output on the terminal and in the transcript file. The hyphenation points determined by TeX are indicated by a hyphen character:

```
[] \OT1/cmr/m/n/10 laryn-gol-o-gist laryn-gopha-ryn-geal
```

If you want to add the missing hyphenation points, you can specify all hyphenation points for one word locally in the text using \-, for example,

```
la\-ryn\-gol\-o\-gist   la\-ryn\-go\-pha\-ryn\-ge\-al
```

Alternatively, you can use a \hyphenation declaration in the preamble:

```
\hyphenation{la-ryn-gol-o-gist   la-ryn-go-pha-ryn-ge-al}
```

The latter technique is particularly useful when you detect a wrong hyphenation, or often use a word for which you know that TeX misses important hyphenation points. Note that such explicit specifications tell TeX how to hyphenate words that are exactly in the form given. Thus, the plural "laryngologists" would be unaffected unless you specify its hyphenation points as well.

The \hyphenation declarations apply to the current language, so if a document uses several languages—for example, by using the methods provided by the babel system—then you need to switch to the right language before issuing the relevant declarations.

Tracing the paragraph algorithm

As TeX uses a global algorithm for optimizing paragraph breaking, it is not always easy to understand why a certain solution was chosen. If necessary, one can trace the paragraph-breaking decisions using the following declarations:[1]

```
\tracingparagraphs=1 \tracingonline=1
```

---

[1] These parameters are also turned on by a \tracingall command, so you may get many lines of paragraph tracing data, even if you are interested in something completely different.

For readers who really want to understand the reasons behind certain decisions, we show some example data with detailed explanations below.

Paragraph tracing will produce output that looks somewhat scary. For instance, one of the previous paragraphs generated data that starts like this:

```
1   @firstpass
2   @secondpass
3   []\T1/cmr/m/n/10 The [] dec-la-ra-tions ap-ply to the cur-rent lan-guage, so
4   @ via @@0 b=3219 p=0 d=10436441
```

Line 2 says that TEX has immediately given up trying to typeset the paragraph without attempting hyphenation. This is due to the value of \pretolerance being set to 100 in the sources for the book; otherwise, TEX may have gotten further or even succeeded (in English text quite a large proportion of paragraphs can be reasonably set without hyphenating[1]). In addition to @secondpass, you sometimes see @emergencypass, which means that even with hyphenation it was impossible to find a feasible solution and another pass using \emergencystretch was tried.[2] Line 3 shows how far TEX had to read to find that first potential line ending that results in a badness of less than $\infty = 10000$. Line 4 gives details about this possible break. Such lines start with a single @; the via gives the previous breakpoint (in this case @@0, which refers to the paragraph start), the line badness (b=), the penalty to break at this point (p=), and the so-called demerits associated with taking that break (a "cost" that takes into account badness, penalty, plus context information like breaking at a hyphen or the visual compatibility with the previous line).

Up to three passes over paragraph data

```
5   @@1: line 1.0 t=10436441 -> @@0
```

In line 5, TEX informs us that it would be possible to form a very loose first line ending in the breakpoint given by line 3 with a total cost (t=) equal to the demerits shown on line 4. This line would be formed by starting at breakpoint @@0. The notation line 1.0 gives the line number being made and the suffixes .0, .1, .2, .3, respectively, stand for very loose, loose, decent, and tight interword spacing in the line. This classification is important when comparing the visual compatibility of consecutive lines.

TEX now finds more and more potential line breaks, such as after "if" in line 6, and after "a" in line 9. Each time TEX tells us what kind of lines can be formed that end in the given breakpoint. If b=* appears anywhere in the trace data, it means that TEX could not find a feasible breakpoint to form a line and had to choose an infeasible solution (i.e., one exceeding \tolerance for the particular line).

```
6    if
7    @ via @@0 b=1087 p=0 d=1213409
8    @@2: line 1.0 t=1213409 -> @@0
9    a
10   @ via @@0 b=334 p=0 d=128336
11   @@3: line 1.0 t=128336 -> @@0
12   doc-
13   @\discretionary via @@0 b=0 p=50 d=2600
14   @@4: line 1.2- t=2600 -> @@0
15   u-
```

---

[1] For the *LATEX Companion* with its many long command names this is less likely.

[2] For this to happen \emergencystretch needs to have a positive value. See also the discussion in Section 3.1.11.

16   @\discretionary via @@0 b=1 p=50 d=2621
17   @@5: line 1.2- t=2621 -> @@0

By hyphenating the word doc-u-ment it finds two more breakpoints (lines 12 and 15). This
time you see a penalty of 50—the value of the parameter \hyphenpenalty (breaking after
a hyphen)—being attached to these breaks. Line 15 is the last breakpoint that can be used
to produce the first line of the paragraph. All other breakpoints would produce an overfull
line. Hence, the next tracing line again shows more text; none of the potential breakpoints
therein can be used as they would form a second line that exceeds \tolerance.

18   ment uses sev-eral languages---for ex-am-ple, by us-ing the meth-
19   @\discretionary via @@1 b=1194 p=50 d=1452116
20   @\discretionary via @@2 b=2875 p=50 d=8325725
21   @@6: line 2.0- t=9539134 -> @@2

Here the breakpoint can be used to form a second line in two different ways: by starting
from breakpoint @@1 (line 19) or by starting from breakpoint @@2 (line 20). If we compare
just these two solutions to form the second line of the paragraph, then the first would be
superior: it has a badness of 1194, whereas the second solution has a badness of 2875,
which results in a factor of 5 in "costs" (d=). Nevertheless, TEX considers the second break
a better solution, because a first line ending in @@1 is so much inferior to a line ending in
@@2 that the total cost for breaking is less if the second alternative is used. TEX therefore
records in line 21 that the best way to reach the breakpoint denoted by line 18 is by
coming via @@2 and results in a total cost of t=9539134. For the rest of the processing,
TEX will not need to know that there were several ways to reach @@2; it just needs to record
the best way to reach it.

More precisely, TEX needs to record the best way to reach a breakpoint for any of the
four types of lines (very loose, loose, decent, tight), since the algorithm attaches different
demerits to a solution if adjacent lines are visually incompatible (e.g., a loose line following
a tight one). Thus, later in the tracing (lines 22–40 are not shown), we get the following
output:

41   by
42   @ via @@3 b=19 p=0 d=10841
43   @ via @@4 b=9 p=0 d=361
44   @ via @@5 b=42 p=0 d=2704
45   @@10: line 2.1 t=5325 -> @@5
46   @@11: line 2.2 t=2961 -> @@4

This output indicates that there are three ways to form a line ending in "by": by starting
from @@3, @@4, or @@5. A line with a badness of 12 or less is considered decent (suffix .2); a
line stretching, but with a badness not higher than 100, is considered loose (suffix .1). So
here TEX records two feasible breakpoints for further consideration—one going through
@@5 and one going through @@4.

Which path through the breakpoints is finally selected will be decided only when
the very end of the paragraph is reached. Thus, any modification anywhere in the paragraph, however minor, might make TEX decide that a different set of breakpoints will
form the best solution to the current line-breaking problem, because it will produce the
lowest total cost. Due to the complexity of the algorithm, minor modifications sometimes have surprising results. For example, the deletion of a word may make the paragraph a line longer. This may happen because TEX decides that using uniformly loose

lines, or avoiding hyphenation of a word, is preferable to some other way to break the paragraph. Further details, describing all parameters that influence the line-breaking decisions, can be found in [82, p.98]. If necessary, you can force breakpoints in certain places with \linebreak, or prevent them with \nolinebreak or by using ~ in place of a space. Clearly, choices in the early parts of a paragraph are rather limited and you may have to rewrite a sentence to avoid a bad break. But later in a paragraph nearly every potential break will become feasible, being reachable without exceeding the specified \tolerance.

Shortening or lengthening a paragraph

Another low-level tool that can be used is the internal counter \looseness. If you set it to a nonzero integer n, TEX will try to make the next paragraph n lines longer (n positive) or shorter (n negative), while maintaining all other boundary conditions (e.g., the allowed \tolerance). In fact, the last paragraph of the previous section was artificially lengthened by one line by starting it in the following way:

```
\looseness=1
Which path through the breakpoints is finally selected
```

Setting the value of \looseness is not guaranteed to have any effect. Shortening a paragraph is more difficult for TEX than lengthening it, since interword spaces have a limited shinkability that is small in comparison to their normal stretchability. The best results are obtained with long paragraphs having a short last line. Consequently, extending a paragraph works best on long paragraphs with a last line that is already nearly full, though you may have to put the last words of the paragraph together in an \mbox to ensure that more than one word is placed into the last line.

B.3.4   Other low-level tracing tools

TEX offers a number of other internal integer parameters and commands that can sometimes help in determining the source of a problem. They are listed here with a short explanation of their use.

We already encountered \tracingonline. If it is set to a positive value all tracing information is shown on the terminal; otherwise, most of it is written only to the transcript file. This parameter is automatically turned on by \tracingall. *On-line tracing*

With \tracingoutput, tracing of page contents is turned on. What is shown depends on two additional parameters: \showboxdepth (up to which level nested boxes are displayed) and \showboxbreadth (the amount of material shown for each level). Anything exceeding these values is abbreviated using etc. or [] (indicating a nested box) in the symbolic display. The LATEX command \showoutput sets these parameters to their maximum values and \tracingoutput to 1, so that you get the most detailed information possible. The \showoutput command is automatically called by \tracingall.

The contents   To see the contents of a box produced with \sbox or \savebox, you can use
of boxes the TeX command \showbox:

```
\newsavebox\test \sbox\test{A test} {\tracingonline=1 \showbox\test }
```

However, the result is fairly useless if you do not adjust both \showboxdepth
and \showboxbreadth at the same time. Hence, a better strategy is to use LaTeX's
\showoutput:

```
{\showoutput \showbox\test }
```

Notice the use of braces to limit the scope of \showoutput. Without the braces
you would see all of the following page boxes, which might not be of much interest.
The same type of symbolic display as discussed in Section B.3.2 will be displayed
on the terminal:

```
> \box26=
\hbox(6.83331+0.0)x27.00003
.\OT1/cmr/m/n/10 A
.\glue 3.33333 plus 1.66498 minus 1.11221
.\OT1/cmr/m/n/10 t
.\OT1/cmr/m/n/10 e
.\OT1/cmr/m/n/10 s
.\OT1/cmr/m/n/10 t
```

If you add \scrollmode or \batchmode before the \showbox command, LaTeX will
not stop at this point. You can then study the trace in the transcript.

Local   To see what values and definitions TeX restores when a group ends, you
restores can set \tracingrestores to a positive value. It is automatically turned on by
\tracingall.

TeX's stack of lists   With \showlists you can direct TeX to display the stack of lists (vertical,
horizontal) that it is currently working on. For instance, putting \showlists into
the footnote[1] of the present paragraph, we obtain the following output in the
transcript file:

```
### horizontal mode entered at line 3066 []
spacefactor 1000
### internal vertical mode entered at line 3066
prevdepth ignored
### horizontal mode entered at line 3060 []
spacefactor 1000
### vertical mode entered at line 0
### current page: []
total height 514.70349 plus 26.0 minus 2.0
 goal height 522.0
prevdepth 1.70349
```

Here the text of the footnote started at line 3066 and the \spacefactor was set to
1000 at its beginning. The footnote itself was started on that same line, contribut-

---

[1]A footnote starts a new vertical list and, inside it, a new horizontal list for the footnote text.

ing the "internal vertical mode", and TEX correctly disregarded the outer value of \prevdepth. The footnote was part of a paragraph that started on source line 3060, which in turn was embedded in a vertical list that started on line 0, indicating that it is the main vertical galley. Finally, the output shows some information about the current page list that is being built, including its current height, its target height, and the value of \prevdepth (i.e., the depth of the last line on the page at the moment).

Because of the default settings for \showboxbreadth and \showboxdepth, the contents of all lists are abbreviated to []. To get more detail adjust them as necessary or use \showoutput\showlists to get the full details.

Not very useful on its own, but helpful together with other tracing options, is \tracingcommands, which shows all primitives used by TEX during processing. A related internal integer command is \tracingmacros, which shows all macro expansions carried out by TEX. If set to 2, it will also display the expansion of conditionals. Both parameters are automatically turned on by \tracingall. *Tracing the processing*

When everything is set up correctly, it is unlikely that TEX will ever access a font position in the current font that is not associated with a glyph. However, some commands, such as \symbol, can explicitly request any font slot, so it is not impossible. Unfortunately, TEX does not consider this event to be an error (which it should). It merely traces such missing characters by writing unsuspicious transcript entries, and it takes that step only if \tracinglostchars is set to a positive value. LATEX tries to be helpful by initializing this internal integer to 1. *Tracing lost characters*

Finally, you can direct TEX to step through your files line by line. When setting \pausing to 1, each source line is first displayed (suffixed with =>). TEX then waits for instructions regarding what to do with it. Pressing ⟨Enter⟩ instructs TEX to use the line unchanged; anything else means that TEX should use the characters entered by the user instead of the current line. TEX then executes and typesets whatever it was passed, displays the next line, and stops again. To continue normal processing you can reply with \pausing=0, but remember that this is used in place of the current source line, so you may have to repeat the material from the current source line as well. *Stepping through a document*

B.3.5   trace—Selectively tracing command execution

The LATEX command \tracingall (inherited from plain TEX) is available to turn on full tracing. There are, however, some problems with this command:

1. There is no corresponding command to turn off tracing. As a consequence, you have to delimit the scope, which is not always convenient or even possible.

2. Some parts of LATEX produce enormous amounts of tracing data that is of little or no interest for the problem at hand.

For example, if LATEX has to load a new font, it enters some internal routines of NFSS that scan font definition tables and perform other activities. And 99.9% of the time you are not at all interested in that part of the processing, but just in the two lines before and the five lines after it. Nevertheless, you have to scan through a few hundred lines of output and try to locate the lines you need (if you can find them).

Another example is a statement such as `\setlength\linewidth{1cm}`. With standard LATEX this gives 5 lines of tracing output. With the calc package loaded, however, it will result in about 60 lines of tracing data—probably not what you expected and not really helpful unless you try to debug the calc parsing routines (which ideally should not need debugging).

To solve the first problem, the trace package [122] by Frank Mittelbach defines a pair of commands, `\traceon` and `\traceoff`. If LATEX is used on top of a TEX engine, then `\traceon` is essentially another name for `\tracingall`: it turns on *More tracing info* the same tracing switches (albeit in a different order to avoid tracing itself). If LATEX *available with eTEX* is run on top of the eTEX engine, then the tracing of assignments and groups is also turned on.[1]

Another difference between `\traceon` and `\tracingall` is that the latter will always display the tracing information on the terminal, whereas `\traceon` can be directed to write only to the transcript file if you specify the option `logonly`. This is useful when writing to the terminal is very slow (e.g., if running in a shell buffer inside emacs).

To solve the second problem, the trace package has a number of internal commands for temporarily disabling tracing. It redefines the most verbose internal LATEX functions so that tracing is turned off while they are executing. For example, the function to load new fonts is handled in this way. If a document starts with the two formulas

```
$a \neq b$   \small  $A = \mathcal{A}$
```

then LATEX will load 22 new fonts[2] at this point. Using standard `\tracingall` on that line will result in roughly 7500 lines of terminal output. On the other hand, if `\traceon` is used, only 350 lines will be produced (mainly from tracing `\small`).

The commands for which tracing is turned off are few and are unlikely to relate to the problem at hand. However, if you need full tracing, you can either use `\tracingall` or specify the `full` option. In the latter case, `\traceon` traces everything, but you can still direct its output exclusively to the transcript file.

---

[1] The corresponding eTEX switches are `\tracingassigns` and `\tracinggroups`; see [27].
[2] You can verify this with the `loading` option of the tracefnt package.

L^AT_EX Software and User Group Information

The files and packages that are described in this book are available in most T_EX distributions, such as the T_EXlive CD-ROM (provided with this book), or on the CTAN CD-ROMs of DANTE. The newest versions can also be directly downloaded from the web. The aim of this appendix is to provide you with the necessary information to obtain current releases of these CD-ROMs and to give hints on how to locate and get the files you need directly from the Internet.

C.1 Getting help

While we certainly hope that your questions have been answered in this book, we know that this cannot be the case for all questions. For questions related to specific packages discussed in the book, it can be helpful to read the original documentation provided with the package. Appendix C.4 suggests ways to find that documentation on your system.

Very valuable resources are the existing FAQ documents. The most important ones are the UK-TUG FAQ by Robin Fairbairns available at `http://www.tex.ac.uk/faq` and the DANTE FAQ by Bernd Raichle et al. available at `http://www.dante.de/faq/de-tex-faq` (in German). Robin's FAQ is also available in HTML format on the CD-ROM in the directory `/texmf/doc/html/faq/index.html`. However, as both documents are constantly being developed further, it is best access the on-line versions if possible.

If precomposed answers are not enough, several news groups are devoted to general TEX and LATEX questions: `news://comp.text.tex` is perhaps the most important one, with usually more than 100 messages posted each day. Many of the authors mentioned in this book are regular contributors on the news groups and help with answering questions and requests. Thus, there is a vast amount of helpful material on the web that can be conveniently searched using any search engine that indexes news entries.

If you post to any of these news groups, please adhere to basic netiquette. The community is friendly but sometimes direct and expects you to have done some research of your own first (e.g., read the FAQ first and searched the archived news) and not ask questions that have been answered several hundred times before. You should perhaps read Eric Raymond's "*How To Ask Questions The Smart Way*", available at `http://www.catb.org/~esr/faqs/smart-questions.html`, as a starter. Also, if applicable, provide a minimal *and* usable example of your problem that allows others to easily reproduce the symptoms you experience—this will save others time and might get you a faster reply.

C.2 How to get those TEX files?

A useful entry point to the TEX world is the TEX Users Group home page (`http://www.tug.org`; see Figure C.1). From there you can reach most information sources about TEX and friends available worldwide.

In particular, from the TEX Users Group home page you can go to one of the CTAN (Comprehensive TEX Archive Network) nodes. CTAN is a collaborative effort initiated in 1992 by the TEX Users Group Technical Working Group on TEX Archive Guidelines originally coordinated by George Greenwade, building on earlier work of Peter Abbott (see [61] for the historical background), and currently maintained by Jim Hefferon, Robin Fairbairns, Rainer Schöpf, and Reinhard Zierke (spring 2004). Its main aim is to provide easy access to up-to-date copies of all versions of TEX, LATEX, METAFONT, and ancillary programs and their associated files.

Presently, there are three backbone machines that act as FTP servers: in the United Kingdom (`cam.ctan.org` or `ftp.tex.ac.uk`), in Germany (`dante.ctan.org` or `ftp.dante.de`), and in the United States (`tug.ctan.org` or `ctan.tug.org`). Moreover, these sites are mirrored worldwide.

The material on CTAN is regularly (currently on a yearly basis) made available on CD-ROMs. One is the TEXlive distribution ([157]; see also `www.tug.org/texlive`), which provides a "runnable" version of TEX for various platforms. TEXlive CD-ROMs have been developed since 1996 through a collaboration between the TEX Users Group (TEX Users Group; United States) and the TEX user groups of the Czech Republic, France, Germany, India, Netherlands, Poland, Slovakia, and the United Kingdom. These user groups distribute the TEXlive CD-ROMs to their members, so you should contact them directly (their addresses are given in Section C.5).

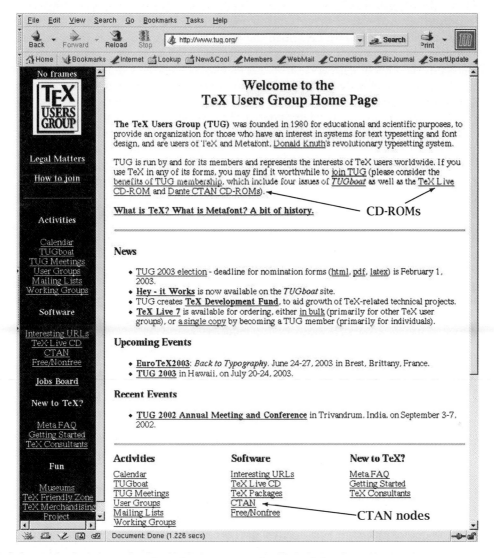

Figure C.1: The TEX Users Group web home page

Another distribution is prepared by the German-speaking TEX user group DANTE (see Section C.5) and contains on several (three in October 2002) CD-ROMs an image of the complete CTAN file tree (almost 2 GB of data). Much like the TEXlive CD-ROMs, these DANTE CTAN CD-ROMs are distributed by most user groups to their members. Thus, the same procedure as for TEXlive should be used if you are interested in getting a copy of the set.

C.3   Using CTAN

In the previous section we described the TEXlive and DANTE CTAN CD-ROM sets. Obtaining the latest version of these CD-ROMs is an optimal way for getting access to recent versions of LATEX software.

Nevertheless, for those readers with an Internet connection, it makes sense to query one of the CTAN nodes every now and then to see whether one of the LATEX components you need has been updated. If you find updates, you can download the latest version of the given package directly from a CTAN archive or one of its mirror sites.

Although network connections get faster all the time, it is often wise to connect to a site that it not too distant geographically from your location. The most convenient way to make an Internet connection is via a web browser, especially since user-friendly interfaces to the CTAN archives have been developed.

C.3.1   Finding files on the archive

The easiest way to find a file on CTAN is using a web interface (the TEX Users Group home page proposes a list of search engines at `http://www.tug.org/ctan.html`). For instance, we use Peter Flynn's server in Ireland, which lets you choose the CTAN node you want to connect to (see Figure C.2).

We connect to the DANTE CTAN Internet node at `http://ftp.dante.de` (upper oval in Figure C.2) and specify the search string "`graphicx`" (second oval in Figure C.2). The search engine returns the list of all files in the CTAN archive matching the given search criterion (for greater clarity, the result of our search is shown inside the rectangle in Figure C.2). By clicking on one of these links you can view (or download) the file in question (in this case we decided to view the file `graphicx.dtx`, whose beginning is shown in the browser window at the bottom of Figure C.2).

C.3.2   Using the TEX file catalogue

A catalogue of TEX- and LATEX-related packages maintained by Graham Williams can be consulted at `http://datamining.csiro.au/tex/catalogue.html`. This interface is especially attractive when you are "surfing" the archive and want to know what a certain package does. Moreover, the interface lets you choose the site from which to download the software, so that you can optimize your connection. When an extended description of the package is available on the Internet, its URL is presented together with the relevant entry.

Several instances of this catalogue, which is regularly updated by its author, are available on the Internet. You can choose the instance closest to where you reside by clicking on one of the flags displayed at the beginning of the catalogue page (see Figure C.3).

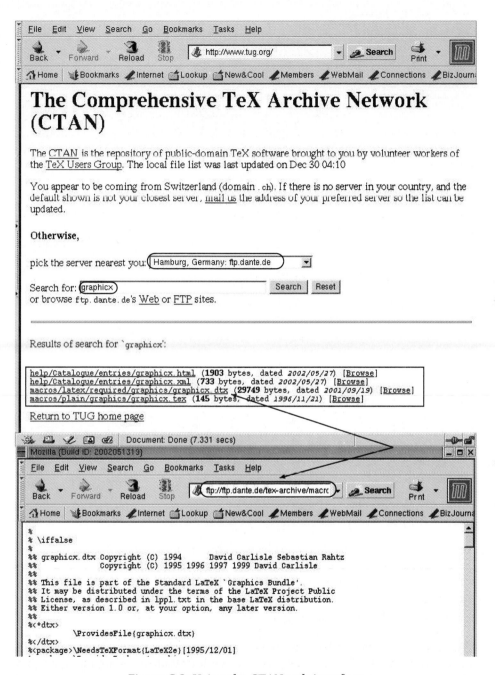

Figure C.2: Using the CTAN web interface

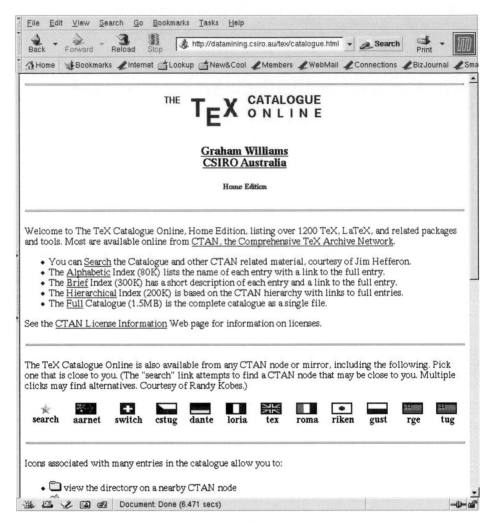

Figure C.3: Graham Williams' TEX catalogue on the web

C.3.3   Getting multiple files

Web interfaces are very handy when you want to check the characteristics of one or more specific files (e.g., date of last modification, size, purpose), but they are not particularly convenient for transferring complete packages consisting of many (sometimes hundreds of) files. In this case it is more appropriate to connect directly via FTP to one of the CTAN nodes or their mirrors. Below is a typical interactive session (commands input by the user are underlined):

```
> ftp ftp.dante.de
Connected to ftp.dante.de (134.100.9.51).
220 nova.dante.de FTP server (Version wu-2.6.2(1) Sat Dec 1 07:52:37 CET 2001).
Name (ftp.dante.de:goossens): ftp
331 Guest login ok, send your complete e-mail address as password.
Password: uuu.vvv@xxx.zz (use your email address here!)
230-Welcome, archive user!  This is an FTP server for the DANTE Archive.
   ...
ftp> quote site index graphicx
>>>>>>> 1.6
200-NOTE. This index shows at most 20 lines. for a full list of files,
200-retrieve /tex-archive/FILES.byname
200-2002/05/27 |        1903 | help/Catalogue/entries/graphicx.html
200-2002/05/27 |         733 | help/Catalogue/entries/graphicx.xml
200-2001/09/19 |       29749 | macros/latex/required/graphics/graphicx.dtx
200-1996/11/21 |         145 | macros/plain/graphics/graphicx.tex
200   (end of 'index graphicx')
ftp> bin
200 Type set to I.
ftp> cd ctan:
250-Machine specific implementations       --> systems
250-Original Knuthian sources:             --> systems/knuth.
250-LaTeX styles, plain macros, MusicTeX:  --> macros.
250-LaTeX2e:                               --> macros/latex.
   ...
ftp> cd macros/latex/required
250-Please read the file README
250-  it was last modified on Wed Mar 24 01:00:00 1999 - 1376 days ago
250 CWD command successful.
ftp> get graphics.zip
local: graphics.zip remote: graphics.zip
227 Entering Passive Mode (134,100,9,51,245,92)
150 Opening BINARY mode data connection for /bin/ZIP.
226 Transfer complete.
127985 bytes received in 0.76 secs (1.6e+02 Kbytes/sec)
ftp> get graphics.tar.gz
local: graphics.tar.gz remote: graphics.tar.gz
227 Entering Passive Mode (134,100,9,51,63,61)
150 Opening BINARY mode data connection for /bin/TARZ.
226 Transfer complete.
118125 bytes received in 0.569 secs (2e+02 Kbytes/sec)
ftp> quit
221-You have transferred 246110 bytes in 2 files.
221-Total traffic for this session was 250149 bytes in 2 transfers.
221-Thank you for using the FTP service on nova.dante.de.
221 Goodbye.
```

After connecting to the site (ftp.dante.de above), you should specify ftp as login name and type *your* e-mail address as the password. Then you can send a query with the command "quote site index ⟨*term*⟩", where ⟨*term*⟩ is the query string. We submitted the same query for the term "graphicx" as in Figure C.2 on page 951; the result is, of course, consistent with the contents of the rectangle in the middle part of that figure. We now decide to transfer the graphics package, so we first position ourself at the root of the CTAN archive tree by issuing the command "cd ctan:" (note the colon at the end, which is necessary!). From our query we know where in the tree the files we want are located, so we change to the directory just one level above (cd macros/latex/required). Then we transfer the directory twice: once as a .zip file and once as a compressed .tar archive (just to show how to specify the commands). The command "quit" ends the FTP session.

C.4   Finding the documentation on your TEX system

When you want to use a LATEX package, it would be nice if you could study the documentation without having to remember where the relevant files are located on your TEX system. Two ways exist to help you in your search: texdoc and its derivative texdoctk.

C.4.1   texdoc—Command-line interface for a search by name

Thomas Esser developed the program texdoc, which is part of the TEXlive distribution. If you know the name of the file describing a package, you can find the relevant documentation files as follows:

```
texdoc -l pspicture
/TeXlive/tl7/texmf/doc/latex/carlisle/pspicture.dvi
/TeXlive/tl7/texmf/doc/html/catalogue/entries/pspicture.html
```

The -l option tells texdoc to list only the path to the files that fulfill the selection criterion (in this case, files called pspicture regardless of their extension). If you do not specify the -l option, texdoc will show you the contents of the documentation file (in this case, pspicture.dvi) with the help of the relevant display program (for instance, xdvi or Windvi).

If you do not know the precise name of the file, you can specify the -s option and provide a wildcard-like specification as a search pattern. For instance:

```
texdoc -s *picture*
/TeXlive/tl7/texmf/doc/generic/mfpic/examples/lapictures.tex
/TeXlive/tl7/texmf/doc/generic/mfpic/examples/pictures.tex
/TeXlive/tl7/texmf/doc/latex/carlisle/pspicture.dvi
/TeXlive/tl7/texmf/doc/html/catalogue/entries/pspicture.html
/TeXlive/tl7/texmf/doc/html/catalogue/entries/pspicture.xml
```

Here we have picked up files that have the string picture in their name—among them the "pspicture" files we found previously.

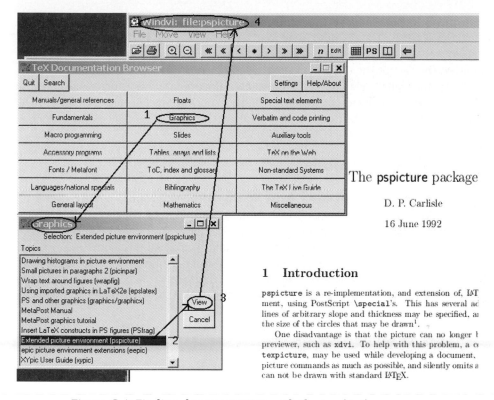

Figure C.4: Finding documentation with the texdoctk program

The texdoc utility is quite useful, but it has a drawback: you must know the name of the file describing the package that you want to use. This is not always just the name of the package itself (as with pspicture in the above examples).

C.4.2   texdoctk—Panel interface for a search by subject

Thomas Ruedas took a somewhat different approach to provide easy access to the documentation for files present on your TeX system. His texdoctk program uses a graphics user interface based on perl and Tk. The program uses a database that groups documentation files present in the Thomas Esser's tetex distribution (TeXlive is based on tetex) into 17 categories, and offers an eigtheenth "user's" category to allow users to add their (local) documentation entries into the database, if needed. As with texdoc, the display or print programs present on the system will be used for viewing (e.g., xdvi, dvips).

Figure C.4 shows how we used the texdoctk system to display the documentation for the pspicture package. In this case we did not have to know the name of the package. In fact, we navigated from the main panel, where we chose the "Graphics" category (1), which opened the "Graphics" menu (lower left), where we selected "Extended picture environment (pspicture)" (2). We then clicked the "View" button (3), which called the .dvi viewer Windvi (4), which displayed the text of the documentation.

On the figure one can see all available documentation categories (note the "Miscellaneous" button in the lower-right corner for special cases) as well as the "Search" and "Help" buttons for more advanced use.

C.5   TeX user groups

TeX users in several countries have set up TeX user groups, mostly based on language affinities. If you need help, you should contact your local user group first, since they might be able to come up with an answer that is most suited to your language-dependent working environment. Below we give some information about groups that have a formal existence (see http://www.tug.org/lugs.html or http://www.servalys.nl/lug/ for up-to-date and more complete lists). They can help you obtain TeX-related material on CD-ROMs or other publications.

cn:	**China PR**
name:	Chinese TeX Users Group
language:	Chinese
web site:	www.rons.net.cn
name:	Hong Feng
address:	RON's Datacom Co., Ltd.
	79, DongWu Ave.,
	Wuhan, Hubei Province
	430040 China P.R.
e-mail:	info@mail.rons.net.cn
phone:	+862783222108
fax:	+862783222108
cz:	**Czech Republic**
language:	Czech
name:	CsTUG
contact:	Petr Sojka
address:	CsTUG, c/o FI MU
	Botanická 68a
	CZ-602 00 Brno
	Czech Republic
e-mail:	cstug@cstug.cz
web site:	www.cstug.cz
phone:	+420541212352
de:	**Germany**
name:	DANTE e.V.
language:	German
contact:	Volker Schaa
address:	Postfach 101840
	D-69008 Heidelberg
	Germany

e-mail:	dante@dante.de
web site:	www.dante.de
phone:	+49622129766
fax:	+496221167906
dk:	**Denmark**
name:	DK-TUG
language:	Danish
contact:	Kaja Christiansen
address:	Department of Computer Science
	Ny Munkegade, Bldg. 540
	DK-8000 Århus C
	Denmark
e-mail:	board@tug.dk
web site:	www.tug.dk
phone:	+4589423220
ee:	**Estonia**
name:	Estonian User Group
address:	Astrophysical Observatory,
	Toravere
	Enn Saar, Tartu
	EE 2444 Estonia
e-mail:	saar@aai.ee
es:	**Spain (CervanTeX)**
name:	CervanTeX
language:	Spanish
e-mail:	secretario@cervantex.org
web site:	www.cervantex.org
esc:	**Spain (Catalan)**
name:	Catalan TeX Users Group
language:	Catalan

contact: Gabriel Valiente
address: Technical University of Catalonia
Jordi Girona Salgado, 1-3
E-08034 Barcelona
Spain
e-mail: valiente@lsi.upc.es
web site: www-lsi.upc.es/~valiente/
tug-catalan.html

fr: France
name: GUTenberg
language: French
address: c/o Irisa
Campus Universitaire de Beaulieu
F-35042 Rennes cedex
France
e-mail: gut@irisa.fr
web site: www.gutenberg.eu.org
phone: +33681665102
fax: +33492579667

fra: France (Astex)
short name: AsTEX
language: French
address: Association AsTEX
BP 6532
45066 Orleans cedex 2
France
e-mail: astex-admin@univ-orleans.fr
web site: www.univ-orleans.fr/EXT/
ASTEX/astex/doc/en/web/html/
astex000.htm
phone: ｜33238640994

gr: Greece
name: Greek TeX Friends Group
language: Greek
contact: Apostolos Syropoulos
address: 366, 28th October Str.
GR-671 00 Xanthi
Greece
e-mail: eft@ocean1.ee.duth.gr
web site: obelix.ee.duth.gr/eft/
phone: +3054128704

hu: Hungary
name: MaTeX
language: Hungarian
address: Institute of Mathematics and
Informatics
University of Debrecen
H-4010 Debrecen, P.O. Box 12
Hungary
e-mail: matex@math.klte.hu
web site: www.math.klte.hu/~matex/

in: India
name: TUGIndia
contact: K.S.S. Nambooripad

address: Kripa, TC 24/548, Sastha Gardens
Thycaud, Trivandrum 695014
India
e-mail: tugindia@river-valley.com
web site: www.river-valley.com/tug/
phone: +91471324341
fax: +91471333186

kr: Korea
name: KTUG
language: Korean
contact: Kim Kangsu
e-mail: info@mail.ktug.or.kr
web site: www.ktug.or.kr

lt: Lithuania
name: Lietovos TeXó Vartotojiø Grupë
contact: Vytas Statulevicius
address: Akademijos 4
LT-2600 Vilnius
Lithuania
e-mail: vytass@ktl.mii.lt
phone: +3702359609
fax: +3702359804

mx: Mexico
name: TeX México
address: Rayon No. 523, Centro 58000
Morelia, Michoacan
Mexico
e-mail: tex@ciencia.dcc.umich.mx
web site: ciencia.dcc.umich.mx./tex/
phone: +52143128724
fax: +52143173945

**nl: Netherlands, Belgium (Flemish
part)**
name: NTG
language: Dutch
contact: Hans Hagen
address: Pragma
Ridderstraat 27
8061 GH Hasselt
The Netherlands
e-mail: info@ntg.nl
web site: www.ntg.nl
phone: +31384775369
fax: +31384775374

no: Nordic countries
name: NTUG
language: Scandinavian languages
discussion: nordictex@ifi.uio.no
contact: Dag Langmyhr
address: University of Oslo
PO Box 1080 Blindern
N-0316 Oslo
Norway
e-mail: dag@ifi.uio.no

web site: `www.ifi.uio.no/~dag/ntug/`
phone: +4722852450
fax: +4722852401

ph: Philippines
name: TUG-Philippines
contact: Felix P. Muga II
address: Ateneo de Manila University
Loyola Heights
Quezon City
Philippines
e-mail: `fpmuga@admu.edu.ph`
phone: +6324266001 ext 2515
fax: +6324266008

pl: Poland
name: GUST
language: Polish
address: UCI UMK
Gagarina 7
87-100 Torun
Poland
e-mail: `sekretariat@gust.org.pl`
web site: `www.GUST.org.pl`

pt: Portugal
name: GUTpt
language: Portuguese
contact: Pedro Quaresma de Almeida
address: Coimbra University
Dep. Matemática, Largo D.Dinis
Apartado 3008, 3001-454
COIMBRA
Portugal
e-mail: `GUTpt@hilbert.mat.uc.pt`
web site: `http://hilbert.mat.uc.pt/~GUTpt/`
phone: +351239791181

ru: Russia
name: CyrTUG
e-mail: `cyrtug@mir.msk.su`
web site: `www.cemi.rssi.ru/cyrtug/`
discussion: `CyrTeX-en@vsu.ru`
subscription: `CyrTeX-en-on@vsu.ru`

si: Slovenia
name: TeXCeH
contact: Vladimir Batagelj
address: Jadranska 19
SI-61111 Ljubljana
Slovenia
e-mail: `Tex.Ceh@fmf.uni-lj.si`
web site: `vlado.fmf.uni-lj.si/texceh/texceh.htm`

uk: United Kingdom
name: UKTUG
language: British English
e-mail: `uktug-enquiries@tex.ac.uk`
web site: `uk.tug.org`
contact: Dr R.W.D. Nickalls
address: Department of Anæsthesia
Nottingham City Hospital NHS
Trust
Hucknall Road
Nottingham, NG5-1PB (UK)
e-mail: `enxtw1@nottingham.ac.uk`
phone: +441159691169 (ext. 45637)
fax: +441159627713

us: TeX User Group (international)
name: TUG
address: P.O. Box 2311
Portland, OR 97208-2311
U.S.A
e-mail: `office@tug.org`
web site: `www.tug.org`
phone: +15032239994
fax: +15032233960

vn: Vietnam
name: ViêtTUG
contact: Nguyên-Ðai Quý
address: LTAS-University of Liège
Rue des Chevreuils, 1
Bât B52, Local 522B
B4000, Liège
Belgium
e-mail: `viettug@eGroups.com`
phone: +3243669098
fax: +3243669311

Appendix D

TLC2 TEX CD

The CD-ROM at the back of this book will enable you to set up a LATEX system that is as close as possible to the descriptions in this book. This appendix explains how we created this CD and gets you started on how to use it.

Origins—The TEX Live system

TEX Live is an "open source" distribution of TEX and LATEX that is sponsored by an international consortium of TEX user groups. The TLC2 TEX CD-ROM is based closely on this distribution and we therefore wish to thank all the individuals involved in the production and maintenance of TEX Live over the years.

The 2003 release of the TEX Live distribution was distributed as three disks: a DVD containing the full distribution and a copy of the CTAN archives, a CD containing (in compressed form) a full TEX Live distribution, and a "demo" disk containing a TEX distribution that may be either installed on a hard disk, or used directly from the CD.

To fit onto one CD, some packages had to be omitted from the "demo" CD, and only the major machine architectures are supported: Linux, Windows and MacOSX.

The TLC2 TEX CD-ROM is a version of the TEX Live "demo" CD. All the binary programs are unchanged, several packages described in this book have been updated or added, and the LATEX format itself is the 2003/12/01 release. In order to keep within the size constraint, some packages had to be removed. A full list of changed packages is contained in the file readme-tlc2.html, which can be found in the top level directory on the CD.

Installing LaTeX from the CD-ROM

Installation and use of this CD-ROM follows exactly the procedures outlined for the TeX Live demo distribution from the original TeX Live documentation. An overview of these procedures is in the file `readme.html`, which has links to more extensive documentation files on the CD. (Much of the TeX Live documentation is available in several languages.)

In brief, the install script `install-tl.sh` in the top level directory should be run by you on Linux or MacOSX. Under Windows the Install program should automatically start (or double click on `autorun.exe`). This process will lead you through some configuration options and then install a LaTeX system on your hard disk. Depending on the options chosen, some lesser used packages may not be installed initially; they may be added to your local installation later, as described in the TeX Live documentation.

If you are already using LaTeX then you may not want to install the whole system but simply use the CD to update your base LaTeX and your chosen packages to more recent versions.

Running LaTeX directly from the CD-ROM

As an alternative to installing the whole system on your local disk, you can opt to run all software directly from the CD-ROM. However, some local disk space will still be required so that TeX can write output files and, if necessary, extra fonts can be generated.

Under Windows this option is taken by choosing the `Explore CD-Rom/Run TeX off CD-Rom` menu option from the TeX Live welcome program. On the other systems you should run `install-tl.sh` as above, but choose the option to run directly from the media.

In addition to giving you a running TeX system, this installation will also set up `xemacs` as an environment for preparing your documents. This provides an extensive set of menu options to help in the editing of LaTeX documents, and in the use of LaTeX and associated programs such as BibTeX.

The LaTeX Companion example documents

Files for all the examples displayed in the book are on the CD-ROM in the directory `Books/tlc2/examples`. The file name is in each case the example number, with extension `.ltx` or `.ltx2` (for two-page examples), as in `1-3-1.ltx` and `2-4-4.ltx2`.

Most of these examples use the class file `ttctexa.cls` which is in the same directory as the examples. This class is a small extension of the `article` class: it defines some extra commands to control the display of preamble commands in this book.

If the TEX system is used directly from the CD then all those packages required for the examples will be available, with the exception of some packages which relate to commercial fonts that cannot be distributed on this CD-ROM.

If the distribution is installed on a hard disk then not all the packages are installed by default. Extra individual packages can be installed using either install-pkg.sh under Linux and MacOSX, or the TEX Live/maintenance option from the Start menu under Windows.

Licenses

The file LICENSE.TL in the top level directory describes the license and copying conditions for TEX Live itself; these also apply to the modified distribution on the TLC2 TEX CD-ROM. All the software contained on this CD-ROM is (to the best of our knowledge) freely distributable, although different licenses are used on the different components, as detailed in the documentation of each package.

Many of the LATEX packages, and all of the example files for this book, are distributed under the LATEX Project Public License, the text of which is on the CD in the file texmf/doc/latex/base/lppl.txt.

The LPPL allows arbitrary use, including copying and modification, so long as you do not distribute modified copies with the same name as the original files.

Bibliography

[1] Adobe Systems Incorporated. *Adobe Type 1 Font Format*. Addison-Wesley, Reading, MA, USA, 1990. ISBN 0-201-57044-0.

The "black book" contains the specifications for Adobe's Type 1 font format and describes how to create a Type 1 font program. The book explains the specifics of the Type 1 syntax (a subset of PostScript), including information on the structure of font programs, ways to specify computer outlines, and the contents of the various font dictionaries. It also covers encryption, subroutines, and hints. `http://partners.adobe.com/asn/developer/pdfs/tn/T1Format.pdf`

[2] Adobe Systems Incorporated. "PostScript document structuring conventions specification (version 3.0)". Technical Note 5001, 1992.

This technical note defines a standard set of document structuring conventions (DSC), which will help ensure that a PostScript document is device independent. DSC allows PostScript language programs to communicate their document structure and printing requirements to document managers in a way that does not affect the PostScript language page description.
`http://partners.adobe.com/asn/developer/pdfs/tn/5001.DSC_Spec.pdf`

[3] Adobe Systems Incorporated. "Encapsulated PostScript file format specification (version 3.0)". Technical Note 5002, 1992.

This technical note details the Encapsulated PostScript file (EPSF) format, a standard format for importing and exporting PostScript language files among applications in a variety of heterogeneous environments. The EPSF format is based on and conforms to the document structuring conventions (DSC) [2].
`http://partners.adobe.com/asn/developer/pdfs/tn/5002.EPSF_Spec.pdf`

[4] Adobe Systems Incorporated. *PostScript Language Reference*. Addison-Wesley, Reading, MA, USA, 3rd edition, 1999. ISBN 0-201-37922-8.

The "red book" can be considered the definitive resource for all PostScript programmers. It contains the complete description of the PostScript language, including the latest Level 3 operators.
`http://www.adobe.com/products/postscript/pdfs/PLRM.pdf`

[5]   Adobe Systems Incorporated. PDF Reference, version 1.4. Addison-Wesley,
      Boston, MA, USA, 3rd edition, 2002. ISBN 0-201-75839-3.
      The specification of Adobe's Portable Document Format (PDF). The book introduces and ex-
      plains all aspects of the PDF format, including its architecture and imaging model (allowing
      transparency and opacity for text, images, and graphics), the command syntax, the graphics
      operators, fonts and rendering, and the relation between PostScript and PDF.   `http://`
      `partners.adobe.com/asn/acrobat/docs/File_Format_Specifications/PDFReference.pdf`

[6]   American Mathematical Society, Providence, Rhode Island. Instructions
      for Preparation of Papers and Monographs: $\mathcal{A}_{\mathcal{M}}S$-LaTeX, 1999.
      This document contains instructions for authors preparing articles and books, using LaTeX, for
      publication with the American Mathematical Society (AMS) to match its publication style speci-
      fications: journals (`amsart`), proceedings volumes (`amsproc`), and monographs (`amsbook`).
                     `ftp://ftp.ams.org/pub/author-info/documentation/amslatex/instr-l.pdf`

[7]   American Mathematical Society, Providence, Rhode Island. Using the
      `amsthm` Package (Version 2.07), 2000.
      The `amsthm` package provides an enhanced version of LaTeX's `\newtheorem` command for
      defining theorem-like environments, recognizing `\theoremstyle` specifications and providing
      a `proof` environment.   `ftp://ftp.ams.org/pub/tex/doc/amscls/amsthdoc.pdf`

[8]   American Mathematical Society, Providence, Rhode Island. User's Guide
      for the `amsmath` Package (Version 2.0), 2002.
      The `amsmath` package, developed by the American Mathematical Society, provides many addi-
      tional features for mathematical typesetting.   `http://www.ams.org/tex/amslatex.html`

[9]   American Mathematical Society, Providence, Rhode Island. User's Guide to
      AMSFonts Version 2.2d, 2002.
      This document describes AMSFonts, the American Mathematical Society's collection of fonts of
      symbols and several alphabets.   `http://www.ams.org/tex/amsfonts.html`

[10] J. André and Ph. Louarn. "Notes en bas de pages : comment les faire en
      LaTeX?" *Cahiers GUTenberg*, 12:57–70, 1991.
      Several special cases of using footnotes with LaTeX are discussed—for example, how to generate
      a footnote referring to information inside a `tabular` or `minipage` environment, and how to
      reference the same footnote more than once.
                        `http://www.gutenberg.eu.org/pub/GUTenberg/publicationsPDF/12-louarn.pdf`

[11] Michael Barr. "A new diagram package", 2001.
      A rewrite of Michael Barr's original `diagram` package to act as a front end to Rose's `xypic` (see [57],
      Chapter 5]). It offers a general arrow-drawing function; various common diagram shapes, such
      as squares, triangles, cubes, and 3×3 diagrams; small 2-arrows that can be placed anywhere in
      a diagram; and access to all of `xypic`'s features.   On CTAN at: `macros/generic/diagrams/barr`

[12] Claudio Beccari and Apostolos Syropoulos. "New Greek fonts and the
      `greek` option of the `babel` package". *TUGboat*, 19(4):419–425, 1998.
      Describes a new complete set of Greek fonts and their use in connection with the `babel` `greek`
      extension.   `http://www.tug.org/TUGboat/Articles/tb19-4/tb61becc.pdf`

[13] Nelson Beebe. "Bibliography prettyprinting and syntax checking". *TUG-
      boat*, 14(4):395–419, 1993.
      This article describes three software tools for BibTeX support: a pretty-printer, syntax checker,
      and lexical analyzer for BibTeX files; collectively called bibclean.
                              `http://www.tug.org/TUGboat/Articles/tb14-4/tb41beebe.pdf`

[14] Barbara Beeton. "Mathematical symbols and Cyrillic fonts ready for distribution". *TUGboat*, 6(2):59–63, 1985.

The announcement of the first general release by the American Mathematical Society of the Euler series fonts. `http://www.tug.org/TUGboat/Articles/tb06-2/tb11beet.pdf`

[15] Frank G. Bennett, Jr. "CAMEL: kicking over the bibliographic traces in BIBTEX". *TUGboat*, 17(1):22–28, 1996.

The camel package provides a simple, logical citation interface for LATEX that allows the bibliographic style of a document to be easily changed without major editing. `http://www.tug.org/TUGboat/Articles/tb17-1/tb50benn.pdf`

[16] Frank G. Bennett, Jr. "User's guide to the camel citator", 1997.

The documentation for version 1 of the camel package. On CTAN at: `macros/latex/contrib/camel`

[17] A. Berdnikov, O. Lapko, M. Kolodin, A. Janishevsky, and A. Burykin. "Cyrillic encodings for LATEX 2_ε multi-language documents". *TUGboat*, 19(4):403–416, 1998.

A description of four encodings designed to support Cyrillic writing systems for the multi-language mode of LATEX 2_ε. The "raw" X2 encoding is a Cyrillic glyph container that allows one to insert into LATEX 2_ε documents text fragments written in any of the languages using a modern Cyrillic writing scheme. The T2A, T2B, and T2C encodings are genuine LATEX 2_ε encodings that may be used in an multi-language setting together with other language encodings. `http://www.tug.org/TUGboat/Articles/tb19-4/tb61berd.pdf`

[18] Karl Berry. "Filenames for fonts". *TUGboat*, 11(4):517–520, 1990.

This article describes the consistent, rational scheme for font file names that was used for at least the next 15 years. Each name consists of up to eight characters (specifying the foundry, typeface name, weight, variant, expansion characteristics, and design size) that identify each font file in a unique way. `http://www.tug.org/TUGboat/Articles/tb11-4/tb30berry.pdf`

[19] Karl Berry. "Fontname: Filenames for TEX fonts", 2003.

The on-line documentation of the latest version of "Fontname", a scheme for TEX font file names; it explains some legal issues relating to fonts in a number of countries.
`http://www.tug.org/fontname/html/index.html`

[20] Javier Bezos. "The accents package", 2000.

Miscellaneous tools for mathematical accents: to create faked accents from non-accent symbols, to group accents, and to place accents below glyphs.
On CTAN at: `macros/latex/contrib/bezos`

[21] The *Bluebook*: A Uniform System of Citation. The Harvard Law Review Association, Cambridge, MA, 17th edition, 2000.

The *Bluebook* contains three major parts: part 1 details general standards of citation and style to be used in legal writing; part 2 presents specific rules of citation for cases, statutes, books, periodicals, foreign materials, and international materials; and part 3 consists of a series of tables showing, among other things, which authority to cite and how to abbreviate properly.
Can be ordered at: `http://www.legalbluebook.com`

[22] Francis Borceux. "De la construction de diagrammes". *Cahiers GUTenberg*, 5:41–48, 1990.

The diagram macros typeset diagrams consisting of arrows of different types that join at corners that can contain mathematical expressions. The macros calculate automatically the length and position of each element. The user can specify a scaling factor for each diagram. `http://www.gutenberg.eu.org/pub/GUTenberg/publicationsPDF/5-borceux.pdf`

[23] Francis Borceux. "Diagram 3", 1993.
       Commutative diagram package that uses LaTeX picture mode.
                                                        On CTAN at: `macros/generic/diagrams/borceux`

[24] Thierry Bouche. "Diversity in math fonts". *TUGboat*, 19(2):120–134, 1998.
       Issues raised when modifying LaTeX fonts within math environments are examined. An attempt
       is made to suggest effective means of accessing a larger variety of font options, while avoiding
       typographic nonsense.   `http://www.tug.org/TUGboat/Articles/tb19-2/tb59bouc.pdf`

[25] Johannes Braams. "Babel, a multilingual style-option system for use with
       LaTeX's standard document styles". *TUGboat*, 12(2):291–301, 1991.
       The babel package was originally a collection of document-style options to support different
       languages. An update was published in *TUGboat*, 14(1):60–62, April 1993.
                    `http://www.tug.org/TUGboat/Articles/tb12-2/tb32braa.pdf`
                         `http://www.tug.org/TUGboat/Articles/tb14-1/tb38braa.pdf`

[26] Neil Bradley. The XML Companion. Addison-Wesley, Boston, MA, USA, 3rd
       edition, 2002. ISBN 0-201-77059-8.
       This book provides a description of XML features without assuming knowledge of HTML or
       SGML, covering also related standards such as Xpath, XML Schema, SAX, DOM, XSLT, Xlink, and
       Xpointer.

[27] Peter Breitenlohner et al. "The eTeX manual (version 2)", 1998.
       The current manual for the eTeX system, which extends the capabilities of TeX while retaining
       compatibility.   On CTAN at: `systems/e-tex/v2/doc/etex_man.pdf`

[28] Robert Bringhurst. The elements of typographic style. Hartley & Marks
       Publishers, Point Roberts, WA, USA, and Vancouver, BC, Canada, 2nd edi-
       tion, 1996. ISBN 0-88179-133-4 (hardcover), 0-88179-132-6 (paperback).
       A very well-written book on typography with a focus on the proper use of typefaces.

[29] Judith Butcher. Copy-editing: The Cambridge handbook for editors, au-
       thors and publishers. Cambridge University Press, New York, 3rd edition,
       1992. ISBN 0-521-40074-0.
       A reference guide for all those involved in the process of preparing typescripts and illustrations
       for printing and publication. The book covers all aspects of the editorial process, from the
       basics of how to mark a typescript for the designer and the typesetter, through the ground
       rules of house style and consistency, to how to read and correct proofs.

[30] David Carlisle. "A LaTeX tour, Part 1: The basic distribution". *TUGboat*,
       17(1):67–73, 1996.
       A "guided tour" around the files in the basic LaTeX distribution. File names and paths relate to
       the file hierarchy of the CTAN archives.
                              `http://www.tug.org/TUGboat/Articles/tb17-1/tb50carl.pdf`

[31] David Carlisle. "A LaTeX tour, Part 2: The tools and graphics distributions".
       TUGboat, 17(3):321–326, 1996.
       A "guided tour" around the "tools" and "graphics" packages. Note that *The Manual* [104] as-
       sumes that at least the graphics distribution is available with standard LaTeX.
                              `http://www.tug.org/TUGboat/Articles/tb17-3/tb52carl.pdf`

[32] David Carlisle. "A LaTeX tour, Part 3: mfnfss, psnfss and babel". *TUGboat*,
       18(1):48–55, 1997.
       A "guided tour" through three more distributions that are part of the standard LaTeX system.
       The mfnfss distribution provides LaTeX support for some popular METAFONT-produced fonts

that do not otherwise have any LaTeX interface. The psnfss distribution consists of LaTeX packages giving access to PostScript fonts. The babel distribution provides LaTeX with multilingual capabilities. `http://www.tug.org/TUGboat/Articles/tb18-1/tb54carl.pdf`

[33] David Carlisle. "OpenMath, MathML, and XSL". *SIGSAM Bulletin (ACM Special Interest Group on Symbolic and Algebraic Manipulation)*, 34(2):6–11, 2000.

Discussion of XML markup for mathematics—in particular, OpenMath and MathML—and the use of XSLT to transform between these languages.
Restricted to ACM members; `http://www.acm.org/sigsam/bulletin/issues/issue132.html`

[34] David Carlisle. "XMLTEX: A non validating (and not 100% conforming) namespace aware XML parser implemented in TeX". *TUGboat*, 21(3):193–199, 2000.

XMLTEX is a an XML parser and typesetter implemented in TeX, which by default uses the LaTeX kernel to provide typesetting functionality.
`http://www.tug.org/TUGboat/Articles/tb21-3/tb68carl.pdf`

[35] David Carlisle, Patrick Ion, Robert Miner, and Nico Poppelier, editors. Mathematical Markup Language (MathML) Version 2.0. W3C, 2nd edition, 2003.

MathML is an XML vocabulary for mathematics, designed for use in browsers and as a communication language between computer algebra systems. `http://www.w3.org/TR/MathML2`

[36] David Carlisle, Chris Rowley, and Frank Mittelbach. "The LaTeX3 Programming Language—a proposed system for TeX macro programming". *TUGboat*, 18(4):303–308, 1997.

Some proposals for a radically new syntax and software tools.
`http://www.tug.org/TUGboat/Articles/tb18-4/tb57rowl.pdf`

[37] Pehong Chen and Michael A. Harrison. "Index preparation and processing". *Software—Practice and Experience*, 19(9):897–915, 1988.

A description of the makeindex system.

[38] The Chicago Manual of Style. University of Chicago Press, Chicago, IL, USA, 15th edition, 2003. ISBN 0-226-10403-6.

The standard U.S. publishing style reference for authors and editors.

[39] Adrian F. Clark. "Practical halftoning with TeX". *TUGboat*, 12(1):157–165, 1991.

Reviews practical problems encountered when using TeX for typesetting half-tone pictures and compares other techniques to include graphics material. Advantages and disadvantages of the various approaches are described and some attempts at producing color separations are discussed. `http://www.tug.org/TUGboat/Articles/tb12-1/tb31clark.pdf`

[40] Matthias Clasen and Ulrik Vieth. "Towards a new math font encoding for (LA)TEX". *Cahiers GUTenberg*, 28–29:94–121, 1998.

A prototype implementation of 8-bit math font encodings for LaTeX.
`http://www.gutenberg.eu.org/pub/GUTenberg/publicationsPDF/28-29-clasen.pdf`

[41] Carl Dair. Design with Type. University of Toronto Press, Toronto, Ontario, Canada, 1967. ISBN 0-8020-1426-7 (hardcover), 0-8020-6519-8 (paperback).

A good survey of traditional typography with many useful rules of thumb.

[42] Michael Downes. "Breaking equations". *TUGboat*, 18(3):182–194, 1997.
       TeX is not very good at displaying equations that must be broken into more than one line. The
       breqn package eliminates many of the most significant problems by supporting automatic line
       breaking of displayed equations.
                                         http://www.tug.org/TUGboat/Articles/tb18-3/tb56down.pdf

[43] Michael Downes. "The amsrefs LaTeX package and the amsxport BibTeX
       style". *TUGboat*, 21(3):201–209, 2000.
       Bibliography entries using the amsrefs format provide a rich internal structure and high-level
       markup close to that traditionally found in BibTeX database files. On top of that, using amsrefs
       markup lets you specify the bibliography style completely in a LaTeX document class file.
                                         http://www.tug.org/TUGboat/Articles/tb21-3/tb68down.pdf

[44] Dudenredaktion, editor. Duden, Rechtschreibung der deutschen Sprache.
       Dudenverlag, Mannheim, 21st edition, 1996. ISBN 3-411-04011-4.
       The standard reference for the correct spelling of all words of contemporary German and for
       hyphenation rules, with examples and explanations for difficult cases, and a comparison of the
       old and new orthographic rules.

[45] Victor Eijkhout. TeX by Topic, A TeXnician's Reference. Addison-Wesley,
       Reading, MA, USA, 1991. ISBN 0-201-56882-9. Out of print. Available free
       of charge from the author in PDF format.
       A systematic reference manual for the experienced TeX user. The book offers a comprehensive
       treatment of every aspect of TeX, with detailed explanations of the mechanisms underlying TeX's
       working, as well as numerous examples of TeX programming techniques.
                                                                       http://www.eijkhout.net/tbt

[46] Robin Fairbairns. "UK list of TeX frequently asked questions on the Web",
       2003.
       This list of Frequently Asked Questions on TeX was originated by the Committee of the U.K. TeX
       Users' Group; it has well over 300 entries and is regularly updated and expanded.
                                                                       http://www.tex.ac.uk/faq

[47] Laurence Finston. "Spindex—Indexing with special characters". *TUGboat*,
       18(4):255–273, 1997.
       Common Lisp indexing program and supporting TeX macros for indexes that include non-Latin
       characters.   http://www.tug.org/TUGboat/Articles/tb18-4/tb57fins.pdf

[48] Shinsaku Fujita and Nobuya Tanaka. "XⓎMTeX (Version 2.00) as imple-
       mentation of the XⓎM notation and the XⓎM markup language". *TUGboat*,
       21(1):7–14, 2000.
       A description of version 2 of the XⓎMTeX system, which can be regarded as a linear notation
       system expressed in TeX macros that corresponds to the IUPAC (International Union of Pure and
       Applied Chemistry) nomenclature. It provides a convenient method for drawing complicated
       structural formulas.   http://www.tug.org/TUGboat/Articles/tb21-1/tb66fuji.pdf

[49] Shinsaku Fujita and Nobuya Tanaka. "Size reduction of chemical struc-
       tural formulas in XⓎMTeX (Version 3.00)". *TUGboat*, 22(4):285–289, 2001.
       Further improvements to the XⓎMTeX system, in particular in the area of size reduction of struc-
       tural formulas.   http://www.tug.org/TUGboat/Articles/tb22-4/tb72fuji.pdf

[50] Rei Fukui. "TIPA: A system for processing phonetic symbols in LaTeX".
       TUGboat, 17(2):102–114, 1996.
       TIPA is a system for processing symbols of the International Phonetic Alphabet with LaTeX. It
       introduces a new encoding for phonetic symbols (T3), which includes all the symbols and dia-
       critics found in the recent versions of IPA as well as some non-IPA symbols. It has full support

for LaTeX 2_ε and offers an easy input method in the IPA environment.
http://www.tug.org/TUGboat/Articles/tb17-2/tb51rei.pdf

[51] Bernard Gaulle. "Comment peut-on personnaliser l'extension french de LaTeX?" *Cahiers GUTenberg*, 28–29:143–157, 1998.
Describes how to personalize the french package.
http://www.gutenberg.eu.org/pub/GUTenberg/publicationsPDF/28-29-gaulle.pdf

[52] Maarten Gelderman. "A short introduction to font characteristics". *TUGboat*, 20(2):96–104, 1999.
This paper provides a description of the main aspects used to describe a font, its basic characteristics, elementary numerical dimensions to access properties of a typeface design, and the notion of "contrast".   http://www.tug.org/TUGboat/Articles/tb20-2/tb63geld.pdf

[53] Charles F. Goldfarb. The SGML Handbook. Oxford University Press, London, Oxford, New York, 1990. ISBN 0-19-853737-9.
The full text of the ISO SGML standard [68] copiously annotated by its author, and several tutorials.

[54] Norbert Golluch. Kleinweich Büro auf Schlabberscheiben. Eichborn, Frankfurt, 1999.
Tecknisches Deutsch für Angefangen.

[55] Michel Goossens, Frank Mittelbach, and Alexander Samarin. The LaTeX Companion. Tools and Techniques for Computer Typesetting. Addison-Wesley, Reading, MA, USA, 1994. ISBN 0-201-54199-8.
The first edition of this book.

[56] Michel Goossens and Sebastian Rahtz. The LaTeX Web Companion: Integrating TeX, HTML, and XML. Tools and Techniques for Computer Typesetting. Addison-Wesley Longman, Reading, MA, USA, 1999. ISBN 0-201-43311-7. With Eitan M. Gurari, Ross Moore, and Robert S. Sutor.
This book teaches (scientific) authors how to publish on the web or other hypertext presentation systems, building on their experience with LaTeX and taking into account their specific needs in fields such as mathematics, non-European languages, and algorithmic graphics. The book explains how to make full use of the Adobe Acrobat format from LaTeX, convert legacy documents to HTML or XML, make use of math in web applications, use LaTeX as a tool in preparing web pages, read and write simple XML/SGML, and produce high-quality printed pages from web-hosted XML or HTML pages using TeX or PDF.

[57] Michel Goossens, Sebastian Rahtz, and Frank Mittelbach. The LaTeX Graphics Companion: Illustrating Documents with TeX and PostScript. Tools and Techniques for Computer Typesetting. Addison-Wesley, Reading, MA, USA, 1997. ISBN 0-201-85469-4.
The book shows how to incorporate graphic files into a LaTeX document, program technical diagrams using several different languages, produce color pictures, achieve special effects with fragments of embedded PostScript, and make high-quality music scores and game diagrams. It also contains detailed descriptions of important packages such as xypic, pstricks, and MetaPost, the standard LaTeX color and graphics packages, PostScript fonts and how to use them in LaTeX, and the dvips and ghostscript programs.

[58] Michel Goossens and Vesa Sivunen. "LaTeX, SVG, Fonts". *TUGboat*, 22(4):269–279, 2001.
A short overview of SVG and its advantages for portable graphics content, conversion of PostScript glyph outlines to SVG outlines, and the use of SVG glyphs in TeX documents.
http://www.tug.org/TUGboat/Articles/tb22-4/tb72goos.pdf

[59] Ronald L. Graham, Donald E. Knuth, and Oren Patashnik. Concrete Math-
      ematics. Addison-Wesley, Reading, MA, USA, 2nd edition, 1994. ISBN
      0-201-55802-5.
      A mathematics textbook prepared with TEX using the Concrete Roman typeface; see also [92].

[60] George Grätzer. Math into LATEX. Birkhäuser and Springer-Verlag, Cam-
      bridge, MA, USA; Berlin, Germany/Basel, Switzerland, and Berlin, Ger-
      many/Heidelberg, Germany/London, UK/ etc., 3rd edition, 2000. ISBN
      0-8176-4131-9, 3-7643-4131-9.
      Provides a general introduction to LATEX as used to prepare mathematical books and articles.
      Covers AMS document classes and packages in addition to the basic LATEX offerings.

[61] George D. Greenwade. "The Comprehensive TEX Archive Network (CTAN)".
      TUGboat, 14(3):342–351, 1993.
      An outline of the conception, development, and early use of the CTAN archive, which makes all
      TEX-related files available on the network.
                                 http://www.tug.org/TUGboat/Articles/tb14-3/tb40green.pdf

[62] Yannis Haralambous. "Typesetting old German: Fraktur, Schwabacher,
      Gotisch and initials". *TUGboat*, 12(1):129–138, 1991.
      Demonstrates the use of METAFONT to recreate faithful copies of old-style typefaces and
      explains the rules for typesetting using these types, with examples.
                                   http://www.tug.org/TUGboat/Articles/tb12-1/tb31hara.pdf

[63] Horace Hart. Hart's Rules; For Compositors and Readers at the University
      Press, Oxford. Oxford University Press, London, Oxford, New York, 39th
      edition, 1991. ISBN 0-19-212983-X.
      A widely used U.K. reference for authors and editors. With the *Oxford Dictionary for Writers and
      Editors* it presents the canonical house style of the Oxford University Press. See also [143].

[64] Alan Hoenig. TEX Unbound: LATEX and TEX Strategies for Fonts, Graphics,
      & More. Oxford University Press, London, Oxford, New York, 1998. ISBN
      0-19-509686-X (paperback), 0-19-509685-1 (hardcover).
      The first part of this book provides a brief but comprehensive overview of TEX, LATEX, META-
      FONT, and MetaPost, with particular emphasis on how everything fits together, how the pro-
      duction cycle works, and what kinds of files are involved. The second part is devoted to details
      of fonts and their use in TEX. Of particular interest are 30 pages of examples showing how
      various combinations of well-known text typefaces might be used together with the few choices
      of math fonts currently available. The final part of the book discusses graphics applications—
      in particular, TEX-friendly methods such as METAFONT and MetaPost, the pstricks package,
      PICTEX, and MFpic.

[65] Berthold K. P. Horn. "The European Modern fonts". *TUGboat*, 19(1):62–63,
      1998.
      The European Modern (EM) fonts are Type 1 fonts based on Computer Modern (CM) that have
      ready-made accented and composite characters, thus enabling TEX hyphenation when using
      languages that use such characters.
                                    http://www.tug.org/TUGboat/Articles/tb19-1/tb58horn.pdf

[66] Jean-Michel Hufflen. "Typographie: les conventions, la tradition, les
      goûts,..., et LATEX". *Cahiers GUTenberg*, 35–36:169–214, 2000.
      This article shows that learning typographic rules—even considering those for French and En-
      glish together—is not all that difficult. It also teaches the basics of using the LATEX packages
      french (for French only) and babel (allowing a homogeneous treatment of most other languages).

Finally, the author shows how to build a new multilingual document class and bibliography style.
`http://www.gutenberg.eu.org/pub/GUTenberg/publicationsPDF/35-hufflen.pdf`

[67] "ISO/IEC 8859-1:1998 to ISO/IEC 8859-16:2001, Information technology—8-bit single-byte coded graphic character sets, Parts 1 to 16". International Standard ISO/IEC 8859, ISO Geneva, 1998–2001.

A description of various 8-bit alphabetic character sets. Parts 1–4, 9, 10, and 13–16 correspond to 10 character sets needed to encode different groups of languages using the Latin alphabet, while part 5 corresponds to Cyrillic, part 6 to Arabic, part 7 to Greek, part 8 to Hebrew, and part 11 to Thai.

[68] "ISO 8879:1986, Information Processing—Text and Office Systems—Standard Generalised Markup Language (SGML)". International Standard ISO 8879, ISO Geneva, 1986.

The—not always easy to read—ISO standard describing the SGML language in full technical detail. An addendum was published in 1988 and two corrigenda in 1996 and 1999. See [53] for an annotated description.

[69] "ISO/IEC 10646-1:2000, Information technology—Universal Multiple-Octet Coded Character Set (UCS)—Part 1: Architecture and Basic Multilingual Plane". International Standard ISO 10646-1 (Edition 2), ISO Geneva, 2000.

This standard specifies the architecture of the Universal Multiple-Octet Coded Character Set (UCS). This 32-bit character encoding standard is for all practical purposes identical to the Unicode standard; see [165]. The layout of the Basic Multilingual Plane (plane 0 or BMP) is described in detail. An amendment in 2002 added mathematical symbols and other characters.

[70] "ISO/IEC 10646-2:2001, Information technology—Universal Multiple-Octet Coded Character Set (UCS)—Part 2: Supplementary Planes". International Standard ISO 10646-2, ISO Geneva, 2001.

Complementing [69], which describes plane 0 (BMP) of the UCS, the present standard details the layout of the supplementary planes; see also [165].

[71] "ISO/IEC 14651:2001, Information technology—International string ordering and comparison—Method for comparing character strings and description of the common template tailorable ordering". International Standard ISO/IEC 14651:2001, ISO Geneva, 2001.

[72] Alan Jeffrey. "PostScript font support in LaTeX 2_ε". *TUGboat*, 15(3):263–268, 1994.

Describes the original psnfss distribution for using PostScript fonts with LaTeX.
`http://www.tug.org/TUGboat/Articles/tb15-3/tb44jeff.pdf`

[73] Alan Jeffrey. "Tight setting with TeX". *TUGboat*, 16(1):78–80, 1995.

Describes some experiments with setting text matter in TeX using Adobe Times, a very tightly spaced text font. `http://www.tug.org/TUGboat/Articles/tb16-1/tb46jeff.pdf`

[74] Alan Jeffrey and Rowland McDonnell. "fontinst: Font installation software for TeX", 1998.

This utility package supports the creation of complex virtual fonts in any encoding for use with LaTeX, particularly from collections of PostScript fonts.
On CTAN at: `fonts/utilities/fontinst/doc/manual`

[75] Alan Jeffrey, Sebastian Rahtz, Ulrik Vieth, and Lars Hellström. "The fontinst utility", 2003.

Technical description of the fontinst utility.
On CTAN at: `fonts/utilities/fontinst/source/fisource.dvi`

[76]   Roger Kehr. "xindy—A flexible indexing system". *Cahiers GUTenberg*,
       28–29:223–230, 1998.
       A new index processor, xindy, is described. It allows for sorting of index entries at a fine
       granularity in a multi-language environment, offers new mechanisms for processing structured
       location references besides page numbers and Roman numerals, and has provisions for complex
       markup schemes.
                    http://www.gutenberg.eu.org/pub/GUTenberg/publicationsPDF/28-29-kehr.pdf

[77]   Brian W. Kernighan. "pic—A graphics language for typesetting". Comput-
       ing Science Technical Report 116, AT&T Bell Laboratories, 1991.
       The user manual for the pic language, which is intended for drawing simple figures on a type-
       setter. The basic objects of the language are boxes, circles, ellipses, lines, arrows, spline curves,
       and text. These may be placed at any position, specified either in an absolute way or with re-
       spect to previous objects.   http://cm.bell-labs.com/cm/cs/cstr/116.ps.gz

[78]   Jörg Knappen. "Release 1.2 of the dc-fonts: Improvements to the Eu-
       ropean letters and first release of text companion symbols". *TUGboat*,
       16(4):381–387, 1995.
       Description of the DC fonts, which were precursors of the EC fonts, which themselves are the
       default fonts for the T1 encoding of LaTeX.
                            http://www.tug.org/TUGboat/Articles/tb16-4/tb49knap.pdf

[79]   Jörg Knappen. "The dc fonts 1.3: Move towards stability and complete-
       ness". *TUGboat*, 17(2):99–101, 1996.
       A follow-up article to [78]. It explains the progress made in version 1.3 in the areas of stability
       and completeness.   http://www.tug.org/TUGboat/Articles/tb17-2/tb51knap.pdf

[80]   Donald E. Knuth. TeX and METAFONT—New Directions in Typesetting.
       Digital Press, 12 Crosby Drive, Bedford, MA 01730, USA, 1979. ISBN 0-
       932376-02-9.
       Contains an article on "Mathematical Typography", describing the author's motivation for start-
       ing to work on TeX and the early history of computer typesetting. Describes early (now obsolete)
       versions of TeX and METAFONT.

[81]   Donald E. Knuth. "Literate programming". Report STAN-CS-83-981,
       Stanford University, Department of Computer Science, Stanford, CA, USA,
       1983.
       A collection of papers on styles of programming and documentation.
                                        http://www.literateprogramming.com/farticles.html

[82]   Donald E. Knuth. The TeXbook, volume A of *Computers and Typesetting*.
       Addison-Wesley, Reading, MA, USA, 1986. ISBN 0-201-13447-0.
       The definitive user's guide and complete reference manual for TeX.

[83]   Donald E. Knuth. TeX: The Program, volume B of *Computers and Typeset-
       ting*. Addison-Wesley, Reading, MA, USA, 1986. ISBN 0-201-13437-3.
       The complete source code for the TeX program, typeset with several indices.

[84]   Donald E. Knuth. The METAFONTbook, volume C of *Computers and
       Typesetting*. Addison-Wesley, Reading, MA, USA, 1986. ISBN 0-201-13445-
       4 (hardcover), 0-201-13444-6 (paperback).
       The user's guide and reference manual for METAFONT, the companion program to TeX for
       designing fonts.

[85] Donald E. Knuth. METAFONT: The Program, volume D of *Computers and Typesetting*. Addison-Wesley, Reading, MA, USA, 1986. ISBN 0-201-13438-1.

The complete source code listing of the METAFONT program.

[86] Donald E. Knuth. Computer Modern Typefaces, volume E of *Computers and Typesetting*. Addison-Wesley, Reading, MA, USA, 1986. ISBN 0-201-13446-2.

More than 500 Greek and Roman letterforms, together with punctuation marks, numerals, and many mathematical symbols, are graphically depicted. The METAFONT code to generate each glyph is given and it is explained how, by changing the parameters in the METAFONT code, all characters in the Computer Modern family of typefaces can be obtained.

[87] Donald E. Knuth. 3:16 Bible texts illuminated. A-R Editions, Inc., Madison, Wisconsin, 1990. ISBN 0-89579-252-4.

Analysis of Chapter 3 Verse 16 of each book of the Bible. Contains wonderful calligraphy.

[88] Donald E. Knuth. The Art of Computer Programming, vols 1-3. Addison-Wesley, Reading, MA, USA, 1998.

A major work on algorithms and data structures for efficient programming.

[89] Donald E. Knuth. Digital Typography. CSLI Publications, Stanford, CA, USA, 1999. ISBN 1-57586-011-2 (cloth), 1-57586-010-4 (paperback).

A collection of Knuth's writings on TEX and typography.

[90] Donald E. Knuth. "Mathematical typography". In Knuth [89], pp. 19–65.

Based on a lecture he gave in 1978, Knuth makes the point that mathematics books and journals do not look as now beautiful as they did in the past. As this is mainly due to the fact that high-quality typesetting has become too expensive, he proposes to use mathematics itself to solve the problem. As a first step he sees the development of a method to unambiguously mark up the math elements in a document so that they can be easily handled by machines. The second step is to use mathematics to design the shapes of letters and symbols. The article goes into the details of these two approaches.

[91] Donald E. Knuth. "Virtual fonts: More fun for grand wizards". In Knuth [89], pp. 247–262. Originally published in *TUGboat* 11(1):13–23, 1990.

An explanation of what virtual fonts are and why they are needed, plus technical details.

On CTAN at: info/virtual-fonts.knuth
http://www.tug.org/TUGboat/Articles/tb11-1/tb27knut.pdf

[92] Donald E. Knuth. "Typesetting concrete mathematics". In Knuth [89], pp. 367–378. Originally published in *TUGboat* 10(1):31–36, 1989.

Knuth explains how he prepared the textbook *Concrete Mathematics*. He states that he wanted to make that book both mathematically and typographically "interesting", since it would be the first major use of Herman Zapf's new typeface, AMS Euler. The font parameters were tuned up to make the text look as good as that produced by the best handwriting of a mathematician. Other design decisions for the book are also described.

http://www.tug.org/TUGboat/Articles/tb10-1/tb26knut.pdf

[93] Donald E. Knuth. "Fonts for digital halftones". In Knuth [89], pp. 415–448. Originally published in *TUGboat* 8(2):135–160, 1987.

This article discusses some experiments in which METAFONT was used to create fonts to generate half-tones on laser printers. The methods also proved useful in several other applications, while their design involved a number of interesting issues.

http://www.tug.org/TUGboat/Articles/tb08-2/tb18knut.pdf

[94] Donald E. Knuth. "Computers and typesetting". In Knuth [89], pp. 555–562. Originally published in *TUGboat* 7(2):95–98, 1986.
Remarks presented by Knuth at the Computer Museum, Boston, Massachusetts, on 21 May 1986, at the "coming-out" party to celebrate the completion of TEX.
http://www.tug.org/TUGboat/Articles/tb07-2/tb14knut.pdf

[95] Donald E. Knuth. "The new versions of TEX and METAFONT". In Knuth [89], pp. 563–570. Originally published in *TUGboat* 10(3):325–328, 1989.
Knuth explains how he was convinced at the TUG Meeting at Stanford in 1989 to make one further set of changes to TEX and METAFONT to extend these programs to support 8-bit character sets. He goes on to describe the various changes he introduced to implement this feature, as well as a few other improvements.
http://www.tug.org/TUGboat/Articles/tb10-3/tb25knut.pdf

[96] Donald E. Knuth. "The future of TEX and METAFONT". In Knuth [89], pp. 571–572. Originally published in *TUGboat* 11(4):489, 1990.
In this article Knuth announces that his work on TEX, METAFONT, and Computer Modern has "come to an end" and that he will make further changes only to correct extremely serious bugs.
http://www.tug.org/TUGboat/Articles/tb11-4/tb30knut.pdf

[97] Donald E. Knuth and Pierre MacKay. "Mixing right-to-left texts with left-to-right texts". In Knuth [89], pp. 157–176. Originally published in *TUGboat* 8(1):14–25, 1987.
TEX was initially designed to produce documents with material flowing left-to-right and top-to-bottom. This paper clarifies the issues involved in mixed-direction document production and discusses changes to TEX that can extend it to become a bidirectional formatting system.
http://www.tug.org/TUGboat/Articles/tb08-1/tb17knutmix.pdf

[98] Donald E. Knuth and Michael F. Plass. "Breaking paragraphs into lines". In Knuth [89], pp. 67–155.
This article, originally published in 1981, addresses the problem of dividing the text of a paragraph into lines of approximately equal length. The basic algorithm considers the paragraph as a whole and introduces the (now well-known TEX) concepts of "boxes", "glue", and "penalties" to find optimal breakpoints for the lines. The paper describes the dynamic programming technique used to implement the algorithm.

[99] Donald E. Knuth and Hermann Zapf. "AMS Euler—A new typeface for mathematics". In Knuth [89], pp. 339–366.
The two authors explain, in this article originally published in 1989, how a collaboration between scientists and artists is helping to bring beauty to the pages of mathematical journals and textbooks.

[100] Markus Kohm and Jens-Uwe Morawski. KOMA-Script: eine Sammlung von Klassen und Paketen für LATEX 2$_\varepsilon$. DANTE, Heidelberg, 2003. ISBN 3-936427-45-3.
KOMA-Script is a bundle of LATEX classes and packages that can be used as replacements for the standard LATEX classes offering extended functionalities. German and English manuals are provided as part of the distribution.
On CTAN at: macros/latex/contrib/koma-script/scrguide.pdf

[101] Helmut Kopka and Patrick Daly. Guide to LATEX. Tools and Techniques for Computer Typesetting. Addison-Wesley, Boston, MA, USA, 4th edition, 2004. ISBN 0-201-17385-6.
An introductory guide to LATEX with a different pedagogical style than Lamport's *LATEX Manual* [104].

[102] Klaus Lagally. "ArabTEX—Typesetting Arabic with vowels and ligatures". In "Proceedings of the 7th European TEX Conference, Prague", pp. 153–172. CsTUG, Prague, 1992. ISBN 80-210-0480-0.

A macro package, compatible with plain TEX and LATEX, for typesetting Arabic with both partial and full vocalization.

[103] Leslie Lamport. "*MakeIndex*, An Index Processor For LATEX". Technical report, Electronic Document in *MakeIndex* distribution, 1987.

This document explains the syntax that can be used inside LATEX's \index command when using *MakeIndex* to generate your index. It also gives a list of the possible error messages.
On CTAN at: `indexing/makeindex/doc/makeindex.dvi`

[104] Leslie Lamport. LATEX: A Document Preparation System: User's Guide and Reference Manual. Addison-Wesley, Reading, MA, USA, 2nd edition, 1994. ISBN 0-201-52983-1. Reprinted with corrections in 1996.

The ultimate reference for basic user-level LATEX by the creator of LATEX 2.09. It complements the material presented in this book.

[105] Olga Lapko and Irina Makhovaya. "The style `russianb` for Babel: Problems and solutions". *TUGboat*, 16(4):364–372, 1995.

This paper describes the language option `russianb`, which includes specific commands to russify captions and alphabetic counters and to allow for Russian mathematical operators. Some problems are mentioned that may occur when using this option (i.e., with different encodings).
`http://www.tug.org/TUGboat/Articles/tb16-4/tb49olga.pdf`

[106] LATEX3 Project Team. "LATEX bug database".

The bug reporting and tracking service run by the LATEX3 team as part of the LATEX 2ε maintenance activity. `http://www.latex-project.org/cgi-bin/ltxbugs2html`

[107] LATEX3 Project Team. "LATEX news".

An issue of *LATEX News* is released with each LATEX 2ε release, highlighting changes since the last release. `http://www.latex-project.org`

[108] LATEX3 Project Team. "Default docstrip headers". *TUGboat*, 19(2):137–138, 1998.

This document describes the format of the header that docstrip normally adds to generated package files. This header is suitable for copyright information or distribution conditions.
`http://www.tug.org/TUGboat/Articles/tb19-2/tb59ltdocstrip.pdf`

[109] LATEX3 Project Team. "LATEX 2ε font selection", 2000.

A description of font selection in standard LATEX intended for package writers who are already familiar with TEX fonts and LATEX. `http://www.latex-project.org`

[110] LATEX3 Project Team. "Configuration options for LATEX 2ε", 2001.

How to configure a LATEX installation using the set of standard configuration files.
`http://www.latex-project.org`

[111] LATEX3 Project Team. "The LATEX project public license (version 1.3)", 2003.

An Open Source License used by the core LATEX 2ε distribution and many contributed packages.
`http://www.latex-project.org`

[112] John Lavagnino and Dominik Wujastyk. "An overview of EDMAC: A plain TEX format for critical editions". *TUGboat*, 11(4):623–643, 1990.

EDMAC is for typesetting of "critical editions" of texts such as the *Oxford Classical Texts, Shakespeare*, and other series. It supports marginal line numbering and multiple series of footnotes and endnotes keyed to line numbers.
`http://www.tug.org/TUGboat/Articles/tb11-4/tb30lava.pdf`

[113] Werner Lemberg. "The CJK package: Multilingual support beyond Babel".
       TUGboat, 18(3):214–224, 1997.
       A description of the CJK (Chinese/Japanese/Korean) package for LaTeX and its interface to mule
       (multilingual emacs).   `http://www.tug.org/TUGboat/Articles/tb18-3/cjkintro600.pdf`

[114] Silvio Levy. "Using Greek fonts with TeX". *TUGboat*, 9(1):20–24, 1988.
       The author tries to demonstrate that typesetting Greek in TeX with the gr family of fonts can be
       as easy as typesetting English text and leads to equally good results. The article is meant as a
       tutorial but some technical details are given for those who will have acquired greater familiarity
       with the font.   `http://www.tug.org/TUGboat/Articles/tb09-1/tb20levy.pdf`

[115] Franklin Mark Liang. Word Hy-phen-a-tion by Com-pu-ter. Ph.D. thesis,
       Stanford University, Stanford, CA 94305, 1983. Also available as Stanford
       University, Department of Computer Science Report No. STAN-CS-83-977.
       A detailed description of the word hyphenation algorithm used by TeX.

[116] Ruari McLean. The Thames and Hudson Manual of Typography. Thames
       and Hudson, London, UK, 1980. ISBN 0-500-68022-1.
       A broad introduction to traditional commercial typography.

[117] Frank Mittelbach. "E-TeX: Guidelines for future TeX". *TUGboat*, 11(3):337–
       345, 1990.
       The output of TeX is compared with that of hand-typeset documents. It is shown that many
       important concepts of high-quality typesetting are not supported and that further research to
       design a "successor" typesetting system to TeX should be undertaken.
                                     `http://www.tug.org/TUGboat/Articles/tb11-3/tb29mitt.pdf`

[118] Frank Mittelbach. "Comments on "Filenames for Fonts" (*TUGboat* 11#4)".
       TUGboat, 13(1):51–53, 1992.
       Some problems with K. Berry's naming scheme are discussed, especially from the point of view
       of defining certain font characteristics independently and the use of the scheme with NFSS.
                                 `http://www.tug.org/TUGboat/Articles/tb13-1/tb34mittfont.pdf`

[119] Frank Mittelbach. "A regression test suite for LaTeX 2_ε". *TUGboat*,
       18(4):309–311, 1997.
       Description of the concepts and implementation of the test suite used to test for unexpected
       side effects after changes to the LaTeX kernel. One of the most valuable maintenance tools for
       keeping LaTeX 2_ε stable.   `http://www.tug.org/TUGboat/Articles/tb18-4/tb57mitt.pdf`

[120] Frank Mittelbach. "Language Information in Structured Documents:
       Markup and rendering—Concepts and problems". In "International Sym-
       posium on Multilingual Information Processing", pp. 93–104. Tsukuba,
       Japan, 1997. Invited paper. Republished in *TUGboat* 18(3):199–205, 1997.
       This paper discusses the structure and processing of multilingual documents, both at a general
       level and in relation to a proposed extension to standard LaTeX.
                                     `http://www.tug.org/TUGboat/Articles/tb18-3/tb56lang.pdf`

[121] Frank Mittelbach. "Formatting documents with floats: A new algorithm
       for LaTeX 2_ε". *TUGboat*, 21(3):278–290, 2000.
       Descriptions of features and concepts of a new output routine for LaTeX that can handle spanning
       floats in multicolumn page design.
                                     `http://www.tug.org/TUGboat/Articles/tb21-3/tb68mittel.pdf`

[122] Frank Mittelbach. "The trace package". *TUGboat*, 22(1/2):93–99, 2001.
       A description of the trace package for controlling debugging messages from LaTeX packages.
                                   `http://www.tug.org/TUGboat/Articles/tb22-1-2/tb70mitt.pdf`

[123] Frank Mittelbach, David Carlisle, and Chris Rowley. "New interfaces for
       LaTeX class design, Parts I and II". *TUGboat*, 20(3):214–216, 1999.
       Some proposals for the first-ever interface to setting up and coding LaTeX classes.
                            http://www.tug.org/TUGboat/Articles/tb20-3/tb64carl.pdf

[124] Frank Mittelbach, David Carlisle, Chris Rowley, et al. "Experimental LaTeX
       code for class design".
       At the TeX Users Group conference in Vancouver the LaTeX project team gave a talk on models
       for user-level interfaces and designer-level interfaces in LaTeX3 [123]. Most of these ideas have
       been implemented in prototype implementations (e.g., template design, front matter handling,
       output routine, galley and paragraph formatting). The source code is documented and contains
       further explanations and examples; see also [121].
                         Slides: http://www.latex-project.org/papers/tug99pdf
                             Code: http://www.latex-project.org/code/experimental

[125] Frank Mittelbach, Denys Duchier, Johannes Braams, Marcin Woliński, and
       Mark Wooding. "The docstrip program", 2003. Distributed as part of the
       base LaTeX distribution.
       Describes the implementation of the docstrip program.
                             On CTAN at: macros/latex/base/docstrip.dtx

[126] Frank Mittelbach and Chris Rowley. "LaTeX 2.09 ↪ LaTeX3". *TUGboat*,
       13(1):96–101, 1992.
       A brief sketch of the LaTeX3 Project, retracing its history and describing the structure of the
       system. An update appeared in *TUGboat*, 13(3):390–391, October 1992. A call for volunteers to
       help in the development of LaTeX3 and a list of the various tasks appeared in *TUGboat*, 13(4):510–
       515, December 1992. The article also describes how you can obtain the current task list as
       well as various LaTeX3 working group documents via e-mail or FTP and explains how you can
       subscribe to the LaTeX3 discussion list.
                             http://www.tug.org/TUGboat/Articles/tb13-1/tb34mittl3.pdf

[127] Frank Mittelbach and Chris Rowley. "The pursuit of quality: How can auto-
       mated typesetting achieve the highest standards of craft typography?" In
       C. Vanoirbeek and G. Coray, editors, "EP92—Proceedings of Electronic Pub-
       lishing, '92, International Conference on Electronic Publishing, Document
       Manipulation, and Typography, Swiss Federal Institute of Technology, Lau-
       sanne, Switzerland, April 7–10, 1992", pp. 261–273. Cambridge University
       Press, New York, 1992. ISBN 0-521-43277-4.

[128] Frank Mittelbach and Rainer Schöpf. "A new font selection scheme for TeX
       macro packages—the basic macros". *TUGboat*, 10(2):222–238, 1989.
       A description of the basic macros used to implement the first version of LaTeX's New Font Selec-
       tion Scheme.   http://www.tug.org/TUGboat/Articles/tb10-2/tb24mitt.pdf

[129] Frank Mittelbach and Rainer Schöpf. "With LaTeX into the nineties". *TUG-
       boat*, 10(4):681–690, 1989.
       This article proposes a reimplementation of LaTeX that preserves the essential features of the
       current interface while taking into account the increasing needs of the various user communi-
       ties. It also formulates some ideas for further developments. It was instrumental in the move
       from LaTeX 2.09 to LaTeX 2ε.   http://www.tug.org/TUGboat/Articles/tb10-4/tb26mitt.pdf

[130] Frank Mittelbach and Rainer Schöpf. "Reprint: The new font family selec-
       tion — User interface to standard LaTeX". *TUGboat*, 11(2):297–305, 1990.
       A complete description of the user interface of the first version of LaTeX's New Font Selection
       Scheme.   http://www.tug.org/TUGboat/Articles/tb11-2/tb28mitt.pdf

[131] Frank Mittelbach and Rainer Schöpf. "Towards LaTeX 3.0". *TUGboat*, 12(1):74–79, 1991.

The objectives of the LaTeX3 project are described. The authors examine enhancements to LaTeX's user and style file interfaces that are necessary to keep pace with modern developments, such as SGML. They also review some internal concepts that need revision.

http://www.tug.org/TUGboat/Articles/tb12-1/tb31mitt.pdf

[132] Gerd Neugebauer. "BIBTOOL: A tool to manipulate BibTeX files", 2002.

Describes the bibtool program for pretty-printing, sorting and merging of BibTeX databases, generation of uniform reference keys, and selecting of references used in a publication.

On CTAN at: biblio/bibtex/utils/bibtool/bibtool.dvi

[133] O. Nicole, J. André, and B. Gaulle. "Notes en bas de pages : commentaires". *Cahiers GUTenberg*, 15:46–32, 1993.

Comments, clarifications, and additions to [10].

http://www.gutenberg.eu.org/pub/GUTenberg/publicationsPDF/15-nicole.pdf

[134] Scott Pakin. "The comprehensive LaTeX symbol list", 2003.

This document lists more than 2800 symbols and the corresponding LaTeX commands that produce them. Some of these symbols are guaranteed to be available in every LaTeX 2_ε system; others require fonts and packages that may not accompany a given distribution and that therefore need to be installed. All of the fonts and packages described in the document are freely available from the CTAN archives.   On CTAN at: info/symbols/comprehensive/

[135] Oren Patashnik. "BibTeXing", 1988.

Together with Appendix B of *The Manual* [104], this describes the user interface to BibTeX with useful hints for controlling its behavior.

On CTAN at: biblio/bibtex/contrib/doc/btxdoc.pdf

[136] Oren Patashnik. "Designing BibTeX styles", 1988.

A detailed description for BibTeX style designers of the postfix stack language used inside BibTeX style files. After a general description of the language, all commands and built-in functions are reviewed. Finally, BibTeX name formatting is explained in detail.

On CTAN at: biblio/bibtex/contrib/doc/btxhak.pdf

[137] John Plaice and Yannis Haralambous. "The latest developments in Ω". *TUGboat*, 17(2):181–183, 1996.

The article describes ΩTimes and ΩHelvetica, public-domain virtual Times- and Helvetica-like fonts based on real PostScript fonts, called "Glyph Containers", which will contain all necessary characters for typesetting with high TeX quality in all languages and systems using the Latin, Greek, Cyrillic, Arabic, Hebrew, and Tinagh alphabets and their derivatives. Other alphabets, such as Coptic, Armenian, and Georgian, will follow, as well as mathematical symbols, dingbats, and other character collections. Ultimately, the Ω font set will contain glyphs for the complete Unicode character set, plus some specific glyphs needed for high-quality typography.

http://www.tug.org/TUGboat/Articles/tb17-2/tb51omeg.pdf

[138] John Plaice, Yannis Haralambous, and Chris Rowley. "A multidimensional approach to typesetting". *TUGboat*. To appear.

Outline of an approach to micro-typesetting that substantially improves on that of TeX and Ω2.0.   http://www.tug.org/TUGboat/Articles/...

[139] Sunil Podar. "Enhancements to the picture environment of LaTeX". Technical Report 86-17, Department of Computer Science, S.U.N.Y, 1986. Version 1.2: July 14, 1986.

This document describes some new commands for the `picture` environment of LaTeX, especially higher-level commands that enhance its graphic capabilities by providing a friendlier and more powerful user interface. This lets you create more sophisticated pictures with less effort than in basic LaTeX.

[140] Rama Porrat. "Developments in Hebrew TEX". In "Proceedings of the 7th European TEX Conference, Prague", pp. 135–147. CsTUG, Prague, 1992. ISBN 80-210-0480-0.
Discussion of available software and macro packages that support typesetting in two directions, and of associated Hebrew fonts.

[141] Bernd Raichle, Rolf Niepraschk, and Thomas Hafner. "DE-TeX-FAQ— Fragen und Antworten über TEX, LATEX und DANTE e.V.", 2003.
Frequently Asked Questions with answers about TEX and the German TEX users' Group DANTE e.V. (in German language).   http://www.dante.de/faq/de-tex-faq

[142] Brian Reid. Scribe Document Production System User Manual. Unilogic Ltd, 1984.
The manual for the system that inspired certain aspects of LATEX.

[143] Robert M Ritter, editor. The Oxford Style Manual. Oxford University Press, London, Oxford, New York, 2003. ISBN 0-198-60564-1.
Reference work incorporating an update to *Hart's Rules* [63], and the *Oxford Dictionary for Writers and Editors*.

[144] Tomas G. Rokicki. "A proposed standard for specials". *TUGboat*, 16(4):395–401, 1995.
A draft standard for the contents of TEX \special commands.
                    http://www.tug.org/TUGboat/Articles/tb16-4/tb49roki.pdf

[145] Tomas G. Rokicki. "Dvips: A DVI-to-PostScript Translator, Version 5.66a", 1997.
The user guide for dvips and its accompanying programs and packages such as afm2tfm.
                    On CTAN at: dviware/dvips/dvips_man.pdf

[146] Emmanuel Donin de Rosière. From stack removing in stack-based languages to BibTEX++. Master's thesis, ENSTBr, 2003.
A description of BibTEX++, a bibliography section creator for LATEX a possible successor of BIBTEX. The program can compile BIBTEX .bst style files into Java code.
        http://www.lit.enstb.org/~keryell/eleves/ENSTBr/2002-2003/DEA/Donin_de_Rosiere

[147] Chris Rowley. "Models and languages for formatted documents". *TUGboat*, 20(3):189–195, 1999.
Explores many ideas around the nature of document formatting and how these can be modeled and implemented.   http://www.tug.org/TUGboat/Articles/tb20-3/tb64rowl.pdf

[148] Chris Rowley. "The LATEX legacy: 2.09 and all that". In ACM, editor, "Proceedings of the Twentieth Annual ACM Symposium on Principles of Distributed Computing 2001, Newport, Rhode Island, United States", pp. 17–25. ACM Press, New York, NY, USA, 2001. ISBN 1-58113-383-9.
Part of a celebration for Leslie Lamport's sixtieth birthday; a very particular account of the technical history and philosophy of TEX and LATEX.

[149] Chris A. Rowley and Frank Mittelbach. "Application-independent representation of multilingual text". In Unicode Consortium, editor, "Europe, Software + the Internet: Going Global with Unicode: Tenth International

Unicode Conference, March 10-12, 1997, Mainz, Germany", The Unicode Consortium, San Jose, CA, 1997.

Explores the nature of text representation in computer files and the needs of a wide range of text-processing software.   http://www.latex-project.org/papers/unicode5.pdf

[150]   Richard Rubinstein. Digital Typography—An Introduction to Type and Composition for Computer System Design. Addison-Wesley, Reading, MA, USA, 1988. ISBN 0-201-17633-5. Reprinted with corrections.

This book describes a technological approach to typography. It shows how computers can be used to design, create, and position the graphical elements used to present documents on a computer.

[151]   Joachim Schrod. "International LATEX is ready to use". *TUGboat*, 11(1):87–90, 1990.

Announces some of the early standards for globalization work on LATEXJoachim Schrod.
                         http://www.tug.org/TUGboat/Articles/tb11-1/tb27schrod.pdf

[152]   Joachim Schrod. "An international version of *MakeIndex*". *Cahiers GUTen-berg*, 10-11:81–90, 1991.

The *MakeIndex* index processor is only really usable for English texts; non-English texts, especially those using non-Latin alphabets, such as Russian, Arabic, or Chinese, prove problematic. In this case the tagging of index entries is often tedious and error prone. In particular, if markup is used within the index key, an explicit sort key must be specified. This article presents a new version of *MakeIndex*, which uses less memory so that it can be used for the creation of very large indices. It allows the automatic creation of sort keys from index keys by user-specified mappings, and supports documents in non-Latin alphabets.
                http://www.gutenberg.eu.org/pub/GUTenberg/publicationsPDF/10-schrod.pdf

[153]   Joachim Schrod. "The components of TEX". *MAPS*, 8:81–86, 1992.

TEX needs a great number of supplementary components (files and programs) whose meanings and interactions often are unknown; the structure of a complete TEX setup is explained.
                                              http://www.ntg.nl/maps/pdf/8_18.pdf

[154]   Paul Stiff. "The end of the line: A survey of unjustified typography". *Information Design Journal*, 8(2):125–152, 1996.

A good overview about the typographical problems that need to be resolved when producing high-quality unjustified copy.

[155]   Anders Svensson. "Typesetting diagrams with kuvio.tex", 1996.

Manual for kuvio system for typesetting diagrams; it uses PostScript code in \specials.
                                      On CTAN at: macros/generic/diagrams/kuvio

[156]   Ellen Swanson. Mathematics into Type. American Mathematical Society, Providence, Rhode Island, updated edition, 1999. ISBN 0-8218-1961-5. Updated by Arlene O'Sean and Antoinette Schleyer.

Originally written as a manual to standardize copyediting procedures, the second edition is also intended for use by publishers and authors as a guide in preparing mathematics copy for the printer.

[157]   The *TUGboat* Team. "TEX live CD 5 and the TEX Catalogue". *TUGboat*, 21(1):16–90, 2000.

The TEX live CD is a ready-to-run TEX system for the most popular operating systems; it works with all major TEX-related programs and contains a complete collection of fonts, macros, and other items with support for many languages. This article describes the TEX live CD 5 distribution with cross-references to Graham Williams' TEX catalogue.
                              http://www.tug.org/TUGboat/Articles/tb21-1/tb66cd.pdf
                              Current version: http://www.tug.org/texlive

[158] Hàn Thế Thành. "Improving TEX's typeset layout". *TUGboat*, 19(3):284–288, 1998.
This attempt to improve TEX's typeset layout is based on the adjustment of interword spacing after the paragraphs have been broken into lines. Instead of changing only the interword spacing to justify text lines, fonts on the line are also slightly expanded to minimize excessive stretching of the interword spaces. This font expansion is implemented using horizontal scaling in PDF. By using such expansion conservatively, and by employing appropriate settings for TEX's line-breaking and spacing parameters, this method can improve the appearance of TEX's typeset layout. http://www.tug.org/TUGboat/Articles/tb19-3/tb60than.pdf

[159] Hàn Thế Thành. "Micro-typographic extensions to the TEX typesetting system". *TUGboat*, 21(4):317–434, 2000.
Doctoral dissertation at the Faculty of Informatics, Masaryk University, Brno, Czech Republic, October 2000. http://www.tug.org/TUGboat/Articles/tb21-4/tb69thanh.pdf

[160] Hàn Thế Thành. "Margin kerning and font expansion with pdfTEX". *TUGboat*, 22(3):146–148, 2001.
"Margin kerning" adjusts the positions of the primary and final glyphs in a line of text to make the margins "look straight". "Font expansion" uses a slightly wider or narrower variant of a font to make interword spacing more even. These techniques are explained with the help of examples. For a detailed explanation of the concepts, see [159]. This feature was used in the preparation of this book. http://www.tug.org/TUGboat/Articles/tb22-3/tb72thanh.pdf

[161] Hàn Thế Thánh and Sebastian Rahtz. "The pdfTEX user manual". *TUGboat*, 18(4):249–254, 1997.
User manual for the pdfTEX system, which extends TEX to generate PDF directly.
http://www.tug.org/TUGboat/Articles/tb18-4/tb57than.pdf

[162] Harold Thimbleby. "'See also' indexing with Makeindex". *TUGboat*, 12(2):290–290, 1991.
Describes how to produce "see also" entries with *MakeIndex* appearing after any page numbers for that entry. Also check [163]. http://www.tug.org/TUGboat/Articles/tb12-2/tb32thim.pdf

[163] Harold Thimbleby. "Erratum: 'See also' indexing with Makeindex, *TUGboat* 12, no. 2, p. 290". *TUGboat*, 13(1):95–95, 1992.
Erratum to [162]. http://www.tug.org/TUGboat/Articles/tb13-1/tb34thim.pdf

[164] TUG Working Group on a TEX Directory Structure. "A directory structure for TEX files (Version 0.999)". *TUGboat*, 16(4):401–413, 1995.
Describes the commonly used standard TEX Directory Structure (TDS) for implementation-independent TEX system files. http://www.tug.org/TUGboat/Articles/tb16-4/tb49tds.pdf
Current version: http://www.tug.org/tds

[165] The Unicode Consortium. The Unicode Standard, Version 4.0. Addison-Wesley, Boston, MA, USA, 2003. ISBN 0-321-18578-1.
The reference guide of the Unicode Standard, a universal character-encoding scheme that defines a consistent way of encoding multilingual text. Unicode is the default encoding of HTML and XML. The book explains the principles of operation and contains images of the glyphs for all characters presently defined in Unicode.
Available for restricted use from: http://www.unicode.org/versions/Unicode4.0.0

[166] Gabriel Valiente Feruglio. "Typesetting commutative diagrams". *TUGboat*, 15(4):466–484, 1994.
Surveys the available support for typesetting commutative diagrams.
http://www.tug.org/TUGboat/Articles/tb15-4/tb4bvali.pdf

[167] Gabriel Valiente Feruglio. "Modern Catalan typographical conventions".
       TUGboat, 16(3):329–338, 1995.

> Many languages, such as German, English, and French, have a traditional typography. However,
> despite the existence of a well-established tradition in scientific writing in Catalan, there are not
> yet any standards encompassing typographical conventions in this area. This paper proposes
> typographical rules that reflect the spirit of ancient Catalan scientific writings while conforming
> to modern typographical conventions. Some of these typographical rules are incorporated in
> Catalan extensions to TeX and LaTeX. The proposal also hopes to contribute to the development
> of standard rules for scientific writing in Catalan.
>
>   http://www.tug.org/TUGboat/Articles/tb16-3/tb48vali.pdf

[168] Michael Vulis. "VTeX enhancements to the TeX language". *TUGboat*,
       11(3):429–434, 1990.

> Description of the commercial VTeX system, which supports a scalable font format.
>   http://www.tug.org/TUGboat/Articles/
>   More recent information available from http://www.micropress-inc.com/enfeat.htm

[169] Graham Williams. "Graham Williams' TeX Catalogue". *TUGboat*, 21(1):17–
       90, 2000.

> This catalogue lists more than 1500 TeX, LaTeX, and related packages and tools and is linked
> directly to the items on CTAN.
>   http://www.tug.org/TUGboat/Articles/tb21-1/tb66catal.pdf
>   Latest version on CTAN at: help/Catalogue/catalogue.html

[170] Hugh Williamson. Methods of Book Design. Yale University Press, New
       Haven, London, 3rd edition, 1983.

> A classic work that has become a basic tool for the practicing book designer. It deals with
> such matters as the preparation of copy, the selection and arrangement of type, the designer's
> part in book illustration and jacket design, and the economics of book production. The book
> also explains the materials and techniques of book production and their effect on the design of
> books.

[171] Peter Wilson. ledmac—A presumptuous attempt to port EDMAC and
       TABMAC to LaTeX, 2003.

> EDMAC and TABMAC are a set of plain TeX macros for typesetting critical editions in the traditional
> way. The ledmac package implements the facilities of these macros in LaTeX—in particular,
> marginal line numbering and multiple series of footnotes and endnotes keyed to line numbers.
> As a new feature the package provides for index entries keyed to both page and line numbers.
> Multiple series of the familiar numbered footnotes are also available.
>   On CTAN at: macros/latex/contrib/ledmac/ledmac.pdf

[172] Reinhard Wonneberger and Frank Mittelbach. "BibTeX reconsidered".
       TUGboat, 12(1):111–124, 1991.

> A discussion of BibTeX and several proposals for its enhancement.
>   http://www.tug.org/TUGboat/Articles/tb12-1/tb31wonn.pdf

[173] Hermann Zapf. "My collaboration with Don Knuth and my font design
       work". *TUGboat*, 22(1/2):26–30, 2001.

> Zapf's story of collaboration with Don Knuth and some thoughts on typography.
>   http://www.tug.org/TUGboat/Articles/tb22-1-2/tb70zapf.pdf

[174] Justin Ziegler. "Technical report on math font encoding (version 2)".
       Technical report, LaTeX3 project, 1994.

> The ground work for a set of 8-bit math encodings for TeX.
>   On CTAN at: info/ltx3pub/l3d007.*

Index of Commands and Concepts

This title somewhat hides the fact that everything except the author names is in this one long index. To make it easier to use, the entries are distinguished by their "type" and this is often indicated by one of the the following "type words" at the beginning of the main entry or a sub-entry:

> attribute, BibTEX built-in function, BibTEX command, BibTEX entry type, BibTEX field, BibTEX style, boolean, counter, document class, env., env. variable, file, file extension, folio style, font, font encoding, function, key, key/option, key value, keyword, length, option, package, page style, program, rigid length, or syntax.

The absence of an explicit "type word" means that the "type" is either a LATEX "command" or simply a "concept".

Use by, or in connection with, a particular package is indicated by adding the package name (in parentheses) to an entry or sub-entry. There is one "virtual" package name, tlc, which indicates commands introduced only for illustrative purposes in this book.

When there are several page numbers listed, **bold** face indicates a page containing important information about an entry, such as a definition or basic usage. A blue page number indicates that use of the command or concept is demonstrated in an example on that page.

When looking for the position of an entry in the index, you need to realize that, when they come at the start of a command or file extension, both of the characters \ and . are ignored. All symbols come before all letters and everything that starts with the @ character will appear immediately before A.

C

People

Biographies

Frank Mittelbach

Frank Mittelbach studied mathematics and computer science at the Johannes-Gutenberg University, Mainz. In 1989 he joined EDS, Electronic Data Systems, working in a newly formed group for document processing using TeX and other tools. In his current position he is responsible for concepts and implementation for remote monitoring and management of distributed systems and networks.

before TLC2...

His interest in the automated formatting of complex documents in general, and in LaTeX in particular, goes back to his university days and has become a major interest, perhaps a vocation, and certainly it is now his "second job". He is author or co-author of many and varied LaTeX extension packages, such as $\mathcal{A}_{\mathcal{M}}S$-LaTeX, doc, multicol, and NFSS: the New Font Selection Scheme.

At the TUG conference at Stanford University in 1989, he gave a talk about the problems with LaTeX 2.09, which led to his taking on the responsibility for the maintenance and further development of LaTeX. This effort is generally known as the LaTeX3 Project and in the capacity of technical director of this project, he has overseen the original major release of LaTeX 2_ε in 1994 and the, by now, 15 subsequent maintenance releases of this software.

His publication of many technical papers on LaTeX and on general research results in automated formatting brought him in contact with Peter Gordon from Addison-Wesley. Peter and Frank inaugurated the book series *Tools and Techniques for Computer Typesetting* (TTCT), with Frank as series editor. *The LaTeX Companion* (1994) was the first book of this series whose titles by now cover LaTeX in all its facets. Forthcoming works will expand that core to cover other typesetting and information processing tools and concepts.

In 1990 Frank presented the paper *E-TEX: Guidelines for further TEX extensions*, which explained the most critical shortcomings of TEX and argued the need for its further development and for research into the many open questions of automated typesetting. This was the first time the topic of change or extension had been openly discussed within the TEX community and, after getting some early opposition, it helped to spawn several important projects, such as eTEX, Omega, and NTS. He is now interested in bringing together the fruits of these TEX extension developments, e.g.,

...and after

the Omega and eTEX projects, to get a stable, well-maintained, and widely available successor of TEX on which a future LATEX3 can be based.

Frank lives with his wife, Christel, and their three sons, Arno (age 19) and the twins Burkhard and Holger (age 6), in Mainz, Germany.

Michel Goossens

After finishing his Ph.D. in high energy physics Michel Goossens joined CERN, the European Laboratory for Particle Physics in Geneva (Switzerland) at the beginning of 1979, where he worked for a few years as a research physicist, and then moved on to software support in the Informatics Technologies Division.

Over the years he has worked with several typesetting systems: LATEX, of course, but also, more recently, HTML/SGML/XML.

As a large international scientific laboratory, a large fraction of the thousands of physicists and engineers working at CERN use LATEX for publishing their papers or for writing their documentation. Therefore, since the late 80s Michel has been involved in developing and supporting tools related to TEX and, especially, LATEX.

A milestone in his LATEX life was a meeting with Frank and Chris at CERN at the end of 1992, where they gave a talk on LATEX3. After their seminar Michel showed them the "Local TEX Guide" that he and Alexander Samarin had written and proposed to extend the material and turn it into a book. This was the birth of the first edition of *The LATEX Companion*, which was published at the beginning of 1994. Using his experience in graphics and web presentation, he also co-authored *The LATEX Graphics Companion* (1997) and *The LATEX Web Companion* (1999), both of which appeared in the TTCT series.

Michel has occupied various positions in the TEX world. He was president of GUTenberg, the French-speaking TEX users Group (1995–2000), as well as president of TUG, the TEX Users Group (1995–1997).

For the past three years he has acted as the CERN Focal Point for the EU-funded TIPS (Tools for Innovative Publishing in Science) project. Within the framework of that project he was responsible for studying how XML tools can be optimally integrated into a framework for efficiently handling electronic information, especially for scientific documents. In particular, he looked at the complementary roles played by LaTeX and MathML for mathematics, SVG for graphics, PDF for typographic quality output, and XHTML or DocBook for structural integration in the Web environment.

He lives in the Geneva area and enjoys reading, watching a good film, walking along the lake or in the beautiful countryside, and visiting museums.

Johannes Braams

Johannes Braams studied electronic engineering at the Technical University in Enschede, the Netherlands. His master's thesis was on video encoding, based on a model of the human visual system. He first met LaTeX at the *dr. Neher Laboratories* of the Dutch PTT in 1984. He was a founding board member of the Dutch speaking TeX User Group (NTG) in 1988 and participated in developing support for typesetting Dutch documents.

He started work on the babel system following the Karlsruhe EuroTeX conference in 1989 and has been a member of the LaTeX3 project since the EuroTeX conference at Cork in 1990. In addition to babel, Johannes is the current maintainer of a number of LaTeX extension packages, such as the ntgclass family of document classes, the supertabular package, and the changebar package.

Johannes is still working for the Dutch PTT, nowadays known as KPN, primarily as a project manager for IT related projects. He lives with his wife, Marion, and two sons, Tycho (age 11) and Stephan (age 9), in Zoetermeer.

David Carlisle

David Carlisle studied mathematics at the University of Manchester and then worked as a researcher in the Mathematics and Computer Science departments at Cambridge and Manchester, where he started using LaTeX in 1987. He joined the LaTeX3 team in 1992, just prior to the start of development work on LaTeX 2_ε.

For the last six years he has worked at NAG Ltd. in Oxford, UK, primarily on projects connected to the development of XML-based languages for the representation of mathematical expressions and documents. He is an editor of the OpenMath specification and was an invited expert on the W3C

Math Working Group responsible for MathML, becoming an editor of the MathML 2 Recommendation. Currently he is an editor of a proposed update to ISO/IEC TR 9573, the "ISO character entities". This allows a wide range of characters to be entered into XML and SGML documents using only ASCII characters, with syntax such as γ to denote γ.

David has also taken an interest in the XSLT language and is a major contributor to the xsl-list discussion group for that language. He has reviewed or acted as technical editor on several XSLT-related books. He lives in Oxfordshire with his wife, Joanna, and their son, Matthew (4 months).

Chris Rowley

When not indulging his addiction to travel, Chris lives in London with his wine cellar, his ceramic collection, and his memories. These last include some now rather hazy ones of the 60s, when he was addicted to mathematics but also dipped his mind into computing, both the theory of programming (pretty wild stuff back then) and number crunching (nice streamers from the paper tape).

at his favourite task

It was not until the early 80s that he discovered, on a newly occupied desk, a TV-like object that was connected to a computer and could help him do creative and useful things, such as producing a single page of beautiful typeset mathematics. That was not done using TeX—so it took two days to complete that single page; but it made him realize what was possible and set him thinking about a better way to achieve it. He is very grateful that he then very soon stumbled across TeX and, not long after, LaTeX; the latter being especially providential, as his colleagues included six mathematical typists who needed something that would work for them too. A few years on he heard about a guy called Mittlebach-and-Schöpf (sic) in Mainz and the rest is ... *to be continued.*

Fifteen years later and Chris Rowley is now a senior member of the Faculty of Mathematics and Computing at the Open University, UK. He has been a manager and active member of the LaTeX3 Project Team since its beginning, when he foolishly believed that it would all be done in two years or so. He has been on too many boards and committees, one of the most pleasant being the editorial board for *Tools and Techniques for Computer Typesetting*, and he has graced various offices in the TeX world, including Chair of UK TUG and a vice-presidency of TUG.

As the largest international player in industrialized mass education for home- and workplace-based university-level customers, the Open University has become a major multi-media publishing corporation with, despite commercial competition, an under-resourced, LaTeX-based production system for its mathematical output. As a mathematician who already understood a fair bit about the production of mathematical texts, Chris was well placed to play a vital rôle in the political, administrative, and technical aspects of establishing this system in the mid-80s.

He is now actively engaged on research into the automation of all aspects of document processing, especially multi-lingual typography for multi-use documents. By contrast, over the decades he has also done his share of practical work on LaTeX-based systems in production environments and acted as consultant on the digitization of mathematical texts to a number of standards bodies, companies, and organizations.

These activities have led Chris to the conviction that TeX has but two important long-term future uses: one is as a vernacular within less formal electronic communications between mathematicians, whilst the other is as a treasure trove of wonderful algorithms, especially for mathematical typesetting. He believes, moreover, that extending the monolithic design and intricate models of the TeX software system will not lead to powerful and flexible typesetting software for the 21st Century, ... but it's more fun than doing crosswords.

Christine Detig & Joachim Schrod

In 1982, Christine Detig met TeX on reel-tape during her computer science studies, resulting in her becoming a founding member of DANTE, the German TeX Users Group. Her early software experiences were gained around the TeX workbench, resulting in the formation of a small business in the provision of TeX distributions. Spreading TeX knowledge as part of her job as a research assistant at TU Darmstadt resulted in a book for TeX beginners: *Der LaTeX Wegweiser*. Meanwhile, visiting lots of international conferences has led to many friendships with the eclectic crowd of TeXies. Meet her there for a nice chat about the Future of TeX!

Joachim Schrod also started to use TeX in 1982 and he is another founding member of DANTE. He wrote and supported the international version of LaTeX until LaTeX 2_ε came along. He has been involved in lots of TeX activities, most of them too long ago to be remembered, but among the more enduring are the creation of CTAN and the TeX Directory Structure. Today he is the CEO of a consulting company, where he strives to translate between business and technical people.

Christine & Joachim live in Rödermark, Germany.

Production Notes

This book was typeset using the LaTeX document processing system, which it describes, together with substantial help from some of the extension packages it covers, and considerable extra ad hoc LaTeX programming effort.

The text body font used is Lucida Bright (Bigelow/Holmes) at 8.8pt/12pt. The other major font is the mono-spaced European Modern Typewriter (Y&Y) 10.06pt/12pt. This particular combination was chosen to get a reasonable amount of material on each page and to optically balance the appearance of the "typewriter font" so that it was distinguishable but without too big a contrast. *Body fonts*

The text in the examples mostly uses Adobe's Times Roman with Helvetica for sans serif. For the mathematical material in the examples we have used the by now classic Computer Modern math fonts, so the symbols will appear familiar to the majority of mathematics users. Of course, examples intended to demonstrate the use of other fonts are exceptions. *Example fonts*

The book was typeset with the base LaTeX release dated 2003/12/01. The pdfTeX program was used as the underlying engine, but it was not set to produce PDF output: we were more interested in its ability to produce "hanging punctuation", and this typographical icing was used for the main galley text (see [159,160] for a description of how this is implemented). For comparison look at pages 941–943, as these are set without hanging punctuation (and in smaller type). *Hanging punctuation*

The production of this book required custom class and package files It also needed a complex "make" process using a collection of "shell scripts" controlled by a "Makefile". One of the major tasks these accomplished was to ensure that the typeset output of each example really is produced by the accompanying example input. *The production cycle*

This "make" process worked as follows:

Generating examples

- When first processing a chapter, LaTeX generated a source document file for each example. These are the "example files" you will find on the CD-ROM.

- The make process then ran each of these "example files" through LaTeX (also calling BibTeX or whatever else was needed) as often as was necessary to produce the final form of the typeset output.

  Finally it used dvips to produce either one or two EPS files containing the "typeset example".

- The next time LaTeX was run on that chapter, each of these EPS output files was automatically placed in its position in the book, next to (or near) the example input. The process was not complete even then because the horizontal positioning of some elements, in particular the examples, depends on whether they are on a verso or recto (the technique from Example A-3-9 on page 876 was used in this case). Thus, at least one or two additional runs were needed before all the cross-references were correctly resolved and LaTeX finally found the right way to place the examples correctly into the margins.

Manual labor

That was about as far as automation of the process could take us. Because of the many large examples that could neither be broken nor treated as floating material, getting good page breaks turned out to be a major challenge. For this and other reasons, getting to the final layout of the book was fairly labor intensive and even required minor rewriting (on maybe 10% of the pages) in order to avoid bad line breaks or page breaks (e.g., paragraphs ending in single word or a distracting hyphenation at a page break). Spreads were allowed to run one line long or one line short if necessary and in several cases the layout and contents of the examples were manually adjusted to allow decent page breaks.

Some statistics

Here are a few approximate statistics from this page layout process: 45 long spreads, 25 short spreads, 230 forced page breaks, 400 adjustments to the vertical spacing, 100 other manual adjustments (other than rewriting).

The index

The "Commands and Concepts" index was produced by printing a version of the book with line numbers and giving that to the indexer, who produced "conceptual index entries" that were then added to the source files for the book. This was a major testament to the quality of the lineno package, as it worked "straight out of the box". For the index processing *MakeIndex* was used as xindy was not then available. However, due to the complexity of the index (the colored page numbers, etc.) it was necessary to use pre- and post-processing by scripts to produce the final form of the index file. This was then typeset using an enhanced version of the multicol package to add the continuation lines—something that perhaps one day can be turned into a proper package.

TOOLS AND TECHNIQUES FOR COMPUTER TYPESETTING

Frank Mittelbach, Series Editor

Helmut Kopka and Patrick W. Daly

Frank Mittelbach and Michel Goossens
with Johannes Braams, David Carlisle, and Chris Rowley

Michel Goossens and Sebastian Rahtz
with Eitan Gurari, Ross Moore, and Robert Sutor

http://www.awprofessional.com

CD-ROM Warranty

Addison-Wesley warrants the enclosed CD-ROM to be free of defects in materials and faulty workmanship under normal use for a period of ninety days after purchase (when purchased new). If a defect is discovered in the CD-ROM during this warranty period, a replacement CD-ROM can be obtained at no charge by sending the defective CD-ROM, postage prepaid, with proof of purchase to:

Disc Exchange
Addison-Wesley Professional
Pearson Technology Group
75 Arlington Street, Suite 300
Boston, MA 02116
Email: AWPro@aw.com

Addison-Wesley makes no warranty or representation, either expressed or implied, with respect to this software, its quality, performance, merchantability, or fitness for a particular purpose. In no event will Addison-Wesley, its distributors, or dealers be liable for direct, indirect, special, incidental, or consequential damages arising out of the use or inability to use the software. The exclusion of implied warranties is not permitted in some states. Therefore, the above exclusion may not apply to you. This warranty provides you with specific legal rights. There may be other rights that you may have that vary from state to state.

More information and updates are available at:
http://www.awprofessional.com/